THE WORKS

OF

HUBERT HOWE BANCROFT.

THE WORKS

OF

HUBERT HOWE BANCROFT.

VOLUME XVIII.

HISTORY OF CALIFORNIA.

VOL. I. 1542–1800.

SAN FRANCISCO:
A. L. BANCROFT & COMPANY, PUBLISHERS.
1884.

PREFACE.

THE past of California, as a whole and in each successive phase, furnishes a record not excelled either in variety or interest by that of any New World province. From the time when it was a mere field of cosmographic conjecture, its position, somewhere on the way from Mexico to India, being vaguely fixed by such bounds as Asia, the north pole, Newfoundland, and Florida, it has drawn upon itself a liberal share of the world's notice. The period of Spanish occupation, of spiritual conquest and mission development growing out of Franciscan effort, of quiet pastoral life with its lively social monotony, is a fascinating subject that in no part of America can be studied more advantageously than here. Even the miniature struggles between church and state, the political controversies of the Mexican régime, the play at war and state-craft, are full of interest to the reader who can forget the meagre outcome. On the ocean, as on a great maritime highway, California was visited by explorers and traders from all parts of the world, thus escaping much of the tedious isolation of inland provinces, to the manifest enlivenment of her annals. Over the mountains presently came adventurous path-finders, followed by swarms of Anglo-Saxon immigrants to seek homes by the Pacific; and their

(iii)

experiences on the overland way, with the dissensions
and filibusterings that followed their coming, from
the 'Graham affair' to the 'Bear Flag' revolt, furnish
matter for a narrative not wanting in dramatic interest. Then came the conquest, the change of flag,
and the interregnum of military rule under the
United States; closely followed by the crowning
excitement of all, the discovery of gold, an event that
not only made California famous among the nations,
but imparted a new interest to the country's past.
The gold-mines with their immense yield, the anoma-
lous social conditions and developments of the 'flush
times,' the committees of vigilance and other strange
phenomena, for years permitted no relaxation of the
world's interest. And then dawned the latest epoch
of industrial progress, of agricultural wealth, of trans-
continental railways, of great towns on the Pacific;
an epoch that in a measure places California side by
side with older states in a career of progressional
prosperity.

My resources for writing a history of California are
shown in the accompanying list of authorities, and in
Chapter II. of the present volume, where a classification of the authorities is given. Existing printed
material for such a history is in the aggregate extensive and valuable. The famous collectors and editors
of old, such as Hakluyt and Purchas, the standard
historians of the Spanish Indies, Torquemada and
Herrera, with Mercator, Ortelius, and all the school
of cosmographers, aided by such specialists as Venegas and Cabrera Bueno, published what was known
and imagined of California in the earliest period of
its annals. Then the early navigators from the time

of La Pérouse and Vancouver gave much attention to the history of the country they visited; and
while few of them made the best use of their opportunities, yet their narratives may be regarded as
the most valuable material in print, unless we except
Palou's missionary annals. Meanwhile Fleurieu and
Navarrete, like Forster and Burney, turned their
attention to the summarizing of early voyages; and
others, like Forbes and Mofras, gave a more practical
scope to their researches. Documentary records were
printed from time to time in Mexico, and even in
California; articles more or less historical found
their way into the world's periodicals, and mention of
the far-off province appeared in general works on
Spanish America. Foreign pioneers, following the
lead of Robinson, described in print the condition and
prospects of their new home; overland immigrants and
explorers, like Bidwell and Hastings and Frémont,
pictured the western coast for the benefit of others to
follow. The conquest was voluminously recorded in
documents printed by the government of the United
States, as well as in such books as those of Colton and
Cutts, also making California a prominent topic of
newspaper mention. From the finding of gold there
has been no lack of books and pamphlets published
in or about the country; while national, state, and
municipal records in type, with the addition of newspapers, have forever abolished the necessity of searching the unprinted state and county archives.

Of late there has been manifest commendable
diligence on the part of early Californians in historic research. Many pioneer reminiscences have
been printed in one form or another, one journal

having been devoted for years almost exclusively to
that labor. A few documents of the older time have
seen the light, with comments by such men as Taylor
and Evans, who, like Stillman, have studied the old
voyages. John T. Doyle, besides publishing several
historical pamphlets, has edited a reprint of Palou's
works. Several men, like Hopkins of San Francisco
and Wilson of Santa Cruz, have brought out small
collections of California documents. Other memorials
of the Mexican time have been translated, printed,
and to some extent utilized in periodicals and legal
records. Some members of the legal profession, such
as Dwinelle, have expanded their briefs into formal
history. Several old narratives or diaries of early
events, as for instance those of Ide and Sutter, have
been recently published. Benjamin Hayes has been
an indefatigable collector of printed items on southern
California. Lancey has presented in crude form a
valuable mass of information about the conquest.
Specialists, like McGlashan on the Donner party,
have done some faithful work. Particularly active
have been the local annalists, headed by Hittell,
Soulé, Hall, and Gilbert, whose efforts have in several instances gone far beyond mere local and personal
records, and who have obtained some original data
from old residents and a partial study of documentary
evidence. And finally there are a few writers, like
Tuthill and Gleeson, who have given the world popular
and creditable versions of the country's general annals.

The services of the lawyers and legal tribunals in
years past merit hearty recognition. My corps of
involuntary legal assistants has been more numerous
than that of the twenty skilled *collaborateurs* employed

directly by me as elsewhere explained; and though they examined but a small part of the archives, yet they employed the finest talent in the profession, labored for more than twenty years, submitted their work to the courts, and collected, I suspect, larger fees than I should have been able to pay. The notes of these workmen were scattered broadcast, and were practically inaccessible in legal briefs, printed arguments, court reports, and bulky tomes of testimony in land and other cases; but I have collected, classified, and used them to test, corroborate, or supplement notes from other sources. This duplication of data, and the comments of the profession on the thousands of documents submitted alternately to partisan heat and judicial coolness in the crucible of litigation, have not only doubled the value of those papers, but have greatly aided me in making proper use of other tens of thousands never submitted to such a test. And to documentary evidence of this class should be added the testimony of pioneers elicited by interrogators who, through personal interests or the *subpœna*, had a power over reticent witnesses which I never possessed.

But while much credit is due to investigators of the several classes who have preceded me, the path, so far as original research on an extended scale is concerned, has to this time remained untrodden. No writer has even approximately utilized the information extant in print. It has now been collected and studied for the first time in its entirety. Yet so much further has the investigation been carried, and so comparatively unimportant is this class of data, that for a large part of the period covered—namely, from 1769 to 1846—the completeness of my record would not be very seriously affected by the destruction of every page that has ever been printed. Never has it been the fortune of any writer, aspiring to record the annals of his country, to have at the same time so new a field and so complete a collection of original and unused material. I may claim without exaggeration to have accumulated practically all that exists on the subject, not only in print but in manuscript. I have copied the public archives, hitherto but very superficially consulted; and I have ransacked the country for additional hundreds of thousands of original documents whose very existence was unknown. I have also taken statements, varying in size from six to two thousand pages each, from many hundreds of the early inhabitants. For details respecting these new sources of information I refer the reader to the list and chapter already cited. It is true that new documents will be found as the years pass by to throw a clearer light on many minor points; but new material—whatever new talent and new theories may do—will necessitate the reconstruction of few if any of these chapters. It is to me a matter of pride that, using the term in the limited and only sense in which it can ever be properly applied to an extended historical work, I have thus been able to exhaust the subject.

Possibly I have at the same time exhausted the patience of my readers; for it is in the HISTORY OF CALIFORNIA that I have entered more fully into details than in any other part of the general work. The plan originally announced carries me from national history into local annals as I leave the south for the north; and among the northern countries of the Pacific States California claims the largest space. That this treatment is justified by the extent and variety of the country's annals, by its past, present, and prospective importance in the eyes of the world, will not probably be questioned. Yet while the comparative prominence of the topic will doubtless be approved, it may be that the aggregate space devoted to it will seem to some excessive. But such would be the case if the space were reduced by one half or two thirds; and such a reduction could only be made by a radical change in the plan of the work, and a total sacrifice of its exhaustive character. A history of California is a record of events from year to year, each being given a space, from a short paragraph to a long chapter, in proportion to its importance. Any considerable reduction in space would make of the work a mere chronological table of events that would be intolerably tedious, or a record of selected illustrative events which would not be history. That the happenings to be chronicled are not so startling as some of the destiny-deciding events of the world's history, is a state of things for which the writer is not responsible; and while from a certain point of view it might justify him in not writing of California at all, it can by no means excuse him, having once undertaken the task, from telling the whole story. The custom has been in writing the annals of this and other countries to dwell at length on one event or epoch recorded in a book or document the writer happens to have seen, and to omit—for want of space!—twenty others equally important which have escaped his research, a happy means of condensation not at my command.

There will be found in these volumes no long-drawn narratives or descriptions. In no part of this series has my system of condensation been more strictly applied. I am firm in the belief that the record is worth preserving, and for its completeness I expect in time the appreciation and approbation of all true Californians. Unless I am greatly in error respecting what I have written, no intelligent reader desiring information on any particular event of early Californian history—information on the founding or early annals of any mission or town; on the development of any political, social, industrial, or religious institution; on the occurrences of any year or period; on the life and character of any official or friar or prominent citizen or early pioneer; on the visit and narrative of any voyager; on the adventures and composition of any immigrant party; on any book or class of books about California; or on any one or any group of the incidents that make up this work—will accuse me of having written at too great length on that particular topic. And I trust the system of classification will enable the reader to select without inconvenience or confusion such portions as may suit his taste.

To government officials of nation, state, and counties, who have afforded me and my agents free access to the public archives, often going beyond their official obligations to facilitate my investigations, most hearty acknowledgments are due. I am no less indebted to Archbishop Alemany of San Francisco and Bishop Mora of Los Angeles and Monterey, by whose authority the parochial archives have been placed at my disposal; and to the curates, who with few exceptions have done much more in appreciation of my work than simply to comply with the requests of their superiors. Acknowledgments are also due to Father Romo and his Franciscan associates at Santa Bárbara for permitting me to copy their unrivalled collection of documents, the real *archivo de misiones*. Nor must I forget the representatives of native Californian and early pioneer families, duly mentioned by name elsewhere in this history, who have generously and patriotically given me not only their personal reminiscences, but the priceless treasures of their family archives, without which documents the early annals of their country could never have been written. Lastly there are the strong, intelligent, and energetic men of Anglo-Saxon origin, conspicuous among the world's latter-day builders of empire, who have laid the foundations of the fullest and fairest civilization in this last of temperate climes—to these for information furnished, with a heart full of admiration and trust, I tender my grateful thanks.

CONTENTS OF THIS VOLUME.

CHAPTER I.

INTRODUCTORY RÉSUMÉ.

CHAPTER II.

BIBLIOGRAPHY OF CALIFORNIAN HISTORY.

CHAPTER III.

THE DISCOVERY OF CALIFORNIA.

1542–1768.

CHAPTER IV.

MOTIVES AND PREPARATIONS FOR SPANISH OCCUPATION.

1767–1770.

CHAPTER V.

OCCUPATION OF SAN DIEGO—EXPEDITIONS BY SEA AND LAND.

1769.

CHAPTER VI.

FIRST EXPEDITION FROM SAN DIEGO TO MONTEREY AND SAN FRANCISCO.

1769.

PAGE

CHAPTER VII.

OCCUPATION OF MONTEREY—FOUNDING OF SAN CÁRLOS, SAN ANTONIO, AND SAN GABRIEL.

1770–1771.

CHAPTER VIII.

PROGRESS OF THE NEW ESTABLISHMENTS.

1772–1773.

CHAPTER IX.

FIRST ANNUAL REPORT; SERRA'S LABORS IN MEXICO.

1773.

CHAPTER X.

RECORD OF EVENTS.

1774.

CHAPTER XI.

NORTHERN EXPLORATION AND SOUTHERN DISASTER.

1775.

CHAPTER XII.

EXPEDITIONS OF ANZA, FONT, AND GARCES.

1775–1776.

CHAPTER XIII.

FOUNDING OF THE PRESIDIO AND MISSION OF SAN FRANCISCO.

1776–1777.

CHAPTER XIV.

MISSION PROGRESS AND PUEBLO BEGINNINGS.

1776–1777.

CHAPTER XV.

CHAPTER XVI.

CHAPTER XVII.

CHAPTER XVIII.

FOUNDING OF SAN BUENAVENTURA AND SANTA BÁRBARA PRESIDIO—
FAGES GOVERNOR.

1782.   PAGE

CHAPTER XIX.

RULE OF FAGES—GENERAL RECORD.

1783–1790.

CHAPTER XX.

RULE OF FAGES, DEATH OF SERRA, AND MISSION PROGRESS.

1783–1790.

CHAPTER XXI.

RULE OF FAGES; FOREIGN RELATIONS AND COMMERCE.

1783–1790.

CHAPTER XXII.

RULE OF FAGES; LOCAL EVENTS AND STATISTICS.

1783–1790.

CHAPTER XXIII.

RULE OF ROMEU.

1791–1792.

CHAPTER XXIV.

RULE OF ARRILLAGA—VANCOUVER'S VISITS.

1792–1794.

CHAPTER XXV.

RULE OF BORICA, FOREIGN RELATIONS, AND INDIAN AFFAIRS.

1794–1800.

CHAPTER XXVI.

RULE OF BORICA—EXPLORATIONS AND NEW FOUNDATIONS.

1794–1800.

CHAPTER XXVII.

MISSION PROGRESS.

1791–1800.

CHAPTER XXVIII.

PUEBLOS, COLONIZATION, AND LANDS—INDUSTRIES AND INSTITUTIONS.

1791–1800.

CHAPTER XXIX.

INDUSTRIES AND INSTITUTIONS.

1791–1800.

CHAPTER XXX.

LOCAL EVENTS AND PROGRESS—SOUTHERN DISTRICT.

1791–1800.

CHAPTER XXXI.

LOCAL EVENTS AND PROGRESS—MONTEREY DISTRICT.

1791–1800.

CHAPTER XXXII.

LOCAL EVENTS AND PROGRESS—SAN FRANCISCO JURISDICTION.

1791–1800.

CHAPTER XXXIII.

CLOSE OF BORICA'S RULE.

1800.

AUTHORITIES QUOTED

IN THE

HISTORY OF CALIFORNIA.

[*There are more than one thousand titles of works actually consulted in these volumes, and many of them named in foot-notes, which do not appear in this list. The catalogue is, however, complete down to the discovery of gold in 1848, and practically so down to 1856. The omissions of later date are general works of reference, cyclopedias, etc.; speeches, addresses, orations, not directly historical in their nature; publications emanating from or relating to various California institutions, associations, companies, orders, churches, banks, courts, schools, etc.; legal briefs, county and municipal regulations, law text-books, briefs, and miscellaneous public documents; works of fiction and science; newspapers, and other similar classes. These works in the aggregate have afforded me much information; indeed there is hardly a Californian book, pamphlet, or paper in my Library which is not in a certain sense historical; but space does not permit a full catalogue, and I am obliged to restrict the list with few exceptions to material that bears directly on history. See chapter ii. of this volume for a classification of the works here named.*]

Aa (Pieter van der), Naaukeurige Versameling. Leyden, 1707. 30 vols.
Abbey (James), A Trip across the Plains in 1850. New Albany, 1850.
Abbott (John S. C.), Christopher Carson. New York, 1876.
Abell (Alexander), Copy of agreement on behalf of U. S. in relation to island of Santa Cruz [32d Cong., 1st Sess., Sen. Ex. Doc. 87]. Washington, 1852.
Abella (Ramon), Correspondencia del Misionero. MSS. in various archives.
Abella (Ramon), Diario de un Registro de los Rios Grandes, 1811. MS.
Abella (Ramon), Noticia de una Batalla entre Cristianos y Gentiles, 1807. MS.
Ábrego (José), Asuntos de la Tesorería. MSS. in various archives.
Ábrego (José), Cartas sobre la Colonia de 1834. MS.
Ábrego (José), Relation. MS.
Acosta (Josef de), Historia Natural y Moral de las Indias. Sevilla, 1590.
Act of Congress Creating the Office of Shipping Commissioner. S. F. 1873.
Actas de Elecciones. MS. In Archivo de California.
Adam (George), Dreadful Sufferings and Thrilling Adventures of an Overland Party of Emigrants to California. St Louis, 1850.
Addresses. See Speeches.
Adventures (The) of a Captain's Wife...to California in 1850. New York, etc., 1877.
Aimard (Gustave), The Gold Seekers. Philadelphia, n.d.
Alaman (Lúcas), Censo de California, 1832. MS.
Alaman (Lúcas), Historia de Méjico. Mexico, 1849–52. 5 vols.
Alaman (Lúcas), Sucesos de California en 1831. MS.
Alameda, Abstract of Title, lots 17–20, survey of Jones. San Francisco, 1873.
Alameda, Argus, Encinal, Messenger, Post, etc.
Alameda County, Historical Atlas. San Francisco, 1878. atlas folio.

Albany (Or.) Register.
Albatross (The ship), Log of a Voyage to the N. W. Coast, 1809–12. MS.
Albatross and *Lydia*, Comunicaciones relativas. 1816. MS.
Alberni (Pedro), Comunicaciones del Teniente Coronel, 1796–1800. MSS. [In different archives.]
Alberni (Pedro), Parecer sobre el sitio de Branciforte, 1796. MS.
Album Mexicano. Mexico, 1849 et seq.
Alcedo (Antonio de), Diccionario Geográfico Histórico de las Indias Occidentales. Madrid, 1786–9. 5 vols.
Alexander (B. S.), G. H. Mendell, and G. Davidson, Report on Irrigation of San Joaquin. Washington, 1874.
Alexander (J. H.), Memoir on the Routes of Communication between Atlantic and Pacific. Washington, 1849.
Alger (Horatio, Jr.), The Young Adventurer. Boston, 1878; The Young Miner. Boston, 1879.
Allsopp (J. P. C.), Leaves from my Log-book. MS.
Allsopp (Robert), California and its Gold Mines. London, 1853.
All the Way Round. London, etc. (1875).
Almanacs. A great number, only a few of which are named in this list as follows: Alta California. S. F., 1868 et seq.; California Merchants and Miners. S. F., 1857 et seq.; California Miners. S. F., 1864; California Pictorial. S. F., 1858 et seq.; California State. S. F., 1854; Californischer Volkskalender. S. F., 1858; Carrie and Damon's California. S. F., 1856; Jacoby (Philo), Almanack für Cal. S. F., 1865 et seq.; Knight (Wm. H.), Handbook for Pacific States. S. F., 1862 et seq.; Langley (Henry G.), Pacific Coast. S. F., 1868 et seq.; *Id.*, State. S. F., 1863; *Id.*, State Register. S. F., 1857 et seq.; San Francisco. S. F., 1859, etc.
Alric (Henry J. A.), Dix Ans de Résidence d'un Missionnaire dans les deux Californies. Mexico, 1866.
Altimira (José), Diario de la Expedicion, 1823. MS.
Altimira (José), Journal of a Mission-founding Expedition, 1823. In Hutchings' Cal. Mag., v. 58, 115.
Alturas, Modoc Independent.
Alvarado (Juan Bautista), Campaña de Las Flores, 1838. MS.
Alvarado (Juan Bautista), Carta Confidencial, 7 de Nov. 1836. MS.
Alvarado (Juan Bautista), Carta en que relata la Campaña de S. Fernando, Enero 1837. MS.
Alvarado (Juan Bautista), Carta en que relata los sucesos de Los Angeles, Feb. 1837. MS.
Alvarado (Juan Bautista), Cartas Relaciones, Revolucion de 1844–5. MS.
Alvarado (Juan Bautista), Comunicaciones al Ayuntamiento de Los Angeles, Enero 1837. MS.
Alvarado (Juan Bautista), El C...Coronel de la Milicia Cívica, etc. [Despacho de Capitan á favor de J. J. Vallejo.] Monterey, 12 Dic. 1836.
Alvarado (Juan Bautista), El C... Gobernador Interino del Estado Libre de Alta Cal. á sus Habitantes, Monterey, Mayo 10, 1837.
Alvarado (Juan Bautista), Gobernador Constitucional, etc. [Suprimiendo los Empleos de Administradores de Misiones.] Monterey, 1 Mayo, 1840.
Alvarado (Juan Bautista), Historia de California. MS. 1876. 5 vols.
Alvarado (Juan Bautista), Instrucciones al Prefecto Castro. 1840. MS.
Alvarado (Juan Bautista), Instrucciones que debe observar el Visitador. 1840. MS.
Alvarado (Juan Bautista), Instrucciones que deberá observar el Visitador Hartnell. 1839. MS.
Alvarado (Juan Bautista), Manifiesto del Gobr., 10 Mayo, 1837.
Alvarado (Juan Bautista), Oficios Varios y Cartas Particulares. MSS. Very numerous in different public and private archives.
Alvarado (Juan Bautista), [Proclama del] Gefe Político 21 Nov. 1838.
Alvarado (Juan Bautista), [Proclama del] Gobernador Interino, 9 Julio, 1837. MS.

Alvarado (Juan Bautista), [Proclama del] Gobernador sobre Destierro de Extrangeros. 1840.
Alvarado (Juan Bautista), Primitivo Descubrimiento de Oro en Cal., 1841. MS.
Alvarado (Juan Bautista), Reglamento de ex-misiones. Monterey, 1843.
Alvarado (Juan Bautista), Reglamento Provisional para Administradores de Misiones, 1839. MS.
Alvarado and Castro, Esposicion contra Micheltorena, 1845. MS.
Alviso (José Antonio), Documentos para la Historia de California. MS., 1817–50.
Alviso (José Antonio), Campaña de Natividad, 1846. MS.
Amador (José María), Memorias sobre la Hist. de Cal. MS.
Amador (Pedro), Diario de la Expedicion para fundar la Mision de S. José, 1797. MS.
Amador (Pedro), Expedicion contra los gentiles Sacalanes, 1796. MS.
Amador (Pedro), Expediente de Servicios, 1765–91. MS.
Amador (Pedro), Papeles del Sargento. MSS. In various archives.
Amador (Pedro), Prevenciones al Cabo de la Escolta de S. José, 1797. MS.
Amador (Pedro), Reconocimiento desde Sta Cruz hasta S. Francisco, 1795. MS.
Amador (Pedro), Salida contra Indios Gentiles, 1800. MS.
Amador County, History. Oakland, 1881. folio.
Amelia Sherwood. Richmond, 1850.
America, Descripcion, 1710. MS.
America, or an Exact Description of the West Indies. London, 1655.
American Antiquarian Society, Proceedings. Worcester, 1820 et seq.
American Educational Monthly. New York, 1864 et seq.
American and Foreign Christian Union. New York, 1851 et seq.
American Geographical and Statistical Society. New York, 1850 et seq.
American Quarterly Register and Magazine. Philadelphia, 1848 et seq.
American Quarterly Review. Philadelphia, 1827 et seq.
American Review. Philadelphia, 1811 et seq.
American State Papers. Boston, 1817–19. 12 vols.; Washington, 1832-4; 1858–61. folio. 39 vols.
Americans at Sea. In Niles' Register, xviii. 417.
Ames (John G.), Report on Mission Indians of California. Washington, 1873.
Amesti (José), Cartas de un Comerciante Español. MSS. In different archives.
Amigo del Pueblo. Mexico, 1827 et seq.
Amulet (The), A tale of Spanish California. London, 1865.
Anaheim, Gazette, Review, etc.
Anaheim, Its People and its Products. New York, 1869.
Anderson (Alexander C.), Northwest Coast History. MS.
Anderson (Alexander D.), The Silver and Gold of the Southwest, etc. St Louis, 1877; The Silver Country, etc. New York, 1877.
Anderson (David C.), Statement of Theatrical Events. MS.
Anderson (Mary E.), Scenes in the Hawaiian Islands and California. Boston [1865].
Annals of Congress. [1st to 18th Congress.] Washington, 1834–56. 42 vols.
Annual of Scientific Discovery. Boston, 1850–67. 1870–1. 19 vols.
Anquetil, Universal History. London, 1800. 9 vols.
Ansted (David T.), The Gold-seeker's Manual. New York, 1849.
Anthony (E. M.), Siskiyou County Reminiscences. MS.
Antioch, Ledger.
Anza (Juan Bautista), Descubrimiento de Sonora á California, 1774. MS.
Anza (Juan Bautista), Diario de una expedicion desde Sonora á S. Francisco, Cal., 1775–6. MS.
Apalátegui y Torres, Averiguacion en Sonora del Tumulto de Los Angeles, 1835. MS.
Apalátegui y Torres, Causa seguida contra los conspiradores, 1835. MS.
Apodaca (Virey), Cartas. MSS. In the archives.
Apostólicos Afanes de la Compañia de Jesus. Barcelona, 1754.

Apponyi (Flora Haines), Libraries of California. San Francisco, 1878.
Arab, Log-book, 1821–5. MS.
Arancel de Precios, 1782. MS.
Arancel de Precios, 1788. MS.
Arce (Francisco), Documentos para la Historia de Cal. MS.
Arce (Francisco), Memorias Históricas y Documentos Originales. MS.
Archbald (John), Why 'California.' In Overland Monthly, ii. 434.
Archer (L.), Speech on Assembly Bill No. 182. n.pl., n.d.
Archivo del Arzobispado de San Francisco. MS. 5 vols.
Archivo de California. MS. 273 vols. and a great mass of loose papers.
    Documents preserved in the U. S. Surveyor-general's office at San Fran-
    cisco. Copies in my Collection. Divided as follows: Prov. St. Pap.;
    Prov. Rec.; Dept. St. Pap.; Dept. Rec.; Leg. Rec.; State Pap.; Sup.
    Govt. St. Pap.; Actas de Elecciones; Brands and Marks; and Unbound
    Doc., q. v. for full sub-titles and further subdivisions.
Archivo de las Misiones. MS. 2 vols.
Archivo del Obispado de Monterey y Los Angeles. MS.
Archivo de Santa Bárbara. MS. 11 vols.
Archuleta (Florentino), Comunicaciones Pedagógicas. MS. In the archives.
Arco Iris. Vera Cruz, 1847 et seq. folio.
Areche, Parecer 14 de Jun. 1773. MS.; also in Palou, Not., i. 572.
Areche, Respuesta 30 de Jun., 1773. MS.
Argelo, Calaveras Mountaineer.
Argüello (Gervasio), Escritos de un Habilitado General y Diputado. MSS. In
    public and private archives.
Argüello (Gervasio), Observaciones, 1816. MS.
Argüello (José), Relacion de lo que declararon los gentiles Sacalanes,1797. MS.
Argüello (José), Relacion que formó sobre Indios huidos de S. Francisco,
    1797. MS.
Argüello (José), Cartas de un Gobernador de las Californias. MSS. In the
    different archives.
Argüello (José), Informe sobre Rancho del Rey en S. Francisco, 1798. MS.
Argüello (José), Instruccion que ha de observar el teniente Luis Argüello en
    S. Francisco, 1806. MS.
Argüello (José), Respuesta á las quince Preguntas sobre abusos de Misioneros,
    1798. MS.
Argüello (Luis Antonio), Cartas del Comandante y Gobernador. MSS. In
    the different archives.
Argüello (Luis Antonio), Hoja de Servicios hasta 1828. MS.
Argüello (Santiago), Correspondencia del Comandante y Prefecto. MSS.
    Archives, passim.
Argüello (Santiago), Correspondencia Particular. MS.
Arman (H. M. Van), The Public Lands of California. San Francisco, 1876.
Armona (Matías), Carta de 1770. In Doc. Hist. Mex. serie iv., tom. ii. p. 156.
Armstrong (William), '49 Experiences. MS.
Arnaz (José), Recuerdos de Un Comerciante. MS.
Arrangoiz (Francisco de Paula), Méjico desde 1808 hasta 1867. Madrid,
    1871–2. 4 vols.
Arricivita (J. D.), Crónica Seráfica y Apostólica. Mexico, 1792. folio.
Arrillaga (Basilio José), Recopilacion de Leyes, etc. Mexico, 1838–50. 16 vols.
Arrillaga (José Joaquin), Borrador de Carta á Vancouver, 1793. MS.
Arrillaga (José Joaquin), Correspondencia del Gobernador. MS. Archives,
    passim.
Arrillaga (José Joaquin), Hojas de Servicio, 1791–8. MS.
Arrillaga (José Joaquin), Informe sobre el estado de Indios, Misiones, etc.,
    1804. MS.
Arrillaga (José Joaquin), Informe al Virey sobre Defensas, 1793. MS.
Arrillaga (José Joaquin), Papel de Puntos para conocimiento del Gobernador,
    1794. MS.
Arrillaga (José Joaquin), Preceptos Generales para Comandantes, 1806. MS.

Arrillaga (José Joaquin), Relacion del estado que guardan los Presidios y Pueblos, 1806. MS.

Arrillaga (José Joaquin), Testamento, 1814. MS.

Arroyo de la Cuesta (Felipe), Cartas del Misionero. MS. In mission and secular archives.

Arroyo de la Cuesta (Felipe), Grammar of the Mutsun Language. New York, 1861; also original MS.

Arroyo de la Cuesta (Felipe), A Vocabulary or Phrase Book of the Mutsun Language. New York, 1861; also original MS.

Arteaga (Ignacio), Tercera Exploracion, 1779. MS.

Ascension (Antonio de la), Descubrimiento de California, 12 Oct. 1620. In Pacheco and Cárdenas, Col. Doc., tom. viii.

Ashburner (William), Report upon the "App." Gold Quartz Mine. San Francisco, 1866.

Ashland (Or.), Tidings.

Ashley (D. R.), Documents for the History of California. MS.

Ashley (D. R.), Records kept during journey made by members of California Association from Monroe, Mich., to Cal., 1849. MS.

Asia y Constante, Tratado de Capitulacion de los Navíos, 1825. MS.

Assembly, Sessions of 1846. In U. S. vs. Bolton, App. Brief U. S. Sup. Court.

Associations. See Institutions.

Astoria, Astorian.

Atanasio, Causa Criminal contra el Indio. Abril 26, 1831. MS.

Atlantic Monthly. Boston, 1858 et seq.

Atlantic and Pacific R. R. Co. Act granting lands. New York, 1866; Circular. New York, 1855; and other documents.

Atleta (El). Mexico, 1829 et seq.

Auburn, Placer Herald, Stars and Stripes, Union Advocate, etc.

Auger (Edouard), Voyage en Californie, 1852-3. Paris, 1854.

Austin (Nev.), Reese River Reveille.

Australian Newspapers in Mechanics' Library of San Francisco and elsewhere.

Autobiografía Autográfica de los Padres Misioneros, 1817. MS.

Averett (T. H.), Speech in U. S. H. of Rep. March 27, 1850, to admit California. Washington, 1850.

Averill (Charles E.), Life in California. Boston. n.d.

Avery (Benjamin Parke), Californian Pictures. New York, 1878.

Ávila (Antonio), y otros, Papeles tocantes á su sedicion, 1832. MS.

Ávila (Juan), Notas Californianas. MS.

Avila (María Inocenta), Cosas de California. MS.

Ávila (Miguel), Documentos para la Historia de California. MS.

Ávila de Rios (Catarina), Recuerdos. MS.

Ayala (Tadeo Ortiz), Resúmen de la Estadística del Imp. Mex. Mexico, 1822.

Ayers (F. H.), Personal Adventures. MS.

Ayuntamientos, Decreto de las Córtes, 23 de Mayo, 1812. In Mexico, Leyes Vigentes, 1829.

Azanza (Virey), Órdenes. MS. In the archives.

Azanza (Virey), Ynstruccion, 1800. MS.

Bacon (L. H.), Memoir of Early Times. MS.

Baird (Spencer F.), Fish and Fisheries [45th Cong., 2d. Sess., Sen. Mis. Doc. 49]. Washington, 1877.

Baker (E. D.), Speech before California Senate Feb. 1st and 2d. 1854. San Francisco, 1854; also other speeches.

Baker City (Or.), Herald.

Bakersfield, Kern County Californian, Kern County Courier, Kern County Gazette, Southern Californian, etc.

Baldridge (William), The Days of '46. MS.

Baldwin (R. S.), Speech in U. S. Sen. March 27, 1850, Admission of California, etc. Washington, 1850.

Ball (N. B.), Sketch by a Pioneer. MS.
Ballenstedt (C. W. T.), Beschreibung meiner Reise nach den Goldminen.
Californiens. Schöningen, 1851.
Ballou (John), The Lady of the West. Cincinnati, 1855.
Ballou (William T.), Adventures. MS.
Baltimore (Md.), Patriot, Sun.
Bancroft (A. L.), Diary of a Journey to Oregon. MS.
Bancroft (Hubert Howe), History of the Pacific States of North America.
San Francisco, 1882 et seq. 28 vols.; Native Races of the Pacific States.
New York, 1875. 5 vols.; Popular Tribunals. San Francisco. 2 vols., etc.;
Bancroft (Hubert Howe), Personal Observations in California, 1874. MS.
Bancroft Library, MS. Scrap-books, containing classified notes used in writing
Bancroft's works.
Bancroft Library, Newspaper scraps classified under the following headings:
Academy of Sciences; Amusements and Celebrations; Art; Authors;
Banks and Banking; Bibliography; Biography; Births, Deaths, etc.;
Charitable Institutions; Chinese; Climate; Constitutional Convention;
Counties; Crimes and Society; Earthquakes; Education and Schools;
Fares and Freights; Fisheries; Floods; Fruit-raising; Indians; Journalism;
Kearneyism and the Workingmen's Party; Lands; Legal; Libraries; Lum-
ber Question; Manufactures; Military Affairs; Mineral Springs; Mining
Stocks; Miscellaneous; Modoc War; New Charter; Oil and Petroleum;
Pioneer Celebrations; Politics; Population and Colonization; Railroads;
Religion; Resources; Revenue and Taxation; Roads and Routes; Ship-
ping and Navigation; Silver Remonetization; State Fairs; Stock-raising;
Stories and Legends; Telegraphs; Trade and Commerce; Trips across the
Continent and Voyages by Sea; United States Mails; Water Supply.
68 vols. 4to.
Bandini (Juan), Acusaciones contra Angel Ramirez, 1834–7. MS.
Bandini (Juan), Apuntes Políticos, 1832. MS.
Bandini (Juan), Carta Histórica y Descriptiva de California, 1828. MS.
Bandini (Juan), Carta Particular á Vallejo sobre cosas políticas. 12 Dic.,
1836. MS.
Bandini (Juan), Carta á Vallejo sobre Revoluciones. 3 Dic., 1836. MS.
Bandini (Juan), Contestacion á la Alocucion de Victoria, 1831. MS.
Bandini (Juan), Correspondencia Particular y Oficial. MSS. A large num-
ber of documents in private and public archives, in addition to those
specially named in this list.
Bandini (Juan), El Diputado de la Alta California á sus Comitentes. 6 Agosto,
1833. Mexico, 1833.
Bandini (Juan), Discurso ante el Ayunt. de Los Angeles. 27 Mayo, 1837. MS.
Bandini (Juan), Documentos para la Historia de California. MS.
Bandini (Juan), Historia de Alta California. MS.
Bandini (Juan), Informacion del Visitador de Aduana, 1835. MS.
Bandini (Juan), Manifiesto á la Diputacion sobre ramos de Hacienda Terri-
torial, 1832. MS.
Bandini (Juan), Proyecto de Misiones, 1846. MS.
Bandini (Juan), Sucesos del Sur, Mayo–Agosto, 1837. MS.
Banfield (J. A.), Historical Sketch of Yolo County. In Woodland Yolo
Democrat, July 6, 1876.
Banker's Magazine and Statistical Register. Baltimore, etc., 1846 et seq.
Banks. See Institutions.
Baránof (Alexander), Shizneopissanie. St Petersburg, 1835.
Barber (John W.), and Henry Howe. History of Western States and Terri-
tories. Cincinnati, 1867.
Barnard (Helen M.), The Chorpenning Claim. n.pl., n.d.
Barnes (Demas), From the Atlantic to the Pacific Overland. New York, 1866.
Barnes (G. A.), Oregon and California. MS.
Barri (Felipe), Oficios del Gobr. de la Baja California, MS. In Prov. St.
Pap. passim.

Barrow (John), The Life, Voyages, and Exploits of Admiral Sir Francis Drake. London, 1843.

Barrow (William), The General; or Twelve Nights in a Hunter's Camp. Boston, 1869.

Barry (W. J.), Up and Down. London, 1879.

Barry (T. A.), and B. A. Patten, Men and Memories of San Francisco. San Francisco, 1873.

Barstow (Alfred), Statement of a Pioneer of 1849. MS.

Barstow (D. P.), Recollections of 1849-51. MS.

Barstow (George), Introductory Address. San Francisco, 1859; other addresses.

Bartlett (John Russell), Personal Narrative of Explorations and Incidents in Texas, New Mexico, California, etc. New York, 1854. 2 vols.

Bartlett, (John Russell), Report on the Boundary Line between the U. S. and Mexico. [32d Cong., 2d Sess., Sen. Ex. Doc. 41.] Washington, 1851.

Bartlett (Washington), Statement of a Pioneer of 1849. MS.

Barton (James R.), Statement of an Early Settler. MS.

Barton (Stephen), Early History of Visalia. Scrap-book.

Basellandschaftlichen Zeitung, 1868.

Bates (D. B.), Four Years on the Pacific Coast. Boston, 1858; Boston, 1860.

Bates (H. W.), Illustrated Travels. London, n.d.

Bates (J. C.), Report of the Proceedings... Will and Testament of Horace Hawes. San Francisco, 1872.

Battle Mountain (Nev.), Messenger.

Bauer (John A.), Statement of a Pioneer of 1849. MS.

Bausman (William), Early California. San Francisco, 1872.

Baxley (H. Willis), What I saw on the Western Coast. New York, 1865.

Beadle (J. H.), The Undeveloped West. Philadelphia [1873]; Western Wilds. Cincinnati, 1879.

Beadle's Monthly. New York, 1865 et seq.

Beale (E. F.), Wagon Road from Fort Defiance to the Colorado River. [35th Cong., 1st Sess., H. Ex. Doc. 124.]

Bean (Edwin F.), see Directories, Nevada County, Cal., 1867.

Bear Flag Papers, 1846. MS.

Beard (Henry), Argument. John Roland... Land Claim, "La Puente." Washington, 1866.

Beckwith (E. G.), Report of Exploration of a Route for the Pacific Railroad near the 38th and 39th Parallels [33d Cong., 1st Sess., H. Ex. Doc. 129]. Washington [1854].

Bee (F. A.), Opening Argument... Chinese Immigration. S. F., 1876.

Bee (Henry J.), Recollections of California from 1830. MS.

Beechey (F. W.), Narrative of a Voyage to the Pacific, etc., in 1825-8. London, 1831, 2 vols.; Philadelphia, 1832.

Beechey (F. W.), Zoölogy of Voyage. See Richardson (J.) et al.

Beers (George A.), Vasquez. New York, 1875.

Belcher (Edward), Narrative of a Voyage round the World in 1836-42. London, 1843. 2 vols.

Belden (David), Speech in Sen. of Cal. Feb. 9, 1866, against the Repeal of the Specific Contract Act. Sacramento, 1866.

Belden (Josiah), Historical Statement. MS.

Belden (Josiah), Letters of a Pioneer of 1841. MS.

Belfast (Me.), Republican Journal.

Bell (A. D.), Arguments in favor of Immigration. San Francisco, 1870.

Bell (Horace), Reminiscences of a Ranger. L. Angeles, 1881; also scrap book.

Bell (J. C.), Obituary Address on Death of. Sacramento, 1860.

Bell (W. A.), New Tracks in North America. London, 1870.

Belleville (Ill.), Advocate.

Bellows (Henry W.), In Memory of Thos. Starr King. Discourse, May 1, 1864. San Francisco, 1864.

Belmont (Nev.), Courier.

Benham (Calhoun), Testimony in behalf of the U. S. vs. Sutter. "New Helvetia." San Francisco, 1861.

Benicia, Chronicle, New Era, Pacific Churchman, Tribune, etc.

Benicia, Official Documents in Relation to Land Titles. Suisun, 1867.

Bennett (H. C.), Chinese Labor. A Lecture. San Francisco, 1870.

Bennett (Henry), Speech in U. S. H. of Rep., May 27, 1850, on Admission of California. Washington, 1850.

Bennett (Nathaniel), The Queue Case. n.pl., n.d.

Bentley (William R.), Pleasant Paths of the Pacific Northwest. San Francisco, 1882.

Benton (J. A.), The California Pilgrim. Sacramento, 1853.

Benton (Thomas H.), Abridgment of Debates in Congress, 1759-1856. New York, 1857-63. 16 vols.; Defence of Frémont. In Niles' Register, lxxi. 173; Speech in U. S. Senate, July, 1848. In Cong. Globe, 1847-8, App. 977; Speech in U. S. Senate, Jan. 15, 1849, on Adjudication of Land Titles, etc., in New Mexico and California. Washington, 1849; Thirty Years' View. New York, 1854. 2 vols.

Berenger (J. P.), Collection de Tous les Voyages faits autour du Monde. Paris, 1788-9. 9 vols.

Berkeley, Advocate, Berkeleyan.

Berkeley Quarterly. San Francisco, 1880-1. 2 vols.

Bermudez (J. M.), Verdadera Causa de la Revolucion. Toluca, 1831.

Bernal (Juan), Memoria de un Californio. MS.

Berreyesa (Antonio), Relacion de sus Recuerdos. MS.

Berreyesa and Carrillo, Quarrel at Sonoma, 1846. MS.

Berry (George), The Gold of California. London, 1849.

Bestard (Buenaventura), Pastoral del Comisario General de Indias. 28 de Agosto, 1816. MS.

Bestard (Buenaventura), Pastoral. 6 de Mayo, 1816. MS.

Betagh (William), A Voyage round the World. London, 1728; London, 1757; also in Pinkerton's Voyages, vol. xvi.; Harris' Col., vol. i.

Beyer (Moritz), Das Auswanderungsbuch. Leipzig, 1846.

Biart (Lucien), My Rambles in the New World. London, 1877.

Bidleman (H. J.), see Directories, Sacramento, 1861-2.

Bidwell (John), California in 1841-8. MS.

Bidwell (John), Journey to California. n. pl. [1842].

Bigelow (John), Les Etats-Unis D'Amérique. Paris, 1863; Memoir of the Life and Public Services of John C. Frémont. New York, 1856.

Biggs, Butte County Register, Silver Bend Reporter.

Bigler (Henry W.), Diary of a Mormon in California. MS.

Bigler (John), Address at a Meeting of Citizens of Santa Clara County. n.pl. [1855]; Scrap Book, 1850-2; Speech at Sacramento July 9, 1867. Sacramento, 1867; and other speeches.

Bigly (Cantell A.), Aurifodina. New York, 1849.

Billings (Frederick), Address, Sept. 23, 1854. San Francisco, 1854.

Bilson (B.), The Hunters of Kentucky, etc. New York, 1847.

Biographical Sketches in S. José Pioneer, 1878-83.

Bird (Isabella L.), Lady's Life in the Rocky Mountains. New York, 1879-81.

Birnie (Robert), Personal Adventures. MS.

Black (George), Report on the Middle Yuba Canal. San Francisco, 1864.

Black (J. S.), Reports of Cases argued and determined in the Supreme Court of the United States. Washington, 1863,

Blaeu (or Jansz), America. (Atlas Maior). Amstelaedami, 1662.

Blagdon (Francis William). The Modern Geographer. London, n.d. 5 vols.

Blake (William P.), Geological Reconnaissance in California. New York, 1858. 4to; The Production of the Precious Metals. New York, etc. 1869.

Blanchet (F. N.), Historical Sketches of the Catholic Church in Oregon. Portland, 1878.

Bledsoe (A. J.), History of Del Norte County. Eureka, 1881.

Bliss (William R.), Paradise in the Pacific. New York, 1873.
Bluxome (Isaac), Vigilance Committee, by '33 Secretary.' MS.
B'nai B'rith. Various pamphlets of different lodges of the Society.
Bodega y Cuadra (Juan Francisco), Comento de la Navegacion, 1775. MS..
Bodega y Cuadra (Juan Francisco), Navegacion y Descubrimiento, 1779. MS.
Bodega y Cuadra (Juan Francisco), Segunda Salida, 1779. MS.
Bodega y Cuadra (Juan Francisco), Viage de 1775. MS.
Bodie, Chronicle, Free Press, Morning News, Standard, etc.
Boggs (William M.), Reminiscences from 1846. MS.
Boggs (William M.), Trip across the Plains in 1846. In Calistoga Tribune,
    1871; Napa Register, 1872.
Bojorges (Juan), Recuerdos sobre la Historia de California. MS.
Bolcof (José), Cartas de un Ruso. MS.
Bonilla (José Mariano), Documentos para la Historia de California. MS.
Bonilla (Mariano), Varias Cartas, 1834–47. MS. Archives, passim.
Bonner (T. D.), Life and Adventures of James P. Beckwourth. N. Y., 1858.
Bonnycastle (R. H.), Spanish America. London, 1818. 2 vols.
Bonwick (James), The Mormons and the Silver Mines. London, 1872.
Booth (Newton), Address, Aug. 8, 1868. San Francisco, 1868; also various
    addresses and letters.
Borbon, Parecer del Fiscal sobre el Proyecto de abrir Comunicacion entre
    California y N. Mexico, 1801. MS.
Borica (Diego), Castigos que han de sufrir los Indios, 1797. MS.
Borica (Diego), Correspondencia del Sr Gobernador, 1794–1800. MS.
Borica (Diego), Informe sobre comunicacion con N. Mexico, 1796. MS.
Borica (Diego), Informe de Nuevas Misiones, 1796. MS.
Borica (Diego), Instruccion de dirigir la fundacion de Branciforte, 1797. MS.
Borica (Diego), Instruccion para la escolta de S. Juan Bautista, 1797. MS.
Borica (Diego), Proyecto sobre Division de Californias, 1796. MS.
Boronda (José Canuto), Notas de California. MS.
Boronda (José E.), Apuntes Históricos. MS.
Borthwick (J. D.), Three Years in California. London, 1857.
Boscana (Gerónimo), Chinigchinich. New York, 1846. With Robinson (Alf.)
    Life in Cal.
Boscana (Gerónimo), Escritos Sueltos del Padre. MSS.
Boston (Mass.), Advertiser, Commercial Bulletin, Journal, Post, Traveller, etc.
Boston in the Northwest, Solid Men of. MS.
Botello (Narciso), Anales del Sur. MS.
Botello (Narciso), Comunicaciones Sueltas de un Angelino. MS.
Botica General de los Remedios Esperimentados. Sonoma, 1838.
Botta (P. E.), Observations sur les Habitans de la Californie. In Nouv. An.
    Voy., lii. 156.
Botta (P. E.), Osservazioni sugli Abitanti della California. In Duhaut Cilly,
    Viag.
Botts (C. T.), Address, Speech, etc.
Bouchacourt (Ch.), Notice Industrielle sur la Californie. Lyon, 1849.
Bouchard Affair, Testimonio de Prisioneros acerca de Insurgentes, 1818. MS.
Bound Home, or the Gold Hunter's Manual. New York, 1852.
Bowen (Asa M.), Statement on San Pascual, 1846. MS.
Bowers (Stephen), Santa Rosa Island. In Smithsonian Report, 1877.
Bowie (Aug. J.). Hydraulic Mining in California. San Francisco, 1878.
Bowie (Richard I.), Speech in U. S. H. of Rep., June 6, 1850, on the Califor-
    nian Question. Washington, 1850.
Bowles (Samuel), Across the Continent. Springfield, 1866; Our New West.
    Hartford, etc., 1869; The Pacific Railroad. Boston, 1869.
Boyer (Lanson), From the Orient to the Occident. New York, 1878.
Boynton (J. S.), Statement of a Pioneer. MS.
Brace (Charles Loring), The New West. New York, 1869.
Brackett (Albert G.), History of the U. S. Cavalry. New York, 1865.
Brackett (Albert G.), Indian War in California and Nevada, 1866-7. MS.

Brackett (Albert G.), List of Officers of California Battalion, 1846-7. MS.
Brackett (Albert G.), Sketch of 1st Regiment New York Volunteers. MS.
Brackett (Albert G.), Sketch of the Mormon Battalion. MS.
Branciforte (villa de), Dictámen del fiscal sobre fundacion, 1797. MS
Branciforte (villa de), El Discretorio de S. Fernando al Virey, 1797. MS.
Branciforte (villa de), Informe del Real Tribunal sobre la fundacion, 1795. MS.
Branciforte (Virey), Autorizacion para la fundacion de Nuevas Misiones, 1796. MS.
Branciforte (Virey), á Borica sobre Baterías de S. Francisco, 1795. MS.
Branciforte (Virey), Instruccion, 1794-7. MS.
Branciforte (Virey), Varios Oficios, 1794-8. MS.
Brands and Marks. MS. 1 vol. In Archivo de California.
Bray (Edmund), Memoir of a Trip to California, 1844. MS.
Breck, Speech in U. S. H. of Rep., March 25, 1850, on the Message of the President relating to California. Washington, 1850.
Breen (John), Pioneer Memoirs. MS.
Breen (Patrick), Diary of one of the Donner Party, 1846. MS.
Brereton (R. M.), Report on Messrs Bensley and Co.'s Canal Project, etc. San Francisco, 1872; other reports.
Brewerton (George D.), A Ride from Los Angeles to New Mexico. In Harper's Magazine. 1853. vol. vii.
Bribery, or the California Senatorial Election. San Francisco, 1868.
Briefe aus den Vereinigten Staaten. Leipzig, 1853. 2 vols.
Briefs of California Supreme Court and other courts, more than 5,000 in number, about 1,000 of which contain items of historical evidence, and over 100 of which are cited in my notes by the names of the cases. Not named in this list.
Briggs (C. P.), Narrative of 1846. In Napa Reporter, Aug. 31, 1872.
Bristow (E. L.), Rencounters with Indians, etc. MS.
Brock (Joseph M.), Recollections of '49. MS.
Brockett (L. P.), Our Western Empire. Philadelphia, etc., 1881.
Brodie (S. H.), Statement of Legal Matters. MS.
Brooklyn, Vidette.
Brooklyn (The) Mormons in California. From a newspaper.
Brooks (B. S.), Alcalde Grants in the City of San Francisco. In Pioneer. vol. i. 129.
Brooks (Charles Wolcott), Chinese in California. S. F., 1877; Early Migrations of Ancient Western Nations. S. F., 1876; Early Migrations, Origin of Chinese Race. S. F., 1876; Japanese Wrecks. S. F. 1876. Newspaper Reports of Papers on Origin of the Japanese Race. Scraps.
Brooks (H. S.), The California Mountaineer. San Francisco, 1861.
Brooks (J. Tyrwhitt), Four Months among the Gold-finders. London, 1849; New York, 1849; Paris, 1849; Vier maanden onder de Goudzoekers in Opper-Californie. Amsterdam, 1849; Vier Monate unter Goldfindern in Ober Kalifornien. Leipzig, 1849; Zürich, 1849.
Brooks (James), A Seven Months' Run. New York, 1872.
Brooks (N. C.), A Complete History of the Mexican War. Phil., 1849.
Brooks (R. S.), Speech in U. S. H. of Rep., June 14, 1854, on Pacific Railroad. Washington, 1854.
Bross (William), Address on Resources of Far West. Jan. 25, 1866. New York, 1866.
Brown (Charles), Early Events in California. MS.
Brown (Elam), An old Pioneer. In San José Pioneer, Jan. 26, 1878.
Brown (H. S.), Early Days of California. MS.
Browne (J. Ross), Address to the Territorial Pioneers of California. In S. F. News Letter, Sept. 11, 1875; Hubert H. Bancroft and his Literary Undertakings. In Overland Monthly; Lower Cal. See Taylor; Relacion de los Debates de la Convencion de California, Set. y Oct., 1849, Nueva York, 1851; Report of Debates in Convention of California. Sept. and Oct., 1849, Washington, 1850; Report upon the Mineral Resources of the States

and Territories West of the Rocky Mountains. Washington, 1867; Washington 1868; San Francisco, 1868; Reports upon the Mineral Resources of the United States. Washington, 1867; Resources of the Pacific Slope, etc., San Francisco, 1869.

Bryant (Edwin), Voyage en Californie, etc. Paris, n.d.; What I saw in California. New York, 1848; New York, 1849.

Bryant (William Cullen), History of the United States. New York, 1876–81. 4 vols.

Bucareli (Virey), Comunicaciones al Com. Gen. y Gob^{r.} de Cal., 1772–9. MS.

Bucareli (Virey), Instruccion al Comandante de Cal^{s.}, 1773. MS.

Bucareli (Virey), Instruccion del Virey. 17 Agosto, 1773. MS.

Bucareli (Virey), Instruccion del Virey. 30 Set., 1774. MS.

Bucareli (Virey), Providencias del Virey. 26 Mayo, 1773. MS.

Buchanan (James), Instructions of the Secretary of State to Thos. O. Larkin as Confidential Agent of the U. S., 1845. MS.

Buchanan (James), Instructions to Vorhies, Oct. 7. 1848. In Cal. and N. Mex., Mess. and Doc. 1850. p. 6.

Buelna (Antonio), Cartas de un Vecino de S. José. MS.

Buelna (Felix), Narracion sobre Tiempos Pasados. MS.

Buffalo (N. Y.), Courier.

Buffum (E. Gould), Six Months in the Gold Mines. Philadelphia, 1850; London, 1850.

Burnett (Peter H.), Recollections and Opinions of an Old Pioneer. N. Y., 1880.

Burnett (Peter H.), Recollections of the Past. MS. 2 vols.

Burney (James), Chronological History of the Discoveries in the South Sea, or Pacific Ocean. London, 1803–17. 4to. 5 vols.

Burns (Aaron), Statement of Vigilance Committee. MS.

Burr (H. T.), Chart showing Age, etc., of Officers of State and Members of Legislature, 1865–6. Sacramento, 1866.

Burris (Davis), Narrative. MS.

Burton (John), Official and Private Letters. MS.

Burton (Mrs M. A.), Biographical Sketch. MS.

Burton (Richard F.), City of the Saints, etc. London, 1861; N. Y., 1862.

Burton (Robert), The English Hero. London, 1687; London, 1710.

Bushnell (Horace), Characteristics and Prospects of California. San Francisco, 1858; Movement for a University in California, etc. San Francisco, 1857.

Bustamante (Anastasio), Escritos del Sr Presidente tocante á California, 1830–2. MS.

Bustamante (Cárlos María), Apuntes para la Historia del Gobierno del General Santa Anna. Mexico, 1841–3. MS. 3 vols.; also print. Mexico, 1845.

Bustamante (Cárlos María), Cuadro Histórico de la Revolucion Mexicana. Mexico, 1823–7. 5 vols.; Mexico, 1832-46. 6 vols.

Bustamante (Cárlos María), Diario de lo especialmente ocurrido en Mexico, Sept. de 1841 á Junio de 1843. Mexico, 1841–3. MS. 4to. 4 vols.

Bustamante (Cárlos María), Gabinete Mexicano. Mexico, 1839–41. MS. 4 vols.; also print. Mexico, 1842. 2 vols.

Bustamante (Cárlos María), Invasion de Mexico de los Anglo-Americanos. MS.

Bustamante (Cárlos María), Medidas para la Pacificacion de la América Mexicana. MS. 1820.

Bustamante (Cárlos María), El Nuevo Bernal Diaz del Castillo ó sea Historia de la Invasion de los Anglo-Americanos en Mexico. Mexico, 1847. 2 vols.

Bustamante (Cárlos María), Suplemento á Los Tres Siglos de Cavo. Jalapa, 1870.

Bustamante (Cárlos María), Voz de la Patria, Continuacion. Mexico, 1837–9. MS. 9 vols.

Butler (A. W.), Resources of Monterey County. San Francisco, 1875.

C (S.), Descripcion Topográfica de Misiones, 1845. In Revista Científ, i. 327.

Caballero (José de), Estadística del Estado Libre de Sonora y Sinaloa. MS.

Cabot (Juan), Expedicion al Valle de los Tulares, 1814. MS.
Cabot (Juan and Pedro), Cartas de dos Frailes. MS.
Cabrera Bueno (Joseph Gonzalez), Navegacion Especvlativa. Manila, 1734.
    folio.
Cabrillo (Juan Rodriguez), Relacion ó Diario. In Florida, Col. Doc., 173; also
    in Pacheco and Cárdenas, Col. Doc., xiv. 165. (Probably by Juan Paez.)
Cahuenga, Capitulacion de 13 de Enero, 1847. MS.
Caldwell (George Alfred), Speech in U. S. H. of Rep. June 7, 1850, on the
    California and Territorial Questions. Washington, 1850.
California, 1799, in Viagero Universal, xxvi.
California Academy of Sciences, Proceedings of the. S. F., 1858 et seq.
California Agriculturist. San José, 1871 et seq. 4to.
California, All about California. San Francisco, 1870; Id., 1873 and Supple-
    ment; Id., 1875 and Supplement.
California, Amount collected from customs. [31st Cong., 1st Sess., H. Ex.
    Doc. 72.] Washington, 1849.
California Anthropographic Chart, 1861 et seq.
California, Appeal in Behalf of the Church, Sept. 1849. New York, 1849.
California, Arrival of the Steamer. Festival in Celebration of the 25th
    Anniversary, Feb. 28, 1874. San Francisco, 1874.
California as it is. San Francisco, 1882.
California Associated Pioneers of the Territorial Days of Cal. in New York.
    Reunion 1875. New York, 1875.
California Bible Society, Annual Reports. San Francisco, 1850, et seq.
California, Biographical Sketches of the Delegates to Convention to frame
    New Constitution. 1878. San Francisco, 1878.
California Characters and Mining Scenes and Sketches. San Francisco, n.d.
California Claims. See Frémont.
California Colored Citizens, Proceedings of Annual Conventions. San Fran-
    cisco, 1856 et seq.
California, Compiled Laws by S. Garfielde and F. A. Snyder, 1850-3.
    Benicia, 1853.
California, Constitution, San Francisco, 1849; also in Spanish.
California, Correspondence relative to the Indian disturbances. [34th Cong.,
    1st Sess., Sen. Ex. Doc. 26.] Washington, 1855.
California, Correspondence and Reports of the Mexican Government, 1843-4.
    n.pl., n.d.
California Culturist. San Francisco, 1858-60. 3 vols.
California se declara Independiente de Mexico. Nov. 7, 1836. (Monterey,
    1836.)
California, Emigrants' Guide to. London, 1849,
California, Establecimiento y Progresos de las Misiones de la Antigua Cal-
    ifornia. In Doc. Hist. Mex., ser. iv., tom. iv.
California, Establishment of Mint and Light-houses. [31st Cong., 1st Sess.,
    H. Ex. Doc. 47.] Washington, 1850.
California, Fresh Water Tide Lands. San Francisco, 1869.
California Geological Survey. Philadelphia, etc., 1864; San Francisco, etc.,
    1867.
California, Gids naar. Amsterdam, 1849.
California Gold Regions, With a full account of the Mineral Resources,
    etc., New York (1849).
California Grape Culture. Report of Commissioners, San Francisco, 1862.
California, Hardy Impeachment. Sacramento, 1862.
California Homographic Chart, 1861 et seq.
California, Illustrated Hand-Book. London, 1870.
California Indians. Report relative to the Colonization of. [33d Cong., 2d
    Sess., Sen. Ex. Doc. 41.]
California, Industrial Interests of. San Francisco, 1862.
California Insurance Commissioners. Annual Reports. S. F., 1868 et seq.
California, Irrigation in San Joaquin and Tulare Plains. Sacramento, 1873.

California, Its Gold and its Inhabitants. London, 1856. 2 vols.

California, Its Past History; Its Present Position, etc. London, 1850.

California, Journals of Assembly and Senate, 1st to 24th sessions, 1850-81; with Appendices—103 volumes in all—containing all public documents printed by the state, which are cited in my notes by their titles and dates, the title consisting of 'California' followed by one of the following headings: Act; Adjutant-general's Report; Agricultural, Mining, and Mechanical Arts College, Reports; Assembly, Rules; Attorney-general, Reports; Bank Commissioners, Reports; Bribery Investigating Committee; Citizen's Hand Book; Common Schools, Acts, etc.; Corporations; Deaf, Dumb, and Blind Institute; Educational Directory; Electors; Fees and Salaries; Fisheries; Inaugural Addresses of Governors; Insane Asylum Reports; Insurance Commissioners; Land Acts; Laws; Memorials; Messages of Governors; Militia; Mines and Mining; Pioneer Silk Growers; Political Code Amendments; Public Lands; Revenue Laws; Sacramento River Drainage District; Sacramento Valley Irrigation and Navigation Canal; School Law; Secretary of State, Reports; Senate and Assembly Bills; Senate Standing and Joint Rules; Special Messages of Governors; State Agricultural Society, Transactions; State Board of Agriculture; State Board of Health; State Board of Equalization; State Capital Commissioners; State Controller, Annual Reports; State Documents; State Geologist, Reports; State Harbor Commissioners; State Library, Reports; State Mineralogist, Annual Reports; State Prison, Reports; State Reform School, Reports; State Superintendent of Public Instruction, Reports; State Teachers' Association; State Teachers' Institute; State Treasurer, Reports; Surveyor-general, Reports; Swamp and Overflowed Lands; Tide Lands; Transportation; Woman's Suffrage.

California, Journal of Education. San José, 1876 et seq.

California Labor Exchange. [Various publications.]

California Land Commission. Correspondence [32d Cong., 1st Sess., H. Ex. Doc. 131]; copy of Instructions [Id., Sen. Ex. Doc., 26]; list of cases in Hoffman's Reports.

California Land Titles, Copies of in U. S. Surveyor-general's Office, 1833-5.

California Land Titles. Remarks of Messrs. Phelps and Sargent in U. S. H. of Rep., June 10, 1862. Washington, 1862.

California, Last Night of the Session of the Legislature. Sacramento, 1854.

California Law Journal and Literary Review. San Francisco, 1862 et seq.

California, Legislative Sketches. Scraps, 1857.

California Legislature. Directory; Sketch Book, etc.

California, Leyes [statutes in Spanish]. Sacramento, 1859-68. 17 vols.

California Magazine and Mountaineer. San Francisco, 1864.

California Mail Bag. San Francisco, 1871 et seq.

California Medical Gazette. San Francisco, 1868 et seq.

California Medical Society, Transactions. Sacramento, 1857 et seq.

California, Memorial of Legislature to Congress on Dangers of Chinese Immigration. San Francisco, 1862.

California Mercantile Journal, 1860. San Francisco, 1860.

California, Message transmitting constitution. [31st Cong., 1st Sess., H. Ex., Doc. 39.] Washington, 1849.

California Nautical Magazine. San Francisco, 1862 et seq.

California, New Constitution. San Francisco, 1879.

California, Northern California, Scott and Klamath Rivers. Yreka, 1856.

California Northern Railroad, Engineers' Report of Surveys, 1859. Sacramento, 1859; other reports.

California, Notes on. New York, 1850.

California, Noticias. See Sales.

California Pacific Railroad Company, Articles and By-laws. Vallejo, 1868; various reports.

California Pioneers (Society of), Anniversaries; Constitution and By-laws; Grand Excursion; Inaugural Ceremonies; Oration and Poem; Reports, etc.

California Pioneers, Copy of Archives. MS.; Portraits in Library of the Society; Scrap-book.
California Pioneers, Sketches of Fifty. MS.
California Prison Commission, Annual Reports. San Francisco, 1866 et seq.
California, Project for Middle Class Colonies. n.pl., n.d.
California, Public Lands of. San Francisco, 1876.
California, Relief of Settlers in. [40th Cong., 2d Sess., H. Mis. Doc. 26.]
California, Reports of Cases in Supreme Court. San Francisco, etc., 1851-81. 58 vols.
California, Round Valley Indian Reservation. [43d Cong., 1st. Sess., H. Ex. Doc. 118.]
California Statistical Chart. Sacramento, Jan. 1, 1855.
California Statutes, 1st to 24th Sess. Sacramento, etc., 1850-81. 24 vols.
California Supreme Court Briefs. San Francisco, etc., 1852 et seq. See also Briefs.
California, Tarif de Douanes de la Californie, 1851. Paris, 1851. 4to.
California Teacher. San Francisco, 1863 et seq.
California Text Book. San Francisco, 1852.
California Volunteers, Correspondence Relative to the Discharge. [39th Cong., 1st. Sess., H. Ex. Doc. 138.] Washington, 1865 et seq.
California Wine, Wool, and Stock Journal. San Francisco, 1863 et seq.
California Workingmen's Party, An Epitome of its Rise and Progress. San Francisco, 1878.
California and New Mexico, Message and Documents, 1848. [30th Cong., 2d Sess., H. Ex. Doc. 1.] Washington, 1848.
California and New Mexico, Message and Documents, 1850. [31st Cong., 1st Sess., H. Ex. Doc. 17.] Washington, 1849.
Californian (The). San Francisco, 1880 et seq.
Californian. See Monterey Californian.
Californias, Reglamento Provisional. 1773. MS.
Californias, 'Junta de Fomento,' q. v.
Californie, Histoire Chrétienne. Plancy, 1851.
Californie, Ses Ressources Générales, etc. San Francisco, 1869.
Californien, Ausfuhrliche Mittheilungen über. San Francisco, 1870.
Californien, Authentische Nachrichten über. Bremen, 1849.
Californien, Rathgeber für Auswanderer nach. Bremen, 1849.
Californien und Seine Goldminen Mittheilungen aus der Geographie. Kreuznach, 1849.
Californien sein Minen-Bergbau, etc. Cassel, 1867.
Calistoga, Calistogan, Free Press, Independent Calistogan, Tribune.
Calleja (Virey), Comunicaciones al Gobr. de Cal., 1813-16. MS.
Calleja (Virey), Respuesta del Guardian al Virey sobre Proyectos de Cal., 1797. MS.
Calvary Presbyterian Church, Historical Sketch. San Francisco, 1869; Manual, etc.
Calvo (Charles), Recueil Complet des Traités de l'Amérique Latine. Paris, 1862-9. 16 vols.
Camden (William), Annales Rervm Anglicarvm et Hibernicarvm, etc. Londini, 1615-27. 2 vols.
Campaign of Los Angeles, 1847. In Monterey, Californian. Jan. 28, 1847.
Campbell, A Concise History of Spanish America. London, 1741.
Campbell (J. F.), My Circular Notes. London, 1876. 2 vols.
Campbell (J. H.), Speech in U. S. H. of Rep., Apr. 8, 1862, on Railroad to the Pacific. April, 1862. Washington, 1862.
Cancelada (Juan Lopez), Ruina de la Nueva España. Cádiz, 1811.
Cancelada (Juan Lopez), El Telégrafo Mexicano. Cádiz, 1813, et seq.
Cancelada (Juan Lopez), Verdad Sabida. Cádiz, 1811.
Cañizares (José), Diario de 1769. MS.
Capron (E. S.), History of California. Boston, 1854.
Cárcaba (Manuel), Informe del Habilitado General, 1797. MS.

Cárcaba (Manuel), Oficios del Habilitado General. MS.
Cardona (Nicolás), Memorial sobre sus descubrimientos, etc., en la California. In Pacheco and Cárdenas, Col. Doc., tom. ix. 42; Relacion del descubrimiento de California. In Id., tom. ix. 30.
Carmany (John H.), A Review of the Year 1866. San Francisco, 1867.
Carr (Ezra S.), The Patrons of Husbandry, etc. San Francisco, 1875.
Carr (John F.) See Anaheim, its People and its Products.
Carriger (Nicholas), Autobiography. MS.
Carrillo (Anastasio) Muchas Cartas del Comandante de Sta Bárbara, etc. MS.
Carrillo (Cárlos Antonio), Cartas del Diputado de Alta Cal., 1831-2. MS.
Carrillo (Cárlos Antonio), Cartas al General Vallejo. Dic. 1836. MS.
Carrillo (Cárlos Antonio), Correspondencia Miscelanea. MS.
Carrillo (Cárlos Antonio), Discurso al tomar el mando político en Los Angeles. 6 Dic. 1837. MS.
Carrillo (Cárlos Antonio), Exposicion sobre el Fondo Piadoso. Mexico, 1831.
Carrillo (Cárlos Antonio), Pedimento de Reos, 1814. MS.
Carrillo (Domingo), Cartas Sueltas. MS.
Carrillo (Domingo), Documentos para la Historia de California. MS.
Carrillo (Joaquin), Escritos en varios Archivos. MS.
Carrillo (José), Documentos para la Historia de California. MS.
Carrillo (José Antonio), Accion de S. Pedro contra los Americanos, 1846. MS.
Carrillo (José Antonio), Comunicaciones Varias del Diputado y Mayor General. MS.
Carrillo (Julio), Narrative. MS.
Carrillo (Mariano), Testamento é Inventario. 1782. MS.
Carrillo (Pedro C.), Documentos para la Historia de Cal. MS.
Carrillo (Raimundo), Los Edificios de Monterey, 1800. MS.
Carrillo (Raimundo), Instruccion que observará el Comandante de Escolta de Sta Inés. MS.
Carrillo (Raimundo), Papeles del Capitan, 1795 et seq. MS.
Carroll (Anna Ella), The Star of the West. New York, 1857.
Carroll (W.), Dr Scott, The Vigilance Committee and The Church. San Francisco, 1856.
Carson (J. H.), Early Recollections of the Mines, etc. Stockton, 1852.
Carson City (Nev.), Appeal, State Register.
Carvalho (S. N.), Incidents of Travel and Adventure in the Far West. New York, 1858.
Cary (Thomas G.), Gold from California, Lecture, March 25, 1856; The San Francisco Vigilance Committee. In Atlantic Monthly. vol. xl. Dec. 1877, 702.
Cassell's Emigrant Handy Guide to California. London, n.d.
Casserly (Eugene), The Issue in California. Letter, Aug. 27, 1861. San Francisco, 1861; Remarks, etc., for the cession to the C. P. R. R. of Cal. of one half of Goat Island. Wash., 1873; Speech on the Chinese Evil. Wash., 1870; and other speeches, etc.
Cassin (Francis), A Few Facts about California. MS.
Castañares (José María), Causa criminal contra...y Ildefonsa Gonzalez por adulterio, 1836. MS.
Castañares (José María), Causa seguida Contra Ana Gonzalez. Adulterio de J. M. Castañares y Alfonsa Gonzalez, 1836. MS.
Castañares (Manuel), California y sus Males, Exposicion 1844. In. Id., Col. Doc., 21.
Castañares (Manuel), Cartas del Administrador de la Aduana. MS.
Castañares (Manuel), Coleccion de Documentos relativos al departamento de Californias. Mexico, 1845.
Castillero (Andrés), Varias Cartas del Capitan y Comisionado. MS.
Castillo (Antonio del), Memoria sobre las Minas de Azogue de America. Mexico, 1871.
Castillo (Felipe), Itinerario desde Sonora hasta Cal., 1845. MS.
Castillo Negrete (Luis), Consejos al Comandante de Sta Bárbara, 1836. MS.

Castillo Negrete (Luis), Escritos del Juez de Distrito. MS.
Castillo Negrete (Luis), Exposicion que dirige el Juez de Distrito al Ayunt.
de Los Angeles sobre el Plan Revolucionario de Monterey, 1836. MS.
Castro (José), Correspondencia oficial y Particular del General, 1826–46. MS.
Castro (José), Decretos de la Diputacion erigida en Congreso Constituyente,
Nos. 1–10. Monterey, 1836.
Castro (José), El C——, Presidente de Congreso Constituyente. (Despacho
de Coronel Expedido á D. Juan B. Alvarado.) Monterey, 11 Dic., 1836.
Castro (José), Órden del Com. Gen. acerca de Emigrados de los E. U., 6 Nov.
1845. MS.
Castro (José), Proclama de 13 de Nov., 1836. Monterey.
Castro (Macario), Cartas del Sargento. MS.
Castro (Macario), Diario de su Expedicion á las Rancherías, 1799. MS.
Castro (Manuel), Carta á D. Pio Pico. Revolucion de Flores, 1847. MS.
Castro (Manuel), Cartas de un Prefecto. MS.
Castro (Manuel), Documentos para la Historia de California. MS. 2 vols.
Castro (Manuel), Informe en Sonora, 7 Junio, 1847. MS.
Castro (Manuel), Relacion de la Alta California. MS.
Castro (Manuel), Sus Servicios Públicos. MS.
Castro (Tiburcio), Papeles de un Juez y Prefecto. MS.
Castroville, Argus.
Catalá (Magin), Carta sobre Nootka, 1794. MS.
Catalá (Magin), Correspondencia del Misionero de Sta Clara. MS.
Catecismo político arreglado á la Constitucion de la Monarquía Española,
1812. MS.
Catholic World. New York, 1865 et seq.
Cauwet (Pierre) and Ch. Duquesnay. Lettres Californiennes. S. F., 1870.
Cavo (Andrés), Los Tres Siglos de Mexico. Mexico, 1836–8. 3 vols.; Mexico,
1852.
Ceballos (Ramon), XXIV. Capítulos en Vindicacion de Méjico. Mad. 1856.
Cedulario, A Collection mostly MSS. folio. 3 vols.
Central Pacific Railroad Company, Annual Reports, By-laws, numerous
pamphlets.
Cerruti (Enrique), Historical Note-books, 1821–46. MS. 5 vols.
Cerruti (Enrique), Ramblings in California. MS.
Cevallos. De el Señor Cevallos, de la situacion actual, del Plan de Jalisco, y
del Gen. Uraga. Mexico, 1853.
Chamberlain (Charles H.), Statement. MS.
Chamberlain (John), Memoirs of California since 1840. MS.
Chamberlain (W. H), and Harry L. Wells. See Yuba County History.
Chamisso (Louis Charles A. von), Adelbert von Chamisso's Werke. Vierte
Auflage. Berlin, 1856. 6 vols.; Reise, included in preceding; Remarks
and Opinions. In Kotzebue's Voy., ii., iii.
Champagnac (Jean B. Joseph), Le jeune Voyageur en Californie. Paris, 1852.
Chandless (William), A Visit to Salt Lake. London, 1857.
Chapin (E, R.), Reminiscences of a Surgeon. MS.
Charton (Édouard), Le Tour du Monde. Paris, etc., 1861. 4to. 2 vols.
Chevalier (Michel), On the Probable Fall in the Value of Gold. New York,
1859.
Chicago (Ill.), Post, Times, Tribune, etc.
Chico, Butte County Press, Butte County Record, Caucasian, Evening
Record, Index, Northern Enterprise, Review, etc.
Chico (Mariano), Alocucion del Gobr. á la Junta Dept. 1 Junio 1836. MS.
Chico (Mariano), El C—— Comandante General y Gefe Político de Alta Cal.
á sus Habitantes. Monterey, Julio 24, 1836.
Chico (Mariano), El C…Gefe Superior Político etc. á sus Habitantes. Mon-
terey, 11 Mayo 1836.
Chico (Mariano), Discurso pronunciado 20 de Mayo. Monterey, 1836.
Chico (Mariano), Discurso pronunciado 27 de Mayo. Monterey, 1836.
Chico (Mariano), Escritos del Gobernador, 1836. MS.

Chico (Mariano), Dos Palabras sobre Memoria del Ex. Gobernador Doblado. Guanajuato, 1847.
Chiles (Joseph B.), Visit to California in 1841. MS.
Chinese in California; Coolie Trade; Immigration; Question; Testimony; etc. Many pamphlets.
Choate (D.) and E. W. Moore. See San Diego and Southern California.
Choris (Louis), Voyage Pittoresque autour du Monde. Paris, 1822. folio.
Chronicle Annual. San Francisco, 1882.
Churches. See Institutions.
Cincinnati (O.), Commercial, Enquirer, Times, etc.
Civil Service Reform Association of California, Purposes of. San Francisco, 1881; other pamphlets.
Clark (Francis D.), A Pioneer of 1847. In S. José Pioneer, July 5, 1879; Roll of Survivors of the 1st Regiment of New York Volunteers. N. Y. 1874.
Clark (Galen), Reminiscences of the Old Times. MS.
Clark (Hiram C.), Statement of Facts from 1851. MS.
Clark (Mrs), Antipodes and Around the World. London, 1870.
Clark (Samuel), Life and Death of Sir Francis Drake. London, 1761. 4to.
Clarke (Asia Booth), The Elder and the Younger Booth. Boston, 1882.
Clarke (Charles E.), Speech on Admission of California in U. S. H. of Rep., May 13, 1850. Wash. 1850; Speech on California Claims in U. S. Sen., Apr. 25, 1848. Wash. 1848.
Claudet (F. G.), Gold. New Westminster, 1871.
Clavigero (Francisco Saverio), Storia della California. Venezia, 1789. 2 vols.
Clemens (J.), California Territorial Governments. Speech in U. S. Sen., May 16 and 20, 1850. Washington, 1850.
Cleveland (Chauncey F.), Speech in U. S. H. of Rep., Apr. 19, 1850...Constitution of California. Washington, 1850.
Cleveland (Richard J.), Narrative of Voyages. Cambridge, 1842. 2 vols.; Boston, 1850.
Clippings from the California Press in regard to Steam across the Pacific. San Francisco, 1860.
Cloverdale, News, Reveille.
Clubs. See Institutions.
Clyman (James), Diary of Overland Journey, 1844-6. MS.
Clyman (James), Note Book, 1844-6. MS.
Coast Review. San Francisco, 1871-80. 15 vols.
Codman (John), The Round Trip. New York, 1879.
Coffey (Titian J.), Argument against McGarrahan's Claim. n.pl., n.d.
Coignet (M.), Rapport sur les Mines de New Almaden. Paris, 1866.
Coke (Henry J.), A Ride over the Rocky Mountains to Oregon and California. London, 1852.
Cole (Cornelius), Australian Mail Line. Speech in U. S. Sen. July 9, 1870. Washington. n.d.; and various Speeches.
Cole (R. Beverly), Statement on Vigilance Committee in San Francisco. MS.
Cole (William L.), California—Its Scenery, Climate, etc. New York, 1871.
Coleccion de Documentos Inéditos para la Historia de España. Madrid, 1842-80. 71 vols. [S. F. Law Library.]
Colegio Seminario de María Santísima de Guadalupe de Sta Inés. Constituciones. MS.
Coleman (William T.), Vigilance Committee of '56. MS.
Colfax (Nev.), Enterprise.
College of California. Oration and Poem; and various pamphlets.
Colonial Magazine. London, 1840 et seq.
Colonizacion, Cédula Real confirmando el Reglamento del Gob.r Neve 1781. MS.
Colton, Advocate, Semi-tropic.
Colton (Walter), Correspondence, 1876-7. MS.
Colton (Walter), Deck and Port. New York, 1850; New York, 1860; The Land of Gold. New York, 1860; Three Years in California. New York, 1850.

Columbia, Citizen, Clipper, 1854, Gazette, 1854, Herald, Mining Dist.
    Gazette, Muggins, 1854, News, Star, Times, Indept. Republic, etc.
Colusa, Independent, Sun.
Colusa County Annual. Colusa, 1878.
Colusa County, History. San Francisco, 1880. folio.
Colvin (Thomas W.), Life of a Pioneer. MS.
Combier (C.), Voyage au Golfe de Californie. Paris, n.d.
Commercial, Financial, and Mining Interests of California. Review for 1876.
    San Francisco, 1877.
Compañía Asiático-Mexicana, Plan y Reglamento, 1825. In Junta de Fo-
    mento de Cal.
Compañía Extrangera de Monterey, Cuaderno de órdenes, 1832. MS.
Companies, Mining, Agricultural, Commercial, etc. See Institutions.
Comstock (A. M.), Statement on Vigilance Committee. MS.
Cone (Mary), Two Years in California. Chicago, 1876.
Conferencia celebrada en el Presidio de S. Francisco entre Sola, Kotzebue, y
    Coscof, 1816. MS.
Congressional Debates [18th to 25th Congress]. Wash. 1824 et seq. 14 vols.
Congressional Globe. Washington, 1836 et seq. 4to.
Congressional Speeches. A Collection.
Conklin (E.), Picturesque Arizona. New York, 1878.
Connor (John), Early California Recollections. MS.
Conquest of California, A very large number of newspaper accounts.
Conquest of California, 1846-7 Various Items and Reports. In Niles' Reg-
    ister, lxxi.–iii. See index, 'Cal.,' 'Kearney,' 'Frémont,' 'Stockton.'
Consejo General de Pueblos Unidos de Cal., Bando de Mayo 13, 1846. MS.
Constitucion Española de 1812, Bandos del Virey sobre su jura, 1820. MS.
Constitutional Convention, Declaration of Rights. Autograph of Members,
    1849.
Contemporary Biography of California's Representative Men. San Francisco,
    1881. 4to. 2 vols.
Conversation, Practical and Philosophical, on the Subject of Currency. San
    Francisco, 1865.
Conway (John), Early Days in California. MS.
Cooke (Philip St Geo.), Conquest of New Mexico and California. New York,
    1878; Journal from Santa Fé to San Diego. [30th Cong., Spec. Sess.,
    Sen. Doc. 2.] Washington, 1849; Scenes and Adventures in the Army.
    Philadelphia, 1857.
Coon (H. P.), Annals of San Francisco. MS.
Cooper (De Guy), Resources of San Luis Obispo County. San Francisco, 1875.
Cooper (Ellwood), Forest Culture, etc. San Francisco, 1876.
Cooper (John B. R.), Accounts, 1827. MS.
Cooper (John B. R.), Cartas Miscelaneas de un Navegante, 1824 et seq. MS.
Cooper (John B. R.), Log of the California, 1839-42. MS.
Copper City, Pioneer.
Copperopolis, Courier.
Córdoba (Alberto), Cartas del Ingeniero, 1796-8. MS.
Córdoba (Alberto), Informe acerca del Sitio de Branciforte, 1796. MS.
Córdoba (Alberto), Informe al Virey sobre Defensas de Cal., 1796. MS.
Cornwallis (Kinahan), The New El Dorado. London, 1858.
Coronel (Antonio F.), Cosas de California. MS.
Coronel (Antonio F.), Documentos para la Historia de California. MS.
Coronel (Ignacio), Cartas de un Maestro de Escuela, 1834 et seq. MS.
Correo Atlántico (El). Mexico, 1835 et seq.
Correo de la Federacion. Mexico, 1826 et seq. folio.
Correspondencia de Misiones. MS.
Cortambert (Richard), Peuples et Voyageurs contemporains. Paris, 1864.
Cortés (Hernan), Auto de Posesion. In Col. Doc. Inéd., tom. iv.; Cartas;
    Historia de N. España; Memorial. In Col. Doc. Inéd., iv.; and Different
    works, as cited in my Hist. Mex.

Corwin (Moses B.), Speech in U. S. H. of Rep., Apr. 9, 1850, to Admit California. Washington, 1850.
Cosmopolitan Monthly. San Francisco, 1874 et seq.
Costansó (Miguel), Diario Histórico de los Viages de mar y tierra hechos al norte de California. Mexico, 1776.
Costansó (Miguel), Historical Journal of the Expeditions by Sea and Land to the North of California. London, 1790.
Costansó (Miguel), Informe sobre el Proyecto de fortificar los Presidios de Cal. 1794. MS. In Pinart, Col. Doc. Mexico.
Cota (Pablo), Diario de Exploracion, 1798. MS.
Cota (Guillermo, Leonardo, Manuel, Pablo, and Valentin), Varias cartas. MS.
Cota (Valentin), Documentos para la Historia de California. MS.
Coulter (John), Adventures on the Western Coast. London, 1847. 2 vols.
Coulter (Thomas), Notes on Upper California, 1835. In Lond. Geog. Soc., Jour., v. 59.
County registers, poll-lists, laws and regulations, and other official publications, cited by name of county but not named in this list.
Courts. See Institutions.
Coutts (Cave J.), Diary of a March to California in 1848. MS.
Covarrubias (José María), Correspondencia del Secretario. MS.
Cox (Isaac), Annals of Trinity County. San Francisco, 1858.
Coxe (Daniel), Description of Carolana. London, 1722; other editions.
Coyner (David H.), The Lost Trappers. Cincinnati, 1859.
Cram (Thomas J.), Report on the Oceanic routes to Cal., Nov. 1856. [34th Cong., 3d Sess., Sen. Ex. Doc. 51.] Washington, 1856; Topographical Memoir on the Department of the Pacific. [35th Cong., 2d Sess., H. Ex. Doc. 114.] Washington, 1859.
Crane (James M.), The Past, Present, and Future of the Pacific. San Francisco, 1856.
Crary (Oliver B.), Statement on Vigilance Committee in San Francisco. MS.
Crescent City, Courier, Herald, 1854, Del Norte Record.
Crespí (Juan), Diario de la Expedicion de Mar., 1774. In Palou, Not., i. 624.
Crespí (Juan), Diario del registro de San Francisco, 1772. In Palou, Not., i. 481.
Crespí (Juan), Primera Espedicion de Tierra al Descubrimiento del Puerto de San Diego, 1769. In Palou, Not., ii. 93.
Crespí (Juan), Viage de la espedicion de tierra de San Diego á Monterey, 1769. In Palou, Not., i. 285.
Croix (Teodoro), Comunicaciones del Com. Gen. de Provincias Internas al Gobr. de Cal., 1777 et seq. MS. In Prov. St. Pap., i.-iv. and other archives.
Croix (Teodoro), Disposiciones para la Guerra á los Yumas, 1782. MS.
Croix (Teodoro), Instruccion sobre Donativos en California para la Guerra con Inglaterra, 1781. MS.
Croix (Teodoro), Instrucciones al Capitan Rivera, 1779. MS.
Cronise (Titus Fey), Natural Wealth of California. San Francisco, 1868; Id. with illustrations and corrections.
Crosby (E. O.), Events in California. MS.
Crowell (J.), Speech in U. S. H. of Rep. June 3, 1850, on Admission of California. Washington, 1850.
Cuesta. See 'Arroyo de la Cuesta.'
Currey (John), Incidents in California. MS.
Cutter (D. S.) See Directories. Sacramento, 1860.
Cutts (James Madison), Conquest of California and N. Mexico. Phila., 1847.

Dall (Caroline H.), My First Holiday. Boston, 1881.
Dall (W. H.), Lords of the Isles. In Overland Monthly, xii. 522.
Dalles (Or.), Mountaineer, Oregon Republican.
Dally (Henry J.), Narrative from 1840. MS.
Dameron (James P.), Autobiography and Writings. San Francisco, 1877.
Dampier (Wm.), New Voyage round the World. London, 1699-1709. 4 vols.

Dana (C. W.), The Great West. Boston, 1861.
Dana (David D.), The Fireman. Boston, 1858.
Dana (Richard H., Jr.), Two Years before the Mast. New York, 1840; New York, 1857; Boston, 1873; Boston, 1880.
Dana (William G.), Letters of a Trader. MS.
Dana (Guillermo G.), and Vicente Moraga, Lista de Extrangeros en Sta Bárbara, 1836. MS.
Dantí (Antonio), Diario de un Reconocimiento de la Alameda, 1795. MS.
Dartin (V.), Reflecciones á los Californios é Hispano-Americanos. San Francisco. [1864.]
Daubenbiss (John), Biographical Sketches. In S. José Pioneer, Mar. 23, 1878.
Davidson (George), Biography and Essay on Irrigation. MS.
Davidson (George), Coast Pilot of California, etc. Washington, 1869.
Davidson (George), Directory for the Pacific Coast. Washington, 1868.
Davis (Horace), An open Letter to. San Francisco, 1880; and various speeches.
Davis (John), World's Hydrographical Description. London, 1595.
Davis (William H.), Business Correspondence. MS.
Davis (William H.), Glimpses of the Past in California. MS. 2 vols.
Davisville, Advertiser.
D'Avity (Pierre), Le Monde ou la Description Generale, etc. Paris, 1637. folio. 5 vols.
Dean (Peter), Occurrences in California. MS.
De Bow (J. D. B.), De Bow's Review and Industrial Resources. New Orleans, etc., 1854-7. 7 vols.; Encyclopedia of Trade and Commerce of the U. S. London, 1854. 2 vols.
Decreto del Congreso Mejicano sobre Colonizacion, 18 Agosto 1824. MS.
Decreto del Congreso Mejicano, secularizando las Misiones. 17 Agosto 1833. In Arrillaga, Recop. 1833, p. 19.
Decreto de las Córtes, 4 Enero 1813, Secularizacion. MS.; also in Mexico, Leyes Vigentes 1879, p. 56; Dwinelle's Col. Hist. Add. 20.
Deer Lodge (Mont.), Independent.
Degroot (Henry), The Donner Party. In Overland Monthly, v. 38.
Del Mar (Alexander), A History of the Precious Metals. London, 1880.
Delano (Amasa), The Central Pacific Railroad, or '49 and '69. San Francisco, 1868; Life on the Plains, etc. New York, 1861; Old Block's Sketch Book. Sacramento, 1856; Penknife Sketches. Sacramento, 1853.
Delessert, Les Mines. In Revue des Deux Mondes. Feb. 1, 1849.
Del Norte County, History of. See Bledsoe, A. J.
Demarcacion y Division de las Indias. In Pacheco and Cárdenas, Col. Doc., xv. 409.
Democratic Members of Legislature of California. Address of the Majority Feb. 1854. San Francisco, 1854.
Democratic State Convention, Proceedings Feb. 1852. Sacramento, 1852.
Dempster (C. J.), Vigilance Committee. MS.
Den (Nicolás A.), Letters of a Pioneer Doctor. MS.
Dent, Vantine, and Co., Claim for Supplies to Indians in California, 1851-2. Washington, n. d.
Departmental Records. MS. 14 vols. In Archivo de Cal.
Departmental State Papers. MS. 20 vols. In Archivo de Cal.; Id., Angeles. 12 vols.; Id., Benicia. 5 vols.; Id., Benicia Custom-house. 8 vols.; Id., Benicia Com. and Treas. 5 vols.; Id., Benicia Prefecturas y Juzgados. 6 vols.; Id., Benicia Military. vols. 53 to 87; Id., Monterey. 8 vols.; Id., San José. 7 vols.
Derby (E. H.), The Overland Route to the Pacific. Boston, 1869.
Derby (G. H.), and R. S. Williamson. Reports on Geology and Topography of California. [31st Cong., 1st Sess., Sen. Ex. Doc. 47.] Wash., 1850.
De Rupert (A. E. D.), Californians and Mormons. New York, 1881.
Diaz del Castillo (Bernal), Historia Verdadera de la Conquista de la Nueva España. Madrid, 1632. 4to.

Diccionario Universal de Historia y de Geografía. Mexico, 1853. 4to. 10 vols.; Madrid, 1846-50. 4to. 8 vols.

Dickinson (John R.), Speeches, Correspondence, etc. New York, 1867. 2 vols.

Dictámen sobre Instrucciones al Gob^{r.} de Californias 1825. In Junta de Fomento de Cal.

Digger's Handbook (The), and Truth about California. Sydney, 1849.

Dilke (Charles Wentworth), Greater Britain. Philadelphia, 1869. 2 vols.

Diputacion de la Alta California (La Ecsma.), á sus Habitantes. Monterey, 6 Nov., 1836.

Directories, Los Angeles; Marysville, Amy; Nevada Co., Bean; Nevada and Grass Valley, Thompson; Oakland, Stillwell; Pacific Coast Business, Langley; Placer County, Steele; Placerville, Fitch; Sacramento, Colville; San Francisco, Bishop, Colville, Gazlay, Harris, Bogardus and Labatt, Judicial, Kimball, Langley, Larkin and Belden, Le Count and Strong, Morgan, Parker, Potter; San Francisco, California, and Nevada; San José, Bishop, Colahan and Pomeroy; San Joaquin County, Berdine; Santa Clara; Solano; Stockton, Bogardus; Tuolumne County, Heckendorn and Wilson; Vallejo, Kelley and Prescott; Watsonville.

Disturnell (J.), Influence of Climate. New York, 1867.

Dittmann (Carl), Narrative of a Seafaring Life from 1844. MS.

Dix (John A.), Speeches and Occasional Addresses. New York, 1864. 2 vols.

Dixon, Tribune.

Dixon (William Hepworth), The White Conquest. London, 1876. 2 vols.

Doctrina para los Padres de Familia. Carta de una Novia de Moda á su futuro. [En verso.] Sonoma [1838].

Documens sur l'Histoire de Californie. In Petit-Thouars, Voy., iv.

Documentos para la Historia. 1846-8. In Los Angeles, Southern California.

Documentos para la Historia de California. MS. 4 vols.

Documentos para la Historia de Mexico. Mexico, 1853-7. 20 vols. 4 series, serie iii., in folio and in four parts.

Domenech (Emmanuel), Seven Years' Residence in the Great Deserts of North America. London, 1860. 2 vols.

Dominguez (Manuel), Escritos de un Ranchero y Prefecto. MS.

Dominguez (Francisco A.), and Silvestre V. Escalante, Diario y derrotero para descubrir el camino de Santa Fé, etc. In Doc. Hist. Mex., serie ii., i. 377.

Donnat (Léon), L'État de Californie en 1877-8. Paris, 1878.

Doolittle (William G.), Journey to San Francisco. MS.

D'Orbigny (Alcide), Voyage Pittoresque dans les deux Amériques. Paris, 1836.

Douglas, Speech in U. S. Sen. June 26, 28, 1850, Public Lands in California. Washington, 1850.

Douglas (David), Letter to Hartnell, 1833. MS.

Douglas (Sir James), Private Papers. 1st and 2d series. MS. 2 vols.; Voyage from the Columbia to Cal., 1841. MS. In Id. Journal.

Douglas City, Trinity Gazette.

Dowell (B. F.), Journal and Letters. MS.

Downey City, Courier, Los Nietos Valley Courier.

Downieville, Democrat, Mountain Messenger, Sierra Advocate, Sierra Age, Sierra County News, Sierra Democrat, Standard, etc.

Dows (James), Statement of Vigilance Committee in San Francisco. MS.

Doyle (John T.), Address at Inauguration of New Hall of Santa Clara College, Aug. 9, 1870. S. F., 1870; Address on the Railroad Policy of California. S. F., 1873; Brief History of the Pious Fund of California. n.pl., n.d.; Memorandum as to the Discovery of the Bay of San Francisco. Worcester, 1874.

Drake (Francis), Drie Voornaame Zee-Togten. In Aa, Naauk. Vers. xviii.; The Famous Voyage. In Hakluyt's Voy., iii.; —Francis Drake Revived. n.pl. [1630]; The World Encompassed. London, 1628. 4to; The World Encompassed [Hakluyt Soc. ed.] London, 1854.

Drama, Copy of a Spanish Drama of 1789. MS.
Druids, Proceedings at Annual Sessions; other pamphlets.
Duarte (Mariano), Causa Criminal contra el Alcalde de S. José, 1831. MS.
Du Hailly (Édouard), Les Américains sur le Pacifique. In Revue des Deux Mondes, Feb. 1859.
Duhaut-Cilly (A.), Viaggio intorno al Globo. Torino, 1841. 2 vols.; Voyage autour du Monde. Paris, 1835.
Dumetz (Francisco), Cartas del Padre Misionero, 1771–1811. MS.
Dunbar (Edward E.), Romance of the Age. New York, 1867.
Duncan, (L. J. C.), Settlement in Southern Oregon. MS.
Dunne's Notes on San Pascual, 1846. MS.
Dunraven (Earl of), The Great Divide. New York, 1876.
Duran (Narciso), Carta al Gobr. Chico, 15 Junio, 1836. MS.
Duran (Narciso), Correspondencia de un Misionero y Presidente. MS.
Duran (Narciso), Crítica sobre las Prevenciones de Emancipacion, 1833. MS.
Duran (Narciso), Informe del Actual Estado de las Misiones, 1844. MS.
Duran (Narciso), Notas á una Circular ó Bando de Echeandía, 1833. MS.
Duran (Narciso), Notas y Comentarios al Bando de Echeandía sobre Misiones, 1831. MS.
Duran (Narciso), Proyectos de Secularizacion, 1833. MS.
Durkee (John L.), Statement on Vigilance Committees in San Francisco. MS.
Dutch Flat, Enquirer, Forum.
Dutch Flat Swindle (The Great). S. F. n. d.
Dwinelle (John W.), Address before the Pioneers. 1866. S. F. 1866; Colonial History of San Francisco. S. F. 1863; S. F. 1867; [Drake's Voyage, a Review of Bryant's Hist. U. S.] In S. F. Bulletin, Oct. 5, 1878; Oration. Oct. 8, 1876. In San Francisco, Cent. Mem., 81.
Dye (Job F.), Pioneer Recollections. In Sta Cruz Sentinel, 1869; Pioneer Scrap-book; Recollections of California. MS.

Eardley-Wilmot (S.), Our Journal in the Pacific. London, 1873.
Earll (John O.), Statement of 1849. MS.
Earliest Printing in California. A Collection of all documents printed before 1848.
Earthquake. The Great Earthquake in San Francisco S. F. 1868.
Eaton (Henry), Pioneer of 1838. MS.
Echeandía (José María), Bando sobre Elecciones, 1828. MS.
Echeandía (José María), Carta que dirige á D. José Figueroa en defensa de lo que ha hecho para secularizar las Misiones, 1833. MS.
Echeandía (José María), Decreto de Emancipacion á favor de los Neófitos, 1826. MS.
Echeandía (José María), Decreto de Secularizacion, 6 Enero, 1831. MS.
Echeandía (José María), Escritos Sueltos del Com. General, 1825–33. MS.
Echeandía (José María), Plan para Convertir en Pueblos las Misiones, 1829–30. MS.
Echeandía (José María), Reglamento para los Encargados de Justicia en las Misiones, 1833. MS.
Echeandía (José María), Reglamento de Secularizacion, 18 Nov. 1832. MS.
Echeveste (Juan José), 'Reglamento,' q.v.
Eco de España. Mexico, 1853–4.
Eco Nacional. Mexico, 1857–8.
Eco de Occidente. Guaymas, 1878 et seq.
Edelman (George W.), Guide to the Value of California Gold. Phil., 1850.
Edinburgh Review. Edinburgh, 1802 et seq.
Edwards (Philip L.), Diary of a Visit to Cal., 1837. MS.
Eliot de Castro (Juan), Papeles Tocantes á su arrestacion, 1815. MS.
Elliot (George H.), The Presidio of San Francisco. In Overland, iv. 336.
Ellis (George E.), The Red Man and the White Man. Boston, 1882.
Emory (W. H.), Notes of a Military Reconnaissance. [30th Cong., 1st Sess., Sen. Ex. Doc. 7.] Washington, 1848.
Escalante (Sylvestre Velez), Carta de 28 de Octubre, 1775. MS.

Escandon (Manuel), and José D. Rascon, Observaciones, Fondo Piadoso. Mexico, 1845.
Escobar (Agustin), Campaña de 1846. MS.
Escobar (Marcelino), Cartas de un Alcalde. MS.
Escudero (José Agustin), Memorias del Diputado de Chihuahua. Mexico, 1848.
Escudero (José Agustin), Noticias Estadísticas de Chihuahua. Mexico, 1837.
España, Constitucion de 1812. MS.
Españoles, Lista de los—que han prestado Juramento, 1828. MS.
Espinosa (Clemente), Apuntes Breves y Notas Históricas. MS.
Espinosa (Rafael), Estudios Históricos. In Soc. Mex. Geog., Bol., v. 429.
Esplandian, Sergas of. 1510, and later editions.
Establecimientos Rusos en California, 1812–41. MS.
Estell (James M.), Speech in Hall of Rep. Sac^to in connection with Vigilance Committee. n.pl. 1857.
Esténega (Tomás), Cartas del Padre Misionero. MS.
Estrada (José Mariano), Correspondencia desde 1783. MS.
Estrada (José Ramon), Comunicaciones Varias. MS.
Estrada (José Ramon), Lista de Extrangeros en Monterey, 1829. MS.
Estudillo (José María), Datos Históricos. MS.
Estudillo (José Joaquin), Documentos para la Historia de Cal. MS. 2 vols.
Estudillo (José María), Hojas de Servicio. MS.
Estudillo (José María), Informe sobre los Frailes, 1820. MS.
Estudillo (José María), Informe sobre Oficios de Capellan, 1820. MS.
Estudillo (José María and José Antonio), Cartas del Padre é Hijo. MS.
Etholin, Letter on Ross, 1841. MS.
Eureka, Democratic Standard, Evening Herald, Evening Star, Humboldt Bay Journal, Humboldt Times, National Index, Northern Independent, Signal, West Coast Signal.
Evangelist (The), San Francisco, 1872 et seq.
Evans (Albert S.), À la California. San Francisco, 1873.
Evans (George M.), A History of the Discovery of Gold in California. In Hunt's Merchants' Mag., xxxi. 385.
Evans (Richard S.) and H. W. Henshaw, Translation, Voyage of Cabrillo. In U. S. Geog. Surv., Wheeler, vii., Arch., 293.
Expediente sobre el modo de dividirse las misiones, 1770. MS.
Expediente sobre las Enfermedades de la Tierra, 1805. MS.
Expediente sobre Recíprocas Quejas del Gobernador y Religiosos, 1787. MS.
Expulsion of Citizens of the U. S. from Upper Cal. President's Mess. [28th Cong., 1st Sess., Sen. Doc. 390.] Wash., 1843.
Ezquer (Ignacio), Memorias de Cosas Pasadas. MS.

Fabian (Bentham), Agricultural Lands of California. San Francisco, 1869.
Fac-símiles de Firmas Californianas. MS.
Facultad de Confirmar, 1781. MS.
Fages (Pedro), Comentario sobre el Informe del Capitan Soler, 1787. MS.
Fages (Pedro), Correspondencia del Comandante y Gob^r., 1781 et seq. MS.
Fages (Pedro), Informe sobre Comercio con Buques de China, 1787. MS.
Fages (Pedro), Informe General de Misiones, 1787. MS.
Fages (Pedro), Informes Particulares al Gob^r. Romeu, 1791. MS.
Fages (Pedro), Instruccion para el Cabo de Escolta de Angeles, 1787. MS.
Fages (Pedro), Instruccion para la Escolta de Purísima, 1788. MS.
Fages (Pedro), Instruccion para la Escolta de S. Miguel, 1787. MS.
Fages (Pedro), Instruccion para su Viage á California, 1769. MS.
Fages (Pedro), Instrucciones al Comandante Interino de Monterey, 1783. MS.
Fages (Pedro), Papel de Varios Puntos. 1791. MS.
Fages (Pedro), Representacion Contra los Frailes, 1785. MS.
Fages (Pedro), Voyage en Californie, 1769. In Nouv. An. Voy., ci.
Fair (Laura D.), Official Report of the Trial. San Francisco, 1871.
Fairchild (John A.), Sketch of Life. MS.
Family Defender Magazine. Oakland, 1881 et seq.

Farnham (Eliza W.), California. In-Doors and Out. New York, 1856.
Farnham (J. T. or Thos. J.), Early Days of California. Phil., 1860; Life, Adventures and Travels in Cal. Pictorial ed. N. Y., 1857; Life, Adventures, and Travels in Cal. N. Y., 1846; N. Y., 1849; N. Y., 1850; N. Y., 1853; Travels in the Californias. N. Y., 1844.
Farwell (James D.), Statement of Vigilance Committees in S. F. MS.
'Far West,' Letters from California. In Honolulu Friend, Nov.–Dec., 1846.
Fay (Caleb T.), Historical Facts on California. MS.
Fédix (P. A.), L'Orégon et les côtes de l'Océan Pacifique. Paris, 1846.
Fernandez (José), Cosas de California. MS.
Fernandez (José), Documentos para la Historia de California. MS.
Fernandez (José Zenon), Cartas Sueltas. MS.
Fernandez (Manuel), Carta del Padre Ministro de Sta Cruz, 1798. MS.
Fernandez de San Vicente (Agustin), Comunicaciones del Canónigo, 1822. MS.
Ferry (Hypolite), Description de la Nouvelle Californie. Paris, 1850.
Fidalgo (Salvador), Tabla de Descubrimientos de 1790. MS.
Fidalgo (Salvador), Viage de 1790. MS.
Field (Stephen J.), Personal Reminiscences of Early Days. n.pl., n. d.; Some Account of the Work of. n.pl., 1881.
Figueroa (José), Anuncia á los Californios su llegada, 16 Enero, 1833. [The first specimen of California printing.]
Figueroa (José), Bando contra Híjar, 1834. MS.
Figueroa (José), Bando en que publica la Resolucion de la Diputacion contra Híjar, 1834.
Figueroa (José), Correspondencia del Gefe Político, 1832-5. MS.
Figueroa (José), Cosas Financieras de California, 1834. MS.
Figueroa (José), Discurso de Apertura de la Diputacion, 1834. MS.
Figueroa (José), El Comandante General, etc., á los Habitantes del Territorio. Monterrey, 16 Marzo, 1835.
Figueroa (José), El Comandante General y Gefe Político de Alta Cal. á sus Habitantes. Monterey, 1835.
Figueroa (José), Informe al Ministro de Guerra sobre Acontecimientos de 1831-2. MS.
Figueroa (José), Informe en que se opone al Proyecto de Secularizacion, 1833. MS.
Figueroa (José), Instrucciones Generales para el Gobierno de Cal., 1832. MS.
Figueroa (José), Manifiesto á la República Mejicana. Monterey, 1835.
Figueroa (José), The Manifesto of. S. Francisco, 1855.
Figueroa (José), Observaciones de un Ciudadano. MS.
Figueroa (José), Plan de Propios y Arbitrios. Monterrey, 6 Agosto, 1834.
Figueroa (José), Prevenciones Provisionales para la Emancipacion de Indios, 1833. MS.
Figueroa (José), Reglamento Provisional para la Secularizacion. Monterrey, 9 Agosto, 1834.
Findla (James), Statement of Events in Early Days. MS.
Findlay (Alexander G.), Directory for the Navigation of the Pacific Ocean. London, 1851; Light Houses in the World. London, 1867.
Fire Underwriters. Annual Reports. San Francisco, 1865 et seq.
First Steamship Pioneers. [San Francisco, 1874.] 4to.
Fisher (Walter M.), The Californians. San Francisco, 1876.
Fitch (Guillermo), Narrativa. MS.
Fitch (Henry D.), Causa Criminal por Matrimonio Nulo, 1830. MS.
Fitch (Henry D.), Letters of a Merchant, 1826 et seq. MS.
Fitch (Henry D. and Josefa C.), Documentos para la Historia de California. MS.
Fitch (Josefa C.), Narracion de una California. MS.
Fitzgerald (O. P.), California Sketches. Nashville, 1879.
Fitzgerald (O. P.), Education in California. MS.
Flagg, Report. [34th Cong., 1st Sess., Sen. Ex. Doc. 107.] Washington, 1855.
Fleurieu (Charles Pierre), Introduction. In Marchand, Voy., i.
Flint. See Pattie's Narrative.

Flores (José María), Cartas varias. MS.
Flores (José María), Informe al Gob^r. de Sonora, 5 Feb. 1877. In Sonorense, Mar. 5, 1847.
Flores (José María), Informe de 5 Feb. 1847, y Correspondencia con las Autoridades de Sonora. MS.
Flores (José María), Oficios del Comandante General, 1846. MS
Flores (Miguel), Recuerdos Históricos de California. MS.
Flores (Virey), Instruccion, 1789. MS.
Flügge (Charles W.), Various Letters, 1841 et seq. MS.
Folsom (J. L.), Correspondence of the Quartermaster, 1846-8. In Cal. and N. Mex., Mess. and Doc., 1850.
Fondo Piadoso de Californias, 1773. MS.
Fondo Piadoso de Californias, Decreto 24 Oct. 1842. MS.
Fondo Piadoso de Californias, Demostracion de los sínodos que adeuda á los Religiosos, 1811-34. MS.
Fondo Piadoso de Californias, Ley y Reglamento. Mexico, 1833.
Fonseca (Fabian) and Cárlos Urrutia, Historia General de Real Hacienda. Mexico, 1845, 1849-53. 6 vols.
Font (José), Varios Escritos del Teniente, 1796 et seq. MS.
Font (Pedro), Journal of a Journey from Sonora to Monterey, 1775. MS.
Foote (H. S.), Speech on Admission of California in U. S. Senate, Aug. 1, 1850. Washington, 1850.
Forbes (Alexander), California, A History of. London, 1839.
Forbes (James A.), Letters, 1833-48. MS.
Ford (Henry L.), The Bear Flag Revolution. MS.
Forest Hill, Placer Courier.
Forsee (Peter A.), Five Years of Crime in California. Ukiah, 1867.
Forster (John), Pioneer Data from 1832. MS.
Forster (John Reinhold), History of Voyages and Discoveries in the North. London, 1786. 4to.
Fort Point and Alcatrazas Island, Information in regard to fortifications being erected. [33d Cong., 1st Sess., H. Ex. Doc. 82.] Washington, 1853.
Foster (G. G.), The Gold Regions of California. New York, 1848; N. Y., 1849.
Foster (Stephen C.), Angeles from '47 to '49. MS.
Foster (Stephen C.), First American in Los Angeles. In Los Angeles Express.
Foster (Stephen C.), Various Writings. MS.
Fourgeaud, The Prospects of California. In California Star, April, 1848.
Fowler (John), Bear Flag Revolt. MS.
Fowler (Orin), Speech in U. S. H. of Rep., March 11, 1850, on Constitution of California. Washington, 1850.
Franklin (Benjamin), Corners, 1849. In S. F. Alta, March 8, 1877.
Fraser (J. D.), Report on the Immense Resources and Natural Wealth of California. New York, 1868.
Frazee (W. D.), San Bernardino County. San Bernardino, 1876.
Free American. Vera Cruz, 1847 et seq.
Freelon (W. T.), Oration before Pioneers. Sept. 9, 1857. San Francisco, 1857.
Fremery (James de), Mortgages in California. San Francisco, 1860.
Frémont (Jessie Benton), A Year of American Travel. n. p., 1878.
Frémont (John C.), California Claims in Congress. In 30th Cong., 1st Sess., H. Rept. 817; Sen. Rept. 75; Houston's Reports;—33d Cong., 1st Sess. H. Ex. Doc. 17; Sen. Ex. Doc. 49;—2d Sess., H. Ex. Doc. 13; Sen. Ex. 8;—34th Cong., 1st Sess., Sen. Doc. 109; Sen. Ex. Doc. 63; Sen. Miscel. 74;—36th Cong. 1st Sess. H. Rept. 7; Id. Court Claims 204, 229; Sen. Rept. 198. Also Cong. Globe 1847-8, 1852-3; and many scattered documents in the various archives; Correspondence 1844-7. MS.; Correspondence 1847-8 in Stockton's Life, App.; Court Martial. Extract in Stockton's Life, App.; Court Martial 1847. In 30th Cong., 1st Sess. Sen. Ex. Doc. 33; Discussions in Congress on his trial and services, 1847-8. Cong. Globe, 1847-8. Index, 'Frémont'; Geographical Memoir upon Up-

per California. Washington, 1848; Philadelphia, 1849. [30th Cong., 1st Sess. Sen. Mis. 148]; Is he honest? Is he capable? n.pl., n.d.; Life of. New York, 1856; Narrative of Exploring Expedition. New York, 1849; Not a Roman Catholic. n.pl., n.d.; Orders and Correspondence, 1847. In Cutt's Conquest; Private and Public Character Vindicated, by James Buchanan. New York, n.d.; Report of Exploring Expedition. Washington, 1845; Pamphlets. A Collection; Fremont Songster. New York, 1856; Boston, 1856.

Frémont (John C.) and W. H. Emory, California Guide Book. New York, 1849.

Frere (Alice M.), The Antipodes and Round the World. London, 1870.

Fresno, Expositor, Republican, Scott Valley News.

Frignet (Ernest), La Californie. Paris, 1865; Paris, 1867.

Frink (George W.), Vigilance Committee. MS.

Froebel (Julius), Central America, Northern Mexico, and Western United States, Seven Years Travel in. London, 1859.

From England to California. Life among the Mormons. Sacramento, 1868.

Frost (John), History of California. Auburn, 1853; New York, 1859; Pictorial History of Mexico. Phil. 1862.

Frost (Thomas), Half-Hours with the Early Explorers. London, etc. [1876.]

Furber (George C.), The Twelve Months' Volunteer. Cincinnati, 1850.

Fuster (Vicente), Registro de Defunciones, 1775. MS.

Gaceta del Gobierno de Mexico, 1728–1821, 1823 et seq.

Gaceta Imperial de Mexico. Mexico, 1821 3. 3 vols.

Galindo (José Eusebio), Apuntes para la Historia de California. MS.

Galitzin (Emmanuel), Notice Biographique sur Baránof. In Nouv. An. Voy., cxxv. 243.

Galvez (José de), Correspondencia con el Padre Lasuen, 1768. MS.

Galvez (José de), Escritos sueltos del Visitador General, 1768–70. MS.

Galvez (José de), Instruccion que ha de Observar D. Vicente Vila, capitan del S. Cárlos, 1769. MS.

Galvez (José de), Instruccion que ha de Observar el teniente D. Pedro Fages, 1769. MS.

Galvez (Virey), Comunicaciones al Gobr. de California, 1783–5. MS.

Galvez (Virey), Instruccion formada en virtud de real órden. Mexico, 1786.

Galvez (Virey), Instrucciones al Gobr. Fages, 1786. MS.

Garcés (Francisco), Diario y Derrotero. In Doc. Hist. Mex., ser. ii., i. 225.

García (Inocente), Hechos Históricos. MS.

García (José E.), Episodios Históricos. MS.

García (Marcelino), Apunte sobre el General Micheltorena. MS.

García Diego (Francisco), Carta Pastoral. Mexico, 1840.

García Diego (Francisco), Carta Pastoral contra la costumbre de azotar á los Indios, Junio 30, 1833. MS.

García Diego (Francisco), Correspondencia de un Misionero y Obispo. MS.

García Diego (Francisco), Parecer del P. Fiscal sobre el Proyecto de Secularizacion, 1833. MS.

García Diego (Francisco), Reglas que propone el P. Prefecto para Gobierno interior de las ex-misiones, 1835. MS.

Garden of the World. Boston, 1856.

Gardiner (Me.), Home Journal.

Garibay (Virey), Comunicaciones al Gobernador de Cal. MS.

Garijo (Agustin), Carta del P. Guardian en que da Noticia de la Revolucion, 1811. MS.

Garner (William R.), Letters of a Pioneer of 1824. MS.

Garnica del Castillo (Nicanor), Recuerdos sobre California. MS.

Garniss (James R.), Early Days of San Francisco. MS.

Gary (George), The Roaming Badgers. MS.

Gasol (José), Expediente sobre Capellanes de Presidios, 1802. MS.

Gasol (José), Letras Patentes del P. Guardian, 1806. MS.

Gay (Frederick A.), Sketches of California. n.pl., n.d.
General Association of California, Minutes of Annual Meetings. San Francisco, 1857 et seq.
German (José and Luis), Sucesos en California. MS.
Genius of Liberty, Vera Cruz, 1847 et seq.
Gerstäcker (Freidrich), Aventures d'une Colonie d'émigrants en Amérique. Paris, 1855; Californische Skizzen. Leipzig, 1856; Gold! Ein Californisches Lebensbild aus dem yahre 1849. Leipzig, 1858; Kaliforniens Gold u Quecksilber-District. Leipzig, 1849; Der Kleine Goldgräber in Californien. Leipzig, n.d.; Kreuz und Quer. Leipzig, 1869. 3 vols.; Narrative of a Journey round the World. Lond. 1853; New York, 1854; Reisen. Stuttgart, etc., 1853-4. 5 vols.; Scènes de la Vie Californienne. Genève, 1860; Travels. London, 1854; Western Lands and Western Waters. London, 1864.
Gibbons (Francis A.), and Francis X. Kelly, Letter relative to appropriation for erection of light-house on Pacific Coast. [33d Cong., 1st Sess., H. Ex. Doc. 113.] Washington, 1853; Resolution calling for Correspondence relative to claim [33d Cong., 2d Sess., Sen. Ex. Doc. 53]. Washington, 1853.
Gibson (H. G.), Address at the Fourth Annual Banquet of New York California Pioneers. In San José Pioneer, Feb. 15, 1879.
Gibson (Otis), Chinaman or White Man, Which? San Francisco, 1873; The Chinese in America. Cincinnati, 1877; other articles on Chinese.
Giddings (George H.), The case of—Contractor on the Overland Mail Route. Washington, 1860.
Gift (George W.), The Settler's Guide. Stockton, 1857.
Gift (George W.), Something about California. Marin County, S. Rafael, 1875.
Gilbert (Frank T.), See Histories of San Joaquin and Yolo Counties.
Gillespie (Archibald H.), Correspondence of a Government Agent. MS.
Gillespie (Charles V.), Vigilance Committee. MS.
Gilman (Daniel C.), Building of the University. Inaugural Address Nov. 7, 1872. San Francisco, 1872.
Gilroy, Advocate, California Leader, Independent, Telegram, Union.
Gleeson (William), History of the Catholic Church in California. San Francisco, 1872. 2 vols.
Glisan (R.), Journal of Army Life. San Francisco, 1874.
Goat Island, Appeal to the California Delegation in Congress, 1872; Proceedings of the Chamber of Commerce. S. F. 1872, etc.
Goddard (Frederick B.), Where to Emigrate and Why. New York, 1869.
Godfrey (John F.), Argument In re City of Los Angeles vs. L. McL. Baldwin et al. San Francisco, 1878.
Gold Fields. Notes on the Distribution of Gold. London, 1853.
Gold-Finder, Adventures of. London, 1850. 3 vols.
Golovnin (V. M.), Voyage of the Kamchatka, 1815-19. In Materialui, pt. iv.
Gomez (José), Diario Curioso, 1776-96. In Doc. Hist. Mex., serie ii., tom. vii.
Gomez (José Joaquin), Cartas, 1831 et seq. MS.
Gomez (Juan), Diario de Cosas Notables, 1836. MS.
Gomez (Juan), Documentos para la Historia de California, 1785-1850. MS.
Gomez (Rafael), Escritos Varios del Licenciado. MS.
Gomez (Vicente P.), Lo que Sabe de California. MS.
Gonzalez (Diego), Cartas del Teniente, 1781 et seq. MS.
Gonzalez (José María de Jesus), Cartas del Padre Zacatecano. MS.
Gonzalez (Mauricio), Memorias Californianas. MS.
Gonzalez (Mauricio), Papeles Originales Históricos. MS.
Gonzalez (Rafael), Correspondencia. MS.
Gonzalez (Rafael), Diario de Mexico á California. MS.
Gonzalez (Rafael), Experiencias de un Soldado. MS.
Gonzalez (Teodoro) Las Revoluciones en California. MS.
Good Templars, Constitution, Proceedings, etc., of various lodges.
Goodrich (Frank B.), The Tribute Book. San Francisco, 1867. 4to.

Goodrich (Samuel G.), History of the Indians of North and South America.
    Boston, 1844; Boston, 1855; Boston, 1864.
Goodyear (W. A.), Coal Mines of the Western Coast.   San Francisco, 1877.
Gottfriedt (Johann Ludwig), Neue Welt.   Franckfurt, 1655. folio.
Gougenheim (Adelaide and Joey), Histrionic Memoirs, etc.   S. F. 1856.
Goycoechea (Felipe), Diario de Exploracion, 1798. MS.
Goycoechea (Felipe), Escritos del Comandante de Sta Bárbara, 1785–1806. MS.
Goycoechea (Felipe), Medios para el Fomento de Californias, 1805. MS.
Goycoechea (Felipe), Oficio Instructivo para el Ten^te. R. Carrillo, 1802. MS.
Goycoechea (Felipe), Respuesta á las Quince Preguntas sobre Abusos de
    Misioneros, 1798. MS.
Graham (J. D.), Report on Boundary Line between U. S. and Mexico [32d
    Cong., 1st Sess., Sen. Ex. Doc. 121.]   Washington, 1851.
Graham (Mary), Historical Reminiscences.   San Francisco, 1876.
Graham (Isaac) and John A. Sutter in New Mexico, Some Facts. MS.
Grajera (Antonio), Escritos del Comandante de S. Diego, 1794–9.
Grajera (Antonio), Respuesta á las Quince Preguntas, 1799. MS.
Grantsville, Weekly Sun.
Grass Valley, Foot Hill Tidings, National, Union.
Gray (A. B.), Resolution communicating report and map relative to Mex.
    Boundary.   [33d Cong., 2d Sess., Sen. Ex. Doc. 55.] Wash. 1853.
Gray (W. H.), History of Oregon, 1792–1849.   Portland, 1870.
Great Registers, cited by name of county.   Not in this list.
Greeley (Horace), Overland Journey.   New York, 1860.
Green (Alfred A.) Life and Adventures of a '47er. MS.
Green (Talbot H.), Letters, 1841–8. MS.
Greenhow (Robert), History of Oregon and California.   Boston, 1844; Lon-
    don, 1844; New York, 1845; Boston, 1845; Boston, 1847.
Greenhow (Robert), Memoir, Historical and Political, of the Northwest Coast
    of North America. [26th Cong., 1st Sess., Sen. Doc. 174.] Wash., 1840.
Greenwood (Grace), New Life in New Lands.   New York, 1873.
Gregory (Joseph W.), Guide for California Travellers.   New York, 1850.
Gregson (James), Statement, 1845–9.   MS.
Grey (William), A Picture of Pioneer Times in California.   S. F. 1881.
Griffin (John S.), Documents for the History of California; San Pascual. MS.
Griffin (John S.), Journal of 1846.   MS.
Grigsby (John), Papers of 1846–8.   MS.
Grijalva (Juan Pablo), Cartas del Teniente, 1794–1806. MS.
Grijalva (Juan Pablo) Explicacion del Registro desde S. Diego.   MS.
Grijalva (Juan Pablo), Informe sobre les Rancherías exploradas por P. Mari-
    ner, 1795. MS.
Grimm (Henry), The Chinese Must Go.   San Francisco, 1879.
Grimshaw (William R.), Narrative of Events, 1848–50.   MS.
Guadalajara, Gaceta de Gobierno.   Guadalajara, 1821 et seq.
Guerra (Francisco), et al.   Investigations of a charge against as Revolutionists,
    1848. MS.
Guerra (José Antonio), Cartas.   MS.
Guerra (Pablo), Comunicaciones.   MS.
Guerra y Noriega (José), Correspondencia del Capitan.   MS.
Guerra y Noriega (José), Determinacion sobre su Ida á Mexico, ó Instruccion,
    1819. MS.
Guerra y Noriega (José), Documentos para la Hist. de Cal.   MS. 6 vols.
Guerra y Noriega (José), Ocurrencias Curiosas de 1830–1.   MS.
Guerra entre Mexico y los Estados-Unidos, Apuntes.   Mexico, 1848.
Guerrero (Francisco), Cartas, 1839–46.   MS.
Guerrero (Vicente), Soberano Estado de Oajaca.   Oajaca, 1833.
Guia de Forasteros.   Mexico, 1797 et seq.
Gutierrez (Nicolás), Carta Oficial del Gefe Político, 4 Nov. 1836.   MS.
Gutierrez (Nicolás), [Publica el Decreto reuniendo los Mandos, y toma
    posesion del Gobierno Político.]   Monterrey, 2 Enero, 1836.

Gutierrez (Nicolás), Varias Cartas del Capitan y Gefe Político, 1832–6.   MS.
Gwin (William M.), Argument on the Subject of a Pacific Railroad. Wash.,
1860; Congress Record. n.pl., n.d.; Land Titles in California. Speech
in reply to Mr Benton in U. S. Sen., Jan. 2, 1851. Wash., 1851; Navy-
yard and Dry-dock in California. Speech in U. S. Sen., March 23, 1852.
Wash., 1852; Remarks in U. S. Sen. Apr. 19 and 20, 1852, on Deficiency
Appropriation Bill. Wash., 1852; Speech in U. S. Sen. Jan. 13, 1853, on
Bill to Establish a Railway to the Pacific. Wash., 1853; Speech in U.
S. Sen. March 2, 1853, on Transportation of U. S. Mails. Wash., 1853;
Speeches in the Senate of the U. S. on Private Land Titles in Cal.
Wash., 1851; other speeches.
Gwin (William M.), Memoirs on History. MS.

Habersham (A. W.), North Pacific Surveying and Expl. Ex.   Phila., 1858.
Hacke (William), Collection of Original Voyages. London, 1699.
Hakluyt (Richard), The Principal Navigations. Lond., 1599–1600. folio. 3
vols.; cited as Hakluyt's Voy.
Hale (Edward Everett), Early Maps of America. Worcester, 1874; His Level
Best, etc. Boston, 1873; The Name of California. In Amer. Antiq. Soc.,
Proc., Apr. 1862, 45; Queen of California. In Atlantic Monthly, xiii.
265.
Hall (Charles Victor), California. The Ideal Italy. Philadelphia, 1875.
Hall (Edward H.), The Great West. N. Y., 1865; N. Y., 1866.
Hall (Frederic), History of San José. San Francisco, 1871; San José History.
Scrap-book. From S. José Pioneer, Jan. 1877.
Hall (John), Remarks on the harbours of Cal. [Being extracts from the log of
the Lady Blackwood, 1822.] In Forbes' Hist. Cal., App.
Hall (William M.), Speech in favor of a National Railroad to the Pacific.
July 7, 1847; New York, 1853.
Halleck (Henry W.), Correspondence of the Secretary of State. 1846–8. In
Cal. and N. Mex., Mess. and Doc., 1850; Mexican Land Laws. MS.;
Report on Land Titles in California. [31st Cong., 1st. Sess., H. Ex.
Doc. 17.] Wash., 1850.
Halley (William), Centennial Year-book of Alameda County. Oakland, 1876.
Hamilton (Nev.), Inland Empire.
Hancock (Samuel), Thirteen Years' Residence on the Northwest Coast. MS.
Hanford, Public Good.
Hansard (T. C.), Parliamentary Debates from 1803. London, 1812–77. [S. F.
Law Library.]
Hardenbergh (J. R.), Answer to charges filed with the Commissioner of the
General Land Office. San Francisco, 1873.
Hardinge (Emma), Funeral Oration on Thomas Starr King. S. F., 1864.
Hardy (Lady Duffus), Through Cities and Prairie Lands. London, 1881.
Hargrave (William), California in 1846. MS.
Haro (Francisco), Cartas Sueltas. MS.
Haro y Peralta (Virey), Comunicaciones al Gobierno de California. MS.
Harper's New Monthly Magazine. New York, 1856 et seq.
Harris (John), Navigantium...Bibliotheca. London, 1705. folio. 2 vols.
Harrison (Henry W.), Battle-Fields and Naval Exploits. Phila., 1858.
Hart (Albert), Mining Statutes of the U. S., Cal., and Nev. S. F., 1877.
Hartman (Isaac), Brief in Mission Cases.
Hartmann (Carl), Geographisch-Statistische Beschreibung von Californien.
Weimar, 1849. 2 vols.
Hartmann (Joh. Adolph), Dissertatio Geographica de vero Californiæ situ et
Conditione. Marburg, 1739. 4to.
Hartnell (Teresa de la G.), Narrativa de una Matrona de Cal. MS.
Hartnell (William E. P.), Convention of '49. Original Records. MS.
Hartnell (William E. P.), Diario del Visitador Gen. de Misiones, 1839–40. MS.
Hartnell (William E. P.), English Colonization in California, 1844. MS.
Hartnell (William E. P.), Miscellaneous Correspondence from 1822. MS.

Harvey (Mrs Daniel), Life of John McLoughlin. MS.
Hastings (Lansford W.), Emigrants' Guide to Oregon and California. Cincinnati, 1845; Letters. 1843-8. MS.; New History of Oregon and California. Cincinnati, 1849.
Haswell (Robert), Voyage of the *Columbia Rediviva*, 1787, 1791-2. MS.
Havilah, Courier, Miner.
Hawes (Horace), Missions in California. San Francisco, 1856.
Hawley (A. T.), Humboldt County. Eureka, 1879.
Hawley (A. T.), The Present Condition, etc., of L. Angeles. L. Angeles, 1876.
Hawley (David N.), Observations of Men and Things. MS.
Hayes (Benjamin), Criminal Trials at Los Angeles. MS.
Hayes (Benjamin), Diary of a Journey Overland, 1849-50. MS.
Hayes (Benjamin), Documents for the History of California. MS.
Hayes (Benjamin), Emigrant Notes. MS. and Scraps.
Hayes (Benjamin), Land Matters in California. MS.
Hayes (Benjamin), List of Vessels. MS.
Hayes (Benjamin), Mexican Laws, Notes. MS.
Hayes (Benjamin), Mission Book of Alta Cal. MS. and Scraps. 2 vols.
Hayes (Benjamin), Notes on California Affairs. MS.
Hayes (Benjamin), Papeles Varios Originales. MS.
Hayes (Benjamin), San Diego, Legal History. Scraps and MS.
Hayes (Benjamin), Scrap Books, 1850-74. 129 vols.; under the following subtitles: Agriculture; Arizona. 6 vols.; California Notes. 5 vols. MS. and Print; California Poets; California Politics. 10 vols.; Constitutional Law; Cuyamaca Case. MS. and Print; Early California Decisions; Indians. 5 vols.; Los Angeles County. 10 vols.; Memorabilia; Mining. 13 vols.; Monterey, Santa Bárbara, etc.; Natural Phenomena. 3 vols.; Pacific Interests; Railroads. 6 vols.; San Bernardino County. 4 vols.; San Diego, Five Years in. 4 vols.; San Diego County, Local History. 3 vols.; Southern California, Historical Items. 2 vols.; Southern California Politics. 2 vols.; Southern California, Wilmington, etc.; Studies in Politics. 7 vols.; Supreme Court, 1868-74.
Haywards, Journal, Alameda Advocate, Plaindealer.
Hazlitt (Wm. Carew), Great Gold Fields of Cariboo. London, 1862.
Healdsburg, Advertiser, Democratic Standard, Enterprise, Review, Russian River Flag.
Heap (Gwinn Harris), Central Route to the Pacific. Philadelphia, 1854.
Hearn (F. G.), California Sketches. MS.
Hebard, Speech, March 14, 1850, on Constitution of Cal. Wash., 1850.
Heceta (Bruno), Diario del Viage de 1775. MS.
Heceta (Bruno), Espedicion Marítima. In Palou, Not., ii. 229.
Heceta (Bruno), Segunda Exploracion, 1775. MS.
Heceta (Bruno), Viage de 1775. MS.
Hecox (Adna A.), Biographical Sketch. In S. José Pioneer, Aug. 1878.
Hecox (Adna A.), A Brief History of the Introduction of Methodism. In S. F. Christian Advocate, 1863.
Helper (Hinton R.), The Land of Gold. Baltimore, 1855.
Henshaw (Josiah S.), Historical Events. MS.
Hernandez (José María P.), Compendio de la Geografía. Mexico, 1872.
Herrera (Antonio de), Historia General de los Hechos de los Castellanos en las Islas i Tierra Firme del Mar Océano. Madrid, 1601. 4to. 4 vols; Madrid, 1726-30. folio.
Herrera (José María), Causa contra el Comisario de California, 1827. MS.
Herrera (José María), Escritos del Comisario. MS.
Herrick (William F.), Current Events from 1853. MS.
Hesperian (The). San Francisco, 1858-64. 11 vols.
Heylyn (Peter), Cosmography. London, 1701. folio.
Hijar (Cárlos N.), California in 1834. MS.
Hijar (José María), Instrucciones del Gefe Político y Director de Colonizacion, 1834. In Figueroa, Man. 11.

Híjar (José María), Instrucciones del Gobierno al Comisionado, 1845. MS.
Híjar (José María), Varias Cartas. MS.
Hinckley (William C.), Life of a Pioneer of 1847. MS.
Hinckley (William S.), Letters of a Sea Captain. MS.
Hinds (Richard B.), Botany of Voyage of the *Sulphur*. London, 1844; Regions of Vegetation, California Region. In Belcher's Nar., ii.; Zoology of the Voyage of the *Sulphur*. London, 1844.
Hines (Gustavus), Voyage round the World. Buffalo, 1850.
Hinton (Richard J.), Handbook of Arizona. San Francisco, 1878.
Historical Magazine and Notes and Queries. Boston, etc., 1857–69. 15 vols.
History of the Bear Flag Revolt. In Niles' Register, lxxiii. 110.
Hitchcock (George B.), Statement of Ramblings. MS.
Hittell (John S.), The Commerce and Industries of the Pacific Coast. San Francisco, 1882. 4to; The History of the Cottonwood Prospecting Expedition. In Alta California; History of San Francisco. S. F. 1878; Limantour. In Overland Monthly, ii. 154; The Limantour Claim. S. F. 1857; Mining Life at Shasta in 1849. In Dietz, Our Boys. 161; Notes of Californian Pioneers. In Hutchings' Cal. Mag. v. 209; Oration at the Nineteenth Anniversary of California Pioneers. S. F. 1869; Papeles Históricos de 1846. MS.; Resources of California. S. F. 1866; S. F. 1867; S. F. 1874; The Resources of Vallejo. Vallejo, 1869; Spoliation of Mexican Grant Holders in California by U. S. In Hesperian. iv. 147.
Hittell (Theodore H.), Adventures of James Capen Adams. S. F. 1860.
Hobbs (James), Wild Life in the Far West. Hartford, 1875.
Hoffmann (Hemmann), Californien, Nevada und Mexico. Basel, 1871.
Hoffman (Ogden), Opinions in Mission Cases. S. Francisco, 1859; Opinions in various other cases; Reports of Land Cases. San Francisco, 1862.
Hoit (C. W.), Fraudulent Mexican Land Claims in California. Sac. 1869.
Holinski (Alex.), La Californie et les Routes Interocéaniques. Bruxelles, 1853.
Holland (Charles), Mines and Mining. In Coast Review. 1873. p. 73.
Hollister, Advance, Central Californian, Enterprise, Telegraph.
Home Missionary (The). New York, 1846 et seq.
Homer (Charles), Memorial for construction of San Francisco Marine Hospital [33d Cong., 1st. Sess., H. Ex. Doc. 54]. Washington, 1853.
Homes (Henry A.), Our Knowledge of Cal. and the N. W. Coast. Albany, 1870.
Homestead Associations. A large number of publications cited by name of the Association.
Honolulu, Friend, 1843 et seq.; Hawaiian Spectator; Polynesian, 1857 et seq.; Sandwich Island Gazette, 1836 et seq.; Sandwich Island News, 1846 et seq.
Hooker (Wm. J.) and G. A. W. Arnott, Botany of Captain Beechey's Voyage. London, 1861. 4to.
Hopkins, Translations of California Documents. n.p., n.d.
Hopkins (C. T.), Common Sense applied to the Immigrant Question. San Francisco, 1870; Taxation in California. S. F. 1881; and other pamphlets.
Hoppe (J.), Californiens Gegenwart und Zukunft. Berlin, 1849.
Hopper (Charles), Narrative of a Pioneer of 1841. MS.
Horn (Hosea B.), Horn's Overland Guide. New York, 1852.
Horra (Antonio de la Concepcion), Representacion al Virey contra los Misioneros de Cal., 1798. MS.
Howard (Volney E.), Speech in U. S. H. of Rep. against Admission of California, June 11, 1850. Washington, 1850.
Howard (W. D. M.), Commercial Correspondence from 1838. MS.
Howe (J. W.), Speech, June 5, 1850, on California Question. Wash. 1850.
Hubner (Le Baron de), A Ramble round the World, 1871. New York, 1874.
Hudson (David), Autobiography. MS.
Hughes (Elizabeth), The California of the Padres. San Francisco, 1875.
Hughes (John T.), California. Its History, etc., Cincinnati, 1848; Cincinnati, 1849; Cincinnati, 1850; Doniphan's Expedition. Cincinnati, 1849.

Huish (Robert), Narratives of Voyages. London, 1836.
Humason (W. L.), From the Atlantic Surf to the Golden Gate. Hartford, 1869.
Humboldt (Alex. de), Essai Politique sur le Royaume de la Nouvelle Espagne. Paris, 1811. folio. 2 vols. and atlas.
Humboldt (Alex. de), Tablas Estadísticas del Reyno de Nueva España en el año de 1803. MS.
Humboldt County. Its Resources, etc. See Hawley, A. T.
Hunt's Merchants' Magazine. New York, 1839 et seq.
Huse (Charles E.), Sketch of the History and Resources of Santa Bárbara City and County. Santa Barbara, 1876.
Hutchings' Illustrated California Magazine. San Francisco, 1857–61. 5 vols.
Hyde (George), Historical Facts on California. MS.

Ibarra (Juan María), Cartas Varias del Teniente. MS.
Idaho City, (Id.) World.
Ide (William B.), Bear Flag Revolt. MS.
Ide (William B.), Biographical Sketch. [Claremont] 1880; Who Conquered California? [Claremont] 1880.
Ilustracion Mexicana (La). Mexico, 1851–3. 4 vols.
Independence (Cal.), Inyo Independent.
Independence (Mo.), Mission Expositor.
Indios, Contestacion al Interrogatorio de 1812 por el Presidente y los Padres sobre costumbres, 1815. MS.
Indios, Interrogatorio del Supremo Gobierno sobre Costumbres, 1812. MS.
Industrial Magazine. San Francisco, 1867 et seq.
Informe de lo mas Peculiar de la Nueva California, 1789. MS.
Informe sobre los Ajustes de Pobladores de la Reina de Los Angeles y demas de las Provincias de Californias. Dec. 30, 1789. MS.
Ingersoll (Ernest), In a Redwood Logging Camp. In Harper's Mag., lxvi. 194–5.
Iniciativa de Ley, 1827. In Junta de Fomento de California.
Iniestra, Expedicion de Cal., 1845. In Amigo del Pueblo, Sept.–Oct. 1845.
Institutions, associations, societies, companies, orders, churches, banks, clubs, courts, etc. Publications cited in notes by name of the institution, etc.; but most of them, not historical in their nature, are omitted in this list.
Instrucciones á que debe sujetarse la Comision nombrada por este Ayuntamiento de Angeles, 30 Mayo, 1837. MS.
Instrucciones para Tribunales de 1ª Instancia. [1824] MS.
Instrucciones que los Vireyes de Nueva Espana. Mexico, 1867.
Investigacion sobre la Muerte de los Religiosos enviados á la reduccion de los gentiles del Rio Colorado, 1781. MS.
Ione, Amador Times, Chronicle, City News, Riverside Independence.
Iriarte (Francisco), Contestacion á la Expresion de Agravios. Mexico, 1832.
Irving (Washington), Adventures of Bonneville. New York, 1860.
Iturbide (Agustin), Cartas de los Señores Generales. Mexico, 1821.
Iturrigaray (Virey), Comunicaciones al Gobr. de California. MS.

Jackson, Amador Dispatch, Amador Ledger, Sentinel, Press.
Janssens (Agustin), Documentos para la Historia de California. MS.
Janssens (Agustin), Vida y Aventuras. MS.
Jay (William), Review, etc., Mexican War. Boston, 1849.
Jenkins (John S.), History of the War between U. S. and Mex. Auburn, 1851; United States Exploring Expeditions. Auburn, 1850.
Jimeno (José Joaquin and Antonio), Cartas de los dos Frailes. MS.
Jimeno Casarin (Manuel), Escritos del Secretario de Estado. MS.
John Bull. [London newspaper.]
Johnson (Daniel H.), and Cornelius Vanderbilt, Correspondence, etc., for Transporting Mails via the Isthmus. [36th Cong., 1st Sess., Sen. Ex. Doc. 45.] Washington, 1859.

Johnson (Theodore T.), California and Oregon, or Sights in the Gold Region. Phil., 1851; Phil., 1857; Phil., 1865; Sights in the Gold Regions. N. Y., 1849; N. Y., 1850.

Johnston (A. R.), Journal of a Trip with the First U. S. Dragoons. 1846. [30th Cong., 1st Sess., H. Ex. Doc. 41.] Washington, 1848; In Emory's Notes.

Jones (John C.), Cartas Comerciales, 1831 et seq. MS.

Jones (Thomas Ap. C.), Agresion en Californias. 1842. In Mexico, Mem. Relac., 1844, An. 87–97; At Monterey in 1842. [27th Cong., 3d Sess., H. Ex. Doc. 166.] Washington, 1842; Miscellaneous Proclamations, 1849; Unpublished Narrative, 1842. From Los Angeles Southern Vineyard, May 22, 1858.

Jones (William Carey), Report on Land Titles in California. Washington, 1850; The Pueblo Question Solved. San Francisco, 1860.

Jonesborough (Tenn.), Sentinel.

Juarez (Cayetano), Notas sobre Asuntos de Cal. MS.

Julio César, Cosas de Indios. MS.

Junta de 5 de Abril de 1791 en Monterey. MS.

Junta Consultativa y Económica en Monterey, 1843. MS.

Junta de Fomento de Californias, Coleccion de los Trabajos. Mex. 1827.

Junta de Guerra y Rendicion de Monterey, 4 Nov. 1836. MS.

Junta Primera de Guerra en Monterey, 4 Oct. 1769. MS.

Kalama, Beacon.

Kearny (Stephen W.), Orders and Correspondence, 1847. In Cal. and N. Mex., Mess. & Doc. 1850; Proclamation, March 1, 1847. Original MS.; also in print; Report to Adjutant-General Jones, March 15, 1847. [31st Cong., 1st Sess., H. Ex. Doc. 17, p. 283.] Washington, 1848; Reports of San Pascual. [30th Cong., 1st Sess., Sen. Ex. Doc. No. 513–16.] Washington, 1848.

Kelley (Hall J.), A History of the Settlement of Oregon. Springfield, 1868; Memoir on Oregon, 1839. [25th Cong., 3d Sess., H. Rept. 101.] Washington, 1838; A Narrative of Events and Difficulties. Boston, 1852.

Kelly (George Fox), Land Frauds of California. Santa Rosa, 1864.

Kelly (William), An Excursion to California. London, 1851. 2 vols.

Kendrick (John), Correspondencia sobre Cosas de Nootka, 1794. MS.

Kern (Edward M.), Journal of Exploration, 1845. In Simpson's Rept., 477.

Kerr (J. G.), The Chinese Question Analyzed. San Francisco, 1877.

Kerr (Robert), General History and Collection of Voyages, Edinburgh and London, 1824. 18 vols.

Keyser (Sebastian), Memoir of a Pioneer. MS.

Khlébnikof (K.), Zapiski o America. St Petersburg, 1861.

King (Clarence), Mountaineering in the Sierra Nevada. Boston, 1874; 1882.

King (Thomas Butler), California; The Wonder of the Age. New York, 1850; Report on California. Washington, 1850 [message of President, March 26, 1851. 31st Cong., 1st Sess., H. Ex. Doc. 59.]

King of William (James), Assassination of, etc. San Francisco, 1856; Family Scrap-book.

King's Orphan, Visit to California, 1842–3, Scrap-book; also in Upham's Notes.

Kinley (Joseph M.), Remarks on Chinese Immigration. San Francisco, 1877.

Kip (Leonard), California Sketches. Albany, 1850.

Kip (Wm. Ingraham), Historical Scenes from the Old Jesuit Missions. New York, 1875; Last of the Leatherstockings. In Overland Monthly, ii. 407; and other works.

Kirchhoff (Theodor), Reisebilder und skizzen. N. Y., 1875–6. 2 vols.

Kirkpatrick (Charles A.), Journal of 1849. MS.

Knight (Thomas), Early Events in California, of a Pioneer of '45. MS.

Knight (Thomas), Recollections. MS.

Knight (Wm. H.), Scrap-books. 40 volumes.

Knight's Ferry, Stanislaus Index.

Knight's Landing, News.
Knox (Thomas W.), The Underground World. Hartford, 1878.
Kohler (Charles), Wine Production in California. MS.
Kotzebue (Otto von), New Voyage round the World. London, 1830. 2 vols.;
    Voyage of Discovery. London, 1831. 3 vols.
Kraszewski (Michael), Acts of the Manilas. MS.
Künzel (Heinrich), Obercalifornien. Darmstadt, 1848.

Labor Agitators; or the Battle for Bread. San Francisco, 1879.
Laet (Joanne de), Novvs Orbis. Batav., 1633. folio.
La Fayette, Democratic Sentinel.
Lafond (Gabriel), Voyages autour du Monde. Paris, 1843. 2 vols.; Paris,
    1844. 8 vols. 4to.
La Harpe (Jean François), Abrégé de l'Histoire Générale des Voyages. Paris,
    1816. 24 vols. and atlas.
Lakeport, Avalanche, Clear Lake Courier, Clear Lake Journal, Clear Lake
    Times, Lake County Bee, Lake County Democrat.
Lakeside Monthly (The). Chicago, 1872.
Lambertie (Charles de), Voyage pittoresque en Californie, etc. Paris, 1854.
Lamotte (H. D.), Statement. MS.
Lancey (Thomas C.), Cruise of the *Dale.* Scrap-book, from S. José Pioneer.
Lander (Frederick W.), Remarks on a double-track Railway to the Pacific.
    Washington, 1854.
Lane (Joseph), Autobiography. MS.
Langley (Henry G.), Trade of the Pacific. San Francisco, 1870. See also
    Directories.
Langsdorff (G. H. von), Voyages and Travels, 1803-7. Lond., 1813-14. 2 vols.
La Pérouse (J. G. F. de), Voyage autour du Monde. Paris, 1798. 4 vols.
    atlas. folio; Voyage round the World, 1785-8. London, 1798. 3 vols.;
    Boston, 1801.
Laplace (Cyrille P. T.), Campagne de Circumnavigation. Paris, 1841-54. 6
    vols.
La Porte, Mountain Messenger, Union.
Lardner (Dionysius), History of Maritime and Inland Discovery. London,
    1830. 3 vols.
Larios (Estolano), Vida de su Padre, Manuel Larios. MS.
Larios (Justo), Convulsiones en California. MS.
Larkin (Thomas O.), Accounts 1827-42. MS. 4 vols.
Larkin (Thomas O.), Accounts 1840-57. MS. 17 vols.
Larkin (Thomas O.), Correspondence Official and Private. MS.
Larkin (Thomas O.), Description of California, 1845. MS.
Larkin (Thomas O.), Documents for the History of California, 1839-56. MS.
    9 vols.
Larkin (Thomas O.), Journal. In Monterey Californian, Feb. 27, '47.
Larkin (Thomas O.), Letter to Mason from San José, May 26, 1848.
Larkin (Thomas O.), Letters to Sec. of State, June 1 and 28, 1848. In
    Foster's Gold Regions.
Larkin (Thomas O.), Notes on the Personal Character of Californians, 1845.
    MS.
Larkin (Thomas O.), Official Correspondence as U. S. Consul and Navy Agent,
    1844-9. MS. 2 vols.
Larkin (Thomas O.), Papers Unbound. MS.
Larkin (Thomas O.), Private Record of Lots sold, 1846-51. MS.
Larkin (Thomas O.), U. S. Naval Agency Accounts. MS. 2 vols.
Lasso de la Vega (José Ramon), Escritos del Alférez, 1784 et seq. MS.
Lasuen (Fermin Francisco), Carta de 1784. MS.
Lasuen (Fermin Francisco), Carta sobre Fundacion de Misiones, 1791. MS.
Lasuen (Fermin Francisco), Cartas al Visitador General Galvez, 1768. MS.
Lasuen (Fermin Francisco), Correspondencia del Padre y Presidente. MS.
Lasuen (Fermin Francisco), Fundacion de Misiones, 1797. Cartas. MS.

Lasuen (Fermin Francisco), Informe de 1783. MS.
Lasuen (Fermin Fran.), Informe sobre Sitios para Nuevas Misiones, 1796. MS.
Lasuen (Fermin Fran.), Informes Bienales de las Misiones, 1793–1802. MS.
Lasuen (Fermin Francisco), Representacion sobre los Puntos representados al
    Gobierno por el P. Antonio de la Concepcion [Horra], 1800. MS.
Latham (Milton S.), Remarks on Overland Mails in U. S. Sen., May 30, 1860.
    Washington, 1860; Speech on Pacific Railroad in U. S. Sen. June 12, 1862.
    Baltimore, 1862; Speech on Steamships between San Francisco and China.
    Washington, 1855; and other Speeches.
Laur (P.), De la Production des Métaux Précieux en Californie. Paris, 1862.
Lauts (G.), Kalifornia. Amsterdam, 1849.
Lawson (James S.), Autobiography. MS.
Lee (John D.), Mormonism Unveiled. St Louis, 1877.
Lee (Daniel) and J. H. Frost. Ten Years in Oregon. New York, 1844.
Leese (Jacob P.), Bear Flag Revolt. MS.
Leese (Jacob P.), Claim for Construction of Monterey Wharf. 1846. [36th
    Cong., 2d Sess., H. Rep. 274.] Wash. 1846.
Leese (Jacob P.), Letters from 1836. MS.
Leese (Rosalía Vallejo), History of the 'Osos.' MS.
Legal publications, law text-books, county and municipal regulations, re-
    ports, etc. See California, San Francisco, Briefs, etc. Many such works
    are not named in this list.
Legislative Records. MS. 4 vols. In Archivo de Cal.
Leidesdorff (William A.), Letters of the U. S. Vice Consul. MS.
Leland (Charles Godfrey), The Union Pacific Railway. Philadelphia, 1867.
Le Netrel (Edmond), Voyage autour du Monde. 1826–9. In Nouv. An. Voy.,
    xlv. 129.
Leslie (Mrs Frank), California. New York, 1877.
Lester (John Erastus), The Atlantic to the Pacific. Boston, 1873; The
    Yosemite, its History, etc. Providence, 1873.
Letts (J. M.), California Illustrated. New York, 1852; Pictorial View of Cal.
    New York, 1853.
Levett's Scrap Book.
Libro de Bitácora, archivo de la Familia Estudillo. MS.
Limantour (José Y.), Apuntes sobre la Causa contra Augusto Jouan. Mexico,
    1855; Opinion delivered by Ogden Hoffman in the Cases of. San Fran-
    cisco, 1858; Pamphlet relating to the Claim of. San Francisco, 1853;
    Limantour Case. MS. volume of documents in S. F. Law Library; and
    various documents.
Linares (Virey), Intendencias. MS.
Linschoten (J. H. van), Reys-Gheschrift Van de Navigatien de Portugaloysers
    in Orienten. Amstelredam, 1604. folio.
Lippincott (Sarah J. C.), New Life in New Lands. New York, 1873.
Lippincott's Magazine. Philadelphia, 1868 et seq.
Lisalde (Pedro), Reconocimiento de Tierras, 1797. MS.
Little (John T.), First Years of Cal. under U. S. MS.
Livermore, Enterprise, Herald.
Livermore (Robert), Occasional Letters from 1829. MS.
Lloyd (B. E.), Lights and Shades in San Francisco. San Francisco, 1876.
Loa á la Vírgen. Papel de Mision. MS.
Lobscheid (W.), The Chinese; What They Are, etc. San Francisco, 1873.
Local histories, see name of county, town, or author.
Lockwood (R. A.), Vigilance Committee Speeches. San Francisco, 1852.
Lodi, Valley Review.
Log-books, Fragments from the Larkin Collection. 3 vols. MS.
Lompoc, Record.
London, Echo, Engineer, Grocer, Mechanic's Magazine, Morning Post, Spec-
    tator, Times, etc.
Lopez (Baldomero), El Guardian á los Padres, prohibiendo el uso de Carrua-
    jes, 1820. MS.

Lopez (Baldomero), El Guardian al P. Presidente sobre cesion de Misiones, 1820. MS.
Lopez (Baldomero), Quejas del P. Guardian al Virey, 1819. MS.
Lopez (Baldomero), and Isidro Alonso Salazar, Carta de los Padres de Sta Cruz, 1791. MS.
Lord (John Keast), The Naturalist in Vancouver Island. Lond., 1866. 2 vols.
Lorenzana (Apolinaria), Memorias de la Beata. MS.
Loreto, Libros de Mision. MS. [In possession of O. Livermore.]
Los Angeles, Archivo, Copies and Extracts. MS. 5 vols.
Los Angeles, Ayuntamiento Records. MS.
Los Angeles, Crónica, Express, Herald, Meridional, Mirror, Morning Journal, News, Republican, Star, Sud. Cal. Post.
Los Angeles, Historical Sketch of (by Hayes, Warner, and Widney). Los Angeles, 1876.
Los Angeles, Homes in. See McPherson, William.
Los Angeles, Instancia de Regidores y Vecinos sobre Tierras, 1819. MS.
Los Angeles, Lista de los Pobladores, Inválidos, y Vecinos, 1816. MS.
Los Angeles, Ordenanzas de la Ciudad. Los Angeles, 1860.
Los Angeles, Padron, 1781. MS.
Los Angeles, Reglamento de Policía, 1827, MS.
Los Angeles, Reparticion de Solares y Suertes, 1786, MS.
Los Angeles, Revised Ordinance of the City of Los Angeles, 1855. Los Angeles, 1860. 2 vols.
Los Angeles County, Historical Sketch of (L. Lewin and Co.) Los Angeles, 1876.
Los Angeles County, History of (Thompson and West). Oakland, 1880. Atlas folio.
Louisville (Ky.), Courier-Journal.
Löw (Conrad), Meer oder Seehanen Buch. Cölln, 1598.
Low (Frederick F.), Observations in Early Cal.. MS.
Lower Lake, Bulletin, Observer, Sentinel.
Ludlow (Fitz Hugh), The Heart of the Continent. New York, 1870.
Lugo (Felipe), Cartas Varias. MS.
Lugo (José del Cármen), Vida de un Ranchero. MS.
Lull (Miguel), Exposicion del Padre Guardian sobre Reduccion de Misioneros en Cal., 1799. MS.
Luyt (Joannis), Introductio ad Geographiam Novam et Veterem. Trajecti ad Rhenum, 1692.

McAllister (Hall), Statement on Vigilance Committee. MS.
McChristian (Patrick), Narrative on Bear Flag. MS.
McClellan (R. Guy), The Golden State. Phil., etc., 1872; Republicanism in America. San Francisco, 1869.
McCloskey (J. J.), The Early Drama in California. In San José Pioneer, Dec. 13 and 14, 1877.
McClure (A. K.), Three Thousand Miles through the Rocky Mountains. Philadelphia, 1869.
McCollum (William S.), California as I Saw it. Buffalo, 1850.
McCue (Jim), Twenty-one Years in California. San Francisco, n.d.
McDaniels (W. D.), Early Days of California. MS.
McDonald (D. G. Forbes), British Columbia. London, 1863.
McDougal (F. H.), The Donner Tragedy. In Pacific Rural Press, Jan. 21, 1871.
McDougall (James A.), Speech on Pacific Railroad in U. S. H. Rep. Jan. 16, 1855. Washington, 1855.
McFarlane (James), The Coal-regions of America. New York, 1873.
McFie (Matthew), Vancouver Island and British Columbia. London, 1865.
McGarrahan (William), The Quicksilver Mines of Panoche Grande. Washington, 1860; Memorial. A Collection of Documents. San Francisco, 1870.

McGlashan (C. F.), History of the Donner Party. Truckee, 1879; San Francisco, 1880.

McGowan (Edward), Facts concerning the Organization known as the 'Hounds' in S. F. Post, Nov. 1, 1878; Narrative of Adventure while pursued by Vigilance Committee. San Francisco, 1857.

McIlvaine (William), Sketches of Scenery and Notes of Personal Adventure in California, etc. Philadelphia, 1850.

McKay (Joseph W.), Recollections of a Chief Trader in the Hudson's Bay Company. MS.

McKinstry (George), Papers on the History of California. MS.

McLean (Finis E.), Speech, June 5, 1850, on Constitution of Cal. Wash. 1850.

McPherson, Letters of Juanita. [In various newspapers.]

McPherson (W.), Homes in Los Angeles. Los Angeles, 1873.

McQueen (John), Speech, June 3, 1850, on Admission of Cal. Wash., 1850.

McWillie (W.), Speech, March 4, 1850, on the Admission of Cal. n.pl., n.d.

Machado (Antonio), Escritos de un Síndico. MS.

Machado (Juana), Tiempos Pasados de California. MS.

Madelene (Henri de la), Le Comte Gaston de Raousset-Boulbon. Paris, 1876.

Maglianos, St Francis and Franciscans.

Maguire (John Francis), The Irish in America. New York, 1868.

Maitorena (José Joaquin), Cartas Sueltas. MS.

Malarin (Juan), Correspondencia. MS.

Malaspina (Alejandro), Nota de Oficiales. MS.

Malaspina (Alejandro) and José de Bustamante, Carta al P. Lasuen, y Respuesta, 1794. MS.

Malte-Brun, La Sonora et ses Mines. Paris, 1864.

Mammoth City, Herald, Homer Mining Index, Lake Mining Review.

Mangino (Fernando J.), Respuesta de 19 de Junio 1773. In Palou, Not., i. 580.

Manrow (John P.), Statement on Vigilance Committees in S. F. MS.

Mans (Matthew), Travels in Mining Districts. MS.

Mansfield (Edward D.), Mexican War. New York, 1849.

March y Labores (José), Historia de la Marina Española. Madrid, 1854. 4to. 2 vols. and atlas.

Marchand (Étienne), Voyage autour du Monde, 1790–2. Paris, n.d. 5 vols.

Marcou (Jules), Notes upon the First Discoveries of California. Wash., 1878.

Marcy (W. L.), Communications of the Secretary of War. 1846–8. In Cal. and N. Mex., Mess. and Doc., 1848; Id., 1850.

Marin County History (Alley Bowen & Co.) San Francisco, 1880.

Mariposa, Free Press, Gazette, Mail.

Mariposa Estate, Its Past, Present, and Future. New York, 1868.

Markleville, Alpine Courier, Alpine Signal.

Markof (Alexey), Ruskie na Vostotchnom. St Petersburg, 1856.

Marquina (Virey), Comunicaciones al Gobr. de Cal., 1800 et seq. MS.

Marquinez (Marcelino), Cartas del Padre al Gobr. Sola, 1821. MS.

Marron (Felipa Osuna), Papeles Originales. MS.

Marron (Felipa Osuna), Recuerdos del Pasado. MS.

Marryat (Frank), Mountains and Mole Hills. New York, 1855; London, 1855.

Marryat (Frederick), Narrative of the Travels, etc. of Monsieur Violet. New York, 1843.

Marsh (John), Letter to Commodore Jones, 1842. MS.

Marsh (John), Letter to Lewis Cass, 1846. In Pacheco Contra Costa Gazette, Dec. 21, 1867.

Marsh (John), Letters of a Pioneer Doctor. MS.

Marshall (H.), Speech, Apr. 3, 1850, on Cal. Message. Wash., 1850.

Marshall (Henry), Statement, 1843. MS.

Marshall (T. W. M.), Christian Missions. New York, 1864. 2 vols.

Marshall (W. G.), Through America. London, 1881.

Martin (Juan), Visita á los Gentiles Tulareños, 1804. MS.

Martin (Thomas S.), Narrative of Frémont's Expedition, 1845–7. MS.

Martinez, Carquinez Enterprise, Express.
Martinez (Ignacio), Defensa Dirigida al Comandante General, 1830. MS.
Martinez (Ignacio), Entrada á las Rancherías del Tular, 1816. MS.
Martinez (Ignacio), Escritos Varios. MS.
Martinez (Luis Antonio), Correspondencia del Padre. MS.
Martinez (Estévan José) and Gonzalo Lopez de Haro, Cuarta Exploracion, 1788. MS.
Marvin (John G.), The Law Establishing Common Schools. S. F., 1853.
Marysville, Appeal, California Express, Herald, North Californian, Northern Statesman, Standard, Telegraph.
Marysville and Benicia National Railroad. Report of Engineers on Survey. Marysville, 1853.
Maseres (Bartholomé), Relacion clara del Nayaríth, 1785. MS. In Pinart, Col. Doc. Mexico. Misiones.
Mason (John Y.), Letters of U. S. Sec. Nav. to Commanders in Cal. 1846-7. In Cutts' Conquest; Speech, May 27, 1850, on Admission of California. Wash., 1850.
Mason's Handbook to California. London, 1850.
Mason (Richard B.), California and her Gold. Report to the secretary of war. Wash., 1850.
Mason (Richard B.), Miscellaneous Proclamations, 1849.
Mason (Richard B.), Orders and Correspondence of the Military Governor, 1847-8. In Cal. and N. Mex., Mess. and Doc., 1850; also, MS. [In archives.]
Mason (Richard B.), Proclamation, Nov. 29, 1847. In English and Spanish. Monterey, 1847.
Massett (Stephen C.), Drifting About. New York, 1863; Experiences of a '49er. MS.
Materialui dhlia Istoriy Russkikh Zasselenig. St. Petersburg, 1861.
Matthewson (T. D.), California Affairs. MS.
Maurelle (Francisco Antonio) Diario del Viage de la Sonora, 1775. MS.
Maurelle (Francisco Antonio), Compendio de Noticias, Viage de, 1774. MS.
Maurelle (Francisco Antonio), Journal of a Voyage in 1775. London, 1780.
Maurelle (Francisco Antonio), Navegacion, 1779. MS.
Maxwell (R. T.), Visit to Monterey in 1842. MS.
Mayer (Brantz), Mexico, Aztec, Spanish, etc. Hartford, 1852. 2 vols.
Mayer Manuscripts. A collection of 30 copies from Mex. archives.
Mayfield, Enterprise, Pastor.
Mayne (R. C.), Four Years in British Columbia. London, 1862.
Mazatlan, Times.
Meade (Edwin R.), The Chinese Question. New York, 1877.
Meadow Lake, Sun.
Meadows (James), The Graham Affair, 1840. MS.
Mechanics' Institute of San Francisco. Report of Industrial Exhibitions. San Francisco, 1857 et seq.
Mellus (Francis), Diary, 1838-40. MS.
Mellus (Francis and Henry), Letters. MS.
Mendocino, Independent Dispatch, West Coast Star.
Mendocino War, Majority and Minority Reports of the Joint Special Committee. San Francisco, n.d.
Mendocino County History. San Francisco, 1880.
Menefee (C. A.), Historical and Descriptive Sketch-book of Napa, Sonoma, etc. Napa, 1873.
Mercado (Jesus María Vazquez), Expediente de Papeles tocantes á la Matanza de Indios hecha por órden del P. Ministro de S. Rafael, 1833. MS.
Mercantile Library Association. Annual Reports of President, etc. San Francisco, 1855 et seq.
Mercator's Atlas. 1569 et seq.
Merced, People, San Joaquin Valley Argus, Tribune.
Merced County History. San Francisco, 1881. 4to.

Merchants' Exchange Prices Current and Shipping List. San Francisco, 1850–2. 4to. 3 vols.

Mercury, Expediente de Investigacion sobre la captura, 1813. MS.

Meredith (W. M.), Miscellaneous Proclamations by Secretary of the Treasury, 1849.

Merewether (Henry Alworth), By Sea and By Land. London, 1874.

Merrill (Annis), Recollections of San Francisco. MS.

Mexican Border Troubles [45th Cong., 1st Sess., H. Ex. Doc. 13]. Wash., 1877.

Mexican Boundary, Resolution respecting adjustment and payment of the $3,000,000 [34th Cong., 1st Sess., Sen. Ex. Doc. 57]. Washington, 1855.

Mexican Ocean Mail and Inland Company, Reports. New York, 1853 et seq.

Mexican War. A Collection of U. S. Government Documents, Scraps, Pamphlets, etc. 12 vols.

Mexican War. Messages of the President [30th Cong., 1st Sess., H. Ex. Doc. 60; Sen. Ex. 1]. Washington, 1847–8. 2 vols.

Mexican War (The). Its Heroes. Phil., 1850; Phil., 1860.

Mexico, Acta Constitutiva de la Federacion Mexicana. Mexico, 1824; Actas de la Junta de Minería, 1846–7. MS.; Acuerdo de la Junta de Guerra y Real Hacienda (Misiones) 1772. MS.; Arancel General de Aduanas Marítimas y Fronterizas. Mexico, 1842 et seq.; Arreglo Provisional de la Administracion de Justicia 23 Mayo 1837. In Arrillaga, Recop. 1837, p. 399; Bases y leyes Constitucionales de la República Mexicana. Mexico, 1837; Coleccion de Decretos y Órdenes de Interes Comun. Mexico 1850; Coleccion de Leyes y Decretos, 1839–41, 1844–8, 1850. Mexico, 1851–2, 6 vols.; Coleccion de Órdenes y Decretos de la Soberana Junta Provis. Gubern. Mexico, 1829. 4 vols.; Constitucion Federal. Mexico, 1824 et seq.; Decreto sobre Pasaportes, etc., 1828. In Schmidt's Civil Law, Spain, 346; Diario del Gobierno de la República Mexicana. Mexico, 1840 et seq.; Estado Mayor General del Ejército, Escalafon. Mexico, 1854; Exposicion del Ministro de Hacienda 1848. Mexico, 1848; Instruccion Provisional Dic. 22, 1824, Mexico, 1824; Leyes Constitucionales. 24 Dic. 1829. In Arrillaga, Recop. 1836, 317; Leyes Vigentes en 1829; Memorias de Guerra, Hacienda, Justicia, Relaciones, etc. Mexico, 1822 et seq. [Annual Reports of the Mexican government in its different departments, cited by name and date. Nearly all contain more or less on California. About 200 vols.]; Providencia de la Suprema Corte, 11 Nov. 1837. In Arrillaga, Recop. 1838, p. 572; Reglamento para la Colonizacion, 1828. MS.; Reglamento de la Direccion de Colonizacion. Mexico, 1846; Reglamento de Elecciones 19 Junio 1843. MS.; Reglamento Provisional, Departmentos, 20 Marzo. In Arrillaga, Recop. 1837, p. 202; Reglamento para el ramo de Pasaportes, 1828. MS.; Reglamento para la Tesorería general. Mexico, 1831. 4to; Reglas para Elecciones de Diputados y Ayuntamiento. 1830. In Arrillaga, Recop. 1830, p. 253.

Meyer (Carl), Nach dem Sacramento. Aaran, 1855.

Meyrick (Henry), Santa Cruz and Monterey. San Francisco, 1880.

Micheltorena (Manuel), Administration in Upper California. n.pl., n.d.

Micheltorena (Manuel), Bando Económico, 19 Junio 1843. MS.

Micheltorena (Manuel), Conciudadanos, etc. Monterey, Dic. 16, 1844.

Micheltorena (Manuel), Correspondencia Miscelánea del Sr Gobernador. MS.

Micheltorena (Manuel), Decreto por el cual devuelve las Misiones á los Frailes, 1843. MS.

Micheltorena (Manuel), Decreto Prohibiendo la Introduccion de Efectos Extrangeros. Monterey, Julio 30, 1844.

Micheltorena (Manuel), Digest of Correspondence, 1843. n.pl., n.d.

Micheltorena (Manuel), El C....[Anuncia la Apertura de las Sesiones de la Diputacion.] Monterey, 28 Agosto, 1844.

Micheltorena (Manuel), El C...[Decreto de la Asamblea, Recursos para la Guerra Probable.] Monterey, 3 Sept. 1844.

Micheltorena (Manuel), Instrucciones, 1842. MS.

Micheltorena (Manuel), Medidas de Defensa contra los E. U., 1844. MS.

Micheltorena (Manuel), Reglamento de Escuelas Amigas, 1844. MS.
Micheltorena (Manuel), Reglamento de Milicia Auxiliar. Monterey, 16 de Julio, 1844.
Millennial Star. Manchester, Liverpool, etc., 1841–79. 41 vols.
Miller (Joaquin), The Danites in the Sierras. Chicago, 1881; Life among the Modocs. London, 1873; First Fam'lies of the Sierras. Chicago, 1876; Shadows of Shasta. Chicago, 1881; A Sierra Wedding. In San José Pioneer, Nov. 17, 1877.
Millville, Shasta County Record.
Miner (The). San Francisco, 1866.
Miners' Own Book (The). San Francisco, 1858.
Mining Companies, Reports, etc. Cited by name of company. Not given in this list.
Mining Magazine. New York, 1853 et seq.
Miscellaneous Historical Papers. A Collection. MS.
Miscellaneous Statements on California History. MS.
Miscellany. A Collection. 9 vols.
Misiones, Cuaderno de Estados, en satisfaccion de los puntos que el Sr Comisionado pide á la Prefectura, 1822. MS.
Misiones, Informes Anuales y Bienales, Índice y Notas. MS. In Arch. Sta Bárbara, v. passim; x. 495–526; xii. 51–129.
Mission Books. See name of the Mission.
Mission Land Grants, Opinions, etc. In Hayes' Mission Book, ii. 35.
Mission Music, An immense parchment folio with introduction by P. Duran, 1813. MS.
Mission Reports, different dates and establishments scattered in the archives. Many cited by name of author or mission.
Mission Statistics. MS.
Modesto, Herald, San Joaquin Valley Mirror, Stanislaus County Weekly News.
Mofras (Eugene Duflot de), Cartas de un Viagero. MS.
Mofras (Eugene Duflot de), Exploration de l'Orégon, des Californies, etc. Paris, 1844. 2 vols. and atlas.
Mohan (H.) et al., Pen Pictures of our Representative Men. Sac., 1880.
Mokelumne, Calaveras County Chronicle.
Möllhausen (Baldwin), Diary of a Journey. London, 1858. 2 vols.
Möllhausen (Baldwin), Tagebuch einer Reise vom Mississippi, etc. Leipzig, 1858. 4to.
Mone (Alexander), A Pioneer of 1847. MS.
Monitor, Alpine Miner.
Montanus (Arnoldus), Die Nieuwe en Onbekande Weereld. Amsterdam. 1671. folio.
Montanus (Arnoldus), Die Unbekannte Neue Welt. [Translated by Dapper.] Amsterdam, 1673.
Monterey, Accounts of the Presidial Company, Rosters, etc. MS. Chiefly in Prov. St. Pap., Ben. Mil.; Dept. St. Pap., Ben. Mil.; and St. Pap., Sac.
Monterey, Actos del Ayuntamiento, 1831–5. MS.
Monterey, Acuerdo del Ayunt. y de la Diputacion contra el Cambio de Capital, 1835. MS.
Monterey, Archivo de. MS. 16 vols.
Monterey, Californian, 1846–8. Also a vol. of MS. extracts.
Monterey, Cuentas de la Compañia Presidial, 1828. MS.
Monterey, Democrat, Gazette, Herald, Recorder.
Monterey, Diario de Sucesos, 1800–2. MS.
Monterey, Extracto de Noticias. Mexico, 1770.
Monterey, Official Account of the Taking of. Pittsburg, 1848.
Monterey, Ordenanzas Municipales, 1828. MS.
Monterey, Padron General, 1836. MS.
Monterey, Parroquia, Archivo. MS.
Mnoterey, Peticion del Ayuntamiento en favor de Frailes Españoles, 1829. MS.

Monterey, President's Mess., Information on taking of, by Com. Jones. [27th Cong., 3d Sess., H. Ex. Doc. No. 166.]
Monterey, Ranchos existentes, 1795. MS.
Monterey, U. S. Consulate Record. MS. 2 vols.
Monterey County, History of. San Francisco, 1881. 4to.
Montesdeoca Document. Nov. 14, 1845. MS.
Montgomery (Richard Z.), Recollections Mining Camps 1853-4. MS.
Montgomery (Zachary), Speech in Assembly of Cal., April 10, 1861, on Common Schools. Sacramento, 1861; Various other Speeches on same Subject.
Moore (Augustin), Pioneer Experiences. MS.
Moore and De Pues. See San Mateo County History.
Mora (José María Luis), Obras Sueltas. Paris, 1837. 2 vols.
Moraga (Gabriel), Cartas. MS.
Moraga (Gabriel), Diario de su Expedicion al Puerto de Bodega, 1810. MS.
Moraga (José Joaquin), Escritos Sueltos. MS.
Moraga (José Joaquin), Informe de 1777 sobre cosas de San Francisco. MS.
Moraga (José Joaquin), Instruccion y órden que debe observar el cabo de Escolta de S. José, 1782. MS.
Morehead (C. S.), Speech, Apr. 23, 1850, on Admission of Cal. Wash., 1850.
Morelli (Ciriacus), Fasti Novi Orbis et Ordinationum. Venetiis, 1776. 4to.
Morenhaut, Correspondence of the French Consul. MS.
Moreno (José Matías), Documentos para la Historia de California. MS.
Moreno (Juan B.), Vida Militar. MS.
Morgan (Martha M.), A Trip across the Plains. San Francisco, 1864.
Morineau (P. de), Notice sur la Nouville Californie. 1834. In Soc. Géog., Bulletin, xv.; Nouv. An. Voy., lxi. 137.
Mormon Battalion, List of Officers and Men. MS.
Morrell (Benjamin W.), Narrative of Four Voyages. New York, 1832.
Morris (Albert F.), Diary of a Crazy Man. MS.
Morris (George B.), The Chinaman as he is. MS.
Morse (J. F.), Illustrated History of California, etc. Sacramento, 1854.
Morskoi Svornik, 1858.
Moulder (A. J.), Commentaries on the School Law. Sacramento, 1858.
Mountaineering on the Pacific. In Harper's Mag., xxxix., 793.
Mowry (Sylvester), The Mines of the West. New York, 1864.
Mugártegui (Pablo), Carta al P. Lasuen, 1794. MS.
Mugártegui (Pablo) and Tomás de la Peña, Parecer sobre el establecimiento de un Convento en S. Francisco, 1797. MS.
Muhlenpfordt (Eduard), Versuch einer getreuen Schilderung der Republik Mexico. Hanover, 1844. 3 vols.
Municipal laws, regulations, reports, and other public documents, cited by name of town, but for the most part not in this list.
Muñoz (Juan Antonio), Cartas del Capitan. MS.
Muñoz (Pedro), Diario de la Expedicion hecha por D. Gabriel Moraga al Tular, 1806. MS.
Murguía (José Antonio), and Tomás de la Peña, Informe de Sta Clara, 1777. MS.
Murphy (Timothy), Letters from 1824. MS.
Murray (Charles Aug.), Travels in North America. New York, 1839.
Murray (E. F.), Miscellaneous Documents. MS.
Murray (Walter), Narrative of a California Volunteer, 1847. MS.
Música de Misiones. MS.

Nacion (La). Mexico, 1856 et seq.
Nanaimo (B. C.), Free Press.
Napa City, Classic, Napa County Reporter, Pacific Echo, Register.
Napa and Lake Counties, History of (Slocum, Bowen, and Co.) San Francisco, 1881. 4to.
National Democratic Quarterly Review. Washington, 1859 et seq.

Nava (Pedro), Comunicaciones del Comandante Gen. de Provincias Internas, 1791 et seq. MS.
Nava (Pedro), Informe sobre Proyecto de Abrir Caminos entre Cal. y N. Mexico, 1801. MS.
Navarrete (Martin Fernandez), Introduccion. In Sutil y Mexicana, Viage; Viages Apócrifos. In Col. Doc. Inéd., xv.
Nayarit, Informe de la Aud. de Guadalajara, 1784. MS.
Neal (Samuel), Notice of a Pioneer of '45. MS.
Neall (James), Vigilance Committee. MS.
Nevada (Cal.) Democrat, Gazette, Herald, Journal, National Gazette, Transcript.
Nevada County, History of. Oakland, 1881. Atlas folio.
Neve (Felipe), Correspondencia Miscelánea del Gobr., 1775 et seq. MS.
Neve (Felipe), Informe de 25 de Abril 1777. MS.
Neve (Felipe), Informe sobre Reglamento, 1778. MS.
Neve (Felipe), Instruccion al Ayudante Inspector Soler, 1782. MS.
Neve (Felipe), Instruccion á Fages sobre Gobierno Interino, 1782. MS.
Neve (Felipe), Instruccion para la Fundacion de Los Angeles, 1781. MS.
Neve (Felipe), Instruccion que ha de gobernar al Comte de Sta Bárbara, 1782. MS.
Neve (Felipe), Reglamento ó Instruccion, 1779. MS.
New Almaden—a great number of briefs, arguments, opinions, documents, etc., in the cases of Castillero, Fossat, and others against the U. S.; also the following pamphlets on the same subject: Correspondence. San Francisco, 1858; The Discussion Reviewed, S. F. 1859; Exploits of the Attorney-General in California. New York, 1860; Further Correspondence in relation to. San Francisco, 1859; (Letter to Hon. J. S. Black, from 'a Cal. Pioneer'). New York, 1860; Letter to the President of the U. S. (by John T. Doyle), New York, 1860; Letters from San Francisco Herald, Dec. 1858; Report of Attorney-General to the President, Resolutions of Cal. Leg., 1860; Smart and Cornered. n. pl., n.d.
Newark (N. J.), Advertiser.
New Haven (Conn.), Journal and Courier.
New Helvetia, Diary of Events in 1845-8. MS.
New Orleans (La.), Advertiser, Bee, Commercial Times, Courier, Picayune, Tropic.
Newspapers of California and other states of the Pacific U. S. The most important are cited under the name of the town where published, and many of them named in this list.
New Tacoma (Wash.), Ledger.
New Westminster (B. C.), Mainland Guardian.
New York, Bulletin, Commercial Advertiser, Commercial Journal and Register, Courier, Graphic, Evangelist, Evening Post, Herald, Journal of Commerce, Mail, Post, Sun, Sunday Times, Times, Tribune, World.
Nicolay (C. G.), Oregon Territory. London, 1846.
Nidever (George), Life and Adventures of an Old Trapper. MS.
Niel (Juan Amando), Apuntaciones á las memorias de Gerónimo de Zárate Salmeron. In Doc. Hist. Mex., ser. iii., tom. iv. 78.
Niles' Register. Baltimore, etc., 1811–49. 76 vols.
Nordhoff (Charles), California: for Health, Pleasure, etc. New York, 1873; Northern California, Oregon, etc. New York, 1874; New York, 1877.
Norman (Lucia), A Youth's History of California. San Francisco, 1867.
North American Review. Boston, 1819 et seq.
North San Juan, Press, War Club.
North Pacific Review. San Francisco, 1862 et seq.
Noticioso General. Mexico, 1815–21. 6 vols.
Nouvelles Annales des Voyages. Paris, 1819–60. 168 vols.
Nueva España, Acuerdos de la Junta Sup. de Real Hacienda, 1794. MS.
Nuevo Mexico, Expediente de Abigeato, 1833. MS.

Nuez (Joaquin Pascual), Diario del Capellan de la Expedicion para los Amajavas, 1819. MS.
Nugent (John), Scraps of Early History. In S. F. Argonaut, April 13, 1878.

Oajaca, Esposicion, 1828.
Oakland, Alameda Democrat, Argus, California Cadet, College Echo, Democrat, Diamond Press, Dominion Press, Herald, Home Journal and Alameda County Advertiser, Homestead, Independent Itemizer, Journal, Mirror, Monthly Review, Nevlæan Review, News, Notes of Warning, Our Paper, People's Champion, Press, Radiator, Semitropical Press, Signs of the Times, Termini, Times, Torchlight, Transcript, Tribune, University Echo.
Oakland Public Schools, Annual Reports. Oakland, 1870 et seq.; many other municipal documents.
Observador Judicial y de Legislacion. Mexico, 1842 et seq.
Occident and Orient. Melbourne, etc.
Odd Fellows. A large number of publications of different lodges of the order, cited under the above title.
Ogilby (John), America. London, 1671. folio.
Olbés (Ramon), Cartas sobre el Tumulto de Sta Cruz, 1818. MS.
Olds (Edson B.), Speech, July 24, 1850, on California Question. Wash., 1850.
Olney (James N.), Vigilance Committee. MS.
Olvera (Agustin), Documentos para la Historia de Cal. MS.
Olvera (Agustin), Varias Cartas. MS.
Olympia, Commercial Age, Echo, Pacific Tribune, Puget Sound Courier.
O'Meara (James), Broderick and Gwin. San Francisco, 1881.
Operacion Cesárea. MS. [A relic of the missions.]
Orations. See Speeches.
Ord (Angustias de la Guerra), Ocurrencias en California. MS.
Ord (J. L.), Reminiscences of '47. MS.
Ordaz (Blas), Cartas del Padre. MS.
Ordaz (Blas), Diario de la Expedicion de Luis Argüello al Norte, 1821. MS.
Ordenanzas Municipales, [1824.] MS.
Orders, secret, benevolent, etc. See Institutions.
Oregon, Spectator. 1846 et seq.
Oregon City, Argus.
Orleans (Cal.), Klamath News, Northern Record.
Oro Molido, en lengua de Indios por Padre Arroyo. MS.
Oroville, Butte County Press, Butte County, Butte Record, Mercury.
Orr (N. M.), The City of Stockton; Its Position, etc. Stockton, 1874.
Ortega (Felipe María), Diario que forma. Reconocimiento de Sitios, 1795. MS.
Ortega (José Francisco), Comunicaciones del Comandante de S. Diego á Rivera y Moncada, 1774–6. MS.
Ortega (José Francisco), Correspondencia. MS.
Ortega (José Francisco), Fragmento de 1769. MS.
Ortega (José Francisco), Informe de 30 Nov. 1775. MS.
Ortega (José Francisco), Memorial sobre sus Méritos y Servicios Militares, 1786. MS.
Ortelivs (Abrahamvs), Theatrvm Orbis Terrarum. Antverpiæ, 1573. folio.
Osborn (W. B.), Narrative of a Visit to S. Francisco, 1844. MS.
Osio (Antonio María), Carta sobre Combinaciones Políticas, 1836. MS.
Osio (Antonio María), Carta á Vallejo. 26 Nov. 1836. MS.
Osio (Antonio María), Escritos Sueltos. MS.
Osio (Antonio María), Historia de California. MS.
Osuna (Juan María), Cartas. MS.
Oswald (H. Fr.), Californien und Seine Verhältnisse. Leipzig, 1849.
Overland Mail Service to California. n.pl. [1857].
Overland Monthly. San Francisco, 1868–75. 15 vols.
Owen (J. J.), Santa Clara Valley. San José, 1873.
Owl (The), San Francisco, 1869 et seq.

P. (D. P. E.)   See California, in Viagero Universal.
Pabellon Nacional (El), Mexico, 1844 et seq.
Pacheco, Contra Costa Gazette, Contra Costa News
Pacheco (Dolores), Cartas. MS.
Pacheco (Romualdo), Cartas, 1825–31. MS.
Pacheco (Salvio), Escritos de un vecino de S. José. MS.
Pacific Coast Educational Journal. San Francisco, 1874.
Pacific Coast Mines. San Francisco, 1876.
Pacific Expositor, San Francisco, 1860–2. 3 vols.
Pacific Mail Steamship Company, Annual Reports. New York, 1854 et seq.;
     and various pamphlets.
Pacific Medical and Surgical Journal. San Francisco, 1858 et seq.
Pacific Railroad. A Collection; also a large number of publications cited by
     this title.
Pacific Railroad Reports. Washington, 1855–60. 4to. 13 vols.
Pacific School and Home Journal. San Francisco, 1877 et seq.
Pacific Wagon Roads, Reports upon [35th Cong., 2d Sess., H. Ex. Doc. 108;
     Sen. Ex. Doc. 36.] Wash., 1858.
Paddock (A. G.), The Fate of Madame La Tour. New York, 1881.
Padrés (José María) Correspondencia de un Republicano. MS.
Padrés (José María), Protesta que dirige al Gefe Político, 1835. MS.
Paez (Juan). See Cabrillo, Relacion.
Pájaro, Monterey Union.
Palmer (J. W.), The New and the Old. New York, 1859.
Palmer (Joel), Early Intercourse. MS. Journal of Travels over the Rocky
     Mountains, 1845–6. Cincinnati, 1852; Wagon Trains. MS.
Palmer (Lyman L.), see Napa and Lake County History.
Palmer (William J.), Report of Surveys across the Continent in 1867–8.
     Philadelphia, 1869.
Palomares (José Francisco), Memoria. MS.
Palou (Francisco), Circular sobre Informes de Misiones, etc., 9 Oct. 1773. MS.
Palou (Francisco), Comunicacion al Presidente sobre Raciones, 1781. MS.
Palou (Francisco), Correspondencia del Misionero. MS.
Palou (Francisco), Defuncion del Padre Junípero Serra, 1784. MS.
Palou (Francisco), Espedicion y Registro de S. Francisco. In Id., Not., ii. 43.
Palou (Francisco), Fondo Piadoso de Misiones de California, etc., 1772. MS.
Palou (Francisco), Informe de 10 Dic. 1773. In Id., Not., ii. 11.
Palou (Francisco), Informe que por el mes de Diciembre de 1773 hizo al Virey
     Bucareli. MS.
Palou (Francisco), Informe sobre Quejas del Gobernador, 1785. MS.
Palou (Francisco), Letter of Aug. 15, 1783. In Hist. Mag., iv. 67.
Palou (Francisco), Noticias de la California. Mexico, 1857. In Doc. Hist.
     Mex., ser. iv., tom. vi.–vii.; San Francisco, 1874. 4 vols.
Palou (Francisco), Relacion Histórica de la Vida etc. de Junípero Serra.
     Mexico, 1787.
Pamphlets. A collection. 5 vols.
Panamá, Star and Herald. Panamá, 1849 et seq.
Panamint, News.
Pangua (Tomás de), Carta al Virey sobre Peligros que amenazan la California,
     1804. MS.
Papeles Varios. A collection of Spanish and Mexican pamphlets. 218 vols.
Parker (Richard), Speech, Feb. 28, 1850, on President's Mess. on Cal. Wash.
     1850.
Parkinson (R. R.), Pen Portraits. San Francisco, 1878.
Parkman (Francis J.), The California and Oregon Trail. New York, 1849.
Parrish (J. L.), Anecdotes of Oregon. MS.
Parrott (John), Business Letters. MS.
Parsons (George F.), Life and Adventures of James W. Marshall. Sacra-
     mento, 1870.
Paschal (George W.), Speech, in the Case of Wm. McGarrahan. Wash., 1869.

Paterna (Antonio) Informes de la Mision de Sta Bárbara, 1787–92. MS.
Patterson (George), Adventures of a Pioneer of 1840. MS.
Patterson (George W.), Across Mexico to California. MS.
Patterson (Lawson B.), Twelve Years in the Mines of California. Cambridge, 1862.
Pattie (James O.), Personal Narratives. Cincinnati, 1833.
Paty (John), Letters of a Sea Captain. MS.
Payeras (Mariano), Circular á los Padres, 1818. MS.
Payeras (Mariano), Circular á los Padres, 1819. MS.
Payeras (Mariano), Circular del Presidente, 1817. MS.
Payeras (Mariano), Circular en que prohibe el uso de Carruajes, 1821. MS.
Payeras (Mariano), Comunicacion sobre la Mision de la Purísima, 1810. MS.
Payeras (Mariano), Cordillera sobre suministracion de Víveres, 1821. MS.
Payeras (Mariano), Correspondencia del Misionero Prefecto. MS.
Payeras (Mariano), Dos Circulares sobre Contrata con McCulloch, Hartnell y Cia, 1822. MS.
Payeras (Mariano), Informe por el Comisario Prefecto del Actual Estado de los 19 Misiones, 1820. MS.
Payeras (Mariano), Informes Bienales de Misiones, 1815–20. MS.
Payeras (Mariano), Instruccion del Vicario Foráneo, 1817. MS.
Payeras (Mariano), Memorial á los Padres, 1821. MS.
Payeras (Mariano), Memorial á los Padres, sobre la Cesion de las Nueve Misiones del Sur, 1820. MS.
Payeras (Mariano), Memorial de 2 de Junio, 1820. MS.
Payeras (Mariano), Memorial sobre Nueva Iglesia en Los Angeles, 1821. MS.
Payeras (Mariano), Noticia de un Viage á S. Rafael, 1818. MS.
Payeras (Mariano), Noticias sobre Ross. Diario de su Caminata con el Comisario del Imperio, 1822. MS.
Payeras (Mariano), Peticion al Gobernador, 1819. MS.
Payeras (Mariano), Representacion sobre Innovaciones del Sr Gobernador, 1821. MS.
Payson (G.), Romance of California. New York, 1851.
Peabody (Alfred), Early Days and Rapid Growth of Cal. Salem, 1874.
Pearce (J. A.), Speech, Apr. 29, 1852, Affairs in California. Washington, 1852.
Pearson (Gustavus C.), Recollections of a California '49er. MS.
Peckham (R. F.), Biographical Sketches. S. José Pioneer, June 9 et seq., 1877.
Peckham (R. F.), An Eventful Life. MS.
Peirce (Henry A.), Biography. San Francisco, 1880.
Peirce (Henry A.), Journals of Voyages, 1839–42. MS.
Peirce (Henry A.), Letter of 1842. In Niles' Register.
Peirce (Henry A.), Memoranda of a Navigator. MS.
Peirce (Henry A.), Rough Sketch. MS.
Peña (Cosme), Escritos de un Abogado. MS.
Peña (Tomás), Cargo de Homicidio contra el Padre, 1786–95. MS.
Peña (Tomás), Diario del Viage de Perez, 1774. MS.
Peña (Tomás), Peticion del Guardian sobre límites de Sta Clara, 1798. MS.
Pensamiento Nacional (El). Mexico, 1855 et seq.
Peralta (Luis), Cartas del Sargento. MS.
Peralta (Luis), Diario de una Expedicion contra Gentiles, 1805. MS.
Perez (Cornelio), Memoria Histórica. MS.
Perez (Eulalia), Una Vieja y Sus Recuerdos. MS.
Perez (Juan), Formulario, Escripturas de Posesion, 1773. MS.
Perez (Juan), Instruccion que el Virey dió á los Comandantes de Buques de Exploracion, 24 Dec. 1773. MS. In Pinart, Col. Doc. Mex.
Perez (Juan), Recuerdos Históricos. MS.
Perez (Juan), Relacion del Viage, 1774. MS.
Perez (Juan), Tabla Diaria, 1774. MS.
Perez Fernandez (José), Cartas del Alférez de Artillería. MS.

Perez Fernandez (José), Cuenta General de la Habilitacion de Mont, 1796. MS.
Perkins (Joseph J.), A Business Man's Estimate of Santa Bárbara County. Santa Bárbara, 1881.
Perry (J. E.), Travels, Scenes, and Sufferings in Cuba, etc. Boston, 1853.
Petaluma, Argus, Courier, Crescent, Journal and Argus, Land Journal, Sonoma County Journal, Standard.
Peters (De Witt C.), Life and Adventures of Kit Carson. New York, 1859.
Petit-Thouars (Abel de), Voyage autour du Monde, 1836-9. Paris, 1840-4. 5 vols.
Peto (Sir S. Morton), The Resources of America. London, etc., 1866.
Peyri (Antonio), Cartas del Fraile. MS.
Peyster (John W.), Personal and Military History of P. Kearny. N.Y., 1869.
Pfeiffer (Ida), A Lady's Second Voyage round the World. New York, 1856.
Phelps (John S.), Speech, June 8, 1850, on Admission of Cal. Wash. [1850].
Phelps (W. D.), Fore and Aft. Boston, 1871.
Philadelphia, American Gazette, Evening Star, Inquirer, Ledger, Press, Record, Times.
Phillips (C. H.), Southern California. San Francisco, 1879.
Phillips (J. Arthur), The Mining and Metallurgy of Gold and Silver. London, 1867.
Photographic Album of California Pioneers. 2 vols.
Pickett (Charles E.), Address to the Veterans of the Mexican War. San Francisco, 1880; Land Gambling versus Mining Gambling. San Francisco, 1879, 1880; Paris Exposition. San Francisco, 1877; and other pamphlets.
Pico (Andrés), Papeles de Misiones. MS. 1828-46.
Pico (José de Jesus), Acontecimientos en California. MS.
Pico (José de Jesus), Mofras at S. Antonio, 1842. MS.
Pico (José María, Dolores, Andrés, Antonio María, José Antonio, José de Jesus, Pio, etc.) Cartas. MS.
Pico (José Ramon), Documentos para la Historia de Cal. MS. 3 vols.
Pico (Pio), Correspondencia con Vocales Recalcitrantes del Norte, 1845. MS.
Pico (Pio), Decreto de Abril 4, 1846. Venta de Misiones. MS.
Pico (Pio), Documentos para la Historia de Cal. MS. 2 vols.
Pico (Pio), Narracion Histórica. MS.
Pico (Pio), Protesta al Manifiesto de D. Manuel Victoria, 1831. MS.
Pico (Pio), Reglamento del Gob^r. para la Enagenacion y arriendo de Misiones, 1845. MS.
Piña (Joaquin), Diario de la Espedicion al Valle de S. José, 1829. MS.
Pinart (Alphonse), Coleccion de Documentos Originales para la Historia de Mexico. MS.
Pinart (Alphonse), Documents on Russian America. MS.
Pinart (Alphonse), Documents for the History of Chihuahua, 1786-1855. MS. and print. 2 vols.
Pinart (Alphonse), Documents for the History of Sonora, 1784-1863. MS. and print. folio. 5 vols.
Pine (George W.), Beyond the West. Utica, 1871.
Pinkerton (John), General Collection of Voyages and Travels. London, 1808-14. 4to. 17 vols.
Pinto (Rafael), Apuntaciones para la Historia. MS.
Pinto (Rafael), Documentos para la Historia de Cal. MS.
Pio VI., Breve Apostólico en que se les concede varias gracias á los Misioneros, 1797. MS.
Pioneer (The). San Francisco, 1854-5. 4 vols.
Pioneer Journalism in California. In Upham's Notes; Rowell's Newspaper Reporter and Advertiser's Guide.
Pioneer Panamá Passengers. Re-union on the 4th of June, 1874. San Francisco, 1874.
Pioneer Perils, Donner Party. In S. F. Call, Oct. 3, 1880, and other papers.

Pioneer Sketches, A Collection. MS.
Pitic, Instruccion que se formó para el establecimiento de la Nueva Villa, 1789. MS.; also print.
Placerville, Courier, El Dorado County Republican, Mirror, Mountain Democrat, News.
Plan para Arreglo de Misiones, 1825. In Junta de Fomento de Cal.
Plan de Colonizacion Estrangera, 1825. In Junta de Fomento de Cal.
Plan de Colonizacion de Nacionales, 1825. In Junta de Fomento de Cal.
Plan de Gobierno adoptado por la Diputacion en Sta Bárbara, 1837. MS.
Plan de Gobierno Provincial. Monterey, 1824. MS.
Plan de Independencia adoptada por la Diputacion, 7 Nov. 1836. Monterey.
Plan de Independencia Californiana, 1836. Monterey, 1836.
Plan Político Mercantil, 1825. In Junta de Fomento de Cal.
Plan de Propios y Arbitrios para Fondos Municipales, 1834. Monterey, 1834.
Plan de S. Diego que proclamaron Zamorano, Bandini, y Otros, 1837. MS.
Player-Frowd (J. G.), Six Months in California. London, 1872.
Plumbe (John), Memorial against Asa Whitney's Railroad Scheme. Washington, 1851.
Point Arena, News, Recorder.
Poll-lists, cited by name of county or town. Not in this list.
Portilla (Pablo), Diario de una Expedicion al Tular, 1824. MS.
Portilla (Pablo), Escritos del Capitan. MS.
Portland (Or.), Bulletin, Catholic Sentinel, Oregonian, Standard, Telegram, West Shore.
Portolá (Gaspar), Diario del Viage á la California, 1769. MS.
Potechin, Selenie Ross, 1859. MS. translation.
Powers (Stephen), Autobiographical Sketch. MS.
Praslow (J.), Der Staat Californien. Gottingen, 1857.
Pratt (Parley Parker), The Autobiography of. New York, 1874.
Presidial Company Accounts, Rosters, etc. San Francisco, Monterey, Santa Bárbara, and San Diego. [Scattered in the archives.]
Presidios, Reglamento é Instruccion, 1772. Madrid, 1772; Mexico, 1773.
Preston (William B.), Speech in U. S. H. of Rep. Feb. 7, 1849. On Formation of a New State. Washington, 1849.
Prieto (Guillermo), Indicaciones sobre el orígen, etc., de las Rentas Generales de la Federacion Mexicana. Mexico, 1850; Viaje á los Estados Unidos. Mexico, 1878-9. 3 vols.
Privilegios Concedidos á Indios, 1803. MS.
Pronunciamiento de Apalátegui en Los Angeles, 1835. In Figueroa, Man.
Pronunciamiento de Monterey contra el Plan de San Diego, 1832. MS.
Pronunciamiento de San Diego contra Victoria, 1831. MS.
Pronunciamiento de Varela y otros contra los Americanos, 1846. MS.
Protesta de los Padres contra Gabelas, 1817. MS.
Providence (R. I.) Journal.
Provincial Records. MS. 12 vols. In Archivo de Cal.
Provincial State Papers. MS. 22 vols. In Archivo de Cal.; Id., Presidios. 2 vols.; Id., Benicia Military. 52 vols.; Id., Benicia Miscel. 2 vols.
Prudon (Victor), Correspondence d'un Français en Californie. MS.
Prudon (Victor), Vigilantes de Los Angeles, 1836. MS.
Purchas, His Pilgrimage. London, 1614. 9 books in 1 vol. folio.
Purchas, His Pilgrimes. London, 1625-6. folio. 5 vols.
Purísima, Cuaderno de Tratados Médicos. MS.
Purísima, Libros de Mision. MS.
Purísima, Peticion de los Padres sobre traslado de la Mision, 1813. MS.
Purkitt (J. H.), Letter on the Water Front Improvement. San Francisco, 1856.
Putnam (Harvey), Speech, July 30, 1850, on Admission of California. Wash. 1850.
Putnam's Magazine. New York, 1863 et seq.

Quarterly Review. London, 1809 et seq.
Queue Ordinance, The Invalidity of the. San Francisco, 1879.
Quicksilver: Facts concerning Mines in Santa Clara Co., Cal. N. Y., 1859.
Quigley (Hugh), The Irish Race in California, etc. San Francisco, 1878.
Quijas (José Lorenzo de la Concepcion), Cartas del Padre. MS.
Quimper (Manuel), Segundo Reconocimiento, 1790. MS.

Rabbison (Antonio B.), Growth of Towns. MS.
Rae (W. F.), Westward by Rail. London, 1870,
Rae (William V.), Investigacion judicial sobre su suicidio, 1845. MS.
Railroad Companies, Reports, etc. See name of company. Many consulted
    are not named in this list.
Railroads and Steamships. A collection.
Ralston (William C.), Affectionate Tribute to. San Francisco, 1875; Memo-
    rial of. San Francisco, 1875.
Ramirez (Angel), Cartas del Ex-Fraile. MS.
Ramsey (Albert C.), The Other Side. New York, 1850.
Randolph (Edmund), Oration before Society of Cal. Pioneers, Sept. 1860.
    In Hutchings' Mag., v. 263; Outline of the History of Cal. S. F., 1868.
Randolph (W. C.), Statement of a Pioneer of 1849. MS.
Raymond (Rossiter W.), Mining Industry of the States and Territories of the
    Rocky Mountains. N. Y., 1874; Silver and Gold. N. Y., 1873; Sta-
    tistics of Mines and Mining. Wash., 1873.
Raynal (G. T.), Histoire Philosophique. Paris, 1820–1. 12 vols. and atlas.
Razonador (El), Mexico, 1847 et seq.
Reading, Independent.
Recopilacion de Leyes de Los Reynos de las Indias mandadas Imprimir y
    Publicar por Cárlos II. Madrid, 1791. folio, 4 vols.
Redding (Benjamin B.), In Memoriam. San Francisco, 1882.
Rednitz (L.), Getreuester und Zuverlässigster Wegweiser und Rathgeber zur
    Reise nach und in Amerika und Californien. Berlin, 1852.
Redwood City, San Mateo Journal, San Mateo Times and Gazette.
Reed (James F.), The Donner Tragedy. In Pacific Rural Press, and San José
    Pioneer, 1877.
Registro de Licencias Militares, 1839. MS.
Reglamento de 24 de Mayo, 1773. In Palou, Not., i. 556.
Reglamento de Contribuciones sobre Licores, 1824. MS.
Reglamento de Defensores de la Independencia, 1845. MS.
Reglamento, Determinacion de 8 de Julio, 1773. In Palou, Not., i. 589.
Reglamento sobre Ganados, 1827. MS.
Reglamento para el Gobierno Interior de la Junta Departmental, 1840. MS.
Reglamento de Misiones Secularizadas, 1834. MS.
Reglamento Provisional para el gobierno interior de la Diputacion. Monte-
    rey, 1834. [The first book printed in California.]
Reid (Perfecto Hugo), Cartas. MS.
Reid (Perfecto Hugo), Los Angeles County Indians. In Hayes Mission Book,
    i., from Los Angeles Star.
Rejon (Manuel C.), Observaciones del Diputado saliente contra los Tratados
    de Paz. Querétaro, 1848.
Relacion de las Embarcaciones que han conducido los Situados, 1781–96. MS.
Rengel (José Antonio), Comunicaciones de Provincias Internas, 1784–6. MS.
Requena (Manuel), Documentos para la Historia de California. MS.
Requena (Manuel), Escritos de un Ciudadano de Angeles. MS.
Restaurador (El), Mexico, 1846 et seq.
Retes (Manuel), Portentosas Riquezas. In Estrella de Occid. Oct. 19, 1860.
Revere (Joseph Warren), Keel and Saddle. Boston, 1871; A Tour of Duty
    in California. N. Y. etc., 1849.
Revilla Gigedo (Virey), Carta de 27 Dic., 1793. MS.
Revilla Gigedo (Virey), Carta sobre Misiones, 1793. In Dicc. Univ., v. 426.
Revilla Gigedo (Virey), Comunicaciones al Gob^r. de Cal., 1790–4. MS.

Revilla Gigedo (Virey), Informe de 12 Abril, 1793. In Bustamante, Suplemento, iii. 112.
Revilla Gigedo (Virey), Instruccion que dejó escrita, 1789–94. MS. 2 vols.
Revista Científica y Literaria de Méjico. Mexico, 1845 et seq.
Revue des Deux Mondes. Paris, 1839 et seq.
Reynolds (J. N.), Pacific Ocean and South Sea. [23d Cong., 2d Sess., H. Ex. Doc. 105.] Wash., 1834.
Reynolds (Stephen), Register of Vessels at Honolulu, 1824–42. In Honolulu Friend, ii., 1849.
Rezánof (Nikolai), Zapiski, 1805–6. In Tikhménef, Istor. Obos., Appen.
Rhoads (Daniel), Relief of Donner Party, 1846. MS.
Richardson (Albert D.), Beyond the Mississippi. Hartford, 1867.
Richardson (Benjamin), Mining Experiences. MS.
Richardson (H. D.), History of the Foundation of Vallejo. MS.
Richardson (William A.), Letters of a Pioneer Sailor. MS.
Richardson (William A.), Salidas de Buques del Puerto de San Francisco, 1837–8. MS.
Richardson (William A.), Tarifa de Fletes y Pasages, S. Francisco, 1846. MS.
Richardson (J.) et al., Zoölogy of Beechey's Voyage. Lond., 1839–40.
Rico (Francisco), Memorias Históricas. MS.
Riesgo and Valdés, Memoria Estadística. Guadalajara, 1828.
Riley (Bennett), Military Correspondence [31st Cong., 1st Sess., Sen. Doc. 52]. Wash., 1849; Miscellaneous proclamations of the Military Governor, 1849; Proclama á los Habitantes de California, 3 Junio, 1848. Monterey, 1848; Tour of the Gold Regions [31st Cong., 1st Sess., H. Ex. Doc. 17].
Ringgold (Cadwalader), Correspondence to Accompany Maps and Charts of Cal. Wash., 1851; A Series of Charts with Sailing Directions. Wash., 1852.
Rio Vista, Enterprise, Gleaner.
Ripalda, Catecismo de la Doctrina Cristiana. Monterey, 1842.
Ripley (R. S.), The War with Mexico. New York, 1849. 2 vols.
Ripoll (Antonio), Levantamiento de Indios en Santa Bárbara, 1824. MS.
Rivera, Nueva Coleccion de Leyes. [Mexico.] 1835.
Rivera (Manuel), Los Gobernantes de Mexico. Mexico, 1872. 2 vols.
Rivera y Moncada (Fernando), Carta al Padre Serra, 1775. MS.
Rivera y Moncada (Fernando), Diligencias en la Toma de posesion del Mando, 1774. MS.
Rivera y Moncada (Fernando), Escritos Sueltos del Comandante General. MS.
Rivera y Moncada (Fernando), Merced de Tierras al Soldado Manuel Butron, 1775. MS.
Roach (Philip A.), Historical Facts from 1849. MS.
Robbins (Thomas M.), Diary, 1843–6. MS.
Roberts (George B.), Recollections of Hudson's Bay Co. MS.
Robinson (Alfred), Life in California. New York, 1846.
Robinson (Alfred), Statement of Recollections from 1829. MS.
Robinson (Fayette), California and its Gold Regions. New York, 1849.
Robinson (Marshall), A Trip in Southern California. Carson, 1879.
Robles (Secundino), Relacion de un Californio. MS.
Rodenbough (Theo. F.), From Everglade to Cañon. New York, 1875.
Roder (Henry), Bellingham Bay. MS.
Rodriguez (Jacinto), Narracion sobre Tiempos Pasados. MS.
Rodriguez (José B.), Recuerdos Históricos. MS.
Rodriguez (Manuel), Lo Acaecido con Tripulantes de la Byrd, 1803. MS.
Rodriguez (Manuel), Correspondencia de un Militar. MS.
Rodriguez (Manuel), Respuesta á las Quince Preguntas, 1798. MS.
Rogers (J. Henry), The California Hundred. San Francisco, 1865.
Rogers (William H.), Statement on Vigilance Committee. MS.
Rogers (Woodes), A Cruising Voyage round the World. London, 1718.
Rollin (M.), Mémoire Physiologique, 1786. In La Pérouse, Voy., iv. 50.
Romero (José), Documentos relativos á su Expedicion para abrir Camino entre Sonora y California, 1823–6. MS.

Romero (José María), Memorias de un Anciano. MS.
Romero (José Mariano) Catecismo de Ortología dedicado á los Alumnos de la
    Escuela Normal de Monterrey. Monterrey, 1836.
Romero (Vicente), Notes of the Past. MS.
Romeu (José Antonio), Cartas al P. Presidente Lasuen, 1791. MS.
Romeu (José Antonio), Correspondencia del Sr Gobernador. MS.
Roquefeuil (Camille de), Journal d'un Voyage autour du Monde, 1816-19.
    Paris, 1823. 2 vols.; Voyage round the World. Lond., 1823.
Rosa (Luis de la), Ensayo sobre la Administracion Pública de Mexico. Mex-
    ico, 1853. 4to.
Rosas (José Antonio), Causa Criminal, 1800-1. MS.
Rosignon (Julio), Porvenir de Vera Paz. Guatemala, 1861.
Ross, Contrat de Vente, 1841. MS.
Ross, Propuesta de Venta é Inventario, 1841. MS.
Ross (Charles L.), Experiences in '47. MS.
Ross (John E.), Narrative of an Indian Fighter. MS.
Ross (Joseph), Sketch of Experiences. MS.
Ross (James) and George Gary. From Wisc. to Cal. and Return. Madison, 1869.
Rossi (L'Abbé), Souvenirs d'un Voyage en Orégon et en Californie. Paris, 1864.
Roswag (C.), Les Métaux Précieux considérés au point de vue économique.
    Paris, 1865.
Rotschef (Alex.), Deed of Ross to Sutter, 1841. MS.
Rouhaud (Hippolyte), Les Régions Nouvelles. Paris, 1868.
Rouset de Jesus, Comunicaciones y Órdenes del Obispo de Sonora. MS.
Rovings in the Pacific from 1837-49. London, 1851. 2 vols.
Rowland (John), Lista de los que le acompañaron en su llegada, 1841. MS.
Rubio (Francisco), Causa Criminal por Asesinato y Estupro, 1828-31. MS.
Ruiz (Francisco María), Cartas del Comandante de San Diego. MS.
Ruschenberger (W. S. W.), Narrative of a Voyage round the World in
    1835-7. London, 1838. 2 vols.
Rush (John R.), Biographical Sketch. MS.
Rusling (James F.), Across America. New York, 1874.
Russ, Remembrances of a Pioneer of 1847. MS.
Russ (Adolph G.), Biography of a Pioneer of 1847. MS.
Russell (William H.), General John A. Sutter. n.pl. n.d.
Russell (William Howard), Hesperothen. New York, 1882.
Russian American Fur Company, Accounts, 1847-50. MS.
Ryan (R. F.), Judges and Criminals. In Golden Era [1853]; Personal Ad-
    ventures in Upper and Lower California in 1848-9. London, 1850. 2 vols.
Ryckman (Gerritt W.), Vigilance Committee. MS.

Saavedra (Ramon), Cartas al Gobr. de California, 1794. MS.
Sacramento, Bee, California Express, California Free Press, California Re-
    publican, Enterprise, Herald, Journal, Leader, News, Phœnix, Placer
    Times, Record, Record Union, Reporter, Rescue, Star, State Capital Re-
    porter, State Fair Gazette, Sun, Transcript, Travellers' Guide, Twice a
    Week, Ubiquitous, Union, Valley Agriculturist, Valley World.
Sacramento Medical Society, Constitution, etc. Sacramento, 1855.
Sacramento, Record of Criminal Court in County Clerk's Office, 1849. MS.
Sacramento, Spanish Archives in Office of Sec. State. MS.
Sacramento County, History. Oakland, 1880. folio.
Sacramento Valley Railroad Company, Reports. S. F., 1855 et seq.
Safford (A. K. P.), Narrative of Political Events. MS.
Saint Amant (M. de), Voyages en Californie et dans l'Orégon. Paris, 1854.
Saint Helena, Star, Yosemite Assembly.
Saint Louis (Mo.), Globe, Reveille, Union.
Sal (Hermenegildo), Cartas Misceláneas, 1777-1800. MS.
Sal (Hermenegildo), Informe. 31 de Enero 1796. MS.
Sal (Hermenegildo), Informe de los Parages que se han reconocido en la Ala
    meda, 1795. MS.

Sal (Hermenegildo), Informes sobre los Edificios de San Francisco, 1792. MS.
Sal (Hermenegildo), Instruccion al Cabo de la Escolta de Sta Cruz, 1791. MS.
Sal (Hermenegildo), Reconocimiento de la Mision de Sta Cruz, 1791. MS.
Sal (Hermenegildo), Respuesta á las Quince Preguntas, 1798. MS.
Sala (George A.), America Revisited. London, 1882. 2 vols.
Salazar (Alonso Isidro), Condicion Actual de California, 1796. MS.
Salem, Oregon Statesman, Willamette Farmer.
Sales (Luis), Noticias de Californias. Valencia, 1794.
Salidas de Buques del Puerto de S. Francisco, 1837-8. MS.
Salinas City, Index, Standard, Town Talk.
Salmeron (Gerónimo de Zárate), Relaciones de todas las cosas que en el Nuevo Mexico. In Doc. Hist. Mex., serie iii. tom. iv.
Salt Lake City (Utah), Deseret News, Herald, Telegraph, Tribune.
Sammlung aller Reisebeschreibungen. Leipzig, 1747-74. 4to. 21 vols.
San Andreas, Advertiser, Calaveras Times, Citizen, Foothill Democrat, Mountain News, Register.
San Antonio, Documentos Sueltos, 1779 et seq. MS.
San Antonio, Extracto del Libro de Difuntos. Muerte de Sarría, 1835. MS.
San Antonio, Libros de Mision. MS.
San Bernardino, Argus, Guardian, Independent, Times.
San Buenaventura, Free Press, Ventura Signal.
San Buenaventura, Libros de Mision. MS.
San Buenaventura, Memorias de Efectos, 1790-1810. MS.
San Buenaventura, Sale and Transfer, 1846. MS.
San Buenaventura, Suministraciones al Presidio, 1810-20. MS.
San Cárlos, Manifiesto de su cargamento para California, 1769. MS.
San Cárlos, Libros de Mision. MS.
Sanchez (José Antonio), Campaña contra Estanislao, 1829. MS.
Sanchez (José Antonio), Correspondencia del Alférez. MS.
Sanchez (José Antonio), Diario de la Caminata que hizo el P. Prefecto Payeras, San Diego á San Gabriel, 1822. MS.
Sanchez (José Antonio), Diario de la Expedicion, Nueva Planta de San Francisco, 1823. MS.
Sanchez (José Antonio), Journal of the enterprise against the Cosemenes, 1826. In Beechey's Voy., ii. 27.
Sanchez (José Antonio), Notas al Reglamento de Secularizacion, 1832. MS.
Sanchez (José Ramon), Notas Dictadas por el Ciudadano. MS.
Sanchez (Vicente), Cartas de un Angelino. MS.
Sanchez, Fidalgo, and Costansó, Informe sobre auxilios que se propone enviar á Cal., 1795. MS.
Sancho (Juan), Informe del Guardian al Virey, 1785. MS.
Sancho (Juan), Informe del P. Guardian al Virey. 20 Agosto, 1785. MS.
Sandels. See 'King's Orphan.'
San Diego, Archivo, 1826-50. MS.
San Diego, Bautismos, 1778-82. MS.
San Diego, Index of Archives, by Hayes. MS.
San Diego, Libros de Mision. MS.
San Diego Presidial Company, accounts scattered in archives. MS.
San Diego, Pueblo Lands of, Exceptions to Survey made by John C. Hays, July, 1858. San Francisco, 1869.
San Diego, Bulletin, Union, World.
San Diego City, Descriptive, Historical, Commercial, Agricultural, and other Important Information. San Diego, 1874.
San Diego and Southern California, The Climate, etc. San Diego, n.d.
San Diego the California Terminus of the Texas Pacific R.R. San Diego, 1872.
San Fernando, Lista Alfabética de Neófitos. MS.
San Francisco, Act to Charter the City. S. F., 1850; many other acts.
San Francisco Baptist Association, Minutes. San Francisco, 1850 et seq.
San Francisco Bulkhead, Address to Members of State Senate. S. F., 1860; and various other pamphlets on same subject.

San Francisco, Chamber of Commerce, Annual Reports. S. F., 1865 et seq.
San Francisco Chronicle and its History. San Francisco, 1879.
San Francisco, Cuentas de la Compañía Presidial, 1813–33. MS. 25 vols.
[Presented by Gen. Vallejo.]
San Francisco Custom House, Certified List of Vessels, etc. S. F., 1873, 1875;
Custom House Correspondence on subject of Appraisements. Wash.,
1852; and other documents.
San Francisco Fire Department, Anniversary of Organization. San Francisco,
1852 et seq.; Reports, etc.
San Francisco, Great Earthquake in. San Francisco, n.d.
San Francisco, History, Incidents, etc. A Collection.
San Francisco, History of the Vigilance Committee. San Francisco, 1858.
San Francisco, Land Titles. A Collection.
San Francisco, Libros de Mision. MS.
San Francisco, Memorial of Holders and Owners of the Floating Debt. San
Francisco, 1857.
San Francisco, Municipal Reports. San Francisco, 1859–82. 21 vols.; also
many separate pamphlets on city affairs and institutions.
San Francisco Newspapers. Advocate, Alta California, American Flag,
American Union, Argonaut, Banner of Progress, California Chronicle,
Cal. Courier, Cal. Farmer, Cal. Leader, Cal. Rural Home Journal, Cal.
Spirit of the Times, Cal. Star, Californian, Call, Catholic Guardian,
Chronicle, Christian Advocate, Coast Review, Commercial Advocate,
Herald and Record, Daily Balance, Herald and Placer Times, Demo-
cratic Press, Despatch, Eco de la Raza Latina, Elevator, Evangel, Even-
ing Bulletin, Examiner, Figaro, Globe, Golden Era, Hebrew, Hebrew
Observer, Illustrated Wasp, Journal, Journal of Commerce, Law Gazette,
Medical Press, Mercantile Gazette, Mining and Scientific Press, Monitor,
National, New Age, News Letter, Occident, Pacific, Pacific Churchman,
Pacific Methodist, Pacific News, Picayune, Pioneer, Post, Scientific
Press, Resources of California, Spectator, Star and Californian, Sun, Sun-
day Despatch, Times, Tribune, True Californian, Wide West, etc.
San Francisco, New City Charter. San Francisco, 1883.
San Francisco, Ordinances and Joint Resolutions of the City. San Francisco,
1854; and other ordinances and regulations.
San Francisco, Our Centennial Memoir. San Francisco, 1877.
San Francisco Presidial Company, Accounts, rosters, etc., scattered in the
archives. MS.
San Francisco, Proceedings of the Town Council, 1849. S. F., 1850.
San Francisco Public Schools, Annual Reports. San Francisco, 1850 et seq.;
and many other Documents on the schools.
San Francisco, Reglamento del Puerto, 1846. MS.
San Francisco, Remonstrance of the City to the Legislature against the Ex-
tension of the City. San Francisco, 1854.
San Francisco, Report of Board of Engineers upon City Grades. San Fran-
cisco, 1854.
San Francisco, Reports of City Surveyor. San Francisco, 1856 et seq.; also
reports of other city officers and boards.
San Francisco, Report in relation to the defence of the harbor [32d Cong.,
2d Sess., Sen. Ex. Doc. 43]. Washington, 1852.
San Francisco, Report for the transportation of mails from New York, New
Orleans, and Vera Cruz [32d Cong., Special Sess., Sen. Ex. Doc. 1].
Washington, 1853.
San Francisco, Resolution in relation to the proceedings of the Vigilance
Committee [34th Cong., 3d Sess., Sen. Ex. Doc. 43]. Washington, 1856.
San Francisco, Supervisors, General Orders. San Francisco, 1869 et seq.
San Francisco, Town Council, Proceedings of. San Francisco, 1849 et seq.
San Francisco del Atí, Libros de Mision. MS.
San Francisco Solano, Libros de Mision. MS.
San Francisco Solano, Padron de Neófitos. MS.

San Gabriel, Libros de Mision. MS.
San Joaquin County, History of. Oakland, 1879. atlas folio.
San Joaquin, Tulare, and Sacramento Valleys, Report of Commissioners on
    Irrigation [43d Cong., 1st Sess., H. Ex. Doc. 290]. Wash., 1873.
San Joaquin Valley, Brief Description of, etc. San Francisco, 1868.
San José, Archivo. MS. 6 vols.
San José, Advertiser, Argus, California Agriculturist, California Granger,
    County Fair Advertiser, Courier, Herald, Independent, Mercury, Morn-
    ing Guide, Patriot, Pioneer, Santa Clara Argus.
San José, Cuestion de Límites, 1797-1801. MS.
San José, Decree confirming Pueblo of. n.pl., n.d.
San José, Libro de Patentes, 1806-24. MS.
San José, Libros de Mision. MS.
San José, Peticion del Ayunt. en favor de los Frailes Españoles, 1829. MS.
San Juan, Central Californian, Echo, Monterey County Journal.
San Juan Bautista, Libros de Mision. MS.
San Juan Capistrano, Libros de Mision. MS.
San Leandro, Alameda County Gazette, Alameda Democrat, Plaindealer,
    Record.
San Luis Obispo, Archivo. MS.
San Luis Obispo, Democratic Standard, Pioneer, South Coast, South Coast
    Advocate, Tribune.
San Luis Obispo, History, Laws, and Ordinances. San Luis Obispo, 1870.
San Luis Obispo, Libros de Mision. MS.
San Mateo, Times.
San Mateo County, Illustrated History. San Francisco, 1878. atlas folio.
San Miguel, Libros de Mision. MS.
San Miguel (Juan Rodriguez de), Documentos relativos al Piadoso Fondo de
    Misiones de California. Mex., 1845; Rectificacion de Graves Equivoca-
    ciones del Fondo Piadoso. Mex., 1845; La República Mexicana en 1846.
    Mex., 1845; Segundo Cuaderno de Interesantes Documentos relativos al
    Fondo Piadoso. Mex., 1845.
San Rafael, Libros de Mision. MS.
San Rafael, Herald, Marin County Journal, Marin County News, Marin County
    Tocsin.
San Rafael and Coast Range Mines, Report. San Francisco, 1879.
Santa Bárbara, Archivo, 1839-49. MS.
Santa Bárbara, Correspondencia entre Virey, Guardian y otros, sobre Padres
    para las Nuevas Misiones del Canal, 1781. MS.
Santa Bárbara, Democrat, Gazette, 1855-7, Independent, Index, News, Post,
    Press, Republican, Times.
Santa Bárbara, Libro de Acuerdos del Ayuntamiento, 1849-50. MS.
Santa Bárbara, Libros de Mision. MS.
Santa Bárbara, Memorias de Efectos Remitidos á la Mision, 1786-1810. MS.
Santa Bárbara Presidial Company, Accounts, Rosters, etc., scattered in the
    Archives. MS.
Santa Clara, Archivo de la Parroquia. MS.
Santa Clara, Index, Journal, News, Union.
Santa Clara, Libros de Mision. MS.
Santa Clara College, Catalogues. San Francisco, etc., 1855 et seq.
Santa Clara County Pioneers, Constitution. San José, 1875.
Santa Clara County, Historical Atlas [Thompson and West]. S.F., 1876. atlas fol.
Santa Cruz, Archivo. [Records in Clerk's Office.] MS.
Santa Cruz, County Times, Courier, Enterprise, Journal, Local Item, Pájaro
    Times, Sentinel, Times.
Santa Cruz, Libros de Mision. MS.
Santa Cruz, A Peep into the Past. Scrap-book. From Sta Cruz Local Item.
Santa Cruz, Records in Parish Church. MS.
Santa Cruz, Testimonio sobre el Tumulto de 1818. MS.
Santa Cruz County, History of [W. Wallace Elliott]. S. F., 1879. atlas folio.

Santa Inés, Exámen de Conciencia en lengua de Indios. MS.
Santa Inés, Libros de Mision. MS.
Santa María (Vicente), Registro de Parages entre S. Gabriel y S. Buenaventura, 1795. MS.
Santa Mónica, The Coming City. San Francisco, 1875; Outlook.
Santa Rosa, Collegian, Democrat, Herald, News, Press, Republican, Sonoma Democrat, Sonoma Index, Times.
Sargent (Aaron A.), Sketch of Nevada County. n.pl., n.d.
Sargent (Aaron A.), Speech in U. S. H. of Rep., April 9, 1862, on Pacific Railroad. How it may be Built. Wash., 1862; and other Speeches.
Sarría (Vicente Francisco), Argumento Contra el Traslado de S. Francisco, 1823. MS.
Sarría (Vicente Francisco), Carta Pastoral, 1817. MS.
Sarría (Vicente Francisco), Defensa del P. Luis Martinez, 1830. MS.
Sarría (Vicente Francisco), Escritos Sueltos del Comisario Prefecto. MS.
Sarría (Vicente Francisco), Exhortacion Pastoral, 1813. MS.
Sarría (Vicente Francisco), Informe del Comisario Prefecto sobre los Frailes de California, 1817. MS.
Sarría (Vicente Francisco), Informe de Misiones, 1819. MS.
Sarría (Vicente Francisco), Sermones en Lengua Vascüense. MS.
Saunders (William), Through the Light Continent. London, etc., 1879.
Savage (Thomas), Documentos para la Historia de California. MS. 4 vols.
Sawtelle (C. M.), Pioneer Sketches. MS.
Sawyer (A. F.), Mortuary Tables of San Francisco. San Francisco, 1862.
Sawyer (Charles H.), Documents on the Conquest of California, 1846. MS.
Sawyer (Eugene T.), The Life and Career of Tiburcio Vazquez. San José, 1875.
Sawyer (L. S. B.), Reports of Cases Decided in the Circuit and District Courts, etc. San Francisco, 1873-80. 5 vols.
Saxon (Isabelle), Five Years within the Golden Gate. Philadelphia, 1868.
Sayward (W. T.), All about Southern California. San Francisco, 1875.
Sayward (W. T.), Pioneer Reminiscences. MS.
Scala (Comte de), Influence de l'Ancien Comptoir Russe en Californie. In Nouv. An. Voy., cxliv. 375.
Schenck (George E.), Statement on Vigilance Committee. MS.
Schlagintweit (Robert von), Californien Land und Leute. Cöln, etc., 1871.
Schmidt (Gustavus), Civil Law of Spain and Mexico. New Orleans, 1851.
Schmiedell (Henry), Statement of California Matters from 1849. MS.
Schmölder (Capt. B.), Neuer Praktischer Wegweiser für Nord-Amerika. Mainz, 1849.
School Scandal of San Francisco. Proceedings before the Investigating Committee. San Francisco, 1878.
Schools, Colleges, Academies, etc. Catalogues, reports, etc., cited by name of the institution. Not in this list.
Schwarz (J. L.), Briefe eines Deutschen aus Kalifornien. Berlin, 1849.
Scribner's Monthly Magazine (later the Century). New York, 1871 et seq.
Seattle, Intelligencer, Pacific Tribune, Puget Sound Despatch.
Secularizacion, Decreto de las Córtes, 1813. MS.
Seddon (J. A.), Speech in U. S. H. of Rep., Jan. 23, 1850, on the Action of Executive in Relation to California. Washington, 1850.
Sedgley, Overland to California in 1849.
Semblanzas de los Miembros del Congreso de 1827 y 1828. Nueva York, 1828.
Semple (Robert), Letters of 1846-9. MS.
Señan (José Francisco de Paula), Cartas Varias. MS.
Señan (José F. de P.), Circular del Vicario Foraneo, 1815. MS.
Señan (José F. de P.), Informes Bienales de Misiones, 1811-14, 1820-2. MS.
Señan (José F. de P.), Respuesta al Virey sobre condicion de Cosas en Cal., 1796. MS.
Sepúlveda (Ignacio), Historical Memoranda. MS.
Sermones de no se sabe cuales predicadores de California, 1790 etc. MS.

Sermones Varios de Misioneros. MS.
Serra (Junípero), Cartas al P. Lasuen, 1778–81. MS.
Serra (Junípero), Correspondencia, 1777–82. MS.
Serra (Junípero), Escritos Autógrafos. MS.
Serra (Junípero), Informe de 1774. MS.
Serra (Junípero), Informe de 5 de Feb. 1775. MS.
Serra (Junípero), Memorial de 22 de Abril, 1773, sobre suministraciones á los Establecimientos de California, etc. MS.
Serra (Junípero), Notas de 1776. MS. In San Diego, Lib. Mision.
Serra (Junípero), Representacion 21 Mayo, 1773. MS.
Serra (Junípero), Representacion 13 Mayo, 1773. In Palou, Not. i., 514; MS.
Serrano (Florencio), Apuntes para la Historia de California. MS.
Serrano (Florencio), Cartas Varias. MS.
Serrano (Florencio), Recuerdos Históricos. MS.
Seward (George F.), Chinese Emigration in its Social and Economical Aspects. New York, 1881.
Seward (William H.), Speech in U. S. Sen. March 11, 1850, on Admission of California. Washington, 1850; and other Speeches.
Seyd (Ernest), California and Its Resources. London, 1858.
Seymour (E. Sanford), Emigrant's Guide to the Gold Mines. Chicago, 1849.
Shaler (William), Journal of a Voyage, 1804. In American Register, iii. 137.
Shasta, Courier.
Shastas and Their Neighbors. MS.
Shaw (William), Golden Dreams and Waking Realities. London, 1851.
Shaw (William), Pioneer Life in Columbia River Valley. MS.
Shaw (William J.), Speech in Sen. of Cal. Feb. 7, 1856, on Constitutional Reform. Sacramento, 1856; and other Speeches.
Shea (John Gilmary), History of the Catholic Missions. New York, 1855.
Shearer, Journal of a Trip to California, 1849. MS.
Shelvocke (George), Voyage round the World, 1719–22. London, 1726.
Sherman (William T.), Correspondence of Lieut., 1847–8. In Cal. & N. Mex., Mess. & Doc., 1850; Memoirs. N. Y., 1875. 2 vols.
Sherwood (J. Ely), California. New York, 1848; The Pocket Guide to California. N. Y., 1849.
Shubrick (W. Branford), Correspondence, 1847. In War with Mex., Reports, etc.; Report to Secretary of the Navy, Feb. 15, 1847. In 30th Cong., 2d Sess., H. Ex. Doc. i. pt. ii. p. 65; and Stephen W. Kearny, Circular of the Naval Commander and Governor, March 1, 1847. English and Spanish.
Shuck (Oscar T.), California Scrap-book, San Francisco, 1869; Representative and Leading Men of the Pacific. S. F., 1870, 1875. 2 vols.
Sierra, Plumas, and Lassen Counties, Illustrated History of. San Francisco, 1882. 4to.
Silliman (Benjamin), American Journal of Science and Art. New Haven, 1819 et seq. 107 vols.
Silver Mountain, Alpine Chronicle, Bulletin.
Simonin (L.), Le Grand-Ouest des États-Unis. Paris, 1869; Les Mines d'Or et d'Argent aux États-Unis. In Revue des Deux Mondes. Nov. 1875. 285; Le Mineur de Californie. Paris, 1866; La Vie Souterraine. Paris, 1867,
Simpson (Sir George), Narrative of a Journey round the World. London, 1847. 2 vols.
Simpson (Henry I.), The Emigrant's Guide to the Gold Mines. New York, 1848; Three Weeks in the Gold Mines. N. Y., 1848.
Simpson (James H.), Report of Explorations across the Great Basin, etc. Wash., 1876; The Shortest Route to California. Phil., 1869.
Sinaloa, Proposiciones de los Representantes sobre clausura de Mazatlan, Mexico, 1837.
Siskiyou County Affairs. MS.
Sitjar (Antonio), Reconocimiento de Sitio para la Nueva Mision de S. Miguel, 1795. MS.

Slacum (William A.), Report on Oregon, March 26, 1837. [25th Cong., 3d Sess., H. Rept. 101.] Washington, 1838.
Sloat (John D.), Despatches on the Conquest of Cal. [29th Cong., 2d Sess., H. Ex. Doc. 4, p. 640; 31st Cong., 1st Sess., H. Ex. 1, pt. ii., p. 2]; also correspondence 1846. MS.
Smiley (Thomas J. L.), Statement on Vigilance Committee and Early Times in San Francisco. MS.
Smith (Jedediah), Excursion à l'ouest des Monts Rocky, 1826. In Nouv. An. Voy., xxxvii. 208.
Smith (Napoleon B.), Biographical Sketch of a Pioneer of 1845. MS.
Smith (Persifer F.), Military Correspondence. [31st Cong., 1st Sess., Sen. Doc. 52.] Washington, 1849.
Smith (Persifer F.), Bennett Riley et als. Reports in Relation to the Geology and Topography of California and Oregon. [31st Cong., 1st Sess., Sen. Ex. Doc. 47.] Washington, 1849.
Smith (Truman), Speech in U. S. H. of Rep., March 2, 1848, on Physical Character of Northern States of Mexico, etc. Washington, 1848.
Smithsonian Institution, Annual Reports. Washington, 1853 et seq.
Smucker (Samuel M.), Life of Col. J. C. Frémont. New York, 1856.
Snelling, Merced Banner, Merced Herald.
Soberanes (Clodomiro), Documentos para la Historia de California. MS.
Sobrantes, Survey of Rancho. San Francisco, 1878.
Sociedad Mexicana de Geografía y Estadística, Boletin. Mexico, 1861 et seq. [Includes Instituto Nacional.]
Societies. See Institutions.
Sola (Pablo Vicente), Correspondencia del Gobernador, 1805–22. MS.
Sola (Pablo Vicente), Defensa del P. Quintana y otros, 1816. MS.
Sola (Pablo Vicente), Informe al General Cruz sobre los Insurgentes, 1818. MS.
Sola (Pablo Vicente), Informe General al Virey sobre Defensas, 1817. MS.
Sola (Pablo Vicente), Informe suplementario sobre los Insurgentes, 1818. MS.
Sola (Pablo), Instruccion General á los Comandantes, contra los Insurgentes, 1818. MS.
Sola (Pablo Vicente), Instrucciones al Comisionado de Branciforte, 1816. MS.
Sola (Pablo Vicente), Noticia de lo acaecido en este Puerto de Monterey, Rebeldes de Buenos Aires, 1818. In Gaceta de Mex., xxxix. 283.
Sola (Pablo Vicente), Observaciones en la Visita desde S. Francisco hasta S. Diego, 1818. MS.
Sola (Pablo Vicente), Prevenciones sobre Eleccion de Diputado, 1822. MS.
Solano County, Historical Atlas. San Francisco, 1877. atlas folio.
Solano County, History of. [Wood, Alley and Co.] San Francisco, 1879.
Soledad, Libros de Mision. MS.
Soler (Nicolás), Cartas del Capitan Inspector. MS.
Soler (Nicolás), Informe sobre Policía y Gobierno, 1787. MS.
Soler (Nicolás), Parecer sobre Comercio con el Buque de China, 1787. MS.
Solignac (Armand de), Les Mines de la Californie. Limoges, n.d.
Solis (Joaquin), Manifiesto al Público, ó sea Plan de Revolucion, 1829. MS.
Solis (Joaquin), Proceso Instruido contra—y otros Revolucionarios, 1829-30. MS.
Sonoma, Compañía de Infantería, Cuaderno de Distribucion, 1839. MS.
Sonoma, Documentos Tocantes á la fundacion de la Nueva Mision, 1823. MS.
Sonoma County, History [Alley Bowen and Co.] San Francisco, 1880.
Sonora (Cal.), American Eagle, American Flag, Herald, Tuolumne Courier, Tuolumne Independent, Union Democrat.
Sonora, Estrella de Occidente. 1859 et seq.
Sonora, Sonorense (El). 1847 et seq.
Soto (Francisco), Expedicion Militar, 1813. MS.
Soulé (Frank), J. H. Gihon, and J. Nisbet, Annals of San Francisco. New York, etc., 1855.
Southern Pacific Railroad Company, Annual Reports. San Francisco, 1877 et seq.; and other documents.

Southern Quarterly Review. New Orleans, etc., 1842 et seq.
Spaulding (E. G.), Speech in U. S. H. of Rep., April 4, 1850, in favor of Gen.
    Taylor's Plan of Admitting Cal. Washington, 1850.
Speeches, orations, addresses, etc., on various occasions, not named in this
    list unless peculiarly historical in their nature. See names of speakers.
Speeches in Congress. A Collection.
Spear (Nathan), Loose Papers of an Early Trader. MS.
Speer (William), China and California, Lecture, June 28, 1853. S. F., 1853.
Spence (David), Historical Notes, 1824–49. MS.
Spence (David), Letters of a Scotchman in California. MS.
Spence (David), List of Vessels in California Ports. MS.
Springfield (Mass.), Republican.
Spurr (George G.), The Land of Gold. Boston, 1881.
Squier (E. G.), New Mexico and California. In Amer. Review, Nov. 1848.
Stanford (Leland), Speech on Pacific Railroad, July 13, 1864. San Francisco,
    1865; also other speeches, etc.
Stanislaus County, History. San Francisco, 1881. atlas folio.
Stanley (E.), Speech, July 6, 1850, on Galpin Claim. Washington, 1850.
Staples (David J.), Incidents and Information. MS.
State Papers, Sacramento, MS., 19 vols. in Archivo de Cal.; Id., Missions, 11
    vols.; Id., Missions and Colonization, 2 vols.; Id., Benicia, 1 vol.
Statistician. San Francisco, 1875 et seq.
Stearns (Abel), Correspondence of a Merchant. MS.
Stearns (Abel), Expediente de Contrabando, 1835. MS.
Steilacoom (W. T.), Puget Sound Express.
Stevenson (Jonathan D.), Correspondence, 1847–8. In Cal. and N. Mex.,
    Mess. and Doc., 1850.
Stevenson (Jonathan D.), Letters in the Archives. MS.
Stevenson's Regiment in Lower California, 1847. In S. José Pioneer, Sept.
    14, 21, 1878.
Steward (William M.), Lecture on the Mineral Resources of the Pacific
    States. New York, 1865.
Stillman (J. D. B.), Did Drake Discover San Francisco Bay? In Overland
    Monthly, i. 332; Footprints in California of Early Navigators. In Id.,
    Seeking the Golden Fleece, 285; Id. In Overland Monthly, ii. 257;
    Observations on the Medical Topography and Diseases of the Sacramento
    Valley. N. Y., 1851; Seeking the Golden Fleece. San Francisco, etc.,
    1877; Statement on Vigilance Committee. MS.
St Louis (Mo.), Globe, Reveille, Union.
Stimson (A. L.), History of the Express Companies. New York, 1858.
Stirling (Patrick James), The Australian and Californian Gold Discoveries.
    Edinburgh, 1853; De la Découverte des Mines d'Or en Australie et en
    Californie. Paris, 1853.
Stockton, Beacon, California Agriculturist, Gazette, Herald, Independent,
    Pacific Observer, San Joaquin Herald, San Joaquin Republican.
Stockton, History of. (See Tinkham George H.)
Stockton (Robert F.), Despatches [29th Cong., 2d Sess., H. Ex. Doc. 4, p. 668];
    Despatches and Orders, 1847. In Cutts' Conquest; Id., Life, Appen.
    [30th Cong., 2d Sess., Sen. Ex. Doc. 31]; also in different Archives. MS.;
    Military and Naval Operations [30th Cong., 2d Sess., Sen. Ex. Doc. 31];
    Miscellaneous Orders and Correspondence. In Id., Life, Appen.; Report
    Feb. 18, 1848. In Id., 24; Report Feb. 18, 1848. In War with Mex.,
    Repts. 33–50; Scattered Communications. MS.; A Sketch of the Life of.
    New York, 1856.
Stockton and Copperopolis Railroad, Engineers' Report, Oct. 1862. Stockton,
    1862; other reports.
Stone (R. C.), Gold and Silver Mines of America. New York, n.d.
Stout (Arthur B.), Chinese Immigration. San Francisco, 1862.
Strahorn (Robert E.) To the Rockies and Beyond. Chicago, 1881.
Streeter (William A.), Recollections of Historical Events, 1843–78. MS.

Stuart (Charles V.), Trip to California in 1849. MS.
Stuart (James F.), Argument on Survey of the Rancho Rio de Santa Clara. Washington, 1872; List showing whereabouts of the governor at different dates. MS.
Studnitz (Arthur von), Gold. Legal Regulations. London, 1877.
Suisun, Solano County Democrat, Solano Herald, Solano Press, Solano Republican, Solano Sentinel.
Sumner (Cal.), Kern County Gazette.
Sumner (Charles A.), The Overland Trip. San Francisco, 1875.
Sun of Anáhuac. Vera Cruz, 1847 et seq.
Suñol (Antonio), Cartas de un Catalan. MS.
Superior Government State Papers. MS. 21 vols. In Archivo de Cal.
Susanville, Farmer, Lassen Advocate, Lassen County Journal, Lassen Sage Brush.
Sutil y Mexicana, Relacion del Viage hecho por las Goletas. Madrid, 1802; atlas. 4to.
Sutro (Adolph), The Mineral Resources of the U. S. Baltimore, 1868.
Sutter (John A.), Correspondence, 1839–48. MS.
Sutter (John A.), Correspondence of the Sub-Indian Agent, 1847–8. In Cal. and N. Mex., Mess. and Doc. 1850.
Sutter (John A.), Diary, 1839–48. Scrap-book from the Argonaut, 1878.
Sutter (John A.), Examination of the Russian Grant. Sacramento, 1860.
Sutter (John A.), Memorial to the Senate and House. Wash., 1876.
Sutter (John A.), Personal Recollections. MS.
Sutter (John A.), Petition to Congress [39th Cong., 1st Sess., Sen. Mis. Doc. 38].
Sutter (John A.), Statistical Report on Indian Tribes. MS.
Sutter County, History of. [Chamberlain and Wells.] Oakland, 1879. folio.
Sutter-Suñol Correspondence, 1840–6. MS.
Sutton (O. P.), Early Experiences. MS.
Swan (John A.), Historical Sketches, 1844, etc. MS.
Swan (John A.), Monterey in 1842. In S. José Pioneer, Mar. 30, 1878.
Swan (John A.), Trip to the Gold Mines, 1848. MS.
Swan (John A.), Writings of a Pioneer. In S. José Pioneer, 1878–9, and other newspapers.
Swasey (William F.), California in 1845–6. MS.
Swasey (William F.), Remarks on Snyder. MS.
Swett (John), History of the Public School System of California. S. F., 1876.

Tapia (Tiburcio), Cartas de un Vecino de Angeles. MS.
Tapis (Estévan), Cartas del Fraile. MS.
Tapis (Estévan), Expedicion a Calahuasa, 1798. MS.
Tapis (Estévan), Informes Bienales de Misiones, 1803–10. MS.
Tapis (Estévan), Noticias Presentadas al Gobr. Arrillaga, 1808. MS.
Tapis (Estévan), Parecer sobre Repartimientos de Indios, 1810. MS.
Tapis (Estévan), and Juan Cortés, Réplica de los Ministros de Sta Bárbara, 1800. MS.
Tarayre (E. Guillemin), Exploration Minéralogique des Régions Mexicaines. Paris, 1869.
Tarbell (Frank), Victoria Life and Travels. MS.
Taylor (Alexander S.), Articles in California Farmer; Bibliografa California. Scrap-book from Sac. Union; Byron, Nelson, and Napoleon in California. In Pacific Monthly, xi. 649; Discoverers and Founders of California. MS. and Scraps; The First Voyage to California, by Cabrillo. S. F., 1853; List of Pioneers. MS.; Hist. Summary of Lower California. In Browne's Min. Res.; Odds and Ends. MS. and Scraps; Sketches connected with California History. n.pl. [1855]; Specimens of the Press [In S. F. Mercantile Library]; The Storehouse of California. n.pl., n.d.
Taylor (Bayard), At Home and Abroad. New York, 1867; El Dorado. N.Y., 1850; N. Y., 1861.
Taylor (Benjamin F.), Between the Gates. Chicago, 1878; Chicago, 1880.

Taylor (Christopher), Oregonians in the California Mines, 1848. MS.
Taylor (Mart), The Gold Digger's Song Book. Marysville, 1856.
Taylor (William), California Life Illustrated. New York, 1858.
Taylor (William), Seven Years' Street Preaching. New York, 1857.
Tehama, Independent, Tocsin.
Temple (Francis P. F.), Recollections, 1841-7. MS.
Temple (John), Letters of a Los Angeles Merchant. MS.
Territorial Pioneers, Annual Meetings. S. F., 1874 et seq.; Constitution and
    By-Laws. San Francisco, 1874; First Annual. S. F., 1877.
Terry (David S.), Trial of, by the Committee of Vigilance. S. F., 1856.
Tevis (A. H.), Beyond the Sierras. Philadelphia, 1877.
Tevis (Lloyd), Address before the American Bankers' Association, Aug. 10,
    1881. n.pl., n.d.
Thomes (R. H.), Life of an Immigrant of 1841. MS.
Thompson (A. B.), Business Correspondence. MS.
Thompson (Ambrose W.), Memorial [to Congress], Steamers between Cali-
    fornia, China, and Japan. n.pl. [1853].
Thompson (Jacob), Speech in U. S. H. of Rep., June 5, 1850, on the Califor-
    nia Question. n.pl., n.d.
Thompson (John R.), Speech on the Conquest of California in U. S. H. of
    Rep. June 5, 1850. Washington, 1850.
Thompson (Robert A.), Historical and Descriptive Sketch of Sonoma County.
    Philadelphia, 1877.
Thompson (Waddy), Recollections of Mexico. New York, etc., 1847.
Thompson and West, Publishers of Several County Histories. See names of
    counties.
Thomson (Monroe), The Golden Resources of California. N. Y., 1856.
Thornton (Harry J.), Opinions on California Private Land Claims. San Fran-
    cisco, 1853; Speech in Cal. Sen., Feb. 8, 1861. Sacramento, 1861.
Thornton (J. Quinn), Oregon and California in 1848. N. Y., 1849. 2 vols.
Thurman (J. R.), Speech in U. S. H. of Rep. June 8, 1850, on the California
    Question. Washington, 1850.
Thurston (S. R.), Speech in U. S. H. of Rep., Mar. 25, 1850, on the admis-
    sion of California. Washington, 1850.
Tikhménef (P.), Istoritcheskoë Obosranie. St Petersburg, 1861. 2 vols.
Tilford (Frank), Argument on San Francisco Outside Lands. Sac., 1868.
Tinkham (George H.), History of Stockton. San Francisco, 1880.
Todd (John), The Sunset Land. Boston, 1870.
Toombs (Albert G.), The Pioneer Overlanders of 1841. In S. F. Bulletin,
    July 27, 1868.
Toombs (R.), Speech in U. S. H. of Rep., Feb. 27, 1850, on President's Mes-
    sage Communicating the Constitution of California. Washington, 1850.
Torquemada (Juan de), Monarquía Indiana. Madrid, 1723. 3 vols. folio.
Torre (Estévan de la), Reminiscencias, 1815-48. MS.
Torre (José Joaquin), Varios Escritos. MS.
Torres (Manuel), Peripecias de Vida Californiana. MS.
Trait d'Union (Le). Mexico, 1861 et seq.
Trask (John B.), Earthquakes in California from 1800 to 1864. In Cal. Acad.
    Science, Proc. vol. iii. pt. ii. 130; A Register of Earthquakes in Califor-
    nia. San Francisco, 1864.
Tratado de las Flores entre Alvarado y Carrillo, 1838. MS.
Tratado de Paz, Amistad, Límites y arreglo definitivo entre la República
    Mexicana y los Estados-Unidos. Mexico, 1848.
Treasure City (Nev.), White Pine News.
Treasury of Travel and Adventure. New York, 1865.
Truckee, Republican, Tribune.
Truett (Miers F.), Statement on Vigilance Committee in San Francisco. MS.
Truman (Benjamin C.), Life, Adventures, etc., of Tiburcio Vasquez. Los
    Angeles, 1874; Occidental Sketches. S. F., 1881; Semi-Tropical Califor-
    nia. S. F., 1874.

Tullidge (Edward W.), Life of Brigham Young. New York, 1876; The Women of Mormondon. New York, 1877.

Tuolumne, Citizen, Courier, News.

Turner (William R.), Documents in Relation to Charges preferred by S. J. Field, etc. San Francisco, 1853; Proceedings of the Assembly of Cal., 1851, for the Impeachment of. Sac., 1878.

Turrill (Charles B.), California Notes. San Francisco, 1876.

Tustin (W. J.), Recollections of an Immigrant of 1845. MS.

Tuthill (Franklin), History of California. San Francisco, 1866.

Twining (Wm. J.), Report of Survey on the Union and Central Pacific Railways [44th Cong., 2d Sess., H. Ex. Doc. 38]. Washington, 1875.

Twiss (Travers), The Oregon Question. London, 1846.

Tyler (Daniel), A Concise History of the Mormon Battalion. n.pl., 1881.

Tyson (James L.), Diary of a Physician in California. New York, 1850.

Tyson (Philip T.), Geology and Industrial Resources of California. Baltimore, 1851; Memoir on Geology and Topography of California. Report March 24, 1850 [31st Cong., 1st Sess., Sen. Ex. Doc. 47]. Wash., 1850.

Tytler (Patrick Fraser), Historical View of the Progress of Discovery. Edinburgh, 1833; New York, 1855.

Ugarte y Loyola (Jacobo), Cartas del Comandante General de Provincias Internas. MS.

Ukiah, City Press, Constitutional Democrat, Democratic Despatch, Mendocino County Press, Mendocino Democrat, Mendocino Herald.

Ulloa (Francisco), Relatione dello Scoprimento, 1539. In Ramusio, Viaggi, iii. 339.

Ulloa (Gonzalo), Instrucciones relativas á la Comision de Estado á ambas Californias, 1822. In Ilustracion Mej. ii. 164.

Unbound Documents. MS. 1 vol. In Archivo de Cal.

United States Exploring Expedition [Wilkes]. Philadelphia, 1844–58. 4to. 17 vols., folio 8 vols.

United States Geological Surveys West of the 100th Meridian. George W. Wheeler. Bulletins, Reports, and Various Publications. Washington, 1874 et seq. 4to. atlas sheets, maps.

United States Government Documents. Accounts; Agriculture; Army Register; Army Meteorological Register; Banks; Bureau of Statistics; Census; Coast Survey; Commerce, Foreign and Domestic; Commerce and Navigation; Commercial Relations; Congressional Directory; Education; Engineers; Finance; Indian Affairs; Interior; Land Office; Life-Saving Service; Light-Houses; Meteorological Reports; Mint; Navy Register; Navy Report of Secretary; Ordnance; Pacific Railroad; Patent Office; Postmaster-General; Post-Offices; Quartermaster-General; Revenue; U. S. Official Register. Cited by their dates.

United States Government Documents. House Exec. Doc.; House Journal; House Miscel. Doc.; House Reports of Com.; Message and Documents; Senate Exec. Doc.; Journal; Miscel. Doc.; Repts. Com. Cited by congress and session. Many of these documents have, however, separate titles, for which see author or topic.

United States Supreme Court, Reports.

United States and Mexican Boundary Survey by Emory. Wash., 1857–9. 3 vols.

Universal (El). Mexico, 1849 et seq.

University of California, Act to Create and Organize. n.pl. n.d.; also many other pamphlets, Reports, Addresses, etc.

Unzueta (Juan Antonio), Informe Presentado al Presidente de los Estados Unidos Mexicanos por el Contador Mayor. Mexico, 1833.

Upham (Charles W.), Life, Explorations, etc., of J. C. Frémont. Boston, 1856.

Upham (Samuel C.), Ye Ancient Yuba Miner of the Days of '49. Philadelphia, 1878; Notes of a Voyage to California. Philadelphia, 1878; Songs of the Argonauts. Philadelphia, 1876.

Urrea (Miguel), Noticias Estadísticas. In Soc. Mex. Geog., Boletin, tom. ii. 42.

Valdés (Dorotea), Reminiscences. MS.
Valdés (José Ramon Antonio), Memorias. MS.
Valle (Antonio del), Correspondencia del Teniente. MS.
Valle (Ignacio del), Cartas. MS.
Valle (Ignacio del), Documentos para la Historia de Cal. MS.
Valle (Ignacio del), Lo Pasado de California. MS.
Vallejo, Advertiser, Chronicle, Independent, Independent Advocate, People's Independent, Recorder, Solano County Democrat, Solano Times.
Vallejo, The Future of. Vallejo, 1868; The Prospects of. Vallejo, 1871.
Vallejo, Resources of. [Rep. from Solano Advertiser, 1868-9.] n.pl., n.d.
Vallejo (Ignacio), Cartas del Sargento Distinguido. MS.
Vallejo (José de Jesus), Libro de Cuentas. MS.
Vallejo (José de Jesus), Reminiscencias Históricas. MS.
Vallejo (Mariano Guadalupe), Campaña contra Estanislao, 1829. MS.
Vallejo (Mariano G.), Carta Impresa al Gob.ʳ 20 de Julio. [Sonoma] 1837.
Vallejo (Mariano G.), Circular Impresa en que anuncia su nombramiento de Comandante General, Nov. 21, 1838. [Sonoma, 1838.]
Vallejo (Mariano G.), Correspondence of Sub-Indian Agent, 1847. In Cal. and N. Mex., Mess. and Doc., 1850.
Vallejo (Mariano G.), Correspondencia Histórica. MS.
Vallejo (Mariano G.), Discourse, 8 Oct. 1876. In S. F., Centen. Mem., 97.
Vallejo (Mariano G.), Discurso Histórico, 8 de Oct. 1876. MS.
Vallejo (Mariano G.), Documentos para la Hist. de California. 1769-1850. MS. 37 vols.
Vallejo (Mariano G.), Ecsposicion que hace el Comandante General de la Alta California al Gobernador de la Misma. Sonoma, 17 Agosto 1837.
Vallejo (Mariano G.), Escritos Oficiales y Particulares. MS.
Vallejo (Mariano G.), Historia de California. MS. 5 vols.
Vallejo (Mariano G.), Informe sobre Nombres de Condados. San José, 1850.
Vallejo (Mariano G.), Informe Reservado sobre Ross, 1833. MS.
Vallejo (Mariano G.), Informes al Ministro de Guerra sobre la Sublevacion de Graham, 1840. MS.
Vallejo (Mariano G.), Males de California y sus Remedios, 1841. MS.
Vallejo (Mariano G.), Oficio Impreso, en que quiere renunciar el Mando. 1 Sept. 1838. [Sonoma, 1838.]
Vallejo (Mariano G.), Oration, 1876. In S. F. Bulletin, July 10, 1876; and in many other papers more or less fully.
Vallejo (Mariano G.), Órdenes de la Comandancia General, 1837-9. [Sonoma, 1837-9].
Vallejo (Mariano G.), Proclama. Monterey, 24 Febrero 1837.
Vallejo (Mariano G.), Proclama en el acto de Prestar el Juramento, 1836. Monterey, 1836.
Vallejo (Mariano G.), Proclama del Comandante Gen., 1837. Sonoma, 1837.
Vallejo (Mariano G.) [Proclama la Conspiracion de Francisco Solano.] Sonoma, 6 Octubre 1838.
Vallejo (Mariano G.), Report on County names, 1850. In Cal. Jour. Sen. 1850, p. 530.
Vallejo (Mariano G.), Sequias en California. MS.
Vallejo (Mariano G.), Tres Cartas Reservadas. Agosto 1837. MS.
Vallejo (Mariano G.), Vida de Wm. B. Ide. MS.
Vallejo (Mariano G.) and Santiago Argüello, Expediente sobre las Arbitrariedades de Victoria, 1832. MS.
Vallejo (Mariano G.) and Juan R. Cooper, Varios Libros de Cuentas, 1805-51. MS.
Vallejo (Salvador), Aviso al Público. Los Rancheros Principales de la Frontern de S. Francisco. Sonoma, 15 Agosto, 1839.
Vallejo (Salvador), Notas Históricas. MS.
Vancouver (George), Voyage of Discovery to the Pacific Ocean. Lond., 1798. 3 vols. 4to. Atlas in folio; Lond., 1801. 6 vols.; Voyage de Découvertes à l'Océan Pacifique, etc. Paris, An., viii. 3 vols. 4to. Atlas in folio.

Van Dyke (Theodore S.), Flirtation Camp. New York, 1881.
Van Dyke (Walter), Statement of Recollections. MS.
Van Voorhies (William), Oration before the Society of California Pioneers. San Francisco, 1853.
Variedades de Jurisprudencia. Mexico, 1850–5. 9 vols.
Vega (Plácido), Documentos para la Hist. de Mexico, 1862–8. MS. 15 vols.
Vega (Victoriano), Vida Californiana, 1834–47. MS.
Véjar (Pablo), Recuerdos de un Viejo. MS.
Velarde (Luis) Descripcion Histórica. In Doc. Hist. Mex., serie iv. tom. i. 344.
Velasco (Francisco), Sonora, its extent, etc. San Francisco, 1861.
Velasco (José Francisco), Noticias estadísticas de Sonora. Mexico, 1850.
Velasquez (José), Diario y Mapa de un Reconocimiento, 1783. MS.
Velasquez (José) Relacion del Viage que hizo el Gob.r Fages, 1785. MS.
Venadito (Virey), Comunicaciones al Gob.r de Cal., 1819. MS.
Venegas (Miguel), Noticia de la California y de su Conquista Temporal, etc. Madrid, 1757. 3 vols.
Venegas (Virey), Comunicaciones al Gob.r de Cal., 1810–12. MS.
'Veritas,' Examination of the Russian Grant. n.p., n.d.
Ver Mehr (J. L.), Checkered Life: In the Old and New World. S. F., 1877.
Verne (Jules), The Mutineers. In Id., Michael Strogoff. New York, 1877.
Vetromile (Eugene), A Tour in Both Hemispheres. New York, etc., 1880.
Viader (José), Cartas del Padre. MS.
Viader (José), Diario ó Noticia del Viage, 1810. MS.
Viader (José), Diario de Una Entrada al Rio de S. Joaquin, 1810. MS.
Viagero Universal (El). Madrid, 1796–1801. 43 vols.
Viages en la Costa al Norte de Californias. Copy from Spanish Archives. MS. [From Prof. Geo. Davidson.]
Victor (Frances F.), Studies of California Missions. In Californian, May 1881
Victor (Frances F.), River of the West. Hartford, 1870.
Victoria (Manuel), Escritos Sueltos del Gobernador, 1831. MS.
Victoria (Manuel), Informe General, 1831. MS.
Victoria (Manuel), Manifestacion del Gefe Político, 1831. MS.
Victoria (Manuel), Manifiesto á los Habitantes de Cal., 1831. MS.
Vigilance Committees in San Francisco, Miscellany. MS.
Vigilantes de Los Angeles, 1836. MS.
Vigneaux (Ernest), Souvenirs d'un Prisonnier de Guerre au Mexique, 1854–5. Paris, 1863.
Vignes (Louis J.), Letters of Don Luis del Aliso. MS.
Vila (Vicente), Instrucciones para el Viage de 1769 á California. MS.
Villa Señor y Sanchez (José Antonio), Theatro Americano. Mex., 1746. 2 vols.
Villavicencio (José María), Cartas. MS.
Vioget (J. J.), Letters of an Early Trader. MS.
Virginia (Nev.), Evening Chronicle, Territorial Enterprise, Union.
Visalia, Delta, Equal Rights Expositor, Iron Age, Tulare Index, Tulare Times.
Vischer (Eduard), Briefe eines Deutschen aus Californien, 1842. San Francisco, 1873; Missions of Upper California. San Francisco, 1872.
Vowell (A. W.), British Columbia Mines. MS.
Voyages, A Collection of Voyages and Travels [Churchill's]. London, 1752. folio. 8 vols.; Curious Collection of Travels. London, 1761. 8 vols.; [Harleian], Collection of Voyages and Travels. Lond., 1745. 2 vols.; Historical Account by English Navigators. London, 1773–4. 4 vols.; Historical Account of, round the World. Lond., 1774–81. 6 vols.; New Collection. London, 1767. 7 vols.; New Universal Collection. London, 1755. 3 vols.; World Displayed. London, 1760. 20 vols.
Voyages au Nord, Recueil. Amsterdam, 1715–27. 8 vols.

Wadsworth (James C.), Statement on Vigilance Committee. MS.
Wadsworth (William), National Wagon Road Guide to Cal. S. F., 1858.
Wakeman (Edgar), The Log of an Ancient Mariner. San Francisco, 1878.
Walker (Joel R.), Narrative of a Pioneer of 1841. MS.

Walla Walla (W. T.), Statesman.
Walpole (Frederick), Four Years in the Pacific, 1844-8. Lond., 1849. 2 vols.
Walton (Daniel), Facts from the Gold Regions. Boston, 1849.
War with Mexico, Reports and Despatches. Operations of U. S. Naval
    Forces, 1846-7. [30th Cong. 2d Sess., H. Ex. Doc. 1, pt. ii.]
Ward (Samuel), Letter to New York Courier and Enquirer, Aug. 1, 1849.
Ware, Emigrant Guide to California. [1849] n.pl.
Warner (J. J.), Biographical Sketch. MS.
Warner (J. J.), California and Oregon. In Colonial Mag., v. 229
Warner (J. J.), Reminiscences of Early California. MS.
Warner, Hayes, and Widney. See Los Angeles History.
Warren (G. K.), Memoir upon the Material used, etc., Railroad Routes to
    Pacific. Pac. R. R. Repts, xi. pt. i.
Washington (Cal.), Alameda Independent.
Washington (D. C.), National Intelligencer, Union.
Watkins (William B.), Statement on Vigilance Committee in S. F. MS.
Watson (Frank), Narrative of a Native Pioneer. MS.
Watsonville, Cal. Transcript, Pajaro Valley Times, Pajaronian, Transcript.
Waverly, Log-Book of, 1828-9. MS.
Weaverville, Trinity Journal.
Webster (Daniel), Speech in U. S. Sen., March 23, 1848, on Mexican War.
    Washington, 1848.
Weed (Joseph), A View of California as it is. S. F., 1874; Vigilance Com-
    mittees of San Francisco. In Overland, xii. 350.
Weeks (William), Reminiscences of a Pioneer of 1831. MS.
Weichardt (Karl), Die Vereinigten Staaten. Leipzig, 1848.
Weik (Johann), Californien wie es ist. Philadelphia, etc., 1849.
Weller (J. B.), Remarks in Sen. of U. S., Aug. 27, 1852, on Mexican Bound-
    ary Commission, etc. Washington, 1852.
Wells (Harry L.), see Nevada County History.
Wells (William V.), Walker's Expedition to Nicaragua. N. Y., 1856.
Werth (John J.), A Dissertation on the Resources of California. Benicia, 1851.
West Indische Spieghel, door Athanasium Inga. [Amsterdam, 1624.]
West Oakland, Press.
Western Scenes and Reminiscences. Auburn, 1853.
Western Shore Gazetteer [Sprague and Atwell]. Woodland, 1870.
Weston (S.), Four Months in the Mines of California. Providence, 1854.
Wetmore (Charles A.), Report of Mission Indians. Washington, 1875.
Whatcom (W. T.), Bellingham Bay News.
Wheatland, Free Press, Recorder, Trinity Press.
Wheaton (William R.), Statement of Facts. MS.
Wheeler (Alfred), Land Titles in San Francisco. San Francisco, 1852.
Wheeler (William), Loss of the *Warren*, 1846. MS.
Whipple (A. W.), Report of Expedition from San Diego to the Colorado.
    [31st Cong., 2d Sess., Sen. Ex. Doc. 19.] Washington, 1850.
White (Elijah), Concise View of Oregon Territory. Washington, 1846.
White (Michael), California all the Way Back to 1828. MS.
Whitney (Asa), A Project for a Railroad to the Pacific. New York, 1849.
Whitney (J. D.), Metallic Wealth of the United States. Phila., 1854.
Widber (J. H.), Statement of a Pioneer of 1849. MS.
Widney, Hayes, and Warner. See Los Angeles County, History.
Wierzbicki (F. P.), California as it is and as it may be. S. F., 1849.
Wiggins (William), Pacific Coast in 1839. In S. José Pioneer, April 6, 1878.
Wiggins (William), Reminiscences of a Pioneer of 1840. MS.
Wight (Samuel F.), Adventures in California. Boston, 1860.
Wilcox (James Smith), Cartas Varias sobre sus viages en la goleta *Caminante*,
    1817. MS.
Wilder (Marshall P.), California. Boston, 1871.
Wiley (James S.), Speech in U. S. H. of Rep., May 16, 1848, on Acquisition
    of Territory. Washington, 1848.

Wilkes (Charles), Narrative of the U. S. Exploring Expedition. Philadelphia, 1844; 4to. 3 vols.; Philadelphia, 1845, 5 vols.; London, 1845.
Wilkes (Charles), Western America. Philadelphia, 1849.
Willey (Samuel H.), Decade Sermons. San Francisco, 1859; An Historical Paper Relating to Santa Cruz. San Francisco, 1876; Personal Memoranda. MS.; Quarter Century Discourse. In Santa Cruz Enterprise March 6, 1874; Thirty Years in California. San Francisco, 1879.
Williams (Albert), Lecture on the Conquest of Cal. Reports in S. F. newspapers of June 1878; A Pioneer Pastorate. San Francisco, 1879.
Williams (Henry F.), Statement of Recollections. MS.
Williamson (R. S.), Report of a Reconnaissance, etc., in Cal. Wash., 1853.
Willie (Roberto Crichton), Mexico; Noticia sobre su Hacienda Pública bajo el Gobierno Español y Despues de la Independencia. Mexico, 1845.
Willows, Journal.
Wilmington, Enterprise, Journal.
Wilson (Benjamin D.), Observations of Early Days, 1841, etc. MS.
Wilson (Edward), The Golden Land. Boston, 1852.
Wilson (Robert A.), Mexico and its Religion. New York, 1855.
Winans (Joseph W.), Statement of Recollections, 1849-52. MS.
Winter, Advocate.
Winthrop (R. C.), Speech, May 8, 1850, on Admission of Cal. Wash., 1850.
Wise, A few Notes on California. MS.
Wise (Lieut.), Los Gringos. New York, 1849.
Wolfskill (William), Story of an Old Pioneer. In Wilmington Journal.
Wood (William M.), Wandering Sketches. Philadelphia, 1849.
Wood, Alley, and Company. See Solano County History, and others.
Woodbridge, Messenger.
Woodbridge (Sylvester), Statement on Vigilance Committee. MS.
Woodland, News, Standard, Yolo Democrat, Yolo Mail.
Woods (Daniel B.), Sixteen Months at the Gold Diggings. N. Y., 1851.
Woods (James), Recollections of Pioneer Work in California. S. F., 1878.
Wool (John E.), Correspondence in regard to his Operations on the Coast of the Pacific [33d Cong., 2d Sess., Sen. Ex. Doc. 16; 35th Cong., 1st Sess., H. Ex. Doc. 88, H. Ex. Doc. 124]. Wash., 1854; Id., 1857.
Worcester (Samuel M.), California—Outlines of an Address, Jan. 14, 1849.
Wozencraft (O. M.), Indian Affairs, 1849-50. MS.
Wright (J. W. A.), The Owens River War. In San Francisco Post, Nov. 15, 1879.
Wright (William), History of the Big Bonanza. Hartford, etc., 1877.
Wytfliet (Corn.), Descriptionis Ptolemaicæ Augmentum. Lovanii, 1597.

Yates (John), Sketch of a Journey to Sacramento Valley, 1842. MS.
Yerba Buena, California Star. See San Francisco.
Yolo County History. San Francisco, 1879. atlas folio.
Young (Ann Eliza), Wife No. 19, Hartford, 1876.
Young (Philip), History of Mexico. Cincinnati, 1855.
Young Men's Christian Association, Annual Reports. S. F., 1854 et seq.
Yreka, Journal, Union.
Yuba City, Journal, Sutter Banner, Sutter County Sentinel.
Yuba County, History [Chamberlain and Wells]. Oakland, 1879. folio.

Zalvidea (José María), Diario de una Expedicion, Tierra Adentro, 1806. MS.
Zalvidea (José María) and José Barona, Peticion al Gefe Político á favor de los Indios, 1827. MS.
Zamacois (Niceto), Historia de Méjico. Barcelona, etc., 1877-80, vols. i.-xi.
Zamorano (Agustin V.), Cartas Sueltas. MS.
Zamorano (Agustin V.), Proclama que Contiene los Artículos de las Condiciones entre él y Echeandía, 1832. MS.
Zamorano (Agustin V.) y Cia., Aviso al Público. Monterey, 1834.
Zavalishin (Dmitry), Delo o Koloniy Ross. MS.
Zúñiga (José), Cartas del Comandante de S. Diego, 1781-95. MS.

MAP
OF
CALIFORNIA

HISTORY OF CALIFORNIA.

CHAPTER I.

INTRODUCTORY RÉSUMÉ.

HISTORY OF THE NORTH MEXICAN STATES, 1520 TO 1769—CORTÉS ON THE
PACIFIC COAST—HIS PLANS—OBSTACLES—NUÑO DE GUZMAN IN SINA-
LOA—HURTADO, BECERRA, AND JIMENEZ—CORTÉS IN CALIFORNIA—DIEGO
DE GUZMAN—CABEZA DE VACA—NIZA—ULLOA—CORONADO—DIAZ—
ALARCON—ALVARADO—MIXTON WAR—NUEVA GALICIA—NUEVA VIZ-
CAYA—MISSION WORK TO 1600—CONQUEST OF NEW MEXICO—COAST VOY-
AGES—SEVENTEENTH CENTURY ANNALS—MISSION DISTRICTS OF NUEVA
VIZCAYA—TEPEHUANES AND TARAHUMARES—JESUITS AND FRANCISCANS—
REVOLT IN NEW MEXICO—SINALOA AND SONORA—KINO IN PIMERÍA—
VIZCAINO—GULF EXPEDITIONS—OCCUPATION OF BAJA CALIFORNIA—
EIGHTEENTH CENTURY ANNALS OF NEW MEXICO, CHIHUAHUA, SONORA,
AND BAJA CALIFORNIA, TO THE EXPULSION OF THE JESUITS IN 1767.

As in the history of Mexico we are referred to
Spain for the origin of affairs, so in the history of
California it is necessary to glance at Mexico in order
properly to understand the course of early events.

Hernan Cortés landed at Vera Cruz in April 1519,
and by August 1521 was in permanent possession of
the Aztec capital. Within ten years Spanish occupation had been pushed south across the isthmus of
Tehuantepec, west to the Pacific, and north to Pánuco,
Querétaro, and Colima; and exploration to the Huas-
tec region of Tamaulipas, the Chichimec territory of
Aguas Calientes, San Luis Potosí, Guanajuato, and
that part of Jalisco below the Rio Grande. Let us
give attention exclusively to the west and north-
west, as Cortés himself was disposed to do whenever

he could avoid the vexatious complications that called him to Mexico, or Central America, or Spain.

Before the middle of May 1522 Cortés had founded a town at Zacatula, and begun to build there an exploring fleet. By this time it had become apparent that the old geographical theories must be somewhat modified. This was shown by discoveries in the Pacific farther south than the conqueror's ship-yard. Evidently the Mexican region was distinct, though not necessarily distant, from Asia, being separated from that continent by a strait in the north; or else it was a south-eastern projection of Asia from a point farther north than the knowledge of the old travellers had extended. Cortés proposed to solve the mystery by simply following the coast, first northward, then westward, and finally southward, round to India. If a strait existed he was sure to find its mouth; and if not, he would at least reach India by a new route, and would at the same time add many rich islands and coasts to the Spanish domain. That such islands existed no one ventured to doubt; and one romancer of the time went so far as to invent a name for one of them, and people it with the offspring of his imagination.

The work of building ships made slow progress. Material had to be transported overland from Vera Cruz; and the tedious operation had to be repeated after a fire which destroyed the Zacatula warehouse. In 1524 it was hoped to have the fleet ready to sail in July of the next year; but Cortés was called away by his Honduras campaign, and exploration must wait. Meanwhile Michoacan had submitted peaceably in 1522; Colima had been conquered after several reverses in 1523; while in 1524 Jalisco, from Lake Chapala to Tepic, was explored by Ávalos and Francisco Cortés, the native chieftains becoming vassals of Spain, though no Spaniards were left in the country. Banderas Valley and a good port, Manzanillo or Santiago, were discovered during this expedition.

The vessels were made ready after the return of Cortés to sail in 1526, and three more were on the stocks at Tehuantepec. Then came Guevara from Magellan Strait to Zacatula; but while Cortés was preparing to send him with Ordaz to India by the northern coast route, a royal order required the vessels to be despatched under Saavedra by a more direct way to the Spice Islands and Loaisa's relief. Yet before starting, the fleet made a beginning of northern exploration by a trial trip up to Santiago in Colima. Work on the other ships was stopped by the captain-general's foes when he went to Spain in 1528; and though building operations were resumed later at Tehuantepec and Acapulco, new impediments were thrown in the explorer's way, and at the end of 1531 he was disheartened at the gloomy prospect.

Meanwhile a rival and foe to the conquistador had appeared on the scene in the person of Nuño de Guzman, president of the royal audiencia. He foresaw that the return of Cortés from Spain would result in his own downfall; and he resolved to wrest triumph from the jaws of disgrace. Having presided at the trial of his enemy, he was familiar with the scheme of northern conquest. As governor of Pánuco he had heard from the natives rumors of great cities in the north. Instead of tamely submitting to trial in Mexico, he would make the northern scheme his own, and by this bold stroke not only turn the tables on his foe, but win for himself lasting power, fame, and riches. At the end of 1529 Guzman marched from Mexico with five hundred soldiers and ten thousand Indian allies. The route was down the Rio Grande de Lerma to the region of the modern Guadalajara. A part of the army under Oñate and Chirinos by a northern detour penetrated to the sites of the later Lagos, Aguas Calientes, Zacatecas, and Jerez; and in May 1530 the divisions were reunited at Tepic. The advance was everywhere marked by devastation; and few native towns escaped burning. No heed was given

to the rights of the former conquerors, Ávalos and
Cortés, but Guzman's policy was to make it appear
that the country had never been conquered at all.
Such Indians as were not hostile at first were therefore provoked to hostility, that there might be an
excuse for plunder, destruction, carnage, and especially for the seizure and branding of slaves.   This
chapter of horrors, one of the bloodiest in the annals
of Spanish conquest, continued to the end; yet outrages were considerably less frequent and terrible in
the far north than in Jalisco.

A garrison was left at Tepic, and Guzman crossed
the great river Tololotlan into unexplored territory,
taking possession under the pompous title of Greater
Spain, designed to eclipse that of New Spain.   In July
the army went into winter-quarters at Aztatlan on
the Rio Acaponeta, remaining until December.   They
suffered severely from flood and pestilence, being
obliged to send back to Michoacan for supplies, and
for Indians to take the place of thousands that had
perished.   After a month at Chametla the march was
continued through Quezala, Piastla, and Ciguatan to
Culiacan in March 1531.   No great cities or golden
treasures being found, the zeal for coast exploration
was at an end after Captain Samaniego had reached
the Rio Petatlan, or Sinaloa, finding a barren country and a rude people.   The president now bethought
him of the inland towns of which he had heard at
Pánuco.   From May to July he made a tedious and
futile trip across the sierra to the confines of Chihuahua.   Oñate and Ángulo crossed the mountains by
different routes, perhaps to the plains of Guadiana, or
Durango, and other minor expeditions were made.
None but savage tribes were found.   The Spanish
villa of San Miguel de Culiacan was founded with
one hundred soldier settlers under Proaño, and then
Guzman started in October with the rest of his army
back to Jalisco.

Guzman was made governor of the new province,

the name of which was made Nueva Galicia, instead
of Mayor España. Compostela was made the capital; and there were also founded within a few years
Espíritu Santo, or Guadalajara, near Nochistlan and
far north of its modern site, and Chametla in Sinaloa,
a mere military camp, sometimes entirely deserted.
The new province had no definite boundaries, being
intended to include the new conquests. Neglecting
the northern regions, to which, as discoverer, he had
some claim, the governor devoted himself chiefly to
encroachments in the south. He became involved in
difficulties that finally overwhelmed him, though he
did not lack opportunity to vent his old spite against
Cortés on one or two occasions. Guzman was summoned to Mexico, and put in prison, and in 1538 was
sent to Spain, where he died six years later in poverty and distress.

Encouraged by the new audiencia Cortés took courage, and in 1532 was able to despatch two vessels
under his cousin Hurtado de Mendoza and Mazuela.
They touched at Santiago; by Guzman's orders were
refused water at Matanchel, or San Blas; discovered
the Tres Marías; and after a long storm landed at an
unknown point on the coast. Provisions were nearly
exhausted, and the men became mutinous. Hurtado
kept on northward, and with all his men was killed
at the Rio Tamotchala, or Fuerte; the malcontents,
returning southward, were driven ashore in Banderas
Bay and killed by the natives, all save two or three
who escaped to Colima, while Guzman seized all that
could be saved from the wreck. To him Cortés attributed the misfortunes of the expedition.

There were still left two vessels at Tehuantepec,
which were despatched late in 1533 under Becerra and
Grijalva. The latter, after discovering the Revilla
Gigedo Islands, returned to Acapulco. Grijalva's
men mutinied, killed Becerra, put his partisans ashore
on the Colima coast, and continued the voyage under
Jimenez. They soon discovered a bay, on an island

coast as they supposed, but really in the peninsula, and probably identical with La Paz; and there Jimenez was killed with twenty of his men.. The few survivors brought the ship to Chametla, where they were imprisoned by Guzman, but escaped with the news to Cortés, carrying also reports of pearls in the northern waters.

The captain-general now resolved to take command in person; and, having sent three vessels from Tehuantepec early in 1535, he set out with a force overland. Guzman wisely kept out of the way, contenting himself with complaints and protests. The sea and land expeditions were reunited at Chametla, and Cortés sailed in April with over one hundred men, about one third of his whole force. Jimenez' bay was reached May 3d, and named Santa Cruz. After a year of misfortunes, during which a part of the remaining colonists were brought over with their families, Cortés went back to Mexico. He intended to return with a new fleet and succor for the colony; but he sent instead a vessel in 1536 to bring away the whole party. He had had quite enough of north-western colonization.

On the main there was occasional communication between San Miguel and the south; indeed, one party of Cortés' colonists went from Chametla to Culiacan by land. In 1533 Diego de Guzman reached the Rio Yaqui; and it was he that learned the fate of Hurtado. There was no prosperity at the villa. The garrison lived at first by trading their beads and trinkets for food; then on tribute of the native towns; and at last, when the towns had been stripped, they had to depend on raids for plunder and slaves.

On one of these excursions to the Rio Fuerte in 1536 a party under Alcaraz were surprised to meet three Spaniards and a negro, who were brought to San Miguel to tell their strange tale of adventure. They were Alvar Nuñez and his companions, the only survivors of three hundred men who, under Narvaez, had landed in Florida in 1528. Escaping in 1535 from slavery on the Texan coast, these four had found their way across Texas, Chihuahua, and Sonora to the Pacific coast. Their salvation was due mainly to the reputation acquired by Cabeza de Vaca as a medicine man among the natives. Alvar Nuñez went to Mexico in 1536, and next year to Spain. He had not, as has sometimes been claimed, reached the Pueblo towns of New Mexico; but he had heard of them, and he brought to Mexico some vague reports of their grandeur.

These reports revived the old zeal for northern conquest. Guzman was out of the field, but Viceroy Mendoza caught the infection. Having questioned Cabeza de Vaca, and having bought his negro, he resolved to send an army to the north. The command was given to Vasquez de Coronado, governor of Nueva Galicia. To prepare the way a Franciscan friar, Marcos de Niza, was sent out from Culiacan early in 1539. With the negro Estevanico, Niza went, "as the holy ghost did lead him," through Sonora and Arizona, perhaps to Zuñi, or Cíbola, where the negro was killed. The friar hastened back with grossly exaggerated reports of the marvels he had seen.

Cortés also heard the reports of Nuñez and Niza, and was moved by them to new efforts, disputing the right of Mendoza to act in the matter at all. He despatched Ulloa with three vessels, one of which was lost on the Culiacan coast, in July 1539. This navigator reached the head of the gulf; then coasted the peninsula southward, touching at Santa Cruz; and rounded the point, sailing up the outer coast to Cedros Island. One of the vessels returned in 1540; of Ulloa in the other nothing is positively known. It seems to have been in the diary of this voyage that the name California, taken from an old novel, the Sergas of Esplandian, as elsewhere explained, was applied to a portion of the peninsula.

Governor Coronado, with a force of three hundred Spaniards and eight hundred natives from Mexico, departed from Culiacan in April 1540. He left a garrison in Sonora; followed Niza's route, cursing the friar's exaggerations, and reached Zuñi in July. Tobar was sent to Tusayan, or the Moqui towns; Cárdenas to the great cañon of the Colorado; and Alvarado far eastward to Cicuye, or Pecos. Then the army marched east to spend the winter in the

NORTHERN NEW SPAIN.

valley of the Rio Grande, the province of Tiguex, later New Mexico. In May 1541, after a winter of constant warfare caused by oppression, Coronado started out into the great plains north-eastward in search of great towns and precious metals never found. He returned in September, having penetrated as he believed to latitude 40°, and found only wigwam towns in the province of Quivira, possibly in the Kansas of to-day. Expeditions were also sent far up and down the Rio del Norte; and in the spring of 1542, when nearly ready for a new campaign, the governor was seriously injured in a tournament, and resolved to abandon the enterprise. Some friars were left behind, who were soon killed; and in April the return march began. Mendoza was bitterly disappointed, but acquitted the governor of blame.

The force left in Sonora, while Coronado was in the north, founded the settlement of San Gerónimo de los Corazones, in the region between the modern Arizpe and Hermosillo; and from here at the end of 1540 Melchor Diaz made a trip up the coast to the Rio Colorado, called Rio del Tizon, and across that river below the Gila. He was killed accidentally and his men returned. San Gerónimo, after its site had been several times changed and most of its settlers had deserted or had been massacred, was abandoned before the arrival of Coronado on his return in 1542.

Also in Coronado's absence and to coöperate with him Mendoza sent two vessels under Alarcon from Acapulco in May 1540. He reached the head of the gulf and went up the Rio Colorado, or Buena Guia, in boats, possibly beyond the Gila junction. Leaving a message found later by Diaz, Alarcon returned to Colima in November. Another voyage was planned, but prevented by revolt.

After a hard struggle to maintain his prestige, and prevent what he regarded as Mendoza's illegal interference with his plans, Cortés went to Spain in 1540 to engage in an equally fruitless struggle before the throne. Another explorer however appeared, in the person of Pedro de Alvarado, governor of Guatemala, who came up to Colima in 1540 with a fleet, eight hundred men, and a license for discovery. But Mendoza, instead of quarrelling with Alvarado, formed a partnership with him.

A revolt of eastern Jalisco tribes, known as the

Mixton War, interrupted all plans of exploration. Many reforms had been introduced since Guzman's time, but too late. Incited by sorcerers on the northern frontiers to avenge past wrongs and regain their independence, the natives killed their encomenderos, abandoned their towns, and took refuge on fortified *peñoles*, believed to be impregnable, the strongest being those of Mixton and Nochistlan. At the end of 1540 Guadalajara, already moved to Tacotlan Valley, was the only place held by the Spaniards, and that was in the greatest danger. Alvarado came to the rescue from the coast, but rashly attacking Nochistlan, he was defeated and killed in July 1541. Soon Guadalajara was attacked, but after a great battle, in which fifteen thousand natives were slain, the town was saved to be transferred at once to its modern site. Mendoza was troubled for the safety not only of Nueva Galicia, but of all New Spain; and he marched north with a large army. In a short but vigorous campaign he captured the peñoles, one after another, even to that of Mixton, by siege, by assault, by stratagem, or by the treachery of the defenders, returning to Mexico in 1542. Thousands of natives were killed in battle; thousands cast themselves from the cliffs and perished; thousands were enslaved. Many escaped to the sierras of Nayarit and Zacatecas; but the spirit of rebellion was broken forever.

There is little more that need be said of Nueva Galicia here. It was explored and conquered. The audiencia was established at Compostela in 1548, and moved with the capital to Guadalajara in 1561. A bishopric was erected in 1544. The religious orders founded missions. Agriculture and stock-raising made some progress. New towns were built. Rich mines were worked, especially in Zacatecas, where the town of that name was founded in 1548. These mines caused the rest of Nueva Galicia to be well nigh depopulated at first, and were themselves almost abandoned before 1600 in consequence of a rush to new mines in the

region of Nombre de Dios.   Some exploring parties
reached Durango, Chihuahua, and Sinaloa.

Ibarra, the leader in inland explorations northward,
was made governor of Nueva Vizcaya, a new province
formed about 1560 of all territory above the modern
Jalisco and Zacatecas line.   Nombre de Dios was
founded in 1558; Durango, or Guadiana, as capital, in
1563.   Before 1565 there were flourishing settlements
in San Bartolomé Valley of southern Chihuahua.
Ibarra also crossed the sierra to Sinaloa and Sonora,
founding San Juan Bautista on the Suaqui or Fuerte,
about 1564; and refounding San Sebastian de Chametla, where rich mines were found.   San Juan was
soon abandoned; but five settlers remained on the
Rio de Sinaloa as a nucleus of San Felipe, the modern
Sinaloa.   Indian campaigns of 1584–9 left a few new
settlers for San Felipe.

Before 1590 the Franciscans had eight or nine missions in Durango and Chihuahua.   When the Jesuits
undertook northern conversion in 1590, fathers Tapia
and Perez, and soon six more, came to San Felipe de
Sinaloa and began work on the rivers Petatlan and
Mocorito.   They had twenty pueblos and four thousand converts before 1600.   Father Tapia reached
the Rio Fuerte and the mountains of Topía, but was
martyred in 1594; yet missions were founded in Topía
in 1600, where the mining towns of San Andrés and
San Hipólito already existed.   San Felipe had become
a kind of presidio in 1596, under Captain Diaz.   East
of the mountains the Jesuits also began work among
the Tepehuanes at Zape and Santa Catalina, and at
Santa María de Parras in the lake region of Coahuila.
Saltillo was founded in 1586; and about 1598 the town
of Parras was built in connection with the Jesuit
mission there.

New Mexico was revisited and finally occupied
before 1600.   In 1581 Rodriguez with two other
Franciscans and a few soldiers went from San Bar-

tolomé down the Conchos and up the Rio del Norte
to the land of the Tiguas, Coronado's Tiguex. The
soldiers soon returned, but the friars remained to be
killed.   In 1582–3 Espejo with a strong force went
in search of Rodriguez, learning at Puara, near
Sandía, of the friars' fate and of Coronado's former
ravages in that region.   Espejo explored eastward to
the buffalo plains, northward to Cia and Galisteo, and
westward to Zuñi and the region of the modern Prescott, returning by way of the Rio Pecos.   In 1590–1
Castaño de Sosa went up the Pecos and across to the
Pueblo towns of the Rio Grande with a colony of
one hundred and seventy men, women, and children.
After receiving the submission of thirty-three towns,
he was carried back to Mexico in chains by Captain
Morlete, on the charge of having made an illegal
entrada, or expedition.   About 1595 Bonilla and
Humaña, sent out against rebellious Indians, marched
without license to New Mexico and sought Quivira
in the north-eastern plains.   Humaña murdered his
chief and was himself killed with most of his party by
the natives.   In 1595 the viceroy made a contract
for the conquest of New Mexico with Oñate, who as
governor and captain-general left Mexico with a large
force of soldiers and colonists in 1596.   Vexatious
complications hindered Oñate's progress and exhausted
his funds, so that it was not until 1598 that he entered
the promised land.   San Juan was made the capital;
all the towns submitted; the Franciscans were stationed in six nations; Oñate visited Zuñi; and the
rebellious warriors of the Acoma peñol were conquered
in a series of hard-fought battles, all before the summer of 1599.

Let us return to the coast and to an earlier date,
since the connection between maritime exploration
and inland progress is very slight.   Mendoza at the
close of the Mixton war in 1542, though not encouraged by the results of past efforts, had a fleet on his
hands, and one route of exploration yet open and

promising, that up the outer coast of the peninsula.
Therefore Cabrillo sailed from Natividad with two
vessels, made a careful survey, applied names that for
the most part have not been retained, passed the limit
of Ulloa's discoveries, and anchored at San Miguel,
now San Diego, in September. Explorations farther
north under Cabrillo and his successor Ferrelo will be
fully given in a later chapter. They described the
coast somewhat accurately up to the region of Monterey, and Ferrelo believed himself to have reached
the latitude of 44°.

Mendoza's efforts on the coast ended with Cabrillo's
voyage; but fleets crossed the ocean to the Philippines, and in 1565 Urdaneta for the first time recrossed the Pacific, discovering the northern route
followed for two centuries by the Manila galleons. Of
discoveries by these vessels little is known; but they
gave a good idea of the coast trend up to Cape Mendocino. They also attracted foreign freebooters. Drake
ravaged the southern coasts in 1579, also reaching
latitude 43°, and anchoring in a California port. Gali,
coming by the northern route in 1584, left on record
some slight observations on the coasts up to 37°.
Cavendish in 1586 made a plundering cruise up as
far as Mazatlan; then crossing over to Cape San
Lúcas he captured the treasure-ship, and bore off
across the Pacific. Maldonado's fictitious trip through
the Strait of Anian and back in 1588, and the similar
imaginary exploits of Fuca in the north Pacific, have
no importance for us in this connection. One Spanish
commander of the many who came down the coast
had orders to make investigations—Cermeñon in
1595; but of the result we know only that his vessel
was wrecked under Point Reyes.

In 1597 Vizcaino was sent to explore anew and
occupy for Spain the Californian Isles. He sailed
from Acapulco with a large force in three vessels,
accompanied by four Franciscan friars. His explorations in the gulf added but little to geographical

knowledge; and the settlement which he attempted
to found at Santa Cruz, by him called La Paz, was
abandoned after a few months from the inability of
the country to furnish food, the departure being
hastened by a storm and fire that destroyed buildings
and stores. Thus close the annals of the sixteenth
century.

· After 1600 Nueva Galicia has no history that can
or need be presented in a résumé like this. Except
one district, Nayarit, the whole province was in permanent subjection to Spanish authority, hostilities
being confined mainly to robberies on the line of travel
from Mexico to Nueva Vizcaya. The president of the
audiencia at Guadalajara was governor, and his judicial authority covered all the north. So did the ecclesiastical jurisdiction of the bishop of Guadalajara
until 1621, when Nueva Vizcaya was separated; but
the north-east to Texas and the north-west to California were retained. The Franciscans alone had missionary authority, and that only in the north, all
establishments depending after 1604 on the Zacatecan
provincia. Mining was profitably carried on notwithstanding an oppressive quicksilver monopoly and
frequent migrations to new discoveries. Agriculture
and stock-raising were the leading industries of the
limited population. The country's only commerce
was the exchange by overland routes of grain and
cattle for supplies needed at the mines. And finally
there were petty local happenings, wholly insufficient
to break up the deadly monotony of a Spanish province when once it becomes a *tierra de paz*, or a land
at peace.

Nueva Vizcaya during the seventeenth century
comprised in a sense northern Durango, Chihuahua,
Sinaloa, and Sonora, besides a part of Coahuila; yet
the connection between coast and inland provinces
was practically very slight, and common usage located
Nueva Vizcaya east of the Sierra Madre. A gover-

nor, and bishop of Guadiana after 1621, resided at
Durango; but save in the larger towns and mining-
camps, the country was for the most part a *tierra de
guerra,* or a land at war; the epoch not one of civil and
ecclesiastic but rather of military and missionary rule.
In general the whole country may be said to have
been divided into eight mission districts.

The Tepehuane missions of Durango prospered from
their beginning in 1594 until the great revolt of 1616
in which eight Jesuit priests and two hundred other
Spaniards lost their lives. All missions and mining-
camps were destroyed, and the capital was seriously
threatened. The massacre was cruelly avenged, and
the natives that survived were driven to the mountains only to be slowly drawn back by missionary zeal.
In 1640 lost ground had been regained, and more,
except in the number of neophytes, of whom there
were eight hundred in 1678, under four Jesuits in nine
towns, with a Spanish population of about three hundred. The Tepehuanes were conquered, except as
individuals or small parties occasionally revolted in
resistance to enforced labor in the mines. In the
south-eastern or Parras district all was peace and
prosperity with the gentle Laguneros, if we except an
occasional pestilence or inundation. Over five thousand natives had been baptized by 1603; the missions
were secularized in 1645; large accessions of Spanish
and Tlascaltec population were received, and early in
the next century under Toboso raids and Spanish
oppression all traces of the missions had disappeared.

In Topía, or western Durango, and south-eastern
Sinaloa, the Jesuits were at work with good success
at first; but the miners were oppressive, and in 1601
five thousand Acaxées took up arms to free their
country, destroying the mining-camps and towns with
forty churches. Brought once more into submission
after a few months, they never revolted again, and
the adjoining tribes were reduced one by one until by
the middle of the century the whole district had passed

permanently under Spanish and Jesuit control. As elsewhere subsequent annals are reduced to statistics and petty items of local record. Fifty thousand natives had been converted before 1644, when eight missionaries were serving in 16 churches. In 1678 there were 1400 neophytes in 38 towns under the care of ten missionaries, with a Spanish population, in mining-camps chiefly, which may be estimated at 500.

The Tarahumara district adjoined that of the Tepehuanes on the north, in northern Durango and the mountains of southern and western Chihuahua. At Parral a Spanish settlement was founded in 1631; and about the same time the Jesuits in their northern tours obtained four or five hundred Tarahumares, and with them founded two towns, San Miguel de las Bocas and San Gabriel, just south of the modern line of Durango; but there were no regular missions in Tarahumara until 1639–40, when fathers Figueroa and Pascual came and founded San Felipe and San Gerónimo Huexotitlan on or near the Rio Conchos below Balleza. In 1648 there were eight pueblos and four missionaries, when war broke out, mainly in consequence of oppressions by Spaniards who wished to use the natives as laborers in their mines, looking with no favor on the mission work. The Tarahumares were always, as the Jesuits maintained, a brave and honorable people, fighting only in defence of their rights or to avenge wrongs. In this first instance the assailants were gentiles, the plot being discovered in time to keep the converts loyal, after five Spaniards and forty neophytes had been killed. Governor Fajardo, defeating the foe, founded a town of Aguilar and a mission at the site of the modern Concepcion. In 1650 the mission was destroyed, a padre killed, and a Spanish force several times defeated; but peace was made in 1651, and the martyr's place was filled. In the outbreak of 1652 mission and town were burned, and not a Spaniard escaped. It required the whole military force of Nueva Vizcaya to restore submission, the Spaniards being often repulsed, and many mission towns and mining-camps being repeatedly destroyed. For twenty years from 1652 upper Tarahumara was abandoned, but was reoccupied in 1673–8 as far north as the Yepomera region, the limit of Jesuit work east of the sierra. There were then about eight thousand Tarahumara converts in the upper and lower districts, living in forty-five towns, and ministered to by twelve Jesuit missionaries. The Spanish population, for the most part engaged in mining, did not exceed five hundred. For the missions the last quarter of the century was a period of constant but not very rapid decadence. They were exposed on the north and east to raids from the fierce Tobosos and Apaches, and there were several attempts at revolt, the most serious being in 1690, when two Jesuits lost their lives.

North-eastern Durango and eastern Chihuahua formed a mission district under the Franciscans. They had a much less favorable field of labor than the Jesuits; their neophytes were inferior in intelligence to the Tepehuanes and Tarahumares, and their establishments had to bear the brunt of savage raids from the north-eastern sierras or Bolson de Mapimi. For over forty years the old convents at Cuencamé, Mapimi, and San Bartolomé were barely kept in existence; and near the latter in the Conchos region four new missions were founded before 1645. Then the Toboso raids became so serious as to imperil all Spanish interests. It was the typical Apache warfare of later times. Not a camp, mission, hacienda, or rancho escaped attack; only Parral and one or two mining-camps escaped destruction. The soldiers were victorious in every engagement, but they could rarely overtake the marauders. The Conchos revolted and destroyed their five missions, killing two friars. At this time the presidio of Cerro Gordo was established, and the fires of war having burned out chiefly for want of fuel, this post served to keep

the southern part of the district in a kind of order
during the rest of the century; the ruined establishments being gradually reoccupied. In the north the
Franciscans extended their operations over a broad
field. Between 1660 and 1670 three or four missions,
with probably a small garrison, were founded in the
region of Casas Grandes; but two of them were destroyed by Apaches before 1700. In 1681–2, an establishment having been formed at El Paso, several
missions sprang up in that region. One was at the
confluence of the Conchos and Rio del Norte, but
was soon destroyed. In 1697 a mission of Nombre
de Dios was founded near the site of the modern city
of Chihuahua. All these northern establishments
maintained but a precarious existence; and but for a
line of presidios erected early in the next century the
whole country would have been abandoned.

Before turning to the coast a glance must be given
at New Mexico beyond the limits of Nueva Vizcaya.
Here prosperity ceased for a time on account of controversies between Oñate, the colonists, and the Franciscan friars. The latter abandoned the province in
1601, but were sent back to reoccupy the missions.
Oñate made some explorations; Santa Fé was founded
and became the capital; and in 1608 eight padres
were at work, having baptized eight thousand natives.
Thirty new friars came in 1629, and the next year
fifty missionaries were serving sixty thousand converts in ninety pueblos. This was the date of New
Mexico's highest prosperity, though the decline was
very slight for fifty years, a period whose history offers
nothing but petty local happenings. But in 1680 a
general revolt occurred, in which four hundred Spaniards, including twenty-one friars, were killed, and the
survivors driven out of the country. While the refu-
gees founded El Paso and did some missionary work
in that region, the New Mexicans fought among themselves and threw away their chances for continued
independence. After several unsuccessful efforts by

different leaders, Governor Vargas reconquered the province after many a hard-fought battle in 1693–4; but two years later a new revolt occurred, in which five missionaries and twenty other Spaniards were killed, and the year 1696 may be regarded as the date of New Mexico's permanent submission to Spanish authority. The western towns were still independent; but except the Moquis all renewed their allegiance before the end of the century.

The coast districts were Sinaloa, extending as far north as the Yaqui River; Sonora, embracing the region of Arizpe and Tepoca; and Pimería, stretching to the Gila. During most of the century all this territory was under a military commandant at San Felipe de Sinaloa; and this office was held for nearly thirty years by Captain Hurdaide, who was popular with the missionaries, and a terror to the natives. His term of office was a continuous campaign for the conquest of new tribes or the suppression of local revolts. In 1600 five Jesuits had founded eight missions, with thirteen towns, on and near the rivers Sinaloa and Mocorito. Very rapidly was the conquest, spiritual and military, pushed northward by the priests and soldiers working in perfect accord. The fierce Suaquis, Tehuecos, and Sinaloas of the Rio Tamotchala, or Fuerte, having been properly chastised by Hurdaide, became Christian in 1604–7. Fort Montesclaros was founded in 1610 on the river, therefore still called Fuerte. The Mayos, friendly from the first, received padres in 1613, and never revolted. The Yaquis, who after defeating the Spaniards in three campaigns had voluntarily submitted about 1610, received Father Ribas in 1617, and were soon converted. In 1621 missions were founded among the Chinipas on the Tarahumara frontier; and the work was extended up the Yaqui to the Sahuaripa region. There were now thirty-four Jesuits at work in this field; and the northern missions, in what is now Sonora, were formed into a new district of San Ignacio. Captain Hurdaïde died about 1626; and during the rule of his successor the only event to be noted was the revolt in the Chinipas district in 1631-2, when two Jesuits were killed, and the missions had to be abandoned.

Father Pascual had labored in this field with great success for years, forming three towns of Chinipas, Varohios, and Guazápares. A chief of the latter was at the head of the revolt, gaining adherents from the Varohios, while the Chinipas remained faithful and tried to protect their missionary. Father Martinez came to join Pascual in 1632, and the two were killed a week later after their house and church had been burned, brutal indignities being offered to their bodies. Fifteen neophytes perished with their martyred masters. Making a raid into the mountains Captain Perea killed many rebels, and new missionaries were sent to the country; but it was finally decided to abandon this field; and the faithful converts were removed to the towns of the Sinaloas.

During the last half of the century the Sinaloa missions have no annals save such as are statistical and purely local. The submission of the natives was complete and permanent, and affairs fell into the inevitable routine. In 1678 there were in the district of San Felipe y Santiago, corresponding nearly to the modern Sinaloa above Culiacan, nine missions, with 23 pueblos, 10,000 neophytes, and nine missionaries. The northern district of San Ignacio de Yaqui, under the same jurisdiction but in modern times a part of Sonora, had 10 missions, 23 pueblos, 10 padres, and 24,000 converts. There had already been a large decrease in the neophyte population. The military force was a garrison of 40 soldiers at San Felipe, and one of 60 men at Fort Montesclaros. The Spanish population, exclusive of soldiers and military officers, was less than 500.

The modern Sonora includes the three ancient provinces of Sonora, Ostimuri, and Pimería; but in the seventeenth century the name Sonora was properly that of the valley in which Arizpe, Ures, and Hermosillo now stand. The name was sometimes extended for a long distance over adjoining regions, especially northward; but never covered the Yaqui missions or Ostimuri in the south. Missionary work was begun in the Sonora Valley by Father Castaño in 1638, near the site of the old and ill-fated San Gerónimo. The Ópatas never gave any trouble; and in 1639 the new district of San Francisco Javier de Sonora was formed with five mission partidos. In 1641 Governor Perea obtained a division of the government, was made ruler of all the country north of the Yaqui towns, styling his new province Nueva Andalucía and his capital San Juan Bautista. In consequence of a quarrel with the Jesuits, he tried to put the Franciscans in charge; but this was a failure, and the new government came to an end in four years; though a garrison remained at San Juan. In 1753 seven Jesuits were serving twenty-five thousand converts in twenty-three towns. In 1678 the new district of San Francisco de Borja was formed of the missions south and west of Opozura; and the two consisted of eighteen missions with forty-nine pueblos and about twenty thousand neophytes. Ten years later there were three districts, the new one of Santos Mártires de Japon extending northward from Batuco and Nacori. The Chinipas missions, which had been reoccupied in 1676, were now part of the Sonora district, and before the end of the century were in a most flourishing condition, under Padre Salvatierra and his associates, though to some extent involved in the troubles with eastern tribes.

Father Kino in 1687 founded the mission of Dolores on the head-waters of the Rio de San Miguel, and thus began the conquest of Pimería, through which Kino hoped to reach northern California. By 1690 he had missions at San Ignacio, Imuris, and Remedios. The Pimas were docile, intelligent, and eager for conversion; but Kino could neither obtain the needed priests, nor convince the military authorities that the Pimas were not concerned in the constant raids of the savages. In 1691 with Salvatierra he reached the modern Arizona line; and later, either alone or with such priests as he could induce to go with him, he explored the country repeatedly to the Gila and gulf coast, first reaching the latter in 1693 and the former in 1694. Three missionaries having been obtained, Tubutama and Caborca were founded; but all were destroyed in the great revolt of 1695, one of the friars being killed. Two years later they had been rebuilt and Suamca added. By 1700 Kino, sometimes with a military escort, had made six entradas, or excursions, to the Gila, some of them by the eastern route via Bac, and others by the coast or Sonoita. In 1700 he first reached the Colorado junction. But he was disappointed in all his schemes for establishing missions in the north. The Rio San Ignacio was the northern frontier, not only of missionary establishments but of all Spanish occupation at the end of the century.

In 1693 Sonora and all the north had been separated practically, perhaps formally, from Sinaloa; and Jironza as capitan-gobernador came with his 'flying company' of fifty men to protect the frontier, his capital being still at San Juan. The next seven years were spent in almost constant warfare against raiding Apaches and other savage bands of the north-east. A garrison was stationed at Fronteras, or Corodeguachi, which in campaigns often acted in union with the presidial force at Janos in Chihuahua, and was often aided besides by the Pimas, whose mission towns were a favorite object of the raids for plunder.

Finally the maritime annals and coast exploration of the century, terminating in the occupation of Baja California, demand our notice. In 1602 Sebastian Vizcaino sailed from Acapulco on a voyage of exploration which will be fully described later in this volume. For more than a century and a half Father Ascension's diary of this voyage was the source of all information extant respecting the western coast up to latitude 40°. Vizcaino's voyage was the end of outer-coast navigation, subsequent efforts being directed exclusively to the gulf and peninsula, though Monterey figured on paper in many of the schemes proposed. The Spanish crown was chary of incurring expense; without money the enthusiasm of neither navigators nor friars could be utilized; and the pearls of the gulf furnished the only incentive to action. A mere catalogue of successive enterprises must suffice here.

Schemes to occupy Monterey in 1607–8 resulted in nothing. In 1615 Cardona and Iturbe went up the gulf to latitude 34° as they reckoned it, saw the strait that made California an island, and landed at several points on that supposed island and the main. Returning, they were captured by the Dutch *pichilingues*. These were Spilberg's freebooters, who vainly sought to intercept the galleon, and had a fight with Spaniards on the Colima coast. Lezama began to build a vessel near San Blas, in 1627, for the gulf; and Ortega, completing it, made a pearl voyage in 1632. He repeated the trip in 1633–4, founding a colony at La Paz. Many natives were baptized; some inland explorations were made, and all went well for several months, until food was exhausted. Then this third attempt at settlement was added to the failures of Cortés and Vizcaino. There were, doubtless, unrecorded and unauthorized pearl-seeking voyages in those times. Carbonel's expedition made by Ortega's pilot in 1636 was an utter failure. It was in 1640 that Fonte sailed through the net-work of straits, lakes, and rivers in the northern continent until he met a Boston ship from the Atlantic! Cañas by the viceroy's orders crossed over from Sinaloa and explored the California coast for some forty leagues in 1642, accompanied by the Jesuit priest, Cortés. Casanate's operations were in 1643–8; but after great expense and much ill-luck the only results were a cruise about San Lúcas by Barriga in the former year, and in the latter a vain

search for a colony site. For twenty years nothing
was attempted, and then Piñadero obtained a commission to reduce California as a pretext for one or
two profitable pearl-seeking trips in 1667. Lucenilla's
expedition in 1668 was not unlike the preceding,
though he had two Franciscans on his ship, who
attempted conversion at La Paz and at the cape.
After fruitless negotiations with other persons the
viceroy made a contract for the settlement of California with Otondo, who was accompanied by Father
Kino and two other Jesuits, sailing from Chacala with
a hundred persons in 1683. The province was now
formally called Californias and the locality of the
colony La Paz. Some progress was made at first;
but presently the men, panic-stricken by reason of
Indian troubles, insisted on abandoning the settlement. Otondo came back before the end of the year,
reëstablishing the colony at San Bruno, above La Paz.
Here it was maintained with difficulty until the end
of 1685, when the enterprise was given up in disgust.
The Jesuits foreseeing the result had baptized none
but dying Indians. The barren peninsula was wholly
unsuited for colonization. In 1685 the British freebooter Swan made an unfortunate cruise along the
coast, failing to capture the galleon, and losing fifty
men who were killed by Spaniards on the Rio Tololotlan. Only one other expedition, that of Itamarra in
1694, is recorded, but very vaguely, before the final
occupation of the peninsula.

The country offered absolutely no inducements to
settlers; and a military occupation, entailing constant
expense without corresponding advantages, did not
accord with the Spanish system of conquest. Only
by a band of zealous missionaries, protected by a
small military guard, with supplies assured from
abroad for years, could this reduction be effected.
The Jesuits understood this, and when the government had been taught by repeated failures to understand it also, the necessary arrangements were

concluded by Salvatierra and Kino; and in 1697 a mission was founded at Loreto, just below the San Bruno of Ortega. Difficulties were formidable at first and for a long time; the savages were stupid and often hostile; the guard was small; vessels came irregularly with supplies, and authorities in Mexico generally turned a deaf ear to appeals for aid. Salvatierra and Piccolo, however, never lost courage in the darkest days, and before 1700 they had two missions and a guard of thirty men.

Eighteenth century annals of Nueva Viscaya and the adjoining regions, so far as they precede the occupation of Alta California in 1769, may be presented with enough of detail for the present purpose very briefly; for throughout those broad territories affairs had fallen into the monotonous routine of peace in the south, of war in the north, that was to characterize them as long as Spanish domination should last, and in many respects longer. To Nueva Galicia as a *tierra de paz* may be added in these times Sinaloa and Durango to the north. The era of conquest, as in a great measure of missionary labor, was past. The authority of the audiencia and civil governors was everywhere respected. Curates under the bishops were in control of spiritual affairs in all the larger settlements. Mining was the leading industry, feebly supplemented by stock-raising and agriculture. Minor political and ecclesiastical controversies, the succession of provincial and subordinate officials, fragmentary statistics of mining and other industries, and petty local happenings of non-progressive localities furnish but slight basis for an instructive résumé, even if such general review were called for here.

There was, however, one exception to the uneventful monotony of Nueva Galicia affairs during this period, which should be noticed here—the conquest of Nayarit. This mountainous and almost inaccessible region of northern Jalisco, near the frontiers of

Sinaloa, Durango, and Zacatecas had been the last
refuge of aboriginal paganism.   Here the bold mountaineers, Nayarits, Coras, and Tecualmes, maintained
their independence of all Spanish or Christian control
till 1721. It was these tribes or adjoining ones directly
or indirectly supported by them, that caused all Indian troubles of the century in Nueva Galicia.   No
white man, whether soldier or friar, was permitted to
enter the narrow pass that led to the stronghold of
the Gran Nayar. A long series of attempts at peaceful conquest resulted in failure; and the difficulties
of forcible entry were greatly exaggerated at the time,
and still more at a later period by Jesuit chroniclers
who sought to magnify the obstacles overcome by
their order. The Nayarits made a brave but fruitless
resistance, and their stronghold fell before the first
determined and protracted campaign of the invaders
in 1721–2. In 1725 the *visitador* or inspector found
about four thousand natives living submissively in ten
villages; and in 1767 seven Jesuits were serving in as
many Nayarit missions.

North of Nueva Galicia, as I have remarked, Durango and Sinaloa require no special notice here. The
provinces at whose annals a glance must be given, are
New Mexico; Chihuahua, or the northern portion of
Nueva Viscaya proper; Sonora, including the lower
and upper Pimería; and the peninsula of Baja California. All this region, though in its industries and
some other phases of its annals very similar to the
southern provinces, was for the most part still a *tierra
de guerra*, or land of war, always exposed to the raids
of savage gentiles, and often to the revolts of Christian converts. The rule was military rather than
civil, missionary rather than ecclesiastic, save in a few
of the larger towns.

New Mexico from 1700 to 1769 was an isolated
community of neophytes, Franciscan missionaries,
Spanish soldiers, and settlers, struggling, not very
zealously, for a bare existence. Each of these classes

was slightly reënforced during the period; and aid, chiefly in the form of agricultural implements, came from time to time for the settlers, as did a salary for the friars, from Mexico. A few mines were opened in different parts of the country; but about them, as about the agricultural and stock-raising industries which furnished the means of provincial subsistence, very little is known. Trade between the different towns, as with outside gentile tribes and with merchants who brought in caravans from the far south needed articles of foreign manufacture, was generally flourishing in a small way. The Pueblo Indians were for the most part faithful converts, though retaining a fondness for the rites and sorceries of their old faith, which gave the missionaries no little trouble. All Spanish inhabitants, with the events of 1680 ever in their minds, were peculiarly sensitive to rumors of impending revolt, which, from one direction or another, were very frequent, but rarely well founded. There were occasional local troubles in frontier towns; Zuñi was long in revolt; and the Moquis, though declaring themselves subjects of Spain, steadfastly refused to become Christians. The Apaches were often troublesome on the south and west; as were the Yutas, Navajos, and Comanches on the north and east—each nation ready to make a treaty of peace whenever prospects for plunder seemed unfavorable. Rarely did a year pass without a campaign against one of these nations, or an expedition to the Moqui towns. Such time as the governor could spare from Indian campaigns was largely devoted to political controversies and defence against charges of corruption or incompetency. The governor was directly responsible to the viceroy, and a Franciscan custodian was in charge of the friars. In the later years of the period now under consideration, the population of native Christians was about ten thousand, in twenty-five towns under fifteen friars. Of Spanish and mixed blood, settlers and soldiers with their families, there were perhaps twenty-five hundred souls, chiefly at

Santa Fé and Alburquerque, but also scattered to some extent on haciendas. Two or three curates under the bishop of Durango attended to their spiritual needs.

Chihuahua during this period, as before and later, was exposed to never ending raids from the murderous Apaches, which for the most part prevented all permanent progress. Though the savages from the Bolson de Mapimi were again troublesome at first, yet the mining settlements of San Bartolomé Valley in the south counted a Spanish population of over four thousand in 1766. Near Nombre de Dios, the rich mines of Santa Eulalia were discovered, and here in the early years of the century the Real de San Felipe, or Chihuahua, sprang into existence. The new town grew rapidly for a time, but in 1766 the population had decreased to four hundred families. A line of half a dozen presidios, or military posts, was established before 1720 in the north as far as Janos and Paso del Norte; and these posts, some of them being moved from time to time according to need, kept the province from utter ruin, though there was hardly a mission, hacienda, or real de minas that was not at one time or another abandoned. The Franciscans continued their struggle against paganism, and in 1714 founded six new missions at the junction of the Rio Conchos and Rio Grande, which, however, had to be abandoned within ten years. In the Spanish settlements curates relieved the friars, and the missions of the region about Paso del Norte were secularized in 1756 only to be restored to the missionaries for a time in later years. Also in 1756 the Jesuit missions of the Tepehuane and Baja Tarahumara districts were secularized. These missions and those of Alta Tarahumara had been constantly declining. Their troubles and those of their Jesuit directors at the hands of savage invaders, revolting neophytes, Spanish settlers and miners, and secular officials, were in every essential respect similar to those of the Sonora establishments to be noticed presently.

The Jesuits were succeeded in 1767 by eighteen Franciscans from Zacatecas.

Sinaloa and southern Sonora in the eighteenth century present little or nothing of importance to our purpose. In the extreme north, Kino continues to labor as before with like discouraging results till his death in 1711. No missionaries can be obtained for the north; his only permanent associates in Pimería Alta are Campos and Velarde. Military authorities still distrust the Pimas, or pretend to distrust them; but the Jesuits believe these officials are really in league with the miners and settlers to oppose the mission work, desiring the hostility of the natives that they may be enslaved and plundered; at any rate a never ending controversy ensues. After Kino's death there is no change for the better; and no increase of missionaries until 1730. Father Campos makes several tours to the gulf coast, but communication with the north becomes less and less frequent; and Apache raids are of constant occurrence. The Spanish population of Pimería in 1730 is about three hundred. The soldiers are said to give more attention to mining than to their proper duty of protecting the province; and an injudicious policy of non-interference with the Apaches is at one time adopted by orders from Mexico. In 1731 three new priests come, and are assigned to the northern missions of Suamca, Guevavi, and San Javier del Bac founded at this time, though the natives of each had been often before visited by the Jesuits. They are supplied irregularly with missionaries from this time. The names of Campos and Velarde presently disappear from the records to be replaced by those of Sedelmair and Keler. In 1736–50 these Jesuits make several tours to the Gila region, in connection with vain projects for the conversion of the Moquis and the occupation of Northern California. It is in these years, 1737–41, that occurs the famous mining excitement of the Bolas de Plata, at a place between Saric and Guevavi called Arizonac, whence

the name Arizona. The presidio of Terrenate is
founded about 1741. The Pimas become perhaps as
bad as they had been accused of being from the first.
They revolt in 1751–2, killing two priests and a hundred other Spaniards; and for five or six years there
is a bitter controversy between the missionaries and
the government touching the causes of the revolt.
But the presidio of Tubac having been established,
and a small garrison stationed at Altar, the missions
are reoccupied, and maintain a precarious existence
during the rest of the Jesuit period. Six priests are
serving in 1767. Near San Javier del Bac there is a
native ranchería, called Tucson, where after 1752 a
few Spaniards have settled; but the place is temporarily abandoned in 1763.

The Apaches of the north are not Sonora's only
savage scourge; but from 1724 the Seris, Tepocas, Sal-
ineros, Tiburon Islanders, and other bands of the
gulf coast above Guaymas, keep the province in almost
constant terror by their ravages. There has been
some mission work done at intervals, by the Californian padres chiefly, in the Guaymas region, but no
permanent missions are established. The Cerro Prieto
is the rendezvous and stronghold not only of the tribes
named, but at intervals of the Pimas Bajos and other
bands of revolting neophytes. The danger from this
direction is generally deemed greater than from the
Apaches, who are somewhat restrained by the hostility of the Pimas Altos. Campaigns to the Cerro
Prieto are frequent, and generally unsuccessful. In
one of them in 1755 Governor Mendoza is killed.

In 1734 the province of Sinaloa y Sonora is separated from Nueva Vizcaya, and put under a governor
and commandant general, whose capital is nominally
still San Felipe de Sinaloa, but really San Juan or
Pitic in Sonora. Under him are the presidio captains.
Civil affairs are administered as before by alcaldes
mayores. The governor's time, or the little that is
left from the almost continuous campaigns against

northern or western savages, is devoted to the defence
of his own policy, to controversies with the missionaries, and to the recommendation of divers measures
for the salvation of the country, few of which are
adopted and none effectual. In 1740–1 there is a serious revolt of the Yaquis and hitherto submissive
Mayos. The presidio of Pitic at Hermosillo is now
founded, afterwards being transferred for a time to
Horcasitas. In 1745 there are estimated to be sixteen hundred Spanish inhabitants, possibly men, in
Sinaloa, Ostimuri, and Sonora, besides about two
hundred soldiers in the different presidios. Visitador
General Gallardo in 1749 reported the province to be
in a most unprosperous and critical condition. The
population is ever shifting with the finding of new
mines, not a single settlement having over ten permanent Spanish families, though a regular town has been
begun at Horcasitas. No remedy is found for existing
evils before 1767, but affairs go on from bad to worse.

The missions share in the general misfortunes.
Before 1730 they had declined about one half in
neophyte population from 1678; and the decline continues to the end. The Jesuits gradually lose much
of their influence except over women, children, and
infirm old men. Indeed there grows up against them
a very bitter popular feeling, and they become involved in vexatious controversies with the authorities and *gente de razon*, or civilized people, generally.
New-comers are largely German members of the company with less patience and less interest in the missions than the old Spanish workers; and all become
more or less petulant in their discouragement under
ever increasing troubles. They are for the most part
good men, and in the right generally so far as the
details of particular quarrels are concerned; but they
cannot obtain the *sine qua non* of continued mission
prosperity, protection in trouble, non-interference in
success; and like missionaries everywhere they cannot
submit gracefully to the inevitable overthrow of their

peculiar system. Settlers and miners, desiring their lands and the labor of their neophytes, preach liberty to the natives, foment hatred to the priests, advocate secularization, and as the Jesuits believe even stir up revolt.

Before secularization or utter ruin befalls the Sonora missions, all of the Jesuit order are expelled from Spanish dominions. The priests had been waiting for a change, and it comes in a most unexpected form. After months of confinement at Guaymas they are banished, thirty-seven in number, at the beginning of 1768. Soon the missions are given to Franciscan friars, who like the Jesuits are faithful; but the change leaves the several establishments in no better condition than before. At the same period comes the grand military expedition of Elizondo under the auspices of Galvez, which is to reduce the savage foes of Sonora to permanent submission, but which is not brilliantly successful. Notwithstanding the radical changes of this period Sonora affairs proceed much as before; but from the exhibition of energy accompanying these changes, as we shall see, results the occupation of Alta California.

Maritime annals of the period have no importance in this connection, consisting almost entirely of the predatory efforts of Dampier, Rogers, Shelvocke, and Anson, who lie in wait at different times for the Manila ship. On the peninsula of Baja California Salvatierra and his associates labor with zeal and success. Gifts from rich patrons, forming the 'pious fund,' enable them to purchase supplies and thus counteract the disadvantages of their barren country. At the same time its barrenness and isolation relieve them from much of the interference suffered in Sonora. Yet there are Spaniards who desire to fish for pearls; and there are others who believe the Jesuits to be engaged secretly in pearl-fishing and thus amassing great wealth. Indeed there are few persecutions suffered by their brethren across the gulf, which in a modified form do not affect them; while they endure many hardships and privations elsewhere unknown. Missions are founded till the chain extends nearly the whole length of the peninsula.   Salvatierra dies in 1717.   In 1718–21 Ugarte builds a vessel and explores the gulf to its head.   The Manila ship touches occa-· sionally after 1734; and this same year marks the beginning of long-continued revolts in the south, during which two priests are killed.   Governor Huidrobo comes over from Sonora for a campaign, and a presidio is founded at San José del Cabo.   In 1742–8 an epidemic destroys several missions.   Father Consag in 1746 and 1751 explores both the gulf and ocean coasts.   About 1750 there is a general revival in commercial, mining, and pearl-fishing industries; but it is not of long duration, bringing blame also upon the Jesuits.   Save the praiseworthy desire to improve the spiritual condition of its inhabitants, there is no encouragement for the Spanish occupation of this country.   Sixteen Jesuits died in the country; sixteen were banished in 1768.   Bitter feelings against the company in the North Mexican provinces, or indeed in America, had but slight influence in causing the expulsion of the Jesuits from the Spanish dominions.

CHAPTER II.

BIBLIOGRAPHY OF CALIFORNIAN HISTORY.

List of Authorities—A Catalogue of California Books—Taylor's List—
Proposed Classification—Periods of History—Sixteen Hundred
Titles before 1848—Printed Material—Epoch of Discovery to
1769—Cosmographies and Voyage Collections—Spanish Epoch
1769-1824—Books of Visitors—Books, Periodicals, and Documents—The Mexican Period, 1824-1846—Voyages—Overland Narratives—First Prints of California—Works of Mexican Authors—
Government Documents—Histories—Local Annals—One Thousand
Titles of Manuscripts—Archives, Public, Mission, and Private—
Vallejo and Larkin—Documentary Titles—Scattered Correspondence—Dictations of Natives and Pioneers—Value of Reminiscences—After the Gold Discovery—Manuscripts—Books Printed
in and about California.

I HAVE prefixed to this volume a list of authorities
cited in the *History of California*, which includes about
four thousand[1] titles of books, pamphlets, newspapers,
printed documents, articles, and manuscripts. It is
something more than a mere list of the works consulted and epitomized in this part of my history,
being practically a complete catalogue of all existing
material pertaining to California, down to the epoch
of the discovery of gold, and of all historical material to a later period. I am of course aware that
a perfectly complete bibliographical list of authorities
on any topic of magnitude does not exist; and I do not
pretend that mine is such a list; hence the limitation, a

[1] Throughout this chapter I employ round numbers, and in most instances
the word 'about' should be understood with each number. The necessity of
printing this summary before the list is put in type prevents absolute accuracy; yet the numerical statements are by no means mere estimates, but may
be regarded as practically accurate, the variation never exceeding two or
three per cent.

(34)

'practically' complete catalogue. Additional research
will add a few items to each, or most, of my subdivisions; and even now, did space permit, several
of them might be greatly extended, as will be presently explained, without really adding much to the
value of the catalogue. As it stands the list is more
complete than any other within my knowledge relating
to any state or territory of our union, or indeed to
any other country in the world.[2]

Respecting each of the titles given there will be
found somewhere in this history a bibliographic note
affording all desirable information about the work and
its author; so that if these notes were brought together
and attached in alphabetic order to the items of the
list, the result would be a *Bibliography of Californian
History*, to which work the present chapter might serve
as an introduction. In it I propose to a certain extent
to classify the works which have furnished data for
this and the following volumes, and briefly to describe
and criticise such of the various classes and subdivisions as may seem to require remark. A few individual works of a general or representative nature may
appropriately be noticed in this connection; but as a
rule the reader must look elsewhere for such special
notices. To the general reader, as must be confessed,
bibliography is a topic not of the most fascinating;

[2] So far as works on California are concerned, the only previous attempt at
anything approaching a complete list is Alex. S. Taylor's *Bibliografa Cali-
fornica* published in the *Sacramento Union* of June 25, 1863, with additions
in the same paper of March 13, 1866. In a copy preserved in the Library of
the California Pioneers in San Francisco, there are manuscript additions of
still later date. This work contained over a thousand titles, but its field was
the whole territory from Baja California to the Arctic Ocean, west of the
Rocky Mountains, only about one half of the works relating to Alta California proper. Dr Taylor's zeal in this direction was most commendable, and his
success, considering his extremely limited facilities, was wonderful; yet his
catalogue is useless. He never saw one in five of the works he names; blunders average more than one to each title; he names many books that never
existed, others so inaccurately that they cannot be traced, and yet others
several times over under different titles. His insufferable pedantry and affectation of bibliographic *patois* unite with the typographic errors of the
newspaper press to destroy for the most part any merit that the list might
otherwise have. I have no doubt there may be a few of Taylor's items representing books or documents that actually exist and are not in my list; but to
select them would be a well nigh hopeless task.

but its novelty in Californian aspects and the brevity
and comprehensiveness of its treatment in this instance
may perhaps be offered as circumstances tending to
counteract inherent monotony.

In point of time bibliography, like the history, of
California is divided into two great periods by the
discovery of gold in 1848.   I have some sixteen hundred titles for the earlier period and over two thousand
for the later; though the division would be numerically
much less equal were printed material alone considered.
And if books and pamphlets only were taken into
account, disregarding newspapers and articles and documents in print, the numbers would stand two hundred
and seventy for the primitive, and more than a thousand for the modern epoch.   Yet there could be no
good reason for restricting my list of authorities to
books; and its extension to manuscript, documentary,
and periodical material is entirely legitimate, as will
be at once apparent to scholars.   Where to stop in
this extension, however, and in the consequent subdivision of documentary data is obviously a point respecting which no two critics would be likely to agree.
The abundance of my material has put me beyond the
temptation to exaggerate; and while some will doubtless regret that in certain directions, notably that of
original manuscripts, I have not multiplied titles, the
ever present necessity of rigid condensation has con-
trolled my course in this matter.[3]

For the years preceding 1848 manuscript authorities greatly outnumber those in print, being 1,030 out
of a total of 1,650; but in later times, the era of newspapers and printed government records, manuscripts
number less than 200, in a total of over 2,000.   I begin naturally with the earlier period, and first give
attention to printed material.

---

[3] The reader is reminded also that in foot-notes of the following pages are
references to thousands of documents in manuscript and print that are not
given titles or mentioned separately in the list.

Titles of printed authorities on this first of the two great periods number, as I have said, something over 600, of which 270 are books or pamphlets, 250 documents or articles, and 90 periodicals or collections that may be so classed. It is well, however, to subdivide the period chronologically, and to glance at the earliest epoch of discovery, namely, that preceding 1769. Up to this date California had not been the exclusive, or indeed the chief, topic of any book; yet my list contains 56 at least, which treat of the distant province and the voyages thereto. The number might be considerably augmented by including all general works, in which California was barely named at second hand; or in like manner lessened by omitting repetitions of Sir Francis Drake's voyage; and indeed eight[4] would suffice to impart all the actual knowledge extant at the time in print, the rest being of interest mainly by reason of their quaint cosmographical conceits or conjectures on the name California. Five of these are general Spanish works alluding to California only as a part of Spanish America, one being a romance naming the province before its discovery.[5] Sixteen are descriptive cosmographical works of the old type, to which may be added four English records of a slightly different class.[6] Then we have sixteen of the once popular collections of voyages and travels, to which as to the preceding class additions might be made without going out of my library.[7] And finally we may notice eight works which treat of special voyages—none of them actually to California—or the lives of special

[4] See in the list the following headings: Cabrera Bueno, Drake, Hakluyt, Herrera, Linschoten, Purchas, Torquemada, and Venegas. It is probable that these list notes will not be deemed of any importance to the general reader; but he can easily pass them by; and it is believed that their value to a certain class of students will more than pay for the comparatively little space they fill.

[5] See Acosta, Apostólicos Afanes, Diaz del Castillo, Esplandian, and Villa Señor.

[6] See America, Blaeu, D'Avity, Gottfriedt, Heylyn, Laet, Löw, Luyt, Mercator, Montanus, Morelli, Ogilby, Ortelius, West Indische Spieghel, and Wytfliet; also Camden, Campbell, Coxe, and Davis.

[7] See Aa, Hacke, Harris, Sammlung, Ramusio, and Voyages.

navigators,[8] and a like number of important documents relating to this primitive epoch, which were not known in print until modern times.[9] As I have said, California was but incidentally mentioned in the books of this early time; a few contained all that visitors had revealed of the coast; while the rest were content with a most inaccurate and superficial repetition eked out with imagination to form the wonders of the Northern Mystery.

The next sub-period was that of inland exploration, of settlement, of mission-founding, of Spanish domination in California, lasting from 1769 to 1824. I have about four hundred titles for this time; but the showing of printed matter is meagre, numbering not above sixty. Yet the number includes three works devoted exclusively to the province, two of them, Costansó's *Diario* and the *Monterey, Extracto de Noticias*, being brief but important records of the first expeditions to San Diego and Monterey, while the third, Palou's *Vida de Junípero Serra*, was destined to be the standard history of the country down to 1784, a most valuable record. Next in importance were ten works in which navigators described their visits to California and to other parts of the western coast.[10] One of these early visitors wrote in English; two in Spanish; three in German; and four in French. Several of them, notably La Pérouse and Vancouver, went far beyond their own personal observations, gleaning material by which the earliest history of the country became for the first time known to the world. To two of the voyage-narratives, unimportant in themselves, were prefixed by competent and well known editors,[11] extensive summaries of earlier explorations.

[8] See Burton, Clark, Dampier, Rogers, Shelvocke, and Ulloa.
[9] See Ascension, Cabrillo, Cardona, Demarcacion, Evans, Niel, and Salmeron. There are many more minor documents of this class relating vaguely to California in connection with the Northern Mystery.
[10] See Chamisso, Choris, Kotzebue, Langsdorff, La Pérouse, Marchand, Maurelle, Roquefeuille, Sutil y Mexicana, and Vancouver.
[11] See Fleurieu and Navarrete.

For the rest we have half a dozen general works on America;[12] a like number of Mexican works with matter on California;[13] and as many collections of voyages and travels.[14]

Of Mexican newspapers containing Californian news during this period, only the official journal, the *Gaceta de Mexico*, requires mention here. And printed documents or articles are only seven in number; though there might be cited very many documents of the Spanish government relating to or naming California simply as a province of Mexico. Two essays by visitors are printed with the books of voyagers that have been named.[15] Captain Shaler had the honor of being the first American visitor whose narrative was printed in the United States; Governor Sola sent a report which was printed in Mexico; two instructions for Californians were put in type;[16] and in one of the Spanish voyage-collections appeared an account of the country's history and condition in connection with Peninsular affairs.[17] Documents of this period not printed until much later are some of them important, especially those published in *Palou, Noticias,* and the *Doc. Hist. Mex.* There are nineteen titles of this class.[18]

The final sub-period extending from 1824 to 1848 may be divided historically into that of Mexican rule to 1846, and that of the conquest and American military rule to the gold discovery; but bibliographically no such subdivision is convenient, and I treat all as one epoch. It claims 700 titles in my list, 475 of which represent printed matter, and 180 books proper.

[12] See Alcedo, Anquetil, Bonnycastle, Burney, Forster, Humboldt, and Raynal.
[13] Arricivita, Clavigero, Cortés, Guia, Presidios, and Rosignon.
[14] Berenger, Kerr, Laharpe, Pinkerton, Viagero Universal, and Voyages.
[15] Chamisso and Rollin.
[16] Galvez and Ulloa.
[17] California en 1799.
[18] Altamira, Armona, Crespí, Dominguez, Garcés, Hall, Heceta, Mangino, Palou, Reglamento, Revilla Gigedo, Serra, and Velarde.

First in importance, with Petit-Thouars at the head of the list so far as history is concerned and Coulter at the foot, are fourteen narratives of voyagers, who visited the coast and in many instances made good use of their opportunities. The works of Mofras and Wilkes are the most pretentious of the number, but not the most valuable.[19] To these should be added four scientific works resulting from some of these voyages;[20] and three official accounts of exploring marches across the continent in book form;[21] with which we may appropriately class a dozen accounts of California by foreign visitors or residents, generally including a narrative of the trip by land or sea.[22] Four foreigners who had never visited the country compiled historical accounts,[23] one of which, by Forbes, has always enjoyed a merited reputation as a standard book. Then there were half a dozen or more works on Oregon with brief mention of California,[24] and half a dozen speeches in congress or elsewhere printed in pamphlet form, a number that might be very greatly increased if made to include all that mentioned California in connection with the Mexican war and the Oregon Question.[25] To all of which titles from foreign sources may be added those of ten general works[26] containing allusions to our province.

Chief among works in Spanish for this period should stand six which, though with one exception not very important for history, were the first books printed in California, most of them being entirely unknown until now.[27] And with these may be named eight other

[19] Beechey, Belcher, Cleveland, Coulter, Dana, Duhaut-Cilly, Huish (not a visitor), Kotzebue, Laplace, Mofras, Morrell, Petit-Thouars, Ruschenberger, Simpson, and Wilkes.

[20] Hinds, Richardson, and U. S. Ex. Ex.—the later including many works by different authors.

[21] Emory and Frémont.

[22] Bidwell, Bilson, Boscana, Bryant, Farnham, Hastings, Kelley, Pattie, and Robinson.

[23] Cutts, Forbes, Greenhow, and Hughes.

[24] Fédix, Lee, Nicolay, Twiss, etc.

[25] Clark, Hall, Thompson, Webster, etc.

[26] Beyer, Blagdon, Barrow, Combier, D'Orbigny, Irving, Lafond, Lardner, Murray, and Tytler.

[27] Botica, Figueroa, Reglamento, Ripalda, Romero, and Vallejo.

pamphlets, printed in Mexico on Californian topics.[28] Then there are sixteen Mexican government documents containing valuable allusions to California,[29] and many more if mere mentions be counted; and finally, we have thirty-five general works on Mexico, with like information often of some value, about a dozen of which are the writings of Cárlos María Bustamante, found also more complete in my library in the original autograph manuscript.[30]

Passing from books to documents, the productions of the Californian press merit first mention. They are fifty-five in number, each separately printed.[31] Three or four are proclamations of United States officials, one is a commercial paper, one an advertisement, and one took a poetical form; but most were official documents emanating from the Hispano-Californian government. Then I note sixteen Mexican government documents in collections or newspapers; and seven others of a semi-official nature;[32] while there are twenty-two topic-collections or separate reports, from United States officers, for the most part printed by the government and relating to the conquest.[33] Three titles belong to matter inserted in the books of navigators already named;[34] six to articles or documents in the *Nouvelles Annales des Voyages*;[35] and twelve are English and American articles in periodicals.[36]

[28] Carillo, Castañares, Fondo Piadoso, García Diego, Junta de Fomento, and San Miguel.

[29] Under the heading 'Mexico.'

[30] Alaman, Ayala, Bermudez, Bustamante, Cancelada, Escudero, Fonseca, Guerrero, Iriarte, Muhlenpfordt, Oajaca, Rejon, Riesgo, Sales, San Miguel, Semblanzas, Thompson, Unzueta, and Willie.

[31] Alvarado, California, Castro, Chico, Diputacion, Doctrina, Figueroa, Gutierrez, Híjar, Mason, Micheltorena, Plan, Pronunciamiento, Riley, Shubrick, Vallejo, and Zamorano.

[32] Ayuntamiento, Compañia, Decreto, Dictámen, Iniciativa, Jones, Mexico, Plan. Also Bandini, 'C.,' Castañares, Chico, Flores, Iniestra, and Sinaloa.

[33] Cal. and N. Mex., Conquest, Cooke, Expulsion, Frémont, Johnston, Jones, Kearny, Kelley, Marcy, Mason, Monterey, Shubrick, Slacum, Sloat, Stockton, War with Mexico. Some of these are the president's messages and documents, containing a very large number of important papers.

[34] Botta, Documens, and Sanchez.

[35] Fages, Galitzin, Le Netrel, Morineau, Scala, and Smith.

[36] Americans, Campaign, Coulter, Evans, Far West, Fourgeaud, Hist. Bear Flag, Larkin, Peirce, Reynolds, Squier, and Warner.

There were some twenty periodicals, or publications that may conveniently be classed as such, some being collections or serial records, that contained material about this province before 1848; at least that is the number that my list furnishes.[37] Of newspapers about seventy titles—forty of them Mexican—appear in my catalogue; but as doubtless many more in different parts of the world contained at least a mention of this country at one time or another, I name only ten published in California, the Hawaiian Islands, and Oregon,[38] all valuable sources of information. *Niles' Register* is the eastern journal that I have found most useful in my task.

Finally I have about 150 titles of books, documents, and articles, which, though printed later, relate to Californian history before 1848, so far as they relate to that subject at all. Seventy-five of the number are in book form, including some valuable monographs on early affairs in California; several collections of documents; some reprints and translations of early works; some treatises on Mexican law as affecting California; several important briefs in land cases, the number of which might easily be multiplied; United States documents relating to the conquest and military rule, but printed after 1848; Russian works containing information on the Ross colony; one or two narratives of visitors; and a number of works on the Mexican war. Those appearing under the names of Dwinelle, Ide, Lancey, McGlashan, and Palou are the most important.[39] Documents and articles of this class are about

[37] American Quarterly Register, American Quarterly Review, American Review, American State Papers, Annals of Congress, Arrillaga, Colonial Magazine, Congressional Debates, Congressional Globe, Edinburgh Review, Hansard's Parl. Debates, Home Missionary, Hunt's Merch. Magazine, London Mechanics' Magazine, North American Review, Nouvelles Annales des Voyages, Quarterly Review, Revista Científica, and Southern Quarterly Review.

[38] In California were four, or rather combinations of two; Monterey Californian, San Francisco Californian, San Francisco Star, and San Francisco Star and Californian. At Honolulu, five; the Friend, Hawaiian Spectator, Sandwich Island Gazette, Sandwich Island News, and Polynesian. In Oregon was the Spectator.

[39] Abbott, Bigelow, California, California Land Titles, California and North

the same in number, and very similar in their nature and variety to the books, including also some titles of pioneer reminiscences in the newspapers, titles that might be multiplied almost without limit.[40]

Of works printed after 1848, relating chiefly to events subsequent to the discovery of gold, and therefore belonging to a later bibliographic period, but yet containing information on earlier annals, I have occasion to cite about three hundred titles in these volumes. Most of them are unimportant in this connection; but some are formal attempts at historical research embracing both chronologic periods. The works of Tuthill and Gleeson, entitled, the one a *History of California*, and the other a *History of the Catholic Church in California*, are the only ones of a general nature requiring notice here. Tuthill's history merits much higher praise than has generally been accorded to it, being the work of a brilliant and conscientious writer. It is a satisfactory popular history, making no claims to exhaustive research, but intelligently prepared from the best accessible authorities. Gleeson is not so able a writer, is somewhat more of a partisan, wrote more hastily, and fell into more errors; yet as a Catholic priest he had some superior facilities. He read more of the old authorities, went more fully into details, and was quite as conscientious; and he has given us a pleasing and tolerably accurate picture of mission life and annals. Neither of these authors had, or pretended to have, any facilities for writing history or annals proper, and

Mexico, Calvo, Cavo, Colton, Cooke, Diccionario, Documentos, Doyle, Drake, Dunbar, Dwinelle, Figueroa, Flagg, Frémont, Furber, Gomez, Guerra, Hale, Halleck, Hartmann, Hawes, Hoffman, Homes, Ide, Jay, Jenkins, Jones, Lancey, Marcou, McGlashan, Mansfield, Mexican War, Palou, Phelps, Ramsay, Randolph, Revere, Ripley, Rivera, Stockton, Taylor, Upham, Vallejo, Velasco, Vischer, Tikhménef, Materialui, Rezánof, Markof, and Khlébnikof.

[40] Archbald, Arroyo, Assembly, Biographical Sketches, Boggs, Bowers, Brooklyn, Brown, Buchanan, Clark, Dall, Daubenbiss, Degroot, Dwinelle, Dye, Elliot, Espinosa, Folsom, Foster, Frémont, Hale, Halleck, Hecox, Hittell, Hopkins, Jones, Kern, Kearny, King's Orphan, Kip, Leese, McDougall, McPherson, Marcou, Marsh, Mason, Mexico, Micheltorena, Peckham, Reed, Sherman, Stevenson, Stillman, Stockton, Sutter, Taylor, Toombs, Trask, Vallejo, Veritas, Victor, Warren, Wiggins, and Wolfskill.

to criticise their failure to accomplish such a result would be affectation.[41] Historical sketches published before 1848, either separately or in connection with narratives of travel, many of them of real value, will be noticed individually in their chronological place. Similar sketches, but for the most part of much less importance, published during the 'flush times' or later, often in connection with descriptive works, such sketches as those found under the headings Capron, Cronise, Frost, and Hastings, require no special notice. They contained no original material, and made but inadequate and partial use of such as was easily accessible.

There is, however, another class of these recent publications that assumes considerable importance, that of local histories, of which my list contains over sixty titles. Each in connection with descriptive matter gives something of local annals for both early and modern times. Some of them are the Centennial Sketches prepared at the suggestion of the United States government, like that of Los Angeles by Warner and Hayes, and of San Francisco by John S. Hittell. This latter work was made also 'incidentally a history of California,' and, like the earlier *Annals of San Francisco* by Soulé and others, it is a work of much merit. The authors were able men, though they had neither time, space, nor material to make anything like a complete record of local events in the earlier times. Hall's *History of San José* should also be mentioned in connection with the *Annals* as a work of merit. And finally there are many county histories, often in atlas form and copiously illustrated with portraits, maps, and views. Each contains a preliminary sketch of California history, with

[41] *The History of California*, by Franklin Tuthill, San Francisco, 1866, 8vo, xvi. 657 pages. About one third of the book is occupied with the period preceding the discovery of gold. Dr Tuthill was connected with the San Francisco press, and died soon after the appearance of his work.

History of the Catholic Church in California, by W. Gleeson, M. A., Professor, St Mary's College, San Francisco, Cal., in two volumes, illustrated. San Francisco. Printed for the author. 1872. 8vo, 2 vols, xv. 446, 351 pages.

more detailed reference to the county which gives
title to the work. Three or four firms have in late
years been engaged in producing these peculiar publications, with a dozen or more different editors. The
books were made of course mainly to sell; yet notwithstanding this and other unfavorable conditions,
some of the editors have done valuable work. As
might be expected they are uneven in quality, abound-
ing in blunders, especially in those parts that depend
on Spanish records; yet in the matter of local annals
after 1840, and of personal details, they have afforded
me in the aggregate considerable assistance. Their
chief defect is—I speak only of those parts relating
to early times—that in their pages valuable information and glaring inaccuracies are so intermingled that
the ordinary reader cannot separate them. They are
not history; but they supply some useful materials
for history. In the results of their interviews with
old residents the editors have furnished some matter
similar and supplemental to the pioneer dictations
which I shall presently mention.

I now come to the thousand and more titles of
manuscript authorities in my list, far exceeding those
in print for this early period, not only numerically, but
in historical value; since the country's annals down
to 1846, at least, could be much more completely
written from the manuscripts alone than from the
print alone. Naturally these authorities lose nothing
of their value in my estimation from the facts that in
most instances no other writer has consulted them,
and that essentially all of them exist only in my collection.

Of the public archives of the Spanish and Mexican
government in California, transferred by copyists to
my library, there are thirteen collections represented
in the catalogue by as many titles, the originals making
about 350 bound volumes of from 300 to 1,000 documents each, besides an immense mass of unbound

papers.[42]   With a view to the convenience of the public, rather than my own, I have made the numbers of my volumes of copies and extracts correspond in most cases to the originals.   For historical purposes these copies are better than the originals on account of their legibility, and the condensation effected by the omission of duplicates and suppression of verbiage in minor routine papers.   The originals are the official papers turned over by the Mexican government to that of the United States in 1846–7, now preserved chiefly in the United States surveyor-general's office at San Francisco, where there are nearly three hundred bulky tomes besides loose papers, but also in less extensive collections at other places, notably at Los Angeles, Salinas City, and San José.   The main *Archivo* is divided into twenty-four sub-collections;[43] but beyond a slight attempt at chronology and the segregation of papers on a few topics involving land titles, the classification is arbitrary and of no value; nor is there any real distinction between the papers preserved in the different archives.   Of the nature of these documents it must suffice to say that they are the originals, blotters, or certified copies of the orders, instructions, reports, correspondence, and act-records of the authorities, political, military, judicial, and ecclesiastical; national, provincial, departmental, territorial, and municipal, during the successive rule, monarchical, imperial, and republican, of Spain, Mexico, and the United States, from 1768 to 1850.   The value of archive records as a foundation for history is universally understood.   Spanish archives are not less accurate than those of other nations; and, since few happenings were so petty as not to fall under the cognizance of some official, they furnish a much more complete record of provincial

[42] Archivo de California, Los Angeles, Monterey, Sacramento, San Diego, San José, San Luis Obispo, Santa Bárbara, and Santa Cruz.

[43] Actas, Brands, Dept. Records, Dept. State Papers, Legislative Records, Provincial Records, Provincial State Papers, State Papers, Superior Govt St. Papers, and Unbound Documents.   For further subdivisions of these titles see list.

annals than would be afforded, for instance, by the
public archives of an English province. Of the
quarter of a million documents consulted in these collections I shall mention later about two hundred
under distinct titles. The early archives of California,
as preserved by the government, are not entirely complete, though more nearly so I think than those of
any other state of our union; but I have taken some
effective steps to supply the defects, as will presently
appear.[44]

Also in the nature of public archives are the missionary records. As the missions by the process of
secularization passed into the control of the church,
the old leather-bound registers of baptisms, marriages, burials, and confirmations at each establishment remained, and for the most part still remain, in
the possession of the curate of the parish. Other
mission papers were gradually brought together by
the Franciscan authorities at Santa Bárbara, where
they now constitute the largest collection extant.
From such documents as were not thus preserved,
remaining in the missions or scattered in private
hands, Taylor subsequently made a collection of five
large volumes, now in the archbishop's library in San
Francisco. A third collection, chiefly of *libros de
patentes*, is that of the bishop of Monterey and Los
Angeles. These have furnished me, under four titles,
eighteen volumes of copies, or not less than 10,000
documents,[45] and my own efforts have resulted in four
volumes of very valuable original documents, about
2,000 in number, under three titles.[46] Then the
twenty-two collections of mission registers already
mentioned as in custody of the curates, the libros de

[44] There are at least seven collections in my list, which are public archives
similar to those before named, except that instead of being copies they are
the originals obtained by me from private sources. See headings, Larkin,
Monterey, San Francisco, Registro, and Sonoma.

[45] Archivo del Arzobispado, Archivo del Obispado, Arch. de Sta Bárbara,
and Correspondencia de Misiones.

[46] Archivo de Misiones, Pico (Andrés), and San Antonio, Documentos
Sueltos.

mision proper with such scattering papers as have remained at some establishments, have been searched for my purposes, each yielding a volume of extracts and statistics;[47] while from private sources I have obtained fifteen originals of similar nature.[48] I give separate titles to about 120 documents from the mission archives; and it should be noted that they contain not a few secular records; while the public, or secular, archives contain many important mission papers.

As I have said, neither the public nor mission archives are complete. Documents were not all turned over as they should have been to the United States and to the church; nearly every Mexican official retained more or less records which remained in his family archives together with his correspondence and that of his ancestors and relations. I have made an earnest effort to collect these scattered papers, and with flattering success, as is shown by about fifty collections of *Documentos para la Historia de California*, in 110 volumes, containing not less than 40,000 documents, thousands being of the utmost importance as containing records nowhere else extant, and 116 of them receiving special titles in my list. About half of all these documents are similar in their nature and historic value—in all save that they are originals instead of copies on my shelves— to those in the public and mission archives; and the rest are in some respects even more valuable for my purpose, being largely composed of the private correspondence of prominent citizens and officials on current public affairs, of which they afford almost an unbroken record. Twenty-nine of these collections of private or family archives bear the names of the

[47] Monterey Parroquia (S. Cárlos), Purísima, S. Antonio, S. Buenaventura, S. Diego, S. Fernando, S. Francisco, S. Gabriel, S. José, S. Juan Bautista, S. Juan Capistrano, S. Luis Obispo, S. Miguel, S. Rafael, Sta Bárbara, Sta Cruz, Sta Clara, Sta Inés, and Soledad. Only the mission books of S. Luis Rey have eluded my search.

[48] Arroyo, Loa, Mission, Música, Oro Molido, Privilegios, Purísima, S. José, Sta Inés, S. Francisco Solano, Sarría, Sermones.

Californian families by the representatives of which they were given to me.[49] Of these by far the largest and most valuable collection is that which bears the name of Mariano Guadalupe Vallejo, in thirty-seven immense folio volumes of not less than 20,000 original papers. General Vallejo, one of the most prominent and enlightened of Californians, was always a collector of such documents as might aid in recording the history of his country; and when he became interested in my work he not only most generously and patriotically gave up all his accumulated treasures of the past, but doubled their bulk and value by using his influence with such of his countrymen as turned a deaf ear to my persuasions. As a contributor to the stock of original information respecting his country's annals, General Vallejo must ever stand without a rival. The second collection in extent, and the largest from the south, is that of the Guerra y Noriega family in Santa Bárbara. But bulk is by no means the only test of value; and many of my smaller collections, from men who gave all they had, contain records quite as important as the larger ones named.

Twenty other collections bear foreign names, in some cases that of the pioneer family whose archives they were, and in others that of the collector or donor.[50] Except that a larger proportion of the documents are in English, they are generally of the same class as those just referred to. At the head of this class in merit stand Thomas O. Larkin's nine volumes of *Documents for the History of California,* presented by Mr Larkin's family through his son-in-law, Sampson Tams. This collection is beyond all comparison the best source of information on the history of 1845-6, which in fact could not be correctly written without

---

[49] See the following headings, each followed by 'Documentos' or 'Papeles;' Alviso, Arce, Ávila, Bandini, Bonilla, Carillo, Castro, Coronel, Cota, Estudillo, Fernandez, Gomez, Gonzalez, Guerra y Noriega, Marron, Moreno, Olvera, Pico, Pinto, Requena, Soberanes, Valle, and Vallejo.

[50] Ashley, Documentos, Fitch, Griffin, Grigsby, Hayes, Hittell, Larkin, Janssens, McKinstry, Monterey, Murray, Pinart, Savage, Sawyer, and Spear.

these papers. Larkin besides being United States consul, and at one time a confidential agent of the national administration in California, was also a leading merchant who had an extensive commercial correspondence with prominent residents both foreign and native in all parts of the country, as also with traders and other visitors at the provincial capital. Business letters between him and such men as Stearns at Los Angeles, Fitch at San Diego, and Leidesdorff at San Francisco, from week to week furnish a running record of political, industrial, social, and commercial annals. The most influential natives in different sections corresponded frequently with the merchant consul; he was on terms of intimacy with the masters of vessels, and with leading men in Mexico and at the islands. The collection contains numerous and important letters from Frémont, Sutter, Sloat, and Montgomery. Autograph communications from James Buchanan, secretary of State at Washington, exhibit the national policy respecting California in an entirely new light. Indeed it is difficult to overestimate the historical value of these precious papers, or the service rendered to their country by the family representatives who have made this material available to the historian. Besides the nine bulky volumes mentioned I have from the same source a large quantity of unbound commercial documents; the merchant's account books for many years, of great value in supplying pioneer names and dates; and, still more important, his consulate records, containing copies of all his communications to the United States government, only a few of which have ever been made known to the public. Larkin and Vallejo must ever stand unrivalled among the names of pioneer and native contributors to the store of original material for Californian history.

My list contains about 550 titles of separate manuscript documents, the number being pretty equally divided between those forming each a volume on my shelves and those to be found in the different private, public, and mission archives. So far as the archive papers are concerned, I might legitimately carry the multiplication of titles much further, since there are thousands of documents, which to a writer with a less abundant store of such material than mine would seem to amply merit separate titles; but here as elsewhere I have preferred to err, if at all, on the side of excessive condensation. Of the whole number three fifths relate to the period preceding, and two fifths to that following, 1824. They may be roughly divided into four general classes.

First there are eighty diaries or journals or log-books, of those who explored the coast in ships, or traversed the interior in quest of mission sites, or marched to attack hostile gentiles, or sought converts in distant rancherías, or came by sea to trade or smuggle, or made official tours of inspection.[51] The second class is that composed of what may be called government documents, one hundred and sixty-three in number. Twenty-seven of these were orders, instructions, reports, and other papers emanating from the viceroy, or other Spanish or Mexican officials.[52] Seventy-five are like official papers written by the governor, comandante general, prefect, or other high officials in California.[53] Thirty-four are similar documents from military commandants and other subordinate California officers;[54] and twenty-seven are Mex-

[51] Abella, *Albatross*, Altimira, Amador, Anza, *Arab*, Arteaga, Bodega, Breen, Cabot, Cañizares, Castillo, Clyman, Cooper, Cota, Coutts, Danti, Douglas, Edwards, Font, Gonzalez, Goycoechea, Griffin, Grijalva, Hartnell, Haswell, Heceta, Libro de Bitácora, Lisalde, Log-books, Malaspina, Martin, Martinez, Maurelle, Mellus, Moraga, Muñoz, Nuez, Ordaz, Ortega, Payeras, Peirce, Peña, Peralta, Perez, Piña, Portilla, Portolá, Robbins, Sal, Sanchez, Santa María, Sitjar, Soto, Tapis, Vallejo, Velazquez, Viader, Yates, and Zalvidea. In many cases more than one diary is found under a single name.

[52] Alaman, Areche, Azanza, Borbon, Branciforte, Bucareli, Cárcaba, Costansó, Croix, Flores, Galvez, Híjar, Montesdeoca, Nava, Revilla Gigedo, and Sanchez.

[53] Alvarado, Argüello, Arrillaga, Borica, Castro, Chico, Echeandía, Fages, Figueroa, Flores, Gutierrez, Micheltorena, Neve, Pico, Rivera y Moncada, Romeu, Sola, Vallejo, and Victoria.

[54] Alberni, Amador, Argüello, Bandini, Carrillo, Córdoba, Estudillo, Gra-

ican and Californian *reglamentos* provincial and municipal, emanating from different authorities.[55] The third class consists of one hundred and four mission documents, of which fifteen are orders, regulations, and reports from guardians of the college of San Fernando, and other high missionary and ecclesiastic authorities in Mexico or Spain.[56] Fifty-two are instructions or reports of the mission presidents and prefects, or from the bishop;[57] while the rest, forty-seven in number, are reports, letters, and miscellaneous writings of the missionary padres.[58] The fifth and last class is that to which may be applied the convenient term 'miscellaneous,' consisting of nearly two hundred titles, and which may be subdivided as follows: Twenty-six items of political correspondence, speeches, and narratives;[59] a dozen or more documents of local record and regulation;[60] twenty-two collections from private sources, equivalent to public or mission archives;[61] twenty-two other collections of material;[62] thirty *expedientes*, or topic collections of documents, including many legal and criminal cases;[63]

jera, Grijalva, Goycoechea, Guerra, Moraga, Ortega, Padrés, Perez Fernandez, Rodriguez, Sal, Soler, and Vallejo.

[55] Alvarado, Arancel, Californias, Colonizacion, Constitucion, Decreto, Echeandía, Galvez, Indios, Instrucciones, Mexico, Micheltorena, Ordenanzas, Pico, Pitic, Plan, Reglamento, and Secularizacion.

[56] Bestard, Branciforte, Calleja, Gasol, Garijo, Lopez, Lull, Pio VI., Pangua, and Sancho.

[57] Duran, García Diego, Indios, Lasuen, Misiones, Payeras, Sanchez, Sarría, Señan, Serra, and Tapis.

[58] Abella, Autobiografía, Catalá, Catecismo, Colegio, Escandon, Expediente, Facultad, Fernandez, Fondo Piadoso, Fuster, Hayes, Horra, Inform, Lasuen, Lopez, Marquinez, Mission, Monterey, Mugártegui, Munguía, Olbés, Palou, Paterna, Peña, Protesta, Purísima, Ripoll, Salazar, San Buenaventura, San José, Santa Bárbara, Serra, Tapis, and Zalvidea.

[59] Alvarado, Argüello, Bandini, Carrillo, Castillo Negrete, Castro, Gomez, Guerra, Osio, and Vallejo.

[60] Estab. Rusos, Los Angeles, Monterey, Ross, Rotschef, and San Francisco.

[61] See notes 44 and 48 of this chapter.

[62] Bear Flag Papers, Boston, California Pioneers, Cerruti, Hayes, Linares, Miscel. Hist. Papers, Nueva España, Pinart, Pioneer Sketches, Douglas Papers, Mayer MSS., Russian America, Sutter-Suñol, Taylor, Viages al Norte.

[63] Ábrego, *Albatross*, Apalátegui, *Asia* and *Constante*, Atanasio, Berreyesa, Bouchard, Carrillo, Castañares, Duarte, Elliot de Castro, Expediente, Fitch, Graham, Guerra, Herrera, Mercado, *Mercury*, Peña, Rae, Rodriguez, Romero, Rubio, San José, Santa Bárbara, Santa Cruz, Solis, Sonoma, and Stearns.

half a dozen old sets of commercial and other account books, some of them of great historical value;[64] fifteen lists of inhabitants, vessels, pioneers, soldiers, etc.;[65] and a like number of old narratives, some being similar to my dictations to be mentioned presently, except that they were not written expressly for my use, and others being old diaries and records;[66] also eight personal records, *hojas de servicio*, and wills;[67] fifteen battles, treaties, juntas, or plans;[68] three very important documents on relations with the United States;[69] four on the Ross Colony;[70] five items of correspondence of visitors or Nootka men;[71] and a dozen, too hopelessly miscellaneous to be classified, that need not be named here.

Thousands of times in my foot-notes I have occasion to accredit certain information in this manner: 'Padre Lasuen's letter of ——, in *Arch. Sta Bár.*, tom. ——, p. ——'; 'Bandini's Speech, in *Carrillo, Doc. Hist. Cal.*, tom. ——, p. ——'; 'Gov. Fages to P. Serra (date), in *Prov. St. Pap.*'; 'Larkin to Leidesdorff, June ——, 1826, in *Id., Doc. Hist. Cal.*, iv.,' etc., etc. Now one of these communications is not worth a separate place in my list; but a hundred from one man form a collection which richly merits a title. That the items are scattered in different manuscript volumes on my shelves, when they might by a mere mechanical operation have been bound in a separate volume, makes no difference that I can appreciate. Therefore from this scattered correspondence of some two hundred of the most prominent men whose writings as used by me are most voluminous, I have

[64] Cooper, Larkin, Russian American Company, and Vallejo.

[65] Dana, Españoles, Estrada, Hayes, Los Angeles, Monterey, Padron, Mormon Battalion, Relacion, Richardson, Rowland, Salidas, Spence, Stuart, and Taylor.

[66] Compañía Extrangera, Ford, Hartnell, Ide, Leese, Marsh, Morris, Murray, New Helvetia, Ortega, Prudon, and Vigilantes.

[67] Amador, Argüello, Arrillaga, Carrillo, Castro, and Ortega.

[68] Cahuenga, Carrillo, Conferencia, Consejo, Instrucciones, Junta, Plan, Pronunciamiento, Solis, Tratado, and Zamorano.

[69] Buchanan and Larkin.

[70] Baránof, Etholin, Potechin, and Zavalischin.

[71] Douglas, Kendrick, Malaspina, Saavedra, Wilcox.

made a like number of titles. The author's name is
followed in each title by *cartas, correspondencia, escritos,* or some similar general term. Seventy belong
to men who wrote chiefly before 1824; one hundred
and thirty to those who flourished later. Of the
whole number, twenty were Spanish or Mexican officials who wrote beyond the limits of California;
twenty were Franciscan friars of the California missions; forty-eight were foreign pioneer residents in
California; and one hundred and eleven were native,
Mexican, or Spanish citizens and officials of California. Several of these collections in each class would
form singly a large volume.[72]

One more class of manuscripts remains to be noticed. The memory of men as a source of historical
information, while not to be compared with original
documentary records, is yet of very great importance.
The memory of men yet living when I began my researches, as aided by that of their fathers, covers in a
sense the whole history of California since its settle-

[72] Spanish and Mexican officials, all before 1824: Apodaca, Azanza, Barry,
Branciforte, Bucareli, Calleja, Cárcaba, Croix, Galvez, Garibay, Haro y
Peralta, Iturigaray, Marquina, Nava, Rengel, Revilla Gigedo, Ugarte y
Loyola, Venadito, and Venegas.

Padres or ecclesiastics, 8 before and 12 after 1824: Abella, Arroyo, Boscana,
Cabot, Catalá, Dumetz, Duran, Esténega, García Diego, Jimeno, Lasuen,
Martin, Martinez, Ordaz, Palou, Payeras, Peyri, Quijas, Rouset, Señan,
Tapis, and Viader.

Foreign residents and visitors: Belden, Bolcof, Burton, Colton, Cooper,
Dana, Davis, Den, Douglas, Fitch, Flügge, Forbes, Foster, Frémont, Garner,
Gillespie, Green, Hartnell, Hastings, Hinckley, Howard, Jones, Larkin,
Leese, Leidesdorff, Livermore, Marsh, Mason, Mellus, Mofras, Morenhaut,
Murphy, Parrott, Paty, Prudon, Reid, Richardson, Semple, Spence, Stearns,
Stevenson, Stockton, Sloat, Sutter, Temple, Thompson, Vignes, and Vioget.

Californian officials and citizens, 36 before and 75 after 1824: Abrego,
Alberni, Alvarado, Amador, Amesti, Archuleta, Argüello, Arrillaga, Ban-
dini, Bonilla, Borica, Botello, Buelna, Carrillo, Castañares, Castillero, Cas-
tillo Negrete, Castro, Chico, Córdoba, Coronel, Cota, Covarrubias, Echeandía,
Escobar, Estrada, Estudillo, Fages, Fernandez, Figueroa, Flores, Font,
Gomez, Gonzalez, Goycoechea, Grajera, Grijalva, Guerra, Gutierrez, Haro,
Herrera, Híjar, Ibarra, Lasso, Lugo, Machado, Malarin, Maitorena, Marti-
nez, Micheltorena, Moraga, Muñoz, Neve, Olvera, Ortega, Osio, Osuna,
Pacheco, Padrés, Peña, Peralta, Perez Fernandez, Pico, Portilla, Ramirez,
Requena, Rivera y Moncada, Rodriguez, Romeu, Ruiz, Sal, Sanchez, Ser-
rano, Sola, Soler, Suñol, Tapia, Torre, Valle, Vallejo, Victoria, Villavicencio,
Zamorano, and Zúñiga.

ment. I have therefore taken dictations of personal reminiscences from 160 old residents. Half of them were natives, or of Spanish blood; the other half foreign pioneers who came to the country before 1848. Of the former class twenty-four were men who occupied prominent public positions, equally divided between the north and the south.[73]

The time spent with each by my reporters was from a few days to twelve months, according to the prominence, memory, and readiness to talk of the person interviewed; and the result varied in bulk from a few pages to five volumes of manuscript. A few spoke of special events; most gave their general recollections of the past; and several supplemented their reminiscences by documentary or verbal testimony obtained from others. They include men of all classes and in the aggregate fairly represent the Californian people. Eleven of the number were women, and the dictation of one of these, Mrs Ord—Doña Angustias de la Guerra—compares favorably in accuracy, interest, and completeness, with the best in my collection. General Vallejo's narrative, expanded into a formal *Historia de California,* is the most extensive and in some respects the most valuable of all; that of Governor Alvarado is second in size, and in many parts of inferior quality. The works of Bandini and Osio differ from the others in not having been written expressly for my use. The authors were intelligent and prominent men, and though their narratives are much less extensive and complete than those of Vallejo and Alvarado, they are of great importance. Those of such men as Botello, Coronel, Pio and Jesus Pico, Arce, Amador, and Castro merit special men-

---

[73] Ábrego, Alvarado, Alviso, Amador, Arce, Arnaz, Ávila, Bandini, Bernal, Berreyesa, Bojorges, Boronda, Botello, Buelna, Burton, Carrillo, Castro, Coronel, Escobar, Espinosa, Estudillo, Ezquer, Fitch, Fernandez, Flores, Galindo, García, Garnica, German, Gomez, Gonzalez, Hartnell, Hijar, Julio César, Juárez, Larios, Leese, Lorenzana, Lugo, Machado, Marron, Moreno, Ord, Osio, Palomares, Perez, Pico, Pinto, Rico, Robles, Rodriguez, Romero, Sanchez, Sepúlveda, Serrano, Torre, Torres, Valle, Valdés, Vallejo, Vega, and Véjar.

tion, and there are many of the briefer dictations which in comparison with the longer ones cited have a value far beyond their bulk.

Of the pioneers whose testimony was taken,[74] twelve wrote on special topics, such as the Bear Flag, Donner Party, or Graham Affair. Twenty of them came to California before 1840. Thirty-five came overland, twenty in immigrant parties, three or four as hunters, and the rest as soldiers or explorers in 1845-8; while twenty came by sea, chiefly as traders or seamen who left their vessels secretly. William H. Davis has furnished one of the most detailed and accurate records of early events and men; and others meriting particular mention are Baldridge, Belden, Bidwell, Bigler, Chiles, Forster, Murray, Nidever, Sutter, Warner, and Wilson. As a whole the testimony of the pioneers is hardly equal in value to that of the native Californians, partly because they have in many cases taken less interest and devoted less time to the matter; also because the testimony of some of the most competent has been given more or less fully in print.

While the personal reminiscences of both natives and pioneers, as used in connection with and tested by contemporaneous documentary evidence, have been in the aggregate of great value to me in the preparation of this work, yet I cannot give them unlimited praise as authorities. A writer, however intelligent and competent, attempting to base the annals of California wholly or mainly on this kind of evidence, would produce a very peculiar and inaccurate work. Hardly one of these narratives if put in print could

[74] Anthony, Baldridge, Bartôn, Bee, Belden, Bell, Bidwell, Bigler, Birnie, Boggs, Bowen, Brackett, Bray, Breen, Brown, Burton, Carriger, Chamberlain, Chiles, Crosby, Dally, Davis, Dittman, Dunne, Dye, Eaton, Findla, Forster, Foster, Fowler, Gary, Greyson, Gillespie, Grimshaw, Hargrave, Hopper, Hyde, Janssens, Knight, Marshall, Martin, Maxwell, McChristian, McDaniels, McKay, Meadows, Mone, Nidever, Ord, Osborn, Parrish, Peirce, Rhodes, Richardson, Roberts, Robinson, Ross, Russ, Smith, Spence, Streeter, Sutter, Swan, Swasey, Taylor, Temple, Tustin, Walker, Warner, Weeks, Wheeler, White, Wiggins, Wilson, and Wise.

escape severe and merited criticism. It is no part of my duty to point out defects in individual narratives written for my use, but rather to extract from each all that it contains of value, passing the rest in silence. And in criticising this material in bulk, I do not allude to the few clumsy attempts in certain dictations and parts of others to deceive me, or to the falsehoods told with a view to exaggerate the importance or otherwise promote the interests of the narrator, but to the general mass of statements from honest and intelligent men. In the statements of past events made by the best of men from memory—and I do not find witnesses of Anglo-Saxon blood in any degree superior in this respect to those of Spanish race—will be found a strange and often inexplicable mixture of truth and falsehood. Side by side in the best narratives I find accounts of one event which are models of faithful accuracy and accounts of another event not even remotely founded in fact. There are notable instances where prominent witnesses have in their statements done gross injustice to their own reputation or that of their friends. There seems to exist a general inability to distinguish between the memory of real occurrences that have been seen and known, and that of idle tales that have been heard in years long past. If in my work I have been somewhat over cautious in the use of such testimony, it is a fault on which the reader will, I hope, look leniently.

The history, and with it the bibliography, of California after the discovery of gold may be conveniently divided into two periods, the first extending from 1848 to 1856 over the 'flush times,' and the second from 1857 to date. For the first period a larger part of the authorities are in manuscript than would at first glance appear, though with the advent of newspapers and printed government records the necessity of searching the archives for the most part disappears; for it is to be noted that most of the documentary collections, public and private, already noticed, contain papers of value of later date than 1849; and, still more important, the reminiscences of natives and the earliest pioneers cited in preceding pages, extend in most instances past the gold discovery. For this period I have also collected in manuscript form the testimony of about one hundred pioneers who came after 1848,[75] the number including a few narratives relating in part to Oregon, and a few miscellaneous manuscripts not quite properly classified with pioneer recollections; there are besides some twenty-five men, 'forty-niners' for the most part, who have devoted their testimony chiefly to the vigilance committees of San Francisco, most being prominent members of those organizations.[76] What has been said of similar narratives on earlier events as authorities for history may be applied to these. In the aggregate they are of immense value, being the statements of men who had been actors in the scenes described. For important additions to this class of material, received too late for special mention here, the reader is referred to the supplementary list of authorities.

Material printed in California during this period, including a few items of 1848 and of 1857–8, is represented by about one hundred titles in my list; to which should be added the legislative journals and the numerous state documents printed from year to year,

[75] See Allsop, Anderson, Armstrong, Ashley, Ayers, Bacon, Ball, Ballou, Barnes, Barstow, Bartlett, Bauer, Bigler, Boynton, Brackett, Bristow, Brock, Brodie, Brown, Burnett, Burris, Cassin, Cerruti, Chamberlain, Chapin, Clark, Colvin, Connor, Conway, Coon, Crosby, Davidson, Dean, Doolittle, Dowell, Duncan, Earll, Fairchild, Fay, Fitzgerald, Garniss, Gwin, Hancock, Hartnell, Hawley, Hayes, Hearn, Henshaw, Herrick, Hinckley, Hitchcock, Hudson, Keyser, Kirkpatrick, Kohler, Kraszewski, Lamotte, Lane, Lawson, Limantour, Little, Low, Mans, Massett, Matthewson, Merrill, Montgomery, Moore, Morris, Palmer, Patterson, Peckham, Powers, Rabbison, Randolph, Richardson, Roder, Ross, Rush, Ryckman, Safford, Sawtelle, Sayward, Schmiedell, Shaw, Shearer, Stuart, Sutton, Tarbell, Taylor, Thomes, Van Dyke, Vowell, Watson, Wheaton, Widber, Willey, Williams, and Winans.

[76] Bluxome, Burns, Cole, Coleman, Comstock, Crary, Dempster, Dows, Durkee, Farwell, Frink, Gillespie, McAllister, Manrow, Neall, Olney, Rogers, Schenck, Smiley, Staples, Stillman, Truett, Wadsworth, Watkins, and Woodbridge.

and preserved as appendices to those journals, as also the series of *California Reports* and *California Statutes*. There are twenty-one books and pamphlets descriptive of the country, with life and events therein during the flush times, most of them having also an admixture of past annals and future prospects.[77] Fifteen pamphlets are records of Californian societies, companies, or associations, the annual publication extending often beyond this period.[78] A like number are municipal records of different towns, besides a dozen directories;[79] and as many more legal, judicial, and other official publications, not including a very large number of briefs and court records which are not named in the list;[80] besides nine speeches delivered in California and published in pamphlet form;[81] and as many miscellaneous publications, including one periodical.[82] Many newspapers might be enumerated besides the *Alta, Herald, Bulletin,* and *Evening News* of San Francisco, the *Placer Times* and *Union* of Sacramento, and the *Gazette* of Santa Bárbara; there are some fifteen articles on early Californian subjects;[83] and a like number of scrap-books in my collection, notably those made by Judge Hayes, contain more or less material on the times under consideration.[84]

[77] Benton, California, Carrol, Carson, Crane, Delano, King of Wm., McGowan, Miners, Morse, San Francisco, Taylor, Terry, Wadsworth, Werth, and Wierzbicki.

[78] Cal. Bible Soc., Cal. Dry Dock Co., First Cal. Guard, Marysville & Ben. R. R., Mechanics' Inst., Mercantile Lib., Mex. Ocean Mail, Overland Mail, Sac. Valley R. R., Sta Clara Col., Univ. Cal., Univ. Pacific, Young Men's Christ. Ass.

[79] Los Angeles, Parkitt, San Diego, San Francisco Act, S. F. Fire Dept., S. F. Memorial, S. F. Minutes, S. F. City Charter, S. F. Ordinances, S. F. Proceedings, S. F. Pub. Schools, S. F. Remonstrance, S. F. Rept., S. F. Town Council, and Wheeler. Directories—Marysville, Sacramento, San Francisco, Stockton, and Tuolumne.

[80] California (Circuit Court, Comp. Laws, Constit., Dist. Court, Sup. Court), Constit. Convention, Crocker, Hartman, Limantour, Marvin, Mason, Riley, Thornton, Turner.

[81] Baker, Bates, Bigler, Billings, Bryan, Freelon, Lockwood, Shaw, Speer.

[82] Cal. Text Book, Gougenheim, Democratic, Limantour, Taylor (song book), Willey, Pioneer, and Almanacs.

[83] Franklin, Hittell, McCloskey, McDougal, McGowan, Nugent, Peckham, Randolph, Reid, Ryan, Victor, Trask, Weed, Willey, Vallejo.

[84] Bancroft Library, Barton, Bigler, Brooks, California, Dye, Hall, Hayes, Knight, Lancey, Levitt, Pac. Mail, Sta Cruz.

Works about California printed elsewhere were three times as numerous as those of home manufacture, and in most respects much more important. First there were over eighty books, similar except in place of publication to those of a class already mentioned, which described California, its mines and towns, its people and their customs, the journey by land or sea to the country with personal adventures of the writers or others, books in different languages owing their existence directly to the discovery of gold.[85] Many of these were to a considerable extent fictitious, but there were others containing little or nothing but fiction.[86] Next among works of real value should be noticed fifty reports on Californian topics, published by the United States government;[87] and in this connection may receive attention the regular sets of U. S. government documents recording the acts of congress from session to session, and containing hundreds of valuable papers, bearing on affairs in the far west, with several other collections of somewhat similar nature.[88] There were a dozen or more pamphlets on various Californian topics not directly connected with the gold discovery and its attendant phenomena.[89] Then

[85] Abbey, Adam, Allsop, Auger, Berry, Ballenstedt, Borthwick, Bouchacourt, Bound Home, Brooks, Bryant, Buffum, Cal. (Emig. Guide, Gold Reg., Gids Naar, Its Gold, Its Past, Notes), Californie, Californien (Ant. Nach., Rathgeber, Und sein Golt, sein Min.), Cassell, Colton, Diggers, Edelman, Farnham, Ferry, Foster, Gerstäcker, Gold-finders, Gregory, Hartmann, Helper, Holinski, Hoppe, Johnson, Kelly, King, Kip, Kunzel, Lambertie, Letts, McCollum, McIlvaine, Marryat, Mason, Meyer, Oswald, Palmer, Parkman, Praslow, Robinson, Ryan, Schwartz, Sedgley, Seyd, Seymour, Shaw, Sherwood, Simpson, Solignac, St Amant, Stirling, Taylor, Thompson, Tyson, Walton, Weil, Weston, Williamson, Wilson, and Woods.

[86] Such as Aimard, Amelia, Ballou, Bigly, Champagnac, Gerstäcker, Payson, and many more.

[87] Abell, Alexander, Bartlett, Beale, Beckwith, California (Amount, Commission, Copy, Dent, Establishment, Indians, Land Com., Message, Volunteers), Cooke, Cram, Derby, Flagg, Fort Point, Frémont, Gibbons, Graham, Gray, Halleck, Homer, Jones, King, Mason, Meredith, Mex. Boundary, Pac. Wagon Roads, Reynolds, Riley, San Francisco, Sherman, Smith, Sutter, Tyson, U. S. and Mex., Warren, Whipple, and Wool.

[88] U. S. Govt Doc. (two series), U. S. Supreme Court Reports, Annals of Congress, Congressional Debates, Cong. Globe, Benton's Abridgment, Smithsonian Reports, and Pac. R. R. Reports.

[89] Atlan. & Pac. R. R., Browne, Cal. Appeal, California, Frémont, Limantour, Logan, Ringgold, Pac. M. S. S. Co., S. F. Custom House, S. F. Land Assoc., Stillman, and Thompson.

we have more than fifty speeches chiefly delivered
in Congress and circulated in pamphlet form, many
of them pertaining to the admission of California as
a state.[90]   Besides the books relating wholly or mainly
to California there were some thirty others on western regions with allusions more or less extended to
the gold regions;[91] and half as many general works
with mention of California.[92]   Both of these classes,
and especially the latter, might be greatly extended
in numbers; and the same may be said of the periodicals and collections that contained articles on our
subject, there being few such publications in the
world that gave no attention to the western El Dorado.[93]

Of works published in and about California since
1856, I attempt no classification. Within my present
limits it would be impossible satisfactorily to classify
so bulky and diversified a mass of material, of which,
indeed, I have not been able even to present the titles
of more than half in the alphabetical list of authorities. The efforts of modern writers to record the history of the Spanish and Mexican periods have already
been noticed in this chapter; but I may add that
these efforts have been much more successful in their
application to events subsequent to the discovery of

[90] Averett, Baldwin, Bennett, Benton, Bowie, Breck, Brooks, Caldwell,
Cary, Clark, Cleveland, Corwin, Crowell, Douglas, Estell, Foote, Fowler,
Gwin, Hall, Hebard, Howard, Howe, Lander, Latham, McDougal, McLean,
McQueen, McWillie, Marshall, Mason, Morehead, Olds, Parker, Pearce, Preston, Putnam, Phelps, Seddon, Seward, Smith, Spaulding, Stanley, Thompson, Thurman, Thurston, Toombs, Van Voorhie, Weller, Wiley, Winthrop,
and Worcester.
[91] Ansted, Briefe, Coke, Combier, Findlay, Gerstäcker, Gold-fields, Heap,
Hines, Horn, Lauts, Perry, Pfeifer, Plumb, Rednitz, Rovings, Schmidt,
Schmölder, Smucker, Stockton, Thornton, Upham, Wells, Western Scenes,
Whiting, Wilkes, Wise, Wood.
[92] Benton, Cevallos, De Bow, Diccionario, Dunlop, Garden, March y Labores, Mayer, Shea, Weichardt, Wilson, Young, Zamacois.
[93] Album Mex., Amer. and For. Christ. Union, Annual of Scientific Discov., Bankers' Mag., De Bow's Review, Edinburgh Review, Hansard, Harper,
Home Missionary, Hunt's Merch. Mag., Ilustracion Mex., Mining Mag.,
Millennial Star, Niles' Register, North Amer. Review, Nouvelles Annales,
Panamá Star, Quarterly Rev., Revue Deux Mondes, Silliman's Amer. Jour.,
etc., etc.

gold, because material has been much more abundant and accessible. This applies particularly to the many works on local and county annals printed in late years, several of which have a standard value.[94]

It is to be noted that the pioneer reminiscences of my collection contain, and are supplemented by, the statements of prominent men on various practical topics connected with the industrial development of California in recent times; that several classes of printed matter already mentioned, such as municipal, state, and national documents, continue to throw light on events of the last thirty years; that travellers have never ceased to print their experiences in, and their views respecting, this western land; that resident and even native writers have contributed largely to our store of books on industrial, literary, educational, religious, legal, political, and historical subjects; that numerous associations and institutions have helped to swell the mass of current pamphlets; and that newspapers—an invaluable source of material for local and personal history—have greatly multiplied. Indeed, California has not only by reason of her peculiar past received more attention at the hands of writers from abroad than any other part of our nation, but in respect of internal literary development she is not behind other provinces of like tender years. In conclusion, I append a short list of works published since 1856, which have somewhat exceptional historic value in comparison with others of the mass.[96] Most of

[94] See in the list, besides the names of counties and towns: Banfield, Barton, Bledsoe, Butler, Cooper, Cox, Dwinelle, Frazee, Gift, Hall, Halley, Hare, Hawley, Hittell, Huse, Lloyd, McPherson, Menefee, Meyrick, Orr, Owen, Perkins, Sargent, Soulé, Thompson, Tinkham, Western Shore, and Willey.

[95] See Alric, Ames, Barry, Bartlett, Bates, Beers, Bell, Blake, Bonner, Brooks, Browne, Bryant, Burnett, Bushnell, California (Arrival, Biog., Hardy, Leyes, Med. Soc.), Carvalho, Chandless, Clark, Contemp. Biog., Cooke, Cornwallis, Cronise, Coyner, Dixon, Gleeson, Fields, First Steamship, Fisher, King, Gray, Grey, Hittell, Hoffman, Hughes, Labatt, McCue, McGarrahan, McGlashan, Möllhausen, Morgan, Moulder, New Almaden, Norman, O'Meara, Palmer, Parsons, Patterson, Peabody, Peirce, Peters, Phelps, Player-Frowd, Randolph, Raymond, Redding, Rossi, Saxon, Schlagintweit, Sherman, Shuck, Simpson, Stillman, Tuthill, Tyler, Upham, Vallejo, Vischer, Wetmore, Willey, and Williams.

them but for the date of their publication might be added to the different classes before named, as pertaining to the period of 1848–56. For further bibliographic information, including full or slightly abridged title, summary of contents, circumstances attending the production, criticism of historic value, and biographic notes on the writer of each work mentioned in the different classes and subdivisions of this chapter, I refer the reader not only to the list at the beginning of this volume but to the foot-notes of all the seven volumes, which may be traced through the alphabetical index at the end of the work.

CHAPTER III.

THE DISCOVERY OF CALIFORNIA.

1542–1768.

ORIGIN OF THE NAME—CONJECTURES—SERGAS OF ESPLANDIAN—MR HALE'S
DISCOVERY—LATER VARIATIONS OF THE NAME—WHO FIRST SAW ALTA
CALIFORNIA?—ULLOA, ALARCON, DIAZ—FIVE EXPEDITIONS—VOYAGE OF
JUAN RODRIGUEZ CABRILLO, 1542–3—EXPLORATION FROM SAN DIEGO TO
POINT CONCEPCION—FERRELO IN THE NORTH—VOYAGE OF SIR FRANCIS
DRAKE, 1579—NEW ALBION—DRAKE DID NOT DISCOVER SAN FRANCISCO
BAY—MAPS—THE PHILIPPINE SHIPS—GALI'S VOYAGE, 1584—CAPE MEN-
DOCINO—VOYAGE OF SEBASTIAN RODRIGUEZ DE CERMEÑON, 1595—THE
OLD SAN FRANCISCO—EXPLORATIONS OF SEBASTIAN VIZCAINO, 1602–3—
MAP—DISCOVERY OF MONTEREY—AGUILAR'S NORTHERN LIMIT—CA-
BRERA BUENO'S WORK, 1734—SPANISH CHART, 1742—THE NORTHERN
MYSTERY AND EARLY MAPS.

THOUGH the California which is the subject of this
work inherited its name from an older country whose
annals have been already recorded by me, yet a statement respecting the origin and application of the name
seems appropriate here. When Jimenez discovered
the peninsula, supposed to be an island, in 1533, he
applied no name so far as can be known. Cortés,
landing at the same place with a colony on the 3d of
May 1535, named the port and the country adjoining
Santa Cruz, from the day. There is no evidence that
he ever gave, or even used, any other name, the name
California not occurring in any of his writings.[1] Ulloa

---

[1] At least I have not found it. The 'puerto y bahía de Santa Cruz' is named
in the original document of 1535. Cortés, Auto de Posesion, in Col. Doc. Inéd.,
iv. 192. After his return to Spain in 1540 in a memorial to the king he testified 'I arrived at the land of Santa Cruz and was in it...and being in the said
land of Santa Cruz I had complete knowledge of the said land.' Cortés, Memorial, in Col. Doc. Inéd., iv. 211. Other witnesses who had accompanied Cortés
testified in Spain about the same time; one, that the country was called Tar-
sis; another, that the country had no name, but that the bay was called Santa
Cruz; several, that they remembered no name. Probanza, in Pacheco and Cárdenas, Col. Doc., xvi. 12, 22, 27.

sailed down the coast in 1539, and the name California first appears in Preciado's diary of that voyage. It was applied, not to the whole country, but to a locality—probably but not certainly identical with Santa Cruz, or La Paz.[2]

Bernal Diaz, writing before 1568, speaks of the island of Santa Cruz, and says that Cortés after many troubles there "went to discover other lands, and came to California, which is a bay."[3] This testimony is not of great weight, but it increases the uncertainty. The difference is not, however, essential. The name was applied between 1535 and 1539 to a locality. It was soon extended to the whole adjoining region; and as the region was supposed to be a group of islands, the name was often given a plural form, Las Californias.

Whence came the name thus applied, or applied by Cortés as has been erroneously believed, was a question that gave rise to much conjecture before the truth was known. The Jesuit missionaries as represented by Venegas and Clavigero suggested that it might have been deliberately made up from Latin or Greek roots; but favored the much more reasonable theory that the discoverers had founded the name on some misunderstood words of the natives.[4] These

---

[2] Printed in 1565, in *Ramusio, Viaggi*, iii. 343. Having left Santa Cruz Oct. 29th, on 10th of Nov. 'we found ourselves 54 leagues distant from California, a little more or less, always in the south-west seeing in the night three or four fires.' (Sempre dalla parte di Garbino vedendo la notte, etc.) Hakluyt's translation of 1600, *Voyages*, iii. 406-7, is 'always toward the south-west, seeing in the night,' etc. From the 9th to the 15th they made 10 leagues; from the 16th to the 24th, 12 or 15 leagues; and were then, having sighted the Isle of Pearls, 70 leagues from Santa Cruz. The author only uses the name California once; Hakluyt's 'point of California' is an interpolation. The definite distance of 54 leagues indicates that California was a place they had passed; it could not be 54 leagues either south-west or north-east of their position, and I suppose the direction refers to the coast generally or the fires. The distances are not out of the way if we allow 6 or 9 leagues for the progress made on Nov. 9th. There is some obscurity of meaning; but apparently California was at or near Santa Cruz. Throughout his voyage up and down the gulf Preciado uses the name Santa Cruz frequently to locate the lands in the west.

[3] *Bernal Diaz del Castillo, Hist. Verdadera*, 233, printed in 1632. This has often been called the first mention of the name. Some have blunderingly talked of Diaz as the discoverer and namer of California.

[4] *Venegas, Not. Cal.*, i. 2–5; *Clavigero, Storia della Cal.*, 29–30. The Latin *calida for ax*, or 'hot furnace,' is the most common of the conjectural derivations, the reference being supposably either to the hot climate, though it was

theories have been often repeated by later writers, with additions rivalling each other in absurdity. At last in 1862 Edward E. Hale was so fortunate as to discover the source whence the discoverers obtained the name. An old romance, the *Sergas of Esplandian*, by Ordoñez de Montalvo, translator of *Amadis of Gaul*, printed perhaps in 1510, and certainly in editions of 1519, 1521, 1525, and 1526 in Spanish, mentioned an island of California "on the right hand of the Indies, very near the Terrestrial Paradise," peopled with black women, griffins, and other creatures of the author's imagination.[5] There is no direct historical evidence of the application of this name; nor is any needed. No intelligent man will ever question the accuracy of Hale's theory. The number of Spanish editions would indicate that the book was popular at the time of the discovery; indeed Bernal Diaz often mentions the *Amadis of Gaul*, to which the *Esplandian* was attached.

Cortés, as we know, was bent on following the coast round to India, and confident of finding rich and wonderful isles on the way. It would have been most natural for him to apply the old fabulous name, if it had met his eye, to the supposed island when first discovered; but it appears he did not do it; and I

not hot compared with others to which the discoverers were accustomed, or to the hot baths, or *temescales*, of the natives. *Calidus fornus, Caliente fornalla, Californo*, and *Caliente horno* are other expressions of the same root, Archibald noting of the last that it would be rather *horno caliente*, making the name 'Fornicalia' instead of California. Another derivation is from *cala y fornix*, Spanish and Latin for 'cove and vault' or 'vaulted cove,' from a peculiar natural formation near Cape San Lúcas. From the Greek we have *kala phor nea, kala phora nea, kala phor neia, kala phorneia, kala chora nea*, or *kalos phornia*—variously rendered 'beautiful woman,' 'moonshine,' or 'adultery;' 'fertile land;' or 'new country.' *Colofon* or *colofonia*, the Spanish for resin, has also been suggested. In Upper California the idea was a favorite one that the name was of Indian origin; but there was little agreement respecting details. According to the Vallejos, Alvarado, and others, all agreed that it came from *kali forno*, the information coming from Baja California natives; but there were two factions, one interpreting the words 'high hill' or 'mountain' and the other 'native land.' E. D. Guilbert, resident of Copala, Sinaloa, told me in 1878 that an old Indian of his locality called the peninsula Tchalifalñi-al, 'the sandy land beyond the water.'

[5] Hale's discovery was first published in the *Amer. Antiq. Soc., Proceed.*, Apr. 30, 1862, 45-53; also in *Atlantic Monthly*, xiii. 265; *Hale's His Level Best*, etc., 234.

strongly suspect the name was applied in derision by his disgusted colonists on their return in 1536. At any rate there can be no doubt the name was adopted from the novel between 1535 and 1539. The etymology of the name and the source whence Montalvo obtained it still remain a field for ingenious guesswork. Indeed most of the old conjectures may still be applied to the subject in its new phase. But this is not an historical subject, nor one of the slightest importance. In such matters the probable is but rarely the true. What brilliant etymological theories might be drawn out by the name Calistoga, if it were not known how Samuel Brannan built the word from California and Saratoga.[6]

The name California, once applied to the island or peninsula, was also naturally used to designate the country extending indefinitely northward to the strait of Anian, or to Asia, except as interrupted in the view of some foreign geographers by Drake's New Albion. Kino at the mouth of the Colorado in 1700 spoke of Alta California; but he meant simply the 'upper' part of the peninsula. After 1769 the northern country was for a time known as the New Establishments, or Los Establecimientos de San Diego y Monterey, or the Northern Missions. In a few

---

[6] In *Webster's Dictionary*, the Spanish *califa*, Arabic *Khalifa*, 'successor,' 'caliph,' is adopted, as indeed suggested by Hale, as the possible root of the name. Archbald, *Overland Monthly*, ii. 440, suggests Calphurnia, Cæsar's wife. Perhaps the coolest exhibition of assurance which this matter has drawn out in modern times is Prof. Jules Marcou's essay on the 'true origin' of the name. The whole pamphlet, although printed by the United States government, with the degree of intelligence too often employed in such cases, perhaps because of an old map attached to it, has about as many blunders as the pages can accommodate. I have no space to point them out; but this is what he says of the name: 'Cortes and his companions, struck with the difference between the dry and burning heat they experienced, compared with the moist and much less oppressive heat of the Mexican *tierra caliente*, first gave to a bay, and afterwards extended to the entire country the name of *tierra California*, derived from *calida fornax*, which signifies fiery furnace, or hot as an oven. Hernan Cortés, who was moreover a man of learning, was at once strongly impressed with the singular and striking climatic differences...to whom is due the appropriate classification of the Mexican regions into *tierra fria, tierra templada, tierra caliente*, and *tierra California*'! *Marcou's Notes upon the first Discoveries of California and the origin of its name*, Washington, 1878. See also *U. S. Geog. Survey, Wheeler, Rept.*, 1878, p. 228.

years, however, without any uniformity of usage the upper country began to be known as California Septentrional, California del Norte, Nueva California, or California Superior. But gradually Alta California became more common than the others, both in private and official communications, though from the date of the separation of the provinces in 1804 Nueva California became the legal name, as did Alta California after 1824. In these later times Las Californias meant not as at first Las Islas Californias, but the two provinces, old and new, lower and upper. Down to 1846, however, the whole country was often called by Mexicans and Californians even in official documents a peninsula.

It is not impossible that Francisco de Ulloa, at the head of the gulf in 1539, had a distant glimpse of mountains within the territory now called California; it is very probable that Hernando de Alarcon, ascending the Colorado in boats nearly to the Gila and possibly beyond it, saw Californian soil in September 1540; and perhaps Melchor Diaz, who crossed the Colorado later in the same year, had a similar view. Thus strictly speaking the honor of the first discovery may with much plausibility be attributed to one of these explorers, though none of them mentioned the discovery, or could do so, boundary lines being as yet not dreamed of. Subsequently Juan de Oñate and his companions, coming down the Colorado in 1604, certainly gazed across the river on California, and even learned from the natives that the sea was not far distant. After 1699 Kino and his Jesuit associates not unfrequently looked upon what was to be California from the Gila junction. No European, however, from this direction is known to have trod the soil of the promised land; therefore this phase of the subject may be dismissed without further remark.

All that was known of California before 1769 was founded on the reports of five expeditions; that of Juan Rodriguez Cabrillo in 1542–3, that of Francis Drake in 1579, that of Francisco de Gali in 1584, that of Sebastian Rodriguez de Cermeñon in 1595, and that of Sebastian Vizcaino in 1602–3. To describe these expeditions—so far only as they relate to the coast of Alta California, for in a general way each has been presented in the annals of regions farther south— with a glance also at a few other voyages bearing indirectly upon the subject, is my purpose in the present chapter.

On the 28th of September 1542, Juan Rodriguez Cabrillo, coming from the south in command of two Spanish exploring vessels,[7] discovered a "landlocked and very good harbor," which he named San Miguel and located in 34° 20′. The next day he sent a boat "farther into the port which was large;" and while anchored here "a very great gale blew from the west-south-west, and south-south-west; but the port being good they felt nothing."[8]

[7] On the fitting-out of the expedition and its achievements south of California, see *Hist. North Mex. States*, this series.

[8] *Cabrillo, Relacion ó diario, de la navegacion que hizo Juan Rodriguez Cabrillo con dos navíos, al descubrimiento del paso del Mar del Sur al norte*, etc. Original in Spanish archives of Seville from Simancas, certified by Navarrete, copy in Muñoz Collection, printed in *Florida, Col. Doc.*, 173–89. 'De Juan Paez' is marked on the Muñoz copy. Another printed original from 'Archivo de Indias Patronato, est. 1, caj. i.,' is found in *Pacheco* and *Cárdenas, Col. Doc.*, xiv. 165–91, under the title *Relacion del descubrimiento que hizo Juan Rodriguez, navegando por la contra costa del mar del Sur al norte hecha por Juan Paez*. Thus it is probable that Juan Paez was the author. Herrera, *Hist. Gen.*, dec. vii. lib. v. cap. iii.–iv., gave in 1600 a condensed account probably from the above original, but with many omissions, and a few additions, which became the foundation of most that was subsequently written on the subject, being followed by Burney and others. In 1802 Navarrete in his introduction to the *Sutil y Mexicana, Viage*, xxix.–xxxvi., gave a narrative from the original, with notes in which he located, for the most part accurately, the points named by Cabrillo. *Taylor's First Voyage to the Coast of California...by Cabrillo*, San Francisco, 1853, was a kind of translation from Navarrete, whose notes the translator attempted to correct without any very brilliant success. Finally in 1879 we have *Evans* and *Henshaw's Translation from the Spanish of the account by the pilot Ferrel of the Voyage of Cabrillo along the west coast of North America in 1542*, printed in *U. S. Geog. Surv., Wheeler*, vii. *Archæology*, 293–314. Richard S. Evans was the translator; H. W. Henshaw, who made antiquarian researches on the coast, was the author of the notes; and H. C. Taylor, U. S. N., of the Coast Survey, aided the gentlemen named with the results of his acquaintance with the coast.

There is no further description; the latitude is wrong; and the port must be identified if at all by its relation to other points visited by Cabrillo. It has usually been identified by those who have followed Navarrete, the earliest investigator, with San Diego; but recently by Henshaw and Taylor with San Pedro further north, San Diego being in that case Cabrillo's San Mateo.[9] Here, as in most parts of this narrative, there is little room for positive assertion; but I prefer to regard San Miguel as San Diego. Difficulties arise at every step which no theory can remove. It is the fault of the narrative, respecting the genuineness of which, however, there is no room for doubt. Without attempting to get over obstacles by ignoring them I shall treat them mainly in notes.[10]

At any rate Cabrillo entered Upper Californian waters, never before disturbed by other craft than Indian canoes, and anchored in San Diego Bay in September 1542. If we suppose this port to have been his San Miguel, he remained six days. The natives

[9] San Mateo was also described as a good and landlocked (*cerrado*) port, with a little lake of fresh water, and with groves of trees like *ceibas*, except that the wood was hard. There were also many drift-logs washed here by the sea, broad grassy plains, high and rolling land, and animals in droves of 100 or more resembling Peruvian sheep with long wool, small horns, and broad round tails. Latitude given 33° 20'.

[10] San Augustin Island, the last point on which Navarrete and Henshaw agree, is identified with San Martin in about 30° 30' on the Baja California coast. Three days with little wind brought the ships, no distance given, to Cape San Martin, north of San Augustin, where the coast turns from north to north-west. This trend, and also the time, if we disregard the calm, favors Henshaw's location of Todos Santos rather than Navarrete's of San Quintin. Next they sailed four leagues N. E., or N. N. E.; but this is not possible from Todos Santos either by the best maps or the trend just noted. Next 21 leagues N. W., and N. N. W. to San Mateo; the distance 25 leagues corresponding better with that from San Quintin to Todos Santos, than with that from the latter to San Diego. On the other hand, the next stage, 32 leagues to San Miguel, better fits that from San Diego to San Pedro than from Todos Santos to the former. But they passed a little island close to the shore on arriving at San Mateo, there being none at Todos Santos so far as the maps show; and on the other hand, on sailing to San Miguel, they passed three *islas desiertas* three leagues from the main, the largest being two leagues long, or possibly in circumference, which agrees better with the Coronados just below San Diego than with San Clemente and Santa Catalina. Moreover the description of San Mateo with its lake, and especially its groves of trees, does not correspond at all to San Diego. The strongest reason why San Miguel must be San Diego and not San Pedro will be noticed presently. The investigator's troubles are not lessened by the non-existence of a perfect chart of the Baja California coast.

were timid in their intercourse with the strangers, whom they called Guacamal; but they wounded with their arrows three of a party that landed at night to fish. Interviews, voluntary and enforced, were held with a few individuals both on shore and on the ships; and the Spaniards understood by their signs that the natives had seen or heard of men like themselves, bearded, mounted, and armed, somewhere in the interior.[11]

Leaving San Miguel October 3d, they sail three days or about eighteen leagues, along a coast of valleys and plains and smokes, with high mountains in the interior, to the islands some seven leagues from the main, which they name from their vessels San Salvador and Vitoria. They land on one of the islands, after the inhabitants, timid and even hostile at first, have been appeased by signs and have come off in a canoe to receive gifts. They too tell of white men on the main. On Sunday the Spaniards go over to *tierra firme* to a large bay which they call Bahía de los Fumos, or Fuegos, from the smoke of fires seen there. It is described as a good port with good lands, valleys, plains, and groves, lying in 35°. I suppose the island visited to have been Santa Catalina, and the port to have been San Pedro.[12]

Sailing six leagues farther on October 9th, Cabrillo anchors in a large *ensenada*, or bight, which is doubtless Santa Mónica.[13] Thence they go on the next day

[11] It is not impossible, though not probable, that the natives had heard of Diaz, Alarcon, and Ulloa, at the head of the gulf. The Indians of San Diego are described as well formed, of large size, clothed in skins.

[12] Henshaw, as we have seen, makes this Bahía de Fumos Bahía Ona (or Santa Mónica), identifying San Pedro with San Miguel, and the island with Santa Cruz. The name San Salvador as mentioned later seems his strongest reason, though he does not say so. He admits the difficulty of identifying Santa Catalina with the Islas Desiertas, hinting that other smaller islands may have disappeared; but a more serious objection still—conclusive to me—is the fact that San Pedro would never have been called a *puerto cerrado*, or landlocked port; nor would it have afforded protection from a south-west gale.

[13] Certainly not the *laguna* near Pt Mugu as Henshaw says. Santa Mónica was exactly what the Spaniards would have called an *ensenada;* indeed, they did often so call it in later years as they did also Monterey Bay, and San Francisco outside the heads from Pt Reyes to Pigeon Point, always the *Ensenada de los Farallones.* Like the navigators of other nations, they were

some eight leagues to an Indian town, anchoring opposite a great valley. The town, called Pueblo de las Canoas and located in 35° 20′, is doubtless in the vicinity of San Buenaventura, the valley being that of the Santa Clara.[14] The Spaniards take formal possession and remain here four days. The natives come to the ships in fine canoes, each carrying twelve or thirteen men, and they report other Christians seven days' journey distant, for whom they take a letter, also indicating the existence of a great river. They say there is maize in the valley, which assertion is confirmed later by natives who talk also of *cae* which the voyagers understand to be cows, calling the maize *oep*. The natives are fishermen; they dress in skins, and live on raw fish and *maguey*. Their name for the town is Xucu, and they call the Christians Taquimine.

Six or seven leagues bring them on the 13th past two islands each four leagues long and four leagues from the coast, uninhabited for lack of water, but with good ports.[15] The next anchorage is two leagues farther, opposite a fine valley, perhaps Santa Bár- bara, where the natives are friendly and bring fish in canoes for barter. The ten leagues of October 15th carry them past an island fifteen leagues in length, which they name San Lúcas, apparently Santa Rosa.[16]

not very strict in their use of geographical terms; but to suppose that the little laguna would have been called by them an 'ensenada grande' is too absurd for even refutation; 'inlet' is not a correct rendering of *ensenada*. Taylor identifies the ensenada with the cove or roadstead of Santa Bárbara. *First Voyage to the Coast of California.* He points out the glaring deficiencies in all that had been written on the subject, and flatters himself that by the aid of men familiar with the coast he has followed the route of the navigators very closely; and so he has, just as far as he copies Navarrete, blundering fearfully in most besides.

[14] Navarrete says in the ensenada of San Juan Capistrano, which is unin- telligible.

[15] Anacapa and the eastern part of Santa Cruz as seen from a distance and as explained by the natives' signs, which were not understood.

[16] Six leagues from the main, and eighteen leagues from Pueblo de Canoas. It was said to have the following pueblos: Niquipos, Maxul, Xugua, Nitel, Macamo, Nimitopal. Later it is stated that San Lúcas was the middle island, having three pueblos whose names do not agree with those here given. There is a hopeless confusion in the accounts of these islands, but no doubt that this was the group visited.

Monday the 16th they sail four leagues to two towns, in a region where there is a place still called Dos Pueblos; and three leagues more on Tuesday. The natives wear their hair long, and intertwined with strings of flint, bone, and wooden daggers. Next day they come to a point in latitude 36°, which they name Cape Galera, now Point Concepcion in latitude 34° 26′. The distance from Pueblo de Canoas is thirty leagues, Xexu being the general name of the province, which has more than forty towns.[17]

The narrative of what Cabrillo saw on the shores and islands of the Santa Bárbara Channel, except a uniform exaggeration in the size of the islands, confusion in locating them, and perhaps the *casas grandes* of Canoas town, agrees very well with the truth as revealed by later mission annals and by the relics exhumed in late years by antiquarians. The region was certainly inhabited in early times by people who used canoes, lived mainly by fishing, and were much superior in many respects to most other natives of California. There was a tendency at first, as is usual in such cases, to ascribe the Channel relics to a prehistoric race;[18] but nothing indicating such an origin

[17] The pueblos, beginning with Canoas, were, Xucu, Bis, Sopono, Alloc, Xabaagua, Xocotoc, Potoltuc, Nacbuc, Quelqueme, Misinagua, Misesopano, Elquis, Coloc, Mugu, Xagua, Anacbuc, Partocac, Susuquey, Quanmu, Gua (or Quanmugua), Asimu, Aguin, Casalic, Tucumu, Incpupu, Cicacut (Sardinas), Ciucut, Anacot, Maquinanoa, Paltatre, Anacoat (or Anacoac), Olesino, Caacat (or Caacac), Paltocac, Tocane, Opia, Opistopia, Nocos, Yutum, Quiman, Nicoma, Garomisopona, and Xexo; and on the islands. On Ziquimuymu, or Juan Rodriguez, or Posesion (San Miguel), Xaco (or Caco) and Nimollollo. On Nicalque, or San Lúcas (Santa Rosa), Nichochi, Coycoy, and Estocoloco (or Coloco). On the other San Lúcas. See note 16. On Limu (or Limun) or San Salvador (Santa Cruz), Niquesesquelua, Pocle, Pisqueno, Pualnacatup, Patiquin, Patiquilid, Ninumu, Muoc, Pilidquay, Lilebeque. These names were those which the Indian natives were understood to apply to towns not visited, and very little accuracy is to be expected. Taylor, *Discoverers and Founders*, i. No. 1, claims to have identified Cabrillo's names in several instances with those found in the mission registers. This is not unlikely, though the authority is not a safe one. He also says that the Indians in 1863 recognized the native names of San Miguel and its towns as given by Cabrillo. None of the many ranchería names which I have met and which will be given in later mission annals show any marked resemblance to the old names.

[18] On the Indians of this region see *Native Races*, i. 402–22; iv. 687–97. See also on archæological researches *U. S. Geog. Survey, Wheeler*, vol. vii. *Archæology*, Washington, 1879, passim.

has ever been found there. Rumors, like those of the cows and maize, were far from accurate.

From Cape Galera they go October 18th to discover two islands ten leagues from the main, and they spend a week of stormy weather in a good harbor in the smaller one which they name La Posesion, probably Cuyler's Harbor in San Miguel. The two are called San Lúcas.[19] Leaving the port Wednesday the 25th the ships are beaten about by adverse winds for another week, making little progress, barely reaching a point ten leagues beyond Cape Galera in 36° 30′. They do not anchor, nor can they find a great river said to be there, though there are signs of rivers, but on the 1st of November they return to the anchorage under Cape Galera, by them named Todos Santos, now Coxo, where is the town of Xexo. They have probably gone as far as the mouth of the Santa María in latitude 35°.[20] Next day they proceed down the coast to the town of Cicacut, or Sardinas, in 35° 45′, where wood and water are more accessible than at the cape. This seems a head town of the province, ruled by an old woman who passes two nights on one of the vessels.[21] Starting the 6th, it takes them till the 10th to get back to the cape anchorage of Todos Santos.

Perhaps they pass the cape on the 10th. At all events on the morning of the 11th they are near the place reached before, twelve leagues beyond the cape; and that day with a fair wind they sail twenty leagues north-west, along a wild coast without shelter, and with a lofty sierra rising abruptly from the shore. The mountains in 37° 30′ are named Sierra de San Martin, forming a cape at their end in 38°, or as is

[19] The islands are said to be 8 and 4 leagues respectively from east to west, twice their real size. Navarrete calls the island San Bernardo, a name that seems to have been applied to San Miguel in later years.

[20] Perhaps not so far, as the point named is nearer 15 than 10 leagues from Point Concepcion. I find no good reason to suppose it was off San Luis Obispo, as Henshaw thinks, which is over 24 leagues.

[21] Sardinas is identified by Henshaw with the present Goleta, which is not unlikely. Taylor loses his head completely, making Todos Santos the modern San Luis Obispo, and identifying Sardinas with San Simeon.

stated later in 37° 30'. The sierra is that now called
Santa Lucía, and I suppose the cape to have been
that still called San Martin, or Punta Gorda in 35°
54', though this is not quite certain.[22] In the night
being six leagues off the coast they are struck by a
storm which separates the ships and lasts all day Sunday and until Monday noon. Under a small fore-
staysail Cabrillo's ships drift slowly and laboriously
north-westward with the wind. Monday evening, the
weather clearing somewhat and the wind shifting to
the westward, the flag-ship turns toward the land,[23] in
search of the consort. At dawn she sights land, and
all day in a high sea labors slowly to the north-west
along a rough coast without harbors, where are many
trees and lofty mountains covered with snow. They
sight a point covered with trees in 40°; and at night
heave to.

Of their course and progress next day, the 15th,
nothing is said, but probably advancing somewhat
farther north-westward they see the consort and join
her at nightfall, when they take in sail and heave to.
At dawn next morning they have drifted back to a
large ensenada in 39° or a little more, the shores of
which are covered with pines, and which is therefore
named Bahía de los Pinos, and one of its points Cabo
de Pinos. They hope to find a port and river, but
after working against the wind for two days and
a night, they are unable to discover either. They

[22] Henshaw makes it Pt Sur in 36° 20'; and it is true that the coast of the
day's sailing corresponds better in some respects with that up to Pt Sur than
to Pt Gorda. However, the latitude 37° 30' with allowance for Cabrillo's
average excess, applies better to Pt Gorda; that point also, according to the
U. S. Coast Survey charts, corresponds much better, from a southern standpoint, to the *remate* of the sierra as described; the distance from Pt Concepcion, 32 leagues, has to be considerably exaggerated even to reach Pt Gorda;
on the return it is noted that about 15 leagues south of the cape the character
of the coast changed and settlements began, which agrees better with Gorda
than Sur, and does not agree with the statement that all of the voyage of the
11th was along a coast where the mountains rise abruptly from the water. I
think the coast from San Luis to Pt Gorda agrees well enough with the
description; and this supposition throws some light on proceedings farther
north.

[23] 'Á la vuelta de la tierra.' Not 'at the turn of the land' as Evans trans-
lates it.

anchor in forty-five fathoms to take possession, but
dare not land on account of the high sea. Lying to
for the night, on the 18th they descend the coast,
under lofty snow-capped mountains so near that they
seem about to fall on them. The Sierras Nevadas,
they are called, and a point passed in 38° 45′ Cabo de
Nieve. Then they proceed to Cape San Martin, and
on the 23d arrive at the old harbor on Posesion, or
San Miguel Island.

Cabrillo had run along the coast, point by point,
from Cape Pinos to the island; from Pinos to San
Martin the coast was wild, rough, without shelter,
and with no signs of inhabitants; but below San Martin fifteen leagues—possibly for a distance of fifteen
leagues—the country became better and inhabited.
Many difficulties present themselves in connection
with this northern navigation; but I am convinced
that the Bahía de Pinos was Monterey Bay; Cabo
de Pinos the cape still so called at the southern end
of that bay; Cabo de Nieve, or Snowy Cape, the
present Point Sur; and the point in 40°, Point Año
Nuevo, Pigeon Point, Pillar Point, or at most not
above Point Reyes in 38°.[24]

[24] Navarrete agrees with this view, except that he does not identify the
cape in 40°, and makes Cape Nieve the same as Año Nuevo, which last of
course is a blunder. Taylor also identifies Monterey Bay, makes Point Reyes
the cape in 40°, but falls into great confusion, especially in locating Point
Martin above Monterey. Herrera makes Point Pinos the cape in 40°. Humboldt, *Essai Pol.*, 329, thinks the cape was Año Nuevo. Venegas, Lorenzana,
and Cavo imply that the cape was Mendocino; and it is probable indeed that
that name was given later to a cape supposed to be this one, as we shall see.
Finally Evans and Henshaw identify the cape in 40° with Point Arenas (38°
57′), the Bay of Pinos with Bodega Bay, Point Pinos presumably the southern point of that bay, and Cape Nieve they pronounce unidentifiable. I find
very little, except the latitudes cited, to justify the conclusions last given, and
I find much against them. Point Arenas is not a wooded point in any sense
not quite as applicable to any of the points further south. Bodega Bay might
possibly be called an *ensenada*, incorrectly translated inlet, but not a large
one; if entered its peculiar ramifications would have called for other remark
than that no port or river could be found; its shores were never covered with
pines; and Point Tomales in no way corresponds to Cabrillo's Point Pinos.
In coasting southward from Bodega, Point Reyes would certainly have been
noted; and assuredly that coast has no mountains overhanging the water.
Evans and Henshaw have to avoid this difficulty by mistranslating *costa deste
dia* the 'coast they passed from this day;' but even that does not suffice, for
there is no such coast for a long distance. Again, Cabrillo claims to have
followed the coast 'point by point,' from Pinos to the islands, finding no

At La Posesion the voyagers remained for nearly two months, and they renamed the island Juan Rodriguez from their brave commander Cabrillo, who died there January 3, 1543. He had had a fall on the island in October, had made the northern trip suffering from a broken arm, and from exposure the injury became fatal. His dying orders were to push the exploration northward at every hazard. He was a Portuguese navigator in the Spanish service, of whom nothing is known beyond the skill and bravery displayed on this expedition, and the fact that his reputation was believed to justify his appointment as commander. No traces of his last resting-place, almost certainly on San Miguel near Cuyler's harbor, have been found; and the drifting sands have perhaps made such a discovery doubtful. To this bold mariner, the first to discover her coasts, if to any one, California may with propriety erect a monument.[25]

On Cabrillo's death Bartolomé Ferrelo, the Levantine piloto mayor, assumes command; but the weather does not permit departure till the 19th. Even then when they start for the main they are driven to the island of San Salvador, or Santa Cruz,[26] and finding no harbor are forced to beat about the islands in veering winds for eight days, until on the 27th they

anchorage and no good inhabited country until past San Martin. This is very absurd when applied to Bodega, but true enough from Monterey. The translators are indeed struck with this absurdity, which they very weakly explain by supposing that Cabrillo trusted to his observations in the storm and fog of the trip northward. There seems never to have been much doubt among the Spaniards about the identity of Cabrillo's Pinos; and I deem it very unwise to plunge into such difficulties as those just mentioned for the purpose of confirming Cabrillo's observations of latitude, which are known to have been very faulty at best.

[25] Taylor, *Discov. and Founders*, i. No. 1, mentions unsuccessful researches by himself, Admiral Alden, and Nidever. In 1875, however, he found two pits on a level near Cuyler's Harbor, about 10 feet in diameter, which he doubts not will prove to be the grave of Cabrillo and his men. At any rate they 'had a very peculiar look!' And an old sailor of Santa Bárbara told this author that in 1872 he opened a Spanish grave on Santa Cruz Island, which had a wooden head-board on which could be deciphered the date of about 1660!

[26] I suppose this was not the San Salvador first named, which was probably San Clemente. That there was confusion in the statements respecting these islands is certain; but in my opinion it is not lessened by Henshaw's theory that San Clemente and Santa Catalina were the islas desiertas, or by Navarrete's that Ferrelo at this time went to San Clemente.

return to the old harbor. Two days later they start again, first for San Lúcas, the middle isle, to recover anchors left there and obtain water, then to Port Sardinas for other supplies, and back to San Salvador, whence they finally sail the 18th of February. With a north-east wind they follow a south-west course in quest of certain islands, which they see at nightfall, six in number,[27] having sailed about twelve leagues. At dawn they are ten leagues to windward of these islands. With a wind from the w. n. w., they stand off south-westward for five days,[28] making a distance of about one hundred leagues. Then they turn their course landward on the 22d with a south-west wind which blows with increasing violence for three days until at dawn on Sunday, the 25th, they sight Cape Pinos, and anchor at night on a bleak coast twenty leagues to windward near a point where the coast turns from n. w. to n. n. w.[29]—that is at Pigeon Point, or thereabout in 37° 12'. Herrera names it Cabo de Fortunas, or Cape Adventure.[30]

From this point the narrative furnishes but little ground for anything but conjecture. There are no longer recognizable landmarks but only courses and winds with one solar observation. The latitude on Wednesday the 28th is 43°. If we go by this alone, deducting the two degrees of excess that pertain to all of this navigator's more northern latitudes, we have 41°, or the region between Humboldt and Trinidad bays, as Ferrelo's position; but if we judge by his starting-point, and probable progress as compared with other parts of the voyage, it is more probable

[27] Of course the islands could have been no others than San Clemente, Santa Catalina, Santa Bárbara, San Nicolás, and Beggs Rock, with Catalina appearing as two to make six; though these are not south-west of the northern group.

[28] By the dates it could not have been quite 4 days.

[29] Evans incorrectly says to the n.w.; and though the point is not identified, it must be the Pt Cabrillo of modern maps just above Pt Arenas according to Henshaw.

[30] Herrera, dec. vii. lib. v. cap. iv. He puts it in 41°, that is 1° beyond C. Pinos, which he identifies with the cape in 40°. He gives the date as Feb. 26th. In other respects Herrera's account contains nothing that might not have been taken from the original narative.

that he is still far below Cape Mendocino, a conclusion that has slight confirmation in the fact that the narrative indicates no change in the general north-west trend of the coast. I append an abridged statement.[31] During the night of February 28th, and most of the next day, they are driven by a south-west gale towards the land, and as they estimate to latitude 44°.[32] They recognize their imminent peril, and appeal to our Lady of Guadalupe. In answer to their cries, a norther comes which sends them far southward and saves their lives. They imagine they see signs of the inevitable 'great river' between 41° and 43°; they see Cape Pinos March 3d; and on the 5th are off the island of Juan Rodriguez, their northern wanderings being at an end.

Of course there is no possibility of determining definitely Ferrelo's northern limit. He thought that he reached 44°, being driven by the gale sixty miles beyond the highest observation in 43°; and there is no reason to suspect any intentional misrepresentation in the narrative, written either by Ferrelo or by one of his associates.[33] But in southern California the latitudes of this voyage are about 1° 30′ too high, increasing apparently to about 2° farther north; thus Ferrelo's northern limit was at most 42° or 42° 30′, just beyond the present boundary of California. This is substantially the conclusion of both Navarrete and Henshaw.[34]

[31] Feb. 25th, midnight to dawn, course w. n. w., wind s. s. w; Feb. 26th, course n. w., wind w. s. w. very strong; Feb. 27th, course w. n. w., with lowered foresail, wind s. s. w. All night ran s. with w. wind and rough sea; Feb. 28th, wind s. w. and moderate; latitude 43°. In the right course n. w. with much labor. March 1, a furious gale from the s. s. w., with a high sea breaking over the ship; course n. e. towards the land. The fog thick, but signs of land in the shape of birds, floating wood, etc., also indication of rivers. At 3 p. m. a n. wind came to save them, and carried them s. all night. March 2d, course s. with rough sea; in the night a n. w. and n. n. w. gale, course s. e. and e. s. e. March 3, cleared up at noon; wind n. w.; sighted C. Pinos.

[32] Herrera says they took an observation in 44° on March 1st. Venegas follows him, but makes the date March 10th.

[33] Perhaps Juan Paez as already explained. Herrera calls Ferrelo Ferrer. The original uses both the forms Ferrelo and Ferrer.

[34] Navarrete puts it ' 43° con corta diferencia segun el error de exceso que generalmente se notó en sus latitudes;' but he himself makes the average excess 1° 30′, so that the limit was 41° 30′. Henshaw was not, as he implies, the first to note the uniform excess. He thinks the southern boundary of Oregon ' not far out of the way.'

But if we disregard Ferrelo's solar observations all other evidence to be drawn from the original narrative points to a latitude much lower even than 42°, particularly if, as I think I have shown beyond much doubt in the preceding pages, the bay and point of Pinos are to be identified with Monterey. It is my opinion that the Spaniards in this voyage did not pass far, if at all, beyond Cape Mendocino in 40° 26′; and there is nothing to support the belief of later years that Ferrelo discovered that cape. It may however have been named indirectly from Cabrillo's supposed discovery; that is, the name may have been given after the return to the cape in 40° which Cabrillo discovered and did not name, though Torquemada says the discovery was made by vessels coming from Manila. Nor is it unlikely that Manila vessels noting the cape in later years may have identified it with Cabrillo's cape and given the name accordingly in honor of the viceroy Mendoza.[35]

Unable by reason of rough weather to enter the old port in the island of Juan Rodriguez, on March 5th Ferrelo runs over to San Salvador where he loses sight of the consort. On the 8th he proceeds to the Pueblo de Canoas, obtaining four natives and returning next day. Two days later he goes down to San Miguel, or San Diego, where he waits six days for the missing vessel, taking two boys to be carried to Mexico as interpreters. On the 17th they are at San Mateo, or Todos Santos; and on the 26th join the *Vitoria* at Cedros Island. They have been in great peril on some shoals at Cabrillo's island; but by

[35] *Torquemada*, i. 693. Venegas, *Not. Cal.*, i. 181–3, seems to have been the first to state that Cabrillo discovered and named the cape. Lorenzana, in *Cortés, Hist. N. España*, 325–6, and Cavo, *Tres Siglos*, i. 135, make the same statement; and it is followed by most later writers. The early writers, however, all imply that the cape was discovered before Cabrillo's death and not by Ferrelo, doubtless identifying it with the nameless cape in 40°, really Año Nuevo or Pigeon Point. Laet, *Novus Orbis*, 306–7, makes C. Fortunas the northern limit of the voyage; and Burney, *Chron. Hist.*, i. 220–5, identifies Fortunas with Mendocino, and is followed by Greenhow, *Or. and Cal.*, 62–3. A very absurd theory has been more or less current that Ferrelo gave his name to the Farallones of San Francisco.

prayers and promises they are saved. They arrive at Navidad April 14th, and the first voyage to Alta California is at an end.[36]

Francis Drake, made Sir Francis later, entered the Pacific by way of Cape Horn in 1578, having in view not only a raid on Spanish treasure, but a return by the long-sought strait of Anian, or, if that could not be found, at least a voyage round the world. His plundering cruise having been most successful, he sailed in April 1579 from Guatulco on the Oajaca coast to find the strait that was to afford him a passage through the continent. He kept well out to sea; but in June he became discouraged on account of the extreme cold, resolved to abandon the northern enterprise, and having anchored in a bad bay, perhaps in latitude 43°, he came down the coast in the *Golden Hind* to refit, when a suitable place could be found, for a voyage round Cape Good Hope and home. The particulars of his operations both in the north and south are fully treated elsewhere; it is only with what he did and saw in California that we are now concerned.[37]

[36] On Cabrillo's voyage, in addition to the works to which I have had occasion to refer, see the following, none of which, however, throws any additional light on the subject, many being but brief allusions to the voyage: *Forster's Hist.Voy.*, 448–9; *Fleurieu*, in *Marchand, Voy.*, i. viii.–ix.; *Montanus, Nieuwe Weereld*, 210–11, 101; *Id.*, *Neue Welt*, 237–8; *Clavigero, Stor. Cal.*, 154–5; *Hist. Magazine*, ix. 148; *Hutchings' Mag.*, i. 111; iii. 146; iv. 116, 547; v. 265, 277; *Cal. Farmer*, May 4, 1860, April 18, 1862, Aug. 14, 21, 1863; *Overland Monthly*, April 1871, 297; *Forbes' Hist. Cal.*, 9; *Findlay's Directory*, i. 314; *Browne's L. Cal.*, 18–19; *Capron's Hist. Cal.*, 121–2; *Domenech's Deserts*, i. 226; *Frignet, L. Cal.*, 9, 26; *Gleeson's Hist. Cath. Ch.*, i. 70–2; *Hines' Voy.*, 352; *Muhlenpfordt, Versuch; Murray's N. Amer.*, ii. 79–80; *Rouhaud, Reg., nouvelles*, 26; *St Amant, Voy.*, 393; *Fédix, l'Oregon*, 55; *Tytler's Hist. View*, 78–9; *Twiss' Oregon Quest.*, 22; *Cronise's Nat. Wealth*, 5; *Marina Española*, ii. 274–7; *Barber's Hist.*, 459; *Mofras, Explor.*, i. 96–7, 328; *Payno*, in *Soc. Mex. Geog., Boletin 2d Ep.*, ii. 199; *Kerr's Col. Voy.*, ii. 112; and a large number of modern mentions in books and newspapers.

[37] See *Hist. North Mex. States*, and *Hist. Northwest Coast*, i., this series, not only for details of Drake's performances, but for bibliographical information touching the original authorities. Of the latter there are only three that narrate the doings in California; *Drake's Famous Voyage*, in *Hakluyt's Voy.*, iii. 440–2; *Drake's World Encompassed*, London, 1628; and *Discourse of Sir Francis Drake's Iorney and Exploytes*, MS. These are all republished in the Hakluyt Society edition of the *World Encompassed*, which is the edition referred to in my notes. Hardly a collection of voyages or any kind of work.

On the 17th of June Drake found a "conuenient and fit harborough" for his purpose in latitude 38° 30′[38] where he cast anchor and remained over a month, until July 23d. Down to this point the coast was "but low and reasonable plaine," every hill being covered with snow; and during all their stay, though in the height of summer, the cold was nipping as farther north, the air for fourteen days being not clear enough by reason of 'stinking fogges' for an observation of the sun or stars, and the fur-clad natives shivering under a lee bank.[39] After a few days the ship was brought near the shore and lightened of her cargo for the purpose of repairs, tents being erected on shore

relating to the early history of California has ever been published that has not contained a narrative or a mention of Drake's voyage; but, particularly so far as California is concerned, they have contained nothing not drawn from the sources named. To point out the many errors resulting from carelessness and other causes would require much space and serve no good purpose. I shall have occasion to name a few works in later notes of this chapter; I refer the reader to the list of authorities on Cabrillo's voyage given in note 36, which with few exceptions also describe Drake's visit; and I also name the following in addition: *Aa*, xviii. 11; *Berenger, Col. Voy.*, i. 63, 117; *Harris, Nav.*, i. 19; *Circumnavigations of Globe*, 85; *Kerr's Col. Voy.*, x. 27; *Laharpe, Abrégé*, xv. 15; *Pinkerton's Voy.*, xii. 169; *Sammlung*, xii. 5; *Voyages, Col. Voy. and Trav.; Voyages, Col. (Churchill's)*, viii. 459; *Voyages, Curious Col.*, v. 153; *Voyages, Harleian Col.*, ii. 434; *Voyages, New Col.*, iii. 15; *Voyages, New Miscel. Col.*, i. 37; *Voyages, New Univ. Col.*, i. 28; *Voyages, Hist. Voy. round World*, i. 1, 45; *Voyages, World Displayed*, v. 150; *Barrow's Life Drake*, 75; *Clarke's Life Drake*, 30; *Purchas his Pilgrimes*, ii. 52; *Gottfriedt, Newe Welt*, 345; *Boss, Leben*, 341; *Ens, West and Ost. Ind. Lustgart*, 113; *Humboldt, Essai Pol.*, 317, 330; *Löw, Meer oder Seehanen Buch*, 44; *Morelli, Fasti Nov. Orb.*, 27; *Laet, Nov. Orbis*, 307; *Navarrete, Introd.*, xcviii.; *Id., Viages Apóc.*, 33; *Burney's Chron. Hist.*, i. 350; *Le Maire, Spieghel*, 77; *Pauw, Recherches*, i. 172; *Edin. Review*, No. clxii. 1879; *Niles' Register*, lxv. 174; *Hunt's Merch. Mag.*, xii. 523; *Hayes' Scraps, Cal. Notes*, iii. 10; *Quigley's Irish Race*, 146; *N. Amer. Review*, June 1839, 132; *Greenhow's Or. and Cal.*, 70; *Id. Memoir*, 36; *Nicolay's Or. Ter.*, 24; *Cavo, Tres Siglos*, i. 214; *Gleeson's Hist. Cath. Ch.*, i. 73, ii. 35; *Belcher's Voy.*, i. 316; *Hazlitt's Great Gold Fields*, 4; *California, Past, Present*, 53; *Frost's Half hours*, 161; *McClellan's Golden State*, 43; *Tuthill's Hist. Cal.*, 17; *Holmes' An. Amer.*, i. 90; *Mayer's Mex. Aztec*, 168; *Meyer, Nach dem Sac.*, 197; *Norman's Youth's Hist.*, 29; *Page's Nouv. Voy.*, ii. 410; *Poussin, Quest. de l'Orég.*, 23; *Id. U. S.*, 237; *Taylor, in Cal. Farmer*, March 29, 1861; April 25, Aug. 15, 22, 29, 1862; *Willard's Last Leaves*, 113; *Douglass' Summary*, i. 35; *Uring's Hist.*, 376; *Farnham's Hist. Oregon*, 11, 21; *Goodrich's Man upon the Sea*, 241; *Delaporte, Reisen*, 457; *Evans' Puget Sd.*, 3; *Falconer's Oreg. Quest.*, 12, 39; *Forbes' Hist. Cal.* 10, 79; *Gazlay's Pac. Monthly*, 227; *Soulé's An. S. F.*, 32; also most of the recently published county histories of California.

[38] *World Encompassed*, 115. 'A faire and good bay' in 38°. *Famous Voy.* 'A harborow for his ship' in 44°. *Discourse*, 184.

[39] The excessive cold here is mentioned only in the *World Encompassed*. The author's absurd statements and explanations are not worth reproducing in detail.

for the men, with a kind of fort for protection. Of
the repairs the two chief authorities say nothing; but
the third tells us that Drake's men "grounded his
ship to trim her," and that they set sail after having
"graved and watred theire ship."[40]

When the ship first anchored a native ambassador
approached in a canoe to make a long speech, bringing
also a tuft of feathers and a basket of the herb called
tabáh.[41] When the Englishmen landed the Indians
came to the shore in great numbers, but showed no
hostility, freely receiving and giving presents, and
soon came to regard the strangers, so the latter believed, as gods. The narratives are chiefly filled with
details of the ceremonies and sacrifices by which they
signified their submission, even crowning Drake as
their *hioh*, or king. The men went for the most part
naked, the women wearing a loose garment of bul-
rushes with a deerskin over the shoulders. Their
houses, some of them close to the water, were partly
subterranean, the upper parts being conical, of wood,
and covered with earth. In details respecting the
people and their habits and ceremonies there is much
exaggeration and inaccuracy; but the descriptions in
a general way are applicable enough to the Central
Californians.[42]

Before his departure Drake made a journey up into
the land, " to be the better acquainted with the nature
and commodities of the country," visiting several villages. " The inland we found to be farre different
from the shoare, a goodly country, and fruitfull soyle,
stored with many blessings fit for the vse of man:
infinite was the company of very large and fat Deere
which there we sawe by thousands, as we supposed,
in a heard; besides a multitude of a strange kinde of
Conies, by farre exceeding them in number: their
heads and bodies, in which they resemble other Conies,

[40] *Discourse*, 184.
[41] Or tobáh, called by the *Famous Voyage, tabacco*. They had also a root
called *petáh* of which they made meal and bread.
[42] See *Native Races*, i. 361 et seq.

are but small; his tayle, like the tayle of a Rat, exceeding long; and his feet like the pawes of a Want or moale; under his chinne, on either side, he hath a bagge, into which he gathereth his meate, when he hath filled his belly abroade...the people eate their bodies, and make great account of their skinnes, for their kings holidaies coate was made of them."[43]

" This country our Generall named *Albion*," or *Noua Albion* according to the *Famous Voyage*, "and that for two causes; the one in respect of the white bancks and cliffes, which lie toward the sea; the other, that it might haue some affinity, euen in name also, with our own country, which was sometime so called." "There is no part of earth here to bee taken up, wherein there is not some speciall likelihood of gold or silver."[44] " Before we went from thence, our Generall caused to be set vp a monument of our being there, as also of her maiesties and successors right and title to that kingdome; namely, a plate of brasse, fast nailed to a great and firme post; whereon is engrauen her graces name, and the day and yeare of our arriual there, and of the free giuing vp of the prouince and kingdome, both by the king and people, into her maiesties hands: together with her highnesse picture and armes, in a piece of sixpence currant English monie, shewing itselfe by a hole made of purpose through the plate; vnderneath was likewise engrauen the name of our Generall, etc.[45] The Spaniards neuer had any dealing, or so much as set a foote in this country, the utmost of their discoueries reaching onely to many degrees Southward of this place." They finally sailed on the 23d of July,[46] on a south-south-west course accord-

---

[43] *World Encompassed*, 131–2. 'We found the whole country to bee a warren of a strange kinde of Conies, their bodyes in bignes as be the Barbary Conies, their heads as the heads of ours, the feet of a Want, and the taile of a rat being of great length: under her chinne on either side a bagge,' etc. *Famous Voyage.*

[44] *Famous Voyage*, the rest being from *World Encompassed.*

[45] In this place Drake set up 'a greate post and nayled thereon a vj[d] ,w[ch] the countrey people woorshipped as if it had bin God; also hee nayled vppon this post a plate of lead, and scratched therein the Queenes name.' *Discourse.*

[46] 'In the latter ende of August.' *Discourse*, 184.

ing to the *Discourse*, and "not farre without this harborough did lye certain Ilands (we called them the Ilands of Saint *James*) hauing on them plentifull and great store of Seales and birds, with one of which we fell *July* 24, whereon we found such prouision as might competently serue our turne for a while. We departed againe the day next following, viz., *July* 25." No more land was seen till they had crossed the Pacific.

It should be noted that no regular diary or log of this voyage is extant or is known to have ever been extant. Of the three narratives which I have cited one was perhaps written from memory by a companion of Drake. The others are compilations from notes of the chaplain, Fletcher, written under circumstances of which we know but little, by a man not noted for his veracity, and from the reminiscences probably of others. Naturally they abound in discrepancies and inaccuracies, as is shown still more clearly in parts not relating to California. They are sufficiently accurate to leave no room for reasonable doubt that Drake really anchored on the coast in the region indicated, touching at one of the Farallones on his departure; but in respect of further details they inspire no confidence.

Yet the identity of Drake's anchorage is a most interesting point, and one that has caused much discussion. There are three bays not far apart on the coast, those of Bodega, Drake, and San Francisco, any one of which to a certain extent may answer the requirements, and each of which has had its advocates. Their positions are shown on the annexed map. The central bay under Point Reyes, the old San Francisco, is almost exactly in latitude 38°, and it agrees better than the others with the south-south-west course to the Farallones as given by one of the narratives; Bodega agrees well enough with the 38° 30′ of the *Famous Voyage*, and more properly than the other may be termed a 'faire and good bay;' while San Francisco, though some twenty minutes south of the

lowest latitude mentioned, is a very much more 'conuenient harborough' than either of the others.

For nearly two centuries after the voyage there
was but slight occasion to identify Drake's anchorage;
yet there can be no doubt that it was to a certain
extent confounded with the old San Francisco men-

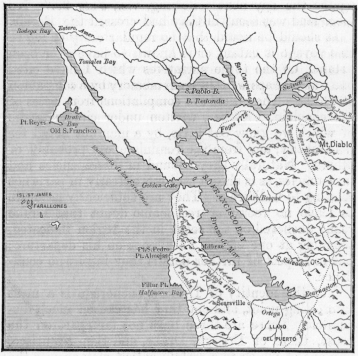

WHERE DID DRAKE LAND?

tioned by Torquemada, and that the confusion was
shown, or increased, by the occasional occurrence of
the name S. Francisco Drak for Sir Francis Drake
on old maps. And later when the new San Francisco
was found, few if any but Spaniards understood the
difference between the two;[47] and therefore, as well

[47] Cabrera Bueno, *Navegacion Especulativa*, Manila, 1734, makes the distinction perfectly clear; but of this work nothing was known to the world
beyond its mere existence till 1874, when one of my assistants in the *Overland Monthly* gave a translation of its contents so far as relating to this subject. Doyle in his reprint of *Palou*, *Noticias*, i. ix.-x., gave the same in
substance later, after consulting my copy.

as on account of the excellence of the new harbor, Drake's anchorage was very naturally identified by most with the bay of San Francisco. The Spaniards, however, never accepted this theory, but were disposed from the first to claim for Portolá's expedition the honor of discovering the new San Francisco, and to restrict Drake's discoveries to Bodega.[48] It cannot be claimed, however, that the Spaniards had any special facilities for learning the truth of the matter; and indeed some of them seem to have declared in favor of the bay under Point Reyes,[49] which has for many years borne Drake's name on the maps, though advocates of both the other bays have not been wanting. The general opinion in modern times

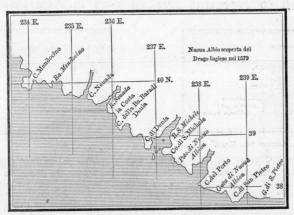

MAP FROM ARCANO DEL MARE, 1647.

[48] In *Bodega y Cuadra, Viage de 1775*, MS., it is clearly stated that Bodega was Drake's bay and that it was distinct from either San Francisco. Fleurieu, *Introd. Marchand, Voy.*, i. lxxvi. et seq., by a blundering reference to *Maurelle's Journal*, 45 et seq., identified Bodega and San Francisco, making some absurd charges against the Spaniards of having changed the name, which charges Navarrete, *Introd. Sutil y Mex. Viage*, xcviii.–ix., refutes, at the same time implying his approval of the identity of Drake's bay and Bodega. Humboldt, *Essai Pol.*, 327, takes the same view of the subject.

[49] Vancouver, *Voyages*, i. 430, in 1792 understood the Spaniards to be of this opinion. Yet I find no evidence that this opinion was ever the prevailing one. The 'Spanish tradition' in California was very strong against new San Francisco; but was not very pronounced as between old San Francisco and Bodega, favoring, however, the latter. Padre Niel, *Apuntaciones*, 78, writing in about 1718 declared his opinion that Drake's bay was at the mouth of Carmelo River!

has been that the great freebooter did not enter San
Francisco Bay, and that he probably did anchor at
Drake Bay.

Early maps, it would seem, should throw some light
on this question, but they fail to do so. With the
exception of Vizcaino's map, to be reproduced presently
and having no bearing on Drake's voyage, I have not
found a single map of the California coast of earlier
date than 1769 bearing the slightest indication of
having been founded on anything but the narratives
still extant and the imagination of the map-maker. I
reproduce two sections of maps from the *Arcano del
Mare* to which Hale attaches some importance in
this connection, with another by Hondius and supposed to represent Drake's port in New Albion.[50]

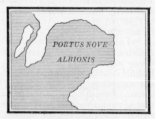

ARCANO DEL MARE.   HONDIUS' MAP.

[50] *Hale's Early Maps of America, and a note on Robert Dudley and the
Arcano del Mare*, Worcester, 1874, a paper read before the American Antiq.
Soc. in 1873. The author is inclined to think that Dudley had some special
authority unknown to us for his maps of this coast. 'Our California friends
must permit me to say that Porto bonissimo (an inscription for Drake's port)
is a very strong phrase for the open road-stead of "Sir Francis Drake's Bay"
as it is now understood.' Of the peculiar 'bottle-shaped loop' of the bay, it
is said, 'the bay of San Francisco after numerous reductions and copyings
would assume much this shape.' And the difficulty arising from the other
bay of like shape just above San Francisco on both maps is thus ingeniously,
if not very satisfactorily, explained away. 'I confess that it seems to me that
more than one navigator of those times probably entered the Golden Gate into
the bay of San Francisco. Each one recorded his own latitude—and these
two bays, almost identical in appearance, are due to an effort of the map-
maker to include two incorrect latitudes in one map'! Hale reproduces one
of the *Arcano* maps and adds the Hondius map in *Bryant's Hist. U. S.*, ii.
570-7. Here he is non-committal about the identity of the bays, admitting
that the maker of the Hondius map had no knowledge of San Francisco Bay,
or indeed of any other bay on the coast. In one of the arguments against
San Francisco that seems to have most weight with him is however in error.
'It is quite certain that the Spaniards, who eagerly tried to rediscover the
port, with this map in their possession, did not succeed until near two hundred years after. Long before they did discover it they were seeking for it,

With due respect for Hale's views, as those of an able and conscientious investigator, I find in them nothing to change my own as just expressed. These maps like all others represent Drake's port from the current narratives as a good bay in about 38° of latitude; all the rest is purely imaginary. For like reasons I cannot agree with another able student of California history who finds proof in the maps given by Hale that Drake anchored in Bodega Bay. I do not object very strongly to the conclusion, but I find no proof, or even evidence in the maps.[51]

calling it the bay of San Francisco, that name probably having been taken from no less a saint than the heretic, Sir Francis Drake.' This is the old confusion already alluded to. Hale knew nothing of the distinction between the old and new San Francisco. The Spaniards were familiar with the position of the former after its discovery and naming by Cermeñon in 1595; Vizcaino entered it without difficulty in 1603; Portolá was approaching it as a perfectly well known landmark when he stumbled on the new San Francisco in 1769. There is no evidence that the Spaniards ever sought San Francisco on any other occasion.

[51] I allude to the writer of a review of *Bryant's Hist. U. S.* in the *S. F. Bulletin*, Oct. 5, 1878, whom I suppose to have been John W. Dwinelle, and whose argument is worth quoting at some length. After some remarks on Hondius' facilities for knowing the truth, Dwinelle writes: 'This map does not accurately describe Bodega Bay. There is now a long spit of sand running from the east at the foot of the bay and nearly shutting it up. But that sand spit did not exist when Captain Bodega discovered the bay in 1775, although he reported his opinion that a bar was forming there. The long, narrow island represented on Hondius' map of the bay as lying on the outside of the coast and parallel to the bay, really lies at the foot of the bay, below the peninsula; but, viewed from the point where Drake's ship is represented as lying, the island appears to lie outside of the peninsula. Drake's ship passed this island only twice, namely, when he sailed in and when he sailed out. But it was in sight every day from the place where his ship lay during the five weeks that he was there, and from that point, we repeat, this island appears to be outside. The bay itself, there at its head, appears to be twice as wide as it is at its mouth some miles below, although the reverse is the fact. But it is just such a map as a good penman ignorant of linear and aerial perspective would have made on the spot, if he had a taste for pen and ink maps, such as Fletcher, Drake's chaplain, is known to have had. We have visited Bodega Bay with a photographic copy of Hondius' map of Drake's Bay, taken from that in the British museum, but enlarged to the dimension of 5 by 6 inches. All the indications called for by Drake's narrative exist there. Those we have mentioned; also the Indian villages; the shell-fish; the seals; the deciduous trees, the "conies" which honey-combed the soil; the elevation of the coast, which commenced at about that latitude; the white sand-hills, which suggested the name of Albion. Also another indication which does not appear in the map as copied in the history, a line of rocks below the beach at the lower right-hand water-line, thus forming a double coast line. We have no doubt that Bodega Bay is Drake's Bay, and that Hondius' map was furnished to him by Fletcher, who made it on the spot. Drake's ship could go in there now and anchor at its head in 15 feet water, 100 feet from the shore, where there is a good sandy beach on which to careen and repair

The main question is, did Drake enter San Francisco Bay? It would serve no good purpose to catalogue the modern writers who have espoused one theory or the other. Able men like Burney, Davidson, Tuthill, and Stillman have maintained that Drake anchored within the Golden Gate, against the contrary opinions of other able men like Humboldt, Soulé, Doyle, Dwinelle, and Hittell. Some have been very positive, others cautious and doubtful. Most

vessels, and where there was an Indian village "on the hill above," as demanded by Drake's narrative. The map from *Arcano del Mar*, edition of 1647, given at page 571 in the history, in our opinion greatly strengthens this view. Directly opposite the mouth of Bodega Bay to the south is the mouth of Tomales Bay. Between the two the Rio Estero Americano of the Spanish Californians debouches into the ocean; a stream whose bed is almost bare in the dry season, but which, during the rainy season and for some time afterwards, poured into the sea a shallow volume of turbulent waters, several hundred feet in width. When Drake was on this coast, the winter or rainy season was unusually protracted, so far that the deciduous trees, which usually resume their foliage in March and April, had not done so as late as July, and it still snowed on the coast. Snow on the coast means rain in the interior at a short distance from the sea. It may be safely assumed that the Rio Estero Americano was swelling full to its margin—probably unusually full. The "bottle-shaped" bay on the reduced scale of the map from *Arcano del Mar* might well represent the two bays, the neck standing for the river. The latitude is precisely that required for Bodega Bay. Following down the map, the coast line corresponds with great exactness with that of the modern maps as given at page 576; C. (Cabo) di San Pietro, Cape St Peter, is Cape Punta de los Reyes, the western point of Jack's, or Drake's bay of modern times; and G. (golfo) di San Pietro, corresponds exactly to Jack's, or Drake's Bay, as it appears from the sea, and also exactly to its latitude. We are of opinion that this map must be regarded as authentic, and also the vignettes engraved upon the same sheet. Two of these represent Drake's ship, the *Pelican*, the first as she lay stranded on the rocks at the Windward Islands, and the other as lying at anchor. They both correspond in all their details. Probably the drawings from which the engraving was executed were made from the ship itself. Drake returned to England in 1580. He never sailed again. The engravings were made between 1590 and 1600. Hondius was in England all this time. If not made from the ship, the engraving may be safely assumed to represent the style of naval architecture of the period. The ship is represented as broad in the beam and round in the bow. Her burden, Drake's narrative informs us, was 100 tons. She was therefore shallow and drew but little water. The ship-builders whom we have consulted inform us that with all her armament she could not have drawn more than from 5 to 6 feet of water. She could therefore have entered Bolinas Bay, Jack's, or Drake's (interior) Bay, Tomales Bay, Bodega Bay, Humboldt Bay, and any or all of the rivers which Drake encountered. Modern navigators and hydrographers who argue that Drake must have entered the Bay of San Francisco because no other bay was deep enough for the entry and repairing of a man-of-war, must have certainly had in their minds a modern 74-gun ship, and not a little caravel of 100 tons carrying six feet of draft.' It will be noticed that the writer attempts no explanation of the two bottle-shaped bays. It is moreover remarkable that he should accept Fletcher's statements about the climate and season as even remotely founded on truth.

have written without a full understanding of the distinction between the two San Franciscos. Few have been sufficiently impressed with the fundamental truth that Chaplain Fletcher was a liar. Besides certain special pleadings often more ingenious than weighty, the convincing arguments have been on the one side that Drake after a stay of five weeks would not have called any other bay but that of San Francisco a good harbor, or have thanked God for a fair wind to enter the same; and on the other, that, having entered San Francisco, he would never have dismissed it with mere mention as a good bay. The former argument is less applicable to Bodega than to the bay under Point Reyes.

The latter appears to me unanswerable. It is one that has naturally occurred to all, but I doubt if any have comprehended its full force. It grows on the student as he becomes acquainted with the spirit of the past centuries in relation to maritime affairs and particularly to the north-west coast of America. I treat this subject fully elsewhere.[52] That Drake and his men should have spent a month in so large and so peculiar a bay without an exploration extending thirty or forty miles into the interior by water; that notes should be written on the visit without a mention of any exploration, or of the great rivers flowing into the bay, or of its great arms; that Drake's companions should have evaded the questions of such men as Richard Hakluyt, and have died without imparting a word of the information so eagerly sought by so many men, is indeed incredible. For sailors in those days to talk of inlets they had never seen was common; to suppress their knowledge of real inlets would indeed have been a marvel.[53] Drake's business

[52] See *Hist. Northwest Coast*, i. chap. ii.–iv., this series.
[53] Stillman says, *Seeking the Golden Fleece*, 300: ' He was not on a voyage of discovery; his was a business enterprise, and he had an eye to that alone. What was not gold and silver was of small consequence to him.' Whence perhaps his minute details of Indian ceremonies! ' Nor does it seem probable that he knew the extent of the bay of San Francisco. He had already concluded...that there could be no northwest passage...and he had aban-

in the North Pacific was to find an interoceanic passage; if he abandoned the hope in the far north, one glance at the Golden Gate would have rekindled it; a sight of the far-reaching arms within would have convinced him that the strait was found; San Pablo Bay would have removed the last doubt from the mind of every incredulous companion; in Suisun Bay the *Golden Hind* would have been well on her way through the continent; and a little farther the only question would have been whether to proceed directly to Newfoundland by the Sacramento or to Florida by the San Joaquin. That a man like Fletcher, who found sceptres and crowns and kings among the Central Californians, who found a special likelihood of gold and silver where nothing of the kind ever existed, who was so nearly frozen among the snow-covered Californian hills in summer, should have called the anchorage under Point Reyes, to say nothing of Bodega, a fine harbor would have been wonderful accuracy and moderation on his part. But supposing San Francisco Bay to have been the subject of his description, let the reader imagine the result. The continent is not broad enough to contain the complication of channels he would have described.

Proof of the most positive nature, more definite than the vague narratives in question could be expected reasonably to yield, is required to overthrow the presumption that Drake did not enter San Francisco Bay. This proof Stillman, who has made himself in these later years champion of the cause,[54] believes himself to have found. First, he declares, and fortifies his position with the testimony of a coast-survey official and other navigators, that Drake could not

doned the hope.' And Tuthill, *Hist. Cal.*, 24: 'They did not go into ecstasies about the harbor. They were not hunting harbors, but fortunes in compact form. Harbors, so precious to the Spaniards, who had a commerce in the Pacific to be protected, were of small account to roving Englishmen.' These are evasions of the issue, or the statements of men not acquainted with the maritime spirit of the time.

[54] *Stillman's Footprints in California of Early Navigators*, in *Id.; Seeking the Golden Fleece*, 285 et seq.; *Id.*, in *Overland Monthly*, i. 332.

have graved his vessel in the bay that bears his name
without the certainty of destruction. Navigators with
whom I have conversde are somewhat less positive
on the subject, simply stating that the beaching of
a vessel there would be venturesome, and a wise
captain would if possible avoid it. It is not at all
uncommon at many places on the coast for vessels to
be beached in a storm, and safely released by the high
tide. Stillman and his witnesses imply that Drake's
ship was grounded to be repaired and graved, but
only one of the narratives, and that the least reliable,
contains such a statement; the others simply mention
a leak to be stopped, perhaps not far below the water-
line, and I am sure that small vessels upon this coast
have been often careened and graved without being
beached at all. The coast survey charts declare the
harbor to be a secure one except in south-east gales.
There is an interior bay, communicating with the
outer by a passage now somewhat obstructed by a
bar, which possibly now, and very probably in 1579,
would afford Drake's small ship a safe anchorage.
And finally this objection would lose its force if applied to Bodega instead of Drake Bay. Thus we find
in this argument nothing of the positive character
which alone could make it valid.

The other argument urged is that Fletcher's 'conies'
were ground-squirrels and that these animals never
existed in the region of Drake Bay. It must be
admitted that the description in several respects fits
the ground-squirrel better than the gopher or any
other animal of this region; but a very accurate description of anything would be out of place, and certainly
is not found, in these narratives; the 'conies'—literally rabbits—were seen on a trip up into the country,
how far we do not know; and no very satisfying proof
is presented that ground-squirrels never frequented
the region of either Drake Bay or Bodega. Therefore whatever weight might be given to Stillman's
arguments as against similar arguments on the other

side drawn from the faulty descriptions available, they are in my opinion entitled to very little consideration as against the overwhelming and irresistible presumption noted that Drake could not have entered San Francisco Bay.[55]

Between Drake Bay and Bodega I have no decided opinion to express. I find no foundation for such an opinion. It is not probable that there will ever be any means of ascertaining the truth. Drake's post and plate were doubtless moved from their original site at an early date. If my supposition that Cabrillo did not pass Cape Mendocino is correct, then the English navigator may perhaps be entitled to the honor of having discovered a portion of the California coast above that point; yet it is by no means certain that he crossed the parallel of 42°.[56]

The Philippine ships from 1565 followed a northern route in returning across the Pacific to Acapulco; but of these trips we have for the most part no records. Their instructions were to keep as near to the line of 30° as possible, and to go no farther north than was necessary to get a wind. It is probable that, while they often reached latitude 37°, or higher, they rarely sighted the coast of Upper California, on account of turning to the south as soon as they found sea-weeds or other indications that land was near. The lower end of the peninsula was generally the first land seen in these early years.

In 1584, however, Francisco Gali, commanding one of these ships returning from Macao by way of Japan, sailed from that island east and east by north about three hundred leagues until he struck the great oce-

[55] Stillman's reference to the Spanish map published by Anson, which I reproduce later, should be noticed. It certainly gives a peculiar form to the bay under Point Reyes; but it has no bearing on Drake's voyage. It simply shows that the draughtsman failed to get a correct idea of the port from the text of Vizcaino and Cabrera Bueno.

[56] On the report of one of Drake's men having been landed in California, and having gone to Mexico overland, a report not founded on fact. See *Hist. Northwest Coast*, i. 60-1, this series.

anic current, which carried him some seven hundred leagues to within two hundred leagues of the American coast. Then, "being by the same course upon the coast of New Spain, under 37° 30', we passed by a very high and fair land with many trees, wholly without snow, and four leagues from the land you find thereabout many drifts of roots, leaves of trees, reeds, and other leaves like fig-leaves, the like whereof we found in great abundance in the country of Japan, which they eat; and some of those that we found, I caused to be sodden with flesh, and being sodden, they eat like coleworts; there likewise we found great store of seals; whereby it is to be presumed and certainly to be believed, that there are many rivers, bays, and havens along by those coasts to the haven of Acapulco. From thence we ran south-east, south-east and by south, and south-east and by east, as we found the wind, to the point called Cabo de San Lúcas, which is the beginning of the land of California, on the north-west side, lying under 22°, being five hundred leagues distant from Cape Mendocino." This is all that Gali's narrative contains respecting the California coast.[57]

Gali's seems to be the first mention of Cape Mendocino, though it is not implied that the name was given by him, as nevertheless it may have been. We have seen that the name was not, as has been generally believed, applied by Cabrillo or Ferrelo in 1542–3; and Torquemada's statement has been noted to the effect that the cape was discovered by the Manila ships. It is possible that it had been thus discovered in an unrecorded voyage preceding that of Gali; but it is quite as likely that the name was given in Mexico,

[57] This narrative was translated into Dutch and published by Linschoten in his famous and oft-reprinted *Itinerario* of 1596. From this source an English translation is given in *Hakluyt's Voy.*, iii. 442–7. A blunder in a French translation by which 57° 30' was substituted for 37° 30' has caused a fictitious importance to be attached to the voyage, not however affecting California. See *Burney's Chron. Hist.*, ii. 58–61; v. 163–4; *Navarrete, Introd., Sutil y Mex.,* xclvi.–ix.; *Id. Viages Apóc.*, 42–3; *Twiss' Or. Question,* 58–62; and mention in many of the works cited on the voyages of Cabrillo, Drake, and Vizcaino.

of course in honor of the viceroy Mendoza, to a point discovered but not named by Cabrillo.

The fourth voyage of Californian annals was like the third one from the far west. The piloto Sebastian Rodriguez de Cermeñon in charge of the *San Agustin* coming from the Philippines in 1595, was ordered by Governor Gomez Perez das Mariñas, in accordance with royal instructions through Viceroy Velasco, to make some explorations on the coast, doubtless with a view to find a suitable station for the Manila ships. Of Cermeñon's adventures we know only that his vessel ran aground on a lee shore[58] behind what was later called Point Reyes, leaving on the land a large quantity of wax and silk in boxes. It is possible that the *San Agustin* was accompanied by another vessel on which the officers and men escaped; but much more probable I think that the expression 'was lost' in the record is an error, and that the ship escaped with a loss of her cargo. One of the men, Francisco Bolaños, was *piloto mayor*, or sailing-master, under Vizcaino in 1603, when he anchored in the same port to see if any trace of the cargo remained, but without landing. The statement of Bolaños as reported incidentally in the narrative of Vizcaino's voyage by Ascension and Torquemada is, so far as I can learn, the only record extant of this voyage.[59]

[58] 'Se perdió, y dió á la costa con vn viento travesía.' 'Que en aquel puerto avia dado á la Costa el año de 1595.'

[59] *Torquemada, Monarq. Ind.*, i. 717–18. 'En la costa reconocimos el puerto de San Francisco, adonde en tiempos pasados se perdió una nao de China que venia con órden de descubrir esta costa, y creo que hoy dia hay mucha cera y losaza [loza?] que el navío traia.' *Ascension, Relacion*, 558. 'Here was where the ship *S. Agustin* was lost in the year 1595, coming to make discoveries, and the cause of her being lost was rather the fault of him who steered than stress of weather.' *Cabrera Bueno, Navegacion*, 303. Venegas, *Noticia*, i. 183, says 'the viceroy Velasco, desirous of making a station for the Philippine ships on the outer coast, sent a ship called *San Agustin*, which soon returned without any results.' And Lorenzana, in *Cortés, Hist. N. Esp.*, 326. Also, from Torquemada, *Salmeron, Relac.*, 20; *Niel, Apunt*, 74; and *Navarrete, Introd.*, lvi.–vii. It does not clearly appear that any of these writers saw anything in addition to the statement in Torquemada. In *Bodega y Cuadra, Viage de 1775*, MS., it is said that Cermeñon was wrecked in a south-east wind, as he could not have been at Bodega or the new San Francisco. Where this information was obtained does not appear.

It is somewhat remarkable that no additional light
has ever been thrown on this voyage; but, slight as
is the record, there is no good reason to question its
accuracy, especially as no grand and impossible discoveries of interoceanic channels are involved. There
can be very little doubt that Cermeñon named the
port of his disaster San Francisco, perhaps from the
day of his arrival. There is nothing to support the
view sometimes expressed that he came in search of
a San Francisco Bay, or of the port discovered by
Drake; though it is not unlikely that rumors of
Drake's fine bay had an influence with other motives
in promoting this exploration. That the Spaniards,
now or at any other time, founded the name of San
Francisco on that of Sir Francis, the English freebooter, is so improbable as to merit no consideration;
but it is certain that subsequently foreign writers and
map-makers confounded the names to some extent, as
was natural enough. That Vizcaino, Cabrera Bueno,
and other Spaniards of the early times mistook the
identity of Cermeñon's bay is hardly possible. The
timely circulation of a paragraph from Cabrera
Bueno's work of 1732 and another from Crespí's
diary of 1769 would have well nigh removed all difficulties in this matter, which has proved so puzzling
to the annalists.

Sebastian Vizcaino, commanding a Spanish exploring fleet of three vessels, anchored in San Diego Bay
on November 10, 1603. He had sailed from Acapulco
in May of the preceding year, with a force of nearly
two hundred men including three Carmelite friars.
His special mission, in addition to that of general exploration and the ever potent purpose of finding an
interoceanic strait, was to find a suitable port for the
Philippine ships. Details of his expedition to the
date mentioned and of his explorations along the outer
coast of the peninsula have been presented in another
part of this work. It is only with his experience on

the coast of Upper California that we are now concerned.[60]

It had been sixty years since Cabrillo had visited this bay and named it San Miguel; but here as elsewhere on the Californian coast Vizcaino pays no heed to the discoveries of his predecessor; giving indeed no indication that they were known to him. The name was now given doubtless with reference to that of the flag-ship, and also to the day of San Diego de Alcalá occurring on the 12th of November. A party landed to explore, climbed to the summit of the hills on the northern peninsula, had a view of the grand harbor and a glimpse of the False Bay, found plenty of wood, and came back to report. The general decided to clean and pay his ship, and to obtain a supply of wood and water. A tent church for the friars was pitched somewhere on the western shore between what are now La Playa and Point Loma. Wells were dug on the opposite sand island, or peninsula, and the work of

[60] *Hist. North Mex. States*, this series. The vessels were the flag-ship, or capitana, *San Diego*, on which sailed Vizcaino as captain-general; the *Santo Tomás*, under Toribio Gomez de Corvan as admiral; and the *Tres Reyes* under Alférez Martin Aguilar and the piloto Antonio Flores. Other officers were Captain Alonso Estévan Peguero, Captain Gaspar Alarcon, Captain Gerónimo Martin Palacios, cosmographer; Alféreces Juan Francisco Suriano, Sebastian Melendez, and Juan de Acevedo Tejeda; pilotos Francisco Bolaños, Baltasar de Armas, and Juan Pascual; sergeants Miguel Legar and Juan Castillo Bueno; and corporals Estévan Lopez and Francisco Vidal. The friars were Andrés de la Asuncion, Tomás de Aquino, and Antonio de la Ascension, the first serving as *comisario* and the latter as chronicler and assistant cosmographer and map-maker. The standard and original authorities are Padre Ascension's account, perhaps but little changed from the original diary, in *Torquemada*, i. 694–726; the same author's *Relacion Breve*, 539–74, written in 1620, and adding not much of importance to the other; *Salmeron, Relaciones,* 14–21, the author of which was personally acquainted with Ascension and other companions of Vizcaino; *Cabrera Bueno, Navegacion,* 302–13, which contains a derrotero of the coast from Cape Mendocino south, drawn from Vizcaino's log and charts; *Venegas, Not.*, i. 193–201; iii. 22–139 and *Navarrete, Sutil y Mex.* ix.–xviii., the author of which saw in the Spanish archives certified copies of all the papers relating to the expedition, including 32 maps, a small reduction from which combined in one he published in his atlas. This map, which I reproduce, was also published in *Burney's Chron. Hist.*, ii. 236–59. It is very much to be regretted that the narratives and maps of this voyage have never been published, and that Navarrete has made so inadequate a use of them. For accounts of the voyage adding nothing to information derived from those mentioned I refer the reader to the account in an earlier volume of my work; it may be added that very many of the works cited in this chapter on the voyages of Cabrillo and Drake contain also a mention of Vizcaino.

refitting went on, though many were sick with the
scurvy of which some had already died. Indians
armed with bows and arrows soon appeared on the
beach but were neither hostile nor very timid, gladly
consenting to an interchange of gifts. They were
understood to say by signs that other bearded men
like the Spaniards were in the interior. All were delighted with the port and its surroundings. Vizcaino
with Fray Antonio and an escort made an expedition
on land, how extensive or in what direction we may
not know, but probably including the eastern shores.
After a stay of ten days, they set sail on the 20th of
November.[61] The islands known as Los Coronados
were noted and named by Vizcaino; and Cabrera
Bueno, giving a full description of the port which he
puts in latitude 34°, names also the Punta de Guijarros, that is the point of cobble-stones, or ballast.[62]

A voyage of eight days against a north-west wind,
the *Tres Reyes* hugging the coast and the others keeping farther out, brought them to an anchorage at the
island which from the day they named Santa Catalina, sighting another large island in the south-west
named San Clemente.[63] Before arriving here they
had gone to a bight on the main, where smoke and
green vegetation were seen, but there seemed to be
no protection from the winds. This was probably
the bay they called San Pedro,[64] a name still retained,

[61] The narratives enter somewhat into descriptive details for which I have
no space. Says Ascension: 'In the sands of the beach there was a great quantity of marcasite, golden (dorada) and spongy, which is a clear sign that in
the mountains round the port there are gold-mines, because the waters when
it rains bring it from the mountains.' They also found in the sand masses of
a gray light substance like dried ox-dung, which it was thought might be am-
ber. Some very heavy blue stones with which powdered and mixed in water
the natives made shining streaks on their faces were thought to be rich in
silver. The fertility of the soil, abundance of game and fish, and indeed all
the natural qualities of the place are highly praised. San Diego was deemed
a fine site for a Spanish settlement.

[62] *Cabrera Bueno, Navegacion*, 305.

[63] Name only in *Cabrera Bueno, Nav.*, 305. The island is not on the map.

[64] On the map it is Ensenada de S. Andrés. Cabrera Bueno names San
Pedro in 34° 30', and mentions the little island there. Nov. 26th is the day
of St Peter, bishop of Alexandria. It will be remembered that Cabrillo had
called this bay Bahía de los Humos.

like those of the islands.   Santa Catalina had a large
population of fishermen and traders, who had large
well built canoes and houses, as well as a temple
where they sacrificed birds to an idol.   They had no
fear and were friendly, though skillful thieves.   One
or two days were spent here,[65] and then they went on
through the waters which they named the Canal de
Santa Bárbara,[66] between the main and a chain of
islands which commanders of the Philippine ships
are said to have regarded before as *tierra firme*.   The

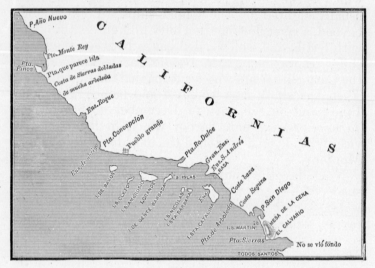

VIZCAINO'S MAP.

country was very attractive on both sides of the
channel, but Vizcaino did not anchor, deeming it
important to take advantage of favorable winds to
reach northern latitudes.   A chief came off in a canoe,
however, and used all his eloquence to induce the
strangers to visit his home, offering ten women for
each man to supply a need that he noted on board
the ships.   I give here a copy of Vizcaino's map of
the coast up to Monterey.   Between the narrative,

[65] Torquemada, i. 713, says they departed on December 25th, but this must
be an error.
[66] The day of Santa Bárbara is December 4th.

the map, and Cabrera's description there is no little confusion in details.[67]

There were other friendly visits from the natives as the Spaniards advanced northward; but after emerging from the channel and passing Point Concepcion the coast was so hidden from view by fogs as to greatly interfere with the search for a harbor.[68] On the 14th of December the fog lifted and revealed to the voyagers the lofty coast range which from the preceding day was named Sierra de Santa Lucía, and which as the chronicler states had been the landmark usually sighted by the China ships. Four leagues beyond, a river flowing from lofty hills enters the ocean with fertile and well wooded banks between the shore cliffs. It was named the Rio de Carmelo in honor of the Carmelite friars who accompanied the expedition.[69] Then Vizcaino's fleet rounded and named Punta de Pinos, and on the 16th of December anchored in a *famoso*, or excellent, harbor which in honor of the viceroy who had despatched the expedition was named Monterey.[70]

Next day the church tent was pitched under the shade of an oak whose branches touched the tidewater, twenty paces from springs of good water in a ravine, which *barranca*, with similar trees not quite so near the shore, is still a prominent landmark at Monterey. There were now but few men on the ships

[67] Map from *Sutil y Mexicana, Viage, Atlas* No. 4. Torquemada gives no names except Santa Catalina Island and Santa Bárbara Canal. Cabrera Bueno, 304, gives a page of not very clear description. He names Punta de Concepcion in 35° 30', Farallon de Lobos, Canal de Sta Bárbara, Punta de la Conversion (perhaps identical with the Punta de Rio Dulce of the map, and with the modern Pt Hueneme) Isla de Sta Bárbara, Isla de Sta Catalina in 34° 30', Isla de San Clemente in 43° (a little less).

[68] On the map is named Ensenada de Roque, which is either San Luis Obispo or Estero Bay; and 'point which looks like an island,' evidently Pt Sur. Cabrera gives no names except Tierra de Santa Lucía, mentioning however the 'morro' corresponding to Pt Sur.

[69] Not shown on the map. Called by Cabrera Bueno a 'famoso puerto que tiene abrigo de todos vientos, y tiene un rio de muy buena agua, y de poco fondo, el qual por las orillas está muy poblado de muchos Alamos negros;' also 'alamos blancos' as the others say.

[70] Often written in early times in two words Monte Rey or Monte-Rei, also Monterei and very commonly Monterrey. Of course the European origin of the name in very remote times was *monte del rey* or 'king's mountain.'

not affected by the scurvy. Many were seriously ill, and sixteen had died. In a council held immediately after religious services it was decided to send back one of the vessels to carry the sick and report progress. Accordingly after such rest and relief as could be obtained from a short stay on shore, the *Santo Tomás* was despatched on the 29th of December for Acapulco, carrying Father Aquino among the disabled. The voyage was one of great suffering; twenty-five men died either on the way or soon after arrival; and only nine survived, among whom were the admiral, Corvan, and Fray Tomás. Five days after Corvan's departure the *San Diego* and *Tres Reyes* having obtained a supply of wood and water sailed from Monterey for the north on January 3, 1603.

The qualities of Monterey as a harbor protected from all winds were somewhat exaggerated, though no minute description was given in the diary; and the explorers were very enthusiastic in their praises of its surroundings, its abundance and variety of animals and fishes, its fertile soil, and plentiful wood and water. It was deemed especially well fitted for a re-fitting station for the Philippine ships, being in the latitude where they often sighted the coast. The natives, respecting whom less information is given than about the fauna and flora of the region, were friendly.[71]

For three days from Monterey no discoveries are recorded; and on the 7th of January the vessels are separated, not to meet again, by some misunderstanding of signals. Vizcaino on the *San Diego* turns back by a point passed on the sixth, and named from the day Punta de los Reyes, to enter the port of San Francisco under that point in search of traces of Cermeñon's visit in 1595. He anchors, but does not

[71] Both Torquemada and Ascension give some details of animals, plants trees, and fishes. The latter mentions the fact that a dead whale was lying on the beach, which bears came down to eat at night. Cabrera Bueno puts the port in 37°, gives a very accurate description of it, and states that the anchorage is well protected except against north-west winds.

land, and next day sails on in quest of the consort, making inconsiderable progress till the 12th, when they sight what they believe to be Cape Mendocino, in latitude 41° 30′.   Next day the ship is hove to in a south-east gale; and as only six men are fit for work, it is decided to return to La Paz in the gulf, but the

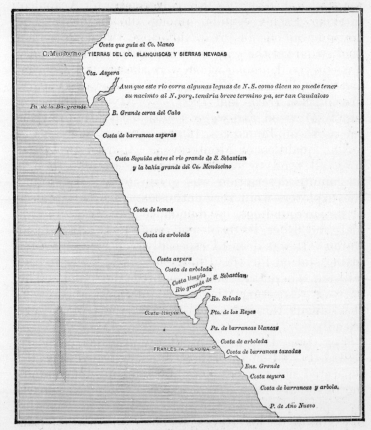

Costa que guia al Co. blanco
Co. Mendocino   TIERRAS DEL CO. BLANQUISCAS Y SIERRAS NEVADAS

Cta. Aspera

Aun que este rio corra algunas leguas de N. S. como dicen no puede tener
su nacimto al N. porq. tendria breve termino pa, ser tan Caudaloso

Pu. de la Ba. grande

B. Grande cerca del Cabo

Costa de barrancas asperas

Costa Seguida entre el rio grande de S. Sebastian
y la bahia grande del Co. Mendocino

Costa de lomas

Costa de arboleda

Costa aspera
Costa de arboleda
Costa limpia
Rio grande de S. Sebastian

Ro. Salado

Costa limpia   Pto. de los Reyes

Pa. de barrancas blancas
Costa de arboleda
FRAYLES IA MENDIDA   Costa de barrancas taxadas

Ens. Grande
Costa segura
Costa de barrancas y arbola.

P. de Año Nuevo

VIZCAINO'S MAP.

gale causes them to drift northward.   On the 14th they are close to Cape Mendocino, but on the 19th the weather clears and they find themselves in latitude 42,° in sight of a white point near high snowy mountains.   They name the point Cabo Blanco de San

Sebastian, and, with a favorable wind, turn southward on St Sebastian's day. They keep near the
shore, but without discoveries that have left any
traces in the narrative, and without anchoring until
they come to Cedros Island on the 7th of January.
The suffering and loss of life from scurvy have been
terrible, but relief is found at Mazatlan.

Meanwhile Aguilar in the *Tres Reyes* advances to
latitude 41° and is then driven by the gale to an
anchorage behind a great cliff near Cape Mendocino.
Continuing his voyage after the storm, he finds his
latitude on the 19th to be 43°, near a point named
Cape Blanco, beyond which the coast turns to the
north-west,[72] and also near a large river. On account
of sickness and because he has already reached the
limit of the viceroy's instructions, Aguilar resolves to
return. Both he and Flores die on the voyage, only
five men surviving. I give a copy of the map representing discoveries above Monterey, not agreeing in
all respects with the narrative, and showing nothing
above Cape Mendocino. The great river, supposed by
Padre Ascension to be the entrance to Anian Strait,
must have been either imaginary or a small stream.
It is not possible to determine accurately the northern
limit of this exploration; but the indications are that
it was not beyond the present Oregon line of 42° and
that Vizcaino's Cape San Sebastian and Aguilar's Cape
Blanco were identical with the modern Trinidad and
St George.[73]

[72] Ascension says north-east and names the river Santa Inés.

[73] See *Hist. Northwest Coast*, i. 147–8. Cabrera Bueno's description of the
northern coast is as follows: 'In latitude 42° is a high cape, apparently cut
down perpendicularly to the sea, and from it runs a lower coast some eight
leagues southward, where the land forms another high point, bare, with some
white cliffs which rise from the water's edge; this point is in 41° 30′ and is
called Cape Mendocino. From here the coast trends s. e. to lat. 39° 30′, the
land being of medium elevation and thickly wooded, with some small hills bare
along the shore. In the said latitude it forms a low point of white cliffs cut
down to the sea; and from here the coast trends s. e. one quarter s. to 38° 30′,
where the land forms a point of medium height, separated from the coast so
as to appear from a distance to be an island, which is called Punta de los
Reyes. It forms a steep cliff (morro), and on its north side affords a good
shelter from all winds, in lat. 38° 30′, and is called San Francisco. In a south
or south-east wind the anchorage is at the end of the beach where it forms an

Except the discovery of Monterey Bay Vizcaino had accomplished no more, and indeed in several respects less, than had Cabrillo sixty years before; but the results of his voyage were clearly recorded, while the expedition of his predecessor had left practically no trace in the world's knowledge. From 1603 the trend and general character of the California coast, together with its chief harbors, always excepting the undiscovered San Francisco, were well known to the Spaniards by these records; but for more than a century and a half there was no addition to this knowledge. No ship is known to have entered the northern waters from the south, while the Manila ships from the far west neither touched at the new ports nor left any record of what they saw as they passed. Vizcaino made strong efforts to be intrusted with a new expedition for the occupation of Monterey; and in 1606 there was a prospect of his success; but attention was diverted to the far west; and though this navigator, returning as a passenger from Japan, on the *San Francisco*, again sighted Cape Mendocino on December 26, 1613, no more attempts were made on the outer coast.[74] There is a perfect blank of one hundred and sixty-six years in the annals of what we call California.

Herrera's history containing an account of Cabrillo's discoveries had been published in 1601–15, and new Spanish editions appeared in 1728 and 1730. Torquemada's great work with a record of Vizcaino's

angle on the N. W.; while on the N. E. are three white rocks very near the sea, and opposite the middle one an *estero* makes in from the sea with a good entrance and no breakers. Inside are found friendly Indians, and fresh water may be easily obtained. S. S. W. from this port are six or seven small white farallones some larger than others, occupying over a league in circuit...About 14 leagues S. E. ¼ S. from Pt Reyes, the land makes a point, before reaching which the land is of medium elevation, bare along the shore, with some steep cliffs, though inland it is high and wooded, until a low point is reached in 37° 30′ called Pt Año Nuevo.' *Navegacion*, 302–3. This author's latitudes are from 30′ to a degree too high. He evidently saw a more minute account of Vizcaino's voyage than the one published, or what is not unlikely, had access to Cermeñon's report.

[74] *Venegas, Not. Cal.*, i. 191, 201; *Clavigero, Storia della Cal.*, 159–60; *California, Estab. y Prog.*, 9, 10; *Doc. Hist. Mex.*, ser. ii. tom. iii. 443; *Cardona, Memorial*, 46; *Vizcaino, Relacion, 1611–13*, p. 199; see *Hist. North Mex. St.*, i. chap. viii. this series.

voyage and Cermeñon's mishaps appeared in 1613 and was republished in 1723. Drake's adventures were related in scores of popular voyage collections besides the original printed accounts. In 1734 Cabrera Bueno's sailing directions were printed across the Pacific, but the work was not widely circulated.[75] In 1742 Anson, the English privateer, found on a captured galleon the Spanish chart of which I reproduce that part showing the coast of California. There is nothing to indicate that the maker had access to any information not given by Vizcaino and

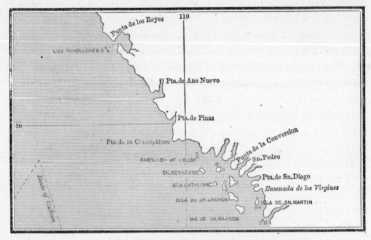

SPANISH CHART, 1742.

[75] *Navegacion Especulativa, y Práctica, con la Explicacion de algvnos instrumentos, qve estan mas en vso en los navegantes, con las reglas necesarias para su verdadero vso*, etc.; *Tabla de las declinaciones del sol, computadas al meridiano de San Bernardino; el modo de navegar por la geometria; por las tablas de rumbos; por la arithmética; por la trigonometria; por el quadrante de reduccion; por los senos logarithmos; y comunes; con los estampas, y figuras pertenecientes á lo dicho, y otros tratados curiosos. Compvesta por el almirante D. Ioseph Gonzalez Cabrera Bueno, piloto mayor de la Carrera de Philipinas, y natural de la isla de Tenerife una de los Canarias, qvien la dedica al M. Ill.tre Señ D. Fernando de Valdés y Tamon*...*Governador y Capitan General de las Islas Philipinas*, etc. Manila, 1792, fol. 11 f. 392 pages. 2 f. The bulk of the work is a treatise on navigation; but Part V., 292–364, is devoted to *derrotas*, containing sailing directions for the various Philippine and Pacific routes; and chap. v., 302–22, relates to the coast from C. Mendocino to Panamá. Portolá and Crespí in 1769 had a copy of this work, or at least were familiar with its contents; but from that time to 1874, when it was described and quoted in the *Overland Monthly* by my assistant, I have found no indication of its having been consulted by any writer.

Cabrera Bueno.[76] In 1757 appeared Venegas' work on Baja California, from which, more than from any other, a popular knowledge of the northern expeditions was derived.[77]

The topic that I designate the Northern Mystery—that is what was thought and written and pictured in maps respecting the coast region above the Californian gulf from 1530 to 1769, the voyages which I have described in this chapter furnishing a slight foundation of actual knowledge on which an imposing structure was reared by imagination, theory, and falsehood—might very plausibly be regarded as a part of the history of California as a country stretching indefinitely from the peninsula to the mythic strait of Anian. Yet much more essential is this subject to the annals of the regions above latitude 42°, and therefore, especially as a general view of the theories involved has already been presented,[78] to avoid undesirable repetition I treat the subject very fully, with a reproduction of many quaint old maps, in another volume relating to the northern countries,[79] confining my remarks here to a very brief statement.

The chief element of the Northern Mystery was the belief in and search for an interoceanic strait separating the Mexican regions from Asia. This strait at first was between South America and the Asiatic main; but was pushed constantly northward by exploration, and was to be found always just beyond the highest latitude visited. Each inlet was the entrance to the strait until the contrary was proved; inlets were discovered or written about that existed only in imagination, and navigators even went so far as to claim boldly that they had sailed through the strait.

[76] *Anson's Voyage*, ed. 1776, 384. Also in *Venegas, Not. Cal.*, iii. 235–6. The dotted line shows the route of the galleons.

[77] Here may be mentioned a report given by the natives of San Luis Obispo to Father Figuer and recorded in *Anza, Diario*, MS., 192–3, in 1776, that 23 years before, in 1753, twelve white men dressed like the Spaniards landed from a boat and were subsequently cast away on the coast and perished.

[78] See *Hist. North Mexican States*, i., this series.

[79] See *Hist. Northwest Coast*, i, chap. ii.–iv., this series.

At first the belief in rich islands on the way to India had been strong, and with reports of the strait, rumors of great kingdoms, cities, amazon isles, gold, and precious stones naturally multiplied.

Next by some strange blunder, apparently of the historian Gomara, the wanderings of Coronado in Arizona, New Mexico, and the far north-east, were transferred to the Pacific coast, and for many years Tiguex, Cicuic, Quivira, and the rest appeared distributed along the shore with names from Cabrillo and Drake. For no other reason apparently than to provide room for all these names, it was customary to make the coast trend but little north of west between 25° and 40°, thence extending north to the strait. One map, however, placed California far north of the strait of Anian, and very near the north pole.

In the third great development of the imaginary geography, California played a more definitely important part than in those mentioned. The New Mexican names were removed from the coast, but California from Cape San Lúcas to latitude 44° became a great island. At first the gulf and peninsula were mapped with remarkable accuracy. But Lok in 1582 turned the coast abruptly eastward above 44°. Ascension in 1603 argued that Aguilar's river in 43° was the entrance of Anian, and probably connected with the gulf. Oñate at the Colorado mouth in 1604 convinced himself that the gulf extended north and east to the Atlantic. Cardona in 1617, having as he believed seen deep water extending far beyond 34°, openly declared the whole country an island. And finally a party of adventurers about 1620 had no difficulty in circumnavigating California. For many years the country was so mapped and described, Nova Albion forming the north end of the island. From 1700 to 1746 the Jesuits labored to restore the belief in a peninsula, and were successful. The last phases of the mystery were those of 1751 and 1774 that the Colorado River sent off a branch to Monterey or San

Francisco, and then the search for northern wonders was transferred to the far north, beyond the farthest limits of our California.

Of the many maps of the early times which I reproduce elsewhere, and of the many more similar ones which I have studied, not one except those presented in this chapter contains any real information about the coast of Upper California. On them the reader will find a coast line varying in its trend from north to west, marked with capes, bays, rivers, and towns, which, except so far as founded on the narratives and maps which I have noted in this chapter, are purely imaginary, the names being traceable to the same narratives and maps, except such as come from Coronado's inland explorations. These maps afford an interesting study, but have no bearing on real discovery. It is not unlikely, however, that useful original maps of Cabrillo's, Cermeñon's, or Vizcaino's explorations may yet come to light, or that in the mean time men will continue to build grave theories of local discovery on the vagaries of the old cosmographers.

CHAPTER IV.

MOTIVES AND PREPARATIONS FOR SPANISH OCCUPATION.

1767–1770.

State of the Spanish Colonies—Accidental Awakening from Apathy—
Revival of Old Motives—Fear of the Russians—Visitador José de
Galvez on the Peninsula—Character and Authority of the Man—
Condition of Affairs in Lower California—Instructions and Plans
of Galvez for the Occupation of San Diego and Monterey—A Four-
fold Expedition by Sea and Land—Vessels, Troops, and Supplies—
Portolá, Rivera, and Serra—Plans for the Conquista Espiritual
—Galvez Consults the Padre Presidente—Sacred Forced Loans—
Active Preparations—Sailing of the Fleet from La Paz and Cape
San Lúcas—March of the Army from the Northern Frontier—
Loss of the 'San José'—Tidings of Success.

In all the historical phases briefly alluded to in the
introductory chapters of this volume, and fully presented in early volumes of this work, I have shown an
epoch of decadence, of varying length in different
provinces, but nowhere much less than half a century
in duration. The adventurous spirit of the conquerors
had for the most part faded away. Poorly equipped
soldiers performed their routine of garrison duty, and
of entradas against frontier savages, in a listless mechanical way that but feebly reflected old-time glories.
Presidios were a kind of public works for the support
of officials, and the drawing of money from the royal
coffers. Missionary zeal had not perhaps materially
abated; but one of the great religious orders had been
driven from the country. The friars were impeded
in their efforts by discouraging difficulties; and the
mission establishments, reduced in number by secularization in the south, by destruction and consolidation

(110)

in the north, decimated in population by pestilence, desertion, and diminished fecundity, ever coveted and disturbed by vicious pobladores, or settlers, had passed the era of their greatest prosperity. The most famous mineral districts had yielded their richest superficial treasures and were now, by reason of savage raids, inefficient working, and the quicksilver monopoly, comparatively abandoned. Commercial, agricultural, and manufacturing industries were now as ever at a low ebb. The native population had lost more than nine tenths of its original numbers, the survivors living quietly in the missions as neophytes, toiling in the mines or on the haciendas practically as slaves, or ranging the mountains as apostates more dreaded than the savages of the frontier. The fables of the Northern Mystery had lost something of their charm, and were no longer potent to inspire at court the fitting-out of armies or fleets. For more than a century and a half no exploring vessel had sailed up the northern coasts. Province after province had settled into that stagnation which sooner or later became the lot of every Spanish colony.

We come now to the partial awakening from this lethargy which caused, or permitted, the occupation of Alta California by Spain in 1769. This occupation was in a certain sense accidental; that is, all the motives leading to it had long existed and had with one exception no new force at this time. For over one hundred and sixty years, or since the voyage of Sebastian Vizcaino in 1602, as much had been known of the country as was now known. This knowledge embraced the general trend and appearance of the coast, the comparative fertility of the country and intelligent docility of its people, the existence, location, and general description of ports San Diego, Monterey, and that under Point Reyes called San Francisco, with a tolerably accurate account of the Santa Bárbara channel and islands. Thus it was no new information about the country that prompted the Californian conquest.

During all those years the Spanish Court had fully realized the importance of extending its dominion over the north and especially over the coast region; but various troubles at home and abroad had encouraged procrastination. Year after year the Manila galleon, coming from the west by the northern route sadly in need of a refitting and relief station, had borne her strained timbers and oriental treasure and scurvy-stricken crew down past the California ports; yet no practical effort was made to possess and utilize those ports, though it was always intended to do so at some future convenient season, and scores of unheeded communications on the subject passed between Mexico and Spain. Tales of the Northern Mystery, of great empires and rich cities, of golden mountains, pearl islands, and giant queens, so effective in the earlier days, had lost, as we have seen, much of their power at court, if not elsewhere; yet little doubt was ever felt that the strait of Anian afforded a northern passage by which a fleet of English cruisers might any day appear from the north-east to seize upon Anian and Quivira, and to ravage more southern coasts. The fear was real enough to the Spaniards, but it was by no means sufficient to rouse them from their apathy, which also successfully withstood the better-founded fear of Russian encroachments from the north-west across rather than through the famous strait; a fear that furnished the only motive for northern conquest which had any new or unusual weight at this time. Finally among operative incentives must be mentioned the missionary ambition to convert northern gentiles. Many times was the king reminded of the rich spiritual harvest to be gathered in California, by friars who never allowed him to forget the secular advantages to be gained by complying with their wishes; but of late the petitions of Jesuits and Franciscans, even for aid and protection in the old frontier districts, had received but little attention. Indeed, it does not appear that the Franciscans were especially urgent at this juncture in their claims to be sent up the coast.

The expulsion of the Jesuits in 1767 fixed the attention of the Spanish and Mexican authorities on the north-west, where were situated the principal missions of the expelled order. California, by reason of the old mysterious charm hanging about the name and country, the strangely exalted value and importance which the Jesuits had always attached to the barren peninsula, and the current tales of immense treasure hidden there by the society, attracted a very large share of this attention. Moreover the explorations of the Russians on the Alaska coasts from 1741 to 1765 were tolerably well known to the Spanish authorities; the danger of Russian encroachment seemed more threatening than in past years; and finally the fitting-out of a military expedition for the relief of Sonora suggested the expediency of taking steps at this time for the protection of the peninsula. Accordingly José de Galvez decided to visit in person the western coast, and not only to superintend preparations for the Sonora campaign, but to cross the gulf, investigate the state of affairs in Baja California, and to adopt such measures as might be found necessary for its safety.

Galvez set out from Mexico for San Blas April 9, 1768. Shortly after his departure Viceroy Croix received from King Cárlos III. orders to the effect that in connection with other precautions against the Russians on the north-west coast, San Diego and Monterey should be occupied and fortified. It had occurred to the monarch, or his advisers, that this would be an opportune time to carry into effect an old scheme, give to the galleons their long-desired harbor, and secure an important coast line from foreign aggression. How the order was worded, whether peremptory in its terms or in the form of a recommendation, does not appear. But that under ordinary circumstances it would have been obeyed with any degree of promptitude may well be doubted. The governor instructed to investigate and report; zealous friars called upon for their views; the Franciscan authorities consulted as to the supply of missionaries; treasury officials questioned about ways and means; preliminary explorations, conflicting reports, petty quarrels—all these with the interminable complication of red-tape communications therewith connected, resulting in vexatious delay, if not in absolute failure, may be readily pictured by the reader of preceding volumes, familiar with the ways of the period.

Fortunately none of these obstacles was in this case interposed. The royal order was clear that San Diego and Monterey should be occupied; the movement was not a complicated or apparently difficult one; it was promptly and effectually executed. The cause of this unusual promptness was in the man who undertook to carry out the order. The whole matter was by the viceroy turned over to José de Galvez, who was, as we have seen, on his way to the Jalisco coast to embark for the peninsula. Galvez had come to Mexico in 1765 as visitador general of New Spain. He was a member of the Council of the Indies, and subsequently minister of state, holding the latter position at the time of his death in 1789. He was invested by Cárlos III. with well nigh absolute powers to investigate and reform the administration of the government in its different branches, particularly in matters pertaining to the royal finances. Independent of the viceroy in many respects by virtue of his position, only nominally subordinate in others, assuming probably some prerogatives that did not belong to him, he was to all intents the highest authority in New Spain. The viceroy Cruillas was removed from office largely because of his opposition to the visitador, and was replaced by the more complaisant Marqués de Croix. If there were any viceregal attributes not originally possessed by Galvez, or arbitrarily assumed by him, they were especially delegated to him by Croix when he started for the west. Thus powerful and independent, Galvez was also remarkable for his practical good sense, business ability, untiring energy, and disregard of all routine formalities that stood in his way. He is entitled to the first place among the pioneers of California though he never set foot in the country.[1]

Galvez sailed from San Blas in May, but was driven to the Tres Marías and back to Mazatlan, not reaching the peninsula till the first week in July. At this time Captain Gaspar de Portolá, an easy-going, popular man, but brave and honest withal, was ruling the country as civil and military governor, while Captain Fernando Javier Rivera y Moncada commanded the garrison of about forty soldiers at Loreto. Portolá was a new-comer of the preceding year; Rivera had been long in the country.[2] The missions were in the

[1] Galvez was 'alcalde de casa y corte, ministro del consejo de Indias, marqués de Sonora, ministro de estado y del despacho universal de Indias.' *Rivera, Gobernantes de Mex.*, 402–16. This is the only authority I have seen for the exact date of the departure from Mexico. In an edict dated Nov. 2, 1768, in Lower California, Galvez signs himself 'del consejo y cámara de Su Magestad en el real y supremo de las Indias, yntendente de exército, visitador general de todos los tribunales de justicia, caxas, y demas ramos de real hacienda de estos reynos, y comisionado con las amplísimas facultades del Ex. Sr. Marqués de Croix.' *Prov. St. Pap.*, MS., i. 6. In his report to the viceroy dated June 10, 1769, he gives as the chief object of the northern expedition the establishment of a presidio to protect the peninsula from the danger always threatened by foreign nations 'y con especialidad las (tentativas) que últimamente han hecho los rusos pretendiendo familiarizarse con la navegacion del mar de Tartaria.' *Palou, Not.*, i. 183. See also for notices concerning Galvez' coming to lower California. *Id.*, i. 248–50. Fear of the Russians as the leading motive for the northern establishment is mentioned in *Armona, Carta*, 1770, in *Doc. Hist. Mex.*, 4th ser., tom. ii. 156–7; *Revilla-Gigedo, Informe de 1793*, according to *Cavo, Tres Siglos*, iii. 117; by Navarrete, introd. to *Sutil y Mex. Viage*, xci.–ii.; and by other writers. Greenhow, *Or. and Cal.*, 105, tells us that Galvez was a man of the most violent and tyrannical disposition. If this be true it is to be regretted that violence and tyranny were not more common qualities in Spanish officials. Hughes, *California*, 119, learns from *Harper's Biog. Cyclopedia*, that Galvez visited California in search of gold-mines discovered by the Jesuits; that his companion, Miguel José de Arenza, became discouraged after a few weeks, recommending the abandonment of the search and accusing Galvez of insanity for continuing it, for which he was cast into prison! Galvez was ill in Sonora after leaving California, and is said to have imprisoned his secretary Azanza, afterward viceroy, for saying that his malady was mental. Such was the origin doubtless of the story. Venegas, *Not. Cal.*, ii. 290, 543–4, iii. 4–14, has something to say on the proposals to settle Alta California and how the matter stood in the middle of the century.

[2] Biographical sketches of these officers will be given later. As authority for the form of Portolá's name I cite his signature in an original letter of 1779

hands of sixteen Franciscan friars from the college of San Fernando in Mexico, who had been in possession only about three months, and were under the direction of Father Junípero Serra as president.[3] There is nothing to show that either governor, or commandant, or president had come to the peninsula with any expectation that their authority was to be soon extended to the northern coast. Yet all doubtless, shared the prevalent impression, amounting to a hope in the minds of the padres, that sooner or later Monterey and San Diego were to be occupied and missionary work begun. Galvez set himself to work most zealously to investigate the condition and supply the needs of the peninsula establishments. His policy and acts in this direction are fully set forth in connection with the annals of Lower California.[4]

But the visitador kept always in mind his project of northern conquest. Rapidly his busy brain matured a plan of action, which had probably been conceived before he left San Blas, and which a few months after his arrival he was ready to carry into execution. Means and methods were fortunately under his exclusive control, and he had resolved on an expedition in four divisions, two by sea and two by land, to start separately, but all to meet at San Diego, and thence press on to Monterey. Thus a practical knowledge of both routes would be gained, transportation economized, and risks of failure lessened. Available for the sea-going divisions were two small vessels, the *paquebotes*, or snows, *San Cárlos* and *San Antonio*, under the command of captains Vicente Vila and Juan Perez, experienced *pilotos* of the royal navy. They had been•built

---

among the MSS. of Molera; *Portolá, Diario del Viage*, 1769, MS., a contemporary copy; Ortega in *Santa Clara, Arch. Parr.*, MS., 48; *Palou, Vida;* and *Monterey, Estracto de Noticias;* though Serra wrote it Portala in *San Diego, Lib. Mision*, MS., 63; and in *Palou, Noticias*, it is printed Portola.

[3] Father Serra was a native of Mallorca, 55 years of age, who had come to America in 1749, had served as a missionary in the Sierra Gorda district for nine years, and about the same time in the college, or travelling as comisario of the inquisition. *Palou, Vida*, 1–13, 43–6. See preceding note.

[4] See *Hist. North Mexican States*, vol. i., this series.

for the transportation of troops to Sonora, and the co-mandante at San Blas had orders to fit them out and send them over to La Paz with the least possible delay. The land expeditions under Portolá and Rivera were to march from Santa María on the northern frontier. An additional military force would be required, to supply which Colonel Elizondo was instructed to send over twenty-five Catalan volunteers[5] under Lieutenant Pedro Fages. The peninsular missions must assist at the birth of the new ones, by furnishing church ornaments, live-stock, and other supplies to the full extent of their ability.

From his head-quarters at Santa Ana Galvez superintended the collection at La Paz and Cape San Lúcas of everything that was to be forwarded by sea. He sent north supplies for the land expedition, and appointed Captain Rivera, a man practically acquainted with the country, as comisario with instructions to proceed northward from mission to mission, and take from each all the live-stock, provisions, and implements that could be spared. Likewise he was to recruit some people for the new settlements, and bring everything to Santa María with all possible despatch. Rivera set out upon this work in August or September 1768.[6]

The proposed occupation of the northern country, however, was to be spiritual as well as military. The natives were to be converted after their subjection, and not only presidios but missions were to be founded. Preparations having been effectually set on foot *en lo secular*, it was now time for the spiritual aspect of the scheme to receive attention. Accordingly the padre president was invited to come down to Santa Ana for a personal interview with the visitador, as he did, arriving at the end of October. Serra doubtless had before this time made himself pretty well acquainted with what Galvez was doing and pro-

[5] The Catalonia company, 1st battalion, 2d regiment, light infantry, had left Cádiz May 27, 1767. *Prov. Stat. Pap.*, MS., i. 2.
[6] Palou, *Not.* i. 252, says August; but in *Vida*, 65, September.

posed to do; but he listened patiently to the visitador's explanations, and then not only expressed his
approval of the scheme, but announced his intention
to join the land expedition in person. It was thought
best to found, besides the missions at San Diego and
Monterey, another at some intermediate point,[7] and
still another on the frontier of Lower California in
order to facilitate communication between the old
establishments and the new. Three priests were to go
north by sea and three by land; and in order that so
many might be spared three were drawn from the
college of San Fernando. Serra agreed with Galvez
that church furniture, ornaments, and vestments,
must be supplied by the old missions. Surplus grain
and other articles of food were to be taken as gifts,
while live-stock and implements must be regarded as
loans, and as such repaid in kind. This burden, although in accord with the past policy of both Jesuits
and Franciscans that old missions must support the
new, might have met with opposition had there been
any to oppose.

The king's and viceroy's representative, the civil
and military governor, and the president of the
missions were in accord on the subject. The natives
were not consulted, and the priests were new-comers,
not very deeply interested in the country or in their
respective missions.[8] Galvez and Serra had only
themselves to convince that the measure was right,
and the task was not a hard one. The Franciscans were bound by their vows, said the visitador,
the president echoing approval, to spread the faith,
not to accumulate wealth or build up grand establishments—a doctrine that subsequently lost something
of its force in the land whither they were going. Serra
took a list of the church property that Galvez had
already collected, and promised to continue this sacred

[7] According to *Palou*, *Vida*, 57, this intermediate mission was to be called
San Buenaventura.
[8] Palou, *Not.*, 1. 43–56, claims also that Galvez, the viceroy, and the king
fully repaid the missions later for all that was taken.

though enforced loan in the north, as he did some months later.[9]

During the month of November, Father Junípero made a tour of the southern missions, completing arrangements for secularization which should release two more priests for duty in the north. A slaughter of wild cattle in the south furnished meat for the first sea expedition. Stores of all kinds were collected at La Paz. Galvez issued a proclamation naming St Joseph the patron saint of the adventure,[10] and shortly after Lieutenant Fages arrived from Guaymas with twenty-five Catalan volunteers of the *compañía franca*, who were to go by sea as a first detachment of the invading army to overcome gentile battalions that might oppose the landing and progress of the Spaniards.

[9] Palou gives long lists of all the church property taken from each mission, which I have thought it worth while to combine into the following, which is as nearly accurate as the author's occasional use of the terms 'several' and 'a few' will permit: 7 church bells, 11 small altar bells, 23 altar cloths, 5 choir copes, 3 surplices, 4 carpets, 2 coverlets, 3 *roquetes*, 3 veils, 19 full sets sacred vestments, different colors, 6 old single vestments, 17 *albas*, albs, or white tunics, 10 *palios*, palliums, or short cloaks, 10 *amitos*, amices, or pieces of linen, 10 chasubles, 12 girdles, 6 *hopas*, or cassocks, 18 altar-linens, or *corporales*, 21 *purificadores*, purificatories, or chalice cloths, 1 pall cloth, 11 pictures of the virgin, 12 silver or gilded chalices, 1 cibary, or silver goblet, 7 *crismeras*, or silver phials for chrism, or sacred oil, 1 *custodia*, or silver casket for holy wafers, 5 *conchas*, or silver conchs for baptism, 6 *incensarios*, or silver censers with incense dish and spoon, 12 pairs of *vinageras*, silver and glass cruets for wine and water, 1 silver cross with pedestal, 1 box containing Jesus, Mary, and Joseph, 1 copper platter for baptismal font, 2 copper baptismal fonts, 29 brass, copper, and silver candlesticks, 1 copper dipper for holy water, 1 silver jar, 1 tin wafer box, 3 statues, 2 silver suns or dazzlers, 4 irons for making wafers, coins and rings for *arras* at marriages, 5 *aras*, or consecrated stones, 4 missals and a missal-stand, 1 Betancurt's Manual; also quantities of handkerchiefs, curtains, and tinsels; with laces, silks, and other stuffs to be made into altar upholstery, taken from the royal *almacen* at Loreto. This church property was for the most part sent by water to the new establishments. Many of the old vestments and church ornaments, some dating back perhaps to this first invoice, are yet preserved in the missions. See *Visit to Southern California*, MS.

[10] In his proclamation, dated Nov. 21st, and preserved in *Arch. Santa Bárbara*, MS., i. 15, 16, Galvez refers to the driving away of the locusts in 1767, at San José del Cabo by aid of St Joseph's image, as a reason why the Monterey expedition is to be under him as patron. He charges the priests to say mass on the 19th of every month, and the rogative litany while the expeditions continue, imploring through the intercession of the saint divine protection, and this in addition to the regular *salve* to María, patron of all the Californian conversions, and also in addition to the regular *fiesta* of San José. On the same day he calls the attention of Padre Lasuen to this matter. Letter in *Id.*, xi. 369-70, with another letter of Nov. 23d, relating to supplies from the Loreto warehouse.

Early in December the *San Cárlos* arrived at La Paz from San Blas. She had been hastily and, like all Pacific coast craft of the time, imperfectly constructed, had encountered stormy weather, and was in a leaky condition. She was already partially laden with effects for the north from the San Blas warehouses; but had to be unloaded, careened, and loaded again, all of which labor Galvez personally superintended, often lending a hand in the stowing of an unwieldy package, greatly to the encouragement of his men and to the admiration of the chroniclers.[11] The 9th of January 1769 the *San Cárlos* was ready. All who were going in her confessed, heard mass, partook of the communion, and then listened to a parting address from Galvez. The visitador reminded his hearers that theirs was a glorious mission, that they were going to plant the cross among the heathen, and charged them in the name of God, the king, and the viceroy to respect their priests and maintain peace and union among themselves. Finally Junípero Serra pronounced a formal blessing on the pilgrims, their vessel, the flag, the crew, and on Father Parron, to whom was intrusted the spiritual care of the company. The ceremony over, the *San Cárlos* put to sea. Galvez in the *Concepcion* accompanied her down the gulf from La Paz to Cape San Lúcas, watching her until she doubled the point and struck bravely northward before a fair wind.[12]

While the president returned to Loreto Galvez gave his attention to the *San Antonio*, which was to follow the *San Cárlos*. Touching at La Paz the 15th of January, she arrived at Cape San Lúcas the 25th.[13]

[11] Palou, *Vida*, 60, notes that Galvez was particularly zealous in packing for San Buenaventura which he called his mission, and was delighted at having done his work quicker than Padre Junípero who packed for his mission of San Cárlos.

[12] Crespí, in Palou, *Not.*, ii. 149, says the *San Cárlos* sailed January 10th. Leaving La Paz on the 9th, she may have been last seen by Galvez on the 10th, though Palou, *Not.*, i. 216, says it was the 11th. For further details respecting the officers, men, cargo, instructions, and plans, see description of the voyage in the next chapter.

[13] Galvez' letter in *Prov. St. Pap.*, MS., i. 44. Palou, *Vida*, 61, tells us that the *San Antonio* had gone to San Lúcas because prevented by the wind from reaching La Paz.

Her condition being no better than that of the *capitana*, or flag-ship, she was unloaded and careened, and so was not ready for sea till the 15th of February. Then, after an exhortation by Galvez and the usual religious ceremonies, Perez shook out his sails and with a fair wind struck northward from San José del Cabo. "God seems to reward my only virtue, my faith," writes Galvez to Fages, "for all goes well." [14]

Meanwhile active preparations for the land expedition were being made in the north. Rivera had left Santa Ana in September, as we have seen. On his way northward he had visited each mission and had taken such live-stock and other needed supplies as he and the different friars thought could be spared. The 200 cattle, 140 horses, 46 mules, and two asses, with various implements and articles of food thus acquired,[15] were collected at first at the frontier mission of Santa María, but the pasturage there being insufficient for his animals, Rivera soon transferred his camp to Velicatá eight or ten leagues farther north.[16] From this point he sent word to Galvez at Santa Ana and to Serra at Loreto that he would be ready to start for San Diego in March. The president had returned to Loreto at the end of January, and had since been busily engaged in his preparations, forwarding such articles as he could get to La Paz or to Santa María according as they were to go by water or by land. On receipt of Rivera's message he at once notified Fray Juan Crespí, who was to accompany the first land expedition, to join the force at Velicatá without delay. Crespí, an intimate personal friend as well as

[14] *Prov. St. Pap.*, MS., i. 46.

[15] The articles, not including the Loreto contribution, were 54 *aparejos*, or pack-saddles, 28 leather bags, 1 case of bottles, 13 sides of leather, 28 arrobas of figs, 1 bale and 4 arrobas of sugar, 340 arrobas *tasajo*, or dried meat, 28 arrobas flour, 35 almudes pinole, 21 fanegas wheat, 23 arrobas raisins, 4 cargas biscuits, 10 arrobas lard, 2 jugs and 12 bottles wine. Eatables were gifts. *Palou, Not.*, i. 43–5. Galvez sent some implements and seeds. *Id. Vida*, 60.

[16] He reached Velicatá before Dec. 20th on which date he wrote to Galvez. *Prov. St. Pap.*, MS., i. 45.

obedient subordinate of Serra,[17] accordingly left his
mission of Purísima the 26th of February and reached
Rivera's camp on the 22d of March, having been
joined at Santa María by Padre Lasuen who had
journeyed from San Francisco de Borja in order to
bestow the customary blessing on the departing pilgrims. Everything was in readiness, and two days
after the coming of the friars Rivera's little army
began its march into the land of gentiles.

Portolá with the second division of the land expedition was already on his way to the northern frontier,
having left Loreto on the ninth of March;[18] but he
was obliged to await at Santa María the transportation from San Luis Bay of supplies which had been
sent up by water.[19] Serra was unable to accompany
the governor because his work of collecting church
utensils and ornaments was not yet completed, and
he was besides suffering from a sore foot, obtained
long before on a walk from Vera Cruz to Mexico,
which made it doubtful to every one but himself
whether he would be able to go with the expedition
at all. However, he promised to follow as soon as
possible, and meanwhile sent Campa from San Ignacio
in his place. At the end of March, though still very
lame, he was ready to start, and after spending several
days at San Javier with Francisco Palou,[20] whom he
appointed president of the old missions during his
absence, he journeyed slowly and painfully northward,
stopping at each mission except Mulegé, and finally

[17] Crespí was like Serra a native of Mallorca, had come to America in the
same vessel, and had served 16 years in the Sierra Gorda missions. He
was at this time 48 years of age. Many old Californians say they were
accustomed to hear his name pronounced by their fathers Crespí, and it is so
written in *Portolá, Diario* and other MSS.

[18] Sergeant José F. Ortega, who was with Portolá on this march, says that
he left Loreto March 14. *Prov. St. Pap.*, MS., vi. 171. According to a fragment in Ortega's handwriting in *Sta. Clara, Arch. Parroquia*, MS., 48, the
date was March 14th or 16th. Palou makes it the 9th.

[19] They had been sent by the *canoas San Ignacio* and *San Borja*, which
returned to San Lúcas before Feb. 14th. *Prov. St. Pap.*, MS., i. 45.

[20] Palou was now 47 years of age. He had been a pupil of Serra in Spain,
was perhaps also a native of Mallorca, had come with him to America, and
had served with him in the Sierra Gorda.

joining the governor's party at Santa María the 5th
of May. The whole company left Santa María on the
11th, and arrived at Velicatá the 14th.[21] The same
day a mission was founded there under the name of
San Fernando, Campa being left in charge; then on
the 15th of May Portolá with the second land expedition set out and followed the track of Rivera.

Thus within a period of four months Galvez had
despatched the four divisions, and only an extraordinary series of misfortunes could prevent the successful
occupation of San Diego and Monterey. He had not,
however, quite reached the limit of his efforts in that
direction, since he had caused to be built at San Blas
a new vessel, especially intended for northern coast
service, and named for the patron saint of the expedition the *San José*. She arrived at Cape San Lúcas on
the 13th of February, two days before the departure
of the *San Antonio*,[22] but it was found necessary to
overhaul her for repairs at the cape harbor, whence
she was convoyed by Galvez in a sloop to Loreto in
April. In May she bore the visitador across the gulf
to the Rio Mayo, and brought back part of a cargo of
supplies to Loreto, where she completed her lading
and sailed for San Diego on the 16th of June.[23] She
was to have touched at San José del Cabo to take on
board Father Murguía and some church ornaments;
but nothing was seen of her there or elsewhere, until
three months later she appeared at Loreto with a
broken mast and otherwise disabled. Word was sent
to Galvez in Sonora, and he ordered her to San Blas
for repairs. The cargo was taken out and sent in
boats to Cape San Lúcas, except a quantity of corn
left on board. A trunk of vestments was sent to
Velicatá by land, and the vessel sailed for San Blas

[21] *Portolá, Diario*, MS., 1, 2. The leader and friars went in advance and
reached Velicatá on the 13th.

[22] Galvez, in *Prov. St. Pap.*, MS., i. 45.

[23] Palou, *Vida*, 63, says the vessel was never heard of again, and it is only
in his other work, *Noticias*, i. 54, 276-9, in which, however, he says nothing
of her trip to Sonora, that he describes her subsequent movements.

in October. The unfortunate *paquebot* came back
next year, and sailed from San José del Cabo in May
with a cargo of supplies and a double crew to reënforce the other vessels, but without Murguía, who
was detained by illness. Nothing was ever heard
subsequently of either vessel or crew. The captain's
name was Callegan.

The proceedings of Galvez and other events in the
peninsula after the departure of the northern expeditions have been fully narrated elsewhere;[24] and there
is but little in connection with those annals for several
years that has any bearing on the new establishments
of San Diego and Monterey. As early as July 1769,
the *San Antonio* returned to San Blas, and on the 7th
of September a schooner brought up to Loreto news
that all the expeditions had reached San Diego.[25] The
25th of February 1770 Rivera returned to Velicatá
for cattle and other supplies left there, with San Diego
news to the 11th of February, and with reports for
Galvez and the viceroy on the failure of the first
attempt to find Monterey. A month later two natives
arrived from San Diego with April letters to Palou
and the viceroy which reached Loreto late in May.[26]
The 2d of August messengers arrived from Monterey
at Todos Santos, bringing to Governor Armona and
Father Palou news of the founding of San Cárlos
mission. The event was celebrated by a mass of
thanksgiving and by a discharge of fire-arms at Santa
Ana. From Portolá who returned by sea the good
news was received in Mexico about the same time.[27]
I have already noticed the despatching of the ill-fated
San José in May 1770. Palou, the acting president,

[24] See *Hist. North Mexican States*, vol. i., this series.
[25] Aug. 20, 1769, Juan B. Anza writes from Tubac, Sonora, to Gov. Pineda
that an Indian from the Gila has reported that a nation beyond the Cocomari-
copas met four Spaniards with guns, whom the writer thinks may be part of
the Monterey expedition. *Doc. Hist. Mex.*, ser. iv. tom. ii. 117-18.
[26] Gov. Armona of Baja California writes from Santa Ana July 19, 1770,
that he arrived June 13th, and found good news of the northern expeditions,
including the discovery of the 'prodigiosísimo puerto' called San Francisco
and which may be Monterey. *Doc. Hist. Mex.*, ser. iv. tom. ii. 156-7.
[27] *Dept. St. Pap., Ben. Mil.*, MS., lxxxvii. 10.

kept himself in constant communication with Serra, and in the midst of all his cares and vexations respecting peninsular affairs, never lost sight of the new northern establishments.[28]

[28] On preparations in the peninsula for the northern expeditions the standard authority is *Palou, Noticias,* i. 29–56, 247–79, and *Id., Vida de Junipero Serra,* 57–75, besides the original sources of information to which I have referred on special points in past notes. So large and complete is my collection of original, and especially manuscript, authorities on California history that I shall not attempt any systematically complete reference to all the printed works which touch upon each point or each brief epoch, but which give information at second hand only. I shall refer to such works to point out errors worth noticing, or for other special purposes; and I shall also for bibliographical purposes give occasional lists of these secondary authorities bearing on definite historic periods. For such a list on the occupation and early mission history of California see end of this volume.

CHAPTER V.

OCCUPATION OF SAN DIEGO—EXPEDITIONS BY SEA AND LAND.

1769.

VOYAGE OF PEREZ IN THE 'SAN ANTONIO'—ARRIVAL IN SAN DIEGO BAY—
A MIRACLE—DISCOVERY OF SANTA CRUZ ISLAND—WAITING FOR THE
CAPITANA—VOYAGE OF VILA IN THE 'SAN CÁRLOS'—FAGES AND HIS
CATALAN VOLUNTEERS—INSTRUCTIONS BY GALVEZ—A SCURVY-STRICKEN
CREW—A PEST-HOUSE AT SAN DIEGO—ARRIVAL OF RIVERA Y MON-
CADA—CRESPÍ'S DIARY—CAMP AND HOSPITAL MOVED TO NORTH SAN
DIEGO—COMING OF PORTOLÁ AND JUNÍPERO SERRA—REUNION OF THE
FOUR EXPEDITIONS—THANKSGIVING TO SAINT JOSEPH—THE 'SAN AN-
TONIO' SENT TO SAN BLAS—PORTOLÁ SETS OUT FOR MONTEREY—FOUND-
ING OF SAN DIEGO MISSION—A BATTLE WITH THE NATIVES—A MISSION
WITHOUT CONVERTS.

TURN now to the northern coasts, to the bay of San
Diego, whose waters had lain for more than a century
and a half undisturbed by European keel, whose
shores had known no tread of iron heel since Sebastian Vizcaino was there. The native inhabitants yet
preserved a traditional remembrance of white and
bearded visitors, kept alive perhaps by an occasional
rumor wafted overland from the south-east, and by
distant glimpses of the white-winged galleon which
year after year bore its oriental treasure down past
this port, which, so far as can be known, was never
entered. And now the aboriginal solitude is destined
to be forever broken.

The 11th of April 1769[1] a Spanish vessel appears
and anchors in the bay. It is the *San Antonio* sometimes called *El Príncipe,* and is commanded by Juan

---

[1] Crespí, in *Palou, Not.,* ii. 149, gives the date as April 14th. Humboldt,
Essai. Pol., 318, says it was in April 1763.

Perez, an experienced Mallorcan who has seen service in the Pacific as *piloto*, or master, of the Manila galleon. She had been despatched from Cape San Lúcas in February, after religious services and a parting address from the visitador general José de Galvez, the highest official who had visited the north-western coast since the days of Hernan Cortés. On board are the friars Juan Vizcaino and Francisco Gomez, a few carpenters and blacksmiths, then there is the crew, whose number is not known, and a miscellaneous cargo of supplies for two settlements which it is designed to found on the upper coast. Under the protecting care of Saint Anthony of Pádua, patron, indeed, of the day of sailing as well as of the vessel herself, the voyage of twenty-four days has been a prosperous one, the only misfortune recorded being the illness of a few seamen who suffered from scurvy, a scourge rarely escaped by voyagers of the period.

The first land made was an island in the Santa Bárbara Channel, which was named Santa Cruz from the honesty of the natives in restoring an iron cross left on shore. Here they received the best of treatment and obtained plenty of fish and water in exchange for beads; but their observations showed that they were above the supposed latitude of San Diego,[2] and Perez accordingly returned southward along the coast until he passed Point Guijarros and entered the desired port, as we have seen, on the 11th of April. Here also the natives are kind to the strangers,[3] but Perez finds no sign of Vila, his superior in command of the

[2] According to observations the vessel was in 34° 40', but really in about 34°; while San Diego, supposed to be in 34°, *Cabrera Bueno, Navegacion*, 305, was nearly a degree and a half further south.

[3] The natives at first took the vessel for a great whale, but soon discovered their error, and regarded it as the forerunner of wonderful things, especially as an eclipse of the sun and an earthquake occurred simultaneously with the arrival of the vessel. This story was told by them later, and is recorded by Serra, *Representacion sobre Misiones, 21 de Mayo 1773*, MS., who says the Spaniards noticed neither eclipse nor *temblor*, and regards it as a miracle by which, though the padres could not yet begin their teachings, 'comenzaron á predicar prodigiosamente á aquellos miseros gentiles las criaturas insensibles del Cielo y de la tierra.' These phenomena are also noticed, from the same source, in the *S. F. Bulletin*, Oct. 12, 1865.

flag-ship, which had sailed from the peninsula more than a month before the *San Antonio,* and which he had hoped to find at San Diego. Neither are there any tidings to be obtained of the overland party to the same port. Under these circumstances the captain's orders call for a stay of twenty days before proceeding to Monterey. As there are no soldiers, and as the instructions of Galvez had been to run no risks, the friars do not land, nor is any attempt made to explore the country. Two days before the twenty days elapse, that is on the 29th of April, the tardy *capitana* comes in sight.

The *San Cárlos,* otherwise called the *Golden Fleece,* is commanded by Vicente Vila, a native of Andalucía, and sailing-master of the first class in the royal Spanish navy.[4] She had sailed from La Paz having on board Vila, a mate not named, Alférez Miguel Costansó[5] acting as cosmographer, and a crew of twenty-three sailors and two boys. Also on board were Lieutenant Pedro Fages, with twenty-five Catalan volunteers, including a sergeant and corporal; Hernando Parron, a Franciscan friar; Pedro Prat, a Frenchman and surgeon of the royal army; four cooks and two blacksmiths—sixty-two persons in all; with supplies for eight months or a year, implements of various kinds, and a quantity of church furniture and other mission property.[6] All the proper religious ceremonies had

[4] Vila's appointment by Galvez, dated La Paz, Dec. 27, 1768, names as 'Capitan, Piloto Mayor, y comandante del *San Cárlos,* á D. Vicente Vila, piloto de los primeros de la Real Armada, por las apreciables circunstancias que en él concurren, con la jurisdiccion y prerogativas que le corresponden por la Real Ordenanza de Marina,' with $120 per month and $30 additional if the voyage is successful. Officers and crews of both vessels are ordered under severe penalties to obey Vila as commander of the capitana. *Prov. St. Pap.,* MS., i. 66–8.

[5] Printed Costansó in *Monterey, Estracto de Noticias,* and so signed by himself in several autographs now before me. Often printed Costanzo or Constanzo.

[6] The manifest of the *San Cárlos* signed by Vila on Jan. 5th is preserved in *Prov. St. Pap.,* MS., i. 13–21. The list of supplies includes: 4,676 lbs. meat, 1,783 lbs. fish, 230 bush. maize, 500 lbs. lard, 7 jars vinegar, 5 tons wood, 1,275 lbs. brown sugar, 5 jars brandy, 6 *tanates* figs, 3 *tanates* raisins, 2 *tanates* dates 300 lbs. red pepper, 125 lbs. garlic, 6,678 lbs. bread, common, 690 lbs. bread, white, 945 lbs. rice, 945 lbs. chickpeas, 17 bushels salt, 3,800 gallons water, 450 lbs. cheese, 6 jars Cal. wine, 125 lbs. sugar, 275 lbs. chocolate, 10 hams,

been attended to at the start; Junípero Serra, president of the California missions, had invoked the blessing of heaven upon this first detachment of pacificators; Miguel de Azanza, subsequently viceroy of New Spain, had acted as shipping-clerk at the embarkation of the supplies; and José de Galvez, the foremost man in America, had not only aided in the lading and delivered a parting address, but had accompanied the vessel to the cape, seeing her safely headed for San Diego.

Yet despite such favorable auspices the *San Cárlos* was unfortunate. The water-casks leaked and nothing but water of a bad quality could be obtained at Cedros Island. This greatly aggravated the scurvy, always prevalent on the coast, and soon no sailors were left with sufficient strength to work the vessel or to launch the boats for fresh water. Vila, in accordance with his instructions,[7] was obliged to go up the coast to 34° as had Perez before him, the increased distance and cold adding greatly to his troubles. At

11 bottles oil, 2 lbs. spice, 25 smoked beef-tongues, 6 live cattle, 575 lbs. lentils, 112 lbs. candles, 1,300 lbs. flour, 15 sacks bran, 495 lbs. beans, 16 sacks coal, hens for the sick and for breeding, $1,000 in money, etc. The brandy and cheese were for stormy weather only, the former being considered conducive to scurvy if used habitually on this coast. The wine was for cabin use, or for the missions. Many of the articles named, or specified portions thereof, were intended for the missions, or for the land expedition; and part of the *panocha* was to be used in sweetening the temper of the natives.

[7] Galvez' instructions to Capt. Vila, dated Jan. 5th, are preserved in *Prov. St. Pap.*, MS., i. 22–31, under the title, 'Instruction to be observed by D. Vicente Vila, first-class master in the royal navy and Captain Comandante of the *paquebot* of his majesty called the *San Cárlos* alias *Toison de Oro* in the voyage which by divine aid this vessel is to make to the ports of San Diego and Monterey, situated on the northern coast of this peninsula of Californias in 33° and 37° of latitude.' The different articles of this document are in substance as follows: 1st. The object is to establish the Catholic faith, to extend Spanish domain, to check the ambitious schemes of a foreign nation, and to carry out a plan formed by Felipe III. as early as 1606. Therefore no pains can be spared without offense to God, the king, and the country. 2d. The vessel being new, strong, and well supplied for over a year, to be followed by the *San Antonio* with additional supplies, having only 300 leagues to make, having a strong military force, and going to a land whose natives are docile, have no arms but bows and arrows, and are without boats, there can be no excuse *en lo humano* for failure. 3d. Vila is to sail Jan. 7th, weather permitting, keep out to sea according to his judgment in search of favorable winds, to take careful observations, and to stand in shore at 34°, San Diego being in 33° according to the cédula of Felipe III., and being easy to find by Vizcaino's narrative enclosed with this document in print in the third volume.

last, however, a tedious navigation of a hundred and
ten days was ended by the *San Cárlos,* almost miraculously it would seem, by turning into San Diego
Bay the 29th of April.[8]

Perez has already deposited a letter at the foot of
a cross on shore, and has completed his preparations
to sail on the 1st of May, when the *San Cárlos* appears and drops anchor, but without lowering a boat.
A visit to the vessel soon reveals the fact that all
hands are down with scurvy. The sick are at once
removed by the crew of the *San Antonio* to the shore,
where they are sheltered by sail tents and receive
from Dr Prat and the three friars such care as circumstances allow. It does not clearly appear that
more than two had succumbed at sea; but now death
begins its ravages in the canvas pest-house on the
beach.[9] Perez' men are attacked by the scourge;

of the *Noticia de Californias* (that is in *Venegas, Not. Cal.,* iii. 85–9). 4th. If
Capt. Rivera be found at San Diego, the mission effects are to be landed, and
such other supplies as Rivera may need, the rest to be taken by sea to Monterey. 5th. If Rivera and the land force have not arrived Vila is to wait 15
or 20 days at most, obtaining wood and water, while Fages and Costansó
explore the country. 6th. After the 20 days, or on Rivera's arrival, the *San
Cárlos* is to sail for Monterey, with the *San Antonio* if she be there. 7th.
The strictest discipline is to be kept, every precaution taken for safety, and
any outrage on the natives to be severely punished. 8th. The sailors are to
aid the soldiers in building a temporary fort at Monterey. 9th. The natives
are to be conciliated with *panocha* and trifles, but to be very closely watched,
and to be induced to look on weapons as a kind of adornment. 10th. *Panocha,*
cloths, etc., are to be given to Fages and Rivera on their demand, a receipt
being taken. 11th. A report is to be sent to Galvez from San Diego by land,
and from Monterey one of the vessels is to return to San Diego with despatches to go overland, or if only one vessel is there she is to come as soon
as safety will permit and return immediately. 12th. Vila to remain in the
best fitted of the two vessels at Monterey until the *San José* shall arrive.
13th. The other vessel is to remain at San Diego long enough to deliver
despatches, etc., and is then to continue her voyage to C. San Lúcas and San
Blas with duplicate despatches. 14th. Coasts about Monterey are to be
explored, especially port and river Carmelo, and if possible the port of San
Francisco said to be in 38° 30'. To this end Vila will give all possible aid to
Costansó and Fages. 15th. On the arrival of the *San José,* Vila in his vessel
will return to San Blas, exploring the coast in order to confirm or correct
Cabrera Bueno's *derrotero,* the best extant. *Navegacion Especulativa y prác-
tica,* Manila, 1734.

[8] According to *Palou, Not.,* i. 262, she anchored on the 30th.

[9] Judge Hayes, *Emig. Notes,* MS., 174, thinks that the vessels were
anchored off what is now New Town, between the two wharves, and that
Punta de los Muertes, or Dead Men's Point, derived its name from the burial

and of about ninety sailors, soldiers, and mechanics considerably less than one third survive, though none of the officers or friars die or are even attacked so far as the records show.[10] Of course the continuation of the voyage to Monterey is not possible under the circumstances. Neither can Fages and Costansó do otherwise than disregard their instructions[11] calling for a preliminary exploration of the surrounding

of the scurvy-stricken sailors. And such is probably the fact, for the name appears on Pantoja's chart of 1784 in *Sutil y Mexicana, Viages, Atlas*, No. 5. See also *Bancroft's Pers. Obs.*, MS., 14.

[10] There is some confusion respecting numbers, increased by our ignorance of the exact force on the *San Antonio*. Palou says, *Not.*, i. 262, that from the *San Cárlos* 5 of the crew and 12 soldiers survived; while of the other crew all but 7 died. Again, ii. 151, he says that before May 14th 9 of the *San Cárlos* had died. Again, i. 282, that the *San Antonio*, sailing July 6th (or 9th), lost 9 men on the voyage, arriving at San Blas *sin gente para marear*. And finally, that 5 sailors and 2 boys remained on the *San Cárlos* after July 14th, at which time 29 sailors and soldiers had been buried on the beach. In a letter dated July 3d, Serra states that all the crew of the *San Cárlos* died except one man and a cook, and 8 died from the *San Antonio*. *Palou, Vida*, 76. He writes in the San Diego death register, *San Diego, Lib. Mision*, MS., 63–5, that half of Fages' soldiers died; that Parron at first and himself later kept a record of deaths which was destroyed with the mission a few years later, and that the deaths within a few months amounted to over 60, including some Indians. The good friar hopes the names are inscribed in the 'book of life.' In *Loreto, Lib. Mision*, MS., 129, the Indian Juan Álvarez is mentioned as having been one of the *San Antonio's* men, who died at San Diego on June 25th.

[11] Galvez' instructions to Fages, dated like those to Vila January 5th, and found in *Prov. St. Pap.*, MS., i. 31–43, are substantially as follows: 1st. Fages, military chief of the sea expedition, is to exercise the same authority on land until Gov. Portolá arrives; that is he is to be Rivera's superior, and is to superintend the economical distribution of rations. 2d. The soldiers are to aid the sailors, and Fages must see that harmony and discipline are preserved. 3d. Three fires on the hill north-west of San Diego will be a signal to the vessel that Rivera has already arrived. 4th. If Rivera has not arrived at San Diego, Fages is to use every possible means by exploration and inquiry to learn his whereabouts and aid his march. 5th. Before Rivera's arrival the natives, and especially chiefs, are to be prepared so far as possible by Fages and Parron for the founding of a mission. 6th. The natives being friendly, and Costansó having selected a proper site, Fages may erect some buildings, and thus prepare for Rivera's coming with soldiers for a mission guard; but if Rivera has already attended to this, Fages is to render any needed aid with the least possible delay to the vessel. 7th. If Rivera has not come, and the *San Antonio* arrives, the latter vessel is to be left at San Diego, with half the soldiers, to attend to the preceding instructions, while the *San Cárlos*, with Fages, goes on to Monterey. Galvez also wrote to Fages on February 14th, *Id.*, 46–7, directing him to put half his men on board the *San Antonio*, 8th. At Monterey the Indians are to be pacified, a landing effected with all caution, and a camp fortified with ditch, *estacada*, and cannons on a site chosen by the engineer, and under the guns of the vessel. 9th. The natives are to be impressed with the advantages of peace and salvation and protection from foreign insult offered by the Spaniards. 10th. The natives, if friendly, to be told of Rivera's approach and induced to send guides. 11th. Fages and

country. For two weeks the well have more than enough to do in caring for the sick and in burying the dead, and then on the 14th of May other Spaniards come to their relief.

These are Rivera y Moncada with his twenty-five *soldados de cuera*,[12] or cuirassiers, from the presidio of Loreto; also the priest Juan Crespí, the *pilotin*[13] José Cañizares, three muleteers, and a band of christianized natives from the northern missions of Baja California. Of these last there were forty-two in number at the outset, whose duty it was to make roads, assist the muleteers, and perform the drudgery. This first division of the land expedition had started from Velicatá in March, and had been fifty-one days on the way, the distance being given at the time as one hundred and twenty-one leagues. Two diaries were kept and are extant, one by Crespí and the other by Cañizares.[14] Both are very complete, but neither affords matter of much interest to the historical student, since it could serve no good purpose to repeat the details of that monotonous march.

Many localities were named and their latitudes

Costansó may, if deemed best, send soldiers with the natives to meet Rivera. 12th. Fages may use force to overcome resistance if necessary. 13th. The natives are never to be fully trusted, but always watched, for the 'common enemy' will surely incite them to mischief. 14th. Both soldiers and sailors to work on the fort. 15th. Constant precautions against danger, notwithstanding peaceful appearances. 16th. Trade with the natives is allowed, but no knives or other weapons must be given them. 17th. Fages is to send full reports to Galvez down to the time of Portolá's taking the command. Great reliance is placed in the 'activity, honor, and prudence' of Fages and Costansó. Galvez adds a note to the effect that the presidio and mission at Monterey are to be called by the glorious name of San Cárlos.

[12] These soldiers derived their name from the *cuera*, or cuirass, which in California was a sleeveless jacket made of 7 or 8 thicknesses of deer or sheep skin quilted. From the Latin *corium*. The metallic cuirass was called in Spanish *coraza*.

[13] A *pilotin* was the master's mate on a vessel. Cañizares accompanied the land force to take observations and write a diary.

[14] *Cañizares, Diario ejecutado por Tierra desde el parage de Villacata á este puerto de San Diego, 1769*, MS. This diary is dated July 3d, and was probably sent south by the *San Antonio* a few days later. *Crespí, Primera Esped. de Tierra al Descubrimiento del Puerto de San Diego*, in *Palou, Not.*, ii. 93-149. This diary extends to July 2d, and probably was completed like the other on July 3d. The writer had before him the diaries of the second expedition under Portolá, from which he takes some material respecting changes in names of places along the route.

fixed, but these geographical details belong to the
peninsula rather than to Alta California. The route
lay west of the main sierra and for the most part near
the coast.[15] The country was barren and unattractive;
water had to be carried for the animals and men for
days at a time; and at times their progress was hindered by showers of rain. At Santa Cruz on Todos
Santos Bay the savages made some threatening demonstrations, and once again there was almost a fight, but
the foe was frightened away by the noise of gunpowder. The Indians of the company soon began to
sicken and die[16] or to desert, and one or more of the
men had usually to be carried on *tepestles*, or litters.
As the party approached San Diego the gentiles
became more numerous, less timid, more disposed to
curiosity and theft, and eager to explain by their sign-
language the recent passing of the Spanish ships. On
the morning of the 14th of May the little army rose
so completely wet through by the rain that had fallen
during the night that mass had to be omitted, much
to the sorrow of Father Crespí because it was the first
day of pentecost. The march began at ten o'clock.
Soon they caught a distant view of the anchored vessels; Crespí says they had seen the mast-tops the day
before; and at four in the afternoon, having travelled
six leagues during the day, they reached the camp on
the beach and were welcomed by a salute from all the
fire-arms that could be manned.[17]

The first thing to be done, now that the coming of
Rivera's men renders it possible, is to prepare for permanent settlement. The old camp, or pest-house, on

[15] At the outset they followed the route of Link in 1766, but the latter soon
turned to the right to cross the mountains.

[16] Serra, in *San Diego, Lib. Mision*, MS., 64, says that 5 died. Nine deserted at one time according to Palou.

[17] Ortega, in *Santa Clara, Arch. Parroquia*, MS., 48–54, gives an account
of this expedition in which he represents the sufferings of the soldiers to have
been very great, three tortillas per day being the rations. Vallejo, *Hist. Cal.*,
MS., i. 83, obtained the same idea from his father's narrative, stating that
the soldiers were glad to barter their jewelry and clothing for the rations of
their Indian companions, while the latter lived on roots, wild fruits, etc.

the bay shore, is probably within the limits of what is now the city of San Diego, locally known as New Town; but the day after his arrival Rivera—so say the chroniclers, although according to the instructions of Galvez, Fages was chief in command—selects a new site some miles north, at what is now Old, or North, San Diego, at the foot of a hill on which are still to be seen the remains of the old presidio. Here camp is pitched and fortified, a corral for the animals and a few rude huts are built, and hither on the seventeenth are transported the sick and their tents. The immediate purpose is that the camp may be near the river which at this point flows into the north end of the bay. For six weeks officers, priests, and soldiers are occupied in attending to the wants of the sick and in unloading the *San Antonio*. Then they await the arrival of Portolá.

In the last days of June Sergeant Ortega with a soldier makes his appearance in camp, announcing that his companions under Portolá are only a few days' march from the port. Ten soldiers are sent back with Ortega to meet the approaching party. On the 29th the governor arrives in advance of his men; and on the first of July, a little before noon, Father Serra and all the rest are welcomed in camp. This second division of the land expedition, consisting of the three officials just named, of nine or ten soldiers *de cuera*, four muleteers, two servants of the governor and president, and forty-four natives of Lower California, had left Velicatá the 15th of May, and had followed the route of Rivera's party. The journey had been an uneventful and comparatively easy one. The gentiles were occasionally threatening, but did no harm. As in the case of the first division most of the neophytes deserted, only twelve reaching San Diego; but there were no deaths.[18] The second day Father

[18] *Portolá, Diario del Viage que haze por tierra Dⁿ Gaspar de Portolá, Capitan de Dragones del regimiento de España, Governador de Californias, á los puertos de San Diego y Monterey situados en 33 y 37 grados, haviendo sido nombrado comandante en gefe de esta expedicion por el Illᵐᵒ Señor Dⁿ Joseph de*

Junípero's foot became so painful that it seemed impossible for him to continue. Portolá wished to send him back, but the president would not think of it. A litter was thereupon ordered to be made, but Serra was much troubled at the extra work this imposed on the poor Indians. Calling an *arriero* he induced him to prepare an ointment of tallow and herbs which, combined with the friar's faith and prayers, so far healed the affected limb in a single night that it gave no more trouble. Listen to the record: "That evening he called the *arriero* Juan Antonio Coronel, and said, 'Son, canst thou not make me a remedy for the ulcer on my foot and leg?' But he answered, 'Padre, what remedy can I know? Am I a surgeon? I am an *arriero*, and have healed only the sores of beasts.' 'Then, son, suppose me a beast and this ulcer a saddle-gall from which have resulted the swelling of the leg and the pains that I feel and that give me no rest; and make for me the same medicament that thou wouldst apply to a beast.'"[19]

Galvez en virtud de las facultades vice-regiasque le ha concedido su Excel[a]. Dicha expedicion se componia de 37 soldados de cuera con su capitan D[n] Fernando de Rivera deviendo este adelantarse con 27 soldados, y el governador con 10 y un sargento. MS., folio, 35 pages. This diary is a copy from the original made in early times. It includes not only the trip to San Diego but the later one to Monterey to be noticed in the next chapter. The entries for each day's march are very brief, containing the number of hours marched, generally 4 or 5 per day, the character of the road and camping-place, and some notes of interviews with gentiles. For example, May 27, 'anduvimos como cinco horas, buen camino, paramos en la cieneguilla, cuio nombre puso el padre jesuita Linc, desde aqui se tomó otro rumbo, y paramos en un arroyuelo aunque seco,' etc. June 21, they were at Todos Santos, and heard of other Spaniards beyond. For the last 3 or 4 days they travelled on or near the shore. Other diaries of this journey, several of which were written, are not extant; but Crespí's journal already referred to was intended to embody all the information worth preserving. Sergt. Ortega, in *Santa Clara, Arch. Parroquia*, MS., 48–54, represents the hardships of the soldiers as very great; but he was evidently writing for an object that required this view of the matter. The same writer gives a brief and rather confused account of the journey in a narrative of his own services dated 1786. *Prov. St. Pap.*, MS., vi. 171–2. Serra, in his letter of July 3d, to Palou, says there was no suffering whatever. *Palou, Vida*, 78; Greenhow, *Or. and Cal.*, 100, erroneously implies that both land expeditions started together and that Portolá arrived last on account of having followed a more difficult route.

[19] From San Diego Serra himself writes, *Palou, Vida*, 73–8: 'Now the foot is all sound like the other, while from the ankle half way up the leg it is as the foot was before, an ulcer; but without swelling or pain except the occasional itching. In fact it is nothing serious.'

Thus are the four branches of the visitador general's grand expedition finally reunited at San Diego, one year after Galvez had begun his preparations on the peninsula. Next day is Sunday, *fiesta de la visitacion*, and the California pilgrims, one hundred and twenty-six in number—out of two hundred and nineteen who had started;[20] or, omitting natives and sailors, seventy-eight of Spanish blood out of ninety who had come to remain—celebrate their safe reunion by a solemn thanksgiving mass to the patron San José chanted with "la solemnidad posible," and to the accompaniment of exploding gunpowder. The ceremonies over, the two comandantes Portolá and Vila meet to consult respecting future movements, the want of sailors necessitating changes in the original plans. The decision is to send the *San Antonio* back to San Blas for supplies, and especially a crew for herself and the *San Cárlos*, which is to await her return. The friars for missionary and hospital work are to be left at San Diego under the protection of a guard of soldiers, while the main force presses on to Monterey by land. Great dependence is placed on the *San José* which on arrival is to be sent up the coast to aid the land expedition. Accordingly the 9th of July Perez sails with a small crew of convalescent sailors for the south,[21] bearing reports from the commandants and president. Five days later Portolá starts on his overland march northward, which will be described in the following chapter.

There are left at San Diego Captain Vila, Surgeon Prat, the mate Cañizares, three friars, a guard of eight

[20] The numbers are not exact, statements of deaths being conflicting. These pioneers included captains Portolá and Rivera, Lieut. Fages, captains Vila and Perez of the vessels, padres Serra, Crespí, Vizcaino, Gomez, and Parron; Surgeon Prat; Costansó, engineer; Cañizares, *piloto;* and sergeants Ortega and Puig. For names of all the band see list at end of this volume.

[21] Palou, *Not.*, i. 282, says that July 6th was the day set for sailing; but this may be a misprint. Nine of the sailors died of scurvy on the voyage. It is probable that these last victims were included in Palou's statement of 12 survivors, 5 of whom were left on the *San Cárlos*, 2 or 3 reached San Blas, and 4 or 5 remained ill at San Diego. The *San Antonio* made the voyage in 20 days.

cuera soldiers, five convalescent Catalan volunteers, a few sick sailors, five able seamen, a carpenter and a blacksmith, three boy servants, and eight Lower California Indians—about forty persons in all. As yet no mission has been formally founded; but this duty is at once attended to by Father Serra, who raises and blesses the cross on Sunday, the 16th of July.[22] This first of the Californian missions is dedicated, as the port had been by Vizcaino long before, to San Diego de Alcalá, being founded on a spot called by the natives Cosoy,[23] now Old Town. The ceremonies are not minutely recorded, but are the usual blessing of the cross, mass, and sermon by which it was hoped "to put to flight all the hosts of Hell and subject to the mild yoke of our holy faith the barbarity of the gentile Dieguinos." Then more huts are built, and one is dedicated as a church.

The new establishment, however, in which Father Parron is associate minister, still lacks one essential element of a prosperous mission, namely, converts, who in this case are difficult to find. The natives are by no means timid, but they come to the mission for gifts material rather than spiritual; and being adroit thieves as well as importunate beggars, their presence in large numbers becomes a nuisance, rendering it impossible for the small force to watch them and give proper attention to the sick. Fortunately the savages will have nothing to do with the food of the Spaniards, attributing to it some agency in the late ravages of the scurvy; but other things, particularly cloth, they deign to steal at any hour of day or night. They even

[22] It is noticeable that in all the general reports after 1823 this date is given as June 16th; but there is no doubt that it is an error. *Arch. Santa Bárbara*, MS., xii. 125. Serra thinks, *Prov. St. Pap.*, MS., i. 125, that April 11th has some claim to be considered the beginning of the mission, since on that day when the *San Antonio* arrived began the spiritual manifestations to the natives, causing them to see an eclipse and feel an earthquake, not perceptible to the Christians.

[23] *San Diego, Lib. de Mision*, MS. St James of Alcalá was an Andalucian Franciscan who lived from 1400 to 1463, and was canonized in 1588 rather for his pious life and the miracles wrought through him before and after death than for any high position held by him. *Alcalá* was rarely attached to the name of the mission in popular usage.

attempt in their tule rafts to pillage the *San Cárlos*, so that two of the eight soldiers are obliged to be on board. Persuasions, threats, and even the noise of fire-arms are met by ridicule.

Naturally matters come to a crisis. The guard is obliged to use force in repelling the intruders, who in their turn determine upon a raid for plunder. The 15th of August, while Parron with a guard of two soldiers is saying mass on the ship, as he is wont to do on feast-days, the savages enter the mission and begin to strip the clothing from the beds of the sick. Two soldiers are on guard and two more hasten to their aid; but when they attempt to drive away the pillagers they receive a volley of arrows which kills a boy and wounds Padre Vizcaino, the blacksmith, a soldier, and a California[24] Indian. The Spaniards in return fire a volley of musket-balls which kills three of the foe, wounds several more, and puts the whole crowd to flight. Serra and Vizcaino have just finished mass and are sitting together in a hut at the time of the attack, and the latter, rising to close the door, receives an arrow in the hand just as the boy servant staggers in and falls dead. The smith greatly distinguishes himself by his bravery, fighting without the protection of a *cuera*.[25]

It is not long before the gentiles come back to seek medical treatment for their wounded, imbued with a degree of faith in the destructive power of gunpowder, and correspondingly improved in manners, but by no means desirous of conversion. A stockade is thrown round the mission and the natives are no longer permitted to bring weapons within musket-shot. Thus safety is assured, but in missionary work

[24] For a long time at San Diego and Monterey the peninsula only was spoken of as 'California.' Either local names or *Nuevos Establecimientos* were applied to the north, although Serra in his first letter from San Diego used the term 'California Septentrional.'

[25] In his *Vida de Junip. Serra*, 84, Palou speaks of previous assaults with intent to kill the Spaniards on Aug. 12th to 13th, which were repulsed. Tuthill, *Hist. Cal.*, 79, erroneously states that a priest was killed. Serra, *San Diego, Lib. Mis.*, MS., 65, says the man killed was a Spanish arriero 20 years old named José María Vegerano.

no progress is made.   One gentile, indeed, is induced
by gifts to live with the Spaniards and becomes a skilful interpreter, but even with his aid no converts can
be gained.   Once the savages offer a child for baptism,
but when the service begins they seize the child and
flee in terror.   Yet we are told that when a painting
of the virgin and child is displayed, the native women
come and offer their breasts to feed "that pretty
babe."   Prior to April 1770, a full year from the first
coming of the Spaniards, and perhaps to a still later
period, for the register was subsequently destroyed,
and thee arliest date is not known, not a single neophyte was enrolled at the mission.   In all the missionary annals of the north-west there is no other
instance where paganism remained so long so stubborn.

Meanwhile new cases of sickness occur and death
continues its ravages, taking from the little band
before the return of Portolá in January, eight soldiers, four sailors, one servant, and six Indians, and
leaving but about twenty persons.   Little wonder
that small progress is made in missionary work.[26]

[26] On the general subject of this chapter, in addition to the special documents already referred to, see for a connected narrative *Palou, Not.*, i. 254-84,
427-32; ii. 93-153; *Id., Vida*, 60-86.   The notes of Serra in *San Diego, Lib.
Mision*, MS., are also a valuable source of information.   These notes were
written to supply as far as possible from memory the loss of the original mission books destroyed with the mission in 1775.   Copies are also found in
Hayes' Miss. Book, MS., i. 99-106, and in *Bandini, Doc. Hist. Cal.*, MS.
Miguel Costansó published in Mexico, 1770, an account of these expeditions as
Diario Histórico de los viages de mar y tierra, hechos al Norte de la California, fol.
56.   It was translated by Wm. Revely and published in 1790 by A. Dal-
rymple as *An Historical Journal*, etc., 2 maps, 4to, 76 p.

CHAPTER VI.

FIRST EXPEDITION FROM SAN DIEGO TO MONTEREY AND SAN FRANCISCO.

1769.

PORTOLÁ MARCHES FROM SAN DIEGO—HIS COMPANY—CRESPÍ'S JOURNAL—
NOTE ON GEOGRAPHY AND NOMENCLATURE—TABLE OF NAMES AND DIS-
TANCES—FIRST BAPTISM IN CALIFORNIA — EARTHQUAKES IN THE LOS
ANGELES REGION—A HOSPITABLE PEOPLE AND LARGE VILLAGES ON THE
SANTA BÁRBARA CHANNEL—ACROSS THE SIERRA AND DOWN THE SALINAS
RIVER—UNSUCCESSFUL SEARCH FOR MONTEREY—CAUSES OF THE ERROR—
NORTHWARD ALONG THE COAST—IN SIGHT OF PORT SAN FRANCISCO
UNDER POINT REYES—CONFUSION IN NAMES—MYSTERY CLEARED—
EXPLORATION OF THE PENINSULA—DISCOVERY OF A NEW AND NAMELESS
BAY—RETURN OF THE EXPEDITION TO MONTEREY AND SAN DIEGO.

I HAVE stated that two weeks after his arrival from
the south Portolá left San Diego[1] July 14, 1769, and
marched with nearly all his force northward. His
intention was to reach Monterey Bay by following
the coast, and either at his destination or on the way
he hoped to be overtaken by the *San José*, and with
the aid brought by her to found a presidio and the
mission of San Cárlos. The company consisted of
himself, Rivera y Moncada in command of twenty-
seven *cuera* soldiers, including Sergeant Joseph Francisco Ortega, Lieutenant Pedro Fages, with six or
seven of his twenty-five Catalan volunteers, all that
the scurvy had left alive and strong enough to undertake the march, Engineer Miguel Costansó,[2] fathers
Juan Crespí and Francisco Gomez, seven muleteers,

---

[1] Mofras, *Explor.*, i. 106, says the expedition had come across Sonora.
[2] Costansó, Fages, and others, according to the *Portolá, Diario*, MS., 10,
were ill, but advised by Prat to undertake the journey as a remedy.

fifteen christianized Lower Californians, and two servants of Portolá and Rivera—sixty-four persons in all.

The expedition is fully described in a diary kept by Crespí[3] and still extant, as are original statements, less complete than Crespí's, of no less than five participants, Portolá, Fages, Costansó, Ortega, and Rivera. As the first exploration by land of a broad extent of most important country it is not without importance and interest; yet as recorded it is in itself singularly unattractive. Crespí's diary, like that of Portolá, is a long and, except in certain parts, monotonous description of petty happenings not worth remembering. It is an almost nedless catalogue of nearly two hundred *jornadas*, or marches, tediously like one another, over hills and vales distinguished as being *con zacate* or *sin zacate*, grassy or barren, with the Sierra ever towering on the right, and the broad Pacific ever stretching to the left. The distance and bearing of each day's march are given, and observations for latitudes were frequent; but the Mexican league was practically a vague measurement, the observations of Crespí and Costansó often differed, and

---

[3] *Crespí, Viage de la Espedicion de tierra de San Diego á Monterey, Copia del diario y caminata que hizo la espedicion desde el puerto de San Diego de Alcalá hasta el de Monterey, saliendo el 14 de Julio de 1769*, in *Palou, Not.*, i. 285-423. Portolá, *Diario del Viage*, MS., 11, et seq., covers the same ground but much more briefly, adding nothing to Crespí's narrative except on a few points to be noticed in their place. 'El 27 handuvimos tres horas, buen camino, mucho pasto y agua' is a fair sample of most entries. Very few names of localities are given. In his *Vida de Junípero Serra*, 80-2, 88-9, Palou gives but a brief account, referring for particulars to Crespí's diary. Lieut. Fages, a member of the expedition, in his *Voyage en Cal.*, in *Nouv. Annales des Voy.*, ci. 147-9, 155-9, 165-71, 176-82, 321-4, 328, gives a very full narrative of it, except from Monterey to San Francisco, including names of places, distances, bearings, latitudes, and description of the country, but omitting names of persons and dates. I shall note variations from Crespí's diary, with which Fages' narrative for the most part agrees. Costansó, in his *Diario Histórico de los viages de mar y tierra*, gives an abridged version differing in no essential respect from Crespí. Costansó's narrative is abridged and quoted in an article signed 'M. P.,' in *Album Mex.*, ii. 37-40. Ortega, *Fragmento*, in *Santa Clara, Arch. Parroquia*, MS., 48-54, gives an original but not very complete or accurate narrative. Capt. Rivera also in a certificate relating the services of Pedro Amador, gives some information respecting this entrada. *St. Pap. Miss. and Colon.*, MS., i. 52-3. John T. Doyle in his pamphlets entitled *Address* and *Memorandum* in 1870 and 1873 gave brief *résumés* of parts from Crespí; and the newspapers since the reprint of Palou's work have had something to say more or less superficially on the subject of the discovery of San Francisco Bay.

worse than all, typographical errors in the printed
diary make the figures unreliable. In a monograph
on the trip I could, I think, trace with much accuracy
each day's course, and such minute treatment would
not be devoid of local interest as showing the original
names applied by the Spaniards, very few of which
have been preserved; but for this of course I have no
space here, and must content myself with a general
narrative and a note on geographical details.[4]

[4] List of places between San Diego and San Francisco as named in
Crespí's diary of the first exploration of the California coast by land, with
distances, bearings, and latitudes. Notes from the return trip in brackets
"[...]"; notes from *Fages' Voyage* in parentheses "(...)"; additional and
self-explanatory notes in *italics*. The *Portolá, Diario* has no distances, or
names, only hours and descriptions.

		Leagues.	Course.
July 14.	San Diego, 32° 30'. *Really 32° 44'.......*		
	Rinconada. *On False Bay.............*		
	Pocitos de la Cañada de San Diego......	2.5 (3)	N.W.
15.	Sta Isabel Valley. 1 league by 400 varas.		
	S. Jácome de la Marca Val. 1 l. by 5 l.,		
	from N. to S. (Posa de Osuna), [7 l.		
	from S. Juan.].................. ...	3.5 (4)	N.N.W.
16.	Encinos Cañada........................		
	S. Alejo. 33°........................	4	
17.	S. Simon Lípnica Val., near sea-shore ...		
	Sta Sinforosa........................	2	N.
18.	S. Juan Capistrano Val. 2 l., N.E. to		
	S.W., ending at shore, 33° 6'. *Really*		
	S. Luis Rey, lat. accurate............	2	N.
20.	Sta Margarita Val. The sierra draws		
	near shore and threatens to stop ad-		
	vance. *Name retained..............*	1.5	N.
21.	Sta Prágedis de los Rosales Cañada, 33° 10'	2	N.E.
22.	Los Cristianos, S. Apolinario, Bautismos		
	[arroyo], (Cañada del Bautismo).....	4	N.W.
23.	Sta María Magdalena Cañada [Quemada],		
	33° 14'.............................	4 (3)	N.N.W.
24.	S. Francisco Solano, 33° 18'. A mesa at		
	foot of sierra with fine stream, oppo-		
	site Sta Catalina Island, said by the		
	explorers to be 5 l. from S. Pedro Bay.		
	At or near S. Juan Capistrano.......	3 [2]	N.W.
26.	S. Pantaleon (Aguada del P. Gomez), on		
	the edge of a large plain............	2.5 [3]	N.W.
27.	Santiago Arroyo, 33° 6'. *Misprint?.....*	3	N.E.
28.	Sta Ana Riv., or Jesus de los Temblores,		
	thought to flow into S. Pedro Bay [9 l.		
	from Rio Porciúncula]..............	1.5 [1]	N.W.
29.	Sta Marta Spring (Los Ojitos and S. Mi-		
	guel)..............................	2	N.W.
30.	(No name), lat. 33° 34'................	6	N.W.
31.	(No name), lat. 34° 10'. *Los Angeles re-*		
	gion............................	2	N.W.

Four days after setting out from San Diego the explorers reached the pleasant valley in which the mission of San Luis Rey was later built. Their progress had been at the rate of from two to four leagues each day, and nothing along the way attracted more attention than the abundance of flowers, especially

Aug.			Leagues.	Course.
	2.	Porciúncula Riv., a large stream, with much good land. *North branch of the S. Gabriel*..........................	3 (2)	N.W.
	3.	Alisos de S. Estévan Spring, near an asphaltum marsh......................	3	W.
	4.	S. Rogerio Spring, or Berrendo (Fontaine du daim moucheté)..................	2	N.W.
	5.	Sta Catalina de Bononia de los Encinos Val., 34° 37′, *really 34° 10′. San Fernando Valley, in which a station still called Encino*........................	3	N.N.W.
	7.	(No name.)............................	3	N.
	8.	Sta Rosa de Viterbo, or Corral ranchería, 3 l. across the plain, and 4 l. over mts., *34° 47′. Near Hart's*...............	4	N.
	10.	Sta Clara stream and cañada............	3	W.N.W.
	11.	Sta Clara, down same stream, 34° 30′, a good site for a mission. 6 l. from Sta Rosa and 10 l. from Sta Catalina. *This must be an error*...............	3	W.S.W.
	12.	S. Pedro Amoliano ranchería, down the stream................................	3	W.S.W.
	13.	Stos Mártires Ipólito y Cuciano ranchería and river, down same stream, which widens out into a river. *Still called Rio Sta Clara*......................	2	S.W.
	14.	Asuncion (Asunta) ranchería, on sea-shore. Fine site for a mission, 34° 36′. *Costansó made it 34° 13′. Doubtless S. Buenaventura*......................	2.5	E.N.E.
	15.	Sta Conefundis (Ranchería Volante), along beach.............................	2	W.(W.N.W.)
	16.	Sta Clara de Monte Talco, or Bilarin, a large pueblo in 34° 40′, on an arroyo, along beach.......................	2	W.(W.N.W.)
	17.	S. Roque, or Carpintería, a large pueblo in a place, 4 l. by 1 l., much asphaltum. *Sta Bárbara region*...........	1	W.(W.N.W.)
	18.	Concepcion Laguna (Pueblo de la Laguna), a very large ranchería, on a point across an *estero. Sta Bárbara was afterwards founded at S. Joaquin de la Laguna.* Coast turns from w.n.w. to w...............................	4 [(3)]	W.(W.N.W.)
	20.	Sta Margarita de Cortona, or Isla, or Mescaltitlan pueblos, 34° 43′. In a marshy region, where the sloughs form an island, with four or five scattered rancherías.............................	3.5 [2.5]	W.(W.N.W.)

of roses similar to those of old Castile, and for that reason delightful to the Spaniards. Crespí notes the plucking of one branch bearing six roses and twelve buds. Thus far all was literally *couleur de rose*. The route followed was very nearly that of the subsequent stage road between San Diego and Los Angeles. It was noticed that much of the grass had been burned

			Leagues.	Course.
Aug.	21.	S. Luis Obispo, 34° 45′, still along shore.	2 [2.5]	W.
	23.	S. Güido de Cortona, along shore, four islands in sight......................	3	W.
	24.	S. Luis Rey, or La Gaviota, along shore, on a slough, 34° 47′. *Perhaps origin of Gaviota Pass.* Three islands in sight: S. Bernardo, *S. Miguel*, farthest west; Sta Cruz, *Sta Rosa*, next; and Sta Bárbara, *Sta Cruz*, farthest east.........	2.5 (3) [2]	W.
	25.	S. Seferino, 34° 30′ (14″), an Indian pueblo, Sta Ana ranchería..................	2	W.
	26.	Sta Teresa, or Cojo, ranchería, 34° 30′, or 34° 51′.............	2.5	W.
		Pt Concepcion, 34° 30′.............	1	W.
	27.	Concepcion, ranchería (Rancho de la Espada), 34° 51′ 30″...................	⎰ 1.5 or ⎱ .5 (1)	N.W.
	28.	S. Juan Bautista, or Pedernales (34° 33′), in sight of another point near by [from which Pt Concepcion bears S.E., 8° E.] *This point must be Pt Argüello, though there are some difficulties......*	2	N.W.
	29.	Sta Rosalía, or Cañada Seca, on a bay between last point and another........	2.5 (2)	N.W.
	30.	S. Bernardo Riv., or Sta Rosa, mouth filled with sand, the largest river yet passed, 34° 55′. *The Rio Sta Inés, though distance and bearing are not correct; just possibly the Sta María, in which case Pt Concepcion was Argüello, Argüello Purísima, the 2d point Purísima, and Sta Rosalía at the mouth of Rio Sta Inés.....................*	.5 (1)	N.W.
	31.	S. Ramon Nonato, La Graciosa, or Baile de las Indias laguna................	2.5 (2)	N.
Sept.	1.	S. Daniel, laguna grande, in a fine valley, 3 l. by 7 l., having in the middle a laguna 500 varas wide ? 34° 13′ ? *Mouth of the Rio Sta María...............*	1.5 (3)	N.
	2.	S. Juan Perucia y S. Pedro de Sacro Terrato, or Real de las Víboras, or Oso Flaco (Laguna Redonda)............	3	N.W. (N.N.W.)
	4.	S. Ladislao, or El Buchon. By varying courses, and finally N. into mts., 35° 28′. *Not clear.....................*	4	
	5.	Sta Elena, or Angosta Cañada, 35° 3′ ?...	2	N.W.
	7.	Natividad, or Cañada de los Osos, down which they went to the sea. *S. Luis Obispo was founded later on this cañada.*	3 (4)	

by the natives to facilitate the capture of rabbits. Few of the inhabitants were met in the south, but when seen they were always friendly, and the 22d of July they permitted to be baptized two dying children, who were named María Magdalena and Margarita. About the same time two mineral deposits, of red ochre and white earth, were discovered. On the 24th the islands

			Leagues.	Course.
Sept.	8.	S. Adriano, near the shore at mouth of Cañada de los Osos. The diary clearly mentions the Estero Bay and Morro Rock of modern maps..............	2	W.
	9.	Sta Serafina Estero, 36°, or 35° 27′, after crossing eight arroyos..............	3	N.W.
	10.	S. Benvenuto, or Osito, 36° 2′, or (35° 33′)	2	N.N.W.
	11.	S. Nicolás, or Cantil, arroyo 35° 35′, along beach.............................	(1)	N.W.
	12.	S. Vicente arroyo (Arroyada Honda), 36° 10′...............................	2	N.W. and N.N.E.
	13.	Sta Umiliana arroyo [35° 45′], at foot of Sierra de Sta Lucía. *In region between S. Simeon and Cape S. Martin.......*	2	N.W.
	16.	Pié de la Sierra de Sta Lucía, up a cañada into the mts., *probably* N.E..........	1	
	17.	Hoya de la Sierra de Sta Lucía, or San Francisco, 36° 18′ 30″, up into the mts. on N. side of a cañon [slightly different route on return]. *In region of the later S. Antonio mission. Probably* N.E..............................	1	
	20.	Real de Piñones, by a mt. way over the summit, N.E.......................	2	
	21.	S. Francisco (Rio de Truchas)..........	1	
	26.	S. Elizario [Elcearo] Rio, or Real del Chocolate, down a cañada to a river believed to be the Carmelo, *but really the Rio Salinas.....................*	4	N.E.
	27.	Real del Álamo, 36° 38′, down the river..	4	N.W.
	28.	Real Blanco, down river................	4	
	29.	Real de Cazadores, down river..........	3.5 (3)	
Oct.	1.	Sta Delfina [Riv.], 36° 44′, or 36° 53′, down river to within 1½ l. of beach. From this point Monterey and Carmelo bays were explored. Pt Pinos, 36° 36′; Pt Año Nuevo, 36° 4′; Carmelo Bay, 36° 36′...............................	5.25	N.W.
	7.	Sta Brígida, or La Grulla, passing several lagoons...........................	2	N.N.W.
	8.	Pájaro, or Sta Ana Riv. *Name still retained*.............................	4	N.
	10.	Nr Sra del Pilar lagunas [corral], 34° 35′?	1	N.W.
	15.	Sta Teresa.............................	1.5	N.W.
	16.	Rosario del Serafin de Asculi arroyo, *near Soquel.........................*	2	N.W.
	17.	S. Lorenzo River—*still retains the name. The camp was near Sta Cruz.........*	2	W.N.W.

of San Clemente and Santa Catalina were sighted. Next day the natives seemed to say that inland were other white men with horses, mules, swords, and hats. On the 28th, when the governor and his followers were on the Santa Ana River, four violent shocks of earthquake frightened the Indians into a kind of prayer to the four winds, and caused the stream to be also named Jesus de los Temblores. Many more shocks were felt during the following week; yet the foreigners were delighted with the region, noting the agricultural possibilities which they and their successors later realized. The 1st of August they began to kill and eat *berrendos*, or antelopes, and next day forded the Rio de Porciúncula on which the city of Los Angeles now stands.

From the Angeles region the route lay through the valley of Santa Catalina de los Encinos, now San Fernando, and thence northward through the mountain pass to the head streams of the Rio de Santa Clara, so called then and now, down whose banks the Spaniards followed to the sea again. Immediately on leaving the Porciúncula more earthquakes were felt, causing the friars to think there were volcanoes in the sierra; springs of *pez brea*, *chapopote*, or asphaltum,

Oct. 18.	Sta Cruz arroyo, and four other streams, the last being S. Lúcas, or Puentes arroyo.................................	Leagues. 2	Course. W.N.W.
	La Olla (Hoya) barranca............		
19.	S. Pedro de Alcántara, or Jumin [Jamon].	2.5	N.W.
20.	S. Luis Beltran, or Salud, arroyo, about 1 l. from Pt Año Nuevo, 37° 22', or 37° 3' [Pt in 36° 4'].................	1	N.W.
23.	S. Juan Nepomuceno, or Casa Grande, ranchería, across a level mesa along shore...........................	2	N.N.W.
	San Pedro Regalado....................		
24.	Sto Domingo, 37° 30'.................	4 or 2	N.
27.	S. Ibon, or Pulgas, ranchería..........	2	N.
28.	S. Simon y S. Judas arroyo, or Llano de los Ánsares, in sight of a point N.N.W. with farallones—*just above Half-Moon Bay, and in sight of Pt S. Pedro*.....	2	
30.	Pt Angel Custodio, or Almejas, 37° 24', 30', 49' [37° 31'].....................	2	N.W.
	To points subsequently visited, no names were applied.		

were also regarded as signs of volcanic action. The natives now spoke not only of bearded men who came from the east in earlier times, but said they had lately observed vessels in the channel—it will be remembered that the *San Antonio* and *San Cárlos* had reached this latitude on their way from Cape San Lúcas to San Diego—and one man even claimed to recognize Gomez, Fages, and Costansó whom he had seen on the vessel. Everywhere the men went naked, but from this region the women dressed more according to European ideas, covering much of their person with skins of deer and rabbits. August 14th Portolá crossed from a point near the mouth of the Santa Clara to the shore farther north, where he found the largest Indian village yet seen in California. The houses were of spherical form thatched with straw, and the natives used boats twenty-four feet long made of pine boards tied together with cords and covered with asphaltum, capable of carrying each ten fishermen. A few old blades of knives and swords were seen. Some inhabitants of the channel islands came across to gaze at the strangers. Previously the inhabitants had bartered seeds, grass baskets, and shells for the coveted glass beads, but now fish and carved bits of wood were added to the limited list of commercial products. Thus more food was offered than could be eaten. This fine pueblo, the first of a long line of similar ones along the channel coast, was called Asuncion and was identical in site with the modern San Buenaventura.[5]

From the middle of August to the 7th of September the Spaniards followed the coast of the Santa Bárbara Channel westward, always in sight of the islands, meeting a dense native population settled in many large towns and uniformly hospitable. Passing Point Concepcion, they turned northward to the site on which San Luis Obispo now stands. On the 18th of August they passed a village called Laguna de la Concepcion in the vicinity of what is now Santa Bár-

[5] See founding of San Buenaventura in a later chapter.

bara, perhaps on the exact site, since the presidio was
founded later at a place said to have been called San
Joaquin de la Laguna by these first explorers.[6]   A
few leagues farther, and in several other places, there
were noticed large cemeteries, those of the men and
women being distinct as the gentle savages explained.
Over each grave a painted pole was set up bearing
the hair of the men, and those of the women being
adorned with *coras,* or grass baskets.   Large whale-
bones were also a distinguishing feature of the burial-
grounds.   Many of these graves have been opened
within the past few years, and the relics thus brought
to light have created in local circles quite a flutter of
archæological enthusiasm, being popularly attributed,
as is the custom in such cases, to 'prehistoric' times
and to races long since extinct.   On the 24th a sea-
gull was killed and the place called San Luis by the
padres was christened La Gaviota by the soldiers—
very many localities along the route being thus doubly
named, whence perhaps the name Gaviota Pass of
modern maps.   Near Point Concepcion the natives
displayed beads of European make, said to have been
obtained from the north.   Here a lean and worn-
out mule was left to recuperate under Indian care.
Crespí's latitudes for the channel coasts were too high,
varying from 34° 30′ to 34° 51′.   Costansó's observations placed Point Concepcion in 34° 30′, about 5′ too
far north.   After turning the point the natives were
poorer and less numerous, but were still friendly.
On the 30th a large stream was crossed on a sand-bar
at its mouth which "served as a bridge."   This was
the Rio Santa Inés,[7] called at its discovery Santa Rosa,
and on September 1st the camp was pitched at the
Laguna de San Daniel, probably at the mouth of the
Rio Santa María.   Next day Sergeant Ortega was

[6] *Prov. Rec.*, MS., ii. 61-2.

[7] There is some confusion in the description of this part of the coast, and
this stream might as well be the Santa María, were it not for the fact that
Purísima Mission was afterward built on Rio de Santa Rosa. *Purísima, Lib.
Mision,* MS., 1; *Prov. St. Pap.*, MS., vi. 112-13.

taken ill, and ten of the men began to complain of
sore feet. Turning inland not far from what is now
Point San Luis, they crossed the hills by a somewhat winding course and on the 7th encamped in
the Cañada de los Osos in the vicinity of the later
San Luis Obispo. Here the soldiers engaged in a
grand bear-hunt, in which one of these fierce brutes,
seen here in groups of fourteen or sixteen, according
to Portolá's diary, was killed after receiving nine bullets, one of the soldiers barely escaping with his life.
The names Los Osos and El Buchon applied at this
time are still preserved in this region.

From San Luis, instead of proceeding north and
inland, which would have been the easier route, the
explorers follow the Bear cañada down to the sea,
where they note Estero Bay and Morro Rock, and
whence they follow the coast some ten leagues to a
point located by Costansó in latitude 35° 45', and
apparently not far below Cape San Martin. The
sierra of Santa Lucía, so named long before, now
impedes further progress, and on September 16th the
travellers turn to the right and begin to climb the
mountain range, "con el credo en la boca," one league
per day being counted good progress in such a rough
country. From the 17th to the 19th they are on the
Hoya, or ravine, de la Sierra de Santa Lucía, on the
head-waters of the Rio de San Antonio near where
the mission of the same name is afterward founded.
On the 20th the lofty range northward is ascended,
and from the highest ridge, probably Santa Lucía
Peak, the Spaniards gaze upon a boundless sea of
mountains, "a sad spectacle for poor travellers worn
out by the fatigues of so long a journey," sighs Crespí.
The cold begins to be severe, and some of the men
are disabled by scurvy; yet for the glory of God and
with unfailing confidence in their great patron St
Joseph, they press bravely on, after remaining four
days in a little mountain cañon dedicated by the friars
to the Llagas de San Francisco, the name San Fran-

cisco proper being reserved for that saint's 'famous port.'
Wending their way down the northern slope, perhaps
by way of the Arroyo Seco, on the 26th they reach
a river which they name San Elizario, or Santa Delfina, believed by the Spaniards to be the Rio del Carmelo. It is the stream, however, since known as
Salinas, and down it Portolá's company march to the
sea, arriving on the 30th at a point near the mouth.
The natives are less hospitable in the Salinas Valley
than south of there.

As the expedition draws near the sea-shore, a point
of land becomes visible in the south, which is correctly
judged to be Point Pinos, one of the prominent landmarks by which Monterey was to be identified. It is
therefore determined to stop here for exploration.
October 1st the governor, engineer, and Crespí, with
five soldiers climb a hill, "from the top of which,"
writes the friar, "we saw the great entrance, and con-
jectured that it was the one which Cabrera Bueno
puts between Point Año Nuevo and Point Pinos of
Monterey." That is to say, believing yet doubting
they look out over the bay and harbor of Monterey
in search of which they had come so far, then pass on
wondering where is Monterey. Rivera with eight men
explores southward, marching along the very shore of
the port they are seeking; then toward Point Pinos
and over to "a small bight formed between the said
point and another south of it, with an arroyo flowing
down from the mountains, well wooded, and a slough,
into which the said stream discharges, and some little
lagoons of slight extent;" but the mountains prevent
further progress southward along the shore. The
places thus explored are Carmelo bay, river, and point;[8]
nevertheless Rivera returns to camp saying that no
port is to be found.

The 4th of October after solemn mass in a brush-

[8] Cypress Point is not noticed in this exploration; but it is certain that if
the bight now visited were not Carmelo Bay, that bay would have been found
and mentioned later when the attempt was made again to find a shore route
southward.

wood tent at the mouth of the Salinas River, a meeting of all the officers and friars is held to deliberate on what shall be done. At this meeting the commandant briefly calls attention to the scarcity of provisions, to the seventeen men on the sick-list unfit for duty, to the excessive burden of labor imposed on those who are well in sentinel duty and continual reconnoissances, and to the lateness of the season. In view of these circumstances and of the fact that the port of Monterey could not be found where it had been supposed to lie,[9] each person present is called upon to express freely his opinion. The decision of officers and priests is unanimous "that the journey be continued as the only expedient remaining, in the hope of finding by the favor of God the desired port of Monterey and in it the *San José* to supply our needs, and that if God should permit that in the search for Monterey we all perish, we shall still have fulfilled our duty to God and men by working together to the death in the accomplishment of the enterprise on which we have been sent." Their hope rests mainly in the fact that they had not yet reached the latitude in which Vizcaino and Cabrera Bueno had placed the port.

[9] 'En visto de lo dicho y de no hallar el puerto de Monterey en la altura que se presumia.' *Crespi, Viage*, 355. This use of the word *altura* is an error of the writer, since Cabrera Bueno, the authority on which dependence was placed, gives the latitude of Monterey as 37°, while Costansó now made it 36° 30'; but the explanation is that this was written after subsequent explorations further north which had an influence on Crespí's words. The *Junta 1ra de guerra de la expedicion de tierra que pasaba en solicitud del puerto te Monterey en 4 de Octubre de 1769* is attached to the *Portolá, Diarro*, MS. In his opening address Portolá says 'what should be the Rio Carmelo is only an *arroyo;* what should be a port is only a little *ensenada;* what were great lakes are *lagunillas;*' and yet to go on and find another Sierra de Sta Lucía would take time; 11 men were sick, and only 50 *costales* of flour remained. Costansó gave his opinion first: that they were in only 36° 42', while Monterey was in 37° or perhaps more; they should not fail to explore up to 37° 30' so as either to find the port or to be sure of its non-existence. Fages followed and also favored going on to 37° or a little more, as the port had certainly not been passed, and they had not yet reached its latitude. Then Rivera, who did not seem to think Monterey would be found, since it was not where it ought to be, but thought they should establish themselves somewhere, but not where they then were. Then Portolá decided to rest 6 days, go on as far as possible, and then select the most eligible place for a settlement if Monterey did not appear. All agreed in writing to this plan, including padres Gomez and Crespí.

It is and must ever remain more or less inexplicable that the Spaniards should have failed at this time to identify Monterey. All that was known of that port had resulted from Vizcaino's visit, and this knowledge was in the hands of the explorers in the works of Venegas and Cabrera Bueno. The description of landmarks was tolerably clear,[10] and in fact these landmarks had been readily recognized by Portolá's party at their first arrival on the bay shore. Moreover, the advantages of the harbor had not been very greatly exaggerated, both Torquemada, as quoted by Venegas, and Cabrera Bueno having called Monterey simply a *famoso puerto*, the former stating that it was protected from all winds, and the latter, from all except north-west winds. Yet with the harbor lying at their feet, and with several landmarks so clearly defined that Vila and Serra recognized them at once from the reports at San Diego, and penetrated the truth of the matter in spite of their companions' mystification, the Spanish officers could find nothing resembling the object of their search, and even were tempted to account for the port's disappearance by the theory that since Vizcaino's time it had perhaps been filled up with sand![11]

[10] See chapter iii., this volume.

[11] Crespí's remarks, in addition to what has been given in the preceding narrative, are as follows: 'In view of what has been said...and of our not finding in these regions the port of Monterey so celebrated and so praised in their time by men of character, skilful, intelligent, and practical navigators who came expressly to explore these coasts by order of the king...we have to say that it is not found after the most careful efforts made at cost of much sweat and fatigue; or it must be said that it has been filled up and destroyed with time, though we see no indications to support this opinion; and therefore I suspend my opinion on this point, but what I can say with assurance is that with all diligence on the part of comandante, officers, and soldiers no such port has been found...At Pt Pinos there is no port, nor have we seen in all our journey a country more desolate than this, or people more rude, Sebastian Vizcaino to the contrary notwithstanding...although this was easier to be misrepresented than a port so famous as was Monterey in former centuries.' *Viage*, 395–6. In a letter buried before the final return it is stated that the expedition 'sighted Pt Pinos and the *ensenadas* north and south of it without seeing any signs of the port of Monterey, and resolved to go on in search of it,' and again on the return 'made an effort to search for the port of Monterey within the mountain range following along the sea, in spite of its roughness, but in vain.' *Palou, Not.*, i. 399–400. According to Palou, *Vida*, 88, P. Crespí wrote him that he feared the port had been filled up; and

There are, however, several circumstances which tend to lessen our difficulty in accounting for the error committed, and which are almost sufficient to remove the difficulty altogether, especially so far as this first visit on the northward march is concerned. First, the Rio Carmelo, seen but once when swollen by winter rains, was on the record as a "river of good water though of little depth," and in geographical discussions of the past had gradually acquired great importance. Portolá's party reaching the Salinas, the largest river in this region, naturally supposed they were on the Carmelo. If it were the Carmelo, Pt Pinos should bear north rather than south; if it were not, then not only was this large river not mentioned in the old authorities, but there was no river in the region to be identified with the Carmelo, for it never occurred to the travellers to apply that name to the creek, now nearly dry, which flowed into the ensenada to the south of the point. Second, Cabrera Bueno's description of the bays north and south of Point Pinos as fine ports, the latter protected from all winds and the former from all but those from the north-west, was exaggerated, perhaps very much so; yet it was not Cabrera's or Vizcaino's exaggerations that

Serra mentioned in one of his letters the same opinion founded on the great sand dunes found where the port ought to be. *Id.*, 92. Fages says: 'We knew not if the place where we were was that of our destination; still after having carefully examined it and compared it with the relations of the ancient voyagers, we resolved to continue our march; for after having taken the latitude, we found that we were only in 36° 44', while, according to the reports of the pilot, Cabrera Bueno, Monterey should be in 37°, and so serious an error was not supposable on the part of a man of well known skill. The configuration of the coast did not agree either with the relations which served us as a guide.' *Voy. en Cal.*, 328–9. Rivera simply says: 'We went in the expedition by land to San Diego and Monterey, and having failed to recognize the latter we proceeded in search of it till we came to San Francisco, whence for want of provisions we returned and the whole expedition slept two nights in Monterey itself and encamped several days on the Rio Carmelo.' *St. Pap.*, *Miss. and Colon.*, MS., i. 52–3. According to Ortega, 'On October 5th or 6th we reached Pt Pinos, and according to the indications of Capt. Vizcaino and the *piloto* Cabrera Bueno—and our latitude as well—we should have thought ourselves already at Monterey; but not finding the shelter and protection ascribed by them to the port caused us to doubt, since we saw a bight over twelve leagues across with no shelter except for small craft at the point, although the said bight is large enough to hold thousands of vessels, but with little protection from some winds.' *Fragmento*, MS., 52.

misled Portolá. Monterey had been much talked and
written about during the past century and a half in
connection with the fables of Northern Mystery, and
while its waters lay undisturbed by foreign keel its
importance as a harbor had been constantly growing
in the minds of Spanish officials and missionaries. It
was not the piloto's comparatively modest description
so much as the grand popular ideal which supported
the expectations of the governor and his companions,
and of which the reality fell so far short. Third, the
very different impressions of storm-tossed mariners
anchoring in the bay when its shores were brightened
and refreshed by winter rains, and of travellers arriving at the end of the dry season from the sunny clime,
large villages, and hospitable population of the Santa
Bárbara Channel must be taken into consideration.
Fourth, the Spaniards had no boats in which to make
soundings and test the anchorage capacities of the
harbor. Fifth, Cabrera's latitude was thirty minutes
higher than that resulting from Costansó's observations.

To these considerations should be added two other
theories respecting the failure to find Monterey. One
is that favored by Palou,[12] who like some of his companions was disposed to regard the concealment of
the port as a miraculous interposition of God at the
intercession and in the interests of St Francis; for
on starting from the peninsula after completing arrangements for the new establishments, Father Junípero had asked Galvez—"and for Our Father San
Francisco is there to be no mission?" to which the
visitador had replied—"if San Francisco wants a
mission let him cause his port to be found and it will
be put there;" and the saint did show his port and left
St Charles to do as much at Monterey later. The

[12] ' Luego que leí esta noticia atribuí á disposicion divina el que no hallando
la expedicion el puerto de Monterey en el parage que lo señalaba el antiguo
derrotero, siguiese hasta llegar al Puerto de N. P. S. Francisco.' *Vida de
Junípero Serra*, 88. Gleeson, *Hist. Cath. Ch.*, ii. 35–8, accepts the view that
it was a miracle.

other theory is one that was somewhat prevalent among the descendants of the first Spanish soldiers and settlers in later years, namely, that the explorers had secret orders from Galvez not to find Monterey, but to go on to San Francisco.[13] Neither this view of the matter nor that involving supernatural agencies seems to demand much comment. It would be very difficult to prove the inaccuracy of either.

It having been determined to proceed, Ortega and a few men advance October 6th to make a rconnoissance which seems to favor former conclusions, since he saw another river and thought he saw another wooded point, which might be the veritable Rio Carmelo and Point Pinos. Next day the whole company set out and in twenty-three days march up the coast to Point Angel Custodio, since called Point San Pedro. Eleven men have to be carried in litters,[14] and progress is slow. On the 8th the Pájaro River is crossed and named by the soldiers from a stuffed bird found among the natives. A week later in the vicinity of Soquel the *palo colorado*, or redwood, begins to be seen. On the 17th they cross and name the Rio de San Lorenzo, at the site of the present Santa Cruz; and on the 23d Point Año Nuevo is passed. Vegetables soon give out as had meat long ago, and rations are reduced to five tortillas of bran and flour a day. Portolá and Rivera are added to the sick list. On the 28th the rains begin, and the men are attacked by diarrhœa, which seems to relieve the scurvy. The 30th they reach a point with detached rocks, or *farallones*, located by Costansó in 37° 31′,

[13] *Vallejo, Hist. Cal.*, MS., i. 39–42; *Alvarado, Hist. Cal.*, MS., i. 19–20; *Vallejo (J. J.), Remin.*, MS., 66–7. All have heard from Ignacio Vallejo and others of his time that Portolá was supposed to have passed Monterey intentionally.

[14] Ortega describes the labors and sufferings of the men more fully than others. He says 16 lost the use of their limbs. Each night they were rubbed with oil and each morning were fastened to the *tijeras*, a kind of wooden frame, and raised to the backs of the mules. The rain however brought some relief. *Fragmento*, MS.

where the hills bar the passage along the shore. It is named Point Angel Custodio and Point Almejas, being that now known as San Pedro.[15]

It is the last day of October. After some preliminary examination by an advance party, the whole company climb the hill and gaze about them. On their left is the ever present sea, rolling off to the west in a dim eternity of waters. Before them is a bay, or bight, lying between the point on which they stand and one beyond extending into the sea far to the northwest. Rising abruptly full before them, high above the ocean, the bold shore presents a dismal front in its summer-soiled robes, as yet undyed by the delicious winter rains, the clouded sun meanwhile refusing its frequent exhibitions of exquisite colorings between the deep blue waters and the dark, purple bluff. Farther to the left, about west-north-west from their position and apparently south-west from the distant point, is seen a group of six or seven whitish farallones; and finally looking along the shore northward they discover white cliffs and what appears to be the mouth of an inlet making toward the north-east. There is no mistaking these landmarks so clearly laid down by Cabrera Bueno.[16] The travellers recognize them immediately; the distant point of land must be Point Reyes, and under it lies the port of San Francisco. The saint has indeed and unexpectedly brought the missionaries within sight of his port. Strong in this well founded conviction, the pilgrims descend the hill northward and encamp near the beach at the southern extremity

---

[15] Mr Doyle, *Address 7*, makes it Corral de Tierra, or Pillar Point, at the northern extremity of Half Moon Bay. I do not know if this was a deliberately formed opinion; but my reasons for identifying Mussel Point with San Pedro are: 1st, the detached rocks or *farallones* not found in connection with the other points, see *Cal. State Geol. Surv. Map of region adjacent to S. F.*, 1867; 2d, the hills cutting off the shore passage as they do not at Pillar Point, see *Id.*; 3d, the clear view of Drake Bay and the Farallones, etc.; and 4th, the fact that in order to put in the number of leagues they did going south along the cañada they must have crossed at San Pedro rather than at Pillar, especially, if as Doyle suggests, their last camp was no farther south than Searsville. There are, however, some difficulties.

[16] For this author's full description of this region see chap. iii. this volume.

of the sheet of water known to the Spaniards from that time as the Ensenada de los Farallones.

There has been much perplexity in the minds of modern writers respecting this port of San Francisco, resulting from want of familiarity with the original records, and from the later transfer of the name to another bay. These writers have failed to clear away the difficulties that seemed to surround the subject.[17] I have no space to catalogue all the erroneous ideas that have been entertained; but most authors seem to have supposed that the matter was as dark in the minds of the Spaniards as in their own, and it has been customary to interpret the reply of Galvez to Serra already quoted somewhat like this: "If San Francisco wants a mission let him reveal the whereabouts of this port of his of which we have heard so much and which we have never been able to find," or in other instances more simply, "let him show a good port if he wants a mission."[18]

[17] Certain exceptions should be noted. My assistant, in the *Overland Monthly*, made known for the first time to the English-reading public the statements of Cabrera Bueno and Crespí, and in a few brief notes put the subject in its true light. Doyle in notes to his reprint of Palou subsequently gave a correct version; and several writers since have partially utilized the information thus presented.

[18] The following from *Dwinelle's Colon. Hist. S. F.*, xi. 24, is a sample of the errors current in the best class of works: 'There was a report in Mexico that such a port existed, yet navigators sent to explore it had not succeeded in finding it, and even at Monterey nobody believed in it. But in 1772 Father Junípero, taking the viceroy at his word, caused an overland expedition to set out for Monterey under the command of Juan B. Ainsa to search for the apocryphal port. They were so successful as to discover the present bay of San Francisco.' Dwinelle's idea seems to be that there was a tradition of such a bay before Drake's time; that Drake and others after him missed the bay on account of fogs, etc.; and that the real bay had thus come to be regarded as apochryphal. Randolph in his famous oration, *Hutchings' Mag.*, v. 269, regards it 'as one of the most remarkable facts in history that others had passed it, anchored near it, and actually given its name to adjacent roadsteads, and so described its position that it was immediately known; and yet that the cloud had never been lifted which concealed the entrance of the bay of San Francisco, and that it was at last discovered by land.' Randolph's error was in supposing that it was the inside bay that 'was immediately known,' rather than the 'adjacent roadstead.' Tuthill, *Hist. Cal.*, 77–9, says that Portolá went on to San Francisco and recognized it as having been before described. Possibly some Spaniards had visited the port and their oral descriptions mixed with that of Drake gave rise to the name and to glowing accounts which were accredited to Monterey! Thus all became confusion between the two bays. Some authors, correctly stating that Portolá discovered the bay of San Fran-

There was, however, nothing mysterious in the matter, save as all things in the north were at one time or another tinged with mystery. The truth is that before 1769 San Francisco Port under Point Reyes had been twice visited by Spaniards, to say nothing of a probable visit by an Englishman, while Monterey had received only one visit; both were located and described with equal clearness in Cabrera Bueno's coast-pilot; and consequently, if less talked about San Francisco was quite as well known to Galvez, Portolá, Crespí, and the rest, as was Monterey. The visitador's remark to Serra meant simply, "if San Francisco wants a mission let him favor our enterprise so that our exploration and occupation may be extended northward to include his port." The explorers passed up the coast, came within sight of San Francisco Port, and had no difficulty in recognizing the landmarks at first glance. The miracle in the padre's eyes was not in the showing of San Francisco, but in the concealment of Monterey. And all this, be it remembered, without the slightest suspicion or tradition of the existence of any other San Francisco, or of the grand inland bay so near which has since made the name famous. St Francis had indeed brought the Spaniards within sight of his port, but his mission was not to be there; and some years later, when the Spaniards found they could not go to San Francisco, they decided that San Francisco must come to them, and accordingly transferred the name southward to the peninsula and bay. Hence the confu-

---

cisco in 1769, also tell us that he named it. See *Gleeson's Hist. Cath. Ch.*, ii. 38; *Capron's Hist. Cal.*, 122; *Soule's Annals of S. F.*, 46, etc.; but the inner bay was not named for some years, and the outer bay had been named long before. That confusion still reigns in the minds of the best writers is shown by the following from *Hittell's Hist. S. Francisco*, 41: 'The Spanish explorers, Portolá and Crespí, did not imagine that they had made a discovery. They saw that the harbor was different from that of Monterey, described by Vizcaino, but they imagined that it was the bay of San Francisco mentioned by their navigators as lying under shelter of Point Reyes. Friar Juan Crespí, who may be considered the head of the expedition, not knowing that he had made a discovery, did on the 7th of November 1769 discover the site and harbor of San Francisco, and he gave to them the name which they now bear.'

sion alluded to. It must be borne in mind that the inner bay was not named during this trip, nor for some years later; while the outer bay had been named for more than a half century.

A few of the company still venture to assert that Monterey has not been passed, and to remove all doubt it is decided to send the explorers forward to Point Reyes. Ortega sets out with a small party on the day following, taking provisions for a three days' trip. Meanwhile the rest remain in camp just north of Mussel Point. But during Ortega's absence, the 2d of November, some of the soldiers, in hunting for deer, climb the north-eastern hills, and return with tidings of a new discovery. From the summit they had beheld a great inland sea stretching northward and south-eastward as far as the eye could reach. The country is well wooded they say, and exceedingly beautiful. Thus European eyes first rest on the waters of San Francisco Bay; but the names of these deer-hunters can never be known. At camp they make one error on hearing the news, by attempting to identify this new "brazo de mar ó estero" with the "estero" mentioned by Cabrera Bueno as entering the land from the port of San Francisco under Point Reyes;[19] that is, at first thought it did not seem possible for an inlet of so great extent to have escaped the notice of the early voyagers; but this erroneous idea does not last long, or lead to any results. It is at once foreseen that Ortega's party will not be able to reach Point Reyes, because he has no boats in which to cross, and no time to go round the inlet. And indeed next day Ortega returns. As had been anticipated, he had not been able to cross the inlet and reach San Francisco. To Ortega, whose descendants still live in California, belongs the honor of having

[19] It must be remembered that, to casual observers like the hunters at least, standing on the San Bruno hills, the connection of the bay with the ocean would seem to be very much farther north than the Golden Gate, and possibly far enough north to reach the bay under Pt Reyes.

first explored the peninsula on which stands the commercial metropolis of the west coast of North America; probably also that of having discovered what is now known as the Golden Gate, and possibly that of being the discoverer of the bay, for he may have climbed the hills on his way north and have looked down on the 'brazo de mar,' before the deer-hunters saw it.[20] Yet we have no details of Ortega's exploration, because he comes back with one idea which has driven all others from his mind, and which indeed turns the thoughts of the whole company into a new channel. He has understood the natives, of whom he found some on the peninsula, to say that at the head of the 'brazo de mar' is a harbor, and in it a vessel at anchor.

Visions of the *San José* and of the food and other necessaries they can now obtain float before them sleeping and waking. Some think that after all they are indeed at Monterey. Obviously the next thing to be done is to seek that harbor and vessel. Henc on the 4th of November they break camp and set out, at first keeping along the shore, but soon turning inland and crossing the hills north-eastward, the whole company looking down from the summit upon the inland sea, and then descending into a cañada, down which they follow southward for a time and then encamp; the day's march being only about five or six miles in all. They have crossed the San Bruno hills from just above Point San Pedro to the head of the cañada in a course due west from Milbrae. Next day they march down the same cañada, called by them San Francisco, now San Andrés and San Raimundo, for three leagues and a half, having the main range on the right, and on the left a line of low hills which obstruct their view of the bay. They encamp on a large lagoon, now Laguna Grande, on San Mateo Creek. On the 6th they continue their march

[20] It must also be noted that among Fages' volunteers there was a Sergeant Puig who may possibly be entitled to all this honor, but probably not.

for other three leagues and a half to the end of the
cañada, pitching their camp on a stream flowing into
the bay—doubtless the San Francisquito Creek in
the vicinity of Searsville.

Here the main force remain four days, suffering
considerably from hunger, and many making themselves ill by eating acorns, while the sergeant and

MOVEMENTS OF THE DISCOVERERS.

eight of the party are absent examining the country
and searching for the port and vessel. On the 10th
of November the men return and report the country
sterile and the natives hostile. There is another large
'estero' communicating with the one in sight, but no
sign of any port at its end, which is far away and
difficult to reach. There is nothing to show how far

this reconnoissance extended along the bay shore; but the new estero is evidently but the south-eastern extension of the main bay; and reports of the country are doubtless colored by disappointment respecting the *San José*. A council of officers and friars is called on the 11th, and after the solemnities of holy mass each member gives his written opinion on what should be done. The decision is unanimous that it is useless to seek Monterey farther north, and that it is best to return to Point Pinos. Portolá makes some objection, probably as a matter of form, but yields to the views of the others.

The same afternoon they set out on their return, and in a march of twenty-six days, over the same route by which they came, and without incidents that require notice, they reach what is really Carmelo Bay. Here they remain from November 28th to December 10th, making some additional explorations, but finding no port, and in fact learning nothing new save that the mountains in the south belong to the Sierra de Santa Lucía and that no passage along the shore is practicable. Grass is now abundant for the animals, but the men can get no game, fish, or even clams. Some gulls are eaten, and a mule is killed which only the Catalan volunteers and Lower Californians will eat. Finally, after religious exercises on the preceding day a council is held on the 7th.[21] Three plans are proposed. Some, and among them the governor, favor dividing the force, part remaining at Point Pinos to wait for a vessel, the rest returning to San Diego; others think it best for all to remain till provisions are exhausted, and then depend on mule-meat for the return; but the prevailing sentiment and the decision are in favor of immediate return, since supplies are reduced to fourteen small sacks of flour, while the cold is excessive and snow begins to cover the hills. Meanwhile two mulatto arrieros desert, and on

[21] The record of this junta and of the former one of Nov. 11th were included in the original *Portolá, Diario*, MS., but are not in the copy.

the 9th an iron band supposed to have come from the mast of some vessel is found on the beach by the natives.

Before leaving Carmelo Bay a large cross is set up on a knoll near the beach, bearing the carved inscription "Dig at the foot and thou wilt find a writing." The buried document is a brief narrative of the expedition with a request that the commander of any vessel arriving soon will sail down the coast and try to communicate with the land party.[22] Recrossing the peninsula they set up, on the shore of the very harbor they could not find, another cross with an inscription announcing their departure. Setting out on their return the 11th they ascend the Salinas and retrace, with a few exceptions, their former route. It is an uneventful journey, but I catalogue a few details in a note.[23] Below the San Luis Obispo region the natives begin to bring in an abundance of fish and other food, so that there is no further suffering, and on January 24, 1770, with many curious conjectures as to the condition in which their friends will be found, they approach the palisade enclosure at San Diego, and announce their arrival by a discharge of musketry. Warm welcome follows and then comparison of notes. Neither party can report much progress toward the conquest of California.

[22] The letter is dated Dec. 9th, and is translated in *Doyle's Address*.

[23] December 16th, a lean mule left in the Sierra de Sta Lucía was recovered fat and well cared for by the natives. 20th, to prevent theft provisions were distributed, 40 tortillas to each man and a little biscuit, ham, and chocolate for each officer and padre. 21st, a man who had deserted at Point Pinos was found among the natives and excused himself by saying that he had gone in search of Monterey in the hope of honor and reward. Another deserter returned later to San Diego. 24th and 25th, the natives began to bring in food. 28th, stuck fast in a mud-hole near San Luis Obispo, and unable to say mass though it was a day of *fiesta*. January 1st, a bear and cubs killed furnishing material for a feast. January 3d, passed Point Concepcion. 4th, another fat mule restored by the natives. Food now abundant. 11th, at Asumpta, or Santa Bárbara. January 12th to 15th, instead of going up the Santa Clara River, they took a more southern route. They could not get through by the first route tried, on which they named the Triunfo ranchería, a name that seems to have survived; but they finally crossed by the modern stage route *via* Simi. January 16th to 18th, their route through the Los Angeles region was also different but not very clear. On the 17th they crossed the Rio Porciúncula and went to a valley which they called San Miguel, where San Gabriel mission afterwards stood; and next day they crossed the Rio Santa Ana 6 long leagues distant.

CHAPTER VII.

OCCUPATION OF MONTEREY—FOUNDING OF SAN CÁRLOS, SAN ANTONIO, AND SAN GABRIEL.

1770–1771.

AFFAIRS AT SAN DIEGO—A DISHEARTENED GOVERNOR—CALIFORNIA TO BE ABANDONED—RIVERA'S TRIP TO THE SOUTH—PRAYER ANSWERED—ARRIVAL OF THE 'SAN ANTONIO'—DISCOVERY OF MONTEREY—IN CAMP ON CARMELO BAY—FOUNDING OF THE PRESIDIO AND MISSION OF SAN CÁRLOS—DESPATCHES SENT SOUTH BY LAND AND SEA—PORTOLÁ LEAVES FAGES IN COMMAND—RECEPTION OF THE NEWS IN MEXICO—TEN PADRES SENT TO CALIFORNIA—PALOU'S MEMORIAL—MISSION WORK IN THE NORTH—ARRIVAL OF THE NEW PADRES—STATIONS ASSIGNED—FOUNDING OF SAN ANTONIO—TRANSFER OF SAN CÁRLOS TO CARMELO BAY—EVENTS AT SAN DIEGO—DESERTIONS—RETIREMENT OF PARRON AND GOMEZ—ESTABLISHING OF SAN GABRIEL—OUTRAGES BY SOLDIERS.

AT San Diego during Portolá's absence no progress had been made in mission work, save perhaps the addition of a palisade and a few tule huts to the buildings. The governor's return in January 1770, from his unsuccessful trip to Monterey, had no effect to brighten the aspect of affairs, since he was much disheartened, and not disposed to afford aid to the president in advancing the interests of a mission that would very likely have to be abandoned. So nothing was done beyond making a new corral for the horses. Serra and Parron were just recovering from the scurvy, and Vizcaino was still suffering from the arrow wound in his hand.[1] Portolá's plan was to make a careful inventory of supplies, reserve enough for the march to Velicatá, and abandon San Diego when the remainder should be exhausted, which would

---

[1] Eight of the volunteers had died. *Portolá, Diario*, MS., 34.

be a little after the middle of April, the 20th being fixed as the date of departure.

The friars, especially Serra and Crespí, were greatly disappointed at the governor's resolution. They were opposed to the idea of abandoning an enterprise so auspiciously begun, though how they expected the soldiers to live does not clearly appear. Portolá was probably somewhat too much inclined to look at the dark side; while the president perhaps allowed his missionary zeal to impair his judgment. So far as they were concerned, personally, Serra and Crespí resolved to stay in the country at all hazards; and for the result they could only trust in providence to send supplies before the day set for departure. They received some encouragement, however, from Captain Vila, who, judging from the description, agreed with Serra that the northern port where a cross had been left was really Monterey. Furthermore it is said that Vila made a secret promise to take the priests on board the *San Cárlos*, wait at San Diego for another vessel, and renew the northern coast enterprise.[2]

On the 11th of February Rivera was despatched southward, with nineteen or twenty soldiers, two muleteers, two natives, eighty mules, and ten horses. He was accompanied by Padre Vizcaino whose lame hand procured him leave of absence; and his destination was Velicatá, where he was to get the cattle that had been left there, and such other supplies as might be procurable. He carried full reports to secular and Franciscan authorities of all that had thus far befallen the expedition, bearing also a letter from Serra to Palou, in which the writer bewailed the prospect of failure and announced his intention to remain to the last. After some skirmishes with the savages, two of whom had to be killed to frighten away the rest, Rivera reached Velicatá February 25th, at once setting about his task of gathering supplies, in which he was zealously seconded by Palou;

[2] *Palou, Vida,* 95-6.

but some months passed before he could be ready to
march northward—indeed, before he was ready the
urgent necessity had ceased.

Meanwhile at San Diego men and officers were
waiting, preparations were being made for departure,
friars were praying, and days were passing one by
one, but yet no vessel came. The only conversation
was of abandoning the northern country, and every
word was an arrow to the soul of the pious Junípero;
but he could only pray unceasingly, and trust to the
intercession of Saint Joseph the great patron of the
expedition. In his honor a *novena*—nine days' public
prayer—was instituted, to culminate in a grand ceremonial entreaty on the saint's own day, March the
19th, the day before the one of final abandonment.

Gently smiled the morning sun on that momentous
morrow as it rose above the hills and warmed to hap-
piness the myriads of creatures beneath its benignant
rays. Surpassingly lovely the scene; the beautiful
bay in its fresh spring border hiding behind the hills
like a sportive girl from briny mother ocean. At an
early hour the fathers were abroad on the heights,
for they could neither eat nor rest. The fulfilment or
failure of their hopes was now to be determined. The
day wore slowly away; noon came, and the hours of
the afternoon, and yet no sail appeared. The suspense
was painful, for it was more than life to these holy
men, the redemption of the bright, fresh paradise;
and so all the day they watched and prayed, watched
with strained eyes, and prayed, not with lips only but
with all those soul-longings which omniscience alone
can translate. Finally, as the sun dropped below the
horizon and all hope was gone, a sail appeared in the
distance like a winged messenger from heaven, and
before twilight deepened into darkness the so ardently
longed-for vessel was in the offing. California was
saved, blessed be God! and they might yet consum-
mate their dearly cherished schemes.

The fourth day thereafter the *San Antonio* anchored in the bay, whence she had sailed the previous July. She had reached San Blas in twenty days, and both Galvez and the viceroy gave immediate orders to provide the needed supplies. After certain vexatious but unavoidable delays, she had again turned her prow northward in December. Perez had orders to sail for Monterey direct, where it was supposed Portolá would be found; but fortunately he was obliged to enter the Santa Bárbara channel for water, and the natives explained that the land expedition had returned southward. Even then Perez in his perplexity would have gone to Monterey had not the loss of an anchor forced him to turn about just in time to prevent the abandonment of San Diego. The *San Antonio* brought abundant supplies, and she also brought instructions from Galvez and Viceroy Croix, one or both of which facts drove from Portolá's mind all thought of abandoning the conquest. He made haste in his preparations for a return to Monterey with Serra and Crespí, setting out overland April 17th, after despatching the *San Antonio* northward the day before.

There were left at San Diego, Vila with a mate and five sailors on the *San Cárlos*, Sergeant Ortega and eight soldiers *de cuera* as a guard, Parron and Gomez as regular ministers in charge of the mission, and ten Lower Californians as laborers. The *San Cárlos* had orders to receive a crew from the *San José* when that most uncertain craft should arrive, and then proceed to Monterey. Simultaneously with the departure of the northern expedition two natives had been sent south with letters which reached Velicatá in nine days, and Loreto late in May. All went quietly with the little company left to struggle spiritually with the southern *gentilidad*. Let it be hoped that before the end of 1770 the missionaries succeeded in making a few converts, as they probably did, but there is no positive record of a single baptism. Rivera with his nineteen or twenty soldiers, over eighty mules laden with supplies, and one hundred and sixty-four head of cattle, having left Velicatá in May,[3] arrived in July. About the same time messengers came down by land announcing the successful occupation of Monterey, and the intention of Portolá to come down by sea and take the *San Cárlos* for San Blas. Vila, accordingly, made ready for departure, obtaining a soldier and two muleteers to reënforce his crew; but as the *San Antonio* did not appear, and his own vessel was being injured by her long stay, in August the worthy captain shook out his idle sails and made for San Blas. He died a little later, and his pioneer *paquebot* had to return to California under a new commander.[4]

Let us turn again toward the north with the expeditions sent out by land and sea to renew the search for Monterey. The *San Antonio* sailed from San Diego April 16th, having on board besides Perez and crew— Miguel del Pino being second officer—Junípero Serra, Miguel Costansó, Pedro Prat,[5] and a cargo of stores for a new mission. Next day Portolá set out by land, his company consisting of Fages with twelve Catalan volunteers and seven *soldados de cuera*, Padre Crespí, two muleteers, and five natives. They followed the same route as before, recovered in the Sierra de Santa Lucía an Indian who had deserted on the former trip, and finally encamped on the 24th of May near the spot where they had left the second cross the winter before on the bay shore. They found the cross still standing, but curiously surrounded and adorned with arrows, sticks, feathers, fish, meat, and clams evidently deposited there by the savages as offerings to the strangers' fetich. And later when the natives

[3] April 14th, according to *Monterey, Estracto de Noticias.*
[4] On San Diego events of 1770 see *Palou, Not.,* i. 423–6, 432–9, 460–1; *Id., Vida,* 88–104.
[5] By computation there should also have been on board 2 mechanics, 5 servants, 3 muleteers, and 6 Lower Californians; but it is doubtful if these figures are correct, especially in the items of Indians and muleteers, not a very useful class of persons on board a ship.

had learned to make themselves understood, to speak as best should please their teachers, some strange tales they told, how the cross had been illuminated at night and had grown in stature till it seemed to reach the heavens, moving the gentiles to propitiate by their offerings this Christian symbol that it might do them no harm. As Portolá, Crespí, and Fages walked along the beach that afternoon returning from a visit to the cross, they looked out over the placid bay, ruffled only by the movements of seals and whales, and they said, all being of one accord, "This is the port of Monterey which we seek, just as Vizcaino and Cabrera ·Bueno describe it"—and so it was, the only wonder being that they had not known it before. Soon for lack of fresh water camp was moved across to Carmelo Bay.

A week later, on the last day of May, the *San Antonio* hove in sight off Point Pinos; fires were lighted on shore for her guidance; and she entered the harbor by Cabrera's sailing directions. She had at first been driven south to latitude 30°, and then north to the Ensenada de los Farallones, where she might have explored the port of San Francisco and the newly discovered inland bay had not Perez' orders required him to steer direct for Monterey. June 1st the governor, friar, and lieutenant crossed over from Carmelo to welcome the new arrival, and the order was given to transfer the camp back to the port of Monterey, about whose identity there was no longer any doubt; for close search along the shore revealed the little ravine with its pools of fresh water, the trees, and even the wide-spreading oak whose branches touched the water at high tide and under which mass had been said by Ascension in 1602,[6] all as in olden time except the crowds of friendly natives.

[6] 'Hizose la Iglesia á la sombra de una grande Encina, que con algúnas de sus ramas llegaba á la Mar, y cerca de ella, en una Barranquilla, á veinte passos, havia unos pozos en que havia agua muy buena.' *Venegas, Not. Cal.*, iii. 101-2, quoted from *Torquemada*. According to Vallejo, *Hist. Cal.*, MS., i. 54, the tree under which Ascension said mass in 1602, and Serra in 1770. is still standing, being that under which a new cross was set up on the 100th anniversary June 3, 1870; but as the latter tree is at some distance from the

On the 3d of June all were assembled on the beach, where an *enramada*, or shelter of branches, had been erected and a cross made ready near the old oak. Water was blessed, the bells were hung, and the *fiesta* began by loud and oft-repeated peals. Then Father Junípero donned his alb and stole, and all on bended knee chanted the *venite creator spiritus*, after which the cross was planted and blessed, and the good friar sprinkled beach and fields with holy water, thus " putting to rout all infernal foes." An image of the holy virgin presented by Archbishop Lorenzana of Mexico having been set up on the altar, mass was said by Serra amidst the thunder of cannon and the crack of musketry, followed by a *salve* to the image and a *te deum laudamus.* The church ceremonies ended, Portolá proceeded to take formal possession in the name of Cárlos III. by hoisting and saluting the royal flag of Spain, and going through the usual forms of pulling grass, throwing stones, and recording all in the prescribed *acta.* Finally the officers and friars ate together under the shade of trees near the shore, while the soldiers and others enjoyed their feast a little apart.

Thus were formally founded on June 3, 1770, the mission and presidio of San Cárlos Borromeo de Monterey.[7] The mission was founded in the name of

tide-water the identity may be questioned. David Spence, an old and well known citizen of Monterey, said that Junípero's tree was shown him in 1824 by Mariano Estrada, and that it fell in 1837 or 1838, the water having washed away the earth from its roots. Spence thought there was no doubt of its identity. *Taylor's Discov. and Founders,* ii., No. 24, 5.

[7] St Charles Borromeo was born at Arona near Milan, Italy, in 1538. He was son of the Count of Arona, nephew of Pope Pius IV., archbishop of Milan, and cardinal. Dying in 1584, he was canonized in 1610. A word is necessary to remove certain difficulties into which modern writers and modern usage have fallen respecting the name of this mission. This name was always San Cárlos; San Cárlos de Monterey was simply San Cárlos at Monterey, that port having been named long before. When the mission was moved to Carmelo bay and river it was naturally spoken of as San Cárlos del Carmelo, or San Cárlos at Carmelo, a port also named long before. But Monterey being a prominent place the mission continued to be often called San Cárlos at Monterey, or San Cárlos at Carmelo near Monterey, as the Spanish preposition *de* may best be translated. But again the full name of the bay and river Carmelo was Nuestra Señora del Monte Carmelo, or Nra. Sra. del Cármen, and hence a new source of confusion arose, all of which, however,

the college of San Fernando; Saint Joseph was named as patron; and Crespí was appointed as associate minister with Serra. A few humble huts were at once erected on a site surveyed by Costansó, a gunshot from the beach and three times as far from the port, on an inlet which communicated with the bay at high water. These buildings constituted both presidio and mission, as at San Diego, being enclosed by a palisade. One of the huts was completed and blessed as a temporary church on the 14th of June, when a grand procession took place; bells were rung, and guns were fired; but thus far no natives appeared, being frightened it is said by the noise of cannon and musketry.

A soldier and a young sailor volunteered to carry despatches with news of success to San Diego and to the peninsula. They started June 14th, met Rivera just below San Diego, were reënforced by five of his men, and finally carried their glad tidings to Governor Armona, who had just succeeded Portolá, and to Padre Palou at Todos Santos, on the 2d of August. Salutes and thanksgiving masses celebrated the occasion at Loreto, Todos Santos, and Santa Ana, while Armona despatched a vessel to carry the news to the main.

In accordance with previous orders from Galvez, Portolá, as soon as a beginning was fairly made at Monterey, turned the government of the new establishments over to Fages as military commandant, and sailed away in the *San Antonio* on the 9th of July. He took with him the engineer Costansó; and Perez

may be removed by bearing in mind that the mission was always San Cárlos, and that other words were used solely to express its locality. Taylor, in *Cal. Farmer*, April 20, 1860, gives the following native names of localities at Monterey; site of modern town *Achiesta* or *Achasta;* beach, *Sukilta;* Fort hill, *Hunnukul;* site of post-office, *Shirista*. About the date of foundation on June 3d, there is no possible error. Palou, Serra, the mission books of San Cárlos, and scores of official reports in later years confirm this. Vallejo, *Hist. Ca'.*, MS., i. 66–8, and Alvarado, *Hist. Cal.*, MS., i. 23–4, are very positive that the mission was not founded till later; but these writers confound the founding with the subsequent transfer. See *S. Cárlos, Lib. Mision*, MS., *Prov. St. Pap.*, MS., i. 109–10. *Arch. Arzobispado*, MS., v. pt. ii. 33.

intended to touch at San Diego to divide his crew with the *San Carlos* if the *San José* had not yet appeared, but, as we have seen, was not able to do so, and arrived at San Blas the 1st of August. Costansó and Perez went to Mexico as bearers of the news, arriving on the 10th, at which date the name of the former disappears from the annals of California for twenty years or more, at the end of which time we shall find him giving some sensible advice on Californian affairs; while of Portolá nothing is known after his landing at San Blas, except that he was governor of Puebla in 1779. He was first in the list of California rulers. His term of office may be regarded as having extended from April 1769 to July 9, 1770, and he is spoken of in the record both as governor and comandante; but, though there is some confusion respecting his exact title, it appears that that of military commandant is used with more propriety than the other.[8]

Leaving the four friars under the protection of Fages and his nineteen men in the north and of Rivera with his twenty-two men in the south,[9] busy in ear-

[8] Portolá came to Lower California in 1768 as governor, the first the peninsula had ever had; but when he volunteered to take command in person of the northern expedition, it seems that Armona was appointed to succeed him in the governorship. I do not know the exact date of Armona's appointment, but he arrived at Loreto in June 1769, and went back to the mainland two weeks later without having taken possession of his office. In the mean time Gonzalez ruled as a kind of lieutenant-governor or military commandant until relieved in October 1769 by Toledo, who governed in the same capacity until Armona, who had failed to get his resignation accepted, returned in June 1770 to rule until November, Moreno ruling, in much the same capacity apparently as Gonzalez and Toledo, until the arrival of Gov. Barri in March 1771. Now while Gonzalez, Toledo, and Moreno cannot be properly credited with any authority in Upper California, their terms as *interinos* render it difficult to define those of the proprietary governors. Thus, though Portolá was in a sense governor of the Californias down to June 1770, since no regular successor had taken possession of the office, I have named him in my list of rulers of Alta California as commandant from the first settlement down to July 9, 1770. In *Monterey, Estracto de Noticias*, he is called comandante en gefe.

[9] Rivera and his men were expected to march to Monterey on their return from the peninsula, but for some unexplained reason, possibly dissatisfaction at Fages' appointment to the chief command, Rivera remained at San Diego. According to *Monterey, Estracto de Noticias*, Fages had a force of over 30 men besides Rivera's force, which is an error.

nest if not very successful efforts to attract and convert
the gentiles of Monterey and San Diego, let us glance
briefly at what was being done in Mexico to advance
Spanish interests in the far north. We have seen
that the news of success at Monterey had arrived by
land at Loreto and by sea at San Blas early in August.
Therefore, the despatches sent by Portolá from San
Blas reached Mexico in advance of the others on the
10th. The news was received with great manifestations of joy; the cathedral bells rang out their glad
peals, those of the churches responding. A solemn
thanksgiving mass was said at which all government
dignitaries were present; and there followed a grand
reception at which Galvez and Croix received congratulations in the royal name for this last extension
of the Spanish domain. Immediate and liberal provision was made for the new establishments. So
favorable were the reports on both country and inhabitants that it was resolved at once to forward all
needed aid and to found five new missions above San
Diego. The guardian of San Fernando was asked to
furnish ten friars for these missions, besides twenty
more for old and new missions in the peninsula. Fortunately a large number of Franciscans had lately
arrived from Spain, and after some deliberation and
discussion resulting in a determination to secularize
the Sierra Gorda missions, the required missionaries
were furnished.[10]

These arrangements were all made within six days
after the news arrived, and under the date of August
16th the viceroy caused to be printed in the government printing-office for general circulation a résumé
in pamphlet form of all that had been accomplished
by the northern expeditions, the present condition
of the new presidios and missions, and of what had

[10] The 10 were Antonio Paterna, president en route, Antonio Cruzado,
Buenaventura Sitjar, Domingo Juncosa, Francisco Dumetz, José Caballer,
Angel Somera, Luis Jaume, Miguel Pieras, and Pedro Benito Cambon. They
were to receive each a stipend of $275 a year, and $400 travelling expenses.
Each new mission received $1,000 and the necessary vestments, including a
specially fine *ornamento*, or set of vestments, for Monterey.

been decided upon respecting aid for further extension.[11] The *San Antonio* was to sail from San Blas
in October with the ten friars and a full cargo of
supplies. The priests set out from the college in
that month, but were obliged to wait at Tepic until
January 20, 1771, before the vessel could be made
ready for sea.[12] The viceroy in his letter to Fages
states that Rivera is ordered to put his men at
the commandant's disposal, and the captain of the
company at Guaymas has orders to send twelve men
to supply the places of those who had died on the
voyage.[13] In 1771 the only thing to be noticed is
the memorial presented in December to the viceroy
by the guardian of San Fernando, at the suggestion
of Palou. Twelve of the eighteen articles of this
document were suggestions for the welfare of the new
establishments,[14] some of them founded on minor disagreements which already began to manifest themselves between the military and missionary authorities.

At Monterey after Portolá's departure little was
accomplished during the year 1770. For want of

[11] *Monterey, Estracto de Noticias del Puerto de Monterey, de la Mision, y
Presido que se han establecido en él con la denominacion de San Cárlos, y del
sucesso de las dos Expediciones de Mar, y Tierra que á este fin se despacharon
en el año proximo anterior de 1769.* Mexico 16 de Agosto de 1770. Con
licencia y orden del Exmo Señor Virrey. En la Imprenta del Superior Govi-
erno. Fol., 3 unnumbered leaves. This rare tract is in my collection, and it
is reprinted also in Palou's *Noticias.* When this notice was printed the
despatches from Loreto had not yet arrived.

[12] Palou, *Vida,* 113–16, says she sailed Jan. 2d.

[13] Letter dated Nov. 12th, in *Prov. St. Pap.,* MS., i. 69–71.

[14] 1st. That the commandants at San Diego and Monterey be made to obey
more closely the instructions of Galvez. (There had been some disagreement
with the friars in connection with the desertion of an arriero.) 2d. That some
families of Christian natives be sent up from Baja California to serve as
laborers. 3d. That a guard or presidio be established at San Buenaventura.
4th. That these natives be kindly treated. 5th. That the train of mules be
increased for service from Sonora and the peninsula. 6th. That presidios and
missions be supplied for 18 months by the service of two snows. 7th. That
San Francisco be explored, Monterey being as some say no harbor. 9th. That
mission temporalities should be wholly under control of the friars, with the
power of removing servants and officials. 14th. Vessels for Monterey should
sail in February or April. 15th. A proper *limosna,* or allowance, should be
granted to friars going or coming. 16th. San Diego, Monterey, and San
Buenaventura should have the $1,000 allowed to new missions. 18th. Sol-
diers should be supplied with rations so as to be able to do escort duty. *Palou,
Not.,* i. 120–3.

priests and of soldiers[15] nothing was done towards the founding of San Buenaventura, although the necessary supplies were lying in readiness at San Cárlos. Meanwhile Serra and Crespí worked among the Eslenes, who under the influence of gifts and kindness were fast losing their timidity. A Baja Californian neophyte who had learned the native dialect rendered great assistance; preaching soon began; and on December 26th the first baptism was administered.[16]

The *San Antonio* anchored at Monterey May 21, 1771, having on board the ten priests already named, except that Gomez from San Diego was in place of Dumetz, with all the necessary appurtenances for the establishing of five new missions. The father president's heart was filled with joy, and he was enabled to celebrate the festival of corpus Christi on the 30th with a community of twelve friars. The five new missions proposed, in addition to San Buenaventura, were San Gabriel, San Luis Obispo, San Antonio,

[15] Palou, *Vida*, 104-6, says it was for want of soldiers, because Rivera did not come up as expected; but he says nothing of the fact that there were no padres available.

[16] Alvarado, *Hist. Cal.*, MS., i. 22, mentions some writings of the soldier J. B. Valdés to the effect that the Baja Californians conversed readily with the Eslenes, and he is disposed to believe after much inquiry that the language was to some extent understood. Vallejo, *Hist. Cal.*, MS., i. 55-6, names the interpreter Maximiano, and states that the Eslen chief lived near the spring called Agua Zarca on what was later the rancho of Guadalupe Ávila. Unfortunately the first book of baptisms for San Cárlos has been lost, and the exact number of converts for the early years is not known. The first burial was on the day of founding June 3d, when Alejo Niño one of the *San Antonio's* crew was buried at the foot of the cross. According to *Palou, Not.*, i. 451, he was a calker; the mission record makes him a *cadete*. The first interment in the cemetery was that of Ignacio Ramirez, a mulatto slave from the *San Antonio*, who had money ready to purchase his freedom. There were four more deaths during the year, three of sailors and one of a Baja Californian. The first marriage did not take place till Nov. 16, 1772. *San Cárlos, Lib. de Mision*, MS., 84; *Taylor's Odds and Ends*, 4. A writer in the *Revista Científica*, i. 328, tells us that the mission of Cármen or Monte Carmelo was founded June 3d on the gulf of Carmelo, but never progressed much. A newspaper item extensively circulated speaks of an Indian woman still living in 1869 who was the mother of two children when the mission church was built. Shea, *Cath. Miss.*, 94, calls the mission Monte Carmel. Tuthill, *Hist. Cal.*, 80-1, says that Portolá retired by water and Rivera by land, leaving Junípero with 5 friars and Fages with 30 soldiers.

Santa Clara, and San Francisco. There were sent
only missionaries sufficient for five of the six, and as
Parron and Gomez, unfitted for duty by the scurvy,
had to be granted leave of absence, still another mission must wait, San Francisco and Santa Clara being
selected for that purpose. The president immediately
announced the distribution of priests to their respective missions,[17] and on the 7th of June the six intended
for the south sailed in the *San Antonio* for San Diego,
Fages accompanying them.

Only one of the northern missions could be founded
until Fages should bring or send north some of Rivera's soldiers, but Serra set out early in July with ar
escort of eight soldiers, three sailors, and a few Indian
workmen for the Hoya de la Sierra de Santa Lucía,
named by the first land expedition, where he proposed
to establish the first mission under Pieras and Sitjar
who accompanied him. His route was probably up
the Salinas River and the Arroyo Seco, and the site
selected was an oak-studded glen named Cañada de los
Robles[18] on a fine stream. Here the bells were hung
on a tree and loudly tolled, while Fray Junípero
shouted like a madman: "Come gentiles, come to the
holy church, come and receive the faith of Jesus
Christ!" until Father Pieras reminded the enthusiast
that there was not a gentile within hearing and that
it would be well to stop the noise and go to work[19]
Then a cross was erected, the president said mass
under a shelter of branches, and thus was founded on
July 14, 1771, the mission of San Antonio de Pádua.[20]

[17] The distribution was as follows: San Diego, Luis Jaume and Francisco
Dumetz; San Buenaventura, Antonio Paterna and Antonio Cruzado; San Luis
Obispo, Domingo Juncosa and José Cavaller; San Gabriel, Ángel Somera and
Pedro Benito Cambon; San Antonio, Miguel Pieras and Buenaventura Sitjar;
San Cárlos, Junípero Serra and Juan Crespí.
[18] The native name of the site was *Texhaya* according to *Dept. St. Pap.*,
Ben. Mil., MS., lxxxi. 49, or *Sextapay* according to Taylor, note on the fly-
leaf of *Cuesta, Vocabulario*, MS.
[19] *Palou, Vida*, 122.
[20] *S. Antonio, Lib. de Mision.* MS., 1; *Prov. St. Pap.*, MS., i. 112–15; Palou,
Not., ii. 24–5, tells us of an old woman who applied for baptism, and who when
a girl had heard her father speak of a padre dressed like these, who came t*

Only one native witnessed the ceremonies, but he soon brought in his companions in large numbers, who brought pine-nuts and seeds, all they had to give, and aided in the work of building a church, barracks, and house for the missionaries, all of which were on a humble scale and protected as usual by a palisade. The natives seemed more tractable than at either San Diego or Monterey, and the ministers had hopes of a great spiritual conquest, the first baptism taking place the 14th of August.[21] Leaving the harvest to the reapers and their guard of six soldiers, I return with Serra to Monterey at the end of July.

Soon after the establishing of San Cárlos Padre Junípero had determined to transfer the mission to Carmelo Valley. His avowed reason was lack of water and fertile soil at Monterey; but it is likely that he also desired to remove his little band of neophytes, and the larger flock he hoped to gather, from immediate contact with the presidio soldiers, always regarded by missionaries with more or less dread as necessary evils tending to corrupt native innocence. The necessary permission for the transfer came up by the *San Antonio* on her third trip,[22] and two days after her departure, before going to found San Antonio, the president crossed over to select the new site. There he left three sailors and four Indians from the peninsula at work cutting timber, and making preparations under the watchful eyes of five soldiers who were charitably supposed to lend occasional assist-

the country flying through the air and preaching Christian doctrines. Gomez, *Lo que sabe*, MS., 53-4, records the tradition that the ringing of the bells frightened away the natives; and that subsequently they refused to eat cheese believing it to be the brains of dead men. San Antonio de Pádua was born in Lisbon in 1195, died at Pádua in 1231, and was canonized in 1232. He was a famous preacher, his sermons affecting even the fishes, and a zealous propagator of the Franciscan order. His day, as celebrated by the church, is June 13th.

[21] P. Serra in his *Representacion*, MS., of May 21, 1773, says the work of building was hurried to get ready for farming, and that it was hindered by Fages taking away the best soldiers. Eight mules were left at the mission.

[22] Nov. 12, 1770, Viceroy Croix writes to Fages that San Cárlos mission is to be established on the Rio Carmelo with a sufficient guard of soldiers. *Prov. St. Pap.*, MS., i. 70.

ance. Back from San Antonio in August he again
went over to Carmelo to hasten the movements of
the workmen, who were proceeding very leisurely;
but it was several months before the palisade square
enclosing wooden chapel, dwelling, storehouse, guard-
house, and corrals could be completed; and it was the
end of December when the formal transfer took place,
the exact date being unknown. The two ministers
took up their permanent residence in their new home,
Juncosa and Cavaller assisting temporarily both at
mission and presidio.[23]

Events at San Diego during the year 1771 were by
no means exciting or important. Beyond the baptism
of a very few natives, the exact number being unknown, no progress in mission work is recorded; but
Rivera with his force of fourteen men, in addition to
Ortega's regular mission guard of eight, would seem
to have passed the time comfortably so far as work is
concerned. In April, when the *San Antonio* touched
at this port with her load of friars, the two ministers
were both disabled by scurvy, and Gomez went up to
Monterey, while Dumetz took his place. On July
14th the vessel returned with six padres besides
Gomez, who had leave of absence and was on his way
to Mexico. Parron retired at about the same time,
overland, to the missions of the peninsula. Captain,
Perez sailed the 21st.[24] Fages came down with the
priests, and the intention was to establish San Gabriel
at once; but local troubles caused delay. The day
after the vessel's departure nine soldiers and a muleteer deserted. Padre Paterna was induced by Fages
to go with a few soldiers and a pardon signed in blank
to bring them back. His mission was successful, and

[23] Vallejo and Alvarado, as I have already noted, insist on regarding this
as the veritable founding of the mission. Taylor, in *Cal. Farmer*, Apr. 20,
1860, says the transfer was in 1772 and that the mission became known as
San Cárlos Borromeo del Carmelo de Monterey.

[24] Serra, *San Diego, Lib. de Mision*, MS., 7, says however that Parron
went, apparently by land, to Baja California; and Palou, *Vida*, 129, says he
went with a party by land, of which party nothing further is known.

after having availed themselves of the ' church asylum'
the deserters returned to duty. Again, the 6th of
August, a corporal and five soldiers deserted, returning on the 24th to steal cattle from the mission. This
time Fages went out to bring them in by force, but
found them strongly fortified and resolved to die
rather than yield, and again, to save life, persuasion
was employed, and Dumetz brought back the fugitives.[25] Respecting the real or pretended grievances
of the soldiers we know nothing, but it is evident
that some misunderstanding already existed between
Fages and the friars, and that Palou's record is intended
to show the agency of the latter in its best light.
Early in the autumn there arrived from Guaymas
twelve Catalan volunteers.

Meanwhile on August 6th Somera and Cambon
with a guard of ten soldiers and a supply-train of
mules under four muleteers and four soldiers, who
were to return, left San Diego to establish their new
mission, following the old route northward. It had
been the intention to place the mission on the River
Santa Ana, or Jesus de los Temblores, but as no suitable site was found there the party went farther and
chose a fertile, well wooded and watered spot near the
River San Miguel, so named on the return trip of the
first expedition three years before,[26] and since known
as the River San Gabriel. At first a large force of
natives presented themselves under two chieftains and
attempted by hostile demonstrations to prevent the
purpose of the Spaniards; but when one of the padres
held up a painting of the virgin, the savages instantly
threw down their arms and their two captains ran up
to lay their necklaces at the feet of the beautiful
queen, thus signifying their desire for peace.[27]

[25] In a letter of Gov. Barri to Fages, dated Oct. 2, 1771, he advises the
commandant not to grieve over the desertion of two soldiers. *Prov. St. Pap.*,
MS., i. 72.
[26] *Palou, Not.*, i. 477. The same author in his *Vida*, 129–30, implies that
the site selected was on the Rio de los Temblores.
[27] It is only in his *Vida*, 129–30, that Palou tells this story.

The raising of the cross and regular ceremonial routine which constituted the formal founding of San Gabriel Arcángel[28] took place on September 8th, and the natives cheerfully assisted in the work of bringing timber and constructing the stockade enclosure with its tule-roofed buildings of wood, continuing in the mean time their offerings of pine-nuts and acorns to the image of Our Lady.[29] Though friendly as yet, the natives crowded into the camp in such numbers that ten soldiers were not deemed a sufficient guard; and Padre Somera went down to San Diego the 1st of October, returning on the 9th with a reënforcement of two men. Next day a crowd of natives attacked two soldiers who were guarding the horses. The chief discharged an arrow at one of the soldiers, who stopped it with his shield, and killed the chieftain with a musket-ball. Terrified by the destructive effects of the gun the savages fled, and the soldiers, cutting off the fallen warrior's head, set it on a pole

[28] The Archangel Gabriel has a place in several religions. To the Israelites he was the angel of death; according to the Talmud he was the prince of fire and ruled the thunder. He set fire to the temple of Jerusalem; appeared to Daniel and Zacharias; announced to Mary the birth of Christ; and dictated the Koran to Mahomet. The last-named prophet describes him very fully, mentioning among other things 500 pairs of wings, the distance from one wing to another being 500 years' journey. His day in the church calendar is March 18th. The mission was often called San Gabriel de los Temblores, the latter word like Carmelo with San Cárlos indicating simply locality. It had been intended to mean San Gabriel on the River Temblores, but when another site was selected the name was retained meaning 'San Gabriel in the region of Earthquakes,' as 'San Gabriel de San Miguel' would have been åwkward. See Serra, in *Prov. St. Pap.*, MS., i. 118; *S. Gabriel Lib. de Mision*, MS. The author of *Los Angeles Hist.*, 5, is in error when he says that the San Gabriel River was called Temblores. The mission was not moved to its present site until several years later. *Arch. Santa Bárbara*, MS., i. 131; *Reid, Los Angeles Co.*, *Ind.*, No. 17. San Gabriel was the only mission at the founding of which Serra had not assisted, and this was because Fages failed to notify him, as he had promised. *Serra, Repres., 21 de Mayo*, MS., 118.

[29] According to Hugo Reid, *Los Angeles Co. Ind.*, No. 16, who derived his information from traditions, the natives were greatly terrified at the first sight of the Spaniards; women hid; men put out the fires. They thought the strangers gods when they saw them strike fire from a flint, but seeing them kill a bird, they put them down as human beings 'of a nasty white color with ugly blue eyes;' and later, as no violence was done, they called them *chichinabros*, or 'reasonable beings.' Women used by the soldiers were obliged to undergo a long purification, and for a long time every child with white blood in its veins was strangled. Food given by the white men was buried in the woods. Brown sugar was long regarded as the excrement of the new-comers.

before the presidio gates. The fugitive assailants came back after a few days to beg for their leader's head; but it was only very gradually that they were induced to resume friendly relations with the friars, and frequent the mission as before. There is little doubt that their sudden hostility arose from outrages by the soldiers on the native women.[30]

A few days after this affair Fages arrived from San Diego with two friars, sixteen soldiers,[31] and four muleteers in charge of a mule train, the force intended for the establishing of San Buenaventura. In consequence of the recent hostilities Fages decided to add six men to the guard of San Gabriel, and to postpone for the present the founding of a new mission. Paterna and Cruzado also remained at San Gabriel where they became the following year the regular ministers on the retirement of Somera and Cambon by reason of ill-health. Mission progress was extremely slow, the first baptism having been that of a child on November 27th, and the whole number during the first two years only seventy-three. This want of prosperity is attributed by Serra largely to the conduct of the soldiers, who refused to work, paid no attention to the orders of their worthless corporal, drove away the natives by their insolence, and even pursued them to their rancherías, where they lassoed

[30] Palou, *Not.*, i. 478–9, says a soldier had outraged a woman in one of the rancherías. The same author in *Vida*, 130–2, tells us that the woman was the wife of the slain chieftain and the guilty soldier the one attacked. Serra in his *Representacion*, MS., of May 21, 1773, says that the first grievance of the natives was an order from Fages that only 5 or 6 of them should be admitted within the stockade at a time, followed by a secret order not to allow any gentiles at all to enter. Serra says decidedly that if he had been there he would have ordered the padres to abandon the mission; for if they could have no intercourse with gentiles for what were they in the country at all? One day the soldiers went out to look for cattle, or more likely for women, and the chief captain was killed, his head being brought to the mission. In Serra's eyes all misfortunes were chargeable to Fages.

[31] Palou, *Not.*, i. 479, says distinctly that he had 26 soldiers, 12 volunteers who had lately arrived from Baja California and 14 soldiers *de cuera;* but I think the last item should be 4 instead of 14, which agrees exactly with the available force at San Diego. Otherwise 10 cuera soldiers must have arrived from the south of which there is no record, or Fages must have brought 10 with him from Monterey, which seems unlikely. A total of 16 also allows San Buenaventura 10 men, the same guard as that sent originally to S. Gabriel.

women for their lust and killed such males as dared to
interfere.[32] Fages, probably with ten Catalan volunteers, continued his march to Monterey at the end of
1771. Rivera y Moncada does not appear at all in
the annals of this period. He probably remained but
a short time at San Diego before retiring to the peninsula. It is not unlikely that he was already preparing
the way by correspondence for the removal of Fages
in his own favor.[33]

[32] *Representacion de 21 de Mayo 1773*, MS. Reform seems to have dated
from a change of corporals, which probably took place late in 1772.
[33] In May 1771 he was at Santa Gertrudis. *St. Pap. Mis. and Col.*, MS., i.
52. On the period covered by this chapter see *Palou, Not.*, i. 98–107, 120–3,
424–80; *Id., Vida*, 88–134.

CHAPTER VIII.

PROGRESS OF THE NEW ESTABLISHMENTS.

1772–1773.

Events of 1772—Search for the Port of San Francisco—Crespí's Diary—
First Exploration of Santa Clara, Alameda, and Contra Costa
Counties—Fages Discovers San Pablo Bay, Carquines Strait, and
San Joaquin River—Relief Sent South—Hard Times at Monterey—
Living on Bear-meat—Fages and Serra Go South—Founding of San
Luis Obispo—Events at San Diego—A Quarrel between Commandant
and President—Serra Goes to Mexico—Cession of Lower Califor-
nian Missions to Dominicans—New Padres for the Northern Estab-
lishments—Palou's Journey to San Diego and Monterey in 1773.

THE year 1772 was marked by an important exploration of new territory in the north. It added a mission to the four already founded, brought three friars
to reënforce Serra's band of workers, and saw arrangements completed for a larger reënforcement through
the yielding-up of the peninsular missions to the exclusive control of the Dominican order. Yet it was a
year of little progress and of much hardship; it was a
year of tardy supply-vessels, of unfortunate disagreements between the Franciscans and the military chief—
disagreements which carried the president in person to
Mexico to plead for reforms before Viceroy Bucareli,
who had succeeded Croix in the preceding autumn.

The *San Antonio* on her last trip had brought
orders from the viceroy to Fages, requiring him to
explore by sea or land the port of San Francisco, and,
acting in accord with Serra, to establish a mission
there, with a view to secure the harbor from foreign
aggression.[1]

---

[1] Dated Nov. 12, 1770, in *Prov. St. Pap.*, MS., i. 70. It was received by
Fages at Monterey in May 1771.

After the spring rains had ceased, the commandant for the first time was able to obey the order as to exploration, but there were neither friars nor soldiers for a mission, though the supplies were lying at San Cárlos.[2] Accordingly with Crespí, twelve soldiers, a muleteer, and an Indian, Fages started from Monterey on the 20th of March and crossed over to the river Santa Delfina, now the Salinas. As the first exploration by Europeans of a since important portion of California, the counties of Santa Clara, Alameda, and Contra Costa, this trip, fully described by Crespí,[3] deserves to be followed somewhat closely.

The second day's march brings the party to the San Benito stream, still so called, near what is now Hollister; and on the 22d they cross San Pascual plain into San Bernardino Valley and encamp a little north of the present Gilroy. Thence they proceed north-westward and enter the great plain of the "Robles del Puerto de San Francisco," in which they have been before, in November 1769, that is, the Santa Clara Valley. Their camp the 24th is near the south-eastern point of the great "brazo de mar," near the mouth of what they call Encarnacion Arroyo, now Penitencia Creek, on the boundary line between Santa Clara and Alameda counties. The peninsula to their left having been previously explored, and the object being to pass round the great inlet and reach San Francisco under Point Reyes, Fages continues to the right along the foot-hills between the shore and Coast Range.

His camp on Wednesday the 25th is beside a large stream, called by him San Salvador de Horta, now

[2] Palou, *Vida*, 134–5, says that Serra proposed the exploration and Fages consented. This is probably accurate enough in a certain sense; but the friars had a noticeable habit of claiming for themselves all the credit for each movement, and omitting any mention of secular orders and agencies—an omission that evidently did not always result from forgetfulness.

[3] *Crespí, Diario que se formó en el registro que se hizo del puerto de Ntro. P. San Francisco*, in *Palou, Not.*, i. 481–501. A brief résumé of the same exploration is given in *Id.*, ii. 46. Among modern writers, Hittell, *Hist. San Francisco*, has given a brief and inaccurate account from Crespí's diary.

Alameda Creek, at a point near Vallejo's Mill. Next day deer and bears are plentiful, and traces are seen of animals which the friar imagines to be buffaloes, but which the soldiers pronounce *burros*, or "jackass deer," such as they had seen in New Mexico. Crossing five streams, two large ones, now San Lorenzo and San Leandro creeks, and two small ones, they reach the Arroyo del Bosque, on a branch of the bay which with another similar branch forms a peninsula, bearing a grove of oaks—the site of the modern town of Alameda. They are near the shore of San Leandro Bay, and probably on Brickyard Slough. On Friday's march they have to climb a series of low hills, Brooklyn, or East Oakland, in order to get round "an estuary which, skirting the grove, extends some four or five leagues inland until it heads in the sierra"— San Antonio Creek and Merritt Lake. Thence coming out into a great plain, they halt about three leagues from the starting-point, opposite the "mouth by which the two great estuaries communicate with the Ensenada de los Farallones"— that is, they stop at Berkeley and look out through the Golden Gate, noting three islands in the bay.[4] Continuing a league the Spaniards encamp on what is now Cerrito Creek, the boundary between Alameda and Contra Costa counties.

For the next two days they follow the general course of the bay coast, note "a round bay like a great lake"—San Pablo Bay—large enough for "all the armadas of Spain," where they see whales spouting. They are kindly received in what is now Pinole Valley, by a ranchería of gentiles, "bearded and of very light complexion." They attempt to pass round the *bahía redonda*, but are prevented by a narrow estuary, the Strait of Carquines. Journeying along the treeless hills that form its shores, they are hospitably treated at five large native villages, some even

---

[4] One of them, Angel, was probably not known to be an island until the party saw it from a point farther north.

coming across from the other shore in rafts, and
finally they encamp on a stream near the shore, probably the Arroyo del Hambre near Martinez.[5] March
30th they advance two leagues to a large stream—
Arroyo de las Nueces, near Pacheco; cross the fine
valley of Santa Angela de Fulgino — Mt Diablo
Creek; pass two rancherías of friendly natives; and
enter a range of low hills—in the vicinity of Willow
Pass. From the summit they look down on the two
broad rivers and valleys, since so well known, with
the various channels, sloughs, and islands about
their junction—all very accurately described in the
diary. Leaving the hills they pass on four or five
leagues across the plain to a small stream on which
they pitch their camp half a mile from the bank of
the great river, "the largest that has been discovered
in New Spain," which is named Rio de San Francisco. They are on the San Joaquin, at or near Antioch.[6]

To carry out the original purpose of "passing on to
Point Reyes to examine the port of San Francisco" it is
now necessary to cross the great rivers, for which they
have no boats, or to "go round them" for which they
lack men and supplies.[7] It is, accordingly, determined
to return to Monterey, but by a shorter route than
that along the bay shore. Recrossing on the last day
of the month the range of hills and the Santa Angela
plain, they turn south-eastward by a pleasant cañada—
San Ramon Creek. During the first and second of
April they pass through what are now known as San
Ramon and Amador valleys into Suñol Valley, which
they call Santa Coleta; thence through a pass to the

[5] Crespí makes the journey of the two days 15 leagues, and leaves his
courses vague, implying that he was travelling always north-west.
[6] Hittell, in his *History of San Francisco and incidentally of California*,
p. 45, tells us that the Spaniards on this trip crossed the strait and traversed the broad hills and valleys intervening until they reached Russian
River!
[7] Palou, *Vida*, 134–5, says the exploration was not concluded on account of
bad news from San Diego; but he means that this news prevented subsequent
trips.

vicinity of Mission San José, and to their former route, encamping one league beyond the Encarnacion Arroyo where they had been March 24th, on a stream called San Francisco de Paula, in the vicinity of Milpitas. From the third to the fourth they return by the former route to Monterey, whence Crespí goes over to San Cárlos and delivers his diary to the president.

Then Padre Junípero, "seeing that it was impossible to found at once the mission of our seraphic father San Francisco in his own port, since, as that port according to Cabrera Bueno was near Point Reyes, it was necessary to go to it by water, passing from Point Almejas to Point Reyes across the Ensenada de los Farallones; or if by land, it was necessary to make a new exploration by ascending the great rivers in search of a ford; and since as it is not known if they extend far inland, or where they rise, a new expedition was necessary; therefore, his reverence determined in view of what had been discovered in this exploration to report to the viceroy" and await his instructions.

During the commander's absence Serra had received letters from San Diego and San Gabriel announcing great want of supplies, the departure of Cambon and Dumetz, and the illness of Somera. He therefore despatched Crespí south, and with him Fages sent an escort and some flour; but food was soon exhausted at Monterey and San Antonio, and, except for a very small quantity of vegetables and milk, the Spaniards were almost wholly dependent for sustenance on the natives.[8] Late in May, when the last extremity was reached, and there was yet no news of the vessels, Fages with thirteen men spent some three months hunting bears in the Cañada de los Osos, thus supplying presidio and mission with meat until succor came.

[8] Oct. 14, 1772, the viceroy acknowledges receipt of Fages' letter of June 26th, complaining of scarcity of food. *Prov. St. Pap.*, MS., i. 75.

At last the two transports arrived on the coast; but by reason of adverse winds they could not reach Monterey and therefore returned to San Diego.[9] Fages and Serra now started for the south late in August to make arrangements for the transportation of supplies to San Cárlos and San Antonio. Padre Cavaller went also, Juncosa and Pieras being left on duty at Monterey, until October or November, when Crespí and Dumetz returned overland. The *San Antonio* also came up with supplies, but there is no record of subsequent events in the north for nearly a year.

Vessels arriving promising relief from pressing needs, the president resolves on his way south to establish one of the new missions in the Cañada de los Osos. He therefore takes with him Padre Cavaller, the mission guard, and the required vestments and utensils. A site, called by the natives Tixlini, being selected, half a league from the famous cañada but within sight of it, on the 1st of September Junípero raises the Christian symbol, says mass, and thus ushers in the mission of San Luis Obispo de Tolosa.[10] Cavaller is left to labor alone at first, with five soldiers, and two Indians to work on the buildings. The natives are, however, well disposed, retaining as they do a grateful remembrance of Fages' recent services in ridding their country of troublesome bears. They are willing to work, offer their children for baptism, and even help with their seeds to eke out the friar's

[9] Letter of Serra to Palou from Monterey, Aug. 18th, in *Palou, Vida,* 136-9.
[10] Saint Louis, bishop of Toulouse, son of Charles II. of Naples, was born in 1275, became a Franciscan in 1294, died in 1298, and was canonized in 1317. His day is August 19th. *San Luis Obispo, Lib. de Mision,* MS. Fages calls the mission San Luis Obispo de los Tichos. *Prov. St. Pap.,* MS., i. 86. According to *Arch. Obispado,* MS., 83, the mission had at first only 50 lbs. of flour and 3 *almudes* of wheat, so that life had to be sustained by seeds obtained from the natives. Dec. 2, 1772, the viceroy writes to Fages approving the founding of the mission in a spot where there is much good land and plenty of game. *Prov. St. Pap.,* MS. i. 76. Serra, in *San Diego, Lib. de Mision,* MS., strangely calls the mission which he founded at this time San Luis Rey. The traditional old Indian woman who aided in building the mission church is not wanting at San Luis. According to newspaper items she was named Lilila and died Aug. 1, 1874.

scanty supply of food. Additional soldiers and provisions are to be left on the return of the train from San Diego, and the associate minister Juncosa is to come down at the end of the year. The day after founding the mission Serra and Fages continue their journey.[11] It is the president's first trip overland and he is delighted with all he beholds, with the prospects at San Luis, with the natives of the channel coast,[12] and with progress at San Gabriel, where he spends September 11th and 12th, and whence Father Paterna goes down to San Diego to return with the supply-train.

Of events at San Diego and San Gabriel, prior to the arrival of Fages and Serra the 16th of September, we know nothing save the illness of Somera, Cambon, and Dumetz, the departure of the last two for the peninsula, the coming of Crespí from the north in May, the return of Dumetz accompanied by Tomás de la Peña sent up by Palou to take Cambon's place, and the arrival of the *San Cárlos* and *San Antonio* in August.

As soon as the *San Cárlos* can be unloaded the mule train is made ready and despatched for the north September 27th, in charge of Crespí and Dumetz, who go to relieve Pieras and Juncosa at San Cárlos. The *San Antonio* is to take her cargo to Monterey, and probably does so, though we have no further notice of her movements during this trip.[13]

Serra now wishes to proceed with the founding of

[11] Serra had great hopes, but says he, 'let us leave time to tell the story in the progress which I hope Christianity will make among them in spite of the Enemy who already began to lash his tail (*meter la cola*) by means of a bad soldier, who soon after arrival they caught in actual sin with an Indian woman, a thing which greatly grieved the poor padre.' *Serra, Repres. 21 de Mayo*, MS., 117.

[12] Yet in his report to the viceroy of April 22, 1773, he refers to a disturbance here between the soldiers and Indians, in which one of the latter was killed and another severely wounded. *Prov. St. Pap.*, MS., i. 101.

[13] Dec. 2, 1772, the viceroy writes to Fages reprimanding him for allowing the vessel to continue her voyage up to Monterey at this season. He should have unloaded her and forwarded her cargo by land. *Prov. St. Pap.*, MS., i. 77–8.

San Buenaventura on the Santa Bárbara Channel, as originally planned by José de Galvez five years before. He had visited its proposed site at Asuncion on his late trip, and has formed some sanguine expectations as to its future. His enthusiasm on this occasion, as on several others, seems to impair his judgment and causes him to forget that, with the present military force, it is impossible to furnish a suitable guard for a new mission, especially for one so far from the others and in so populous a region. I suppose that Fages very properly refused to furnish a guard until more soldiers should be sent to California.[14] At any rate a bitter quarrel ensued between the two, respecting the merits of which few details are known, but in the course of which the hot-headed Fages, in the right at first, may very likely have exceeded the bounds of moderation and good taste; while the president, though manifestly unjust in his prejudice against the commandant, was perhaps more politic and self-contained in his words and acts at the time, and has, moreover, the advantage of having left his side of the question more fully recorded than that of his antagonist.[15]

[14] Palou, *Vida*, 146, says that Serra 'consulted with comandante Fages about an escort and other assistance necessary for the founding, but he found the door closed, and that he (Fages) went on giving such directions that if they should be carried into effect, far from being able to found (the mission) they threatened the risk of losing what it had cost so much work to accomplish. To prevent such a result, from which serious misfortunes might issue, the venerable padre used all the means suggested by his great prudence and well known skill; but in no way was he able to accomplish his purpose.' The same author in *Noticias*, i. 509–10, says: 'They spoke of the number of soldiers who were to remain, and of the manner in which the mission was to be managed, because he (Fages) had already meddled in the government of the missions, already pretending that all belonged to him and not to the padres; so that the missions, instead of progressing, retrograded, and if the thing went on the reduction might be rendered impossible.'

[15] Palou had alluded, in his *Memorial* of December 1772, to misunderstandings between the military and missionary authorities. March 18, 1772, the viceroy in a letter to Fages, *Prov. St. Pap.*, MS., i. 74–5, urges him to maintain harmony, to listen to all complaints, to aid the padres with guards and supplies, to treat converts well, and to promote the mission work in every possible way. October 2d, Serra says to Fages that the padres are unwilling to take charge of the troops' provisions, fearing quarrels, but will do it temporarily if military supplies be delivered in separate packages. *Arch. Arzobispado*, MS., i. 3. October 8th, Fages transcribes to Serra a communication from the viceroy, dated November 3, 1771, on the duty of president and

The charges of the president against Fages were embodied in his *Representacion* of the following year. According to this document his offences were as follows: Bad treatment of and haughty manners toward his men, causing them to hate him, as Serra had learned by long experience; incompetence to command the *cuera* soldiers, since he belonged himself to another branch of the service; refusal to transfer soldiers for bad conduct at the padres' request; meddling with mission management and the punishment of neophytes as he had no right to do except for *delitos de sangre*, or grave offences; refusal to allow the padre a soldier to serve as majordomo, the soldier being transferred as soon as he became attached to a padre, on the plea that such attachment was subversive of the military authority; irregular and delayed delivery of letters and property directed to the padres, according to his whim, thus preventing the distribution of small gifts to the Indians; insolence and constant efforts to annoy the friars, who were at his mercy; delaying mission work by retaining at the presidio the only blacksmith; opening the friars' letters, and neglect to inform them in time when mails were to start; taking away the mission mules for the use of the soldiers; and the retention under charge of the presidio of cattle intended for new missions.[16] Some of these charges were doubtless unfounded, or at least exaggerated.

It was partly on account of this difficulty with Fages that Serra determined to go in person to Mexico, but there were other motives that made such a trip desirable. The mission work in California had now been fairly begun, and from the actual working of the system the need of some changes had become

padres to set a good example by obedience to the orders of the commandant. *Id.* October 12th, Serra assures Fages that neither he nor his subordinates ever have failed or ever will fail in respect to the commandant's orders. *Id.*, 4.

[16] *Serra, Representacion de 13 de Marzo 1773*, in *Palou, Not.*, i. 518–34, passim. He hints that he could say much worse things about his foe if it were necessary. There is also much against Fages in *Serra, Repres., de 21 de Mayo 1773*, MS.

apparent, changes which the president could advocate
more effectually in person than by correspondence;
and what made a visit to Mexico the more imperative
in the padre's opinion was the news that a new viceroy, presumably ignorant of northern affairs, had come
to New Spain the preceding autumn to succeed Croix,
and that Galvez, California's best friend, had also
gone to Spain. Only the most active efforts could
keep up the old enthusiasm; and at least it was well
to learn of what stuff Bucareli was made.

Serra accordingly sailed on the *San Cárlos* the 19th
or 20th of October, taking with him a neophyte from
Monterey who afterward received the rite of confirmation at the hand of Archbishop Lorenzana. Of the
president's doings in Mexico I shall have something
to say in the next chapter.[17] Shortly before the vessel sailed, Padre Somera had started for the peninsula;[18] a little later Fages set out overland for Monterey; and in November the friars Juan Figuer and
Ramon Usson arrived from the south, sent up by
Palou at Serra's request for the proposed mission of
San Buenaventura.

At a consultation between the Dominican vicar
general and Rafael Verger the guardian of San Fernando College, an agreement was formed April 7,
1772, by which all the missions of the peninsula were
given up by the Franciscan to the Dominican order.
The long series of negotiations and intrigues which
led to this result has been presented elsewhere in connection with the annals of the peninsula,[19] and need
not be repeated here. The Dominicans had worked
hard for a division of the missions, which the Fran-

[17] He arrived at San Blas Nov. 4th, was at Tepic Nov. 10th, had very
severe and dangerous attacks of illness at Guadalajara and Querétaro, and
finally arrived in Mexico in February 1773. Serra, in *Bandini, Doc. Hist. Cal.*,
MS., 1, says he went to Mexico to plead for the extension of missions, etc.
Fages in letter of Dec. 22, 1772, affirms that the padre left for Mexico ' on
mission business.' *Prov. St. Pap.*, MS., i. 86-7.

[18] Possibly several months before, since he sailed from Loreto for San Blas
on Oct. 19th.

[19] See *Hist. North Mexican States*, this series.

ciscans had strenuously resisted. At first the new establishments of the north were hardly taken into the account by either party; but as the struggle continued, additional knowledge of the new country was constantly accumulating; and finally, when it was no longer possible to prevent a division, so flattering were the reports from Alta California that the peninsula was regarded as hardly worth the keeping, and was gladly relinquished by the guardian of the mother college. The followers of Saint Dominic were pleased, for they obtained more than they had ever asked for. So far as is shown by the records Palou and Serra knew nothing of the cession until it was consummated, the latter first learning of it from retiring Franciscans whom he met at Tepic; yet it is difficult of belief that the guardian did not act on the direct advice of the two presidents, or that Padre Junípero did not know what was brewing when he left San Diego. However that may have been, all three were satisfied with their bargain, as they had every reason to be. Later the division would have been on a very different basis.

In August Palou received information of the agreement at Loreto. His acts in the final delivery of the missions have been noticed elsewhere. The guardian's instructions required four friars to be assigned to duty in the north, while the rest were to return to their college. But in the mean time two, Cambon and Somera, had returned ill, two others had asked leave of absence, one was needed for the Monterey presidio, and one or two extra helpers would be convenient for emergencies. Besides, it seemed much better to send the friars up to San Diego, whence, if not needed, they could return by sea to San Blas, than to send them back to the college to undertake, if needed in the north, a long and dangerous voyage. He wrote forthwith to Guardian Verger on the subject, and also to Serra, sending two of the padres, Usson and Figuer, up to San Diego with the letter, in September.

Paterna, acting president in Serra's absence, wrote

back that ten friars would not be too many; Serra
wrote from Tepic, November 10th, that at least eight
or ten should be sent to California if it could be done
without disobeying very positive orders of the guardian, and that he hoped to see Palou himself among
the number; and finally Verger wrote approving the
idea of sending eight or ten friars, but expressing
doubts as to his ability to obtain a stipend for the
one destined to presidio service, and hoping that Palou
would decide to come back to the college. The latter
of course fixed upon the outside number, and immediately selected eight in addition to the two already
sent north; neither could he resist the temptation to
include his own name in the list.[20] It was his plan
to leave behind temporarily Father Campa, who was
to act in his own absence as president, and to come
north later with a drove of cattle, which by authority
of the viceroy were to be taken from the missions of
the peninsula.

Palou was also authorized to take twenty-five native families from the frontier missions for the northern
establishments, and during the autumn of 1772 and
the spring of 1773, while occupied with the final details of the transfer, he made a beginning of the work,
meeting many obstacles through the lukewarmness
of the Dominicans and the open hostility of Governor
Barri.[21] In July while at Velicatá, with six of his
friars, he received information from Campa that the
San Cárlos had arrived at Loreto laden with supplies
for San Diego, which it was proposed to unload at
Loreto while the vessel returned to San Blas for repairs. Foreseeing that this delay was likely to cause
great want in the new missions, the president resolved
to suspend his recruiting and press on to San Diego
immediately with all the maize his mules could carry.

[20] The eight were: Francisco Palou, Pedro Benito Cambon, Gregorio Amurrio, Fermin Francisco Lasuen, Juan Prestamero, Vicente Fuster, José Antonio Murguía, Miguel de la Campa y Cos.
[21] Yet Barri writes to Fages Jan. 7, 1773, that he has sent up 30 horses and
40 mules, all he could collect in the peninsula. *Prov. Stat. Pap.*, MS., i. 138.

Cambon was left in charge of Indian families, cattle, and a considerable amount of church property, respecting which there was much subsequent difficulty, as we shall see. He wrote to Governor Barri urging him to forward to San Luis Bay as much maize as possible, for which he would send back mules from San Diego, and with the six padres and a guard of fourteen men he set out for the north the 21st of July.

As the Californian annals of 1772, beginning in the extreme north, were made to follow, so to speak, the progress of President Serra southward, so may the little that is recorded of 1773 be most conveniently attached to the march of President Palou northward from Velicatá to Monterey. On the 26th three soldiers were sent out in advance to announce their coming, and Paterna and Peña came down far on the way to meet the travellers, with all the mules that could be spared. The only event in the journey requiring notice was the raising of a cross, with appropriate ceremonies, to mark the boundary between Franciscan and Dominican territory, on the 19th of August. The cross was placed on a high rock five leagues above the Arroyo of San Juan Bautista and about fifteen leagues below San Diego.[22] Arriving at the latter port on the morning of the 30th, the newcomers were welcomed with a discharge of fire-arms and with every demonstration of joy.

Palou's advance messengers had gone on to Monterey to obtain from Fages mules to bring up the supplies from Velicatá. While awaiting a reply the president busied himself in studying the condition of affairs and in making a temporary distribution of the new friars, since nothing could be done in the new establishments until the vessels came with supplies and soldiers.[23] The native families expected from the

[22] The cross bore the inscription, *Division de las misiones de Nuestro Padre Santo Domingo y de Nuestro Padre San Francisco; año de 1773.*

[23] The missionary force after this distribution was as follows: San Diego—Luis Jaume, Vicente Fuster, and Gregorio Amurrio as supernumerary. San

south were also apportioned in advance among the missions according to their apparent need.[24] Paterna, Lasuen, and Prestamero started for their stations on the 5th of September. On the 19th came a letter from Fages with all the mules that could be obtained, eighty-two in number, which were sent forward three days later under Ortega and a guard for Velicatá.[25] On the 26th Palou, Murguía, and Peña started for the north, after having baptized fifteen new converts from El Rincon, a league and a half north of the mission.

The journey northward presents nothing of interest, Palou simply stationing his companions at their respective missions according to the plan already given, and making close observations to be utilized in his forthcoming report. At San Luis the party was met by Fages, and a league from Monterey Crespí came out to greet his old friend and school-mate. At the presidio on November 14th they were welcomed with the customary salute and ringing of bells, to which Palou replied with a *plática*, expressing to the soldiers his joy at seeing that they had come to serve God in so distant a land, where he hoped they would set a good example to the natives. Then they went over to San Cárlos and were greeted by the ministers and Indians. Palou was very enthusiastic over his arrival at Monterey, a place which he had desired to visit ever since he read Torquemada's description of Vizcaino's voyage over twenty years ago, and a place where he was willing to devote his life to the saving of precious souls, his own included.

Gabriel—Antonio Paterna, Antonio Cruzado (both of whom had asked leave to retire), Juan Figuer, and Fermin Francisco Lasuen. San Luis Obispo—José Cavaller, Domingo Juncosa (anxious to retire), later José Antonio Murguía, with Juan Prestamero and Tomás de la Peña as supernumeraries. San Antonio—Miguel Pieras, Buenaventura Sitjar, and Ramon Usson as supernumerary. San Cárlos—Juan Crespí, Francisco Dumetz, and Francisco Palou.

[24] San Diego was to have one family; San Gabriel 6 families, and most of the unmarried; and San Luis Obispo 3 families and some *solteros*. It is possible that these Indians came up with Palou.

[25] I suppose that the 14 soldiers who had come up with Palou also returned, though there is no record of it. It is a point, moreover, of some importance in tracing the names of the earliest settlers in California.

It is recorded that some time during 1773 Comandante Fages, while out in search of deserters, crossed the sierra eastward and saw an immense plain covered with *tulares* and a great lake, whence came as he supposed the great river that had prevented him from going to Point Reyes. This may be regarded as the discovery of the Tulare Valley. Thus close the somewhat meagre annals of an uneventful year, so far as internal affairs in California are concerned, but there were measures of much moment being fomented without, to which and to a general report on the condition of the country the following chapter will be devoted.[26]

[26] On the events of this chapter see *Palou. Not.*, i. 180–245, 481–513; *Id. Vida*, 134–51.

CHAPTER IX.

FIRST ANNUAL REPORT; SERRA'S LABORS IN MEXICO.

1773.

THE resolution of the *junta de guerra y real hacienda*, dated April 30, 1772, giving the missions of the peninsula to the Dominicans, required the Franciscans to render an annual report on the condition of their new establishments; and on May 12th the viceroy had ordered such report from the president.[1] Therefore Palou, president in Serra's absence, gave his attention to the matter during his stay at San Diego and his trip northward, devoting himself, on arrival at Monterey in November, to the task of forming from the results of his observations a complete statement for the viceroy. The document was completed the 10th of December 1773, and was forwarded to Mexico overland with a letter to the

---

[1] The first document is given in full in *Palou, Not.*, i. 190–5; and the second is referred to in *Id.*, ii. 9.

guardian of San Fernando.[2] Under date of May 21st of the same year Serra in Mexico had included in his report to the viceroy a detailed statement of the actual condition of the missions at the time of his departure the preceding September, supplemented by information derived from later correspondence. This report[3] covers substantially the same ground as that of Palou and the two combined may be regarded as one document. Later annual and biennial reports of the missions, preserved in my Library, will be utilized for the most part in local chapters and statistical appendices, being noticed in my text only in a general manner or for special reasons. But this first report being a very complete statement of California's condition at the end of what may be regarded as the first period of her mission history, deserves fuller notice here. Historical items proper respecting the founding of each mission gathered from this source as from others having been given in the preceding chapters, I now invite the reader's attention to the new establishments as they were at the end of 1773, the fifth year of Spanish occupation.

The 'New Establishments,' 'Establishments of San Diego and Monterey,' the 'Missions of Monterey,' 'New California,' 'Northern California,' 'California Superior,' 'Alta California,' and the 'Peninsula'—for all these names had been or were a little later applied, and continued in use for many years—include at this time five missions and a presidio.[4] These are San

---

[2] Palou, Informe que por el mes de diciembre de 1773 se hizo al Exmo Señor Virey del estado de las cinco misiones de Monterey, in Palou, Not., ii. 11-42. Fages, in his Voyage en Cal., a report addressed to the Viceroy on Nov. 30, 1775, used this first report of Palou, to which he, however, gives the date of Nov. 24th, instead of Dec. 10th.

[3] Serra, Representacion del P. Fr. Junípero Serra sobre las Misiones de la Nueva California, 21 de Mayo de 1773, MS. This report is in two parts, one respecting the needs of the country from a military point of view, and the other on the actual condition of the missions.

[4] It is to be noted that Palou in his report does not name San Diego as a presidio, and there is no evidence that it was in these earliest years considered as such except in the sense that every post guarded by soldiers, like any of the missions, is spoken of as a presidio. San Diego had no larger regular force than some other missions. It became, however, a regular presidio in 1774 when the new reglamento went into effect.

Diego de Alcalá at Cosoy on the port of San Diego in 32° 43′, built on a hill two gunshots from the shore, and facing the entrance to the port at Point Guijarros; San Gabriel Arcángel, forty-four leagues north-west of San Diego, in the country of Los Temblores in 34° 10′, on the slope of a hill half a league from the source of the Rio de San Miguel, six leagues west of the River Jesus de los Temblores, and a league and a half east of the River Nuestra Señora de Los Angeles[5] de Porciúncula; San Luis Obispo de Tolosa, about seventy leagues from San Gabriel in 35° 38′, on an eminence half a league from the Cañada de los Osos and three leagues from the Ensenada de Buchon, in the country of the Tichos; San Antonio de Pádua, twenty-three leagues above San Luis, in 36° 30′, in the Cañada de los Robles of the Sierra de Santa Lucía, at first on the River San Antonio, but moved a league and a half up the cañada to the Arroyo de San Miguel; San Cárlos Borromeo, on the River Carmelo, one league from Monterey and twenty-five leagues from San Antonio; and, finally, the presidio of San Cárlos de Monterey on the bay and port of the same name.

The five missions are under the care of nineteen Franciscan friars of the college de propaganda fide of San Fernando in the city of Mexico, whose names and distribution have been given,[6] and who are subject locally to the authority of a president residing at San Cárlos, the cabecera, or head mission of the five.[7] The military force to which is intrusted the protection of the missions is sixty men, thirty-five soldados de cuera and twenty-five Catalan volunteers, under a commandant residing at the presidio of Monterey, each mission having a guard of from six to sixteen under a corporal or sergeant, while about twenty

[5] This is the first application of the name Los Angeles to this region, and is doubtless the origin of the name as afterward applied to the pueblo and city.
[6] See note 23, chap. viii. of this volume.
[7] A full description of the mission system in all its parts and workings will be given elsewhere; also of the presidio or military system, and of civil government.

men garrison the presidio under the commandant's direct orders. The civil and political authority is blended theoretically, for there is no record of the practical exercise of any such power in these earliest days, with the military, and vested in the commandant, who is in civil matters responsible and subordinate to the governor of the Californias, residing at Loreto. The population consists of military officials and soldiers, friars and their neophytes, a few mechanics under government pay, servants and slaves—all these of Spanish, negro, Indian, and mixed blood—some natives of Baja California serving as laborers without other wages than their sustenance, and, finally, thousands of gentile natives. There are as yet no colonists or settlers proper.[8]

Glancing first at the mission work *par excellence*, the conversion of the heathen to Christianity, we find a total of 491 baptisms for the first five years, 29 of them having died, and 62 couples, representing doubtless nearly all the adult converts, have been united in marriage by Christian rites.[9] The two northern missions with 165 and 158 baptisms are far above the southern establishments, which are 83 and 73 respectively, while the newly founded San Luis has only twelve converts.[10] It is to be noted, however, that the friars have not in several of the missions baptized so many as they might have done, preferring that the candidates should be well instructed, and often restrained by an actual or prospective lack of supplies, since they are unwilling to receive formal neophytes whom they may not be able to supply with food. Again, more than half the whole number have been baptized during the year and a half since Serra's departure. The gentiles are now everywhere friendly

[8] The matter of the preceding paragraph has not been drawn from the reports of Palou and Serra.

[9] Complete statistics of baptisms, marriages, deaths, and population for every mission and every decade from the beginning will be given in their proper place.

[10] So say the general reports; yet the mission baptismal register shows a total of 34 baptisms in 1772 and 4 in 1773.

as a rule, and have for the most part overcome their original timidity, and to some extent also the distrust caused by outrages of the soldiers.[11] Only at San Diego have there been unprovoked hostilities. Near each mission, except San Luis, is a ranchería of gentiles living in rude little huts of boughs, tules, grass, or of whatever material is at hand. Many of these savages come regularly as catechumens to *doctrina,* and often those of more distant rancherías are induced to come in and listen to the music and receive trifling gifts of food and beads. The neophytes are generally willing to work when the friars can feed them, which is not always the case; but it does not appear that at this early period they live regularly in the mission buildings as in later times. At San Diego there are eleven rancherías within a radius of ten leagues, living on grass, seeds, fish, and rabbits. A canoe and net are needed that the christianized natives may be taught improved methods of fishing.[12] At San Gabriel the native population is larger than elsewhere, so large in fact that more than one mission will be needed in that region. The different rancherías are unfortunately at war with each other, and that near the mission being prevented from going to the sea for fish is often in great distress for food. Here the conduct of the soldiers causes most trouble, but the natives are rapidly being conciliated. At San Luis the population is also very large and the natives are from the first firm friends of the Spaniards; but as they have plenty of deer, rabbits, fish, and seeds, being indeed far better supplied with food than the Spaniards, it is difficult to

[11] That the irregular conduct of the soldiers was one of the chief obstacles to missionary success there can be little doubt; yet it is not likely that the comandante was so much to blame as Serra says. His dislike for Fages colors his report. Have misfortunes of any kind occurred at a mission, they were entirely due to the mismanagement of 'a certain official;' has another mission been prosperous, it was in spite of that mismanagement.

[12] According to Serra nearly all in the ranchería that had formerly attacked the mission had been converted. The 'oficial' was displeased that so many had been baptized, and he had wished to remove the natives to a distance on pretence of danger to the presidio, but Serra had objected strenuously and every one else ridiculed the proposal!

render mission life fascinating to them, articles of clothing being the chief attraction. They come often to the mission but do not stay, having no ranchería in the vicinity. At San Antonio the natives are ready to live at the mission when the priests are ready for them, and far from depending on the missionaries for food they bring in large stores of pine-nuts, acorns, rabbits, and squirrels.[13] At San Cárlos converts are most numerous, but for want of food they cannot be kept at the mission. Here and also at San Antonio three soldiers have already married native women.

It is a rude architecture, that of pre-pastoral California, being stockade or palisade structures, which were abandoned later in favor of adobe walls. At every mission a line of high strong posts, set in the ground close together, encloses the rectangular space which contains the simple wooden buildings serving as church and dwellings, the walls of which also in most instances take the stockade form. The buildings at San Cárlos are somewhat fully described by Serra. The rectangle here is seventy yards long and forty-three wide, with ravelins at the corners. For want of nails the upright palisades are not secured at the top, and the ease with which they can be moved renders the strong gate locked at night an object of ridicule. Within, the chief building, also of palisade walls plastered inside and out with mud or clay, is seven by fifty yards and divided into six rooms. One room serves as a church, another as the minister's dwelling, and another as a storehouse, the best rooms being whitewashed with lime. This building is roofed with mud supported by horizontal timbers. A slighter structure used as a kitchen is roofed with grass. The quarters

[13] They had revealed, as Serra says, the locality of the cave where their idols were kept, so that those idols could be destroyed at any time. The assessor of Monterey County in his report to the surveyor-general, according to an item going the rounds of local newspapers, mentions a large cave in this region covered on the inside with hieroglyphics and having a cross cut in its walls traditionally by the hands of Serra himself. Near the cave is a hot sulphur spring. It would be difficult to prove the non-identity of the two caves.

of the soldiers are distinct from the mission and are enclosed by a separate palisade, while outside of both enclosures are the simple huts of the ranchería. Between the dates of the two reports it is found that the mud roofs do not prove effective against the winter rains; and a new church partly of rough and partly of worked timber is built and roofed with tules. The timber used is the pine and cypress still so abundant in that region. At San Luis and San Gabriel the buildings are of the same nature, if somewhat less extensive and complete, there being also a small house within the stockade for each of the Baja Californian families. At San Diego, where the stockade is in a certain sense a presidio, two bronze cannons are mounted, one pointing toward the harbor, and the other toward the ranchería. Here, in addition to wood and tules, or rushes, adobes have also been used in constructing the friars' house.[14] Four thousand adobes have been made, some stone have been collected, and the foundation laid of a church ninety feet long; but work has been suspended on account of the non-arrival of the supply-vessels in 1773. At San Antonio the church and padres' dwelling are built of adobes, and the three soldiers married to native women have each a separate house. The presidio at Monterey is also a stockade enclosure with a cannon mounted in each of its four ravelins at the corners. The soldiers' quarters and other rooms within are of wood with mud roofs, except a chapel and room for the visiting friar, which are of adobe, as in the commandant's house and the jail.

But slight progress has been made in agriculture; though by repeated failures the padres are gaining experience for future success, and a small vegetable garden at each mission, carefully tended and irrigated by hand, has been more or less productive. At San Diego, at first, grain was sown in the river-bottom and the crop entirely destroyed by a rising of the stream.

[14] Serra says that a large part of the buildings were of adobes.

Next year, it was sown so far away from the water that it died from drought all but five or eight fanegas saved for seed. The river now dried up, affording no running water as we are assured even in the rainy season, though plenty of water for the cattle and for other uses could always be found in pools or by slight digging in the bed of the stream. Irrigation being thus impossible the rain must be depended on, and while Palou was here a spot was selected for the next experiment in the river-bottom, about two leagues from the mission, at a spot called Nuestra Señora del Pilar, where rain was thought to be more abundant and the risk of flood and drought somewhat less.[15] San Gabriel is in a large, fertile, well watered plain, with every facility for irrigation. Though the first year's crop, according to Serra, had been drowned out and entirely lost, the second, as Palou tells us, produced one hundred and thirty fanegas of maize and seven fanegas of beans, the first yielding one hundred and ninety-five fold and the latter twenty-one fold. Planting the next year was to be on a much larger scale with every prospect of success. San Luis has also plenty of fertile, well watered, and well wooded land which has yielded a little maize and beans the first year, and promised well for the future. At San Antonio two fanegas of wheat are to be sown on irrigated land. San Cárlos has some good land, and though there are no advantages for irrigation, it is thought maize and wheat can be raised. By reason of late sowing only five fanegas of wheat were harvested in 1772.

Pasturage is everywhere excellent, and the little live-stock distributed among the missions has flourished from the beginning. Each mission has received 18 head of horned cattle and has now from 38 to 47 head, or 204 in the aggregate, with 63 horses, 79 mules, 102 swine, and 161 sheep and goats at San Diego and

---

[15] *Palou, Not.*, i. 240–1. The place must have been near the site of the later mission. Serra says it was the crop of 1772 that was destroyed by flood, only 8 fanegas being saved.

San Gabriel alone. Some memoranda of farmers' and mechanics' tools are given in connection with each mission; but there are no mechanics save at the presidio. Palou has something to say of the missions to be founded in the future, but nothing that requires attention here, except perhaps that the proposed Santa Clara is not identical with the mission that is later founded under that name, but is to be on the Santa Clara River in the southern part of the province.[16]

Having thus laid before the reader the condition of California in 1773, the end of the first period of her history, I have now to consider the important measures for her welfare, urged and adopted at the capital of New Spain during the same year. First, however, a royal order of September 10, 1772, must be briefly noticed in which the king issued a series of regulations and instructions for the new line of royal presidios, to be formed along the northern frontier of his American possessions.[17] These regulations, the military law in California as in all the north-west for many years, will require to be studied somewhat in detail when I come to describe the presidio system; but as an historical document under its own date it did not affect California as it did other provinces, where it abolished or transferred old presidios, established new ones, and effected radical changes in their management. Its last section is as follows: "I declare that

[16] The receipt of Palou's report was acknowledged by the viceroy in a letter of May 25, 1774, received July 6th, and answered July 28th; but there is nothing of importance in this correspondence. A résumé with extracts of Palou's report was published in the *S. F. Bulletin*, Oct. 12, 1865. In *San Gabriel, Lib. de Mision*, MS., 6–8, is a circular letter addressed to the padres of California by Palou, requiring each of them, or each pair of them, at the end of every December to send in full reports of their respective missions to the president, from which he might form his general report to the viceroy, since it would be impossible for him to visit each mission annually. This letter was dated San Gabriel, Oct. 9, 1773, while the writer was at work on his first report.

[17] *Presidios, Reglamento é Instruccion para los Presidios que se han de formar en la linea de frontera de la Nueva España. Resuelto por el Rey N. S. en cédula de 10 de Septiembre de 1772*, Madrid, 1772. Sm. 4to, 122 pages. My copy was presented by Viceroy Bucareli to Melchor de Peramas. I have also the edition of Mexico, 1773. 8vo, 132 pages.

the presidios of California are to continue for the present on their actual footing according to the provisions made by my viceroy after the conquest and reduction had been extended to the port of Monterey; and on the supposition that he has provisionally assigned the annual sum of thirty-three thousand dollars for the needs and protection of that peninsula, I order and command that this sum be still paid at the end of each year from the royal treasury of Guadalajara, as has been done of late; and that my viceroy sustain and aid by all possible means the old and new establishments of said province, and inform me of all that he may deem conducive and useful to their progress, and to the extension of the new reductions of gentile Indians."[18]

President Serra, having left California in the preceding September, arrived at the city of Mexico in February 1773. The objects of his visit were to see to it that California was not neglected through ignorance or indifference on the part of the new viceroy, to urge certain general measures for the good of his province suggested by his experience of the past five years, to get rid of the commandant, Fages, his bitter foe and the cause, from the friar's point of view, of all that was not pure prosperity in the missions, and to procure such regulations as would prevent similar troubles with future commandants by putting all the power into the friars' hands and reducing the military element to a minimum.[19] He found Bucareli not less favorably disposed than had been his predecessor Croix, and was by him instructed to prepare a memorial, in which were to be embodied his views on the questions at issue. Being authorized to do so by his superior, the guardian of San Fernando, and having

[18] *Presidios, Reglamento*, 120-1.
[19] Serra had received from California a certificate from Fages dated Monterey, Dec. 22, 1772, to the effect that the missions were all supplied with padres and that Serra had left on business connected with his work. *Prov. St. Pap.*, MS., i. 86. It seems strange that Serra did not get this certificate at his departure if necessary, and that Fages should have sent it voluntarily, for there was no time to send back for it.

hastened the sailing of the *San Cárlos* with supplies, Padre Junípero set himself diligently to work, completed the required document on March 13th, and presented it two days later to the viceroy.[20]

His suggestions or claims were thirty-two in number, formed without any attempt at classification into as many articles of the memorial. I shall avoid much confusion and repetition by referring to the several points in the order in which they were acted upon rather than as they were presented. His first and second claims were for a master and mate to aid Perez on the transports, since Pino had leave of absence, and Cañizares was too young to have full charge of a vessel; and that the new vessel be made ready as soon as possible. He soon found, however, that in order to cut down expenses to agree with the royal order of September 10, 1772, already alluded to, it had been determined in Mexico to give up the San Blas establishment and to depend on mule trains for the forwarding of supplies to San Diego and Monterey.

Against this policy the California champion sent in a new memorial dated the 22d of April.[21] In this document he argued that the conveyance of supplies by land would be very difficult if not impossible, that it would cost the royal treasury much more than the present system, and that it would seriously interfere with the spiritual conquest. Besides at least a hundred men and horses, there would be required eleven hundred, and probably fifteen hundred, mules for the service, which it would be impossible to obtain in time to prevent much suffering in California if not its total abandonment, to say nothing of the excessive. cost. The great expense of the San Blas establishment had been largely due to the building of new vessels and warehouses, not necessary in the future. There had possibly been some mismanagement that

[20] *Serra, Representacion de 13 de Marzo 1773*, MS.; also in *Palou, Not.*, i. 514–38; and elsewhere in fragments and abridgments.
[21] *Serra, Memorial de 22 de Abril, sobre suministraciones á los Establecimientos de California y conduccion de ellas*, MS.

might be avoided; in any case some kind of a marine establishment must be kept up for the transport of supplies to Loreto, and the muleteers would be quite as numerous and expensive as the sailors. Moreover, the oft-repeated passage of large caravans of careless, rough, and immoral men across the long stretch of country between Velicatá and Monterey could not fail to have a bad effect on the natives along the route. These arguments proved unanswerable, and the viceroy ordered that for the present, until the king's pleasure could be known, the San Blas transports should continue their service, with the slight changes suggested by Father Junípero, who thus gained the first two points of his original demand.

The thirty remaining points of the *representacion* were by the viceroy submitted to the *junta de guerra y real hacienda*[22]—board of war and royal exchequer —which august body on May 6th granted eighteen of them and part of another, denying only a part of article 32, in which Serra asked to have paid the expenses of his journey to Mexico. Thus twenty-one of the original points were disposed of almost entirely in Serra's favor.[23] Four of these bore upon the past troubles between the Franciscan and military authorities, and were designed to curtail the powers which, as the former claimed, had been assumed by the latter. By the decision the commandant was required to transfer from the mission guard to the presidio, at the minister's request, any soldier of irregular conduct and bad example, and this without the padre being obliged to name or prove the soldier's offence; the missionaries were to have the right to manage the mission Indians as a father would manage his family, and the

[22] The document had, however, previously, March 16th to April 5th, been in the hands of the fiscal Areche, whose report was favorable; and had then been passed to the proper bureau to be prepared for presentation to the junta. *Prov. St. Pap.*, MS., i. 88–9.
[23] Those were 1–4, 8, 9, 12, 15–25, 27, 28, and 32, leaving 11 points yet undecided. The junta was composed of Viceroy Bucareli, Valcárcel, Toro, Areche, Barroeta, Abad, Toral, Valdés, Gutierrez, Mangino, Arce, and José Gorraez.

military commandant should be instructed to preserve perfect harmony with the padres;[24] property
and letters for the friars or missions were to be forwarded separately instead of being enclosed to the
presidio commander; and the friars' correspondence
was not to be meddled with, passing free of mail
charges like that of the soldiers. By the terms of
the decision on the other points Serra was to receive
his regular pay as a missionary, during his whole
absence from California. Contributions of food from
the Tepic region were to be forwarded expressly for
the missions, and Governor Barri was not to hinder
the removal of the church property at Velicatá. Sailors might be enlisted at San Blas and employed as
laborers at the missions, receiving rations for one
year as if on board vessels, but they could not be
forced to remain after the year had passed, and the
regular crews of the transports must not be interfered with. Two blacksmiths, two carpenters, with
some tools and material were to be sent from Guadalajara for the exclusive use of the missions. Seven
additional bells were to be furnished, four of them
having already been sent to Monterey. Additional
vestments were to be sent to take the place of soiled,
worn, and 'indecent' articles contained in some of the
cases from Baja California. San Blas measures were
to be adjusted on a proper basis and a full set of
standards sent to each mission. Greater care was to
be taken in packing food for California, where it often
arrived in bad condition. Cattle for the proposed
missions were to be under the temporary care of the
missionaries, who might use their milk. A new surgeon was to be sent in the place of Prat, deceased,
and finally a copy of the junta's decision was to be

[24] This was hardly what had been asked for by Serra, who wished officers
and soldiers notified that the entire management of the Indians belonged
exclusively to the padres, and that the military had no right to interfere in
matters of discipline or punishment except in the case of *delitos de sangre.*
The junta was very careful not to commit itself very decidedly in the quarrel
between Serra and Fages. The viceroy, however, in subsequent instructions
came nearer to Serra's views.

given to Serra, that the missionaries might hereafter
act understandingly.

The president was charged to return as soon as
possible to his post, after having made a complete
report on the condition of each mission.[25]

Several points of Serra's petition connected with
the military and financial aspects of the subject under
consideration had been left by the junta to be provided for in a new regulation for the Californias.
This document was drawn up on May 19th by Juan
José Echeveste, deemed an expert in the matter, since
he had superintended for some years the forwarding
of supplies.[26] This plan provided for California a captain, a lieutenant, eighty soldiers, eight mechanics,
two store-keepers, and four muleteers, with salaries
amounting to $38,985 per year; for Baja California a
commissary, a lieutenant, and thirty-four soldiers,
with a governor of both Californias, all at an annual
cost of $16,450; a commissary and dock-yard depart-
ment at San Blas to cost, including rations for soldiers
and employés in both Californias, $29,869; and a
transport fleet of a *fragata* and two *paquebotes* serving
both Californias at an annual cost for wages and
rations of $34,038, forming a grand total of $119,342.
Payment was to be made, however, to officers and
men in the Californias, save to the governor and commissary, in goods at an advance on the original cost
of one hundred per cent for the peninsula, and of one
hundred and fifty per cent for New California; a
regulation which reduced the total cost to $90,476.
To meet this expense[27] there were the $33,000 prom-

[25] May 12th, the viceroy decreed the execution of the junta's resolutions,
the issuance of the necessary orders, and the preparation of records in
duplicate. May 13th, the secretary Gorraez certifies the delivery of a copy
to Serra. May 14th, a certified copy was made for the king. *Copia de lo
determinado por la Real Junta de Guerra y Real Hacienda*, in *Palou, Not.* i.,
540–53; also in *Prov. St. Pap.*, MS., i. 89.

[26] *Reglamento é instruccion provisional para el auxilio y conservacion de los
nuevos y antiguas establecimientos de las Californias con el departamento de San
Blas*, etc., MS.; also in *Palou, Not.* i., 556–71. The printed copy is, however,
full of errors in figures. Also in *Arch. Col., St. Pap. Ben.*, MS., 1–24.

[27] This part of the *reglamento* is omitted in Palou's printed copy.

ised by the king in his order of September 10, 1772;
$25,000, estimated yield of the salt-works near San
Blas, which had, it seems, been assigned to the Californias; and a probable net revenue of $10,000 from
the pious fund, still leaving a balance of $22,476 to
be paid from the royal treasury.

Echeveste added to his plan seventeen *puntos in-
structivos*, suggestive and explanatory, from which it
appears that in the author's judgment, the state of
the treasury and pious fund did not warrant the granting of other aid than that provided, which must therefore suffice for new missions if any were to be founded;
that the sailors enlisted as mission laborers, according
to the recommendation of the junta, should be paid
sailor's wages for two years and receive rations for five
years; that instead of the previous system by which
each mission received a stipend of $700 and certain
supplies it would be better to give a stipend of $800,
being $400 for each minister, and double rations for
five years to all the friars, including those waiting for
the foundation of new missions, the double rations
amounting to $1,779 being charged to the pious fund
as an addition to the stipend; that the commissary at
San Blas should buy maize and meat instead of raising
it, selling the rancho and sending the mule train to
Loreto or San Diego; and finally, in addition to some
suggestions about minor details of business management, that Echeveste's successor[28] should be allowed a
salary of $2,000, thus raising the amount to come out
of the treasruy to $24,476.

On the 21st of May Serra presented, as required,
a full report on the California missions, giving the
history of each from its foundation and its condition
in September 1772, the date of the writer's departure. The substance of this statement has been
already presented to the reader. The writer included,
however, an argument respecting the number of
soldiers needed in California. In article 10 of his

[28] Exactly what Echeveste's office was does not appear.

original petition he had demanded one hundred men; but that number had seemed too great to the junta, which had reserved its decision and called for more information. Echeveste, as we have seen, reduced the number to eighty, and now Serra, by giving up the proposed mission of Santa Clara[29] and reducing the guard of San Buenaventura, assented to the reduction in the aggregate; but objected to the distribution. Echeveste had assigned twenty-five men to each of the two presidios and a guard of six men to each of the five missions, or of five to each of six missions;[30] but Serra would assign to Monterey fifteen men, to San Buenaventura fifteen, to San Diego thirteen, to San Cárlos seven, and to each of the other missions ten. He argued that in a country of so many inhabitants with missions so far apart, a guard of five men was not sufficient for adequate protection. The wily friar's policy—or rather, perhaps, the enthusiastic missionary's hope—was by securing a double guard to be enabled to double the number of his missions without being obliged to ask the presidio commanders for soldiers allowed them by the regulation.[31]

On May 26th the viceroy addressed to Fages a series of instructions, provisional in their nature, pending the final approval of the regulations. These instructions covered the same ground as the decision of the junta on May 6th, but also granted two additional requests of Serra by authorizing Fages to issue a pardon to all deserters in California; and to replace with new men such soldiers as had families far away, from whom they had been long separated.[32]

[29] It is to be noticed that no mention is made of San Francisco in any of these calculations.

[30] The idea of moving San Diego mission was doubtless already entertained, though nothing is said of it here.

[31] Serra, Repres. de 21 de Mayo, MS. Also translated by Taylor, and printed in Cal. Farmer, Sept., Oct. 1865, and pasted in Taylor's Discov. and Found., ii. 49. This Representacion with that of April 22d was referred to the fiscal on June 10th.

[32] Bucareli, Providencias de 26 de Mayo 1773, MS. Serra had asked for leave of absence in behalf of eight soldiers either on account of long separation from their wives, or unfitness for duty. From several of these he brought

Bucareli referred Echeveste's regulation on May 24th to his legal adviser, Areche, who in his opinion of June 14th repeats all the articles of the document with a general approval. He calls attention, however, to the fact that no provision is made for the expense of ammunition, nor for the surgeon promised by the junta. He also suggests a doubt as to the ability of the pious fund to pay the $11,779 required of it in addition to the large sum expended in the missionaries' stipends; and he recommends a reference of the matter to the director of the fund before its final consideration by the junta.[33]

In accordance with Areche's suggestion, Fernando J. Mangino, director of the pious fund, was called upon for a report, which he made on June 19th, showing that the available product of the fund was $20,687, though a large part of that amount being the yield of sheep ranchos, was subject to some variation; that the present liability for missionary stipends was $14,879; and that there would remain but $5,808 with which to pay the $11,779 called for; though the amount might be increased by $2,662 if the colleges were obliged to pay five per cent on loans.[34]

On the 8th of July the board met to finally decide on the whole matter. The decision was to put Echeveste's plan in force from January 1, 1774, the only changes being an order that the San Blas mule train be sold and not transferred to California; a recommendation that the four extra vessels at San Blas be sold and not used in the gulf; and some suggestions

petitions which are given in *Prov. St. Pap.*, MS., i. 87. These instructions probably went up on the *San Cárlos* to Loreto and were carried to San Diego by Palou, reaching Fages in September 1773.

[33] *Areche, Parecer sobre Reglam. de Cal. 14 de Junio 1773*, MS.; also in *Palou, Not.*, i. 572–80. Areche made a supplementary report June 30th on Serra's *representaciones* of April 22d and May 21st; but adds nothing to the subjects treated, beyond expressing regret that the mission work in America does not prosper as in days of old, and suggesting that it would be better if the California missions were not so far apart. *Areche, Respuesta Fiscal de 30 de Junio 1773*, MS.

[34] *Mangino, Respuesta sobre Fondo Piadoso, 19 de Junio 1773*, MS.; and also less accurately in *Palou, Not.*, i. 580–6. The report contains much additional information about the pious fund which will be utilized elsewhere.

respecting minor details of business management. As
to the ways and means, however, in view of Mangino's report, the pious fund was to furnish from
moneys on hand $10,000 for the first year only, and
the remaining expense, $59,476, would be borne by
the treasury, aided by the San Blas salt-works.[35] The
surgeon's salary was also to be paid; but nothing was
said about the expense of ammunition. On July 23d
the viceroy decreed the execution of the decision,
ordered nine certified copies made, thanked Echeveste
for his services, and directed him to hunt up a surgeon.

Three points of Serra's original memorial, on which
a decision had been reserved, were settled by the
board's last action. These were a petition that routes
be explored to California from Sonora and New Mexico, not acted on by the junta but granted by the
viceroy; a demand for one hundred soldiers, eighty of
whom were granted by the regulation; and a request
for Spanish or Indian families from California denied
by non-action. Four other points had been left to
be settled by the *reglamento;* the establishment of a
storehouse at Monterey, the right of each mission to
a soldier acting as a kind of majordomo, a demand
for mules, and a reward in live-stock to persons marrying native women. The first was practically granted
by the appointment of store-keepers at Monterey and
San Diego, while the third was practically denied by
the order to sell the mule train at San Blas.[36] The
others do not seem to have been acted upon.

One important matter was still in abeyance, and
this was now settled by Bucareli in accordance with
Serra's wishes, by the removal of Fages and the
appointment of another officer to succeed him. In
selecting a new commander, however, the president's

[35] *Reglamento, Determinacion de 8 de Julio 1773*, in *Palou, Not.*, i. 589-94.
[36] Yet the viceroy soon ordered 100 mules to be distributed among the
missions, and ordered Captain Anza to open communication by land between
Tubac and Monterey.

choice was not followed, since Ortega, his favorite for the place, was not deemed of sufficiently high military rank, and Captain Rivera y Moncada was named as California's new ruler.[37] Ortega was brevetted lieutenant and put in command of San Diego, which was now to be a regular presidio.

The exact date of Rivera's appointment I do not know, but it probably preceded by only a few days that of his instructions, which were issued on the 17th of August. These instructions in forty-two articles are long and complete,[38] and some portions will be given more fully elsewhere when I come to treat of the institutions to which they refer. The purport of the document is as follows:

Copies of the regulations and action of the board are enclosed. Great confidence is felt in Rivera's ability, and knowledge gained by long experience, which experience must have taught him how important it is to preserve perfect harmony, so that both commander and friars may devote themselves exclusively to their respective duties. The first object is of course the conversion of the natives; but next in importance is their gathering in mission towns for purposes of civilization. These little towns may become great cities; hence the necessity of avoiding defects in the beginning, of care in the selection of sites, in the assignment of lands, laying out of streets, etc.

The commander is authorized to assign lands to communities, and also to such individuals as are disposed to work; but all must dwell in the pueblo or mission, and all grants must be made with due regard to the formalities of law. Missions may be converted

---

[37] In a letter to Serra dated Nov. 8, 1774, the guardian warns him not to quarrel with the new governor, who doubtless had secret instructions and would cause any contrarieties to react upon the padres. Serra's weakness was not unknown to his superiors. *Arch. Sta Bárbara*, MS., xi. 191-2.

[38] *Bucareli, Instruccion que debe observar el Comandante nombrado para los Establecimientos de San Diego y Monterey*, 1773, MS., also copy from the original in *Mayer*, MS., No. 18. Translated extracts chiefly on pueblos and colonization in *Halleck's Report*, 133; *Dwinelle's Colon. Hist. Add.*, 2.

into pueblos when sufficiently advanced, retaining the name of the patron saint. New missions may be founded by the commander, acting in accord with the president, whenever it can be done without risk to the old ones. Rivera is to report to the viceroy on needs of the royal service in his province.

The captain is charged with recruiting soldiers to complete the full number. Married recruits must take their families, and unmarried ones the papers to prove that they are single. The Catalan volunteers are to return with their lieutenant by the first vessel. Strict discipline and good conduct must be enforced among soldiers, employés, and civilians, vicious and incorrigible persons being sent back to San Blas. The commandant must be subordinate to the governor at Loreto only to the extent of reporting to him and maintaining harmonious relations. Communication with the peninsula by land should be frequent. Good faith must be kept with the Indians, and the control, education, and correction of neophytes are to be left exclusively to the friars, acting in the capacity of fathers toward children.

No vessels are to be admitted to Californian ports except the San Blas transports and the Philippine vessels, and no trade with either foreign or Spanish vessels is to be permitted. The captains of the transports are not to be interfered with in the management of their vessels, but they cannot admit on board or take away any person without a written request from the commandant, who is to grant such requests only for urgent reasons. San Francisco should be explored as soon as practicable, and the mission of San Diego may be moved if it be deemed best. A complete diary of all events and measures must be kept in a book, and literal copies forwarded to the superior government as often as opportunity occurs. Three complete inventories are to be made on taking possession of government property, one for the viceroy, one for Fages, and one to be kept by Rivera. All

records and archives to be carefully cared for, and
finally these instructions to be kept profoundly secret.

These instructions, with the regulations that precede
and similar instructions of the next year to the governor, constituted the law of California for many years.
Rivera was in Guadalajara when appointed, though it
does not appear from the record when he had come down
from San Diego. He went to Mexico to receive his
instructions in person and then hastened to Sinaloa to
recruit soldiers and families for his command, finishing
his task and arriving with fifty-one persons, great
and small, in March 1774 at Loreto, whence he soon
started northward overland.[39] At about the same
time that Rivera received his orders, that is in
August, Bucareli also authorized Captain Juan Bautista de Anza to attempt the overland route from
Sonora to Monterey, and that officer after some delays
began his march from Tubac in the following January.
Early in September, after Rivera and Anza had received their instructions, the viceroy wrote to Fages,
announcing the appointment of Rivera, and ordering
him to give up the command, and to return by the
first vessel with his company of Catalan volunteers to
join his regiment at the Real de Pachuca.[40]

And now Father Serra, having successfully completed his task in Mexico, is ready to return homeward to utilize the aid and put in practice the reforms
for which he has toiled. Kissing the feet of every
friar at the college, begging their pardon for any bad
example he has set, and bidding them farewell forever, the good friar, with Padre Pablo Mugártegui,
sets out in September for the west coast. At Tepic
he waits until the new vessel, the *Santiago* or *Nueva
Galicia*, is ready for sea, which is not until January 24,
1774. In addition to the articles granted by the gov-

[39] Letter of Rivera to viceroy, dated Loreto, March 25th, in *Arch. Sta Bárbara*, MS., xi. 378-9; *Palou, Not.*, i. 609-10.
[40] Bucareli to Fages, Sept. 7, 1773, in *Prov. St. Pap.*, MS., i. 140.

ernment Padre Junípero has obtained from the viceroy a liberal *limosna*, or alms, of supplies for the
exclusive use of the missions,[41] invoiced separately to
gratify the friar's pride and avoid complications with
Fages who is still in command.   The regular supplies
for the northern missions, with a part of the pittance,
are taken by the *Santiago*, Captain Perez, who has
orders to undertake explorations to the north of Monterey.   Supplies for San Diego and the southern
missions are left for the *San Antonio*, to sail later.[42]

[41] The articles officially granted were: 3 cases of vestments for San Gabriel,
San Antonio, and San Luis, 5 nests, or sets, of measures, 6 in each, one forge
with appurtenances, and 5 quintals, 3 arrobas of iron.   The *limosna* to suffice
for 5 years was 5 packages of cloths for Indians as follows: 107 blankets, 29
pieces *manta poblana*, 488 yds striped sackcloth, 389 yds blue baize, 10 lbs
blue maguey cloth for little girls; also 4 reams fine paper, 5 bales red pepper,
100 arrobas tasajo, 16 boxes panocha, 4 boxes beads, 10 boxes hams, 6 boxes
chocolate, 3 bbls lard, 9 bales lentils, 1 bale and 9 jugs olive-oil, 4 bbls Cas-
tilian wine, 3 bbls brandy, 9 bales chickpeas, 6 bales rice, 160 bales flour,
900 fanegas maize, 250 fanegas beans. *Palou, Not.*, i. 603-5.

[42] Respecting Serra's work in Mexico in addition to the authorities cited,
see *Palou, Vida*, 150-9.   It is related that when Serra arrived in San Blas
from California and saw the *Santiago* in the dock-yard, he remarked that he
would return in her, a remark that excited some ridicule, because everybody
thought the San Blas establishment on the point of being abandoned.

CHAPTER X.

RECORD OF EVENTS.

1774.

WE have seen that Anza from Sonora, Serra from
Mexico *via* Jalisco, and Rivera from Sinaloa *via* the
peninsula were all en route for Monterey under viceregal orders in the spring of 1774. California annals
for that year may be most clearly presented by following those expeditions, in the order named, as a
thread to which may be attached all recorded events.
Previous to their arrival there is nothing known of
matters in the north, save that great want was experienced through the non-appearance of the vessels
due the year before.[1]

When Galvez was preparing the first expeditions
to the north in 1769, Captain Juan Bautista de Anza,
commander of the Tubac presidio in Sonora, a brave
officer like his father, as we have seen in the annals

---

[1] A 'cruelísima hambre,' Palou calls it, *Vida*, 153, 159–60, the greatest ever
experienced. No bread, no chocolate, only milk and herbs 'salted by tears.'
Milk had to be eaten by all from the commandant down. They had some
very strange ideas of what constituted a famine. Soup of peas or beans took
the place of tortillas, and coffee had to do instead of chocolate. The natives
all left the mission to seek for food. *Id., Not.*, i. 608.

of Pimería, became interested in the scheme, and offered to make the trip by land at his own expense to meet the sea expedition. The route up to the Colorado and Gila junction had often been traversed, and it had long been a favorite plan, especially among the old Jesuit pioneers, to reach the northern coasts from this direction; but for some reason not explained the visitador declined the offer. Anza, however, renewed his proposition later, when San Diego and Monterey had been occupied, and finally Bucareli, authorized by the king to pay the expense from the royal coffers,[2] and urged by Father Junípero in his memorial of March 1773—in which he also urged the exploration of a route from New Mexico—gave the required license, probably in September 1773.

Anza obtained twenty soldiers and had nearly completed his preparations for departure, when the Apaches made one of their characteristic raids, stealing his horses and killing some of his men. This caused delay and obliged the captain to start with less force than he had intended; but as a compensation he unexpectedly obtained a guide. This was a Baja California neophyte, Sebastian by name, who had deserted from San Gabriel in August, and, keeping far to the east to avoid meeting soldiers, had reached the Colorado River rancherías and had been brought by the natives to Altar, thus entitling himself to the honor of having been the first Christian to make the overland trip.[3] Under his guidance Anza set out from Tubac January 8, 1774, with Francisco Garcés and Juan Diaz, Franciscan friars from the Querétaro college. There were in all 34 men with 140 horses and 65 cattle.

In a month they had reached the Gila, by way of Sonoita through Papaguería. Palma, a famous Yuma

[2] Ortega in a letter to Rivera, dated San Diego, May 5, 1775, says that Anza's expedition cost from 25,000 to 30,000 pesos. *Prov. St. Pap.*, MS., i. 162-3.

[3] According to one of the two chief authorities Sebastian had started from San Gabriel with his parents and wife, all of whom had perished.

chief, entertained the Spaniards at his ranchería at San Dionisio, Isla de Trinidad, a kind of island formed by a double channel of the Gila at its junction with the Colorado,[4] and received from Anza a badge of office under Spain. He accompanied the explorers across the Colorado and some eight or nine leagues south-westward to the lagoon of Santa Olaya. To this lagoon the whole party was obliged to return on the 19th of February, after having wandered for six days through a country destitute of grass and water.[5] But they started again on the 2d of March, leaving with Palma a large part of the animals in charge of three soldiers, three muleteers, and three Indian servants. The route through the country of the Cojat, Cajuenches, and Danzarines, cannot be traced exactly; but as this was the first exploration of this region and of the great route into California, I append the details, confusing as they are, in a note.[6] Anza would

[4] One of the channels no longer carries water, and perhaps did so then only at high water. In Kino's map of 1701 San Dionisio is not represented as an island. Emory, *Notes*, 95-6, in 1846 noted that the Gila once flowed to the south of its present channel, and says: 'During freshets it is probable the rivers now discharge their surplus waters through these old channels.' Another discovery of Anza is less intelligible. In a letter of Feb. 9th from San Dionisio to the viceroy, *Prov. St. Pap.*, MS., iii. 190-1, he says he had crossed the Colorado and Gila, and had found a branch of the former extending north and west, and entering probably the South Sea—perhaps at San Francisco Bay.

[5] Padre Garcés claimed to have been in this region, the north-east section of Baja California, in 1771; but the narrative of his trip in that year, in *Arricivita, Cron. Seráf.*, 420 et seq., does not show clearly that he crossed the Colorado at all.

[6] The most complete, and indeed the only, authority in print is *Arricivita, Crónica Seráfica*, 450 et seq.; but it is very unsatisfactory. The best account of the expedition seems to be Anza, *Descubrimiento de Sonora á Californias año de 1774*, MS. This appears to be an abridged copy of the original diary made soon after the date of the expedition by some one who did not accompany it. The route was as follows, items from the return march being in brackets: Feb. 9th. At junction of the Gila and Colorado, near the site of the later Concepcion. Feb. 10th to 12th. 5 l. w. N. (s.) w. and 4.5 l. s. w. and s. to Laguna de Sta Olaya, formed by the Colorado in time of flood. Lat. 32° 34'. [According to the return trip Sta Olaya was 4 l. w. of the river and 8 l. w. s. w. of S. Dionisio, or Isla de Trinidad.] Feb. 13th to 19th. Off into the desert and back to Sta Olaya. March 2d. 4 l. w. s. w. to Laguna del Predicador. Mar. 3d to 5th. 3 l. w. s. w.; 6.5 l. w. N. w.; 6 l. w. N.w. with low sierra on left; 3 l. N. w. across the hills; 2 l. w.; 1.5 l. N. and N. w., in sight of an estero, to Pozos de San Eusebio. Mar. 6th. 4 l. w. to Sto Tomás, in middle of sierra. Mar. 7th and 8th. 4 l. N. w. and 1 l. N. E. to Pozos de Sta Rosa de las Lajas (18 l. in a direct line from Sta Olaya). Mar. 9th and 10th.

seem at first to have kept far to the south of the modern railroad route, but to have returned to it before reaching the San Gorgonio Pass, which he named San Cárlos. He crossed the Santa Ana River on a bridge of boughs the 20th of March, and on the 22d arrived at San Gabriel.

The travellers had exhausted their supply of food; and they found equal destitution at San Gabriel; but the friars Paterna and Cruzado entertained them as best they could after a mass, te deum, and sermon of welcome. A cow was killed, and in ten days four of Anza's men returned from San Diego with supplies that had come on the *Santiago*.[7] In a few days all but six of the men were sent with Father Garcés back to the Colorado, having some slight trouble with the savages on the way, and, according to Arricivita, finding that the men left with the animals had become frightened and retired to Caborca. Anza with his six men made a trip up to Monterey and back from the 10th of April to the 1st of May; and two days later he started with Diaz for the Colorado, which he reached in eight days. Palou tells us that some of Fages' men went with him to become acquainted with the route, and returning reported that they had been attacked by the natives as had been the men left at the Colorado. The explorers reached Tubac on the 26th of May, and in July Anza went to Mexico to report.

His expedition had accomplished all that it had

11 l. N. to S. Sebastian Peregrino, a large *ciénega* in the Cajuenche nation [22 l. w. and w. N. w. from Sta Olaya]. Mar. 11th. 1.5 l. w. on same ciénega. Mar. 12th. 6 l. w. N. w. to S. Gregorio. Mar. 14th. 6 l. N. [N. w.] to Sta Catarina [10 l. from S. Sebastian]. 6 l. N. N. w. to Puerto de S. Cárlos, following the cañada [33° 42′]. Mar. 16th and 17th. 3 l. N. w. and N. N. w. to Laguna and Valley of Principe [or S. Patricio, 8 l. w. N. w. from Sta Catarina]. Mar. 18th. [4] l. N. and N. N. w. to Valle de S. José [33° 46′] on a fine stream. Mar. 19th. 6 [5] l. N. w. to Laguna de S. Antonio de Bucareli. Mar. 20th. 5 l. N. w. and 2. 5 l. w. N. w. to Rio Sta Ana. Mar. 21st. 7 l. w. N. w. to Arroyo de Osos [or Alisos]. Mar. 22d. To S. Gabriel [10 l. w. and 5 l. w. N. w. from S. Antonio]. See also, in chap. xii. of this volume, the account of Anza's second trip.

[7] On March 24th Anza was godfather to a child baptized by P. Diaz. *S. Gabriel Lib. Mis.*, MS., 7.

been intended to do, in showing the practicability of the new route.[8]

President Serra sailed from San Blas January 24th in the new transport[9] *Santiago* or *Nueva Galicia*, built expressly for the California service, commanded by Juan Perez, and laden with supplies for San Cárlos, San Antonio, and San Luis. Serra was accompanied by Pablo Mugártegui, a new missionary; and the *Santiago* also brought to California Juan Soler, the store-keeper for Monterey, a surgeon José Dávila with his family, three blacksmiths and families, and three carpenters. After a comparatively prosperous voyage the vessel anchored in San Diego Bay the 13th of March.[10] It had been the intention to go direct to Monterey, but an accident caused a change of plan, and fortunately, for Serra by landing a small portion of the cargo was enabled to relieve the pressing need of the southern missions. He had quite enough of the sea, and besides was anxious to visit the friars; therefore he went up by land, starting on April 6th, having an interview with Captain Anza on the way, and reaching Monterey on the 11th of May after an absence of nearly two years. On account of ill-health Mugártegui also landed and remained at San Diego, Amurrio taking his place on the *Santiago*, which sailed on the same day that Serra started, and anchored at Monterey two days before the president's arrival the 9th of May.[11]

[8] Mofras, *Explor.*, i. 282, mentions this expedition, giving the date of starting incorrectly as Sept. 1773. See also brief account in *Velasco, Sonora*, 150; *Id.*, in *Soc. Mex. Geog., Boletin*, x. 704.

[9] She is called both *fragata* and *corveta*.

[10] According to *Perez, Relacion*, they reached the Santa Bárbara Islands on March 6th. The northern group are named from west to east Santa Rosa (San Miguel), Santa Margarita (Santa Rosa), Santa Cruz (still so called), and Santo Tomás (Anacapa). Thence they sailed southward between the coast and San Clemente, reaching San Diego March 10th (another copy makes it March 11th), sailing April 5th, and arriving at Monterey May 8th. Palou, *Vida*, 153–62, gives the latter date as May 9th.

[11] *Palou, Not.*, i. 606–8; *Id., Vida*, 156–61; *Serra*, in *Bandini Doc. Hist. Cal.*, MS., 1.

We left Rivera y Moncada at Loreto in March with fifty-one persons, soldiers and their families, recruited in Sinaloa for his new command.[12] Lieutenant Ortega was in the south at Santa Ana, with other families, whom he was ordered to bring up to Velicatá to join the rest, and was to remain in command of the camp until supplies and animals for the northern journey could be sent back. Rivera then started northward by land and reached Monterey on the 23d of May. Respecting the details of his march and the number of men he took with him nothing is known; but he left all the families and some of the new soldiers at Velicatá. On the 25th he assumed the duties of his new office in place of Pedro Fages,[13] who prepared, as ordered by the viceroy, to go south with his company of Catalan volunteers.[14] The first opportunity to sail was by the *San Antonio*, which, leaving San Blas in March under Cañizares as master, had arrived on June 8th, this being the first trip ever made direct to Monterey without touching at San Diego.

The feeling between Rivera and Fages was by no means friendly, the former having considered himself aggrieved by Galvez' act in preferring the latter at the beginning notwithstanding the disparity of rank, and a second time by Portolá's choice of a commander in 1770. Triumphant at last, he was not disposed to adopt a conciliatory policy toward his vanquished rival, whom, without any unnecessary expenditure of courteous phrases, he ordered to prepare his accounts

[12] March 20th, Rivera writes to the viceroy from Loreto that he has arrived from Sinaloa and will proceed by land to San Diego and join Anza. *Arch. Santa Bárbara*, MS., xi. 378–9; but as we have seen he was too late to meet Anza.

[13] The viceroy, on Jan. 2, 1775, acknowledges receipt of Rivera's letter of June 14th, stating that he had taken possession of the command on May 25th. *Prov. St. Pap.*, MS,, i. 168. Palou, *Not.*, i. 609–13, makes the date May 24th. May 4, 1771, Fages was made a captain. *Id.*, i. 74.

[14] In addition to the general instructions to Rivera and Fages already noticed, there was a special order of the viceroy dated Sept. 30, 1774, for Fages with his volunteers and all of the cuera company not expressly ordered to remain to be sent to San Blas by the first vessel. *St. Pap., Miss. and Colon.*, MS., i. 313.

and get ready to sail on the *San Antonio*, taking with him all his men except ten who were to be retained until the new force arrived from the peninsula. Fages, though of course obliged to obey the viceroy's orders, was not the man to quit the country without making a show of independence and an effort for the last word. A caustic correspondence followed, little of which is extant, but in which Rivera with the vantage-ground of his superior authority by no means carried off all the honors. Fages claimed the right to embark from San Diego, wishing to obtain certain receipts from padres and corporals at the several missions. Rivera replies, "The viceroy does not order me to allow the volunteers and you to embark at San Diego, but simply by the first vessel. His excellency knows very well that this presidio is the capital where you reside; therefore, this is the place he speaks of, and from this place you must sail." Whereupon Don Pedro, as he might have done before, showed a permit from the viceroy to sail from San Diego, of later date than the commander's instructions; and Rivera was forced to yield.

Again Fages announced that he had some animals set apart for his own use which he proposed to take away with him to San Diego, and, after Rivera's prompt refusal to allow any such outrageous use of the king's property, proceeded to prove that the mules were his own. Then he pleaded for more time to arrange his accounts, which could not be completed before the sailing of the *San Antonio;* but after getting an insolent permission to wait for the *Santiago*, he decided to start at once and leave the accounts to a clerk. Having gathered thus much from Rivera's own letters, it is hard to resist the conclusion that if Fages' letters were extant they would show the writer, with perfect *sang froid*, if not always with dignity, engaged in a deliberate epistolary effort to annoy his exultant and pompous rival. If this was not the case, all the more discreditable to himself was the tone adopted in Rivera's communications.[15] The *San Antonio* sailed from Monterey on July 7th, with thirteen of the volunteers, and with Rafael Pedro y Gil the new store-keeper for San Diego. Fages started by land with two soldiers on the 19th and sailed on the 4th of August from San Diego. We shall hear again from this gallant officer. Fathers Prestamero and Usson also sailed for San Blas on the *San Antonio*, being forced to retire by ill-health.

Perez in the *Santiago* was meanwhile engaged in another important service, that of exploring in the far north. There still existed among Spanish authorities a fear of Russian encroachments on the Pacific coast, or at least a spirit of curiosity to know what the Russians were doing. Bucareli had orders from the king to give this matter his attention as soon as it might be convenient.[16] It is said to have been Serra who first suggested that the California transport might be advantageously used for purposes of geographical discovery, and opening up a new field for spiritual conquest. He also urged that no man was better fitted to take charge of the enterprise than his friend and compatriot Juan Perez, who had been the first in these later times to reach both San Diego and Monterey. Perez was accordingly instructed, after landing the supplies at Monterey, to explore the northern coast up to 60°, with a view to discover harbors and to make such observations respecting the country and its inhabitants as might be practicable. The expense was borne by the king.

It was the intention that Mugártegui should go as chaplain, but in case of his illness Serra had been requested[17] to name a substitute, and appointed Crespí and Peña to act as chaplains and to keep diaries of

[15] *Rivera y Moncada, Testimonio de diligencias en la toma de posesion del mando, 1774*, MS., consisting of two letters dated June 21st and 22d.

[16] *Revilla-Gigedo, Informe de 12 de Abril 1793*, 117-19.

[17] Bucareli's letter of Dec. 24, 1773, in *Prov. St. Pap.*, MS., i. 137-8.

the voyage, as they did, both journals being still extant. The surgeon Dávila went along, the vessel's surgeon, Costan, remaining temporarily at Monterey. June 6th everything being ready at Monterey the padres went on board, and next day the *Santiago* attempted to sail, but was prevented by contrary winds. On the 8th the arrival of the *San Antonio* from San Blas, already noted, caused a new delay. Two days later solemn mass for the success of the expedition was said under the old oak that had witnessed the rite in 1602 and 1770, and on the 11th, just before noon, the vessel sailed from the bay. Adverse winds still baffled the navigators, driving them southward, so that for seventeen days they did not get above the latitude of Monterey, being driven back and forward along the coast between that latitude and that of the Santa Bárbara Islands. On the 9th July, when they were again able to make observations, they were in latitude 45°, beyond the limits of the modern California of which I now write. The details of the voyage in northern waters, during which the Spaniards reached a latitude of 55°, making some observations and naming some points along the coast, dealing with the natives, who came off in canoes, but not landing, belong to another volume of this series, in which I shall narrate the annals of more northern lands.[18]

Reëntering California waters on the return trip the 17th of August, they sighted on the 22d what was supposed to be Cape Mendocino in latitude 40°, on the 26th they saw the Farallones, and next day at 4 P. M. anchored at Monterey. The prevalence of fogs had prevented exploration of the Californian coast, beyond a mere glimpse of Mendocino and the Farallones. It is to be noticed that in speaking of the latter islands as a landmark for San Francisco the diarists clearly locate that port under Point

[18] For a full account of this voyage, with references to the original diaries, see *Hist. Northwest Coast*, i. 150–8.

Reyes, and speak of the other bay discovered five years before as the *grande estero*, not yet named.[19]

Two important events in California must be added to the record of 1774 before I call attention to certain other events on the peninsula and in Mexico nearly affecting the interests of the New Establishments. One was the moving of San Diego Mission in the extreme south in August; the other an exploration of San Francisco Bay in the extreme north at the close of the year. The site on which the mission at San Diego had been originally founded, and the presidio a little later, had not proved a desirable one for agricultural purposes since the drying-up of the river; and in fact for several years seed had been sown for the most part at an inconvenient distance. The first proposition toward a change of site came early in 1773 from Fages, who favored a removal of the ranchería containing all the neophytes as well as many gentiles from the vicinity of the stockade, for the reason that the huts would give the natives an advantage in hostile operations. This was not exactly a removal of the mission, since it does not appear that the friars were to accompany their neophytes; the fear of danger was deemed unfounded and even absurd; and, moreover, the measure was recommended by a man whose approval was enough to condemn any measure in Serra's eyes. Consequently he opposed the change most strenuously in his report to the viceroy.[20]

Jaume, the minister, however, addressed a letter in April 1773 to the president, in which he favored a removal of the mission. Experience had clearly shown, he thought, that want of water would always prove a drawback to prosperity at the original site; it

[19] Crespí in his *Diario* makes a long and confusing argument to prove that the *farallones* seen at this time were not those seen in 1769, the former being 50 leagues from Pt Reyes, and the latter much nearer. The reason of the friar's confusion is not clear. The authorities on this voyage are: *Crespí, Diario; Peña, Diario*, MS.; *Perez, Relacion*, MS.; and *Perez, Tabla Diario*, MS.

[20] *Serra, Repres. 21 de Mayo, 1773*, MS.

was always better for a mission to be a little removed from presidio influences; and he had a report
from the natives confirmed by a soldier, of a very
favorable site some six or seven leagues distant across
the sierra.[21] The matter having been referred to the
viceroy he authorized Rivera to make a change if it
should seem expedient to himself and to Serra.[22] Of
the subsequent consultations and explorations which
doubtless took place we have no record; but the
change was decided upon and effected in August
1774. The new site was not the one which Jaume
had in mind, but a nearer one called by the natives
Nipaguay,[23] about two leagues up the valley north-
eastward from Cosoy, and probably identical or nearly
so with that of the later buildings whose ruins are
still visible some six miles from the city and port.
We have no account of the ceremonies by which the
transfer was celebrated, nor do we know its exact
date; but both friars and neophytes were pleased with
the change, and worked with a will, so that by the
end of the year the mission buildings were better than
at Cosoy, including a dwelling, storehouse, and smithy
of adobes, and a wooden church with roof of tules,
measuring eighteen by fifty-seven feet. At the old
site all the buildings were given up to the presidio,
except two rooms, one for the use of visiting friars
and the other for the reception and temporary storage
of mission supplies coming by sea.[24] Nothing further
is known of San Diego events during the year, except
that Ortega came up from below with the remaining

[21] Jaume's letter of April 3d (or 30th), in *Mayer MSS.*, No. 18, pp. 4, 5.

[22] *Bucareli, Instruccion de 17 de Agosto 1773*, MS.

[23] San Diego de Nipaguay—that is, San Diego at Nipaguay—was a common name for the mission afterwards. Serra called it so in his second annual
report.

[24] *Serra, Informe de 5 Feb. 1775*, MS., 124–7. An unfinished church built
four or five feet above the foundations, with adobes all made ready to finish
it, was also delivered. In a letter of October 3d the commandant of the presidio says he was uncertain whether to accept the building, for how was it to
be finished? *Prov. St. Pap.*, MS., i. 156–7. Lasuen in his report of 1783
says the new site was but little better than the old so far as fertility was concerned. *Lasuen, Informe de 1783*, MS.; see also Serra, in *San Diego, Lib. de
Mision*, MS., 3, 4.

force and families recruited by Rivera in Sinalóa, arriving at San Diego on September 26th, and despatching a part of the company to Monterey on the 3d of October. The new troops gave Ortega some trouble by their tumultuous conduct, complaining of the quantity and quality of the food.[25]

The occupation of the port of San Francisco and the founding of a mission there, though a matter still kept in abeyance, was one by no means forgotten, and one often mentioned in communications passing between Mexico and Monterey. Portolá and Crespí when they had almost reached the port in 1769, had, as we have seen, discovered a large bay before entirely unknown, and had explored to some extent its western shore. Galvez and the viceroy on hearing of Portolá's near approach to San Francisco had ordered the captain of the *San Antonio*, when she brought ten new friars to California in 1771, in case she should reach San Francisco first, to leave there two of the padres and all that was required for an immediate foundation, under a temporary guard of sailors;[26] but the vessel touched first at Monterey and Saint Francis was obliged to wait. In 1772 Fages and Crespí had again attempted to reach San Francisco by passing round the newly discovered bay, thus exploring the eastern shore, although prevented from accomplishing their main object by a great river which they could not cross.[27]

In his instructions of August 17, 1773, Bucareli had ordered Rivera to make additional explorations of San Francisco, and with the approval of Serra to found a mission there.[28] Before either Rivera or his instructions reached California, however, Palou in his first annual report spoke of the proposed mission of San Francisco "in his own port supposed to be in

[25] Ortega to Rivera, in *Prov. St. Pap.*, MS., i. 154–6.
[26] *Palou, Vida*, 88–9.
[27] See Chap. viii. of this volume.
[28] *St. Pap., Miss. and Colon.*, MS., i. 333.

the Ensenada of the Farallones toward Point Reyes," of the attempt recently made to arrive there, of the obstacles in the way, and of the determination that had been formed. This determination was to explore the country northward from Monterey, and to establish the proposed mission wherever a suitable place could be found, since it could not be exactly known where the port was until explorations were made by sea; and later, if the port were found on the other side of the new bay, another mission might be established there.[29] It must be borne in mind that the name of San Francisco had not yet been applied to the newly found body of water, although the latter was by some vaguely supposed to be connected with the port so long known; neither had the bay been explored as yet with boats so that it might be known whether it contained a 'port' at all; or if so, in what part of the broad expanse the harbor was to be found.

In obedience to the viceroy's orders,[30] and with a view, perhaps, to test the necessity or expediency of Palou's plan, a new exploration was undertaken by Rivera as soon as his new recruits arrived at Monterey, which was early in November. He took with him sixteen soldiers, two servants, and a mule train laden with supplies for a journey of forty days. Palou accompanied him, by order of the president, to perform a chaplain's duty and keep a diary.[31] Setting out on November 23d the party followed Fages' route of 1772, via what are now Hollister and Gilroy, until, on entering the grand valley about the bay, they bore to the left instead of to the right as Fages had done, and on the 28th encamped at the very spot where Rivera had spent four days in 1769, that is, on what is now San Francisquito Creek below Searsville.[32] The

[29] *Palou, Not.*, ii. 32.

[30] These orders had, it seems, been repeated in a letter dated May 25, 1774, and directed to Palou.

[31] *Palou, Espedicion y Registro que se hizo de las cercanías del puerto de Nuestro Seráfico Padre San Francisco*, in *Id.*, *Not.*, ii. 43-92.

[32] As distances are not given in this diary it is of little or no help in fixing exact locations. The party was now about one league from the shore, about a

natives were hospitable and not so shy as they had been along the way. This seemed a fitting place for a mission, and a cross was erected as a sign of the Spaniards' purpose to locate San Francisco here. I suppose that from this circumstance originated the name San Francisquito later applied to the stream.

Next day the explorers started on north-westward, soon crossing the low hills into the cañada that had been followed in 1769, to which, or to a locality in which, they now gave the name Cañada de San Andrés which it still bears. Rancherías were numerous, and the natives uniformly well disposed. On the 30th they left the glen, climbed some high land, and encamped on a lagoon in the hills, not improbably that now known as Laguna de San Bruno. From a lofty hill Rivera and Palou obtained a view of the bay and valley to the south-eastward, but could not see the outlet, on account of another hill intervening. December 1st Rivera with four soldiers climbed that hill and on his return said he had been very near the outlet, which could be conveniently reached from the camp by following the ocean beach. Delayed for a few days by cold, rainy weather, they started again on the fourth, proceeded north over low hills and across cañadas, in three of which was running water, and encamped before noon on a stream which flowed into a large lake stretching toward the beach, known later as Laguna de la Merced.

Taking with him four soldiers and accompanied also by Palou, Rivera continued north-westward over hill and vale into the sand dunes and down to the beach, at a point near where the Ocean Side House later stood. Thence he followed the beach, as so many thousands have done since in conveyances somewhat more modern and elegant than those of the gallant captain and friar, until stopped by the

day's journey from the end of the peninsula, and in 37° 46′ by their own reckoning. That they were below Searsville is shown by the fact that on starting north-west they at first crossed a plain.

steep slope of a lofty hill, in sight of some pointed rocks near the shore, this being the first visit to the Seal Rocks since famous, and to the site of the modern 'Cliff.' They climbed the hill and gazed around on what was and is still to be seen, and described by Palou as it might be described now, except in the matter of artificial changes. A cross was set up on the summit, and the explorers returned by the way they had come to their camp on Lake Merced after an absence of only four hours.

It was now resolved to postpone the exploration of the Rio de San Francisco, the San Joaquin, until after the rainy season, and to return to Monterey by the shore route of 1769. Three hours' journey southward, over grassy hills, brought them on the 5th into the old trail, by which, having crossed the San Lorenzo and Pájaro rivers on the 11th, they arrived at the presidio the 13th of December.[33] On the trip Palou had found six sites which he deemed suitable for missions. These were, in the valley of San Pascual near the modern Hollister, in the 'plain of the great estuary' where the cross was left on San Francisquito Creek, in the vale of San Pedro Regalado and that of San Pedro Alcántara between Spanish Town and Pescadero, on the River San Lorenzo at Santa Cruz, and on the River Pájaro at Watsonville. "God grant that in my day I may see them occupied by missions, and in them assembled all the gentiles who inhabit their vicinities, and that none of the latter die without holy baptism, to the end that the number of the children of God and of his holy church be increased, and also of the vassals of our

[33] The lack of distances in this diary renders it of little use in fixing exact localities, although the route is somewhat more fully described in several respects than in the diary of the former expedition. The fact that three hours' journey southward from the head of Lake Merced brought Rivera into the old trail confirms my former conclusion—see chap. vi.—that the first expedition crossed from Pt San Pedro rather than from Half Moon Bay. Now the travellers visited a lagoon in the hills near the shore, about a league above Pt Angel—probably Laguna Alta.

catholic monarch," adds the good padre in closing his journal.[34]

When Palou left the peninsula in the summer of 1773, he left Campa and Sanchez at Loreto to attend to the forwarding of certain cattle from the old missions, which had been assigned to the new ones, but which he had been unable to obtain on account of the never ending excuses of Governor Barri and President Mora, who, however, had agreed to settle the matter definitely in October of the same year. Nothing being done, excuses following excuses, and there being some evidence that the recalcitrant governor was causing delay in the hope of breaking up the whole arrangement by communications with the viceroy, Campa wrote Palou how he was situated, and sailed on April 5, 1774, for Mexico to consult the guardian, Sanches starting about the same time to join Cambon at Velicatá. In Mexico Campa made but little progress. Some cattle and horses purchased for the missions the viceroy had already ordered to be sent up, as they were early in 1775; but the Dominicans had convinced him, as was probably true, that their missions had no cattle to spare, and, therefore, stock for California must be sought elsewhere.[35]

At Velicatá Cambon had been left by Palou in charge of vestments and other church property collected from the southern missions by the order of Galvez. The quarrel between the Franciscans and Barri, for which the removal of this property served largely as a motive, or at least a pretence, was now at its height. The governor had taken advantage of the fact that the agreement by which the Franciscans had voluntarily ceded the Lower California missions was not popularly known, to circulate a report that his own influence had forced the friars to quit the

[34] Rivera sent a diary of the trip to the viceroy on Jan. 5, 1775, as appears from Bucareli's acknowledgment on May 24th, in *Prov. St. Pap.*, MS., i. 172.

[35] *Palou, Not.*, ii. 156–7, 207–8.

·country. He labored hard to win over the Dominicans to his side, and was practically successful so far
at least as the president was concerned, and he insisted
that the property in question had been stolen. The
details and merits of the general controversy need not
be repeated here. It is evident enough that Barri
allowed his bitterness toward the Franciscans to get
the better of his judgment, and that he neglected no
opportunity to annoy his foes.

From San Diego Palou sent back mules to bring up
supplies and part of the church property, but Barri
sent an order to the officer in command at Velicatá to
load the animals with corn, but by no means to allow
the vestments to be taken, pretending that a new
examination of the boxes was necessary. Governor
and president were now acting in full accord and causing delay by throwing the responsibility of every new
hinderance each upon the other. Mora claimed to have
full faith in Franciscan honor, but had consented to
the proposed search merely to convince Barri of his
error! Cambon was instructed to submit to the search
if required, but to insist on exact inventories and certificates. Thus things remained until Serra returned
from Mexico with a positive order from the viceroy
for the removal of the goods, an order which was sent
south and reached Velicatá July 16, 1774.

A correspondence ensued between Cambon and the
military officer in charge, in which the latter professed
to be utterly ignorant of any embargo on the removal
of the property, and to have received no orders whatever from Barri on the subject, although the contrary
was well enough known to be true. Preparations
were made for Padre Sanchez to take the property
with Ortega's force, but a new difficulty arose; for
Hidalgo, the Dominican in charge of Velicatá, had
positive orders from President Mora to stop the goods.
He was in much perplexity, and begged for delay.
Finally, however, after obtaining a certificate from the
commandant that he would furnish no troops to pre-

vent the removal, Hidalgo gave his permission, and it was found that after all there were only three mules to carry the vestments, most of which had therefore to be left behind. They were carried up, however, early in the next year by Father Dumetz, who came down from Monterey with a mule train for the purpose.[36]

There was now but small opportunity left for quarrels between Barri and the Franciscans, but it seems there were also dissensions with the Dominicans. It was evident to the viceroy, that only harmonious relations between the political and missionary authorities could ensure the prosperity of the peninsula, and that under Barri's rule such relations could not be maintained. Bucareli, therefore, decided, as he had done before in the case of Fages, without committing himself decidedly respecting the points at issue, to appoint a new governor, as in fact Barri had several times asked him to do. His choice of "a person endowed with wisdom and love for the service to establish, maintain, and firmly implant good order," fell upon Felipe de Neve, major of the Querétaro regiment of provincial cavalry.[37] He was summoned to Mexico and received his instructions September

[36] *Palou, Not.*, ii. 158–205. With the first collection of vestments there went up to Rivera a letter from Gov. Barri, simply stating that application for the property, in order to prevent delays, should have been made to President Mora rather than himself, and the same mail carried a letter from Mora with the assurance that all the blame for delays belonged exclusively to Barri! Palou adds a short 'reflexion' making excuses, as was his duty, for all concerned. Mora probably was accused of complicity in robbing the missions, and favored a search in order to vindicate his own honor and that of the Franciscans. The viceroy consented from the same motives and to avoid litigation, and Gov. Barri's charges and actions were, perhaps, from ' excess of zeal' to protect the missions of Baja California. It would seem that there was also a quarrel between Barri and Rivera arising in some way from the opening by the commandant of a despatch addressed to the governor. Ortega in letters of July 18th and Oct. 3d—*Prov. St. Pap.*, MS. i. 148–9, 155—advises Rivera that the governor is hostile and disposed to wrangle about superiority; that he had been taking testimony; and that it was only President Mora's efforts which had prevented Rivera's arrest on arrival at Loreto.

[37] The only item of information that I have found respecting Neve before he came to California, is the fact that when his regiment was formed in 1766 he was sent to raise a squadron in Michoacan; but both at Valladolid and Patzcuaro the people resisted the draft, liberated several recruits by force, wounded a sergeant, and forced Neve to return. *Rivera, Gob. de Mex.*, i. 407–8.

30th from the viceroy. These instructions were similar in their general purport to those before issued to Rivera and already noticed. The only points relating to Upper California were those defining the official relations between Neve and Rivera, requiring special attention to the forwarding of despatches from the north and keeping open the routes of communication, and the forwarding of the church property at Velicatá. The commander of Monterey was only nominally subordinate to the governor, being required to maintain harmonious relations with that official, and to report in full to him as he did to the viceroy, but not in any sense to obey his orders. Bucareli was careful to avoid future dissensions by causing Neve to understand Rivera's practical independence.[38] Neve's appointment may be said to have begun with the date of his instructions on September 30th; but his final orders were received October 28th[39] and he started from Mexico the next day, although he did not reach Loreto and assume command until March 4th of the following year.[40] Of Barri after he left Loreto March 26, 1775, nothing is recorded. His term of office had been from March 1771 to March 1775, but he had exerted, as we have seen, no practical authority over Alta California.

Serra's second annual report for the year 1774, completed in February of the following year, is almost entirely statistical in its nature, containing in addition to figures of agriculture, stock-raising, mission buildings, baptisms, marriages, and deaths, long lists of church ornaments, agricultural implements, and other property. The year would seem to have been fairly prosperous, with no disasters. At San Diego the mission had been moved to a new site and new buildings had been erected at least equal to the old ones. It was proposed to move San Gabriel also for a short distance,

[38] *Bucareli, Instrucciones al Gobernador de Californias, 30 de Septiembre 1774*, MS.
[39] *Prov. St. Pap.*, MS., i. 191; *Id.* xxii. 2.
[40] *Prov. Rec.*, MS., i. 1.

and for that reason but very slight additions had been made to the buildings. At the other missions many small structures had been put up for various uses. At San Luis Obispo a new church of adobes, eight by twenty varas, but as yet without a roof, was the most prominent improvement. At San Antonio an adobe storehouse had been built, a bookcase made for a library, and an irrigating ditch dug for about a league. San Cárlos had seven or eight new houses of adobe and palisades, besides an oven.

Agricultural operations had been successful, and the grain product had exceeded a thousand fanegas, the seed having yielded forty fold. San Gabriel took the lead, close followed by San Cárlos. San Luis raised the most wheat, while sterile San Diego showed a total return of only thirty fanegas of wheat. Nowhere was there a total failure of any crop. In the matter of live-stock, horned cattle had increased from 205 to 304; horses from 67 to 100; mules from 77 to 85; sheep from 94 to 170; goats from 67 to 95; swine from 102 to 131; while asses remained only 4. The mission records showed a total of 833 baptisms, 124 marriages, 74 deaths, and an existing neophyte population of 759; or for the year a gain of 342 baptisms, 62 marriages, 45 deaths, and 297 in population. San Cárlos was yet at the head with 244 neophytes, and San Diego came in last with 97.[41]

---

[41] *Serra, Informe de los Augmentos que han tenido con todo el año de 1774 las cinco misiones del Colegio Apostólico de Propaganda Fide de San Fernando de Mexico de órden de N. P. S. Francisco y del estado actual en que se hallan á últimos de Diciembre del año de 1774*, MS. The report was dated San Cárlos, Feb. 5, 1775.

CHAPTER XI.

NORTHERN EXPLORATION AND SOUTHERN DISASTER.

1775.

A California-bound Fleet—Franciscan Chaplains—Voyage of Quiros
in the 'San Antonio'—Voyage of Ayala in the 'San Cárlos'—
Voyage of Heceta and Bodega y Cuadra to the Northern
Coasts—Discovery of Trinidad Bay—Discovery of Bodega Bay—
Death of Juan Perez—Exploration of San Francisco Bay by
Ayala—Trip of Heceta and Palou to San Francisco by Land—
Preparations for New Missions—Attempted Founding of San
Juan Capistrano—Midnight Destruction of San Diego Mission
Martyrdom of Padre Jaume—A Night of Terror—Alarm at San
Antonio.

A FLEET of four vessels was despatched from San
Blas in the spring of 1775, all bound for Californian
or yet more northern waters. The king had sent out
recently from Spain six regular naval officers, one of
whom was to remain at San Blas as commandant,
while the rest were to assume charge of the vessels.
The viceroy was to supply chaplains, and, no clergy-
men being immediately accessible, he called upon the
college of San Fernando to furnish friars for the duty,
on the plea that all was intended to advance the work
of converting heathen, a plea which the guardian
could not disregard, and he detailed four Franciscans
for the new service temporarily, though it was foreign
to the work of the order.[1]

[1] The friar chaplains were Campa, Usson, Santa María, and Sierra. Life
on the ocean wave had no charms for them, and on return from the first
voyage they asked permission to quit the service and to resume their legitimate work as missionaries. The first two were successful, but the others had
to 'sacrifice themselves' again, and José Nocedal was sent also as a companion.
The only consolation of each was the hope of being able to take the place of
some retiring friar in California. *Palou, Not.*, ii. 216-17, 257-8.

All sailed from San Blas on the same day, the 16th
of March.[2] The *San Antonio* was under Lieutenant
Fernando Quirós, and her chaplain was Ramon Usson.
She was laden with supplies for San Diego and San
Gabriel. Quirós' voyage was a prosperous one, and
having landed the cargo at San Diego he was back at
San Blas by the middle of June. The other transport, the *San Cárlos*, bearing the supplies for Monterey and the northern missions, set sail under the
command of Miguel Manrique, but was hardly out of
sight of land when he went mad and Lieutenant Juan
Bautista de Ayala took his place, Vicente Santa María
serving as chaplain. Her trip, though longer from
adverse winds, was not less uneventful and prosperous
than that of the *San Antonio*. Anchoring at Monterey June 27th, she discharged her cargo, and after
having made an exploration of San Francisco Bay,
for which Ayala had orders, and of which I shall
have more to say presently, the *Golden Fleece* set out
on her return the 11th of October.[3]

The other vessels were the ship *Santiago*, under
Captain Bruno Heceta, with Juan Perez and Chris-
tóbal Revilla as master and mate, and with Miguel
de la Campa and Benito Sierra as chaplains; and the
schooner *Sonora* alias *Felicidad*, commanded, after
Ayala's removal by Lieutenant Juan Francisco de
Bodega y Cuadra, with Antonio Maurelle as sailing-
master.[4] The full crew was one hundred and six
men, and the supply of provisions was deemed suffi-

[2] Some authorities say the 15th, and Palou, probably by a misprint, has it
the 26th.

[3] May 5th, Ortega writes from San Diego to Rivera that the *San Cárlos*
was stranded in leaving San Blas, and that the cargo will probably be transferred to the *Santiago*. This idea probably came from some rumor brought
by the *San Antonio*, respecting the delay occasioned by Manrique's madness.
Prov. St. Pap., MS., i. 162.

[4] Heceta, Quirós, and Manrique were *tenientes de navío*, or lieutenants in
the royal navy, the former being acting captain and comandante of the
expedition. Ayala and Bodega were *tenientes de fragata*, a rank lower than
the preceding and obsolete in modern times save as an honorary title in the
merchant marine. Perez and Maurelle held the rank of *alférez de fragata*,
still lower than the preceding, besides being, as was Revilla, *pilotos*, or sail-
ing-masters.

cient for a year's cruise. Sailing from San Blas
March 16th, the schooner being towed by the ship,
they lost sight of the *San Cárlos* in a week, and were
kept back by contrary winds at first, only beginning
to make progress northward early in April. May
21st they were in nearly the latitude of Monterey,
but it was decided in council not to enter that port,
since the chief aim of the expedition was exploration,
and it was hoped to get water at the river supposed
to have been discovered by Aguilar, in latitude 42° or
43°.

On the 7th of June, in latitude 42° as their observations made it, the vessels drew near the shore,
which they followed southward to 41° 6′,[5] and found
on the 9th a good anchorage protected by a lofty
headland from the prevalent north-west winds. Two
days later they landed and took formal possession of
the country with all the prescribed ceremonial, including the unfurling of the Spanish flag, a military salute,
raising the cross, and a mass by Father Campa.
From the day the name of Trinidad was given to the
port, which still retains it, and the stream since known
as Little River was named Principio. The natives
were numerous and friendly, and by no means timid.
They were quite ready to embrace the padres; they
did not hesitate to put their hands in the dishes; and
they were curious to know if the strangers were men
like themselves, having noted an apparent indifference
to the charms of the native women. More than a
week was spent here, during which some explorations
were made, water and wood were obtained, and the
disposition and habits of the natives studied. One
sailor was lost by desertion, and a new top-mast was
made for the *Santiago*. Finally, on the 19th, the
navigators embarked and left the port of Trinidad
with its pine-clad hills, and, much to the sorrow of
the savages, bore away northward, in which direction

---

[5] 41° 8′, 41° 18′, 41° 7′, and 41° 9′ are given by different authorities. The
true latitude is about 41° 4′.

no more landings or observations were made on Californian territory.

The explorations of Heceta and Bodega in northern waters receive due attention in another volume of this series. The ship and schooner, the latter no longer in tow, kept together till the end of July, when they parted in rough weather. Heceta in the *Santiago* kept on to latitude 49°, whence on August 11th he decided to return, many of his crew being down with the scurvy. He kept near the shore and made close observations down to 42° 30′; but on reëntering California waters on the 21st, the weather being cloudy, little was learned of the coast. Passing Cape Mendocino during the night of the 25th, the commander wished to enter San Francisco, but a dense fog rendered it unsafe to make the attempt, though he sighted the Farallones, and the 29th anchor was cast in the port of Monterey. Now were landed some mission and presidio supplies which had come to California by a roundabout way.

The schooner *Sonora*, after parting from her *capitana*, kept on up to about 58°, and then turning followed the coast down to Bodega Bay, so named at this time in honor of Bodega y Cuadra,[6] though there was much doubt among the officials at first whether it were not really San Francisco. They anchored October 3d, and without landing held friendly intercourse with the natives, who came out to them on rafts. The harbor seemed at first glance a good one, and as in the part since called Tomales Bay it extended far inland, apparently receiving a large river at its head, it seemed likely to have some connection with the great *bahia redonda*, San Pablo Bay, which had been discovered to the south. Next day, however, a sudden gale proved the harbor unsafe, breaking a boat, which prevented proposed soundings. Narrowly escap-

[6] Many suppose the name to have come from the fact that the Russians in later times had their cellars—in Spanish, *bodegas*—here. Strangely enough ex-governor Alvarado, *Hist. Cal.*, MS., ii. 8, 10, takes this view of it, and also derives the name Farallones from Cabrillo's pilot Ferrelo!

ing wreck in leaving the bay, the *Sonora* headed
southward; the Farallones were sighted on the 5th,
and on the 7th Cuadra anchored at Monterey, to the
great joy of his former companions who had given
the schooner up for lost.   Nearly all were down with
the scurvy, but they rapidly recovered under the
kindly care of the missionaries and the good-will of
Our Lady of Bethlehem, to whose image in the mission church of San Cárlos the whole crew tendered a
solemn mass of intercession a week after their arrival.
The return voyage from Monterey to San Blas lasted
from the 1st to the 20th of November.[7]   Juan Perez,
who had been the first in these later expeditions to
enter both Monterey and San Diego from the sea,
died the second day out from port, and funeral honors
were paid to his memory a year later when the news
came back to San Cárlos.

At the end of 1774 the viceroy writes both Rivera
and Serra, of his intention to establish a new presidio
of twenty-eight men at San Francisco, under a lieutenant and a sergeant.   This establishment will serve
as a base of operations for a further extension of
Spanish and Christian power, and under its protection
two new missions are to be founded at once, for which
Serra is requested to name ministers.   It is announced
that Anza will recruit the soldiers in Sonora and Sinaloa and bring them with their families, to the number
of one hundred persons or so, by the overland route
explored by himself the same year, coming in person
to superintend the ceremonies.   The comisario at San

[7] The authorities for these voyages, for particulars of which in the north
see *Hist. Northwest Coast*, i. 158 et seq., are *Heceta, Viaje de 1775; Diario de la
Santiago*, MS.; *Bodega y Cuadra, Viage de 1775; Diario de la Sonora*, MS.;
Maurelle, Diario del Viage de la Sonora 1775, MS. (with *Reflexiones, tablas*,
etc.); *Bodega y Cuadra, Comento de la Navegacion y Descubrimiento 1775*, MS.;
Heceta, Segunda Exploracion de la costa Septentrional de Ca'ifornia 1775,
MS.; *Heceta, Expedicion maritima hasta el grado cincuenta y ocho de las costas
del Mar Pacífico*, in *Palou, Not.*, ii. 219–57; *Maurelle, Journal of a Voyage in
1775; Palou, Vida*, 162–5; *Navarrete*, in *Sutil y Mex., Viage*, xciii.–ix.;
Mofras, Explor., i. 107–9; *Greenhow's Or. and Cal.*, 117–20; *Forster's Hist.
Voy.*, 455–8.

Blas has orders to send by the next year's transports
supplies sufficient for the new colony, and the commander of the vessel which brought these letters is
instructed to make a preliminary survey of San Francisco Bay.[8] Details are left to the well known discretion and zeal of the commandant and president,
who are directed to report minutely and promptly on
all that is done. The substance of these communications is duplicated in others written at the beginning
of 1775;[9] one set and perhaps both reaching Monterey
the 27th of June by the *San Cárlos.*

Lieutenant Ayala, as I have said, has orders to explore San Francisco by water. His instructions refer
more directly to the new bay than to the original San
Francisco. As is natural in the case of two bodies of
water so near together and probably connected, there
is no further effort in Mexico to distinguish one from
the other, the lately discovered grandeur of the new
absorbing the traditional glories of the old. For a
time the friars and others in California show a feeble
tendency to keep up the old distinction, but it is practically at an end. From 1775 the newly found and
grand bay bears the name San Francisco which has
before belonged to the little harbor under Point
Reyes. Ayala's mission is to ascertain if the mouth
seen by Fages three years before from the opposite
shore is indeed a navigable entrance, and also to learn
by examination if the bay is a 'port,' or if it contains
a port. He is also to search for a strait connecting
the bay with the San Francisco of old. Rivera is to
coöperate by means of a land expedition, and the two
are to make all possible preparations for the reception of Anza's force soon to be on its way. Rivera
cannot send his party till his men return from the

[8] Letters dated December 15, 1774. Of that to Serra I have the original,
partly in the handwriting of Bucareli himself. *Arch. Misiones*, MS., i. 49-56;
Arch. Santa Bárbara, MS., i. 119-22; *Prov. St. Pap. Ben. Miscel.*, MS., ii.
20-5.

[9] Letters dated January 2, 1775. Original addressed to P. Serra, in *Doc.
Hist. Cal.*, MS., iv. 25-7. See also *Prov. St. Pap.*, MS., i. 166-7; *Id.*, xxii. 3.

south, whither they have gone to escort Dumetz to Velicatá and back in quest of church property. Father Junípero names Cambon and Palou for the proposed mission, and Ayala busies himself in constructing a *cayuco*, or 'dugout,' from the trunk of a redwood on the River Carmelo, a beginning in a small way of ship-building on the Californian coast.

Ayala, with his two pilotos, José Cañizares and Juan Bautista Aguirre, and his chaplain Santa María, sail from Monterey, probably on the 24th of July,[10] beginning with the voyage a novena to Saint Francis, at the termination of which on the 1st of August just at night the *San Cárlos* is off the entrance to San Francisco Bay. The boat is sent in first, and as she does not immediately return, the paquebot follows in the darkness, and anchors without difficulty in the vicinity of what is now North Beach. Next morning she joins the boat and both cross over to the Isla de Nuestra Señora de los Angeles, so named as I suppose from the day, August 2d, and still known as Angel Island.[11] There they find good anchorage, with plenty of wood and water. Ayala remains at anchor in the bay for over forty days, making careful surveys and waiting for the land expedition, which does not make its appearance. It is unfortunate that neither the map nor diary of this earliest survey is extant. Cañizares is sent in the boat to explore the northern branch, the 'round bay,' now called San Pablo, going up to fresh-water rivers,[12] and bartering beads for fish with many friendly natives. Aguirre makes a similar reconnoissance in the southern branch

[10] Palou, *Not.*, ii. 218, 248–9; *Vida*, 201–3, the only authority extant, says July 27th, but this I think is a misprint, since it would not allow the anchorage at Angel Island August 2d.

[11] The fact that it is called 'la isla que está en frente de la boca' would agree better with Alcatraz, but Font, *Journal*, MS., a little later mentions another island agreeing with Alcatraz, removing all doubt.

[12] As nothing is said of the bodies of water corresponding to Suisun Bay and Carquines Strait, it would seem likely that the rivers were Petaluma, Sonoma, or Napa creeks, and not the San Joaquin and Sacramento; but in his *Vida*, 203, Palou says they noted the mouth of the great river San Francisco formed by five other big rivers.

of the bay, noting several indentations with good anchorage; but he encounters only three natives, who are weeping on the shore of what is now Mission Bay, called from that circumstance Ensenada de los Llorones. Santa María and the officers land several times on the northern shore toward Point Reyes, visiting there a hospitable ranchería. The conclusion reached is that San Francisco is indeed a port, and one of the best possessed by Spain, "not merely one port, but many with a single entrance." There is an aboriginal tradition that the bay was once an oak grove with a river flowing through it, and the Spaniards think they find some support for the theory in the shape of oak roots there found.[13] On the 22d of September the *San Cárlos* is back at Monterey.

In the mean time the *Santiago* has arrived from the north, and Heceta, who had been unable by reason of fogs to enter San Francisco by water, resolves to make the attempt by land. He obtains nine soldiers, three sailors, and a carpenter, places on a mule a canoe purchased from the northern Indians, and with Palou and Campa sets out the 14th of September. Following Rivera's route of the preceding year the party arrive on the 22d at the sea-shore, and find on the beach below the cliff Ayala's canoe wrecked. This first product of home ship-building, after fulfilling its destiny in the first survey of California's chief harbor, had broken loose from its moorings and floated out with the tide to meet its fate where more pretentious craft have since stranded.

On the hill-top, at the foot of the old cross, are found letters from Santa María directing the land party to go about a league inland, and light a fire on the beach to attract the notice of the *San Cárlos* anchored at Angel Island. Heceta does so, but finds no vessel, and returns to encamp on Lake Merced, so named from the day, September 24th, on which he left it. Next day he returns to North Beach, but finds no

[13] *Arch. Santa Bárbara*, MS., iv. 153.

ship; and, supposing correctly that she has left the
bay, departs on the 24th for Monterey, where he
arrives the 1st of October.[14] Thus no buildings are
yet erected for Anza's expected force.

Before receiving the viceroy's instructions regarding
San Francisco, Serra had desired to found some new
missions under the regulations of 1773; that is, by
diminishing the old guards and taking a few soldiers
from the presidio. But Rivera declared that no soldiers could be spared, and the president had to content
himself with writing to the guardian and asking that
officer to intercede with the viceroy for twenty men.
Had he known of the force already assigned to the
new presidio, it is doubtful if even he would have had
the effrontery to ask so soon for a reënforcement.
The guardian, unable to get the soldiers, asked permission to retire the supernumerary padres, which was
granted at first but immediately countermanded; and
Bucareli wrote to both Serra and Rivera, authorizing
the former and instructing the latter, in view of
Anza's expected arrival, to establish two or three new
missions on the old plan, depending on future arrangements for additional guards.[15]

The viceroy's letter just alluded to reached Monterey on the 10th of August. At a consultation held
two days later it was resolved to establish at once a
mission of San Juan Capistrano between San Diego
and San Gabriel, under Fermin Francisco de Lasuen
and Gregorio Amurrio, with a guard of six men, four
from the presidial force and two from the missions of
San Cárlos and San Diego.[16] The friars from Monterey and San Luis, where they had been waiting,
went down to San Gabriel in August, Lasuen continuing his journey to San Diego, whence he accom-

[14] *Palou, Not.*, ii. 243–8.
[15] *Palou, Not.*, ii. 259–61; Bucareli to Rivera, May 24, 1775, in *Prov. St.
Pap.*, MS., i. 174–5.
[16] Rivera announced this to the viceroy in a letter of Aug. 22d. *Prov. St.
Pap.*, MS., i. 191–2. Gov. Neve notified the viceroy of the padre's appointment, on Dec. 10th. *Prov. Rec.*, MS., i. 156–7.

panied Ortega to explore a site for the new mission. This done, Lasuen returned from San Diego with Ortega, a sergeant, and twelve soldiers, sending word to Amurrio to come down from San Gabriel with the cattle and other church property. Lasuen formally began the mission on the 30th of October.[17] The natives were well disposed, work on the buildings was progressing, Father Amurrio soon arrived, and prospects were deemed favorable, when on the 7th of November the lieutenant was suddenly called away by tidings of a disaster at San Diego. By his advice the new mission was abandoned, the bells were buried, and the whole company set out for the presidio.[18]

Of affairs at San Diego, before the event that called the company back from San Juan, we have no record, save a few letters of Ortega to the commandant, relating for the most part to trivial details of official routine. There is some complaint of lack of arms and servants in the presidio. Several mule trains arrive and depart; there are hostile savages on the frontier; the lieutenant is sorry because Rivera wishes to leave, doubts if he can obtain permission to resign, which is the first we know of any such intention on the part of the commandant.[19]

At the new mission, six miles up the valley, prospects are bright. New buildings have been erected, a well dug, and more land made ready for sowing. On the 3d of October sixty new converts are baptized. Then comes a change. On the night of November 4th the mission company, eleven persons of Spanish

[17] So says Palou; but Ortega, in a letter to Anza dated Nov. 30th, says it was Oct. 19th. *Arch. Cal. Prov. St. Pap., Ben. Mil.*, MS., i. 2, 3.

[18] Thus Anza on his arrival Jan. 8, 1776, found the site and unfinished buildings unoccupied. *Anza, Diario*, MS., 90.

[19] *Prov. St. Pap.*, MS., i. 142-7, 163-6; *Prov. Rec.*, MS., i. 144-5. In one of his letters Ortega speaks of the landing-place of goods for the presidio as being at least two leagues distant. It would be interesting to know just where this landing was and what was the necessity of landing goods so far off. In fact without crossing to the peninsula it would seem impossible to find a spot so far away.

blood, retire to rest in fancied security. A little after
midnight they awake to find the buildings in flames
and invested by a horde of yelling savages. The two
ministers, Luis Jaume and Vicente Fuster, with two
boys, a son and a nephew of Ortega,[20] rush out at the
first alarm. Jaume turns toward the savages with his
usual salutation *Amad á Dios, hijos*, 'Love God, my
children.' Thereupon he is lost sight of by Fuster,
who with the young Ortegas succeeds in joining the
soldiers at their barracks.

Two blacksmiths, José Manuel Arroyo and Felipe
Romero, the former being on a visit from the presidio,[21]
were sleeping in the smithy. Arroyo is the first to be
roused, and though ill he seizes a sword and rushes
forth. Receiving two arrows in his body he staggers
back into the shop to rouse his companion, and falls
dead. Romero, awakened by the cry, "Compañero,
they have killed me!" springs from his bed, seizes a
musket, and from behind his bellows as a barricade
kills one of the assailants at the first shot. Then,
taking advantage of the confusion which follows, he
escapes and joins the soldiers. The carpenter, José
Urselino, was in the barracks and at once joins the
soldiers; but in doing this, or immediately after, he
receives two arrow wounds which some days later
prove fatal.

The mission guard consisting of three soldiers,
Alejo Antonio Gonzalez, Juan Álvarez, and Joaquin
Armenta,[22] under Corporal Juan Estévan Rocha, in the
absence of a sentinel are aroused from their slumber
by the flames, and by the yells of the assailants.

[20] These were not the Juan and José María of the list given at the end of
this volume. Their age at this time is not stated. The records are strangely
silent about these boys during the rest of this eventful night.

[21] Palou, *Not.*, ii. 264–71, and *Vida*, 176–87, one of the leading authorities
on this affair, erroneously speaks of the three mechanics as two carpenters
and one smith, one of the two room-mates being the carpenter Urselino.

[22] Francisco Peña, the fourth man, was ill at the presidio. The names of
the guard with many other interesting particulars are given in *Ortega, Informe
de Nov. 30, 1775*, MS., this document being a communication addressed to
Lieut.-Col. Anza, and one of the most valuable sources of original information
respecting the disaster, embodying as it does all the results of Lieut. Ortega's
investigations down to date.

Reënforced by the blacksmith, the wounded carpenter, and the surviving friar, the Spaniards defend themselves for a time; but the fire soon forces them to seek other shelter.[23] They first repair to a room of the friars' dwelling, where Father Fuster makes a hazardous but ineffectual attempt to find Jaume.

The fire soon renders the house untenable. In their dire extremity they bethink themselves of a small enclosure of adobes in which they take refuge, there to fight to the death. In one wall is an opening through which arrows are shot; but the soldiers erect a barricade with two bales or boxes and a copper kettle brought from the burning house at great risk. But by the time the opening is closed, all are wounded, and two soldiers besides the carpenter disabled. A fast of nine Saturdays, a mass for each of the soldiers and mechanics, and a novena for the priest are promised heaven for escape; and thereafter not an arrow touches them, though sticks and stones and burning brands are still showered on their heads.[24] Ursclino and the disabled soldiers strain their feeble strength to ward off the missiles, Fuster covers with his body, his cloak, and his prayers the sack containing fifty pounds of gunpowder, while the blacksmith and one soldier load and reload the muskets which Corporal Rocha discharges with deadly effect into the ranks of the foe, at the same time shouting commands in a

[23] It may be noted that according to the last annual report—Serra, *Informe de 1774*, MS.—the mission buildings on the new site had not been enclosed in the usual stockade defences. The barracks are not described in that report, but were of wood; the church was not of adobe; and all the adobe buildings except the granary had tule roofs. The padres' house, or the smithy, or the granary with their adobe walls would seem to have afforded better protection than the building chosen; but the progress of the flames or some other unrecorded circumstance doubtless determined their action.

[24] For this night's struggle I have followed for the most part Fuster, *Registro de Defunciones*, MS., in *San Diego, Lib. de Mision*, 67–74, an original record by a survivor of the fiery ordeal left by Fuster in the mission register of deaths. This author calls the structure which afforded shelter a 'cercadito de adobes, como de tres varas,' and does not imply that it had a roof. Palou says it was a kind of kitchen with walls but little over three feet high and roofed with branches and leaves, the burning of which added to the peril. This author also gives some indications of the padre's bravery which modesty prompted the other to conceal.

stentorian voice as if at the head of a regiment. What a subject for a painting! Thus the hours slowly pass until at dawn the savages withdraw. The survivors, or such of them as can move, crawl from behind the adobe battlements, and the Baja Californians and neophytes make their appearance.

The latter come fully armed with bows and arrows, and claim to have been largely instrumental in putting the foe to flight. The first solicitude of the survivors is to learn the fate of Father Jaume, of whom the neophytes say they know nothing. His body is soon discovered in the dry bed of the creek at some distance, naked, bruised from head to foot with blows of stones and clubs, his face disfigured beyond recognition, and with eighteen arrow wounds.[25] It is subsequently ascertained from the natives that the friar fell calling on Jesus to receive his spirit.

Two Indians were now sent to the presidio, though not without serious misgivings, since it was understood that one party of savages had gone to attack the garrison. The force at the time, during the absence of Ortega and Sergeant Mariano Carrillo at San Juan, consisted of Corporal Mariano Verdugo and ten soldiers, four of whom were on the sick-list and two in the stocks. They were found safe and entirely ignorant of what had happened up the river. On receipt of the news Verdugo hastened with his four men to the mission, where he arrived about eight o'clock in the morning; and a few hours later the whole company started in sorrowful procession back to the presidio, carrying the disabled with the body of Jaume and the charred remains of the blacksmith, Arroyo, and driving the few animals that were left of the mission herds. A small band of neophytes, all that had shown themselves since the attack, was left behind to battle with the flames and save, if possible, something from the general wreck.

[25] Palou says his consecrated hands alone were uninjured, preserved doubtless by God to show his innocence; but Fuster says nothing of this.

On the sixth, after letters from Verdugo and the store-keeper, Pedro y Gil, had been sent by a courier to recall the commandant, Fuster performed funeral rites to the memory of his martyred associate, and buried the body in the presidio chapel. He had died without the last sacrament, but he had said mass the day before his death, had confessed only a few days before, and it could hardly be doubted that all was well with him. The same day Arroyo's body was buried.[26] In the forenoon of the 8th Ortega arrived, soon followed by Carrillo with the remainder of the San Juan party. On the 10th the carpenter, Urselino, was buried by Fuster, having died from the effects of his wounds the day before, after receiving the sacrament, and having left all the pay due him to be used for the benefit of his murderers.

From investigations set on foot as soon as the presidio had been put in a state of defence, some information was brought to light repecting the revolt and its attendant circumstances. Just after the baptism of October 3d two brothers Francisco and Cárlos, both old neophytes,[27] and the latter chieftain of the San Diego ranchería, had run away and had not returned when Ortega went north to found San Juan. It was learned that they had visited all the gentiles for leagues around, inciting them to rise and kill the Spaniards. No other cause is known than that a complaint of having stolen fish from an old woman was pending against them, and so far as could be learned they made no charges against the friars except that they were going to convert all the rancherías, pointing to the late baptism of sixty persons as an indication of that purpose. Some rancherías refused to participate in the plot; but most of them promised their aid,[23] and the

[26] *San Diego, Lib. de Mision*, MS., 74–5. Arroyo's widowed mother had been buried here before. Her name was Petrona García.

[27] So Palou calls them, but I think there may be some doubt about this.

[28] Ortega in his *Informe*, MS., 5, names the Christian rancherías of San Luis, Matamó, Xamachá, Meti, Xana or Xanat, Abascal, Abuscal or Aguscal, and Magtate or San Miguel; and the gentile rancherías of La Punta, Melejó,

assailants were estimated at from eight hundred to a thousand. They were divided into two bodies and were to attack mission and presidio simultaneously; but the mission party began operations prematurely, and the others, seeing the light of the burning buildings, which they supposed or feared would rouse the garrison, abandoned their part of the scheme.

At the mission the savages first went to the neophyte's huts and by threats and force, as the latter claimed, or by a previous understanding, as many Spaniards believed, insured their silence while they proceeded first to plunder and then to burn. About the part taken by the neophytes in this revolt there is some disagreement among the authorities. All the evidence goes to show that some renegade converts were concerned in it; but Palou, reflecting doubtless the opinions of the other friars,[29] accepts the plea of those in the huts that they were kept quiet by force, and that the mass of the Christians were faithful. Others, however, and notably Anza, an intelligent and unprejudiced man well acquainted with the facts, believed, as there was much testimony to prove, that it was the neophytes who planned the rising, convoked the gentiles, and acted treacherously throughout the whole affair.[30]

Otai, Pocol, Cojuat, and El Corral, as among those involved in the movement. Chilcacop, or Chocalcop, of the Xamachá ranchería, a Christian, is said to have aided in the killing of Jaume, in connection with the pagans, Tuerto and the chief of the Maramoydos, both of Tapanque ranchería. St. Pap. Sac., MS., ix. 72. Those who led the attack were Oroche, chief of Magtate or Mactati, Miguel, Bernardino of Matamó, 'and two others. Zegotay, chief of Matamó, testified that 9 rancherías were invited, and that among the leaders were Francisco of Cuyamac, himself, and another. The southern rancherías assembled at La Punta, the mountaineers at Meti. Chief Francisco plotted the revolt, and he, Zegotay, had invited 10 rancherías. Arch. Cal., Prov. St. Pap., MS., i. 228–32. Very little satisfactory information can be gathered from the reports of these investigations. Rafael of Xanat and the chief of Aguscal were also leaders, according to Ortega.

[29] Lasuen, however, in his Informe de 1783, MS., says that most of the neophytes took part in the revolt.

[30] Anza, Diario, MS., 90–6. Anza, as we shall see, arrived early in the next year. He calls attention to the cool lying of the neophytes with a view to exonerate themselves, they even claiming that when liberated from their confinement they had turned upon the gentile foes, driving them to the mountains. There was evidence of some understanding between the natives of San Diego and those of the Colorado River. Garcés on the Colorado in 1776

To insure safety at the presidio a roof of earth was rapidly added to the old friars' dwelling, to which families and stores were removed. The tule huts were then destroyed and other precautions taken against fire. Letters asking for aid were despatched to Rivera at Monterey, and to Anza approaching from the Colorado region, and both, as we shall see, arrived early the next year. Then parties of soldiers were sent out in different directions to learn something of the enemy's plans, and several leaders were captured and made to testify. Thus, in suspense and fear of massacre, the little garrison of San Diego passed the rest of the year.[31]

Serra at San Cárlos received a letter announcing the disaster the 13th of December. "God be thanked," exclaimed the writer, "now the soil is watered; now will the reduction of the Dieguinos be complete!" Next day the six friars paid funeral honors to the memory of Jaume, whose lot, we are told, all envied. They doubted not he had gone to wear a crown of martyrdom; but to make the matter sure, "si acaso su alma necesitase de nuestros sufragios," each promised to say twenty masses. Serra wrote to the guardian that the missionaries were not disheartened, but did not fail to present the late disaster as an argument in favor of increased mission guards.[32]

heard of the disaster, and from his intimate acquaintance with the tribes of that region he believes that they would have joined the San Diego rancherías in a war against the Spaniards later, had it not been for the favorable impression left by Anza. *Garcés, Diario,* 264-285.

[31] See also on the San Diego revolt *Serra, Notas,* in *San Diego, Lib. de Mision,* MS., 4; *Lasuen, Informe de 1783,* MS.; *Id.,* in *Arch. Santa Bárbara,* MS., ii. 197; *St. Pap., Miss. and Colon.,* MS., i. 16, 127; and investigations of Ortega and Rivera in April to June 1776, in *Prov. St. Pap., Ben. Mil.,* MS., i. 22-3. Ortega credits privates Ignacio Vallejo, Anastasio Camacho, and Juan de Ortega with great gallantry in these trying times, *Informe,* MS., 3; and Alvarado, *Hist. Cal.,* MS., i. 83, goes so far as to say that Vallejo was the chief cause of the Spanish triumph, thus becoming a great favorite among the padres. Gleeson, *Hist. Cath. Ch.,* ii. 68-76, is somewhat confused in his account of this affair, making the natives destroy San Cárlos and attack the presidio in 1779.

[32] *Palou, Not.,* ii. 272-5; *Id., Vida,* 184-7. Dumetz now went to San Antonio and Cambon and Pieras returned to San Cárlos Dec. 23d.

Rivera set out for the south on the 16th of December, with thirteen men, one of whom was to be left at San Antonio while two were to remain at San Luis.

In August there had been an alarm at San Antonio. A messenger came to the presidio on the 29th with the news that the natives had attacked the mission, and shot a catechumen about to be baptized. Rivera sent a squad of men who found the wounded native out of danger. They captured the culprits and held them after a flogging, until the commandant ordered them flogged again, when after a few days in the stocks they were released.[33]

[33] *Palou, Not.*, ii. 244-5.

CHAPTER XII.

EXPEDITIONS OF ANZA, FONT, AND GARCÉS.

1775-1776.

ANZA AND HIS COLONY—PREPARATIONS IN MEXICO AND SONORA—TWO HUN-
DRED IMMIGRANTS—ORIGINAL AUTHORITIES—MARCH TO THE RIO COLO-
RADO—MISSIONARIES LEFT—ITINERARY—MAP—A TEDIOUS MARCH TO
SAN GABRIEL—ANZA GOES TO THE RELIEF OF SAN DIEGO—RIVERA EX-
COMMUNICATED—ANZA BRINGS HIS FORCE TO MONTEREY—HIS ILLNESS—
RIVERA COMES NORTH AND ANZA GOES SOUTH—A QUARREL—RIVERA
VERSUS ANZA AND THE FRIARS—STRANGE ACTIONS OF THE COMMANDANT—
HIS MARCH SOUTHWARD—INSANITY OR JEALOUSY—ANZA'S RETURN TO
THE COLORADO AND TO SONORA—EXPLORATIONS BY GARCÉS—UP THE
COLORADO—ACROSS THE MOJAVE DESERT—INTO TULARE VALLEY—A
REMARKABLE JOURNEY—DOMINGUEZ AND ESCALANTE.

CAPTAIN ANZA, returning from his first exploration
of an overland route to California, went to Mexico to
lay before the viceroy the results of his trip. Very
soon, by royal recommendation, the projects of establishing missions in the Colorado region and a new
presidio at San Francisco were taken into consideration. In November 1774 the board of war and finance
determined to carry out or advance both projects by a
single expedition to California, by way of the Colorado, under the command of Anza.[1] This determination, as we have seen, was announced to Rivera and
Serra at Monterey by Bucareli in December and January. Anza was advanced to the rank of lieutenant-
colonel and hastened homeward to raise the required

---

[1] Anza states that the decree of the viceroy, under which he acted, was
dated Nov. 24th. Garcés says the expedition, or his part of it, was determined
on by the junta on Nov. 28th, was ordered by the viceroy by letter of Jan.
2d, and by the letters of the guardian of Santa Cruz College Jan. 20th and
Feb. 17th.

force of thirty soldiers with their families for California.

Bucareli was very liberal with the king's money on this occasion; giving four mule trains and many horses and cattle for the new establishment, and also providing that families of settlers, like those of the soldiers, were to be transported at government expense, receiving pay for two years and rations for five. The expense of each family was about eight hundred dollars. Anza took with him from Mexico animals, arms, and clothing, and began his work immediately by recruiting on the way. He clothed his recruits, men, women, and children, from head to foot, and allowed their pay and rations to begin with the date of enlistment. At San Felipe de Sinaloa a regular recruiting-office was opened, Anza's popularity, with his liberal display of food and clothing, insuring success both here and in the north, until in September 1775 most of the company were assembled at the appointed rendezvous, San Miguel de Horcasitas. They were ready the 29th of September, all being united in time to start from the presidio of Tubac the 23d of October.[2]

The force that set out from Tubac consisted, first, of Anza, commander, Pedro Font of the Querétaro Franciscans as chaplain, ten soldiers of the Horcasitas presidio, eight muleteers, four servants, and Mariano Vidal, purveyor—twenty-five persons in all who were to return to Sonora; second, Francisco Garcés and Tomás Eixarch,[3] destined to remain on the Rio Colorado with three servants and three interpreters; and third, Alférez José Joaquin Moraga, and Sergeant Juan Pablo Grijalva, twenty-eight soldiers, eight from the presidio force and twenty new recruits; twenty-nine women who were wives of soldiers; 136

[2] Arricivita, *Crón. Seráf.*, 461, says they left Horcasitas on April 20th, and Tubac Oct. 21st. The rendezvous of the friars connected with the expedition was at the mission of Tumacacori near Tubac.

[3] So Font calls him. Garcés writes the name Eixarth; Arricivita, Eyzarch; and Anza, Esiare.

persons of both sexes belonging to the soldiers' families
and to four extra families of colonists;[4] seven muleteers, two interpreters, and three vaqueros—altogether 207 destined to remain in California,[5] making
a grand total of 235, to say nothing of eight infants
born on the way. The live-stock of the expedition
consisted of 165 mules, 340 horses, and 320 head of
cattle.[6]

Our Lady of Guadalupe, Saint Michael, and Saint
Francis of Assisi were selected as patrons of the expedition, and after the celebration of mass on Sun-

[4] Palou says there were 12 of these families and that the whole force for
California was 200 souls.

[5] There may be some slight inaccuracy respecting the vaqueros, muleteers,
and interpreters, the numbers given being those not otherwise disposed of
definitely in the diaries. The names are included in the list at end of this
volume. There are no means of separating most of them from other parties.

[6] *Anza, Diario del Teniente Coronel Don Juan Bautista de Anza, Capitan del
Presidio de Tubac, Sonora, de su expedicion con familias desde dicho presidio, al
reconocimiento del puerto de San Francisco de Alta California; y de su vuelta,
desde este puerto al Presidio de San Miguel de Horcasitas*, MS., 232. Completed at Horcasitas on June 1st. This official journal kept by the comandante
from day to day throughout the whole expedition is of course the chief
authority on the subject. There is an occasional ambiguity of expression
which causes confusion, notably so at the beginning where the company is
described; but otherwise the diary leaves nothing to be desired. The author
was a man of great ability and force of character, besides being very popular
with his men. Another original authority is *Font, Journal made by Padre
Pedro Font, Apostolic Preacher of the College of Santa Cruz de Querétaro,
taken from the minutes written by him on the road, during a journey that he
performed to Monterey and the Port of San Francisco, in company with Don
Juan Bautista de Anza, etc.*, MS., 52. Completed at Ures, Sonora, June 23d.
This translation was made from the original in the parochial archives of Guadalajara, or, more probably, from a copy of the same, apparently about 1850,
under circumstances of which I know nothing, but evidently with considerable
care. The original, which I have not seen, is cited in *Prov. St. Pap.*, MS.,
xiii. 206, among other documents as *Diario que firma el P. Font...con dos
mapas.* A copy of the translation was obtained in California by Bartlett,
and is cited in that author's *Personal Narrative*, ii. 78, 278–80. Another
copy, probably made from that in my possession, is preserved in the library
of the Territorial Pioneers in San Francisco, and an abridgment was published by that society. *Territorial Pioneers of Cal., First Annual*, 81–107.
The maps are not copied in the translation, though there are a few rude pen
drawings, and though the numbers on one of the maps, representing days'
journeys, are given in the diary. Fortunately this map, a very interesting
and important one, has been found, and a lithographic copy of it—though
with many blunders in lettering—published in *Hinton's Hand-Book of Arizona*,
of which book, recently printed, it is the sole meritorious feature so far as
history is concerned. I reproduce the map, or that part of it representing
California, in this chapter. Font's diary, though less complete and extensive
than that of Anza, is still of very great value as an authority on this expedition. Still another original authority is *Garcés, Diario y Derrotero que siguó
el M. R. P. Fr. Francisco Garcés en su viaje hecho desde Octubre de 1775 hasta 17*

day, they began their march on Tuesday, the 23d of October. Details of the route and march, through Pimería and the country since known as Arizona, belong rather to the annals of those territories than to those of California, but there is little to record anywhere. The route was by San Javier del Bac and Tucson to the river Gila, and down that river generally along the southern bank to the Colorado junction, a route often travelled in the old Jesuit era. The march was not a difficult one. The natives were uniformly hospitable, and ready both to receive trifling gifts and to have the authority of their chieftains confirmed by Spanish appointments. The only misfortunes were the death of a woman in childbirth, the desertion of one or two muleteers brought back by natives, and the loss of a few horses from bad water and excessive cold. The only delays were caused by an examination of the famous Casa Grande, by an occasional halt for rest, and by other detentions of a day or two by the birth of young immigrants. They reached the Gila the last day of October and were about a month on the march down to the Colorado junction.

Crossing the Gila to the northern bank near its mouth November 28th, Anza and his company were given a hospitable and even enthusiastic welcome by the Yuma chief, Palma, whose domain lay, it seems, on both sides of the Colorado, and who had built a large house of branches especially for the use of the travellers.[7] Four soldiers were met here, who had been sent in advance, and had been searching during the past six days, on the California side of the Colo-

de Septiembre de 1776, al Rio Colorado para reconocer las Naciones que habitan sus márgenes, y á los pueblos del Moqui del Nuevo-México, in Doc. Hist. Mex., serie ii. tom. i. 225–348. This diary is nearly as complete as Anza's, and more so than Font's, down to the time when Anza's expedition left the Colorado for the north-west. Other authorities are Palou, Not., ii. 213–15, 277–82; Id., Vida, 204–5, 186–7; Arricivita, Crón. Seráf., 461–90, the last being a very full account but with some errors respecting minor details.

[7] P. Font's map is incorrect in representing the ford of the Colorado as below the Gila, while all three diaries say that it was a little way above.

rado, for a more direct route than that followed the year previous; but without success, as neither water nor grass could be found. The first task, and by no means an easy one, was to get the large company with cattle and stores safely across the river. The Yumas said the Colorado was not fordable, and must be crossed by means of rafts, a slow and tedious process, but one which Anza was inclined to think necessary for the families and supplies at least. At seven o'clock in the morning of the 29th he went down to the bank to reconnoitre. He ordered the necessary timber for rafts, and then with a soldier and a Yuma determined to make one final search for a ford, which he found about half a mile up the river, where the water was diverted by islands into three channels. The afternoon was spent in opening a road through the thickly wooded belt along the bank; and on the 30th before night all the families and most of the supplies were landed on the western side, without the use of rafts.

The travellers remained in camp on the right bank for three days, partly on account of the dangerous illness of two men, and also to make certain needful preparations for the comfort and safety of the two friars who were to remain here until Anza's return. Father Garcés was requested to select the place where he would reside, and chose Palma's ranchería about a league below the camp and about opposite the mouth of the Gila. So earnest were Palma's assurances of friendship and protection that it was deemed safe to leave the missionaries with their three servants and three interpreters. Before starting Anza built a house, and left provisions for over four months, and horses for the use of the remaining party, whose purpose was to explore the country, become acquainted with the natives, and thus open the way for the establishing of regular missions at an early date. I shall presently have more to say of their travels in California. Setting out December 4th from Palma's ranchería, Anza

marched slowly down the river, the way made difficult
by the dense growth of trees and shrubs, by cold, and
by illness in the company. The first halt was at the
rancherías of San Pablo, or of Captain Pablo as Font
says; the second was at the lagoon of Coxas, or Cojat,
the southern limit of Yuma possessions and of Palma's
jurisdiction; and the third, on the 6th of December,
was at the lagoon of Santa Olaya, the beginning of
Cajuenche territory, about twelve leagues below the
mouth of the Gila.[8]

During the stay at Santa Olaya Garcés overtook
the party, having already set out to explore the country toward the mouth of the Colorado. Anza divided
his force into three parties under the command of
himself, Grijalva, and Moraga, who started on the
9th, 10th, and 11th, respectively, and were reunited
December 17th. at San Sebastian. I give some details of names and distances in a note.[9] I also append
a copy of Font's map, substituting names for numbers
in the case of important places and where space permits. The route followed was nearly the same as
in Anza's former trip, and substantially that of the
modern railroad through Coahuila Valley and San
Gorgonio Pass. The journey, every petty detail of

[8] Font, *Journal*, MS., 16, 17, makes the distance 14 leagues with some
winding, and the latitude 32° 33' which by the distances is very nearly accurate.
Garcés, *Diario*, 244, calls the lagoon Santa Eulalia. By Anza and Font the
name is written Olalla. See chap. x. for Anza's trip of 1774.

[9] Route from Palma's ranchería on the west bank of the Colorado near
mouth of the Gila to San Gabriel. The courses are from *Font's Journal*,
Anza's agreeing with them generally but being definitely expressed. The
distances in parentheses, differing widely from Anza's, are from Font, whose
leagues were about 2 miles. The numbers refer to Font's map: 42. Laguna
of San Pablo, or Capt. Pablo, 4½ l. (5) w. ¼ s. w.; 43. Laguna of Coxas, or
Cojat, 3 l. (4) s. w., Laguna of Santa Olalla, 32° 33', 4 l. (5) s. w.; 45. Pozo
del Carrizal, or Alegría, 5 l. (7) w. n. w.; 46. Dry Gulch, 5 l. (7) w. n.w.; 47.
Pozos de Santa Rosa de las Lajas, 10 l. (14) w. n. w., w., w. s. w.; 48. Dry Creek,
4 l. (3) n.; San Sebastian, 33° 8', 5½ l. (7) n. n. w.; 51. Pozo de San Gregorio,
7½ l. (9) w. ¼ n. w.; 52. Arroyo of Santa Catalina del Vado, Sink, 4 l. n. w. ¼ w.;
53. Id., source, 1½ l. (1) n. w. ¼ w.; 54. Danzantes ranchería in same cañada, 3 l.
(4) w. n. w.; San Cárlos Pass (San Gorgonio?) 2½ l. (3) n. n. w.; [123. Portezuelo on return;] 56. San Patricio Cañada, source of stream, 33° 37'; 57. San
José Arroyo, 6 l. (7) n. w. ¼ w.; 58. Laguna of San Antonio Bucareli, down
San José Valley, 4 l. (5) w. n. w.; Santa Ana River, 9 l. (8) w. n. w.; 60. Arroyo
de los Alisos, 6 l. w. n. w.; 61. River San Gabriel, branch, 5 l. (6) w. n. w.,
San Gabriel, 34° 35', 2 l. w. s. w.

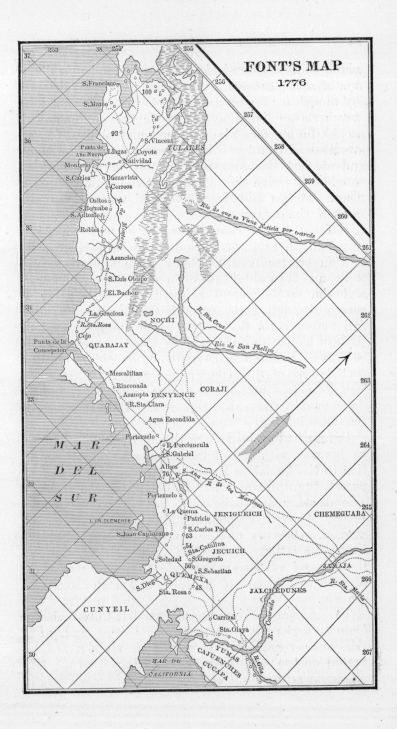

FONT'S MAP
1776

which is fully described in the commandant's diary, was a slow, tedious, and difficult one, requiring a full month for its accomplishment; and the fact that it was accomplished at all under the circumstances speaks highly for Anza's energy and ability. Long stretches of country without water must be crossed, and at first the company must be divided that all should not arrive the same day at the same watering-place. It was midwinter, the cold was intense, and most of the company were not accustomed to a cold climate. Storm followed storm of snow and hail and rain, and an earthquake came to increase the terrors of San Gorgonio pass. They were obliged to dig wells, and then obtained only a small supply of water, and the cattle were continually breaking away in search of the last *aguage*. There was much sickness; and yet, beyond the loss of some hundred head of live-stock, there was no serious disaster, owing to the skill and patience of Anza and his aids. On the first day of 1776 the new pioneers of California and San Francisco forded the River Santa Ana, and on January 4th the expedition reached the mission of San Gabriel.

Rivera had arrived from the north the day before, on his way with ten or twelve men to afford protection to the threatened presidio of San Diego, and to punish the Indians who had destroyed the mission. The disaster and danger at San Diego seemed to justify Anza in suspending his own expedition for a time, especially as the season was not favorable for the immediate exploration of San Francisco. At the request of Rivera, therefore, he determined to proceed with a part of his force to punish the southern foe.

The company of immigrants was left to rest at San Gabriel under the command of Moraga, and, after religious ceremonies of gratitude for safe arrival celebrated on the 6th, Anza set out at noon on the 7th, accompanied by Font and seventeen of his soldiers in addition to Rivera's force, for San Diego, where he arrived the 11th.[10]

Naturally, the coming of reënforcements caused great relief to Ortega and his little garrison, who were in constant fear of an attack from the gentiles. There seems to have been some foundation for these fears besides the exaggerated rumors always prevalent on such occasions ; but, whatever may have been the plans of the savages, their hostile purposes did not long survive the arrival of new forces. One of Rivera's first acts was to send six soldiers to the peninsula with communications for the viceroy and a demand for reënforcements, in view of the recently developed dangers threatening the permanency of the Spanish establishments in California. Then followed investigations respecting the late outbreak, lasting the remainder of the year ; they were imperfectly recorded, and of slight importance. Raids were made to different rancherías; gentile chiefs were brought in, made to testify, flogged, liberated, or imprisoned, but nothing was learned in addition to what has been already stated.[11]

It was not long before a difference of opinion arose between the two commanders which later developed into a quarrel. As we have seen Anza had consented to postpone temporarily the special business the viceroy had intrusted to him, in view of the danger threatening San Diego. He found the danger somewhat less than had been represented. He had come to San Diego for a brief, vigorous, and decisive campaign against the savages, but he found Rivera disposed to a policy of delay and inaction. Anza's chief concern

[10] Anza, *Diario*, MS., 89–90, says he took 17 men ; Font, *Journal*, MS., 22, says 20 men ; Palou, *Not.*, ii. 275–6, makes it 18 men ; and the same author, *Vida*, 186–7, implies that there were 40 men. The route from San Gabriel was: 63. River Santa Ana 6 l. (10 according to Font); Arroyo de Santa María Magdalena, or La Quema, 11 l. (14) ; River San Juan Capistrano, 11 l. (14) ; La Soledad ranchería, *via* San Dieguillo and 68 Agua Hedionda, 9 l. (12); San Diego, 3 l. (4).

[11] *Anza, Diario*, MS., 97–100, 104, 106; *Prov. St. Pap., Ben. Mil.*, MS., i. 22–3; *Prov. St. Pap.*, MS., i. 215–32.

was naturally the founding of San Francisco, while in
Rivera's mind the protection of San Diego was the
only subject at present to be thought of. Anza at
first yielded to the captain's views, realizing that as
ruler of the province he naturally felt for its safety,
but at last tidings came from San Gabriel which turned
Anza's attention again to his own affairs. Five men
arrived February 3d with a despatch from Moraga and
the purveyor Vidal, to the effect that the mission
could no longer furnish food for the immigrants except to the injury of its own neophytes, Father Paterna
having distributed rations for eight days and given
notice that these would be the last.

On receipt of this intelligence Anza resolved to take
his military colony without delay up to Monterey.
He agreed, however, with Rivera, to leave ten of his
soldiers at San Gabriel, thus relieving a portion of
the old guard at that mission for service at San Diego
if needed,[12] and with the other seven, having sent in
advance a mule train laden with maize and beans, he
set out on the 9th, still accompanied by Font, and
arrived at San Gabriel on the 12th. Only one event
occurring at San Diego after Anza's departure requires notice in this connection. Cárlos, an old neophyte but a ringleader in the late revolt, returned in
real or assumed penitence, and, prompted doubtless by
the missionaries, took refuge in the church. Rivera
sent a summons to Fuster to deliver the culprit on the
plea that the right of church asylum did not protect
such a criminal, and moreover that the edifice was not
a church but a warehouse used temporarily for worship. Fuster by the advice of his comrades of the
cloth refused, and warned the commandant to use no
force. Rivera then entered the church sword in hand
with a squad of soldiers and took the Indian out, paying no heed to the expostulations of the three padres,

---

[12] *Anza, Diario*, MS., 108. He did leave 12 instead of 10. Palou, *Not.*, ii.
275–6; *Vida*, 186–7, implies that the 12 men were left at San Diego instead
of San Gabriel.

Fuster, Lasuen, and Amurrio. The priests proceeded to excommunicate the commander and the soldiers who had aided him, and ordered them to leave the church before beginning service on the next day of mass. The friars reported to Serra, sending the report up to Monterey by Rivera himself.[13]

Arriving at San Gabriel on February 12th Anza found that the night before three of his muleteers and a servant with a mission soldier had deserted, taking twenty-five horses and other property, part of which belonged to the mission and part to the expedition. The colonists proper, however, seemed content and showed no disposition to desert. Moraga was sent with ten men to capture the fugitives, and before his return Anza resolved to set out for the north. Leaving twelve men and their families under Grijalva to reënforce the mission guard, and ordering Moraga on his arrival to follow with eight men, the commandant started on the 21st with seventeen men, the same number of families,[14] the mule train, and the live-stock. Heavy rains had swollen the streams and rendered many parts of the route well nigh impassable. Observations respecting the natives of Channel rancherías are omitted by Anza as having been given in the diary of his former trip, a diary which unfortunately is no longer in its entirety extant. Font gives merely an outline of distances and directions.[15] With no other

[13] *Palou, Not.*, ii. 292–5.

[14] The full division of the forces was as follows on Anza's departure: At San Gabriel, 8 California soldiers, 12 families, Sergeant Grijalva, and 4 soldiers of Anza's guard waiting for Moraga; with Moraga, 8 California soldiers (2 of the 10 having returned before Anza started); with Anza, 11 California soldiers, 17 families, and 6 of Anza's men—total 29 out of the 30 soldiers who were to remain in California, one not being accounted for. This explanation is necessary on account of the confused statements of Anza, who had no head, or pen at least, for figures.

[15] The route was as follows; the earlier part to the sea-shore being apparently further south than that followed by the first Spanish explorers in 1769, and Anza's distances being as before considerably less than Font's. The numbers refer to Font's map, q. v.: San Gabriel; 119. Rio Porciúncula, 2 l.; 72. Portezuelo, 6 l.; 73. Agua Escondida, 7 l. (10); 74. Rio Santa Clara, 9 l. (15); 75. Rincon or Rinconado ranchería, past Carpintería, 6 l. (9); [117.] Assumpta River]; 76. Mescaltitlan ranchería, 7 l. (9); Ranchería Nueva, 8 l. (9); 78. Cojo ranchería, 7 l. (10); 79. River Santa Rosa, past Pt Concepcion, rancherías of

notable occurrence than an occasional miring of the train, in the midst of which it became necessary to unload the animals, the women meanwhile being compelled to walk,[16] the immigrants were welcomed March 2d at San Luis Obispo, where next day, as shown by the mission records, Anza stood as godfather to several native children baptized by Font.[17] From this place they passed directly north by the modern stage route to the Salinas River, or Rio de Monterey as they called it, reaching San Antonio on the 6th, and feasting on two fat hogs magnanimously killed for their use by order of the friars. Moreover, they were delighted to receive intelligence from the south, having been in great anxiety since they heard of the late disaster. Here Moraga came up, having captured the deserters near the Colorado River, and having left them tied at San Gabriel. On the 10th all arrived safely at Monterey.[18]

Next morning Padre Junípero came over from San Cárlos to congratulate Anza on the safe termination of his march, and to assist with his three companions at the religious ceremonial of thanksgiving, on which occasion Father Font delivered an address of encouragement with advice to the newly arrived company. Anza and Font went over to the mission by invitation of the president, where the commandant was confined to his bed for more than a week by a painful illness. On the 18th eight of the presidio soldiers were sent south to reënforce Rivera at San Diego, with a request to that officer to take immediate steps

Pedernales and Espada, 9½ l. (12); 81. Buchon ranchería, 9 l. (13); San Luis Obispo, 35° 17½′, 3 l. (4); over mountains and down Rio Santa Margarita to (83) Ascencion on Rio de Monterey (Salinas), 7 l. (10); 84. First ford of Rio San Antonio, 8 l. (10); [111. Cañada de Robles]; San Antonio, 36° 2½′, 8 l. (10); 86. Los Ositos, on Rio de Monterey, past Roble Caido (in Cañada de S. Bernabé) 7 l. (9); 87. Los Correos, on the river, 8 l. (10); [109. S. Bernabé Cañada; 108. Buena Vista;] Monterey, 7 l. (10).

[16] Hundreds of travellers over the coast stage route in winter, myself among the number, have no difficulty in identifying this place near San Luis.

[17] San Luis Obispo, Lib. de Mision, MS., 31.

[18] On the journey to Monterey see Anza's Diario, MS., 112-34; Font's Journal, MS., 25-9.

for the founding of San Francisco. On the 23d, against the surgeon's advice, Anza insisted on mounting his horse and setting out to explore San Francisco Bay, returning April 8th from this exploration, which may be most conveniently described in connection with other San Francisco matters in the next chapter.

Back at Monterey the commandant was disappointed in finding neither Rivera in person nor any message from him. He accordingly sent Sergeant Góngora with four men[19] south with letters requesting Rivera to meet him at San Gabriel on the 25th or 26th for consultation respecting important matters. Two days later, on the 14th of April, having turned over his company and all connected with the San Francisco establishment to Moraga, he began his return march with Font, Vidal, seven soldiers of his escort, six muleteers, two vaqueros, and four servants. The parting with the soldiers and their families, whom he had recruited in Sonora and brought to their new home, is described by Anza as the saddest event of the expedition. All came out as their leader mounted to leave the presidio, and with tearful embraces bade him god-speed. Font affirms that according to the list, which he consulted just before starting, there were one hundred and ninety-three souls of the new colony left at Monterey.

Next day between Buena Vista and San Bernabé, less than twenty miles from Monterey, they met Góngora, who announced that Rivera was close behind him, and revealed certain strange actions of this officer. He had met Rivera between San Antonio and San Luis, and in reply to questions had told his business and presented Anza's and Moraga's letters, which the captain refused to take, simply saying "Well, well; retire!" Góngora followed his superior officer north, keeping at a little distance, and a day or two later Rivera suddenly called for the letters, received

[19] Two of the men were of Anza's guard, and the others of the Californian troops. Palou, *Not.*, 288-90, says that Góngora had but two men.

them without breaking the seals, and gave in return two letters for Anza which the sergeant was to deliver in all haste. As Góngora called Anza aside and delivered the letters he stated his belief that Rivera was mad. The letters contained a simple refusal to effect or permit the establishing of San Francisco. Góngora was ordered to go on to Monterey, and after proceeding another league Anza met Rivera on the road, saluted him, and asked about his health. Rivera said his leg troubled him, heard Anza's expressions of regret, and started on, as if it were a casual meeting, with a simple *adios*. "Your reply to my letter may be sent to Mexico or wherever you like," called out Anza, and Rivera answered, "It is well." Calling on the friars who accompanied him,[20] to witness what had occurred, Anza, considerably offended by actions which seemed to him attributable to impoliteness and a "great reserve" rather than madness, went on his way, arriving at San Luis Obispo the 19th of April.

In the mean time Rivera went on to Monterey, arriving on the 15th, and sending word to Serra to come over from the mission for his letters, which he wished to deliver in person and was too unwell to visit him. Serra came, and thought Rivera's illness, which was a slight pain in the leg, greatly exaggerated. He found his letters likewise broken open, though Rivera assured him it was accidental and they had not been read. He then told the president of his excommunication at San Diego, and Serra, after consultation with the San Cárlos friars, approved what Fuster had done, refusing to grant the captain's request for absolution, until he should give satisfaction

---

[20] Pieras was returning in his company to San Antonio. Anza, *Diario*, MS., 185, says he took a written certificate from the padres. Font, *Journal*, MS., 43, says: 'We supposed that he had returned to speak with Capt. Anza before his departure and treat about the affairs of the expedition, and that we should probably have to return to Monterey or at least stay where we were; but we soon found that his arrival did not cause us any detention whatever, for when we fell in with Capt. Rivera, a short time afterward, the two captains saluted each other on passing, and without stopping to speak about anything Capt. Rivera immediately went on to Monterey, and we continued our journey toward Sonora.'

to the church by returning the Indian Cárlos to the sanctuary, on which condition the San Diego ministers could grant absolution without necessity of Serra's interference. He also wrote the guardian about the matter, and after much difficulty in getting an escort from Rivera, who put him off with frivolous pretexts, he sent Cambon with the letter to overtake Anza. The next day, April 19th, Rivera himself started south again, refusing Serra's request to go with him on the plea of very great haste.[21]

Cambon overtook Anza at San Luis on the 19th, bringing besides the president's letters for Mexico one in which he announced his purpose to come down with Rivera if possible, and asked Anza to wait a little; another from Moraga telling of Rivera's arrival at Monterey, and volunteering the opinion that the commandant was insane; and still another from Rivera himself announcing his immediate departure, asking for a delay and consultation, and apologizing for past discourtesy on the plea of ill-health.[22] On the afternoon of the 21st some soldiers came in saying that Rivera had encamped for the night but a little way off. Anza at once sent a message that he would consult with him on matters affecting the service, but that all communication must be in writing. Next day came back a letter naming San Gabriel as the place of consultation. Anza was there on the 29th,[23] and

[21] *Palou, Not.*, ii. 291–7. Another serious cause of trouble between Rivera and Serra was the action of the former respecting the mules which were sent for mission use. One hundred mules were sent *via* Baja California, and 89 were sent up by Gov. Barri to Rivera, who, knowing that they belonged exclusively to the missions, distributed them all the same among his soldiers, except 40 which he brought to Monterey, admitting when questioned that the mules were not his, but pleading military service. Subsequently, a letter came to Serra for Rivera ordering the distribution of the mules. The letter was open, and was sealed and delivered after being read, but Rivera never mentioned the matter again. *Id.*, 209–11.

[22] Palou, *Not.*, ii. 297–300, says that Anza was induced by the padres to read the letter, but would not answer it. According to this author Rivera's apology was in the subsequent letter.

[23] This is Anza's own version, *Diario*, MS., 189–97. Font, *Journal*, MS., 44, tells us that Rivera came to San Luis on the 22d, and after staying a while without seeing Anza started for San Gabriel. Palou also says that Rivera came to San Luis, got angry because Anza refused to communicate

found that Rivera had arrived two days before him. Here the two commandants had no personal interview, but exchanged several letters, Anza sending to Rivera a description and map showing his survey of San Francisco, and giving him three days in which to prepare such reports or other communications as he might wish to forward to the viceroy. When the time had passed Rivera was offered more time, but replied that no more was needed and that his despatches would soon overtake Anza.[24] The latter finally set out for Sonora May 2d, with the same company he had brought from Monterey and the remainder of his ten soldiers.

Next day there came from Rivera, not his report to the viceroy on matters connected with his command, but a private letter to Anza in which he said that he "lacked a paper bearing upon a criminal who took refuge in the place where mass is said at San Diego," and asked Anza to present his excuses to the viceroy. He also enclosed a letter to the guardian of San Fernando. Anza sent back both letters to the writer, and went on to the Colorado; while Rivera went immediately down to San Diego. The quarrel is certainly a curious item in the annals of California, being a subject which it is difficult fully to comprehend. Rivera was evidently a weak man. Whether he was insane, or influenced solely by a spirit of childish jealousy, of which we have seen manifestations in a previous quarrel with Fages, is a question. Both officers were subsequently reprimanded by Bucareli

except in writing, and went on to San Gabriel followed by Anza. Here may be mentioned a tradition of the natives recorded by Anza as having been told to P. Figuer, of the arrival and wreck, 23 years before, of a vessel bearing 12 white men like the Spaniards, who before their death in the wreck had landed and gave the Indians beads and other articles, including the knives found by the Spaniards in 1769. 'Qué gente seria esta queda al discurso de quien está mas instruido que yo,' writes Anza, and I can do no better than follow his discreet example.

[24] Palou says that Anza did not stop at the mission but encamped at a little distance, fearing a controversy with Rivera; and that he subsequently sent back Rivera's letters with the message that 'he was not the mail.' The correspondence between the two was sent by Anza to the viceroy but has not, so far as I know, been preserved.

for allowing a quarrel in matters of etiquette to interfere with the public service; but Rivera's early removal to Lower California put an end to the matter, as it did to his quarrel with the friars.

The return march of Anza's party to the Colorado presents nothing of importance. They followed the same route as before, except between San Sebastian and Santa Olaya, where they kept more to the north, and arrived May 11th at the Portezuelo de la Concepcion, just below Palma's ranchería, and nearly if not exactly identical with the site of the modern Fort Yuma. Here they found Padre Eixarch in safety and added him to the company; but of Garcés nothing could be learned except that he had gone up the river to the country of the Jalchedunes, whither a letter was sent ordering him to return. Palma with three other natives also joined the party, being allowed at the earnest solicitation of himself and nation to go with Anza to Mexico to present his petition for missionaries. They crossed the swollen river on rafts just below the Gila, followed the banks of the latter stream for two days, and then, turning to the right, returned to Horcasitas by way of Sonoita, Caborca, and Altar, arriving the 1st of June.[25]

I have now to narrate briefly the Californian wanderings of Father Francisco Garcés, whom Colonel Anza had left on the 4th of December 1775 at Palma's ranchería opposite the mouth of the Gila, and whom he had subsequently seen at Santa Olaya on the 9th, the friar being already on his way to explore the country and learn the disposition of the natives toward the Christians. This first trip lasted till January 3d, and in it the friar wandered with

[25] *Anza, Diario,* MS., 198–232; *Font's Journal,* MS., 45–52; *Arricivita, Crón. Seráf.,* 464–8, 490. The last author affirms that Palma was well received at Mexico, but there was some hesitation about sending missionaries, as he was chief of one ranchería only. I should add that one of the deserting muleteers condemned by Anza to remain in California escaped from San Diego and crossed the country eastward alone and unmolested, joining Anza on the Colorado. The name of this first explorer on this route is not recorded.

three Indian interpreters in all directions over the country between Santa Olaya and the mouth of the Colorado,[26] everywhere kindly received, everywhere showing his banner with a picture of the virgin on one side and of a lost soul on the other. The natives invariably looked with pleasure on the former painting, pronouncing it *muy buena*, but turned with horror from the latter as something very bad, to the unceasing delight of Garcés, who regarded their preferance as a token of predestination to salvation. The diary contains much useful information respecting the aboriginal tribes.

On the return of Garcés early in January the two padres moved their residence from Palma's ranchería to what they called the Puerto, or Portezuelo, de Concepcion, the site, as already stated, of the modern Fort Yuma. They also examined the ranchería, or *puerto*, of San Pablo below on the river, and pronounced it a suitable site for a mission. Visitors came in from different nations, and among others from those dwelling in the mountains toward San Diego. The people called Quemeyabs announced that those on the coast had already killed a priest and burned his house, that war was expected, and that in case it came all the nations would combine against the Spaniards, asking the Colorado tribes to remain neutral. Garcés paid, however, very little attention to this story, knowing of course nothing about the massacre at San Diego; yet he lost no opportunity to insist on the necessity of maintaining the most friendly relations with these tribes, in order to insure the safety of the coast establishments and communication with them.

On February 14th Garcés started up the river, always to the west of it, with two or three interpreters to visit the Yamajabs, as the Mojaves were orig-

[26] The general route is indicated by dotted lines on Font's map, but must have been added after the diary was finished, for then Font had heard nothing of Garcés. This part of the padre's wanderings might, indeed, have been reported by Eixarch, but not his northern travels, also shown on the map.

inally called, arriving on the 28th in their country, or rather opposite, for they lived on the east of the river, between what are now the Needles and Fort Mojave.[27] During his short stay two thousand natives came across the Colorado to visit the first white man who had ever been in that region. Here the adventurous friar conceived the idea of crossing the country westward to visit the friars who lived near the sea, and was encouraged by the natives, who had traded with the coast tribes and said they knew the way. Leaving some of his not very bulky effects and one of his interpreters, he started with the rest and a few Yamajabs March 1st and arrived on the 24th at San Gabriel.[28] The route was substantially that of the modern road from Los Angeles to Mojave, up the Mojave River and through the Cajon Pass; and the journey was without incident requiring special mention.

Garcés was warmly welcomed by the priests at San Gabriel, where it will be remembered he had been with Anza in 1774, finding that establishment "muy adelantada en lo espiritual y temporal," and remaining for

[27] This being the first exploration of most of this region, or of all west of the river, I give the route in full. See also Font's map route marked —·—·—. Puerto de la Concepcion, 6½ l. N. W.; 2 l. W. N. W. through pass in Sierra de San Pablo to San Marcelo watering-place; 5 l. N. W. in sight of Cabeza del Gigante in the east, Grande Medanal, and vicinity of San Sebastian, passing near Peñon de la Campana; 8 l. N. and N. N. W. through pass in the sierra on north of the Medanal to San José watering-place 33° 28′; 3½ l. N. N. W. and E. N. E., across sierra to a valley; 6 l. N. N. W. and E. N. E.; 6 l. E. N. E. and N. into Sierra of Santa Margarita to banks of Colorado, across valley to watering-place in 33° 25′(?); 1½ l. W.; 6 or 11 l. N. W. and N. W. to Tinajas del Tezquien, one day's journey from river; 8 l. (or 6 l.) N. N. W. and N. across a sierra, to Santo Angel springs 34° 31′ (in Chemehueves country); 6 l. N. E. and N. W.; 7 l. N. N. E. across a sierra to Yamajab nation, whose rancherías, La Pasion, were across the river. (35° on Font's map.)

[28] The full route over a country which Garcés was the first, as also for many years the last, to traverse is worth recording as follows. (See also map): 3 l. N. W. to rancherías of Santa Isabel; 3 l. N. W. and E. N. W. (sic) to San Pedro de los Yamajabs in 35° 1′, still near the river; 2½ l. s. w. to San Casimiro wells; 8 l. W. ¼ W. S. W. to wells; 5 l. W., 3 l. W. S. W. to Sierra de Santa Coleta; 4 l. W. N. W. across sierra (Providence Mts.) to Cañada de Santo Tomás; 6 l. W. S. W. to wells of San Juan de Dios, where the country of the Beñemés begins; 5 l. to Pinta Pass and Arroyo de los Mártires (Rio Mojave); 12½ l. W. S. W. on same stream; 2 l. W. N. W., and 2 l. S. W. and S. 34° 37′; 5 l. S. W. up the stream; 8½ l. up the stream; 3 l. S. W. and S. to San Benito ranchería; 3 l. S. S. W. across sierra (Cajon Pass?) in sight of sea, and 3 l. E. S. E. to Arroyo de los Alisos; 2½ l. W. S. W. into Anza's trail, and 8 l. W. N. W.; 2 l. W. N. W. to San Gabriel.

over two weeks.[29] It had been his intention to reach
San Luis instead of San Gabriel, but the natives had
refused to guide him in that direction. He now determined to go up to San Luis by the highway, and
thence to return eastward to the Colorado across the
tulares. He applied to the corporal of the mission
guard for an escort and supplies for the trip, and was
refused, being subsequently refused also by Rivera to
whom he wrote at San Diego. The commandant soon
arrived, however, on his way to Monterey, and a discussion ensued on the matter, which finally elicited
from Rivera, after various excuses, the declaration
that he was not in favor of any communication between
the natives of the Colorado and those of the missions,
having already taken some measures to prevent it by
ordering the arrest of eastern Indians coming to the
missions to trade. Garcés deemed Rivera's views
erroneous, but he was obliged to submit, receiving,
however, from the missionaries supplies which enabled
him to partially carry out his plans, though he did not
venture along the Channel shores.

Setting out on the 9th of April, the padre crossed
the San Fernando Valley—I use here for convenience
modern names, referring to a note for those applied
at the time[30]—and the Santa Clara River; entered

---

[29] It appears by the mission record that Garcés on April 6th baptized an
Indian of 20 years named Miguel Garcés, Sergeant Grijalva being godfather.
San Gabriel, Lib. de Mision, MS., 10. It is very strange that neither Anza
nor Font in their diaries mention Garcés' visit to San Gabriel, though the
route is indicated on the latter's map, which, as I have said, must have been
made after the completion of the diary.

[30] See also Font's map. San Gabriel; 1½ l. N. W. and W. N. W.; 5½ l. N. W.
at foot of sierra; 2½ l. N. W. to ranchería in 34° 13′ (vicinity of San Fernando
mission); 2 l. N. to Santa Clara Valley and 1½ l. W. N. W. to a *ciénega;* 9 l. W.
and N. across (?) the Sierra Grande; ¼ l. N. E. to a lake where Fages had been
(Elizabeth Lake?); 5 l. across valley to Sierra de San Márcos; 2½ l. N. and 3½ l.
W. across the Sierra to San Pascual ranchería of the Cuabajay nation (in
edge of Tulare Valley, but this nation farther west on map); 1½ l. W. N. W. to
ranchería in 35° 9′; 8 l. N. to Arroyo de Santa Catarina in country of the
Noches; 1 l. N. W. to a great river San Felipe flowing with rapid current from
eastern mountains (Kern River above Bakersfield?) and 3 l. N. W. and N. to
smaller stream Santiago (Posa Creek?); 4½ l. N.; 2½ l. N. to River Santa Cruz
(White River?); 1 l. E. to ranchería. Back to San Miguel at junction of two
branches of River San Felipe; back to San Pascual ranchería; 2 l. E. and N. E.
in sierra to lagoon of San Venancio; 3½ l. N. W. and S. E.; 1½ l. S. E. to Arroyo

the great Tulare Valley by way of Turner's and Tejon
passes; crossed Kern River, which he called San
Felipe, near Bakersfield; went up nearly to the latitude of Tulare Lake, which he did not see, being too
far to the east; left the valley, probably by the Teha-
chepi Pass but possibly by Kelso Valley; and thence
went across to the Mojave, and back by nearly his
original route to the starting-point on the Colorado.
Thus he had been the first to explore this broad
region, the first to pass over the southern Pacific
railway route of the thirty-fifth parallel. His petty
adventures with the ever friendly natives in the Tulare
Valley are interesting, but cannot be sufficiently condensed for insertion here. Seven days' journey north
of the limit of his trip he heard of another great
river which joined the San Felipe, and which Garcés thought might be that flowing into San Francisco Bay, the San Joaquin, as it doubtless was. At
one place the priest was greeted by a native who
asked him in Spanish for paper to make *cigarritos*, who
said he came from the west, and who was, doubtless,
a runaway neophyte from San Cárlos or San Antonio.
Everywhere the natives were careful to inquire of
the guides whether the friar was a Spaniard of the
west or of the east, the latter bearing a much better
reputation than the former.

On the Colorado Garcés received Anza's letter
requiring his return if he wished to accompany the
party to Sonora. But it was already too late; there
was much to be done in his favorite work of making
peace between hostile tribes, the Indians desired him
to stay, and there were other regions to explore.
Consequently, although he had once started down the
river, he suddenly changed his mind and decided to
visit the Moqui towns. Parting from his last inter-

de la Asuncion; 6½ l. s. s. w. out of mountains and over plains; 7 l. s. s. w.
to Rio Mártires at old station in 34° 37'; back to San Juan de Dios by old
route; 2 l. E. N. E. to Médano; 4½ l. E. S. E. across Sierra of Santa Coleta; 3 l.
E. N. E. to well of San Felipe Neri; 5 l. N. E.; 1½ l. N. E. to Trinidad; 1½ l. N. E.;
9 l. E. and S. E. to San Casimiro; 2 l. E. S. W. (sic) to starting-point.

preter he crossed the river and started June 4th with a party of Hualapais for the north-east, reaching the Moqui towns the 2d of July. Here his good-fortune deserted him. The Moquis did not harm him, but would not receive him in their houses, would not receive his gifts, looked with indifference on his paintings of hell and heaven, and refused to kiss the Christ. Having passed two nights in a corner of the court-yard, and having written a letter to the minister at Zuñi, Garcés turned sorrowfully back and retraced his steps to the country of the Yamajabs, where he arrived on the 25th. He was a month in going down the river to the Yuma country, and reaching San Javier del Bac, on the 17th of September.[31]

The expedition of Dominguez and Escalante may be alluded to here as an unsuccessful attempt to reach California. They went in 1776 from Santa Fé, New Mexico, to Utah Lake. But winter was near, food became scarce, reports of the natives were not encouraging, and they soon gave up their plan of reaching Monterey, returning to Santa Fé by way of the Moqui towns.[32]

[31] *Garcés, Diario*, 246–348. Signed at Inbutama Jan. 30, 1777. Forbes, *Hist. Cal.*, 157–62, saw this diary in MS., at Guadalajara. Journey mentioned in *Prov. Rec.*, MS., i. 47–8; vi. 59. Palou, *Not.*, ii. 281–2, mentions rumors that Garcés had been killed by savages.

[32] *Dominguez* and *Escalante, Diario y Derrotero, 1776*. In his *Carta de 28 de Octubre 1775*, MS., Escalante favors a route from Monterey to the Moquis and to Santa Fé. He has heard of some light-colored natives somewhere on the route, who had probably reached the interior from Monterey, by the great rivers.

CHAPTER XIII.

FOUNDING OF THE PRESIDIO AND MISSION OF SAN FRANCISCO.

1776–1777.

The expedition of Anza, described in the preceding
chapter, was planned and executed with almost exclusive reference to the establishment of a presidio at
San Francisco, and of one or two missions in the same
region under its protection. Though I have not found
the text of Bucareli's instructions to Anza, it was
probably the intention that the foundation should be
accomplished during that officer's stay in California,
and to a certain extent under his supervision. The
expedition, however, for various reasons, did not reach
California so early as had been intended. The matter
was delayed by the critical state of things at San
Diego, and still farther delayed by Rivera's idiosyn-
crasies; and Anza was obliged to leave the country
before his colonists had been settled in their new
home. Yet he did not go until he had made every
possible effort to forward the scheme by repeatedly

(279)

urging its importance upon the dilatory and obstinate commandant, and by making in person a new examination of the San Francisco region. This examination, minutely described in the original records,[1] was omitted from its chronological place as a part of Anza's expedition, and must now receive attention.

With Moraga, Font, a corporal, and two soldiers from the presidio, eight of his own men, and provisions for twenty days, Anza left Monterey for San Francisco the 23d of March 1776, having been but two days from his sick-bed at San Cárlos.[2] The party followed the route of Rivera and Palou in their journey of December 1774,[3] to the Arroyo de San Francisco, now known as San Francisquito Creek, at a spot where the Spaniards had first encamped in December 1769, and which Palou had selected two years previously as a desirable site for the mission of San Francisco. The cross set up in token of this selection was still standing, but intermediate exploration, as Anza tells us, referring presumably to Heceta's trip of the year before, had shown a lack of water in the dry season, very unfortunately, as in respect of soil, timber, and *gentilidad* the place was well adapted for a mission.

Instead of entering the cañada of San Andrés Anza seems to have kept nearer the bay shore—though neither he nor Font states that the bay was kept in sight; but after crossing the Arroyo de San Mateo, so called at the time and since, there are but slight data, save the general course, between north-west

[1] *Anza, Diario*, MS., 139–78; *Font's Journal*, MS., 30–43.

[2] Palou, *Not.*, 285–7, says the start was March 22d, and the total number of soldiers 10. Anza wished Palou to go with him, but Serra objected. Two of the soldiers, however, had been over the route before.

[3] See chap. x. of this volume. The itinerary, with Font's distances in parentheses, was as follows: From Monterey, $7\frac{1}{2}$ l. (7) to Asuncion or Natividad across the River Monterey or Santa Delfina: 8 l. (12) to Valley of San Bernardino or Arroyo de las Llagas (still called Llagas Creek) across Arroyo de San Benito and Pájaro River (?); 8 l. (12) to Arroyo de San José Cupertino (93 on Font's map) in sight of bay; 4 l. (6 ?) to Arroyo de San Francisco. At one place on the way the poles used to support the altar on a previous visit of the Spaniards were found decorated with offerings of arrows, feathers, food, etc., recalling the similar occurrence at Monterey in 1770.

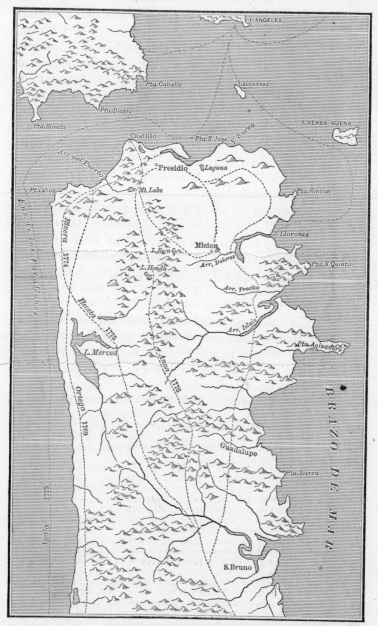

PENINSULA OF SAN FRANCISCO.

and north, from which to determine the exact route,[4] until, on March 27th, he encamped at about 11 A. M. on a lake near the "mouth of the port," out of which was flowing water enough, as the writer says, for a mill. This was what is now Mountain Lake, to which the Spaniards at this time gave no name,[5] though they called the outlet Arroyo del Puerto, now known as Lobos Creek. As soon as the camp was pitched Anza set out exploring toward the west and south, spending the afternoon, and finding water, pasturage, and wood, in fact all that was required for his proposed fort except timber.

Next morning he went with the priests to what is now Fort Point, "where nobody had been," and there erected a cross, at the foot of which he buried an account of his explorations.[6] Here upon the table-land terminating in this point Anza determined to establish the presidio. Font presently returned to camp,[7] while Anza and Moraga continued their explorations toward the east and south-east, where they found, in addition to previous discoveries, a plentiful supply of oak timber which, though much bent by the north-west winds, would serve to some extent for building purposes. About half a league east of the camp they

[4] From the topography of the region, and from the fact that no mention is made of seeing or being near either the bay or Lake Merced, it is most likely that Anza followed the route of the present county road and railroad from San Bruno to the vicinity of Islais Creek, thence turning to the left past the present Almshouse tract.

[5] The lake is called Laguna del Presidio on La Pérouse's map of 1786. That the lake on which this party encamped was Mountain Lake, an identity that no previous writer has noticed, is proved not only by Anza's subsequent movements, but by the following in Font's *Journal*, MS., 31: 'The coast of the mouth (of San Francisco Bay) on this side runs from N. E. to S. W., not straight, but forming a bend, on the beach of which a stream, which flows from the lagoon where we halted, empties itself, and we called it the Arroyo del Puerto.' No other part of the shore corresponds at all to this statement.

[6] Misled, perhaps, by this mention of the cross, Palou, *Not.*, ii. 286, says that Anza followed his, Palou's, route of 1774 until he reached the cross planted at that time.

[7] Font in his diary gives a long and accurate description of San Francisco Bay. He clearly mentions Alcatraz Island, though without applying any name. It is to be noted that he mentions Punta de Almejas, or Mussel Point, still so called; but this was not the original Mussel Point of 1769, though Font very likely thought so.

found another large lagoon, from which was flowing
considerable water, and which, with some artificial improvements, they thought would furnish a permanent
supply for garden irrigation. This was the present
Washerwoman's Bay, corner of Greenwich and Octa-
via streets. About a league and a half south-east of
the camp there was a tract of irrigable land, and a
flowing spring, or *ojo de agua*, which would easily
supply the required water. Anza found some well
disposed natives also, and he came back at 5 P. M. very
much pleased, as Font tells us, with the result of his
day's search.

Next morning, the 29th, they broke camp, half the
men with the pack animals returning by the way they
had come, to San Mateo Creek, and the commander
with Font and five men taking a circuitous route by
the bay shore. Arriving at the spring and rivulet discovered the day before, they named it from the day,
the last Friday in lent, Arroyo de los Dolores.[8]
Thence passing round the hills they reached and
crossed the former trail, and went over westward into
the Cañada de San Andrés in search of timber, of
which they found an abundance. They followed the
glen some distance beyond where the San Mateo
creek flows out into the plain, killed a large bear,
crossed the low hills, and returned northward to join
their companions on the San Mateo.

The next objective point was the great River San
Francisco, which had in 1772 prevented Fages from

---

[8] It is to be noted that Anza calls it simply an 'ojo de agua ó fuente' and
Font an 'arroyo,' but neither mentions any lagoon. Palou, however, says,
'on reaching the beach of the bay which the sailors called De los Llorones
(that is Mission Bay, called Llorones by Ayala's men on account of two weeping natives, see chap. xi.), he crossed an arroyo by which empties a great
lagoon which he named Dolores, and it seemed to him a good site for the mission,' etc. This may be punctuated so as to apply the name to the stream
rather than the lagoon; but I suspect that the lagoon—subsequently known
as The Willows—with its stream was entirely distinct from Anza's stream of
Dolores. Of this more in note 26 of this chapter. Font from an eminence
noted the bearing of the head of the bay E. S. E., and of an immense spruce,
or redwood, afterwards found it to be 150 feet high and 16 feet in circumference, on the Arroyo de San Francisco, S. E.

reaching Point Reyes.[9] Save that in going round
the head of the bay they named Guadalupe and
Coyote streams, and further on the Arroyo de San
Salvador, or Harina, there is nothing of value or
interest in the diaries until April 2d when the explorers reached the mouth of "the fresh water port
held hitherto to be a great river," that is, to the
strait of Carquines and Suisun Bay. The water was
somewhat salt; there was no current; this great
River San Francisco was apparently no river at all,
but an extension of the bay. The matter seems to
have troubled them greatly, and their observations
were chiefly directed to learning the true status of
this body of water. There was no reason for it,
but they were confused. Crespí's diary of the former trip had described the body of water accurately enough, and had not at all confounded the
strait and bay with the River San Francisco, or San
Joaquín; but, possibly, Fages had also written a
diary in which he expressed the matter less clearly.[10]

The camp on the 2d was on a stream supposed to
be identical with the Santa Angela de Fulgino[11] of
Fages. On the 3d they continued eastward past the
low range of hills, from the summit of which, near
Willow Pass, like Fages and Crespí before them, they
had a fine view of a broad country, which they describe
more fully, but not more accurately, than their predecessors.[12] The long descriptions are interesting, but
they form no part of history and are omitted, strange
as it may seem, on account of their very accuracy, as
is also true regarding Font's description of San Francisco Bay. They described the country as it was and

[9] It is noticeable that Anza several times implies that more than one exploration had been made in this direction, but only one, that of Fages, is
recorded.

[10] See account of Fages' trip in chapter viii. According to *Arricivita,
Crón. Seráf.*, 465–7, Font named the body of water Puerto Dulce.

[11] No. 100 of Font's map.

[12] See also Font's map in preceding chapter, on which 'a' is 'the hill to
which Fages arrived;' 'b' a 'ranchería at edge of the water;' 'c,' a 'hill from
which we saw the tulares;' 'd' the 'summit of the sierra;' and 'e' some 'mineral hills.'

is; it is only with the annals of their trip and such
errors in their observations as had or might have
had an effect on subsequent explorations that I have
to deal.   There are, however, errors and confusion to
be noted.   It is evident that for some reason they had
an imperfect idea of Fages' trip.   On the strait they
had labored hard to prove it not a river, as it certainly
was not, and as it had never been supposed to be, so
far as can be known.   Now that they had reached the
river and were looking out over the broad valleys of
the San Joaquin and Sacramento from the hills back
of Antioch, they still flattered themselves that they
were correcting errors of Crespí and Fages, and they
still labored to prove that the broad rivers were not
rivers, but 'fresh water ports' extending far to the
north and south, possibly connecting by tulares in the
former direction with Bodega Bay.   In all this, however, Anza was not so positive; but in correcting an
error Crespí never made respecting the Strait of Carquines, Font was singularly enough led into real error
left on record for others to correct.

Like Fages, Anza descended the hills and advanced
some leagues over the plain to the water's edge,[13]
but instead of turning back and entering the hills by
the San Ramon Cañada, as Fages had done, after
some rather ineffectual attempts to follow the miry
river-banks, he kept on over the foot-hills, noting vast
herds of elk, or jackass deer, passed to the left of
what is now Mount Diablo, and crossed the moun-

[13] Font in one place calls the hill the terminus of Fages' exploration, and
says: 'From said hill which may be about a league from the water, Captain
Fages and P. Crespí saw its extent and that it was divided into arms which
formed islands of low land; and as they had previously tasted the water
on the road further back and found it to be fresh, they supposed without
doubt that it must be some great river which divided itself here into three
branches...without noticing whether it had any current or not, which was
not easy for them to do from said hill at such a distance.'   Font counted
seven islands.   Anza, *Diario*, MS., 168, says of the body of water 'nos pareció
ser mas una gran laguna que rio,' and 172, 'Me hizo esta noticia (the statement of two soldiers that the tulares were impassable even in the dry season)
y lo que yo observaba acabarme de conceptuar que lo que se ha tenido por rio
es puramente una gran laguna.'   San Ricardo was the name given to the
ranchería in the Antioch region.

tains by a difficult route not easy to locate, on which
he named the Cañada de San Vicente and the Sierra
del Chasco, finding also indications of silver ore.
April 6th the party encamped on Arroyo del Coyote,[14] and on the 8th arrived at Monterey. As before
related, Anza started south on the 14th, and his final
exhortation to Rivera on the importance of prompt
action in the San Francisco matter was accompanied
by a diary and map of the exploration just described.[15]

With the arrival of the colony at Monterey from
the south, there had come instructions from Rivera
to build houses for the people, since there would be
at least a year's delay before the presidio could be
founded.[16] And such were the orders in force, notwithstanding Anza's protest, when that officer turned
over the command to Moraga,[17] and left the country.
But Rivera, coming to his senses perhaps after a little
reflection, or fearing the results of Anza's reports in
Mexico, or really taking some interest in the new
foundation now that the object of his jealousy had
departed, changed his policy, and the day after his
arrival in San Diego, on May 8th, despatched an order
to Moraga to proceed and establish the fort on the
site selected by Anza. He could not, however, neglect the opportunity to annoy the priests by saying
that the founding of the missions was for the present
suspended, as Moraga was instructed to inform the
president. Truly the latter had not gained much in
the change from Fages to his rival. At the same
time Rivera sent an order to Grijalva at San Gabriel
to rejoin the rest of the colony at Monterey with the

[14] No. 104 of the map.
[15] The route of Anza's trip is shown, but of course in a general way, on
Font's map. See chapter xii. The natives had been as usual friendly in every
ranchería visited.
[16] *Palou, Not.,* ii. 283. From the viceroy Rivera had permission dated
Jan. 20th, to delay the exploration only until Anza's arrival. *Prov. St. Pap.,*
MS., i. 193–4. But of course the viceroy knew nothing yet of the San Diego
affair.
[17] Feb. 4th, Rivera orders Moraga to take command of the expedition
after Anza's departure. *Prov. St. Pap.,* MS., xxii. 19.

twelve soldiers and their families. Anza's departure had, it seems, greatly lessened the danger at San Diego.

Góngora brought the order to San Gabriel, and Grijalva, setting out at once with his company, carried it to Moraga at Monterey. It was resolved to start north in the middle of June, and though the mission must wait, Serra thought it best that Palou and Cambon, the friars destined for San Francisco, should accompany the soldiers to attend to their spiritual interests and be ready on the spot for further orders. Meanwhile the transport vessels arrived on their yearly voyage, having sailed from San Blas together on the 9th of March. The *San Antonio*, Captain Diego Choquet, with Francisco Castro and Juan B. Aguirre, as master and mate, and Friar Benito Sierra as chaplain, arrived May 21st, unloading supplies for Monterey and waiting for some pine lumber for San Diego. The *San Cárlos*, a slower vessel, arrived the 3d of June,[18] under Captain Quirós, Cañizares and Revilla as master and mate, with Santa María and Nocedal as chaplains. She brought supplies for Monterey and also for San Francisco, and many articles were put on board to go up by water and save mule transportation; but as two cannons were to be taken from the presidio an order from Rivera was necessary, and the vessel was obliged to wait until this order could be obtained.

On June 17th Moraga with his company of soldiers, settlers, families, and servants[19] set out in company with the two friars by the old route, moving very slowly, halting for a day on San Francisco

[18] June 5th, Moraga to Rivera, announcing arrival of the transports. *Prov. St. Pap.*, MS., i. 232–3.

[19] About the number of soldiers there is much confusion. Rivera's orders, *Palou, Not.*, ii. 300, had been to take 20 of them, but the same author says, page 307, that Moraga had 13; and elsewhere, *Vida*, 205–7, that there were 17. He still claims that 12 of Anza's force were at San Diego, but there is no doubt that all the 29 were at Monterey and that about 20 of them started. There were 7 settlers with their families, 5 vaqueros and muleteers, 2 Lower Californians, 1 San Cárlos neophyte, a mule train, and 200 head of cattle.

Arroyo, noting the abundance of deer and antelope, and finally encamping, June 27th, on the Laguna de los Dolores in sight of the Ensenada de los Llorones and of the south-eastern branch of the bay. An altar was set up and mass was said on the 29th, as on every succeeding day. Here Moraga awaited the coming of the *San Cárlos*, because the exact location of the presidio site was to depend to some extent on her survey for anchorage. A month was passed in explorations of the peninsula, in cutting timber, and in other preparations of which no detailed record was kept, and still no vessel came. The lieutenant finally determined to go over to the site selected by Anza, and make a beginning by erecting barracks of tules and other light material. Thus far all had lived in the field tents, and the camp was transferred on the 26th of July. The first building completed was intended for a temporary chapel, and in it the first mass was said on July 28th by Palou.[20] The priests, however, did not change their quarters. They as well as Anza thought the first camp in a locality better fitted for a mission than any other part of the peninsula; and though by Rivera's orders the mission was not yet to be founded, the spot was so near the presidio, and the natives were so friendly, that it was deemed safe and best for the two friars to remain with the cattle and other mission property, guarded by six soldiers and a settler, who might without disobedience of superior orders make preparations for their future dwellings. Things continued in this state for nearly another month.

To their great relief on the 18th of August the *San Cárlos* arrived and anchored near the new camp. After leaving Monterey she had experienced contrary winds and had been driven first down to the latitude of San Diego, then up to 42,° anchoring on the night of the 17th outside the heads and north of

---

[20] The camp was pitched July 26th, and building begun July 27th. Letter of Sal to Governor in 1792. *Prov. St. Pap.*, MS., xi. 52, 54.

the entrance. Quirós and the rest having approved the choice of sites, work was immediately begun on permanent buildings for the presidio, all located within a square of ninety-two yards, according to a plan made by Cañizares. Quirós sent ashore his two carpenters and a squad of sailors to work on the storehouse, commandant's dwelling, and chapel, while the soldiers erected houses for themselves and families. All the buildings were of palisade walls, and roofed with earth. They were all ready by the middle of September, and the 17th was named as the day of ceremonial founding, being the day of the 'Sores of our seraphic father Saint Francis.'[21] Over a hundred and fifty persons witnessed the solemn ceremony. The *San Cárlos* landed all her force save enough to man the swivel-guns. Four friars assisted at mass, for Peña had come up from Monterey, and the prescribed rites of taking possession, and the *te deum laudamus*, were accompanied and followed by ringing of bells and discharge of fire-arms, including the swivel-guns of the transport. The cannon so terrified the natives that not one made his appearance for some days.[22] Thus was the presidio of San Francisco founded, and after the ceremonies its commandant, Moraga, entertained the company with all the splendor circumstances would allow.[23]

While the presidio supplies were being transferred to the warehouse, a new exploration of the head of the bay and of the great rivers was made by Quirós, Cañizares, and Cambon in the ship's boat, and by

[21] 'On that same 17th of September on the other side of the continent Lord Howe's Hessian and British troops were revelling in the city of New York.' Elliot, in *Overland Monthly*, iv. 336–7.
[22] So says Palou, and it reads well. It must be added, however, that according to the same author all had left the peninsula a month before.
[23] In connection with the founding of the presidio it may be noted that Moraga in his preliminary search found one or two fine springs which Anza had not mentioned. Gen. Vallejo, in his *Discurso Histórico*, pronounced at the centennial celebration of the founding of the mission, notes that some remarkable qualities were popularly attributed to the spring called El Polin. Women drinking the water were, it seems, made more than usually prolific, giving birth to twins in many instances. Several other Californians mention this old popular belief.

Moraga with a party of soldiers by land. The two expeditions were to meet beyond the 'round bay,' or at the mouth of the river, on a certain day, apparently September 26th, whence by water and land they were to go up the river as far as possible. They started on the 23d, the land party carrying most of the supplies, while the boat took only enough for eight days. On the 29th Quirós returned. He had reached the rendezvous at the appointed time, but not meeting Moraga, he had been obliged after waiting one day to turn back for want of provisions. Although prevented from exploring the great river, he was able to settle another disputed question and prove that the 'round bay' had no connection with Bodega. For sailing in that direction he had discovered a new estuary and followed it to its head, finding no passage to the sea, and beholding a lofty sierra which stretched toward the west and ended, as Quirós thought, at Cape Mendocino. This was, probably, the first voyage of Europeans up the windings of Petaluma Creek.[24] Respecting the region at the mouth of the great rivers he had done no more than verify the accuracy of previous observations by Fages and Anza.

Meanwhile Moraga, on arriving at the south-eastern head of the bay, had changed his plans, and instead of following the shore had conceived the idea that he could save time and distance by crossing the sierra eastward. This he accomplished without difficulty by a route not recorded, but apparently at an unexpected cost of time; for on reaching the river he concluded it would be impossible to reach the mouth at the time

[24] Palou, *Noticias*, states that Quirós sailed two days on the new estero, and he might with unfavorable winds have spent that time on Petaluma Creek; but if he waited a day for Moraga the two days must include the whole return voyage. He had not, however, disproved Font's theory that the bay communicated with Bodega by way of the great 'fresh water port,' or lagoon, now called the Sacramento River. In his *Vida*, 210–14, Palou gives rather vaguely additional details. At the mouth of the great river was a fine harbor, as good as San Diego, named Asuncion (Suisun Bay?). The lofty sierra stretching to Cape Mendocino was called San Francisco. The estuary on the west of Round Bay, up which they sailed one day and night, was named Merced.

agreed on, and resolved to direct his exploration in the other direction. Marching for three days rapidly up the river he reached a point where the plain in all directions *le hizo horizonte*, that is, presented an unbroken horizon as if he were at sea! The natives pointed out a ford, and Moraga travelled for a day in the plain beyond the river, seeing in the far north lines of trees indicating the existence of rivers. But he had no compass, and fearing that he might lose himself on these broad plains he returned by the way he had come, arriving at the presidio the 7th of October.

Let us now return to the other camp at the Laguna de los Dolores, where since the end of July Palou and Cambon, reënforced after a time by Peña appointed to Santa Clara, had been making preparations for a mission. Six soldiers and a settler had built houses for their families, and the establishment lacked only certain dedicatory formalities to be a regular mission. True, there were no converts, even candidates, but the natives would doubtless come forward in due time. Their temporary absence from the peninsula dated from the 12th of August, before which time they had been friendly though apparently unable for want of an interpreter to comprehend the aims of the missionaries. On the date specified the southern rancherías of San Mateo came up and defeated them in a great fight, burning their huts and so filling them with terror that they fled in their tule rafts to the islands and *contra costa*, notwithstanding the offers of the soldiers to protect them. For several months nothing was seen of them, except that a small party ventured occasionally to the lagoon to kill ducks, accepting also at such visits gifts of beads and food from the Spaniards. Two children of presidio soldiers were baptized before the founding of the mission.[25] As soon as Quirós arrived he had

[25] *San Francisco, Lib. de Mision*, MS., 3. These are the first entries in the mission books; the first on August 10th was the baptism of Francisco José de los Dolores Soto, infant son of Ignacio Soto; the second that of Juana Maria Lorenza Sanchez 15 days of age, on Aug. 25th. Both were baptized *ad instantem mortem* without ceremony, the latter by a common soldier.

given his attention to the mission as well as the presidio, and immediately set six sailors at work to aid the priests in constructing a church and dwelling, so that the work advanced rapidly.

No orders came from Rivera authorizing the establishing of a mission, but Moraga saw no reason for delay and took upon himself the responsibility. A church fifty-four feet long and a house of thirty by fifteen feet, all of wood, plastered with clay, and roofed with tules, were finished and the day of Saint Francis, October 4th, was the time set for the rites of foundation. On the 3d the church, decorated with bunting from the vessel, was blessed; but next day only a mass was said, the ceremony being postponed on account of the absence of Moraga. He arrived, as we have seen, on the 7th, and on October 9th the *solemne funcion* was celebrated in presence of all who had assisted at the presidio a month before, save only the few soldiers left in charge of the fort. Palou said mass, aided by Cambon, Nocedal, and Peña; the image of Saint Francis, patron of port, presidio, and mission, was carried about in procession. Volleys of musketry rent the air, aided by swivel-guns and rockets brought from the *San Cárlos*, and finally two cattle were killed to feast the guests before they departed. Thus was formally established the sixth of the California missions, dedicated to San Francisco de Asis on the Laguna de los Dolores.[26]

[26] The patron of this mission, it is needless to say, was the founder of the Franciscan order of friars. He was born in the city of Assisi, Italy, in 1182, in a stable, and on the shoulder was a birth-mark resembling a cross. With a slight education and somewhat dissolute habits he was employed in trade by his father until 25 years of age. Taken prisoner in a petty local war, his captivity caused or was followed by an illness during which his future vocation was revealed to him in dreams. Useless thereafter for business and regarded as insane by his father, he renounced his patrimony, vowed to live on alms alone, and retired to the convent of Porciúncula near Assisi, where he laid the foundations of his great order. This organization was approved by the pope in 1209, and at the first chapter, or assembly, in 1219 had over 5,000 members in its different classes. The founder gave up the generalship as an example of humility, and went to Egypt in 1219 in search of martyrdom; but the Sultan, admiring his courage, would not allow him to be killed. Among the many miracles wrought by or through him, the most famous is that of the *stigmata*, or *llagas de Jesus*, the wounds of the nails and spear inflicted on the

The annals of San Francisco for the first months, or even years, of its existence are meagre. The record is indeed complete enough, but there was really very little to be recorded. On October 21st

body of Christ imprinted by an angel on Saint Francis as he slept. Though in feeble health he continued preaching until his death on Oct. 4, 1226. He was canonized in 1228, and his festival is celebrated on the day of his death, October 4th.

As to the exact date of the foundation there is a degree of uncertainty, it lying between the 8th and the 9th. True, Palou, *Not.*, ii. 320, in a statement which from its connection with the date of Moraga's return (p. 318) cannot be a slip of the pen or typographical error, is the only authority for the former date, while Palou himself, *Vida*, 214, and all other authorities (excepting of course a few very recent writers who follow the *Noticias*), including the annual and biennial reports of missionaries so far as they have been preserved, agree on Oct. 9th. Yet this evidence is not so overwhelming in favor of the latter date as it seems, since all printed works have doubtless followed Palou's *Vida*, and it is not certain that the regular reports alluded to did not follow the same authority. I have seen no report preceding 1787, the date when Palou's work was published, which gives the date at all. Ordinarily the writers of official reports obtained such dates from the mission books, on the title-pages of which the date of founding is in every other mission correctly given; but strangely enough in this instance *San Francisco, Lib. de Mision*, MS., 2, the date is given in Palou's own handwriting as August 1st, which is not only incorrect but wholly unintelligible. Lacking this source of information I suppose the friars may have used Palou's work, which was in most if not all the mission libraries. To name the writers who have given one date or the other would not aid in settling the question, and it must be left in doubt. Since it is only conjecture that the source of information for official reports was Palou's printed book, the balance of evidence is of course in favor of Oct. 9th. Vallejo, in his *Discurso Histórico*, MS., states that the founding was on Oct. 4th, but in a note appended to the translation of his discourse, *San Francisco, Centennial Mem.*, 105-6, as in conversation, he explains his meaning to be that as Oct. 4th was the day appointed for the ceremony, as it was the day of San Francisco, and as it was the day annually celebrated by the Californians, it ought still to be the day celebrated as an anniversary. Whatever may be said of the theory, it has no bearing on the actual date as an historical fact. Vallejo's suggestion that both Oct. 8th and Oct. 9th in Palou may be typographical errors is scarcely sound.

Respecting the locality of the mission there was a theory long current that it was first founded on Washerwoman's Bay, the lagoon back of Russian Hill, and subsequently moved to its present site. *Soule's Annals of S. F.*, 46-7; *Tuthill's Hist. Cal.*, 85-6; and many other modern writings in books, magazines, and newspapers. This supposition was unfounded, except in the statements of Palou, *Vida*, 209-10, the only authority extant until quite recently, that Moraga's expedition encamped June 27th 'on the bank of a great lagoon which emptied into the arm of the sea of the port which extends inland 15 leagues toward the south-east,' and that a mission site was selected 'in this same place at the lagoon on the plain which it has on the west.' To John W. Dwinelle, *Colon. Hist. S. F.*, p. xiii., belongs, I believe, the credit of having been the first to show the inaccuracy of the prevalent opinion as early as 1867, and without the aid of Palou's *Noticias* which he had never seen. By the aid of the *Vida*, of La Pérouse's map (which I reproduce in chap. xxii.) and the testimony of Doña Cármen Cibrian de Bernal, an old lady at the mission, he identified the Laguna de los Dolores with 'The Willows,' a lagoon, filled up in modern times, which lay in the tract bounded by 17th, 19th, Howard, and Valencia streets, discharging its waters into Mission

the *San Cárlos* sailed for San Blas, leaving four sailors as laborers at the new mission, who completed
the buildings and brought water in a ditch from the
stream. Meanwhile Rivera, having received at San

Bay. Gov. Neve in his report to the viceroy of Feb. 25, 1777, in *Prov. Rec.*,
MS., i. 141, says the mission was 1¼ leagues from the fort and near Lake
Dolores. Vallejo, in his *Discurso Histórico*, advanced the theory that Laguna
de los Dolores was a small lake situated between two hills to the right of the
old road from the presidio to the mission. In the translation and accompanying notes, *San Francisco, Centennial Mem.*, 25, 107, the lake is located, osten-
sibly on Vallejo's authority, 'in Sans Souci Valley, north of the Mission...
and immediately behind the hill on which the Protestant Orphan Asylum
now stands.' Dwinelle in his oration delivered on the same day and printed
in the same book (p. 86) declared in favor of 'The Willows' and maintains his
position in a supplementary argument (pp. 187–91). There can be no doubt, I
think, that the Laguna de Dolores of Palou was identical with the pond of
the Willows, formerly the head of an estuary, according to the testimony of
Sra Bernal and other old residents, though fed by springs, and not with the
pond to which Vallejo alludes. The statement of Palou that the mission was
on the plain westward of the laguna, together with La Pérouse's map which
gives the same relative position, seems conclusive. But while Dwinelle's
argument against Vallejo is conclusive, it contains some curious errors.
Palou, *Not.*, ii. 309, says the Spaniards encamped on June 27th 'á la orilla
de una laguna que llamó el Señor Anza de Nuestra Señora de los Dolores que
está á la vista de la ensenada de los Llorones y playa del estero ó brazo de
mar que corre al Sudeste,' that is, 'on the bank of the lake which Anza
named Dolores, which is in sight of the Ensenada de los Llorones and of the
beach of the estuary, or arm of the sea, which runs to the south-east.' Now
the 'Ensenada de los Llorones,' as we have seen, was Mission Bay, the name
having been given by Aguirre in 1775 (see p. 247 of chap. xi.) from three
'weeping Indians' standing on the shore. Dwinelle, however, translated
Llorones as 'weeping willows,' which but for the circumstance alluded to
would be correct; and having the willows on his hands, must have fresh
water for their roots, which he obtains by translating *ensenada* as 'creek,' and
thus identifying Ensenada de los Llorones with a stream of fresh water flowing from a ravine north-west of the mission and into the bay at what was
in later years City Gardens, a stream which supplied the mission with water
for all purposes, being 'in sight of' the mission, and moreover lined in Dwinelle's own time with willows. Then having fitted the name of one of the
objects seen from the mission site to the fresh-water stream, it remained to
identify the other, the 'playa del estero ó brazo de mar que corre al
Sudeste' with Mission Bay, which he does by a peculiar system of (unwrit-
ten) punctuation and by changing *de* to *del*, making it read 'shore of the inlet, or arm, of that sea which trends to the south-east'! The meaning of the
original was 'in sight of Mission Bay and of the south-eastern branch of San
Francisco Bay.' Dwinelle's reasoning is a very ingenious escape from difficulties that never existed.

After all I have an idea that Palou made the first blunder in this matter
himself. It will be remembered that Anza applied the name Dolores to an
ojo de agua, a spring or stream, which he thought capable of irrigating the
mission lands, making no mention of any *laguna*. I suppose that this was
the fresh-water stream alluded to by Dwinelle which did, as Anza had
thought it might, supply the mission with water. Later when Palou came
up, for some unexplained cause he transferred the name of Dolores to the pond
at the Willows, too low to be used for irrigation and probably at that time
connected with tide-water.

Respecting the name of this mission it should be clearly understood that

Diego communications from the viceroy in which that official spoke of the new missions in the north as having been already founded, concluded that it was time to proceed north and attend to their founding. On the way at San Luis Obispo he learned that his orders had been disobeyed at San Francisco, and said he was glad of it and would soon go in person to found the other mission. From Monterey accompanied by Peña, who had in the mean while returned, he went up to San Francisco, arriving November 26th and cordially approving the choice of sites and all that had been done. Three days later he set out with Moraga to make a new exploration of the great river and plain, leaving Peña at the mission, and promising on arrival at Monterey to send up soldiers for the founding of Santa Clara. Rivera's expedition accomplished nothing, for after fording the river he did not go so far as Moraga had done, fearing that a rise in the stream might prevent his return. On his way back he was met by a courier with news of trouble at San Luis, which claimed his attention, whereupon Moraga returned to his presidio, and Peña was obliged to wait.

In December the self-exiled natives began to come back to the peninsula; but they came in hostile attitude and by no means disposed to be converted. They began to steal all that came within reach. One party discharged arrows at the corporal of the guard; another insulted a soldier's wife; and there was an attempt to shoot the San Cárlos neophyte who was still living here. One of those concerned in this

it was simply San Francisco de Asis and never properly anything else. Asis was dropped in common usage even by the friars, as was Borromeo at San Cárlos and Alcalá at San Diego. Then Dolores was added, not as part of the name but simply as the locality, like Carmelo at San Cárlos, and, more rarely, Nipaguay at San Diego. Gradually, as San Francisco was also the name of the presidio, and there was another mission of San Francisco Solano, it became customary among settlers, soldiers, and to some extent friars also, speak of the *Mision de los Dolores*, meaning simply 'the mission at Dolores.' No other name than San Francisco was employed in official reports. Dolores was in full Nuestra Señora de los Dolores, one of the virgin's most common appellations, and a very common name for places in all Spanish countries.

attempt was shut up and flogged by Grijalva, whereupon the savages rushed up and discharged a volley
of arrows at the mission buildings, attempting a
rescue, though they were frightened away by a discharge of musketry in the air. Next day the sergeant
went out to make arrests, when a new fight occurred,
in which a settler and a horse were wounded, while
of the natives one was killed, another wounded, and
all begged for peace, which was granted after sundry
floggings had been administered. It was some three
months before the savages showed themselves again
at the mission.

Events of 1777 may be very briefly disposed of,
and as well here as elsewhere. The natives resumed
their visits in March, gradually lost their fears, and
on June 24th three adults were baptized, the whole
number of converts at the end of the year being
thirty-one.[27] Some slight improvements were made
in buildings at both establishments; but of agricultural progress we have no record. José Ramon Bojorges was the corporal in command of the mission
guard. In April San Francisco was honored by a
visit from the governor of the Californias, who had
come to live at Monterey, and wished to make a personal inspection of the famous port.[28] May 12th the
Santiago, under Ignacio Arteaga, with Francisco Castro
as master, and Nocedal as chaplain, entered the harbor
with supplies for the northern establishments and San
Blas news down to the 1st of March. This was the
first voyage to the port of San Francisco direct without touching at intermediate stations. Arteaga set
sail for Monterey on the 27th. In October the good

[27] San Francisco, Lib. de Mision, MS. The first convert was named Francisco Moraga, the commandant of the presidio standing as godfather. The
first burial of a neophyte was on October 20th. There had already been eight
deaths of Spaniards, but there were no more for two years. The first marriage
was that of Mariano A. Cordero, a soldier, and Juana F. Pinto on November
28, 1776; the first burial that of María de la Luz Muñoz, wife of J. M. Valencia, a soldier.

[28] His report to the viceroy dated February 25, 1777, is in Prov. Rec., MS.,
i. 140-2.

padre presidente on his first visit to San Francisco arrived in time to say mass in the mission church on the day of Saint Francis in the presence of all the 'old residents' and of seventeen adult native converts. Passing over to the presidio October 10th, and gazing for the first time on the blue waters under the purple pillars of the Golden Gate, Father Junípero exclaimed: "Thanks be to God that now our father St Francis with the holy cross of the procession of missions has reached the last limit of the Californian continent. To go farther he must have boats."[29]

[29] Comprehensive references on the general subject of this chapter are *Palou, Not.*, ii. 285–347; *Id.*, *Vida*, 201–24. A few additional notes on minor topics of San Francisco history are as follows: February 25, 1777, the governor reports that Moraga has been ordered to enclose the presidio, and has begun the work. The commandant's house and the warehouse are of adobe, though very unsubstantial; all the other structures are mere huts. *Prov. Rec.*, MS., i. 142. On June 4th the governor notes the arrival of a picture of St Francis for the presidio chapel, *Id.*, 69, which it seems was sent at Moraga's request. *Arch. Santa Bárbara*, MS., vi. 139. The value of effects received in the warehouse in 1776 was $14,627. *St. Pap. Sac.*, MS., vi. 60. The expense of building the presidio down to 1782 had been in goods as per Mexican invoice $1,200. *Id.*, iii. 230. Eight servants at the mission at end of 1777, names given. *Id.*, *Ben.*, i. 11. The force of the San Francisco district, including San José, at the end of 1777, was as follows: Lieutenant Moraga; Sergeant Juan Pablo Grijalva; corporals Domingo Alviso, Valerio Mesa, Pablo Pinto, Gabriel Peralta, and Ramon Bojorges; 33 soldiers, including mission guards at San Francisco and Santa Clara; settlers Manuel Gonzalez, Nicolás Berreyesa, Casimiro Varela, Pedro Perez, Manuel Amézquita, Tiburcio Vasquez, Francisco Alviso, Ignacio Archuleta, and Feliciano Alballo; *sirvientes* of the presidio, including mechanics, etc., Salvador Espinosa, Juan Espinosa, Pedro Lopez, Pedro Fontes, Juan Sanchez, Melchor Cárdenas, Tomás de la Cruz, Miguel Velez, Felipe Otondo; *sirvientes* of the mission, Diego Olvera, Alejo Feliciano, Victoriano Flores, Joaquin Molina, Angel Segundo, José Rodriguez, José Castro, José Gios; *sirvientes* of Santa Clara, 9 (see chapter xiv.); padres, Francisco Palou, Pedro Benito Cambon, José Antonio Murguía, and Tomás de la Peña; store-keeper, Hermenegildo Sal. Total 80 men. Moraga's report in MS. *Moraga, Informe de 1777*, MS.

CHAPTER XIV.

MISSION PROGRESS AND PUEBLO BEGINNINGS.

1776–1777.

INDIAN AFFRIGHT AT MONTEREY—FIRE AT SAN LUIS OBISPO—AFFAIRS AT
SAN DIEGO—RIVERA AND SERRA—REËSTABLISHMENT OF THE MISSION—
THE LOST REGISTERS—FOUNDING OF SAN JUAN CAPISTRANO—FATHER
SERRA ATTACKED—FOUNDING OF SANTA CLARA—CHANGE OF CAPITAL
OF THE CALIFORNIAS—GOVERNOR NEVE COMES TO MONTEREY—RIVERA
AS LIEUTENANT-GOVERNOR AT LORETO—PROVINCIAS INTERNAS—GOV-
ERNOR'S REPORTS—PRECAUTIONS AGAINST CAPTAIN COOK—MOVEMENTS
OF VESSELS—NEVE'S PLANS FOR CHANNEL ESTABLISHMENTS—PLANS FOR
GRAIN SUPPLY—EXPERIMENTAL PUEBLO—FOUNDING OF SAN JOSÉ—IND-
IAN TROUBLES IN THE SOUTH—A SOLDIER KILLED—FOUR CHIEFTAINS
SHOT—THE FIRST PUBLIC EXECUTION IN CALIFORNIA.

ALL that is known of Monterey affairs during the
year 1776 has been told in connection with the founding of San Francisco, except a rumor of impending
attack by gentiles on San Cárlos in the spring, which
filled Father Junípero's heart with joy at the thought
of possible martyrdom—a joy which, nevertheless, the
good friar restrained sufficiently to summon troops
from Monterey; but the rumor proved unfounded.[1]

Of San Antonio nothing is recorded save that the
mission was quietly prosperous under the ministrations
of Pieras and Sitjar. At San Luis Obispo there was
a fire on November 29th which destroyed the buildings, except the church and granary, together with
implements and some other property. The fire was
the work of gentiles who discharged burning arrows
at the tule roofs, not so much to injure the Spaniards

---

[1] *Palou, Vida,* 318–20. Anza in his report, *Diario,* MS., 135, represented
San Cárlos as in a very prosperous condition, with over 300 neophytes.

as to revenge themselves on a hostile tribe who were the Spaniards' friends. Rivera hastened to the spot, captured two of the ringleaders, and sent them to the presidio.[2] Cavaller and Figuer were in charge, assisted much of the time by Murguía and Mugártegui; while at San Gabriel, of which mission something has been said in connection with Anza's expedition, Paterna, Cruzado, and Sanchez were serving.

In the extreme south as in the extreme north the year was not uneventful, since it saw the mission of San Diego rebuilt and that of San Juan Capistrano successfully founded. Rivera returned to San Diego in May, to resume his investigations in connection with the disaster of the year before; but he seems to have had no thought of immediate steps toward rebuilding the destroyed mission. His policy involved long investigations, military campaigns, and severe penalties, to be followed naturally in the distant future by a resumption of missionary work. Such, however, was by no means the policy of Serra or of the missionaries generally. Throughout the northwest both Jesuits and Franciscans had from the first, on the occurrence of hostile acts by the natives, favored prompt and decisive action, with a view to inspire terror of Spanish power; but long-continued retaliatory measures they never approved. Condemnation and imprisonment were sometimes useful, but mainly as a means of increasing missionary influence through pardon and release. This policy, though sometimes carried too far for safety, was a wise one,

[2] *Palou, Not.*, ii. 339-40. Neve's Report of Sept. 19, 1777, in *Prov. Rec.*, MS., i. 19. The mission register of marriages was destroyed. Note of Serra in *S. Luis Obispo, Lib. de Mision*, MS., 57. The mission was twice again on fire within ten years, which caused the use of tiles for roofs to be universally adopted. *Palou, Vida*, 142-3. Alvarado, *Hist. Cal.*, MS., i. 83, says that Ignacio Vallejo, the author's grandfather, was at the intercession of the padres allowed to quit the service temporarily to superintend the rebuilding of the mission and the construction of irrigation works; and in fact Vallejo's name appears as witness in a marriage which took place the day after the fire, as 'carpenter and employé of the mission.' *San Luis Obispo, Lib. de Mision*, MS., 57.

and indeed the only one by which the friars could have achieved their purpose.[3]

The viceroy on hearing of the massacre at San Diego had given orders for protective measures, including a reënforcement of twenty-five men; but a little later he expressed his opinion, agreeing with that of the missionaries, that it would be better to conciliate than to punish the offending gentiles, and that the reënforcement ordered should be employed rather to protect the old and new establishments than to chastise the foe.[4]   Bucareli's communications, though dated in the spring of 1776, seem to have been delayed; at any rate Rivera was doing nothing towards reëstablishment, and the southern friars were becoming discouraged.   Serra therefore determined to go down in person.   As we have seen, he had wished to accompany Rivera, but that officer had pleaded necessity for a more rapid march than was suited to his advanced age and feeble health.   Now he sailed on the *San Antonio* which left Monterey the last day of June, and arrived at San Diego the 11th of July.   Father Nocedal was left at San Cárlos; Serra took the latter's place as chaplain; and Santa María accompanied the president, who intended to substitute him for some southern missionary whose discontent might not impair his usefulness, for three had already applied for leave to retire.[5]

Serra found the natives peaceable enough; in fact Rivera had reported them to the viceroy as 'pacified;' but though the military force was idle in the presidio, the friars for want of a guard could not resume their

[3] In a communication to Rivera Serra urges a suspension of hostilities, which would do more harm than good, and a light punishment to captives. Let the living padres be protected 'as the apple of God's eye,' but let the dead one be left to enjoy God, and thus good be returned for evil. *St. Pap.*, MS., xv. 14, 15.

[4] Bucareli's letters to Serra of March 26th and April 3d, in *Arch. Santa Bárbara*, MS., vi. 1–3, and Palou, *Vida*, 187–90.   It is stated in the letters that instructions of similar purport were sent to Rivera.

[5] These were probably Fuster, the survivor of San Diego, and Lasuen and Amurrio destined for San Juan.   Their petition to retire was simply a protest against Rivera's inaction, and not improbably had been suggested by Serra himself.

work. The president at once made an arrangement with Captain Choquet of the *San Antonio*, who offered to furnish sailors to work on the mission, and go in person to direct their labors. Then Rivera, asked in writing for a guard, could not refuse, and detailed six men for the service. On August 22d[6] the three friars, Choquet with his mate and boatswain and twenty sailors, a company of neophytes, and the six soldiers went up the river to the old site and began work in earnest, digging foundations, collecting stones, and making adobes. The plan was to erect first an adobe wall for defence and then build a church and other structures within the enclosure. Good progress was made for fifteen days, so that it was expected to complete the wall in two weeks and the buildings before the sailing of the transport, with time enough left to put in a crop. But an Indian went to Rivera with a report that the savages were preparing arrows for a new attack, and though a sergeant sent to investigate reported, as the friars claim, that the report had no foundation[7] the commandant was frightened, and on September 8th withdrew the guard, advising the withdrawal of the sailors. Choquet, though protesting, was obliged to yield to save his own responsibility, and the work had to be abandoned, to the sorrow and indignation of the missionaries.

About this time a native reported that Corporal Carrillo was at Velicatá with soldiers en route for San Diego. Serra was sure they were the soldiers promised him for mission guards, and Rivera equally positive that they were destined to reënforce the presidio; but he refused to send a courier to learn the truth until a letter came from Carrillo on the 25th.

[6] Lasuen in his report of 1783, in *Bandini, Doc. Hist. Cal.*, MS., 2, states that the mission was reëstablished in June 1776. There may, however, be an error of the copyist.

[7] The governor in a later report says that investigations had proved a second convocation of 21 rancherías for hostile operations. *Prov. Rec.*, MS., i. 60–1. It is not certain however that the allusion is to this occasion.

Three days later the viceroy's despatches arrived and proved favorable to Serra's claims, directing the troops, which arrived on the 29th, to be used for the restoration of the missions.   The president celebrated his triumph by a mass and the ringing of bells.   Rivera was obliged to modify his plans, assigning twelve of the twenty-five men to the mission, ten to San Juan, two to San Gabriel, and the remainder to the presidio.   He also released the Indian captives whom he had intended to exile to San Blas.[8]   On the 11th he started north to establish the missions near San Francisco, learning on the way, as we have seen, that one of them had already been founded in spite of his orders to the contrary.[9]

Work was at once resumed at the mission, and the buildings were soon ready for occupation.   Three friars, Fuster, Lasuen, and probably Santa María, moved into their new quarters and under the protection of an increased escort renewed their labors, the date being apparently the 17th of October.[10]   Already the lost mission registers of baptism, marriages, and deaths had been replaced with new ones in which the missing entries were restored, so far as possible, from the memory of priests, neophytes, and soldiers, by Serra himself, who added some valuable notes on the past history of the mission, at various dates from August 14th to October 25th; Fuster also added an interesting narrative of the tragedy of November 5, 1775.   These records, which I have had occasion to

[8] But this release would seem not to have been immediate, for the governor in a letter of Feb. 27, 1777, says that there were still 13 prisoners at San Diego implicated in the revolt. *Prov. Rec.*, MS., i. 143.   In a letter of June 3d he states that on receipt of the viceroy's orders of Feb. 2d, the troops were drawn up, the prisoners called out and harangued on the enormity of their offence meriting death, warned that if they abused the present clemency they must expect the severest penalty, and then they were dismissed with an exhortation by the priests, both soldiers and criminals uniting in a cheer, and a salute from two cannons celebrating this termination of a painful matter. *Id.*, 60–1.   One of the prisoners had strangled himself on Aug. 15th, the anniversary of the day when six years before he had attempted to kill Father Serra in the first attack on the mission. *Palou, Vida,* 87.

[9] *Palou, Not.* ii, 325–37; *Id., Vida,* 191–3, 196–7.

[10] Ortega to Rivera, Dec. 3d, in *Prov. St. Pap.*, MS., i. 151.

use freely in the preceding chapters, are among the
most valuable original authorities on the early history
of California.[11] Palou asserts that progress in the
work of conversion was rapid from the first, whole
rancherías coming in from far away to ask for baptism.
The only additional record for the year at San Diego
is in letters of Ortega to Rivera complaining of some
minor matters of the presidio routine, among others
of want of clothing and tortillas.[12]

In the last days of October, leaving San Diego
affairs in a satisfactory condition, Serra started northward with Gregorio Amurrio, and the escort of ten
soldiers[13] to establish the new mission of San Juan
Capistrano,[14] on the site abandoned the year previous.
The buried bells were dug up to be hung and chimed;
mass was said by the president, and thus the seventh
mission was founded the 1st of November[15] on or near
the site where stood the ruins of a later structure
a century after,[16] near a small bay which offered good
anchorage and protection from all but south winds, and
which long served as the port for mission cargoes. Lasuen, originally assigned to this mission, had remained

[11] *Serra, Notas*, MS.; *Fuster, Registro de Defunciones*, MS.
[12] Ortega to Rivera, in *Prov. St. Pap.*, MS., i. 152-3.
[13] The mission guard under Corporal Nicolás Carabanas included the
soldiers Jacinto Gloria, José Antonio Peña, Francisco Peña, Pio Quinto
Zúñiga, Nicolás Gomez, Matias Vega, José Dolores Dominguez, Julian Acebedo, and José Joaquin Armenta. It is to be noted that many early Californians wrote their names 'Joseph' rather than José.
[14] The patron saint of this mission was born at Capistrano in the kingdom
of Naples in 1385, was educated as a lawyer, became a judge, and in 1415
took the habit of St Francis. He was noted thereafter for his austere life and
his zeal against heretics, occupying high positions in the Inquisition. He also
travelled extensively in Europe on diplomatic business for the pope. He took
part in the crusades, and hated Jews and Turks no less than heretics. He was
prominent in the siege and Christian victory of Belgrade in 1456, and died in
October of that year, to be canonized in 1690. He was the author of many
ecclesiastical works, and his festival is celebrated by the church the 31st of
October.
[15] *S. Juan Capistrano, Lib. de Mision*, MS., title-page; *Ortega*, in *Prov. St.
Pap.*, MS., i. 151.
[16] According to *Los Angeles, Hist.*, 5, the first mission was located some
miles north-easterly from the present location, at the foot of the mountain,
the place being still known as *Mision Vieja;* but this can hardly agree with
Palou's statement, *Vida*, 197-200, that the mission stood half a league from
the bay, on a stream running into it, and in sight of it as at present.

in Jaume's place at San Diego, and Pablo Mugártegui, appointed in his place, soon came down from San Luis. A few days after the founding Serra made a trip to San Gabriel. While returning in company with a pack-train and a drove of cattle he went a little in advance with a soldier and a neophyte, and was met on the Trabuco stream by a horde of painted and armed savages who approached with shouts and hostile gestures, but were induced to desist by a few judicious falsehoods applied by the San Gabriel neophyte, who affirmed that there was a large body of soldiers close behind who would take terrible vengeance for any harm done to the friar.[17] There were no further demonstrations of the kind. The natives near the mission were not averse to christianity, and Amurrio administered baptism December 15th, and Mugártegui again on Christmas, the whole number during the year being four, and during the next year forty. The native name of the mission site was Sajirit.[18]

As soon as Rivera arrived from the south in the autumn of 1776, he gave his attention to the two new missions which the viceroy in his late communications had spoken of as already founded, and which the commandant now realized to have been too long neglected. One of them had indeed been established; Tomás de la Peña and José Murguía had long since been assigned to the other; mission guard, church paraphernalia, and all needed supplies were ready; and Peña had already been over the northern country and

[17] Nov. 12th Corporal Beltran reports the hostile demonstrations against Serra and the soldier Peña, and adds that the natives are at the mission ready to fight. Nov. 15th Ortega reports having sent Mariano Carrillo to investigate. He adds that two soldiers and a servant have deserted from the new mission. Nov. 23d Carrillo reports that all is quiet since the original demonstration; all round the mission were peaceable, and two pagan chiefs had come to ask permission to settle at San Juan. One chief complains that a soldier has taken his wife, but the soldier will be sent to San Diego. *St. Pap. Sac.*, MS., vii. 5–13.

[18] *San Juan Capistrano, Lib. de Mision*, MS. In several of the mission registers the aboriginal name was written *Quanis-Savit*, which was, in all but one, erased and Sajirit substituted.

made up his mind about the most desirable site. Setting out in November to inspect the establishments at San Francisco, and accompanied by Peña, Rivera visited on the way the proposed site near the banks of the Guadalupe River in the broad San Bernardino plain, since known as Santa Clara Valley.[19] Subsequently Friar Tomás was left at San Francisco with the understanding that Rivera on his return to Monterey should send up the men and supplies, with the other priest, and orders to proceed at once to the founding. On account of the alarm at San Luis Obispo already noticed, these orders were delayed, but they came late in December, and on the 6th of January 1777, Moraga with Peña and a company of soldiers[20] started southward.

A cross having been erected and an *enramada* prepared, Father Tomás said the first mass on January 12th, dedicating the new mission to Santa Clara,[21] virgin, on the site called aboriginally Thamien, among the natives known as Tares, who had four rancherías in the vicinity.[22] In respect of agricultural advantages this valley was thought to be hardly inferior to the country of San Gabriel, but it was feared, and with reason as it proved, that the mission site might be liable to occasional inundations.[23] The work of build-

[19] Palou, *Not.*, ii. 341-3, implies that the site was formally selected by Moraga later; but this is not probable; at any rate the site had doubtless been long before fixed upon more or less definitely by the priests.

[20] The soldiers destined for the new mission were the remaining ten of Anza's company who had been all this time at Monterey. Palou, *Vida*, 218-20, implies that these soldiers with their families came up to San Francisco; which may be true, but it seems more likely that they met Moraga at the head of the bay, the latter taking with him a few men from his own presidio.

[21] Santa Clara was the daughter of a rich and noble family of Assisi, Italy, born in 1193, and wholly devoted to the fashionable frivolities of her class, until at the age of 17 she was converted by the preaching of Saint Francis, retired to the convent of Porciúncula, and became as famous for the austerity and piety of her life as she had been for her wit and beauty. She founded an order of *religiosas* named for herself, died in 1253, and was canonized in 1255. Her day is celebrated on the 12th of August.

[22] Peña's Report of Dec. 30th, in *Arch. Santa Bárbara*, MS., ix. 505-9. Tares was the native word for *men*. A newspaper scrap says the place was called *Socoisuka* from the abundance of laurels. The governor on Feb. 25th writes that the mission was located on Jan. 4th. *Prov. Rec.*, MS., i. 141.

[23] In January and February 1779 the mission was twice flooded. Several

ing was at once begun within a square of seventy yards.   Father Murguía arrived with cattle and other mission property on the 21st, and Moraga went back to San Francisco.   The latter however was soon recalled, for the natives, though friendly at first, soon developed a taste for beef, which flogging and even the killing of three of their number did not entirely eradicate.[24]   In May an epidemic carried off many children, most of whom were baptized, and missionary work proper was thus begun.[25]

According to the minister's report at the end of the year there had been sixty-seven baptisms, including eight adults, and twenty-five deaths.   Thirteen Christians and ten catechumens were living at the mission, and the rest at the rancherías with their parents.   In the way of material improvements the new establishment could show a church of six by twenty varas, two dwellings of six by twenty-two and five by thirty-one varas respectively, divided into the necessary apartments, all of timber plastered with clay and roofed with earth.   There were likewise two corrals and a bridge across the stream.[26]

Since March 1775 Felipe de Neve had been ruling at Loreto as governor of the Californias, though his authority over Upper California had been merely nominal, the commandant of the new establishments

houses fell and all had to be moved to higher ground.   Governor's report of April 4th, in *Prov. Rec.*, MS., i. 125–6.

[24] Gov. Neve in a report of Sept. 19, 1777, in *Prov. Rec.*, MS., i. 19–20.

[25] *Santa Clara, Lib. de Mision*, MS.   The first baptism of a child *de razon* on July 31st was that of an illegitimate son of José Antonio Gonzalez and of a woman whose marriage with another man the next year is the first recorded.   The first death was that of José Antonio García in Jan. 1778.   Both Ramon Bojorges and Gabriel Peralta are named as corporals of the mission guard during the first year.   *Prov. St. Pap., Ben. Mil.*, MS., i. 11.

[26] *Murguía and Peña, Informe de Santa Clara*, 1777, MS.   The *sirvientes* of the mission—not all 'servants' as we use the word, but including mechanics, vaqueros, etc.—were Francisco Ibarra, Cristóbal Armenta, Agustin Soberanes, Antonio Romero (1st and 2d), Joaquin Sanchez, Manuel Antonio, Joaquin Puga, Cirilo Gonzalez.   Moraga, in *Prov. St. Pap. Ben.*, MS., i. 9, and Gleeson, *Hist. Cath. Ch.*, ii. 80–2, say the founders reached Santa Clara Jan. 1st.   Shea, *Cath. Miss.*, 100, tells us the mission was founded Jan. 6th.   For account of founding from Palou, see *Hall's Hist. San José*, 416–18; *The Owl*, Jan. 1871.

being directly responsible to the viceroy and subordinate to the governor only in being required to report fully to that official. Soon however a change was ordered, due largely it is believed to the influence of José de Galvez, now in Spain and filling the high position of minister of state for the Indies. The 16th of August 1775 the king issues a royal order that Governor Neve is to reside at Monterey as capital of the province, while Rivera is to go to Loreto and rule Baja California as lieutenant-governor. At the same time, perhaps, Neve's commission as governor is forwarded, for his office down to this time had been merely provisional under appointment of the viceroy requiring the king's approval. A second royal order of April 19, 1776, directed the change to be made immediately.[27] It is difficult to ascertain in the absence of original instructions of king and viceroy exactly what effect the change of residence had on the respective powers of Neve and Rivera, especially those of the latter. But it is evident that while Rivera's authority as lieutenant-governor on the peninsula was less absolute and his subordination to the governor greater than in Upper California as commandant, Neve's authority in the north was practically the same as Rivera's had been; that is, in California the only change in government was in the title of the ruler. The new establishments were recognized by Cárlos III. as more important than the old. In six years the child had outgrown its parent. Monterey was to be capital of the Californias as it had always been of California Setentrional.[28]

[27] The order of Aug. 16th is merely referred to in a list of documents in *Prov. St. Pap.*, MS., xxii. 3, and may possibly be an error. The order of April 19th is referred to in a letter of the viceroy in *Id.*, i. 203. Neve's commission as governor was forwarded to him by the viceroy on Dec. 20, 1775. *Prov. Rec.*, MS., i. 39.

[28] The formation of the Provincias Internas de Occidente under Teodoro de Croix as commandant general with viceregal powers was nearly simultaneous with the change in California; and to this new official Gov. Neve became responsible instead of to the viceroy as Rivera had been. March 8, 1777, Croix writes to Neve that Art. 20 of royal instructions requires the governor and officials of California to render individual reports of acts and events to

For the first time so far as the record shows, Viceroy Bucareli transmitted the king's orders to Neve at Loreto the 20th of July 1776. During this month and the next a correspondence took place between the two officials,[29] which, from its fragmentary nature as preserved, is unsatisfactory, but from which it appears that Bucareli was desirous that Neve should start as soon as possible, that orders to Rivera were enclosed to the governor, that a herd of live-stock was to be taken from the peninsula, and that twenty-five soldiers were sent by the *Concepcion* to Loreto to accompany Neve northward. Though Bucareli had nothing to do with the change in rulers and capitals, he could not fail to be well pleased with the order received from Spain, since it came just in time to relieve him from the undesirable task of deciding several quarrels. Rivera's troubles with the Franciscans and with Anza are fresh in the reader's mind, and Neve's relations with the Dominicans were but little less uncomfortable. Complaints to the viceroy were frequent, and it was an easy reply to say that the impending change would probably remove all reason for dissatisfaction and prevent the necessity for any specific measures.[30] Had Rivera's peculiar conduct been known in Spain it is not likely that he would have been retained in office; but the viceroy hoped that in a new field he might succeed better.

The troops referred to in the viceroy's communications were probably those whose arrival at San Diego in September 1777 has been already noticed, since there

him. *Prov. St. Pap.*, MS., i. 245. Dec. 25, 1776, the viceroy notified Neve of the appointment of Croix, to whom he is to report directly on occurrences in California; but for supplies, etc., he is still to communicate with the viceroy. *Prov. Rec.*, MS., i. 66–7. Neve had written to the viceroy for certain instructions, which were transmitted to Croix. The latter writes to Neve Aug. 15, 1777, that his duties in other provinces will prevent his attention to California, and he has therefore turned the whole matter over to the viceroy for the present. He, however, asks for Neve's suggestions respecting reforms, etc., for a new *reglamento* for California. *Prov. St. Pap.*, MS., i. 252–3.

[29] *Prov. St. Pap.*, MS., i. 203–7.

[30] Bucareli wrote on Dec. 25, 1776, to Serra, announcing the change ordered. *Palou, Vida,* 194–5.

is no record of any soldiers having come up with Neve except an escort of six who returned with Rivera.[31] Indeed, respecting Neve's journey to California nothing is known beyond the facts that it was made by land *via* San Diego; that he made close observations, as shown by his later reports, of the condition and needs of each establishment on the way; and that he arrived at Monterey February 3, 1777.[32] His first act after a review of the troops and a consultation with Serra, was to send to Mexico a report on February 25th that the new presidio and the four new missions, including San Diego, had been successfully founded and were in a condition more or less satisfactory.[33] In March Rivera started for Baja California. Then in April Neve made a tour in the north, visiting San Francisco and Santa Clara. It had been proposed by Rivera to move the presidio of Monterey to the river since called Salinas, chiefly because of the insufficient supply of water at the original site. The viceroy approved the measure;[34] but the royal orders to Neve expressly forbade the removal, declaring that the presidio must be maintained where it was at any cost, for the protection of the port. Still another matter had been intrusted to the patriotic zeal of the new ruler, though one that did not prove a very severe tax on either ability or time. He had an order from the king to be on the watch for Captain Cook's two vessels that had been despatched from England on a voyage of discovery in the South Sea, and by no means to

[31] According to a communication of some official on Feb. 10, 1776, in *Prov. Rec.*, MS., i. 139, the cattle from the old missions amounted to 1,209, and were to be sent up to the frontier, with 80 mules and 36 horses for the 25 San Diego recruits.

[32] Letter of Neve to viceroy, Feb. 26th, in *Prov. Rec.*, MS., i. 139–40, in which he notes the bad condition in which he found the San Diego force in respect of clothing, arms, and horses. March 2d he writes, *Id.*, i. 59, that he has given Rivera full instructions, and the latter will depart to-morrow. Rivera writes Feb. 6th, that Neve has arrived, and that he is about to retire to Loreto. *Prov. St. Pap.*, MS., xxii. 20. See also *Palou, Not.*, ii. 344–5.

[33] *Neve, Informe de 25 de Feb. 1777*, MS., in *Prov. Rec.*, i. 140–2. There are several other minor communications of the governor written about this time.

[34] Letter of Jan. 2, 1775, in *Prov. St. Pap.*, MS., i. 169.

permit that navigator to enter any Californian port.[35]
The transports of 1777 were the *San Antonio* and
the *Santiago*. The former under Francisco Villaroel,
with Serra as chaplain, arrived at San Diego in May
with supplies for the south, and having unloaded sailed
at once for San Blas. The latter, whose arrival at
San Francisco has already been noted, came down to
Monterey and sailed for San Blas the 8th of June.
By her Neve sent a report on the Santa Bárbara
Channel and its tribes, giving his views of what was
necessary to be done in that region to control and
convert a large native population, that might in the
future become troublesome by cutting off land communication between the north and south, which from
the peculiar nature and situation of their country they
could easily do. His plan included a mission of San
Buenaventura at Asuncion at the southern extremity
of the channel, another of Purísima near Point Concepcion at the northern extremity, and a third of
Santa Bárbara with also a presidio in the central
region near Mescaltitlan. The military force required
for the three establishments would be a lieutenant
and sixty-seven soldiers. This report was dated June
3d, and next day the governor wrote asking permission to resign and join his family in Seville whom he
had not seen since 1764, being also in ill-health growing out of seven years' service in administering the
colleges of Zacatecas.[36]

The shipment of grain from San Blas for the military establishments of the Californias was a very
expensive and uncertain method of supply, and officials had been instructed from the first to suggest
some practicable means of home production to be

[35] Royal order, July 14, 1776; sent by viceroy Oct. 23d. *Prov. Rec.*, MS., i.
13; *Prov. St. Pap.*, MS., i. 213. The governor acknowledges receipt of the
order on June 6th. *Prov. Rec.*, MS., i. 76.

[36] There are 22 communications of Neve to Bucareli, written during the
first half of 1777, preserved in *Prov. Rec.*, MS., i. 59–79. His correspondence
for the last six months has for the most part been lost.

introduced as soon as possible. In June 1776, before leaving Loreto, Neve in a communication to the viceroy proposed an experimental sowing for account of government on some fertile lands of the northern frontier, both to supply the usual deficiency on the peninsula, and especially to furnish grain at reduced cost for the new establishments. Bucareli in August approved the proposition in a general way, but stated that in view of the proposed change in the governor's residence it would be impossible for Neve to attend personally to the matter, and suggested that the scheme might be carried out with even better chances of success in the fertile lands of New California, referring also to Anza's favorable report on the Colorado River region as a source of grain supply in case of special need.[37]

Accordingly Neve kept the matter in view during his trip northward, closely examining the different regions traversed to find land suited to his purpose. The result of his observations was that there were two spots eminently fitted for agricultural operations, one being on the Rio de Porciúncula in the south, and the other on the Rio de Guadalupe in the north; and he also made up his mind that the only way to utilize the advantages offered was to found two pueblos on the rivers. To this end he asked for four laborers and some other necessary assistance.[38] Without waiting, however, for a reply to this communication, and possibly having received additional instructions from Mexico, the governor resolved to go on and make a

[37] Neve's letter of June 21st is not extant, but is referred to with a résumé of its contents in the viceroy's letter of August, in *Prov. St. Pap.*, MS., i. 205–6.

[38] Neve's letter is missing as before, but is alluded to in a subsequent letter of April 1778, in *Prov. Rec.*, MS., i. 7–9. In another letter of June 4th, the day after the first, Neve says that he has made no formal distribution of lands to either settlers or soldiers, except to one soldier (Butron?) to whom Rivera in past years had given a title to a lot of land near San Cárlos mission. Also that as there are no suitable lands near the presidio he cannot for the present carry out the sowing order. *Id.*, i. 68. From this it would seem likely that he had received some more direct order from Bucareli to sow near the presidio.

beginning of the northernmost of the two pueblos. He selected for this purpose nine of the presidio soldiers of Monterey and San Francisco, who knew something of farming, and five settlers, who had come to California with Anza,[39] and the fourteen with their families, sixty-six persons in all, started on November 7th from San Francisco under Moraga for their new home.   A site was chosen near the eastern bank of the river, three quarters of a league south-east of Santa Clara, and here the new pueblo, the first in California, was founded on the 29th under the name of San José de Guadalupe, that is San José on the River Guadalupe.   The name was apparently selected by Neve as an honor to the original patron of the California establishments, as named by Galvez in 1768.[40]

The first earth-roofed structures of plastered palisades were erected a little more than a mile north of the centre of the modern city.[41]   The settlers received

[39] Palou, *Not.*, ii. 348–50, says that all were of Anza's company, lying idle at San Francisco.   Neve, letter of April 15, 1778, in *Prov. Rec.*, MS., i. 8, says he took 3 of those who had come as pobladores and 'recruited' 2 more, from what source it does not appear.   We have no list of the San José settlers until the more formal distribution of lands in 1781, when the number was 9 instead of 14.   The names of all the first settlers of 1777 cannot therefore be given; but from Moraga's list of all the pobladores in the San Francisco district in December 1777, in *Prov. St. Pap.*, MS., i. 8, 9, and from an examination of the Santa Clara records, *Santa Clara, Lib. de Mision*, MS., I conclude that 4 of the 5 original pobladores of San José were José Ignacio Archuleta, Manuel Francisco Amézquita, José Manuel Gonzalez, and José Tiburcio Vasquez, while the fifth was not improbably a lady, Gertrudis Peralta.   Of 9 soldier settlers I can give the names of only 4; Valerio Mesa, corporal in command, Seferino Lugo, Juan Manuel Marcos Villela, and José Antonio Romero.   Gabriel Peralta was the corporal in 1779.   Romero was the only soldier who remained, and the 4 pobladores mentioned make up 5 of the 9 names on the list and map of April 1781. See *St. Pap. Miss. and Colon.*, MS., i. 243.   Of the other 4, Claudio Alvires was a servant before 1780, while Bernardo Rosales, Sebastian Alvitre, a soldier in 1769–74, and Francisco Ávila were new names.

[40] See chapter iv. of this volume.   In the heading of one document in the archives I find the pueblo called San José de Galvez.   This name—though perhaps a copyist's error—would have been a most appropriate one.   In later times an effort was made to christen the town San José de Alvarado, in honor of the governor; but it was unsuccessful so far as common usage was concerned.

[41] Near the little stream crossed by the first bridge on the road leading from the city to Alviso.   *Hall's Hist. San José*, 14–19, 46.   This modern work contains a tolerably accurate and complete history of San José.   Documents on the early years are not numerous, and the author seems to have consulted most of them.   There are a few errors in names and translation, but the book

each a tract of land that could be irrigated sufficient for planting about three bushels of maize, with a house-lot, ten dollars a month, and a soldier's rations. Each also received a yoke of oxen, two horses, two cows, a mule, two sheep, and two goats, together with necessary implements and seed, all of which were to be repaid in products of the soil delivered at the royal warehouse. The mission of Santa Clara being near, the ministers consented to attend for the present to the settlers' spiritual interests, and accordingly the names of the latter are frequently found in the mission-book entries. In April of the next year Neve reported to the viceroy what he had done.[42]

The first work in the new pueblo after building houses to shelter the families was to dam the river above, bring down water in a ditch, and prepare the fields for sowing; but the attempt was not successful, and the sowing of over fifty bushels of corn was a total loss, since it was necessary to change the site of the dam, and the new one was not completed and water brought to the fields till July. The second sowing yielded between six and eight hundred bushels. A second dam was built above the first to protect it in time of freshet, and the irrigation system thus completed was planned to supply thirty-six *suertes*, or sowing-lots, of two hundred varas each. As early as 1778 the governor complained that the lands were nearer those of the mission than he had intended, and badly distributed. In 1779 much damage was done by high water both at San José and Santa Clara, among other

is far above the average of what has been given to the California public as history. *Hall's San José*, from the *San José Pioneer*, Jan. 1877, being an address by the author on July 4th, is full of errors, many of which are doubtless due to the newspaper and not the writer.

[42]April 15th, *Prov. Rec.*, MS., i. 7–8. A duplicate was sent to General Croix. *Id.*, 9, 10. See an English translation of this report in *Dwinelle's Colon. Hist. S. F.*, addenda, 8. The viceroy's acknowledgment of this report and approval of Neve's acts was dated July 22, 1778. *St. Pap. Miss. and Colon.*, MS., i. 28–9. He mentions a servant besides the 5 settlers, and makes the whole population 68 instead of 66. He also speaks of a dam not alluded to by Neve. Croix's acknowledgment and approval was dated July 19, 1779, and included that of the king dated March 6th. *Hall's Hist. San José*, 14–19.

things the new dam at the pueblo being washed away. At this early date also the governor notes the influence of the friars as adverse to pueblo progress. Before founding San José he had considered the prospects of obtaining supplies from the missions, and had concluded that for some years, at least, the products of the missions would not increase faster than the mouths of neophytes to be fed. The missionaries well knew that such was the prospect; but on general principles they were opposed to all establishments in the country save their own. The presidios were a necessary evil, and the soldiers must be fed, therefore the government should feed them until the missions could do so. As soon as Serra realized that Neve was in earnest about founding pueblos, he began to be very certain that his missions could have supplied the presidios; "but he forgets," says Neve, "that this would not people the land with Spanish subjects." There is nothing more to be recorded concerning San José for several years, and down to 1781 the establishment may be regarded as to a great extent provisional or experimental.[43]

Certain troubles with the southern savages, during this year and in the spring of the following, remain to be noticed in this chapter. They seem to have begun in June 1777 when the Alocuachomi ranchería threatened the neophytes of San Juan Capistrano, and Corporal Guillermo Carrillo was sent with five men to chastise the offenders, which he did by killing three and wounding several. Sergeant Aguiar was sent by Ortega to investigate, and his report showed the existence of disorders among the soldiers, in their relation to the natives, by no means creditable to Spanish discipline in California. A native chieftain who was in league with the offenders and who furnished women to the guard, was deemed to merit

---

[43] Neve's communications in *Prov. Rec.*, MS., i. 90-2, 125-6, ii. 21-2; *Prov. St. Pap.*, iii. 145.

fifteen lashes and an admonition from the minister;
and two culprit soldiers were taken south to San
Diego. It was, perhaps, in connection with these
disturbances that the Indians of San Gabriel came in
arms to the mission to avenge some outrage; but they
were subdued, as by a miracle, when the friars held
up a shining image of our lady, kneeling, weeping, and
embracing the missionaries.[44] Hardly had the excitement of the disturbances alluded to died out, when
on August 13th four soldiers bearing despatches from
General Croix to Neve were surprised at midnight,
at a place called San Juan just above San Diego, by
a party of savages who killed the corporal in command,
Antonio Briones. The rest escaped with their horses,
after having repulsed the foe in an hour's fight. Sergeant Carrillo was ordered to make a retaliatory campaign, but the result is not recorded beyond the
statement that a chief was arrested. In February
of 1778 Carrillo was obliged to make a new expedition to San Juan Capistrano, where several rancherías,
Amangens, Chacapamas, and Toban Juguas were
assembled and threatening. A chieftain's wife had
eloped with a Lower Californian, and the outraged
husband made his grievance a public one by appealing
to the natives to avenge the death of their comrades
slain the year before; also charging that the Spaniards
were really devils come to destroy the crops by
drought.

In March it was reported that the people of Pamó,
one of the San Diego rancherías, were making arrows
to be used against the Spaniards, counting on the aid
of three neighboring bands and of one across the
sierra, and having already murdered a San Juan
Indian. Ortega sent a message of warning and
Aaaran sent back a challenge to the soldiers to come
and be slain. Carrillo's services were again called
into requisition and he was sent with eight soldiers to

[44] This story is told by Hugo Reid and Benjamin Hayes, and it is also the
subject of a poem by Miss M. A. Fitzgerald. *Hayes' Mission Book*, i. 197.

chastise this insolence, capture the chiefs, and to give thirty or forty lashes each to such warriors as might seem to need them. In carrying out his orders the sergeant surprised the foe at Pamó, killed two of the number, and burned a few who refused to come out of the hut in which they had taken refuge. The rest surrendered and took their flogging, while the four chieftains were bound and carried to San Diego. Captured in this battle were eighty bows, fifteen hundred arrows, and a large number of clubs. The four chiefs, Aachil, Aalcuirin, Aaaran, and Taguagui were tried on April 6th, convicted of having plotted to kill Christians in spite of the mercy shown them in the king's name for past offences, and condemned to death by Ortega, though that officer had no right to inflict the death penalty, even on an Indian, without the governor's approval. The sentence was: "Deeming it useful to the service of God, the king, and the public weal, I sentence them to a violent death by two musket-shots on the 11th at 9 A. M., the troops to be present at the execution under arms, also all the Christian rancherías subject to the San Diego mission, that they may be warned to act righteously." Fathers Lasuen and Figuer were summoned to prepare the condemned for their end. "You will coöperate," writes Ortega to the padres, "for the good of their souls in the understanding that if they do not accept the salutary waters of holy baptism they die on Saturday morning; and if they do—they die all the same!" This was the first public execution in California.[45]

[45] On these Indian troubles see reports of Neve and Ortega in *St. Pap. Sac.*, MS., vii. 61–3, viii. 31–52; *Prov. Rec.*, MS., i. 19, 96–7; *Prov. St. Pap.*, MS., ii. 1–6; *Prov. St. Pap., Ben. Mil.*, MS., i. 41–4.

CHAPTER XV.

A DECADE COMPLETED—PRESIDENT SERRA VERSUS GOVERNOR NEVE.

1778—1780.

A Period of Preparation—Schemes for the Future—Government Reforms—Pueblos—Channel Establishments—Neve Wants to Resign and is made Colonel—Sacrament of Confirmation—Episcopal Powers Conferred on Padre Serra—Tour of the Missions—Quarrel with Neve—Ecclesiastic Prerogative and Secular Authority —A Friar's Sharp Practice—Serious Charges by the Governor— Movements of Vessels—Arrival of Arteaga and Bodega from a Northern Voyage—The First Manila Galleon at Monterey— Local Events and Progress—Presidio Buildings.

THE years 1778 and 1779, completing the first decade in the annals of Alta California as a Spanish province, together with 1780, formed a period rather of preparation than of accomplishment, of theories rather than practice, in matters affecting the general interests of the country; though there was a satisfactory showing of local progress at the several missions. One of the most important general subjects which claimed Governor Neve's attention, was the preparation of a new *reglamento*, or system of military government for the Californias; the new establishments having in a general sense outgrown Echeveste's regulation of 1773, and some articles of that document having in practice proved unsatisfactory. The king's order of March 21, 1775, for the reform of the system was, on August 15, 1777, forwarded by General Croix to Neve with a letter in which he says: "Lacking knowledge on the subject, I need that you report to me at length and in detail what are the faults that impair the usefulness of the old regulation, and what you deem necessary for its reform, so that I may be enabled to decide when consulted about the country." This request came by the *Santiago* in June, and on December 28, 1778, Neve dated the required report.[1] We hear no more of this subject till the appearance of the regulation itself, full fledged, and with all its reforms, accredited to Neve, as author, under date of June 1, 1779.[2]

That the preparation of so extensive and important a state paper, and especially of those portions relating to colonization which was a new and difficult subject, should have been intrusted *in toto* to the governor, seems strange, and equally so the fact that no correspondence on the subject has been preserved; but both Croix and Galvez in signifying the king's approval accredit Neve with the authorship. It was certainly a mark of great confidence in his ability, and a still greater compliment was the adoption of his plan without, so far as appears, a single modification. September 21, 1780, General Croix writes to the governor from Arizpe that the plan has been forwarded by the viceroy to the king, and that provisionally, pending the royal approval, it is to go into effect in California from the beginning of 1781.[3] The subject-matter of the reglamento, and the new system of government resting on it, may be properly deferred until the beginning of the next period, when the changes went into practical effect.

An important and new feature of Neve's plan was that relating to pueblos and colonization, enforced in connection with the redistribution of lands in the hitherto informal pueblo of San José, and the founding of a new pueblo of Los Angeles on the Rio Porciúncula. It is therefore in connection with these

---

[1] *Neve, Informe sobre Reglamento, 28 de Dic. 1778*, MS.
[2] *Neve, Reglamento é Instruccion para los Presidios de la Península de California, Ereccion de Nuevos Misiones y fomento del pueblo y estension de los Establecimientos de Monterey*, MS.
[3] Croix to Neve, Sept. 21, 1780, in *Prov. St. Pap.*, MS., ii. 114.

events, which took place in 1781, that the general
subject may be best considered. Another matter
pending was the occupation by Spain of the rich and
densely populated central region along the Santa Bárbara channel. From observations made during his
first trip northward Neve had sent in a report in June
1777, urging the importance of such occupation and
the dangers of its postponement; also giving his views
as to the best methods of its accomplishment. He
favored the establishing of three missions and of
a central presidio, requiring a force of sixty-two men.
Croix approved his views[4] and they were embodied in
the plan of June. A correspondence respecting details followed during 1779–80. Meanwhile, Rivera
was sent to recruit settlers in Sinaloa and Sonora, as
well for the Channel establishments as for the pueblos
of Los Angeles and San José; but of these special
preparations I shall speak as before stated in the
chapters devoted to results. At first, as we have seen,
Neve was wearied with long service or dissatisfied with
his position, and had asked leave to retire and go to
Spain. On January 14, 1778, the viceroy writes that
the request has been forwarded to the king and will
probably be entertained with favor. At the end of
May Neve sent in his formal resignation, and in
August thanked Bucareli for a favorable report
thereon; but in October he requests the viceroy to
keep back his memorials and petitions respecting resignation. The reason of his change of purpose is
perhaps to be found in another letter of the same
date, in which he thanks the king for promotion to the
rank of colonel in the Spanish army, he having been
only major before.[5]

The right to administer the rite of confirmation belonged exclusively to bishops, and could be exercised
even by the highest officials of the religious orders

[4] Sept. 1778, *Prov. Rec.*, MS., ii. 6, 7.
[5] *Prov. Rec.*, MS., i. 85–96; *Prov. St. Pap.*, MS., ii. 8, 9.

only with special authorization from the pope. It was of course desirable that mission neophytes should not be deprived of any privileges and consolations pertaining to the new faith they had embraced; but in isolated provinces like the Californias, episcopal visits must of necessity be rare, so that most neophytes, to say nothing of *gente de razon*, must live and die unconfirmed but for some special exercise of the papal power. In fact Alta California, though included successively in the bishoprics of Durango and Sonora, never was visited by a bishop until it had one of its own in 1835. When Father Junípero first came to Lower California he found in the Jesuit archives a bull of Pope Benedict XIV. conceding the power of confirmation to missionary officials of the company. Anxious that the neophytes should lose nothing of their privileges under Franciscan management, he soon forwarded the old bull to the guardian of San Fernando, with a request that a similar favor be obtained from the pope in behalf of himself and his flock.[6] The Franciscan authorities exerted themselves in bringing this matter before the pope, and obtained under date of July 16, 1774, a papal decree, approving that rendered by the sacred congregation of propaganda fide on July 8th, which authorized the comisario prefecto of the colleges for a period of ten years to administer confirmation and to delegate his power in this respect to one friar connected with each of the four colleges in America. Both church and crown in Spain were zealous defenders of their respective prerogatives; and as not even a bishop could exercise the functions of his office until his appointment had received the royal approval, of course this special concession of episcopal

---

[6] Palou, *Vida*, 226-8, is careful to explain that Serra was too humble to have sought the episcopal power for the dignity involved; in fact hearing that a great honor was in store for him he had made a vow to accept no honor that would separate him from his mission work, and had directed the influence of his friends in Spain toward the obtaining of the episcopal power in behalf of his neophytes.

powers must be submitted to the king's royal council
of the Indies.   It was so submitted, and received the
sanction of that body December 2, 1774, being also
approved by the audiencia of New Spain September
27th, and by Viceroy Bucareli October 8, 1776.[7]

On October 17, 1777, the commissary and prefect of
the American colleges, Father Juan Domingo de
Arricivita, well known to my readers as the chronicler of his college,[8] issued from Querétaro in ponderous latin the desired 'faculty to confirm' to President
Junípero Serra.   The patent with instructions came
up on the *Santiago* and reached Serra's hands in the
middle of June 1778.   No time was lost in exercising
the newly acquired power, and at different dates from
the 29th of June to the 23d of August, the president
confirmed one hundred and eighty-one persons at San
Cárlos.   Then, notwithstanding his infirmities, he embarked for San Diego, and from the 21st of September
to the 13th of December administered confirmation,
with all its attendant solemnities and ceremonies, to
the neophytes at each of the five missions on his way
back to Monterey, resuming the work in the north at
the beginning of 1779 and extending his tour to Santa
Clara and San Francisco.   Two thousand four hundred and thirty-two persons in all received the rite
in 1778-9, about one hundred of the number being
gente de razon.[9]

But now the president encountered obstacles in his
way.   As we have seen, the apostolic brief conceding

[7] *Facultad de Confirmar*, 1774-7, MS., containing the *Decretum Sacræ
Congregationis Generalis de Propaganda Fide habite die 8 Julij*, etc., with
the other documents referred to and much additional correspondence on the
same subject.

[8] *Arricivita, Crónica Seráfica del Colegio de Santa Cruz de Querétaro.*

[9] Register of confirmations in *San Cárlos, Lib. de Mision*, MS., 56-64, with
an explanation of the authority to confirm and citation of documents recorded
by Serra himself, and in the books of the other missions.   It will be remembered that one neophyte, Juan Evangelista, was carried to Mexico by Serra
in 1773 and received the rite of confirmation from the Archbishop of Mexico
on August 4th.   Serra entered this fact in the book of confirmations at San
Cárlos when such a book was opened in 1778.   In a letter of March 23, 1781,
Facultad de Confirmar, MS., 270, Serra says he had confirmed 2,455 before
the power was suspended, and the mission books make the number 2,457.

the right to confirm had required sanction of the
royal council, a requirement which the Franciscan
authorities understood perfectly, and to which as an
unfortunate necessity they had submitted. Whether
this approval of the secular authorities was certified
in due form in the document forwarded to Serra in
1778, and from which he derived his powers, there
are no means of knowing; but Neve, as representative
of the crown in California, had a right to know whether
the required formalities had been observed, and it was
clearly the duty of Serra to satisfy him on this point
before exercising his new power. Serra, however, had
no idea of humbling his pride of ecclesiastical prerogative before any Californian representative of royalty;
in fact to him secular authority in the province was
something to be used rather than obeyed. Exactly
when or how the inevitable quarrel broke out the
records very strangely do not show; but it would
seem that in the middle of 1779, soon after Serra's
return from his first tour of confirmation in the south,
the governor summoned him to show the authority
under which he was acting.

Whether Serra from pride, or knowledge of their
defective nature, refused to show his papers, or whether,
being shown, they were pronounced insufficient by
Neve, I am not sure; neither is it certain that the
governor ordered an absolute suspension of confirmations;[10] but the indications are that Serra refused to
show his papers, and that Neve to save his responsibility ordered confirmations to cease, and refused to

---

[10] In an opinion on the matter dated April 17, 1780—*Facultad de Confirmar*, MS., 259—it is stated that Serra confirmed in all the missions except
San Francisco and Santa Clara, in which places he did not, because Neve
refused him an escort and required him to suspend confirmation until he could
show the papal bull approved by the Council of the Indies, which Serra could
not do, since he had no document to prove it. The same statement is made in
a communication from Bonilla to Croix on Apr. 20, 1780. *St. Pap. Sac.*, MS.,
viii. 53.   This is however partially erroneous, for Serra did go to Sta Clara
and San Francisco with or without an escort. The guardian simply says, *Id.*,
253, that Neve had raised a doubt whether the apostolic brief has the proper
sanctions. Had Serra's papers been defective he would have known it and
would have hesitated to administer a sacrament which might prove illegal.

authorize a continuance even by supplying the escort demanded, but did not of course attempt to enforce his order, referring the whole matter to General Croix in Sonora. At all events Serra paid no heed to Neve's orders or protests, but went on confirming through the year, even administering the sacrament to twenty-four or twenty-five persons in 1780. In October 1779, however, he reported from San Francisco to the commandant general, and also to the guardian of San Fernando, taking the precaution to forward to the latter all the documents he had bearing on the matter in dispute, having doubtless a shrewd and well founded suspicion that an order might come to deliver the papers to the governor.

Croix on receipt of despatches from California, which had been forwarded by Arteaga's exploring fleet to be noticed later in this chapter, referred the subject in dispute to his *asesor*, or legal adviser, Pedro Galindo Navarro, in accordance with whose counsel he sent April 20, 1780, an order to Neve to take possession of the original patent and instructions which had been sent by the guardian to Serra and must still be in possession of the latter; and, furthermore, under no pretext whatever to permit the president to go on administering the sacrament till new orders should be given. The papers were to be sent at once to Croix, who would communicate with the viceroy respecting the original concession by the pope, and would settle the matter as soon as possible. To Serra Croix communicated the purport of the order to Neve, "charging and entreating" him to obey the order punctually by giving up the papers.[11]

The details of what took place between Neve and Serra on receipt of these orders must be left to the imagination of the reader. The president could not give up the papers because he had taken the precau-

[11] The order to Neve is not extant, but its purport is given in the communication to Serra in *St. Pap. Sac.*, MS., viii. 28; and *Facultad de Confirmar*, MS., 258-60.

tion to get rid of them; and he suspended confirmations, as he flattered himself, at the 'entreaty' of
Croix and not the 'command' of Neve.   The 20th of
July Serra replied to the letter of Croix "about a continuation of administering the sacrament of confirmation which I solicited." He has the day before
received Neve's letter containing the general's order
to suspend confirmation, which of course he will cheerfully obey; though he regrets that the legal adviser has
not given more weight to his argument on the gossip
and wonder that a suspension of the power to confirm
will cause among ignorant people.   In order, however,
to prevent this gossip as far as possible, he will absent
himself on some pretext or other, when he hears that
the vessel is coming, though that will be just the time
when his presence will be most needed.   As to the
papers, he has sent them nine months ago to his college, and as a tribulation sent upon him by an all-wise
God, the vessels are late this year and the documents
have not come; but they will soon be here and will
be delivered to the governor for the purposes indicated, though with a little delay they might be delivered in a more complete and satisfactory state.[12]

[12] *Facultad de Confirmar*, MS., 260–6.   There are two copies of the letter,
both in Serra's handwriting, but differing somewhat in the closing portions.
The variations are not however in substance essential.   It is but fair to the
padre to say that in speaking about the documents his language is not clear,
and might possibly bear a different construction from that I have given in the
text; that is, he may mean to say in substance, 'I have sent copies of my
papers' (though it reads 'remitiendo allá todos mis papeles que hacian al
caso') to Mexico for completion by the addition of missing ones, and by a
little delay I could send them in a completed state; but as it is I give up the
originals as they are to the governor.   Or he might mean that he had sent
the most important papers to Mexico and would give up what were left.   There
is however no evidence outside of this letter that he ever gave up any papers,
but it appears rather that he gave up none.   It is not impossible that his
language was intentionally made vague.   Governor Neve in a subsequent
letter to Croix, March 26, 1781, in *Prov. Rec.*, MS., ii. 81, speaks very plainly
on the subject, saying that Serra claimed to have sent his patent to Mexico,
and he does not deem it wise to take possession of and search his papers, because if he has not sent the document away he will have hid it 'with his
unspeakable artifice and shrewdness;' and the only result will be trouble
with the padres and delay in the Channel foundations, for which they will
refuse to contribute supplies.   Being exasperated there is nothing these friars
'with their immeasurable and incredible pride' will not attempt, since on
more than four occasions it has required all Neve's policy and moderation to

The commandant general, on receipt of Serra's letter, simply repeated on November 29th his previous order that the papers were to be given up at once. This brought out from the venerable friar under date of March 23, 1781, a letter in which he protests that his patent is not in his possession nor indeed in California, but was sent to Croix by way of Mexico, since Neve was absent in Baja California and the date of his return uncertain. He swears *in verbo sacerdotis* and *tacti pectori sacerdotali* that he tells the truth, and wonders greatly that Croix has not received from Mexico all needed papers and proofs to settle the whole matter permanently.[13] For an explanation of this extraordinary reply it is necessary to turn back a little. The guardian, Rafael Verger, on receipt of Serra's first letter of October 1779, had written to Viceroy Mayorga—Bucareli having died in April of the same year—stating the case and instituting proceedings to obtain certified copies of all documents bearing on the subject of confirmation.[14] This was on December 17th; the required certificates were obtained without difficulty, and on February 16, 1780, the guardian sent them in due form to Serra to be shown to Neve, at the same time facilitating a settlement of the matter in dispute by forwarding a copy to General Croix. The president received the papers by the vessel which arrived at Monterey October 6th, and, in the confident expectation of an order from Croix to resume confirmations, felt very independent, so much so that he deemed it safe to disregard the orders both of Croix and of the guardian requiring the delivery of the documents to Neve. Circum-

turn them from surreptitious conspiring against the government. At a more fitting time it will be well to carry out certain measures which he has deemed it best for the present to defer as the only means of bringing 'this president to a proper acknowledgment of the authority which he eludes while pretending to obey.' This is very strong language from a man who was not prone to excitement or exaggeration.

[13] *Facultad de Confirmar*, MS., 269-71. This is the first use, by the way, of the name Baja California that I have noticed.

[14] The guardian says nothing of having received any papers from Serra; but of course this is not very strong evidence that he did not get them.

stances favored his plans, for Neve was at the time
absent from the capital on a visit to the frontier missions of the peninsula. Accordingly, apprehending
the receipt of more positive orders from the general,
and resolved to take no risk of eventual discomfiture,
the venerable friar despatched his patent forthwith to
Croix, *via* Mexico, probably by the very vessel that
had brought it.

Soon the governor returned to Monterey and on
December 30th demanded the documents in order
that he might forward them as ordered to Croix.
Serra did not deign to say whether he had the papers
or not, but coolly replied on the same date by saying
in substance: 'The whole matter has been settled by
higher authorities; the papers proved to be all right;
I have written to General Croix, and he will doubtless be satsified with what I have said. You and I
have only to wait for orders." Neve for reasons
already mentioned did not enforce his demand, and
Serra was happy in the thought that he had snubbed
his enemy. Then, as the president had anticipated,
came the order of Croix dated November 29th, and
written before he had received despatches from Mexico. Serra's reply was an easy one and has been
already given. Meanwhile, Croix on receipt of the
Mexican despatches, sent as a matter of course the
corresponding instructions dated the 23d of December. They were received by Neve at San Gabriel,
whence in a letter dated May 19, 1781, he informed
Serra that as the apostolic brief had been shown to
have the requisite approval of the council, there was
no longer any obstacle to his administering the sacrament.[15]

During the continuance of this quarrel the president took advantage of another opportunity to show
his independence of the government. The governor
had been ordered to send in connection with his an-

[15] All the communications referred to are found in the *Facultad de Confirmar*, MS.

nual reports inventories of the missions; but Serra refused to render any account of the missions, claiming that he was acting according to orders from the guardian, and would send the inventories direct to Mexico.[16]

This episode of California history, now for the first time made public, exhibits the character of Junípero Serra in a new and, considering the previous character of the man, in a startling light. And though from this distance nothing can be seen in the controversy which might affect the interests of Christianity, of the Franciscan order, or of the California missions, we must conclude that Serra was conscientious in his belief that principles of the gravest character were involved or he never would have manifested the firmness and the stubborn pertinacity he did from the beginning to the end of this dispute with the governor. The great battles between the royal prerogative and the *fuero eclesiástico* had been fought in Spain; it certainly could have been no trifling matter that would induce this man of peace to renew them in California. On the other hand Neve claimed what he regarded as a well known right, nothing in the slightest degree humiliating to the president, and so far as can be known he urged his claims in a courteous and respectful manner; and when obedience to his demands was refused nothing but his moderation and cool-minded patriotism prevented a scandal which would have been unfortunate to the country, and perhaps disastrous to the missions. No ardent churchman entertains a more exalted opinion of the virtues of Junípero Serra, his pure-mindedness, his self-sacrificing devotion, his industry and zeal than myself. Nor would I willingly detract from the reputation of a man who has been justly regarded as an ideal missionary, the father of the church in California; but I am writing

[16] Neve to Croix June 4, 1779, in *Prov. Rec.*, MS., i. 127-8. The governor says that the natives are taught that the padres are supreme and the secular officials are to be regarded with indifference.

history, and I must record the facts as I find them and leave my readers to form their own conclusions.[17] The license to confirm for ten years expired with the life of Serra in 1784, before which time he had confirmed 5,309 persons. The privilege was again given at Rome in 1785 and forwarded by the bishop of Sonora in 1790 to President Lasuen, who confirmed within five years about 9,000 persons. The license was never again renewed.

The transport vessels of 1778 were the *San Cárlos*, which arrived at San Diego in May, returning at once to San Blas; and the *Santiago*, under Captain Juan Manuel de Ayala, pilotos Castro and Aguirre, and chaplain Nocedal, which anchored at San Francisco June 17th, one hundred and five days out from San Blas. Besides more material supplies she brought an unusual budget of news. An exploring fleet for the northern coast was fitting out at San Blas; Teodoro de Croix had been appointed commandant general of the Interior Provinces; a change was proposed in mission government, making California a custodia, though this was never carried out; and the right to confirm had been granted to President Serra. The *Santiago* on her return touched at Monterey at the end of July and at San Diego.

The *Santiago* returned to San Francisco in 1779, but we have no further information about her trip than that several of her officers served as godfathers at the baptism of natives on the 6th of July. The officers included Captain Estévan José Martinez, Piloto José Tobar, and Chaplain Nicolás de Ibera.[18]

[17] Palou, *Vida*, 235-6, alludes to the quarrel very briefly, admitting that Neve was not actuated by malice. In his *Noticias* he does not mention the subject at all. Shea, *Cath. Miss.*, 100, says that Serra was for a time prevented by the government from exercising his right. Taylor, *Discov. and Founders*, ii. No. 28, affirms that P. Junípero had a serious fright soon after beginning to confirm on account of a rumor from Mexico that there was something irregular in his papers; but on assurance from all the prominent men accessible that there was nothing wrong he was comforted! Gleeson, *Hist. Cath. Ch.*, ii. 84-6, attributes the hindrance to the Chevalier de Croix who was opposed to the missions, and would not allow Serra to confirm until the viceroy was appealed to and told him to let the padres alone.

[18] *San Francisco, Lib. de Mision*, MS., 10. She came back next year with

Entered San Francisco Bay the *Favorita* September
14th, followed next day by the *Princesa*. They were
exploring vessels commanded by lieutenants Bodega
y Cuadra and Ignacio Arteaga respectively, the latter
being chief in command.[19] They had left San Blas in
February, and had been up the coast to latitude 60°,
and on the return had explored the old bay of San
Francisco under Point Reyes where the *San Augustin*
was cast away, this being the first visit since the time
of Vizcaino. The men were many of them sick with
scurvy and the ships remained for six weeks in port
for their benefit. In Cuadra's possession was an
image in bronze of Nuestra Señora de los Remedios,
copied from the original in Mexico, which he presented
to the mission and which was placed on the altar with
proper ceremonies the 3d of October. Next day the
festival of the patron saint was celebrated, and in
connection with the ceremony three natives brought
from the northern coasts were baptized. Serra could
not come up in time for the festival on account of
etiquetas with Neve; but a little later he was met by
the naval officers at Santa Clara and came to San
Francisco to administer confirmation as we have seen,
insisting on walking all the way and refusing to have
his ulcerated leg treated after arrival. A courier now
arrived overland with tidings of Viceroy Bucareli's
death and of the war with England. This hurried the
vessels away, and after hasty preparations in view of
possible hostilities on the high seas, they sailed October 30th, bearing important despatches from Serra,
and leaving Matias Noriega in place of Father Cambon, who retired on account of ill-health.[20]

the same officers, except that Miguel Dávalos was chaplain, entering Monterey in October and unloading there, to the great inconvenience of San Francisco, whither the cargo had to be carried by land. *Palou, Not.*, ii. 368-9;
Prov. Rec., MS., ii. 32-3.

[19] According to *S. Francisco, Lib de Mision*, MS., 11–12; *Palou, Vida*,
231–3. Lieut. Quirós y Miranda was one of the officers. Cañizares and
Maurelle were also on the vessels.

[20] *San Francisco, Lib. de Mision*, MS., 11; *Bodega y Cuadra, Navegacion*,
etc., 1779, MS.; *Arteaga, Tercera Exploracion, 1779*, MS.; *Maurelle, Nave-*

There is yet another maritime event to be included in the annals of 1779, namely: the arrival of the first Manila galleon. Off Monterey harbor the 11th of October arrived the *San José*, and the commander, José Imparan, sent a boat ashore asking for a pilot and that buoys be placed to mark deep water, alluding to the royal orders for the galleons to get water and food here.[21] Neve's reply the records fail to show. Palou states that the ship's boat took off a sheep and basket of vegetables from Carmelo Bay, while the officer went across to the presidio. There a bull was given and the key of the storehouse, also the required pilot, or a soldier who knew the harbor; but the boat was upset just as the men boarded the ship and a sudden wind forced her to depart without anchoring, taking the soldier with her to Cape San Lúcas.[22] Imparan was however blamed subsequently for his action in this affair; for General Croix writes to Neve on July 17, 1782, that the king has been notified of Imparan's refusal to anchor at Monterey;[23] and indeed Minister of State Galvez writes in February of the same year that though signal fires were lit at Monterey the galleon paid no attention, sailing for Cape San Lúcas in defiance of royal orders; that the king is much displeased; and that in future galleons must call at Monterey under a penalty of four thousand dollars, unless prevented by contrary winds.

Besides the arrival and departure of vessels, and Father Junípero's visits to the different missions for the

gacion, MS.; *Bodega y Cuadra, Segunda Salida*, MS.; *Prov. Rec.*, MS., i. 132–4; *Prov. St. Pap.*, MS., ii. 49–50; *Palou, Not.*, ii. 356–64; *Id., Vida*, 165–71; *Bustamante, Suplemento*, 34–5. There are some differences about the date of departure. The rumor of war with England caused the two California transports *San Cárlos* and *San Antonio* to be sent in the autumn of 1779 over to Manila to give notice of danger and carry $300,000 in money. Padre Font went as chaplain on the *San Cárlos*. Cambon recovered his health, resolved to return, and bought maize and sugar with his earnings as chaplain. The supplies he sent up on the *Santiago*, but he was obliged himself to make a trip to Acapulco and perhaps to Manila under Heceta on the *Princesa. Palou, Not.*, ii. 365–7.
[21] Imparan's letter in *Prov. St. Pap.*, MS., ii. 38.
[22] *Palou, Not.*, ii. 363–4.
[23] *Prov. St. Pap.*, MS., iii. 228.

purpose of administering confirmation, there is but little to be noted in the way of local events. Neophyte alcaldes and regidores were chosen in 1779 for the older missions; two of each for San Cárlos and San Diego, and one for San Antonio, San Luis, and San Gabriel. Neve at his coming had found the so-called presidios to be mere collections of huts, enclosed in slight fences of sticks called palisades, altogether inadequate to purposes of defence, even against the poorly armed Californians. He gave special attention to this matter and with such success that on the 3d of July 1778 there was completed at Monterey a wall of stone 537 yards in circumference, 12 feet high and four feet thick, enclosing ten adobe houses each 21 by 24 feet, with barracks 136 by 18 feet not quite finished. At San Francisco walls were also being built, but of adobe, which the rains of January and February of 1779 undermined and destroyed, showing that here also stone must be used. At San Diego stones were being collected for foundations in 1778, but we hear nothing definite of progress for several years. At San Francisco presidio a new chapel was in course of erection at the beginning of 1780;[24] while at San Diego mission a new adobe church, strengthened and roofed with pine timbers, was this year completed. It was ninety feet long by seventeen feet wide and high. The farmers of San José were prospering in a quiet way, raising over 700 bushels of grain in 1780, and having at that date nearly 600 head of live-stock, large and small. San Gabriel and San Luis had some 2,000 bushels of surplus maize.[25]

At the end of this first decade of its history the Spanish settlements in California consisted of three presidios, one pueblo, and eight missions. There were at these establishments besides the governor, two lieu-

[24] A house was burned at the presidio Oct. 11, 1779, and with it the hospital tent of the two vessels *Princesa* and *Favorita*.

[25] On local matters 1778–80 see *Arch. Sta Bárbara*, MS., x. 495–513; *Prov. Rec.*, MS., i. 18, 51, 83, 89, 104, 117, 120, 122–5, 127–8; ii. 21–2; *Prov. St. Pap.*, MS., ii. 36–7.

tenants, three sergeants, 14 corporals, about 140 soldiers, 30 *sirvientes*, 20 settlers, five master-mechanics, one surgeon, and three store-keepers, 16 Franciscan missionaries, and about 3,000 neophytes. The total population of Spanish and mixed blood was not far from 500. The annual expense to the royal treasury of keeping up these establishments was nearly $50,000, or some $10,000 more than was provided for by the regulation of 1773.[26]

[26] For a list of male inhabitants of California from 1775 to 1800, see end of this volume.

CHAPTER XVI.

A NEW REGLAMENTO—COLONISTS AND RECRUITS—LOS ANGELES FOUNDED.

1781.

AT the beginning of 1781 the new regulation for
the government of California went into effect provisionally by order of Comandante General Croix of
the Provincias Internas de Occidente, receiving the
formal approval of King Cárlos III., October 24th
of the same year,[1] but dating back to the 1st of June
1779, in its original drawing-up by Neve. Echeveste's
regulation of 1773,[2] resulting chiefly from the labors
of President Serra in behalf of California during his
visit to Mexico, had been designed as a temporary
expedient rather than a permanent system; and the
aim in preparing the document to supersede it was to
bring the Californian establishments, so far as possible,

---

[1] *Neve, Reglamento é Instruccion*, MS. For the Reglamento in print see
Arrillaga, Recopilacion, 1828, 121–75. Orders of Croix of Sept. 21, 1780, in
Prov. St. Pap., MS., ii. 114. Neve acknowledged receipt of preceding order
Jan. 20, 1781. *Id.*, ii. 38–9. See first pages of chapter xv. of this volume.
[2] *Reglamento de 24 de Mayo 1773*, and *Id., Determinacion de 8 de Julio*, MS.,
5; *Palou, Not.*, i. 556–71, 589–94. See chapter ix. of this volume.

under the general system prevalent in the other
interior provinces, and embodied in the royal regulation for frontier presidios,[3] with such modifications
as were rendered necessary by the distance and peculiar
circumstances of California as shown by experience
under the old system. Elsewhere in this series I
devote some space to a careful study of the presidio
system in all its workings and details. Hence to enter
here into the minutiæ of the new regulation would
serve no useful purpose. I therefore notice the document briefly in its main features as the beginning of
a new epoch; its practical workings will in a general
way be apparent in the course of events from year to
year. The reader will thus be led to peruse with
interest, qualified to study with profit, or enabled to
omit altogether the later analysis necessary in a work
of this character for purposes of reference, but not
interesting to a large class of general readers.

The distance and isolation of California preventing
regular visits of the royal inspector of frontier presidios, the governor was made provincial inspector,
responsible by virtue of this new commission for the
enforcement of the regulations. But that the duties
of the new position might not interfere with other
official duties, the actual work of inspecting the presidios was given to an adjutant inspector acting under
the inspector's orders.[4] Supplies of all kinds were as
before to be shipped from San Blas, being purchased in
accordance with annual *memorias* of articles required,
forwarded through governor to viceroy, and delivered
to soldiers and servants in payment of their wages.
There was, however, an important change in one respect; for the former profit of a hundred and fifty per
cent was relinquished by the government, and supplies were furnished to the men at their cost in San
Blas, no addition being made for transportation by

---

[3] *Presidios, Reglamento é Instruccion de 10 de Sept. 1772.*
[4] Nicolás Soler first held this position from November 1781 under Inspect-
or Neve.

sea. As an offset to this reduction the pay of soldiers was reduced about forty per cent,[5] they were obliged to submit to losses and damage incurred on the voyage, and they were obliged to pay two per cent to an *habilitado*. This last named official took the place of the old *guarda-almacen*, or store-keeper, and had charge, subject to the inspection of his commandant, of the reception and distribution of pay and rations and the keeping of company accounts. The habilitado was chosen from among the subaltern officers by each presidial company, and the company was responsible for any deficit in his accounts.[6] While supplies were yet to be imported from abroad as a matter of necessity, the habilitado was authorized to purchase California productions whenever offered, and it was expected that all grain consumed would soon be grown in the country, or in 'the peninsula,' as even Upper California was still called.

The new regulation provided for the occupation of the Santa Bárbara Channel region, in accordance with Neve's original idea, by the founding of a new presidio and mission of Santa Bárbara in the centre, and two missions, San Buenaventura and Purísima, at the extremities of the Channel coast. It also made provision for two pueblos, the one already founded at San José, and another to be established on the Rio Porciúncula and called Nuestra Señora de los Angeles. For the four presidios, and the eleven missions and two pueblos under their protection, a force of four lieutenants, four sub-lieutenants, or alféreces, six sergeants, sixteen corporals, one hundred and seventy-two soldiers, one surgeon, and five master-mechanics was allowed at an annual expense for salaries of $53,453. From this force a sergeant

---

[5] A sergeant's pay was reduced from $400 to $262; corporal, $400 to $225; soldier, $360 to $217.50; mechanic, $300 to $180. A lieutenant was to get $550 instead of $500; an alférez $400; and a surgeon $450.

[6] The first habilitados, in 1781, were Mariano Carrillo at Monterey, Hermenegildo Sal at San Francisco, José de Zúñiga at San Diego, and José F. Ortega at Santa Bárbara.

and fourteen men were to be stationed temporarily
at San Buenaventura and Purísima; a corporal and
five men at each of the other missions; four soldiers
at each of the pueblos for two years; and the rest to
be retained for presidio service proper.[7]

Section xiv. of the regulation deals with the new
and important subject of pueblos and colonization. As
the foundation of pueblo land-titles this section has
played an important part in the subsequent litigations
of Californian courts, and has often been republished
and translated.[8] The system of distributing pueblo
lands, left somewhat vague at first, not reduced to an
exact science in the practical application of later
years, and almost inextricably confused by the voluminous explanations of lawyers since 1849, need not
be closely analyzed here. It was only in its strictly
legal aspects that the pueblo system was vague or
complicated. Historically all was clear enough. According to the new regulations settlers were to be
obtained from the older provinces and established in
California; to be granted each a house-lot and a tract
of land for cultivation; to be supplied at the beginning
with the necessary live-stock, implements, and seed,
which advance was to be gradually repaid within five
years from the produce of the land; to be paid each an
annual sum $116.50 for two years, and of $60 for the
next three years, the payment to be in clothing and
other necessary articles at cost prices; to have as
communities the use of government lands for pasturage and the obtaining of wood and water; and, finally,
to be free for five years from all tithes or other taxes.
Government aid in the way of money and cattle was to
be given only to colonists who left their own country to
come to California; but in respect of lands other colo-

[7] This left 27 men to San Diego, 23 to Santa Bárbara, 27 to Monterey,
and 19 to San Francisco.
[8] For translation see *Halleck's Report, 21st Cong., 1st Sess., H. Ex. Doc.
17*, p. 134; *Jones' Report*, No. 4; *U. S. Sup. Court Repts.*, i., Rockwell, 445;
Dwinelle's Colon. Hist. S. F., addenda, 3; *Hall's Hist. San José*, 460–73;
besides references more or less complete in many legal briefs.

nists, such as discharged soldiers, were entitled to equal privileges.

In return for aid thus received the colonists were simply required to sell to the presidios exclusively the surplus products of their lands, at fair prices to be fixed from time to time by the government, in accordance with market rates in the southern provinces. In the total absence of other purchasers this requirement would for many years at least prove a decided benefit rather than a burden. Each settler must keep himself and horses and musket in readiness for military service in an emergency. Other conditions were imposed, but all more directly advantageous to the settler than to the government. Thus the pobladores must take their farms together within pueblo limits of four square leagues according to the Spanish law and custom; they could not alienate their land, nor in any way encumber it with mortgages or otherwise; they must build houses, dig irrigating ditches, cultivate, own, and keep in repair certain implements, and maintain a certain number of animals; they could not kill or otherwise dispose of their live-stock except under certain regulations to insure its increase; neither could one person own more than fifty animals of a kind and thus monopolize the pueblo wealth; and finally, each pueblo must perform certain community work in the construction of dams and irrigating canals, on roads and streets, in a church and the necessary town buildings, in tilling the *propios*, or pueblo lands, from the product of which municipal expenses were to be paid. Municipal officers were at the beginning appointed by the governor but afterwards chosen by the people. This system of colonization was in every respect a wise one and well adapted to the needs of the country. If it was not successful, it is to the character of the colonists, the mildness of the climate, and the opposition of the missionaries that we must look for the causes of failure.

The regulation provided in its last section for the

establishment in the future of new missions, in addition to the three to be immediately founded. By the line of eleven missions located along the coast at intervals of from fourteen to twenty-five leagues, with four protecting presidios at greater intervals, communication would, it was thought, be sufficiently secured; and new missions should be located on a second line farther inland, each new establishment being as far as possible equidistant from two of the old ones, and from fourteen to twenty leagues east. Two ministers as before were to be left in each of the old and of the three Channel missions, but the places of those who died or retired were not to be filled so long as one padre was left at each mission, except that at presidio missions there were to be two friars until some other provision should be made for chaplains. New missions were to have but a single minister with an annual stipend of four hundred dollars; and this sum, with the $1,000 allowed each new foundation, must suffice for all needs both religious and temporal. The old establishments were, however, to contribute animals and seed, and they might also supply a companion minister for a year. No necessity for an increased military force was anticipated, since the temporary pueblo guards and the extra force at San Buenaventura and Purísima would provide for at least four new guards without diminishing the presidial garrisons. It will be noted that this section of the regulation shows less indications of missionary influence in its shaping than did Echeveste's which was inspired by Serra; but we shall also see that most of the present provisions were of no practical effect until modified by Franciscan influences.

Meanwhile preparations for the proposed new establishments were going on slowly, preparations that had begun with Neve's arrival in the country, his report of June 1777 on the means and importance of controlling the eight or ten thousand natives of the twenty-one Channel rancherías,[9] and his provisional founding of San José. General Croix approved the governor's schemes for new establishments in September 1778, and some correspondence on minor details followed.[10] Neve as we have seen included his plans in the regulation of June 1779, which Croix approved in September. Actual operations toward a carrying-out of the plans were begun at the end of the year by Rivera y Moncada, lieutenant governor of Lower California,[11] who at Neve's order crossed the gulf and went to Arizpe to receive from Croix certain instructions which bore date of December 27, 1779, and by which Rivera was intrusted with the recruiting in Sinaloa and Sonora of soldiers and settlers for California;[12] the former for the Santa Bárbara presidio and missions, the latter for the new pueblo on the Rio Porciúncula to be called Queen of the Angels.

In a preliminary letter Rivera's attention is called to the importance of his mission and he was flattered, as was the custom in such documents, with expressions of confidence in his ability and with prospective approval by the king. He is also reminded of a popular idea that Californian wages, while looking well on paper, are liable to a woful shrinkage in actual practice; an idea that of course will seriously interfere with recruiting, and must be dispelled by a careful explanation of the exact terms offered, without exaggeration. The settler must understand that he is to receive ten dollars a month and regular rations for

[9] *Prov. Rec.*, MS., i. 70–3.

[10] *Prov. St. Pap.*, MS., ii. 6, 7; *Prov. Rec.*, MS., i. 122–3. Neve on Sept. 23, 1778, announced to the king what he had done, and the king's approval was forwarded by Croix July 19, 1779. *Prov. St. Pap.*, MS., ii. 47.

[11] 'Rivera y Marcado, Comandante of the presidio of Monterey,' is what Hall calls him. *Hist. San José*, 19–24. This is a fair sample of the way in which Californian affairs are treated by modern writers, Hall as I have said being above the average of his class.

[12] *Croix, Instruccion que debe observar el Capitan D. Fernando Rivera y Moncada para la recluta y habilitacion de familias, pobladores y tropa, acopia de monturas, trasporte de todas y demas auxilios que ha solicitado y se conceden al Coronel D. Felipe de Neve, Gobernador de Californias, para el resguardo, beneficio y conservacion de los nuevos y antiguos establecimientos de aquella Península.* MS.

three years,[13] beginning with the date of enlistment,
and subject to no discount; but the advance of clothing, live-stock, seed, and implements must be gradually repaid, not by a discount on wages, but from the
surplus products of the land. Soldiers on the contrary, having a permanent and larger salary, must
repay by 'prudent discounts' the sums advanced in
aid of themselves and families.

Coming now to the body of the instruction, we
learn that the subaltern officers required for the increased force of California, with one exception, had
been selected and commissioned,[14] and that twenty-
five soldiers had been selected from the volunteers of
the presidial companies of Sonora to serve out their
time in California, their service beginning February
1st when they were to assemble at Horcasitas. There
were to be recruited twenty-four settlers and fifty-
nine soldiers, and to obtain them Rivera was allowed
to go beyond the limits of the Provincias Internas,
as far as Guadalajara if necessary. Twenty-five of
the new recruits were to fill the places of those taken
from the presidios, so that only thirty-four soldiers
were to go to California. These and the twenty-four
settlers must be married men, accompanied by their
families, healthy and robust, likely to lead regular
lives, and to set a good example to the natives. The
settlers must include a mason, a carpenter, and a
blacksmith. All must bind themselves to ten years'
service. Female relatives of the pobladores, if unmarried, should be encouraged to accompany the families with a view to marriage with bachelor soldiers

[13] This, strangely enough, does not agree exactly with the regulation,
which offers $116 per year for two years and $60 for the next three, these
sums including rations; neither was the pay to begin according to the reglamento, until the grant of a lot in one of the pueblos.
[14] These were lieutenants Alonso Villaverde and Diego Gonzalez, and
alféreces Mariano Carrillo, Manuel García Ruiz, and Ramon Lasso de la
Vega, one alférez remaining to be appointed after consultation with Gov.
Neve. Lieut. José Zúñiga was a little later substituted for Villaverde, who
never came to California; Alférez José Darío Argüello was also sent in place
of Ruiz; and José Velasquez was appointed to fill the vacant place of the
fourth alférez.

already in California. The rendezvous for the whole company was to be at Álamos, except such as might be obtained in Guadalajara, who were to go by sea from San Blas. From Álamos the recruits and their families were to be forwarded by sea or land as might be decided later. Nine hundred and sixty-one horses and mules were to be purchased and were to go by way of the Gila and Colorado.[15]

On February 10, 1780, General Croix sent to Neve a copy of his instructions to Rivera, with the information that the latter had already begun his work, that the recruits would probably come in three divisions, and that the land expedition would start, if nothing happened, in September or October.[16] The general also enclosed copies of his communications to the viceroy on the same subject, from one of which it appears that the plan of obtaining volunteer soldiers from the Sonora presidios had been a failure, so that all the new recruits must go to California. In another communication Croix called on the viceroy for various measures in behalf of the new establishments, including a resurvey of the channel with a view to find a suitable landing-place for supplies. He also called attention to the fact that for the three new missions six friars would be needed, four of whom should sail from San Blas and accompany the land expedition. San Buenaventura had already an allowance of $1,000, and the same sum should be allowed the others, being expended in sacred vestments, vessels, and utensils to be shipped from San Blas. Six peons with pay and rations for three years should also be furnished to each of the new missions.

By the 1st of August Rivera had recruited forty-five soldiers and seven settlers, and thought he would have to go to Guadalajara; but by the 25th he had so nearly completed his full number at Rosario, in Sinaloa,

---

[15] At the end of the *Instruccion* (pp. 80–4) are given full lists of the articles, chiefly of clothing, to be furnished each recruit, soldier or poblador, man or woman, boy or girl.

[16] Croix to Neve, Feb. 10, 1780, in *Prov. St. Pap.*, MS., ii. 89–99.

that he thought it best to abandon the southern trip, and returned to the north.[17] He obtained, however, but little more than half the full number of settlers. In a letter of December 18th Croix explains that one party under Gonzalez and Lasso will cross over to Loreto, proceed to San Luis Bay by water, and thence by land to San Diego; while the rest, forty-two soldiers with their families, will march by way of the Colorado under Rivera in person, escorted above Tucson by sixty-five men from the Sonora presidios under Lieutenant Andrés Arias Caballero. This escort was to be sent back from the Colorado except such a detachment as Rivera might deem necessary to go farther, under Alférez Cayetano Limon.[18] The date when Rivera and his land expedition left Álamos in Sonora is not exactly known, but was probably in April 1781. With it went also Lieutenant Gonzalez who had been transferred from the other party, and Alférez José Darío Argüello. Thirty of the soldiers were accompanied by their families, but there were no settlers proper with this expedition. Of events along the way there is no record. Progress was very slow, in accordance with the orders of Croix, to avoid needless fatigue and hardship to families, and also to keep the live-stock in good condition. Neve, hearing of Rivera's approach, sent Sergeant Juan José Robles with five or six soldiers from San Diego and Monterey to meet him on the Colorado. Joined by this guard Rivera sent back most of the Sonora troops; despatched the California-bound company—except five or six men whom he retained—to their destination under Gonzalez escorted by Limon and nine soldiers;

[17] Croix to Neve September 21st, mentioning letters from Rivera, in *Prov. St. Pap.*, MS., ii. 89–99. Nov. 15th, Governor Neve asks the viceroy for $3,000 with which to purchase grain from San Gabriel and San Luis. The *memorias* asked for Santa Bárbara amount to $12,952, much of the amount being in implements, etc., to be charged to settlers. *Prov. Rec.*, MS., ii. 33.

[18] Croix to Neve, December 18, 1780, in *Prov. St. Pap.*, ii. 117–25. Probably 42 soldiers—possibly one or two less—did start by this route as intended, and 17 by the other route, completing the full number of 59. The settlers all seem to have come *via* Loreto, and so far as the records show there were only 14 of them, two of whom ran away before reaching California.

while he with Robles and nine or ten men encamped
near the river, on the eastern or Arizona bank, with
a view to afford needed rest to a part of the live-stock
and then resume his journey westward. Gonzalez,
Limon, Argüello, thirty-five soldiers, thirty families,
and the Sonora escort arrived at San Gabriel the 14th
of July. As it was deemed impossible to transport supplies and complete other preparations before the rainy
season, Neve decided to postpone the Channel foundations until the next year.[19] Limon with his nine men
soon started back for Sonora by way of the Colorado.

Meanwhile the rest of the recruits crossed the gulf
from Guaymas to Loreto, under command of Lieutenant José Zúñiga substituted for Gonzalez. Seventeen
men, probably soldiers, with their families, left Loreto
March 12th under Alférez Lasso and reached San
Luis Bay by water April 24th, soon followed by the
rest under Zúñiga, this last division including apparently eleven settlers and their families, two of the
original number having deserted and one remaining
for a time at Loreto. All were en route for the north
on May 16th, when Neve communicated the preceding facts to General Croix,[20] and all arrived August
18th at San Gabriel, where they were obliged to
encamp in quarantine for a time, at a distance of a
league from the mission, some of the children having
recently recovered from the small-pox.[21]

That section of the regulation relating to pueblos
and colonization had already been made public in California in a special *bando* dated March 8, 1781.[22]

[19] Neve to Croix, July 14, 1781, in *Prov. Rec.*, MS., ii. 87–8. Some other
unimportant correspondence on the general subject of the new foundations is
found in *Id.*, ii. 14, 40–1; *Prov. St. Pap.*, *Ben. Mil.*, MS., ii. 41; *Prov. St.
Pap.*, MS., iii. 265.
[20] Neve to Croix, May 16, 1781, in *Prov. Rec.*, MS., ii. 82. In this letter
Neve announces his intention to send Robles with 12 men to meet Rivera. I
have already stated that he sent only 5 or 6 men. Palou, *Not.*, ii. 381, says
the number was 5. Rivera certainly had 11 or 12 men and all may have been
those sent with Robles; but if he started with 42 and only 35 arrived, Palou's
version accounts for the discrepancy.
[21] Neve to Croix, Oct. 29, 1781, in *Prov. Rec.*, MS., ii. 89–90.
[22] *St. Pap. Miss. and Colon.*, MS., i. 105–19. This document is literally
identical with section xiv. of the reglamento already referred to and found in

Though for reasons already given the foundation of the Channel missions and the Santa Bárbara presidio was postponed, there was no reason for delay in establishing the pueblo, since the site was near at hand and the settlers had arrived. Even when Limon arrived unexpectedly at San Gabriel late in August with seven survivors of his nine men, himself wounded, bringing news of the terrible massacre on the River Colorado in which Rivera had been killed, as will be related in the following chapter, the resulting excitement furnished no motive for delay at Los Angeles.

Governor Neve issued his instructions for founding the pueblo of La Reina de los Angeles from San Gabriel on the 26th of August. While agreeing with, or literally copying the clauses of the regulation which I have translated in the preceding note, this document contains many additional particulars re-

Id., 209–24, and elsewhere. The clauses relating to the distribution of lands are as follows: 'The *solares* (house-lots) granted to the new settlers must be designated by the government in respect of location and extent according to the ground on which the new pueblos are established, so that plaza and streets be formed as prescribed by the laws of the kingdom, conformably to which there shall also be designated for the pueblo a suitable *egido* (commons or vacant suburbs, to be divided into additional house-lots and given to new settlers if required) and *dehesas* (outside pasture-grounds used in common by the settlers) with the sowing-lands needed for *propios* (lands rented for a revenue to pay municipal expenses). Each *suerte* (planting-lot) of land, whether irrigable or depending on rainfall, must be 200 varas long and wide, this being the area generally occupied by a *fanega*, a bushel and a half, of maize in sowing. The distribution of said *suertes*, which like that of the *solares* must be made in the king's name, will be made by the government with equality and with proportion to the irrigable land, so that, after making the corresponding demarcation and after reserving as *baldíos*, or vacant, one fourth of the number which results from reckoning the number of settlers, they (*suertes*) shall be distributed, if there are enough of them, at the rate of two *suertes* of irrigable land to each settler and two more of dry; and of the *realengas* (royal lands including the lots left vacant as above) there shall be set apart such as may be deemed necessary for the pueblo's *propios* (municipal lands as above), and from the rest grants shall be made by the governor in the name of his majesty to such as may come to settle later,' especially to discharged soldiers, etc. The original is somewhat vaguely worded and badly punctuated, hardly two of the copies in manuscript and print, or of the many translations extant, being punctuated alike. The above is the meaning of the clauses as clear as I can make it. I see no good reason for reproducing the original vagueness of expression where the meaning is clear, and in my opinion the semicolon objected to by Mr Dwinelle, *Colon. Hist. S. F.*, addenda, No. 4, brings out the signification better than a comma. In learning the meaning of a sentence even so frail a thing as Mexican punctuation may be studied; having discovered the meaning, there is no further use for the stops.

specting the survey and distribution of lots.[23] Of subsequent proceedings for a time we only know that the pueblo was founded September 4th, with twelve settlers and their families, forty-six persons in all, whose names are given and whose blood was a strange mixture of Indian and negro with here and there a trace of Spanish.[24] Two of the original recruits, Miguel Villa and Rafael Mesa, had deserted before reaching the country, one was still absent in the peninsula, and

[23] *Neve, Instruccion para la Fundacion de Los Angeles, 26 de Agosto 1781,* MS. After selecting a spot for a dam and ditch with a view of irrigating the largest possible area of land, a site for the pueblo was to be selected on high ground, in sight of the sowing-lands, but at least 200 varas distant, near the river or the main ditch, with sufficient exposure to the north and south winds. Here a plaza of 200 x 300 feet was to be laid out with its corners facing the cardinal points, and with three streets running perpendicularly from each of its four sides; thus no street would be swept by the wind, always supposing that the winds would confine their action to the cardinal points, but I think the Angeles winds have not always been well behaved in this respect. The house-lots are to be each 20 x 40 varas, and their number is to be equal to that of the available *suertes* of irrigable ground, that is, more than double that of the present inhabitants. The eastern side of the plaza is to be reserved for public buildings. After the survey and reservation of *realengas* as prescribed, the settlers are to draw lots for the *suertes*, beginning with those nearest the pueblo.

[24] *Los Angeles, Padron de 1781,* MS.; *Ortega,* in *St. Pap., Miss. and Colon.,* i. 104–5. The settlers were as follows: José de Lara, Spaniard, 50 years of age, wife Indian, 3 children; José Antonio Navarro, mestizo, 42 years, wife mulattress, 3 children; Basilio Rosas, Indian, 68 years, wife mulattress, 6 children; Antonio Mesa, negro, 38 years, wife mulattress, 2 children; Antonio (Felix) Villavicencio, Spaniard, 30 years, wife Indian, 1 child; José Vanegas, Indian, 28 years, wife Indian, 1 child; Alejandro Rosas, Indian, 19 years, wife coyote (Indian); Pablo Rodriguez, Indian, 25 years, wife Indian, 1 child; Manuel Camero, mulatto, 30 years, wife mulattress; Luis Quintero, negro, 55 years, wife mulattress, 5 children; José Moreno, mulatto, 22 years, wife mulattress; Antonio Miranda, chino, 50 years, 1 child. The last-named was at first absent at Loreto. He was not a Chinaman, nor even born in China, as has been stated by some writers, but was the offspring probably of an Indian mother by a father of mixed Spanish and negro blood. From a later padron of 1785, *Prov. St. Pap.,* MS., xxii. 29, it appears that Navarro was a tailor, and the age of several is given differently. From *Los Angeles, Hist.,* 11, 12, we learn that two were born in Spain, one in China, and the rest in Sinaloa, Sonora, or Baja California, a very mild way of putting it, though true enough except in the case of the chino; but the same work erroneously states that the 12 settlers had previously been soldiers at San Gabriel. In the same work the plaza is located between Upper Main, Marchessault, and New High streets of the modern city, the N. E. bound not being named. The goods delivered to settlers on government account to the end of 1781, amounted to $4,191. *Prov. St. Pap.,* MS., iii. 265–7. According to accounts in *Prov. St. Pap., Ben. Mil.,* MS., ii. 4–7, 21–2, the contracts of 11 had been made in 1780, and of one in February 1781. They were engaged at $10 per month for 3 years, and rations of one real per day for 10 years, though this does not agree with the reglamento; $2,546 was furnished them in Sonora and $500 in California, and there was due to them December 31, 1781, $2,303. See also *Id.,* iii. 13; *Prov. Rec.,* MS., ii. 65.

three were described as useless. But the rest went to work, and soon the governor reported satisfactory progress in their irrigating ditch and mud-roofed huts of palisades, the latter before the end of 1784 being replaced by adobe houses, the needed public buildings having also been erected, and a church begun of the same material.[25] Some changes also took place among the settlers during these few years.[26]

I have recorded the preceding items of local Angeles annals beyond the chronological limits of this chapter because they may as well be recorded here as elsewhere, and because a still later event of 1786 seems to belong here properly. I allude to the formal distribution of lands to the settlers. Some kind of a grant in the king's name must have been made at the beginning,[27] and there is nothing to show that the survey and distribution made at that time were not permanent. The fact that formal possession, or renewal of possession, was given in 1786, just five years after the founding, when according to the regulations government aid to settlers was to cease and advances were to be repaid, has probably some significance, though there is nothing in the regulation to show that full titles were to be given only at the expiration of five years.[28]

[25] For scattered references to buildings, see *Prov. Rec.*, MS., i. 175–6, 184; iii. 23; *Prov. St. Pap.*, MS., iv. 91.

[26] Early in 1782 Lara, Mesa, and Quintero, a Spaniard, and two negroes, were sent away as useless to the pueblo and themselves, and their property was taken away by order of the governor. The record does not show that Miranda, the 'chino,' ever came to Los Angeles at all, unless he be identical with another 'useless' settler said to have been sent away in 1783. José Francisco Sinova, who had lived a long time as a laborer in California, applied for admission as a settler in 1785, and was admitted, receiving the same aid as the original colonists in the way of implements and live-stock, save in respect of sheep and goats, which the government had not on hand. One of the deserters, Rafael Mesa, seems to have been caught and brought to California, but there is no evidence that he settled at Los Angeles. Two grown-up sons of Basilio Rosas appear on the list of 1785, as does also Juan José Dominguez, a Spaniard; but all three disappear from the next year's list. *Prov. Rec.*, ii. 79; iii. 185; *Prov. St. Pap.*, MS., v. 144–5; xxii. 29–30; *Prov. St. Pap., Ben. Mil.*, MS., iii. 1.

[27] In fact the titles given to settlers seem to have been approved by the commandant general on Feb. 6, 1784. *Prov. St. Pap.*, MS., x. 152.

[28] Art. 17, sect. xiv., simply provides that the governor or his comisionados shall give titles and cause the same, with register of brands, to be recorded and kept in the archives—impliedly at the beginning.

However this may have been, Governor Fages, of
whose accession to the rule more hereafter, on August
14, 1786, without any preliminary correspondence so
far as the records show, as if this was unquestionably
the natural and proper thing to be done at this particular time, commissioned Alférez José Argüello to
go to Angeles and put the settlers in possession of
their lands in accordance with section xiv. of the
regulation.[29]

Argüello accepted the commission September 4th
and on the same day appointed Corporal Vicente
Félix and private Roque de Cota as legal witnesses.
On the 18th he reports his task completed and
duly recorded in the archives. This was perhaps
the first important public service rendered by a man
who was later governor and father of a governor. In
the performance of his duty Argüello with his witnesses summoned each of the nine settlers in succession and in presence of all granted first the house-lot,
then the four fields, and finally the branding-iron by
which his live-stock was to be distinguished from
that of his neighbors. In both house lots and fields
the pretence of a measurement was made. In each
case the nature of the grant was fully explained, the
grantee assented to the conditions involved, and for
each of the twenty-seven grants a separate document
was drawn up, each bearing, besides the signatures of
Argüello and his witnesses, a cross, for not one of the
nine could sign his name. I give herewith a map
showing the distribution of lands.[30] Argüello's survey of the various classes of reserved lands is not
very clearly expressed; the *propios*, however, are
said to extend 2,200 varas from the dam to the limit

[29] *Los Angeles, Reparticion de Solares y Suertes*, 1786, MS. The document
contains Argüello's appointment, his acceptance, the appointment of two
witnesses, three *autos de diligencias*, or records of granting house-lot, field,
and branding-iron respectively to each of 9 settlers, one *auto* of survey of
municipal and royal lands, and a final certificate of having completed his task
and deposited the records in the archives.
[30] *Prov. St. Pap.*, MS., iii. 55; *Id.*, *Ben.*, ii. 2; signed by Argüello Dec.
21, 1793. The map of the pueblo is on a scale five times larger than that

of distributed lands, and the royal lands were on the
river's opposite bank.

At San José de Guadalupe, notwithstanding the
informality of its original foundation, nothing was
done under the new regulation until 1783, or five years
after the beginning, as in the south. Some of the
settlers, not having been among the original founders
in November 1777, were still receiving rations from

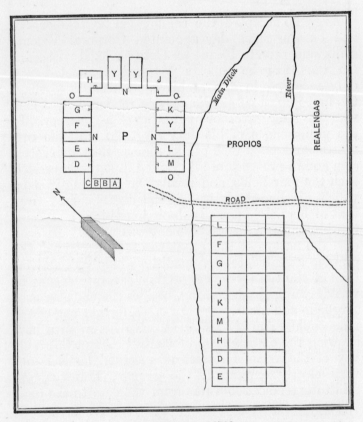

LOS ANGELES IN 1786.

of the fields. The distribution is shown by the letters as follows: A, guard-
house; B, town-houses; C, *trozo del posito;* D, Pablo Rodriguez; E, José
Vanegas; F, José Moreno; G, Félix Villavicencio; H, Francisco Sinova; Y,
vacant; J, Basilio Rosas; K, Alejandro Rosas; L, Antonio Navarro; M,

the government.[31] In December 1782 Governor Fages
commissioned Moraga of San Francisco to put the
settlers in formal possession of their lands.[32] After

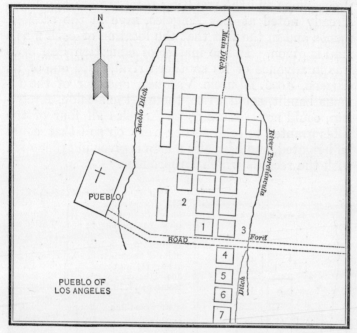

Manuel Camero; N, O, streets; P, Plaza. Two other maps are given—*St.
Pap., Miss. and Col.*, MS., i. 103, 307—one of which I reproduce. For the
third transfer 1 to 2; add a lot at 3; and move 4, 5, 6, 7 one tier to the east.
I suppose these maps to have been of earlier date than 1786.

[31] According to documents in *Prov. St. Pap., Ben. Mil.*, MS., iii. 23, the pay
or rations of 6 of the 9 settlers ceased Nov. 1, 1782; one had rations to Nov. 3d;
and 2 had rations all the year. According to other records in *Prov. St. Pap.*,
MS., v. 25–6, 28, 4 had rations during 1783, and 3 at beginning of 1784. In *Id.*,
iii. 244–7, Moraga says that from June to Dec. 1781 three settlers had pay
and rations, while 2 had rations only.

[32] In *Prov. Rec.*, MS., iii. 154–6, this document is given under date of
Dec. 2d, and is preceded, *Id.*, 153–4, by a letter of instructions dated Dec.
12th, and ordering that the *mandamiento* (the document of Dec. 2d) be placed
at the head of each title. On Jan. 4, 1783, Moraga writes that he cannot
attend to the distribution at once as ordered by the governor in letter of
Dec. 6th, but will do so at an early date. *Stat. Pap., Miss. and Colon.*, MS.,
i. 30. In the regular record, however, *Id.*, 244–71, Moraga's appointment as
comisionado, differing very slightly from the doc. of Dec. 2d, is dated Dec.
24th, being followed by Moraga's *auto de obedecimiento* dated May 13th and
containing most of the land clauses of the reglamento, and this by the 27
diligencias de posesion by which the 9 settlers were granted their lots, fields,
and branding-irons; then comes the measurement of public lands, and finally
Moraga's final certificate of Sept. 1st at San Francisco.

some delay Moraga appointed Felipe Tapia and Juan
José Peralta as witnesses and began his task at San
José May 13, 1783, completing it on the 19th. The
proceedings and the resulting records were like those
already noted at Los Angeles, save in the settlers'
names and in the fact that the location of each man's
land is given. In the matter of education San José
was in advance of its southern rival, since one of its
citizens, José Tiburcio Vasquez, ancestor of the famous bandit, could write, though the alcalde, Archuleta, could not. Here as at Angeles all four of the
fields granted to each settler were on soil that could
be irrigated, and here also a map is given in connection
with the records which I reproduce.[33]

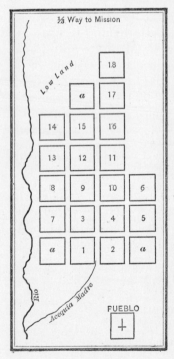

MAP OF SAN JOSÉ.

[33] *St. Pap., Miss. and Colon.*, MS., i.
243. On the original the names are written on their respective lots. I refer to
them as follows: a, a, a, Realengas;
1, 2, Manuel Amézquita; 3, 4, Claudio
Alvires; 5, 6, Sebastian Alvitre; 7, 8,
Manuel Gonzalez; 9, 10, Bernardo Rosales; 11, 12, Francisco Avila; 13, 14,
José Tiburcio Vasquez; 15, 16, Antonio
Romero; 17, 18, Ignacio Archuleta. As
I have before noted, four of these names
differ from those of the original founders.
Alvitre was a pioneer soldier of the earlier
years; Alvires had been a laborer or servant before 1780; Ávila and Rosales appear here for the first time. This map
in the archives is dated at San Francisco
June 1, 1782, and contains a statement
by Moraga that he distributed the lots
on April 23, 1782, all of which is altogether unintelligible. Evidently however the map was made before 1783 since
it shows only two fields for each man.
Here as at Los Angeles there is nothing
to show that at this final distribution any
change was made. The map so far as it
goes agrees with Moraga's location of
lots, and the new lots seem to have extended in different directions from the
original. Hall, *Hist. San José*, 26–31,
gives a pretty full account of Moraga's
proceedings, and alludes to the map as
being dated April 23, 1783, and as showing 19 *suertes*. After granting the private
lands, Moraga went, apparently, to the
west bank of the river, where he measured 1,958 varas from the dam down to

Beyond what has been recorded in connection with the new establishments, there is very little to be said of the year 1781. The natives were troublesome on the frontier below San Diego, and Neve had planned to march against them with forty men, but other duties prevented the campaign.[34] Father Mugártegui also wrote from San Juan Capistrano that there were reasons to fear a rising of the gentiles reënforced from the Colorado, and that two of the six soldiers on guard were unfit for duty.[35] At Santa Clara August 12th the festival of the patroness was celebrated with the aid of Dumetz from San Cárlos and Noriega from San Francisco. The latter, after accompanying Serra to San Antonio, took temporarily the place of Crespí at San Cárlos while Crespí went with Serra to San Francisco on his tour of confirmation, this being the venerable friar's first visit to the northern missions, and his last journey on earth. Returning by way of Santa Clara, they officiated with Murguía and Peña on November 19th in laying the corner-stone of a new church dedicated to "Santa Clara de Asis, virgin, abbess, and matriarch of her most famous religion." The soldiers of the guard were present, and Alférez Lasso de la Vega from San Francisco acted as secular godfather. Under the stone were placed a cross with holy images and pieces of money.[36] The building was completed in 1784.

The supply-ship did not arrive this year, because on account of troubles with England[37] the *Santiago* was obliged to make a trip to Lima for quicksilver. A small transport was laden at San Blas, but proved to

the Santa Clara boundary, designating half the space (no width is given) as *propios* and the rest as *realengas*. Then the *egidos* 1,500 x 700 varas were located on the eminence where the pueblo stood.

[34] *Prov. St. Pap.*, MS., iii. 130–1.

[35] Letters of Sept. 25th and 28th in *Monterey Co. Arch.*, MS., vii. 3, 4.

[36] *Santa Clara, Lib. de Mision*, MS., 10, 11; *Palou, Not.*, ii. 369–70; *Arch. Sta. Bárbara*, MS., xi. 131; *Palou, Vida*, 236–7. A scrap in *Levett's Scrap-book* says the site was called by the natives Gerguensen, or 'valley of the oaks.'

[37] Orders for a war tax circulated by Gen. Croix and sent to California, *Arch. Misiones*, MS., i. 59–70.

be so worm-eaten that she could not safely be trusted
to sail. In December the *San Cárlos de Filipinas*
from Manila touched at San Diego. The old *San
Cárlos* had remained at the Philippines and the new
vessel had been built to take her place. Father Cambon was on board as chaplain, and being unwell was
allowed to remain at San Diego. He had some vestments and other articles for San Francisco which he
had bought with his wages, but they were invoiced
for San Blas and could not be unloaded.[38] Cambon
brought by a roundabout course the tidings that six
friars had been appointed for the three Channel missions, at which Serra rejoiced greatly, but about which
there is more to be said hereafter.

[38] *Palou, Not.*, ii. 369–73.

CHAPTER XVII.

PUEBLO-MISSIONS ON THE RIO COLORADO.

1780-1782.

THE reader of Sonora history will remember the
expeditions of Father Kino and his companions to
northern Pimería during the Jesuit period, their
flattering reports of prospects both spiritual and
temporal, and their efforts oft repeated but always
unsuccessful to establish missions in the Gila and
Colorado region. The natives were always clamorous
for friars; but the necessary combination of circumstances could never be effected. The requisites were
a favorable disposition on the part of the government,
a favorable condition of European and Mexican affairs,
money to spare in the royal treasury, and quiet among
the Sonora tribes. What Kino's zeal in time of peace
could not do, was impossible to the comparative lukewarmness of his successors in times of constant rebellion and warfare with the Apaches. The Franciscans,
if somewhat less enthusiastic than the earlier Jesuits,
and notwithstanding their greater difficulties, never

allowed the matter to drop.   The record of their efforts,
as of earlier attempts, belongs in detail to another
part of this work; but there was little or no actual
progress down to the time of Anza's expeditions, made
with a view to open communication by land with California.[1]

With the second of these expeditions in 1775–6
Francisco Garcés and Thomas Eixarch had gone to
the Colorado and had been left on the western bank
of the river with a few Indian attendants and under
the protection of Palma, a prominent Yuma chieftain
noted for his friendship for the white men.   Both friars
were Franciscans from the Queretaro college.   During
Anza's absence in the west, Eixarch remained on the
river, at or near the site of the modern Fort Yuma;
while Garcés travelled extensively down and up the
Colorado, west and east to San Gabriel and the Moqui
towns, well received by all natives except the Moquis.
So well were the Colorado Indians pleased with Anza's
treatment that, as Garcés was led to believe, they
refused aid to the hostile San Diego tribes.   The
only source of possible danger was believed to be in
Rivera's tendency to ill treat those who for one purpose or another visited the coast establishments.   In
their explorations the two friars fixed upon the Puerto,
or Portezuelo, de la Concepcion and the Puerto, or
Ranchería, de San Pablo as the most desirable sites
for future missions.   The former, Concepcion, was, as
I have said, identical in site with Fort Yuma, while
the latter, San Pablo, was eight or ten miles down
the river on the same side in what is now Baja Californian territory.[2]   Eixarch went back to Sonora with

[1] See chapters x. and xii. of this volume.
[2] I suppose that San Pablo was identical with the Ranchería or Laguna of
San Pablo, or Capt. Pablo, 4½ or 5 leagues below Concepcion, visited by Anza
and mentioned in his diary and in that of P. Font.   Arricivita gives the distance between the two as three leagues.   Taylor, in *Browne's L. Cal.*, 51, 71,
doubtless following Arricivita, says the two were 9 miles apart.   P. Sales, in
his *Noticias de Cal.*, carta iii. 65–7, says that the Franciscan missions were
on territory conceded to the Dominicans, so that they were even then in a
sense considered to be in Lower California.   The author would seem almost

Anza, and Garcés followed a little later. Palma also accompanied Anza to Mexico to present in person the petition of his people for missionaries. All the returning travellers were impressed with the feasibility and great importance of founding on the Colorado one or more missions under the protection of a strong presidio.[3]

The viceroy favored the views of Garcés and Anza. He promised early in 1777 to transfer northward the presidios of Horcasitas and Buenavista as a protection to the proposed missions, and recommended the whole matter to the favorable consideration of General Croix.[4] Palma in the mean time was kindly entertained; and after being baptized as Don Salvador, he was sent home with promises of friars and other favors to his country and people.[5]

Croix it is said entertained an idea of going in person to the Colorado and to Monterey, but he was detained by illness in Chihuahua and had, besides, a broad territory to attend to. Colonel Anza was about this time sent to New Mexico as governor, and thus the northern enterprise lost one of its most effective supporters. In March 1778 Palma, seeing no sign that the promises made him were to be fulfilled, came down to Altar to ascertain the reason. He was more or less satisfied with the excuses offered by the pre-

to entertain the idea that the Franciscans, in their zeal to get the rewards offered, brought upon themselves the resulting misfortunes by intruding on Dominican ground.

[3] Garcés suggested a route by water by way of the gulf and river, or by the ocean to San Diego. He also recommended that San Diego be subject to the Colorado presidio instead of Monterey, so as to protect communication and prevent conflicts with the California authorities. Thus his views in behalf of his college were somewhat ambitious. Whether they resulted in some degree from his own treatment by Rivera, or whether Rivera's policy was influenced by the views of Garcés, there is no means of knowing.

[4] In 1778 Croix writes to Galvez on the importance of conciliating the Colorado and Gila tribes, and of founding settlements on the route to California. *Ugalde, Documentos*, MS., 5.

[5] *Arricivita, Crónica Seráfica y Apostólica del Colegio de Propaganda Fide de la Santa Cruz de Querétaro*, 491–514. This important work, the official chronicle of the Querétaro College, is the leading authority for the contents of this chapter, in fact the only continuous narrative of the whole subject, though as will be seen there are other authorities that throw much light on certain parts of it.

sidio captain and went back to wait. Still no Spaniards came, and Palma's people began to taunt him,
and to more than hint that all the stories he had
brought from Mexico were lies. Palma endured it
for a while and then went again to Altar and then to
Horcasitas to explain his difficulties.

General Croix, still at Chihuahua, hearing of Palma's
visit and knowing that his complaints were just, wrote
in February 1779 to the president asking him to send
Garcés and another friar to the Colorado to begin the
work of conversion, at the same time ordering the
authorities of Sonora to furnish supplies and soldiers.
Juan Diaz was selected to accompany Garcés. The
governor gave an order for supplies, but the commandant could not furnish a proper guard, for his
force was small and the natives were unusually bitter.
In obedience to orders, however, he told Garcés to
select the smallest number of soldiers that would meet
immediate necessities. The friars realized that in
establishing a distant mission under these circumstances there was danger. But delay was also for
many reasons undesirable, and the early establishment of a presidio was confidently hoped for. Therefore after much discussion, including a reference to the
viceroy and college, the two friars chose seventeen
soldiers from Tucson and Altar, though when they
started in August for their destination they had but
thirteen. After passing Sonoita in the Pápago country, they were forced to turn back for want of water;
but Garcés with two soldiers soon continued and
reached the Colorado at the end of August. He
found Palma and those of his ranchería very friendly,
but other Yumas considerably disaffected, the Jalchedunes and other tribes being also somewhat hostile to
the Yumas.

On September 3d the two soldiers were sent back
with letters for Diaz and for Croix, leaving Garcés alone
with the Yumas. Rumors were rife of hostilities on
the part of the Pápagos, and the soldiers at Sonoita

were disposed to abscond. Father Diaz sent to Altar
for aid, and received from a new commandant a letter
advising the friars to abandon the enterprise for the
present. Diaz declined the advice. He succeeded in
removing the soldiers' fears, and joined Garcés on the
2d of October. The two friars with their guard of
twelve men and a sergeant now found themselves in
an embarrassing position. Promises had been lavishly
bestowed on Palma by the viceroy and by Croix in
Mexico, promises which had not lost color in transmission, and which had roused expectations of lavish gifts.
Long delay had lessened somewhat the native faith in
Palma's tales; but even now the contrast between
expectation and reality was great, and at sight of two
friars bearing trinkets hardly sufficient to buy their
daily food, the natives regarded themselves as victims
of a swindle. Nor did they take pains to conceal their
disgust. The two padres could barely maintain themselves in Palma's ranchería, that chieftain's authority
proving to be limited, and his position being hardly
more agreeable than their own. Entreaties for aid
were sent south, but the soldiers so sent were usually
retained in the Sonora presidios on some excuse, thus
lessening the escort and increasing the danger.

In November Croix arrived at Arizpe, whither
Diaz proceeded to report in person, and Juan Antonio
Barreneche was sent as companion to Garcés. The
general listened to the padre's report, and resolved on
the establishment of two mission-pueblos on the Colorado, in accordance with a new system devised for this
occasion, the formal instructions for which were issued
March 20, 1780. There was to be no presidio, mission,
or pueblo proper, but the attributes of all three were
to be in a manner united. The soldiers, under a sub-
lieutenant as commandant, were to protect the settlers,
who were to be granted house-lots and fields, while
the friars were to act as pastors to attend to the
spiritual interests of the colonists, but at the same
time to be missionaries. The priests were to have

nothing to do with temporal management, and native converts were not to be required to live in regular mission communities, but might receive lands and live in the pueblos with the Spaniards. Each pueblo was to have ten soldiers, ten settlers, and six laborers.

This was certainly a change in the mission system. Palou italicizes it as a *nuevo modo de conquistar*, and passes on without further comment to relate results.[6] Arricivita denounces both the system and its author, charging Croix with having been influenced by *políticos arbitristas* who knew nothing of the subject, and by false notions of economy. And further with having paid no heed to the advice of the only men who were qualified to give it; with giving instructions to the friars in matters entirely beyond his jurisdiction; with direct opposition to the laws of Spain, especially in uniting Spaniards and Indians in the same pueblo, and with having in his stupid pride and ignorance exposed over fifty families to sure destruction. A large part of the bitter feeling exhibited by Franciscans on the subject may be fairly attributed to the tragedy that followed and to the removal of the temporal management from their hands, a matter on which they were very sensitive; yet it must be admitted that Croix acted unwisely. The time and place were not well chosen for such an experiment. Anza, a warm advocate of the Colorado establishments, a man of great ability and experience, and one moreover who had seen the Yumas and their neighbors at their best, had expressed his opinion that missions could not safely be founded in this region except under the protection of a strong presidio. At the time of Anza's return it would have been hazardous to try the experiment, but in the light of the friars' reports it was a criminally stupid blunder.

As soon as he heard of the plan Garcés sent in repeated protests and warnings that the aspect of affairs was worse then ever, but all in vain. The

[6] *Palou, Not.*, ii. 374-88.

colonists reached their new homes in the autumn
of 1780 under the command of Alférez Santiago de
Islas. The pueblo of La Purísima Concepcion was
at once founded, and the adjoining lands were distributed, Garcés and Barreneche being its ministers.
Very soon the second pueblo, San Pedro y San Pablo
de Bicuñer, was established under the care of Diaz

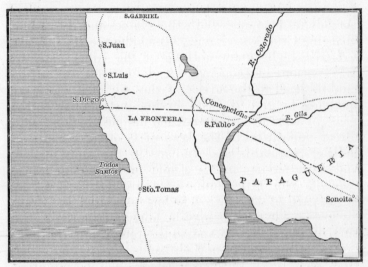

THE COLORADO MISSIONS.

and Matías Moreno. The names of the twenty soldiers and of fourteen settlers have been preserved.[7]

[7] They are as follows, those of persons who escaped from the subsequent
massacre being italicized: P. Francisco Garcés, P. Juan Diaz, Alférez Santiago Islas, Corporal Pascual Rivera, P. Juan Barreneche, P. Matías Moreno,
Sergt. José (or Juan) de la Vega, Corporal Juan Miguel Palomino.

Soldiers: Cayetano Mesa, Gabriel (or Javier) Diaz, Matías de la Vega, José
Ignacio Martinez, Juan Gallardo, Gabriel (or Javier) Romero, Pedro Burques,
José Reyes Pacheco, Juan Martinez, Gabriel (or Javier) Luque, Manuel Duarte,
Bernardo Morales, Ignacio Zamora, Faustino Sallalla, *Pedro Solares*, *Miguel
Antonio Romero*.

Settlers: Manuel Barragan, José Antonio Romero, Juan Ignacio Romero,
José Olgin, Antonio Mendoza, Ignacio Martinez, *Matías de Castro*, Cárlos
Gallego, Juan Romero, José Estévan, Justo Grijalva, Gabriel Tebaca, Nicolás Villalba, *Juan José Miranda, José Ignacio Bengachea*, servant, *José Urrea*,
interpreter. These names come chiefly from the subsequent examination of
survivors recorded in *Prov. St. Pap.*, MS., iii. 319-32. So far as soldiers and
settlers are concerned the list is probably complete. All, or nearly all, had
families.

The coming of the colonists naturally afforded temporary relief to the friars, for a small stock of articles
suitable for gifts brought a brief renewal of Spanish
popularity; but even at the beginning Garcés and his
companions seem to have foreseen disaster, though it
is hard to tell how much was foresight and how much
may be attributed to the despondency of the friars
when their privileges were curtailed. In addition to
the old causes of disaffection among the natives, new
and more serious ones began to work. In the distribution of lands along the river but little attention
was paid to the rights of the aborigines, whose little
milpas, if spared in the formal distribution, were
rendered useless by the live-stock of the Spaniards.
This great wrong, added to the ordinary indifference
of soldiers and settlers to native rights, and their
petty acts of injustice, soon destroyed any slight feeling of friendship previously existing. The friars with
difficulty and by patient kindness retained for a time
a degree of influence even in the midst of adverse influences. They established a kind of missionary station at some distance from the pueblo, where the
natives were occasionally assembled for religious instruction. Some of them were faithful notwithstanding the unpopularity brought upon themselves by
friendship for the friars; but their influence amounted
to nothing against the growing hatred among the
thousands of Yumas and neighboring tribes.

After the provisions brought from Sonora had
been exhausted there was much suffering among the
families, the natives refusing to part with the little
corn in their possession and asking exorbitant prices
for the wild products gathered. In their great
need they sent over to San Gabriel for succor and
were given such articles of food as the mission could
spare.[8] We have no chronological record of events

---

[8] Palou, Not., ii. 375, says that in asking for this aid they declared that if
it were not sent they would have to abandon the Colorado establishments.
Neve reports on June 23, 1781, having sent the succor asked for by Alférez
Islas. Prov. Rec., MS., ii. 85.

during the winter and spring of 1780–1. The settlers
lived along in the lazy improvident way peculiar to
Spaniards of that class, attending chiefly to their live-
stock. Neither they nor the soldiers had any fears
of impending danger, and rarely had either of the
pueblos more than two or three soldiers on duty.
They found time, however, to administer an occasional flogging or confinement in the stocks to offending natives. The friars went on with their duties,
aware that trouble was brewing, and perhaps deriving
a certain grim satisfaction from their prospect of being able to prove by their own death that Croix was
wrong in interfering with missionary prerogative.[9]
Meanwhile a few leading spirits among the Yumas
were inciting their people to active hostilities, with a
view to exterminate the intruders. Palma himself
was among the number, as were one or two of his
brothers and several chieftains who had accompanied
him to Mexico. Francisco Javier, an interpreter, is
also named as having taken a prominent part. Ignacio Palma, Pablo, and Javier were the leaders.
With a view to conciliate the disaffected Alférez Islas
made Ignacio Palma governor of the lower Yumas
about San Pedro y San Pablo, and a little later arrested him and put him in the stocks, thus adding
fuel to the flame of the revolt.

Late in June Rivera y Moncada arrived from
Sonora with his company of about forty recruits and
their families bound for Los Angeles and the Santa
Bárbara channel. From the Colorado he sent back
most of his Sonoran escort, and after a short delay
for rest, despatched the main company to San Gabriel
under the escort of Alférez Limon and nine men.
Having seen the company started on its way, Rivera
recrossed the Colorado and with eleven or twelve men,

[9] According to Arricivita the priests for many days devoted almost their
whole attention to labor among the Spanish population, striving to reawaken
interest in religious exercises and thus to prepare the souls of the unsuspecting
men, women, and children for death. In these efforts they were also said to
have been remarkably successful.

including Sergeant Robles and five or six men sent to meet him from the California presidios, encamped near the eastern bank opposite Concepcion, where he proposed to remain for some weeks to restore his horses and cattle to a proper condition for the trip to San Gabriel. Rivera's coming contributed nothing to the pacification of the natives, but had rather the contrary effect, for his large herd of live-stock destroyed the mesquite plants, and he was by no means liberal in the distribution of gifts.[10] From his choice of a location for his camp it is clear that he attached no importance to the friars' apprehensions.

Early in July the natives became somewhat more insolent in their actions, often visiting the towns in a quarrelsome mood. On Tuesday, July 17th, the storm burst.[11] Early in the morning the lower village of San Pedro y San Pablo was attacked by the savages, who, meeting no resistance, killed the two priests, Diaz and Moreno, besides Sergeant Vega, and most of the soldiers and settlers. Only five men, including two Indians more or less in sympathy with the savages, are known to have survived. These were made captive as were all the women. After the Indians had taken everything they desired they burned the buildings and destroyed all other property. The bodies of the victims were left to lie where they fell, except those of the friars, which, as there is some reason to believe, were buried.[12]

[10] Neve in a letter to Croix of Nov. 18, 1781, says that the Jalchedunes sent word to Rivera that as no gifts were made, they did not wish to retain the badges of office formerly given their chiefs by Spaniards. *Prov. Rec.*, MS., ii. 69.

[11] Arricivita, followed by other writers, erroneously states that it was on Sunday. The surviving witnesses testified that it was Tuesday, and the 17th was certainly Tuesday.

[12] Arricivita, 529–54, gives some details respecting the lives of the missionaries. Juan Marcelo was born in 1736 in the city of Alajar, Spain, taking the name of Diaz when he became a Franciscan. He came to Mexico in 1763; in 1768 became minister of Caborca mission in Pimería Alta; and accompanied Anza as we have seen on his first expedition to California. José Matías Moreno was born in 1744 at Almarza, Spain; became a Franciscan in 1762; and came to Mexico in 1769. His first missionary service, save as supernumerary, was at the place of his death. Francisco Tomás Hermenegildo Garcés was born in 1738 in Morata del Conde, Aragon; came to the Querétaro

On the same day and at about the same hour when Father Garcés was saying mass,[13] the town of Concepcion was invaded and the commandant, Islas, and a corporal, the only soldiers there at the time, were killed, as were indeed most of the unarmed men scattered in the adjoining fields. Some of the houses were sacked, but the friars were spared, and a part of the men were not found, the ravages being suspended about noon. Next morning the savages attacked the camp across the river. Rivera had hastily thrown up some slight intrenchments and his men made a gallant defence, but the numbers against them were too great. One by one the soldiers fell under the arrows and clubs of the foe until not one was left.[14] Thus died Captain Fernando Javier de Rivera y Moncada, one of the most prominent characters in early Californian annals, who had come in the first land expedition of 1769, had been military commandant of the Monterey establishments, and who at the time of his death was lieutenant-governor of Baja California. All that is known of his life and character has been recorded in the preceding chapters. He was not the equal, in ability and force, of such men as Fages and Neve, but he was popular and left among the old Californian soldiers a better reputation probably than any of his contemporaries.[15]

College in 1763; and became minister of San Javier del Bac in 1768. He travelled extensively among the gentile tribes, from his first coming to Sonora down to the time of his death. Juan Antonio Barreneche was born in Lacazor, Navarre, in 1749, and came when a child to Habana. He became a Franciscan in 1768; joined the Querétaro College in 1773. His first missionary work was in the Colorado pueblos where he died at the early age of 32 years. The author in connection with these facts repeats much of the history told in this chapter, and adds many details of the lives and Christian virtues of these four martyrs for which I have no space.

[13] It is not impossible that Arricivita draws on his imagination for details about the religious services, supposing the day to have been Sunday.

[14] In *Prov. St. Pap., Ben. Mil.*, MS., iii. 19, 22, are *revistas* of 1782 showing the following soldiers of the San Diego and Monterey company who had died besides Sergt. Robles: Manuel Cañedo, Tomás María Camacho, Rafael Marquez, Joaquin Guerrero, José M. Guerrero, Nicolás Beltran, Juan Angel Amarillas, Francisco Peña, Joaquin Lopez, Joaquin Espinosa, Antonio Espinosa, and Pablo Victoriano Cervantes. These 12 names doubtless include the Colorado victims.

[15] Father Consag—*Zevallos, Vida de Konsag*, 14—writing in 1753 of his third expedition says of Rivera: 'No perdonó ningun trabajo personal de

The natives returned to Concepcion the same afternoon. The priests on their approach escaped with the families and took refuge with some of their convert friends. The buildings were sacked and burned as at the lower village, and next day the two priests were killed notwithstanding the efforts made by certain Indians in their behalf. Only two men are known to have saved their lives at Concepcion, and the whole number of the slain at the two pueblos and Rivera's camp was at least forty-six, probably more. We hear of no killing of women and children. The captives were made to work, but no further outrage is recorded.[16]

Alférez Limon after escorting the California colony to San Gabriel started back for Sonora by the old route with his nine men. Drawing near the Colorado he was informed by the natives that there had been a

modo que al Padre ya le faltaban palabras y trazas paraque se ciñese á trabajos proporcionados á su carácter.' His wife was Teresa de Dávalos. A son, Juan Bautista Francisco María, was baptized Oct. 5, 1756, by Father Bischoff at Loreto; another son, José Nicolás María, May 8, 1758, by Father Ventura; and still another March 9, 1767. *Loreto, Libro de Mision*, MS., 174, 177, 195. Alvarado, *Hist. Cal.*, MS., ii. 106–7, says that his memory was long honored by anniversary funeral masses at San Diego, and that Gov. Echeandía in 1825 proposed a monument in his honor.

[16] The information that the hostilities lasted three days comes from Arricivita. Most other authorites state or imply that the bloody work was begun and ended on July 17th; but Croix in a note dated July 17, 1782, and in correction of a report from Neve that Rivera died on July 1st, states that it was on July 18th, thus sustaining Arricivita. *Prov. St. Pap., Ben. Mil.*, MS., iii. 10. Neve in a letter to Croix of March 10, 1782, *Prov. Rec.*, MS., ii. 76–8, says that the savages attacked the two villages and Rivera's camp simultaneously and by 8 o'clock had completed their work at the former; that they found Rivera's men scattered and at first entered the encampment as friends, attacking before the soldiers could be gathered, and killing the last man at night after fighting all day. In another letter of Sept. 1st, *Id.*, 88–9, Neve mentions a report brought by Limon that Corporal Pascual Bailon (this Bailon is mentioned by others, but I suspect that he and Pascual Rivera are the same person), with 9 soldiers, one settler, and a muleteer, was killed while bringing supplies from Sonora. Sales, *Noticias, Carta* iii. 65–7, tells us the assailants were 20,000 in number. Velasco, *Son.*, 151; *Soc. Mex. Geog., Boletin*, x. 704, gives the number of killed as 53. Taylor in *Browne's L. Cal.*, 71, says the massacre took place in the fall of 1782. Bartlett, *Pers. Nar.*, ii. 183–4, tells us that a mission established by P. Kino at the mouth of the Gila was in existence as late as 1776! also that Garcés established a mission among the Moquis which was soon destroyed! See further for brief mention of the subject, *Mofras, Explor*, i. 284–6; *Revilla-Gigedo, Informe de 12 de Abril 1793*, 122; *Escudero, Not., Chih.*, 229; *Gleeson's Hist. Cath. Ch.*, ii. 87–93; *Taylor*, in *Cal. Farmer*, March 7, 1862; *Shea's Cath. Miss.*, 101–2.

massacre; but, doubting the report, he left two men in charge of his animals and went forward to reconnoitre. The blackened ruins at Concepcion and the dead bodies lying in the plaza told all. His own party was attacked the 21st of August and driven back by the Yumas, one of whom wore the uniform of the dead Rivera. Limon and his son were wounded, the two men left behind had been killed, and the survivors hastened back to San Gabriel with news of the disaster. Governor Neve sent Limon and his party to Sonora by way of Loreto with a report to General Croix dated September 1st.[17]

Meanwhile the news was carried by the Pimas of the Gila to Tucson, and by one of the captives who managed to escape to Altar, and thus reached the ears of Croix in August.[18] On the 26th of that month Croix wrote to Neve of the reports that had reached him, warning him to take precautions. The 9th of September a council of war was held at Arizpe, and decided that as the Yumas after urging the establishment of missions had risen without cause, they must according to the laws be proceeded against as apostates and rebels. A sufficient force must be sent to the Colorado to investigate, ransom, and punish, and peace be made on condition that the natives voluntarily submit, and deliver the captives and their property; the ringleaders should then be put to death on the spot. If they would do this, well; if not, war should follow, and the neighboring tribes might be employed against the foe. The commander of the expedition must report to Neve on arrival at the Colorado.[19] In accordance with this resolution the

[17] *Prov. Rec.*, MS., ii., 88-9; *Prov. St. Pap., Ben. Mil.*, MS., ii. 23; *Palou, Vida*, 242. Palou, *Not.*, ii. 377, says that Limon wanted to take 20 men and go to chastise the Yumas, but Neve did not approve the plan. The author is inclined, apparently unjustly, to blame the governor for his inaction. This Limon was a soldier at Altar in 1760, when his daughter was baptized by Padre Pfefferkorn. *S. Francisco del Ati, Lib. Mision*, MS.

[18] Arricivita, page 509, says that at first the report was not believed and that a soldier sent up to the Colorado to learn the truth was killed.

[19] *St. Pap. Sac.*, MS., vi. 123-33.

general despatched a force to the Colorado under the command of our old friend Pedro Fages, about whose life since he sailed from San Diego in 1774 we know little beyond the fact that he left California a captain and now returns a lieutenant-colonel. He was accompanied by Captain Fueros of the Altar presidio.[20]

Fages and Fueros marched with a hundred soldiers of their respective companies and many friendly natives to the Colorado, and forded the river to the ruined villages. They buried the bodies of the victims which were found lying as they fell in the plaza and in the fields. . The Yumas had abandoned the vicinity, but were found some eight leagues down the river in a densely wooded tract where it was deemed unadvisable to attack them. All or nearly all of the captives, however, were ransomed,[21] and both they and the natives stated that the latter had been frightened away by a procession of white-robed figures that with crosses and lighted candles had marched through the ruins chanting strange dirges each night after the massacre. With the rescued captives Fages retraced his steps to Sonoita, where he arrived late in October.

Here were found orders from the general, given at the petition of the father president, to recover and bring back the bodies of the slain friars. These orders had been intended to reach Fages earlier and not to necessitate another journey; but as he had made no special search for the bodies, he deemed it best to return.[22] Before setting out he held an exam-

[20] In a record of certain California documents existing in Mexico in 1795, *Prov. St. Pap.*, MS., xiii. 205–6, is mentioned the original account of the expedition. *Diario del viaje de tierra hecho al Rio Colorado de órden del Comandante General, El Caballero de Croix, al mando del Teniente Coronel D. Pedro Fages*, etc., dated at Altar Sept. 16, 1781 (it should probably be Sonoita Dec. 20th), a document I have been unable to find.

[21] Palou, *Vida*, 247–54, who saw the original narrative, seems to be the authority for the finding of the Yumas down the river. He is quoted by Arricivita, who, however, implies erroneously that the captives were ransomed on a subsequent visit.

[22] Arricivita is the only authority who directly mentions this second expe-

ination at Sonoita October 31st and took the testimony of six men who had survived the massacre, material which I have already utilized in describing that event.[23] At San Pedro y San Pablo on December 7th the bodies of Diaz and Moreno were discovered in a good state of preservation, though the head of Moreno had been cut off. At Concepcion the remains of Garcés and Barreneche could not be found at first and some hope was felt that they had not been killed; but in continuing their search at a distance the soldiers finally saw a bright green spot in the desert, and there, marked by a cross, under a bed of verdure and flowers, they found the grave where the two martyrs had been buried by some of their converts. Respecting this miraculous verdure, the supernatural procession at the ruined pueblos, and the utter blamelessness of the friars before and during the disaster, properly attested certificates were drawn up and forwarded to the Santa Cruz College in Querétaro by Croix at the request of the Franciscans. The remains of the four martyrs were carried south and buried in one coffin in the church at Tubutama.

On September 10th Croix had forwarded to Neve the resolutions of the council of the day before, to the end that he, as the proper official to direct all military operations in California, might on hearing of Fages' arrival at the Colorado send orders or go in person to take command. Neve did prepare a force, composed chiefly of the men waiting to found Santa Bárbara, which he held in readiness; and he seems also to have sent Alférez Velasquez with a small party to make inquiries about Fages' coming. But Velasquez brought back nothing but an unintelligible rumor from the natives about some white and black

dition; but his statement is partially corroborated by certain circumstantial evidence in official communications in the archives.

[23] *Investigacion sobre la muerte de los religiosos, etc.*, *enviados á la reduccion de los gentiles del Colorado*, 1781, MS. One of the witnesses was an Indian interpreter named Urrea, whom Arricivita names as a traitor to whom the murder of the padres was largely due.

horsemen who had come four moons ago to burn
and kill.[24]   Fages' diary of his expedition was dated
Sonoita, the 20th of December.

Another council had been held at Arizpe the 15th
of November, on receipt of news respecting the first
return of the expedition to Sonoita. Fages' report of
October 31st was read, announcing his intention to
return to the Colorado on the arrival of certain pack-
mules with supplies. His action in ransoming the
captives and sending them to Altar was approved, and
he was instructed to march without delay to attack
the Yumas. He was to announce his arrival to Neve,
and if his first attack on the foe were not decisively
successful in securing the death of the Yuma leaders
and establishing a permanent peace, the command was
to be transferred to Neve, and military operations
were to be continued. After the enemy was fully
conquered the governor must select a proper site for
a presidio on the Colorado, which would afford adequate protection to future settlements, and report
in full as to the number of men and other help required. Government aid was to be furnished to the
families who had survived the massacre.[25]

These resolutions of the council not having been
received by Fages until he had returned from his
second trip, or at least until it was too late to carry
them into execution, the same body met again January 2, 1782, and modified somewhat its past action.
Fages was to press on as rapidly as possible with
forty men to San Gabriel, where he would receive
instructions and aid from Neve. Meanwhile Fueros
with a sufficient force was to arrive on the Colorado
by April 1st at the latest and there to await orders
from Neve, holding himself meanwhile strictly on the
defensive unless some particularly good opportunity

[24] Croix to Neve, Sept. 10, 1781, in *St. Pap.*, *Sac.*, MS., vi. 120-2; Neve to
Croix, Nov. 18, 1781, and Mar. 10, 1782, in *Prov. Rec.*, MS., ii. 68, 77-8.
[25] *Prov. St. Pap.*, *Sac.*, MS., iv. 21-8; duplicate in *Id.*, xv. 5-10. Neve
acknowledged the receipt of the documents of Nov. 15th, on March 2, 1782,
also that of the subsequent orders of Jan. 2d. *Prov. Rec.*, MS., ii. 56.

should offer of striking a decisive blow. The governor was instructed to take all the available troops in California, suspending the Channel foundations temporarily for the purpose, and to begin the campaign by the 1st of April.[26]

Fages seems to have arrived at San Gabriel late in March and a messenger soon brought Neve back from the Channel, where he had gone to superintend the new foundations.[27] Receiving the despatches brought by Fages the governor decided that it was too early in the season for effective operations on the Colorado, by reason of high water, and postponed the campaign until September, when the river would be fordable, and when the Yuma harvest would be desirable spoils for native allies. Fages was sent to the Colorado to give the corresponding instructions to Fueros, who was to proceed to Sonora and wait, while Fages returned to wait in California. Croix seems to have approved the change of plan, and on May 16th the council met once more at Arizpe to issue thirteen resolutions respecting the fall campaign, the substance of which was that about one hundred and sixty men were to be on the east bank of the Colorado on the morning of September 15th to meet the Californian troops and show the rebellious Yumas the power of Spanish arms.[28]

The resolutions were to a certain extent carried into effect, but about the result there is little to be said.

[26] *Prov. St. Pap.*, MS., iii. 236–9. Croix communicated the plan to Neve Jan. 3d and Jan. 6th. *Id.*, 236, 182–3. Neve acknowledged receipt March 2d. *Prov. Rec.*, MS., ii. 57. March 18th Croix announces that Fages is on the march. *Prov. St. Pap.*, MS., iii. 185. April 30th Neve wrote to Croix that Fages had arrived at San Gabriel and that the Yumas had left their own country and retired to that of the Yamajabs. *Id.*, 233. And still earlier on March 29th he had written in answer to Croix's letters of January, announcing a postponement of the campaign until September. *Id.*, 198; *Prov. Rec.*, MS., ii. 53.

[27] Palou, *Not.*, ii. 383, says that the messenger overtook Neve March 26th, the same day he had left San Gabriel to found San Buenaventura.

[28] *Prov. St. Pap.*, MS., iii. 198–207, including a letter of Croix of May 18th, communicating to Neve the junta's action, and another letter announcing the sending of 200 horses and 40 mules to mount the Californian troops.

Captain José Antonio Romeu [29] with a force of one hundred and eight men reached the seat of proposed war at the specified time.   Neve, having intrusted his adjutant inspector, Nicolás Soler, with the temporary government of California, departed from San Gabriel August 21st, [30] with Fages and sixty men.   Some three days' journey before reaching Concepcion a messenger met the party with despatches for Fages which caused him to return and assume the governorship of California, [31] while Neve proceeded and joined Romeu on the 16th, not returning to San Gabriel, but going to Sonora after the campaign to assume his new office of inspector general of the Provincias Internas. About the campaign we know little save that it was a failure, since the Yumas were not subdued, peace was not made, and the rebel chiefs Palma and the rest were not captured.   Yet there was some fighting in which a few Yumas were killed. [32]   The nation remained independent of all Spanish control, and was always more or less hostile.   Neither presidio, mission,

[29] Romeu, afterwards governor of California, had been with Fueros on the Colorado earlier in the year, and had written a diary of that expedition, which by resolution of the junta was sent to Neve for his instruction.

[30] Neve's instructions to Soler, July 12, 1782. *Prov. St. Pap.*, MS., iii. 120. Neve to Croix, Aug. 3, 1782, receipt of letter announcing approval by the junta of the suspension of Yuma campaign. *Prov. Rec.*, MS., ii. 65–6.   Neve to Croix, Aug. 12, 1782, announcing march of troops on Aug. 21st, and his own departure on Aug. 25th or 26th. *Id.*, 47.

[31] *Palou, Not.*, ii. 390–2.   More of this change of governors in a later chapter.

[32] In *Prov. St. Pap.*, MS., xiii. 205–6, there is mentioned as existing in Mexico in 1795 a *Diario de las marchas y ocurrencias...desde 21 de Agosto 1782*, which my search of the archives has not brought to light.   A short letter of Neve to Croix dated Sonoita Oct. 16th—*Prov. Rec.*, MS., ii. 53—is the only original account extant.   He says he sent an alférez with 8 men to reconnoitre, heard firing, and hurried up to support the alférez, but the enemy fled. Then Romeu attacked a Yuma ranchería and inflicted some loss, having 4 soldiers wounded.   He vaguely states that he should have subdued the Yumas and left communication by that route secure, had it not been for distrust caused partly by the imprudent actions of preceding expeditions.   Arricivita, *Crón. Seráf*, 514, says 108 natives were killed, 85 taken prisoners, 10 Christians freed from captivity, and 1,048 horses recovered, but all without pacifying the foe.   Palou states that after receiving his appointment as inspector, Neve did not care to march against the Yumas.   The enemy, however, came out boldly to taunt and challenge the Spaniards until one of the Sonora captains (Romeu) could endure it no longer, and obtained Neve's permission to punish the Yuma insolence, which he did in three days' fighting in which many natives fell.

nor pueblo was ever again established on the Colorado; and communication by this route never ceased to be attended with danger. Truly, as the Franciscan chroniclers do not fail to point out, the old way was best; the innovations of Croix had led to nothing but disaster; the *nuevo modo de conquistar* was a failure.

CHAPTER XVIII.

FOUNDING OF SAN BUENAVENTURA AND SANTA BÁRBARA PRESIDIO—FAGES GOVERNOR.

1782.

READY TO BEGIN—MISSIONARIES EXPECTED—NEVE'S INSTRUCTIONS TO OR-
TEGA—PRECAUTIONS AGAINST DISASTER—INDIAN POLICY—RADICAL
CHANGES IN MISSION SYSTEM—SAN BUENAVENTURA ESTABLISHED—PRE-
SIDIO OF SANTA BÁRBARA—VISIT OF FAGES—ARRIVAL OF THE TRANS-
PORTS—NEWS FROM MEXICO—NO MISSION SUPPLIES—NO PRIESTS—
VICEROY AND GUARDIAN—SIX FRIARS REFUSE TO SERVE—CONTROL OF
TEMPORALITIES—FALSE CHARGES AGAINST NEVE—CHANGES IN MISSION-
ARIES—FAGES APPOINTED GOVERNOR—NEVE INSPECTOR GENERAL—IN-
STRUCTIONS—FUGITIVE NEOPHYTES—LOCAL EVENTS—DEATH OF MARI-
ANO CARRILLO—DEATH OF JUAN CRESPÍ.

THE new establishments of the Channel, of which
so much has been said, were not yet founded. The
required force had arrived late in the summer of 1781,
but it was deemed best to delay until the rainy season
had passed, and moreover the disaster on the Colorado
had resulted in orders to suspend all operations and
settlements that might interfere with measures against
the Yumas. The forces had therefore remained in
camp at San Gabriel, where some slight barracks had
been erected for their accommodation,[1] under Ortega
who had been chosen to command the new presidio,
Lieutenant Zúñiga taking his old command at San
Diego.

[1] Oct. 29, 1781, Neve writes to Croix that he has taken a corporal and 7
men from Monterey and the same number from San Diego to form a basis for
the Santa Bárbara company, and also that he has built 40 small huts to shelter
the men and their families during the rainy season. *Prov. Rec.*, MS., ii. 89,
91. Reviews during the winter show a lieutenant, Ortega, an alférez, Argüello, 3 sergeants, 2 corporals, and 49 or 50 soldiers. *Prov. St. Pap.*, MS., iii.
261, 264; *St. Pap., Miss. and Colon.*, MS., i. 104.

In the spring of 1782 it seemed to the governor that he might proceed in the matter without prejudice to other interests, and accordingly in February he wrote to President Serra, announcing his intention and asking for two friars, for San Buenaventura and Santa Bárbara respectively. Serra had but two supernumerary friars in all California, one of whom was needed at San Cárlos during his own occasional absence. But he was extremely desirous that the new missions should be established, and he expected six new friars by this year's transport; so he went south himself, administering confirmation en route at San Antonio and San Luis, reaching Angeles on March 18th, and San Gabriel the next day. Here he he met Father Cambon, who at his order had come up from San Diego, and the two agreed to attend to the spiritual needs of the two new establishments till the coming of the six missionary recruits.[2]

Meanwhile on March 6th Governor Neve had issued his instructions to Ortega, indicating the line of policy to be followed at the new presidio and the missions under its protection and jurisdiction.[3] Like all the productions of Neve's mind these instructions were models of good sense in substance, though diffuse as usual. The first duty urged was that of vigilance and precaution. Late events on the Colorado would have suggested extraordinary vigilance anywhere; but the comparatively dense native population in the Channel country rendered it especially necessary there. The erection of defensive works must be the commandant's first care, and beyond a few temporary shelters of brushwood for the families, and a warehouse for the supplies, no structures could be built

[2] *Palou, Not.*, ii. 380–9; *Id.*, *Vida*, 243–7. February 8, 1782, Minister Galvez communicated to Croix, who forwarded it on July 24th, the royal order approving Neve's acts and propositions respecting the three new foundations as made known to him in letter and documents of February 23, 1780. *St. Pap. Sac.*, MS., iv. 30–1.

[3] *Neve, Instruccion que ha de gobernar al Comandante del presidio de Santa Bárbara*, 1782, MS. This document was examined by Fages at Santa Bárbara on October 1st, and Ortega was ordered anew by him to obey its requirements.

until the square was safely enclosed by a line of
earthworks and palisades.   The natives were not to
be allowed within the lines except in small numbers
and unarmed.   The utmost efforts were to be made
to win and retain the respect and friendship of the
native chiefs, and to this end a policy of kindness and
strict justice must be observed.   Soldiers must be
restrained by the strictest discipline from all outrage,
oppression, or even intermeddling.   They were not
to visit the rancherías under severe penalties, such
as fifteen consecutive days of guard duty wearing four
cueras, unless sent with definite orders to escort a
friar or on other necessary duty.

The natives were to be interfered with in their
ranchería life and government as little as was possible.   They were to be civilized by example and precept and thus gradually led to become vassals of the
king; but they were not to be christianized by force.
Any outrages they might commit must be punished
firmly by imprisonment and flogging with full explanation to the chiefs; but to remove the strongest
temptation to Indian nature, the soldiers could at
the beginning own no cattle.   Trade with the natives was to be encouraged by fair treatment and fair
prices.   In a word they were to be treated as human
beings having rights to be respected.   In that part
of Neve's instructions relating to the friars and the
missions, however, there appeared a palpable trace of
the policy inaugurated by Croix on the Colorado,
with the most dangerous features omitted.   In fact
I am inclined to think that the Colorado experiment,
so far as it affected the relations between padres and
the temporalities, was largely inspired by Neve, an
intimate friend, whose advice had great weight with
the general.   In the Channel missions the priests
were to be virtually deprived of the temporal management, because there were to be no temporal interests to manage.   They were to attend exclusively to
the instruction and conversion of the natives, and to

this end were to be afforded every facility by the military; but the natives must not be taken from their rancherías or required to live in mission communities, except a few at a time, who might be persuaded to live temporarily with the missionaries for instruction.

The reasons given for these regulations were the small area of tillable land in proportion to the number of inhabitants, rendering agricultural mission communities impracticable, and the great danger that would be incurred by any attempt to break up or rearrange the numerous and densely populated native towns or rancherías along the Channel. Without doubt also another motive, quite as powerful, was a desire on the part of the governor to put a curb on missionary authority. The new system which it was now proposed to introduce was a good one in many respects, and was at least worth a trial; but it was nevertheless a complete overthrow of the old mission system in one of its most important features, and the wonder is that it did not provoke a general and immediate outburst of Franciscan indignation throughout the whole province. No such demonstration, however, is recorded, though much was written on the subject later. It is probable that the friars, attributing the proposed innovations to the local authorities, strong in the result of recent experiments on the Colorado, and believing they could interpose such obstacles as would prevent any very brilliant success of the new experiment, determined that quiet and prolonged effort would be more effective than open denunciation, trusting to their influence in Mexico and Spain to restore the old state of affairs. Their practical success was rapid and not very difficult, as we shall see.[4]

All being ready the company[5] set out from San

[4] There are three copies of these instructions, in one of which they are preceded by some preliminary remarks of a general nature respecting past intercourse with the Channel tribes, their intertribal quarrels which will favor the Spanish settlement, and the general policy to be followed.

[5] Palou, *Vida*, 245, says it was the largest expedition ever seen in Cali-

Gabriel the 26th of March. At the first encampment Fages' courier arrived with orders for Neve, who was obliged to return with his escort; but the company continued and arrived on the 29th at the first ranchería of the channel, named Asuncion, or Asumpta, by Portolá's party in 1769. This had long ago been selected as a suitable locality for one of the three missions. A site was chosen near the beach and adjoining the native town with its neat conical huts of tule and straw, and here next day a cross was raised with the required shelter of boughs for the altar. With the usual ceremonies, including a sermon from Serra, on the 31st of March the mission was founded and dedicated to the 'seraphic doctor' San Buenaventura,[6] in the presence of a large attendance both of Spaniards and of natives, the latter expressing much pleasure at what had been done, and cheerfully aiding in the work of building.

About the middle of April Neve came up from San Gabriel and expressed his satisfaction with the progress made.[7] Cambon remained in charge of the new mission until the coming of Dumetz and Santa María, assigned to San Buenaventura as regular

fornia, including besides officers 70 soldiers with their families, to say nothing of Neve's escort of 10 men from Monterey. The 70 should however include the 10.

[6] *San Buenaventura, Lib. de Mision*, MS. On the day of foundation Serra writes to Lasuen expressing his joy at witnessing the foundation. *Arch. Sta. Bárbara*, MS., ix. 288. Gen. Croix congratulates Serra in letter of July 22, 1782. *Id.*, i. 261–2. April 24th, Neve writes to Croix that by April 12th the enclosure of 40 by 50 varas, of palisades 4 varas high with two ravelins, a gate, and a small warehouse had been completed. Facilities were good for irrigation and for obtaining building material. *Prov. Rec.*, MS., ii. 61. Giovanni di Fidanza was born at Bagnarea in Tuscany in 1221. St Francis of Assisi, meeting him one day and foreseeing his future greatness, exclaimed 'O buona ventura!' and the name, Buenaventura in Spanish, clung to him. He became bishop, minister-general of the Franciscan order, and cardinal. His title of seraphic doctor was founded on his skill in mystic theology, to which a large part of his numerous writings was devoted. He died in 1274. His day is July 14th.

[7] Palou, *Vida*, 254–5, says that the mission had been established on the old footing though Neve had entertained the idea and had been instructed, as it afterward proved, to found it on the Colorado plan; but late events had changed his mind and he made no objection. This sounds somewhat strange, in connection with the instructions already noted. Possibly the nature of the instructions was not made public at first, and this accounts for the quiet of the priests.

ministers in May. Only two adults received the
rite of baptism in 1782.[8]

About the middle of April the governor, president,
commandant, and the whole company of soldiers,
except a sergeant and fourteen men left as a guard
for the mission just founded, started up the coast to
establish the presidio of Santa Bárbara. The site
chosen was on the shore of a small bay affording tolerably secure anchorage, at a place said to have been
called San Joaquin de la Laguna in the first expedition of 1769,[9] and near a large native town, which,
like its *temi*, or chief, was called Yanonalit. Near
the lagoon were found springs of a peculiar water,
and an eminence suitable for the fort. The formal
establishing was on April 21st, when Serra said mass
and chanted an *alabado*. The natives were more
friendly than had been anticipated, and Yanonalit was
willing to exchange presents. Work was at once
begun and oak timber felled for the requisite shelters,
and particularly for the palisade enclosure, sixty varas
square, which was later to be replaced by a solid wall
enclosing an area of eighty yards square.[10] The natives
were hired to work and were paid in articles of food
and clothing. Yanonalit had authority over some
thirteen rancherías, and his friendship proved a great
advantage.

Affairs progressed favorably, and Ortega even
found time to construct irrigation works and prepare for farming on a small scale. Serra, on ascertaining that there was no immediate prospect of
founding another mission, wrote to Fuster at San
Juan Capistrano to come up for temporary service at

[8] In December 1782 a Frenchman, Pierre Roy, was a *sirviente* at the mission. *S. Buenaventura, Lib. Mision*, MS., 2.

[9] The original diary gave no such name. See chap. vi. of this volume.
But the place was called Pueblo de la Laguna and Concepcion Laguna.

[10] On foundation of Santa Bárbara presidio see letter of Neve to Croix
April 24, 1782, in *Prov. Rec.*, MS., ii. 61-2, 64; Serra, April 29, 1782, in
Arch. Santa Bárbara, MS., ix. 293-4; baptismal book of presidio in *Id.*,
vii. 32-3; Croix to Neve, July 22, 1782, approving foundation, in *Prov. St.
Pap.*, MS., iii. 232-3; *Id.*, iii. 128-9; iv. 38; vi. 172-3; Neve to Fages August
25, 1783, in *St. Pap., Sac.*, MS., xv. 18.

Santa Bárbara,[11] and himself returned to Monterey. During the months of May and June Lieutenant-colonel Fages made a tour of unofficial inspection from San Diego to San Francisco, including in his route the new presidio of Santa Bárbara.[12]

Just before Serra reached Monterey from the south, May 13th, the transports *Favorita* and *Princesa,* under captains Echeverría and Martinez,[13] brought full cargoes of supplies for the three presidios and also for the old missions, together with Cambon's gift for San Francisco, purchased in China, as already related, with his earnings as chaplain on the *San Cárlos.* There also came by these vessels many items interesting to the friars, with other unrecorded news doubtless of equal interest to other Californians. There came the report that Antonio Reyes of the Querétaro college had been made bishop of Sonora and California; that Rafael Verger, the ex-guardian of San Fernando, had been also made a bishop in Spain;[14] and that it was again proposed to divide the Franciscan missions into four independent *custodias,* a measure that was never carried out.[15]

What the transports of 1782 did not bring, greatly

[11] *Palou, Vida,* 255–6. The same author says, *Not.,* ii. 388–9, that Cambon was to come to the presidio while Fuster was to take his place at San Buenaventura. It is not certain that Fuster ever came.

[12] *Palou, Noticias,* ii. 390–1.

[13] The officers of the *Favorita* were Agustin de Echeverría, captain; José Tobar, second; and José Villaverde, a clergyman, as chaplain. Those of the *Princesa* were Estévan Martinez, captain; Juan Pantoja, second; and Miguel Dávalos, also a *clérigo,* as chaplain. Both vessels had left San Blas the same day, and, though they anchored the same day at Monterey, had not seen each other after the first few days of the trip. *Palou, Not.,* ii. 386–9. The two vessels were at Sta. Bárbara Aug. 4. *Prov. St. Pap., Ben. Mil.,* MS., iii. 17.

[14] Verger was bishop of Nuevo Leon in 1785–7. Letters in *Pinart, Col. Doc. Mex.,* MS., 153–5.

[15] Bishop Reyes was consecrated at Tacubaya on Sept. 15, 1782. He remained for some time at the two colleges, where there was much discussion about his future plans and considerable opposition on the part of the colleges to giving up the missions to *custodios.* The bishop finally proceeded north to establish the *custodia* of San Cárlos de Sonora, and proposed later to go over and establish that of San Gabriel de California. In connection with this movement the Dominicans were to give up Lower California. Such was the news that came to California in June 1783. *Palou, Not.,* ii. 394–5. Bishop Reyes was vicar general of the Californian troops. *Prov. Rec.,* MS., iii. 183; *Prov. St. Pap.,* MS., iv. 121.

to the surprise of all, was the six expected friars, and supplies for the missions of Santa Bárbara and Purísima. The reason of their non-arrival came, however, and that carries us back to an interesting dispute and correspondence in Mexico. Viceroy Mayorga at the request of General Croix, December 7, 1780, called on the college of San Fernando for six friars to serve in the three Channel missions about to be established. Four of the number should be sent to San Blas to go by sea, while two should proceed to Sonora to accompany Rivera by the Colorado River route. The viceroy announced his readiness to furnish such aid as might be required.

The guardian, Francisco Pangua, replied December 18th by stating that the aid required for the new missions was the same as that furnished the old ones, that is, a full complement of church vestments and utensils including bells; a proper supply of live-stock and seed grain; an outfit of implements for house, shop, and field; and one thousand dollars to be expended in clothes and various articles useful in attracting the good-will of the natives. A full list of the articles needed was annexed. A year's stipend must be paid in advance. The friars could not walk eight hundred leagues, nor were they accustomed to ride on horseback, and the viceroy was entreated to permit that all might go by sea. It was also suggested that if there was any doubt about the transports of 1782 being able to carry supplies for all the new establishments, it would be better to attend to the wants of the old missions and let the establishing of new ones be postponed. After these preliminaries the guardian named six friars selected for duty in California,[16] who would be ready to sail from San Blas with the supplies asked for and expected.

Mayorga's reply was dated April 5th, and in it he

[16] The friars were Antonio Aznar, Diego Noboa, Juan Rioboo, Manuel Arévalo, Mateo Beavide, and José Esteves. Only the second and third ever came to California.

declines to furnish either church paraphernalia or the
implements of house and field as requested; the former
because they had already been ordered as a matter of
course for the new missions by General Croix, who alone
had control of the matter; the latter because neither
general nor governor, though well acquainted with
the country, had indicated that any such implements
were needed. If after the friars have begun work
they find that the necessity exists, they can report,
and the subject will receive due attention. The viceroy not only consents to an advance of stipends, but
authorizes the payment of two hundred dollars to each
friar for travelling expenses. He urges the guardian
to act with the least possible delay. The Franciscan
authorities now saw clearly what they had previously
more than suspected, that an attempt was to be made
in California to overthrow the old mission system.
No implements of house and field signified no agricultural and mechanical industries, no communities of
laboring neophytes, no temporalities for the friars to
control. Pangua notified the viceroy on April 7th
that, while the right to the implements in question
was not relinquished but would be pressed at a future
time, he would despatch the missionaries on the terms
proposed. This signified nothing, however, for the
guardian was not inclined to take ventures; and two
days later he sent to Mayorga a communication from
the six friars, in which they flatly refused to serve in
California on the proposed basis, Pangua expressing
his opinion that no others could be induced to go in
their place, but promising to write more fully after
easter.

The promised communication was dated the 19th
of April. In it the writer, after calling attention to
the fact that under the laws no friar could be compelled to serve as a missionary against his will, proceeds to justify the refusal of the six. The argument
is that only by gifts can the missionaries gain the
good-will of the savages as shown by experience; that

the only way to the native heart is through the native stomach and pride of personal adornment; that not only are laborious habits essential to civilization, but such habits can be formed only under the friar's influence based on their having the exclusive right to distribute the fruits of neophyte labor; and that while at best the work of conversion is difficult and discouraging, without the old advantages of material rewards to native faithfulness coming exclusively from the padres, permanent progress will be impossible, friars' efforts will amount to nothing, and their support will be a useless expense to church and crown. The soldiers are not only fed and clothed but armed and equipped for their work of conquest and defence; why should the militia of Christ be denied arms and ammunition for spiritual warfare?

Yet another point *de no menor consideracion* is brought forward in this document, which is signed not only by Pangua but by the other five members of the college *discretorio*. This is the "irregular manner in which missionaries are regarded and treated in those establishments" of California. So pronounced is Neve's aversion to the friars that the soldiers are warned not to become *fraileros*, not to perform any service for the missionaries, and not to aid in bringing back fugitive neophytes. The natives lose their respect for the priest when they find he is not supported by the civil and military authority, and the result is of course disastrous. Again, subaltern officers and the soldiers under them, encouraged to disregard alike the teachings and chidings of the ministers, form scandalous connections with native and other women, and thus, with the tacit approval of the governor, they entirely neutralize all missionary effort and teach the natives to despise Christianity.[17] It is impossible to arrive at any other conclusion than that these charges

---

[17] The priests go so far as to charge that on one occasion the governor and his escort on the march from one mission to another deliberately stopped and waited while one of the number *se separó para ir á sus liviandades.*

against Governor Neve, resting on the bare assertion of the authors, were in part exaggerated, and in part false. There is nothing in Neve's preserved writings or in the annals of his time to show dislike to the friars, disinclination to aid them in their work of conversion, or a tendency to overlook immorality on the part of his subordinates. He favored a change in the mission system because he believed the missionaries were inclined to abuse the powers given them under the old *régime*, and this to the prejudice of the royal authority which he represented in California.[18]

The viceroy allowed the matter to rest here but reported to the king for instructions. Such were the facts that came to the knowledge of Junípero Serra at Monterey in May 1782. Clearly the proposed foundations must be postponed; in fact, instructions soon came from the college that neither Santa Bárbara nor any other mission must be established except in accordance with the laws, that is, under the old system.[19] San Buenaventura, however, need not be disturbed, for it had been provided for long ago, and the supplies of different kinds had been in readiness. Neither Neve nor Fages seems to have made any special effort to enforce the new regulations here. Like the viceroy, they were content to await the decision of the king. Fathers Dumetz and Santa María were appointed to the new mission; Cambon returned to San Francisco; Fuster went back to San Juan, or possibly had never left that mission; there were now just eighteen padres for the nine missions; and Santa Bárbara presidio had no chaplain.[20]

[18] The preceding correspondence is found in *Arch. Santa Bárbara*, MS., i. 231-46; vi. 266-71. It is a fact worthy of notice that Palou, *Not.*, ii. 388, does not argue the case, and that while opposed to Neve's policy he makes no charge against him either of immorality or of bitter feeling against the friars. Gleeson, *Hist. Cath. Ch.*, ii. 93-4, tells us that Governor Croix of California wanted to found missions on the Colorado plan, but the priests refused to serve.

[19] Guardian to Serra, Jan. 8, 1783, in *Arch. Sta. Bárbara*, MS., xii. 158-9.

[20] July 22, 1782, General Croix refers to Serra's request for live-stock, servants, and other aid for the San Buenaventura padres, and seems to favor granting the request, although contrary to the reglamento. *Prov. St. Pap.*,

On leaving San Gabriel for the Yuma campaign,
Neve left Captain Soler, his adjutant-inspector, in
command. His instructions to Soler as temporary
ruler were attached to others of July 12th relating to
his duties in connection with the presidial inspections,
and they contained but little beyond the technicalities
of routine duty. They enjoined care and kindness
in dealing with gentiles, but discouraged the use of
force in bringing back runaway neophytes.[21] Neve and
Fages, as we have seen, marched together from San
Gabriel on or about August 21st for the Colorado.
Whether either of them anticipated an early change
in his official position I have no means of knowing;
but shortly before their arrival at the river in the first
days of September they were met by a courier, who
among his despatches bore a promotion for both, from
Croix, who had appointed Neve inspector general
of the Provincias Internas, and Fages governor of
California.[22] At the camp of Saucito September 10th
the office was formally turned over to Fages, whose
governorship dates from that day.[23] Neve's instruc-

MS., iii. 231. December 30th he writes to Serra that beyond the six sailor
sirvientes allowed by him to the Channel missions and the $1,000 allowed by
the junta for live-stock and implements, no further aid can be granted not
even rations to the padres. The stipend is sufficient and older missions can
help the new. *Arch. Santa Bárbara*, MS., i. 277–8.

[21] *Neve, Instruccion al Ayudante Inspector Nicolás Soler, 12 de Julio 1782*,
MS. At the beginning of the year Soler had been in Lower California as shown
by letters of Neve in *Id.*, 2–20. Aug. 7, 1782, Neve announces to Croix that
Soler will come to San Gabriel and take his place. *Prov. Rec.*, MS., ii. 50–1.

[22] The appointments, both provisional or requiring confirmation from the
king, were dated July 12, 1782. *Prov. Rec.*, MS., i. 179; ii. 48. Neve announces the news of the appointments Sept. 4th, which was perhaps the date
they were received. *Prov. St. Pap.*, MS., xxii. 20–1. Also in Sept. Croix
announced that by a royal order Neve had been rewarded with the cross of the
order of San Cárlos. *Prov. Rec.*, MS., ii. 48–9; *Prov. St. Pap.*, MS., iii. 224.

[23] Neve to Gonzalez Sept. 10, 1782, in *Prov. St. Pap.*, MS., iii. 24–6. Fages
to P. Hidalgo Dec. 9, 1782, in *Prov. Rec.*, MS., iii. 69, 72, announcing his
taking possession, and his salary of $2,500, which he thinks will be $4,000
when it is confirmed. See also *Prov. Rec.*, MS., ii. 92, and *Id.*, iii. 227, in the
latter of which Fages seems to say that he took possession on Sept. 12th.
Feb. 28th Fages thanks Neve for his influence in getting his pay increased to
$4,000, and also thanks Gov. Corbalan of Sonora for his influence in his favor.
Prov. Rec., MS., iii. 85. The royal confirmation of Fages' appointment was
dated July 6, 1783. *Prov. St. Pap.*, MS., v. 247. Aug. 19, 1783, Fages is
granted by royal order the subdelegation of the *vice regis patronato. Id.*, xxii.
5. Feb. 16, 1783, Fages orders Neve to be proclaimed as inspector-general of
all troops in California. *Id.*, iv. 39.

tions, or memoranda, for the guidance of his successor
had been dated at Saucito three days earlier; but
there is very little in the document that requires notice,
save that he repeats the advice already given to Soler
respecting the necessity of taking every precaution to
maintain friendly relations with the gentiles, and disapproves the use of soldiers to bring back fugitive
converts, who should rather be persuaded to return by
the friars and by Christian Indians. In this last of
his official papers Neve shows more opposition to the
friars than ever before, for he implies that they are
wont to ask for escorts on frivolous pretexts. He
thinks that a priest actually going to administer sacraments should have a guard of two soldiers, who
should, however, never pass the night away from the
mission, and no friar should be allowed to accompany
the soldiers on their expeditions to the rancherías.
Moreover, care should be taken to enforce the laws
forbidding missionaries to board the galleon, showing
that even at this early day they were suspected of a
willingness to indulge in clandestine trade. If the
governor was somewhat severe at the last, it must be
admitted that his patience had been sorely tried. All
the varied interests of presidio, mission, and pueblo
are commended to the watchful care of his successor.[24]

Governor Fages returned westward to San Diego,
and during the month of October made another tour
from south to north, visiting and studying the interests and needs of each mission, personally exhorting
the neophytes to good behavior, promising pardon to
such runaways as would voluntarily return to duty,
but threatening severe punishment to those who
might refuse. His efforts in this direction, as Palou
asserts, were successful, most of the fugitives returning. At the end of October the governor reached
San Francisco, whence he turned back to Monterey,

[24] *Neve, Instruccion que da sobre gobierno interino de la península,* 7 de Set.
1782, MS. Neve speaks of the instructions as secret in *Prov. Rec.,* MS., ii.
48. Soler was still to be ayudante inspector and comandante de armas. *Prov.
St. Pap.,* MS., iii. 26.

the capital. It must have been a severe blow to Serra to see his old enemy, whom he had worked so hard to remove from the command when he was but a simple lieutenant, returning as lieutenant-colonel to assume the governorship of the province. Much as the friars hated Neve, a change in favor of Fages can hardly have been welcome; but their feelings on the subject at this time are not on record. So far as Fages was concerned his policy respecting runaway neophytes showed a disposition on his part to let the old quarrels drop.

On the 25th of April there was laid at San Francisco mission the corner-stone of a new church, with all the ceremonies prescribed for such occasions by the Roman ritual. Murguía officiated as prester, assisted by Palou and Santa María and in the presence of Lieutenant Moraga, his son Gabriel, Alférez Lasso de la Vega, Surgeon Dávila, the mission guard, and a body of troops from the presidio. "There was enclosed in the cavity of said corner-stone the image of our holy father St Francis, some relics in the form of bones of St Pius and other holy martyrs, five medals of various saints, and a goodly portion of silver coin." [25]

In May of this year the old presidio church at San Diego was burned; and in November fire destroyed a large part of the mission buildings at San Luis Obispo with some six hundred bushels of maize.[26] At Monterey in January there occurred the death of two prominent men. One was Mariano Carrillo, a pioneer soldier of 1769, who from the first had been Ortega's most efficient aid as corporal and sergeant, in the military service required for the protection of Spanish interests in the south, and who had lately been transferred to the north and had been given the commission of alférez.[27] The other death was that of the

---

[25] *S. Francisco, Lib. de Mision*, MS., 16, 17. There is no evidence that this corner-stone has ever been disturbed.

[26] *Monterey Co. Arch.*, MS., vii. 11; *Prov. Rec.*, MS., iii. 158–9; *Prov. St. Pap.*, MS., iv. 90–1.

[27] Carrillo was a native of Loreto and entered the service as a private in

venerable missionary Father Juan Crespí, whose pen
has left original records of the first explorations by
land of California from the peninsular frontier to the
Strait of Carquines.   It is as the chronicler of those
first expeditions that his memory will live; of his subsequent life as a missionary, chiefly at Monterey, we
know but little save that he was a faithful worker,
beloved by his neophyte flock and by his companion
friars.   In the disputes between secular and missionary
authorities his name never appears.   He died at San
Cárlos January 1st at the age of not quite sixty-one
years.[23]

the presidio company on July 26, 1756.   He came to San Diego in 1769 as a
corporal; was made sergeant in April 1771; and alférez in Feb. 1780.   He
was also habilitado of the Monterey company at the time of his death, which
occurred on Jan. 27th, being buried by P. Serra on Jan. 28th.   His *hoja de
servicio*, *St. Pap. Sac.*, MS., i. 108-9, represents him as of 'medium' valor,
application, and capacity, of good conduct, and unmarried.

[28] Juan Crespí—there is a shadow of doubt whether it should be so written
and pronounced, or without the accent—was born in 1721 on the island of
Mallorca, where he was also educated, being a school-mate of Francisco Palou.
He was distinguished from the first for humility and piety, if such expressions
from a priestly biographer and eulogist mean anything, and was sometimes
called by fellow-students El Beato or El Místico.   He came to San Fernando
de Mexico in 1749 and was sent two years later to the Pame missions of the
Sierra Gorda, where he served over sixteen years, particularly distinguishing
himself by the erection of a large stone church in the Valle del Tilaco, the
mural decorations of which he paid for out of his own scanty salary.   He
arrived in Baja California in April 1768, and served on the peninsula at La
Purísima.   He accompanied the first land expedition which reached San Diego
in May 1769, and a little later was one of the party that searched for Monterey
and discovered San Francisco Bay.   His diaries of both these trips are extant
and have been utilized in my narrative.   Returning from San Diego to Monterey in 1770 he assisted in founding the mission of San Cárlos in June, and served
there as minister until March 1772.   Then he went with Lieutenant Fages to
the San Joaquin River, of which exploration his diary is the only record.   He
was now sent south to serve with Jaume at San Diego from May to September,
and returning resumed his duties at San Cárlos, where with the exception of
two short periods of absence, he toiled until his death.   From June to August
1774 he served as chaplain on board the *Santiago* in northern waters, writing
a diary of the voyage; and in the autumn of 1781 he accompanied Serra to
San Francisco and Santa Clara.   On his return from this last journey he was
attacked by a fatal illness.   It was from his old friend, companion, and
superior Father Junípero, that Crespí received the last consolatory rites of
his religion, and his body was interred in the mission church within the
presbytery on the gospel side, with the assistance of commandant and garrison, and amid tears from his flock of neophytes, who lost a true friend in
Padre Juan.

CHAPTER XIX.

RULE OF FAGES—GENERAL RECORD.

1783–1790.

An Uneventful Decade—Statistics of Progress—Missions, Presidios, and Pueblos—Population, Padres, and Neophytes—Pedro Fages Brings his Family to California—Doña Eulalia—A Jealous Catalan—A Monterey Court Scandal—Fages and Soler—Inspection of Presidios—Soler's Proposed Reforms—Troubles with Habilitados—Governor and Franciscans—A Never Ending Controversy—General Reports of Palou and Lasuen—Charges and Counter-charges—Franking Privilege—Cruelty to Natives—Chaplain Service—Patronato—Prices for Mission Products—Inventories—License to Retire—Natives on Horseback—Mission Escorts—Native Convicts and Laborers.

The rule of Pedro Fages as governor of California extended from 1782 to 1790. It was an uneventful period, the annals of which include little beyond petty local happenings; yet it was a period not of stagnation but rather of silent unfolding, as may be seen from the following statistical view. The nine missions[1] were increased to eleven before the close of Fages' rule by the founding of Santa Bárbara and Purísima. In round numbers the neophyte population under missionary care and living in mission communities grew from 4,000 in 1783 to 7,500 in 1790, this being an average gain per year of 500. In the mean time 2,800 had died, 6,700 had been baptized; while about 400 had apostatized and fled to the old delights of savagism. In temporal matters progress had been yet more pronounced. The mission herds of horses,

[1] These were in their order from south to north: San Diego, San Juan, San Gabriel, San Buenaventura, San Luis, San Antonio, San Cárlos, Santa Clara, San Francisco.

mules, and horned cattle multiplied in the seven
years from 4,900 to 22,000 head, while sheep, goats,
and swine increased from 7,000 to 26,000. Agricultural products, chiefly wheat, maize, and barley,
amounted in 1783 to 22,500 bushels; in 1790 there
were 37,500 bushels, though these figures give no
accurate idea of progress, since the harvest of several
intermediate years had been larger than in 1790.
Improvement in buildings, corrals, fences, and irrigating works was constant, though not to be so briefly
indicated in figures. Several new churches were
erected, few of which, however, were the permanent
structures still to be seen in different stages of ruin.
In 1782 there were nineteen friars in charge of the
nine missions—the full complement of two to each
establishment, besides the president. Before 1790
sixteen new padres came, five retired, and four died at
their posts, leaving twenty-six still on duty.[2]

No new pueblos were founded, nor did any new
immigration of settlers take place. A few pobladores
left the country; a few soldiers became pobladores,
and a few boys growing up adopted an agricultural
in preference to a military life. Hence the united
population of San José and Angeles varied from 185
to 220, men, women, and children of so-called gente
de razon. The pueblo herds increased from 750 to
4,000 head of cattle and horses, while the small stock
remained at about 1,000 head. Agricultural products
were 3,750 bushels in 1783, and over 6,750 in 1790,

[2] The 19 serving in 1783 were: Cambon, Cavaller, Crespí, Cruzado, Dumetz,
Figuer, Fuster, Lasuen, Mugártegui, Murguía, Noriega, Palou, Paterna,
Peña, Pieras, Sanchez, Santa María, Serra, and Sitjar. The 16 new-comers
were: Arroita, Arenaza, Calzada, Danti, García, Giribet, Mariner, Noboa,
Orámas, Rioboo, Rubí, Santiago, Señan, Sola, Tapis, and Torrente. Left
California: Mugártegui, Palou, Noriega, Sola, and Rioboo. Died: Cavaller,
Figuer, Murguía, Serra, and Crespí. In 1785, Aug. 20th, Father Sancho, the
guardian, made a full report to the viceroy on the Californian missions. *Sancho,
Informe, 1785*, MS. It was largely devoted to a description of the system
and routine to be utilized elsewhere; it predicts that 'many years' will elapse
before the Indians will be fit for any other system; enters somewhat into
the controversies to be noted presently; and states that up to date there had
been 5,808 baptisms, 5,307 confirmations, and 1,199 marriages. There were
12,982 head of live-stock, and 12,119 fanegas of grain at the last harvest.

more than the average at the missions; while in 1790 Angeles produced more grain than any mission except San Gabriel. But the pueblos were not yet on the whole a success. They were far from fulfilling the high expectations with which they had been founded; they had by no means repaid the government for their cost. At the four presidios there was no change that can be statistically expressed. The regulation allowed a military force of 205 men for garrisons and mission guards, and the ranks were generally full, never lacking more than ten men. The places of such as died or served out their term, were filled for the most part from boys who became of age in California, and though individuals were doubtless recruited from other provinces and from the transport vessels, there is no record that any body of recruits was ever sent to replenish the ranks. Most of the soldiers were married men, and their families, added to the pueblo inhabitants, the priests, and the sirvientes from other provinces, made the total population of gente de razon in round numbers one thousand souls.[3]

Having thus presented a statistical view of the period under consideration, I pass on to a study of certain events connected with the provincial government and its officials, which have something more than a strictly local signification.

Fages came to Monterey as we have seen late in the autumn of 1782; but in the spring of 1783 he went south again to Loreto to meet his wife Doña Eulalia de Callis and his little son Pedrito whom he had left behind in Sonora. The lady had consented at the solicitation of General Neve and Captain Ròmeu, and on their assurance that California was not altogether a land of barbarism, to live at Monterey.[4] Leaving

[3] According to a *Resúmen de Poblacion* for 1790, in *St. Pap.*, *Miss.*, MS., i. 72, the neophytes were 7,353, and the gente de razon 970.
[4] Dec. 9, 1782, Fages writes to his mother-in-law Doña Rosa Callis, that Neve has undertaken to attend to his wife's departure; and on Dec. 21st he asks Romeu to use his influence to induce Doña Eulalia to come. *Prov. Rec.*,

Monterey in March the Governor reached Loreto in May. He set out on his return in July, and on November 13th was congratulated by Palou on his safe arrival with wife and son at San Diego,[5] and by the middle of January was back at Monterey. The journey was delightful. Everywhere along the route, writes the governor to his wife's mother Rosa, padres, Domínicos and Fernandinos, troops, settlers, and even Indians vied with each other in showering attentions upon the travellers. "The Señora Gobernadora is the Benjamin of all who know her; she is getting on famously, and Pedrito is like an angel; so rest assured, for we live here like princes."[6] Doña Eulalia, a native of Catalonia, like her husband,[7] belonged apparently to a family of considerable position and influence, a fact which I suspect had something to do with Don Pedro's rapid promotion and invariable good-fortune at court. She was perhaps the first woman of her quality who ever honored California with a visit. It is related that on arrival she was shocked, and at the same time touched with pity, at the sight of so many naked Indians, and forthwith began to distribute with free hand her own garments and those of her husband. She was induced to suspend temporarily her benevolence in this direction by a warning that she might have to go naked herself since ladies' clothing could not be obtained in the country. Nevertheless after a long residence at Monterey she left a reputation for her charities and kindness to the poor and sick.[8]

MS., iii. 72. For further correspondence on this subject see *Id.*, 86–9, 96, 105. It seems that Captain Cañete was sent over from Loreto to escort the lady, who, as the fond husband affirmed, was to have in California a reception befitting a queen.

[5] Palou writes from San Francisco Nov. 13. *Arch. Arzob.*, MS., i. 7. There are however some documents to show that Fages was at San Fernando de Velicatá in December, the lady being delayed by a miscarriage at Mulege. See also Fages' trip. *Prov. Rec.*, MS., iii. 101, 108, 111, 122, 138, 200-25, 249; *Prov. St. Pap*, MS., iv. 94; *Palou, Not.*, ii. 392.

[6] *Prov. Rec.*, MS., iii. 127.

[7] *San Francisco, Lib. de Mision*, MS., 20.

[8] *Vallejo, Hist. Cal.*, MS., i. 90-1.

It would be pleasing to record a continuance of tranquillity in domestic life at the gubernatorial mansion; but the archives contain records revealing the presence of a skeleton in the household, a court scandal at Monterey which cannot be passed over without notice. At the end of a year's life in California the 'señora gobernadora,' having in the mean time borne to her husband a daughter, whose birth is recorded in the mission register of San Francisco under date of Aug. 3, 1784, expressed herself satiated with California, and wished to leave the country. Don Pedro was by no means disposed to give up his lucrative and honorable position for a woman's whim, and a quarrel ensued, during which for three months the governor was exiled by his spouse to a separate bed. Finding this treatment, however, less effective than she had anticipated in overcoming the executive obstinacy, Doña Eulalia set herself to work to learn the cause of his lonely contentment, and found it as she suspected in the person of an Indian servant-girl whom her husband had rescued from barbarism on the Colorado and brought to the capital. On the morning of February 3, 1785, the irate gobernadora followed Don Pedro when he went to call the servant, accused him of sinful intent, heaped on his head all the abusive epithets in the vocabulary of an angry and jealous Catalan, and left the house vowing divorce, and ringing out upon the wind her wrongs.

The governor went over to San Cárlos and enlisted the services of the friars to bring his wife to reason, but she was not to be moved. All the more she scandalized their reverences by flatly declaring that the devil might carry her off before she would live again with her husband. The padres examined witnesses and decided, so says Fages, that there was no ground for divorce; but sent the case to the bishop and ordered the lady to remain meanwhile in the retirement of her own apartments, separated from the gubernatorial bed and board, and not at liberty to

repeat her charges throughout the capital. Things
remained in this state for a week, when the governor,
obliged to go south on business and unwilling to leave
his wife alone in the *casas reales,* wrote to Father
Noriega, who had acted as ecclesiastical judge in the
past investigations, asking him to remove the lady to
the mission where she might be kept in the seclusion
customary in such cases. Noriega sent an alférez on
the 12th of February with the proper documents to
effect the removal; but this caused a new outbreak,
for Doña Eulalia not only refused to go, but shut
herself up with Pedrito in her private apartments.
The door was forced open by the husband, who after
threats to have the lady tied, carried her to San
Cárlos. At the end of the month he set out for
the south taking his son with him to be left at San
Antonio.[9]

During the governor's absence Captain Soler was
applied to by both parties, by the wife to defend her
honor and innocence from outrage; by the husband
to effect a reconciliation. Soler's letters are not altogether intelligible, but they show that the priests had
found the lady by no means an easy subject to manage. There had been new outbursts of fury and food
for scandal, occurring apparently in church, and the
prisoner was threatened with flogging and chains. He
warns Doña Eulalia that she must moderate her
actions and restrain her wrath; while he urges Don
Pedro to return as soon as possible, and claims that
the lady whether guilty or not should not, in consideration of her position and breeding, be subjected to
such indignities. Fages writes from San Gabriel in
May that, while he admits the superior station and
birth of his wife, he cannot forget the outrage and
contumely she has publicly heaped upon him. Subsequent links in this chain of family discord are miss-

[9] Fages to Rosa Callis, Feb. 8, 1785; to Gov. Corbalan of Sonora, same
date; to P. Noriega, Feb. 11th; to P. Palou, Feb. 21st, in *Prov. Rec.,* MS., ii.
105–6.

ing; but on September 1st Fages writes to Bishop Reyes that his wife has returned to him, satisfied that the charges against him were unfounded. It must not be supposed, however, that Doña Eulalia gave up her original scheme of quitting California and taking the governor with her, for in October he writes that she has sent to the audiencia a petition asking his removal on the plea that the climate was injurious to his health. He begs a friend to interfere and prevent the document from being forwarded to Spain.[10] We know nothing further of Don Pedro's domestic affairs; let us hope that all quarrels ended with the year 1785.

There were, however, other difficulties in the ruler's path, though none of them assumed serious proportions. Among these minor troubles were the actions of Soler, the inspector of presidios. When Neve departed from San Gabriel for the Colorado he left Soler as temporary governor and inspector, and a little later, on Fages taking the governorship, Neve wrote to Soler that he was still to retain the military command. Why it was that Fages, especially when his appointment had received the royal confirmation, did not become, as prescribed by the regulation, commandant inspector, I am unable to explain; yet he frequently admits that he has nothing to do with the military command,[11] only claiming a kind of civil jurisdiction over Soler as a citizen of the province which he ruled. The two were personal friends and compadres; and, so long as their jurisdictions were separate, seem to have made an earnest effort to avoid an open quarrel; yet all the

[10] Soler to Fages April 14, 1785; to Sra. Fages April 9th, in *Prov. St. Pap.*, MS., v. 254–5; Fages to Garrido, May 2d; to Sra. Fages May 3d, in *Prov. Rec.*, ii. 107–8; Fages to bishop, *Id.*, iii. 144; to Garrido, Oct. 25th; *Id.*, ii. 111.

[11] In a communication to Romeu dated Dec. 21, 1782, Fages says 'the reglamento keeps me in a chaos of confusion since it supposes the government and inspection united, and as the latter has been separated I find myself very much embarrassed in my projects and measures, in order not to make them impertinent and cause discord with the ayudante.' Then he goes on to ask some information about the respective duties of the two offices. *Prov. Rec.*, MS., iii. 72–3. Additional correspondence on this subject in *Prov. Rec.*, MS., i. 170; ii. 99, 106, 112–15, 131; *Prov. St. Pap.*, MS., v. 45, 186, 251, 253.

same neither was ever entirely satisfied that the other was not encroaching on his prerogatives. No one of the petty disagreements is of sufficient importance to be noticed here.

At last the respective powers of the two dignitaries were fixed by an order of the commandant general, dated February 12, 1786, which arrived August 8th, making Fages commandant inspector as prescribed by the reglamento. Late in the year Soler accordingly turned over the office to his chief and resumed his old position as ayudante inspector, in which subordinate capacity he still ventured to disagree with his compadre to such an extent that on one occasion he was put under arrest at Monterey with orders to go on with his duties, but to enter the presidio always by the little door, and to pass back of the church to his office![12]

In November 1787 Soler made a long report to the general in reply to a request of that officer for his views on needed reforms in the administration of Californian affairs.[13] The author was not a man overburdened with ideas, and such as he had were pretty effectually suffocated in a mass of unintelligible verbiage, but the leading points in his proposed reform were as follows: The presidio of San Francisco should be abandoned and its company transferred to Santa Bárbara, which, as well as San Diego, should be under a captain instead of a lieutenant. The missions should furnish supplies to the presidios at fixed prices, and thus the expense of the San Blas transports be avoided, since articles necessarily imported could be furnished at prices to include freight, the missions and presidios being equally benefited by the change. Garrison soldiers should be relieved of the care of live-stock,

---

[12] *Prov. St. Pap.*, MS., vi. 21–2, 136, 138, 154, 189–93; xxii. 31; *Prov. Rec.*, MS., i. 30–1, 200–2, ii. 137.

[13] *Soler, Informe al Comandante General sobre Policía y Gobierno*, 3 de Nov. 1787, MS. At the beginning the author says, 'I confess, Señor, that I have had no head to present any project or circumstantial plan,' which may be taken as a résumé of the whole document with its 35 articles.

and thus be left free to master the duties of their proper service; and to this end the presidio stock should be greatly reduced in numbers, and the practice of supplying cattle to the southern frontier should be stopped. Some adequate provision must be made for the descendants of the present population. The government can furnish no increase of military force, and it is useless to found new missions which cannot be protected. The prohibition of killing cattle by private individuals, established by church influence in the interest of the tithe revenue, ought not to be enforced. It would also be better to grant grazing-lands, requiring the grantee, if necessary, to pay the natives for damage to their food supply; since under the present system soldiers who have served out their term leave the country for want of facilities to establish themselves in California. The natives have been neophytes long enough; they are fitted for civilized life, and the government has spent all the money on them that can be afforded. The pobladores have more land than they can cultivate; the pueblo *realengas* should be ganted to native families; Spaniards should be granted lands at the missions, and the military escorts should be withdrawn from both missions and pueblos. Then the gentiles will be attracted by the good fortune of the old converts to follow their example, the work of the priests being thus simplified and promoted.

To Soler therefore must be accorded the authorship of the first direct proposition to secularize the California missions, although some of Neve's propositions had tended more or less in the same direction. Soler's plan involved a complete overthrow of the old mission system, putting Spaniards and natives on the same footing as citizens, dependence on persuasion and good example for future conversions, dependence for supplies on home products, and restriction of the soldiers to garrison duty proper and the keeping in check such gentiles as might fail to appreciate the advantages of civilized life. Whether under his plan the new converts were to undergo a preliminary training as neo-phytes under the friars' care, or were to pass directly to the state of citizens and land-owners, does not clearly appear.

This series of recommendations was sent to the general through the governor, who with them for-warded also his own comments. I have no need to say that Fages opposed any plan suggested by his compadre.[14] There is no record respecting the fate of the propositions as annotated after they left Cali-fornia; but they at any rate were not adopted as the law of the province.

Soler had other troubles besides those with the governor, especially with the habilitados, few of whom escaped his criticism and few deserved to escape it. It was very hard to find officers with sufficient quali-fications for keeping the not very complicated presidial accounts, and it took time and patience to distribute the abler ones, Zúñiga, Sal, Goycoechea, and Argüello in the four presidios, especially as Argüello was the only one in whose ability Soler had confidence, and as it was well nigh impossible for him and Fages to agree respecting the merits of any one. Though by the regulation the soldiers had a vote in choosing the habilitado, for whose deficits they were responsible, yet practically the governor and inspector gave the

[14] *Fages, Comentarios sobre Informe del Capitan Soler, 8 de Nov. 1787*, MS. While approving Soler's views respecting the existence of certain minor evils in the present system, and claiming to have already suggested measures for the removal of those evils—for instance, annual slaughters and exportation of meats to San Blas to reduce the excessive number of presidio cattle—he de-clares that it would be folly to abandon San Francisco and leave the northern missions unprotected; that there is no reason for transferring the Loreto cap-tain to San Diego in order to get rid of Zúñiga, who cannot be spared; that the soldiers' work in caring for cattle, though considerable, is exaggerated by the adjutant, and the existence of wild cattle would be a great evil to the country; that the cattle of settlers as yet do no harm to the natives; that inducements to remain in the country are good, and more discharged soldiers remain than go away; that the natives are kept in order as neophytes only by the unremitting efforts of the friars, and are as yet wholly unfit to become citizens; that the pobladores can and do cultivate all the lands given them and often more; and finally that the introduction of Spanish settlers into the missions would interfere with the laws of the Indies providing that the mis-sion lands are to belong to the natives eventually when they shall be fitted to profit by their possession.

appointment to either the lieutenant or alférez of the company according to the relative fitness of those officers. They divided all the officers into two classes, the intelligent and stupid, according to ability as accountants, for as a rule there was no question of integrity, and were careful not to assign to any presidio two from the same class. With all possible precautions deficits occurred frequently, as we shall see in local annals, and Soler was always ready to suspect and charge irregularities, sometimes where none existed. At last the inspector and his aid could no longer get along together; Fages asked for Soler's removal, and Soler demanded a court-martial and a full investigation, being unable to discharge properly his duties under the governor's orders. The result was that the office was abolished, Soler was summoned to Arizpe in 1788, and was made commandant of Tucson, dying about 1790. Strangely enough after all his fault-finding and his constant search for defalcations on the part of others, he left California with a deficit of about $7,000 in his own accounts; that is, he owed that amount[15] to the presidios, and it is difficult to

[15] On troubles with habilitados' accounts see chapter xxi. of this volume; also *Prov. St. Pap.*, MS., vii. 114–16. Fages writes to Soler that he wants no discussion to embitter friendly intercourse, but prefers to leave all questions to superior authorities. *Id.*, vii. 143–5. July 14, 1787, Soler, who has been accused by Fages of carelessness, defends himself with unintelligible verbiage made worse by Latin. *Id.*, vii. 121. Before coming to California Soler had served as lieutenant-governor at El Paso, Chihuahua. *Prov. Rec.*, MS., ii. 75. He was only brevet captain, for the general recommends June 24, 1787, that he take command of a presidio in case of a vacancy if he ranks the other lieutenants. *Prov. St. Pap.*, MS., vii. 56. Being sick in 1786 he induced the captain of the *Princesa* to leave his surgeon, Carbajal, for his convenience, at which the Mexican authorities find fault and order the surgeon back to San Blas. *Id.*, vii. 2, 108. His private troubles with Sal arose from the jealousy of the latter who suspected him of an intrigue with his wife, and threatened to kill him. Soler was arrested by Fages to protect him from Sal's wrath. *Id.*, vii. 124–5. About his relations with the padres we have only his own remark, 'suelen (los padres) criar muy mal humor y mi naturaleza es muy propensa al contagio.' *Id.*, vii. 135. April 17, 1788, he writes to the general demanding a court-martial. May 20th he acknowledges receipt of order to proceed to Arizpe. August 30th he writes to Fages announcing his departure and the end of the inspectorship, and referring to slurs cast upon his character. *Id.*, viii. 50, 56–61. June 18, 1790, Gen. Ugarte writes to Fages that the king has approved the suspension of the inspectorship; that Soler is to be captain of Tucson; and that the governor is hereafter to inspect the troops, going down to Loreto once in two years for that purpose. *Id.*, ix.

account for such a debt except on the theory that he took improper advantage of his official position. The debt had to be paid out of his half-pay after his death.

The controversies between church and state were never ending, and though not particularly bitter during this period, ever require attention as a leading feature in early Californian history. The regulation of 1781, it will be remembered, provided for founding the Channel missions on a new basis very unfavorable to the friars' plans; but by refusing to serve in California the Franciscans carried their point and the new missions were put on the same footing as the others. The number of priests was to be gradually reduced to one for each mission with certain exceptions; but after several emphatic protests this regulation was also rendered of no effect.[16]

Thus the features most objectionable to the priests were eliminated practically from the law, but there

351–3. Fages alludes to Soler's death in letter of Feb. 26, and Gen. Nava on June 25th. *Id.*, x. 115, 164–5. His debt caused some trouble before he left California, and the matter was not settled until long after his death. Three thousand five hundred dollars of his pay was by order of the viceroy on June 8, 1787, secured for the benefit of his wife Doña Josefa Rodriguez de Vargas. *Id.*, vii. 9, 10. A large part of his debt was owing to the presidios and missions. *Prov. St. Pap., Presidios*, MS., ii. 51–3. March 4, 1797, the governor received $3,000 on the debt. *Prov. Rec.*, MS., iv. 209. Nov. 7, 1797, the habilitado general pronounces the decision in favor of Soler's widow unjust, but says an appeal to the king would be very costly. *Id.*, iv. 163. Finally in 1806 Capt. Zúñiga of Tucson is ordered to pay $1,062 of Soler's debt to the San Diego company. *Prov. St. Pap.*, MS., xix. 150, 153.

[16] Jan. 8, 1783, the guardian writes to Serra complaining that the government in the new reglamento seems to aim at the destruction rather than support of the missions. No more missions will be founded till the regulation is modified. It is better to abandon a mission than leave it in charge of one priest, and any priest left alone may refuse to serve without fear of consequences. *Arch. Santa Bárbara*, MS., xii. 155–8. I have an original letter of Lasuen to the guardian, apparently written in 1784, in which he protests most earnestly against the reduction, explaining the difficulties involved, and declaring his intention to resign his position, quit California, and if necessary sever his connection with the college rather than serve alone; for nothing save the commission of sin could be so terrible. The author of the project must' have misunderstood the king's intentions. *Lasuen, Carta de 1784*, MS. In his report of Oct. 1787 he says 'no one can convince me that I am bound to remain solitary in the ministry.' *Arch. Santa Bárbara*, MS. viii. 61. Aug. 16, 1786, the guardian writes to the president that he has reliable information that the objectionable clause in the reglamento is abolished. *Id.*, xii. 37–40. Palou, in *Id.*, viii. 40, says the clause was annulled by the king's order of May 20, 1782, providing that each mission must have two priests.

were left still some grounds on which to base a quarrel. Fages on assuming command and during his whole term of office seems to have made an earnest effort to conciliate the priests and prevent a reopening of the old troubles. Considering his rather irritable nature and the bitterness of the old feud with Serra, he was not altogether unsuccessful; still he was the successor of the hated Neve, the originator of the *reglamento*, largely committed to Neve's policy, and responsible to the king for the execution of the laws. Perfect accord was impossible, and causes of complaint on one side or the other were not infrequent.[17]

Postal charges and especially the franking privilege of the friars furnished occasional matter for dispute.

[17] 'Es ya declarada la oposicion del P. Serra á toda providencia gubernativa, significada no solo en palabras sino con obras y por escrito,' says Fages to the inspector general on March 1, 1783. He charges the president with too great severity not only toward Indians but the padres. *Prov. Rec.*, MS., iii., 87. On Sept. 15, *Id.* 124–5, he says that Serra 'tramples upon the measures of the government and bears himself with much *despotiquez* and total indifference.' The padres commit many abuses in opposition to the government. *Id.*, ii. 128. Sept. 26, 1785, Fages writes to the bishop on the padres' neglect of chaplain service, and avers that they cannot be spoken to on the most trivial matters without showing disdain. *Id.*, ii. 109. On the same day to the viceroy he protests against the fatal consequences of the missionary policy, which is diametrically opposed to the reglamento. *Id.*, ii. 95. Dec. 7, 1785, Fages complains to Cambon of Palou's sullen and cold behavior, and of the padres at San Cárlos who have twice received him (the governor) with disrespectful cries and stamping of feet. Yet he has been so devoted to the padres as to have drawn upon himself the name of *frailero*. Several friars have told him to his face that they doubted his word, forgetting the respect due him as governor. Letters are written him without proper politeness. He will no longer endure this, even if he be termed a persecutor of friars; yet he will never cease to venerate them. *Id.*, iii. 60–3. July 9th and 10th, Fages gives orders forbidding public murmurs against the padres and orders the arrest of soldiers who make public comments on their conduct. *Prov. St. Pap.*, MS., vi. 160; xxii. 24. Aug. 16, 1786, the guardian informs the president that projects for the weal of California have been presented to the viceroy, and the opinion of the fiscal and his agent is that the proposals should be carried out and the governor restrained. Fages is warned that he must have a care and that on the least complaint of the padres he will lose his position and honors. *Arch. Santa Bárbara*, MS., xii. 37–40, Aug. 23, 1787. Fages to Lasuen, regrets that he can make no provision without being suspected, 'que no se haga misteriosa.' *Prov. Rec.*, MS., iii. 64–5. Nov. 19, 1790, Lasuen to the padres, a secret letter referring vaguely to a *bando* which the padres must obey because they can't help themselves, though he has *representado* on the subject. *Arch. Arzobispado*, MS., i. 15, 16. May 28, 1791, Fages recounts the troubles to his successor. He says quarrels with the Fernandinos have been frequent, since they are very much opposed—*opuestísimos*—to the maxims of the reglamento, wishing to be wholly independent. At San Buenaventura it even came to blows with Padre Santa Maria. *Prov. St. Pap.*, MS., x. 149–50.

One of the privileges obtained by Serra for the missionaries in 1773 was that of sending letters to the college free of cost, and certain other letters to and from the president were also exempt from postage as official communications. The friars were inclined to include much private correspondence in the privileged mail matter, and not much attention was given to the subject ordinarily. In these later years, however, officials by the governor's orders became more strict, imposing on the missionaries what was deemed by them a heavy and unjust burden. Hence much discussion without practical result, since the law was clear enough, and was not changed, the strictness of its enforcement depending on the disposition of the local officials. As a rule the friars gained nothing by agitating the subject, though in some instances they obtained a decision in their favor from Mexico or Arizpe.[18] In real or affected pity for the natives, the governor complained of excessive severity on the part of the missionaries toward their neophytes. Doubtless there were instances of cruelty, but not many could be cited in these early years.[19]

[18] January 12, 1783, Fages writes to Sal that Serra's claim for free sending of his letters to college and to the padres cannot be granted, referring to royal cédula of October 25, 1777, and viceroy's instructions of April 26, 1780. Serra pleaded poverty and told Sal to keep his letters if he would not forward them free. Subsequently, however, Fages consented to have the letters forwarded, and an account kept of them until superior instructions could be received. The expense seems to have been finally charged to the government. *Prov. Rec.*, MS., iii. 80–1, 88, 163; *St. Pap. Sac.*, MS., i. 128–9, 134; *Prov. St. Pap.*, MS., iv. 32, 122–3. August 16, 1786, the guardian says the junta real has allowed letters between padres and the college to pass free. They must be in a separate package and directed 'Contador General de Correos.' *Arch. Santa Bárbara*, MS., xii. 37. July 22, 1791, President Lasuen issues a circular stating that last year the formalities were not observed, and the result was a cost of $18 for postage. *Id.*, ix. 314. October 22, 1795, he issues another circular to the effect that private letters had been sent in the padres' package, and this must be stopped, for there is a danger of losing the franking privilege. *Id.*, ix. 325–6. See also *Id.*, xi. 194; xii. 19–24; *Palou, Not.*, i. 532.

[19] Putting neophytes in irons and forced labor very frequent in all the missions, and particularly at San Cárlos. Fages, 1783, in *Prov. Rec.*, MS., iii. 87. June 11, 1785, Fages writes to Noriega that the natives accuse him of beating them with chains for trifling faults, charges which he has investigated and found to be true. Implores him in the name of humanity and of the king to change his course. *Id.*, iii. 51. Lieutenant Zúñiga complained in 1788 that the natives of San Diego were overworked and too severely pun-

Fages sent a document to the viceroy the 26th of September 1785, in which he made a formal complaint against the priests for their opposition to the law, an opposition which was injurious to the royal service and to the spiritual good of the troops. He enumerated five grounds of complaint which I shall notice presently.[20] By the government the matter was referred to the college of San Fernando, and a report was made by Guardian Palou, who denied all the allegations and presented counter-charges in behalf of the missionaries.[21] The audiencia was puzzled by contradictory evidence. A few recommendations were made on different points, and on January 12, 1787, the *expediente* was sent to Commandant General Ugarte y Loyola with instructions to make further investigations and pacify the contending parties as best he could.[22] General Ugarte wrote on April 22d to President Lasuen, ordering compliance with the suggestions of the audiencia and calling for a full report on the disputed points, which was rendered on the 25th of October.[23]

From the documents just mentioned we learn the foundation of the controversy. Fages' first charge was that the presidio of San Francisco had been deprived of mass for three years notwithstanding the obligation of the friars to serve as chaplains. Palou's reply was a denial that the friars were required to serve gratuitously as chaplains; a claim that such service if rendered was to be voluntary; and that the article treating this point, also reducing the number

ished. *Id.*, iii. 67. Fages has seen P. Peña draw blood by pulling a boy's ear, and the natives accuse him of having killed one of their number. *Prov. St. Pap.*, MS., x. 167. An unsigned scrap of 1785 speaks of irregular conduct of a padre and objects to mode of chastisement. *Id.*, v. 256.

[20] *Fages, Representacion contra los Frailes, 26 de Set. 1785*, MS.; alluded to with general statement of its purport in *Prov. Rec.*, MS., ii. 95.

[21] *Palou, Informe sobre Quejas del Gobernador, 1786*, MS.

[22] *Expediente sobre reciprocas quejas del Gobernador de Californias y Religiosos misioneros, 1787*, MS. Addressed to Gen. Ugarte on Jan. 12, 1787, by José Antonio de Urizar and other oidores.

[23] *Lasuen, Informe y satisfaccion al Sr. Comandante General sobre quejas del Gobernador, 25 de Oct. 1787*, MS.

of priests, had been annulled by royal order. Lasuen states that the padres have never refused or hesitated to attend to the spiritual welfare of the soldiers; that he personally served the presidio of San Diego when a minister of that mission, though six miles distant; that at Santa Bárbara the missionaries of San Buena-ventura served though eight leagues distant; and that the lack of service at San Francisco was because there was until recently no decent place for it, and the mission was so near that the soldiers could easily go there for spiritual care. The friars, however, were offended because the soldiers insolently claimed their service as regular chaplains, when it was really a mat-ter of voluntary charity. The viceroy's order on this subject was that a proper allowance be made to the friars for their services at presidios.[24]

The governor's second charge was that the padres refused to recognize the government in matters per-taining to property and the *patronato*. Lasuen states that the friars manage the mission temporalities by order of the king, though the management was at first reluctantly assumed; that the *vice regio patronato* has little or no application in a country like California, but that they will gladly observe any rules that may be prescribed. Palou charged the governor with a disposition to interfere illegally and despotically in the management of temporalities, and declared that

[24] In a correspondence between Gen. Ugarte and Lasuen in March 1786, the latter makes the same reply on the San Francisco matter as in his informe. *Arch. Santa Bárbara*, MS., i. 285–7. March 5, 1783, the padres of San Francisco to Fages excuse themselves for failure to say mass on the plea that the place is unhealthy, there are no proper implements, the soldiers have no regard for the missionaries, and stigmatize their friends as *fraileros*. The corporal had even ordered that no soldier must approach the padres' house. Fages directs the commandant to be indifferent until orders come from the general. *Prov. Rec.*, MS., iii. 91–2. Several communications respecting fail-ure to say mass at San Francisco in *Prov. Rec.*, MS., i. 192; iii. 24, 166, 209, all written by Fages. Orders from commandant that the reglamento must be enforced. *Prov. St. Pap.*, MS., vi. 115; *Arch. Sta. Bárbara*, MS., viii. 132; xi. 375–6. In these orders it is charged that fees are being collected by the friars; and Fages makes the same statement. *Prov. Rec.*, MS., iii. 87. The governor also complains on several occasions that the other presidios are neglected, and the pueblo of San José, where P. Peña has refused confession. *Id.*, ii. 109; iii. 171; *St. Pap. Sac.*, MS., ix. 83–4.

he had no proper understanding of the *patronato*, claiming the right to require or permit work on days of festival.

Thirdly the padres were accused of refusing to sell mission produce at the prices fixed by the government. Palou claims that there is no proof that the tariff rates have ever been approved by the king; that those prices ought to be regulated by scarcity or abundance; and that the president should have a voice in the matter. Lasuen, however, knows of no instance where the missionaries have refused to sell at the prescribed prices when they had grain to sell at all; though during several years of scarcity the prices have been kept down to a figure barely endurable in years of plentiful harvests.[25] The next cause of complaint was the refusal of the friars to furnish inventories of property, yearly increase, and the disposition made of mission products. Lasuen in reply says that the reports furnished to the governor are exactly the same as those rendered by the padres to the president, and by the latter to the college; that until now these reports have been satisfactory to all; and finally that there are no laws requiring the missionaries, who are not mere treasury officials, to render itemized accounts of what has been done with each bushel of maize.[26]

[25] Lasuen admits that P. Peña suggested an increase in price, for which he was duly reproved; and he says that the governor himself increased the price of corn, which is shown to be true by a letter of Fages in *Prov. St. Pap.*, MS., vi. 160–1, in which Sal is ordered to pay two reales extra for maize from S. Cárlos, Sta. Clara, and San José. Also Jan. 2, 1787, Fages modifies the tariff prices. *Id.*, vii. 168–9; and July 20, 1787, he asks Lasuen for harvest returns that he may regulate prices. *Arch. Sta. Bárbara*, MS., vi. 19. Fages complains of Peña's refusal to furnish grain on November 8, 1785, and March 27, 1786. *Arch. Sta. Bárbara*, MS., x. 25–39. Lasuen's replies being that he is sorry and has reproved P. Peña or will write to him. Fages also says on Sept. 26, 1785, that a mule train was sent back from San Cárlos without maize. *Prov. Rec.*, MS., ii. 128–9.

[26] May 2, 1786, Fages complains to the general that the padres are reluctant to show their inventories, do not make them out according to rule, and omit the register of inhabitants. *Prov. Rec.*, MS., ii. 136. Feb. 7th he complains to the president that P. Peña refused his aid and the mission books for a census. The president explains that the commandant had not asked in a proper manner. He has requested all padres to give the required aid. *Arch. Sta. Bárbara*, MS., xi.

Finally it was alleged that in defiance of the law the Franciscans insisted on retiring to their college without obtaining permission from the governor. Palou replies that by an order of the viceroy dated March 29, 1780, a friar had only to show the governor a license from his prelate. Lasuen goes more fully into the subject. In Neve's time, he says, a priest retired with his prelate's license and the viceroy decided that there was no law to prevent it. Palou departed in the presence of Fages, who is responsible for any irregularity in the proceeding. The next year Fages on being consulted made no objection to the departure of Rioboo; but finally there came a decree of Viceroy Galvez, forbidding the entry or departure of any friar without his license. This order has been obeyed in the case of Noriega, and it will be obeyed; but the president goes on to argue earnestly against the justice and policy of such a requirement, subjected to which the friars will serve only with reluctance.[27]

Fages had also found fault, though apparently not in his formal complaint, because neophytes were allowed to ride too much, the policy of the government being opposed to this, in fear that like the Apaches the Californians might become skilful warriors. The friars admitted the danger, declared that their interest was identical with that of the government, but claimed

[27] The viceroy's communications of Mar. 29, 1780, which are given in *Arch. Sta. Bárbara*, MS., vi. 272–6, xi. 25–6, are not correctly cited by Palou. The viceroy, while approving the claims of the college, turns the matter over to the commandant general, who he says may have had good reasons for his orders. The decree requiring the viceroy's permission for any padre to come or go was dated Dec. 7, 1786. *Prov. St. Pap.*, MS., vi. 202–3. In April 1787 the fiscal of the royal treasury explained that as the movements of the padres were paid from the missionary fund, their going to California if not needed or retiring for a mere whim would cause useless expense; therefore, the government had a right to know the reasons. April 23d the audiencia decreed in conformity to the fiscal's opinion; May 21st the archbishop communicated the decision to Palou; and June 22d and 23d Fages gave corresponding orders, though the president of Baja California protested that this was contrary to royal orders. *Arch. Arzobispado*, MS., i. 8, 9; *Arch. Sta. Bárbara*, MS., xi. 53. July 9, 1788, the viceroy informs the governor that the viceregal authorities and not the general will determine the sending and recalling of friars even if the command becomes independent of Mexico. *Prov. St. Pap.*, MS., viii. 1–3.

that there were none but natives to serve as vaqueros, and that the work could only be done on horseback.

Having replied to the governor's specific charges, Lasuen proceeds to lay before the government certain complaints on the part of the missionaries, namely: that the soldiers, being occupied largely with matters outside of their proper duty—that of affording protection to the friars in their work of christianizing the natives—neglected that duty; that in consequence of a long peace they were becoming careless and neglecting precautions against disaster; that an insufficient guard was given to the missions, the most useless and the worst equipped soldiers being detailed for that duty, and only one soldier being allowed to escort the friars on long journeys;[28] that the soldiers of the guards kept much live-stock to the prejudice of mission interests; that Indians were condemned to work as

[28] This subject of mission guards and their duties was really one of the most serious in the whole controversy. The padres wished entire control of the soldiers to use as they deemed best, and particularly in pursuing runaway converts. Neve had opposed the employment of soldiers to hunt fugitives in ordinary cases, because he deemed other means better fitted for the purpose, and because men enough could not be spared for effective and safe service. *Prov. St. Pap.*, MS., iii. 123–4. The French voyager La Pérouse praises Neve highly for his position on this point. *La Pérouse, Voy.*, ii. 297–8. In his instructions to Fages, Sept. 7, 1782, Neve advised that not more than two soldiers should accompany a padre to confess, etc., at a ranchería, and that they should not be absent overnight. The Indians must not learn to fight with and kill soldiers. *Prov. St. Pap.*, MS., iii. 138–9. Yet Fages did not rely entirely on persuasion to bring back fugitives, but favored a resort to arms only after all other means had failed, such as persuasions by padres, sending of neophytes, appeal to chiefs, offer of presents to gentiles, etc. See Fages' instructions to soldiers sent after runaways in *Prov. Rec.*, MS., iii. 151–2. In 1784 Fages repeats the order forbidding an escort of more than two soldiers, who must not be absent over night. The safety of the mission demands the presence of all, and the king has confirmed orders to that effect. *Prov. Rec.*, MS., iii. 47–8. The latest orders do not permit him to let the troops pursue *cimarrones* except in extreme cases. Fages to Dumetz, Jan. 5, 1785, in *Prov. Rec.*, MS., ii. 103–4. Oct. 17, 1785, Fages to Sal. No escort to be given to padres except when they go to say mass at presidios, or to confess or baptize. *St. Pap., Sac.*, MS., ii. 51. Escoltas refused, except as above, at San Antonio and Santa Bárbara. *Prov. St. Pap.*, MS., v. 142, 167. P. Dumetz at San Buenaventura being refused an escort to go to San Gabriel says, Feb. 4, 1786, in substance: 'Very well, since we are to be thus restricted to our missions we can no longer visit the presidio, which is beyond our jurisdiction.' *Prov. St. Pap.*, MS., vi. 45–6. March 3, 1786, however, Fages orders an escort to be furnished when the padres of San Buenaventura wish to visit San Gabriel and Santa Bárbara. *Id.*, vi. 72. Aug. 16, 1788, in a long letter to Lasuen Fages explains the policy of the government respecting escorts, and the forcible capture of cimarrones. *Arch. Sta. Bárbara*, MS., i. 167–73.

peons at the presidios for stealing cattle and for other offences, the punishment of which should rest exclusively with the friars, the sole object being to get free laborers;[29] that the settlers of San José employed pagans to do their work, demoralized them by bad example, and even persuaded them to avoid Christianity and its attendant slavery; that the disposition to make mission alcaldes independent of the friars in punishing offences greatly impaired their usefulness, the law having been intended only for curates and not for missionaries; that illegal and unequal measures were 'used for mission produce; that the raising of cattle by the presidios and the preference given to the pueblos in buying supplies would soon deprive the missions of all means to procure needed articles for the neophytes, especially as the articles most needed were often refused by the habilitados, or prices made too high in proportion to those of mission products, and yet the padres would submit humbly to the decisions of the commandant general.

Palou in addition to the preceding charges, declares that the regulation was never proclaimed in California until September 1784, and was not really in force, that of Echeveste being much better adapted to the needs of the country. He says that the regulation was not carried out, the articles on the inspection of presidios and on pueblo management being notably disregarded, and that not only were the pueblos in a sad state of decadence, but that San José, on the rapid road to ruin, was by its aggressions under the governor's policy dragging the mission of Santa Clara to ruin with it. Finally, the governor, instead of obeying the law, had not given the missions the slightest

---

[29] The secular authorities, in the light of past experience in other provinces, seem to have regarded the stealing of cattle as a much more serious offence, and one much more dangerous to Spanish domination in California, than did the padres. It was by no means one of the trivial faults in which the friars had exclusive jurisdiction. Fages has something to say on this subject in the letter last alluded to. Still there is no doubt the military authorities did abuse their power in this direction with a view to get workmen free of cost.

encouragement or aid either in spiritual or temporal affairs.

The reader who has followed this and preceding quarrels between the political and missionary author-

PALOU'S MAP, 1787.

ities in California, will have noted that they were often petty in all their phases, and such as might easily have been avoided by slight mutual concessions and efforts to promote harmony. It is not necessary to decide on the merits of the respective parties in each dispute, even if it were possible; yet it is apparent that the friars were determined not to yield a single point of their claimed prerogatives until forced to do so, and then to yield only to the highest authorities, to the king if possible, or to the viceroy, but never to so insignificant an official as the governor, whose presence they regarded as an outrage if he had a will of his own, and whose authority they practically disregarded in a way very hard to bear. Yet in his general report on missions rendered in 1787,[30] Governor Fages speaks in the highest terms of the zeal and efficiency of the missionaries, and his personal relations with them were for the most part pleasant. It was only as governor and president, as representatives of Cárlos III. and St Francis, that they quarrelled, save in the case of a few individuals or in the ruler's irritable moods. One of the friars, however, in an interesting report on the missions in 1789 could not deny himself the satisfaction of stating that while the king's provisions had been all that they could desire, there had been great and even culpable remissness on the part of the royal representatives, or agents, in California.[31]

[30] *Fages, Informe General de Misiones, 1787,* MS. This is an excellent résumé of the past progress and present condition of the Californian establishments, containing a separate notice of each mission and some general suggestions of needs, but with no reference to current controversies. A statistical presentation of the subject seems to have accompanied the original, which was made in answer to an order of the general of December 1, 1786. The date in 1787 is not given, and it may have been after the receipt of the king's order of March 21, requiring governors to render such reports every two or three years. Of this cédula I have an original in print with autograph signatures in *Doc. Hist. Cal.,* MS., iv. 31–3.

[31] *Informe de lo mas peculiar de la Nueva California, 1789,* MS. This report was probably directed to the bishop or archbishop, but there is nothing, in my copy at least, to indicate the author. The document contains general information about the Indians and the mission system, without much of chronological annals.

CHAPTER XX.

RULE OF FAGES, DEATH OF SERRA, AND MISSION PROGRESS.

1783-1790.

PRESIDENT SERRA'S LAST TOURS—ILLNESS AND DEATH—BURIAL AND FUNERAL
HONORS—HIS LIFE AND CHARACTER—SUCCESSION OF PALOU AND LASUEN
—MUGÁRTEGUI AS VICE-PRESIDENT—CONFIRMATION—NOTICE OF PALOU'S
HISTORICAL WORKS—VIDA DE JUNÍPERO—NOTICIAS DE CALIFORNIA—
MAP—PROPOSED ERECTION OF THE MISSIONS INTO A CUSTODIA—NEW
MISSIONS—FOUNDING OF SANTA BÁRBARA—INNOVATIONS DEFEATED—
FIVE YEARS' PROGRESS—MISSION OF LA PURÍSIMA CONCEPCION FOUNDED
—EARLY ANNALS.

IN 1784 the Californian missionaries were called
upon to lose their well beloved master. President
Junípero Serra died at San Cárlos on the 28th
of August. In January he had returned from his
last tour of confirmation in the south, during which
he visited every mission from San Diego to San
Antonio. In June he came home from a last visit to
the northern missions of San Francisco and Santa
Clara. He left Monterey by sea for the south so ill
that all, including himself, deemed his return doubtful.
He was near death at San Gabriel, and when he left
Santa Clara it was with the avowed intention to prepare for the final change. He had long been a sufferer from an affection of the chest and ulcers on the
legs, both aggravated if not caused by self-inflicted
hardship and a pious neglect of his body. The death
of his old companion Crespí had been a heavy blow;
his sorrow had been deep at partial failure in his
efforts to place California exclusively under missionary control, and to revive under better auspices the
Jesuit epoch of the peninsula. The return of Fages

to power was not encouraging to his plans and hopes. His license to confirm, under which he had administered the sacrament to over five thousand persons, expired in July, and discouraging news came at the same time from Mexico about the prospect of obtaining new friars. The death of Father Murguía broke another link that bound him to this world, and the venerable apostle felt that his work was done, his reward was near at hand. To all the Franciscans was despatched a letter of eternal farewell, in every word of which seemed distilled, drop by drop, the very soul of the dying man, while from each of the nearer missions a padre was summoned to take leave in person. Palou from San Francisco, the only one who arrived before Father Junípero's death, was obliged to say on August 19th the regular monthly mass in honor of St Joseph, California's great patron, but in other religious services the saintly sufferer insisted on taking his usual part. Irritants were applied to his chest by the presidial surgeon on the 23d without any beneficial effect. On the 26th he made a general confession, and next day walked to church to receive the last sacrament in the presence of friars, officers, troops, and natives, having ordered the carpenter to make his coffin. The night was passed by the dying man on his knees, or a part of the time reclining in the arms of his neophytes. Having been anointed, and recited with the others the litany, toward morning he received absolution and the plenary indulgence of his order. In the morning of the 28th he was visited by Captain Cañizares and other officers of the vessel in port, and he asked that the bells might be tolled in honor of their visit. Then he conversed with his old friend Palou, requested to be buried in the church near Crespí, and promised to pray for California when he should come into the presence of the trinity. At one moment a fear seemed to oppress his mind, but soon all was calm, and he went out of doors to gaze for the last time upon the face of nature. Returning at one P. M. he lay down after prayers to rest, and was thought to be sleeping, but within an hour Palou found that he was dead. The bells announced the mournful intelligence. Clad in the friar's simple robe in which he died and which was the only garment he ever wore, save when travelling, the body was placed in the coffin, with six candles beside it, and the weeping neophytes came to cover the remains of their beloved master with flowers, and touch with their medals and rosaries the lifeless form. Every article of clothing save the one that served as a shroud was distributed in small fragments as precious relics among the people, and notwithstanding all vigilance a part of the robe was taken also. On Sunday, the 29th, the body was buried in the mission church by Palou in the presence of all the inhabitants of Monterey, and with all possible ceremonial display, including military honors and the booming of guns from the fort and Cañizares' vessel at anchor in the bay.[1]

The life of Father Junípero Serra is so closely

[1] A full account of Serra's sickness, death, and burial, much longer and more detailed than I have space to reproduce, is given in *Palou, Vida*, 261–305. Another good authority, including a sketch of Serra's life is *Palou, Defuncion del R. P. Fr. Junípero Serra*, MS.; translation in *Arch. Misiones*, i. 73–6. There are some slight differences in the two accounts not worth noticing here, except perhaps the statement in the latter that Serra died just before 4 P. M. Gov. Fages was not present at the funeral, being absent from Monterey. Capt. Soler was the highest official who took part in the ceremonies. Palou was aided by PP. Sitjar and Noriega, and by Diaz the chaplain of the *San Cárlos*. On Sept. 4th there was a renewal of funeral honors with the same crowded attendance as before, and with the additional assistance of P. Paterna of San Luis. Now the relics were blessed. The crew of the *paquebot* secured Serra's tunic which was made into scapularies; the small clothes were distributed by lot among the troops and others; and the surgeon obtained a handkerchief, which cured a sailor of a headache, as did a girdle cure P. Paterna of the colic. P. Serra's body was buried in the presbytery of the church on the epistle side before the altar of our lady of Dolores. When the new church was built the remains of both Serra and Crespí were probably transferred, but so far as I know there is no record of such transfer or of the place where they finally remained. Taylor, in *Hutchings' Mag.*, May 1860, and in *Cal. Farmer*, Nov. 28, 1862, says that the body lies near the altar covered by the débris of the roof, which fell in 1852. The parish priest made an unsuccessful search for it in 1855. Vischer, *Missions of Cal.*, pp. i.–ii., says the remains are supposed to have been taken to Spain, shortly after 1784; and that the priest in his 'antiquarian mania' found the remains of another friar which believers seized upon as precious relics. There is no doubt the bodies still rest at San Cárlos, and in 1882 they were identified to the satisfaction of the parish curate.

blended with the first fifteen years of California mission history that any attempt to present it here would result in an unnecessary résumé of the preceding chapters. I subjoin however in a note[2] for convenient

[2] Miguel José Serra, son of Antonio Serra and Margarita Ferrer, was born at Petra on the island of Mallorca Nov. 24, 1713, took the Franciscan habit at Palma Sept. 14, 1730, and made his profession Sept. 15, 1731, on which occasion he assumed the name Junípero. In early boyhood he served as chorister and acolyte in the parish church greatly to the delight of his parents, a God-fearing couple of lowly station. The lives of the saints were his favorite reading, and his fondest ambition was to devote his life to religious work. He was an earnest and wonderfully proficient student, and taught philosophy for a year before his ordination in the chief convent of Palma, then obtaining a degree of S. T. D. from the famous Lullian University with an appointment to the John Scotus chair of philosophy which he held with great success until he left Spain. He was also noted for his doctrinal learning and still more so as a sensational preacher. He was wont to imitate San Francisco Solano and often bared his shoulders and scourged himself with an iron chain, extinguished lighted candles on his flesh, or pounded his breast with a large stone as he exhorted his hearers to penitence. Thus he is represented in the engraving which Palou has attached to his life, but which has probably little or no merit as a portrait.

March 30, 1749, after repeated applications he obtained his *patente* to join the college of San Fernando and devote himself to missionary work in America. With Palou he left his convent April 13th and sailed *via* Málaga to Cádiz where he arrived May 7th. On the way to Málaga he maintained a continuous disputation on dogmatic theology with the heretic master of the vessel and would not yield even to the somewhat forcible though heterodox arguments of a dagger at his throat and repeated threats to throw him overboard. Sailing from Cádiz Aug. 28th, he touched at Puerto Rico where he spent 15 days in preaching, anchored at Vera Cruz Dec. 6th, and walked to Mexico, reaching the college Jan. 1, 1750. Assigned the same year to the Sierra Gorda missions of Querétaro and San Luis Potosí, he made the journey on foot and reached Santiago de Jalpan on June 16th. For nine years he served here, part of the time as president, devoting himself most earnestly and successfully to the conversion and instruction of the Pames. In 1759 or 1760 he was recalled and appointed to the so-called Apache missions of the Rio San Sabá in Texas; but the plans being changed he was retained by the college and employed for seven years in preaching in Mexico and the surrounding bishoprics, in college service, and in performing the duties of his office of comisario of the inquisition held since 1752.

July 14, 1767, Serra was named president of the Baja Californian missions, arrived at Tepic Aug. 21st, sailed from San Blas March 12, 1768, and reached Loreto April 1st. March 28, 1769, he started—always on foot—for the north, founded San Fernando de Velicatá on May 14th, reached San Diego July 1st, and founded the first California mission July 16th. April 16, 1770, he sailed for the north, reached Monterey May 31st, and founded San Cárlos June 3d. July 14, 1771, he founded San Antonio. Aug. 20, 1772, he started south by land, founded San Luis Sept. 1st, and reached San Diego Sept. 16th. On Oct. 20th he sailed from San Diego, reached San Blas Nov. 4, and Mexico Feb. 6, 1773. Leaving Mexico in September, he sailed from San Blas Jan. 24, 1774, arrived at San Diego March 13th, and went up to Monterey by land, arriving May 11th. From June 30, 1776, to Jan. 1, 1777, he was absent from San Cárlos, going down to San Diego by water, returning by land, and founding San Juan Capistrano on Nov. 1st. In September and October 1777 he visited San Francisco and Santa Clara. From Sept. 15, 1778, to Jan. 5, 1779, he made another trip south, confirming at all the mis-

reference an outline of dates with some items illustrative of his character and habits taken from his

sions on his way back; and in October and November he visited Santa Clara
and San Francisco on the same business. In September and October 1781 he
again visited San Antonio, San Francisco, and Santa Clara. In March 1782
he went to Los Angeles and San Gabriel, founded San Buenaventura March
31st, was present at the founding of Santa Bárbara presidio in April, and
returned to San Cárlos *via* San Luis and San Antonio about the middle of
June. In August 1783 he sailed for San Diego, arriving in September, returning by land, visiting all the establishments, and arriving at home in January.
Between the end of April and the early part of June 1784 he visited San
Francisco and Santa Clara.

In the last chapter of his biography Palou recapitulates 'the virtues which
were especially brilliant in the servant of God, Fr. Junípero,' declaring that
'his laborious and exemplary life is nothing but a beautiful field decked with
every class of flowers of excellent virtues.' First in the list was his profound
humility, as shown by his use of sandals and his abnegation of self. He always
deemed himself a useless servant; deemed other missionaries more successful
than himself; and rejoiced in their success. He avoided all honors not actually
forced upon him, shunned notice and praise, sought the lowest tasks, kissed
the feet of all even to the lowest novice on leaving Spain and Mexico, ran
away from the office of guardian, and was in constant fear of honors from his
order or from the church or king. Then came the cardinal virtues of prudence, justice, fortitude, and temperance, resting like columns on his humility as a base, and supporting the 'sumptuous fabric of Christian perfection.'
His prudence was shown in his management as president of the missions,
though he was always modest and ready to consult with the lowest about
him; his justice was shown by his kindness and charity to all, his exact obedience to the commands of superiors, and his patience with enemies as exempli-
fied particularly in his writing a letter in favor of Fages to the viceroy; and
only four days before his death he gave a blanket to an old woman who at the
founding of San Cárlos had induced a boy to kill the friar's only chickens.
His fortitude appeared in his resistance to physical pain and constant refusal
of medical treatment, in his self-restraint, in his steadfast adherence to his
purposes, in his resolution to remain at San Diego alone if need be when it
was proposed to abandon the conquest, in his conflict with the indifference or
opposition of the military authorities, and in his courage in the presence of
hostile Indians—for he only feared death or ran from danger because of the
vengeance that would be taken on the poor Indians; and finally his temperance was such that he had no other passion than that for the propagation of
the faith, and constantly mortified the flesh by fasting, vigils, and scourging.
On these columns rested a superstructure of theological virtues, faith, charity,
and religion, of which a mention must suffice. The author, however, does not
claim for his hero the gifts of contemplation, of tongues, revelation, prophecy,
miracles 'and all that apparatus of the *gracias gratis datas* which make admir-
able and striking the saintliness of some servants of God,' but which are not
essential to holiness.

During his novitiate Padre Junípero was small and sickly, but he says,
'with the profession I gained health and strength and grew to medium
stature.' Of one of his sermons an able critic said: 'It is worthy of being
printed in letters of gold.' A woman *endemoniada* shouted during one of
his sermons, 'thou shalt not finish the lenten season,' and then the padre
was exceeding glad, for of course the father of lies could inspire no truth.
Suffering from want of water on the voyage to Mexico he said to complainers,
'the best way to prevent thirst is to eat little and talk less so as not to waste
the saliva.' In a mutiny and a storm threatening death to all he was perfectly
calm, and the storm ceased instantly when a saint chosen by lot had been addressed in prayer. On the way from Vera Cruz to Mexico several miracles

biography by Padre Palou, and his letters in the
mission archives.[3]

Serra doubtless owes much of his fame to his position as first president of the California missions and
to the publication of a biography by a warm personal
friend. But it did not require Palou's eulogistic pen

were wrought in his favor. Coming to a swollen stream by a town in a dark
night there was a man on the other bank to show the ford and guide him to a
lodging. A man, perhaps the same, met Junípero and his companion next
day and gave them a pomegranate which had a refreshing effect, and still
later a man gave them a bit of corn-bread of excellent savor. It was on this
journey that his legs first became swollen, from the effects of mosquito-bites
as was supposed, resulting in ulcers that lasted all his life. 'Oh, for a forest
of Junipers!' exclaimed a friar at the college when Serra arrived. In one of
his revival meetings in Huasteca he was beating himself with a chain, when
a man took the chain from him and with it beat himself to death as a miserable sinner in presence of the crowd. Sixty persons who neglected to attend
his meetings were killed by an epidemic which did not cease until religious
duties were generally attended to. On his way back from Huasteca he was
well lodged and entertained in a cottage by the way; but later he learned
that there was no such cottage on the road; and of course concluded that his
entertainers were Joseph, Mary, and Jesus—in fact he had noticed an extraordinary air of neatness about the place. Poisoned once in taking the communion he refused the antidote and was cured by a simple dose of oil, perhaps
miraculously as he thought. It was at Velicatá in May 1769 that he first
saw and baptized pagans.

[3] Serra, Correspondencia, 1777–82, MS., is a collection of his letters to different missionaries and officials. It is impossible by means of extracts to
give any proper idea of these long, rambling, and peculiar epistles. Palou
has selected the very best of his letters for publication, if indeed he has not
changed and improved them. Large portions of some of them are utterly
unintelligible and were apparently intended to be so for the ordinary reader.
Sea todo por Dios and similar pious expressions are used in great profusion
whether the subject be important or trivial. To Pieras he gives the most
minute directions how to answer the governor's letter and how to make out
mission reports and inventories, leaving nothing in manner or matter to the
padre's judgment. He wishes all made ready for signatures because the
most serious part of it is to feed the governor's agents while doing the business.
He expresses deep pity for some condemned criminals, and directs a padre to
attend to their spiritual needs. 'It will be some work, but very holy and
meritorious.' To Lasuen, announcing the governor's refusal to increase an
escort, he says, 'and this the result of all my efforts and all a viceroy's recommendations, and in response to an affectionate and humble suggestion made
with all the honey my mouth would hold. Believe me, of all the draughts
I have to swallow none is so bitter.' 'I and your Reverences—for this once
I name myself first.' In the matter of escoltas, however, he directs the padres
to 'go on as if they had a legion of soldiers; punish whoever merits chastisement; and if in the exact performance of the holy ministry trouble
arises not to be repressed with the force at hand, then retire to the presidio,
write me the facts in detail; then dirán y dirémos.' He writes a long letter
to induce Figuer to give up his intention of retiring, reminding him that
'patience and suffering are the inheritance of the elect, the coin with which
heaven is bought.' He begins by an anecdote of a friar at matins who
wished to retire to his cell not feeling in a good-humor, and to whom the
prelate replied that if such an excuse were admitted all would retire, 'and I
among the first.' Then he compares San Diego life with that at other mis-

to prove him a great and a remarkable man. Few
who came to California during the missionary régime
were his equal in devotion to and success in his work.
All his energy and enthusiasm were directed to the
performance of his missionary duties as outlined in
the regulations of his order and the instructions of his
superiors. Limping from mission to mission with a
lame foot that must never be cured, fasting much and
passing sleepless nights, depriving himself of comfortable clothing and nutritious food, he felt that he was
imitating the saints and martyrs who were the ideals
of his sickly boyhood, and in the recompense of absti-
nence was happy. He was kind-hearted and charitable
to all, but most strict in his enforcement of religious
duties. It never occurred to him to doubt his absolute right to flog his neophytes for any slight negligence
in matters of the faith. His holy desires trembled
within him like earthquake throbs; in his eyes there
was but one object worth living for, the performance
of religious duty, and but one way of accomplishing
that object, a strict and literal compliance with Franciscan rules; he could never understand that there
was anything beyond his narrow field of vision. In
an eminent degree he possessed the faculty of applying spiritual enthusiasm to the practical affairs of life.
Because he was so grand a missionary he was none the
less money-maker and civilizer, yet money-making and
civilizing must ever be subordinate to missionary
work, and all not for his glory, but the glory of God.
A St Augustine in his religion, he was a Juvenal in his
philosophy. He managed wisely the mission interests
both spiritual and temporal; and his greatest sorrow
was that the military and political authorities were

sions, showing that each has its advantages and disadvantages. He suggests
the question which is worse 'to be hungry and have nothing to eat or plenty
to eat and no appetite.' When San Francisco and Santa Clara had nothing
to eat they attributed to this want 'el no hacer prodigios de conversiones;'
but now that there is food there is nobody to eat it. 'Therefore, my brother,
let us go on with our matins to the *sancto sanctore*.' 'Adonde irá el buey
que no are? sino va á Campeche?' Some who have gone away would perhaps
gladly take what they left.

not so easily managed as padres and neophytes. In his controversies with the governors he sometimes pushed diplomacy to the very verge of inconsistency, but all apparently without any intention of injuring them, though he knew he was dealing with men who cast obstacles in the way of his great work. His letters were long, verbose, and rambling, but left no minute detail of the subject untouched. The loss of a sheep from a mission flock evoked a communication of the same style and length, with the same expressions of trust in heaven, as the conversion or destruction of a whole tribe; and it is to be noted that in writing to his friars, especially about his political quarrels, he adopted a peculiar and mysterious style wholly unintelligible, as it was doubtless intended to be, to all but the initiated. On the whole the preceding remarks fail to do him justice; for he was a well meaning, industrious, enthusiastic, and kind-hearted old man; his faults were those of his cloth, and he was not much more fanatical than others of his time, being like most of his Californian companions a brilliant exception in point of morality to friars of some other lands and times.[4]

At the death of Serra the presidency of the missions naturally fell temporarily to Palou as the senior friar in California, who had also held the position

[4] Nearly all the books that have been written about California have something to say of Junípero Serra, and it is not necessary to refer to the long list. It is somewhat remarkable, however, that there are very few if any official communications respecting his death preserved in the archives either secular or missionary. Hittell, *Hist. S. F.*, 33–9, gives a very good account of the padre's life, concluding that 'his cowl covered neither creed, guile, hypocrisy, nor pride. He had no quarrels and made no enemies. He sought to be a simple friar, and he was one in sincerity. Probably few have approached nearer to the ideal perfection of a monkish life than he.' I have his autograph signatures in *S. Antonio, Doc. Sueltos*, 9, 13, 17. See a poem by M. A. Fitzgerald on his death in *Hayes' Miss. Book*, 152. Palou's *Vida* contains a portrait more likely to be like the original than any other extant. Gleeson, *Hist. Cath. Ch.*, ii. frontisp., has one copied from a painting in the library of the California pioneers, about the authenticity of which nothing is known. Dr Taylor, *Discov. and Founders*, ii. 41, claims to have obtained in 1853 a photograph from an original painting at the college of San Fernando, of which a caricature was published in *Hutchings' Mag.* in 1860.

before in Serra's absence. Palou at first declined to act as president, partly from real or affected modesty, but chiefly because he desired to leave the country as soon as possible. He had, however, to yield to the unanimous wish of his companions, who claimed that a vacancy would prove injurious to mission interests, and reluctantly assumed the duties until a successor could be appointed.[5] The choice of the college fell on Fermin Francisco Lasuen of San Diego; his patent was forwarded February 6, 1785; and he took possession of the office probably in September. Father Mugártegui was named to succeed Lasuen in case of accident, and August 16, 1786, was appointed vice-president of the southern missions.[6] By a later patent of March 13, 1787, issued in accordance with a decree of the sacred congregation at Rome, March 4, 1785, which extended the power to administer the rite of confirmation for ten years, Lasuen received the same powers that Serra had held; but he did not obtain the document until July 13, 1790, and had consequently less than five years for the exercise of his privilege. During that time, however, he confirmed 10,139 persons.[7]

In connection with the departure of Palou, the completion of his historical writings on California deserves notice as a prominent and important event in the country's annals. The notice however need not be long, because the reader of the preceding chapters is already familiar by constant reference with the

[5] The records are very meagre on Palou's term and I find no official act by him as president. Payeras, writing in 1818, gives substantially the version of my text. *Arch. Sta. Bárbara*, MS., xii. 453. Mugártegui writes March 8, 1785, that Palou declined to serve. *Doc. Hist. Cal.*, MS., iv. 29. May 29, 1785, Fages urges Palou to accept for the good of the country, regretting his ill-health. *Prov. Rec.*, MS., iii. 50. See biography of Palou in next chapter.

[6] *Arch. Sta. Bárbara*, MS., ix. 306-9; xii. 35-6, containing the patents of Lasuen and Mugártegui. Lasuen's first record as president was Jan. 27, 1786; but he seems to have served from Palou's departure, which was probably in September or a little later. *Prov. Rec.*, MS., i. 180, ii. 128-9.

[7] *S. Cárlos, Lib. Mision*, MS., 66-8; *S. Diego, Lib. Mision*, MS., 45. March 2, 1790, Gen. Ugarte orders Fages to interpose no obstacles. *Prov. St. Pap.*, MS., ix. 350.

scope and contents of this author's literary works. There was no man so well qualified by opportunities and ability to write the early history of California as Palou, and he made excellent use of his advantages. As early as 1773, and probably before that date, he began the accumulation of material by copying original documents and recording current events, without any definite idea, as it would seem, of publication. He continued this labor of preparing careful historical notes down to 1783, devoting to it such time as could be spared from his missionary duties at San Francisco. During the years 1784–5, having apparently suspended work on his notes, he gave his attention to the preparation of a life of Serra, his prelate, former instructor, and life-long friend. This work he completed in February 1785 and carried it to Mexico later in the same year, where it was published in 1787. It was extensively circulated for a book of that epoch, though since considered rare, and it has been practically the source of all that has ever been written on California mission history down to 1784. Very few of modern writers have, however, consulted the original, most contenting themselves with a weak solution of its contents at second hand; hence the numerous errors extant in books, pamphlets, and newspapers. The manuscript of the historical notes after lying for some years in the college vaults, was copied into the Mexican archives and finally printed in 1857, though it was utterly unknown to writers on California until 1874, since which date it has been as carelessly and superficially used as was the life of Padre Junipero before. The *Noticias* is far the more extensive and complete work of the two,[8] though both cover

[8] *Palou, Relacion Histórica de la Vida y Apostólicas Tareas del Venerable Padre Fray Junípero Serra y de las Misiones que fundó en la California Septentrional, y nuevos establecimientos de Monterey. Escrita por el R. P. L. Fr. Francisco Palou, Guardian actual del Colegio Apostolico de S. Fernando de México, y Discípulo del Venerable Fundador: dirigida á su Santa Provincia de la Regular Observancia de Nro. S. P. S. Francisco de la Isla de Mallorca. A expensas de Don Miguel Gonzales Calderon, Síndico de dicho Apostólico Colegio. Mexico, 1787, 8vo 14 l. 344 pages, with map and portrait.* The author's

substantially the same ground. While my researches among original manuscript authorities have brought to light a large amount of material not given by Palou, yet his writings contain a few diaries which I have not found elsewhere. I have sometimes been

dedicatory letter and protesta is dated San Francisco, Feb. 28, 1785. The license of the audiencia to print is dated Dec. 7, 1786; and the latest of the various approvals of Franciscan authorities on March 12, 1787. In his prologue the author, after explaining that the work, written for the province of Mallorca, is published at the urgent request of certain friends of Serra who bear the expense, goes on to say: 'I well know that some who read new things expect the historian to indulge in theories and to clear up all difficulties. This method although tolerated and even applauded in profane histories, in those of saints and servants of God written for edification and to excite imitation, is deemed by the best historians a fault, the which I have aimed to avoid. As the soul of history is simple truth, thou canst have the assurance that almost all I relate I have witnessed, and the rest has been told me by other padres worthy of faith.' On Aug. 16, 1786, Palou writes to Lasuen, *Arch. Sta. Barbara*, MS., xii. 41–2, that everything is going well with the book, which he is told will circulate all over Europe, where all are curious to learn about California. He thinks it has been heard of at court, will send some copies to California, and asks Lasuen to pray for its success. It was sent to California, where each mission library had a copy. The work has become less rare and costly of late years than formerly. I have three copies, the most expensive of which cost less than $25. I have also the edition of Mexico, 1852, in which it was published with Clavigero's history of Lower California in a volume of the *Biblioteca Nacional y Estrangera*. It was also reprinted in a newspaper of southern California and in the form of scraps is found in *Hayes' Mission Book*, i.

Palou, Noticias de la (Antigua y) Nueva California. Escritas por el R. P. Fr. F. Palou (tom. i. ii.), in *Doc. Hist. Mex.*, serie iv. tom. vi.–vii. Mexico, 1857, 8vo, 688, 396 pp. The latest date mentioned is in July 1783, about which time it was doubtless concluded. A passage in tom. i. 269, shows that chap. v. of part ii. was written as early as 1773 at Monterey. It is evident that the author collected material from his first arrival, and wrote up the record to date at intervals as allowed by his duties. The original manuscript in the college of San Fernando has disappeared; but by royal order of 1790 a copy was made under the direction of P. Francisco Garcia Figueroa, who certified to its accuracy December 3 and 4, 1792. This copy, a duplicate of which was sent to Spain, has since been preserved in Mexico with other documents copied under the same order, which form the first 32 volumes of the *Archivo General*, an invaluable collection, all the volumes of which (except tom. i., which has been lost from the archives) are in my Library, some in print, others copied for the Maximilian Imperial Library, and the rest copied expressly for my collection. Palou's work formed tomes xxii.–iii. of the collection. In 1857 (not 1846 as Doyle says), it was printed in the form of a *folletin* of the *Diario Oficial*, forming the last two of a set of 20 volumes of Documents for the History of Mexico printed in the same way and selected largely from the same source. This collection, though badly printed, is the most important source of information extant on the history of Sonora, Chihuahua, and New Mexico, as well as California; but it is very rarely to be found complete, and has been utterly unknown to modern writers on history. Palou's work is divided into four parts. Part I. includes the annals of Baja California, under the Franciscans from 1768 to 1773, and extends over 245 pages of the first volume in 40 chapters; Part II. describes the expeditions to Monterey and the foundation of the first five missions, extending from page

tempted to entertain a selfish regret that Palou wrote,
or that his writings were ever printed, yet all the
same he must be regarded as the best original authority for the earliest period of mission history.
I have copied his map of Upper California.[9]

The missions had a narrow escape from ruin or from
what the friars believed would result in ruin, in the
form of their erection into a custody. Sonora and the
Californias had been formed into a bishopric in 1779,
and Bishop Reyes came in 1783, with full authority

247 to 688, in 50 chapters, and covering the period from 1769 to 1773; Part
III. is a collection of original documents on events of 1773-4, not arranged in
chapters, and filling 211 pages of tom. ii.; and Part IV. continues the narrative in 41 chapters, pages 213-396, from 1775 to 1783. At the beginning of
tom. i. the author gives the following prefatory notice: 'Jesus, Mary, and
Joseph. Summary (of the annals) of Old California during the time that
those missions were administered by the missionaries of the Regular Observ-
ance of Our Seraphic Father San Francisco of the Apostolic College of San
Fernando in Mexico—and of the new missions which the said missionaries
founded in the new establishments of San Diego and Monterey, written by
the least (the most unworthy) of said missionaries, who worked in Old California from the time it was intrusted to said College down to its delivery to
the reverend fathers of the sacred religion of Our "Cherubic" Father Santo
Domingo, and who later with other missionaries of the same College of San
Fernando went up to Monterey, having no other aim in this material work
which I undertake than that allowed me by the apostolic ministry, which is
to leave on record all that has happened and may happen while God gives me
life and health to work in this new vineyard of the Lord, so that when the
chronicler of our apostolic colleges may demand from that of San Fernando
notes of its apostolic labors I may have them compiled in a volume, or more
should there be enough to note, leaving it to the skill of the chronicler to put
them in the style for publication, and to his prudence and "religiosity" to
leave to the secrecy of the archives those which are written only because they
may be needed to shut the mouth of those rivals in the apostolic ministry who
are never lacking in new conversions, so that if they should talk some day of
missionary achievements there may be had in readiness all the events as they
really occurred in California, both old and new, all of which with all sincerity
and truth I will narrate in this summary, divided into four parts,' etc. This
gives an idea of the author's purpose, but hardly of his style, which was tolerably good. The book has many typographical defects, but few or none
which may not be corrected in substance from the archives. I have referred
constantly to this original edition, using for convenience tom. i. and ii., instead
the tom. vi.-vii. of the Collection. In 1874-5, Mr John T. Doyle issued in
San Francisco a reprint of Palou's *Noticias* in four 8vo volumes, one volume
to each part, well printed on good paper, and with a few corrections of typographical errors. The prefatory notice just quoted is omitted in the reprint;
there is a transfer of a diary from one part to another; some photographs of
mission buildings and other Californian scenes are added; and the whole is
prefaced by a long and ably written note by Mr Doyle on Palou's life, the mission system, the pious fund, etc.

[9] *Californias. Antigua y Nueva* . . .Longitude reckoned from San Blas. Diego
Francisco, sc., Mexico, 1787. Many strange inaccuracies will be noticed,
especially in the location of Santa Clara, San Antonio, and the Colorado
missions. For map see p. 408, this vol.

from the king and the Franciscan commissary general
to make the change, which though it was to leave the
friars in control and give the bishop but little if any
increased authority, was doubtless intended as a step
toward secularization. By it the connection between
missions and the colleges was to cease; the missions
were to become hospices and *pueblos de visita*, the
president would be replaced by a custodian, who with
his council of *definidores* took the place also, in a certain sense, of the college guardian and *discretorio*; and
the system was to be supported largely by the begging of alms. The colleges naturally protested against
the change, claiming that new friars would have to be
brought from Spain at great expense, since the old
missionaries would not sever their connection with their
colleges; that the new system made no provision for
new conversions; that, in California particularly, there
were none to give alms; and that there were many
of the custody regulations which it would be absolutely
impossible to enforce in these provinces. These protests were of no avail so far as Sonora was concerned, where the custody of San Cárlos was formed
in October 1783; but the college of San Fernando
succeeded in postponing action in the erection of San
Gabriel de California until the practical result elsewhere could be known. As the system proved to work
very badly in Sonora, California escaped the experiment which would almost certainly have proved destructive of mission prosperity. I hear nothing of
the scheme in California after 1787.[10]

---

[10] For a full account of the experiment in Sonora see *Arricivita, Cron.
Seráf.*, 564–75. The royal order in favor of custodies was dated May 20, 1782.
Aug. 17, 1792, after numerous petitions, the king, on advice of general, governor, bishop, and audiencia, issued an order which restored the old system.
Jan. 8, 1783, the guardian sends to Serra the brief and laws for custodies with
the remark that they contain many falsehoods and impossibilities, saying, 'we
work here with all our might to overthrow these projects in the beginning, realizing that merely to attempt them will cause great mischief.' The bishop will
try the experiment in Sonora, and we shall be left in peace for a while at any
rate. If you get orders from the bishop you must reply that your superior is to
be consulted. *Arch. Sta. Bárbara*, MS., xii. 156–8. Feb. 3, 1783, the guardian
of San Fernando and agents of Santa Cruz and Guadalupe colleges unite in a
protest to the viceroy. *Id.*, xii. 212–13. Jan. 14, 1784, Galvez informs the

Not only did the missions escape separation from
the control of San Fernando, but their number was
increased by the founding of two new establishments,
Santa Bárbara and Purísima, the long-talked of missions of the Channel. In 1782 these establishments
had been suspended as will be remembered because of
a plan of the secular authorities to break up the old
system and take from the friars the management of
temporalities, and the consequent refusal of the friars
to serve. The matter was referred to the king, but
I find no record of definite action thereon. The guardian instructed President Serra and his successor
Lasuen not to allow any new establishments except
on the old basis;[11] a good excuse was accordingly ready
whenever any suggestion was made by governor or
general; and finally by the tacit agreement of their
opponents the friars were allowed to have their own
way. In April 1786 the guardian informed the president that friars will come to California this year, and
Santa Bárbara may be founded, if the old system be
allowed, but not otherwise.[12]

viceroy that notwithstanding the opposition it is the king's will that the custodies be promoted. April 12, 1785, guardian informs Lasuen that there is
nothing for it but to be silent and cautious. *Id.*, 214–15. It seems that general Neve had favored the custody in California. *Prov. St. Pap.*, MS., vii.
13–14. March 21, 1787, the king ordered that if there were not enough friars of
San Fernando for the California missions, others might be taken from Michoacan. *Arch. Sta. Bárbara*, MS., x. 287; *Doc. Hist. Cal.*, MS., iv. 32.

[11] April 1, 1784, the general wrote to Fages authorizing the founding of a
mission at Montecito near the presidio of Santa Bárbara. The governor notified
Pres. Serra on July 27th from San Francisco. *Arch. Sta. Bárbara*, MS., vi.
194, xi. 5. No notice seems to have been taken of this. March 9, 1785, Gen.
Rengel, presuming that the padres sent for have arrived, orders Fages to proceed at once to found a mission at Montecito. Instructions have been given
to pay the $1,000 allowed each new mission. *St. Pap., Sac.*, MS., iv. 34–5.
Sept. 30th Fages notifies Lasuen that in company with P. Santa María he has
explored the Montecito site three fourths of a league from the presidio and
found it suitable for a mission. He has informed the general who orders an
immediate foundation. *Prov. Rec.*, MS., iii. 55. The same day Fages also
writes to Lasuen that as the two padres (Noboa and Rioboo) have arrived, he
hopes he will proceed at once to found the mission. *Arch. Sta. Bárbara*, MS.,
xi. 386–7. Lasuen replies that the padres are destined elsewhere and there
can be no foundation yet. *Id.*, 389–90. PP. Mariner and Giribet came in 1785,
but still nothing was done.

[12] Guardian to Lasuen April 1, 1786, in *Arch. Sta. Bárbara*, MS., viii. 133–
4; xi. 214. On the same date he forwarded instructions, not extant, and directs
Lasuen to show them to the governor if necessary, but on no account to allow

President Lasuen went down to the presidio at the end of October with two of the newly arrived friars, and superintended active preparations for the new mission which was to be formally dedicated the 4th of December.[13] On that day the cross was raised and blessed, and that day, the festival of Santa Bárbara Vírgen y Martyr,[14] is regarded as the day of the mission's regular foundation, though the ceremonies were not completed on account of the governor's absence and his order to suspend operations until his arrival. Possibly Fages had some thought of insisting on the innovations which had caused so much controversy, but if so he changed his mind, for after his arrival on December 14th the friars were allowed to go on in their own way. On the 16th the first mass was said by Father Paterna, a sermon was preached by Lasuen, and thus the foundation was completed.[15]

Fathers Antonio Paterna from San Luis, and Cristóbal Orámas, one of the new-comers, were the *ministros fundadores*, the latter being replaced in 1790 by José de Miguel.[16] The rainy season did not permit

---

[13] any infringement on the old system, or any experiments like those on the Colorado River, which he fears are still intended. *Id.*, xii. 24–5. April 9th he communicates the royal orders that older missions are to contribute stock and grain for Santa Bárbara. *Id.*, xi. 6. The new padres, six in number, were Arenaza, Arroita, Orámas, Santiago, Sola, and Torrente.

[13] Oct. 27, 1786, the commandant writes to Fages asking him to be present at the ceremony, and stating that the president and padres are about to arrive. Nov. 13th, he writes that timber has been cut and preparations have been made for sowing. *Prov. St. Pap.*, MS., vi. 51, 58.

[14] Santa Bárbara, the virgin and martyr, is a saint whose existence is traditionary and very doubtfully authenticated. She was the daughter of one Dioscoro who lived once upon a time in Asia Minor, a cruel idolater who gave his daughter to be tortured for her adherence to Christianity, and cut off her head with his own hand after she had borne unflinchingly the most cruel torments. She was and still is the patron saint of artillerymen in the Spanish army, and the powder-magazine on men-of-war often bears her name.

[15] Title-pages of mission-books signed by Lasuen in *Sta. Bárbara, Lib. de Mision*, MS., 43; *Arch. Sta. Bárbara*, MS., xii. 3, 4, 15–17. In the first annual report of the mission the date of the first mass is given as Dec. 15th, and the site is called Pedragoso, one fourth of a league from the presidio. *Id.*, v. 3, 4. Dec. 11th Lasuen writes to the general about the governor's order suspending the foundation. *Id.*, xi. 7. April 11th the general acknowledges receipt of news of founding, and in June of progress. *Prov. St. Pap.*, MS., vii. 43, 58–9.

[16] See lists of padres at Santa Bárbara from the beginning, compiled from the records by E. F. Murray, in *Arch. Sta. Bárbara*, MS., vii. 8–10, 25–9, 39–43, 68–70, 75–7.

the erection of buildings at first, and the first baptism on December 31st was administered at the presidio. On account of the proximity of the presidio only the ordinary guard of six men was allowed.[17] By the end of 1787 there had been 188 baptisms, which number was increased to 520 in 1790, with 102 deaths, leaving 438 existing neophytes. At this time large stock numbered 296 and small stock 503 head, while products of the soil amounted to about 1,500 bushels. A church 18 by 90 feet was completed in 1789, and by the end of 1790 other mission buildings of adobes with tile roofs were sufficiently numerous and in good condition.[18]

Respecting the founding of the third Channel mission little material is preserved in the archives. As early as 1779–80 it had been determined to locate the mission at the western extremity of the Santa Bárbara channel in the region of Point Concepcion, and that, not improbably with some reference to the name of the cape, it should be dedicated to La Purísima Concepcion, that is, "to the singular and most pure mystery of the immaculate conception of the most holy virgin Mary, mother of God, queen of heaven, queen of angels, and Our Lady." The foundation was suspended like that of Santa Bárbara, and operations were resumed when certain restrictions obnoxious to the friars were removed. In June 1785 Governor Fages recommended a site on the Santa Rosa River, now called the Santa Inés; and in March 1786 General Rengel instructed the governor to proceed with the establishment.[19] At last President Lasuen, doubtless

[17] *Fages, Informe de Misiones*, MS., 135–6.

[18] Full statistics of baptisms, deaths, etc., with inventories of mission property, and lists of buildings as completed from year to year in *Paterna, Informes de la Mision de Santa Bárbara, 1787–92*, MS. Want of water a great drawback in agricultural operations. *Fages, Informe de Misiones*, 136–7. First sowing of wheat did not come up. *Prov. St. Pap.*, MS., vii. 65. Owing to lack of means to support Indians only voluntary converts were admitted at first. *Id.*, vii. 59.

[19] Fages to Rengel June 2, 1785, in *Prov. Rec.*, MS., i. 192–3. Rengel to Fages March 24, 1786, in *Prov. St. Pap.*, MS., vi. 112–13. He calls the site

accompanied by a military guard, went up from the presidio of Santa Bárbara to the site selected, called by the natives Algsacupí, where on December 8, 1787, he blessed the spot, raised the cross, celebrated mass, and preached a sermon. Thus the mission was nominally founded, and the day was afterward given in mission reports as the anniversary date; but there was in reality no beginning of the mission work proper at this time. The day was that of La Purísima Concepcion and was therefore selected for the ceremony; but the spot was subsequently abandoned for several months, all returning to the presidio on account of the rainy season, as had doubtless been the intention. In the middle of March 1788 the mission escort, probably under Sergeant Pablo Antonio Cota, with a band of laborers and servants, went up to prepare the necessary buildings, and early in April President Lasuen returned with the two *ministros fundadores*, Vicente Fuster from San Juan and José Arroita a new-comer of 1786.[20] The former was succeeded late in 1789 by Cristóbal Orámas from Santa Bárbara. As early as August 1788 seventy-nine neophytes were enrolled. In September Corporal José M. Ortega took command of the mission guard.[21] The site as we shall see was changed in later years.[22]

selected Santa Rosa de la Gaviota, and says he will apply for the $1,000 allowed each new mission.

[20] Title-page of baptismal register signed by Lasuen, in *Purísima, Lib. de Mision*, MS., 1–3. Fages' instruction to the sergeant in command are dated at San Gabriel on April 7th. They are very complete and carefully prepared, enjoining great caution, kind treatment to the natives, and harmonious relations with the missionaries, the conversion of gentiles being the chief aim of the conquest. *Fages, Ordenes generales que debe observar el Sargento encargado de la Escolta de la Nueva Mision de la Purísima Concepcion, 1788*, MS. The sergeant is ordered to explore for the shortest way and best road to the Laguna Larga.

[21] *Prov. St. Pap.*, MS., viii. 87, 110. By the end of 1790, 301 natives had been baptized, 23 had died, and the number existing was 234. Small stock had increased to 731 and large to 257 head. The mission crops in 1790 were 1,700 bushels.

[22] List of over 50 rancherías in Purísima district, in *Purísima, Lib. Mision*, MS., 10.

CHAPTER XXI.

RULE OF FAGES; FOREIGN RELATIONS AND COMMERCE.

1783-1790.

No Fears of Foreigners—Isolation of California—War Contributions against England—Visit of the French Voyager La Pérouse—His Instructions—An Hospitable Reception—The Strangers at San Cárlos—Fate of the Expedition—Observations on the Country and the Mission System—Commerce—The Salt-trade—The Fur-trade—Vasadre's Project—A Failure—The Manila Galleon—Current Prices—Arrival of Transport Vessels—Northern Voyages of Martinez and Elisa—General Washington's Ship the 'Columbia'—The Chigoes—Ex-governor Neve and the Provincias Internas.

ALTHOUGH fears of foreign encroachments had been a principal motive for the Spanish occupation of California, and these fears were still entertained in Spain and Mexico respecting the far north, there was little anxiety on the subject in California. True, orders had been received occasionally from the king requiring precautions in view of special dangers real or imaginary,[1] and such orders had been made public with

---

[1] July 26, 1778, Croix to Neve, strict neutrality to be observed in the Anglo-French war by royal order of March 22. *Prov. St. Pap.*, MS., ii. 28. Aug. 6, 1779, Gen. Croix forwards to Gov. Neve royal orders for defence and reprisals against the English with whom Spain was at war. *Prov. St. Pap.*, MS., ii. 49. Feb. 11th and 18th, Croix to Neve forwarding orders for non-intercourse, reprisals, etc., *Id.*, ii. 102, 108. Aug. 25, 1780, Croix to Neve warning him of Admiral Hughes' departure from England in March 1779 with a fleet to operate on west coast of America. *Id.*, ii. 112–13. Sept. 22, 1780, Croix expresses to Neve the remarkable, not to say idiotic, opinion that to stop the breeding of horses in California and other frontier provinces would keep foreigners away 'pues difícilmente lo emprenderan (internarse) faltando los ausilios principales para transitar los desiertos que promedian.' *Prov. St. Pap., Ben. Mil.*, MS., iv. 14. March 22, 1781, Neve orders Carrillo to drive away the live-stock in case the English fleet should appear, in order to be free

all due formality, but always without producing the slightest ripple of excitement. There was not even the occasional appearance of a strange sail off the coast which produced such a tempest in a teapot at the south. No foreigner was seen in California during the first sixteen years of her history. Knowledge of current events was limited apparently to the names of ruling king in Spain and pope at Rome. If they knew more the records do not show it, and there is no evidence that the great conflict on the Atlantic side of their own continent was heard of until long after it was over.

Yet in the war between Spain and England, lasting, so far as knowledge of it in this far north-west was concerned, from 1780 to 1784, the Californians were called upon to aid their sovereign with their money and their prayers, and they responded very freely to the call. In 1780 Cárlos III. called upon his American subjects for a donation, fixing the contribution of each Spaniard at two dollars and of each Indian vassal at one dollar. A year later General Croix forwarded this order to California with instructions for its publication and enforcement.[2] Nominally the contribution was to be voluntary, but in reality was so managed as to leave no convenient method of escape. All persons under eighteen years of age were exempt. Neophytes might contribute produce which was to be sold at tariff prices; but it was of course a mission contribution made by the friar in charge from the community property in proportion to the number of male neophytes. Places that had suffered from epidemic or other special disaster might be declared exempt; but

to defend Monterey. *Prov. St. Pap.*, MS., iii. 305. March 17, 1784, treaty of peace between Spain and England sent to California. *Prov. St. Pap.*, MS., v. 56. Nov. 15, 1784, Fages to commandant general, has learned that a foreign power intends to send disguised emissaries to Mexico; will arrest any such who may come to California. *Prov. Rec.*, MS., i. 182. Nov. 15th, Id. to id. understands that no foreigners must be allowed in the country, especially at the ports. There are none here now. *Id.*, i. 181.

[2] Royal order of Aug. 17, 1780. Forwarded by Gen. Croix Aug. 12, 1781. *Arch. Sta. Bárbara*, MS., xii. 223–9; vii. 147–53; *Croix, Instruccion sobre Donativo en California para la guerra con Inglaterra, 1781*, MS.

full lists and records of the contributors in each establishment were to be made and forwarded to Spain. It was the opinion of General Croix that the soldiers should not be required to aid in the donation, but might do so if they wished. The missions of San Diego and San Juan Capistrano pleaded poverty at first,[3] but seem to have borne their part of the burden at last, since for any missionary to refuse was to put his mission in an unfavorable light for the future. The whole amount raised was over four thousand dollars, of which the governor personally contributed two thousand.[4]

The first intercourse of the Californians with subjects of a foreign power was with the French under Jean François Galaup de La Pérouse in the autumn of 1786. This distinguished navigator had sailed from Brest in August 1785 on the frigate *Boussole* with the *Astrolabe* under M. de Langle, on a scientific exploring expedition round the world, fitted out and despatched by the French government. A full corps of scientific specialists accompanied the expedition; minute and carefully prepared instructions were given, accompanied by reports and charts of all that had been accomplished by the explorers of different nations; the commanders were carefully selected for their ability and experience; and in fact every possible precaution was taken to make the trip a success. In the king's general instructions dated June 26, 1785, occurred

[3] *Arch. Sta. Bárbara*, MS., i. 259–60; xii. 230–2. President Serra approved the plea of San Diego. According to *Prov. Rec.*, MS., iii. 132–3, several missions sought exemption.

[4] The sums paid by each establishment were as follows: San Francisco presidio and two missions, $373; Monterey, $833; San Cárlos, $106; San Antonio, $122; San Luis, $107; Sta. Bárbara presidio, $249; Los Angeles, $15; San Gabriel, $134; San Juan and San Diego, $229; San Diego Pr., $515; total, $2,683, but there is some variation in the records. Dec. 7, 1782, Gen. Croix names the total amount as $4,216. Besides Gov. Neve, Ignacio Vallejo, majordomo at San Cárlos, is the only contributor named. He gave $10. San José would seem to have done nothing. See *Prov. St. Pap., Ben. Mil.*, MS., ii. 5, iii. 11, 27–9; viii. 4; *Prov. St. Pap.*, MS., iv. 76; *Prov. Rec.*, MS., ii. 70, 74–5. In accordance with a cédula of June 15, 1779, received in California June 13, 1780, prayers both public and private were ordered by the padre presidente on June 24th. *Arch. Sta. Bárbara*, MS., ix. 277–80; x. 273.

some passages relating more or less directly to California.[5]

La Pérouse brought with him, besides the historical work of Venegas, a printed account of the Spanish expeditions of 1769–70,[6] and other narratives in manuscript or print of subsequent Spanish voyages up the coast, several of which are translated and published with the journal of this expedition.

Having doubled Cape Horn, visited Easter Island and the Hawaiian group, the *Boussole* and *Astrolabe* crossed to the American coast, anchoring July 4, 1786, in the Port des Français in 58° 37′.[7] The navigator's instructions had been to visit Monterey first and thence to explore the coast up to the Aleutian Isles; but a knowledge of the prevailing wind had led him to a higher latitude; delays at Port des Français left no time for a northern voyage; and it was decided to run down the coast without stopping, obtain supplies at Monterey, and hasten back to the China coast, where the expedition was due in the early spring. On the voyage southward no observations were made on the California coast on account of the dense fogs, save that one night there was seen what seemed to be a

[5] ' If in the survey which he is to make of the north-west coast of America he finds at any points of that coast forts or trading-posts belonging to His Catholic Majesty he will scrupulously avoid everything which might give offence to the commandants or chiefs of those establishments; but he will use with them the ties of blood and friendship which so closely unite the two sovereigns in order to obtain by means thereof all the aid and refreshment which he may need and which the country may be able to furnish. . . So far as it is possible to judge from the relations of those countries which have reached France, the actual possession of Spain does not extend above the ports of San Diego and Monterey, where she has built small forts garrisoned by detachments from California or from New Mexico. The Sieur de La Pérouse will try to learn the condition, force, and aim of these establishments; and to inform himself if they are the only ones which Spain has founded on those coasts. He will likewise ascertain at what latitude a beginning may be made of procuring peltries; what quantity the Americans (Indians) can furnish; what articles would be best adapted to the fur-trade,' what facilities there might be for a French establishment, all this relating of course chiefly to the northern coast. *La Pérouse, Voyage de (Jean François Galaup) de la Pérouse autour du monde, publié conformément au décret du 22 Avril 1791, et rédigé par M. L. A. Milet-Mureau*. . .Paris, 1798, 8vo, 4 vol. with atlas in folio, tom. i. 28–9. It does not seem desirable to mention here the various translations and abridgments of this narrative and its accompanying documents.

[6] Doubtless the *Monterey, Estracto de Noticias,* or *Costansó, Diario Hist.*

[7] On the northern explorations see *Hist. Northwest Coast*, i. 174–7.

volcano in active operation below 41°, until they
entered Monterey Bay September 14th, anchoring
next day among the whales which came boldly within
pistol-shot to spout vile-smelling water round about
the vessels.

The French navigators had been expected. The
authorities had received orders to accord to the foreign
fleet the same welcome as to vessels of their own nation,
so that La Pérouse had little need to show his open
letter from the minister of Spain. The transports of
this year, the *Princesa*, Captain Estévan Martinez, and
the *Favorita*, Captain José Tobar, were now in port,
and their boats were promptly taken out by their captains to pilot the visitors into the harbor, seven guns
from the fort saluting them as they dropped anchor.
Don Pedro Fages not only carried out the orders of
his superiors, but says La Pérouse "he put into their
execution a graciousness and air of interest which
merit from us the liveliest acknowledgment. He did
not confine himself to obliging words; cattle, vegetables, and milk were sent on board in abundance.
The desire to serve us well nigh caused a disturbance
of the harmony between the commandants of fort and
corvettes; for each wished the exclusive right to supply our needs; and when it came to settling the score,
we had to insist on their receiving our money. Vegetables, milk, poultry, all the garrison's labor in helping
us to wood and water were free; and cattle, sheep,
and grain were priced at so low a figure that it was
evident an account was furnished only because we had
rigorously insisted on it. M. Fages joined to his gen-
erosity the most gentlemanly demeanor; his house was
ours, and we might dispose of all his servants."

"The padres of San Cárlos mission two leagues
from Monterey soon came to the presidio; as kind to
us as the officers of fort and frigates they insisted on
our going to dine with them, and promised to acquaint us in detail with the management of their
mission, the Indian manner of living, their arts and

customs, in fact all that might interest travellers. We accepted with eagerness... M. Fages wished to accompany us... After having crossed a little plain covered with herds of cattle... we ascended the hills and heard the sound of bells announcing our coming. We were received like lords of a parish visiting their estates for the first time. The president of the missions, clad in cope, his holy-water sprinkler in hand, received us at the door of the church illuminated as on the grandest festivals; led us to the foot of the altar; and chanted a te deum of thanksgiving for the happy issue of our voyage. Before entering the church we had crossed a plaza where Indians of both sexes were ranged in line; their faces showed no surprise and left room to doubt if we should be the subject of their conversation for the rest of the day."[8] After leaving the church the visitors spent a short time in examining the mission and in making a careful, though necessarily brief, study of the Franciscan régime and its effects on the natives. They probably visited San Cárlos more than once.

"As the soldiers had rendered us a thousand little services, I asked leave to present them a piece of blue cloth; and I sent to the mission some blankets, stuffs, beads, tools, etc. The president announced to all the village that it was a gift from their faithful and ancient allies who professed the same faith as the Spaniards; which announcement so aroused their kind feeling toward us that each one brought us the next day a bundle of hay or straw for the cattle and sheep. Our gardener gave to the missionaries some potatoes from Chili, perfectly sound; I believe this is not one of the least of our gifts and that this root will succeed perfectly around Monterey." M. de Langle also presented San Cárlos with a handmill for grinding grain which would enable four of the neophyte women to do the work of a hundred in the old way.[9]

[8] *La Pérouse, Voyage,* ii. 291–4.
[9] *Id.,* ii. 315, 299.

During the brief stay of ten days the crew were busy in obtaining wood and water; while the botanists, geologists, and other specialists pursued their studies, made drawings, and gathered specimens. Three short letters were written by La Pérouse and one by M. de Langle, to be sent to France by way of Mexico.[10] On the 22d all was ready for departure, and farewell was said to governor and missionaries. Next day the winds were contrary, but early on the 24th the navigators parted from Martinez, who came off in his longboat, and set sail for the far west. Then California's relations with the outside world were for a time suspended.[11]

[10] *Id.*, iv. 176–86. In a note of Sept. 14th (?) the commander says: 'Nos vaisseaux ont été reçus par les Espagnols comme ceux de leur propre nation; tous les secours possibles nous ont été prodigués; les religieux chargés des missions nous ont envoyé une quantité tres-considérable de provisions de toute espèce, et je leur ai fait présent, pour leurs Indiens, d'une infinité de petits articles qui avaient été embarqués à Brest pour cet objet, et qui leur seront de la plus grande utilité.' Again Sept. 19th: 'Nous sommes arrivés à Monterey le 15 septembre; les ordres du roi d'Espagne nous y avaient précédes, et il eût été impossible, dans nos propres colonies, de recevoir un meilleur accueil.' M. de Langle says on Sept. 22d, of Capt. Martinez: 'Il a prévenu nos besoins avec un zèle infatigable, et nous a rendu tous les services qui dépendaient de lui. Il m'a chargé de vous supplier de le recommander à son ministre...Je pars d'ici sans avoir un malade.' Again from Macao Jan 3d, *Id.*, iv. 235, La Perouse writes: 'I send the chart of Monterey made by ourselves; I have met at Monterey officers of the little San Blas establishment who certainly are not without ability and who seemed to me very capable of making charts with exactitude.'

[11] La Pérouse's visit left but a slight record in the Californian archives, yet it is alluded to in several official communications. See *Prov. St. Pap., Ben. Mil.*, MS., viii. 14; *Prov. St. Pap.*, MS., vii. 6, 42, 135; letter of Governor Fages of September 28th, in *Gaceta de Mex.*, ii. 286–8. September 18th, P. Lasuen writes to La Pérouse sending him three pieces of reed and a stone worked by the Santa Bárbara Indians. Will send 70 fanegas of grain. *Arch. Sta. Bárbara*, MS., xii. 364. Taylor, *Discov. and Found.*, No. 31, ii. 193, tells us that a picture of La Pérouse's vessels by one of his officers was preserved for many years at San Cárlos, but disappeared after 1833, having been carried away as the old settlers say by Petit-Thouars. This writer is very likely wrong about the subject of the picture. An anonymous Spanish writer in 1845, *C. S., Descripcion Topográfica de las Misiones, Pueblos, y Presidios del Norte y de la Nueva-California*, in *Revista Científica y Lit.*, i. 327–9, says that one of La Pérouse's officers made a sketch of his reception at San Cárlos by Palou (Lasuen) and two padres, which was kept in the mission *locutorio*. Captain Beechey wished to buy it, but P. Abella refused to part with it. When Petit-Thouars came it had disappeared. The writer made every effort to find it, offering as high as $1,000, but in vain. It was thought to have been stolen. The writer found at San Cárlos (no date) two Indians who remembered all about La Pérouse's visit. Finally Mrs Ord, *Occurrencias en California*, MS., 57–9, says that P. Moreno, soon after his arrival (1833), gave the painting to her brother, Juan de la Guerra, who on his death-bed presented it to her. In

Crossing the Pacific the Frenchmen visited the Philippine Islands in February 1787; then they coasted Japan and China, and reached Kamchatka in September; at the Navigator Islands in December, M. de Langle, with eleven of his men, was killed by the Indians; and the last that was ever known of vessels, commander, or crew, they were at Botany Bay on the coast of New Zealand, where La Pérouse's journal ends with January 24, 1788, a subsequent letter being dated February 8th, at the same place.

Though the stay of the ill-fated navigators at Monterey was brief and uneventful, I have deemed it worthy of somewhat extended notice, not only as the first visit of a foreigner to California, but on account of the remarkable accuracy, comprehensiveness, and kindly fairness of La Pérouse's observations on the province and its institutions. "His account of the natural resources of the country and its characteristics," says a modern writer of scientific attainments,[12] "was never surpassed in fidelity by his successors. His observations on the administration of the missions especially arrest our attention as the testimony of a Catholic concerning people of his own faith."

The navigator's observations can be only very briefly alluded to here, since they are in part scientific and beyond the province of history, and because many of the institutions mentioned have been or will be fully treated elsewhere in this work by the aid of this and other original testimony; yet a general glance at these impressions of an enlightened traveller seems appropriate. La Pérouse's geographical explorations on the Californian coast amount to nothing. His atlas contains the whole coast laid down from Spanish sources in his general maps, showing little detail and

1838 or 1839 it was stolen from her trunk, and in spite of all her efforts has never been recovered. She describes the painting as showing P. Noriega and two other friars at the door of the church, naked Indians ringing the bells and looking on as spectators, and La Pérouse, a tall, thin gentleman, with long gray hair in a queue, with some officers of his suite.

[12] *Stillman*, in *Overland Monthly*, ii. 257-8.

not requiring notice, yet copied here because of its date, being the first to show certain parts of the seaboard. Additional charts are given of San Diego, Monterey, and San Francisco, that of Monterey only partially from original surveys, the first from Spanish sources and accurate, and the last a rude sketch which is reproduced in the following chapter. The features

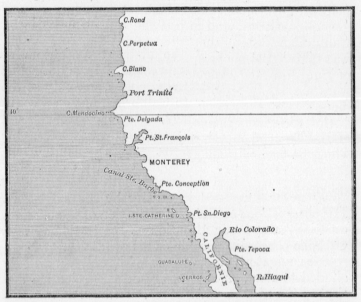

LA PÉROUSE'S MAP.

of the country round Monterey with its plants and animals, are however fully described, and a page in the atlas is devoted to an excellent engraving of a pair of California quails.

Of the country and its resources La Pérouse speaks in the most flattering terms, as also of its ultimate prospects, though he believes that under Spanish control its progress will be slow, the fur-trade being the most promising interest in the near future.[13] To the

[13] 'The salubrity of the air, the fertility of the soil, the abundance of all kinds of peltries give this part of America infinite advantages over the old California.' 'No country is more abundant in fish and game of all kinds.' 'This land is also of an inexpressible fertility; vegetables of every kind suc-

aboriginal inhabitants he gives much attention and finds in them physically, mentally, or morally but little to praise. The author is in error when he states that these Indians cultivated a little maize before the Spanish settlement. A vocabulary of the Monterey languages is included in the journal.[14] A brief but accurate account is presented of the military and political government with some items of history and general statistics; and in fact the only element in the Californian system that this writer failed to notice was that of the pueblos. He evidently did not hear of San José and Angeles, for he states that there were absolutely no Spanish inhabitants but the soldiers.

But what more than all else attracted the attention of the Frenchman was the mission system, respecting which he made a wonderfully exhaustive and accurate

ceed perfectly. Crops of maize, barley, wheat, and peas can be compared only to those of Chili, wheat yielding on an average 70 to 80 fold. The climate differs little from that of our southern provinces in France, but the heat of summer is much more moderate on account of the constant fogs which will give this land a moisture very favorable to vegetation.' California 'would be in no wise behind Virginia, which is opposite, if it were nearer Europe, but its proximity to Asia might indemnify it, and I believe that good laws, and especially free trade, would soon bring it some inhabitants; though the possessions of Spain are so broad that it is impossible to think that for a long time population will increase in any of her colonies. The large number of celibates of both sexes who as a principle of perfection have devoted themselves to this condition, with the constant policy of the government to admit but one religion and to employ the most violent means to maintain it, will ever oppose a new obstacle to increase. M. Monneron, in a note on Monterey, tom. iv. 122-3, says: 'A century will probably pass, and perhaps two, before the Spanish establishments situated to the north of the Californian peninsula can attract the attention of the great maritime powers. That which is in possession will not think perhaps for a long time of establishing colonies susceptible of great progress. Yet its zeal for the spread of the faith has already founded there several missions; but it is to be believed that not even the pirates will interfere with the friars.'

[14] The number of natives in both Californias is estimated at 50,000. 'These Indians are small, feeble, and do not show the love of independence which characterizes the northern nations, of which they have neither the arts nor the industry; their color is very similar to that of negroes, with straight hair.' The governor said the Indians plucked out the hair on face and body; while the president thought it was naturally lacking. They are very skilful hunters. M. de Lamanon obtained the vocabularies chiefly from two Indians who spoke Spanish. M. Rollin, surgeon-in-chief of the expedition, wrote a *Mémoire physiologique et pathologique, sur les Américains*, joined to La Pérouse's journal, tom. iv. 50-77, which relates largely to the natives of California and is of great importance.

study, considering the brief time at his disposal. Doubt-less the fact that he represented a Catholic nation did much to open the hearts and mouths of the friars, who seem to have held nothing back. The author not only presents a general view of the system, and of the mis-sions in their material aspects with statistics of the condition of each establishment, but he gives an excel-lent picture of the neophytes and their routine of daily life. Of the missionaries personally, of their character and their zeal and their motives, he speaks in terms of the highest praise;[15] but their efforts for the civilization of the natives did not seem likely to succeed. The neophyte was too much a child, too much a slave, too little a man. The mission régime was not fitted to dispel ignorance, missionary efforts were directed exclusively to the recompenses of another life, the present being disregarded. The community system based on the prejudices and ambition of the Jesuits was too servilely imitated. "The government is a veritable theocracy for the Indians; they believe that their superiors are in immediate and continual communication with God." "The friars, more occupied with heavenly than temporal interests, have neglected the introduction of the most common arts." La Pé-rouse saw in the *tout ensemble* of the Franciscan establishments an unhappy resemblance to the slave plantations of Santo Domingo. "With pain we say

---

[15] 'La piété espagnole avait entretenu jusqu' au présent, et à grands frais, ces missions et ces présidios, dans l'unique vue de convertir et de civiliser les Indiens de ces contrées; système bien plus digne d'éloge que celui de ces hommes avides qui semblaient n'être revêtus de l'autorité nationale que pour commettre impunément les plus cruelles atrocités.' 'It is with the sweetest satisfaction that I shall make known the pious and wise conduct of these friars who fulfil so perfectly the object of their institution; I shall not conceal what has seemed to me reprehensible in their interior régime; but I shall announce that individually good and humane, they temper by their gentleness and charity the harshness of the rules that have been laid down by their superiors.' 'I have already made known freely my opinion on the monks of Chili, whose irregularity seemed to me generally scandalous. It is with the same truth that I shall paint these men, truly apostolic, who have abandoned the idle life of a cloister to give themselves up to fatigues, cares, and anxieties of every kind.' 'They are so strict toward themselves that they have not a single room with fire though the winter is sometimes rigorous; and the greatest anchorites have never led a more edifying life.'

it, the resemblance is so perfect that we have seen men
and women in irons or in the stocks; and even the
sound of the lash might have struck our ears, that
punishment being also admitted, though practised with
little severity." Like Governor Neve, speaking of the
custom of hunting neophytes with soldiers, he "thought
that the progress of the faith would be more rapid,
and the prayers of the Indians more agreeable to the
supreme being if they were not under constraint."

"I confess," to give a final quotation from the
French navigator, "that, friend of the rights of man
rather than theologian, I should have desired that to
principles of Christianity there might be joined a leg-
islation which little by little would have made citizens
of men whose condition hardly differs now from that
of the negroes of our most humanely governed colonies. I understand perfectly the extreme difficulty
of this new plan; I know that these men have few
ideas, and still less constancy, and that if they are
not regarded as children they escape those who have
taken the trouble to instruct them. I know also that
reasonings have almost no weight with them, that it
is absolutely necessary to strike their senses, and that
corporal punishment with recompense of double rations has been so far the only means adopted by their
legislators; but to ardent zeal and extreme patience
would it be impossible to make known to a few families the advantages of a society based on mutual
rights, to establish among them a right of property
so attractive to all men; and by this new order of
things to induce each one to cultivate his field with
emulation, or to devote himself to some other class
of work? I admit that the progress of this new
civilization would be very slow; the pains which it
would be necessary to take, very hard and tiresome;
the theatres in which it would be necessary to act
very distant, so that applause would never make itself
heard by him who might consecrate his life to being
worthy of it; and therefore I do not hesitate to de-

clare that human motives are insufficient for such a ministry, and that only the enthusiasm of religion with its promised rewards can compensate the sacrifices, the *ennui*, the risks of such a life. I have only to desire a little more philosophy on the part of the men, austere, charitable, and religious, whom I have met in these missions." M. de La Pérouse longed for the existence of qualities and views that have rarely been possessed by missionaries in California or elsewhere.

Previous to 1786 California, beyond furnishing occasional supplies to the Philippine galleon, and sending to San Blas by the returning transports now and then a cargo of salt,[16] exported nothing; and little or no advantage was taken of a royal order of this year by which trade with San Blas was made free for eight years, and duties were reduced one half for five years more.[17]

The publication of Cook's voyage of 1778–9 on the Northwest Coast first opened the eyes of Spain to the importance of the fur-trade and led to some feeble attempts on her part to prevent so rich a treasure from passing into the hands of foreign nations and to utilize it for herself. A scheme was projected by the government in 1785 for the opening of a trade between California and China, the intention being to exchange peltries for quicksilver, and to make the fur-trade a government monopoly as that in quicksilver had always been. With this view Vicente Ba-

[16] The records are meagre about this salt supply. There are several orders in the archives requiring that salt be shipped from Monterey, and some indications that it was so shipped. Sept. 1, 1784, Capt. Cañizares at Monterey informs Gov. Fages that he has orders to load with salt. *Prov. St. Pap.*, MS., iv. 151. Order of the commissary at San Blas to same effect. *Id.*, 152. July 2, Gen. Neve orders Fages to have the salt ready so that no detention may occur. *Id.*, v. 62. Order given by Mexican government March 8, 1784, and repeated Jan. 11, 1787. *Id.*, vii. 11, 12. Nov. 15, 1784, governor understands that salt must be collected at Monterey. *Prov. Rec.*, MS., i. 182. Sept. 11, Fages tells Cañizares that as sailors are refused to get the salt none can be furnished. *Id.*, ii. 112. As early as 1770 the *San Antonio* was ordered to load with salt in California. *Prov. St. Pap.*, MS., i. 71.

[17] *Fonseca* and *Urrutia, Hist. Gen.*, ii. 84.

sadre y Vega was sent as a commissioner to California
to investigate the matter and to make a beginning of
collecting otter and seal skins.[18]

Don Vicente came up on one of the transports of
1786 which left San Blas in June, bringing with him
his credentials and instructions to Fages from Viceroy
Galvez, which were made public in the governor's proclamation of the 29th of August.[19] The skins were to
be collected from the natives by the missionaries, who
were to deliver them to Basadre at the tariff prices
ranging from $2.50 to $10, according to size and color.
Neophytes must relinquish to the friars all the skins
in their possession; skins obtained from neophytes
by soldiers or settlers were liable to confiscation, the
informer receiving one third of their value; those
legitimately obtained from gentiles must be sent at
once to the nearest authorities; all trade by private
persons was prohibited; and any skins reaching San
Blas through other than the regular channel would
be confiscated. The aim was to make the government
through the commissioner the sole purchaser, though
peltries were to be received and forwarded by commanders of presidios after Basadre's departure. The
friars favored the scheme since it put into their hands
a new branch of mission temporalities.[20]

[18] A good account of the project and its results is given in *Fonseca* and
Urrutia, Hist. Gen. Real Hacienda, i. 372–81.
[19] The royal cédula was dated June (July ?) 2, 1785; the viceroy's letter announcing Basadre's coming to Fages, Jan. 23, 1786; viceroy's letter to Lasuen
on same subject March 1, 1786; Fages' proclamation Aug. 29, 1786, including
regulations for the collection of skins. *Prov. St. Pap.*, MS., vi. 38–9, 52, 140–
5, 204–6; *Arch. Sta. Bárbara*, MS., i. 283–4, x. 8–10. Curiously the earliest
document in the archives relating to the otter is dated Oct. 24, 1785, after
the king's order was issued but before it could have reached California. It is
an order from Fages to Ignacio Vallejo at San José that if any one goes out to
trade with the Indians for otter-skins he is to be punished. *Dept. St. Pap. S.
José*, MS., i. 6, 7.
[20] March 8, 1787, the audiencia complained that the prices were too high,
since skins could formerly be bought for from one *real* to $1 each; besides
otter, other skins should be collected. *Arch. Sta. Bárbara*, MS., x. 1, 2. Sept.
24th, Lasuen replies that the former cheapness resulted from great abundance
and no demand; competition (!) reduced the otters and raised prices; if the
missions were allowed to trade with China the prices would be still higher; he
intimates that the missions should have a monopoly of the catch; and states
that there are no beavers or martens. *Id.*, x. 3–7, 13–16. Sept. 15th and 20th,

We have seen that La Pérouse had been instructed by the French government, prompted like the Spanish by Cook's narrative, to make a special investigation of the fur-trade and its possibilities. When he arrived at Monterey he found Basadre already there and the country considerably interested in the subject of his commission. Don Vicente is spoken of as "a young man of intelligence and merit, who is to depart soon for China for the purpose of making there a treaty of commerce in otter-skins." La Pérouse believed that the new branch of trade might prove 'to the Spaniards more profitable than the richest gold-mine of Mexico. Fages told him he could furnish 20,000 skins each year, or by means of new establishments north of San Francisco many more.[21] Yet notwithstanding the temporary enthusiasm of all concerned, this attempt of Spain to build up a profitable peltry trade in California was a failure.

Basadre, though complaining of obstacles thrown in his way by Fages, obtained 1,600 otter-skins, with

Fages issued a decree prohibiting gente de razon from acquiring otter-skins, giving the right exclusively to the Indians and missions. *Id.*, xii. 3; *Prov. Rec.*, MS., i. 35-6. July 30, 1788, Lasuen complains to the viceroy that prices are too low, and on Sept. 7th Fages seems to have issued a new tariff. *Arch. Sta. Bárbara*, MS., i. 289-92, ii. 1. March 18 (or possibly May 18), 1790, a new price-list with regulations in detail was issued in Mexico. The prices were to range from $2 to $7; and neither soldiers nor settlers were prohibited from gathering skins provided they dispose of them properly; but these regulations probably had no effect in California. *Id.*, ii. 4-8; *Dept. St. Pap. S. José*, MS., i. 31-5.

[21] 'We cannot fail to be astonished that the Spaniards, having so close and frequent intercourse with China through Manila, should have been ignorant until now of the value of this precious fur. Before this year an otter-skin was worth no more than two rabbit-skins; the Spaniards did not suspect their value; they had never sent any to Europe; and Mexico was so hot a country it was supposed that there could be no market there. I think there will be in a few years a great revolution in the Russian trade at Kiatcha from the difficulty they will have to bear this competition. The skins in the south are a little inferior in quality, but the difference is...not more than ten per cent in the sale price. It is almost certain that the new Manila Company will try to get possession of this trade, which will be a lucky thing for the Russians, because it is the nature of exclusive privileges to carry death or sluggishness into all branches of commerce and industry.' *La Pérouse, Voy.*, ii. 309-11. The Spaniards 'do not cease to keep their eyes open to this important branch, in which the king has reserved to himself the right of purchase in the presidios of California. The most northern Spanish establishment furnishes each year 10,000 otter-skins(?); and if they continue to be sold advantageously to China, it will be easy for Spain to obtain even 50,000, and thus to destroy the commerce of the Russians at Canton.' *Id.*, iv. 177-8.

which he returned to Mexico at the end of the year
and proceeded to Manila early in 1787. Before 1790
the whole number of otter-skins from both Californias
sent to Manila on account of the royal treasury under
Basadre's system was 9,729, the total cost at Manila,
including Basadre's salary, being $87,699.[22] In 1786
the Philippine Company had applied through the
house of Cosío for an exclusive privilege of the fur-
trade; and the government had been willing to grant
it on condition of past expenditures being reimbursed;
but the company did not accept the terms. Basadre
returned to Spain, and the government finally decided in 1790 to drop the project and pay money for
quicksilver, leaving the fur-trade to private enterprise.[23]

[22] *Fonseca* and *Urrutia, Hist. Gen.* The records of the skins collected are
meagre and incomplete. Oct. 7, 1786, Lieut. Zúñiga of San Diego speaks of
having some time in the past shipped $2,000 worth to José María Arce. *Prov.
Stat. Pap.*, MS., vi. 38. Sept. 15, 1787, José Soberanes charged $55 for dress-
ing 95 otter-skins. *Prov. St. Pap., Ben. Mil.*, MS., ix. 6. Oct. 6, 1787, there
were shipped on the *San Cárlos* and *Favorita* 267, of which 97 belonged to
presidio of Monterey, 62 to Lieut. Ortega, 56 to San Cárlos, and 52 to San
Antonio. *Id.*, ix. 14. July 30, 1788, Lasuen says to viceroy that Basadre collected from the mission 64 otter-skins worth $405. *Arch. Sta. Bárbara*, MS.,
i. 289. Nov. 9, 1789, commandant of Santa Bárbara to governor. He has collected and delivered to Cañizares of the *Aranzazu* 74 otter-skins from Purísima,
79 from Santa Bárbara, 81 from San Buenaventura, besides 32 fox-skins.
Prov. St. Pap., MS., ix. 146. Aug. 10, 1790, the Procurador Sampelayo has
collected for otter-skins remitted 1786–9, $1,472 on 169 skins to king; $132
on 18 skins to Basadre. *Arch. Sta. Bárbara*, MS., xii. 4, 5.

[23] Date March 29th, *Prov. St. Pap.*, MS., ix. 144. The following notes
from the archives are all I have found for the period of 1790–1800, and some
of them indicate that notwithstanding the royal order of 1790 some skins
were still bought on government account. Aug. 3, 1791, Sal to Romeu asking
for $823 for 97 skins in Mexico. *Prov. St. Pap.*, MS., x. 21. 1792, treasury
paid $439 for 59 skins from Santa Bárbara Company. *Id.*, xxi. 86. Dec. 30,
1793, viceroy to court of Spain says some otter and seal skins are sold to
vessels visiting the ports. *St. Pap., Miss. and Colon.*, MS., i. 17. Feb. 1794,
by order of viceroy otter-skins may be exported free of duty. *Prov. Rec.*, MS.,
viii. 141; *Prov. St. Pap.*, MS., xi., 159. June 8, 1795, governor to commandant. King allows Nicolás Manzaneli of San Blas to take otter-skins to
China from California and trade for goods. *Prov. Rec.*, MS., iv. 134. Feb.
23, 1795, the governor explains that the privilege of taking otter along the
coast amounts to nothing since they cannot buy China goods at Canton, a
privilege monopolized by the Philippine Company; yet that company might
advantageously take up the fur-trade. It is known that the English are
intriguing for it. By the treaty of Oct. 28, 1790, between Spain and England,
the latter power was prohibited from taking otter within ten leagues of any
part of the coast occupied by the former—that is, all of California below San
Francisco—and from engaging in illicit trade with the Spanish establishments. *Caloo, Recueil complet des Traités*, iii. 356–9.

The causes of failure, without going into petty details, were mainly as follows: the furs obtained in California were less numerous than had been expected, the natives lacking both skill and implements for otter-hunting; the quality was not equal to that of the furs brought to China from the Northwest Coast; the tariff of prices fixed by Basadre at first was thought too high; the royal fur-traders were not content with a fair profit; the Spaniards had no experience or skill in preparing, assorting, and selling the furs; and there were some diplomatic obstacles to be overcome in China. No private company ventured to engage in the trade thus abandoned by the crown; but skins in small quantities continued for many years to be collected by natives for the friars, who sent them by the transports to San Blas, whence they found their way to the Philippines. Later the American smugglers afforded the California traders a better market.

In other branches of commerce there was no development whatever. The Philippine galleon was required to touch at Monterey on each eastward trip, and was furnished with needed supplies on account of the royal treasury; but the commanders often did not stop, preferring to pay the fine imposed;[24] but all trade with this vessel by the missions or by private persons was strictly forbidden and, except in the form of occasional smuggling, prevented.[25] Governor Neve when he left California had in mind a project for trade with the galleons, which was further agitated by his successors; but after unfavorable reports had

[24] 'Dans la vue, sans doute, de favoriser le préside de Monterey, on oblige depuis plusieurs années, le galion revenant de Manille à Acapulco, de relâcher dans ce port; mais cette relâche et cet atterrage ne sont pas si nécessaires, que, même en temps de paix, ce vaisseau ne préfère quelquefois de continuer sa route, et de payer une certaine somme, par forme de dédommagement du bien qu'il aurait fait en y relâchant.' *Monneron*, in *La Pérouse, Voy.*, iv. 122.

[25] For orders against trade with the galleon in 1777, 1782, 1783, and 1787, see *Prov. Rec.*, MS., i. 64–5; *Prov. St. Pap.*, MS., iii. 154–6; iv. 99–100; vii. 38–9. Nov. 15, 1784, the governor asks for information on the charge that a padre and other persons went on board the galleon and brought off four bales of goods. *Prov. Rec.*, MS., i. 182. In December 1785 P. Noriega denies that there has been any trading between missions and galleon. *Monterey, Parroquia*, MS., 23.

been received from both Soler and Fages, the general
decided to continue the prohibition.[26]   I annex in the
form of a note a list of the prices current in California at this epoch.[27]

[26] *Soler, Parecer sobre comercio con el Buque de China, 14 de Enero 1787*, MS.
Fages, Informe sobre Comercio con Buques de China, 18 de Febrero 1787, MS.
The reasons urged against free trade were, that so far as the soldiers were
concerned better goods were received with greater regularity and at more
uniform prices by the present system; as the galleon could not touch at
all the presidios, a monopoly and inequality would be caused; the soldiers
becoming traders would be distracted from their regular duties; avarice and
pride would be engendered in California; China goods were not fitted for the
California trade; and there was no money to pay for them.   Yet Soler
favored the trade if the barter of peltries could be included; and Fages was
disposed to favor taking no notice of the barter of trifling articles by individuals.   July 14, 1786, Gen Ugarte asks Fages for his views on the matter.
Prov. St. Pap., MS., vi. 134–5. June 23, 1787, having received the reports, he
renews the old prohibition. *Id.,* vii. 38–9.

[27] Jan. 1, 1781, Gov. Neve formed a new *arancel* in accordance with royal
order of March 21, 1775, and decree of audiencia of Jan. 11, 1776. *Prov. St.
Pap.,* MS., vi. 14, 15; announced to Gen. Croix March 4th. *Prov. Rec.,* MS.,
ii. 41–2; approved by Croix July 27, 1781, and by king Feb. 22, 1782, and
royal approval published by Fages Jan. 12, 1784. *Prov. St. Pap.,* MS., iv.
156–8. This arancel given in full under date of Aug. 12, 1782, in *Arancel de
Precios,* 1782, MS. January 2, 1788, Gov. Fages issued a new *arancel* which,
however, only included live-stock and agricultural products, or articles likely
to be purchased by the government. *Arancel de Precios,* 1788, MS. Manuscript copy certified by Gov. Borica, in *Estudillo, Doc. Hist. Cal.,* i. 7; *Savage,
Doc. Hist. Cal.,* MS., 2; *Prov. St. Pap.,* MS., viii. 36–8. In the following
list the prices of 1788 are given in parentheses—*reales* expressed in 'cents':
Horses, $9 ($3–$9); asses ($6–$7); calves ($1.50); bulls ($4); sheep (75c.–$2);
swine ($1–$4); cocks (12c.–25c.); quail, per doz. (25c.); hares (12c.); mules,
$16–$20 ($14–$20); horses (unbroken, colts, mares, $3); cows ($4); oxen ($5);
goats (75c.–$1); hens (25c.–37c.)!; pigeons, per pair (25c.); rabbits (12c.)
Beef, jerked, per 25 ℔s.¦(75c.); beef, fresh, per 25 ℔s. (25c.); eggs, per doz. 24c.;
hides, untanned (37c.); hides, tanned, $2.75 ($2.25); wool, per 25 ℔s. ($1.25–
$2); tallow, per 25 ℔s. ($1.25–$2.50); candles, per 25 ℔s., $3 ($2.50); lard,
per 25 ℔s. $3 ($3); sheep-skin, 50c.; deer-skin (25c.); dog-skin, 75c.; buckskin, or antelope, tanned ($1.25–$1.50); cheese, per ℔., 6¼c. Wheat, per
fanega ($2); barley, per fan. ($1); lentils, per fan., $2.50; maize, per fan.,
$1.50; beans, per fan. ($2.50); peas, per fan. ($1.50–$3); flour, per 25 ℔s.
($1.25–$2); $2 per 25 ℔s. to $6 per fanega. Sugar, ℔., 25c.; panocha, ℔., —;
brandy, pt., 75c.; saffron, oz., 50c.; olive-oil, jar, $4.37; figs, ℔., 12c.; gun-
powder, ℔., $1; soap, ℔., 18c.; chocolate, ℔., 37c.–56c.; cloves, oz., 62c.;
cinnamon, oz., 62c.; cumin, oz., 3c.; red pepper, ℔., 18c.; pepper, oz., 6c.;
tobacco, ℔., $1.25. Anquera, $1.50; awl, 12c.; shield, $2; kettles (calde-
reta), $1; stirrups, wooden, $1; gun-case, $1.50; saddle-irons, $1; lance, 87c.;
penknife, 25c.; earthen pot., 12c.–18c.; plates, 4c.–18c.; comb, 6c.–50c.;
rosary, 3c.; ear-rings, pr., 75c.; saddle, $12–$16; punch, 25c.; cup, 18c.;
dagger, 22c.; anquera trappings, $2.50; earthen pan, 18c.; wooden spoon,
6c.; spurs, pr., $1; sword, $4.50; gun, $4.50–$16; bridle, $1; horseshoes, set,
$1; pocket-knife, 50c.; razor, 62c.; copper pot, $3.50; paper, quire, 45c.;
needles, paper, $1.28; needles, per 24, 12c.; bridle-lines, 50c.; Holy Christ,
$1.75; chisel, 12c.; scissors, 37c.–62c.; screw of gun, 25c.; jug, 12c. Baize,
yd., 50c.; coarse linen (Cotense), yd., 37c.–75c.; gold-lace, oz., $1.62; silver-
lace, oz., $1.62; ribbon, yd., 12c.–75c.; cotton cloth, yd., 25c.–37c.; pita twist,
10c.; linen (Platilla), yd., 62c.; Britannia (linen), yd., 82c.–$1.25; Bramant

Each year two of the four transports arrived from San Blas with supplies for presidios and missions, one usually visiting San Diego and Santa Bárbara, and the other San Francisco and Monterey. The *Favorita* from 1783 to 1790 made five trips; the *Princesa* and *San Cárlos*, or *Filipino*, each four trips; and the *Aranzazu* three. The commanders were Martinez, Aguirre, Camacho, Tobar, and Cañizares. These annual voyages present nothing requiring attention, save that in 1784 after the *Favorita* had sailed from San Francisco rumors were current of a wreck and four or five men killed at the mouth of the Pájaro River, rumors which proved unfounded. The Manila galleon touched at Monterey in 1784 and 1785; and in 1784 the *Princesa* arrived from the Philippines under Capt. Maurelle.[28]

In 1788 Martinez with the *Princesa* and the *San Cárlos* made a voyage to the Alaska coast and on his return touched at Monterey, where he remained with one vessel from September 17th to October 14th, the *San Cárlos* having gone back to San Blas without stopping.[29] In his northern voyage to Nootka the next year, in which he captured several English vessels and very nearly provoked a European war, Martinez did not touch on the California coasts; but in 1790 the *San Cárlos* and *Princesa*, under Fidalgo and Quimper, touched at Monterey on their return from Nootka in September, and perhaps brought the Californian *memorias* by this

---

(linen), yd., 82c.; Frieze (jerga), yd., 37c.; silver-thread, oz., $2.25; linen, domestic, yd., 62c.; linen (glazed), yd., 37c.; cloth (ordinary woollen), yd., $1.25; silk twist, 82c.; sackcloth, yd., 25c. Shirt (crea), $3.75; shirt (linen), $6.00; blankets (pastoras), $1; blankets (cameras), $2; medals, oz., 12c.; silk shawl, $6; hat, $1.12; handkerchiefs, silk, $1.50; stockings (thread), $1.50; stockings (woollen), 75c.; stockings (silk), $4–$4.50; shoes, 75c.

[28] For records of arrival and departure of the vessels each year see *Prov. St. Pap.*, MS., iv. 69, 133–4; v. 104–5, 161, 166; vi. 50, 53; vii. 4, 70; viii. 68, 89, 91–100; ix. 100, 243–4; *Prov. Rec.*, MS., i. 177–8; ii. 95; iii. 124, 200; *Prov. St. Pap., Ben. Mil.*, iv. 21; *St. Pap. Sac.*, MS., i. 52, ii. 16, 17; *S. Buenaventura, Lib. Mision*, MS., 4; *Gaceta de Mex.*, i. ii.; *Palou, Not.*, ii. 393–6.

[29] See *Hist. Northwest Coast*, i.; and *Hist. Alaska.* See also references of preceding note.

somewhat roundabout course.[30] The Nootka voyages will demand our attention in a subsequent volume of north-western annals.

As a continuation of Californian maritime history for this period the following order issued by Governor Fages to Commandant José Argüello of San Francisco May 13, 1789, explains itself, chronicles California's first knowledge of the United States, alludes to what might have been, but was not, a conflict between the Pacific province and the infant republic of the Atlantic, and indicates the foreign policy of Spain. "Should there arrive at the port of San Francisco a ship named *Columbia*, which they say belongs to General Washington of the American states, and which under the command of John Kendrick sailed from Boston in September 1787 with the design of making discoveries and inspecting the establishments which the Russians have on the northern coasts of this peninsula;—you will take measures to secure this vessel and all the people on board, with discretion, tact, cleverness, and caution, doing the same with a small craft which she has with her as a tender, and with every other suspicious foreign vessel, giving me prompt notice in such cases in order that I may take such action as shall be expedient." [31]

But Kendrick, in the *Columbia*, had sought a more northern port than San Francisco, and no narrative of a naval conflict has place in this chapter. Kendrick's associate, Gray, in the *Lady Washington*, however, had sighted California in latitude 41° 28′ in August 1788,

[30] *Hist. Northwest Coast*, i. 239, etc.; *Fidalgo, Viage*, 1790, MS.; *Id., Tabla*, MS.; *Quimper, Segundo Recon.*, MS.; *Navarrete*, in *Sutil y Mex., Viage, Introd.*, cxii.

[31] Copy certified by Argüello July 14, 1789, in *St. Pap., Miss. and Colon.*, MS., i. 53–4. Also printed translations in *Randolph's Oration; Hutchings' Mag.*, v. 310; *Elliot*, in *Overland Monthly*, iv. 337; *S. F. Evening Post*, July 21, 1877. A translation in the Library of the California Pioneers seems to have been followed by all writers, who have copied the error by which the *Columbia's* tender is taken for the boat of the presidio by the aid of which Argüello was to effect the capture! Several writers, including Randolph, Tuthill, *Hist. Cal.*, 117, and Frignet, *Californie*, 52, have also softened the governor's stern decree into an order merely to 'examine delicately' or 're-ceive with great reserve' the suspicious craft.

and passing northward had strangely identified a cape
in 43° with Mendocino.[32]

Similarly ineffective though well meant was an order that came all the way from the court of Spain in
1787, to be published in all parts of California, pre-
scribing an application of cool olive-oil as a remedy
for *niguas,* or chigoes, sometimes less elegantly termed
'jiggers,' a troublesome insect of tropical America;
but the chigoes, like the Yankees, avoided California,
and the order of Cárlos III. remained a nullity in this
part of his possessions.[33]

A birth, marriage, or death in the royal family was
usually announced with all due formality in this remote corner of the world; and on one occasion a deserter at Monterey, whose descendants still live in
California, took advantage of the general pardon accompanying the news of the happy delivery of the
princess.[34]

The death of Cárlos III. was announced in February 1789, and orders were issued for the *salva fúnebre*
and other rites at the presidios, with prayers by all
the padres.[35]

Felipe de Neve, ex-governor, went to Sonora in
the autumn of 1782, as we have seen, to take the position of inspector general with the rank of brigadier.
Early in 1783 he succeeded Don Teodoro de Croix as
commandant general of the Provincias Internas, a
position second only to that of viceroy among Spanish
officials in America, though Neve, like his prede-

[32] *Haswell's Voyage,* 1787–9, MS.; *Hist. Northwest Coast,* i. 187.
[33] A royal order of Nov. 20, 1786, forwarded by commandant general,
Apr. 22, 1787. *St. Pap., Miss. and Colon.,* MS., i. 51–2.
[34] *Prov. Rec.,* MS., i. 159. In 1784 the *Princesa* was illuminated at
news that royal twins had been born; and the president was ordered to announce the birth and give thanks therefor. *Prov. St. Pap.,* MS., v. 117;
Arch. Sta. Bárbara, MS., xi. 385. Aug. 1st, Fages notifies commandants that
congratulations may be sent in. *Prov. St. Pap.,* MS., iv. 165. Oct. 14,
1785, the king orders thanksgiving everywhere for birth of Prince Fernando
María. *St. Pap., Sac.,* MS., xv. 26. Nov. 4, 1780, Santa Barbara ordered to
fire 21 guns with 23 lbs. of powder on San Cárlos day. *Prov. St. Pap.,* MS.,
viii. 89. Oct. 15, 1785, general pardon published in California on account of
birth of twins Don Cárlos and Don Felipe. *St. Pap., Sac.,* MS., iv. 5.
[35] *Arch. Sta. Bárbara,* MS., xii. 306.

cessor, was independent of viceregal authority.[36] The choice was a merited recognition of Neve's abilities, but his rule was cut short by death at the end of 1784.[37] All that is known of Neve's life has been told in the preceding chapters, and the reader is already aware of what manner of man he was, able, patriotic, and dignified. Devoted to the royal service and to the true interests of California, he formed and followed a well defined policy, rising above the petty obstacles thrown in his way by the friars. The dislike of the latter was caused almost wholly by Neve's great influence in Mexico and Spain, and by his opposition to their far-reaching schemes of unlimited control. Personally he was courteous and agreeable, more so than many other officials; but while others followed more or less faithfully the policy laid down in superior instructions, he largely dictated that policy. Finding that the friars would not submit to amicable recognition of the secular authorities he proposed to restrict their control of the mission temporalities and of the natives in the interests of colonization, of real civilization, and the rights of man. Whether his system or any

[36] On appointment as inspector see chap. xviii. Made commandant general Feb. 15, 1783. Acknowledges Fages' congratulations Feb. 6, 1784. April 5, 1784, Fages learns that Neve has been granted $8,000 salary as commandant inspector. July 12, 1783, royal cédula confirming Neve's appointment dated July 12, 1783. See *Prov. Rec.*, MS., i. 166, 188; iii. 182; *St. Pap.*, *Sac.*, MS., xv. 18; *Prov. St. Pap.*, MS., iv. 62-4; v. 25, 88.

[37] He died probably on November 3d, and his death was announced to Gov. Fages on Nov. 30th. *Prov. St. Pap.*, MS., v. 63-4. Fages speaks of his death on Feb. 1, and April 22, 1785. *Prov. Rec.*, MS., i. 201, ii. 93. Don Felipe de Neve was a major of the Querétaro regiment of provincial cavalry from its organization in 1766 until September 1774, when he was selected by Viceroy Bucareli to succeed Gov. Barri in the Californias. He assumed the office at Loreto on March 4, 1775. When the capital was changed he came to Monterey, arriving on Feb. 3, 1777. He made a beginning of colonization in 1777; offered his resignation, and was made colonel in 1778; prepared in 1779 his new reglamento; and had his quarrel with Serra in 1780. Subsequently he spent most of his time at San Gabriel superintending the foundation of Los Angeles and making preparations for the Channel missions. On Aug. 21, 1782, he started for the Colorado River on a campaign against the murderers of Rivera, but on the way, unexpectedly as it would seem, he received notice of his promotion dated July 12th to be inspector general. In September he received the cross of the order of San Cárlos and at the same time or a little later the rank of brigadier general. He was made commandant general Feb. 15, 1783, probably; was confirmed July 12, 1783; and died Nov. 3d of the next year.

possible system could have been successful, considering
the class of colonists obtainable, the character of the
natives, the isolation of California, and the general current of Hispano-American affairs, I seriously doubt;
but unlike some Mexican governors who affected a like
position in later times, Neve was honest in his views
and worked calmly and intelligently for their realiza-
tion.   Such men would have done all that it was possible to do with half-breed colonists, stupid aborigines,
and opposing priests.

At Neve's death José Antonio Rengel was appointed by the audiencia of Guadalajara to the temporary command; and by royal order of October 6,
1785, General Jacobo Ugarte y Loyola was placed in
command,[38] where he remained until 1790.   During
this period there were several subdivisions of the internal provinces, but Ugarte always possessed power
over those of the west, including California.   During
the term of Viceroy Galvez, 1785–7, he had authority
over the commandant general, who had before been
independent; and after his death the dependence continued, though not very clearly defined, until 1788.
In 1790 Ugarte was succeeded by Pedro de Nava
under whose rule all subordination of the command
was removed, and in 1792 or 1793 all the provinces
were reunited in one independent command.[39]

Viceroy Flores in his instructions to his successor

---

[38] *Prov. St. Pap.*, MS., iv. 154–5; v. 63–4; vi. 106; *Galvez, Instruccion
formada de real órden, 1786*, pp. 1–56.

[39] Ugarte commanded in person in Sonora and California; had a subordinate in N. Vizcaya and New Mexico, and another in Coahuila and Texas; was
subordinate to Viceroy Galvez; but became independent at his death. *Instrucciones de Vireyes*, 124–5; *Mayer MSS.*, No. 8.   February 10, 1787, Ugarte informs Fages that by death of Galvez his command again becomes independent.
Prov. St. Pap., MS., vii. 43–5.   March 2, 1787, royal order giving Viceroy Flores
the same authority that Galvez had held. *Id.*, vii. 31, viii. 40–1.   December
3, 1787, comandancia divided into eastern and western provinces. *St. Pap.,
Miss. and Colon.*, MS., i. 58, 61.   May (or March) 11, 1788, king gave viceroy increased and full powers over Provincias Internas. *Mayer MSS.*, No. 1;
San Miguel, Rep. Mex., 13.   July 9, 1788, Viceroy Flores gives Ugarte full
powers. *Prov. St. Pap.*, MS., viii. 5, 6.   March 7, 1790, Ugarte succeeded
by Nava and Ugalde (in eastern provinces) by Rengel. *Mayer MSS.*, No. 2;
November 28, 1790, Nava announces his appointment. *Prov. St. Pap.*, MS.,
ix. 348.   1792, all provinces reunited. *Escudero, Not. Sonora*, 71.   1793, *Instrucciones de Vireyes*, 201.

Revilla Gigedo in 1789 devoted considerable attention to California and to the importance of its defence and further colonization, recommending war-vessels to protect the coast, since an attack by foreigners was possible and the reconquest would be extremely difficult. A reënforcement of soldiers who would later become settlers was likewise proposed for consideration; and the viceroy had also asked the king for a few families from the Canary Islands to take care of a large number of foundlings whom he intended to send to California.[40] During the period, however,. there was practically nothing done in behalf of colonization, beyond allowing discharged sailors in the ports to be enlisted as settlers or soldiers; yet Fages reported strongly in favor of colonization, since the missions with their increasing number of neophytes could not be depended on to supply grain for the presidios.[41]

The old desire for overland communication with California had pretty nearly died out. Fages at the beginning of 1785 proposed to lead an expedition and to open communication with New Mexico; but the scheme met with no favor, and was positively forbidden by Viceroy Galvez in his instructions to General Ugarte in 1786, on the ground that small parties would be exposed to great danger on the route, and large ones could not be spared.[42]

[40] *Instrucciones de Vireyes*, 139–40; *Florés, Instruccion*, MS., 22–5.

[41] *Prov. Rec.*, MS., i. 203–4; *St. Pap., Sac.*, ii. 17; *Prov. St. Pap.*, MS., v. 164. Feb. 15, 1785, Gen. Rengel forwards orders of king for weather reports every 6 months. *St. Pap., Sac.*, MS., xv. 26. Dec. 31, 1785, the governor renders the only report extant for this decade, describing the climate as cold and humid, especially at San Francisco, but better for Spaniards than natives; yet the region is fertile and attractive with ample resources for colonies. The spring rains are as in Spain, and this year have been very abundant. *Relacion de Temperamento 1785*, MS.

[42] Fages to Gen. Rengel, Jan. 14, 1785. *Prov. Rec.*, i. 186, ii. 104–5; Rengel to Fages, July 1st. *St. Pap., Sac.*, MS., xv. 23; *Galvez, Instruccion*, 1786, MS., 31; *Escudero, Not. Son.*, 70; *Mayer MSS.*, No. 8. In the diary of an expedition to the Tulare region in 1806 P. Muñoz mentions a report by the chief of a San Joaquin ranchería that some twenty years before—1786—a party of soldiers had arrived from the other side, killed some of the natives when attacked, and retired. The padre thinks this must have been a party from New Mexico. *Arch. Sta. Bárbara*, iv. 25–6.

CHAPTER XXII.

RULE OF FAGES; LOCAL EVENTS AND STATISTICS.

1783-1790.

DURING the era of exploration, conquest, and foundation, which was for the most part ended soon after the beginning of the second decade, the local history of each new establishment has been a link in the chain of provincial development so closely united with affairs of government and the general march of events as to be susceptible of strict chronological treatment. Local annals will be to the end an important and deservedly prominent element in Californian history, as in any provincial history properly so called; but hereafter it will be best, that is, most conducive to a clear presentment and easy study of the subject, to group these annals in decades, or other convenient periods, and to present them side by side with and to some extent independently of the more formal and

(450)

general narrative which they support and illustrate. The present chapter I devote to purely local annals of the missions, presidios, and pueblos during the rule of Pedro Fages, from 1783 to 1790, a period which may, however, be regarded practically in most respects as beginning a year or two earlier, and thus comprising the second decade of Spanish occupation.

To begin in the extreme south; the presidio of San Diego from 1781 to 1790 and for three years more was under the command of Lieutenant José de Zúñiga, who, as habilitado, was also intrusted with the company accounts. So far as the records show no complaint was ever made against him in either capacity, and he not only enjoyed the entire confidence of both governor and commandant general, but was popular with his men, and efficient in keeping the savages quiet.[1] The second officer was at first Alférez José Velasquez, who like Zúñiga was one of the new officers sent to California under the regulation of 1781, who did good service among the southern and frontier savages, some of whose explorations I shall have occasion to mention later, but who died at San Gabriel November 2, 1785.[2] During 1786 the position was vacant,

[1] Fages to Gen. Ugarte Nov. 8, 1787, in *Prov. St. Pap.*, MS., v. 4, urges that it would be unsafe to remove Zúñiga in view of his success in ruling the natives. Capt. Soler wished to put him in command at Santa Bárbara so that under his supervision a stupid alférez might be utilized as habilitado. *Id.*, vii. 114–16. Lieut. Ortega, Zúñiga's predecessor, had practically commanded at San Diego since its foundation, at first as sergeant in charge of the *escolta*, and after March 1774, *Id.*, i. 149, as lieutenant and commandant of the presidio. Rafael Pedro y Gil, who as *guarda-almacen* had charge of the accounts before Zúñiga's time, gave them up on Oct. 19, 1781, and went to San Blas under arrest to account for a deficit of $7,000. *Prov. Rec.*, MS., i. 118; ii. 70–1. Pedro y Gil was a native of Baroca in Aragon, married to Doña Josefa de Chavira y Lerma, a native of Jalisco, by whom he had several children, three of them born at San Diego. *S. Diego, Lib. de Mision*, MS., 12, 18, 20. He came as store-keeper in 1774, asked to be relieved the same year, had a deficit of $333 in 1775, and asked again for dismissal before he was ruined. *Prov. St. Pap.*, MS., i. 234–5, 238. In 1782 his deficit was $6,300. *Monterey Co. Arch.*, MS., vii. 6. In 1791 he was a revenue-officer in Etzatlan, Jalisco, and again in debt to the government. *Nueva España, Acuerdos*, MS., 16.

[2] He was buried Nov. 3d by Sanchez in the mission church. *San Gabriel, Lib. de Mision*, MS., 8; *Prov. St. Pap., Ben. Mil.*, MS., vii. 2. His death was caused by a sore hand. *Prov. St. Pap.*, MS., v. 160. In *Prov. Rec.*, MS., ii.

but early the next year Sergeant Pablo Grijalva of
the San Francisco company was made alférez, or sub-
lieutenant, and sent down to take the place, which he
held for the rest of the period.[3]

Grijalva, it will be remembered, had come from
Sonora with Anza's San Francisco colony in 1776.
The sergeant of San Diego had been Juan José Robles,
a victim of the Colorado River massacre, and after
his death Guillermo Carrillo served for a time, but
died in December 1782,[4] and after a vacancy of two
years Ignacio Alvarado was promoted from among
the corporals to fill the place from 1784. The presidial force under these officers was by the regulation
to be five corporals and forty-six soldiers, and the
ranks never lacked more than three of being full. Six
men were constantly on duty at each of the three
missions of the district, San Diego, San Juan Capistrano, and San Gabriel; while four served at the
pueblo of Angeles, thus leaving a sergeant, two
corporals, and about twenty-five men to garrison the
fort, care for the horses and a small herd of cattle,
and to carry the mails, which latter duty was the
hardest connected with presidio service in time of
peace. There were a carpenter and blacksmith constantly employed, besides a few servants, mostly
natives. The population of the district in 1790, not
including Indians, was 220.[5]

132, it is implied that Velasquez had been habilitado, that the office fell to
Zúñiga at his death, and that Raimundo Carrillo was to be sent to aid Zúñiga
in his new duties; but this is certainly an error.

[3] His commission as alférez of the San Diego company was sent by the general Feb. 9, 1787. *Prov. St. Pap.*, MS., vii. 45.

[4] *San Diego, Lib. de Mision*, MS., 79.

[5] Company rosters, containing the names of all officers and men, were
made out monthly for each presidio. In the early years only a few of these
rosters for each year have been preserved; but in later times they are nearly
complete. The reglamento gave San Diego $13,000 per year; but the aver-
age annual expense as shown by the company accounts was about $16,000.
The average pay-rolls were $12,000; Mexico *memorias*, $8,000; and San Blas,
$3,500. In 1786 supplies to the amount of $3,653 were bought of the missions. Between $400 and $500 were retained from soldiers' pay each year for
the *fondo de retencion*. Military accounts in *Prov. St. Pap., Ben. Mil.*, MS.,
ii. 21; iii. 14; vi. 4; v. 9; viii. 3–5; xx. 6, 7; *St. Pap., Miss. and Colon.*, MS.,
i. 169–70; *Monterey Co. Arch.*, MS., vii. 6. For lists of arms and ammunition see *St. Pap., Sac.*, MS., ii. 26–7, v. 25; *Prov. St. Pap.*, MS., v. 176–9.

Respecting the presidio buildings during this period the records are silent; but in view of Governor Neve's efforts in this direction, of the fact that the work of collecting foundation stones was begun as early as 1778, and especially because the correspondence of the next decade speaks of extensive repairs rather than original construction, I suppose that the palisades were at least replaced by an adobe wall enclosing the necessary buildings, public and private. Here on the hill lived about one hundred and twenty-five persons, men, women, and children. Each year in summer or early autumn one of the transport vessels entered the harbor and landed a year's supplies at the embarcadero several miles down the bay, to be brought up by the presidio mules. Every week or two small parties of soldier-couriers arrived from Lóreto in the south or Monterey in the north with ponderous despatches for officials here and to the north, and with items of news for all. Each day of festival a friar came over from the mission to say mass and otherwise care for the spiritual interests of soldiers and their families; and thus the time dragged on from day to day and year to year, with hardly a ripple on the sea of monotony.

There was an occasional rumor of intended hostilities by the natives, but none resulted in anything serious, most of the trouble occurring south of the line in Baja Californian territory and requiring some attention from Fages during his southern trip in the spring of 1783. Here in the south, as in fact throughout the country, the natives were remarkably quiet and peaceful during Fages' rule. This is shown by the meagre records on the subject in connection with the well known tendency of the Spaniards to indulge in long correspondence on any occurrence that can possibly be made to appear like an Indian campaign.[6]

[6] June 30, 1783, Fages to Padre Sales, in *Prov. Rec.*, MS., iii. 218, says that he has ordered a sally against the Colorado Indians; and Oct. 26, *Id.*, 201, he orders Sergt. Arce with a guard of 4 or 5 men to watch those Indians,

Neve's instructions on leaving California had included a recommendation to open a new and safer route from San Diego to the peninsula. The exploration seems to have been made, and the result, saving ten or twelve leagues of distance and avoiding some dangerous bands of coast natives, was approved by General Rengel in 1786.[7] At the end of May 1783 Alférez Velasquez made a reconnoissance eastward from San Diego with a view to examine a new route to the Colorado River recommended by Lasuen. He went no farther than the summit of the mountains, found the route impracticable, and returned by another way after an absence of four days.[8] In October of the same year Velasquez had instructions from Fages to visit the Colorado, to examine a ford said by the natives to exist near the mouth, to recover as many horses as possible without using force, and to keep a full diary of the trip;[9] but it seems that no such exploration was made. In 1785, however, Fages in person made a similar reconnoissance accompanied by Velasquez, whose diary has been preserved.[10] This trip was made from the frontier where Fages had been searching for a mission site, the outward march being in what is now Lower California, but a portion

the guard to be relieved every 15 days. Aug. 21st, Zúñiga to Fages states that the Serranos have killed a neophyte and threaten to attack the mission. He has taken steps to keep them in check. *Prov. St. Pap.*, MS., iv. 77. Nov. 15, 1784, governor to general, that a deserter, Hermenegildo Flores (an Indian probably) has been killed by the Indians. *Prov. Rec.*, MS., i. 181–2. Oct. 7, 1786, Zúñiga to Fages, that he has sent 7 men to reconnoitre Tomgayavit. *Prov. St. Pap.*, MS., vi. 38. Dec. 21, 1788, the soldier Mateo Rubio seriously injured while loading a gun. *Id.*, viii. 68.

[7] *Prov. St. Pap.*, MS., iii. 131–3; *Id.*, *Ben. Mil.*, MS., iv. 18; vi. 113–14. Some details respecting the new route are given.

[8] *Velasquez, Diario y Mapa de un Reconocimiento desde S. Diego, 1783*, MS., with a rude sketch of the route, which although the earliest map of this region extant, I do not deem worth reproducing.

[9] *Prov. Rec.*, MS., iii. 188–90.

[10] *Velasquez, Relacion del Viaje que hizo el Gobernador Fages, 1785*, MS. A continuation of the title explains the document: 'Diary made by order of Gov. Fages of the exploration made by him in person from the frontier, crossing the sierra, wandering from the mouth of the Colorado River to the gulf of California, passing through the country of the Camillares, Cucupaes, Guyecamaes, Cajuenches, and Yumas; and his return across said sierra to this presidio.' Dated San Diego, April 27, 1785. The trip lasted from April 7th to 20th.

of the return north of the line across the sierra to
San Diego. There was one fight in which the natives
were punished for having killed a horse as well as for
previous offences with which they were charged. The
narrative is long and filled with petty details, without
value for the most part, but which might be of some
geographical interest if presented in full and studied
in connection with an accurate topographical map, did
such a thing exist. It may be noted here that Fages
in 1782 had crossed directly from the Colorado to San
Diego, the first recorded trip over that route. I append a chart made by Juan Pantoja in 1782, which
was copied by La Pérouse in substance.[11]

At the mission six miles up the river there was a
total change in the missionary force about the middle
of the decade, caused by the death of one of the
ministers and promotion of another. Juan Figuer
after seven years of service in this field died December 18, 1784,[12] and was buried in the mission church
next day. For about a year Fermin Francisco de
Lasuen served alone, until in November 1785 the
duties of his new position as president called him to
San Cárlos, and his place was taken by Juan Mariner.
Juan Antonio García Rioboo was associate until October 1786, and was then succeeded by Hilario Tor-

[11] *Sutil y Mexicana, Viage, Atlas; La Pérouse, Voy., Atlas.* I omit the
soundings.
[12] *San Diego, Lib. de Mision,* MS., 80, containing his *partida de entierro*
signed by Lasuen. Figuer was a native of Anento in Aragon, and became a
Franciscan at Zaragoza. Of his coming to America and to San Fernando college I have found no record. With 29 companion friars for the Californias
he arrived at Tepic from Mexico at the end of 1770, and with about 19 of the
number sailed for Loreto in February 1771. The vessel was driven down to
Acapulco and in returning was grounded at Manzanillo. Most of the padres
returned to Sinaloa by land, but Figuer and Serra intrusted themselves again
to the sea, when the *San Cárlos* was got off, and after a tedious voyage
reached Loreto in August 1771. Figuer was assigned to the Baja Californian
mission of San Francisco de Borja. In November 1772 he was sent up to
San Diego by Palou in company with Usson, both being intended for the
proposed mission of San Buenaventura; but that foundation being postponed
Figuer became minister of San Gabriel in May 1773. He served at San
Gabriel 1773–4; at San Luis Obispo Oct. 1774 to June 1777; and at San Diego
until his death in Dec. 1784. He was buried in the mission church on Dec.
19th, by his associate Lasuen. In 1804 his remains, with those of the martyr
Jaume and of Mariner, were transferred with all due solemnity to a new sepulchre under an arch between the altars of the new church.

rens.   The three last named friars were new-comers,
Rioboo having been sent up by the guardian in the
vessel of 1783 at Serra's request for supernumeraries,
and the other two having arrived in 1785 and 1786,

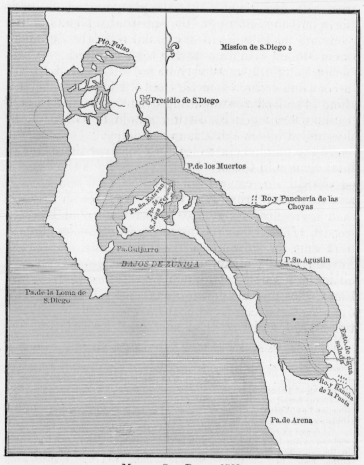

MAP OF SAN DIEGO, 1782.

doing their first work at San Diego.   Rioboo is not
heard of after he left this mission, and I suppose him
to have retired to his college at the end of 1786.[13]

[13] Juan Antonio García Rioboo, who should properly be spoken of as
García-Rioboo, whose last name should perhaps be written Rióbó, and of

In June 1783 Lasuen sent to Serra a report on the
mission of San Diego, which included an outline of its
past history, already utilized in the preceding chapters, and a statistical statement of agricultural progress, intended to show that the place was wholly unfit
for a mission, although the spiritual interests of the
converts made it necessary to keep up the establishment, there being no better site available.   A description of the mission buildings then in existence
accompanied the other papers.[14]   There were at this
time 740 neophytes under missionary care, and Lasuen
estimated the gentiles within a radius of six or eight
leagues at a somewhat larger number.   In 1790 the
converts had increased to 856, of this number 486
having been baptized and 278 having died.   Large
stock had increased from 654 to 1,729 head, small
stock from 1,391 to 2,116, and the harvest of 1790
had aggregated about 1,500 bushels.   In his general
report of 1787 on the state of the missions Fages,
repeating the substance of Lasuen's earlier statements
respecting the sterility of the soil, affirms that only
about one half of the neophytes live in the mission,
since they cannot be fed there, that the gentiles are

whose early life I know nothing, came from San Fernando college to Tepic
probably in the same company as Figuer (see note 12), in October 1770.   He
crossed over to the peninsula with Gov. Barri in January 1771, and was put
in charge of the two pueblos near Cape San Lúcas.   In May 1773 he sailed
from Loreto on his way to his college.   We hear nothing more of him until
he was assigned to the Santa Bárbara Channel missions, but refused to serve
under the new system proposed.   Later, however, he was sent up with Noboa
as supernumerary, arriving at San Francisco June 2, 1783, and spending his
time at San Francisco, San Juan, and San Gabriel until he came to San
Diego in 1785.   It is probable that even here he was not regular minister.

[14] *Lasuen, Informe de 1783*, MS.; *Hayes' Mission Book*, 89–98.   The report
was first dated May 10th, but Serra having ordered it kept back—probably
in the fear that he might have to show it to the secular authorities—the
author made some additions under date of June 21st.   The buildings were:
Church, 30 x 5.5 varas; granary, 25 x 5.5 varas; storehouse, 8 varas; house
for sick women, 6 varas; house for men, 6 varas; shed for wood and oven; 2
padres' houses, 5.5 varas; larder, 8 varas; guest-room; *hato;* kitchen.   These
were of adobe and from 3 to 5.5 varas high.   With the soldiers' barracks
these buildings filled three sides of a square of 55 varas, and the fourth side
was an adobe wall 3 varas high, with a ravelin a little higher.   Outside, a
fountain for tanning, 2 adobe corrals for sheep, etc., and one corral for cows.
Most of the stock was kept in San Luis Valley 2 leagues away, protected by
palisade corrals.

numerous and dangerous, and that it is only by the
unremitting toil and sacrifice of the padres in connection with the vigilance of governor and commandant
that this mission has managed to maintain a precarious existence. He adds, however, that notwithstanding all difficulties San Diego was the first mission
to register a thousand baptisms.[15]

Of San Juan Capistrano there is little to be said
beyond naming its ministers and presenting a few
statistics of conversion and of industrial progress.
Lands ·were fertile, ministers faithful and zealous,
natives well disposed, and progress in all respects satisfactory. Fages in his report of 1787 alludes briefly
to this establishment as in a thoroughly prosperous condition. The number of converts was nearly doubled
prior to 1790, and an occasional scarcity of water was
the only drawback, apparently not a serious one, to
agricultural operations.[16] Of the original ministers
who served at San Juan from the founding in 1776,
Gregorio Amurrio had left the mission and probably
the country in the autumn of 1779,[17] and had been succeeded by Vicente Fuster, who at the end of 1787
was transferred to Purísima, his place being filled by
Juan José Norberto de Santiago, who had come from
Mexico the year before and from Spain in 1785.

[15] *Fages, Informe General sobre Misiones*, 1787, MS. Owing to peculiar traits
of the San Diego Indians they were left more completely under missionary
control than at other missions, there being no alcaldes. *Id.*, 77–8.

[16] Converts in 1783, 383; in 1790, 741; new baptisms, 569; deaths, 140.
Large stock had increased from 473 to 2,473; and small stock from 1,175 to
5,500. Agricultural products for 1790 were over 3,000 bushels.

[17] Amurrio was one of the party who with Figuer (see note 12) was wrecked
at Manzanillo in attempting to cross from San Blas to Loreto in 1771. He
came back to Sinaloa by land, reached Loreto in November, and served at Santa
Gertrudis during the brief occupation of the peninsula by the Franciscans.
At the cession he came with Palou to San Diego in August 1773. Here he
remained until April 1774, when he sailed for Monterey, subsequently serving
most of the time as supernumerary at San Luis Obispo until the attempted
foundation of San Juan in October 1775. The next year he spent chiefly at
San Diego, was present as minister at the successful foundation of San Juan on
Nov. 1, 1776; and his last entry in the books of that mission was in September
of 1779. I think he sailed in the transport of that year for San Blas, retiring
on account of impaired health.

Pablo de Mugártegui, the other founder, left California at the end of 1789,[18] Fuster having returned in September to serve with Santiago during the last year of the decade.[19]

At San Gabriel, the third mission of the San Diego military jurisdiction, Antonio Cruzado and Miguel Sanchez served together throughout this decade as in the next and a large part of the preceding, the former having begun his service in 1771 and the latter in 1775, while both died at their posts after 1800. They had José Antonio Calzada as a supernumerary associate from 1788 to 1790. They baptized on an average a hundred converts each year, half of whom soon died. In neophyte numbers San Gabriel was second only to San Antonio, while in live-stock and farm products this mission had in 1790 far outstripped all the rest.[20] The governor alludes to it as having often relieved the necessities of other establishments in both Californias, and as having enabled the government to carry out important undertakings that without such aid would have been impracticable. Prosperity did not however carry in its train much excitement in the way of local events, and the calm of this mission of

[18] Pablo de Mugártegui came to California with Serra on that friar's return from Mexico, arriving at San Diego March 13, 1774. Being in poor health he remained for some time unattached to any mission, first serving as supernumerary at San Antonio from January to July 1775. He was minister at San Luis Obispo from August 1775 until November 1776, and at San Juan as we have seen from November 1776 until November 1789. He writes to Lasuen on Jan. 30, 1794, from the college, that he had been very ill but was now out of danger. From Aug. 16, 1786, he held the office of vice-president of the California missions, having charge of the southern district. Taylor, in *Cal. Farmer*, July 24, 1863, says, erroneously I suppose, that he died on March 6, 1805, at San Buenaventura.

[19] Much of the information respecting the friars in charge I have obtained from *San Juan Capistrano, Lib. de Mision*, MS. Among the visiting padres who officiated here during the period and before were Serra, Oct. 1778; Figuer, June 1780; Miguel Sanchez, May 1782; Lasuen, Oct. 1783; Rioboo, Feb. 1784; Mariner, Oct. 1785; José Arroita, Dec. 1786; José Antonio Calzada, April 1788; Torrens, Oct. 1788; and Cristóbal Orámas, Dec. 1788 to Jan. 1789. Thus we see that San Juan for some not very clear reason was much less isolated in respect of visitors than San Diego.

[20] Neophytes in 1783, 638; in 1790, 1,040. Baptisms during period, 818; deaths, 466. Increase of large stock, 860 to 4,221; small stock, 2,070 to 6,013. Harvest in 1790, 6,150 bushels.

the great archangel on the river of earthquakes was
disturbed only by one or two slight troubles, or rumors
of trouble, with the natives. In October 1785 the
neophytes and gentiles were tempted by a woman, so
at least said the men, into a plan to attack the mission and kill the friars. The corporal in command
prevented the success of the scheme without bloodshed, and captured some twenty of the conspirators.
Fages hurried south from the capital, put the four
ringleaders in prison to await the decision of the
commandant general, and released the rest with fifteen
or twenty lashes each. Two years later came General
Ugarte's order condemning one native, Nicolás, to six
years of work at the presidio followed by exile to a
distant mission. The woman was sent into perpetual
exile, and the other two were dismissed with the two
years' imprisonment already suffered.[21] Again in July
1786 a gentile chieftain was arrested on a charge presented by the chief of another ranchería that he had
threatened hostilities, but the accusation proved to
have little or no foundation.[22]

The annals of the adjoining pueblo, Our Lady,
Queen, or Saint Mary, of the Angels on the Rio de
Porciúncula have already been brought down in a
general way to the distribution of lands in the autumn
of 1786.[23] By the end of the decade the number of
settlers had been recruited, chiefly from soldiers who
had served out their time, from nine to twenty-eight,
who with their families made up a total population of
one hundred and thirty-nine.[24] All of the original
pobladores who received a formal grant of their lands
in 1786 remained except Rosas.[25] Sebastian Alvitre

[21] Fages to Gen. Ugarte Dec. 5, 30, 1785, in *Prov. Rec.*, MS., ii. 131–2;
Ugarte to Fages, Dec. 14, 1787, in *Arch. Sta. Bárbara*, MS., vi. 116–17.
[22] Zúñiga to Fages, Aug. 15, 1786, in *Prov. St. Pap.*, MS., vi. 35–6.
[23] See chapter xvi., this volume.
[24] An *estado* of August 17, 1790, makes the total 141. Males, 75; females,
66. Unmarried, 91; married, 44; widowed, 6. Under 7 years, 47; 7 to 16
years, 33; 16 to 29 years, 12; 29 to 40 years, 27; 40 to 90 years, 13; over
90 years, 9. Europeans, 1; Spaniards, 72; Indians, 7; mulattoes, 22; mestizos,
39. *Prov. St. Pap.*, MS., ix. 152.
[25] The 20 new settlers were: Domingo Aruz, Juan Álvarez, Joaquin Ar-

had proved unmanageable at San José and after four or five years of convict life at the presidio had been sent to Angeles for reform. The settlers were not a very orderly community, but they seem to have given some attention to their fields, since the pueblo produced in 1790 more grain than any of the missions except San Gabriel, its neighbor. Their dwellings, twenty-nine in number, were of adobes, like the public town hall, barrack, guard-house, and granaries; and all were enclosed within an adobe wall, there being also a few buildings outside the wall.[26]

Vicente Félix was at first corporal of the pueblo guard furnished by the San Diego presidio; but he soon developed special ability and interest in general management and was made a kind of director before 1784. Though some complaints were made against him by the settlers, and Zúñiga at one time favored his removal, the governor's confidence was not shaken, and he finally made him comisionado, intrusting to him the management not only of the pueblo but of its alcalde and regidores,[27] he being responsible to the governor through the commandant of Santa Bárbara for any failure of those officials to attend properly to their duties. Fages' instructions to Félix were dated Jan. 13, 1787, and required the latter to see that the

menta, Juan Ramirez Arellano, Sebastian Alvitre, Roque Cota, Faustino José Cruz, Juan José Dominguez, Manuel Figueroa, Felipe Santiago García, Joaquin Higuera, Juan José Lobo, José Ontiveros, Santiago de la Cruz Pico, Francisco Reyes, Martin Reyes, Pedro José Romero, Efigenio Ruiz, Mariano Verdugo, José Villa, besides Vicente Félix, corporal and comisionado. In 1789 there had been 5 additional names: José Silvas, Rejis Soto, Francisco Lugo, Melecio Valdés, and Rafael Sepúlveda, or at least lands were ordered to be granted to these men. Nine only drew pay and rations in 1789. *Prov. St. Pap.*, MS., v. 29–36; ix. 120, 159–63; *Prov. St. Pap., Ben. Mil.*, MS., x. 2–6; *St. Pap., Miss.*, i. 66–72. Large stock had increased from 340 to 2,980 head; small stock from 210 to 438; and the crops of 1790 amounted to 4,500 bushels.

[26] *Prov. St. Pap., Miss.*, MS., i. 68, 71. Aug. 10, 1785, 35 pounds powder and 800 bullets sent to Angeles as reserve ammunition for settlers. *Prov. Rec.*, MS., ii. 7. Nov. 9, 1786, Goycoechea to Fages, will take steps to stop excesses. *Prov. St. Pap.*, MS., vi. 57. May 8, 1787, commandant general congratulates Fages on progress reported. *Id.*, vii. 41. Pueblo called Santa María de los Angeles. *St. Pap., Miss. and Colon.*, MS., i. 125.

[27] *Prov. Rec.*, MS., i. 163–4; *Prov. St. Pap.*, v. 180; ix. 105, 119–20, 225–6. José Vanegas was the first alcalde in 1788; José Sinova the second in 1789, with Felipe García and Manuel Camero as regidores; and Mariano Verdugo the third in 1790.

settlers performed all the duties, complied with all
the conditions, and enjoyed all the privileges enjoined
by the regulation; to watch and instruct and coöperate
with the alcalde in his efforts to insure good order and
justice and morality; and to attend to the carrying-
out of some very judicious regulations which are
included in the document respecting the treatment
of the natives and their employment as laborers.[28]

At the Channel presidio of Santa Bárbara the force
maintained was from fifty to fifty-four privates, two
corporals, two or three sergeants, an alférez, and a
lieutenant. Of this force fifteen men at first and
later ten were stationed at San Buenaventura, fifteen
at Purísima, and from three to six at Santa Bárbara
after those missions were founded, and two generally
at Los Angeles. The so-called white population of this
presidial district was about two hundred and twenty,
or three hundred and sixty with Los Angeles.[29]

Lieutenant José Francisco Ortega, the original
commandant, retained his position together with that
of habilitado, until January 1784, when he was sent
to the peninsula frontier and Lieutenant Felipe de
Goycoechea came up to take his place, which he held
until 1804. Ortega was removed by the general at
the request of Soler, who alone found fault with the
lieutenant, and who as we know was a chronic fault-
finder. Soler subsequently complained of the new
commandant's lack of application, and wished to put
in the place Zúñiga with a stupid habilitado or Ortega

---

[28] *Fages, Instruccion para el cabo de la Escolta del pueblo de Los Angeles como
Comisionado por el gobierno para dirigir al alcalde y á los regidores, 1787,* MS.
  [29] The Santa Bárbara *situado* by the reglamento was $14,472; average pay-
roll, $13,500; average *memorias* of supplies, $12,500; average total of habilitado's accounts, $26,000, of which about $6,000 was a balance of goods on
hand; *fondo de gratificacion,* $2,000, and *fondo de retencion,* $1,000 in 1784;
fondo de inválidos and *Montepio,* $427 in 1782. Company accounts in *Prov. St.
Pap., Presidios,* MS., i. 2, 90; *Prov. St. Pap., Ben. Mil.,* MS., ii. 1, 8, 20–2,
38–9; iii. 18; iv. 22; vi. 3; viii. 13; ix. 3, 4; xiv. 6, 7. Inventories of armament in *Prov. St. Pap.,* MS., v. 96–9; vii. 86; *St. Pap., Sac.,* MS., i. 6, 7.
A list of inhabitants with families, age, etc., showing 67 male heads of families, dated Dec. 31, 1785, in *St. Pap., Miss.,* MS., i. 4–9.

with an able one, but Fages could not spare Zúñiga
from San Diego. In 1786, however, in consequence
of the vacancy caused by the death of Moraga at San
Francisco, the governor offered Ortega his choice of
the presidios, and he at first chose Santa Bárbara, but
finally took command of Monterey. José Argüello
was company alférez from the beginning down to
April 1787, when he was promoted to the command
of San Francisco, leaving a vacancy not filled until
after 1790. The sergeants were Pablo Antonio Cota
and Ignacio Olivera, with Raimundo Carrillo after
1781,[30] perhaps from 1783.

Work on the presidio buildings was pushed forward, in the Hispano-Californian sense, throughout
the period, and the commandant's communications to
Fages on plans and progress, on delays and accidents,
on the making of adobes and tiles or the receipt of
beams, on laborers and their wages, and on other
matters connected with the structure were very numerous.[31] The building material was chiefly adobe,
though mortar, or cement, was used in some buildings, and the outer or main wall stood on a foundation of stone. Roofs were for the most part of tiles,
supported by timbers which were brought down by
the transports from the north. The laborers were

[30] Ortega appointed commandant of Sta. Bárbara Sept. 8, 1781. *Prov. St.
Pap., Presidios*, MS., i. 1, 2. Ortega removed for incompetency, not understanding his own accounts. Soler, June 7, 1787, in *Prov. St. Pap.*, MS., vii.
115. Ortega and Goycoechea ordered to change places. Soler to Fages, May
14, 1783, in *Prov. Rec.*, MS., iv. 120-1, 132. Goycoechea's commission sent to
him Jan. 17, 1783. *Id.*, iii. 55. Goycoechea arrived at San Diego en route
north Aug. 24, 1783. *Prov. St. Pap.*, MS., iv. 78. Ortega gave up command
Jan. 25, 1784. *Prov. Rec.*, MS., i. 162; ii. 4. Ortega thanks Fages for offer
of any presidio, and selects Santa Bárbara Jan. 3, 1787. *Prov. St. Pap.*, MS.,
vii. 175. Soler's complaints against Goycoechea and suggestion of changes.
March and June, 1787. *Id.*, 114-15, 135. Argüello left for San Francisco in
April, 1787. There was some correspondence about Goycoechea giving up the
habilitacion. Id., 59, 67. Ugarte to Fages Oct. 25, 1787. The viceroy will
fill the vacant place of alférez. *Id.*, 31. Hermenegildo Sal was one of the
sergeants at the foundation but left the company very soon. *Prov. St. Pap.,
Ben. Mil.*, MS. It would serve no useful purpose to refer here to the hundreds of company rosters and similar documents scattered through different
archives and which have afforded me much information.

[31] *Prov. St. Pap.*, MS., iv. 143-44; v. 155, 167; vi. 48, 50, 55, 59, 62-3, 68,
72; vii. 6, 7; viii. 90, 114; ix. 108, 168, 173; xii. 60-1.

the soldiers themselves, some thirty sailors obtained at different times from the San Blas vessels, and natives who were paid for their work in wheat. The soldiers and officers contributed about $1,200 for the work from 1786 to 1790, an amount which seems however to have been returned to them later as a

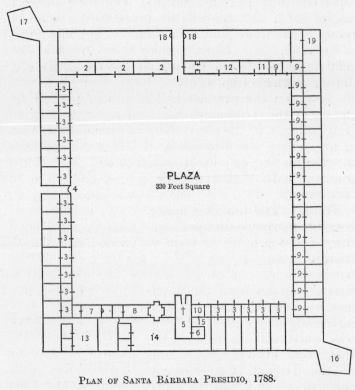

PLAN OF SANTA BÁRBARA PRESIDIO, 1788.

gratuity. The best description of the result is the annexed plan which was sent by Goycoechea to Fages in September 1788. At that time the western line of houses were not roofed and the outer walls were not yet begun; but before the end of 1790 at least three sides of the main wall had been built.[32] The natives

[32] 1, chief entrance, 12 ft.; 2, storehouses, 16 x 61 ft.; 3, 18 family houses, 15 x 24 ft.; 4, false door, roofed, 9 ft.; 5, church 24 x 60 ft.; 6, sacristy, 12 x

as hired laborers worked well, and the grain raised at
the presidio to be dealt out in wages was so abundant
that in 1785 orders came from the general not to sow
any that year.[33]

The discovery of a so-called volcano in 1784 was
the source of some local excitement, and was duly
reported to Mexico and Arizpe. The volcano was a
league and a half west of the presidio at a bend or
break in the shore line, and about a thousand varas
in circumference. The ground was so hot that the
centre could not be approached; fire issued from thirty
different places with a strong fume of sulphur; and
the heat of the rocks caused the water to boil when
the spot was covered at high tide. There was no
crater proper, or rather it was covered up with fragments of rock and with ashes. Fages went in person
to examine the sulphurous phenomenon and learned
from the natives that the volcano had been long in
operation.[34]

The aborigines in this district gave the Spaniards
very little trouble beyond the occasional theft of a
cow or sheep from the mission herds, engaging in
hostilities among themselves, or rarely committing
outrages on neophytes which called for Spanish interference. In August 1790 Sergeant Olivera with eight
men went in search of an Indian deserter, and were
instructed also to prospect for mines. While the force
was scattered somewhat in the search for minerals,
they were attacked by a large number of Indians
of the Tenoqui ranchería and driven away with
the loss of two soldiers killed, Espinosa and Carlon. Goycoechea was blamed by Fages for having

15 ft.; 7, alférez' suite, 3 rooms; 8, commandant's suite, 4 rooms; 9, 15 family
houses, 15 x 27 ft.; 10 chaplain's 2 rooms; 11, sergeant's house, 16 x 45 ft.;
12, quarters and guard-room; 13, corrals, kitchen, and *dispensa* of alférez;
14, corrals, kitchen, and *dispensa* of commandant; 15, chaplain's corral; 16,
western bastion; 17, eastern bastion; 18, corrals.

[33] *Prov. St. Pap.*, MS., v. 244; *Prov. Rec.*, MS., i. 171, 185. In 1787,
however, the wheat crop was destroyed by rain and snow, which caused the
seed to rot. *Prov. St. Pap.*, MS., vii. 65.

[34] *Prov. Rec.*, MS., i. 181; ii. 119–20; *St. Pap., Sac.*, MS., xv. 19.

engaged in mining operations at the risk of his soldiers' lives.[35]

At San Buenaventura, the southernmost of the Channel missions, Dumetz and Santa María, the first regular ministers, served with much zeal and success throughout the decade, increasing the list of neophytes from 22 to 388, baptizing 498, and losing 115 by death. Large stock increased from 103 to 961; small stock from 44 to 1,503; and the crops of 1790 were over 3,000 bushels.   The surrounding gentiles were always friendly, but on account of their large numbers a larger guard was stationed there than at other missions, 15 men at first, and later only 10.   Sergeant Pablo Antonio Cota commanded until the end of 1788, when on complaint of the padres Sergeant Raimundo Carillo was put in his place.[36]

The missions of Santa Bárbara and Purísima, belonging to this military district, as new establishments have been disposed of in the preceding chapter.

The regulation called for a presidial force at Monterey of fifty-two men under a lieutenant and

[35] Goycoechea to Fages, Sept. 2, 1790, in *Prov. St. Pap., Ben. Mil.*, MS., ix. 6–8; Fages to Romeu, in *Prov. St. Pap.*, MS., x. 148. Sept. 17, 1783, Attack on Conejo and Escorpion rancherías, who have stolen cattle, to be deferred. *Prov. Rec.*, MS., iii. 130. Indian Captain Chico killed by captain of Najalayegui ranchería and others May 27, 1785. *Prov. St. Pap.*, MS., v. 157. July 1787, Four neophytes fled and with pagans attacked a ranchería, killing 5 in retaliation for the killing of 13 of their kinsmen. *Id.*, vii. 92. July 26th, Playanos have killed some cattle at Angeles, but sickness in the company prevents chastisement at present. *Id.*, 68. Oct. 30th, When Lieut. Gonzalez passed through Espada ranchería a woman was cut in pieces—or perhaps in several places—for refusing to yield to the wishes of a soldier. *Id.*, 70–1, 91. In August 1787 there was an expedition to punish pagans for outrages on neophytes. Several arrests were made and some fugitives brought in. The Calahuasat ranchería was the principal one involved. *Id.*, 76–7. Jan. 1788, Sergt. Cota went to the Tachicos ranchería in the mountains to catch a neophyte thief, but was attacked and had to kill 3 and wound 8. *Id.*, viii. 123.

[36] Fages in his report of 1787 refers to San Buenaventura as having made very satisfactory progress in all respects except that the church is a very poor affair. *St. Pap., Miss. and Colon.*, MS., i. 133–5. Seven houses for families completed by May 12, 1788. *Prov. St. Pap.*, MS., viii., 109. Olivera replaced by Carillo, Oct. 1788. *Id.* 118, 122. See *S. Buenaventura, Lib. de Mision*, MS., for names of soldiers, children, etc.

alférez, and the number during this decade never fell below fifty, though, including invalids, it was sometimes as high as sixty-two; and there were, besides, a surgeon and two or three mechanics. A guard of six men was kept at each of the three missions of San Cárlos, San Antonio, and San Luis Obispo; and four men were furnished for San José pueblo beyond the limits of the district, which had in 1790 a population of gente de razon numbering two hundred. At the same time the presidio herds numbered four thousand head of live-stock great and small.[37]

Lieutenant Diego Gonzalez, like Zúñiga one of the new officers who came under the regulation of 1781, was commandant until July 1785, when he was sent to San Francisco. The commandant at Monterey played a less prominent part in history, or at least in the records, by reason of the governor's presence, and little is known of Gonzalez' acts here save that he was arrested at the governor's orders for insubordination, gambling, and smuggling; but we shall hear of him again. The alférez of the company, and also habilitado, was Hermenegildo Sal, who had come to California as a private with Anza in 1776. Sal became acting commandant on the departure of Gonzalez, and held that position until 1787. He would probably have kept the command had it not been for his quarrels already alluded to with Captain Soler, whose ill-will he incurred and who claimed to have discovered a serious deficit in his accounts. It was in August 1787 that the charge was made, and Sal was placed under arrest by order of the governor, his property being attached and two thirds of his pay being kept back at first, and later all but two reals per day. Correspondence on this matter was quite extensive,[38] and

---

[37] Situado allowed by reglamento, $17,792; pay-roll, about $13,000; total of habilitado's yearly accounts, $35,000. Company accounts in *Arch. Cal.*, passim.

[38] Letters of Sal, Soler, and Fages in *Prov. St. Pap.*, MS., vii. 60–1, 120, 130, 143, 167–8; viii. 41–2, 54–5; ix. 140–1; x. 162–3; *Prov. St. Pap., Ben. Mil.*, MS., x. 10, 11; iii. 9; *Prov. Rec.*, MS., i. 33–4.

shows that though Sal was personally somewhat involved in debt, the charge of defalcation in connection with the company accounts was unfounded. Instead of owing the company $3,000, the company owed him about $600. It required three years to set Don Hermenegildo right, and in the mean time Ortega, whom it had been intended to restore to his old presidio of Santa Bárbara, came to take the command and the office of habilitado at Monterey instead, from September 1787.[39] The sergeant of the company was Mariano Verdugo until 1787, succeeded by Manuel Vargas. The surgeon was José Dávila.[40]

Beyond matters connected with the government, with the visit of La Pérouse, and with other events of general interest recorded in preceding chapters there is nothing to be said of this presidio except to note a conflagration that occurred August 11, 1789. In firing a salute to the *San Cárlos* on her arrival in port the wad of the cannon set fire to the tule roofing, and about one half of the buildings within the square were destroyed. Repairs were far advanced by the end of 1790.[41]

At the three missions of this presidial district, San Cárlos, San Antonio, and San Luis Obispo, there is nothing in the way of local events to be noted during the period covered by this chapter; but the statistics

[39] Ortega gave up his command on the frontier to Gonzalez May 3d, left San Miguel in May, was at San Diego on June 5th, arrived at Santa Bárbara June 27th, and started north Aug. 21st. *Prov. St. Pap.*, MS., vii. 71, 76, 78, 81, 105–6. After his accounts were settled Sal did not resume the place of habilitado at Monterey, but was sent to San Francisco in April 1791, Argüello coming to the capital.

[40] Surgeon Dávila came to San Diego in July 1774 and to Monterey in December. As early as 1781 Gov. Neve favored granting his petition for leave to quit the country as being incompetent and captious. *Prov. Rec.*, MS., ii. 68. The exact date of his departure does not appear, but it was before December 1783. *Prov. St. Pap.*, MS., v. 57–8. Dávila's first wife, Josefa Carbajal, died at San Francisco in November 1780. *San Francisco, Lib. de Mision*, MS., 12, 64, and in January 1782 he married María Encarnacion Castro, a daughter of Isidoro Castro. *Sta. Clara, Lib. de Mision*, MS., 40.

[41] *Prov. St. Pap.*, MS., ix. 1, 2; x. 166; xiii. 191; xxii. 87; *Id., Ben. Mil.*, i. 9. The old presidio chapel stood in the middle of the square, and April 14, 1789, Fages had ordered adobes made for a new one.

as given in connection with other missions are as follows: At San Cárlos Junípero Serra and Matías Antonio de Santa Catarina y Noriega served until August 1784, when the former having died, the latter served till October 1787,[42] and José Francisco de Paula Señan from that time on, having Pascual Martinez de Arenaza as associate from 1789, and Lasuen as president from 1790. The friars named were the regular ministers so far as the records show, but other priests arriving by sea from San Blas or coming in from other missions often spent some time here, so that there were nearly always two and often more.[43] At San Antonio de Pádua the founders of 1771, Miguel Pieras and Buenaventura Sitjar, served throughout this decade, having at its close 1,076 neophytes under their charge—the largest mission community in California.[44] At San Luis Obispo José Cavaller served continuously from the foundation in 1772 to his death on December 9, 1789.[45] His associate was Antonio Paterna until December 1786, when he went to found Santa Bárbara, and Miguel Giribet came in December 1787. Between the two I find that Faustino Sola had charge of the mission

[42] Matías Antonio de Santa Catarina (written also Catharina and Catalina) y Noriega, who was best known by the name Noriega, came up as chaplain on the transport of 1779, and took Cambon's place at San Francisco. He remained there until 1781, and then served at San Cárlos until 1787, when he retired to his college.

[43] Increase of converts 1783 to 1790, 614 to 733; baptisms, 639; deaths, 425; large stock, 628 to 1,378; small stock, 245 to 1,263. Crops in 1790, 3,775 bushels. Fages in his general report of 1787 alludes to the climate with its sudden changes of heat and cold, as having something to do with the great mortality. Crops have been good, though arrangements for irrigation have not yet been completed. *St. Pap., Miss. and Colon.*, MS., i. 139–40.

[44] Increase in neophytes, 585 to 1,076; baptisms, 773; deaths, 333; large stock, 429 to 2,232; small stock, 466 to 1,984; crops in 1790 only 1,450 bushels. Fages says the soil is tolerably good though irrigation is difficult, and the mission has raised enough for her own use and a surplus for sale. San Antonio had the best church in California excepting, perhaps, Santa Clara. *St. Pap., Miss. and Colon.*, i. MS., 145–7.

[45] José Cavaller was a native of the town of Falcet in Catalonia. He left the college in Mexico in October 1770, sailed from San Blas in January 1771, reached San Diego in March and Monterey in May, remaining there as supernumerary until he went to found San Luis in Sept. 1772. His remains were buried in the mission church, and he left the reputation of a zealous and successful missionary. *S. Luis Obispo, Lib. de Mision*, MS., 38; autograph in *S. Antonio, Doc. Sueltos*, MS., 4.

for a few months, but am unable to completely fill the vacancy even with one padre.[46]

Lieutenant José Moraga was commandant and habilitado of San Francisco until his death, which occurred on July 13, 1785,[47] from which date Gonzalez, transferred from Monterey, became commandant for two years, and José Ramon Lasso de la Vega, the alférez, served as habilitado. During the two years there was trouble with both these officials. Before leaving Monterey Gonzalez had once been put under arrest for insubordination, gambling, failing to prevent gambling, and for trading with the galleon. At San Francisco his irregular conduct continued in spite of warnings and re-arrest; and in 1787 the governor was obliged to send him to the frontier. He never returned to California.[48]

[46] Increase in neophytes, 492 to 605; baptisms, 332; deaths, 130; large stock, 815 to 3,810; small stock, 960 to 3,725; crops for 1790, 2,340 bushels. Want of water was the chief drawback according to Fages' report.

[47] Of José Joaquin Moraga, or as he always signed his name, Josseph Moraga, little is known beyond what has been told in the text. He came with Anza in 1776, and was commandant of San Francisco from the first, founding the presidio, the two missions, and the pueblo of San José. He was godfather of the first neophyte at San Francisco, who received his name; and he was secular sponsor at the laying of the corner-stone of the mission church still standing, as also at the dedication of the Santa Clara church. His record as an officer was an honorable and stainless one. His wife was María del Pilar de Leon y Barceló, who died in October 1808 and was interred in the San Francisco cemetery, her husband's remains resting in the church. He brought a son Gabriel to California who afterwards became a lieutenant, a famous Indian fighter, and the ancestor of a family still surviving. Don José's niece, María Ignacia, was the wife of José Argüello. The commandant is described as having been 5 ft. 2 inches and 2 lines in height; but there is reason to suppose that the *pié del rey* used in measuring the height of soldiers was longer than the ordinary Spanish foot, which was 8 per cent shorter than our foot.

[48] Gonzalez' arrest at Monterey in August 1784. *Prov. Rec.*, MS., i. 186; ii. 102–3; *Prov. St. Pap., Ben.*, MS., i. 41. Soler alludes to his *mucha ridiculez* Nov. 14, 1786, and proposes Argüello as a successor. *Prov. St. Pap.*, MS., vi. 198; vii. 114–16. Gonzalez arrested at San Francisco by Lasso at Soler's order Feb. 4, 1787, and sent south to meet Fages March 18th. *Id.*, vii. 98–9; *Prov. Rec.*, MS., iii. 39. Fages tells the story to his successor, Romeu, Feb. 26, 1791. *Prov. St. Pap.*, MS., x. 162–3. General approves measures against Gonzalez. *Id.*, vii. 50. Gonzalez was born at Ceste del Campo in Spain, and enlisted as a private at about the age of 26 in 1762. He served 3 years as a private, 2 as corporal, 10 as sergeant, and a little over one year as alférez. Having seen much service in Indian campaigns in the Provincias Internas, he was promoted to be lieutenant for California service in December 1779. *Hoja de Servicios*, in *Prov. St. Pap., Ben. Mil.*, MS., ii. 12–13; iv. 15. Fages says of

Lasso the habilitado was a stupid fellow, though neither dishonest nor dissipated, always in trouble with his accounts, and always recommended to the executive clemency. During his first brief term in 1781–2 he managed to leave a deficit of about $800; and early in 1787 Captain Soler discovered a still more serious and inexcusable defalcation. His usual excuses of forgetfulness, stealing by soldiers and convicts, and the melting-away of sugar during transportation would no longer save him; he was suspended from office, placed under arrest, and obliged to live on twenty-five cents a day, the rest of his pay as alférez being reserved to make up the deficit in his accounts. This state of things continued for over four years, and then, the amount having been in great part repaid, he was dismissed from the service; but the king subsequently granted him retirement and half-pay.[49] José Argüello was taken from Santa Bárbara and promoted to be

him after he was sent to the frontier 'no tiene narizes ní asiento.' *Prov. St. Pap.*, MS., x. 148. In Nov. 1791 the king's permission was sent to the governor to put Gonzalez on the retired list. *Id.*, 94. He retired as *inválido* to Rosario in Sonora, and his name was dropped from the company rolls after Jan. 1, 1793. *Prov. Rec.*, MS., ii. 157.

[49] On Lasso's San Francisco troubles see correspondence in *Prov. Rec.*, MS., ii. 136–9; iii. 35–7; *Prov. St. Pap.*, MS., vi. 93–4; vii. 114–17, 121–3, 128, 141–2; viii. 7–9; xi. 179; xxi. 157; *Prov. St. Pap., Ben. Mil.*, MS., xiii. 10. Sept. 16, 1786, Fages speaks of the appointment of Sergt. José Perez Fernandez as alférez of San Francisco; but it was not done before 1790. On same date he orders the deficit charged to the company. July 6, 1787, Fages blames Soler for not having been more strict in Lasso's case. Soler went up to straighten out Lasso's accounts, but himself made a blunder, probably in 1782. Aug. 9, 1788, the general orders Lasso's dismissal when the deficit is paid. Dec. 1, 1791, Gov. Romeu suspends him from rank and pay. Lasso was commissioned alférez Feb. 10, 1780. *Prov. St. Pap., Ben. Mil.*, MS., iv. 14–15. In 1790 he was 34 years old and single. *St. Pap. Miss.*, MS., i. 84, though he had wanted to marry in 1781, and Gov. Neve had been ordered to dismiss him from the service if he persisted in his intention. *Prov. Rec.*, MS., ii., 84. Again in 1787 in the midst of his troubles he wished to take a wife, but his petition forwarded by Lasuen was refused. *Arch. Sta. Bárbara*, MS., xii. 364–5. The royal order of retirement was forwarded by the viceroy, applied for in 1794, viceroy to Fages in *Prov. St. Pap.*, MS., xi. 179, April 11, 1795, and by the governor Aug. 24th. *Prov. St. Pap.*, MS., xiii. 105; *Prov. Rec.*. MS., v. 61; and Aug. 27th the governor writes to Arrillaga 'our poor Lasso has received his retirement with half-pay as alférez, as petitioned by you, for which may God reward you.' *Prov. Rec.*, MS., v. 320–1. Though 'quiso la naturaleza negarle una precisa parte de espiritu'—*Prov. St. Pap.*, MS., vii. 114—yet by birth he was entitled to be called 'Don.' He was of Spanish blood and a native of Chihuahua. He was school-master at San José in 1795–6, as late as Aug. 19, 1797, is urged to pay a balance still due, *Prov. Rec.*, MS., v. 266, and he died Nov. 30, 1821, at the age of 64, being buried at San Rafael. *Arch. Misiones*, MS., i. 905.

lieutenant from June 1787, taking charge at the same time of the accounts.[50]   Juan Pablo Grijalva was the company's sergeant until 1787, when he was sent as alférez to San Diego, and Pedro Amador was promoted to fill his place.

The presidial force was thirty-four men besides the officers, from fifteen to twenty of whom served in the garrison while the rest did guard duty at the mission, at Santa Clara, and at San José.   With their families they amounted to a population of about one hundred and thirty.   Of the presidio buildings there is nothing to be said beyond the fact that from want of timber, bad quality of adobes, and lack of skilful workmen no permanent progress was made during the decade. Some portion of the walls was generally in ruins, and the soldiers in some cases had to erect the old-fashioned palisade structures to shelter their families.[51] Local events as recorded were neither numerous nor very exciting.   The natives gave no trouble save by the rare theft of a horse or cow, for which offence they were chastised once or twice in 1783; and in 1786 neophytes were arrested and flogged for ravages among the soldiers' cattle.[52]   These cattle became so numerous as to be troublesome, and slaughter was begun as early as 1784 to reduce the number to eight or nine hundred.[53]   Captain Soler complained much of the bad climate of the place, and even advocated, as we have seen, its abandonment; but in the eyes of higher officials the importance of the location on San Francisco Bay, and the duty of protecting the mission, outweighed the peculiarities of the peninsula climate.[54]

[50] Argüello's commission was forwarded by the general Feb. 9, 1787. *Prov. St. Pap.*, MS., vii. 45.   He left Santa Bárbara April 12th. *Id.*, 67.   Took possession of office at San Francisco June 12th.

[51] *Prov. St. Pap.*, MS., x. 166; xi. 53.   In January 1784 the corner of the presidio was blown down in a gale. *Id.*, v. 69.

[52] *Prov. St. Pap.*, MS., iv. 21, 30; *Prov. Rec.*, MS., ii. 134.

[53] Sergeant Grijalva had over 50 head, and was ordered to remove the surplus where they would not interfere with the mission herds. *Prov. Rec.*, MS., i. 173, 181.   January 23, 1788, Fages says that he will send men to build a corral at San Mateo and there to gather stock from San Bruno to Santa Clara if pasturage grows scarce. *Id.*, iii. 40.

[54] *Prov. St. Pap.*, MS., vii. 117; v. 4, 5.

There was some trouble about the performance of a chaplain's duties at the presidio, and for over two years the soldiers heard no mass unless at the mission; but in February a chapel was completed, after which time the friars made occasional visits.[55] San Francisco was honored by several visits from the governor, and in August 1784 was the birthplace of his daughter.[56] A sailor from the *Princesa,* who had served out his time, remained at San Francisco in 1784, intending to establish a school; but it does not appear that he succeeded.[57]

The mission of San Francisco in respect of neophytes was the smallest of the old establishments, having increased in the eight years from 215 to 438. Baptisms had been 551, and deaths 205.[58] The increase of herds was, of large stock from 554 to 2,000, and of small from 284 to 1,700. Notwithstanding the small area and barren nature of the soil, which, as Fages states in his general report, had yielded but small crops, we find that the yield in 1790 was 3,700 bushels, excelled by only four in the list of missions. It appears, however, that the sowing was done mostly at a spot ten or twelve miles distant down the peninsula.[59]

In the ministry Pedro Benito Cambon, the founder, served throughout the whole period; and Francisco Palou, also a founder, until 1785, when he retired to his college at a ripe old age.[60] Miguel Giribet was

---

[55] *Prov. St. Pap.,* MS., vii. 99; *Prov. Rec.,* MS., i. 192.

[56] *S. Francisco, Lib. de Mision,* MS., 20–1.

[57] *Prov. Rec.,* MS., i. 183.

[58] In 1784 the governor reports it also as having one of the poorest churches. *St. Pap., Miss. and Colon.,* MS., i. 145–7.

[59] *St. Pap., Miss. and Colon.,* MS., i. 143.

[60] Francisco Palou, sometimes written with an accent Paloú, without any good reason so far as I know, was born at Palma in the Island of Mallorca, probably in 1722. Mr Doyle in his introduction to the reprint of *Palou, Noticias,* i. iii., infers that the date was about 1719; but in a letter dated 1783, *Hist. Mag.,* iv. 67–8, the padre calls himself 61 years of age. Taking the habit of San Francisco he entered the principal convent of the city, and in 1740 became a disciple of Junípero Serra, with whom and with Juan Crespí of the same convent he contracted a life-long friendship. With his master he volunteered for the American missions in 1749, left Palma in April, Cádiz in August, and landed at Vera Cruz in December. Joining the college of San

stationed here in 1785–7; Santiago in 1786–7; Sola and García in 1787–90; and Dantí from 1790.

Before leaving San Francisco I present a map which belongs to the period under consideration, being a copy of a Spanish chart published in La Pérouse's atlas and probably obtained by that voyager at Monterey in 1786.

At Santa Clara Mission the new adobe church was dedicated on Sunday, May 15, 1784, by Serra, Palou, and Peña, in the presence of Fages and Moraga, the

Fernando, he was assigned to the Sierra Gorda missions, where he served from 1750 to 1759, subsequently living at the college for 8 years. Appointed to Baja California he arrived at Loreto in April 1768, took charge of San Francisco Javier; and in 1769 after Serra's departure for the north became acting president. In May 1773 he surrendered the missions to the Dominicans and soon started north, arriving at San Diego at the end of August and at Monterey in November of the same year, sending in the first annual report on the missions, and acting as president until Serra's return at the beginning of 1774. For two years and a half he served at San Cárlos, and in June 1776 went to found the San Francisco establishments, having previously visited the peninsula twice, in Nov. 1774 and Sept. 1776. His first entry in the mission registers bears date of Aug. 10, 1776, before the mission was formally founded, and his last was on July 25, 1785, and not July 20, 1784, as Doyle says. See *S. Francisco, Lib. de Mision*, MS., 2. There is another entry of July 13, 1785. About 1780, by reason of ill-health, he asked leave to retire, which was granted; but which he could not profit by at first for want of transportation, then for want of a substitute, and finally on account of new instructions connected with the foundation of a custody; but in 1783, fearing by longer delay to be incapacitated for so long a voyage, he wrote to Don José de Galvez to obtain from the king new permission to retire. Letter of Aug. 15, 1783, in *Hist. Mag.*, iv. 67–9. The result was a royal order of Oct. 5, 1784, and a corresponding decree of the audiencia of Feb. 18, 1785, that Palou return to his college. *Id.*, 69. Meanwhile Serra died in Aug. 1784 and Palou as senior missionary was obliged against his own wishes to serve as acting president, residing part of the time at San Cárlos, but chiefly at San Francisco engaged in writing his Life of Serra, until Lasuen received the appointment in Sept. 1785. Palou was now free to go, and sailed, I suppose, on the *Favorita* late in September, which touched at Santa Bárbara with a load of lumber, *Prov. St. Pap.*, MS., vi. 166, and arrived at San Blas on Nov. 14. *Gaceta de Mex.*, i. There is, however, a difficulty; for the *Favorita* touched at Santa Bárbara Oct. 1st, and Fages in Monterey wrote on Oct. 3d, wishing the padre a pleasant voyage. *Prov. Rec.*, MS., iii. 55. There may be an error in one of these dates, or else possibly Palou departed in the Manila galleon *San José* which touched at Monterey in November. *Prov. Rec.*, MS., ii. 95. In any case he reached the college on Feb. 21, 1786. *Arch. Sta. Bárbara*, MS., xii. 29; and on July 1st was elected guardian. *Id.*, xi. 214–15. Sometime before Jan. 12, 1787, he presented a report to the government on the state of affairs in California. *Id.*, viii. 39. Nothing further is known of him, but he seems to have lived only a few years. I think he died before 1790. The guardian in 1798, mentioning the death of Viceroy Galvez, which occurred in Nov. 1786, says that Palou died 'a little later,' and implies that it was before Romeu's rule which began in 1790. *St. Pap., Miss. and Colon.*, MS., i. 48. The earliest communication that I have seen signed by his successor as guardian is dated November 1792, though it is of course possible that

LA PÉROUSE'S MAP OF SAN FRANCISCO.

former serving as *padrino*, with all the solemnities prescribed by the Roman ritual.[61]

This church was the finest yet erected in California; yet its dedication was a sad occasion, since under the edifice lay the body of its architect and builder, the founder of the mission, Father Murguía, who had died only four days before, a missionary well beloved and mourned by all.[62] His companion founder, Tomás de la Peña, served until 1794, although there were complaints against him for cruelty to the neophytes under his charge.[63] Murguía was succeeded by Diego de Noboa, and President Lasuen seems to have resided

Palou resigned. Taylor, *Discov. and Founders*, ii. No. 28, 171, says he seems to have died about 1796. For a sample of his handwriting with autograph signature see *S. Antonio, Doc. Sueltos*, MS., 13.

It is chiefly through his writings, the *Vida de Junípero Serra* and the *Noticias de California*, both of which have been noticed fully in a preceding chapter, that Palou's fame will live; yet as a missionary and as a man he deserves a very high place among the Californian friars. I regard him as but little inferior to Serra in executive ability and in devotion to his work, while in every other respect, save possibly in theological and dogmatic learning, he was fully his equal. His views as expressed in his writings are notably broad, practical, and liberal. Palou, Serra, and Crespí presented three good types of the missionary. Their friendship did not result from similarity of character, but rather from opposite qualities; and 'their reciprocal confidence and zeal for a common object,' as Doyle remarks, 'could not fail to prove most beneficial to the enterprise in which they all felt the greatest interest.'

[61] *Santa Clara, Arch. Parroq.*, MS., 12. Roof of beams 'labradas y curiosa lo posible.' Fages to general, in *Prov. Rec.*, MS., i. 172; *Hall's Hist. S. José*, 418-20; *Levett's Scrap Book*. The date has been incorrectly given as May 16th.

[62] Joseph Antonio de Jesus María de Murguía was born Dec. 10, 1715, at Domayguia, Álava, Spain. He came to America as a layman, but became a Franciscan at San Fernando college June 29, 1736; was ordained as a priest in 1744; and was assigned to the Pame missions of the Sierra Gorda in 1748. Here he toiled for 19 years and built the first masonry church in the district; that of San Miguel. Transferred in 1767 to Baja California he reached Loreto April 1, 1768, and was assigned to Santiago mission, where he served until March 1769. In June he was at San José del Cabo waiting to embark for California; but sickness saved his life by preventing him from sailing on the ill-fated *San José*. He subsequently served at San Javier, but in July 1773 joined Palou at Santa María and accompanied him to San Diego, arriving Aug. 30th. Residing for a while as supernumerary at San Antonio, he became minister of San Luis Obispo in October 1773, and in January 1777 founded Santa Clara where he served continuously until his death. He died while preparing for dedication the church on which he had worked so hard as architect, director, and even laborer. He was buried on May 12th in the presbytery of the new edifice by Palou, *Santa Clara, Lib. de Mision*, MS., 33-4, by whom as by Serra and others he had been regarded as a model friar. *Palou, Vida*, 265-6.

[63] Fages in a report to the general in 1786 speaks of these complaints, stating that one or two Indians have died from the effects of his severity, and that he will be retired to his college. *Prov. St. Pap.*, MS., ii. 136.

here much of the time from 1786 to 1789. There were no serious troubles with the natives, though the neophytes were sometimes inclined to take part in the petty wars of the gentiles.[64] In agricultural advantages Santa Clara was deemed superior to any other mission except San Gabriel, and crops of grain and fruit were usually large, although in 1790 the harvest of 2,875 bushels was less than that of San Francisco. Large stock had increased since 1783 from 400 to 2,817, and small stock from 554 to 836 head. Baptisms had been 1,279, many more than elsewhere, but deaths had been 639, a proportionally large figure; yet with an increase from 338 to 927, Santa Clara stood third in the list in respect of the number of converts.

Of the nine settlers of San José to whom lands were formally distributed in 1783, but who had become settlers in 1780 or earlier, the term of the last one, Claudio Alvires, expired in August 1785, and no rations were subsequently supplied by the government. Sebastian Alvitre had been expelled for bad conduct; but in 1786 eight of the original nine remained, and ten new names had been added as soldiers or *agregados*. Ten more were added before 1790. This latter class was composed of discharged soldiers who became settlers, differing from the pobladores in receiving no pay or rations. The soldiers of the guard were practically settlers from the first, men being selected for the duty usually whose time of discharge was near, and who intended to remain permanently at the pueblo.[65] In 1790 the total population

---

[64] Two or three neophytes were chastised by the padres for being present at a gentile fight, and Sergt. Amador was sent to warn the pagans not to tempt the converts. A pagan laborer of San José was flogged and imprisoned for inciting hostilities. This in 1786. Argüello to Fages, in *Prov. St. Pap.*, MS., viii. 76–7. Sergt. Cota ordered to explore from Santa Clara to Santa Rosa on the other side of the sierra, May 2, 1785. *Prov. Rec.*, MS., ii. 7.

[65] The ten names of 1786 were: Manuel Butron, Ignacio Castro, Manuel Higuera, Ignacio Linares, Seferino Lugo, Hilario Mesa, Nasario Saez, Ignacio Soto, Felipe Tapia, Atanasio Vazquez. *Prov. St. Pap.*, MS., v. 24–5, 27–8. Four received rations during the year, doubtless as invalids. See also *St. Pap., Sac.*, MS., i. 36. Manuel Valencia was a settler who died in 1788. *Prov.*

LOCAL EVENTS AND STATISTICS.

was about eighty. Agricultural products amounted to about 2,250 bushels; while large stock had increased from 417 to 980, and sheep had decreased from 800 to 600.

San José was less prosperous than Los Angeles, at least during the first half of the decade. Several causes contributed to this result, one of which was inefficient management and local government. The regulation allowed the governor to appoint alcaldes the first three years, after which time they were to be elected by the people. Fages, however, permitted an election, Ignacio Archuleta was chosen for 1783, and Mesa, corporal of the guard, was removed in September of that year for inharmonious relations with the alcalde. Who held the position of alcalde in 1784 the records fail to show; but by reason of irregularities and slow progress the governor was obliged to resume the power of appointment, naming Manuel Gonzalez as alcalde for 1785 with Romero and Alvires as regidores, and also appointing a comisionado to manage these officials. Corporal José Dominguez, the successor of Mesa, was at first made comisionado but died probably before the appointment reached him.[66] Ignacio Vallejo, who had been sent to San José in January to make a survey for a new dam or reservoir, remained as corporal to succeed Dominguez, and in May was appointed comisionado by Fages, with duties

St. Pap., MS., viii. 71. Mesa, Tapia, Higuera, and Lugo were soldiers in 1784 and the question came up whether they ought like the original settlers to be exempt from tithes since they cultivated lands like the rest. Prov. Rec., MS., i. 163-4. July 30, 1788, Argüello reports having gone to San José to put Ignacio Castro and Seferino Lugo in possession of lands, but did not do so because they claimed pay and rations, only allowed to the original settlers. St. Pap., Miss. and Colon., MS., i. 50-1. In the list of 1790 the name of Tapia disappears and there appear those of Joaquin Castro, Antonio Alegre, Antonio Aceves, Ignacio Higuera, and Pedro Cayuelas, agregados; Gabriel Peralta, Ramon Bojorges, and Juan Antonio Amézquita, inválidos; and Macario Castro, corporal of the guard. Argüello's report in St. Pap., Miss., MS., i. 18, 60-3.

[66] Fages to general Feb. 1, 1785, in Prov. Rec., MS., i. 187-8. He announces the changes mentioned in my text, and asks if he cannot reappoint Gonzalez the next year. The records do not show if this was permitted, the next alcalde mentioned being Antonio Romero in 1790. Dominguez died on Jan. 31st, the day before the date of Fages' letter. Sta. Clara, Lib. de Mision, MS., 35.

like those of Vicente Félix at Angeles.[67]   Vallejo had
some special fitness for directing agricultural operations, was allowed to cultivate vacant lands on his own
account, and held his position for seven years though
not without opposition.   To him, or rather to the wise
instructions given him, Fages attributed the pueblo's
later prosperity.[68]

The pueblo did not make much advance in the
matter of buildings, since nothing but palisade structures with roofs of earth were erected; but there was
good reason for this.   The site at first selected for
the house-lots proved to be too low, and exposed to
inundation in wet seasons.   There was a proposition
in 1785 to move the town a short distance to a higher
spot.   In 1787 General Ugarte authorized the transfer, and it was made soon after, certainly before 1791,
the slight nature of the buildings making the operation an easy one.[69]

One of Fages' first acts on taking command was to
march in January 1783 against the gentiles of the
San José region who had stolen some horses from

[67] Vallejo's appointment dated July 18, 1785.   Instructions in *Prov. Rec.*,
MS., ii. 121–5.   Jan. 24th, Vallejo named to make explorations for the reservoir. *Dept. St. Pap., S. José*, MS., i. 2.

[68] Fages to Romeu, Feb. 26, 1791, in *Prov. St. Pap.*, MS., x. 153.   In
October 1787 Capt. Soler went to San José to investigate certain charges of
the people against the comisionado.   All that the fault-finding inspector could
find against Vallejo, in his official capacity at least, was a *mando insípido*,
whatever that may be.   He recommended that he be put to personal labor in
the fields; but nothing was done in the matter. *Id.*, vii. 132.

[69] Hall, *Hist. San José*, 46–50, erroneously states that there was a long correspondence on the subject in 1797, and that the removal was effected in that
year; but the quarrel of that year was about boundaries between mission and
pueblo, and in the correspondence the site of the 'old town' is mentioned;
moreover Fages in his instructions of 1791 to Romeu speaks of the change
as already effected. *Prov. St. Pap.*, MS., x. 152.   Vallejo first urged the
removal on Feb. 20, 1785, in a communication to Moraga.   The latter found
it difficult to decide because the land on the proposed site had already been
distributed to settlers.   He accordingly addressed Fages on April 1st. *Prov.
St. Pap.*, MS., v. 26.   On March 9th Fages writes to Vallejo approving the
scheme. *Dept. St. Pap., S. José*, MS., i. 25; and on July 7th he assures the
people of San José that they shall be at no expense in the removal, and that
the pueblo shall lose no land—for it seems there was a fear that to move the
pueblo would also move the boundary between the pueblo and mission lands.
Prov. Rec., MS., iii. 30–1.   Fages refers the matter to Ugarte on Aug. 5th,
Id., ii. 126; and that official on June 21, 1787, grants the petition of the
settlers, and orders that there be no change in the boundary lines. *St. Pap.,
Miss. and Colon.*, MS., i. 274.

the settlers. The warlike governor killed two of the enemy, frightened the rest into complete submission, and for years after attributed to this campaign the prevailing quiet among gentiles. But again in 1788 it was necessary to place fifteen natives, including three chiefs, at work in the presidio, for horse-stealing.[70] There is little more to be said of local happenings at San José for this period. Some of the settlers were imprisoned and put in irons for refusing to work on a house for the town council, Ignacio Archuleta, ex-alcalde, being ringleader. The river broke through the old dam and the governor resolved to build a new one of masonry. Two boys drowned an Indian to amuse themselves, but in consideration of their tender years were dismissed with twenty-five lashes administered in presence of the natives. All this in 1784; the tithes for which year amounted to $428.[71]

[70] *Palou, Not.*, ii. 392; *Prov. Rec.*, MS., ii. 98; *Id.*, iii. 98, 170. Thirty-five lbs. powder, 800 bullets, and 100 flints sent to San José as reserve ammunition in August 1785. *Id.*, iii. 31.

[71] *Prov. Rec.*, MS., i. 168, 172; iii. 22-3. A wooden granary had been completed in December 1782. *Prov. St. Pap.*, MS., iii. 166-7. A settler put in the stocks in 1788 for assaulting his corporal, and corporal reprimanded for his violence. *Id.*, vii. 134.

CHAPTER XXIII.

RULE OF ROMEU.

1791-1792.

PEDRO FAGES, worn down by work, and more by
the anxieties imposed on a nervous temperament
growing out of the responsibilities of his position as
governor, asked to be relieved of the office and to be
granted leave of absence that he might revisit Spain.
In May 1790 his resignation was accepted by Viceroy
Revilla Gigedo, and he was ordered to Mexico to
receive twelve months' advance pay as colonel with
which to defray his expenses in Spain; José Antonio
Romeu was named as his successor. This information reached Fages at Monterey in September, and
was all the more agreeable from the fact that Romeu
was his personal friend. In February 1791 Fages,
who had awaited letters announcing his successor's
coming to Monterey, received orders from the viceroy
by which, after setting the commandants and habilitados at work upon their respective presidio accounts,
he was to proceed to Loreto and there make formal

delivery of his office to Romeu; or, if not able to do this, he was to send orders to Arrillaga, the commandant at Loreto, to surrender the office in the governor's name. As the state of Fages' health would not permit a journey overland to the peninsula, he forwarded the necessary orders to Arrillaga, lieutenant governor of the Californias, who accordingly transferred the command to Romeu at Loreto on April 16, 1791, which is therefore the date when Fages ceased to rule.[1]

With his orders to Arrillaga under date of February 26th, Fages transmitted the instructions which it was customary for a retiring governor to prepare for the use of his successor, outlining the country's past history and present condition, and embodying the results of his own experience in recommendations respecting future policy. The historical portions of this important document have already been utilized largely in the preceding chapters; but a brief consideration of the paper as a whole, will throw light on the condition of affairs at the time of Romeu's accession. The development of the two pueblos, says the retiring governor, and the settlement in them of retired soldiers, has received and still merits the deepest attention. Their products are purchased by the presidios and paid for in goods and drafts. The distribu-

---

[1] The viceroy's order granting Fages' request and appointing Romeu, dated May 16, 1790. *Prov. St. Pap., Ben.*, MS., i. 8–10. May 27th seems to have been the date of the viceroy's communication to king; but of the king's approval and confirmation of Romeu we only know that it reached Mexico before May 18, 1791. *Prov. St. Pap.*, MS., x. 139. September 1, 10, 13, 1790, the viceroy instructs Fages about the transfer. *Id.*, ix. 308, 346–7. September 14, 1790, Fages to Romeu, expressing his pleasure at the latter's appointment, describing the presidio, saying something of the condition of the country, and saying: 'You will find in this casa real, which is sufficiently capacious, the necessary furniture; a sufficient stock of goats and sheep which I have raised; and near by a garden which I have made at my own expense, from which you will have fine vegetables all the year, and will enjoy the fruits of the trees which I have planted.' He asks for information as to when and by what route Romeu will come. *Prov. St. Pap., Ben.*, MS., i. 8–10. Romeu takes possession April 16, 1791. *Prov. St. Pap.*, MS., x. 124; *St. Pap., Sac.*, MS., v. 86–7; *Arch. Sta. Bárbara*, MS., xi. 414–15. February 26, 1791, Fages notifies Romeu that he has ordered Arrillaga to make the transfer, and has directed presidial accounts, etc., to be made ready. *Prov. St. Pap.*, MS., x. 144–5.

tion of lands has been made in due form, and—together with certain changes at San José rendered necessary by the moving of the houses—approved by the superior authorities. It was intended at first to remove the pueblo guards after two years, but they are to be maintained as long as necessary. In the first years, on account of bad management, San José made little progress; but the appointment of a comisionado as at Angeles and the subjection of the alcalde to him, have restored prosperity; and these measures were approved in 1785–6.

In the missions great care must be taken to guard against the increase of veneral diseases which are causing such ravages in the peninsula. The sending of soldiers for escaped neophytes is extremely dangerous, and should be avoided, being resorted to only after other means—the best being for the friars to send other natives with flattery and trifling gifts to enlist the services of chiefs—have failed, and then with every possible precaution. The granting of escorts whenever asked for has also proved dangerous and inconvenient, since only two men could be spared, leaving the mission exposed and the friar only slightly protected. It has therefore been restricted, and the soldiers are not allowed to pass the night away from the mission. This policy, notwithstanding protests, and in consequence of Neve's confidential reports, has been approved by superiors and by the king.

In the case of mail-carriers and escorts passing from one presidio to another, careful orders have been given to prevent disaster and at the same time to insure humane treatment of the gentiles. Each presidio has in its archives properly indexed the orders that have been issued for its government and the prevention of all disorder. The abundance of products in proportion to consumers has led to a reduction of some of the prices affixed by Neve to grain and meat. Cattle belonging to the crown are kept from excessive increase and consequent running wild by annual slaugh-

ters for the supply of presidios and vessels with beef.
The breeding of horses and mules, just beginning to
prosper, should be encouraged. The friars often wish
to buy these animals, but have been uniformly refused.
All trade with the Manila ship is strictly prohibited;
but trade with San Blas is free for five years from
October 1786, and subject to only half duties for five
years more—a trade which is bad in its effects, leading to 'immoderate luxury,' for the inhabitants can
buy all they really need at cost prices from the *memorias*. To provide the wasting of clothing and other
useful articles in barter with the sailors, Fages has
forbidden the opening of the bales uñtil the vessel
leaves the port.

In articles 21–3 of his *papel*, Fages tells the tale
of three or four incorrigible rogues, Alvitre and Navarro of Angeles, Ávila of San Jose, and Pedraza, a
deserter from the galleon, whose scandalous conduct
no executive measure has been able to reform. Articles 24–7 are devoted to past troubles between Captain Soler and the habilitados, with which the reader
is already familiar; and finally, after devoting some
attention to the condition of the different presidios,
the author closes by alluding to the charges of cruelty
pending against Father Peña of Santa Clara, and to
the orchard of six hundred fruit-trees, besides shrubs
and grape-vines, to which since 1783 he has given
much of his attention.[2]

[2] *Fages, Papel de varios puntos concernientes al Gobierno de la Península de
California é Inspeccion de Tropas, que recopila el Coronel D. Pedro Fages al
Teniente Coronel D. José Antonio Romeu, 26 de Febrero 1791, MS.* On May
28th Fages wrote again to Romeu a most interesting letter in which he gives
his opinion of various persons with whom his successor will come in contact.
He speaks very highly of Arrillaga, Zúñiga, and Argüello, deems Goycoechea
somewhat prone to carelessness, says nothing of Ortega, and pronounces
Gonzalez fit only for his present position on the frontier. None of the sergeants are suitable for habilitados, though Vargas is faithful and can write.
With the Dominicans there has been no serious trouble, and President Gomez
is disposed to sustain harmonious relations; but with the Fernandinos quarrels have been frequent, since they are '*opuestísimos* á las máximas del reglamento y gobierno' and insist on being independent and absolute each in his
own mission. Fages doubts that Romeu will be able to endure their independent way of proceeding. The priests at San Francisco and Santa Clara
are forming separate establishments at some distance from the mission, which

Don Pedro sent his wife and children southward in advance of his own departure, probably on board the *San Cárlos,* or *Princesa,* which left Monterey for San Blas in the autumn of 1790.[3] He remained at Monterey, though he made a visit to San Francisco in May,[4] and still exercised by common consent a kind of superintendence over the actions of his former subordinates, though now addressed as colonel instead of governor. There are letters of his in the archives dated at Monterey July 13th.[5] His intention was to remain until October or November, and I suppose he embarked on the *San Cárlos* for San Blas November 9, 1791, though possibly his departure was a month earlier.[6] In 1793 he made a report on the California presidios, and in October 1794 was still residing in Mexico. Of Pedro Fages before he came to California in 1769 and after his departure in 1791 we know little; with his career in the province the reader is familiar,[7] and will part with the honest Catalan, as I do, reluctantly.

matter needs looking after. Mission stock is increasing too much, and the neophytes are becoming too skilful riders and acquiring 'Apache insolence.' Some advice is given about the journey north. A promise is made of more letters, and Fages closes by making a present of his famous orchard, well pleased that the fruits of his labors and expenditures are to be enjoyed by his friend. *Fages, Informes Particulares al Gobr. Romeu 28 de Mayo 1791,* MS. On May 1st he had written to Romeu that he was permitted to take away with him six mules and as many horses if the commander of the vessel had no objections. *Prov. St. Pap.,* MS., x. 147. There are also communications of Fages to Romeu on matters of trifling importance dated May 26th, 30th, June 1st, July 4th, 13th. *Id.,* 141–70.

[3] In his letter of May 28, 1791, Fages expresses his pleasure that Romeu on his journey—probably at San Blas or between there and Mexico—had met his family. He states his intention of staying at Monterey until October or November. *Prov. St. Pap.,* MS., x. 148, 150.

[4] *Id.,* x. 44.

[5] *Id.,* x. 142–3, 169. In one of the letters he says that, suffering in his foot, he is unable to review the troops at Santa Bárbara.

[6] Sailing of the *San Cárlos* Nov. 19th. *St. Pap., Sac.,* MS., v. 91. According to a letter in *Prov. St. Pap.,* MS., x. 134, however, the schooner *Saturnina* from Nootka was at Monterey on Oct. 14th and ready to sail for San Blas, so that Fages may have sailed in her; yet if there is no error it is strange that while the arrival of the *San Cárlos* was announced to Gen. Nava on Nov. 30th, that of the *Saturnina* was not announced until Dec. 22d. *St. Pap., Sac.,* MS., iv. 3.

[7] Pedro Fages, a native of Catalonia, and first lieutenant of a company of the 1st battalion, 2d regiment, of the Catalan Volunteer Light Infantry, probably left Spain with his battalion in May 1767, and soon after his arrival in Mexico

He was a peculiar man; industrious, energetic, and
brave, a skilful hunter and dashing horseman, fond of
children, who were wont to crowd round him and
rarely failed to find his pockets stored with *dulces*.
Of fair education and executive abilities, hot-tempered

was sent with Col. Elizondo's expedition against the Sonora Indians. In the
autumn of 1768 by order of the visitador general, Galvez, he was sent over from
Guaymas to La Paz by Elizondo with 25 men of his *compañía franca* for the
California expedition. In January 1769 he embarked with his men on the *San
Cárlos* and arrived at San Diego May 1st. Fages was military chief of the sea
branch of the expedition, and commandant on shore from May 1st to June
29th, thus being California's first ruler. After Portolá's arrival on June 29th,
he was second in command and Capt. Rivera's superior. With seven of his
men, all that the scurvy had not killed or disabled, he accompanied the first
land expedition from San Diego to Monterey and San Francisco from July 14,
1769, to Jan. 24, 1770. He started north again April 17th with Portolá and
reached Monterey May 24th. When Portolá left Monterey July 9th, Fages
was left as commandant of the Californian establishments, a position which
he held until May 25, 1774. His commission as captain was dated May 4,
1771, and in the same year he went down to San Diego by water, returning
by land. In March and April 1772 he led an exploring expedition up to what
are now Oakland, San Pablo Bay, Carquines Strait, and the mouth of the San
Joaquin. In May 1772 he proceeded to the San Luis region and spent some
three months hunting bears to supply the Monterey garrison with meat.
Perhaps it was here that he gained the sobriquet of El Oso often applied to
him in later years, though there is a tradition that the name Old Bear was
given him for other reasons. He went to San Diego in August, and there
incurred Padre Serra's displeasure by refusing a guard for the founding of a
new mission. The object of Serra's journey to Mexico was chiefly Fages' removal. The friar represented him as a man hated by all the soldiers, incompetent to command, and a deadly foe to all mission progress. The charges
were largely false, but they served Serra's purpose whether believed or not,
for the government could not afford at the time a quarrel with the missionaries; and Rivera was sent to supersede Fages, taking command on May 25,
1774. Subsequently Serra wrote a letter to the viceroy in which he expressed
regret at Fages' removal, commendation of his services, and a desire that he
be favored by the government. *Arch. Sta. Bárbara*, MS., xi. 379–80. The
friars regarded this as a praiseworthy return of good for evil; others might
apply a different name.

Fages sailed from San Diego Aug. 4, 1774, on the *San Antonio* with orders
to join his regiment at Pachuca. On the way to Mexico at Irapuato, Guanajuato, he was robbed of a box containing his money, by his own servants as it
seems. *Prov. St. Pap.*, MS., i. 190. He reached Mexico before the end of
1774 in poor health. He dated in Mexico, Nov. 30, 1775, a report on California, addressed to the viceroy, and devoted chiefly to a description of the
province, its natives, animals, and plants; but also giving a tolerably complete
sketch of the first expeditions and the condition of the missions at the author's
departure. This document, of great importance and interest, was translated
from the original in the library of M. Ternaux-Compans and published as
Fagès, Voyage en Californie, in *Nouv. Ann. des Voy.*, ci. 145–82, 311–47. At
the beginning the author says: 'Ayant été chargé du commandement militaire
du poste de Monterey, depuis le commencement de l'année 1769, et mon chef
don Diego Portola qui s'embarqua le 9 de Juillet à bord du paquebot le *San
Antonio*, m'ayant fortement recommandé de m'occuper des établissements
situés dans la partie septentrionale de la Californie, je m'y suis livré pendant
plus de quatre ans. J'ai rassemblé le plus de renseignements qu'il m'a été

and inclined to storm over trifles, always ready to quarrel with anybody from his wife to the padre presidente, he was withal kind-hearted, never feeling and rarely exciting deep-seated animosities. He was thoroughly devoted to the royal service and attended with rare conscientiousness to every petty detail of his official duty; yet his house, his horse, and above all his garden were hardly second in importance to his office, his province, and his nation. He possessed less breadth of mind, less culture, and especially less dignity of manner and character than Felipe de Neve, but he was by no means less honest and patriotic. The early rulers of California were by no means the characterless figure-heads and pompous nonentities that modern writers have painted them, and among them all there is no more original and attractive character than the bluff Catalan soldier Pedro Fages.

José Antonio Romeu, a native of Valencia, Spain, had served in the Sonora Indian wars with Fages in and before 1782 as captain. As we have seen, he took part in the campaigns following the Colorado

possible sur ces provinces éloignées, sur les nations qui les habitent, la nature de leur territoire, ses productions, les moeurs et coutumes de la population, et beaucoup d'autres sujets dont je traiterai dans le cours de cette relation.'

Capt. Fages was in garrison with his company at Guadalajara, when he was ordered, perhaps in 1777, to the Sonora frontier; and there he served in the wars against Apaches and other savages for five years, receiving in the mean time a lieut. colonel's commission. In 1781–2 he made several expeditions from Sonora to the Colorado to avenge the death of his former rival, Rivera; and visited California twice in 1782 before he came as governor, making the first trip from the Colorado direct to San Diego. He was in the Colorado region when on Sept. 10th, by an appointment of July 12, 1782, he took possession of his office as governor, and reached Monterey in November. 1783 was spent chiefly in a journey to Loreto whence he brought his wife, Doña Eulalia de Callis, and son to the capital. He had at least two children born in California. In 1785 he had trouble with his wife, which does not seem however to have outlasted the year. From August 1786, by Gen. Ugarte's order of Feb. 12th, Fages became inspector of presidios. His commission as colonel was dated Feb. 7, 1789. His governorship ended April 16, 1791, and he sailed from Monterey in the autumn of the same year. Taylor, *Discov. and Founders*, ii. 179, says he died in Mexico before 1796, but it is by no means certain that he had any authority for the statement. Aug. 12, 1793, he makes a report on Monterey Presidio buildings at Mexico. *Prov. St. Pap.*, MS., xiii. 191; and in Oct. 1794 he resided in the city of Mexico. *Costansó, Informe*, MS.

disaster. In May 1790, when appointed governor he was major of the España dragoon regiment, also holding the rank of lieutenant colonel. He was probably in Mexico at the time of his appointment and proceeded to his province by way of San Blas, since he met the family of his predecessor and friend on their way from California. Accompanied by his wife, Josefa de Sandoval, and daughters Romeu arrived March 17, 1791, at Loreto by the schooner *Santa Gertrudis*. On April 16, as already stated, he took formal possession of the governorship, Captain Arrillaga representing Fages in the transfer of the necessary papers.[8] The reason why the new governor was ordered to assume his office at Loreto instead of proceeding directly to the capital was that he might attend to his duties as inspector of presidios in the south, thus avoiding a useless repetition of the journey, and that he might make certain investigations of presidial accounts. These Californian accounts had been in some confusion since 1769. Details it is undesirable as well as impossible to explain; but many men had unsettled accounts running back to the earliest period of Spanish occupation. The treasury officials in Mexico, attributing the prevalent confusion to the incompetence of habilitados, were themselves greatly puzzled,[9] and Romeu seems to have been selected with a special view to his fitness for unravelling past financial complications and effecting a final adjustment.

Whatever may have been his abilities in this special direction, he had very slight opportunity to show them; for from the moment of embarking on the *Santa Gertrudis* his health failed; indigestion, sleepless nights, and an oppressive pain in the chest left

[8] See references in note 1 of this chapter. Also letter of Arrillaga to Fages March 21, 1791, announcing Romeu's arrival. *Prov. St. Pap.*, MS., x. 38.

[9] The *Informe sobre los ajustes de Pobladores de la Reina de Los Angeles y demas de las Provincias de Californias*, MS., a report of the contador mayor dated Mexico, Dec. 30, 1789, and filling above 60 pages, is a specimen of the many wordy communications on the subject which are extant in the archives. I have made no attempt to reach the bottom of this financial puzzle. Viceroy's orders to Romeu on this subject Sept. 1, 1790. *Prov. St. Pap.*, ix. 313–19.

him but little opportunity of attending to public duties.[10] Yet he did not lose courage, and late in the summer, after communicating his instructions to presidal officers and satisfying himself of Arrillaga's entire competence, he proceeded north, reached San Diego in August,[11] and arrived at Monterey October 13th, doubtless before the departure of his predecessor.[12] Through the winter his ill-health continued, and he was barely able to attend to the routine duties of his office. His official communications in the archives are few, brief, and unimportant. His correspondence with President Lasuen both at Loreto and Monterey, though containing little more than the formal expressions required by courtesy, indicate a desire on his part, such as most rulers entertained when they first came to California, to preserve harmonious relations with the missionaries.[13] In fact either by natural disposition or by reason of feeble health he was evidently more *frailero* than Fages or Neve. On December 1st he received the royal confirmation of his appointment as governor.[14]

Late in March 1792 Romeu's condition became critical, and after a series of convulsions it became evident that he had but a few days to live. The surgeon, Pablo Soler, made a written report to this effect on April 5th, and the last rites of religion were administered by the friars in attendance. He died at Monterey April 9th and was buried at San Cárlos

[10] *Romeu, Carta al Virrey, 21 de Nov. 1791*, MS., in *St. Pap., Sac.*, v. 91-2.
[11] He was at San Diego from Aug. 20th to 31st if not longer. *Prov. St. Pap.*, MS., x. 40-3.
[12] Nov. 28, 1791, the viceroy acknowledges the receipt of his letter of Oct. 14th, announcing his arrival on the 13th. *Prov. St. Pap.*, MS., x. 134.
[13] *Romeu, Cortas al Presidente Lasuen, 1791*, MS. On July 16th from Rosario he writes: 'Aunque mi caudal de mérito no es otro que el tener unos buenos y constantes deseos de llenar el cumplimiento de mi obligacion, y ser útil y sin embargo de carecer de aquellas apreciables circunstancias conducentes á su logro de que la bondad de V. R. me supone acompañado, espero merecerlo de la piedad del Altísimo al verme auxiliado de las fervientes oraciones de V. R. y de esos RR. PP. misioneros á los que de nuevo me encomiendo correspondiendo con iguales á las expresiones finas conque me honran.'
[14] *St. Pap., Sac.*, MS. v. 92. The confirmation was dated Feb. 15th.

the day following. By his will the widow was made
executrix of his estate and guardian of their daughters. Doña Josefa embarked for San Blas in October. Alférez Sal in a letter says that California·was
not worthy of a governor like Romeu. At his funeral
all who knew him displayed deep grief.[15]

Local annals as well as certain general topics of
commercial, industrial, and mission development, I
shall treat collectively for the decade from 1791 to
1800, in subsequent chapters. Besides such topics
the visit of a scientific exploring expedition and the
founding of two new missions are to be noted during
Romeu's short rule. The expedition referred to was
that of Alejandro Malaspina in command of the royal
corvettes *Descubierta* and *Atrevida*,[16] the latter being
under the immediate command of José de Bustamante
y Guerra, and the scientific corps including Bauzá
and Espinosa.[17] Malaspina sailed from Cádiz in July
1789, for a tour round the world, and after making
explorations on both coasts of South America, and
from Panamá to Acapulco, left the latter port in May
1791 for the Northwest Coast, which he struck a little
above 60° and carefully explored southward, sighting

[15] *Prov. St. Pap.*, MS., xxii. 7–9, 14; x. 139; xxi. 71, 89; *St. Pap., Sac.*,
MS., vi., 76; *Prov. Rec.*, MS., ii. 152; *San Cárlos, Lib. de Mision*, MS.; *Taylor's Discov. and Founders*, ii. 179; *Vallejo, Hist. Cal.*, MS., i. 96–7.
[16] The vessels had, like nearly all in the Spanish navy, each a double name,
being called respectively *Santa Justa* and *Santa Rufina. St. Pap., Sac.*, MS.,
v. 96.
[17] A full list of officers made at Monterey, is as follows: Captains Alejandro Malaspina and José de Bustamante y Guerra; lieutenants Dionisio Galiano,* José Espinosa, Cayetano Valdés, Manuel Novales,* Fernando Quintano,
Juan Bernaci, Secundino Salamanca, Antonio de Tova, Juan Concha, José
Robredo, Areaco Zeballos, Francisco Viana, and Arcadio Lineda;* alféreces
Martin Olavide,* Felipe Bauzá, Flavio Aleponzoni, and Jacobo Murphy; con-
tadores Rafael Rodriguez de Arias and Manuel Esquerra; chaplains José de
Mesa and Francisco de Paula Añino; surgeons Francisco Flores and Pedro
Gonzalez; pilotos Juan Diaz Maqueda, José Sanchez, Gerónimo Delgado, Juan
Inciarte y Portu, and Joaquin Hurtado; apothecary Luis Nee* and Tadeo
Haenek; pintor de perspectiva Tomás Suria; disecador y dibujante de plantas
José de Guio.* The names marked with a star remained behind in Mexico.
*Malaspina, Nota de Oficiales de Guerra y Mayores, Naturalistas, Botánicos,
Dibujantes, y Disecadores, que tienen destino en las corbetas de S. M. nombra-
das Descubierta y Atrevida, que dan vuelta al Globo...que salieron de Cádiz en
30 de Julio de 1789*, MS.

Cape Mendocino September 6th, being off San Francisco the 10th,[18] and anchoring the 13th at Monterey, where his vessels remained till the 25th, thence continuing the survey down to Cape San Lúcas, San Blas, Acapulco, and returning to Spain by the Philippines and Cape Good Hope.[19]

Of the stay at Monterey, of scientific observations there, of Malaspina's impressions of California and its people we know little. The archives contain only the merest mention of the arrival and of courtesies exchanged between the visitors and Lasuen, who aided in gathering specimens,[20] Malaspina seems entitled to the honor of having brought to California the first American who ever visited the country, and he came to remain, his burial being recorded on the mission register under date of September 13th, and name of John Groem, probably Graham, son of John and Catherine Groem, Presbyterians, of Boston. He had shipped as gunner at Cádiz.[21] The reports of this expedition were never published. The commander was imprisoned for certain crimes or irregularities, and it is only through Navarrete's brief résumé, and an abridged narrative by one of the officers, that anything is known of results.[22]

As early as 1789 it was determined to found two new missions, in honor of 'our lady of solitude' and

[18] At least 4 or 5 shots were heard from a fog-hidden vessel on that date. Bustamante, in *Cavo, Tres Siglos*, iii. 106-7, says he left Nootka August 25th, and anchored at Monterey September 11th.

[19] For account of Malaspina's explorations in the north, see *Hist. N. W. Coast*, i. 249; and *Hist. Alaska*, this series.

[20] Sept. 21, 1791, Malaspina and Bustamante to Lasuen thanking him for aid. Lasuen in reply gives thanks for presents. The letters are full of flattering expressions, and the voyagers promise to make the king and the world acquainted with their favorable impressions of California and with the success and zeal of the padres. *Malaspina* and *Bustamante—Carta al P. Lasuen y respuesta de dicho Padre*, Sept. 1791, MS. March 27, 1792, Gen. Nava has learned of Malaspina's visit. *Arch. Arzobispado*, MS., i. 19.

[21] *Taylor*, in *Pacific Monthly*, xi. 649-50, from *San Cárlos, Lib. de Mision*.

[22] *Navarrete, Viages Apócrifos*, 94-8, 268-70, 313-20; *Id.*, in *Sutil y Mexicana, Viage, Introd.*, cxxii.-iii. Taylor, in *Pacific Monthly*, xi. 649, and *L. Cal.*,

of the holy cross. The necessary preliminaries were arranged by correspondence between president, guardian, and viceroy, and four new friars were selected to take charge, or enable others to do so, of the new establishments.[23] The information reached California at the end of July 1790 together with the friars, Dantí, Miguel, Rubí, and Tapis; and all the necessary effects except the church vestments and utensils. This omission caused delay, for the priests were not disposed to take anything on trust in dealing with the government, and it was not until July 1791 that a positive assurance came from the viceroy that the sacred utensils would be sent, together with an order to proceed at once, borrowing the needed articles from the other establishments.[24] Subsequent preliminary work is best described in the words of Lasuen, who writes the 29th of September: "In view of the superior order of his excellency I at once named the missionaries. I asked and obtained from the commandant of this presidio the necessary aid for exploring anew the region of Soledad, and there was chosen a site having some advantages over the two previously considered. I applied to the missions for vestments and sacred vessels; and as soon as the commander of the *Aranzazu* furnished the sirvientes allowed for the new establishments I proceeded to Santa Clara in order to examine anew in person the site of Santa Cruz. I crossed the sierra by a long and rough way,

41, says that Malaspina, through the jealousy of Godoy, was imprisoned for 14 years and finally liberated when Marshal Soult took Coruña in 1809.

[23] Guardian Noriega to viceroy, Sept. 22, 1789; viceroy to guardian, Oct. 31; guardian to Lasuen, Dec. 10, in *Arch. Sta. Bárbara*, MS., vi. 280–2. Two thousand eight hundred dollars was to be paid to the síndico, $1,000 for each mission, and $200 for travelling expenses of each friar. April 1, 1790, the síndico, Fr. Gerónimo de Sampelayo, sends provisions and tools for Santa Cruz to value of $1,021. *Sta. Cruz, Lib. de Mision*, MS., 3.

[24] Aug. 3, 1790, Lasuen to Fages, announces arrival of padres; nothing lacking but for the government to deliver the sacred vessels; he is ready. *Arch. Arzobispado*, MS., i. 10; Jan. 20, 1791. Viceroy to Lasuen and to governor, *ornamentos*, etc., will be sent; let the old missions lend. July 15th, Lasuen replies: all right. *Arch. Sta. Bárbara*, MS., xi. 8–10; *Prov. St. Pap.*, MS., x. 138. July 22, 1791, Lasuen issues a circular to the padres making known viceroy's orders; let each padre mark on the margin the articles that he can lend. *Arch. Sta. Bárbara*, MS., ix. 316–17.

and I found in the site the same excellent fitness that had been reported to me. I found, besides, a stream of water very near, copious, and important. On the day of San Agustin, August 28th, I said mass, and a cross was raised in the spot where the establishment is to be. Many gentiles came, large and small, of both sexes, and showed that they would gladly enlist under that sacred standard, thank God! I returned to Santa Clara by another way, rougher but shorter and more direct. I had the Indians improve the road and was perfectly successful, because for this as for everything else the commandant of San Francisco, Don Hermenegildo Sal, has furnished with the greatest activity and promptness all the aid I have asked for. I ordered some little huts made, and I suppose that by this time the missionaries are there. I found here in Monterey the two corvettes of the Spanish expedition, and the commander's power of pleasing obliged me to await their departure. I endeavored to induce them to transport the Santa Cruz supplies by water, but it could not be accomplished. Day before yesterday, however, some were sent there by land, and with them a man from the schooner which came from Nootka under Don Juan Carrasco.[25] The plan is to see if there is any shelter for a vessel on the coast near Santa Cruz, and there to transport what is left. To-morrow a report is expected. This means is sought because we lack animals. To-day eleven Indians have departed from here with tools to construct a shelter at Soledad for the padres and the supplies. I and the other padres are making preparations, and my departure thither will be, by the favor of God, the day after San Francisco, October 8th, at latest."[26]

The preliminaries having been thus arranged Alférez Sal started from San Francisco September 22d with

---

[25] This schooner was the *Horcasitas*, which under Narvaez had taken part in Elisa's northern explorations. See *Hist. N. W. Coast*, i. 244–250. The *Aranzazu* had also made a trip to the north, under Matute.

[26] Lasuen, *Carta al Sr. Gobernador Romeu, sobre fundacion de Misiones, 29 de Sept. 1791*, MS.

Corporal Luis Peralta and two privates, arriving at
Santa Clara in the afternoon.[27] Next morning he
proceeded to Santa Cruz, his force being increased by
fathers Alonso Salazar and Baldomero Lopez, while
the rest of the mission guard with six or seven servants
were left to bring supplies and cattle. On the 24th
some Christian Indians of Santa Clara were set at
work cutting timber and building a hut for the friars,
who busied themselves seeking a spot for sowing
twenty-five fanegas of wheat. A fine plain was found
well adapted for the purpose, capable of irrigation
from a small stream called by the explorers of 1769
Arroyo de San Pedro Regalado. The mission site
was about five hundred yards from the Rio San
Lorenzo, also named in 1769. The chief Sugert came
in with a few of his followers, and promised to become
the first Christian of his tribe, Sal agreeing to be
godfather. On Sunday, September 25th, as soon as
the soldiers and horses arrived from Santa Clara,
Sugert and his people having been fortified by assurances against the noise of exploding gunpowder, and
the friars having donned their robes, Don Hermenegildo took formal possession as he says, "in such words
as my moderate talent dictated," and at the conclusion
the guns were discharged. Five more salutes were
fired while the padres said mass and chanted a te

[27] Sept. 17, 1791, Sal to Romeu, excusing himself for sending, without
having awaited Romeu's arrival or orders, at Lasuen's request, a guard and
mule train for the new mission. *St. Pap., Sac.*, MS., vii. 18–20. The corporal
of the mission guard was fully instructed respecting his duties under date of
Sept. 17th. *Sal, Instruccion al Cabo Luis Peralta al cargo de la Escolta de la
Mision de Santa Cruz, 1791*, MS. The general purport was, constant precautions, kindness to gentiles, harmony with padres, strict performance of
religious duties, and the details of routine. The details were much the same
in all missions. It is to be noticed, however, that in the matter of escorting
the priests the soldiers were strictly limited, and were not allowed to pass
the night away from the mission. If a priest desired to go to a distant mission, word must be sent to San Francisco and a guard obtained from the
presidio. On the 29th or 30th of each month a report to Sal must be sent by
two soldiers to Santa Clara, where the two must wait till two Santa Clara
men carried the despatch to San Francisco and returned. As the rainy season
was drawing near, the gentiles might be induced to work on the warehouse
and guard-house by presents of food, etc., even against the wishes of the
padres.

deum, and thus the mission of Santa Cruz was founded.[28]

Local annals of Santa Cruz to 1800 are best presented here and may be briefly recorded. Often there were apprehensions of trouble with the natives, but the fears of the friars rested for the most part on nothing more solid than rumor, the occasional flight of a neophyte, or the loss of an animal. To keep the soldiers of the guard on the alert they were once ordered to hunt bears for target practice.[29] The neophytes numbered 84 at the end of the year 1791. They had increased to 224 in another year; in 1796 the number was 523, the highest ever reached, and in 1800 they were 492. There had been 949, according to the registers, baptized, 271 couples married, and 477 buried. Large stock increased during the decade from 202 to 2,354 head; small stock from 174 to 2,083. Agricultural products in 1792 were about 650 bushels;

[28] *Sal, Diario del Reconocimiento de la Mision de Santa Cruz, 1791*, MS. Certificate on foundation of the mission, dated Sept. 25th, and signed by Sal, Corp. Peralta, and soldier Salvador Higuera. *St. Pap., Sac.*, MS., ii. 137. Sal returned to Santa Clara Sept. 26th, and San Francisco Sept. 27th. Sept. 25th, the padres announce the foundation to-day in a letter to Romeu; site fine and prospects flattering. *Lopez and Salazar, Carta de los Padres de Santa Cruz al Gobernador, 1791*, MS. Title-pages of mission registers. *Santa Cruz, Lib. de Mision*, MS., 28. Santa Clara furnished for Santa Cruz 64 cattle, 22 horses, 76 fanegas of grain, and 26 loaves of bread; San Francisco, 5 yoke of oxen, 70 sheep, and 2 bushels of barley; San Cárlos, 7 mules and 8 horses. The guard furnished the padres $42.50 worth of provisions, to be repaid. A list of the church vestments and sacred vessels is also given. Copy from mission records in *Vallejo, Doc. Hist. Cal.*, MS., xxviii. 102–3. See also *Willey's Centennial Sketch of Santa Cruz*, 11, 12. *Santa Cruz Sentinel*, Aug. 12, 1865. Another record makes the contribution of Santa Clara 151 cattle, 19 horses, 18 fanegas of grain; San Francisco, 6 yoke of oxen, 100 hogs, 12 mules; and other missions 8 beasts of burden. *Salazar, Condicion actual de California, 1796*, MS.

[29] This was in 1797. *Prov. Rec.*, MS., v. 106. Jan. 1794, Mission guard increased to 8 men, but reduced to 5 before May 1795. *Prov. St. Pap.*, MS., xiii. 231; xii. 77. April 1798, 90 fugitives gathered in by Corp. Mesa. *Id.*, xxii. 101. Road from Monterey threatened; a soldier *nearly* attacked in 1792, *St. Pap., Sac.*, MS. vi. 70–1. Feb. 1793, 9 neophytes brought in 9 pagans. Mountain Indians said to be making arrows. *Prov. St. Pap.*, MS., xi. 152-3. Dec. 1793, the corporal and a soldier wounded; two parties sent from San Francisco to punish the natives. *Id.*, xxi. 176. Jan. 1795, Sergt. Amador sent to capture 2 Indians who were making trouble on the Rio Pájaro. *Prov. St. Pap., Ben. Mil.*, MS., i. 47. March 7, 1796, P. Sanchez asks for aid. Indians threatening. *St. Pap., Sac.*, MS., viii. 3. Feb. 29th, Amador sent to investigate a rumor that the Indians would rise and kill the padres. *Prov. St. Pap.*, MS., xiv. 18.

3,400 in 1796, and 800 in 1799; in 1800 were 4,300 bushels; total yield of the decade, 17,590 bushels.

The church, whose corner-stone had been laid with due ceremony on February 27th of the preceding year, was formally dedicated to its holy use the 10th of May 1794, by Father Peña from Santa Clara, with the aid of Gili and Sanchez, besides the ministers of the mission. Alférez Sal was present and as godfather of the church received its keys. All the ceremonies prescribed by the Roman ritual were solemnly performed in presence of neophytes, servants, and troops, and next day a mass was celebrated in the new edifice. The church was about thirty by one hundred and twelve feet and twenty-five feet high. The foundation walls to the height of three feet were of stone, the front was of masonry, and the rest of adobes.[30] There is some evidence that the site of the mission had been slightly changed in 1792 to avoid danger from inundation.[31] About the mission buildings but little is recorded except that the last two sides of the square were completed in 1795; and a flouring-mill was built and began to run in the autumn of 1796, but was badly damaged by the rains of

[30] A full account of the ceremony and of the building, signed by the six persons named and by Francisco Gomez, José María Lopez, Ignacio Chumazero, and José Antonio Sanchez, is given in *Sta. Cruz, Lib. de Mision*, MS., 38–40. Mr Willey, *Centennial Sketch Sta. Cruz*, 12, gives the date as March 10th, and this may possibly be correct, as it is often difficult to distinguish in old Spanish manuscript *Marzo* from *Mayo*. Progress made on church in 1793, and it was finished in 1794. *St. Pap., Miss.*, MS., i. 122; ii. 17. Being damaged by rains in 1797. *Id.*, ii. 122. Account of dedication in *Sta. Cruz Sentinel*, Aug. 12, 1865. According to a scrap in *Hayes' Mission Book*, i. 130, some coins and relics deposited in the corner-stone gave rise to rumors of treasure for which search was made when the building fell in 1856; but not even the stone was found.

[31] Sept. 12, 1792. Letter of the governor in *Prov. Rec.*, MS., ii. 139. Inhabitants in 1795: Corporal José Antonio Sanchez; soldiers Joaquin Bernal, José Acéves (whose marriage with a neophyte woman was the first recorded at Santa Cruz on March 3, 1794, *Sta. Cruz, Lib. de Mision*, MS., 29), Ramon Linares, Joaquin Mesa, and José Vizcarra; sailor sirvientes, Lopez, Carrillo, Arroyo, Barajas, Rodriguez, and Soto; and the artisan Antonio Henriquez. All but the sailors had families. *Prov. St. Pap.*, MS., xiii. 234. Nov. 1, 1794, the padres complain that the sailor laborers know nothing of their work and should be transferred to the presidio. *Id.*, xii. 40. Supplies to presidios in 1795–6, about $2,000. *Id.*, xvi. 203, 206; *Prov. Rec.*, MS., v. 76. Due from presidio to mission in 1800, $183. *Sta. Cruz, Lib. de Mision*, MS., 19.

December.[32] The annual election of mission alcaldes, which was required by the regulation, but had been for a long time neglected here as elsewhere, began by Borica's orders in 1797.[33]

In these later years the mission prospects were far from encouraging, if we may judge from the tone of missionary correspondence. At the beginning of 1798 Fernandez writes that everything is in a bad way. A hundred and thirty-eight neophytes have deserted, leaving only thirty or forty to work, while the land is overflowed and the planting not half done. The church has been damaged by the flood; the live-stock is dying; and a dead whale on the beach has attracted an unusual multitude of wolves and bears.[34] The establishing of Banciforte across the river, of which I shall speak in another chapter, had much to do with the friars' despondency.

The missionary founders, Lopez and Salazar, served here, the latter till July 1795 and the former to July 1796, at or about which dates they departed from the country to seek the retirement of their college.[35]

---

[32] In March artisans were sent to build the mill and instruct the natives. In August a smith and miller were sent to start the mill. *Prov. Rec.*, MS., iv. 224, 232; v. 50, 58, 65-6, 98, 115; vi. 68; *Arch. Sta. Bárbara*, MS., ii. 78; *St. Pap., Sac.*, MS., vii. 30. Four millstones were ordered made at Santa Cruz for San Cárlos. A house for the mill was also built; and in 1793 a granary of two stories and a house for looms had been finished. *St. Pap., Miss.*, MS., ii. 17, 78.

[33] *Santa Cruz, Parroquia*, MS., 15, 16.

[34] *Fernandez, Carta del Padre Ministro sobre la condicion de Santa Cruz, 1798*, MS. Aug. 1, 1798, Engineer Córdoba reports that Santa Cruz has 3,435,600 sq. varas of irrigable lands of which 1,120,000 are *sin abrir*. Pastures 1.5 x 8 or 9 leagues with seven permanent streams. *Prov. Rec.*, MS., vi. 99.

[35] Of Alonso Isidro Salazar we know nothing till he became minister of Santa Cruz in Sept. 1791, having probably arrived from Mexico a little earlier in the same year. He and Lopez did not get along amicably together, and the archives contain an order of the guardian to the president to send Salazar to some other mission since he and his confrère would not 'listen to reason,' and in order ' to reduce their pride.' *Arch. Sta. Bárbara*, MS., xi. 251-2. He never served at any other mission, and his license to retire, dated by the viceroy Jan. 23, 1795, reached him before June 10th of the same year. *Prov. Rec.*, MS., vi. 47. *St. Pap., Sac.*, MS., i. 50. No reason for his retirement is given. He doubtless sailed in the transport of that autumn; and on May 11, 1796, he wrote at the college of San Fernando a long report on California, of which I shall have something to say elsewhere. *Condicion Actual de Cal.*, MS.

Baldomero Lopez, like Salazar, came to California in 1791, like him served

They were succeeded by Manuel Fernandez and José de la Cruz Espí, the latter being replaced in May 1797 by Francisco Gonzalez, while the former left the country in October 1798 and was replaced by Domingo Carranza.[36]

We come finally to the other new mission of 1791, La Soledad. True to the condition expressed in the name, 'Our Lady of Solitude' has left but a meagre record either of foundation or subsequent career. As we have seen, Lasuen had personally selected a site. The 29th of September a party of natives departed from San Cárlos to erect a shelter. The friar, delayed by Malaspina's visit, intended to go to Soledad again by October 9th at the latest.[37] He did go on that date or perhaps the day before, for on the 9th with the aid of Sitjar and García, and in the presence of Lieutenant José Arguello, the guard, and various natives, he sprinkled holy water on the site, blessed and raised the cross which all adored, and performed all the necessary rites by which the mission of Nuestra Señora de la Soledad was ushered into existence. The site was called by the natives Chuttusgelis and the region

only at Santa Cruz, and like him was ill-tempered to such an extent that his constant bickerings with his companion received the reproof of his superiors. His temper was, however, largely the result of ill-health. He was the victim of hypochondria which unfitted him for missionary duties and he retired in August 1796. *Arch. Sta. Bárbara*, MS., vi. 228, xi. 56–7; *Prov. Rec.*, MS., vi. 163. In Mexico it seems his health was restored, for on Aug. 8, 1818, he was elected guardian of San Fernando.

[36] P. Manuel Fernandez was a native of Tuy in Galicia, Spain, born in 1767, who became a Franciscan at Compostela in 1784, and joined the college of San Fernando in 1793, being sent to California in 1794. *Arch. Sta. Bárbara*, MS., xi. 248. He was one of five priests who came recommended by Mugártegui as of a different kind from several who had exhausted Lasuen's patience, these being in fact model missionaries. *Mugártegui, Carta al P. Lasuen 30 de Enero 1794*, MS. An original letter. He was impetuous, violent, cruel, and a bad manager of neophytes. *Prov. Rec.*, MS., vi. 103; or at least over-zealous in converting pagans, and was admonished by the president to moderate his zeal. *Prov. St. Pap.*, MS., xii. 125–32. This was at Santa Clara where he served in 1794. He was much at San Francisco in the early part of 1795. During his service at Santa Cruz in 1795–8 we hear no complaint against him, and in October 1798 he obtained license to retire on account of sickness. *Arch. Arzobispado*, MS., i. 52.

[37] See p. 493, this volume.

had been known to the Spaniards as Soledad since the first occupation of the country.[38]

Beyond the names of officiating missionaries and the usual statistics Soledad has no recorded history for this first decade. One entry in the mission books however deserves mention, by which it appears that on May 19, 1793, there was baptized a Nootka Indian, twenty years of age, "Iquina, son of a gentile father, named Taguasmiki, who in the year 1789 was killed by the American Gret (Gray) captain of the vessel called *Washington* belonging to the Congress of Boston." [39]

Fathers Diego García and Mariano Rubí were the first ministers of Soledad, the former being present at the founding and the latter arriving shortly after. Rubí left the mission in January and the country in February or March 1793. García left Soledad in February 1792, but he returned, serving there from December 1792 to March 1796, when he was transferred to San Francisco. These two were of the class alluded to by Mugártegui as having exhausted the president's patience. They were even worse than Salazar and Lopez at Santa Cruz, for Rubí was an immoral man, while García, if not partially insane, was unpopular and disobedient.[40] After the terms of

[38] *Soledad, Lib. Mision*, MS., 1, 2. Narrative signed by Lasuen. Romeu to viceroy Dec. 1, 1791, in *St. Pap. Sac.*, MS., v. 93. The first baptism of an aboriginal was on Nov. 23d. The following names from the mission records are those of the soldiers and sirvientes during the decade: Soldiers, Macario Castro, corporal in 1792, Ignacio Vallejo, corporal in 1793, José Dionisio Bernal, Leocadio Cibrian, Teodoro Gomez, José Ignacio Mesa, Antonio Buelna, Marcos Villela, Manuel Mendoza, Salvador Espinosa, Miguel Espinosa, Cayetano Espinosa, Marcos Briones, Bartolomé Matéo Martinez, José María Soberanes, Juan María Pinto, and Manuel Rodriguez. Servants: Antonio Santos, Leocadio Martinez, Matias Solas, Pedro Bautista Leonardo, José Bernardino Flores.

[39] *Soledad, Lib. Mision*, MS., 4.

[40] Mariano Rubí was one of the four padres who arrived in California in July 1790 sent expressly for the new establishments. He served at San Antonio 1790 to Sept. 1791, and from Oct. 1791 to Jan. 1793. He retired under a provisional license, being in ill-health. *Arch. Arzobispado*, MS., i. 33; *Prov. Rec.*, MS., ii. 160. In Oct. 1793 and again in Feb. 1794 the guardian wrote to the president asking for detailed reports on Rubí's conduct and excesses, and an official certificate on the nature of his disease, which was doubtless venereal. He was to be expelled for the honor of the college. *Arch.*

these first ministers the following missionaries served for brief periods: Father Gili, like Rubí more *muge-riego* than was well for his reputation and health, in 1793, Espí in 1794–5, Martiarena in 1795–7, and Carnicer in 1797–8. At the end of the decade the ministers were Antonio Jaime and Mariano Payeras, since March 1796 and November 1798 respectively. In neophyte population Soledad counted eleven converts only at the end of 1791, but 493 in 1800, the baptisms having aggregated 704, deaths 224, and marriages 164. Large stock gained from 194 to 1,383 head; small stock from 213 to 3,024. Agriculture yielded 525 bushels in 1792; 350 in 1794; 2,000 in 1797, and 2,600 in 1800. Total yield of decade 14,800 bushels. In 1797 this mission possessed an adobe church with roof of straw.[41]

Sta. Bárbara, MS., xi. 229–31, 255. Of García's shortcomings I shall have more to say hereafter. At Soledad he once neglected to sow grain on some frivolous pretext, and the neophytes were near starving in consequence.

[41] *St. Pap., Miss.*, MS., ii. 120. Supplies to the presidio in 1796 $418. *Prov. St. Pap.*, MS., xvi. 203.

CHAPTER XXIV.

RULE OF ARRILLAGA—VANCOUVER'S VISITS.

1792–1794.

In view of the governor's illness a council was held at Monterey April 5, 1792, by call of Lieutenant Argüello,[1] to decide on whom the command should fall in the event of Romeu's death, which Surgeon Pablo Soler pronounced to be near. The council consisted of Argüello, Ortega, Goycoechea, and Alférez Sal. The decision was that according to the regulation the governorship *ad interim* would belong to Captain José Joaquin de Arrillaga, commandant at Loreto and lieutenant-governor of the Californias; that the provincial archives should be kept temporarily by the council, and that Arrillaga should be notified at once of the state of affairs. Goycoechea and Sal should return to their presidios, and Ortega

---

[1] Argüello had succeeded Ortega in the spring of 1791, and Alférez Sal had been put in command at San Francisco.

(501)

on Romeu's death should proceed directly to Loreto.[2] This decision was communicated on the same day to Arrillaga and to the commandants not present at the council. The date of Arrillaga's accession may therefore be considered as identical with that of Romeu's death the 9th of April. On May 4th Arrillaga announced his succession to the viceroy, and on the 7th to the officials in California, who acknowledged the receipt in June.[3]

Arrillaga chose to take a modest view of his own abilities and a rather exalted one of his new duties, asking for counsel and suggestions from his subordinates. "From this moment I unload my conscience upon each, and hold him responsible for results," writes the new ruler, "since an officer must be directed in his acts more by his own honor then by fear of authority." Viceregal authority for his exercise of the chief command bore date of the 8th of July. It was his intention to remain at Loreto; but on September 28th he was ordered to Monterey, where he arrived early in July 1793, soon visiting San Francisco and returning to the capital the 17th of September.[4]

Arrillaga's attention was given almost exclusively, during this first term of office and long after, to the inspection of the presidios and to the adjustment of the old presidial accounts in continuation of the task that had been intrusted to Romeu. He worked diligently

[2] *Junta de 5 de Abril de 1791 en Monterey*, MS. Argüello's letters to commandants Zúñiga and Gonzales, same date. *Prov. St. Pap.*, MS., xxii. 13–15.

[3] *Prov. St. Pap.*, MS., xi. 4, 7, 8. May 4th, Arrillaga to viceroy. *Id.*, xxi. 71. May 7th, *Id.*, to Goycoechea and Argüello. *Id.*, xi. 25; *St. Pap., Sac.*, MS., i. 115. May 7th, *Id.*, to Lasuen, and the padre's congratulations on June 25th. *Arch. Arzobispado*, MS., i. 27–8. May 10th Gen. Nava sends to the governor a copy of Neve's previous instructions to Fages; but this document was probably intended for Romeu since Nava first announces knowledge of Romeu's death on June 17th. *St. Pap., Sac.*, MS., i. 72–3; *Prov. St. Pap.*, MS., xi. 59.

[4] June 8, 1792, Arrillaga to commandants in *St. Pap., Sac.*, MS., vi. 76–8. Viceroy to governor, July 8, 1792, in *Prov. St. Pap., Ben. Mil.*, MS., xx. 3. Sept. 28, 1792, Arrillaga ordered to Monterey. *Ib.* At San Diego in March 1793; at Monterey, before July 8th; went to San Francisco July 27th; returned Sept. 17th. *Prov. St. Pap.*, MS., xxi. 92–3, 101, 109, 116. His last communication from Loreto is dated Dec. 29th.

at the complicated task and with much success, though many years passed before it was completed. Beyond the details of this adjustment, and the ordinary routine of official correspondence with commandants, general, or viceroy—for early in 1793 California became by royal order separated from the Provincias Internas and subordinate directly to the viceroy[5]—the archives contain but little on this administration, which continued until 1794.

Arrillaga carried out conscientiously the instructions of general and viceroy on the strengthening of coast defences and assistance to north-coast establishments. He met the English navigator Vancouver on his second visit to Monterey, leaving a not very favorable impression on the mind of his visitor, and urged the viceroy to put the presidios under captains, who should have nothing to do with the financial accounts.[6] He granted lands provisionally to three or four men in the Monterey region,[7] issued in the interests of agriculture a proclamation forbidding the natives to kindle fires in the fields, and in the direction of public works opened a new road and ford at the Pájaro River. By Arrillaga's advice the proposition of the clergyman, Alejandro Jordan, to found a colony in California for the supply of San Blas with products at cheaper rates, was declined by the king in 1794.[8] Besides

[5] The king resolved in council of Sept. 7, 1792, on making the Provincias Internas independent of the viceroy; but the Californias and some eastern provinces were excepted in military and political matters. *Revilla Gigedo, Bandos*, 63. Feb. 12, 1793, viceroy gives corresponding orders to the governor. *Prov. St. Pap.*, MS., xxi. 106.

[6] July 18, 1792. *Prov. St. Pap.*, MS., xxi. 108–9. In 1791 the office of habilitado general of the Californian Presidios had been created with Manuel Carcaba as first incumbent. *Id.*, x. 136–7.

[7] Arrillaga says that his predecessors had not granted any lands, he favors it and has granted ranches to several invalids on the river 3 or 4 leagues from Monterey. *Prov. St. Pap.*, xii. 45–7, 189; xxi. 132. It was in his rule, 1793, that General Nava's order, allowing commandants of presidios to grant lands within 4 leagues, was approved by the viceroy. *St. Pap., Miss. and Colon.*, MS., i. 320–1, 341–2.

[8] Arrillaga to viceroy, November 8, 1792, in *Prov. St. Pap.*, MS., xxi. 85–6. Jordan is said to have spent 8 months in Alta California at some previous time, and to have caused some dissatisfaction by his intrigues, though I find no other record of his presence than Arrillaga's statement. Jordan asked for

ordering the appropriate manifestations of rejoicing at the queen's happy delivery in 1793, the governor continued the collection of alms for the Capuchin nuns of Granada authorized before his accession, and in 1794 had the pleasure of forwarding California's contribution of $154 for so pious an object.[9]

From what has been said it will be apparent to the reader that little occurred to distract Arrillaga's attention from his figures. The period was one of quiet prosperity for the missions, and no new establishments were founded. The governor was liked by the friars, with whose management he made no attempt to interfere. He had no quarrels; introduced no reforms; met with no disasters, but regarding himself as merely an accidental and temporary ruler he was content with the performance of routine duties until a successor could be selected. We shall hear more of him later. Local events during this and the preceding and following administrations I shall group into the annals of a decade. General topics of provincial progress I shall group practically in the same way by attaching the little that belongs to Romeu and Arrillaga to the much that is to be said of Borica's time.

Maritime affairs and foreign relations, or the dread of foreign relations and consequent precautions, form the only general topic of Arrillaga's term which demands extended notice. The subject is somewhat closely connected with the annals of the Northwest Coast, fully recorded in another volume of this work,

$4,000 salary, 18 men, and a supply of implements. Arrillaga thought that the expense of a colony would outweigh its advantages, since the supply-ships might take south produce obtained from the settlers. August 7, 1794, the viceroy communicates to the governor the king's decision against the proposal, on the ground that free trade with San Blas would of itself accomplish quite as satisfactory results. *Id.*, xi. 192–3; *Prov. Rec.*, MS., viii. 145. The king's order was dated March 7, 1794. *Nueva España, Acuerdos*, MS., 179.

[9] May 8, 1793, order for te deum on queen's delivery. *Prov. Rec.*, MS., i. 210; *Arch. Arzobispado*, MS., i. 34. December 1, 1791, authorization of Capuchin collection by general. *Prov. St. Pap.*, MS., xi. 23. June 6, 1794, viceroy acknowledges receipt of $154 collected at Monterey and San Francisco. *Id.*, xi. 172–3; $32 at San Francisco. *Id.*, x. 14, 40; xxi. 116, 132, 164; *Prov. Rec.*, MS., i. 213.

and therefore briefly referred to here.[10] Spain no longer attached the same importance as in former years to her exclusive claims in the far north, now that the geographical relations of America and Asia were approximately known, and the occupation of California had furnished suitable ports for the Philippine trade. After the explorations of 1774–9 to latitude 60° nothing was done for a decade. Had it not been for the possible existence of an interoceanic strait and the ever present fear of foreign encroachment from the north, the Spaniards would have given no more thought to these far-off coasts. New rumors came, however, that the Russians were advancing southward, rumors proved to be of no serious importance by the expedition of 1788; but this expedition brought the more alarming report of a British plan to occupy Nootka. Therefore Martinez was sent in 1789 to prevent this step and establish a Spanish post at that place. In the execution of his duty Martinez seized several English vessels as prizes. This led to complications between the two nations which nearly plunged Europe in war, but were settled by a treaty of 1790. By this treaty Spain virtually relinquished all her claims to exclusive sovereignty on the Northwest Coast, the right of navigation, fishery, and settlement being made common to both nations.

The establishment at Nootka was kept up, however, from the spring of 1790, before the date of the treaty, and was regularly supplied from San Blas by the California transports which often went direct to the northern post and touched at Monterey on the return. Nootka was simply an extension of the Californian establishments. Spain had, as already explained, no desire for northern possessions, but she maintained the post for five years for two reasons—first, because if a strait or an inlet leading to New Mexico could be found it would be important to hold it, and to that end exploration was zealously prosecuted; and second,

[10] See *Hist. Northwest Coast*, i. chap. v.-ix.

because if there were no strait the position could be used in diplomatic negotiations to secure a favorable boundary further south, such as the strait of Fuca, the main object being to secure a broad frontier between San Francisco and the first foreign post. It is only certain voyages connected with the explorations and negotiations referred to that have a bearing on California history. The touching on the coast of several Nootka vessels connected with the expeditions of Elisa, Fidalgo, Quimper, Saavedra, Matute, and Malaspina in 1790–1 has already been noticed.

In the spring of 1792 three vessels sailed from San Blas for Nootka, one of them bearing Juan Francisco de la Bodega y Cuadra as Spanish commissioner to settle certain questions still pending with England. At Nootka he met Vancouver, the British commissioner. By the treaty Spain had agreed to restore all lands of which England had been dispossessed. Cuadra claimed, as was indeed the fact, that there were no such lands and therefore proposed to fix a boundary, offering to give up Nootka and make Fuca Strait the line. Vancouver demanded the unconditional surrender of the port, and declined to treat on the boundary question at all. The commissioners not being able to agree, left the matter to be settled by their respective governments, and soon all the vessels, Spanish and English, sailed for the south.

The *Sutil* and *Mexicana* had been sent from Acapulco in March under captains Dionisio Galiano and Cayetano Valdés to explore the strait of Juan de Fuca and the coast to the south. After exploring the sound in company with Vancouver's fleet the two vessels returned to Monterey[11] where they arrived September 22d and remained till the 26th of October.

[11] For northern explorations see *Hist. N. W. Coast*, i. 270, etc. Previous arrivals of 1792 had been the *Concepcion*, Captain Elisa, from Nootka, leaving supplies at Monterey July 9th, at Santa Bárbara, Sept. 8th, and at San Diego, Oct. 8th; the *Santa Gertrudis*, Capt. Torres, from Nootka, touching at Monterey Aug. 11th to Oct. 26th, en route for San Blas; and the *Saturnina*, which arrived from San Blas at San Francisco Sept. 10th and at Monterey Oct. 17th. For arri-

The author of the diary devotes two chapters to California, which contain a description of Monterey and its surroundings, a somewhat extended account of aboriginal manners and customs, and a superficial but not inaccurate view of the provincial establishments, including a table of mission statistics. He speaks highly of the country and of the missionaries; but there is nothing in his observations on California that possesses any special value as throwing new light on her condition or institutions. He presents, however, the following not very well founded complaint: "These deserving soldiers, and not less useful colonists, live with the affliction that when with failing strength they can no longer support the fatigues of their profession, they are not permitted to settle there and devote themselves to agricultural occupations. This prohibition of building houses and tilling lands near the presidio seems directly opposed to all the purposes of utility, security, and prosperity of those establishments, and contrary perhaps to what good policy should dictate. Were the soldiers permitted while in the service to employ their savings and moments of leisure in forming a hacienda and raising cattle, both for their families' convenience and as a resource against poverty...it is very likely that within a few years there would be planted a flourishing colony most useful for its inhabitants and of great service to Spanish navigators." After leaving Monterey Galiano and Valdés sailed down the coast, making some observations without anchoring, and communicating with the transport *Concepcion* as they passed San Diego. Most of their stay in California had been spent in preparing their reports and charts of northern regions.[12] I reproduce the general map of the California coast.

vals and departures of vessels see *Prov. St. Pap.*, MS., xxi. 75–6, 88–9, 159, 162–3; *St. Pap., Sac.*, MS., iii. 17; vi. 68, 72; ix. 82–3; *Prov. Rec.*, MS., ii. 141, 157; *Navarrete, Introd.*, cxxiii.–xxxi. There is some confusion respecting duties.

[12] *Sutil y Mexicana, Relacion del Viage hecho por las goletas Sutil y Mexicana en el año de 1792 para reconocer el Estrecho de Fuca; con una Introduccion,*

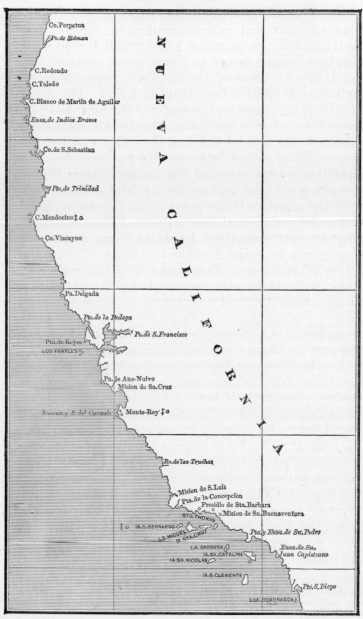

MAP OF 1792.

The probable arrival of the Spanish and English commissioners had been announced in advance, and the Californian authorities were instructed to maintain by a cordial reception the Spanish reputation for hospitality.[13] Cuadra on the *Activa* from the north arrived at Monterey the 9th of October. The *Saturnina*, bearing important despatches for him, had been lying at San Francisco for a month and came down as soon as his arrival was known. These despatches, in accordance with a late royal order, contained new instructions from Revilla Gigedo by which Nootka was not to be surrendered as the viceroy had at first proposed. Since the proposal had not been accepted, there was no special haste about the new orders; yet they were sent up to Fidalgo at Nootka by the *Horcasitas*,[14] and Cuadra remained in California through the winter. Before the end of October the *Aranzazu*, under Caamaño, arrived at Monterey from the north.

etc. Madrid, 1802, 8vo, 7 l. clxviii. 185, 20 pages with folio atlas. Chapters on California, 157–77. The atlas contains a general map of the whole coast, including California, and a chart of Monterey, made by these explorers; a chart of San Diego, made by Pantoja in 1782 (given in chap. xxii. this vol.); and a map of the coast from Vizcaino's survey of 1602–3 (see chap. iii. this vol.) The most valuable part of this work, however, is *Navarrete, Introduccion en que se da noticia de las Expediciones executadas anteriormente por los Españoles en busca del Paso del Noroeste de la América*, i.–clxviii. This work, which has often been cited by me, is probably the best *résumé* of Spanish voyages on the Pacific coast. It was written by Martin Fernandez de Navarrete, whose name does not appear as the author, but whose facilities were of the best, by reason of access to Spanish archives and of ability. Greenhow's charge, *Or. and Cal.*, 241, of 'gross and palpable misstatements of circumstances, respecting which he undoubtedly possessed the means of arriving at the truth,' has, I believe, no just foundation. Galiano, Valdés, and Álava who visited Monterey a little later, all fell at the famous naval battle of Trafalgar. The viceroy had at first intended Lieut. Maurelle to make this exploration. *Revilla-Gigedo, Informe de 12 de Abril 1793*, 141; *Prov. St. Pap.*, MS., xi. 40.

[13] Arrillaga, still at Loreto, communicated this order to the presidio commandants on Sept. 16, 1792. *Prov. St. Pap.*, MS., xi. 35; *St. Pap., Sac.*, MS., i. 42–3. Orders had also been given in the spring of 1792 for the friendly reception and aid of the French expedition in search of La Pérouse, which never arrived. *Prov. St. Pap.*, MS., xxi. 73; *St. Pap., Sac.*, MS., i. 112.

[14] *Revilla-Gigedo, Informe de 12 de Abril 1793*, 137. Oct. 31st, Sal writes to Gov. Arrillaga that he judges from Cuadra's remarks that the English want the mouth of San Francisco Bay for a boundary. *St. Pap., Sac.*, MS., i. 119. Sept. 9th, Sal had written to Arrillaga that he had seen a suspicious vessel off the port on the 7th, and fired 6 shots at her. She anchored for the night about a league from Mussel Point. *Id.*, i. 69–71.

In April of this year Captain George Vancouver in the *Discovery* with the *Chatham* under Lieutenant Broughton, on a grand exploring voyage round the world, had crossed over from the Sandwich Islands and made observations on the California coast as he sailed northward from just below Cape Mendocino.[15] Now six months later, coming from Nootka, the English navigator sailed down the coast without anchoring, and on November 14th, in the *Discovery*, entered San Francisco Bay at nightfall and anchored in front of Yerba Buena Cove, having received a salute of two guns as he passed the fort.[16] Next day he was visited in the morning by Sergeant Pedro Amador and Padre Landaeta, and later by Commandant Sal and Father Dantí; while on the 16th by advice of the Spaniards, Private Miranda serving as pilot, the *Discovery* was transferred to the usual anchorage nearer the presidio.[17]

Vancouver's reception at San Francisco was most cordial and satisfactory. Every attention was shown and every possible aid furnished the visitors by Commandant Sal and his wife and the friars at the mission. Couriers were despatched to Monterey with a message for Cuadra. Facilities were afforded for obtaining wood and water; feasts were given at both presidio and mission, and meat and vegetables were sent on board the vessel. Indeed everything the Spaniards had in this the most poverty-stricken of their establishments was at the disposition of the strangers. On the 20th of November Vancouver and seven of his officers made an excursion on horseback to Santa Clara, being the first foreigners who had ever penetrated so far into

[15] *Vancouver's Voyage*, i. 196–200. For his northern explorations with maps, see *Hist. N. W. Coast*, i. 274, et seq.

[16] *Id.*, i. 432; Sal to Arrillaga Nov. 14, 1792, in *St. Pap., Sac.*, MS., i. 115–17; *Id.* to *Id.*, Nov. 30th, in *Id.*, iii. 22. It is strange that Sal makes the day of arrival Nov. 13th, while the voyager's diary has it Nov. 14th. The same discrepancy exists respecting the date of changing anchorage. On the location of Yerba Buena, see chap. xxx. of this volume.

[17] The commander of the *Santa Gertrudis* had left a note for Vancouver, and a horseman had therefore been stationed at the heads to give notice of his approach. *St. Pap., Sac.*, vi. 72.

the interior. They were escorted by Amador with a squad of five soldiers, and were delighted with much of the intermediate country. After most hospitable treatment by fathers Peña and Sanchez at Santa Clara, they returned to San Francisco on the 22d. The *Chatham* had meanwhile arrived, and preparations were hastened for departure. For supplies furnished[18] Don Hermenegildo would take no pay, acting as he said under instructions from Bodega y Cuadra; but he accepted from Vancouver some implements and ornaments besides a hogshead each of wine and rum, all to be distributed to the presidio and two missions. The two vessels sailed away the 26th and anchored next morning at Monterey.[19]

Vancouver found lying at anchor in the harbor of Monterey the *Dædalus*, his store-ship which had joined the fleet at Nootka, the *Activa* bearing Cuadra's broad pennant, the *Aranzazu*, and the *Horcasitas*. The presidio and Cuadra's flag each received a salute of thirteen guns and each returned the compliment. From Cuadra, Argüello, Caamaño, and all the Spanish officials the Englishmen received the same courteous attentions as at San Francisco, and a series of social entertainments followed on shore and on deck which were mutually agreeable and productive of good-feeling. Orders recently received from Spain not to molest English vessels but to capture all those of other nations led both commanders to believe that the Nootka difficulties had been settled by their respective governments; consequently Vancouver made arrangements with Cuadra to send Broughton to England *via* San Blas and Mexico, to

---

[18] These supplies were, according to a list in *St. Pap., Sac.*, MS., iii. 21–2, for acct. of Cuadra—11 cows, 7 sheep, 10 arrobas of lard; free from Sal—2 cows, 2 calves, 4 sheep, 190 pumpkins, 10 baskets vegetables, a cart-load of ditto, 95 fowl, 400 eggs.

[19] On Vancouver's stay at San Francisco, visit to Santa Clara, and voyage, see *Voyage*, ii. 1–30. Argüello reports to Arrillaga on Nov. 30th, the arrival of the *Dædalus* on the 22d 'commanded by Geo. Anson,' and of the *Discovery* and *Chatham* on the 25th, one day before Vancouver's date, as at San Francisco. *St. Pap., Sac.*, MS., v. 97. The date is given as Nov. 25th also in *Prov. St. Pap.*, MS., xxi. 93.

which end the Spanish commander offered every facility. The *Discovery* and the *Chatham* remained at
Monterey for about fifty days for reloading and
repairs. A tent and observatory for astronomical
observations were set up on the beach, and the *Dædalus* sailed in December for New South Wales with
a load of cattle and other supplies generously furnished by the Spaniards.

Vancouver and party went over to San Cárlos the
2d of December, and were hospitably entertained, as
La Pérouse had been six years before, by President
Lasuen and the other friars. The natives gave an
exhibition of their skill in killing deer by stratagem.
Back at the port a dinner was given on board the
Discovery which proved agreeable until Señora Argüello and other ladies as well as some gentlemen were
forced by sea-sickness to retire to *tierra firme*. A pic-
nic dinner at the presidio garden several miles away
was another day's programme. Subsequently a display of fireworks delighted the Spaniards and astonished the aborigines. When this pleasant intercourse
was over and the day of departure drew near Bodega
y Cuadra, who in addition to constant kindness had
prolonged his stay at Monterey for no other purpose
than to carry Broughton to San Blas, refused to take
pay for cattle or other stores supplied to the fleet;
and Vancouver was obliged to be content with a new
distribution of such useful utensils as his vessels could
supply.[20] At last January 15, 1793, after an ineffectual
pursuit of two deserters[21] and the reluctant acceptance

[20] Revilla-Gigedo, *Informe de 12 de Abril*, 139, says Vancouver's gifts were
worth about $2,000. Salazar, *Condicion actual de Cal.*, MS., 67, estimates
all of Vancouver's presents in his three visits at $10,000, and says that Santa
Cruz received $1,000 with which a mill was built. By the viceroy's order of
Sept. 30, 1794, any debts on Vancouver's account except expenses for securing deserters were charged to the San Blas department as expenses of the
boundary commission. *Prov. St. Pap.*, MS., xi. 200.

[21] About these deserters there is no lack of information in the archives.
Besides the 2 from the *Chatham* there were 3 from the *Dædalus*. Governor
to viceroy March 16, 1793, says that 3 are Catholics and deserted because not
allowed to attend mass; the others desire to become Catholics. They were
prisoners at Monterey. Cuadra on Jan. 19th had ordered them sent, if
caught, to Nootka *via* Loreto. *Prov. St. Pap.*, MS., xxi. 94-7. Gov. to Ar-

by Vancouver of the only smith at the presidio in place of the lost armorer, the fleet of five sail, two English and three Spanish, disappeared in the south-west behind Point Pinos and left to Monterey its usual solitude.[22]

Governor Arrillaga was not pleased when he heard of the excessive freedom that had been allowed Vancouver, and especially did he disapprove of the Englishman's visit to Santa Clara. He felt that a kind reception to the boundary commission according to viceregal instructions did not include such extraordi-

güello March 27th, Deserters not to be delivered to any English vessel except Vancouver's and then only on his paying the expenses. The 2 not to be admitted to Catholic faith until further orders, except in danger of death. To be supplied at rate of 18 cents per day for rations and clothes. May be employed at their trades. Arrillaga disapproves sending them to Loreto. *St. Pap., Sac.*, MS., i. 107, 109–10 ; vii. 82 ; *Prov. Rec.*, MS., ii. 161–2. Aug. 10th, They must be given up to an English vessel or sent to San Blas. Clothes furnished to be charged to account of boundary commission. *Prov. St. Pap.*, MS., xi. 95–6. In Sept. 1793 the 5 deserters were sent to San Blas on the *Princesa. Prov. St. Pap.*, MS., xxi. 117. Jan. 9, 1794, viceroy tells gov. that they will be sent back for delivery to Vancouver. Jan. 22d, Vancouver is charged with $250 expenses at San Blas. He must return the three borrowed sailors. *Id.*, xi. 153, 158, xxi. 142. May 16th, viceroy to gov., The 5 have been sent by the *Concepcion;* charges $228 to be paid by Vancouver; else they are to be sent to Nootka for delivery to some English vessel. *Id.*, xi. 171–2. June 9th, Id. to Id. Another deserter taken at San Diego is to be given up. *Id.*, xi. 173–4. June 12th, Gov. to viceroy, As Vancouver had no Spanish money he has presented the amount in the name of the Spanish nation. *Id.*, xxi. 144. Sept. 12th, Arrillaga to Argüello, Arrival of the 6 in *Concepcion*, the $288 and rations to be collected from Vancouver. *Id.*, xii. 167–9. Sept. 30th, Argüello to Arrillaga, keeps the 6 under surveillance; will deliver them to Vancouver, to an English vessel, or to a Spanish vessel bound for Nootka. Some want to be Catholics and some to enlist. *Id.*, xii. 148–9. Nov. 5th, Argüello to Capt. Puget of *Chatham*, surrendering 2 of the 6. Total bill $747. *Id.*, xii. 170–1. Nov. 16th, Vancouver to gov., Finds that 3 of the 6 are not British subjects and will not claim them. Has no instructions to pay the bill but will lay the account before the admiralty. *Id.*, xii. 154–5. Nov. 16th (or 17th), Gov. to Vancouver interceding for the 3 deserters given up and charging $325 for expenses. The three not given up were 2 Portuguese and one Dane. *Id.*, xii. 172–3. The purport of 2 preceding communications in *Vancouver's Voyage*, iii. 333–4. Nov. 20, 1794, Fidalgo takes the 3 remaining deserters on board his vessel to work out the $421 of charges. *Id.*, xii. 171–2, 174.

[22] *Vancouver, A Voyage of Discovery to the North Pacific Ocean, and round the World...1790–5.* London, 1798, 3 vols. 4to, and folio atlas. On this visit to Monterey, see vol. ii. 29–49, 99–105. Other editions and translations of Vancouver's voyage with numerous abridged narratives and references all drawn from this original source I do not deem it necessary to notice here. Dec. 15, 1792, Lasuen writes to Vancouver thanking him for his gifts to the missions. *Arch. Sta. Bárbara*, MS., vi. 260–1. March 13, 1793, Viceroy to Vancouver, has given Lieut. Broughton all possible aid, and with the greatest pleasure. *Prov. St. Pap.*, MS., xi. 93–4.

nary license to a foreign power. He was only temporary governor and he entertained a nervous dread
of overstepping the literal instructions of his superiors.
He feared that what had taken place would be disapproved, and that he would be held responsible. His
trouble was increased by an order from the viceroy
dated November 24, 1792, to be on his guard against
English ships, and especially to prevent the weakness
of the Spanish establishments from becoming known
to foreigners.[28] No wonder he was alarmed and that
on his way up to Monterey in the spring of 1793 he
wrote to chide Sal for having permitted Vancouver to
gain a knowledge of the country, at the same time
instructing him and other commandants to limit their
courtesies to foreign vessels in the future to the mere
granting of needed supplies as demanded by the laws
of hospitality.[24] The presence of two English vessels
on the coast in March did not tend to allay the governor's fears.[25] Sal humbly confessed that in permitting
the visit to Santa Clara he had committed an inex-
cusable fault. "I am human and I fell into an error
which I cannot mend," says he. But he claims that
with Father Landaeta he endeavored to dissuade his
guest from his purpose, thus exciting his displeasure,
and that there was no other way to prevent the intru-
sion but to remove the horses. This differs materially
from Vancouver's account, where no trouble is hinted

[23] *Prov. St. Pap., Ben. Mil.*, MS., xix. 1, 2; xx. 3, 4.

[24] Arrillaga to Sal, March 26, 1793. Only the commander or his representative must be permitted to land. *Prov. Rec.*, MS., ii. 142–4. May 2d, Arrillaga says he has given orders not to let any English land. *Prov. St. Pap.*,
MS., xxi. 98–9. April 1st, meat and vegetables to be supplied sparingly as a
matter of policy only. *Prov. Rec.*, MS., ii. 162.

[25] March 16, 1793, Sal to governor, announces the arrival of an English
vessel under Captain Brown, asking for water, wood, and meat. She had a
suspicious appearance, said she came from Monterey and was bound for
Nootka, and was said by the natives to have been hanging about the coast for
two months. *St. Pap., Sac.*, MS., ii. 131–2. Two English vessels, one of them
the *Princess*, obtained wood and water at Monterey early in March. *Prov.
Rec.*, MS., ii. 162. March or February, an English vessel at mouth of San
Francisco, and another at Bodega with guns landed. The presidios are unde-
fended and the English have noticed it, saying that pirates are numerous and
an invasion not unlikely. So sa s the governor to the viceroy. *Prov. St. Pap.*,
MS., xxi. 94.

at, and it is only said that in consequence of despatches received by Sal, and the indisposition of one of the friars, they begged leave to decline the engagement.[26]

Together with his order requiring precautions against the English and other foreigners with a special view of keeping Spanish weakness from their knowledge, and subsequently, the viceroy announced his intention of remedying that weakness by strengthening the four presidios and by the immediate occupation of Bodega. The 16th of July Arrillaga sent in a report on the state and needs of Californian defences.[27] Vancouver, unwisely permitted to investigate, had been surprised to find California so inadequately protected, and the Spaniards seem to have realized the utter insufficiency of their coast defences at about the same time; but nothing was accomplished in 1793 beyond an unsuccessful effort to occupy Bodega Port. Their Bodega scheme and the whole project of strengthening the Californian defenses were devised by Viceroy Revilla Gigedo, and urged most ably in his report of April 12, 1793, a document which covers the whole northern question from a Spanish standpoint, and although little consulted by modern writers is really a most important authority.[28] After giving

[26] April 30, 1793, Sal to Arrillaga in *St. Pap., Sac.*, MS., v. 6; *Vancouver's Voyage*, ii. 16. I suspect that a night's sleep calmed the Spaniards' enthusiasm somewhat, and showed them that they were going too far; therefore they made excuses intended as a hint which the Englishman did not care to take.

[27] *Arrillaga, Informe al Virey sobre defensa de la Costa, 1793*, MS. Feb. 16, 1793, viceroy to governor, approves fortification of the presidios and has ordered artillery and other material sent. *Id.*, xx. 4. The governor says that Monterey has 8 guns and 3 pedreros; San Francisco 2 useless guns; Santa Bárbara 2 guns and a pedrero with nobody to manage them; and San Diego 3 guns dismounted. The nominal force free for action in the 4 presidios is 35, but after deductions only one or two men to each fort. He recommends a force of 264 men; wants a vessel at Monterey or San Francisco; and approves the occupation of Bodega.

[28] *Revilla Gigedo, Informe de los Sucesos ocurridos en la Península de Californias y departamento de San Blas, desde el año de 1768. Mexico 12 de Abril de 1793*, in *Bustamante, Suplemento á la Hist. de los Tres Siglos de Mexico*, iii. 112-64. Another important work belonging to this year and written by the same author is *Revilla Gigedo, Carta dirigida á la corte de España contestando á la real órden sobre establecimientos de misiones, Mexico, 27 de Diciembre de 1793*, in *Diccionario Universal*, v. 426-70. The part relating to the California

a complete history of his subject the distinguished author argues that distant and costly outposts in the north are not desirable for Spain; and attention should be given exclusively to the preservation and utilization of the establishments now existing in California, and to the prevention of too near approach by any foreign power. To this end Bodega should be held and the English plan of making a boundary of San Francisco Bay be thus defeated. Probably this one measure may suffice in the north; Nootka may be given up, and Fuca, and also the Entrada de Heceta, or Columbia River, unless it should prove to afford a passage to the Atlantic or to New Mexico. Meanwhile the presidios should be put in an effective condition; a new one should be founded on the Rio Colorado, and an able successor to Romeu be selected as governor. The department of San Blas should be transferred to Acapulco, and certain reforms be introduced in the management of the pious fund and of the salt-works.

Because of its supposed excellence as a harbor, and because of its vicinity to San Francisco, making its occupation by England equivalent to an occupation of that harbor for purposes of contraband trade, it was decided to found a Spanish settlement at Bodega. Moreover there were rumors that foreigners were already taking steps in that direction.[29] To this end the 10th of February the viceroy announced the giving of orders to the commandant at San Blas to despatch a schooner and long-boat for the service, and Arrillaga was directed to go to San Francisco to meet the vessels. He gave orders the 20th of March to have

missions is found on pp. 427–30; and this portion in manuscript is also in *St. Pap., Miss. and Colon.*, MS., i. 2–28. See also extracts in *Jones' Report on Land Titles*, No. 6; *Hayes' Mission Book*, 176. This report is a careful statement of the mission condition and system at the time, and is used in another chapter.

[29] Oct. 8, 1792, Sal informs the governor that according to Indian reports two vessels—presumably English, for the men wore red—were at Bodega, got wood, water, and deer, and asked the natives to get cattle for them. *St. Pap., Sac.*, MS., vi. 67–8. Jan. 15, 1793, two English ships said to be at Bodega. Five shots heard off San Francisco on 16th and 17th. *Id.*, vi. 98.

a road opened from San Francisco across to Bodega.
These instructions came up on the *Aranzazu*, which
arrived at San Francisco the 24th of July.[30] Arrillaga
obtained boats from the vessels, set across some thirty
horses, and on the 5th of August Lieutenant Goycoechea with a sergeant and ten men set out to open the
road and to meet at Bodega Matute, who with the
Sutil and *Mexicana* had probably been sent direct to
that port from San Blas.   Unfortunately I have not
found Goycoechea's diary which was sent to Mexico,
and we know absolutely nothing of either the exploration by sea or land, save that Matute returned to San
Francisco on August 12th, and five days later Arrillaga informs the viceroy that the occupation of Bodega
is put off for this year.   The postponement proved to
be a permanent one, for some unexplained cause, and
the ten soldiers and five mechanics with some stores
intended for Bodega were retained by Sal at San
Francisco.[31]

Coming from the Hawaiian Islands Vancouver
touched again the shores of California, or of New
Albion as he is careful to call it, in the spring of 1793.
From the 2d to the 5th of May the *Discovery* was at

[30] The *Princesa*, Fidalgo, from Nootka, arrived at San Francisco June 21st,
San Diego, Oct. 24th; *Aranzazu*, Menendez, from San Blas, San Francisco,
July 24th, Monterey, Aug. 25th, San Diego, Oct. 24th; *Activa*, Elisa, from
San Blas, San Francisco, Aug. 11th, San Diego, Oct. 24th; *Sutil* and *Mexicana*, Matute, from San Blas, San Francisco, Aug. 12th—Oct. 16th; Vancouver's vessels, Trinity Bay, May 2d, San Francisco, Oct. 19th, Monterey,
Nov. 1st, Santa Bárbara, Nov. 9th, San Diego, Nov. 27th.   On the arrivals
and departures of vessels for 1793, there being as usual some confusion in the
dates, see *Prov. St. Pap.*, MS., xii. 163; xxi. 101, 109, 111, 121–2; *St. Pap.*,
Sac., MS., i. 61; *Prov. Rec.*, MS., ii. 162.
[31] Governor to viceroy, July 16th, Aug. 17th, 20th, in *Prov. St. Pap.*, MS.,
xxi. 107, 111, 113.   Aug. 3d, gov. orders Sal to receive the men and stores.
Prov. Rec., MS., ii. 144–5. Aug. 4th, gov. instructs Goycoechea to use caution, treat the Indians well, etc. *Id.*, i. 206.   Sept. 24th, gov. to viceroy,
asking for a boat for Bodega to carry timber; so that the project was not
yet quite abandoned. *Prov. St. Pap.*, MS., xxi. 117.   Feb. 28, 1794, viceroy
has heard that the *Sutil* and *Mexicana* have sailed, leaving the 10 soldiers and
a bricklayer for Bodega. *Id.*, xi. 160.   As late as July 6, 1793, the viceroy
repeated the orders to open a road. *Id.*, xi. 92; but June 9, 1794, he answers
the request for a boat by saying that it will not be needed, as the new establishment is suspended. *Id.*, xi. 175.   July 25, 1794, Sal mentions the suspension. *Prov. St. Pap., Ben. Mil.*, MS., xix. 5.

anchor in Trindad Bay, where Vancouver found the
cross set up by Cuadra in 1775 with its inscription
Carolus III. Dei G. Hyspaniorum Rex. Obtaining
water, surveying and sketching the region, after some
intercourse with the natives the voyagers departed
with a very unfavorable idea of the harbor, and sailed
northward.[32]

Returning southward some months later the *Discovery* anchored at San Francisco the 19th of October.[33] Commandant Sal came on board, courteous
as before, with welcome European news; but mindful
of his former indiscretion[34] he sent letters asking a
formal statement, for the governor, of Vancouver's
object, the length of his stay, the supplies needed;
also making known the current orders respecting foreign vessels, and politely informing the visitor that
only himself and one officer could be permitted to
land and visit the presidio. This restriction seemed
to Vancouver "ungracious and degrading, little short
of a dismission from San Francisco," due as he was
given to understand to "sentiments apparently not
the most favorable towards foreign visitors" entertained by "a captain named Arrillaga," who had taken
command the preceding spring, and whose orders Sal
seemed to obey with reluctance. It was a chilling
reception certainly in comparison with that of the
year before and with the Englishman's glowing expectations. But he complied with the formalities,
and on the 24th as soon as he had been joined by the
Chatham, which had been exploring Bodega and had
obtained a supply of water, he sailed for Monterey.[35]

Having anchored at Monterey November 1st, Van-

[32] *Vancouver's Voyage,* ii. 240–50. *Hist. N. W. Coast,* i. 291, for northern
voyage.

[33] Strangely enough in this case as in that of the former visit the Spanish
records make the arrival a day earlier than the voyager's narrative.

[34] Oct. 21st, the governor had ordered Sal to furnish Vancouver what he
absolutely needed, and to insist on his sailing at once without visiting any
other port. *Prov. Rec.,* MS., ii. 145–6.

[35] *Vancouver's Voyage,* ii. 432–8. Puget in a slight examination of Bodega
had understood from the natives that the Spaniards were then in possession
of a part of the bay. Just out of San Francisco the *Dædalus* from across

couver held a short interview with Arrillaga, and a written correspondence followed, in which the governor explained the hospitalities to which foreign vessels were entitled in Californian ports, asked for a formal statement of the voyager's aims, and, while desiring harmony, insisted on the enforcement of orders that only the commander with one or two officers could land. Vancouver replied explaining the scientific nature of his voyage, and the benefits to be derived from its results by Spain as well as England, alluding to his kind reception of the year before, inclosing letters of the viceroy which approved the attentions previously shown him, and stating his desire to refit his vessels, transfer stores, make astronomical observations, and give his men some exercise and recreation on shore. Arrillaga's answer was that the viceroy had sent no orders respecting a second visit, that there were no royal orders in Vancouver's favor as in the case of La Pérouse, and that Cuadra even had left instructions that the former attentions were for that time only and need not be repeated.[36] Yet as he desired to render all possible aid to so worthy a cause, he would permit the landing of stores, which might be deposited in the warehouse at the landing under lock and key or elsewhere if the warehouse were not deemed suitable, in care of one or two men from the vessels and protected by a Spanish guard; but on the condition that all the rest of the Englishmen retire to the vessels at night. Astronomical observations must have been well advanced during the former long stay, yet an observatory, to be used in daytime only, might be

the ocean joined the fleet. Mention of arrival and departure from San Francisco in *St. Pap.*, *Sac.*, MS., ii. 90–1, iv. 9; *Prov. St. Pap.*, MS., xi. 160; xxi. 121–2. A fourth vessel, the *Vucas*, is mentioned. Supplies amounting to $737 were furnished. Sal says the vessels left on Oct. 29th.

[36] These instructions or similar ones dated Jan. 12, 1793, and addressed to Argüello are in *Prov. St. Pap.*, MS., xii. 163. The letter of the viceroy to Vancouver dated Feb. 18, 1793, in answer to Vancouver's letter of Jan. 13th is found in *Id.*, xi. 112–13. In it the writer says: 'I am glad that as you say in your letter of Jan. 13th of this year all the subjects of His Majesty under my orders and residing in the regions of New Orleans (sic) of this America where you have been have treated you with the greatest hospitality and friendship.'

erected near where the cargo was deposited. The naturalists might make their investigations and the men might take exercise on foot in the vicinity of the presidio. Water and wood might be procured without restriction save that the men must not pass the night on shore and the work must be completed with all possible despatch. In his official capacity this was, he said, as far as he could go; but to personal service he placed no limit, being desirous of proving his regard.[37]

The governor thus courteously tendered to Vancouver all the hospitalities that he had a right to offer, or the navigator to expect; but the contrast was so great between them and those previously tendered by Cuadra in the absence of any responsible authority, that Vancouver was offended. "On due consideration of all these circumstances," he says, "I declined any further correspondence with, or accepting the incommodious assistance proffered by Señor Arrillaga; and determined, after finishing our investigation of these shores, to retire to the Sandwich Islands, where I had little doubt that the uneducated inhabitants of Owyhee, or its neighboring isles, would cheerfully afford us that accommodation which had been unkindly denied us at San Francisco and Monterey."[38]

He did, however, here as at San Francisco accept some live-stock and other supplies, payment for which, according to the records, he was obliged to defer until

---

[37] *Arrillaga, Borrador de Carta al Capitan Vancouver, Nov. 1793*, MS. I have given the purport of this letter somewhat at length because Vancouver misrepresents it by stating that there was no choice offered of a spot to deposit the cargo, the place suggested being the slaughter-house in the midst of putrid offal and inconvenient on account of high-running surf; by omitting to state that an English guard for the stores was permitted; and by other slight changes not favorable to the Spanish governor. Blotters of Arrillaga's and translations of Vancouver's other letters in *Prov. St. Pap.*, MS., xi. 100–4.

[38] *Vancouver's Voyage*, ii. 442. In other parts of his narrative the author treats Arrillaga very unjustly, accusing him of having misrepresented the viceroy's orders, and making him responsible for matters over which he had no control. In a letter of Feb. 28, 1794, the viceroy fully approves Arrillaga's policy and orders a continuance of it, though he desires harmonious relations with Vancouver. *Prov. St. Pap.*, MS., xi. 162–3.

some more convenient occasion;[39] and on the 5th of
November he sailed southward to make further explorations on the coast of this inhospitable province
before he departed to take advantage of barbaric hospitality.

If Vancouver was offended at Arrillaga's actions,
the governor had his suspicions aroused by those of
his visitor in departing without water and leaving
some supplies that had been prepared for him. It
seemed to him that Vancouver's displeasure was exaggerated, and he feared that his object was not so
much to obtain necessary supplies as to make observations respecting the Spanish establishments. Accordingly he despatched orders to the commandants
of presidios forbidding the furnishing of aid or facilities for investigation.[40] Vancouver continued his
observations along the coast southward, naming Point
Sal and Point Argüello in honor of his friends, received visits from the Channel aborigines, and anchored
November 10th at Santa Bárbara. Here he found
Goycoecha very friendly, for at first he had not received Arrillaga's strict orders and was inclined to
construe preceding ones liberally. Hence as Van-

[39] Nov. 5th, Vancouver to Arrillaga, regrets that he has to depart without
paying for supplies obtained at Monterey and San Francisco. He may be able
to get the money from some English vessel. *Prov. St. Pap.*, MS., xi. 98.
Arrillaga to Vancouver, urges him to feel no anxiety about leaving the debt
unpaid; returns the draft in favor of Sal; and asks him to accept some calves
as a present. *Id.*, xi. 99–100.

[40] While the vessels were in port Arrillaga sent to the commandants an
order in which he says: 'I have offered all the aid they need to undertake
their voyage; therefore if they touch at any of the ports under the pretext
of getting food or water their request is to be denied, and with politeness
they are to be made acquainted with the orders that require them to retire.'
Prov. St. Pap., MS., xi. 97. Attached to this order is a document which
seems to be secret—*reservadísimas*—instructions to the governor from the
viceroy requiring him in the most positive terms to allow no intercourse with
any foreign vessel except to furnish, in case of urgent need, such relief as is
demanded by the law of nations—and especially to prevent any knowledge
of the country being acquired. There is little doubt therefore, though this
paper is unsigned and undated, that Arrillaga acted under direct orders from
his superiors. See also *Id.*, xxi. 121. Jan. 15, 1794, Arrillaga says to the
viceroy that Vancouver apparently did not want supplies but merely to explore,
and he has warned the commandants accordingly. *Id.*, xxi. 130. Nov. 14,
1793, Arrillaga to Goycoechea of Santa Bárbara, Vancouver is to be refused
supplies since he has declined them at Monterey. *Prov. Rec.*, MS., i. 207.

couver's anticipations were less high than formerly
the Englishman was in good-humor.   True Goycoechea required the men to retire to their ships at night,
and Vancouver himself ordered his men to keep always in sight of the presidio in their recreations; and
though personal kindness from officials with permission to obtain wood and water and meat and vegetables
were the only hospitalities extended, yet the visitor
was delighted with his reception, and it never occurred
to him that it was not so very different from that in
the north.   Fathers Miguel and Tapis were very kind,
though it does not quite appear that they entertained
their guest at the mission; and Santa María hastened
up from San Buenaventura with a flock of sheep and
as many vegetables as twenty mules could carry.
After spending a most agreeable week the navigators
set sail on the 18th.

Santa María returned to San Buenaventura in the
Discovery, and Vancouver spent a day at that mission,
where he had the good fortune to intercept a courier
bound for Monterey with the latest European news.
Naming on the way points Felipe, Vicente, Dumetz,
Fermin, and Lasuen, he arrived at San Diego November 27th and was kindly welcomed by Grajera and
Zúñiga, who had, however, received from Arrillaga
"many severe and inhospitable injunctions" which
they were obliged against their inclinations to obey,
though they received some packets to be forwarded to
San Blas and Mexico.   Lasuen arrived from San
Juan Capistrano just before the departure of the vessels, too late to bring supplies from San Juan as he
wished, but in time to receive a handsome barrel-
organ as a gift for his San Cárlos church.   Vancouver
left the port of San Diego December 9th to cross the
Pacific.   During this second visit to the coast he had
learned nothing respecting the Nootka question;
neither had he recovered his deserters, who had been
sent to San Blas as already related.[41]   In March of

[41] On this voyage after leaving Monterey, see *Vancouver's Voy.*, ii. 443–76.

this year Don Juan Francisco de la Bodega y Cuadra, commander at San Blas, and discoverer of the Californian bay that bears his name, died, and was succeeded by General José Manuel de Álava.

Once more did Vancouver visit the coast, and besides his visit there is not much to be said of maritime affairs or foreign relations during the year 1794. The viceroy approved Arrillaga's policy and acts toward foreign vessels.[42] A report was received from Saavedra, now commanding at Nootka, that a forty-gun ship was coming from England to relieve Vancouver and settle the northern question; but Arrillaga replied that a treaty had been formed and no danger need be apprehended.[43] The *Concepcion*, Menendez in command, brought up the supplies and five padres to San Francisco in June, and during the year visited all the Californian ports. Two Manila vessels, the *Valdés* under Bertodano, and *Horcasitas*, under Mondojia, touched at Monterey in July and August.[44] The *Aranzazu* made two trips down from Nootka arriving in July and September. On the former voyage she was under an American commander, John Kendrick. He came for supplies and also for the men that had been destined for Bodega; but the latter had already been shipped on the *Concepcion*. Father Magin Catalá came down with Kendrick and refused to return to Nootka, though the president had no authority to send another chaplain in his place and though the pious captain vowed he would hold the padres responsible before God and the king for the lack of spiritual rations on board his vessel. The difficulty seems to have been settled by Gili going on board the

[42] June 11, 1794, viceroy to governor, approving the reception of Vancouver and orders given to commandants to prevent an examination of the country and the shipment of cattle to foreign establishments. *Prov. St. Pap.*, MS., xi. 177–8; but the day before he had forwarded a royal order of March 25, 1793, granting shelter to English vessels in Spanish ports. *Id.*, 176.

[43] Saavedra to Arrillaga, June 15, 1794, in *Prov. St. Pap.*, MS., xii. 207. Arrillaga to Saavedra, July 15th. *Id.*, 208.

[44] On movements of vessels for 1794 see *Prov. St. Pap.*, MS., xi. 160, 195–6; xii. 12, 14, 106–7, 121, 150–1, 198, 201–2, 211; xxi. 146–7; *Prov. Rec.*, MS., vi. 28, 30, 43; viii. 146.

Concepcion, whose regular chaplain was transferred to
the *Aranzazu.* Kendrick was unable to obtain all
the supplies he desired, especially in hogs and medicine; neither were there men enough that could be
spared as substitutes for the sick he brought down,
though two or three were sent.[45]

About the Nootka settlement in connection with
California I have only to say here that the reasons for
its maintenance by Spain had ceased to exist, and by
the terms of a treaty of January 11, 1794, it was
abandoned by both powers in March, 1795, California
obtaining apparently a few of the retiring soldiers.[46]

Vancouver came back across the Pacific and arrived at Nootka in September 1794. He found there
Álava, the successor of Cuadra.[47] Álava's instructions
had not however arrived, and after waiting till the
middle of October both commissioners went down to
Monterey, in the *Princesa, Discovery,* and *Chatham,*
arriving on the 2d, 6th, and 7th of November.[48] The
old slights were still weighing on the English com-

---

[45] *Kendrick, Correspondencia con el Gobernador Arrillaga sobre cosas de
Nootka,* 1794, MS; *Catalá, Carta sobre Nootka,* 1794, MS. See also *Prov. St.
Pap.,* MS., xii. 198–9, 209–13; xxi. 195. There had been some minor corre-
spondence that has not been mentioned about supplies, etc., for Nootka in 1791.
Sta. Bárbara, MS., xi. 118; *Prov. St. Pap.,* MS., x. 1, 2, 45–6, 140.

[46] See *Hist. N. W. Coast,* i. 300–1, this series. Dec. 10, 1794, governor to
viceroy asking that the unmarried soldiers from Nootka be retained to fill
vacancies in California. *Prov. Rec.,* MS., vi. 32. Granted March 14, 1795.
Prov. St. Pap., MS., xiii. 122–3. The *Activa,* Capt. Bertodano, arrived at
Monterey, Feb. 13, 1795, and sailed March 12th, having on board Pierce and
Álava, the English and Spanish commissioners for the 'disoccupation.' The
Princesa under Fidalgo left Monterey for San Blas April 8th. The *San Cárlos*
under Saavedra arrived from Nootka May 12th, and sailed for San Blas in June.
Saavedra brought down 21 natives from Nootka who were baptized at San
Cárlos as 17 others had been in November 1791. *Gaceta de Mex.,* vii. 266;
Prov. St. Pap., MS., xiii. 80, 89; *Prov. Rec.,* MS., vi. 37, 46; *Taylor's Dis-
coverers and Founders,* No. 25, p. 141, No. 28, p. 177; *Id.,* in *Cal. Farmer,* April
20, 1860. Taylor repeats a groundless story that the Nootka chief Maquinna
came down with a son and daughter; Gregorio and José Tapia, living at Santa
Cruz in 1854, being his grandsons.

[47] May 10, 1794, viceroy to governor, Álava to sail in the *Princesa* and to
receive all aid and attention in California. *Prov. St. Pap.,* MS., xi. 171. Aug.
20, 1794, this order communicated by governor to commandants. *Prov. Rec.,*
MS., iv. 117.

[48] Nov. 3d, Argüello to governor, announcing the *Chatham's* arrival on
Nov. 2d and Nov. 7th, that of the *Discovery* on Nov. 5th; delivery of deserters; sending a courier to San Diego. *Prov. St. Pap.,* MS., xii. 144–7.

mander's mind; but he was comforted by learning from Álava that the viceroy's "very humane and liberal intentions had no doubt been materially misunderstood by Señor Arrillaga;" and still more when he knew that, "Arrillaga having been ordered to some inferior establishment," Argüello was temporarily in command until the governor should arrive. Argüello placed everything at his visitor's disposal, and as the latter had now learned not to construe Spanish expressions of courtesy too literally, all went well.[49] No instructions for either Vancouver or Álava had arrived, and a courier was sent to San Diego. On November 11th Governor Borica arrived to confirm and continue the courtesies offered by the commandant. The same day despatches came for Álava, who confided the information that the Nootka question had been amicably adjusted at court, and that a new commission had been issued relieving Vancouver. Borica received similar information from the new viceroy, Branciforte, with instructions to receive the new commissioner.[50]

Remaining at Monterey till December 2d Vancouver was chiefly engaged in preparing his reports and charts, a copy of which was sent to England through Mexico. In the mean time his deserters were recovered, the vessels were overhauled, and an excur-

[49] Nov. 12th, the governor writes to the viceroy that while harmony was preserved, Vancouver was given to understand that his admission to the fort was a special favor, and adds that on account of Vancouver's past curiosity precautionary orders had been given to commandants and padres. *Prov. Rec.*, MS., vi. 29. Dec. 20th, the governor says Vancouver was satisfied with his treatment, but was not allowed to make observations on those matters that were to be kept from him. *Prov. St. Pap.*, MS., xxi. 210–12. A circular order dated Nov. 12th was sent to the missions forbidding any intercourse with foreign vessels, or any furnishing of supplies, except in cases of urgent necessity, when the corporal of the guard may furnish what is absolutely necessary and demanded by the laws of hospitality. Vancouver has been supplied and must receive nothing more. *Arch. Arzobispado*, MS., i. 41, 43; *Prov. Rec.*, MS., vi. 141–2. The padres promised obedience; at least all but those of Soledad, who said they would be glad to carry out the governor's instructions 'should it ever please divine providence to favor their inland mission with a port!'

[50] May 16, 1794, viceroy to governor, mentions appointment of a new commissioner. *Prov. St. Pap.*, MS., xi. 171–2. Nov. 12th, gov. to viceroy, acknowledges receipt. *Prov. Rec.*, MS., vi. 29.

sion was made into what is now known as Salinas
Valley. A large amount of supplies was obtained
from Monterey and Santa Cruz.[51] This done, and
having left on the beach certain articles of iron-ware
which the governor had refused to accept, the English navigator bade adieu to California and sailed for
England by way of Cape Horn, giving the commandants of presidios no occasion to exercise the precautions still ordered in case of trading at any other
port.[52]

Captain Vancouver was an intelligent and honest
British sailor, a good representative of a good class
of explorers and writers, plain of speech, and a reliable
witness on matters which fell under his personal observation, and in which his national pride and prejudices
were not involved. His statements of the condition
of the different establishments visited have a special
value and will be utilized in my chapters on local progress. His geographical and scientific researches, much

[51] Vancouver says that Swaine was sent with three boats to Santa Cruz
Nov. 27th for garden stuff, and was tolerably successful. The archives contain, however, several documents on the subject. Nov. 25, 1794, governor
to padres, Vancouver having sent three boats instead of one the padres must
not visit them but send supplies by Indians and wagons. *Prov. Rec.*, MS., vi.
142–3. Nov. 25th, gov. to corporal at Sta. Cruz, Three boats will come for
supplies; don't let them land, for the padres will send Indians with the supplies. *Id.*, v. 23. Nov. 29th, Corporal Sanchez to gov., he ordered the English
commander not to let any sailors go to the mission and obedience was promised. The natives brought the supplies and the English departed in peace.
Prov. St. Pap., MS., xii. 43. Nov. 30th, Sal to gov., Nov. 26th, the corporal reported the English boats approaching, and Sal sent five men from San
Francisco, who returned saying that the foreigners had retired Nov. 28th
without disorder. The soldier who brought the news was put in irons for
reporting incorrectly. *Id.*, xii. 32–3.
[52] Dec. 3, 1794, governor says that Vancouver left on the shore $505 worth
of iron-ware. *Prov. Rec.*, MS., vi. 32. He left well supplied and contented.
Id., vi. 31. Dec. 1st, Argüello certifies a list of goods including 24 blankets
left in spite of governor's excuses. *Prov. St. Pap., Ben. Mil.*, MS., xxi. 5.
Dec. 1794 and Feb. 1795, some not very clear communications of the commandant of Santa Bárbara about the gifts made. *Prov. St. Pap.*, MS., xii.
87; xiii. 23. Dec. 1st, gov. to Sal, repeats the old orders forbidding intercourse
with foreign vessels. *Prov. Rec.*, MS., v. 26–7. Feb. 23, 1795, viceroy to gov.,
approving the restrictions imposed. Vancouver should regard his admission
as a special favor. *Prov. St. Pap.*, MS., xiii. 11. April 11, 1795, viceroy forwards royal decree commending the governor's acts in not allowing Vancouver
to examine the country or to take breeding cattle for English colonies. Vancouver is alluded to as having visited Santa Bárbara and San Diego 'under
pretence' of wanting wood and water. *Id.*, xiii. 103–4.

iess extensive in California than in the far north, need no further attention here.[53] His persistence in ignoring the name California and extending New Albion down beyond San Diego by virtue of Drake's so-called 'discovery' is an amusing and harmless idiosyncrasy. His ignorance of the Spanish language and the peculiarly delicate position in which he was placed on account of international jealousies led him into many errors respecting matters with which he became acquainted by conversation with the Spaniards, his narrative in this respect presenting a marked contrast with that of La Pérouse; yet his errors are mostly confined to names and dates and minor details, and his general statements are more accurate and comprehensive than might have been expected. With the natural advantages of the country he was favorably impressed, and of them he left a fair record. Of the Spanish people with whom he came in contact, always excepting Arrillaga with whom he was unjustly but naturally offended, he speaks in kind and flattering terms, though criticising their inactivity and indisposition to take advantage of the possibilities by which they were surrounded. The natives, except some in the Santa Bárbara Channel, seemed to be a race of the most miserable beings ever seen possessing the faculty of human reason, and little if any advantages had attended their conversion. Yet he testified to their affectionate attachment to their missionary benefactors, whose aims and methods, without attempting a discussion of the mission system, he approves, looking for gradual success in laying foundations for civil society. For the friars personally he had nothing but enthusiastic praise.

What was needed to stimulate true progress in California was a friendly commercial intercourse with foreigners, to create new wants, introduce new com-

[53] Vancouver's atlas contains a carefully prepared map on a large scale, better than any of earlier date, of the whole California coast, which I reproduce. There are charts of Trinidad Bay, San Diego, and the entrance to San Francisco, and seven views of points along the coast.

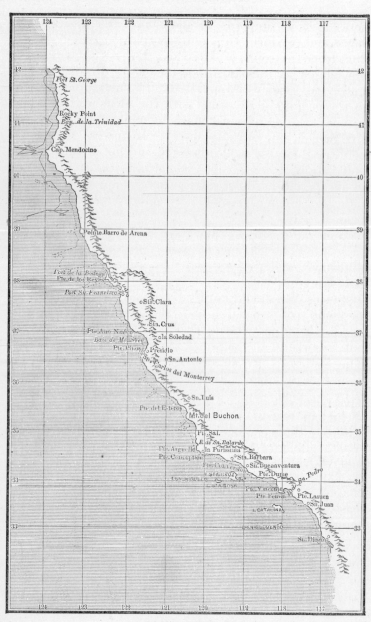

VANCOUVER'S MAP, 1794.

forts, give an impetus to industries and a value to lands and produce; this and a proper degree of attention from the court of Madrid. For with California considered as a Spanish possession the English navigator was greatly disappointed. The actual condition of the people "ill accorded with the ideas we had conceived of the sumptuous manner in which the Spaniards live on this side of the globe." "Instead of finding a country tolerably well inhabited and far advanced in cultivation, if we except its natural pastures, flocks of sheep, and herds of cattle, there is not an object to indicate the most remote connection with any European or other civilized nation." At the weakness of Californian defenses Vancouver was particularly surprised. "The Spanish monarchy retains this extent of country under its authority by a force that, had we not been eye-witnesses of its insignificance in many instances, we should hardly have given credit to the possibility of so small a body of men keeping in awe and under subjection the natives of this country, without resorting to harsh or unjustifiable measures." The soldiers "are totally incapable of making any resistance against a foreign invasion, an event which is by no means improbable." "Why such an extent of territory should have been thus subjugated, and after all the expense and labour that has been bestowed on its colonization turned to no account whatever, is a mystery in the science of state policy not easily to be explained."[54] I shall chronicle in the succeeding chapters a series of efforts, not very brilliantly, or at least permanently, successful, to remedy the evils complained of by Vancouver.

[54] For general remarks, in addition to those scattered through the narrative, see *Voyage*, ii. 486–504.

HIST. CAL., VOL. I. 34

CHAPTER XXV.

RULE OF BORICA, FOREIGN RELATIONS, AND INDIAN AFFAIRS.

1794–1800.

Diego de Borica—Arrival at Loreto—Branciforte Viceroy—Borica's Journey to Monterey—Arrillaga's Instructions—Charms of California—Résumé of Events in Borica's Term of Office—Coast Defences—Promised Reënforcements—French War Contribution—Foreign Vessels—Precautions—The 'Phœnix'—Broughton's Visit—The 'Otter' of Boston—A Yankee Trick—Arrival of Alberni and the Catalan Volunteers—Engineer Córdoba's Surveys—War with England—Coasting Vessels—War Contribution—Distribution of Forces—Map of California—The 'Eliza'—The 'Betsy'—War with Russia—Indian Affairs—Minor Hostilities—Campaigns of Amador, Castro, and Moraga.

"The new governor whom his Majesty is to appoint in place of the deceased Lieutenant-colonel Don José Romeu must have the advantages of good talent, military skill, and experience, robust health for the greatest hardships, prudent conduct, disinterestedness, energy, and a true zeal for the service; since all these he needs in order to traverse frequently the broad territories of the peninsula, strengthen defences, regulate the presidial troops, prevail by skill, or if that suffice not by force, over the ideas and aims and prejudicial introduction of the English, and contribute to the advancement of pueblos and missions." Such were the views of Viceroy Revilla Gigedo;[1] such were the qualities sought in Romeu's successor, and believed with much reason to have been found in Lieutenant-colonel Don Diego de Borica, adjutant-inspector of presidios in Chihuahua, who early in 1794 was appointed gov-

---

[1] *Revilla Gigedo, Informe de 12 de Abril 1793*, 152–3.

ernor, political and military, and commandant-inspector
of the Californias. He took possession of his office
at Loreto the 14th of May, having arrived two days
before by sea from San Blas accompanied by his wife
and daughter. On the same day he communicated his
accession to officials in Alta California and sent Arrillaga instructions to continue acting as governor until
he should arrive at Monterey.[2] Shortly after Borica
assumed office his friend the viceroy, to whom probably he owed the appointment, was replaced by the
Conde de Branciforte, who on July 12th took possession of the office. His succession was announced in
California in November.[3]

Borica remained two months and more at Loreto,
attending as may be supposed to affairs of state, but in
the mean time by no means neglecting the friends left
in Mexico, to whom he wrote long epistles narrating
in a witty and jocose vein, for he was "a fellow of
infinite jest," the details of his journey to California
with its attendant sea-sickness, which had rendered
the mere mention of the ocean a terror to the ladies.
At Loreto, where the governor represented himself
as "haciendo en esta Barataria mas alcaldadas que
Sancho Panza en la suya," health was regained and all
went well. The 1st of July he sent to the king a
petition for a colonel's commission, which he received in
the autumn of 1795.[4] It was his intention as announced
in several letters to complete the journey to Monterey
by land, but as the ladies regained their health and

[2] Letters of Borica in May 1794 to various persons in *Prov. St. Pap.*, MS.,
xxi. 196, 198–205; xii. 174; *Prov. Rec.*, MS., iv. 115–16; vi. 23. There seems
to be little or no doubt about May 14th as the date of taking possession; but the
day of arrival is given by Borica himself in different letters as May 11th, 12th,
and 13th. May 31st, Lasuen from Santa Bárbara congratulates the new governor. *Arch. Arzobispado*, MS., i. 36. July 31st, Commandant of San Diego
has received the announcement and proclaimed it in his district. *Prov. St.
Pap.*, MS., xii. 20. Arrillaga to same effect Aug. 4th. *Id.*, xxi. 196. Viceroy has received the news Aug. 5th. *Id.*, xi. 190–1. Aug. 2d, Argüello orders
Borica proclaimed as governor at San José. *San José, Arch.*, MS., iii. 23.

[3] July 5, 1794, Revilla Gigedo announces the arrival of his successor. He
will be glad to keep up a private correspondence with Borica. *Prov. St. Pap.*,
MS., xi. 183. July 12th, Branciforte announces his accession. *Id.*, xi. 189.

[4] *Prov. St. Pap.*, MS., xi. 197; xiii. 55; xiv. 29; *Prov. Rec.*, MS., v. 71;
vi. 26; *St. Pap., Sac.*, MS., xvii. 2.

courage, and were made acquainted with the prospective difficulties of the peninsula route in time of drought, the plan was changed. All went on board the *Saturnina* July 20th, and four days later set sail for San Luis Bay far up the gulf. The winds and other circumstances seem to have been unfavorable, for on the 28th the governor decided to land at Santa Ana and make his way to San Fernando and across the frontier by land.[5] With the exception of some correspondence about the furnishing of escorts and animals by the different commandants along the way we know nothing of the journey until he reached San Juan Capistrano in the middle of October.[6]

Here he met Arrillaga, who had left Monterey in September, and spent four days in consultation with that officer, starting northward the 17th of October.[7] Here I suppose were delivered by Arrillaga the instructions left by each retiring governor for the guidance of his successor, though the document as preserved bears no date. It was intended to acquaint the new ruler with the condition of affairs in the province; but it is devoted almost entirely to local and minor details, containing nothing of general interest with which the reader is not already acquainted,

[5] On embarkation and voyage, see *Prov. St. Pap.*, MS., xii. 75; *Prov. Rec.*, MS., vi. 134. July 10th, governor writes to viceroy on the difficulties of the land journey. *Id.*, vi. 26. I think the name Santa Ana may be an error, or that there may have been a locality of that name north of Loreto; for it seems hardly probable that the vessel was driven far south, or that Borica visited Loreto again on his way north. Vancouver, *Voyage*, iii. 330–1, tells us that Borica had come all the way from Mexico on horseback.

[6] July 28th, Borica to P. Calvo, asks for 24 mules and 24 natives, for his journey to San Fernando. *Prov. Rec.*, MS., vi. 134. August 6th, Grajera to Borica, Has sent 29 mules, 35 horses with 8 soldiers under Corporal Olivera from San Diego. *Prov. St. Pap.*, MS., xii. 19. Sept. 8th, 'N.' from San Fernando to commandant at Sta Bárbara, asks for 10 men and 54 animals to be sent at once; similar demand enclosed for commandant at Monterey for escort to be sent to San Luis. *Prov. Rec.*, MS., iv. 1. Sept. 15th, Goycoechea wishes a pleasant journey and a safe arrival to Borica and his wife and daughter. 'C. P. B.' *Prov. St. Pap.*, MS., xii. 102. Oct. 1st and 2d, Argüello to Borica and to Arrillaga, Has sent 60 animals with 10 men to San Luis. *Id.*, xii. 147.

[7] Arrillaga was at Monterey Sept. 16th, and left before Sept. 22d. *Prov. St. Pap.*, MS., xii. 152–3. Oct. 16th, Borica to viceroy announcing conference with Arrillaga and intention to start next day. *Prov. Rec.*, MS., vi. 28. Dec. 17th, viceroy's acknowledgment of above. *Prov. St. Pap.*, MS., xi. 207.

therefore I do not deem it necessary to reproduce it
here even en résumé.[8]   Arrillaga proceeded to Loreto
to resume his duties as lieutenant-governor; while
Borica continued his journey northward to the capital
where he arrived the 9th of November.[9]   With Monterey the new ruler was delighted, deluging his
friends and relatives with letters in praise of the
country immediately on his arrival.   "To *vivir mucho*
and without care come to Monterey," he tells them.
"This is a great country; climate healthful, between
cold and temperate; good bread, excellent meat,
tolerable fish; and *bon humeur* which is worth all the
rest.   Plenty to eat, but the most astounding is the
general fecundity, both of rationals and irrationals.
The climate is so good that all are getting to look
like Englishmen.   This is the most peaceful and quiet
country in the world; one lives better here than in
the most cultured court of Europe."   He was busy
with routine duties at first, but he found time for
convivial pleasures with Vancouver, Puget, Álava, and
Fidalgo, all jolly good fellows, and not one of whom
was more than a match for Borica "before a dozen of
Rhine wine, port, or Madeira."[10]

The Spanish authorities were now somewhat aroused
to the importance of strengthening Californian coast
defences, and this subject was therefore still more
prominent in Borica's term of office than it had been
during Arrillaga's administration.   To compensate
the soldiers for labor begun on the presidio buildings
in Fages' time an appropriation of $5,200 had been
made from the royal treasury to be expended in supplies.[11]   In the middle of 1793 some guns and work-

---

[8] *Arrillaga, Papel de Puntos para conocimiento del Gobernador de la
Peninsula, 1794.* MS.

[9] In three letters Borica says he arrived on Nov. 9th. *Prov. St. Pap.*, MS.,
xxi. 207–8; but Vancouver, *Voyage*, iii. 330–1, affirms it was on the 11th. It
is difficult to understand how either could mistake.

[10] Borica's Letters in Nov.–Dec. 1794. *Prov. St. Pap.*, MS., xxi. 207–12.

[11] Oct. 26, 1791, viceroy to governor, Has ordered the $5,200 paid to the
habilitado general; $1,600 for Monterey, and $1,200 for each of the other

men had been brought up from San Blas, and at
Borica's arrival in the autumn of 1794 work had been
going on for over a year on the San Francisco defences,
besides some slight preparations at Monterey and San
Diego.   Details of progress at the different presidios
may be more appropriately given in connection with
local annals in another chapter, and it is only in a
general way that I propose to treat the subject here.[12]

Viceroy Revilla Gigedo earnestly recommended
the fortification of the coast in his instructions of
1794 to his successor Branciforte,[13] who called upon
Colonel Costansó, the same who had visited California with the first expedition of 1769, for a report on
the subject.   Costansó's report was rendered October 17th of the same year, and was to the effect that
the difficulties in the way of adequate fortification
were insuperable.   The author had no faith in forts
situated in a distant province without home resources.
The only way to protect the country was to encourage
settlement and commerce.[14]   In this report, however,

presidios.   Jan. 15, 1792, V. R. to gov., Gen. Carcaba says that $5,200 is not
enough, since Fages had estimated $12,000 for three presidios.   The V. R.,
however, claims that Fages' estimate was on the basis of 150 per cent advance
on goods, or $5,200 without that advance; though Fages later raised the esti-
mate to $12,000, but this had no approval of general and king.   He therefore
refuses to give more than the $5,200 with $400 for package and freight. *St.
Pap., Sac.*, MS., i. 46–7; *Prov. St. Pap.*, MS., x. 112.   Some details about
the distribution of the amount among the presidios. *Id.*, xi. 54, 57; xii. 57–9;
Prov. Rec., iv. 3, 4.
    [12] Beginning of work at San Francisco announced in August 1793. *Prov.
St. Pap.*, MS., xxi. 113.   March 18, 1793, commandant of San Blas writes
that he has ordered fortification of Bodega and the presidios (except Sta Bárbara, supposed to be already in good condition).   The vessels will bring the
needed aid and the work is to begin at San Francisco.   July 8th, governor has
heard of the viceroy's approval and order for vessels to carry material. *Prov.
St. Pap.*, MS., xxi. 106–7   Jan. 22, 1794, V. R. to gov., says the Junta
Superior, after consulting the fiscal determined on Dec. 28, 1793, to conclude
the presidio works, the cost to be paid from the tobacco revenue.   The governor must form estimates and finish the work as solidly and economically as
possible. *Id.*, xii. 180–1.   The document of Dec. 28th, in *Nueva España, Acuerdos*, MS., 13, 14.   June 9th, V. R. to gov., has ordered supply-vessels to
transport timber from Monterey for the southern defences. *Prov. St. Pap.*,
MS., xi. 175–6.   Arrillaga, *Papel de Puntos*, MS., 192, explained his plan that
the workmen at San Francisco should come to Monterey to prepare timber
for that place and for the south.
    [13] *Revilla Gigedo, Instruccion*, MS. i. 530.
    [14] *Costansó, Informe sobre el Proyecto de fortificar los Presidios de la Nueva
California, 1794*, MS.   This officer seems to have been prominent in his pro-

and in another of July 1795 made by a committee composed of Costansó, Fidalgo, and Sanchez, batteries of eight twelve-pounders were recommended with eighty gunners for the ports, with a view solely to protection against corsairs. Defence against a hostile squadron was pronounced impracticable, and in case of attack nothing was to be done but to withdraw the people and live-stock to the interior. Vessels should, however, be furnished for coasting service, for which purpose three very small ones were available at San Blas.[15] As we shall see it was decided to send reënforcements.

During 1795 while some slight progress was being made with the fortifications, the war in France was inciting the government in Spain and Mexico to still further measures of defence. Borica had asked early in this year for armorers, guns, and munitions for the batteries being constructed; and on July 25th the viceroy replied, promising not only what had been asked but also a strong reënforcement of troops. He announced that a company of seventy-two Catalan volunteers under Lieutenant-colonel Pedro Alberni would soon embark from San Blas, picked men, robust, well behaved, and for the most part married, with the best arms and outfit obtainable. With this *compañia franca* there were to be sent seventeen or eighteen artillerymen and three armorers. The commandant general had orders to furnish needed aid from Sonora and the commandant of San Blas to send up the required armament. Moreover two small vessels were to run up and down the coast to bring news every six months. The viceroy concluded by a repetition of the old orders respecting foreign vessels visiting the coast, English ships to be treated more hospitably than

fession. I have before me several original reports on government works in different parts of Mexico from 1788 to 1800. He is mentioned by Viceroy Azanza. *Ynstruccion*, MS., 159. He reported on the fortifications of Vera Cruz as late as 1811. *Mexico, Mem. Guerra, 1840*, 26.

[15] *Sanchez, Fidalgo,* and *Costansó, Informe sobre auxilios que se propone enviar á la California, 13 Julio, 1795*, MS.

others, but none to be permitted a long stay or any inspection of the country.[16]

The news that war had been declared between Spain and France came to California in October 1793, with a decree of the viceroy calling on faithful subjects of Cárlos IV. for a contribution. The decree being duly published the Californians responded with $740, as was announced by Borica in March 1794; but the amount was declined with thanks by the viceroy in June, and thereupon redistributed to the donors.[17] In April 1795, however, things in Europe assuming a darker aspect for Spain, Branciforte again changed his mind and indicated his willingness to accept the Californian donation, and even urged in June a special effort on the governor's part to increase its amount. Borica published the appeal, and calling on officers, friars, soldiers, and neophytes to assist, headed the list himself with $1,000. The missionaries still professed their inability to give any but spiritual aid; but other classes responded generously, and contributions reached $3,881. In the early spring of 1797 the return of peace was made known in California.[18]

[16] *Branciforte á Borica sobre fortalecer las Baterías de San Francisco, Monterey, etc., 1795*, MS. On same date, July 25th, viceroy to governor, of same purport, mentioning the sending of an engineer, and also declaring it impossible to fortify and defend the whole coast against superior forces. In emergencies aid must be sought from Sonora. *Prov. St. Pap.*, MS., xiii. 53–4. The actual force in California was 225 men; Arrillaga's plan called for 271; and Borica's, 335. *Prov. St. Pap., Ben. Mil.*, MS., xix. 3, 4. Sept. 22, 1795, the V. R. announces that the company of volunteers was inspected at Mexico on Sept. 11th by Col. Salcedo, and found in good condition. *Prov. St. Pap.*, xiii. 83; Nov. 11th, he speaks of the artillerymen, and says the royal treasury at Vera Cruz pays the expense to the end of 1795. *Id.*, xiii. 74; *St. Pap., Sac.*, MS., vii. 44–5.

[17] June 22, 1793, viceroy's decree. *Prov. St. Pap.*, MS., xi. 129. Oct. 9th, Arrillaga to commandant of Monterey, mentioning decree of June 19th. *St. Pap., Sac.*, MS., i. 113. Oct. 28th, Lasuen says the padres will contribute what they can—that is their prayers. *Arch. Arzobispado*, MS., i. 36. Dec. 7th, decree has been published in Loreto. *Prov. St. Pap.*, MS., xi. 149. March 4, 1794, Gov. to V. R. announces $740 as the amount. *Id.*, xxi. 133; xii. 93; *Prov. Rec.*, MS., vi. 31; *Gaceta de Mex.*, vi. 578. June 26th, V. R. declines with thanks in the king's name. *Id.*, xii. 35; xi. 180, 182; *Prov. Rec.*, MS., viii. 144. Nov. 11th, Gov. announces the restitution. *Prov. Rec.*, MS., iv. 120.

[18] April 4, 1795, viceroy to governor, accepting the donation. *Prov. St. Pap.*, MS., xiii. 114–15. June 17th, V. R. to gov. and other later corre-

The orders respecting precautions against foreign
vessels were duly promulgated;[19] but opportunities for
carrying them into execution were rare in 1795. The
visit of the English merchant vessel *Phœnix*, Captain Moore—if that may be taken as a satisfactory
average from the Mor, Mayor, Moor, Murr, and Morr
of the archives—was the only sensation of the year,
and was indeed a mild one. She touched at Santa
Bárbara in August from Bengal for supplies, affording
the provincial authorities an excellent opportunity to
repeat the old orders, and the local powers to carry
out the hospitable but strict policy in such cases prescribed. They were fortified with the treaty of 1790
and other formidable material for a discussion on international obligations; but the *Phœnix* was content to
receive a few needed supplies and sail away. Moore
left with Goycoechea a Boston lad who desired to remain in the country and 'become a Christian;' but he
was sent to San Blas a few months later.[20]   Six letters

spondence on subject. *St. Pap., Sac.*, MS., v. 99–105. July 19th, Oct. 12th,
16th, Gov. to commandants and padres. *Prov. Rec.*, MS., iv. 30–1, 135, 137; vi.
151.   Oct. 18th, Lasuen to gov. explaining the poverty of the padres, the great
services they are rendering the king, and their inability, with the best wishes,
to give anything but their prayers for the victory of Spanish arms. *Arch. Sta
Bárbara*, MS., xii. 234; *St. Pap. Sac.*, MS., ix. 88–93.   March 12, 1796,
announcement of results, showing that San Francisco gave $707; Monterey
and San José, $554; Santa Bárbara and Angeles, $930, and San Diego, $639.
St. Pap., Sac., MS., v. 98; viii. 75; *Prov. Rec.*, MS., iv. 153.   Jan. 17, 1797,
viceroy's thanks for aid, including the prayers. *Arch. Sta Bárbara*, MS., xii.
234; *Prov. Rec.*, MS., vi. 181.   Peace announced by V. R. Nov. 29, 1795,
and solemn mass of thanksgiving ordered. *Prov. St. Pap.*, MS., xiii. 73.
Published by gov. Feb. 29, 1796. *Prov. Rec.*, MS., iv. 144.   Original letter
of Lasuen asking padres to say mass at each mission. *Doc. Hist. Cal.*, MS.,
iv. 55–7.   General amnesty and pardon on account of peace, and of marriage
of princesses. *Prov. Rec.*, MS., vi. 82; *Prov. St. Pap.*, MS., xv. 40.

[19] Jan. 6, 1795, governor orders that even in the case of San Blas vessels,
the first persons landing must be closely examined to be sure they are really
Spaniards. *Prov. St. Pap.*, MS., xiii. 16–17.   Nov. 2d, Sal to comisionado
of S. José urging strict compliance with the V. R's orders of July 25. *S. José
Arch.*, MS., iv. 26.   Nov. 14th, Goycoechea to Borica. No foreigners will be
allowed to visit the country on horseback or to get breeding animals. *Prov.
St. Pap.*, MS., xiv. 29–30.

[20] Portrait of Thomas Murr sent to viceroy (?). *Prov. Rec.* MS., viii. 166.
Sept. 5th, Goycoechea to Borica, Says the boy's name was Bostones and he
was of good parentage, a pilot and carpenter. *Prov. St. Pap.*, MS., xiv. 69–
70.   Capt. Matute is asked to carry the young Bostonian to San Blas. *Id.*, xxi.
230.   His name was Joseph O'Cain, an Irishman, and he went in the *Aranzazu*
(perhaps in 1796). *Prov. Rec.*, MS., iv. 22–3, 30–1. 'This Englishman is a native
of Ireland and his parents live now in Boston.' *Prov. St. Pap., Ben. Mil.*,

with English addresses were taken from the mail this year and forwarded to the viceroy by Borica's order.[21]

Throughout the year 1796 precautionary orders against foreign vessels continued to be issued, presenting no variation in matter or manner from those of former years, yet it may be well to notice an order of Borica to the effect that large war-ships, able to seize San Diego, were not to be permitted to enter the port, supplies being sent out in boats. Just how they were to be kept out does not clearly appear, since no such ship came to that harbor.[22] In July a report reached Monterey, coming from an American captain at Nootka, who received it from an English captain at Botany Bay, that the Englishmen had orders to attack Spanish vessels; but the report did not receive much credit, and the viceroy's orders dated November 30th to make reprisals on all English craft entering the ports, did not reach California till the next year.[23]

Only two foreign vessels made their appearance on the coast this year. The first was the English man-of-war *Providence*, under Captain Broughton who had visited California before with Vancouver. She anch-

[21] MS., xxi. 11. There is a José Burling also mentioned as an Irishman who arrived in or about this year. *St. Pap., Sac.*, MS., xix. 8, 9. See also on the visit of the *Phœnix. Prov. St. Pap.*, MS., xiii. 17–68; xiv. 67; *St. Pap., Sac.*, MS., xvii. 1; *Prov. Rec.*, MS., iv. 22–3. Another English vessel, the *Resolution*, Capt. Lochi (Locke?), was reported by Grajera of San Diego as having touched at Todos Santos Bay in August. *Prov. St. Pap.*, MS., xiii. 66–70.

[21] *Prov. St. Pap.*, MS., xiii. 175. The only Spanish vessels of the year seem to have been the *Concepcion*, Melendez, and the *Aranzazu*, Matute, with the *memorias*.

[22] Jan. 1796, viceroy to governor, no person from a foreign vessel to be admitted into California. *Prov. Rec.*, MS., viii. 158; *St. Pap., Sac.*, MS., xvii. 7. March 30th, Sal to Borica, for supplies furnished a receipt to be taken and sent to gov. *Prov. St. Pap.*, MS., xiv. 104. No goods to be taken in return for supplies. *St. Pap., Sac.*, MS., iv. 69. April 7th, Borica to commandant of San Diego, war-vessels not to be admitted into the ports. *Prov. Rec.*, MS., v. 242. April 18th, Indians to be sent to Bodega to look out for foreign vessels. *Prov. St. Pap., Ben. Mil.*, MS., xxiv. 11. Nov. 2d, Borica to V. R. *St. Pap. Sac.*, MS., iv. 61. June 18th, viceroy orders strict precautions. *Prov. St. Pap.*, MS., xiv. 151.

[23] July 15, 1796, governor to commandant, private. *Prov. Rec.*, MS., iv. 149. Aug. 25th, Grajera to gov. *Prov. St. Pap.*, MS., xiv. 115. Nov. 30th, viceroy to gov. *Id.*, xiv. 173. Oct. 19th, a courier arrived at Monterey from San Diego, announcing that 18 sail had been sighted. *St. Pap., Sac.*, MS., vi. 89.

ored at Monterey, obtained some needed supplies, left some instruments which had been intended for Bodega y Cuadra, but which Borica received and paid for, and then sailed away. It is recorded not very clearly, that Broughton after raising his anchor attempted in boats some exploration of the Rio San Antonio, or Salinas, and that his boats were fired at.[24] The other vessel, the first from the United States to anchor in a Californian port, was the *Otter* of Boston, commanded by Ebenezer Dorr.[25] She carried six guns and twenty-six men, arriving at Monterey on October 29th, after having cruised in the vicinity for nearly a week. Having obtained wood and water, freely supplied by the Spaniards on sight of her passport from General Washington signed by the Spanish consul at Charleston, she sailed on the 6th of November. Dorr asked permission to land some English sailors who had secretly boarded his vessel at Port Saxon.[26] His request was refused, but he landed five men on the beach at night, and the next night five more and a woman on the Carmelo shore, forcing them from the boat, they said, by the use of a pistol. Dorr's conduct naturally seemed to the Spaniards ungrateful; but his position was doubtless a difficult one, and the necessity of getting rid of his convict passengers was urgent. Governor Borica regarded it as a dishonorable trick on the part of the Yankee; but he had to

[24] Sept. 10, 1796, viceroy to Borica, approves of his having fired at the boats, suspecting that the aim was to explore the *salinas*, and he will send a vessel to prevent such attempts. *St. Pap., Sac.*, MS., viii. 74. The *Providence* fired a salute of 11 guns on entering and the battery responded. According to *Id.*, vi. 85-6, she sailed June 18th; but according to *Prov. St. Pap., Ben. Mil.*, MS., xxiii. 3, 5, it was July 8th. The instruments left were worth £250. According to *Id.*, xxiv. 6, the vessel appears to have been at San Francisco on June 10th. Alberni is ordered not to let Broughton land. Orders were sent to other ports not to permit a landing or to furnish any more supplies. *Prov. Rec.*, MS., iv. 67. Supplies furnished amounted to $308, the bill being sent to Mexico. *Id.*, iv. 206. The instruments were sent to San Blas. *Prov. St. Pap.*, MS., xxi. 242.

[25] She is called by the Spaniards the *Otter Boston*, *El otro Boston*, and *Loter Boston*; and their captain, Dow, Dour, Dor, Daur, Door, and Dore.

[26] Herbert C. Dorr, son of this captain, a well known *littérateur* residing in San Francisco, tells me that these men were convicts from Botany Bay, and that he has often heard his father tell the story of this voyage and of his

provide for the new-comers. They were set at work as carpenters and blacksmiths at nineteen cents per day, and they proved so industrious and well behaved that Borica would fain have retained them in the country; but in obedience to royal orders he was obliged to send them the next year to San Blas en route for Cádiz.[27]

On March 23d and April 1st the *Valdés* and *San Cárlos* arrived at Monterey and San Francisco respectively with most of the compañía franca, and of the artillerymen, the rest coming up the following spring, and the military force in California being thus increased by nearly one hundred men.[28] Lieutenant-

troubles with these reckless men who used the *Otter* as a means of escape. The Dorr family furnished several masters and owners of vessels engaged in the fur-trade in northern waters, as will be seen in the *Hist. N. W. Coast*, this series.

[27] Nov. 5, 1796, Borica to viceroy, announcing arrival and stating that no irregularities have been committed by the Americans. *St. Pap., Sac.*, MS., iv. 62–3; vi. 86–8. Nov. 10th, Borica to V. R., describing the subsequent 'irregularities.' *Id.*, iv. 63–4. Dec. 6th, Has received order to send the Irishman Burling and all other foreigners to Cádiz, will therefore send by first vessel the men left by Dorr. *Id.*, iv. 68–9. Dorr obtained supplies to the value of $187. *Prov. Rec.*, MS., iv. 288. Five Englishmen kept as prisoners until the *Aranzazu* arrives. *Prov. St. Pap.*, MS., xxi. 244. Aug. 1796, V. R.'s order to send Burling and foreigners to Cádiz. *Prov. Rec.*, MS., viii. 165; iv. 147. I suppose this Burling and the Boston boy, and O'Cain to have been possibly the same person. Oct. 6, 1797, Borica to V. R., sends the 11 to San Blas. *Prov. Rec.*, MS., vi. 56. Oct. 19th, Borica asks Capt. Caamaño to take them. *Prov. St. Pap.*, MS., xxi. 270. Feb. 3, 1798, V. R. approves. *Id.*, xvii. 17. Oct. 23d, a strange vessel anchored off Santa Cruz. *Prov. Rec.*, MS., v. 94. Doubtless the *Otter*. The Spanish vessels of the year were the *Valdés* and *San Cárlos* which brought troops, etc., from San Blas in April, touching at San Francisco, Monterey, and Santa Bárbara; the *Sutil*, Capt. Tobar, from a tour in the north; the *Concepcion*, Capt. Salazar from Manila at Santa Bárbara in April; and the *Aranzazu*, Capt. Cosme Bertodano, with the *memorias* at Monterey and San Francisco in July, and at Santa Bárbara in September. *Prov. Rec.*, MS., iv. 60–1, 74, 77, 148; *Prov. St. Pap.*, MS., xiv. 24, 86, 133; xxi. 236; *St. Pap., Sac.*, MS., xvii. 6. According to the *Relacion de las Embarcaciones que han conducido los Situados de los 4 presidios de la Nueva California, con espresion de los nombres de sus comandantes, desde el año de 1781, hasta 1796*, MS., it appears that since 1788 only one vessel each year had come especially with the regular *memorias* of supplies, though as we have seen several vessels arrived for one purpose or another.

[28] Arrival of the vessels. *St. Pap., Sac.*, MS., xvii. 6. Arrival of *Concepcion*, 1797, with Lieutenant Suarez and 4 privates. *Prov. St. Pap.*, MS., xvii. 148. The compañía franca of Catalan volunteers consisted of captain, 2 lieutenants, 3 sergeants—Joaquin Ticó, Francisco Gutierrez, and Juan Iñigues—8 corporals, 2 drummers, and 59 privates—75 men in all. Full list of names in *Prov. St. Pap., Ben. Mil.*, MS., xxiv. 1–4. The artillery detachment consisted of a sergeant—José Roca—3 corporals, and 14 privates—18 men in all. Total 93. *Id.*, xxiii. 11.

colonel Pedro Alberni, captain of the Catalan volunteers, became at once commandant at San Francisco, where twenty-five of his men were stationed. Twenty-five were sent to San Diego under Lieutenant José Font, and eight under sub-lieutenant Simon Suarez remained at Monterey, a sergeant and thirteen men being scattered in various duties. The artillery detachment under Sergeant José Roca was also distributed between the three presidios.[29] With the troops came the lieutenant of engineers, Alberto de Córdoba, who proceeded to make an inspection of the coast defences. In September he reported to the viceroy, chiefly on the works at San Francisco, which he found exceedingly defective and well-nigh useless. The battery at Monterey was also useless so far as the defence of the port was concerned, since vessels could easily anchor and land men out of range of the guns. Córdoba believed that effective forts and enough of them could not be erected except at an enormous expense, and he favored rather an increase of troops and one or more cruising vessels on the coast. He subsequently visited the south, and found the defences not more effective than those in the north, as the governor informed Branciforte at the beginning of 1797. Borica, however, found some comfort in the thought that the foes from whom attack might be feared were probably ignorant how weak the fortifications really were.[30]

[29] July 8, 1793, the presidios had 161 muskets, 59 pistols, 177 swords, 223 lances. *Prov. St. Pap.*, MS., xxi. 150–3. July 10th, received from San Blas 158 muskets, 142 swords, 96 lances—value $2,650. *Id.*, xxi. 194; *Prov. St. Pap., Ben. Mil.*, MS., xxv. 1. Sept. 15, 1795, 170 cwt. powder sent. *Prov. St. Pap.*, MS., xiii. 81. Dec. 1796, Feb. 1797, 200 muskets, 200 pistols, 200 cartridges, 200 musket-cases, 16,000 flints. *Prov. Rec.*, MS., viii. 170, 173; iv. 157; vi. 58; *Prov. St. Pap.*, MS., xv. 223; xvi. 240; xvii. 146; xxi. 253.

[30] *Córdoba, Informe al Virey sobre defensas de California, 1796*, MS. Dec. 27, 1796, viceroy to gov. has received Córdoba's plans of San Francisco, Monterey, and Santa Cruz, has ordered the fitting-out of two cruisers, and has taken measures for the proper strengthening of San Francisco. *St. Pap., Sac.*, MS., vii. 32–5. Jan. 20, 1797, Borica to V. R. *Prov. Rec.*, MS. vi. 78. Córdoba's first report was sent to Mexico by Borica with his communication of Sept. 21st, enclosing five plans and approving Córdoba's suggestions. *St. Pap., Sac.*, MS., iv. 56–7. Borica's instructions to Córdoba for his southern trip, Oct. 8, 1796. *Prov. St. Pap.*, MS., xxi. 246–7. He was to gather material for

The transport *San Cárlos*, Captain Saavedra, arrived at San Francisco March 11, 1797, and probably brought the news of actual war with England, though the communication of the viceroy does not appear in the archives;[31] for the 13th of March despatches began to circulate throughout the province, ordering the seizing of English vessels, instructing commandants to redouble their precautions, and calling upon friars to give not only prayers but Indians if needed. On the first alarm of invasion notice was to be sent to Monterey, the military forces were to concentrate at the threatened point, and live-stock was to be driven inland. Men were drilled in the use of arms; messengers were kept in constant motion; Indians were harangued on the horrors of an English invasion; sentinels were posted wherever an anchorage or landing was deemed possible; able-bodied men were gathered at the presidios, while the disabled ones were detailed to protect women and children; and strict economy was practised, since a non-arrival of the supply-ship was feared. This state of things lasted several months, but the popular excitement was considerably allayed by the arrival of the *Concepcion* and *Princesa* in April and May, and by the delay of the English invasion, nothing more alarming having occurred in the mean time than the rumored finding of some bodies of white men in the surf at Point Reyes.[32]

[31] Arrival of *San Cárlos*, *Prov. St. Pap.*, MS., xxi. 249; *Prov. St. Pap., Ben. Mil.*, MS., xvi. 62. There is a letter of the viceroy to Borica dated Jan. 25th, in which he alludes to some vague rumors of trouble with England, and recommends precautions. *Prov. St. Pap.*, MS., xv. 218–19.

[32] March 13th, Borica to Lasuen, *Prov. Rec.*, MS., vi. 183. Borica to commandants. *Id.*, iv. 155. March 13th to 14th, Lasuen to padres ordering prayers, litany on Saturdays, mass once a month, and exhortations such as Maccabeus gave during the campaign against Nicanor. *Arch. Sta Barbara*, MS., xi. 141–4; *Doc. Hist. Cal.*, MS., iv. 83–4. March 17th, Borica to commandants. *Prov. Rec.*, MS., iv. 155–6. March 19th, 24th, Sal to B. *Prov. St. Pap.*, MS., xvi. 220–22. March 22d, B. to commandant S. F. Cautious with strange vessels, war-ships to be menaced. *Prov. Rec.*, MS. v. 82–3. March 28th, April 10th, 2d, Goycoechea to B., Santa Bárbara defences in a very bad state to resist attack. Is suspicious of the Indians to whom the British have given beads.

During the months of July, August, and September all seems to have been quiet,[33] but in the middle of October there came a report from the peninsular mission of San Miguel that five, ten, or even sixteen vessels had been seen making for the north. The falsity of the report was ascertained before a week had passed, but not before it had been published with all the precautionary orders of old throughout the province, and had been sent to Mexico.[34] This emergency elicited from Governor Borica peremptory instructions which went all the rounds, to the effect that in case he were taken prisoner by the English no attention was to be paid to any orders purporting to come from him, whatever their nature; but the commandants were to go on in defence of California as their duty and circumstances might dictate.[35]   A

Families to be gradually removed to Angeles. *Prov. St. Pap.*, MS., xv. 40, 43–5, 188–9. March 31st, Sal to B., all care taken. Provisions to be destroyed and not allowed to fall into the hands of the foe. *Id.*, xvi. 220. March 31st, April 6th, May 11th, Grajera to B., a sentinel on the beach at San Juan Capistrano, Invalids of Angeles, San Gabriel, and Nietos rancho ready. If the Presidio has to be abandoned, shall it be destroyed or not? *Id.*, xvi. 267–9, 211–12. April 5th, Fidalgo to B. from San Blas. The *Concepcion*, Captain Manrique, and the *Princesa*, Captain Caamaño, will protect the California coast. *Id.*, xvii. 147. April 24th, B. to Goycoechea, Target-shooting every Sunday. Indians must be imbued with anti-English sentiments, taught that the foe are hostile to religion, violators of women. *Prov. Rec.*, MS., iv. 88. April 25th, B. to commandants, economize, for the supplies of 1798 cannot come. *Id.*, iv. 158. April 30th, Alberni to B., Indians refuse to go to Bodega from fear. *Prov. St. Pap.*, MS., xvii. 152. May 25th, *Princesa* at Sta Bárbara with supplies. Will remain as a coast-guard. *Id.*, xxi. 261–2. June 8th, B. to commandants. If Presidio is abandoned, guns to be spiked and powder burned. *Prov. Rec.*, MS., v. 254–5. Finding of bodies at Pt Reyes in April. *Prov. St. Pap.*, MS.. xv. 116. Two years later it was learned that San Diego Bay had been surveyed by the English in 1797 on a moonlight night. *Prov. St. Pap., Ben. Mil.*, MS., xiii. 20.

[33] Oct. 1st, Vallejo, writing from San José, mentions the arrival of an English ship at Santa Cruz, *Prov. St. Pap.*, MS., xv. 155, but nothing more is heard of the matter.

[34] Oct. 15th, Grajera to Borica. Oct. 20th, contradiction. *Prov. St. Pap.*, MS., xvi. 190–1. Oct. 19th, B. to all, Spread the news in all directions *á mata-caballo*. Vigilancia!! *Prov. Rec.*, MS., iv. 160; v. 259. Dec. 3d, 4th, viceroy to B. He doubts the accuracy of the report, since the *Concepcion* and *Princesa* came down the coast without seeing any vessels. *Prov. St. Pap.*, MS., xv. 273–5.

[35] Oct. 20th, Borica to commandants. *Prov. Rec.*, MS., iv. 161. Oct. 22d, Alberni to comisionado of San José. *San José, Arch.*, MS., v. 28. Nov. 3d, Goycoechea to B. *Prov. St. Pap.*, MS., xv. 100. Nov. 9th, Grajera to B. *Id.*, xvi. 195–6.

large war-ship arrived at Santa Bárbara on Dec. 17th, but she proved to be the Spanish *Magallanes*, Captain Espinosa, from Manila, and had come to protect rather than to invade the country. Finding no foes in California waters, she sailed for the south, as the *Concepcion* and *Princesa* had done a little earlier.[36]

The only subsequent events of the war, so far as California was concerned, were the contribution for the relief of his Majesty's exchequer, called for by Viceroy Azanza through bishop and governor in the fall of 1798 and paid in the summer of 1799,[37] and a new fright, also in 1799, resulting in the usual precautionary orders, and caused by the report of from fifteen to nineteen English frigates in and about the gulf of California.[38]

[36] Of the *San Cárlos* we know nothing beyond her arrival on March 11th at San Francisco. The *Concepcion* left San Blas in March with $1,088 of provisions; she brought also 9 settlers, 2 smiths, 4 soldiers, and 11 padres, having on board Alférez Lujan and Lieut. Suarez; arrived at San Francisco April 14th; was at Monterey June 28th; left Monterey Sept. 4th; left San Diego Nov. 8th; arrived S. Blas Nov. 22d. The *Princesa* arrived at Sta Bárbara May 27th with 100 men, many sick with scurvy; was at San Diego from June to October; and sailed with the *Concepcion*. The *Magallanes* remained only a few days at Sta Bárbara and sailed for Acapulco. The only other vessel of the year was the *Activo*, Captain Salazar, from Manila, which arrived at Monterey Sept. 27th, and sailed Oct. 7th. The vessels of 1798 were the *Concepcion*, Caamaño, and the *Activo*, Leon y Luna. The former arrived at Santa Bárbara in May with 8 padres and 24 convicts, and left Monterey in June. The latter arrived at San Francisco in June. On movements of vessels: *Prov. Rec.*, MS., iv. 90–1, 94, 105, 157, 162; vi. 52, 54, 56, 76, 87, 92–4, 104, 256; *St. Pap., Sac.*, MS., viii. 76; *Prov. St. Pap.*, MS., xv. 52, 68, 113–14; xvi. 54, 62, 175, 192, 197; xvii. 1; xxi. 249, 253–5, 281.

[37] Oct. 20, 1798, viceroy to gov. *Prov. St. Pap.*, MS., xvii. 82. Nov. 13th, bishop to padres, and Lasuen's refusal. *Arch. Sta Bárbara*, MS., x. 67–72; xii. 235–7; vi. 296–7. Jan. 31st, Borica to V. R., sends $1,000 as a personal contribution. *Prov. Rec.*, MS., vi. 118. Same date to commandants. *Id.*, iv. 170. June 26, account of results. Settlers and Indians of the missions (perhaps an error for Monterey including Borica's amount?) $1,853; San Francisco, $242; Angeles, $175; Santa Bárbara, $375; San Diego, $519; Catalan volunteers, $257; artillery, $39; total, $3,460. *Prov. St. Pap., Ben. Mil.*, MS., xxvii. 7. Another account makes $1,853 the total. *Prov. Rec.*, MS., vi. 128.

[38] July 4, 1798, Borica to commandants, 19 frigates in the Pacific. *Prov. Rec.*, MS., iv. 172. July 12th, 15th, Sal to comisionado of San José, forwarding orders and 1,000 cartridges. *S. José, Arch.*, MS., vi. 48–9. July 19th, B. to commandant Sta Bárbara, a place to be prepared at San Fernando for archives, reserve arms, and church vessels. *Prov. Rec.*, MS., iv. 112. Aug. 3d, V. R. to B., the Manila galleons must remain at Monterey until the way is cleared of privateers. *Prov. St. Pap.*, MS., xvii. 237. Governor's orders in accordance. *Prov. Rec.*, MS., iv. 176; vi. 131. Sept. 18th, two Spanish vessels reported as captured, not in Cal. *Id.*, iv. 173.

From 1797 to 1800 the military force and distribution remained practically the same as in 1796 after the arrival of the Catalan volunteers and the artillery. In April 1797 Borica asked for twenty-five recruits per year to fill vacancies and for an increase of thirty infantry and fifty cavalry, besides three war-vessels. At the beginning of 1799 the total expense of the military establishment as given by the governor, was $73,889 per year. In March Borica urged an increase of $18,624 in the annual expense, by the addition of three captains and an adjutant inspector, and the substitution of one hundred and five cavalry for the Catalan volunteers. Nothing was accomplished, however, in these directions until after 1800.[39] In the mean time some slight progress was made on local fortifications, and the engineer Córdoba, having completed his surveys and made a general map of California, had returned to Mexico in the autumn of 1798.[40]

At the end of 1798 four sailors who had been left in Baja California by the American vessel *Gallant* were brought up to San Diego and set to work while awaiting a vessel to take them to San Blas.[41] In May 1799 James Rowan in the *Eliza*, an American ship, anchored at San Francisco and obtained supplies under a promise not to touch at any other port in the province.[42] In August 1800 the American ship *Betsy*,

[39] *Prov. Rec.*, MS., vi. 86–8; *Prov. St. Pap.*, MS., xvii. 180, 188–9.

[40] Oct. 17, 1795, viceroy to Borica, speaks of Córdoba's appointment. He is able, well behaved, and energetic. *Prov. St. Pap.*, MS., xiii. 46. Jan. 1797, Córdoba at work on a map of California. *Prov. Rec.*, MS., vi. 78. Nov. 26, 1797, Borica forwards the map to the viceroy; received in March (or Nov.) 1798. *Id.*, vi. 62; viii. 189; *Prov. St. Pap.*, MS., xvii. 3. Nov. 27, 1797, Córdoba ordered by V. R. to return to Mexico. He sailed in October 1798. *Id.*, xv. 272–3; xxi. 286.

[41] *Prov. Rec.*, MS., v. 283, 285; vi. 111; *Prov. St. Pap.*, MS., xvii. 197–202. They were examined carefully but no information of importance was elicited. Wm. Katt, Barnaby Jan, and John Stephens were natives of Boston 'in the American colonies.' Gabriel Boisse was a Frenchman.

[42] May 27, 1799, Rowan to commandant. Gives the promise required; will pay cash; would sail to-day if it were less foggy. *Prov. St. Pap.*, MS., xvii. 206–8. June 3d, Borica to viceroy. The *Eliza* had 12 guns; gave a draft on Boston for $24. *Prov. Rec.*, MS., vi. 125–6. Aug. 3d, V. R. to B., Approves his course; names John Kendrick as supercargo, and says he wished to winter at Monterey.

Captain Charles Winship, obtained wood and water at San Diego.[43]   In October there anchored a large vessel, of suspiciously English appearance and carrying twenty-six guns, off the mouth of the Rio San Antonio in Monterey Bay; but she sailed without committing hostilities.[44]

In the spring of 1800 there had come news of war between Spain and Russia.   This brought out the usual orders for precautionary measures and non-intercourse, but it failed to arouse even a ripple of excitement.   An invasion from Kamchatka seems to have had no terrors for the Californians after their success in escaping from the fleets of Great Britain.[45]

Precautions taken to guard against invasion by a foreign foe having thus been narrated, it is necessary to give some attention to the dangers that threatened from within at the hands of the natives.   Although this subject of Indian affairs, in this as in most other periods of California history, is prominent in the archives, I do not deem it necessary to devote much space to it here.   The Spaniards, few in number and surrounded by savages of whose numbers and disposition little was known, were peculiarly situated.

[43]*Prov. Rec.*, MS., viii. 132; xii. 6; *Prov. St. Pap.*, MS., xxi. 44; *St. Pap., Sac.*, MS., ix. 12, 13.   She arrived on the 25th and sailed Sept. 4th; she had 19 men and 10 guns; she asked aid later at San Blas, but was frightened away by the approach of Spanish vessels, leaving her supplies, papers, captain, supercargo, and some sailors.

[44]Nov. 30, 1800, governor to commandant. *Prov. Rec.*, MS., xi. 146–7. Gov. to viceroy. *Prov. St. Pap.*, MS., xviii. 67.   Dec. 18th, V. R's orders to look out for returning whalers. *St. Pap., Sac.*, MS., ix. 50.   The *Concepcion* brought the *memorias* with nine padres to San Francisco in May 1799, being kept in quarantine 13 days, and not leaving California until January 1800. Coming back she arrived at Monterey in August 1800 with supplies, padres, and children, convoyed by the armed *Princesa*, Capt. Vivero.   They were at Santa Bárbara in September, and left San Diego in November. *Prov. St. Pap.*, MS., xviii. 9, 69; xxi. 30, 43–4, 48, 54; *Prov. Rec.*, MS., ix. 12; xi. 84, 144; *St. Pap., Sac.*, MS., iii. 20; vii. 76–7.

[45]Dec. 21, 1799, viceroy to Borica.   Newspapers announce war. *St. Pap., Sac.*, MS., ix. 54.   Feb. 8, 1800, B. to commandants.   War not certain; but the province must be ready for an invasion from Kamchatka. *Prov. St. Pap.*, MS., xviii. 23; *Prov. Rec.*, MS., x. 5.   March 31st, declaration of war known at Monterey.   Intercourse with Russia forbidden. *Id.*, ix. 2, 7. Oct. 9, 1802, mass ordered for peace. *St. Pap., Sac.*, MS., vii. 1.

They fully realized the dangers to which they would be exposed in case of a general uprising among the natives; and the consequence was that any unusual action on the part of the aborigines, the rumor of impending hostilities, gave birth to long investigations and a mass of correspondence out of proportion to the cause. Nine tenths of the rumors investigated proved to be groundless, and the few that had real foundation rested for the most part on petty events of no interest save in the mission or pueblo where they happened. Therefore I shall have something to say of these matters in connection with local annals, but in this chapter shall enter but slightly into the details either of events or correspondence.

In September 1794 fifteen or twenty neophytes of San Luis Obispo and Purísima were arrested with some gentiles for making threats and inciting revolt at San Luis. Five of the culprits were condemned to presidio work. Throughout the year there was some apprehension of trouble at San José and Santa Clara, caused mainly by the natives suddenly leaving certain rancherías. Lieutenant Sal went in person to make investigations, and the natives disclaimed any idea of revolt, but Father Fernandez was admonished to be somewhat less zealous, not to say cruel, in his treatment of the natives.[46]

In March 1795 a party of neophytes were sent from San Francisco across the bay northerly in search of fugitive Christians. After marching two nights and a day in that direction they were attacked by the gentiles and eight or ten slain. The friars were blamed for having sent out the party, and the governor deemed it unwise to avenge the loss and make enemies of these warlike and hitherto friendly tribes. In the south Alférez Grijalva had some trouble with the natives on the frontier between San Diego and San Miguel. This was in June and one or two savages lost their lives. Near Santa Bárbara there was

[46] *Prov. St. Pap.*, MS., xii. 33, 49–53, 100–4, 124–32, 194.

a fight in October between pagans and neophytes in which lives were lost on both sides.[47]

In June 1797 thirty neophytes were sent across the bay from San Francisco, in a direction not clearly indicated, in search of fugitives, and they were rather roughly treated by a tribe of Cuchillones though none were killed. This affair caused a long correspondence and finally brought positive orders from the viceroy forbidding the friars to send out such parties. In July after many preliminaries Sergeant Amador made an expedition against both the Cuchillones and the Sacalanes, who had committed the outrage of 1795. He brought in nine of the gentile culprits and eighty-three fugitive Christians. The savages are said to have dug pits which prevented the use of horses, and obliged Amador to fight on foot hand to hand, seven or eight of them being killed. At San Luis Obispo a neophyte was murdered by a gentile and there was a temporary excitement and fear that the mission would be attacked. Depredations continued on the southern frontier and San Diego as usual was deemed in danger.[48]

In 1798 the savages are said to have surrounded San Juan Bautista by night, but they retired after killing eight Indians of an adjoining ranchería. In the resulting expedition to the sierra under Sergeant Macario Castro, one chief was killed, four captives were taken, and a soldier was badly wounded. There was a false alarm of impending attack on San Miguel, San Luis, and Purísima by the Tulare and channel Indians. Around San Francisco Bay and especially at San José Mission there were constant rumors of preparations for hostilities that never occurred.[49]

[47] Prov. Rec., MS., v. 227–8; iv. 35–6; vi. 48–50, 56, 146; Prov. St. Pap., MS., xiii. 82, 177–8, 215–16, 241–2, 275–6; xvi. 71. According to Calleja, Respuesta, MS., 12, the ranchos of four men in the Monterey district were destroyed by Indians this year.

[48] Prov. St. Pap., MS., xv. 19–27, 122–5, 173–8, 282–3; xvi. 70–3, 90, 239, 249; Prov. Rec., MS., iv. 88; v. 206–7, 267.

[49] Prov. Rec., MS., iv. 285; v. 210; vi. 106–7, 100; ix. 9; Prov. St. Pap., MS., xvii. 97, 100, 106–7.

The only recorded event of 1799 was an expedition of Macario Castro in June to the various rancherías of the Monterey district. His object was to collect fugitives from San Cárlos, Soledad, and San Juan Bautista, and also to warn the gentiles against harboring runaways. Fortified by long and explicit instructions from Borica, and accompanied by thirteen soldiers and as many natives, Castro was successful. In May 1800 Pedro Amador made a raid from Santa Clara into the hills. He killed a chief, broke many weapons, and took a few captives and runaways. The natives again committed some depredations at San Juan Bautista, and in July Sergeant Moraga, marching against them, captured fourteen.[50] From the preceding paragraphs it appears that Borica's rule was a period of peace so far as Indian hostilities against the Spaniards are concerned. Naturally there were conflicts between neophytes and pagans, especially when bands of the former were sent out by the friars to scour the country for fugitives, and here and there a theft or other petty depredation was committed; but the natives were not yet hostile, though they resisted the soldiers on several occasions in the hills, and showed that in case of a general war they might prove formidable.

[50] *Prov. St. Pap.*, MS., xvii. 325–30; xviii. 33; *Id., Ben. Mil.*, MS., xxviii. 10–12; *Prov. Rec.*, MS., ix. 9, 10; *St. Pap., Sac.*, MS., viii. 70–1.

CHAPTER XXVI.

RULE OF BORICA—EXPLORATIONS AND NEW FOUNDATIONS.

1794–1800.

Search for Mission Sites—Exploration of the Alameda—San Benito—Las Pozas—Encino—Palé—Lasuen's Report—Foundation of Mission San José at the Alameda—Local Annals to 1800—Mission San Juan Bautista at Popeloutchom—Earthquake—Mission San Miguel at Vahiá—Padre Antonio de la Concepcion Horra—Mission San Fernando on Reyes' Rancho, or Achois Comihavit—Mission San Luis Rey at Tacayme—A New Pueblo—Preliminary Correspondence—Search for a Site—Reports of Alberni and Córdoba—San Francisco and Alameda Rejected in Favor of Santa Cruz—Arrival of Colonists—Founding of the Villa de Branciforte—Protest of the Franciscans—Plan to Open Communication with New Mexico—Colorado Route to Sonora.

It had long been the intention to found a series of new missions, each equidistant from two of the old ones, or as nearly so as practicable, and all somewhat farther inland than the original line. The friars of course were familiar with the general features of the country, and had made up their minds long ago about the best sites. In 1794–5, however, explorations were made by the priests, assisted in each instance by a military officer and guard of soldiers. In some cases this was a real search for new information; in others it was a formality, that the choice of sites might be officially confirmed. This matter settled, the necessary correspondence between governor, president, viceroy, and guardian took place in 1795–6, and in 1797–8 the new missions, five in number, were put in operation.

In 1794 the eastern shores of San Francisco Bay were almost a tierra incógnita to the Spaniards. It would perhaps be too much to say that those shores had not been visited for nearly twenty years, since the time of Anza; but there is no record of any previous raid against the gentiles in that region, much less of any exploring expedition. In November of this year, four natives were sent across to work with the pagans, but one of the two tule-rafts composing this armada was swept out and wrecked on the Farallones, where two of the navigators were drowned. In the same month the friars wished to go with a small guard up the eastern bay-shore from Santa Clara to conquer the gentiles, taking advantage of their short supply of food resulting from drought, but the commandant at San Francisco refused, because the country was "almost unknown," the natives perverse, and the adventure too hazardous.[1] Before June Sergeant Pedro Amador visited the southern part of this territory, and in his report used the name of Alameda, still applied to county and creek.[2] November 15, 1795, in accordance with Borica's orders of the 9th, Alférez Sal and Father Dantí set out from Monterey. On the 16th they explored the San Benito region, on the stream of the same name, where they found all that was required for a mission; and next day they found another suitable location on the edge of the San Bernardino plain near Las Llagas Creek, or what is now the vicinity of Gilroy. Having arrived at Santa Clara on the 21st, they were joined by Alférez Raimundo Carrillo, and started next day to examine the Alameda previously explored by Amador, whose diary they had. The river of the Alameda was also called by Dantí Rio de San Clemente. The explorers continued their journey up to a point which they state to have been opposite or in sight of San Francisco

[1] Nov. 30, 1794, Sal to Governor, in *Prov. St. Pap.*, MS., xii. 28–9.

[2] Amador's report is not extant, but the governor's acknowledgment of its receipt is dated June 2, 1795. *Prov. Rec.*, MS., v. 54. I suppose he applied the name, or it had been applied before, to a grove on the stream, since it is so applied a little later. Alameda was subsequently used for the southern section as was Contra Costa for the northern, though much less commonly.

Mission and Yerba Buena Island, nearly or quite to the site of the modern Oakland perhaps, and then turned backward, discovering some important salt-marshes, and finally erected a cross at a spot some-what south of the Alameda and called San Francisco Solano, arriving at Santa Clara, well soaked with the rain, on the 25th of November. Both commandant and friar kept a journal of this expedition. The documents still exist and contain many interesting local details, but are somewhat vaguely written. At all events I have no space for their reproduction, and the still longer explanation that would be required.[3]

In August 1795 Father Sitjar of San Antonio made an examination of the country between his mission and San Luis Obispo, finding no better place for a mission than Las Pozas, where farming-ground for three hundred fanegas of seed might be irrigated from the arroyos of Santa Isabel and San Marcos. He was accompanied on his trip by Macario Castro and Ignacio Vallejo.[4]

[3] Sal, Informe que hace de los Parajes que se han reconocido en la Alameda, 1795, MS. Dated San Francisco, Nov. 30th. Left San Francisco, Oct. 16th. St. Pap., Miss., MS., ii. 60–1. Danti, Diario de un Reconocimiento de la Alameda, 1795, MS. Dated San Francisco, Dec. 2, 1795. It may be noted that Macario Castro, of San José, had a herd of mares at this time in the Alameda. Also that one of the northern streams visited was called San Juan de la Cruz. Sal, Informe en el cual manifiesta lo que ha adquirido de varios sugetos para comunicarlo al gobernador, 31 de Enero 1796, MS., contains the following geographical information about the great interior valley—unintelligible for the most part: About 15 leagues north from Santa Clara is the Rio del Pescadero where salmon are caught. A quarter of a league further the Rio San Francisco Javier still larger. Two leagues beyond, the Rio San Miguel, larger than either. These three have no trees where they cross the tulares valley. Five leagues farther is the Rio de la Pasion. Between the last two is an encinal in that part of the Sierra Madre which stretches north and is called the Sierra Nevada. Keeping in the encinal and leaving the tulares to the left there is a region of fresh-water lakes. The four rivers run from east to west and empty into the ensenada of the port of San Francisco, tide-water running far up. The Sierra Madre is about eight leagues from Rio de la Pasion. Before coming to the rivers, on the right is the Sierra of San Juan, a short distance from the Sierra Nevada, and in sight from the presidio. The four rivers were named by Captain Rivera in December 1776.

An Indian said his people traded with a nation of black Indians who had padres. Another spoke of the Julpones, Quinenseat, Taunantoe, and Quisitoe nations, the last bald from bathing in boiling lakes. An Indian woman said that five days beyond the rivers there were soldiers and padres. Lovers of mystery will find food for reflection and theory in the preceding remarks.

[4] Sitjar, Reconocimiento de Sitio para la Nueva Mision de San Miguel, 1795, MS. Dated Aug. 27th, and addressed to Lasuen. See also St. Pap., Miss., MS., ii. 56–7.

The region between San Buenaventura and San Gabriel was explored in August 1795, in accordance with the governor's instructions of July 23d, by Father Santa María, Alférez Cota, and Sergeant Ortega with four men. The Encino Valley, where Francisco Reyes had a rancho, was the spot best suited for a mission among the many visited, but the gentiles being attached to the pueblo of Los Angeles or to the private ranchos, showed no desire for missionaries.[5] In the preceding June Sergeant Ortega had explored the country northward from Santa Bárbara and found a fertile valley on the Rio Santa Rosa, probably near where Santa Inés was founded in later years.[6] In the southern district Father Mariner with Alférez Grijalva and six men started from San Diego on August 17th to search for a mission site between San Diego and San Juan Capistrano. His report was in favor of the valley of San José, called by the natives Tacopin, a league and a half beyond Pamó toward the sierra.[7]

The results of the various explorations were summed up by President Lasuen in a report of January 12, 1796, which was incorporated by Governor Borica in a report to the viceroy in February.[8] The sites ap-

[5] *Santa María, Registro que hizo de los Parages entre San Gabriel y San Buenaventura, 1795*, MS. Dated Feb. 3, 1796. The padre visited in this tour Cayegues ranchería, Simi Valley, Triunfo, Calabazas, Encino Valley with rancherías of Quapa, Tacuenga, Tuyunga, and Mapipinga, La Zanja, head of Rio Santa Clara, and Mufin ranchería. The document is badly written, and also I suspect badly copied, and the names may be inaccurate. In some spots the pagans cultivated the land on their own account. Corporal Verdugo owned La Zanja rancho. Governor's order of July 23d, in *Prov. Rec.*, MS., iv. 19. In *St. Pap., Miss.*, MS., ii. 55-6, it is stated that Santa María made an unsuccessful survey.

[6] *Ortega, Diario que forma Felipe María de Ortega, Sargento de la Compañía de Santa Bárbara en cumplimiento á la comision que obtuvo de D. Felipe de Goycoechea saliendo con tres hombres á reconocer los sitios por el rumbo del norte en el dia 17 á las 8 de la mañana del mes de Junio, y es como signe, 1795*, MS. The same diary includes an examination of the Mojonera region on June 26th to 28th. Some explorations in 1798 will be given later in connection with the foundation of Santa Inés.

[7] July 23, 1795, governor's order. *Prov. Rec.*, MS., v. 229-30. Aug. 14th and 28th, Sept. 1st and 9th, communications of Mariner and Grajera. *Prov. St. Pap.*, MS., xiii. 19-20; *St. Pap., Miss.*, MS., 53-5.

[8] *Lasuen, Informe sobre Sitios para Nuevas Misiones, 1796*, MS.; *Borica, Informe de Nuevas Misiones, 26 de Feb., 1796*, MS.

proved were San Francisco Solano, seven or eight leagues north of Santa Clara; Las Pozas, equidistant between San Antonio and San Luis Obispo; and Palé, fourteen leagues from San Diego and eighteen from San Juan. The other two required additional examination, since two sites had been recommended between San Cárlos and Santa Clara, and that between San Buenaventura and San Gabriel was not altogether satisfactory. Borica hoped that by means of the new missions all the gentiles west of the Coast Range might be reduced and thus $15,060, the annual expense of guards, might be saved to the royal treasury. He did not deem it safe to expose the friars with a small guard of soldiers east of the mountains. The viceroy if he consents to the foundations should send friars and the $1,000 allowed to each new establishment; but no increase of military force will be needed, since the presence of the volunteers and the artillerymen will release some soldiers, and the guards of some old missions may be reduced. The saving of $15,060 and the unusual circumstance that no additional force was needed, were strong arguments in Mexico, and on the 19th of August 1796 the viceroy, after consultation with the treasury officials, authorized the carrying-out of Borica's plan.[9] On September 29th Nogueyra, the guardian, announces that he has named the ten friars required. He asks for the usual allowances, and begs that a vessel may sail with the missionaries as soon as possible, but protests against any reduction of the guards at the old missions. Borica received the viceroy's orders before the end of the year, and on May 5, 1797, Lasuen announced that the friars were coming and all was ready.[10]

[9] *Branciforte, Autorizacion del Virrey para la fundacion de cinco nuevas misiones, 1796*, MS. Sept. 29th, guardian consents. *Prov. St. Pap.*, MS., xiv. 128-9.
[10] Dec. 23, 1796, Borica to viceroy, *St. Pap., Sac.*, MS., iv. 71-2. May 5, 1797, Lasuen to B., *Id.*, vii. 28-31. Lasuen says it will be hard for the old missions to contribute for so many new ones at the same time; yet he will do his best. San Cárlos, Santa Clara, and San Francisco will be called upon to aid the two northern establishments and to lend Indians and tools. Livestock must be given outright. Santa Cruz certainly and Soledad probably must be excused.

Preliminaries being thus arranged, I come to the actual founding of the five missions, chronological order in this instance agreeing with that of localities from north to south. Desiring to avoid any unnecessary scattering of material I shall join to the establishing of each mission its local annals to the end of the decade, as I have done before in the case of new establishments.

Borica sent orders to the commandant of San Francisco, the 15th of May, to detail Corporal Miranda and five men for the mission of San José to be founded at the Alameda. On June 9th the troops under Amador and accompanied by Lasuen started for the spot, where next day a temporary church, or *enramada*, was erected. The native name of the site was Oroysom, and the name of the mission, San José, in honor of the patriarch husband of the virgin Mary, had been included in the orders from Mexico. On June 11th, Trinity Sunday, the regular ceremonies of foundation—blessing the ground, raising the cross, litany of all saints, mass, sermon, te deum, and the burning of one pound of gunpowder—were performed by or under the superintendence of Father Lasuen, the only friar present. The same day all returned to Santa Clara leaving the new mission to solitude and the gentiles. Five days later Amador and his men came back to cut timber and prepare the necessary buildings. By the 28th this work was so far advanced that the guard, as was thought, could complete it. Water was brought to the plaza, and the soldiers, all but Miranda and his five men, retired to the presidio. The same day the ministers, Isidoro Barcenilla and Agustin Merino, arrived and took charge.[11]

---

[11] *Amador, Diario de la Expedicion para fundar la Mision de San José, 1797*, MS.; *Amador, Prevenciones al Cabo de la escolta de San José, 1797*, MS. Dated June 28th, *San José, Lib. de Mision*, MS., title-pages. May 15th, governor's order to commandant. *Prov. Rec.*, MS., v. 107. June 11th, Lasuen to gov. *Arch. Sta Bárbara*, MS., vi. 21–2; *St. Pap., Sac.*, MS., xviii. 29–30; *Prov. Rec.*, MS., vi. 190. July 2d, Gov. to viceroy. *Id.*, vi. 94. June 29th, Miranda to commandant. *Prov. St. Pap.*, MS., xvi. 91. The Indian name of the site is also written Oroyjon, Oroyson, and Oryson. Contributions

In July 1797 there were rumors of impending attack by the savages, and such rumors were prevalent to the end of the decade; but there was no disaster, and I shall have occasion elsewhere to speak further of Indian troubles round San Francisco Bay.[12] The first baptism was administered September 2d by Father Catalá. By the end of 1797 there were 33 converts, and in 1800 the number had increased to 286, the baptisms having been 364 and the burials 88. Meanwhile the large stock came to number 367, and there were 1,600 sheep and goats. Crops in 1800 were about 1,500 bushels, chiefly wheat. Total for the three years 3,900 bushels. Padre Barcenilla, a man who, by reason of ill-health as was believed, was extremely irascible and always in a quarrel with somebody, particularly with the corporal,[13] remained at San José till after 1800. Merino was replaced in 1799 by José Antonio Uría. All three were new-comers, and none remained long in the country. A wooden structure with grass roof served as a church. Miranda was replaced by Luis Peralta in 1798.[14]

from the three northern missions for San José were 12 mules, 39 horses, 12 yoke of oxen, 242 sheep, and 60 pigs. *Arch. Misiones*, MS., i. 57.

[12] See Chapter xxxi. of this volume. July 3, 1797, Corp. Miranda to commandant, says that on account of the danger, the padres wished to abandon the mission, but he has dissuaded them. *Prov. St. Pap.*, MS., xvi. 90. Aug. 17, 1797, Amador to Borica. Some gentiles want to come near the mission to live because the Sacalanes threaten to kill them for their friendship to the Christians. *Id.*, xv. 173–4. April 6, 1798, Argüello to B., Indians making arrows to attack the mission. Reënforcements sent. The corporal has orders not to force Indians to come to the mission. *Id.*, xvii. 97. April 17th, Amador says 26 Indians consented to come and be made Christians. *Id.*, xvii. 101. The making of arrows seems to have been for hunting purposes. *Id.*, xvii. 100. June 6th, Gov. to Corporal Peralta ordering great caution and prudence, but the Indians must be punished if fair words have no effect. *Id.*, xvii. 106–7.

[13] Sept. 27, 1797, Barcenilla writes to the commandant that the soldiers will not lend a hand even in cases where 'the most barbarous Indian would not refuse his aid.' Private Higuera does nothing but wag his tongue against such as assist the padres. Corp. Miranda is much changed and will not work even for pay. Miranda explained that the padres were angry because the soldiers would not act as vaqueros. *Prov. St. Pap.*, MS., xvi. 47–8. Details of the trouble in *Id.*, xvi. 35–8, 46–7.

[14] *St. Pap. Miss.*, MS., ii. 122. Soldiers of the guard before 1800, according to *S. José, Lib. de Mision*, MS., Juan José Higuera, Salvador Higuera, Juan García, Cornelio Rosales, Rafael Galindo, Juan José Linares, Ramon Linares, Francisco Flores, José María Castillo, Miguel Salazar, Hilario Miranda, and Hermenegildo Bojorges.

For the second mission Borica instructed the commandant of Monterey on May 18th to detail Corporal Ballesteros and a guard of five men.[15] Next day
were issued Borica's instructions to the corporal, similar in every respect to documents of the same class
already noted in past chapters. It is to be noted,
however, that the matter of furnishing escorts to the
friars is left more to the corporal's discretion than
before, the absence of soldiers at night being declared
inexpedient but not absolutely prohibited. Sending
soldiers after fugitive neophytes was, however, still
forbidden. These instructions, though prepared especially for this new mission, were ordered published at
all the missions.[16]

The site chosen was the southernmost of the two
that had been examined, called by the Spaniards for
many years past San Benito, but by the natives
Popeloutchom.[17] Here as early as June 17th, Corporal
Ballesteros had erected a church, missionary-house,
granary, and guard-house,[18] and on June 24th, day of
the titular saint, President Lasuen with the aid of
fathers Catalá and Martiarena founded the new mission of San Juan Bautista,[19] the name having been

[15] *Prov. St. Pap.*, MS., xvii. 144–5. A list of supplies furnished the
escolta is given as follows: 12 fan. maize, 4 fan. beans, 1 butt of fat, 1 barrel,
1 pot, 1 pan, 1 iron ladle, 1 metate, 1 earthern pan, 1 frying-pan, 2 knives, 5
axes, 3 hoes, 1 iron bar, 1 machete, 6 knives for cutting grass and tules, 10
hides, 2 muskets, 1,000 cartridges, No. 14, 1,000 balls, 200 flints, 50 lbs. powder, 1 pair of shackles, 2 fetters, 1 door, 1 padlock, weights and measures.
List also in *St. Pap., Miss.*, MS., ii. 51–2. May 19th, Borica gives some general orders about the two new missions. *Prov. St. Pap.*, MS., xvii. 137.

[16] *Borica, Instruccion para el Comandante de la Escolta destinada á la fundacion de la Mision de San Juan Bautista, 1797*, MS.

[17] Written also Poupeloutehun and Popelout. The 23 rancherías belonging to this mission were Onextaco, Absayruc, Motssum, Trutca, Teboaltac,
Xisca, or Xixcaca, Giguay, Tipisastac, Ausaima, Poytoquix, Guachurrones,
Pagosines or Paycines, Calendaruc, Asystarca, Pouxouoma, Suricuama, Ta-
marox, Thithirii, Uñijaima, Chapana, Mitaldejama, Echantac, and Yelmus.

[18] *Prov. Rec.*, MS., vi. 190–1.

[19] Lasuen both on the title-page of *S. Juan Bautista, Lib. de Mision*, MS.,
and in a letter of June 27th, to the governor, *Arch. Sta Bárbara*, MS., vi.
22–3, commits the strange error of making the foundation on June 21st. In
another letter dated June 27th, he gives the date correctly. *St. Pap., Sac.*,
MS., xviii. 28–9. July 2d, governor announces the foundation to viceroy.
Prov. Rec., MS., vi. 94. See also *Id.*, iv. 250; *Arroyo de la Cuesta, Gram.
Mutsun*, p. vii.–viii.

indicated in the orders of the viceroy, and the day having been selected as appropriate.

José Manuel Martiarena and Pedro Adriano Martinez were the first ministers, both new arrivals of 1794 and 1797 respectively, the latter serving at San Juan until the end of 1800, the former leaving the mission in July 1799, and Jacinto Lopez coming in August 1800. The first baptism took place on July 11th, and before the end of the year 85 had received the rite, as had 641 before the end of 1800, 65 having died in the mean time, and 516 remaining as neophytes. Livestock increased to 723 large animals and 2,080 small; agricultural products for 1800—much the largest crop that had been raised—amounted to about 2,700 bushels.[20]   A mud-roofed wooden structure was the mission church before 1800.

Beyond the statistics given there is nothing to be noted in the local annals of San Juan Bautista except certain Indian troubles and the earthquake of 1800. The Ansaimes, or Ansayames, were the natives who caused most trouble. They lived in the mountains some twenty-five miles east of San Juan. In 1798 they are said to have surrounded the mission by night, but were forced to retreat by certain prompt measures of the governor not specified. In November another band known as the Osos killed eight ranchería Indians, and Sergeant Castro was sent to punish them. They resisted and a fight occurred, in which the chief Tatillosti was killed, another chief and a soldier were wounded, and two gentiles were brought in to be educated as interpreters. In 1799 the Ansaimes again assumed a threatening attitude and killed five Moutsones, or Mutsunes, who lived between them and the mission. Acting under elaborate instructions from Borica, Castro visited several rancherías, recovered over fifty fugitives, administered a few floggings

[20] The soldiers named in the mission-books before 1800 were Corporal Juan Ballesteros, Antonio Enriquez, José Manuel Higuera, José Guadalupe Ramirez, Matías Rodriguez, Manuel Briones, Lúcas Altamirano, Isidro Flores, and José Ignacio Lugo.

with no end of warnings, found some of the prevalent rumors of past misdeeds to be unfounded, and brought in a few captives for presidio work. Again in 1800 the Ansaimes killed two Mutsunes at San Benito Creek, burned a house and some wheat-fields, and were with difficulty kept from destroying the mission. Sergeant Gabriel Moraga marched with ten men and brought in eighteen captives including the chieftains of the Ansaime and the Carnadero rancherías.[21]

There were shocks of earthquake from the 11th to the 31st of October, sometimes six in a day, the most severe on the 18th. Friars were so terrified that they spent the nights out of doors in the mission carts. Several cracks appeared in the ground, one of considerable extent and depth on the banks of the Pájaro, and the adobe walls of all the buildings were cracked from top to bottom, and threatened to fall. The natives said that such shocks were not uncommon in that vicinity, and spoke of subterranean fissures, or caverns, caused by them, from which salt water had issued.[22]

The site of the third mission, between San Antonio and San Luis Obispo, was called Las Pozas by the Spaniards and Vahiá by the natives.[23] "Here," says

[21] *Prov. Rec.*, MS., ix. 9–11; vi. 106–7; *Borica, Instruccion al Sargento Castro sobre recorrer las Rancherías de Gentiles, 1799*, MS., in *Prov. St. Pap.*, xvii. 325–8. Dated Monterey, June 7th. *Castro, Diario de su Expedicion á las Rancherías, 1799*, MS. Dated June 29th. It seems that the Spaniards were in the habit of going to the Ansaime country after *tequesquite*, or saltpetre. Besides those named in the text the Orestaco and Guapo rancherías are mentioned. See also *St. Pap., Sac.*, MS., viii. 80–1; *Prov. St. Pap.*, MS., xviii. 33. In 1800 the San Juan Indians sent 3 wagons, 9 yoke of oxen, 9 horses, and 15 Indians to Monterey when an attack from foreign vessels was feared. For this they were remunerated by order of the viceroy to encourage zeal in like cases. *Id.*, xix. 7.

[22] Comandante Sal. to governor, Oct. 31, 1800, in *St. Pap., Miss.* and *Colon*, MS., i. 40–2. Nov. 29th, governor acknowledges receipt. *Prov. Rec.*, MS., xi. 147. Dec. 5th, governor to viceroy. *Prov. St. Pap.*, MS., xxi., 51. Feb. 10th, V. R. to gov. *Id.*, xviii. 69. This earthquake has been noticed also in *Randolph's Oration; Vallejo, Hist. Cal.*, MS., i. 107; *Tuthill's Hist. Cal.*, 116; *Trask*, in *Cal. Acad. Nat. Science*, iii. 134. On Nov. 22d a shock was felt in the extreme south. *Prov. St. Pap.*, MS., xxi. 54.

[23] There is much doubt about this aboriginal name. Different copyists from Lasuen's original letters and entries in the mission-books make it: Vaticá, *Savage*, in title-page of *S. Miguel, Lib. de Mision*, MS.; Vahca, another from

Lasuen on July 25, 1797, "with the assistance of the Reverend Padre Apostolic Preacher, Fr. Buenaventura Sitjar, and of the troop destined to guard the new establishment, in presence of a great multitude of gentiles of both sexes and of all ages, whose pleasure and rejoicing exceeded even our desires, thanks to God, I blessed water, the place, and a great cross, which we adored and raised.   Immediately I intoned the litany of the saints, and after it chanted the mass, in which I preached, and we concluded the ceremony by solemnly singing the te deum.   May it all be for the greater honor and glory of God our Lord. Amen." Thus was founded the mission of San Miguel, in honor of "the most glorious prince of the heavenly militia," the archangel Saint Michael, for which Sitjar and Antonio de la Concepcion Horra, a new-comer of 1796, were appointed ministers.   José Antonio Rodriguez was corporal of the guard.[24]

A beginning of missionary work was made by the baptism of 15 children on the day of foundation; at the end of 1800 the number had increased to 385, of whom 53 had died and 362 were on the registers as neophytes.[25]   The number of horses and cattle was 372, while small animals numbered 1,582.   The crop of 1800 was 1,900 bushels; and the total product of the three years, 3,700 bushels.[26]   Sitjar left San Miguel and returned to his old mission of San Antonio in

same original; Vahiá, *Murray*, from Lasuen's letters of July 25th, in *Arch. Sta Bárbara*, MS., vi. 23–4; Vaheá, *Piña*, from Borica, July 31st, in *Prov. Rec.*, MS., vi. 94–6.

[24] *San Miguel, Lib. de Mision*, MS.; Rodriguez' letter of July 25th. *St. Pap., Sac.*, MS., xviii. 27–8; Lasuen's letter of Aug. 5th, referring to the unusually favorable disposition of the natives, but suggesting caution. *Id.*, vi. 96–7; *Prov. Rec.*, MS., vi. 193. See also references of preceding note. Contributions from San Antonio, San Luis, and Purísima were 8 mules, 23 horses, 8 yoke of oxen, 128 cattle, 184 sheep. *Arch. Misiones*, MS., i. 201.

[25] I give the figures as they stand on the records. The sum of the deaths and *existentes* is rarely the same as the baptisms. When less, the deficiency may be attributed to runaways; but when greater it is inexplicable save on the theory of an error in the register.

[26] The soldiers of the guard were José Antonio Rodriguez, corporal, Manuel Montero, José María Guadalupe, and Juan María Pinto, according to the mission-book. According to the report of 1797–8, the bell at San Miguel was soon after its hanging found to be cracked and worthless. *Arch. Sta Bárbara*, MS., xii. 66.

August 1798. Juan Martin began a very long term of ministry in September 1797, and Baltasar Carnicer a short one in May 1799. Horra, better known by the name of Concepcion, served only about two months, when, being charged with insanity, he was enticed to visit Monterey on some pretended business of importance and sent to his college by order of Lasuen and consent of the governor, sailing on the *Concepcion* or *Princesa*, which left Monterey in September.[27] He is said to have been a very able and worthy friar before he came to California; and in proof of his insanity nothing more serious is recorded than baptizing natives without sufficient preparation and neglecting to keep a proper register. There is no special reason to doubt, however, that the charge was well founded. After his return to the college, on July 12, 1798, he made a long report in which he charged the California friars with gross mismanagement, with cruelty to the natives, and with inhuman treatment of himself. This report I shall have occasion to notice more fully elsewhere. In the mission-books of San Miguel this padre's signature appears but once—on the title of the death-register, where his statement that he was one of the founders was subsequently struck out. The original mud-roofed wooden church was not replaced by a better structure until after 1800.

For the fourth mission, between San Buenaventura and San Gabriel, additional exploration revealed no better location than that of Reyes' rancho in Encino Valley, called by the natives Achois Comihavit. A quarrel between Reyes and the friars respecting the ownership of the land would be an appropriate introduction to the narrative of this foundation; but no

[27] Aug. 20th, Lasuen to governor in *St. Pap., Sac.*, MS., vi. 93–4. Sept. 4th, governor to viceroy. *Id.*, viii. 4. Sept. 2d, Gov. to Lasuen. *Prov. Rec.*, MS., vi. 196. Horra seems to have been transferred subsequently to the Querétaro college, for which the guardian thanks God in a letter to Lasuen, May 14, 1799. *Arch. Sta Bárbara*, MS., xi. 280–1.

such controversy is recorded, though the ranchero's
house was appropriated as a dwelling for the missionaries. Lasuen had gone down from San Miguel to
Santa Bárbara, whence he started at the end of August
with Sergeant Olivera and an escort. With the aid of
Father Francisco Dumetz, on the 8th of September, in
the presence of the troops and a great crowd of natives,
he performed the usual ceremonies, and dedicated the
new mission, as required by instructions from Mexico,
to San Fernando, Rey de España.[23] Francisco Javier
Uría was the associate of Dumetz, and both served
until the end of 1800 and later. Ten children were baptized the first day, and thirteen adults had been added
to the list early in October. There were 55 neophytes
at the end of 1797, and 310 at the end of 1800, baptisms having amounted to 352 and deaths to 70. Five
hundred and twenty-six was the number of cattle,
mules, and horses; and 600 that of sheep. Products
of the soil in 1800 were about 1,000 bushels, though
they had amounted to 1,200 bushels the year before,
the total yield for three years being 4,700 bushels.

The fifth and last of the new establishments was not
founded until the next year. In October 1797 a new
exploration was made between San Juan Capistrano
and San Diego by Corporal Lisalde, with seven soldiers and five Indians, escorting fathers Lasuen and

---

[23] St Ferdinand was Fernando III., King of Spain, who reigned from 1217
to 1251, under whose rule the crowns of Castile and Leon were united. He
was canonized in 1671 by Clement X. Aug. 28th, Goycoechea to Borica announcing Lasuen's departure for Reyes' rancho. *Prov. St. Pap.*, MS., xv.
82. Sept. 8th, Lasuen's report of foundation. *St. Pap.*, *Sac.*, MS., xviii. 26–7;
Arch. Sta Bárbara, MS., vi. 24–5. Sept. 8th, certificate of Sergt. Olivera; he
calls the site Achoic. *Prov. Rec.*, MS., iv. 92; vi. 191, 196. Oct. 4th, Goycoechea to Borica, sends Olivera's diary. Guard-house and store-house finished.
Two houses begun, church soon to be begun. *Prov. St. Pap.*, MS., xvi. 246–7;
Prov. Rec., MS., iv. 92. Contributions from Santa Bárbara, San Buenaventura, San Gabriel, and San Juan were 18 mules, 46 horses, 16 yoke of oxen,
310 cattle, 508 sheep. *Arch. Misiones*, MS., i. 202. The mission-books of San
Fernando I examined at the mission in 1874. They consisted of baptismal
register 1 vol., 1798–1852, 1st entry April 28, 1798, signed by Dumetz; marriage register, 1 vol. 1797–1847, first entry, Oct. 8, 1797; and the *Libro de
Patentes y de Inventarios*. In the legal difficulties that followed the death of
Andrés Pico the books disappeared and could not be found by Mr Savage in
1877.

Santiago from San Juan. The party separated to
return north and south at the old Capistrano, which
they doubtless selected at the time, October 6th, as
the best mission site, for we hear no more of the Palé
of former expeditions.[29] During December there was
a correspondence between Borica and Lasuen on the
subject, by which it appears that the large number
of docile natives was the chief inducement to found a
mission in this region, but that agricultural and other
advantages were believed to be lacking. The governor insisted on the foundation, and prophesied that
difficulties in the future would be less serious.[30]

The governor issued orders the 27th of February
1798 to the commandant of San Diego, who was to
furnish an escolta and to require from the soldiers
personal labor in erecting the necessary buildings,
without murmuring at site or work, and with implicit
obedience to Lasuen.[31] The records show no subsequent proceedings till the 13th of June. On that
date at the spot called by the natives Tacayme, and
by the Spaniards in the first expedition of 1769 San
Juan Capistrano, or later, Capistrano el Viejo, in the
presence of Captain Grajera, the soldiers of the guard,
a few neophytes from San Juan, and a multitude of
gentiles, and with the aid of fathers Santiago and
Peyri, President Lasuen with all due solemnity, supplemented by the baptism of fifty-four children,
ushered into existence the mission of San Luis, Rey
de Francia, it being necessary hereafter to distinguish

[29] *Lisalde, Reconocimiento de las tierras para situar la Mision de San Luis,
1797,* MS. The places named are Las Animas, Las Lagunitas, Temeca ranchería, Pauma, Pullala, and San Juan Capistrano. In *Grijalva, Informe
sobre las rancherías que se hallan en las tierras exploradas por el Padre Mariner, 1795,* MS., there are named the following rancherías: Mescuanal, To-
napa, Ganal, Mocoquil, and Cuami, in a little valley called Eschá; Tagui, Gante,
Algualcapa, Capatay, Tacupin, Quguas, Calagua, Matagua, and Atá, in
another valley three leagues distant; Curila, Topame, Luque, Cupame,
Páume, and Palé, three leagues from former valley, and speaking language
of San Juan; Palin, Pamame, Pamua, and Asichiqmes, lower down; Chacápe
and Pamamelli in Santa Margarita Valley; Chumelle and Quesinille in Las
Flores.

[30] Lasuen to Borica. *Arch. Arzobispado,* MS., i. 44; to Lasuen, *Prov. Rec.,*
MS., vi. 201.

[31] *Prov. Rec.,* MS., v. 273-4.

between the establishment of San Luis, king, and San Luis, bishop.[32] All was prosperity at first. In a week Antonio Peyri, the energetic founder, had seventy-seven children baptized and twenty-three catechumens under instruction. By the first of July he had six thousand adobes made for the mission buildings. In July he was joined by José Faura, who was succeeded in the autumn of 1800 by José García. José Panella was assigned to this mission, and served for a short time in 1798, during the absence of one of the ministers, who went to the baths of San Juan Capistrano for his health. Panella made himself unpopular by his harsh treatment, and so great was the discontent of the natives and the clamor for a change, that Lasuen was obliged to send him away and promise the return of the other padre, probably Peyri, who was greatly beloved.[33] The baptisms in 1798 were 214; before the end of 1800 there were 337 neophytes, 371 having been baptized, and 56 being the number of burials. There were 617 horses, mules, and cattle in 1800, besides 1,600 sheep. Products of the soil were 2,000 bushels of wheat, 120 of barley, and six of maize, the latter being just the amount sown, while eight bushels of beans produced nothing. The mission-books of San Luis Rey are the only ones in California which I have not examined. Their whereabouts is not known.

It had long been deemed desirable to promote colonization in California, and the prevalent fears of foreign aggression did much to cause definite action

[32] Saint Louis was Louis IX., king of France, who reigned from 1226 to 1270, and earned his reputation for piety both at home and in the crusades. June 13th, Lasuen to Borica reporting the foundation. *Arch. Sta Bárbara*, MS., vi. 25–7; xi. 11; *Arch. Arzobispado*, MS., i. 47–9. July 12th, B. to Lasuen. *Prov. Rec.*, MS., vi. 218–19. Aug. 1st, B. to viceroy. *Id.*, v. 279; vi. 98–9. Contributions of Santa Bárbara, San Gabriel, San Juan, San Diego, and San Luis Rey: 64 horses, 28 yoke of oxen, 310 head of cattle, 508 sheep. *Arch. Misiones*, MS., i. 202.

[33] The governor in a communication to Lasuen on the subject calls the absent missionary Juan Martinez, but there was no such padre in California. *Prov. Rec.*, MS., vi. 222–3. Dec. 7, 1798, Borica also writes a letter of warning and advice to the friar. *Id.*, 227–8.

to be taken at this epoch. The completed line of missions as planned was rapidly to civilize the natives, but a larger Spanish population was desirable and new pueblos of gente de razon were to be founded as well as new missions. This subject was doubtless included in a general sense in Borica's original instructions; but the first definite action is seen in a report of the royal tribunal of accounts to the viceroy, dated November 18, 1795. In this document it is recommended as a most important measure for the welfare and protection of the Spanish possessions in California that the governor, with the aid of Engineer Córdoba and other officers, proceed to select a site and to found a pueblo, or villa, to be called Branciforte in honor of the viceroy. This establishment as a coast defence should be put on a military basis, securely fortified, and settled with soldiers as pobladores. The site must be selected and the lands divided according to existing pueblo regulations and the laws of the Indies. Each officer and soldier is to have a house-lot, and between those of the officers lots are to be assigned to chieftains of rancherías who may be induced to live with the Spaniards, thus assuring the loyalty of their subjects. Live-stock and implements may be furnished by the government as hitherto. Instead of an habilitado there is to be a town-treasurer; and Alberni may command, acting as lieutenant-governor. As the time of the infantry soldiers expires they are not to be reënlisted, but new recruits obtained from New Spain will create an immigration without the heavy cost of bringing in settlers as such.[34]

It is to be supposed that the viceroy approved this plan in its main features at least, and sent corresponding orders to Borica, though no such order appears in the archives.[35] It had been indicated in the plan

[34] Branciforte, Informe del Real Tribunal sobre fundacion de un pueblo que se llamará Branciforte, 1795, MS. This report was prepared by Beltran on Nov. 17th, and approved by the tribunal Nov. 18th.

[35] The order dated Dec. 15, 1795, and enclosing the auditor's report given above is alluded to by Borica on June 16, 1796. St. Pap., Miss. and Colon., MS., i. 364.

that the new establishment should be on or near San
Francisco Bay, and in the spring of 1796, on receipt
of the viceroy's instructions, whatever they may have
been, the governor began to move in the matter,
though in January 1795 he had instructed the commandants to report on suitable sites for new pueblos,
and though Sergeant Amador seems to have explored
with the same view as early as July of the same year
the coast region from San Francisco to Santa Cruz.[36]
On May 21st Borica requested Alberni and Córdoba
with an escort of six men to meet him at Santa Cruz
on the 28th. During the next few weeks, the three
made some personal explorations not described in
detail, and June 16th the governor asked the others
to report on the best place for the town, and to give
their ideas generally in connection with the plan of
foundation. Private letters of similar purport were
written on the 17th and 18th.[37]

Alberni's report was dated at San Francisco July
1st, and that of Córdoba the 20th, the two being in
substance identical. Three sites were considered: the
Alameda, San Francisco, and Santa Cruz. The first
was pronounced unsuitable for a pueblo, not only because the bed of the creek was so low as to prevent
irrigation, but because there was no wood, timber,
stone, or pasturage, except at a great distance. San
Francisco was declared to be the very worst place in

[36] Jan. 9, 1795, Borica to commandants. *Prov. Rec.*, iv. 126–7. *Amador,
Reconocimiento de Terreno desde Santa Cruz hasta San Francisco, 1795*, MS.
Dated July 4th, he describes particularly four fertile spots with more or less
advantages for settlements at distances of 8, 12, 15½, and 20 leagues from San
Francisco, the last being 5 leagues from Santa Cruz. July 23d, has received
the report of July 4th, and orders Amador to improve the road with the aid
of commandants at Santa Cruz and Santa Clara (San Francisco?). *Prov. Rec.*,
MS., v. 57–8. May 11, 1796, Salazar in his report to the viceroy mentioned
a spot suitable for a pueblo about midway between San Francisco and Santa
Cruz where there is an anchorage. San Benito was also a good site, but there
were many Indians requiring a mission, as there were not at the former
spot. *Arch. Sta Bárbara*, MS., ii. 75–7.

[37] *Prov. St. Pap., Ben. Mil.*, MS., xxiv. 6, 7; *St. Pap., Miss. and Colon.*,
MS., i. 364–5, 374–5; Translation in *Sta Cruz, Peep*, 51; *Prov. St. Pap.*,
MS., xxi. 241. In his letter to Córdoba, Borica says that the viceroy cannot
entertain the request of the Catalan volunteers to have lands granted them,
but instead will found a new town and give them lands therein as a recompense when their term expires.

all California for the purpose in view, since the peninsula afforded neither lands, timber, wood, nor water, nothing but sand and brambles and raging winds. The Santa Cruz site, across the river from the mission, had all the advantages which the others lacked, and had besides proximity to the sea, affording facilities for export, plenty of fish, with an abundance of stone, lime, and clay for building. The establishment of a town here could moreover do no possible harm to the mission. The settlers should be practical farmers from a cold or temperate climate, and should have houses and a granary built for them at expense of the government in order that they might apply themselves at once to agriculture. The soldiers and invalids are entitled to more assistance than other settlers by reason of their past services. The scheme of adding Indian chiefs to the town is impracticable, since there are no chiefs; some mission Indians, however, might be profitably attached to the settlement to work and learn in company with Spaniards.[33]

August 4th Borica transmitted these reports to the viceroy with his own enthusiastic approval, pronouncing the Santa Cruz site the best between Cape San Lúcas and San Francisco, and giving some additional particulars about the anchorage. He recommends that an adobe house be built for each settler so that the prevalent state of things in San José and Los Angeles, where the settlers still live in tule huts, being unable to build better dwellings without neglecting their fields, may be prevented, the houses to cost not over two hundred dollars each.[39] On September 23d another communication of the governor

[38] *Alberni, Parecer sobre el sitio en que debe fundarse el nuevo Pueblo de Branciforte, 1796*, MS. A part is translated in *Dwinelle's Col. Hist. S. Francisco, App.* 18. *Córdoba, Informe acerca del sitio de Branciforte, 1796*, MS. Very inaccurately translated, and dated July 2d, in *Sta Cruz, Peep*, 53–5. Brief mention of the decision against San Francisco in *Randolph's Oration*, 309; *Tuthill's Hist. Cal.*, 105; *Elliot*, in *Overland Monthly*, iv. 337–8.

[39] *St. Pap., Miss. and Colon.*, MS., i. 258–60. The volunteers should have a year's pay, and as a *reintegro*, 2 mares, 2 cows, 2 sheep, 2 goats, a yoke of oxen, plough, harrow, hoe, axe, knife, musket, and 2 horses; other *vecinos* besides the house, stock, tools, etc., and $10 per month for a year.

to the viceroy contained suggestions of similar purport, and asked for four classes of settlers: first, robust
country people from cold or temperate climes; second,
carpenters, smiths, stone-cutters, and masons; third,
tailors, tanners, shoemakers, and tile-makers; and
fourth, shipwrights, and a few sailors, to take advantage of the abundance of whales.[40]   Having received
Borica's report and also the opinion of the legal
adviser of the royal treasury, the viceroy on January
25, 1797, in accordance with that opinion, ordered
Borica to proceed immediately with the foundation.
He had already sent a list of eight men who had
volunteered at Guadalajara as settlers.[41]   The beginning was to be made with such settlers at San José or
Angeles as had no lands and might be induced to
change their residence to Branciforte.   New settlers
and artisans were to be sent as soon as possible; in
fact, orders had already been issued for the collection
of vagrants and minor criminals to be shipped to California.   The president of the missions was ordered to
render all possible assistance; and Borica must forward at once an estimate of cost and a memorandum
of needed implements and other articles.[42]

The receipt of the viceroy's orders was acknowledged
by Borica on April 29, 1797, and three days later he
sent the necessary orders to the commandant of Santa
Bárbara and the comisionado of San José in order
that recruits for the new establishment might be obtained from the settlers and rancheros at and near the
two old pueblos.   At the same time Lasuen directed
his friars to afford the required aid, though he had
received no instructions on the subject from his college,
and deemed it strange that the king should have permitted the foundation of a villa so near a mission

[40] *St. Pap., Sac.*, MS., iv. 57–8.
[41] Oct. 24, 1796. *Prov. St. Pap.*, MS., xiv. 169.
[42] *Branciforte, Dictámen del Fiscal de Real Audiencia sobre la fundacion de
la Villa de Branciforte, Aprobado por el Virrey en 25 de Enero 1797*, MS.;
inaccurate translation of copy certified by Borica May 9th in *Sta Cruz, Peep*,
57. Mention in *Dept. St. Pap., S. José*, MS., i. 76–7.

established with royal approval.[43] The *Concepcion* arrived at Monterey May 12th with a party of colonists on board in a pitiable state of destitution and ill-health.[44] It was necessary to provide some kind of a home for them; and before the end of May Gabriel Moraga was sent as commissioner to erect temporary shelters at Branciforte, since Córdoba, who was to superintend the formal establishment, had other duties which would keep him busy for a time. It is impossible to give the exact date when Moraga began his work, when the first settlers took possession of their new homes, or when the formal foundation occurred.[45]

The 17th of July, possibly at or about the time that the settlers left Monterey for Branciforte, Borica issued instructions to Comisionado Moraga for the internal management of the villa. The townsmen must be made to live in peace and harmony; no concubinage, gambling, or drunkenness, which offences, like

[43] April 29th, Borica to viceroy. *Prov. Rec.*, MS., vi. 91–2. May 2d, B. to commandant. *Id.*, iv. 89–90. B. to comisionado S. José. *Id.*, iv. 211–12. May 5th, Lasuen to B. *St. Pap., Sac.*, MS., vii. 27–8.

[44] They were José Antonio Robles, Fermin Cordero, José Vicente Mojica (or Morico), wife and five children, José María Arceo, José Barbosa and wife, José Silvestre Machuca and wife, José Acevedo, José Miguel Uribes, José Agustin Narvaez. The different lists of arrival, departure, and settlement differ somewhat. The first lacks the last four names and has Gallardo and Guzman which never appear again. The nine colonists with their families, 17 persons, were of the vagabond and criminal class, but they differed from the first settlers of the other pueblos in being for the most part so-called Spaniards. They included 2 farmers, 2 tailors, 1 carpenter, 1 miner, 1 merchant, 1 engraver, and 1 with no trade. *St. Pap. Miss. and Colon.*, MS., i. 384–5; *Prov. Rec.*, vi. 92; *Prov. St. Pap.*, MS., xv. 223–4; xiii. 277–8; xvii. 31, 89–90; xxi. 256.

[45] May 12, 1797. Borica to commandant. When the settlers go to Branciforte, cattle, implements, etc., will be furnished, an account being opened with each. *Prov. St. Pap.*, MS., xvii. 31. May 15th, B. to Córdoba. Directs him after completing the work at S. Francisco, the survey of the Sta Clara boundary, and that for a removal of S. José, to go to Sta Cruz and make careful surveys and plans for the town of Branciforte and its buildings public and private, with an estimate of expenses. *Id.*, xxi. 260–1. May 26th, B. to Moraga. Instructions to build some temporary huts for himself and the guard and to take his family there to live; then to build some large huts to accommodate 15 or 20 families each, also temporary. The soldiers must work and the colonists also if they arrive before the work is done. Implements, stock, etc., will be sent by Sal. Córdoba is to be obeyed when he comes. *Sta Cruz, Arch.*, MS., 67–8; *Prov. Rec.*, MS., iv. 247; *Sta Cruz, Peep*, 3, 5. May 27th, Sal acting as secretary for Borica forwards blank-books, paper, and materials for making ink. *Sta Cruz, Arch.*, MS., 69.

neglect of public work, must be punished. Mass must
be attended on holidays, on penalty of three hours in
the stocks; prayers and the rosary must close the day's
labor; and certificates of compliance with the annual
communion and confession must be forwarded regularly to the governor. All intercourse with the mission Indians and gentiles was prohibited; and the most
friendly relations must be maintained with the friars
of Santa Cruz. The greatest precautions must be
taken to insure proper care of the colonists' clothing,
implements, and other property, and to prevent sales,
which were to be void. And finally all labor, before
Córdoba's arrival, was to be directed to the preparation
of the needed shelters for men and animals, monthly
reports of progress being sent to the governor.[46] By
August 12th Córdoba was on the spot, had surveyed
the lands, done some work on the temporary houses,
begun an irrigating canal, and was in search of suitable stone and timber for the permanent edifices. He
also furnished Borica with an estimate of cost, $23,-
405, which early in October was forwarded to the viceroy, and a little later by order of October 24th, the
work at Branciforte was suspended for want of funds,
Córdoba retiring to the presidio.[47]

Thus the proposed greatness of the Villa of Branciforte was indefinitely postponed; but there remained
the temporary huts, the nine pobladores, the comisionado, and the military guard. The colonists, though
not convicts, were of a class deemed desirable to get
rid of in and about Guadalajara whence they came.
They had been aided at the beginning to the extent
of from $20 to $25 each; and they were to receive
from the government $116 annually for two years,

[46] Borica, Instruccion de dirigir la fundacion de la Nueva Villa de Branciforte, 1797, MS.
[47] Aug. 12th, Córdoba to Borica. Prov. St. Pap., MS., xvii. 149; xxi. 265–6.
The irrigable lands were 1,300 x 1,500 varas; those depending on rain 2,000
to 3,000 varas. Oct. 7th, Gov. to viceroy with estimate of cost. Prov. Rec.,
MS., vi. 56. Oct. 24th, to Córdoba ordering suspension of works, though he
is to leave the mission mill in good shape. Prov. St. Pap., xxi. 272. Aug.
22d, Borica orders a 'model fence' to be erected at Branciforte. Id., xxi. 266.

and $66 for the next three years,[48] besides the live-
stock and implements for which they were obliged
gradually to pay. They were thus enabled to live after
a fashion, and they never became noted for devotion
to hard work. There was no change in the number
of regular pobladores down to 1800, though half a
dozen invalids and discharged soldiers were added to
the settlement,[49] perhaps more, for the records on the
subject are meagre. Corporal Moraga remained in
charge until November 1799, when Ignacio Vallejo
was ordered to take his place as comisionado, arriving
about the 20th.[50] The settlers raised in 1800 about
1,100 bushels of wheat, maize, and beans; and their
horses and cattle amounted to about 500 head. I
append in a note a few minor items which make up
all that Branciforte has of history down to the end
of the decade and century.[51]

[48] *Prov. St. Pap.*, MS., xvii. 31, 41, 89–90.
[49] Feb. 1, 1798, the governor states to the viceroy that there were, besides
the 9, two invalids and one discharged soldier. *Prov. Rec.*, MS., vi. 65. In
a list of 1799, *Prov. St. Pap.*, xvii. 264, six invalids; Marcelino Bravo, Marcos Briones, Marcos Villela, José Antonio Rodriguez, Juan José Peralta, Joaquin Castro. The population tables make the number of men in 1800, 17, or
66 persons in all; but I suppose this may have included besides those just
mentioned from 3 to 5 soldiers of the guard with their families. Yet 21 settlers, one an Indian, are reported by Vallejo on Dec. 31, 1799. *St. Pap., Miss.*,
MS., iii. 6.
[50] *Prov. Rec.*, MS., iv. 302; *Santa Cruz, Arch.*, MS., 65.
[51] The work called *Sta Cruz, A Peep into the Past, The Early Days of the
Village of Branciforte*, should be noticed here. It is a series of articles published in the *Sta Cruz Local Item* from July 1876 to Aug. 1877, which I have
collected in a scrap-book. Each of the 42 articles contains the translation of
an original document from the archives with preliminary remarks of considerable interest by the translator, Mr Williams, an old resident of Santa Cruz.
The plan of this work is so praiseworthy, and the result so far superior to
what newspapers usually furnish in the way of local history, that the numerous inaccuracies of detail may almost be pardoned.
In the following I omit many items of no importance or interest. Dec. 14,
1797, Sal to Moraga, Sends 6 varas of *jerga* for each settler for bedclothes.
Sta Cruz, Arch., MS., 69. Jan. 28, 1798, Borica to Moraga, Must teach the
Guadalajareños agriculture and strive against their natural laziness; treat
them with charity and love, but punish grave faults and malicious failure to
work. *Id.*, 71; *Sta Cruz, Peep*, 7–9; *Prov. Rec.*, MS., iv. 264. March 3d, Bo-
rica says the community must till the field of Narvaez if he is ill. *Id.*, iv. 266,
May 30th, cows and sheep promised. Each settler got three cows. *Id.*, iv. 271,
274. July 27th, a settler to attend to no other work than tilling his own fields.
Sta Cruz, Arch., MS., 70; *Sta Cruz, Peep*, 11. Oct. 29th, Cordero and Arceo,
runaways, if caught must work in irons. *Id.*, 71 and 13. Oct. 28th, Borica orders
Moraga to inspect the wardrobe of settlers' wives and report what is needed.
Prov. Rec., MS., iv. 282. Expense for wages and rations to end of 1798,

Meanwhile in Mexico August 30, 1797, the San Fernando college sent to the viceroy a protest against the choice of a site so near that of the mission. The utility of the new establishment was not to be questioned; but the villa site was on the pasturage-ground of the natives; troubles would surely result; the laws allowed a mission at least one league in every direction; and, according to a report by Father Señan, there were good lands nearer San Francisco. The only result of this protest before 1800 seems to have been a reply of the governor dated February 6, 1798, in which he gave statistics to show that the mission had more land and raised more grain than could be attended to; that the neophytes were dying off and there were no more pagans to convert; and there was no better site between Santa Cruz and San Francisco than that at Branciforte.[52]

$1,720. *Prov. St. Pap.*, MS., xvii. 41. Feb. 4, 1799, a close watch to be kept on the coast. *Sta Cruz, Peep*, 13. Moraga must go on with his duties, for his chance of promotion depends on it. Better times coming if the wheat crop is cared for. The king will send his troops where they are needed, not where they wish to go. *Sta Cruz, Arch.*, MS., 62–3. March 6th, Borica wants information about a site for a rancho for horses and cattle near the villa. March 27th, if the settlers object, let nothing be done; the only object was to aid them. *Id.*, 61–2, 66; *Peep*, 15, 19. April 3d, Borica consents to dividing of sowing-lands. Will hold Moraga responsible for remissness of any settler in caring for his land. *Sta Cruz, Arch.*, MS., 62. May 12th, the settlers' two years at $116 per year expire to-day. *St. Pap., Miss. and Colon.*, MS., i. 380–1, 383. Oct. 16th, two settlers may go to San José and return on a fixed day. *Sta Cruz, Arch.*, MS., 65–6; *Peep*, 23. Nov. 21st, Sal notifies Moraga that Vallejo will supersede him as comisionado. *Id.*, 25. Dec. 26th, Sal to Vallejo, guns of the battery at Monterey to be fired. Don't be alarmed. *Id.*, 25, 27. Dec. 31st, Sal assures Borica that Vallejo will perform his duties faithfully. *Prov. St. Pap.*, MS., xvii. 289. Settlers must not make pleasure trips to San José. *San José, Arch.*, MS., iii. 59; *Sta Cruz, Arch.*, MS., 18. Jan. 3, 1800, settlers in need of corn and beans. The comisionado of San José to make a contract with some person to furnish these supplies at the expense of the government. *San José Arch.*, MS., iii. 55. Feb. 10th, Sal to Vallejo, at the end of 1799 the settlers owed the treasury $558; the appropriation for 1800 is $540, so that receiving nothing they would still be in debt. The delivery of cigarritos and other articles not rations and tools has been suspended. *Sta Cruz, Arch.*, MS., 63. Oct. 9th, aid to be furnished to the padres if asked for. *Sta Cruz, Peep*, 31. Dec. 5th, governor to viceroy, the Branciforte settlers are a scandal to the country by their immorality, etc. They detest their exile, and render no service. Daily complaints of disorders. *Prov. St. Pap.*, MS., xxi. 50–1. Dec. 11th, death of Comandante Sal announced at Branciforte. *Sta Cruz, Peep*, 45. The nine pobladores received in 1800 rations at $60 each. *Prov. St. Pap., Ben. Mil.*, MS., xxvi. 16.

[52] *Branciforte, El Discretorio de San Fernando al Virrey sobre el sitio de la Nueva Villa, 1797*, MS., Feb. 6th, Borica to viceroy, in *Prov. Rec.*, MS., vi. 70.

Independent of the explorations made with a view to new establishments, Borica had a scheme of opening communication with New Mexico, where, as he had heard from Governor Concha through General Nava, there were fifteen hundred gente de razon with neither lands nor occupation. He sent to Mexico early in 1795 for copies of Garcés' diary and map. Having obtained these he instructed Goycoechea of Santa Bárbara at the end of the year to make inquiries about the eastern country and to suggest some way to send a letter across to the governor of New Mexico by the natives, who could at the same time explore the route. In January 1796 Goycoechea sent to the governor such vague and unreliable rumors as he could gather from the natives of the channel respecting the country beyond the Tulares; and in February he informed Borica that he had made arrangements with the native chief, Juan María, and four companions to carry the letter, but that Father Tapis had forbidden their departure, at least until an order could be obtained from Lasuen.[53]

This state of the matter was reported to the viceroy in Borica's communication of October 2d,[54] and the attorney-general having reported favorably on the scheme of intercommunication as useful to California's commerce, development, and defence, the viceroy requested Borica to send to Mexico the maps and papers on which his project rested; that the project be also sent to the commandant general for his inspection; and that Lasuen forward his views about the employment of the Santa Bárbara Indians. This was in January 1797, and in April Lasuen answered,

[53] April 29, 1795, Borica to viceroy. *Prov. Rec.*, MS., vi. 44. Dec. 14th, Borica to Goycoechea. *Id.*, iv. 41, 46–7. Jan. 18th, Goycoechea to Borica. *Prov. St. Pap.*, MS., xiv. 16, 17. Feb. 16th, Id. to Id., *St. Pap., Sac.*, MS., iv. 74–7. Sept. 28th, Borica orders the padres to use gentle measures with the Tulare Indians so that there may be no difficulty on the proposed route. *Prov. Rec.*, MS., vi. 174. Sal's report of Jan. 31st, already alluded to, was probably in answer to similar inquiries sent him by the governor.

[54] *Borica, Informe sobre comunicacion con Nuevo Mexico, 1796*, MS. A similar communication dated October 5th is given in *Arch. Sta. Bárbara*, MS., x. 73–6.

arguing that it was dangerous to send a party of natives so far among foreign and hostile tribes, since on one side or the other excesses would surely be committed. Moreover the chief it was proposed to send was very useful to the mission and any accident to him would lead to trouble with his people; and finally Tapis had not forbidden the expedition, but had simply refused to urge the neophytes to undertake it.[55] Here, so far as the archives show, correspondence on this matter ceases. It is probable that more was written, but not likely that any actual expedition was made, and certain that communication was not opened with New Mexico. Neither was there anything accomplished toward opening the Colorado River route between California and Sonora, a subject slightly agitated during this period.[56]

[55] Jan. 11, 1797, viceroy to Lasuen. *Arch. Sta. Bárbara*, MS., x. 76-7. April 25th, Lasuen to V. R., *Id.*, 77-83. Feb. 14, 1798, V. R. calls for Arrillaga's ideas on the project and the best way to execute it. *Prov. St. Pap.*, MS., xvii. 9.

[56] April 16, 1795, Borica to viceroy, asks to have Fages send his papers relating to his expedition to the Colorado. *Prov. Rec.*, MS., vi. 44. Sept. 4, 1797, Borica thinks no party of less than 35 can safely pass to Sonora. *Id.*, vi. 53. Dec. 22, 1797, refers to Arrillaga's report and schemes of Oct. 26, 1796; 1st, a presidio of 100 men at Sta Olaya with 20 at S. Felipe and 20 at Sonoita; 2d, a presidio on California side at mouth of Colorado, to be crossed in canoes. Borica prefers the latter, and advises that all attention be given at present to pacification of the Indians between Sta Catalina and the Colorado. *Prov. Rec.*, MS., vi. 65-6. April 24, 1798, Amador says that the padre of San José went to the Colorado, and that the Indians fled, fearing enforced baptism. *Prov. St. Pap.*, MS., xvii 123. Reference to the general topic in *Azanza, Ynstruccion*, MS., 90.

CHAPTER XXVII.

MISSION PROGRESS.

1791–1800.

At the beginning of this decade the missions were eleven in number; at its end they had been increased by new establishments, as recorded in the preceding chapters, to eighteen—within three of the highest number ever reached.[1] In 1790 there were twenty-six friars on duty. Before 1800 there came up from the college thirty-eight new missionaries; twenty-one retired—some on the expiration of their regular term of ten years, others on account of failing health, four virtually dismissed for bad conduct, and four sent away more or less afflicted with insanity; while three died at their posts. This left forty still in the service, or two ministers for each of the eighteen missions and four supernumeraries. Six of the old pioneers who had come before 1780 were still left.[2]

[1] The seven new missions in the order of their founding were: Santa Cruz, Soledad, San José, San Juan Bautista, San Miguel, San Fernando, and San Luis Rey. There were subsequently founded Santa Inés, San Rafael, and San Francisco Solano. For a general statistical view of the missions in 1790 see chapter xix. of this volume.

[2] The original 26, the names of pioneers being italicized, were: Arroita, *Arenaza*, Calzada, *Cambon*, *Cruzado*, *Dumetz*, Dantí, *Fuster*, García, *Giribet*,

The average of integrity, zeal, and ability among the new friars was lower than in the case of Junípero Serra's companions, since a dozen or more were either refractory, immoral, inefficient, or insane; yet the list included such eminent names as Peyri, Payeras, Viader, Martinez, and Catalá, together with many faithful and efficient Christian missionaries.

The eleven old missions in 1790 had in round numbers 7,500 converts; in 1800 they had 10,700, a gain of 3,200 for the decade, 320 a year on an average, or about 30 a year for each mission. During the period the priests had baptized 12,300 natives, and buried 8,300, leaving 800 to be regarded as approximately the number of deserters and apostates. Meanwhile in the seven new establishments baptisms had been 3,800 and deaths 1,000, leaving 2,800 converts on the rolls. Thus for old and new missions together

Lasuen, Mariner, Miguel, Noboa, Orámas, Paterna, Peña, Pieras, Rubí, *Sanchez*, *Santa María*, Santiago, Señan, *Sitjar*, Tapis, and Torrens.

The new-comers, 38 in number, were: Abella, Barcenilla, Barona, Carnicer, Carranza, Catalá, Catalan, Ciprés, Cortés, Espí, Estévan, Faura, Fernandez (3), García, Gili, Gonzalez, Horra, Iturrate, Jaime, Landaeta, Lopez (2), Martiarena, Martin, Martinez, Merelo, Merino, Panella, Payeras, Peyri, Puyol, Salazar, Uría (2), Viader, and Viñals.

The deaths were Mariner, *Paterna*, and *Fuster*. There left California, 21: Arroita, Arenaza, Catalan, Dantí, Orámas, Espí, Fernandez (2), García, Rubí, Salazar, Gili, Giribet, Horra, Lopez, Torrens, Cambon, Noboa, Peña, Pieras, Merino. Lists of friars in different years, with general statements of numbers, in *St. Pap.*, *Miss.*, MS., ii. 4, 77–8, 100–2, 107–8; iii. 3–5; *Arch. Sta Bárbara*, MS., xii. 55–6, 61, 66, 68, 235; *St. Pap.*, *Sac.*, MS., iv. 14–17; *Prov. St. Pap.*, MS., xvii. 83–4. These lists, however, afford but a very small part of the *data* from which I have formed my local tables and biographies of padres, *data* which I have had to collect little by little from a thousand sources.

Arrivals in 1791 were Gili, Landaeta, Baldomero Lopez, and Salazar, intended for Santa Cruz and Soledad, or to replace others who were to be sent to those new missions while Cambon retired. In 1792 came Espí; and in 1793 Catalá, the latter as chaplain on a Nootka vessel. This same year Orámas and Rubí—the latter a black sheep of the Franciscan flock—departed, and Paterna, an old pioneer, died in harness. In 1794 five new priests were sent to California—men of a different stamp, it was thought, from those who had given the president so much trouble. *Mugártegui*, in *Doc. Hist. Cal.*, MS., iv. 39–40. These were Martin, Martiarena, Estévan, Manuel Fernandez, and Gregorio Fernandez. The departures were Noboa, Pieras, Peña, and Gili—the latter another source of scandal—who sailed on the *Concepcion*, Aug. 11th. *Prov. St. Pap.*, MS., xi. 157, 175, 202; xxi. 142, 146–7; *Arch. Arzobispado*, MS., i. 39. Viceroy's license dated Jan. 10th; governor's, May 31st. In 1795 Jaime, Ciprés, and Puyol came; while Salazar and Señan retired, the latter temporarily. *St. Pap.*, *Sac.*, MS., i. 50; *Prov. Rec.*, MS., vi. 47; *Prov. St. Pap.*, MS., xxi. 230. Dantí, Lopez, Calzada, and Arroita sailed in July

we have a total population of 13,500, a gain of 6,000 in ten years, during which time the baptisms had been 16,100 and the deaths 9,300.   There is no doubt that the deaths were largely in excess of the births, though there are no available means of accurately estimating the latter.[3]

The mission herds and flocks multiplied about three-fold during the decade.   Horses, mules, and horned cattle increased from 22,000 to 67,000; small stock, almost exclusively sheep—goats having diminished very rapidly and swine being comparatively few—from 26,000 to 86,000.   Agricultural products had been 30,000 bushels in 1790, the smallest subsequent crop being also 30,000 in 1795, and the largest 75,000 in 1800.   About three fifths of the whole crop in 1800 was wheat, which was less proportionately than usual, one fifth corn, and one tenth barley, the remainder being beans, pease, and various grains.   Wheat yielded

or August 1796. Other priests wished to retire, but the guardian thought, as they had been eager to come to California, it was best not to permit them to leave without the most urgent reasons. *Arch. Sta Bárbara*, MS., xi. 56–7, 274; *St. Pap.*, *Sac.*, MS., xvii. 8; *Prov. St. Pap.*, MS., xxi. 246; *Prov. Rec.*, MS., vi. 163. The new-comers of 1796, arriving in June by the *Aranzazu*, were: Payeras, José María Fernandez, Peyri, Viader, and Cortés. *Prov. St. Pap.*, MS., xiv. 139; *Prov. St. Pap.*, *Ben. Mil.*, MS., xxiv. 7; also Catalan and Horra. In April 1797 the *Concepcion* is said to have brought 11 priests. *Prov. St. Pap.*, MS., xvii. 145–6; xxi. 254; but there were really only 7: Barcenilla, Carnicer, Gonzalez, Martinez, Merino, Uría, and Panella. The same vessel carried back to San Blas in September, García and Arenaza, who were ill and had served out their term; and also the insane priests José María Fernandez and Concepcion de Horra. *Prov. Rec.*, MS., vi. 94, 98, 192; *Prov. St. Pap.*, MS., xxi. 264; *Arch. Sta Bárbara*, MS., xi. 57–8; *St. Pap.*, *Sac.*, MS., vi. 107–8. On her next trip the *Concepcion* brought to Santa Bárbara in May 1798 Señan and Calzada, returning from a visit to Mexico, and also the six new friars: Barona, Faura, Carranza, Abella, Martinez, and Viñales. *Arch. Arzobispado*, MS., i. 47; *Prov. Rec.*, MS., vi. 75–6; *Prov. St. Pap.*, MS., xvii. 19; xxi. 279; *St. Pap.*, *Sac.*, MS., viii. 13. Manuel Fernandez and Torrens retired this year, as did PP. Landaeta and Miguel temporarily. *Arch. Sta Bárbara*, xi. 60; *St. Pap.*, *Sac.*, MS., vi. 107. *Prov. St. Pap.*, MS., xvii. 2, 3. In 1797 Merelo, Jacinto Lopez, and José Uría arrived; while Espí, Giribet, Merino, and Catalan, the last two afflicted with insanity, obtained leave to retire, sailing in January 1800. This last year of the decade Fuster and Mariner died; Landaeta and Miguel came back; and García and Iturrate were added to the force, some of them apparently against their wishes. *Prov. Rec.*, MS., vi. 127–9, 243; ix. 12; xi. 144; xii. 1; *Prov. St. Pap.*, MS., xxi. 30, 44, 292; *St. Pap.*, *Sac.*, MS., vii. 77; *Arch. Sta. Bárbara*, MS., ix. 24; xi. 61–2; 281–2, 284.

[3] The governor in a report of 1800 states that the number of deaths is almost double that of births. *Bandini, Doc. Hist. Cal.*, MS., No. 3.

on an average fifteenfold, barley eighteenfold, and corn
ninety-threefold for the ten years.

Fermin Francisco Lasuen remained at the head of
the Franciscan community as president, performing
his duties to the satisfaction of all classes, loved and
respected by friars, officers, soldiers, settlers, and
neophytes. He received no pay for his services, being
a supernumerary friar, and no stipend being allowed
except to the two regular ministers of each mission.
The duties of the supernumeraries were as arduous,
and those of the president more so, than those of the
ministers, yet though petitions were made and the
viceroy was disposed to grant them in Lasuen's favor,
the attorney general always interposed objections.
Dumetz and Peña held patents after Mugártegui's
departure to assume the presidency in case of accident.[4] The power to administer the sacrament of
confirmation, granted by the pope in May 1785,
expired May 4, 1795, although Lasuen had actually
exercised it only since 1790, or half the full period.
The privilege was never renewed, and there were no
more confirmations until California possessed a bishop
of her own.[5] The ordinary episcopal powers of administering sacraments other than confirmation were
conferred on the president by the bishop of Sonora.
As *vicario foraneo* Lasuen exercised those powers
toward the civilians, and as *vicario castrense* toward
the military; that is to say, as a kind of chaplain

[4] *Arch. Sta Bárbara*, MS., xi. 220, 260–3. Viceroy Revilla Gigedo in
his report of 1793, *St. Pap., Miss. and Colon.*, MS., i. 18, 24, implies that
missionaries are often removed unnecessarily by their prelate; but it does
not clearly appear that he refers particularly to California, where he says
the friars perform their duties in a most commendable manner. See pope's de-
crees of July 8, 1794, and Dec. 12, 1797 on qualifications, duties, honors, etc., of
friars of the Propaganda Fide colleges, in *Arch. Sta Bárbara*, MS., x. 109–
36; ix. 37–40; *Prov. St. Pap.*, MS., xiii. 272–3.

[5] Sept. 9, 1792, pope's license forwarded from Mexico. *Arch. Sta Bárbara*,
MS., x. 289; yet Lasuen says he received the power on July 13, 1790. *S. Diego,
Lib. de Mision*, MS., 45. Expires May 4, 1795. *Arch. Sta Bárbara*, MS., xi.
233; *Prov. St. Pap.*, MS., xx. 284. April 3, 1795, Borica to Lasuen, learns
that the president is hurrying through the province to use his privilege
while it lasts. *Prov. Rec.*, MS., vi. 144–5.

general. The new bishop renewed the concession in 1796, and Lasuen subdelegated the authority to his subordinate missionaries.[6] Lasuen was also comissary of the holy inquisition for California after 1795, but so far as the records show his only duties in this capacity were to receive and publish an occasional edict on general matters.[7]

In an exhaustive report on the missions of New Spain Viceroy Revilla Gigedo presented to the king in 1793 an historical, descriptive, and statistical view of the Californian establishments, which is an interesting and important document, though expressing only *en résumé* what I have presented in detail from the same original papers on which this report was founded. An effort was made also about this time by the Spanish and Mexican authorities to insure greater regularity and thoroughness in reports of missionary progress.[8] Father Salazar having returned

[6] Sept. 30, 1796, bishop to Lasuen, confirming faculties. Dec. 16th, Lasuen to bishop, expressing thanks. March 20, 1797, Lasuen takes the oath as vicario foraneo before P. Arenaza. June 19th, bishop reserves the right of granting divorce and some other episcopal faculties. *Arch. Sta Bárbara*, MS., xii. 192–8. Dec. 18, 1796, Lasuen's circular to the padres. *Id.*, xi. 139–41. March 20, 1797, Lasuen notifies Borica. Is only awaiting the license and blessing of the guardian. *Arch. Arzobispado*, MS., i. 45. March 22d, B. to Lasuen, will proclaim him juez vicario eclesiástico in the presidios. *Prov. Rec.*, MS., vi. 184–5. June 20th, B. says the title of vicar must be presented to the government. *Id.*, vi. 192–3. It appears that *castrense* powers were conferred by Lasuen on only seven friars. *Arch. Sta Bárbara*, MS., xi. 145–6.

[7] Oct. 15, 1795, Lasuen's *patente de Comision del Santo Oficio* sent from Mexico. *Arch. Sta Bárbara*, MS., xi. 56. Several edicts of 1795, 1797, and 1800 in *Arch. Misiones*, MS., i. 187–8, 228; *Doc. Hist. Cal.*, MS., iv. 67–8. In offences of which the inquisition had cognizance the natives were not directly subject to that tribunal but to the provisor de Indias, who, with the knowledge of the inquisition, acted as judge. *Privilegios de Indios*, MS., 6. Some additional items on ecclesiastical matters are given later in this chapter.

[8] *Revilla Gigedo, Carta sobre misiones de 27 de Diciembre de 1793*, in *Dicc. Univ.*, v. 427–30; also MS., i. See also chap. xxiv. of this volume. Oct. 22, 1794, viceroy to governor, urging compliance with royal order of March 21, 1787, which required attention to mission welfare and reports every two or three years on mission progress. *Prov. St. Pap.*, MS., xi. 203. July 28, 1795, Branciforte sends Borica a copy of his predecessor's report of 1793 to serve as a guide for new reports; and also calls for suggestions. *St. Pap., Miss. and Col.*, MS., i. 1. Jan. 2, 1795, Lasuen in a circular says the council of the Indies have read the mission reports and thank us in king's name for progress made, which is great compared with other missions with better advantages. The guardian sends the thanks of the college. *Arch. Sta Bárbara*, MS., ix. 320–1.

from California was called upon by the viceroy for a report on the condition of the country, which was rendered May 11, 1796, but contained little of value respecting the missions. Salazar estimated the wealth of the Franciscan establishments at $800,000 in buildings and chattels; but he complained that progress was impeded by the excessive labors imposed upon the friars; also by the preference shown to settlers in the purchase of supplies.[9]

On the subject of secularization, not referring particularly to California, Revilla Gigedo expressed his dissatisfaction with the condition of such missions as had been given up to the clergy. He would take no steps in that direction without a better prospect of success. Curates could do no better than friars in the instruction and improvement of the natives.[10] In a letter of 1796 Governor Borica says that according to the laws, the natives are to be free from tutelage at the end of ten years, the missions then becoming *doctrinas;* "but those of New California at the rate they are advancing will not reach the goal in ten centuries; the reason, God knows, and men know something about it."[11]

Two special projects for the advancement of Californian interests were devised in Mexico during the decade; and both, being opposed by the Franciscan authorities, seem to have been given up at the end of 1797. The first was to establish a Carmelite monastery at San Francisco, which was to consist of twelve friars, and cost from $25,000 to $30,000. It was to be supported by an agricultural establishment, become the nucleus of a settlement, and thus promote both the colonization of the country and the civilization of the natives, to say nothing of the usefulness of the monastery towers to navigators as landmarks. This matter was referred to two friars who had been in

[9] *Salazar, Condicion Actual de Cal., Informe General al Virey, 11 de Mayo 1796,* MS.
[10] *Revilla Gigedo, Carta de 1793,* MS., 25.
[11] Aug. 3, 1796, Borica to Alberni. *Prov. St. Pap., Ben. Mil.,* xxiv. 7, 8.

California and who reported adversely. The second project was to establish a hacienda of the pious fund in Jacopin Valley near San Diego, but the guardian of San Fernando pronounced the scheme impracticable if not absurd. The general argument of the Franciscans on these questions was, that so far as the conversion of the natives was concerned the old methods were sufficient, and any innovation would be dangerous; and that for the promotion of settlement by gente de razon the new establishments would have no advantages over the old, which were far from prosperous.[12]

The regulation of 1781, as we have seen, provided for the gradual reduction of the ministers to one at each mission. Until this was effected friars retiring or dying were not to be replaced. This regulation was disregarded by the friars and the secular authorities made no attempt to enforce it. The subject came up and was discussed during this decade, but nothing was effected. The law remained unchanged, and was practically disregarded as before.[13] Respecting the re-

[12] Dec. 4, 1795, viceroy to governor, in *Prov. St. Pap.*, MS., xiii. 34; *Mugártegui* and *Peña, Parecer sobre el Establecimiento de un Convento en el Puerto de San Francisco, 28 de Enero de 1797*, MS. These padres declare that aid from the Carmelites in founding new missions would be acceptable. *Calleja, Respuesta del Guardian al Virey sobre Proyectos de California, 1797*, MS. This report, dated Oct. 23d, is chiefly devoted to another subject, of which more anon. It is noticeable that the guardian speaks very ironically of the 'domesticated' gentiles whose services it was proposed to utilize in the new establishments, greatly exaggerating the danger of the old missions and pueblos from the natives, and implying without intending to do so that not much had been effected by nearly 30 years of missionary work. Borica also disapproved of the hacienda because there would be no market for produce. *Prov. Rec.*, MS., vi. 61.

[13] Revilla Gigedo, *Carta de 1793*, 24, disapproves the reduction, among other reasons because it would favor immorality on the part of the friars. April 30, 1796, the guardian writes to Lasuen that the fiscal wants to know the reasons for non-compliance with the reglamento; consequently all the documents on the subject are needed, only one or two being in the college archives. *Arch. Sta Bárbara*, MS., xi. 275–6. Nov. 16, 1797, Borica to viceroy, thinks the matter should be settled, as there is a deficit of $52,142 in the mission fund. He suggests that two padres be allowed to each mission, but that only one *sínodo* of $400 be divided between them, since they now spend no more than that on themselves. *Prov. Rec.*, MS., vi. 60–1. Sept. 3, 1699, Padre Lull, *Exposicion del Guardian sobre la reduccion de Misioneros en California, 1799*, MS., presents the usual arguments against reducing the number of missionaries, and also opposes Borica's scheme of reducing the *sínodo*, not only because it is contrary to the king's intentions, but because, while, as Borica says, the

tirement of friars to Mexico there was now no controversy between the secular and Franciscan authorities,
because the latter were considerably troubled to keep
the missionaries at their posts, and welcomed even
secular interference to aid in the task.   In 1795 there
came a royal order that the governor and president
might grant license to retire for due and certified
cause without waiting for a report from Mexico; but
before the end of this decade this rule seems to have
been modified.[14]   Since 1787 and down to 1794 friars
coming to or returning from California were allowed
two hundred dollars for travelling expenses on land
and ninety-five cents per day while on the water.
Subsequently their stipends were allowed to cover the
time consumed on the journey provided there were
no unnecessary delays.[15]

two priests spend less than $400 on themselves they spend the remainder for
the natives, and this is practically the only way of obtaining necessary articles since there is no market for mission produce. In 1800, or perhaps later,
Lasuen in a letter to the guardian argues the same side of the case most
earnestly, speaks rather bitterly of any scheme to economize on the pay of
poor over-worked friars when the king is so liberal in other expenses, and repeats his old determination to retire if the change be insisted on. *Lasuen, Correspondencia*, MS., 329–33.

[14]1793, a priest retired on a provisional license of the comandante at Monterey. *Arch. Arzobispado*, MS., i. 33.   1794, the 10 years of service to count
from the date of embarking from Spain. *Arch. Sta Bárbara*, MS., vi. 294–
5. Royal orders referred to in my text dated Sept. 16, 1794. Sent from Mexico June 8, 1795. *Prov. St. Pap.*, MS., xiii. 124–5. Just before the receipt
of this order Borica refuses Danti's petition to retire until leave is obtained
from Mexico. *Prov. Rec.*, MS., vi. 149. Dec. 9, 1797, viceroy to the guardian, friars must not go to Mexico to solicit license to retire to Spain. *Arch.
Sta Bárbara*, MS., xi. 59. Sept. 1, 1800, governor to viceroy, understands
that no leave to retire is to be given, even on expiration of term, until substitutes arrive. The priests are not pleased at this. *Prov. St. Pap.*, MS., xxi. 42.
[15] On measures adopted 1786–8, see *Arch. Sta Bárbara*, MS., x. 267–70;
xi. 52–3, 241–2; xii. 40–1; *Prov. St. Pap.*, MS., vi. 202–3; viii. 1–3. It
seems that the $200 was to be paid, like the stipend, from the pious fund, which
in 1787 was charged with $3,944 for friars' travelling expenses for the past 20
years. In December 1793 the guardian attempts to secure travelling expenses
for supernumerary friars going to California, and succeeds after some correspondence in getting an advance of their stipend to pay those expenses,
though their stipend would cease on arrival until assigned to a mission. From
this correspondence it appears that by royal order of April 20, 1793, the stipend began on the date of departure from Mexico. *Arch. Sta Bárbara*, MS.,
xi. 246–51. By order of Sept. 16, 1794, the stipend was extended to date of
arrival in Mexico on return and all gratuities for travelling expenses were
abolished. *Prov. St. Pap.*, MS., xiii. 124–5; *Arch. Sta Bárbara*, MS., ix.
324–5; *Vallejo, Doc. Hist. Cal.*, MS., xxviii. date July 20, 1795. The friars
subsequently had much trouble on account of the naval authorities who
demanded $2.25 per day instead of 95 cts. Moreover the government in some

Many of the old matters of dispute still remained open, but as a rule they gave rise to no very bitter controversy during this period. No regular chaplains were appointed, though Borica made an effort to secure such appointments; neither does it appear that the friars got any pay for attending to the spiritual interests of soldiers and settlers.[16] In the matter of mission escorts and their duties there were no radical changes and few disputes. The soldiers were instructed to treat the padres always with respect and evidently did so, the chief complaint being that they would not always serve as vaqueros and servants of all work, a refusal the padres could never quite understand. The guard furnished to a friar engaged in his several duties abroad was still regulated by the governor's or commandant's instructions, or in some cases left to the corporal's discretion. The friars desired discretionary powers, but submitted. The strict rule of Fages that no soldier on escort duty should sleep away from the mission was relaxed somewhat in urgent cases by the viceroy's orders; but the order that no soldier should be sent after fugitive natives or allowed to visit the rancherías of gentiles without superior command was strictly enforced, and the friars, now that their temper had cooled a little, doubtless recognized the necessity of such a rule. The instructions of Borica to the guards show an earnest desire to maintain harmonious relations with the missionaries, as well as a prudent and wise policy toward the gentiles. Doubtless the patience of the friars was often sorely tried by the indolence

cases when the return voyage was very long by no fault of the priests refused to pay the full stipend as per royal order. *Arch. Sta Bárbara*, MS., ix. 41–5, 23–5.

[16] Sept 26, 1793, governor to viceroy asking for a friar for each presidio, as the missionaries have too much to attend to. *Prov. St. Pap.*, MS., xxi. 117. June 18, 1794, viceroy must have more information before deciding. *Id.*, xi. 181–2. November 28th, gov. circulates nine questions on the performance of chaplain's duties by padres; and April 3, 1795, explains more fully to the V. R. asking again for chaplains at a salary of $400. *Prov. Rec.*, MS., iv. 122; vi. 41–2. Nothing more is heard from Mexico. June 17, 1796, Comandante Goycoechea complains of the padres having declined to hear confessions. *St. Pap., Sac.*, MS., ix. 73.

and insolence of individual soldiers, but of the government they had no cause to complain. The guards
were reduced in most of the old missions on the establishing of new ones, and this brought out a protest
from the Franciscans, which was in some instances
successful.[17]

Desertion of neophytes became prevalent, especially
in the northern missions, the pretended motive of the
fugitives, and in some instances the real one, being
ill-treatment, overwork, and hunger; but oftener the
true cause of apostasy was a longing for the old freedom and dread of the terrible death-rate in the mission communities. As we have seen, the soldiers of
the guard were not allowed to pursue runaways;
neither was the practice of sending neophytes after
them, approved by Fages, allowed during Borica's
rule. Gentiles might be bribed to bring them in;

[17] Borica, Instruccion para la Escolta de San Juan Bautista, 1797, MS. This
document was ordered to be posted in every mission for the guidance of the
corporal. Sal, Instruccion al Cabo de Sta Cruz, 1791, MS.; Fages, Instruc.
para la Escolta de Purísima, 1788, MS.; Id., Instruc. para S. Miguel, 1787,
MS. Prohibition of escorts for long distances, approved by king, Jan. 13,
1790. Fages, Papel de Puntos, MS., 155. 1794, soldiers to be alternated in
escolta and presidio service. Prov. St. Pap., MS., xii. 8; Prov. Rec., MS.,
v. 48. Muskets to be fired and reloaded once a week. Some complaint of
failure to keep watch at night. No escorts for long distances. Arrillaga,
Papel de Puntos, MS., 196–7. May 15, 1795, escorts of padres must return
to mission same day. Prov. Rec., MS., iv. 133. June 3d, Borica to viceroy.
The padres still ask for escorts to visit rancherías; but I attribute present
tranquillity to the measures of my predecessor and refuse. We must not risk
our peace in the hands of a careless soldier. Prov. Rec., MS., vi. 52. Oct.
5th, approval of V. R. Prov. St. Pap., MS., xiii. 42–3; but on Nov. 7th the
V. R., on petition of the guardian, recommends concessions in urgent cases,
always with due prudence. Id., xiii. 65–6. On this ground, Lasuen, March
5, 1796, informs the padres that the old restriction has been removed, the
matter never having been properly understood in Mexico before. Doc. Hist.
Cal., MS., iv. 56; Arch. Sta Bárbara, MS., xi. 137. Corporal at Soledad
had to give monthly reports on manufactures, etc. Prov. Rec., MS., iv. 179.
Must keep a diary of events to be sent in every month. St. Pap., Sac., MS.,
vi. 1. Escoltas to build themselves houses to save paying rent. Prov. St.
Pap., MS., xiv. 175. June 9, 1796, padres to have escorts on journeys, or
on going to confess, etc., but not to pursue fugitives. Prov. Rec., MS., iv.
64; v. 86. No aid to padres to punish Indians unless two agree; but to alle-
viate suffering the request of one to suffice. Id., v. 89. April 29, 1797,
Argüello reprimands a corporal for having furnished only one soldier to escort
seven padres. Prov. St. Pap., MS., xvi. 57. Lasuen, Informe Bienal, 1797–8,
MS., 67–8, objects to the reduction of the guard in the old missions. Oct.
11, 1799, the guardian complained to the V. R. that the escoltas were too
small; and the report was sent to Borica on Dec. 17th. Prov. St. Pap., MS.,
xviii. 148–9.

and occasionally an expedition of presidio soldiers was sent out to make a wholesale collection of apostates, but such raids were not yet very frequent. Kind treatment of returned fugitives was required by the governor, and was to a large extent enforced. Neophytes sometimes stowed themselves away on the San Blas vessels, or escaped by land to Sonora.[18]

The laws required an alcalde and several regidores to be elected annually in each mission, a policy which had in earlier times met with considerable opposition from the padres, who insisted that the natives were by no means fitted for self-government even to this slight extent. After 1792 these elections ceased altogether until Borica brought up the matter in 1796 and insisted with the viceroy's approval on the enforcement of the law. President Lasuen obeyed, but in his instructions to the padres he clearly indicated that the election was to be a mere formality and the authority of the native officials merely nominal, the whole system being intended simply for the instruction of the neophytes in the forms of civil government with a view to the time when the missions should be secularized. After 1796 the elections were regularly reported to the governor each year, and the padres sometimes caused the choice to fall on a trusty neophyte who could be allowed to exercise slight authority as a kind of overseer. The gov-

[18] 1791, Fages' policy of sending neophytes. *Fages, Papel de Puntos*, MS., 154-5. Jan. 15, 1794, governor to viceroy. Progress has been made in the reduction of gentiles and fugitives by gentle measures. A chief has even brought in fugitives voluntarily. *Prov. St. Pap.*, MS., xxi. 131. 1795, Borica approves sending pagans after fugitives. *Prov. Rec.*, MS., v. 69. 1796, fugitives to be treated well. *Prov. St. Pap.*, MS., xix. 176. 1797, viceroy forbids any Indian being taken to Mexico. *Prov. Rec.*, MS., vi. 195. 1798, ninety fugitives of Santa Cruz recovered by soldiers. *Prov. St. Pap.*, MS., xvii. 101. Nov. 8, 1798, viceroy to Lasuen, disapproves the sending of neophytes after fugitives, except in extreme cases after consultation with the governor. *Arch. Sta Bárbara*, MS., vi. 75. Mar. 4, 1799, Lasuen instructs the padres accordingly. *Id.*, xi. 146-7; Lasuen's original order in *Doc. Hist. Cal.*, MS., iv. 71-3. July 22, 1799, governor to padres of San Juan. They may send Indians after fugitives to peaceful rancherías. *Prov. Rec.*, MS., vi. 242. Flight of Indians to San Blas and Sonora. *Prov. St. Pap.*, MS., xi. 209; xxi. 185; *Prov. Rec.*, MS., iv. 58. On fugitives from San Francisco where the most trouble occurred see chapter xxxi. of this volume.

ernment did not choose to interfere so long as the prescribed formalities were complied with.[19] The secular authorities still found fault because the neophytes were permitted to ride and thus fitted to be formidable foes in the future; but the friars, while appreciating the danger and admitting that one white man was equal to six or eight Indians to care for their herds, claimed that as there were no Spaniards to be had even if the missions were able to pay for their services, they must necessarily employ natives as vaqueros.[20] In two local controversies elsewhere narrated, that is to say at Santa Clara respecting boundary lines between mission and pueblo and at San Francisco respecting the establishment of the rancho del rey, the friars were victorious in the first and defeated in the second, receiving strict justice at the hands of the authorities in California as well as in Mexico. Indeed, throughout this decade there was an evident disposition on the part of viceroy and governor to promote friendly relations; while guardian and president, especially the latter, were much more disposed than formerly to conciliatory methods.[21]

[19] On mission alcaldes before 1790 see *Prov. Rec.*, MS., i. 120; iii. 71, 170; *Arch. Sta Bárbara*, MS., x. 94–6. Sept. 22, 1796, Borica to Lasuen and to the padres, requiring compliance with the law. *Prov. Rec.*, MS., vi. 173; *Sta Cruz, Parroquia*, MS., 16; *Arch. Arzobispado*, MS., i. 44. Nov. 2, 1796, Lasuen's circular to the padres. *Arch. Sta Bárbara*, MS., xi. 138–9; vi. 118–19. Nov. 19, 1796, Borica to viceroy stating his action in the matter. *St. Pap., Sac.*, MS., iv. 66–7. Dec. 20, 1797, viceroy to Lasuen. *Arch. Sta Bárbara*, MS., x. 90–3. Dec. 2, 1796, Borica to Lasuen, approving the election of neophyte alcaldes and regidores who are to act generally under the padres' direction, but in criminal matters under the corporal of the escolta. *Prov. Rec.*, MS., vi. 178–9. Jan. 7, 1797, Borica orders padres of San Diego to depose a bad alcalde and elect a new one. *Id.* March 30, 1798, Borica tells padres of Soledad they were wrong in changing alcaldes without submitting the case to the government. *Prov. Rec.*, MS., vi. 210.

[20] This matter was pretty well settled before 1796 so far as the missions were concerned. *Prov. Rec.*, MS., iii. 64–5, 87; *Arch. Sta Bárbara*, MS., xi. 392–6; viii. 63. May 28, 1791, the governor says the Indians are getting too much meat to eat, are becoming too skilful riders, and are acquiring the insolence of Apaches. *Prov. St. Pap.*, MS., x. 150. Strict orders against any gentile or any Indian servant of soldier or settler being allowed to ride or to have arms. *S. José, Arch.*, MS., ii. 86; iii. 65.

[21] For the controversies at Santa Clara and San Francisco see chapter xxxi., this volume. Revilla Gigedo, *Carta de 1793*, MS., 24–5, dwells on the importance of promoting harmony with the friars. Jan. 2, 1795, Lasuen in a circular orders the padres to forward to him all consultations of the gov-

The leading controversy of the decade in Franciscan circles resulted from certain charges made against the missionaries by one of their own number, though in subsequent investigations the secular authorities became involved. The results of these investigations present the best information extant respecting the details of the mission routine in certain of its phases, and they will be used elsewhere in a chapter devoted to the subject; but here I present the matter only in a general way as a prominent historical event and as illustrating the missionary policy of the time. In 1797 Padre Antonio de la Concepcion Horra, who had come to California the same year, was sent back to Mexico by President Lasuen on a charge of insanity. Back at the college on July 12, 1798, Horra addressed a memorial to the viceroy in which, besides complaining bitterly of the treatment to which he had been personally subjected on a false charge of insanity, he made some serious charges against the Californian friars of cruelty and mismanagement. There was nothing in the document to indicate that the writer was of unsound mind, unless it was his closing request to be sent away because his life would be in danger if it were known that he had revealed prevalent abuses to the viceroy.[22]

ernor. *Arch. Sta Bárbara*, xi. 135. Catalá's reported hostility to settlers rebuked. *Prov. Rec.*, MS., vi. 169–70. In case of innovations the padres to be cautious and consult the president. *Lasuen, Correspondencia*, MS., 318–19. Dec. 14, 1796, Borica to Goycoechea, he must give the padres all needed aid by viceroy's order. *Prov. Rec.*, MS. iv. 86. Jan. 1797, corporals Moraga and Vallejo forced to apologize to Catalá for their rudeness. *Id.*, vi. 179–80; iv. 204–5. A padre must settle his troubles with a companion or appeal to the prelate; the governor will not interfere in such matters. *Id.*, vi. 197.

[22] *Horra, Representacion al Virey contra los Misioneros de California, 1798*, MS. Sitjar, Lasuen, and Miguel were the particular objects of Horra's wrath. Sitjar, offended at Padre Concepcion's criticisms, went to his intimate friend Lasuen, who believed the absurd story of insanity, and sent Miguel who treated him as a maniac, even laying violent hands on him and maltreating him all the way from San Miguel to Monterey where he was thrown into a fever, all of which could be proved by Peyri, the soldiers, and the surgeon. He cites many witnesses including Gov. Borica to prove that he is not mad, and others to prove his past services; but he can get no justice at the college because all there are friends of Lasuen. See also chapter xxvi., on Padre Horra's life and experience in California.

On August 31st the viceroy sent the representations of Horra to Borica, who was ordered to investigate and report on the truth of the charges. Borica accordingly despatched private instructions to the four commandants to send in answers to fifteen questions propounded on the manner in which the friars were discharging their duties.[23] This was on December 3d, and before the end of the month the required reports were made by Argüello, Goycoechea, Sal, and Acting Comandante Rodriguez; while Grajera sent in his reply in March 1799. These replies, especially those of Goycoechea and Sal, went far to support some of the mad friar's accusations.[24] The report which Borica probably made to the viceroy on receipt of his subordinates' statements is unfortunately not extant.[25] It was not apparently until this report, including those of the commandants, reached Mexico that anything whatever was known at the college of Horra's representation against the friars or of the resulting investigations. In February 1799 the guardian sent Lasuen a statement of the charges,[26] and a little later copies of other documents which were lost in crossing the gulf of California, and Lasuen did not receive the fifteen questions and the commandants' replies until September 1800. In October Tapis and Cortés of Santa Bárbara sent in to the president a long and complete reply to Goycoechea, whose statements had been more full than those of the others and slightly

[23] Aug. 31st, viceroy to Borica, in *Prov. St. Pap.*, MS., xvii. 49; *Borica, Quince Preguntas sobre Abusos de Misioneros, 1798*, MS.

[24] *Argüello, Respuesta á las Quince Preguntas sobre Abusos de Misioneros, 1798*, MS. Dated San Francisco, Dec. 11th, and more favorable to the padres than the others. *Goycoechea, Respuesta*, etc., MS., Sta Bárbara, Dec. 14th; *Sal, Respuesta*, etc., MS., Monterey, Dec. 15th; *Rodriguez, Respuesta*, etc., MS., San Diego, Dec. 19th; *Grajera, Respuesta*, etc., MS., San Diego, March 21, 1799.

[25] On Oct. 30, 1798, however, Borica in a letter to the viceroy expresses his opinion that the best way to insure the advancement of the natives was to form a reglamento for the whole mission routine, including instruction, food, dress, dwellings, care of sick, labor, punishments, and amusements, and to hold the president responsible for exact compliance with the rules; for at present his authority is sometimes disregarded. *Prov. Rec.*, MS., vi. 105–6.

[26] Feb. 6, 1800, guardian to president, in *Arch. Sta Bárbara*, MS., xi. 284–7.

less favorable to the friars.[27]   And finally president
Lasuen devoted himself from November 12, 1800, to
June 19, 1801, to the preparation of a comprehensive
exposition of the whole subject, which is not only the
leading production of the venerable author's pen, but
the most eloquent and complete defence and presentment of the mission system in many of its phases
which is extant.[28]   It is in a chapter on the mission
system and routine that the details of all these documents must be chiefly utilized as already intimated;
but it seems necessary to present here a general view
of the questions at issue, which difficult task I proceed to perform as briefly as possible.

It was the policy of the government and the duty
of the friars to introduce the Spanish language in place
of the vernacular, thus fitting the natives for future
citizenship.   Padre Concepcion accused the friars of
an almost total neglect of this duty.   According to
the commandants religious services and some teachings
of Christian principles were conducted daily in the
north in Spanish; in the south the natives were taught
in their own language, though the doctrina was often
repeated to them in Spanish.   In general intercourse
the vernacular was used wherever the friars had learned
it, and in some missions exclusively.   Nowhere were
the natives compelled to learn Spanish, and everywhere the friars were more or less indifferent on the
subject.   Padres Tapis and Cortés affirmed that at
Santa Bárbara the doctrina at mass was taught in
Spanish and in the afternoon either in one language
or another; but they admitted that the natives were
not required, only persuaded, to use the Spanish.
And finally Lasuen, while maintaining that it was use-

[27] *Tapis* and *Cortés, Réplica de los Ministros de Sta Bárbara á la Respuesta
que dió el Comandante Goycoechea á las quince preguntas de Borica sobre abusos
de Misioneros, 1800,* MS.   Dated Oct. 30th.   Other padres, not unlikely one
from each mission, sent in similar reports on the subject, but I have found
none of the documents except this.

[28] *Lasuen, Representacion sobre los Puntos representados al Superior Gobierno
por el P. Fr. Antonio de la Concepcion (Horra) contra los misioneros de esta
Nueva California, 1800,* MS., with autograph signature.

less to preach to the natives in a language they did
not understand, claimed that an honest effort was made
to teach Spanish, that exercises were conducted in
that language once a day, that the natives were compelled to use it in their petitions, that premiums were
offered for acquiring it, and moreover that the natives
were inclined to learn it.[29]

Respecting Horra's statement that natives were
baptized without sufficient instruction in the faith, and
then often allowed to return to the forest, to be re-
baptized perhaps at a later date, the commandants
thought the preliminary teaching of eight days or
more and rarely less might be sometimes too little,
some padres being more careful than others, and that
rebaptism might occur, though they knew of no instances where it had occurred. The padres claimed
that eight days was the minimum, that the instruction
was ample, and that a second baptism could never
happen under their system of registers. Lasuen knew
of but three cases of rebaptism out of 27,000 converts. All but Goycoechea agreed that neophytes
were never allowed to return to the woods and mountains except for definite periods and purposes. In
answer to the charge of insufficient food many details
were given of the rations actually served, which
though insipid and unvarying in quality seem to have
been sufficient in quantity. Sal and Goycoechea
deemed the amount of food too small for laboring
men; but Lasuen affirmed most earnestly that the
natives had all they wanted, not only of the everlast-
ing *atote* and *pozole*, but regular allowances of meat
and milk, with fish occasionally, and always a plate

[29] Revilla Gigedo understands that the natives permanently settled use
Spanish; but the friars learn the vernacular to advance their instruction.
Carta de 1793, MS., 14, 15. Feb. 19, 1795, Borica to president, enclosing
royal order that natives be taught Spanish. *Prov. Rec.*, MS., vi. 143. Feb.
23d, circular of president requiring padres to promote learning Spanish and
forbid the use of vernacular. *Arch. Sta Bárbara*, MS., xi. 120. Dec. 1798,
Borica says that Sitjar of San Miguel teaches in the vernacular. *Prov. Rec.*,
MS., vi. 115. March 21, 1799, Grajera says the natives at San Diego are
taught the doctrines in their own language by educated Indians, no effort
being made to teach Spanish. *Prov. St. Pap.*, MS., xvii. 192.

from the padres' table if asked for. The mission Indians were always fatter than the gentiles, their work was easier than that required to gain a subsistence in the old way, and the gentiles greatly preferred the Spanish grains to their wild seeds and fruits. Still, as the president admits, the neophytes did desert and plead hunger, and they were always glad to get permission to go to the *monte* for a time to live in the old way. Such permissions were given more freely in times of short supplies; but no Indian was ever compelled to go. As to the clothing of the neophytes there was a substantial agreement on the one or two blankets, breech-clouts or petticoats, and shirts given to each native every year or two, and no expression of opinion that the supply was not adequate to their wants, except by Sal.

The dwellings of the neophytes were, as Lasuen admitted, in many places like those of the gentiles, but cleaner, better on the Channel than elsewhere, and in some missions already replaced by adobe houses with tile roofs. These dwellings like the presidios and other buildings went through successive stages, and were improved as fast as possible. Unmarried females it was found necessary to lock up at night and to watch closely, but they were given generally the best room in the mission, and subjected to no hardships. In only a few missions were bachelors locked up or forced to sleep in the mission. On these points Horra had made no special charges except as they were included in the general one of ill-treatment.

On the subject of labor there was a radical difference of opinion. According to the commandants the working hours were from six to nine hours per day, varying with the season, with extra work on special occasions as in harvest-time. Task work was also common, but the tasks were so heavy that the time was not materially reduced. Women must carry adobes, stones, and bricks, and when with child or giving suck their tasks were not sufficiently dimin-

ished.   Children were employed at driving away birds
or at other lighter labor; the aged and sick were
exempt.   The friars on the contrary affirm that working hours were from four to six hours; that not more
than half the natives worked at the same time, the
rest escaping on some reason or pretext, for they were
always excused even when their plea was doubtful;
that many did little even when pretending to work;
that tasks were assigned whenever it was possible,
and so light that the workers were usually free in the
afternoon or a day or two in every week, and finally
that all proper allowances were made for women in
their various conditions.   Lasuen compares the mission tasks with those imposed on such natives as were
sent to work at the presidios where they were obliged
to toil from morning till night; and he ventures to
doubt the sincerity of the commandants' compassion
for the poor overworked neophytes.

The commandants in answering Borica's questions,
and indeed the governor in asking them, touched on
several points not included in Horra's accusations.
One complaint was that too short a time was allowed
to the neophytes for gathering wild fruits.   The
answer was that at Santa Bárbara one fifth of the
whole number were allowed every Sunday to go to the
monte for a week or two, and elsewhere a similar system was adopted.   If the converts are to be freed
from every restraint like the pagans, says Lasuen,
when are they to become civilized?   Another charge
of Sal and Goycoechea was that the natives were
carefully restricted from all intercourse with the gente
de razon, and were not allowed to visit the presidios
or to afford any aid to the soldiers, the missionaries
being afraid of losing their services.   These statements the friars denied as false and calumnious.
There was no effort to restrict intercourse except in
special cases with vicious persons; any neophyte was
free to visit the presidio on holidays or with leave of
absence, and none had ever been punished for helping

the soldiers, except sometimes for absconding. Moreover the presidios had always been supplied with servants of all kinds for no compensation save what the employers chose to pay, and neither missions nor natives had ever been benefited by this intercourse. The aborigines did not like to work at the presidios, where they were ill-treated and often cheated out of their pay; yet most of the work on the presidios had been done by laborers furnished from the missions.

"The treatment shown to the Indians," says Padre Concepcion, "is the most cruel I have ever read in history. For the slightest things they receive heavy floggings, are shackled, and put in the stocks, and treated with so much cruelty that they are kept whole days without a drink of water." The commandants, without expressing an opinion as to the propriety or undue severity of the punishments inflicted, simply specify those punishments, administered by the padres at will, as flogging, from fifteen to fifty lashes, or sometimes a novenary of twenty-five lashes per day for nine days, stocks, shackles, the *corma*—a kind of hobble—and imprisonment in some of the mission-rooms, for neglect of work or religious duties, over-staying leave of absence, sexual offences, thefts, and quarrelling among themselves. Rarely or for serious offences were the natives turned over to the military, or assistance asked from the soldiers. The friars admitted all this, except that they denied that more than twenty-five lashes were ever given,[30] affirming moreover that only at Santa Bárbara were women put in the stocks, and that they were very rarely flogged. They claimed that according to the laws they stood *in loco parentis* to the natives, must necessarily restrain them by punishments, and inflicted none but proper penalties, pardoning first offences, and always inclining to mercy and kindness. The soldiers were

[30] Sept. 26th, 1796, Borica says to a padre that only 25 lashes may be given; beyond this the matter belongs to royal jurisdiction. *Prov. Rec.*, MS., vi. 174.

not asked to render aid because Governor Neve had
opposed it; and natives were not sent to the presidio
because there they were ill-treated, used merely as
peons, could easily escape, and always came back
worse than ever.   Lasuen admits that there may have
been instances of undue severity, and that one missionary had been removed; but he denies the charges
of cruelty at San Francisco, which had had most
weight with Borica, and insists that for every instance
of apparent severity there have been many where the
commandants have blamed the friars for excessive
tolerance and yielding.[31]

Father Concepcion renewed the old complaint that
the padres in selling mission products to the presidios
disregarded the tariff of prices established by the
government. Although the president indignantly denied any variation from the legal rates, and although
the different statements are somewhat confusing in
detail, yet from the testimony of the officers and
from the admissions of Tapis and Cortés it is evident
enough that, except in the articles of wheat and corn
in ordinary years, and in the more ordinary qualities
of animals, little attention was paid to the price-lists
either by missionaries or any other class in California.
It was easy for the friars by pleading the needs of
the neophytes or the choice quality of the article
desired, to avoid selling or obtain an extra price; but
grain and ordinary live-stock they were almost always
glad to sell, and sometimes at less than the legal rates.
That wines and liquors were bought by the friars at
high prices in addition to the quantities obtained in
Mexico, was unsupported by any evidence. Finally
the missionaries were accused of having accumulated
wealth, though they pleaded poverty. To this the
commandants replied that they knew nothing of the

[31] See chapter xxxi. of this volume for the charge of cruelty at San Francisco, which Borica believed to be well founded; also *Prov. Rec.*, MS., v. 266;
vi. 97–8, 115, 172, 176; *Prov. St. Pap.*, MS., xvi. 88; *Id.*, *Ben. Mil.*, xxiv.
8–10. Instructions of the viceroy in 1793 and 1797, in favor of kindness and
mercy to the Indians so far as justice and caution may allow. *St. Pap.*, *Miss.
and Col.*, MS., i. 23–4.

mission wealth, because the friars kept the matter secret, and simply gave some figures respecting amounts paid and due for mission supplies to the presidios during the past year or two. The padres made no reply to the main charge, though announcing their readiness to reply when required to do so by their superiors; but they indignantly repelled the insinuation that there was anything in their financial management or condition kept secret from the government.[32]

Such was the controversy and such the statements presented on the leading points by both parties, though the résumé does but scanty justice to the subject, and especially to Lasuen's report, many of the minutiæ being necessarily omitted. The author manifests some dissatisfaction that the charges of a man who left California under such peculiar circumstances should have been made the basis of this investigation without a preliminary taking of testimony as to the state of his mind. He is indignant at the commandants, not only for what he regards as misstatements on certain details, but chiefly for what they failed to say and for what their silence implied. They had failed to refute

[32] Of the supplies furnished by missions to presidios the accounts preserved are very meagre and fragmentary, some of them being presented with local annals. Perhaps an average of $1,200 per year for each mission during this decade would be a fair estimate. This amount and the stipend of $800 for each mission was all the revenue of the padres to support themselves and keep their churches in order. So far as can be judged from the partial accounts of the procurador extant, the annual *memorias* of supplies ordered by the friars were fully equal to their credits. I think there was little foundation for the charge that the padres were accumulating money either at the missions or in Mexico in these early years. Balance against the missions Sept. 6, 1800, $11. Procurador's accounts in *Sta Cruz, Parroquia*, MS., 18. May 11, 1796, Salazar estimates the mission wealth, in buildings, etc., at $800,000. *Salazar, Condicion actual de Cal.*, MS., 66–7. Dec. 1798, Borica to viceroy, he never interferes in mission finances, and is merely informed at end of each year of produce existing. Both he and the commandants believe the padres to have large surpluses at Mexico and in the coffers at San Diego, San Juan, Capistrano, and San Gabriel. He advises investigation in Mexico. The president aids new missions abundantly. There are complaints of not following the tariff, but Borica expresses no opinion. *Prov. Rec.*, MS., vi. 116–17. Aug. 16, 1795, Lasuen to Borica, representing the injustice of keeping grain at the same low prices as in years of plenty. *Arch. Sta Bárbara*, MS., vi. 97–101. In 1793, Pedro A. de Anteparaluceta, canon of Puebla, left a legacy of $500 to the California missions, $36 apiece with $40 for Sta Bárbara and Soledad, and $60 for Sta Cruz. *Id.*, xi. 235. On mission trade for this period see next chapter. Lists of increase in church vestments, etc., 1794–5. *St. Pap., Miss.*, MS., ii. 15–27, 78–9.

the statements of ever-complaining neophytes whom their own observations must have shown to be unreliable witnesses; and because of certain petty quarrels about the services of the natives as peons at the forts, they had given weight to the charge of a madman and had done great wrong to the missionary cause. Lasuen claimed that he and his band of friars were working honestly for the conversion of the natives according to the well known rules of their order and the regulations of the Spanish government, by which they stood in the position of parents to the aborigines. He admits that, being but men, they differed from one another in judgment and patience, and consequently that errors were committed; but he affirms most earnestly that the natives were shown all the kindness that was consistent with the restraint implied in the missionary and parental relation. The venerable friar's words and manner impress the reader most forcibly, and a close study of the subject has convinced me that he was right; that down to 1800 and considerably later the natives were as a rule most kindly treated. We are by no means to conclude that the friars were now free from all blame in their quarrels with the secular authorities, or that they had lost the arbitrary spirit that had distinguished them in the days of Serra and Fages. Neither are their protestations of a scrupulous regard for the regulation in the details of business management to be implicitly credited; but in the matter of neophyte labor at presidio, pueblo, and rancho the friars here as elsewhere were usually right and the military wrong; and so far as they touched this point, cruelty to natives, or accumulation of wealth, Horra's charges must be regarded as for the most part unfounded. After reference to the fiscal and the usual delays, in April 1805 the viceroy rendered his decision, completely exonerating the missionaries.[33]

[33] April 19, 1805, viceroy to governor, the padres are cleared and are to continue in the same course of zeal and brotherly love, etc. Commandants

There are a few miscellaneous topics connected with the ecclesiastical administration of the province that may appropriately receive brief notice here. There were as yet no regularly appointed chaplains, and the friars continued to care for the spiritual interests of soldiers and settlers, apparently without any compensation. An income was, however, derived from the saying of masses for souls in purgatory, some soldiers leaving a large part of their small property to be thus expended, or during their own life paying fees for members of their families.[34] Most of the missions

are urged to promote harmony. *Prov. St. Pap.*, MS., xix. 2, 3. Same date, V. R. to guardian to same effect, the good name of the padres is nowise tarnished by P. Concepcion's charges—the emanations of an unsound mind. (Original document in my collection, reference lost.) A fragment of the fiscal's opinion is also extant. *Prov. Rec.*, MS., ii. 1–3. He advises that there be no sweeping decision because a few points may be proved. There is a natural conflict of interests between padres and commandants, since the latter have to come to the former for supplies, and the careful management and strict dealings of the friars are attributed to meanness or spite. Moreover there are dissensions between the Indians and soldiers, and on the reports of corporals punishments are inflicted which seem to the padres too severe. It is difficult to obtain testimony from disinterested parties in California. It is a pity the poor Indian has to be all his life in the service of others, never owns anything, and is fed on rations, yet it cannot now be helped.

It appears that early in the decade there had been an attempt to take from the padres the management of the temporalities, originated by some of the friars themselves. Jan. 30, 1794, P. Mugártegui, formerly of California, writes to Lasuen expressing in strong language his opposition to the proposition advocated by some members of the college to give up the temporalities. It would be a pity 'for the disconnected reasonings of two Mallorcan charlatans to stop the work begun by a holy Mallorcan.' Fortunately, however, the projects of the would-be reformers meet with but little encouragement, and the same may be said of the complaints of two other padres, Gili and Rubí, who have spoken against the California missionaries. *Mugártegui, Carta de 1794*, MS. April 30, 1791, the bishop of Sonora calls Lasuen's attention to the royal order of March 6, 1790, granting an ecclesiastical tax on all revenues, including those of missionaries; and asks him to collect 6 per cent. for four years on the stipends of all the friars and all other revenues. Lasuen replies that the California padres have no revenue, except the stipend of $400 each, given as alms, and even with that they have nothing to do except to name the articles needed for the churches. A *síndico* at the college collected the stipends and with them paid for the invoices. If the king wants to reduce the stipend by a tax, let the matter be arranged at the college; Franciscan friars have nothing to do or say about revenue matters. He sends a sworn statement, though regretting that his word does not suffice. *Arch. Sta Bárbara*, MS., x. 61–8. I hear no more of this matter. Sept. 19, 1799, Borica says that a royal order decides that temporalities are to be incorporated in the royal hacienda. *Prov. Rec.*, MS., iv. 174. 1795, 1798, director-general of temporalities (for America) appointed. *Prov. St. Pap.*, MS., xxi. 232, 289. 1792, 1796, governor signs certificates for the padres to get their stipends. *Arch. Arzobispado*, MS., i. 28; *Prov. Rec.*, MS., vi. 168.

[34] Santa Bárbara Mission received alms for 757 masses said from 1794 to 1800. *Arch. Sta Bárbara*, MS., ii. 134. The friars had also masses to say

had now a palisade or adobe enclosure serving as a cemetery. No pueblo, and of the presidios only San Diego, had a cemetery. It was customary to bury gente de razon in the churches or chapels, but the friars made an effort to break up the practice.[35]   Both soldiers and natives often escaped a flogging by taking advantage of their right of church asylum, and occasionally this taking refuge in the sacred edifice led to petty misunderstandings between the officers and friars, though there were no notable instances during this decade.[36]

The performance of religious duties by the people was rigidly enforced, as is shown by many orders in the archives.[37]   Papal bulls or indulgences were sent to California every two years, and such as were not sold were burned at the end of a specified time. The habilitado of Monterey was general administrator of this branch after 1797, and each commandant attended

for members of their order abroad.   Oct. 22, 1795, Lasuen says in a circular that the numerous deaths of friars at San Fernando and other colleges and *en route*, have burdened the community with over 7,000 masses.   Each padre is to say how many he can take. *Id.*, ix. 323–4.   Dec. 7, 1800, Lasuen orders mass and te deum on the accession of Pope Pius VII. *Id.*, xi. 148–9.

[35] Dec. 20, 1792, Lasuen to Arrillaga. *Arch. Arzobispado*, MS., i. 28–9. 1790, Señan refuses to bury María del Cármen Alviso in the presidio chapel. *Prov. St. Pap., Ben. Mil.*, MS., xx. 5, 6.   Two soldiers buried in the chapel at San Diego. *Prov. St. Pap., Presidios*, MS., i. 53, 60.

[36] July 29, 1794, governor orders an Indian culprit to be taken out of the church at Santa Clara by force since his offence was not subject to ecclesiastical immunity. *Prov. Rec*, MS., ii. 150.   Dec. 6, 1798, Lasuen certifies that he found a soldier in the church claiming asylum for having struck a woman. He was ordered on guard, and as there was no one to replace him Lasuen gave him a *papel de iglesia* to protect his right of asylum. *Arch. Arzobispado*, MS., i. 53.   Mar. 29, 1800, commandant of Monterey orders a soldier to be given up for trial on bail. *Id.*, ii. 5–6.

[37] March 28, 1793, Arrillaga to commandants.   All officers and men by 3d day of Pentecost are to show certificates of having complied with church rules. *St. Pap., Sac.*, MS., i. 113.   April, 1795, Padres of Sta Cruz, Sta Clara, and S. Francisco certify to those who have complied with the annual precept of confession and communion. *Prov. St. Pap.*, MS., xiii. 234–8, 242–4. Sept. 29, 1795, Sal to comisionado of San José.   Tobar is sent to the pueblo; if he does not confess within 15 days he is to be sent to Monterey in irons. He must also go to work. *San José, Arch.*, MS., iv. 27.   Jan. 14, 1798, Lasuen in a circular regrets the carelessness of many.   All must commune on easter and be examined in the doctrina. *Arch. Sta Bárbara*, MS., xi. 144–5.   June 6th, Corporal Peralta is to arrest any of the San José Mission guard and keep them so until they perform their duties. *Prov. St. Pap.*, MS., xvii. 107. Roman, the tailor, must be kept handcuffed until he complies. *Prov. Rec.*, MS., iv. 110.   Arrellano to be shackled. *Prov. St. Pap.*, MS., xxii. 24.

to his own district. Some statistics on the subject are given in connection with local annals. So far as can be determined from the records the annual revenue from this source was from fifty to a hundred dollars.[38] A sacred image of our lady of Guadalupe sent to California in 1795 was by license of the highest ecclesiastical authorities allowed to be touched by the original picture. In one instance the soldiers established a kind of rancho where was raised a herd devoted to decorating the image of the virgin.[39]

[38] *Prov. Rec.*, MS., iv. 148, 296; *Prov. St. Pap.*, MS., ix. 241; xv. 42–3, 48, 77–8; xvi. 98, 220; *Id., Ben. Mil.*, MS., xxviii. 9; *St. Pap. Miss.*, MS., ii. 65; *S. José, Arch.*, MS., vi. 42. The bulls sent sold from 2 reals, or 25 cents, to $2 each. The different kinds were *vivos, laticinios, composicion,* and *difuntos.*

[39] *Prov. St. Pap.*, MS., ix. 194–5; xiii. 79.

CHAPTER XXVIII.

PUEBLOS, COLONIZATION, AND LANDS—INDUSTRIES AND INSTITUTIONS.

1791–1800.

PUEBLO PROGRESS—STATISTICS—JORDAN'S PROPOSED COLONY—EFFORTS OF GOVERNMENT—MARRIAGE ENCOURAGED—INNS—VIEWS OF SALAZAR, SEÑAN, AND COSTANSÓ—WOMEN WANTED—CONVICTS—FOUNDLINGS—TENURE OF LANDS—PUEBLO AND MISSION SITES—CHRONOLOGICAL STATEMENT, 1773–90—PRESIDIAL PUEBLOS—PROVISIONAL GRANTS—LAND-TITLES AT END OF CENTURY—LABOR—INDIAN LABORERS—SAILORS—ARTISAN INSTRUCTORS—MANUFACTURERS—MINING—AGRICULTURE—FLAX AND HEMP—STOCK-RAISING.

THE missions, as may be seen from the preceding sketch, if we regard only the primary object for which they were founded, were successful and prosperous. Given a band of earnest and able missionaries, a friendly native population, and a military force for protection if needed, there was nothing to prevent success and prosperity in a land so blessed by nature. The government had nothing more to do in the matter. If the towns were less successful in their efforts at colonization and progress it was not because they were deemed of less importance or received less attention. Nor was it because the colonization system was less judiciously managed by the crown than the missionary system by the Franciscans. It was because this problem was more complicated than the other. It would not solve itself, and faithful provincial officers with wise regulations could not solve it. It is not necessary to claim that the king's officers were as devoted to the welfare of the towns as the friars to that of their missions, for they had other duties and lacked the incentive of holy zeal; but had their opportunities, their authority, and their enthusiasm corresponded to and exceeded those of the missionaries, they never could have made the pueblos prosper. Two fatal obstacles to success were the worthless character of the original settlers, most of them half-breeds of the least energetic classes of Nueva Vizcaya and Nueva Galicia, and the lack of provincial commerce to stimulate industry; for before 1800 the settlers could not have sold additional products of their fields.

I give elsewhere the local annals of the three Californian pueblos, San José, Los Angeles, and Branciforte—the latter honored with the title of villa—during this decade.[1] The united population of the three towns in 1800 was about 550 in something over a hundred families, including a dozen or fifteen men who raised cattle on ranchos in the vicinity and whose families for the most part lived in the pueblos. About thirty families had been brought from abroad as settlers and had been paid wages and rations and otherwise aided for a term of years; while the increase came from children who grew to manhood and from soldiers who had served out their term of enlistment and retired, often with pensions. These, although generally old men, were as a rule the most successful farmers. The only industries of the settlers were agriculture and stock-raising. They had 16,500 head of cattle and horses, about 1,000 sheep, and they raised about 9,000 bushels of grain each year, surplus products being sold to the presidios. Each settler had his field which he was required to cultivate, and he had to contribute a certain quantity of grain each year to the common fund from which municipal expenses were paid. Each pueblo had a small guard of soldiers, who were practically settlers also; and each in addition to its alcalde and regidores had a comi-

[1] See chapter xxix. of this volume for Angeles; chapter xxxii. for San José, and chapter xxvi. for Branciforte.

sionado, generally corporal of the guard, who represented the governor and reported directly to the commandant of the nearest presidio. Labor was largely done by hired gentiles. Los Angeles was more populous and prosperous than either of the others, while Branciforte was as yet but a burden to the government.

A Spanish visitor in 1792 stated in his narrative that soldiers in California when too old for service were not allowed to settle as farmers, and he criticised this state of things very unfavorably; but needlessly, for no such conditions existed. Many of the invalids went to live in the pueblos, a few obtained ranchos, and others remained at the presidios, performing a certain amount of military service. It was even permitted them to settle near the presidio but outside the walls, though it does not appear that any did so at this early period.[2] Alejandro Jordan's project for a colony to be established in the interests of trade under govermental protection and with somewhat extravagant emoluments for himself, was disapproved by the king on Arrillaga's advice, as already noted, after negotiations lasting from 1792 to 1794.[3] Revilla Gigedo in 1793 favored the settlement of some Spanish families at the missions, though he admitted the great difficulty of finding families possessing the required moral qualifications.[4] Costansó in his report of 1794 says: "The first thing to be thought of, in my opinion, is to people the country. Presidios to support missions are well enough for a time, but there seems to be no end of them. Some missions have been for a hundred years in charge of friars and presidial guards. The remedy is to introduce gente de razon among the natives from the beginning. Cali-

[2] *Sutil y Mexicana, Viage,* 162-3. Oct. 24, 1792, governor orders that no quiet *vecino* is to be prevented from settling at the presidio of Monterey. *Prov. Rec.,* MS., ii. 156. Vancouver gives a rather superficial and inaccurate account of the pueblos, which he did not visit. *Voyage,* ii. 495-6.

[3] See chapter xxiv., this volume.

[4] *Revilla Gigedo, Carta de 1793,* 23-4.

fornians understand this, and clamor for industrious
citizens. Each ship should carry a number of families
with a proper outfit. The king supplies his soldiers
with tools, why not the farmer and mechanic as well?
They should be settled near the missions and mingle
with the natives. Thus the missions will become
towns in twenty-five or thirty years."[5]

In 1795 Borica made some special efforts to promote marriage among soldiers and settlers by favorable
regulations, and he even discouraged the enlistment
of the sons of settlers in the presidio companies;
but an absurd proposition from Mexico to establish
inns for the convenience of travellers at ten suitable
spots in California met with no favor from Borica
and the project died a natural death.[6]

In 1796 a special agitation of this subject of colonization began in Mexico, with the founding of Branciforte as a result, as elsewhere narrated. Father
Salazar, lately from California, was called upon for
his views on the condition of the country. His report
on the pueblos was not an encouraging one. The inhabitants were idlers, paying more attention to gambling and playing the guitar than to tilling their lands
and educating their children. The pagans did most

---

[5] *Costansó, Informe, 1794,* MS.

[6] April 13, 1795, Borica to commandants, marriages to be promoted by
all honorable means. Soldiers to be aided with arrears of pay, with what
they have in the *fondos,* or even by an advance of $40. Parents of contract-
ing parties to be aided with such effects as can be paid for from their crops in
a year. *Estudillo, Doc. Hist. Cal.,* MS., i. 11; *Prov. Rec.,* MS., iv. 129–30;
Prov. St. Pap., MS., xiii. 227–8. Goycoechea's reply, May 15th. *Id.,* xiv.,
76. Nov. 19, 1796, B. directs the commandant of San Francisco to try and
prevail on María Simona Ortega, a widow, to remain in the country; for sooner
or later some soldier or civilian will ask her hand in marriage. *Prov. St. Pap.,*
Ben. Mil., MS., xxiv. 10, 11. Feb. 14, 1795, Grajera has received B.'s order
not to accept any recruit from Angeles, 'in order that the population may
not be lessened.' *Id.,* xxi. 7. March 12, 1795, B. to viceroy, explaining that
the population of California, which he gives as 1,275, is much too small for
the 10 inns proposed; also that travellers have to sleep out of doors to care
for their animals, etc. *St. Pap., Sac.,* MS., xvii. 3–6. Oct. 5th, the *tribunal
de contaduría* advises the V. R. to submit the scheme, recommended by Beltran, to a council before adopting it. *Prov. St. Pap.,* MS., xiii. 197–9. Oct.
15, 1796, B. asks for a list of settlers living on ranchos and for an opinion
whether they should be allowed to do so. Dec. 29th, he decides that unless
the rancheros will keep sheep they must live at the pueblo. *Prov. Rec.,* MS.,
iv. 79, 86.

of the work, took a large part of the crop, and were so well supplied thereby that they did not care to be converted and live at the missions. The friars attended to the spiritual needs of the settlers free of charge, and their tithes did California no good. Young men grew up without restraint, and wandered among the rancherías, setting the Indians a bad example and indulging in excesses that were sure sooner or later to result in disaster. The great remedy was to build up commerce and give the colonists an incentive to industry. Now they could not sell all their produce; they obtained a small price for what they did sell, and often they could not get the articles they wanted in payment, or had to pay excessive rates for them.

Without the encouragement of trade the country could never prosper; but other reforms were also needed. There should be a settlers' fund similar to the military funds, in which each settler should deposit annually a sum varying according to the size of his family. In the sale and purchase of supplies an officer should stand between the settlers and the habilitados; each pueblo should moreover support a priest and a teacher.[7] Father José Señan was temporarily in Mexico, and a report was also obtained from him which agreed with that of Salazar in most respects. This writer, however, attached special importance to the introduction of a better class of settlers. He would appoint to each pueblo a director, or comisionado, of better abilities and not related to the inhabitants, and he would enforce residence of all settlers in the towns, and not on distant ranchos out of reach of spiritual care and exposed to dangers. Above all, towns should not be placed too near the missions.[8]

[7] *Salazar, Condicion Actual de Cal. 1796*, MS., 73-82. The author also advocates the transfer of the San Blas naval station and ship-yards to San Francisco or Monterey. This would be for the interest of the department, since wages and food would be cheaper than at San Blas, and it would develop the industries of California.

[8] *Señan, Respuesta del Padre al Virey sobre Condicion de Cosas en California, 1796*, MS.. Dated at college of San Fernando May 14, 1796. March 19,

In his correspondence of 1797, Borica still urges colonization, substantially approving the ideas of Salazar and Señan, and issuing orders which compelled retired soldiers to live in the pueblos.[9] We have seen that nine persons, though rather of a worse than better class compared with the rest, were obtained from Guadalajara and settled at Branciforte. In 1797–8 an effort was made to obtain a reënforcement of marriageable women, in which the governor was seconded by the viceroy, but in which he does not seem to have been successful.[10]

There was another class of colonists much more easily obtained and by no means beneficial to the country. Unfortunately California was from this time to a considerable extent a penal colony for Mexico. Governor Fages was perhaps responsible for the beginning of the plague. In 1787 he proposed that artisans imprisoned in Mexico and Guadalajara should have their sentence commuted to exile to California on condition of working out their term at the presidios or missions, and subsequently remaining as settlers. Nothing was done on this proposition; but in 1791 three *presidiarios*, or convicts, were sent up to

1797, Borica to viceroy, refers to voluntary enrolment of settlers at Guadalajara. *Prov. Rec.*, vi. 83.

[9] Nov. 16, 1797, Borica to viceroy, favoring commerce and admitting that the pueblos have a surplus of 2,000 fanegas of grain for which there is no market. Twelve sailors from the *Concepcion* and *San Cárlos* have volunteered to remain at Monterey. *Prov. Rec.*, MS., vi. 61–2. Oct. 15th, B. to commandant at Monterey, invalided or discharged soldiers must live in the towns and not on ranchos nor in the presidio, unless they wish to continue military service. *Guerra, Doc. Hist. Cal.*, MS., i. 109–10. May 1799, Settler Rosales petitions the viceroy for permission to leave California with his family. *Prov. Rec.*, MS., vi. 125. Branciforte in his *Instruccion*, MS., 32–8, speaks of California's need of colonists, and of his efforts in her behalf.

[10] Sept. 17, 1797, Borica to viceroy, wants good wives, strong young spinsters, especially for criminal settlers, since the padres objected to the native women marrying such husbands. Besides good health the girls must bring good clothes, so that they may go to church and be improved. A *sine qua non* of a California female colonist must be a serge petticoat, a *rebozo corriente*, a linen jacket, two woollen shifts, a pair of stockings, and a pair of strong shoes. *Prov. Rec.*, MS., vi. 55–6. Jan. 25, 1798, viceroy says orders have been given to procure young, healthy, single women for the pobladores, but the task presents some difficulties. *Prov. St. Pap.*, MS., xvii. 19–20. June 1, 1798, Borica says one hundred women are wanted. *Prov. Rec.*, MS., vi. 75.

Monterey to labor with shackled feet for rations; and the same year we hear of a convict blacksmith teaching the natives at San Francisco.[11] In 1798 the *Concepcion* brought twenty-two convicts, of various grades of criminality, some of them merely vagrants like those formerly destined for Branciforte. They were set at work by Borica to learn and teach trades, a saving of nine thousand dollars being thereby effected as the governor claimed.[12] Three convicts had arrived the year before, and subsequently such arrivals were of frequent occurrence. Some artisan instructors sent to the country by the government will be noticed a little later. In 1800 nineteen foundlings were sent from Mexico under the care of Madre María de Jesus, nine boys under ten years of age, and ten girls some of them already marriageable, who were distributed in respectable families in the different presidios.[13]

[11] There was a royal order forbidding convicts from settling in pueblos until their sentences were served out. *Prov. St. Pap.*, MS., vi. 98. Fages' proposition in his *Informe Gen. de Misiones*, MS., 154. The three presidiarios of 1791 were Ignacio Saenz, Rafael Pacheco, and Felipe Álvarez, sent up by Romeu from Loreto. *Prov. St. Pap.*, MS., xxii. 15. Smith at San Francisco, *Id.*, x. 41.

[12] The three of 1797 were Rafael Arriola, Tomas Escamilla, and José Franco. *Prov. St. Pap.*, MS., xvii. 134. Correspondence on the 22 sent in 1798, in *Prov. St. Pap.*, MS., xv. 249–50; xvii. 7, 88–9, 182; xxi. 275, 280, 285; *Prov. Rec.*, MS., vi. 91–2, 101–2; *St. Pap., Sac.*, viii. 11–13, 68–9; ix. 75–6. Four or five lists are given, the following being the names: José de los Reyes, José María Perez, José Vazquez, Juan Hernandez, José Velasquez, Cornelio Rocha, José Chavez, José Salazar, Antonio Ortega, Juan Lopez, José Balderrama, Pedro Osorno, José Calzado, José Ávila, José Hernandez, José Igadera, José Ramos, José Rosas, José Chavira, Casimiro Conejo, Pablo Franco, María Petra Aranda, José Bárcena, Felipe Hernandez, Rafael Gomez, Juan Blanco, 26 in all, though the number is spoken of as from 17 to 24, and 22 are said to have landed. They arrived in August. The expense of sending them was $405. There were 3 hatters, 3 miners, 1 shoemaker, 1 silversmith, 1 trader, 3 bakers, 1 tailor, 1 blanket-maker, 1 laborer, 1 overseer, 3 without trade, and 1 woman. There were 4 Spaniards only. There were a saddler and 2 carpenters, not convicts, perhaps included in the list I have given. Several friars also came on the same vessel. After the arrival of these convicts all persons not having passports were ordered to be arrested. *Prov. Rec.*, MS., iv. 166. Feb. 26, 1799, Borica publishes a series of rules for the conduct of the convict workmen. They were subjected to strict surveillance and allowed few privileges. *Prov. St. Pap.*, MS., xvii. 243–4. August 1800, Hernandez allowed to earn wages by his trade as saddler. *Prov. Rec.*, MS., ix. 13. Nov. 1800, José Cris. Simental sentenced to 6 years as settler in California, to be accompanied by his wife. *St. Pap., Sac.*, MS., ix. 57–8; *Prov. St. Pap.*, MS., xxi. 53–4.

[13] Twenty-one children left Mexico for San Blas and one died on the sea-voyage. The expense is said to have been $4,763. There was a plan to send

The tenure of lands is an interesting topic of California history, both in itself and especially in view of the litigation of later times. In its earliest phases the subject falls more naturally into the annals of this decade than elsewhere, though a general statement with but few details is all that is required here. As soon as the territory was occupied by Spain in 1769 the absolute title vested in the king. No individual ownership of lands, but only usufructuary titles of various grades, existed in California in Spanish times. The king, however, was actually in possession of only the ground on which the presidios stood and such adjoining lands as were needed in connection with the royal service. The natives were recognized as the owners, under the king, of all the territory needed for their subsistence; but the civilizing process to which they were to be subjected would greatly reduce the area from that occupied in their savage state; and thus there was no prospective legal hinderance to the establishment of Spanish settlements. The general laws of Spain provided for such establishments, and the assignment to each of lands to the extent of four square leagues.[14] Meanwhile neither the missions, nor the friars, nor the Franciscan order, nor the church owned any lands whatever. The missionaries had the use of such lands as they needed for their object, which was to prepare the Indians to take possession as individuals of the lands they now held as communities. When this was accomplished, and the missions had become pueblos, the houses of worship would naturally become the property of the church, and the friars would move on to new spiritual conquests. Each mission and each presidio was at the proper time to become a pueblo; other pueblos were expected to be

60 boys and the same number of girls. Two of the girls were married before the end of the year. *St. Pap., Sac.,* MS., iv. 74; vii. 74–6; *Prov. St. Pap.,* MS., xviii. 9, 18, 31; xxi. 34, 47; *Id., Ben. Mil.,* MS., xxviii. 22; *Prov. Rec.,* MS., ix. 11, 12; *Arch. Sta Bárbara,* MS., xii. 307; *Bustamante, Suplemento,* 181; *Azanza, Instruccion,* MS., 88–9.

[14] *Recopilacion de Indias,* lib. iv. tit. v. ley. vi., x. I intentionally avoid conditions and details in this chapter.

founded from time to time; and four square leagues
of land was the area to be assigned under ordinary
circumstances to each; but the fixing of boundaries
was tacitly left until the future increase in the number
of establishments should render it a necessity, nothing in the mean time being allowed to interfere with
the area to which each pueblo would be entitled,
though the missions in their temporary occupation
were not restricted.

In his instructions of 1773 Viceroy Bucareli authorized Captain Rivera to make a beginning of the future
pueblos by distributing lands to such persons, either
natives or Spaniards, as were worthy and would dedi-
cate themselves to agriculture or the raising of stock.[15]
Rivera did grant a piece of land in 1775 to Manuel
Butron, a soldier who married a neophyte of San
Cárlos; but the land was subsequently abandoned, and
if any other similar grants were made by Rivera there
is no record of the fact. In November 1777 the
pueblo of San José was founded and a somewhat informal distribution of lands to settlers was made by
order of Governor Neve. In 1781 Neve's regulation
went into effect, and one of its sections regulated the
distribution of pueblo lands; prescribed the assignment to each settler of four fields, each two hundred
varas square, besides a house-lot; specified the lands to
be devoted to various uses of the community; and
made provision for the gradual extension of the town
by the granting of new lots and fields. Under this
regulation the pueblo of Los Angeles was founded in
the same year of 1781. The formal distribution of
lands, however, and the giving of written titles took
place for San José and Los Angeles in 1783 and 1786
respectively.[16] These titles were the nearest approach
to absolute ownership in California under Spain; but
the lands were forfeited by abandonment, failure to
cultivate, and non-compliance with certain conditions.

[15] *Bucareli, Instruccion de 17 de Agosto de 1773*, MS.
[16] On foundation of San José and Angeles and the distribution of lands,
see chapters xiv. and xvi. of this volume.

They could not be alienated; and one instance is recorded of lands being taken for hemp culture from a settler, who was given others in their place. New grants of pueblo lands to new settlers were of constant occurrence hereafter. Neither in the regulation nor in the proceedings under it was any attention paid to exterior pueblo limits, save the vague establishment of a boundary, at San José at least, with the adjoining mission. This matter was practically and naturally left to be agitated by the crown should there ever in the distant future be danger of the town exceeding its four leagues, or by the pueblo itself in case of encroachments by other towns or by individuals.

In 1784 application was made to Fages by private individuals for grants of ranchos. He granted written permits to several men for temporary occupation of the lands desired,[17] and wrote to the commandant general for instructions. General Ugarte replied in 1786, on the recommendation of his legal adviser, Galindo Navarro, by authorizing the granting of tracts not to exceed three leagues, always beyond the four-league limits of existing pueblos, without injury to missions or rancherías, and on certain other conditions including the building of a stone house on each rancho and the keeping of at least two thousand head of livestock.[18] The instructions required the immediate assignment by clear landmarks of the four leagues to each pueblo; but there is no evidence that any such survey was made, that any documents were given in place of the temporary permits, or that the few provisional grants subsequently made differed in any respect from those permits.

[17] The ranchos since known as Los Nietos and San Rafael were thus granted to Manuel Nieto and José María Verdugo in 1784. In the case of Nieto his long possession until 1804 and that of his children after him was urged as affording presumption of a complete title; but the supreme court held that Fages' written permit destroyed this presumption. The land commission had already taken a similar view. *Nieto vs. Carpenter*, 21 Cal. 456.

[18] Fages' report to Ugarte Nov. 20, 1784. Navarro's opinion, Oct. 27, 1785. *St. Pap., Miss. and Colon.*, MS., i. 325-7. Ugarte's order June 21st. *Id.*, i. 343.

In 1789 a series of instructions was issued with royal approval for the establishment of the Villa of Pitic in Sonora since called Hermosillo, instructions which were to be followed also in the founding of similar establishments throughout the northern provinces. Omitting details unimportant to my present purpose, each pueblo was to have assigned to it with definite bounds four square leagues of land in rectangular form; the land given to each settler to depend somewhat on his character and needs, but might be fifty per cent larger than that already given in California; and after four years the ownership might become absolute. I do not find that this regulation ever had any effect at Los Angeles or San José.[19] In 1790 a pensioned corporal, Cayuelas, who had married a neophyte of San Luis Obispo, asked in the name of his wife for lands at Santa Margarita belonging to that mission; but the grant was opposed, probably with success, by the friars, on the ground that the land was needed for the community, to which the neophyte in question had rendered no service.[20]

A beginning of the presidial pueblos was made by General Nava in 1791, when he authorized commandants of presidios to grant lots and fields to soldiers and settlers desiring them within the prescribed four square leagues,[21] but there is no clear evidence

---

[19] Pitic, Instruccion aprobada por S. M. que se formó para el establecimiento de la nueva Villa de Pitic, y mandada adaptar á las demas nuevas poblaciones proyectadas, 1789, MS. Dated Chihuahua, Nov. 14, 1789.

[20] Arch. Sta Bárbara, MS., xi. 398-9, 400-2; Prov. St. Pap., MS., ix. 163-6. This instance and that of Butron are the only ones recorded of land being asked for by neophytes before 1800. In fact only 24 neophyte women had married gente de razon since 1769. Lasuen, in Arch. Sta Bárbara, MS., ii. 192.

[21] Nava's decree, dated Oct. 22, 1791, at Chihuahua, and approved provisionally by the viceroy before Jan. 19, 1793. St. Pap., Miss. and Colon., MS., i. 320-2, 341-2; Prov. St. Pap., MS., xi. 27-8. This decree has been often translated and referred to in legal reports, sometimes erroneously under the date of March 22d. According to the Ordenanza de Intendentes of 1786, the royal intendentes had been intrusted with the distribution of royal lands; but this order shows that the four leagues belonged to the pueblo and were not included in the king's lands. Dwinelle's Colon. Hist. S. F., 34-5. In U. S. Sup. Court Repts., 9 Wallace, 639, it is stated that the words 'the extent of 4 leagues measured from the centre of the plaza of the presidios in every direction,' found in an order of Nava of June 21, 1791, and in other papers, caused Los Angeles to claim before the land commission 16 square leagues

that any such grants were made. Arrillaga reported
to the viceroy in 1793 that no grants had been made
by his predecessors under the order of 1786, and that
on account of this failure to act, and because of the
ultimate right of the natives to the best sites—
although he was constantly asked for ranchos and
believed that it would be well for the country to
grant them—he would not act without further instructions.[22] Yet early in 1794 he reported that he
had permitted several persons to settle on the Rio de
Monterey from three to five leagues from the presidio, the permission being only provisional.[23] In
April 1795 Borica sent to the viceroy his views on
the subject. He did not know why his predecessors
had failed to grant sites for cattle-raising, but he did
not favor such concessions. It would be difficult to
tell what lands the missions really needed, since new
converts were constantly made. Troubles between
the owners of ranchos and ranchería Indians would
lead to excesses and war; the animals of the settlers
would do injury to the food-supply of the gentiles;
the rancheros would be far removed from spiritual
care and from judicial supervision; and finally the
province had already live-stock enough, there being
no export. Borica therefore proposed that no ranchos
should be granted for the present, but that settlers
of good character be allowed to establish themselves
provisionally on the land asked for near a mission or
pueblo, to be granted them later if it should prove
best. In fact several ranchos already existed under
those conditions.[24]

instead of 4. This would literally be 64 square leagues; but the original
'4 l. measured from the centre of the plaza, 2 in each direction,' might—like
the corresponding definition in the *Recopilacion de Indias*—be interpreted
naturally 16 square leagues. It is a curious complication; but that an area
of 4 square leagues, either in square or rectangular form, was what was
intended, and in hundreds of cases actually surveyed for each Spanish pueblo,
there can be, I suppose, no doubt.

[22] *Prov. St. Pap.*, MS., xii. 45-7. This report was sent back to Borica
for his opinion on Aug. 25, 1794. Arrillaga recognizes the four-league limit
even in the case of missions.

[23] *Prov. St. Pap.*, MS., xxi. 132; xii. 189.

[24] April 3, 1795, Borica to viceroy. *Prov. Rec.*, MS., vi. 39-41.

There was certainly a degree of force in some of Borica's arguments, though most of them were quite as conclusive against his substitute for land-grants. Indeed there is something mysterious about the preference of successive governors for provisional permits of occupation over the regular concessions authorized by superior authority. I suspect that the preference may have been largely on the part of the settlers themselves, who did not like to comply with the conditions attached to a regular grant. There were some sixteen ranchos in the regions of Los Angeles and Monterey thus provisionally held by some twenty men in 1795. Two and doubtless more similar permissions were given before the end of the decade.[25] In 1796 a part of the land which Fages had allowed Nieto to occupy was taken from him, on the claim of San Gabriel mission that it was needed by the natives. In 1797 the Encino Rancho, held by Francisco Reyes, was taken from him, and both land and buildings were appropriated by the new mission of San Fernando. This same year the Villa de Branciforte was founded, presumably on the plan of Pitic, though there is no positive information extant respecting the distribution of lands in that famous town. In 1798 Borica gave some kind of a confirmation to the title of Verdugo at San Rafael, but we know nothing of its nature. The condition of land matters in California at the end of the decade and century was then briefly as follows: There were eighteen missions and four presidios, each without settlers,[26] but each intended to become a pueblo, and each entitled to four square leagues of land for distribution to settlers in house-lots and sowing-lands, or for other pueblo uses; three pueblos of Spaniards already established, entitled like the pros-

[25] See chapters xxx. and xxxi. for lists of the ranchos with additional details. Borica, whatever may have been his real motives, opposed even the provisional concessions in several instances.

[26] It is noticeable, however, that some of the tracts occupied near Monterey under the provisional permits were probably within the limits of the prospective presidio-pueblo, where there was no legal authority for granting lands for stock-raising.

pective ones to four leagues of land, though like them
as yet without fixed boundaries, inhabited by over
one hundred settlers, each of whom held about four
acres of land still subject to conditions and not to
be alienated or hypothecated; and finally twenty or
thirty men raising cattle on ranchos which they occupied temporarily by permission of the authorities,
without any legal title, though some of them or their
children subsequently became owners of the land.

Besides the missions and pueblos, conversion and
colonization, there are various institutions and industries of the province whose progress during this period
merit brief notice here; though in most respects that
progress was great only in comparison to that of other
epochs of California history. The order in which the
several topics are treated being a matter of no moment, I begin with that of manufactures and labor.
At the first occupation of Upper California some
Christian Indians from the peninsula; the only persons for many years who were honored with the name
of Californians, were brought north as servants of all
work in the new missions. The presidial companies
usually had a few smiths, armorers, and carpenters
whose services were available at times, as well for the
friars as for the soldiers; the soldiers themselves
were obliged to render assistance in building and
some other kinds of work. Gentiles were hired from
the first, especially on the Channel coast. After 1773
men were enlisted and paid as sailors to serve in California as laborers, and among the settlers at the
pueblos were persons of various trades, on which,
however' none seem to have depended for subsistence. This was the condition of mechanical industry down to 1790. Besides the repairs executed on
arms, implements, and articles of clothing, there
were rude attempts at tanning and various other
simple and necessary processes suggested by the
needs of the soldiers and ingenuity of the friars; but

progress in this direction was slight and is but vaguely recorded.

During the last decade of the century all the classes of laborers mentioned continued to be employed, except that no new natives were brought from Baja California. Neophytes were extensively hired from the friars for all kinds of presidio work, the mission and not the Indian receiving the pay, and there were few Spanish families without a native servant. This question of neophyte labor was, as we have seen, a fruitful source of misunderstanding between friars and officers. Gentiles were also hired in large numbers to work both at presidios and pueblos, being paid chiefly in grain, but also with blankets and other articles of clothing. Negotiations for laborers were made for the most part with chiefs who contracted to supply the required number. It is not improbable that the chiefs were already so far advanced in civilization as to make a profit on the contracts. Spanish regulations required kind treatment and fair compensation to all Indian laborers, and any notable or habitual abuses in this respect would in these early times have largely cut off the supply. The friars complained that the gentiles earned so much grain and clothing that one of their chief incentives to become Christians was lost.[27] The sailor *sirvientes*, several of whom were

[27] Nov. 10, 1791, Sergt. Ortega wanted men to build a house, etc., at San Gabriel; but the padres refused to furnish any even for wages. *Prov. St. Pap.*, MS., x. 4, 5. The gentiles, though lazy, offer themselves to work for a *manta* and daily rations of meat and boiled maize. The best are chosen, who take their blankets, lay down their arms, and go to work bringing building-materials. *Sutil y Mex.*, *Viage*, 164–5. Great care taken in employing Indians, and a daily sum of money paid. *Vancouver's Voyage*, ii. 497. May 7, 1794, governor to Sal, if padres want a gratuity for Indians above wages it must be refused. At Sta Bárbara they get 19 cents per day, and an *almud* of corn per week. San Antonio Indians at the Rancho del Rey get a *coton* and *manta* per month. Even if content with little they should be given all they deserve. *Prov. Rec.*, MS., ii. 147–8, 163. Dec. 1794, at San Diego Indians got one real and rations. *Prov. St. Pap.*, MS., xii. 7. Indians must be treated well and work equally. *Prov. Rec.*, MS., iv. 15, 16. April, 1796, Indian laborers not to be obtained without governor's permission. *Prov. St. Pap.*, MS., xiv. 176. 1796, Sal sends 30 blankets to San José with which to hire 30 Indians. They will be treated well. Any *capitanejo* helping to get them may be given a *gratificacion*. Travelling expenses paid. Later some invalids are sent to look after the 30; who were to be treated with *alguna comiseracion*. *S. José,*

furnished to each of the new missions, did not in many instances give satisfaction. There was also some difficulty about their wages being paid by the royal treasury, and they were all sent back to San Blas in 1795, though sailors were subsequently allowed to remain in California as workmen at the presidios and as settlers.[28]

In the promotion of manufactures, however, a decided effort was made in this decade, and with considerable success. The plan adopted was to send skilled artisans from Mexico under government pay to teach their trades to neophytes and to white apprentices. About twenty of these artisan instructors were sent to California, chiefly in 1792 and 1795, a few of whom remained permanently as settlers, but most retired on the expiration of their contracts before 1800.[29]

Arch., MS., ii. 75. Wages paid to mission, not to Indians. *Prov. St. Pap.*, MS., xxi. 158. 1800, mission Indians get two reals per day, one in extra food and one in cloth, or sometimes money from presidios. Private persons pay in corn or meat. *Arch. Sta Bárbara*, MS., ii. 119.

[28] *Prov. St. Pap.*, MS., xii. 193–4; xiii. 69, 123–4; xvi. 2; *Prov. Rec.*, MS., iv. 232; v. 5. The sailor *sirvientes* got $10 per month and 19 cents for rations. One slave is mentioned during the decade. He was owned by Col. Alberni, and was tried for robbery in 1798. *Prov. Rec.*, MS., vi. 102.

[29] Their names were: Santiago Ruiz, Manuel D. Ruiz, Toribio Ruiz, Salvador Rivera, Joaquin Rivera, and Pedro Alcántara, masons; Mariano Tapia, potter; Cayetano Lopez, mill-maker; José A. Ramirez and Salvador Véjar, carpenters; Miguel Sangrador, tanner and shoemaker; Joaquin Ávalos, tanner; Mariano Tapinto and Joaquin Botello, tailors; Pedro Gonzalez García, José Arroya, and José F. Arriola, blacksmiths; Antonio Dom. Henriquez and Mariano José Mendoza, weavers; Manuel Muñoz, *listonero*, ribbon-maker; José de Los Reyes and Antonio Hernandez, saddlers. One or two of these names may have been those of settlers who had trades; and one or two of convicts. A few of the *maestros* got $1,000 per year, and the journeymen from $300 to $600. The contracts were for four or five years. Sept. 10, 1790, Fages specifies 51 mechanics needed, besides teachers, millers, and a surveyor. *St. Pap., Sac.*, MS., xv. 13; *St. Pap., Miss.*, MS., i. 82. 1790 and 1792, lists of trades existing. *Id.*, i. 96, 98, 101–2. Salvador Rivera, the stone-cutter, was at first left at Nootka in 1791. *St. Pap., Sac.*, MS., v. 95. Four mechanics arrived in Dec. 1791. *Prov. St. Pap., Ben. Mil.*, MS., xv. 6. Viceroy says a carpenter must teach his trade to at least 12 Indians in the four years. *Prov. St. Pap.*, MS., x. 137. In 1791 tailor at Monterey did $135 worth of work for private parties. *Prov. St. Pap., Ben. Mil.*, MS., xiii. 3. June 20, 1792, opinion of the fiscal on the project, including provision for granting the artisans land and making permanent settlers of them. The engineer Miguel Costansó appears as one of the advisers in the matter. *St. Pap., Sac.*, MS., ix. 62–8. March 1793, three artisans sent back as useless. *Prov. Rec.*, MS., ii. 163. Jan. 1794, no visible progress made though the artisans work well. *Prov. St. Pap.*, MS., xxi. 178–9. Of the value of work done by the artisans half goes to the treasury, one third to apprentices, and one sixth to artisans. *Id.*, xi. 158; *Prov. Rec.*, MS., viii. 140. April 29, 1795, V. R. wonders that though wages have been paid, $10,000 is yet due the artisans. *Id.*, iv. 227. July 19, 1795, new opinion of

At first the artisans were distributed in the missions and presidios, or in some cases travelled from one place to another giving instruction. The friars were of course pleased, for they thus received almost without cost instructions for themselves and their neophytes which in the future must contribute largely to the prosperity of their establishments. But they were deeply grieved when they found that the king's mechanics were by no means disposed to regard themselves as mere mission servants to be utilized according to the orders of the padres, and at the necessity of paying something for the work done by the artisans in the course of their teaching. As usual they wanted all the benefits of the enterprise and its management, but pleaded poverty when payment was asked. The government was not willing to do so much for the missions, and after 1795 the friars were obliged to pay for the work done, to pay the artisans' salaries, or to send their neophytes to the presidios to be taught. In many cases they refused to do either, and quite a controversy ensued. But the difficulty settled itself as the terms of contract expired, and before 1800 the neophytes had acquired a stock of instruction which it was thought would suffice for the mission needs.[30]

the fiscal on details. *Prov. St. Pap.*, MS., xiii. 56–60. Aug. 24, 1795, B. says V. R. has ordered work of artisans to cease at missions. *Prov. Rec.*, MS., v. 61. Pay began when artisans left Mexico. *St. Pap., Sac.*, MS., vii. 41–3. Fifty dollars advanced for travelling expenses. The married ones to be given in California a male and female Indian servant for each family, to be fed and educated. *Prov. St. Pap.*, MS., xiii. 202–4; *Prov. Rec.*, MS., iv. 184. Dec. 4, 1795, fiscal's report, with details of contracts. *Id.*, xiii. 34–42. Jan. 1796, the missions must be asked to support the new artisans expected. *Prov. Rec.*, MS., v. 78. 1796, effort to obtain white apprentices. *Prov. Rec.*, MS., iv. 53–4, 72–3; v. 249; *Prov. St. Pap.*, MS., xiv. 16. July 1796, lands ordered granted (in pueblos) to several artisans. *Prov. Rec.*, MS., viii. 164. 1797, the basis of pay was changed in later years, one eighth of the value of work done going to the artisan, and seven eighths to the treasury. *Prov. Rec.*, MS., vi. 90–1 (and many other references). See also for voluminous correspondence on this subject—chiefly on the names, salaries, engaging, distribution, arrival and departure of the artisans—*Prov. St. Pap.*, MS., x. 41; xii. 192–3; xiii. 40–2, 52–3, 60, 107, 126–7; xiv. 6; xvi. 202, 213; xvii. 40, 135; xxi. 36–7, 44, 73–4, 89–90, 229, 236, 238, 253, 280, 287; *Id., Ben. Mil.*, MS., xxi. 9; xxiii. 3; *Id., Presidios*, MS., ii. 4, 5, 82–3; *St. Pap., Sac.*, MS., ii. 9, 10; iv. 2, 62; vii. 47–9; xvii. 8; *Prov. Rec.*, MS., ii. 157; iv. 190, 210; v. 14; vi. 32, 35, 76; *Arch. Arzobispado*, MS., i. 33.

[30] Dec. 21, 1792, Lasuen to Arrillaga, some of the artisans show a ten-

Some white apprentices were obtained and taught, though instances were not wanting where parents deemed it degrading to put their sons to a trade.

The results of all these efforts were that before 1800 rude looms were set up in many of the missions, on which by Indian labor the wool of the country was woven into blankets and coarse fabrics with which the neophytes were clothed;[31] hides were tanned and made into shoes, some of the coarser parts of saddles and other leather goods being also manufactured, though

dency to act as *officers* rather than *instructors*. The tailors don't amount to much, in fact tailors are not much needed in a country where each native is tailor for himself. It is not well to send the natives to the presidios for instruction; but it would be a good idea to let certain artisans travel from mission to mission. *Arch. Arzobispado*, MS., i. 30–2. 1793–4, several San Cárlos Indians instructed in stone-cutting, bricklaying, etc. *Arch. Sta Bárbara*, MS., xii. 59. Dec. 1795, Borica orders missions to send each four or five Indians to presidios. They will be supported and will have a soldier to teach them religion. *Prov. Rec.*, MS., v. 235–6. July 28, 1796, Lasuen in a circular regrets the restrictions, but orders the padres to send the neophytes to the presidios, not however expecting any good results. *Arch. Sta Barbara*, MS., xi. 138. Aug. 8, 1796, B. says to Lasuen seven eighths of products of work must go to treasury and one eighth to artisan. An Indian boy and girl must be supplied, as servants, or appeal will be made to the viceroy. *Prov. Rec.*, MS., vi. 166–7, 163–4. Dec. 20, 1796, V. R. says that the artisans are engaged to teach the natives and not to serve at missions. The missions must pay. *Arch. Sta Bárbara*, MS., ix. 167–8. April 26, 1797, Lasuen to V. R. protesting against giving the artisans one eighth of the value of their work when the mission furnishes all the material, and also against sending Indians to the presidios as being subversive of all subordination. *Id.*, ix. 169–72; *Prov. St. Pap.*, MS., xv. 281–2. Nov. 12, 1798, B. has given a mission the free use of a smith and carpenter for a year. *Prov. Rec.*, MS., vi. 226. Sept. 21, 1799, V. R. to gov. and president, asking them to come to some conclusion how best to instruct neophytes without risk to Christian duties. *Arch. Sta Bárbara*, MS., ix. 173–4; *Prov. St. Pap.*, MS., xvii. 339; *Prov. Rec.*, MS., viii. 193. Jan. 22, 1800, Lasuen to V. R., neophytes ought not to be sent to the presidios where they are used as peons and often run away; still something may be effected by sending docile youth and requiring a strict watch over them. The objection to the artisans coming to the missions, is the required payment for the articles made by them which the mission cannot afford, especially after furnishing servants and material, and as the objects made are not sold. *Arch. Sta Bárbara*, MS., ix. 175–80.

[31] For items about weaving see *Prov. Rec.*, MS., ii. 162–6; iv. 98–9, 251, 300; v. 206. 245–7; vi. 3, 79, 81, 117, 230; ix. 5; *Prov. St. Pap.*, MS., xii. 24; xv. 67–8; xvi. 233, 261–2; xviii. 18, 19; xxi. 189; *Id.*, *Ben. Mil.*, xxv. 14; *St. Pap.*, *Miss.*, MS., ii. 100; *St. Pap.*, *Sac.*, MS., vi. 103–5; *Arch. Sta Bárbara*, MS., ii. 68, 96–7; ix. 168–9; *Vancouver's Voyage*, ii. 11–13. No blankets were brought from Mexico after 1797. A little cotton cloth was woven from material brought from San Blas. The Indians had some natural skill at dyeing. The ribbon-maker was found to be of no use. There was a proposition in 1797 to make the learning of a trade obligatory. Weaving was a failure at Monterey. Some hemp was used for neophytes' garments. P. Espí wanted to establish a fulling-mill, but the governor disapproved the scheme. The pueblos got none of the instructors, but some weaving was done there.

not enough as yet to avoid importation from Mexico.[32]
Soap was made of suitable quality and quantity to
supply home needs after 1798;[33] coarse pottery was
produced at San Francisco and several other places;[34]
and water-power flouring-mills were built at Santa
Cruz and San Luis Obispo, possibly also at San
Gabriel and San José, which with the *tahonas* worked
by horse or man power and the *metates* of the neophyte women, supplied the province with flour.[35]
Some details of these different branches of manufactures will be found in local annals of the different
towns, missions, and presidios.[36]

In the way of public improvements, repairs were
several times ordered to be made on the roads, especially at the crossings of streams where couriers were
liable to be delayed. There were several supposed
discoveries of rich mineral deposits, including one of
quicksilver in the black mud at Santa Bárbara in 1796.
In fact Father Salazar reported that the province was
supposed to be very rich in metals, which were not
developed for fear that foreigners would rush in, but
actual mining operations were confined to an occasional
trip after *tequesquite,* or saltpetre, and the extraction
of *brea,* or asphaltum, from the pitch-wells of the
Channel coast, used to some extent for roofing.[37]

[32] *St. Pap., Ben.,* MS., i. 46–7; *Prov. Rec.,* MS., iv. 50, 220; *Arch. Sta
Bárbara,* MS., ii. 72–3, 129. Some 2,000 hides were tanned at Santa Clara as
early as 1792, but very few of them could be sold. At Sta Bárbara the corporal of the guard was paid $150 per year to attend to the tanning.

[33] *Prov. Rec.,* MS., iv. 33, 48, 50, 95, 105, 303; v. 211; ix. 5; *Prov. St.
Pap.,* MS., xvii. 110. About $1,000 worth of soap was required each year.
There was a manufactory of this article at the rancho del rey in Monterey.

[34] *Prov. St. Pap.,* MS., xvi. 25; xviii. 259; *Prov. Rec.,* MS., iv. 75; v. 88;
Arch. Sta Bárbara, MS., ix. 313.

[35] *Prov. Rec.,* MS., ii. 162–3; iv. 177, 187–8, 224, 232, 253, 283; v. 50; vi. 6,
68; *Arch. Sta Bárbara,* MS., xii. 59; *Los Angeles Hist.,* 7. *Hall's Hist. S.
José,* 114.

[36] See also general communications on the progress of the various industries
between governor and viceroy in *Prov. Rec.,* MS., vi. 67–8, 89–90, 117; *St.
Pap., Miss. and Col.,* MS., i. 79; *Dept. St. Pap., S. José,* MS., i. 46; *St.
Pap., Miss.,* MS., ii. 6.

[37] *Prov. St. Pap.,* MS., xiv. 107, 175; xxi. 176–7; *Prov. Rec.,* MS., iv. 57–8;
Arch. Sta Bárbara, MS., ii. 64–5. The only ship-building industry recorded
is the building of a large boat by the sailors left by Capt. Dorr in 1796. *Prov.
Rec.,* MS., vi. 79.

Agricultural statistics are given elsewhere in chapters devoted to missions, pueblos, and to local progress; but it is well here to give the grand total of production, which was on an average 56,000 bushels of grain per year during the decade. Of this yield 36,000 bushels were wheat; 11,700 bushels, corn; 5,400 bushels, barley; 1,800 bushels, beans; and 1,200 bushels, miscellaneous grains such as pease, lentils, etc. Of other crops no statistical records were kept, though each establishment had a vegetable garden, a fruit-orchard, or a vineyard, most having all of these in a prosperous condition supplying the wants of the country. There have been some interesting discussions in modern times respecting the dates at which grapes, oranges, and other fruits were introduced in California; but there are no records which can throw light on the matter. Many varieties of fruit, including probably grapes, were introduced from the peninsula by the earliest expeditions between 1769 and 1773; nearly all the varieties were in a flourishing condition on a small scale before Junípero Serra's death in 1784; and very few remained to be introduced after 1800.[38]

Borica gave and required his commandants to give much personal attention to the advancement of agricultural interests, using various expedients of reward and threat to accustom the settlers—for there was rarely any occasion to interfere with the friars and their subjects—to habits of industry and to precautions against possible famine in years of drought.

[38] Information on these matters is very meagre and of a general nature. Vallejo has heard from his father and others of the *fundadores* that vines were brought up in 1769, and planted at San Diego. *Vallejo, Doc. Hist. Cal.*, MS., xxxvi. 288. Palou, *Vida de Junípero Serra*, 199, 220, etc., mentions grapes, vegetables, fruits, etc., as flourishing in 1784. Yield of Monterey garden sufficient to pay for a gardner in 1784. *Prov. St. Pap.*, MS., v. 54. La Pérouse left the first potatoes in California in 1786. There are some traditions of wild grapes found in the country near San Antonio, and improved by cultivation. *Gomez, Lo que sabe*, MS., 105–6. Fages' garden in 1783–91 with 200 fruit-trees, vines, etc. *Prov. St. Pap.*, MS., x. 167. Vancouver names many kinds of fruit raised in 1792. Wine manufactured in the southern missions in 1797–8. *Arch. Sta Bárbara*, MS., xii. 66, 70, 1798. The culture of vines and olives must be encouraged. *Prov. Rec.*, MS., iv. 106.

Regular weather reports were insisted on, though very few of them have been preserved.[39]   The hardest years for the province were 1794 and 1795; but even in those years the drought did not extend over all the territory, so that more than half the average crop was produced.   In 1793 the governor seconded by President Lasuen prohibited the kindling of fires by neophytes and gentiles which had in several instances caused considerable damage in the grain-fields.[40]   In 1795 owners of gardens were required to fence them, or at least to make no complaints of ravages by cattle.[41]   The chief enterprise, however, of an agricultural nature in which the government took an interest was the attempt to introduce the cultivation of flax and hemp.   The establishment of this industry in the American colonies of Spain had been ordered by the king in 1781, and the orders had been promulgated in California as elsewhere, without receiving any practical attention; but in 1795 special orders and a package of seed having been sent up to Monterey, the experiment was undertaken in earnest by Borica's directions, San José being selected as the spot and Ignacio Vallejo as the superintendent, with the aid of a soldier who knew something of flax-culture.   Some details of the experiment will be found in connection with the local history of San José for this period. There were some failures of crops, and others resulting from inexperience in the various processes to which the product was subjected; but several lots of the staple sent to Mexico gave satisfaction, and in 1800 the prospects of the new industry were considered encouraging, and preparations were made to send Joaquin Sanchez to superintend it in California.[42]

[39] Minor communications of the governor on agriculture. *Prov. Rec.*, MS., iv. 52–3, 69–186; v. 63; vi. 67, 80; *Dept. St. Pap. S. José*, MS., i. 52. Borica offered a premium of $25 for the largest crop in 1796.

[40] *Prov. St. Pap.*, MS., xii. 187–8; *Id., Ben. Mil.*, xx. 5; *Arch. Arzobispado*, MS., i. 34; *Arch. Sta Bárbara*, MS., vi. 210–14.

[41] *Prov. Rec.*, MS., iv. 16, 17, 29, 33–4, 272, 293; *Prov. St. Pap.*, MS., xiv. 77.

[42] Nov. 13, 1781, royal orders published by Neve. *Prov. St. Pap.*, MS.,

The companion industry to agriculture, and the favorite occupation of Californians from the first, as requiring less hard work than tilling the soil, was stock-raising. California had in 1800 in round numbers 187,000 animals in her herds and flocks: 74,000 cattle, 24,000 horses, 1,000 mules, and 88,000 sheep, not to mention the comparatively few asses, goats, and swine. Of the total number the missions had 153,000; the presidios 18,000; and the pueblos 16,000. The increase had been uninterrupted from 1769 except in the year 1794–5 when there was a slight decrease. The king's rancho at Monterey with branches at San Francisco and San Diego furnished to the presidial companies a very large part of the meat consumed and nearly all the cavalry horses employed in the service, the proceeds of sales on royal account varying from $1,000 to $3,000 per year. The missionaries always looked with much hostility on these establishments as depriving the missions of the best and almost the only market for their produce; but having founded

iii. 247–53. 1785, other orders of the audiencia published. *Id.*, v. 250–1. Sept. 13, 1785, José de Galvez to Fages on aiding the enterprise. *St. Pap. Sac.*, MS., iv. 35. Sept. 6, 1793, viceroy orders flax-culture to be promoted in all the missions. *Arch. Sta Bárbara*, MS., xi. 263–4. Sept. 7th, guardian also recommends the matter, saying that a wild flax is found on the California coast. *Id.*, xii. 14, 15. Aug. 13, 1794, two fanegas of hemp-seed sent to Lasuen. *Id.*, xi. 267–8. Instructions for hemp-culture. Instruments sent 1795. *St. Pap.*, *Sac.*, MS., xv. 15–17; *Dept. St. Pap.*, *S. José*, MS., i. 53–6; *Prov. Rec.*, MS., iv. 140. See chapter xxxii. for experiments at San José. May 21, 1796, flax and hemp to be free of duty, and implements free from taxes. *Gaceta de Mex.*, viii. 95–8; *Prov. St. Pap.*, MS., xiv. 194. Dec. 19, 1796, Borica to V. R., 30 fanegas of seed harvested. Missions as a rule will not be able to raise hemp. No success yet in working the material. *St. Pap.*, *Sac.*, MS., iv. 70. Hemp exported in 1796–7 of no use. *Prov. Rec.*, MS., iv. 272. 1798, samples sent to Mexico and approved. *Id.*, vi. 103; viii. 189–90. *Prov. St. Pap.*, MS., xxi. 272, 287. May 3, 1798, hemp sent to P. Viader to try experiments in spinning. *Prov. Rec.*, MS., vi. 213. 1799, 25 arrobas of hemp sent to Mexico. Price $350. Prospects favorable. *Prov. St. Pap.*, MS., xviii. 83–4; xvii. 213. Culture must be introduced at Branciforte. *Id.*, xvii. 314–15. San Cárlos using hemp for ordinary cloth for neophytes. *Prov. Rec.*, vi. 117. 1800, crops not good. *Id.*, ix. 15; *S. José Arch.*, MS., iii. 70. Arrangements in Mexico to continue to encourage the new industry and to send Joaquin Sanchez to California. *S. José*, *Arch.*, MS., v. 20; *St. Pap.*, *Miss. and Col.*, MS., i. 55–7; *St. Pap.*, *Sac.*, MS., ix. 102–4. By these arrangements the *memoria* ships were to take flax and hemp in good condition and pay for it in cash. Sanchez did not sail for California. *Guerra*, *Doc. Hist. Cal.*, MS., iii. 176–9. Vague indications that cotton was also tried. *Prov. Rec.*, MS., iv. 108; vi. 209; ix. 6.

the ranchos at a time when the missions had no live-
stock to sell, the government was not disposed to
abandon them later; and indeed it was claimed that
only by means of the rancho del rey and of the fixed
tariffs of prices were the friars kept from maintaining
an oppressive monopoly.[43]

In 1796–7 Borica made a special effort to promote
the raising of sheep in connection with the manufacture of cloth. Statistical reports do not show that
the increase in the mission flocks was much greater
in those than other years, though it was uniformly
rapid; while in the pueblos, to which Borica gave his
attention more particularly, very little was accomplished.[44] The Californian cattle were very prolific,
and, under the early regulations forbidding the
slaughter of cows, multiplied with wonderful rapid-
ity. The pueblos were not allowed to let their large
stock increase beyond fifty head to each settler; the
rancheros had no very large herds before 1800; and
in the missions during the last decade efforts were
directed rather to restrict than encourage further
increase; yet in spite of all restrictions, and of the
ravages of bears, wolves, and Indians, and of the
constantly increasing slaughter for meat and tallow,
cattle were becoming too numerous for the needs of

[43] *Prov. St. Pap.*, MS. x. 91; xii. 30, 97; xvi. 92; xvii. 14–16; *Id., Ben.
Mil.*, xiii. 1–7; xvii. 1; xviii. 4, 5; xxv. 2–4; *Prov. Rec.*, MS., i. 208; iv. 16,
117, 134, 255–6, 273, 285; v. 64, 68, 85, 269; vi. 100, 104, 109; *St. Pap., Miss.*,
MS., i. 73–4; *St. Pap., Miss. and Col.*, MS., i. 68–78. See also chapters xxx.
and xxxii. for local items respecting the rancho del rey. 1795, cattle lost on
the road were charged to the consumption of the troops. 1790, 4,000 cattle
belonging to the real hacienda, from which many private persons were supplied. 1795, each soldier might have two milch cows. There seem to have
been some sheep on the rancho. After 1797 an account was made of the
hides, which before had been left to the soldiers.
[44] Efforts at Sta Bárbara. *Prov. Rec.*, MS., iv. 66. Rancheros must keep
sheep or live in the pueblos. *Id.*, iv. 86. Introduced at Angeles, S. José,
and San Francisco. *Id.*, vi. 79. Every settler should have at least 11 sheep,
for which they may pay in grain. *Id.*, iv. 147. Breeding-sheep to be purchased and sent to Monterey. *Id.*, iv. 62. Six hundred and fourteen sheep
at 7 reals, wethers $2, received from San Diego. *St. Pap., Sac.*, MS., vi. 6.
Wool at S. Gabriel 20 reals per arroba. *Id.*, vi. 6. Two hundred sheep distributed at Angeles August 1796. *Id.*, vi. 1. Every settler at San José must
keep 3 sheep for every larger animal. *Dept. St. Pap., S. José*, MS., i. 73–4.
The breed at San Francisco was merino, and better than elsewhere. *Prov. St.
Pap.*, MS., xv. 8, 9.

the country. Horses, not being used for food, nor as yet stolen extensively by Indians, were largely in excess of all demands at four or five dollars each. Mules at fifteen dollars were generally in demand, comparatively few being yet raised. Tithes of all live-stock except in the missions were branded each year in October or November and added to the rancho del rey.[45]

[45] 1791, mission stock should be reduced to prevent dispersion. The Indians eat too much meat. Missions not allowed to buy animals from the troops. The raising of horses and mules should be promoted. Yearly slaughter for meat ordered. Fages to Romeu, in *Prov. St. Pap.*, MS., x. 150, 157, 170. 1792, no more fat to be shipped from San Blas, and 200 cows to be killed each year. It is better to make monthly distributions of meat. Arrillaga, in *Id.*, xi. 37–8; *Prov. Rec.*, MS., ii. 156. Vancouver took some cattle away for Botany Bay and the Sandwich Islands. *Vancouver's Voy.*, ii. 99; *Prov. St. Pap.*, MS., xxi. 122. 1794, no market for horses. Mules promise better. Pueblo stock much exposed to Indians. Soldiers allowed only three or four cows. King's stock not much affected by the removal of females. Adobe houses built for soldiers guarding stock, in place of huts of hides. *Arrillaga, Papel de Puntes*, MS., 189–91. 1795, rancheros have but little stock and it must not increase. *Prov. St. Pap.*, MS., xiii. 269, 219, 224–5. 1796, wild beasts troublesome, preventing the increase of tithes. A lion attacked a corporal, soldier, and Indian woman at Ranchería Nueva. *Prov. Rec.*, MS., ix. 6, iv. 63. 1797, no settler to have over 50 head of large stock, for each of which three head of small stock must be kept. *Id.*, iv. 204, 284; *Dept. St. Pap.*, S. *José*, MS., i. 73–4. Two reals to be paid on each head of cattle killed. *S. José, Arch.*, MS., v. 31. Tithe cattle to be branded with royal rancho brand applied crosswise to prevent confusion. *Id.*, v. 31. Over 12,000 horses on the Monterey ranchos in 1800 (evidently an error). *Arrillaga, Estado de 1800–1*, MS., in *Bandini, Doc. Hist. Cal.*, 3, 4.

CHAPTER XXIX.

INDUSTRIES AND INSTITUTIONS.

1791–1800.

Commerce—Trade of the Transports—Otter-skins—Projects of Marquez, Mamaneli, Inciarte, Ponce, Mendez, and Ovineta—Provincial Finances—Habilitados—Factor and Commissary—Complicated Accounts—Supplies and Revenues—Taxes—Tobacco Monopoly—Tithes—Military Force and Distribution—Civil Government—Pposed Separation of the Californias—Administration of Justice—A Cause Célèbre—Execution of Rosas—Official Care of Morals—Use of Liquors—Gambling—Education—Borica's Efforts—The First Schools and School-masters.

California had as yet no commerce. Not a trading-vessel proper touched on the coast before 1800, though there had been some little exchange of goods for meat and vegetables on several occasions between the Californians and such vessels as arrived for purposes other than commercial. "It is sad to not see a single ship-owner on the Pacific coast," wrote Costansó in 1794; no trade in the South Sea, and therefore no revenue, a lack of population, and great expense to the crown. The Cádiz merchants from mistaken motives stifled the coast trade in its infancy. A grand commerce might be developed, affording California colonists a market for their products, including fish and salted meats.[1] The Spanish laws strictly forbade all trade not only with foreign vessels and for foreign goods, but with Spanish vessels and for Spanish-American goods except the regular transports and articles brought by them. At first the transports were forbidden to bring other goods than those included in the regular invoices to the habilitados, and great pre-

[1] Costansó, Informe de 1794, MS.

cautions were insisted on to prevent smuggling by friars, soldiers, and sailors. After 1785, however, trade was free on the transports except that from 1790 to 1794 one half the regular rates of duties mu&t be paid, and that at no time could foreign goods be introduced. The methods of conducting this traffic are not clearly indicated, but apparently the officers and even sailors of the transports brought up from San Blas on private speculation such articles as they could barter with the soldiers. In the absence of money this trade could not have assumed large proportions; but the soldiers formed the habit of exchanging the regularly furnished goods needed by their families for liquors, bright-colored cloths, and worthless trinkets. To prevent this the governor sometimes delayed opening the regular supplies till after the vessel had departed. The supply-ships continued during this decade as before to take an occasional small quantity of salt or salt meat to San Blas, besides receiving the needed supplies for their return trips. The importation of mission produce from Lower California was allowed, but naturally little was done in this direction, though one or two lots of brandy, figs, and raisins for the friars were sent up overland.[2]

[2] Feb. 26, 1791, Fages disapproves the free trade with San Blas because the soldiers sacrifice useful articles in barter for luxuries and liquor. *Papel de Puntos*, MS., 158–9. 1793, the viceroy thinks no branch of commerce is likely to succeed unless it may be the shipment of grain to San Blas. *Revilla Gigedo, Carta de 1793*, MS. 1794, Gov. allows importation from Baja California, except of mescal and other liquors. *Prov. St. Pap.*, MS., xii. 110–11. Nov. 1794, publication of the king's renewal of license (of Feb. 18, 1794), for free trade with San Blas for 10 years. *Id.*, xi. 186–7; xii. 9, 10, 177–8. May 27, 1795, V. R. has learned that the habilitados have paid the half duties on San Blas imports down to Nov. 21, 1794. This would indicate perhaps that this duty was paid on the regular *memorias*, as well as on extra goods. *Id.*, xiii. 91–2; xii. 135. June 8, 1795, all foreign goods except such as are included in the regular invoices of the habilitado general are to be confiscated by V. R.'s order. *Id.*, xiii. 208; *Prov. Rec.*, MS., vi. 47; *S. José, Arch.*, MS., iv. 31. July 7, 1795, Perez Fernandez of San Francisco wants instructions how to carry out this order. *St. Pap., Sac.*, MS., i. 21–2. 1796, royal order not to admit goods from foreign vessels. *Prov. Rec.*, MS., viii. 165. Aug. 17, 1796, V. R. transmits royal order of May 5th approving certain restrictions imposed on the leaving of cloth, etc., in payment for supplies by captains Moore and Locke. English cunning and pretexts for trade must be watched. *St. Pap., Sac.*, MS., v. 30–1. 1798–9, brandy, figs, and raisins sent up from Baja California. *Prov. Rec.*, MS., vi. 216, 238.

Within the limits of California trade consisted in the delivery of goods from the presidio warehouse to the soldiers for their pay and rations and to the settlers in payment for grain and other supplies, the habilitados being required to purchase home productions rather than to order from Mexico. Money was paid but rarely, but goods were delivered at cost. For the benefit of the pueblos Borica urged not only the exportation of grain that the settlers might have a market, but the sending by the government of special invoices of goods to be sold to them at a small advance on cost, in order that they might not be compelled to purchase inferior articles at exorbitant prices from the San Blas vessels.[3] The missions also sold supplies to the presidios, and sometimes received goods in payment; but they preferred as a rule to keep an open account which was settled once a year by a draft of the habilitado on Mexico, with which special invoices of articles needed by the friars for themselves or their neophytes or their churches were purchased and sent to California free of all duties. The friars still sent a few otter-skins to Mexico, and an occasional cargo of tallow found a market at San Blas.[4]

[3] 1794, orders to try all possible home products, paying in goods at cost. *Prov. St. Pap.*, MS., xiii. 163–4; xii. 91, 99; xiv. 76–7; *Prov. Rec.*, MS., ii. 127–8; iv. 118. 1796, care must be taken to prevent the settlers selling too much of their grain, and keeping none for seed. *S. José, Arch.*, MS., ii. 73–4. Correspondence between governor, viceroy, and habilitado general about the project of special invoices of goods for the pueblo trade. The matter was taken under consideration. *St. Pap., Sac.*, MS., ix. 18–29; *Prov. Rec.*, MS., vi. 7, 103–4. The settlers were disposed to cheat the government by selling damp flour. *S. José, Arch.*, MS., vi. 46.

[4] The only communication which I find respecting the fur-trade in this decade is a somewhat remarkable circular of President Lasuen dated July 22, 1791, in *Arch. Sta Bárbara*, MS., ix. 314–15, 317, in which he says that advices from Mexico promise better prices for otter-skins, which may therefore be accumulated. They can be sent to the Mission síndico so packed and mixed with other goods that the contents of the packages may not be apparent; but the guardian or procurador should be notified as to the details of marks, etc.! Lasuen in the same circular, *Id.*, ix. 315–16, says that too much tallow has been sent to San Blas and the price is lower; therefore the remainder may be disposed of to private persons. 1794, the guardian gives the bad quality of the tallow as the reason why the ships have refused it. They will take 500 or 600 arrobas yearly at $2.50 if well prepared. He sends directions for preparing it. *Doc. Hist. Cal.*, MS., iv. 51–2; *Arch. Sta Bárbara*, MS., xi. 258, 264–7, 271–3. Salazar complains that pueblos have the preference as sellers, and also of the long time that the missions have to wait.

In 1793 the king granted to Roman Marquez of
the Comercio de Indias license to make an experimental trading voyage from Cádiz to San Blas and
California, with the privilege of introducing Spanish
goods free of all duties, though foreign goods must
pay seven per cent. Californian products exchanged
for these goods might also be exported free of duties.
Due notice was forwarded to the viceroy, and by him
to Borica and Lasuen, who notified friars and commandants to be ready for the expected commercial
visitor. It was announced in November 1794 that
the vessel, the *Levante*, had actually sailed. A year
later came the notice that as Marquez had failed to
carry out his enterprise it would be undertaken by
Ignacio Inciarte. Here the matter seems to have
dropped out of view.[5] Meanwhile the king and viceroy in 1794–5 approved the petition of Nicolás Mamaneli who proposed to make a trading voyage from
California and return; but nothing more is heard of
the scheme.[6] Permission was also granted to Antonio
Ponce to build a schooner and open a trade between
San Blas and California.[7]

I have alluded to Borica's recommendation in favor
of the sending of special invoices by the government
for pueblo trade. In May 1797 the habilitado general made a long report in favor of the project, explaining that nothing but a market for produce could
arouse Californian industries from stagnation to prosperity; enumerating the facilities for a profitable
exportation of furs, hides, fish, grain, flax, oil, and
wine, and especially sardines, herring, and salmon, and
insisting that the government must take the initiative
in opening this provincial commerce, since the pros-

Condicion Actual de Cal., MS., 71–3. 1799, contracts not to be made with
Mission majordomos without consent of padre. *S. José, Arch.*, MS., vi. 40.

[5] Viceroy's communication of April 2, 1794, enclosing royal order of Oct.
1, 1793, and other papers. *Prov. St. Pap.*, MS., xi. 168, 188–9; xii. 21–2;
Prov. Rec., MS., iv. 116–17, 119, 140; *Arch. Arzobispado*, MS., i. 40; *Cedulario*, MS., i. 249.

[6] Feb. 28, 1795, viceroy to governor, in *Prov. St. Pap.*, MS., xiii. 12.

[7] *Nueva España, Acuerdos*, MS., 92–3.

pects at the first were not sufficiently flattering to attract private companies. He urged the sending of an experimental invoice of $6,000, and gave many details respecting the management of the business. Here so far as the records show the matter ended without practical benefit to Los Angeles and San José.[8] Two other commercial schemes in behalf of California were devised in 1800 and were still in abeyance at the end of this decade. Juan Ignacio Mendez, who had brought some goods to California for sale on the supply-ship in 1798 and had worked in the country as a carpenter, asked for a license to export California productions on private account by the same vessels. Juan Bautista Ovineta asked for the approval of a contract which he had made with the settlers of San José and Branciforte for one thousand fanegas of wheat each year at two dollars and a half a fanega. The viceroy and fiscal were disposed to favor both projects, but called on the governor for his opinion.[9]

---

[8] *Cárcaba, Informe del Habilitado General sobre la remision de memorias de Efectos para los Pueblos de California, 1797*, MS.

[9] Oct. 3, 1800, viceroy to governor, on the Mendez proposition. *St. Pap., Sac.*, MS., ix. 104–6. Dec. 18, 1800, fiscal to V. R., on Ovineta's contract. *Prov. St. Pap.*, MS., xviii. 72–5. Viceroy Azanza in his *Ynstruccion*, MS., 91–2, speaks of a proposal of Tepic merchants to supply California with merchandise. On prices I append the following items: Feb. 26, 1791, Fages suggests a reduction in some of the tariff prices for grain and meat. *Prov. St. Pap.*, MS., x. 156–7. Prices at Sta Bárbara and S. Buenaventura, 1794 to 1821. *Arch. Sta Bárbara*, MS., vii. 44–66, 80–111; ix. 485–7. Sept. 22, 1795, Borica gives a list of articles which could be advantageously sold in California, including hats costing $22 and selling at $30 per dozen; stockings, $9–$12 per dozen; handkerchiefs, $13–$18 per dozen; gold lace, $28–$50 per pound; chocolate, 1.75 reales to 3.5 reales per pound. *Prov. St. Pap., Ben. Mil.*, MS., xxii. 2. 1796, *cojinillos*, saddle-pads, 50 cents a pair. *Prov. Rec.*, MS., vi. 160. Wheat, $3 per fanega. *Dept. St. Pap., S. José*, MS., i. 69. Freight on grain from Angeles to Sta Bárbara 7 reals. *Prov. Rec.*, MS., iv. 82–3. 1797, wool 18 reals per arroba (9 cents per pound). *Id.*, iv. 91; $3 at Monterey. *Dept. St. Pap., S. José*, MS., i. 78; *Prov. Rec.*, MS., iv. 214. Lambs offered, 7 reals; asked by padres, $1. *Prov. St. Pap.*, MS., xv. 86. 1798, tiles $20 per thousand. *Id.*, xvii. 97. Bulls, $4. *Id.*, xvii. 103. Calves, $4; cows, $5. *Prov. Rec.*, MS., iv. 102, 105. 1799, blankets $4.50; brandy, $1.07 per *cuartillo;* figs, 30 cents per pound; olive-oil, 40 cents per pound. *Prov. Rec.*, MS., iv. 110; vi. 233. Chickens, 50 cents per dozen. *S. José, Arch.*, MS., vi. 41. June 26, 1799, Borica favors reduction in price of horses from $9 to $7; mares, $4 to $3; and colts, $5 to $3.50. Other tariff prices fair enough. *Prov. Rec.*, MS., vi. 126–7. Soap, 15 cakes for $1. Tithe wheat may be sold for 13 reals for cash or on 4 months' time. *S. José, Arch.*, MS., vi. 48, 41.

The matters of provincial finance, presidial supplies, and habilitado's accounts are closely allied to that of commerce, since the distribution of supplies constituted for the most part the traffic of the country. There were no radical changes in the system of financial management during this decade. Each year an appropriation from the royal treasury was made in Mexico to cover all Californian expenses, according to the pay-roll of officers, soldiers, artisans, and settlers. Before 1796 it was about $64,000; subsequently by reason of the reënforcements of Catalan volunteers and artillerymen, of artisan instructors, and of the settlers of Branciforte, the amount was raised to about $81,000.[10] Each year in March or April a list was sent from California of all the articles which would be needed for the following year and which could not be purchased in the province. From the appropriation was deducted the amount of drafts on Mexico with which supplies obtained in California had been paid for, and also the amount of various royal revenues retained in California and represented by drafts. Then there was added the amount of supplies furnished in California to vessels or by due authority to native laborers, or otherwise properly disposed of. Finally, the memorias of needed articles were purchased at Mexico and San Blas and shipped regularly to the north. The accounts of each presidial company and of the volunteers and artillery were kept separate, and there was usually a balance of a few hundred or a few thousand dollars for or against each company, according as the memorias were less or greater than the net appropriation. The habilitados were not allowed to include in their lists articles of luxury. Some coin was sent with each invoice, enough to pay the salaries

<hr/>

[10] For separate presidial accounts see chapters xxx.–xxxii. The following references are somewhat general in their nature, embracing accounts and fragments relating to all the presidios: *St. Pap., Sac.,* MS., i. 47–8; ii. 35, 38; vi. 115; ix. 48, 58–60, 74–6; xv. 10–12; *Prov. St. Pap., Ben. Mil.,* MS., xiv. 8; xix. 5, 7–9; xxvi. 5; xxvii. 5, 6; xxviii. 21–2; *Prov. Rec.,* MS., ii. 160; v. 6, 7, 10; vi. 120–1; *Prov. St. Pap.,* MS., xvii. 35–43; *Prov. St. Pap., Presidios,* MS., ii. 76–88.

of the governor and one or two other officers, with a small amount for the soldiers. There was at one time an order that all balances due the companies be sent in coin, but I find no evidence that anything of the kind was ever done.[11]

Until 1791 the purchase of supplies and general management of California business in Mexico was in the hands of a factor, Pedro Ignacio Aríztegui being the last to hold that position, preceded by Ramon Manuel de Goya from 1776, and his place taken by José Avila from 1785 for several years. Francisco Hijosa as commissary attended to the business at

[11] From the voluminous correspondence on the topics treated in this and the next paragraph I present the following items: 1790, full details on forms of accounts. *Prov. St. Pap.*, MS., ix. 289–99, 305. Viceroy's orders for reports, etc., to aid Romeu in his investigation of presidial accounts. *Id.*, ix. 313–19. Sept. 26, 1790, Revilla Gigedo's letter to court recommending the appointment of Cárcaba as habilitado general, and explaining the desirability of the new office. *Estudillo, Doc. Hist. Cal.*, MS., i. 8, 9. May 14, 1791, royal order creating the office. *Prov. St. Pap., Ben. Mil.*, MS., xxv. 2. Oct. 3, 1791, viceroy communicates royal approval of Cárcaba's appointment to governor. *Prov. St. Pap.*, MS., x. 136–7. Sept. 20th, habilitado's deficits to be charged to the company pro rata, and he is to live on 25 cts per day under arrest, his property also being sold. *Id.*, x. 76. Some clerical fees had to be paid from California on statements of account. *Id.*, xii. 105. Damaged effects charged to the factor; expenses to company. *Prov. Rec.*, MS., ii. 158, Jan. 4, 1793. Sending of supplies suspended until accounts are cleared up. *Prov. St. Pap., Ben. Mil.*, MS., xx. 4. Jan. 23, 1794, habilitado general, his appointment, accounts, etc. *Nueva España, Acuerdos*, MS., 40–3. May 12th, gov. complains to V. R. of lack of system in the accounts. *Prov. St. Pap.*, MS., xxi. 138–40. 1794, Col. Alberni was refused 50 arrobas of flour, because it could be bought in California. *St. Pap., Sac.*, MS., ix. 41–2. Articles of luxury not to be included in memorias. Balances in coin, one fourth in small change. *Prov. Rec.*, MS., iv. 124–5; *Prov. St. Pap.*, MS., xii. 182–3. Dec. 1795, 10 per cent advance to be charged on goods distributed to Indians. *Id.* The habilitados had to send with their memorias an account of the condition of arms, dress, and other kinds of property. *Prov. St. Pap.*, MS., xii. 91. Jan. 1, 1795, Borica to Cárcaba, complaining of the inefficiency of his officers especially as habilitados. Grajera is named as an exception. *Prov. St. Pap.*, MS., xxi. 213–14. April, $6,000 in silver coin sent to California. *Prov. St. Pap., Ben. Mil.*, MS., xxi. 10. Report of Feb. 19, 1795, on the accounts of the expedition of 1769–74. *Prov. St. Pap.*, MS., xiii. 5–9. Habilitado general considered as agent and apoderado of the California Indians. *Prov. Rec.*, MS., vi. 2. Company accounts must bear the signature of commandant and alférez besides that of the habilitado. *St. Pap. Sac.*, MS., vii. 40. 1797, precautions against counterfeit money, with indications that some of it was in circulation in California. *Prov. Rec.*, MS., iv. 154; vi. 78; *Prov. St. Pap.*, MS., xvi. 245. March 19, 1797, Borica asks for a release of habilitados from some duties, and the appointment of administrators. *Prov. Rec.*, MS., vi. 83–4. Gov. still at work on the accounts of 1781–92. *Id.* Cárcaba succeeded by Columna. *Guerra, Doc. Hist. Cal.*, MS., iii. 168–9; *Prov. St. Pap.*, MS., xvii. 209, 322–3; *Prov. Rec.*, MS., iv. 112; viii. 224. Arrears of pay at San Diego. *Prov. St. Pap.*, MS., xxi. 34, 60–3.

San Blas until 1795 and perhaps throughout the decade. In 1791 Manuel Cárcaba, at the recommendation of Revilla Gigedo, was put in possession of the newly created office of habilitado general with the rank of captain and the pay of $1,200 a year. He was to devote his whole attention to California business as the factor had not done. The office was to be elective; and in 1799, Cárcaba obtaining leave of absence, Eucario Antonio Columna was appointed to succeed him *ad interim* in May, and the choice was duly ratified by the presidial companies in August and September. It is not certain that Columna ever took possession of the office, there being some indications that Cárcaba held it again in 1802. Through want of skill on the part of the habilitados the accounts were always in confusion. Deficits during this decade are noticed in local chapters. In 1793 the forwarding of supplies was once suspended till the accounts could be adjusted. In 1795 the final orders were issued for settling the old accounts of the first expeditions of 1769–74. Many of the soldiers were now dead and their descendants scattered. Whenever the sum due was large, the heirs were to be sought; otherwise the money was to be spent in masses for the souls of the dead pioneers. In 1797 Borica in the north and Arrillaga at Loreto were still at work on the accounts of the past decade. There had been $12,000 due the presidio of Santa Bárbara in 1792, and in 1801 the governor expressed doubts whether a settlement would ever be reached. Truly there was little inducement to the soldiers to live economically and to leave large balances in the hands of the government. The procuradores at San Fernando college, charged with the transaction of business for the California missions, were José Murguía and Tomás de la Peña, whose duties were simply to collect the friars' stipends and drafts sent from California, and with the proceeds to purchase supplies for shipment according to the orders received. Of the pious fund, source of the stipends, nothing in particular is known pertaining directly to this epoch; but Revilla Gigedo in his report of 1793 represents the fund as rapidly running to decay, and predicts that the royal treasury will have to make new sacrifices in behalf of the missions.[12]

The Californians were free from *alcabalas*, or excise tax, on articles bought and sold for five years from 1787 to 1792, and again for ten years from 1794. From 1792 to 1794 one half the regular tax of six per cent was paid, but statistics are insufficient to show the revenue from this source, which was very small. There was also a tribute of one fanega of corn per year paid by the settlers, which yielded to the king something over $100.[13] From $100 to $200 a year resulted from the sale of papal indulgences, an ecclesiastical revenue, but managed by the treasury officials.[14] Another ecclesiastical revenue belonging to the bishop of Sonora, but by him sold to the royal treasury, was that of *diezmos*, or tithes. This tax of ten per cent on all products must be paid by settlers after five years and by the rancho del rey, only the missions being exempt. The treasury gained five per cent by the purchase from the bishop, the habilitados received ten per cent of gross receipts for collection, and it was customary to sell the tithes for a year in advance at auction whenever a purchaser could be found, the price being the probable proceeds, and the purchaser making his profit by a more careful collection than the officials would enforce. This tax was collected in kind for grain and even for live-stock when the animals could be used at the presidios. The net proceeds, paid by drafts into the branch treasury at Rosario, or at Guadalajara after 1795, were over $1,200.[15]

[12] *Revilla Gigedo, Carta de 1793*, MS., 18, 19.
[13] *Prov. St. Pap.*, MS., x. 178; xi. 8, 9; *Id., Ben. Mil.*, xviii. 6, 7; xxv. 6, 7; *S. José Arch.*, MS., iii. 21. Tributes paid at Monterey in 1793, were $12, and in 1794, $22. In 1797, 24 men paid $97. *Alcabalas* at Monterey in 1793–4, $236.
[14] See chapter xxvii.; also local items in chapters xxx.–xxxii. this volume.
[15] 1794, tithes paid into real caja de Rosario. *Prov. St. Pap.*, MS., xii.

The largest item of royal revenue in California, as in all other Spanish provinces where no rich mines were worked, was that produced by the sale of tobacco, always monopolized by the government. The net product of cigars, cigaritos, and snuff, little or no tobacco being used for chewing or smoked in pipes, was not less than $6,000 a year on an average.[16] Postal revenue amounted to about $700 a year, the habilitados serving as post-masters at their respective presidios, and receiving eight per cent of gross receipts as a compensation for their services.[17]

The management of all branches of the revenue was

135. Sta Bárbara tithes for 1794 were $328. The governor authorizes the commandant to sell them for two years at $400. *Prov. Rec.*, MS., iv. 9, 10, 20. Capt. Ortega bid $200 (per year) on condition that the presidio purchase grain and cattle at tariff prices. *Prov. St. Pap.*, MS., xiii. 173-4. Oct. 1795, tithes and quicksilver revenue of California transferred to Guadalajara. *Id.*, xiii. 44-5; xiv. 5; *Prov. Rec.*, MS., iv. 143; *St. Pap., Sac.*, MS., xvii. 2. 1796, items showing that the tithes on live-stock, when paid in money or grain, were from 10 to 25 cents per head, or for mules 50 cents. *Prov. St. Pap.*, MS., xvi. 178, 244; *Id., Presidios*, i. 8; *S. José Arch.*, MS., v. 29. Habilitados allowed 10 per cent. *Prov. St. Pap.*, MS., xvi. 178. No offers to rent the tithes of Sta Bárbara in 1799. *Prov. Rec.*, MS., iv. 109. Jan. 22, 1800, Sal to comisionado of San José, urging him in no gentle terms to hasten the branding. Excommunication is the penalty for failure to pay tithes. *S. José, Arch.*, MS., iii. 57. Twenty-five ewes claimed out of every thousand killed. *St. Pap. Mis.* and *Colon*, MS., i. 38. Tithe cattle sold at $1.25 each. *S. José, Arch.*, MS., iii. 66.

[16] Product in 1789, $6,019. Consumption in 1790, 7,751 pckgs. cigars, 71,323 pckgs. cigaritos, and 13 lbs. of snuff. *St. Pap., Sac.*, MS., iii. 3, 5, 7. Revenue in 1793, $4,018. *Prov. St. Pap.*, MS., xi. 183; xxi. 136. In 1796, $7,918. *Prov. St. Pap., Presidios*, MS., ll. 89-90. In 1800, $7,981. *Prov. St. Pap., Ben. Mil.*, MS., xxviii. 8. The habilitados received 5 per cent on gross sales, and the habilitado of Monterey as administrator got $545 a year. *Id.*, xxvii. 8.

[17] In the numerous communications in the archives respecting the management of the mails during this decade there is very little matter of interest or value. 1790, $250 paid for a special express from Nootka. *Prov. St. Pap., Ben. Mil.*, MS., xix. 10. 1792, couriers to leave San Francisco on 1st of each month. *Prov. Rec.*, MS., ii. 152. 1793, a courier sent from Monterey Nov. 16th, arrived at San Diego Nov. 23d, and at Loreto Dec. 7th. The day and hour of arrival and departure at each mission are given. The stay at each station was generally an hour. *Prov. St. Pap.*, MS., xi. 77-80. In 1794 a change was made in route, mails going via Chihuahua and Buenavista instead of Álamos and Guadalajara. *Prov. Rec.*, MS., vi. 25; viii. 145-6; *Prov. St. Pap.*, MS., xi. 194. English letters taken from the bags and sent to Mexico in 1794-5. *Prov. Rec.*, MS., iv. 9, 121; *Prov. St. Pap.*, MS., xii. 134; xiii. 175. 1795, mails leave Monterey on 3d of each month for south. *Prov. Rec.*, MS., v. 304. Net proceeds in 1796-7 were $758. *Prov. St. Pap., Ben. Mil.*, MS., xxv. 14. New mail-bags in 1797. *Prov. St. Pap.*, MS., xvi. 193. Administrators of P. O. got 8 per cent. *Prov. St. Pap., Ben. Mil.*, MS., xxviii. 14. Vessel carrying the mail across the gulf lost in 1800. *Prov. St. Pap.*, MS., xviii. 86.

in the hands of the habilitados for their respective jurisdictions, the accounts being sent to Monterey for transmission to Mexico; until in 1799 Hermene-gildo Sal, as habilitado of Monterey, was formally appointed administrator general of royal exchequer revenues for New California.[18]

The military force maintained in California during this decade was 280 men of the presidial companies, besides governor and surgeon, and 90 Catalan volunteers and artillerymen after 1796. There were 12 commissioned officers, 35 non-commissioned officers, 260 private soldiers, 60 pensioners, and four or five mechanics. Grades and salaries I append in a note.[19] In 1799 an effort was made by the officers, supported by the governor, to obtain an increase of pay to the extent of $150 per year. It was claimed that the sum received was insufficient to supply food and clothing to the officer's family, his children going barefoot and in rags, while his wife had to take in washing and sewing. No immediate result is recorded. With their pay the cavalry soldiers must buy food, clothing, arms, and horses; but the latter were taken back and

[18] Nov. 7, 1799, Sal declared administrator. *Prov. Rec.*, MS., iv. 176; *Prov. St. Pap.*, MS., xvii. 285, 315. 1795, tobacco accounts sent to habili-tado of Monterey, as also cattle accounts; tithes to Rosario; mail accounts to administrator general at Mexico; *bulas* to the respective branch of the treasury. *Prov. St. Pap.*, MS., xiii. 26; *Prov. Rec.*, MS., iv. 133.

[19] Salaries paid were as follows: governor (lieut.-col.), $4,000; captain Cat. vol., $840; alférez or sub.-lieut., $400; alférez Cat. vol., $384; sergeant, $262.50; sergeant artillery, $240; sergeant Cat. vol., $192; soldiers, $217.50; soldiers Cat. vol., $132; soldiers artillery, $180; invalid alférez, $200; invalid corporal, $96; surgeon, $840; lieutenant, $550; lieutenant Cat. vol., $480; bleeder, $360; corporal, $225; corporal artillery, $204; corporal Cat. vol., $156; mechanics, $180; drummer Cat. vol., $144; armorer, $217; invalid sergeant, $120; invalid soldier, $96. Nov. 5, 1792, Arrillaga to viceroy, urging a provision for sending the soldiers' pay in advance, as was done in some other presidios, though contrary to the reglamento. The delays, especially in fitting out new recruits and in paying off soldiers whose term had expired, caused great hardship. *Prov. St. Pap.*, MS., xxi. 80–4. Oct. 2, 1793, viceroy orders two payments in advance to lieutenants Grajera and Parrilla for travelling expenses. *St. Pap., Sac.*, MS., ix. 71. 1797, sailors employed in defensive duty get 25 cents per day. *Prov. St. Pap.*, MS., xxi. 256. 1799, correspondence between commandants, governor, and viceroy respecting an increase of pay for the presidial officers. *St. Pap., Sac.*, MS., i. 123–4; *Prov. Rec.*, MS., iv. 113; vi. 120–1.

credited at the expiration of the term. The Catalan
volunteers received less pay, and had no horses to
buy. For them and for the artillerymen separate invoices of effects were sent from Mexico, to the amount
of about $15,000 per year. This infantry company
was not deemed a very useful addition to the forces
of the country, and it was hoped that most of the
members at the expiration of their term might be
induced either to reënlist in the cuera companies or
remain in the country as settlers.[20]

I explain elsewhere the military and presidio system. Here it is my purpose to note briefly the condition of military affairs and the slight modifications
that occurred during the decade. The regular term
of enlistment was ten years,[21] but at least eighteen
years' service was required for retirement as an invalid on half-pay pension, and the pensioners were
often retained a long time in the service for want of
recruits to fill their places. From the pay of each

[20] The compañía de voluntarios de Cataluña was also called the compañía
de fusileros de montaña. *Prov. St. Pap.*, MS., xiii. 186. Dec. 1795, the petition of the volunteers for travelling expenses denied. *Prov. Rec.*, MS., viii.
158; *St. Pap., Miss. and Colon.*, MS., i. 363. June 1797, volunteers may
enlist in the companies on expiration of their term, but not before, and enjoy
the advantages of their previous services. They were encouraged to marry
christianized natives as a means of retaining them in the country. *Prov. St.
Pap.*, MS., xv. 252–3; *Prov. Rec.*, MS., viii. 175. July 1, 1796, Alberni
argues that the volunteers desiring to become settlers should receive double
allowances, on account of their 15 or 20 years of service and because it is hard
for an old soldier to bend his body to the axe, hoe, and plow. *St. Pap., Miss.
and Colon.*, MS., i. 368–9, 379. March 1799, Borica favors an increase of
cavalry in place of infantry. *Prov. Rec.*, MS., vi. 121–2. Aug. 1799, B. says
the artillery-men live at the batteries and alternate with the infantrymen in
their duties. When free they promenade about the presidios. No complaints of injustice heard. *Id.*, vi. 128.

[21] There are no records that any recruits were obtained from abroad during this decade—certainly there were but very few; neither do the archives
show how many recruits were obtained in California to keep the companies
full; but many of the young men chose a military career. There was no
bounty paid. *Prov. St. Pap.*, MS., ix. 192–3; *Vallejo, Doc. Hist. Cal.* MS.,
xv. 3–66, 69, 72, 85, 92. Jan. 15, 1794, governor says he found many useless
men at the presidios and tried to promote recruiting so as to fill the vacancies
with good men. *Prov. St. Pap.*, MS., xxi. 132. March, 1795, Gov. orders
commandant of Fronteras to enlist 15 or 20 young men. *Prov. Rec.*, MS., v. 310.
Dec. 1797, corporal sent to Angeles to recruit 6 youths so that as many invalids
may be released. *Id.*, v. 261; *Prov. St. Pap.*, MS., xvi. 184. June 1799. Sal
wants a healthy robust man from San José to fill a vacancy. Not a widow's
son. *S. José, Arch.*, MS., vi. 47.

soldier was kept back a certain sum constituting the *fondo de retencion,* to be paid him on his discharge. This was fifty dollars till 1797, when it was raised to one hundred dollars, to be made up in four annual retentions.[22]

In military discipline there was nothing notable at this time.[23] In 1793 the governor recommended that San Francisco, Santa Bárbara, and San Diego be commanded by captains who should have nothing to do with the presidial accounts,[24] but the suggestion was not followed, though several of the lieutenants were brevetted captains before 1800. In 1794 the presidios were reported to have no flags and no material with which to make them; accordingly one flag for each establishment was sent from Mexico the next year.[25] In the matter of uniform and equipments buckskin *chupas,* or jackets, and breeches were allowed to be worn on active duty, and *anqueras,* heavy leather coverings for horses' haunches, were prohibited in 1794.[26] In 1795 the royal tribunal,

[22] *Prov. St. Pap.,* MS., xvi. 63, 223; xv. 50. The other military 'funds' were the *fondo de gratificacion,* an allowance of $10 for each man in the companies per year for miscellaneous company expenses; the *fondo de inválidos,* a small discount on soldiers' wages, 8 maravedís on a dollar, for the payment of pensions; and the *fondo de montepio,* a discount of officers' pay for similar purposes. Feb. 1795, the king ordered $5 per month as alms paid to the old carpenter Lorenzo Esparza. *Prov. St. Pap., Ben. Mil.,* MS., xxv. 16. This sum was paid to Esparza until his death. April 1795, 70 persons in the four presidios entitled to retirement but no recruits to replace them. *Prov. St. Pap.,* MS., xxi. 221–2. Dec. 6, 1796, royal order regulating details of pensions. *Prov. Rec.,* MS., iv. 151–2. Oct. 1797, invalids declining to live in the pueblos must stand guard at the presidios. *Prov. St. Pap.,* MS., xvi. 86–7, 184; xv. 99–100; *Prov. Rec.,* MS., iv. 159–60. Oct. 1798, retired officers who held government positions get no half-pay. *Prov. Rec.,* MS., vi. 104.

[23] 1795, Sergt. Ruiz reports that the soldiers at San Buenaventura have to be treated with severity. Their insubordination has reached such a point that they have to be threatened with kicks. *Prov. St. Pap.,* MS., xiv. 45. But Ruiz was arrested for offensive language to private Lugo. *Id.,* xiii. 14. Albino Tobar sent out of the country for bad conduct. *Prov. Rec.,* MS., v. 62. Two soldiers given two hours of extra guard duty per day, wearing their *cueras,* for eight days, having allowed some Indian prisoners to escape. *Prov. St. Pap.,* MS. xvi. 173.

[24] *Prov. St. Pap.,* MS., xxi. 108–9. A captain also proposed for Santa Bárbara in 1799. *Prov. Rec.,* MS., vi. 121.

[25] *Prov. St. Pap.,* MS., xi. 200; xiv. 58; xxi. 190.

[26] *Prov. St. Pap.,* MS., xii. 28, 143; xvii. 98. *S. José, Arch.,* MS., ii. 79; *Prov. Rec.,* MS., iv. 8; v. 24.

through Contador Beltran, reported to the viceroy that the California soldiers had too many duties not belonging to their profession, serving as vaqueros, farmers, couriers, artisans, and butchers, so that but little time was left for rest or for their proper duty of protecting and advancing the spiritual conquest.[27] The governor also urged the necessity in 1795, and again in 1799, of appointing an adjutant-inspector to relieve him of some of his duties.[28] In connection with the apprehensions of attack by foreigners in 1797, a slight attempt was made to organize the militia of California, and a distribution of arms and ammunition was made among the settlers, the employment of the natives as auxiliary forces being also contemplated.[29]

Civil and political government had but a nominal existence at this epoch, consisting mainly in the facts that the comandante de armas was also political governor of the province and that each pueblo had its alcalde. This is not the place to attempt an analysis of the relations between military and civil authority, in which there was substantially no change from the beginning down to the end of Spanish power in California. The only topic that requires notice in the annals of this decade is the proposed separation of the two Californias hitherto forming a single province under one governor. This separation was recommended in March 1796, by Beltran of the court of exchequer in Mexico, who based his argument on the great distance between Loreto and Monterey, and the consequent delays in the transaction of all public business. Arrillaga at Loreto could take no action until he had communicated with Borica at Monterey. Orders from Mexico for Loreto must make the jour-

[27] *Prov. St. Pap.*, MS., xiii. 185-6.
[28] April 3, 1795, March 18, 1799, Borica to viceroy. *Prov. Rec.*, MS., vi. 121; *Prov. St. Pap.*, MS., xxi. 221. There had been no such officer since the time of Capt. Nicolás Soler.
[29] *Prov. Rec.*, MS., iv. 87, 93, 165; *Prov. St. Pap.*, MS., xv. 101-2; xvi. 55, 222.

ney to Monterey and back, and reports from Loreto made the same circuit on their way to Mexico. The inconvenience of all this was apparent, and the separation in military and political rule was greatly facilitated by that already existing in mission affairs. Borica made a full report in favor of the change in September, declaring that the interests of both parts of the province could not be properly attended to by a governor at Monterey, favoring in connection with the change a transfer of the capital of the peninsula from Loreto to the frontier, expressing the greatest confidence in Arrillaga's ability, and suggesting an increase of his salary. No one had anything to say in opposition to the separation, which we shall see was accomplished during the next decade.[30]

On the administration of justice, we learn that in 1794 Ignacio Rochin was shot for murder at Santa Bárbara, on a sentence coming from the audiencia of Guadalajara.[31] A soldier was sentenced to ten years public labor at San Blas for incest in 1799, while his daughter and accomplice was condemned to seclusion for two years.[32] There were six or seven cases of murder among the natives, the culprits being condemned by the viceroy to terms of four to eight years of presidio work or imprisonment together with floggings.[33]

[30] March 7, 1796, Beltran's proposition. *Prov. St. Pap.*, MS., xiv. 140-4. March 21st, viceroy to Borica transmitting the proposition. *Id.*, 140; *Prov. Rec.*, MS., v. 344; viii. 159. July 11th, Borica to Arrillaga on the subject, in which he calls Beltran 'El Tuerto.' *Id.*, v. 343. Aug. 18th, Arrillaga favors the change. *Id.*, iii. 268. Sept. 11th, Borica's report to viceroy. *Borica, Proyecto sobre division de las Californias en dos provincias, 1796*, MS.

[31] See chapter xxx. In 1801 Cristóbal Simental is mentioned as having arrived at Monterey for the audiencia of Guadalajara; but nothing is known of his business. *Prov. Rec.*, MS., x. 11.

[32] *St. Pap., Sac.*, MS., i. 122; *Prov. Rec.*, MS., iv. 109; viii. 187.

[33] 1796, four natives for murder of another, four years of prison with 50 to 100 lashes. *Prov. Rec.*, MS., iv. 43-4, 84. 1797, Indian who undertook to punish his wife and through ignorance 'overdid it,' four years on public works. *Prov. St. Pap.*, MS., xv. 277. 1799, wife-murderer at Santa Bárbara, eight years of hard labor in chains. I append some minor cases of interest: 1800, Rafael Gomez, apparently for lying, condemned by P. Catalá, commissioned by Lasuen, to sweep the church daily and attend mass, besides asking a padre's pardon, being put in irons to await the governor's approval of this sentence. *San José, Arch.*, MS., iii. 55-7. 1799, no cases pending which belong to the

The most striking criminal case of the period, though by no means a pleasing one to describe, was that of José Antonio Rosas. He was a native of Los Angeles, only eighteen years of age, and a private soldier in the Santa Bárbara company in the guard of San Buenaventura. In June 1800, while in charge of the animals at La Mesa, he was seen to commit a *crímen nefando* by two Indian girls, who reported the matter. Criminal proceedings were at once instituted by order of Comandante Goycoechea, Alférez Pablo Cota being prosecuting attorney, the cadet Ignacio Martinez acting as clerk, the soldier José María Dominguez as interpreter, and the retired sergeant José María Ortega as defender of the accused. Rosas made a confession, pleading only that he was tempted by El Demonio. Cota demanded the death penalty, Ortega made an eloquent appeal for mercy, and in July the case went to the viceroy. The sentence rendered in September, after consultation with the auditor de guerra, was that Rosas must be hanged and the body burned together with that of the mule, "en quien cometió tan horrible delito." The execution took place on Feb. 11, 1801, at Santa Bárbara presidio in the presence of the whole garrison; but there being no hangman in California, the boy had to be

audiencia. *Prov. St. Pap.*, MS., xxi. 290. 1797, natives for assault on neophytes sentenced to work on presidio in shackles for a month or two. *Prov. St. Pap.*, MS., xvi. 77–8. 1796, carpenter Martinez exiled to San José for eight years for assault and wounding. *Prov. Rec.*, MS., iv. 198. 1797, Cristóbal Rey prosecuted for assault, with some details of proceedings. *Prov. St. Pap.*, MS., xvi. 251–2. Natives sentenced by Borica to from 10 to 30 lashes for stealing. *Id.*, *Ben. Mil.*, MS., xxvii. 4. 1799, slave Máximo sentenced to four years service on the royal vessels for stealing silver-ware from his master Alberni; and the soldier Oseguera to five years for receiving the goods. *Prov. Rec.*, MS., vi. 119. Four hundred dollars stolen from the warehouse at Monterey. *Id.*, iv. 171. 1798, two soldiers at San Francisco put in irons for stealing a calf and sheep from the mission. *Prov. St. Pap.*, MS., xvii. 111. 1795, twenty-five lashes and three months' work in shackles for stealing clothes. A Sinaloa Indian at San José. *Prov. Rec.*, MS., v. 49. 1800, two soldiers sentenced to a year's presidio work for breaking open a trunk. *Prov. St. Pap.*, *Ben. Mil.*, MS., xxix. 1. 1796, viceroy sends sentence of 50 lashes and 4 years' labor against three neophytes and a pagan. *St. Pap.*, *Sac.*, MS., xiv. 13. A settler of San José received 25 blows with a stick. *Prov. St. Pap.*, *Ben. Mil.*, MS., xxvi. 14. Cordero, a settler of Branciforte, sentenced to a month of hard work for striking the commandant, who was reprimanded for his hasty action. *Santa Cruz, Arch.*, MS., 69–70.

shot after receiving from Father Tapia the last comforts of religion and reciting the service in a firm voice. On a burning heap of wood near at hand the rest of the sentence was carried out, and the charred remains of the victim, fitted by the purification of flame for rest in consecrated ground, was buried in the presidio cemetery.[34]

Thus we see that the morality of the Californians was somewhat closely looked after by the authorities. The settlers at the pueblos gave more trouble than any other class, being free from military discipline and enjoying greater facilities for sinful dissipations. Sebastian Alvitre of Los Angeles and Francisco Ávila of San José were usually in prison, in exile, or at forced work for their excesses with Indian women and with the wives of their neighbors; and there were other settlers who were scarcely less incorrigible. Concubinage and all irregular sexual relations were strictly prohibited and the authorities seem to have worked earnestly in aid of the friars to enforce the laws.[35]

[34] *Rosas, Causa Criminal*, MS., 1800–1. Certificate of execution. *Prov. St. Pap., Ben. Mil.*, xxviii. 17. Goycoechea begs the governor for a postponement on account of a prevailing illness which renders it difficult to spare a man. *Id.*, xxix. 4. Burial. *Sta. Bárbara, Lib. Mision*, MS., 23. Aug. 11, 1804, governor says a mule is to be given to the owner of the one burned. *Prov. Rec.*, MS., xi. 102. The author of *Romero, Memorias*, MS., was present at the execution. He says the boy's body was merely passed through the flames as a formality of purification; while the mule was entirely consumed.

[35] Shortcomings of Alvitre and Ávila. *Prov. St. Pap., Ben. Mil.*, MS., xiv. 6; *Prov. St. Pap.*, MS., ix. 215–16; x. 161. Navarro exiled from Los Angeles to San José, and relapsing, to San Francisco. *Id.*, x. 160–1. 1793, Higuera living improperly. Men in such cases to be handcuffed; women must not go to the pueblo when their husbands were absent; men and women who go to the mission without leave to sleep to be put in the stock. *St. Pap., Sac.*, MS., iii. 2. 1795, Goycoechea to Borica, 'Como solo se castiga á los hombres amancebados, que se ha de hacer con las mugeres que hacen gala de ello?' *Prov. St. Pap.*, MS., xiv. 33. Borica replies—warnings, threats, exposure to husbands, and finally seclusion in respectable houses with hard work. *Prov. Rec.*, MS., iv. 38. 1797, concubinage strictly forbidden. *St. Pap., Miss. and Colon.*, MS., i. 360. 1798, adulterers to be warned and then punished. The governor will decide about the women. *Prov. Rec.*, MS., iv. 277. 1799, 30 lashes for a man who abused Indian women. *Id.*, v. 114. Adultery case at San Miguel. *Prov. St. Pap.*, MS., xvii. 250. Ruiz found in bed with his corporal's wife at San Diego. Put in irons and the woman sent to Los Angeles. *Id.*, xvii. 253. Investigation of the case of an Indian woman at San Juan Capistrano who gave birth to a dog. *Id.*, xvii. 239; *Prov. Rec.* MS., v. 286–7.

The people were also closely restricted in the use of intoxicating liquors. Borica not only exercised his authority through his commandants to prevent and punish excesses and drunkenness, but restricted the introduction and sale of liquors so far as was possible under national commercial regulations. Wine and brandy made in either Upper or Lower California were of free sale. There is no positive proof that any brandy was manufactured in Upper California before 1800; but Ortega had a still, and it is probable that a beginning was made in this deadly industry. Toward the close of the decade it was decided that the introduction of brandy and mescal from abroad could not be prevented, but the governor could still regulate the sale to soldiers and others under government pay.[36] Gambling was another weakness prevalent in California as elsewhere in Spanish America, and requiring frequent attention from the authorities.[37]

[36] 1794, no mescal or even permitted liquors to be introduced by traders who barter at the missions. *Prov. St. Pap.*, MS., xii. 111. 1795, two barrels of wine brought from Santa Bárbara to Monterey. *Prov. Rec.*, MS., iv. 13. Borica to commandants, drinking and gambling must be stopped. *Prov. St. Pap.*, MS., xiii. 240; *San José, Arch.*, MS., iv. 24. 1796, sergeant at Monterey has some Spanish brandy for sale. Can only sell two reals worth in morning and one real in evening to one person, to be drunk in his presence. *Prov. Rec.*, MS., v. 333. 1797, commandants must promote manufacture of brandy from sugar-cane. *Id.*, iv. 90. Free introduction since Nov. 1797 of home-made liquors; but no debt can be collected for liquor furnished to troops, etc. *Prov. St. Pap.*, MS., xv. 112; xvi. 180; *Prov. Rec.*, iv. 163. Jan. 1797, general pardon to all imprisoned for contraband making of *chinquirito*, probably of no effect in California. *Prov. St. Pap.*, MS., xv. 18, 217–18. April, 1797, Brandy 'es de venta lícita.' *Prov. Rec.*, MS., iv. 158. Oct. 1798, Borica solicited a provision forbidding the introduction of mescal on account of the *inconvenientes y escándalos* resulting; but the viceroy in May 1799 declared that trade in mescal and aguardiente (Californian aguardiente was brandy; but the imported article may have been—though it probably was not—rum, whiskey, or other alcoholic liquor, the name being common to all) was free, and therefore other ways must be devised to stop drunkenness. *Prov. St. Pap.*, MS., xviii. 309; xvii. 209; *Prov. Rec.*, MS., vi. 104. 1799, some wine made at southern missions, and soon brandy enough will be produced for moderate consumption. *Prov. Rec.*, MS., vi. 130. Padres receive from San Blas the mescal they need. *Prov. St. Pap.*, MS., xvii. 78–9, 195. Sept. 3, 1799, Borica prohibits selling mescal. *Dept. St. Pap., San José*, MS., i. 96. Aug. 29, Borica asks that only two barrels of mescal be imported for each mission. Eighteen barrels of aguardiente from Baja California imported this year. *Prov. Rec.*, MS., vi. 130.

[37] Miscellaneous communications, nothing important. *Prov. Rec.*, MS., iv. 128; *San José, Arch.*, MS., ii. 78; iv. 23; *Prov. St. Pap.*, MS., xv. 127; *St. Pap., Miss. and Colon.*, MS., i. 360. 1798, Borica granted the petition of citizens of San José to be allowed to play *malilla* on Sundays in the guard-house. *Dept. St.*

There were no schools in California before Borica came as governor, at a time when many natives, of Spanish blood, had become parents of children growing up as they had done in ignorance. Few of the soldiers could read or write, and in fact this continued to be the case throughout the whole Spanish period.[33] Officers taught their children, and occasionally a woman acted as *amiga*, and instructed not only her own children but those of her neighbors, or even an ambitious soldier who aspired to be a corporal. In 1793 a royal order was issued and published in California requiring the establishment of a school in each pueblo, but referring apparently to the education of Indians only. Nothing was done under it, except to render a formal promise of compliance[39] at the end of 1794.

Borica began to agitate the matter by making inquiries respecting available teachers and sources of a school fund. Before the end of December the retired sergeant Manuel Vargas had started the first school in the public granary at San José.[40] The governor's communications continued through 1795; the old alférez Ramon Lasso de la Vega was sounded as to the terms on which he would become a teacher;

Pap., San José, MS., i. 139. The trader Gallego forbidden to hold raffles. *Prov. Rec.*, MS., iv. 108. 1799, *malilla* and *tururu* to be played only on feast days; no player must lose over $2; and no credit is to be given. *Id.*, iv. 291. Governor orders a sum lost at *albures* to be returned to Larios. Rebukes Comisionado of San José for habitual gambling at his house. *Id.*, iv. 293-4. *Porrazo, tururu, malilla*, and *cientos* may be played Sundays, if stakes are not over $1, and the sexes are kept separate. *Id.*, iv. 294. Children gambled for buttons, some of them cutting off the buttons from their clothing. Prominent men often looked on and made bets on the children's game of *tángano*. *Amador, Memorias*, MS., 227-8.

[38] 1781, alcalde of San José unable to write. *Pico, Doc. Hist. Cal.*, MS., i. 13. 1785, only 14 out of 50 of the Monterey company could write. *Prov. St. Pap., Ben. Mil.*, MS., vii. 1. 1786, seven out of 30 at San Francisco. *Id.*, vii. 2. 1791, two out of 28 at San Francisco. *Id.*, xv. 3. 1794, not a man at San Francisco can write. The commandant asks that one be sent from Santa Bárbara. *Prov. St. Pap.*, MS., xii. 41. 1800, many soldiers acting as corporals could not be promoted because they could not read. *Amador Mem.*, MS., 219.

[39] *Arch. Sta. Bárbara*, MS., vi. 293-4; *Prov. St. Pap.*, MS., xiv., 60; *Prov. Rec.*, MS., iv. 128.

[40] *Dept. St. Pap., S. José*, MS., i. 45; *Prov. Rec.*, MS., iv. 219.

José Manuel Toca, apparently a *grumete,* or ship-boy, from one of the transports, arrived at Santa Bárbara; Vargas was offered $250 a year contributed by citizens to go to San Diego; compulsory attendance and a tax of thirty-one cents a month per scholar were ordered at San José; Santa Bárbara was required to pay $125, each soldier paying one dollar; soldiers, corporals, and sergeants were ordered to go over their studies and prepare for promotion; and primary teachers were asked for from Mexico.[41] No doubt before the end of the year Vargas was teaching at San Diego, Lasso at San José, and Toca at Santa Bárbara. The *doctrina cristiana* was first to receive attention by the governor's orders, and afterward reading and writing were to be taught. Paper was furnished by the habilitados, and after being covered with scholarly pothooks, was collected to be used in making cartridges. In 1796 the above-named teachers continued their labors. Corporal Manuel Boronda, serving also as carpenter, taught the children of San Francisco gratuitously; the soldier and carpenter José Rodriguez did the same at Monterey, and Borica continued to interest himself greatly in the schools, requiring frequent reports to be sent him with copybooks for examination.[42]

In 1797 Toca was called away from Santa Bárbara to attend to his duties on board ship, being replaced by José Medina, another *grumete;* and Boronda was

[41] *Prov. Rec.*, MS., iv. 31–2, 136, 221, 229; *Prov. St. Pap.*, MS., xiii. 19, 34–5; xiv. 27; *Id., Ben. Mil.*, MS., xxi. 11; *Dept. St. Pap., San José*, MS., i. 50.

[42] Feb. 18, 1796, 27 children attending Lasso's school at San José: four pay nothing, and the rest two and one half reals per month. *Prov. St. Pap.*, MS., xiv. 101. Feb. 20th, Borica to Lasso, urges great care. His pay will be advanced from the tobacco revenue and collected from the settlers. A house to be furnished for L. and family. *Prov. Rec.*, MS., iv. 181. Feb. 25th, children attending Santa Bárbara school, 32. *Prov. St. Pap.*, MS., xiv. 101. May 6th, Borica speaks of Boronda and Rodriguez teaching at San Francisco and Monterey, Lasso at San José, a teacher at Santa Bárbara at $125 per year, and Vargas at San Diego at $100. *Prov. Rec.*, MS., v. 338–9. Sept. 20th, San Diego school has 22 pupils. *Prov. St. Pap., Presidios*, MS., i. 64. Governor orders reports, copybooks, etc., to be sent him every two, three, or six months. *Prov. Rec.*, MS., iv. 50; *St. Pap. Sac.*, MS., vi. 7.

succeeded at San Francisco by the artilleryman José
Álvarez, who for his services received an addition of
two dollars per month to his pay. Evidently the
schools went on with considerable prosperity this
year,[43] but of their progress for the rest of the decade
we know little or nothing.[44] .

[43] *Prov. St. Pap.*, MS., xvi. 41, 168–9; xxi. 262–3; *Prov. Rec.*, MS., v.
101, 108. Randolph, *Oration*, speaks of copybooks sent from Santa Bárbara, Feb. 11, 1797, still preserved in the archives, the samples being scrip-
ture texts in a fair round hand.

[44] Dec. 1798, Vargas transferred to Sta Bárbara. *Prov. Rec.*, MS., iv.
109. Borica complains that few pupils attend at San Diego. Parents must
be stimulated. *Id.*, v. 263. 1801, complaints of children growing up in
ignorance, and of great need of teachers. *Prov. St. Pap.*, MS., xviii. 54–5;
xxi. 65. Says Judge Sepúlveda: 'They could learn very little in those days;
schools were few, books rare, and the pursuits of the people required not a
very extensive book-learning. When any writing was needed they could
easily apply to the few who were the depositaries of legal form or epistolary
ability.' *Sepúlveda, Hist. Mem.*, MS., 3, 4. Many mission libraries had
Palou's Life of Serra and perhaps one or two other historical works before
1800, besides a few theological books. A few French books were given to
Borica by Capt. Dorr's French pilot in 1797. *Prov. Rec.*, MS., vi. 76–7.

CHAPTER XXX.

LOCAL EVENTS AND PROGRESS—SOUTHERN DISTRICT.

1791-1800.

San Diego Presidio—Lieutenants Zúñiga and Grajera—Military Force —Population—Rancho del Rey—Finances—Presidio Buildings— Vancouver's Description—Fort at Point Guijarros—Indian Affairs—Precautions against Foreigners—Arrivals of Vessels— Mission San Diego—Torrens and Mariner—Statistics—San Luis Rey—San Juan Capistrano—Fuster—Buildings—Pueblo de Los Angeles—Private Ranchos—San Gabriel—Orámas—San Fernando —Presidio of Santa Bárbara—Officers, Forces, and Population— Buildings and Industries—Local Events—First Execution in California—The 'Phœnix'—A Quicksilver Mine—Warlike Preparations—Death of Ortega—Mission of Santa Bárbara—Paterna— Rancherías of the Channel—New Church—San Buenaventura— La Purísima Concepcion—Arroita.

Lieutenant José de Zúñiga remained in command of the San Diego presidio[1] till October 1793. In May of the preceding year he had been promoted to captain and appointed commandant of Tucson in Sonora; but he was obliged to wait the arrival of his successor, who assumed the offices of comandante and habilitado on the 19th of October. Zúñiga was preparing for departure in November when Vancouver visited this port, and but little is known of his subsequent career. He had been a faithful and efficient officer, one of the few who in the performance of military duties, and especially in keeping presidial accounts, had given no cause of complaint.[2] His successor was Lieutenant

---

[1] For annals of San Diego from 1780 to 1790, which I here continue to 1800, see chap. xxii., this volume.

[2] José de Zúñiga enlisted as a *soldado distinguido* October 18, 1772; went through the grades from corporal to alférez in 1778-9; was made lieutenant,

Antonio Grajera, of the España dragoon regiment, who had arrived at San Francisco from San Blas in July, and who assumed the duties of his office on the day of his arrival at San Diego.

Though fifteen years a soldier Grajera had seen no active service, but he was an able and faithful man, and performed his official duties to the satisfaction of all during a term of six years in California. His private and social record is less favorable. He had no family, and it was not long before his *liaisons* with women of the presidio gave rise to scandal. His excessive use of intoxicating liquors finally affected his mind, and broke his constitution. He gave up his office temporarily in August 1799, and never resumed it, having, however, been made a brevet captain in 1797. Obtaining leave of absence to visit Mexico he sailed on the *Concepcion* and died two days out of port January 18, 1800.[3] From August 23,

April 21, 1780; commandant of San Diego, Sept. 8, 1781; habilitado, Oct. 19, 1781. Before coming to California he had seen much service in Indian campaigns in Sonora and Chihuahua. *Prov. St. Pap., Ben. Mil.*, MS., xiv. 9; xvi. 1. In 1790 he was granted leave of absence on petition of his mother to visit Mexico and attend to a legacy; but seems not to have left his post. He showed much attention to Vancouver, who named Pt Zúñiga on the lower coast in his honor, and who speaks of shoals in San Diego Bay called on a Spanish chart of 1782 'Barros de Zooniga' (Bajíos de Zúñiga). See Pantoja's map, p. 456, this vol.; *Vancouver's Voy.*, ii. 470, 473, 482. Letter of viceroy announcing his appointment as captain of Tucson dated May 29, 1792. *Prov. St. Pap.*, MS., xxi. 75. By a letter of May 30, 1810, it appears that he still held the same position, and had been made lieutenant-colonel. *Prov. St. Pap., Ben. Mil.*, MS., xliv. 1.

[3] Antonio Grajera enlisted as a private Aug. 13, 1772; served 4 years as private, 4 as corporal, 7 as sergeant, and 1 as flag-bearer; was made alférez April 15, 1789; and was appointed lieutenant to command San Diego July 14, 1792. *Prov. St. Pap.*, MS., xxi. 161, 174; *St. Pap., Sac.*, MS., iv. 18; i. 34. He arrived at San Francisco July 25, 1793, and at San Diego Oct. 15. Charges of licentiousness and drunkenness by an officer on the *Concepcion* Nov. 1794. *Prov. St. Pap.*, MS., xii. 11, 12; xvii. 251-2. 1797, a corporal asks for transfer on account of Grajera's disgraceful connection with his wife. *Id.*, xvi. 193. Royal order of promotion to brevet captain, June 12, and viceroy's despatch Oct. 28, 1797, acknowledged by Borica Feb. 26, 1798. *Id.*, xv. 265; *Prov. Rec.*, vi. 70-1; *Arch. Arz.*, MS., i. 201. Nov. 11, 1799, permission from Borica to go to Mexico. *Prov. Rec.*, MS., v. 236-7. Departure Jan. 16th, and death Jan. 18, 1800. *Id.*, v. xii. 1.; *Prov. St. Pap.*, MS., xxi. 30, 35. Feb. 11, 1800, decree of V. R. to put Grajera on the retired list, and naming Alférez Manuel Rodriguez of the San Francisco company to replace him. *Prov. St. Pap., Ben. Mil.*, MS., xxvi. 18; *St. Pap., Sac.*, MS., iv. 72-3; *Prov. St. Pap.*, MS., xxi. 36. Vancouver in November 1793 was very kindly treated by Grajera, and applied his name to a point below San Diego. *Vancouver's Voyage*, ii. 470-1, 478.

1799, by order of Borica, Alférez Manuel Rodriguez became acting commandant of the company, while Lieutenant José Font of the Catalan volunteers, ranking Rodriguez, was made temporary comandante of the military post. Rodriguez had been habilitado since the middle of 1798 and had really performed the functions of commander; and his regular appointment, dated in Mexico Feb. 11, 1800, reached San Diego in May, though his commission as lieutenant did not leave Mexico until July 1801.[4]

Pablo Grijalva was alférez of the company until December 1796, when he was retired, after thirty-three years of service, on half-pay of alférez and with rank of lieutenant, spending the remaining twelve years of his life in California. His successor, who served throughout the decade, was Alférez José Lujan, a new-comer from Mexico. Ignacio Alvarado,[5] the company sergeant, having become a pensioner of the Santa Bárbara company, was replaced in 1796 by Antonio Yorba, one of Fages' original Catalans and a son-in-law of Grijalva, who was retired as an invalid and succeeded by Francisco Acebedo in 1798. The corporals and privates, with generally an armorer and carpenter, varied but slightly in number from fifty-seven during the ten years, not including the retired soldiers, or invalids, who gradually increased from four in 1792 to fifteen in 1800.[6] From this force from

[4] Rodriguez habilitado from July 31, 1798. *Prov. St. Pap., Ben. Mil.*, MS., xvii. 1. Perhaps appointed in May. *Prov. Rec.*, MS., v. 276. Borica's order of Aug. 23, 1799. *Id.*, v. 293–4. Rodriguez' appointment as comandante by viceroy Feb. 11, 1800. *Prov. St. Pap., Ben. Mil.*, MS., xxviii. 15. Became full comandante May 24, 1800. *Id.*, xxvi. 18. Commission as lieutenant sent from Mexico July 17, 1801. *Prov. St. Pap.*, MS., xviii. 96. Rodriguez had never been alférez of the San Diego company, belonging nominally to that of San Francisco.

[5] Ignacio Rafael Alvarado, not an ancestor of the later governor, enlisted in 1773 at the age of 23. He came to San Diego in 1774, was made a corporal in 1781, and sergeant in 1783. In 1795 the governor complained of his lack of resolution, and in 1797 his *cédula de inválido* was received. He was still on the list of pensioners in 1805.

[6] The Lower Californian mission of San Miguel belonged at this period to San Diego, as did Los Angeles as late as 1796, at least so far as the military guard was concerned, though in other respects the pueblo was subject to Santa Bárbara. San Gabriel had its guard from San Diego throughout the dec-

twenty-seven to thirty-three men were constantly detached to form the five or six guards of the jurisdiction. After 1796 Lieutenant Font with twenty-five Catalan volunteers of the new reënforcements was stationed here, as were six artillerymen under Sergeant José Roca, increasing the effective force to nearly ninety men.[7] The white population of this southern district, consisting of the soldiers and their families, was about three hundred at the end of the decade, or two hundred and fifty exclusive of San Gabriel and Los Angeles, more conveniently classed with the Santa Bárbara district.[8] About one hundred and sixty lived at the presidio; and the rest were scattered in the missions, or lived as pensioners at the pueblo. Eight foundling children from Mexico were sent to San Diego to live in 1800.[9] The native neophyte population, excluding that of San Gabriel and San Miguel, was not quite three thousand.

There is no record of any agricultural operations whatever at or near the presidio, nor were there any private ranchos in the whole region before 1800. That some of the soldiers came down from Presidio Hill and cultivated small patches of vegetables would seem not unlikely, but the archives contain nothing on the subject. There were kept here, however, from 900 to 1,200 head of live-stock, including the company's horses, from 30 to 50 mules, two or three asses, possibly a few milch cows by the soldiers, and from 300 to 700 horned cattle in a branch of the rancho del rey

ade. *Prov. St. Pap.*, MS., xvii. 192. Feb. 1, 1796, Borica ordered escoltas to be as follows: San Miguel, 8; San Diego, 3; San Juan Capistrano, 8; San Gabriel, 4; Los Angeles, 4. *Prov. Rec.*, MS., v. 240. San Luis Rey, founded in 1798, probably had 6 men at first. According to orders, *Prov. St. Pap.*, MS., xii. 8, it was customary to have soldiers serve alternately in escoltas and presidio, though it caused much inconvenience on account of their families.

[7] Company rosters and statements of force and distribution scattered in the archives, chiefly in *Prov. St. Pap., Ben. Mil.*, MS., xiii.–xxvii., and *St. Pap., Sac.*, MS., i. vi.

[8] In the various reports on the population of the southern district in 1799 and later, the escorts and families are credited to the missions instead of the presidio as before and as in other parts of the country. List of rank and file of the presidial company in 1798, in *Prov. St. Pap., Ben. Mil.*, MS., xvii. 14–16.

[9] *Prov. St. Pap., Ben. Mil.*, MS., xxviii. 22.

maintained here during the last half of the decade.[10] Each year in Mexico an appropriation was made from the royal treasury for the presidio expenses, varying from $14,000 to $15,000; and invoices of goods, based on the habilitado's estimate of needs, were sent with a small amount of coin by the transports from San Blas, varying in amount from $11,000 to $17,000 per year. San Diego usually had a credit balance of from $1,000 to $3,000 in its favor. The *situado*, or allowance, for the volunteers and artillery was not included in the amounts above mentioned. Supplies to the amount of about $15,000 per year were sent to California for them, and San Diego received not quite one third.[11] There are no records of the annual supplies obtained from missions, but during the last three years of the decade the presidio was indebted to the missions about $10,000.

"The Presidio of St Diego," says Vancouver, who visited it in November 1793, "seemed to be the least of the Spanish establishments. It is irregularly built, on very uneven ground, which makes it liable to some inconveniences, without the obvious appearance of any object for selecting such a spot. With little difficulty

[10] The records are fragmentary and contradictory. Statistical reports sometimes include the king's cattle and sometimes not. There is no evidence that the rancho at this period included any horses; in fact it had been established to avoid driving cattle from the north. In 1797 it contained 681 cattle; increase for the year 137; sales, 30; killed by natives and wild beasts, 27; proceeds of sales, $125; tithes paid, $26; net profit to treasury, $99. *Prov. St. Pap., Ben. Mil.*, MS., xxv. 4. The total amount of tithes in the jurisdiction was $34. *Prov. St. Pap.*, MS., xvi. 178; and this difference of $8 is the only indication I find of the possible existence of a private rancho. Cattle at end of 1798, 531; proceeds of sales, $539. *Id.*, xvii. 1. 1800, cattle, 690; proceeds, $342. *Id.*, xviii. 5.

[11] San Diego Company accounts in *Prov. St. Pap.*, MS.. xiv.–xxxiii.; *St. Pap. Sac.*, MS., i. ii. vi. ix. Loss sustained on the government forge and carpenter's shop for 1797, $70. *Prov. St. Pap.*, MS., xvi. 179. *Fondo de gratificacion* for 1797: income $3,075, expended $2,641. *Prov. St. Pap. Presid.*, MS., i. 102–3. *Fondo de Retencion* for 1800: $3,750. *Prov. St. Pap., Ben. Mil.*, MS., xxviii. 18. Inventory of effects in warehouse 1798, $13,992. *Id.*, xvii. 4. Papal bulls on hand Nov. 1795, $4,339. *Id.*, xiii. 5, received from Zúñiga with the office by Grajera. *Prov. Rec.*, MS., v. 227. Bulls needed for 1796–7, 100 at 25 cents for *vivos;* 100 at 25 cents for *difuntos;* 50, *lacticinio;* 2 or 3 *composicion. Prov. St. Pap., Ben.*, MS., i. 12. Net revenue of San Diego post-office for 1794, $71; for 1796, $95. *Prov. St. Pap., Ben. Mil.*, MS., xxi. 2; xxiii. 8. Accounts of presidio with missions 1797–1800. *Id.*, xxxiii. 13; *Prov. St. Pap.*, MS., xvi. 265; xvii. 195.

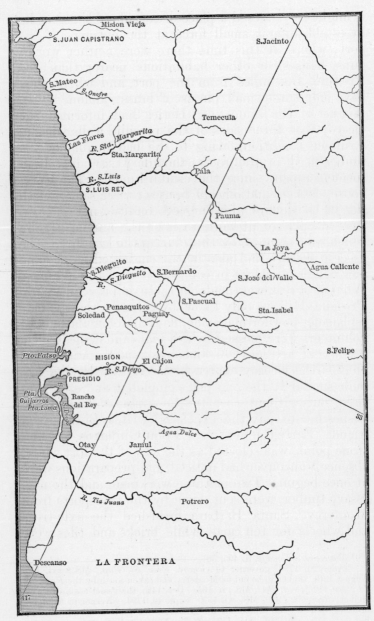

MAP OF SAN DIEGO DISTRICT, 1800.

it might be rendered a place of considerable strength, by establishing a small force at the entrance of the port; where at this time there were neither works, guns, houses, or other habitations nearer than the Presidio, five miles from the port, and where they have only three small pieces of brass cannon."[12] In August of the same year Borica had informed the viceroy that three sides of the presidio walls were in a ruinous condition, owing to the bad quality of the timber used in the roofs, though $1,200 had been spent in repairs since the establishment. The warehouse, church, and officers' houses forming the fourth side of the square were in good condition. Workmen were at once set at work to cut timber at Monterey which was shipped by the *Princesa* in October to be used in repairs and also in the construction of some new defensive works in connection with the old ones. What progress was made in these improvements on Presidio Hill we only know by a vague record that esplanade, powder-magazine, flag, and houses for the volunteers were blessed by the friars and dedicated by a salute of artillery November 8, 1796.[13] At the end of 1794 the viceroy expressed a desire to have a fort built similar to the one just completed at San Francisco, but without cost to the king. "Perhaps he wishes me to pay the expenses" writes Borica to a friend. Early the next year Point Guijarros, Cobblestone point, was selected as the site of the fort whose absence Vancouver had noticed, and preparations were at once begun. Two or three workmen, and the necessary timber, were sent down by the transports from Monterey. Santa Bárbara furnished the axle-trees and wheels for ten carts, while bricks and tiles were

---

[12] *Vancouver's Voyage*, ii. 495, 501.

[13] Aug. 20, 1793, governor to viceroy. *Prov. St. Pap.*, MS., xxi. 115. August 18th, timber to be cut at Monterey and taken south by the *Princesa*. *Id.*, xxi. 112; *Prov. Rec.*, MS., ii. 165. Oct. 14th, the vessel has sailed with timber. *Prov. St. Pap.*, MS., xi. 157. Sept. 16, 1794, governor to Argüello, ordering him to send timber in the *Aranzazu* for esplanade and bastions; but none were sent. *Id.*, xii. 150, 152-3. Nov. 17, 1796, governor to the friars, blessing of the works. *Prov. Rec.*, MS., v. 247b.

hauled from the presidio to the beach and taken across to the point in a flatboat. In December 1796 the engineer Córdoba arrived to inspect the San Diego defences, in which he found no other merit than that an enemy would perhaps be ignorant of their weakness. But the fort had evidently not been built yet, for early in 1797 Borica approved Córdoba's idea that the form should not be circular. Nothing more is known of this fortification till after 1800, save that it was intended to mount ten guns; that on battery, magazine, barrack, and flatboat $9,020 had been expended before March 1797; and that in 1798 there was a project under consideration to open a road round the bay to connect Point Guijarros with the presidio.[14]

The natives gave the commandant and people of San Diego but little trouble, the few depredations committed being chiefly directed against the Dominican establishment in La Frontera. In 1764 three natives were held as prisoners, one of whom, a neophyte, had been leader in a proposed attack on San Miguel. Several bands had approached the mission by night, but finding the guard mounted and ready had retreated.[15] In May or June 1795 Alférez Grijalva while returning from San Miguel with three natives arrested on a charge of murder was attacked by some two hundred savages, one of whom was killled and two were wounded in the skirmish, Grijalva having a

[14] Prov. St. Pap., MS., xiii. 69, 165; xiv. 168; xvii. 9, 10; xxi. 212, 216–17, 248; Prov. Rec., MS., iv. 20–1; v. 238, 272, 278; vi. 46, 79. Water had to be carried from the presidio, where a well long abandoned was reopened. One hundred and three planks, 22 feet long, were among the timber shipped from Monterey. A few industrial items are as follows: For a time after May 1793 there was no armorer, the old one having left after a service of 20 years. Prov. St. Pap., MS., xiii. 56–8. In 1795 the missions of this district were requested to send each four or five Indians to the presidio to learn stone-cutting and bricklaying. Prov. Rec., MS., v. 235–6. Jan. 1796, a weaver was to go to San Diego to teach. Id., v. 78. The comandante tried to induce Spanish youth to learn trades, but without success, some of them deeming the request an insult. Prov. St. Pap., MS., xiv. 16. The forge and carpenter shop did $93 worth of work for soldiers and missions in 1797; but as expenses, including two apprentices, were $163, the king's exchequer was not perceptibly benefited. Id., xvi. 179.

[15] Arrillaga, Papel de Puntos, 195, MS.

horse killed under him. This affair caused some fear and precautions at San Diego, redoubled a few days later on rumors of new hostilities; but Grijalva went south and found all quiet. Raids on the cattle of San Miguel again required the attention of a sergeant and eight men in April 1797.[16]

San Diego did not come much into contact with the outside world. The first foreign vessels that ever entered this fine harbor were those of the English navigator Vancouver, which remained at anchor some three miles and a half from the presidio from November 27th to December 9th 1793. Vancouver was courteously received by Grajera and Zúñiga, who, however, on account of Arrillaga's " severe and inhospitable injunctions" were not able to allow the foreigners such privileges as were desired. The Englishman, though he visited the presidio, spent most of his time on board in preparing journals and despatches to be sent to England by way of Mexico, having little opportunity for observations.[17] In the early part of 1797 an English invasion was supposed to be imminent, and all possible preparations were made by Grajera. Great reliance was placed on the battery at Point Guijarros; but Grajera was also careful to obtain instructions respecting what was to be done should the enemy succeed in entering the bay, or should it be necessary to abandon the presidio. In case of such disasters it was decided to spike the guns and burn the powder and provisions, but to leave the buildings intact. A reserve of ammunition was stored at San Juan, whither the sacred vessels, archives, and other valuables were to be carried if necessary. The English did not appear; the armed frigate *Princesa* lay in port from June to October; and San Diego escaped destruction.[18] At the end of 1798 the port was a second time visited by foreigners, this time by four

[16] *Prov. Rec.*, MS., v. 227-8; iv. 88; vi. 50; *Prov. St. Pap.*, MS., xiii. 215-16; xvi. 249.

[17] *Vancouver's Voyage*, ii. 469-76.

[18] *Prov. Rec.*, MS., v. 254-5; *Prov. St. Pap.*, MS., xxi. 197, 211-12, 267-9.

Boston sailors who had been left on the lower coast and were put to work in the presidio to earn their living until a vessel came to carry them to San Blas.[19] Yet once more was the port visited by the Americans during this decade, when in August 1800 the *Betsy*, Captain Charles Winship, obtained wood and water here, remaining ten days in the bay. Later, on November 22d, there came an earthquake which in six minutes did more damage to the adobe buildings than had been done by either the British or Yankees.[20]

At San Diego mission Juan Mariner and Hilario Torrens served as associate ministers until the last years of the decade. The latter left California at the end of 1798, dying early in the next year; while the former died at San Diego on January 29, 1800.[21] Their sucessors were padres José Panella and José Barona, both recent arrivals who had lived at San Diego, the former since June 1797, and the latter

[19] *Prov. Rec.*, MS., v. 283, 285; vi. 111; *Prov. St. Pap.*, MS., xvii. 197–202. Their names were Wm. Katt, Barnaby Jan, John Stephens, and Gabriel Boisse. The captors of a Spanish vessel in 1799 claimed that some of their men, being on the coast in 1797, as part of the crew of two (English) ships had entered San Diego and made soundings by moonlight. *Prov. St. Pap., Ben. Mil.*, MS., xiii. 20.

[20] *Prov. Rec.*, MS., viii. 132; xii. 6; *Prov. St. Pap.*, MS., xxi. 44, 54; xviii. 67; *St. Pap., Sac.*, MS., ix. 12, 13. The earthquake occurred at 1:30 P. M., and the soldiers' houses, warehouse, and the new dwelling of the volunteers were considerably cracked. The drought of 1795 and an epidemic diarrhœa in 1798 are the only other natural afflictions noted. *Prov. St. Pap.*, MS., xiii. 4; xvii. 69.

[21] Hilario Torrens—thus he signed his name, but by his companions it was more frequently written Torrente or Torrent, to say nothing of several other variations—was a native of Catalonia, where he was for a long time predicador, for three years guardian, and also vicar. He came to California in 1786 with the highest recommendations from his college for talent, experience, and *circunstancias*. Serving at San Diego from November 1786 to November 1798, he had but slight opportunity to distinguish himself save by a faithful performance of his missionary duties. His license to retire was signed by the viceroy March 17, 1798. He sailed in the *Princesa* on Nov. 8th, and May 14, 1799, the guardian wrote that he had died in a convulsion. *Arch. Sta. Bárbara*, MS., xi. 281; xii. 26–7; *Prov. St. Pap.*, xvi. 187. Of Juan Mariner still less is known. He came to California in 1785, served at San Diego from November of that year, made a trip with Grijalva in July 1795 to explore for the new mission site of San Luis Rey. He died Jan 29, 1800, and was buried in the presbytery by Padre Faura on Jan. 30th. Finally April 26, 1804, his remains were removed and placed, together with those of Jaume and Figuer, in a sepulchre constructed for the purpose under the small arch between the two altars of the new church. *San Diego, Lib. de Mision*, MS., 81, 89.

since May 1798. Another supernumerary was Pedro de San José Estévan, from April 1796 to July 1797. The only one of the missionaries with whose conduct any fault was found, so far as the records show, was Panella, who was accused of cruelty to the neophytes and was reprimanded by President Lasuén, who declared that he would not permit one of his subordinates to do injustice to the natives.[22]

During the decade the neophytes of San Diego increased from 856 to 1,523. There had been 1,320 baptisms and 628 deaths. San Diego had thus passed San Gabriel and San Luis Obispo, and now was the most populous mission in California. In the number of baptisms for the ten years it was excelled only by Santa Clara. The baptisms in 1797 were 554, the largest spiritual harvest ever gathered in one year with one exception, that of the year 1803 at Santa Bárbara, when 831 new names were added to the register. The deaths moreover at San Diego were less in proportion to baptisms than elsewhere except at Purísima and Santa Bárbara, though the rate was frightfully large, over fifty per cent, even here. The greatest mortality was in 1800 when 96 natives died.[23] This comparative prosperity was, however, more apparent than real in some respects, since the San Diego converts were left more at liberty in their rancherías

---

[22] Sept. 30, 1798, Lasuen to Borica. *Arch. Arzobispado*, MS., i. 51. July 14, 1799, Lujan instructed to report confidentially on the treatment of the natives. *Prov. St. Pap.*, MS., xvii. 247. July 17, 1797, Grajera explains his treatment of the natives. Does not allow them to have much intercourse with those of other missions, to prevent illicit intercourse. *Id.*, xvi. 172. 1796, padres to depose misbehaving alcaldes and appoint others. *Prov. Rec.*, MS., vi. 178–9. Jaime Samop and Antonio Pellau were alcaldes in 1799. *Arch. Arzobisbado*, MS., i. 220. Three neophyte stowaways were found on the *Concepcion* eight days out of port in 1794. They did it, they said, in sport, and were sent back from San Blas. *Prov. St. Pap.*, MS., xiii. 216–17; *Prov. Rec.*, MS., v. 226; xi. 209. Again in 1798 a runaway neophyte was sent back from Tepic. *Prov. St. Pap.,*, MS., xxi. 289. In the mission registers appear the names of fathers Cayetano Pallas, Mariano Apolinario, José Conanse, and Ramon Lopez, Dominicans from the peninsula who officiated here at different times; also presbyters Loesa and Jimenez, chaplains of San Blas vessels, and a dozen Franciscans from different missions. *San Diego, Lib. de Mision*, MS.

[23] Lasuen confirmed 656 persons between 1790 and 1793. *S. Diego, Lib. de Mision*, 45.

than in other establishments, Christianity being therefore somewhat less a burden to them. Meanwhile the mission herds multiplied from 1,730 to 6,960 head, and its flocks from 2,100 to 6,000. The harvest of agricultural products in 1800 was 2,600 bushels, the largest crops having been 9,450 bushels in 1793 and 1799, surpassed only by those of San Gabriel and San Buenaventura in 1800, and the smallest 600 bushels in 1795, a year of drought: average crops 1,600 bushels.

Respecting material improvements in and about the mission we have but fragmentary data. In 1793 a tile-roofed granary of adobes, ninety-six by twenty-four feet, was built. In 1794, besides some extensive repairs, one side of a wall which was to enclose and protect the mission was constructed, and a vineyard was surrounded by five hundred yards of adobe wall. In 1795 work was begun on a newly discovered source of water-supply for irrigation.[24] Whether this was the beginning of the extensive works whose ruins are still to be seen, and which Hayes supposes with some plausibility to have been constructed before 1800, I know not, for there are no further records extant.[25] Of manufacturing and other industries during this period nothing is known, nor are there any means of ascertaining if the teachings of the artisan instructors sent by government to California penetrated to this southern establishment. In respect to commerce nothing further appears than that there was due the

[24] *St. Pap., Miss.*, MS., i. 113; ii. 26, 29. The neophytes' huts at San Diego as late as 1798 were like those of the gentiles of wood and grass, considered by the comandante as sufficient protection against the weather, if not against fire. *Prov. St. Pap.*, MS., xvii. 73. Names of rancherías in the *Lib. Mision*, MS., 3, 4: Cosoy, San Francisco, Soledad, S. Antonio or Las Choyas, Santa Cruz or Coapan in San Luis Valley, Purísima, or Apuoquele, S. Miguel, or Janat, San Jocome de la Marca or Jamocha, San Juan Capistrano or Matamo, and San Jorge or Meti.

[25] *Hayes' Emigrant Notes*, 153, 477, 603. Hayes gives from personal observation a most interesting description of this dam and aqueduct, which I shall notice in a subsequent chapter, as I am inclined to think without having any very strong evidence that the works were built or completed in the next decade. In a report of March 1799 Grajera speaks of an attempt to bring in water, at which the Indians had been overworked, but which was not a success. *Grajera, Respuesta*, MS., 193–4.

mission at the end of each of the later years about $3,500 for supplies to the presidio.[26]

San Luis Rey, a new establishment of 1798, where Padre Peyri was at work building up one of the grandest of the Californian missions, has been disposed of for this period in a preceding chapter.[27] At San Juan Capistrano, next northward Fuster and Santiago were the associate ministers until 1800, when the former died,[28] and José Faura from San Luis Rey took his place. These missionaries baptized in the decade 940 converts and buried 668, the community being increased from 741 to 1,046. Horses and cattle from 2,500 became 8,500, San Juan being third in the list, while in sheep with 17,000 it was far ahead of any other mission. Crops in 1800 were 6,300 bushels; the average, 5,700; the best crop, in 1792, 7,400, and the smallest, in 1798, 3,700 bushels. In 1797, there was due San Juan for supplies furnished to San Diego and Santa Bárbara presidios over $6,000.[29]

In 1794 there were built at San Juan two large adobe granaries roofed with tiles, and forty houses for neophytes, some with grass roofs and others tiled. In

[26] *Prov. St. Pap.*, MS., xvi. 195, 197, 265.

[27] See chapter xxvi. of this volume.

[28] Vicente Fuster was a native of Aragon, who had originally left Mexico in October 1770, arrived at Loreto in November 1771, served at Velicatá, and came up from the peninsula with Palou, arriving at San Diego August 30, 1773, where he served until 1776. He was with Jaume on the terrible night of November 5, 1775, when the mission was destroyed and his companion was murdered. His pen has graphically described the horrors of that night. After living at San Gabriel and other missions as supernumerary he was minister of San Juan Capistrano from November 1779 until December 1787, when he founded Purísima and remained there till Aug. 1789. Then he returned to San Juan and served until his death on Oct. 21, 1800. He was buried by Estévan, Santiago, and Faura in the mission church. He had received the last sacrament, writes Estévan, 'with the most perfect corformity to the divine will, giving us even to the last moment of his life the most illustrious example of the resignation and love to God our Lord and his holy law which he had preached in his life, both by works and words.' Sept. 9, 1806, with all due solemnity Fuster's remains were transferred to their final resting-place in the presbytery of the new church on the epistle side. *San Juan Capistrano, Lib. de Mision*, MS., 28, 39–40.

[29] Due San Juan from Sta Bárbara $1,628. *Prov. St. Pap.*, MS., xvii. 80–1. From San Diego in 1797, $4,785; in 1798, $4,553. *Id.*, xvi. 195, 265. Mar. 15, 1797, draft on Mexico in favor of the padres for $3,000. *Prov. Rec.*, MS., vi. 184. July 1794, draft drawn by Grajera for $2,000. *Prov. St. Pap.*, MS., xii. 17.

February 1797 work was begun on a new stone church which was to be the finest edifice in California. A master mason was obtained from Culiacan and the structure rose slowly but steadily for nine years.[30]

Mariano Mendoza, a weaver, was sent from Monterey in the summer of 1796 to teach the natives. If he neglected his business, he should be chained at night, for he was under contract with the government at thirty dollars a month. A loom was set up with other necessary apparatus of a rude nature, with which by the aid of natives coarse fabrics and blankets were woven. Early in 1797 the friars were notified that if they wished the services of Mendoza for a longer time they must pay his wages; but they thought his instructions not worth the money, especially now that they had learned all he knew, and the weaving industry had been successfully established. Besides home manufactures San Juan supplied from its large flocks quantities of wool for experiments at other establishments.[31]

Vancouver, sailing down the coast in the autumn of 1793, noted San Juan as "erected close to the water-side, in a small sandy cove; very pleasantly

[30] *St. Pap., Miss.*, MS., ii. 26. A mason sent up by Arrillaga, who reports to the viceroy Jan. 11, 1799. *Prov. St. Pap.*, MS., xxi. 15. Lasuen in report of 1799–1800 says the church has been building four years. *Arch. Sta Bárbara*, MS., xii. 128. Date of beginning, *S. Juan Cap., Lib. de Mision*, MS., 26. Dec. 1797, church of masonry with arches being built 53 x 10 varas. *St. Pap., Miss.*, MS., ii. 110.

[31] May 1796, a weaver (*tejedor de ancho*) sent. *Prov. Rec.*, MS., v. 79, 245, 247. April 16, 1797, Pedro Poyorena's report to Grajera. Blankets, wide woollen cloths, *mangas* for vaqueros, 30 yards of *manta*, 30 yards of baize successfully woven. Not so perfect as Mexican goods, but good enough for this country. The native women spin and pick wool and cotton, and also dye tolerably well. *Prov. St. Pap.*, MS., xvi. 261–2. April 17th, report of padres on progress. The weaver's attempts at dyeing with vinegar, etc., not equal to what the natives could do much, but he will pay what Lasuen deems just. June 26th, Borica to commandant of Monterey. Make an arrangement with Lasuen and pay one eighth to Mendoza and seven eighths to royal treasury. *Prov. St. Pap., Ben. Mil.*, MS., xxv. 15; *Prov. Rec.*, MS., vi. 185–6, 189. Wool purchased for Monterey and Santa Bárbara. *Id.*, ix. 5; *St. Pap., Sac.*, MS., vi. 2.

situated in a grove of trees, whose luxuriant and diversified foliage, when contrasted with the adjacent shores, gave it a most romantic appearance; having the ocean in front, and being bounded on its other sides by rugged dreary mountains, where the vegetation was not sufficient to hide the naked rocks. The buildings of the mission were of brick and stone, and in their vicinity the soil seemed to be of uncommon and striking fertility. The landing on the beach in the cove seemed to be good."[32] In the fear of English invasion which agitated the whole country in 1797 a sentinel was posted on the beach at San Juan to watch for suspicious vessels, since it was not doubted that England had her eyes upon the cove anchorage. Whether a four-pounder was mounted here as recommended by Captain Grajera does not appear. The arrest of a neophyte Aurelio for the murder of his wife in 1797, and the earthquake of November 22, 1800, which slightly cracked the rising walls of the new church, complete the annals of the decade.[33]

Respecting the pueblo of Los Angeles from 1791 to 1800, the information extant is exceedingly slight. The number of families residing here increased from thirty to seventy, and the white population from 140 to 315, chiefly by the growing-up of children and the aggregation of invalids from the different presidios. Horses and cattle increased from 3,000 to 12,500, a larger number than is accredited to any other Californian establishment. Sheep numbered 1,700 only, though a special effort had been made since 1795 to increase the pueblo flocks with a view to the industry

---

[32] *Vancouver's Voyage*, ii. 467. This description seems to locate the mission much nearer the shore than it really is, but it could hardly have been moved before 1797 when the new church was begun, and certainly not later. See chapter xiv. this vol.

[33] *Prov. St. Pap.*, MS., xvi. 155–6, 170, 249–50; xxi. 54. The Indian Aurelio was not severely punished. In a fit of jealousy he proceeded to administer some conjugal discipline, and in his zeal overdid the duty as he frankly confessed. He had no intention of killing her. The authorities decided it not a matter for criminal process.

of weaving.   Crops in 1800 were 4,600 bushels, the
largest having been 7,800 in 1796, and the smallest
2,700 in 1797.   Seven eighths of the entire harvest
was usually maize, though the inhabitants offered in
1800 to contract for the supply of 3,400 bushels of
wheat per year at $1.66 a bushel for the San Blas
market.[34]

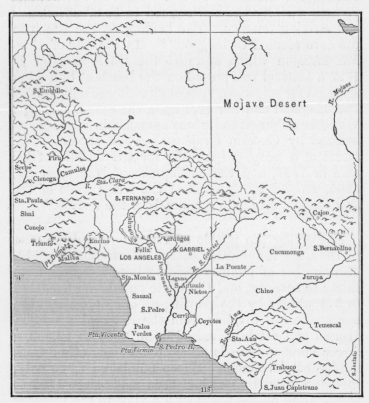

MAP OF LOS ANGELES REGION IN 1800.

[34] From 9 to 12 pobladores in 1793.   Expense of pay and rations $1,528.
Prov. St. Pap., Ben. Mil., MS., iii. 16.   List of 42 names of male settlers in
1799. *St. Pap., Miss.*, MS., iii. 9, 10.   Two hundred sheep distributed in
August, 1796. *Prov. Rec.*, MS., iv. 74; vi. 79; *St. Pap., Sac.*, MS., vi. 1.
1796, Borica orders that land be given to heads of families who have none,
but they must cultivate it. *Prov. Rec.*, MS., iv. 44–5.   1795, correspondence
and orders requiring seeded lands to be fenced.   In one case a willow fence
is mentioned. *Prov. Rec.*, MS., iv. 12, 16, 17, 29. *Prov. St. Pap.*, MS., xiv. 77.
The same year especial effort was made by the governor through Commandant
Goycoechea to encourage the settlers to raise good crops in view of the general

Vicente Félix remained in charge of the pueblo as comisionado throughout the decade, except perhaps for a brief period in 1795–6 when Javier Alvarado seems to have held the office. The successive alcaldes were Mariano Verdugo, elected in 1790; Francisco Reyes, 1793–5; José Vanegas, 1796; Manuel Arellano, 1797; Guillermo Soto, 1798; Francisco Serrano, 1799; and Joaquin Higuera for 1800. The pueblo was in the jurisdiction of Santa Bárbara, the comisionado receiving his orders from the commandant of that presidio, though as we have seen the small military guard was furnished by the San Diego company. Of local events from year to year there is practically nothing in the records.[35]

It is in connection with the pueblo of Los Angeles that the most interesting topic of early land-grants in this southern central region may most conveniently be noticed. In February 1795 there were five ranchos in private possession, held under provisional grants and supporting several thousand head of live-stock.[36] The first was San Rafael, granted by Fages October 20, 1784, to the retired corporal of the San Diego company José María Verdugo. It was also known as

drought. *Id.*, xix. 38–40; *Prov. Rec.*, MS., iv. 15. Proposal to furnish wheat for the San Blas market. *Prov. St. Pap.*, MS., xviii. 50. 1787, grain sold to Santa Bárbara, $358. *Prov. St. Pap., Ben. Mil.*, MS., ix. 4. Each settler must give annually two fanegas of maize or wheat for a *fondo de proprias* to be spent for the good of the community. *Prov. Rec.*, MS., iv. 98–9.

[35] Arrillaga reported that Los Angeles was in quiet in 1792, but certain unruly persons were ordered to leave, and though they did not go, the warning proved effective. *Prov. St. Pap.*, MS., xii. 188. Oct. 11, 1795, Borica to comandante, if the comisionado is not active enough he must be removed. *Prov. Rec.*, MS., iv. 29–30. Alvarado comisionado 1795–6. *Id.*, iv. 39; *Prov. St. Pap.*, MS., xxi. 234; *Id., Ben. Mil.*, xv. 7. 1796, Francisco Ávila drowned in the tulares. Suspicions of murder proved groundless. *Prov. Rec,* MS., iv. 66, 71. Dec. 7, 1797, the settlers Ávila and Arellano must be chastised and turned out if they continue to disturb the pueblo. *Id.*, iv. 93–4. 1798, allusions to speedy completion of a jail. *Prov. Rec.*, iv. 108. Padre Salazar relates that when he was here in 1795 a man who had 1,000 mares and cattle in proportion came to San Gabriel to beg cloth for a shirt, for none could be had at pueblo or presidio. *Arch. Sta Bárbara*, MS., ii. 77.

[36] Feb. 24, 1795, Goycoechea's report to Borica in *Prov. St. Pap., Ben. Mil.*, xxii. 7, 8. April, 1795, Borica to viceroy. *Prov. Rec.*, vi. 40–1. The former important report seems not to have been seen by either writers or lawyers in the past.

La Zanja, described as across the river and four leagues from Los Angeles, and was confirmed by Borica January 12, 1798.[37] The second rancho was that of Manuel Nieto, held under Fages' permission of November 1784, the largest and best of all, supporting 1,100 head of cattle and large enough for a pueblo, since well known as Los Nietos, and formerly granted in several tracts to Nieto's heirs by Figueroa in 1834.[33] The third was the famous San Pedro, or Dominguez, rancho, occupied by Juan José Dominguez with about a thousand head of cattle under a permission given very likely by Fages, but the date of which is not known. It was regranted by Sola in 1822, and is one of the few Californian ranchos that have remained in the possession of the original grantees and their descendants.[39] Fourth in the list was the rancho at Portezuelo, smaller but fertile and well watered and stocked with cattle on a small scale, situated about four leagues from Los Angeles on the main road, and occupied by the old veteran Sergeant Mariano de la Luz Verdugo.[40] The fifth and last was the Encino rancho, where

[37] According to *Reg. Brands*, MS., 39-3. Fages permitted Verdugo on Oct. 20th to keep his cattle at Arroyo Hondo, one and a half leagues from San Gabriel on the road to Monterey, on condition that no harm was done to mission or pueblo, and care taken with the natives. Jan. 12, 1798, in answer to petition of Nov. 4, 1797, Borica permitted him to settle with his family, relatives, and property, under like conditions, and the new one of raising sheep, at La Zanja. This rancho was visited in August 1795 by the party seeking a mission site. *Sta María, Registro*, MS.

[38] In 1795-6 the mission of San Gabriel laid claim to Nieto's land, called at the time La Zanja. After an investigation Borica allowed Nieto to retain what land he had actually under cultivation and in use, the rest to be used by the mission without prejudice to Nieto's legal rights. *Prov. Rec.*, MS., iv. 45, 51-2, 61-2. It would seem that other persons besides Nieto were living here in 1797, when the inhabitants were called on to be ready to resist English invasion. *Prov. St. Pap.*, MS., xvi. 249-50. This grant came before the U. S. land comission in later times in five separate tracts: Los Cerritos, Los Coyotes, Las Bolsas, Los Alamitos, and Santa Gertrudis, aggregating 33 sq. leagues. *Hoffman's Land Cases.*

[39] Granted by Sola Dec. 31, 1822, to Sergt. Cristóbal Dominguez as nephew and heir of Juan José. *Reg. Brands*, MS., 35. The author of *Los Angeles, Hist.*, 8, 9, supposes this grant to have been originally made before 1800, chiefly on the testimony of Manuel Dominguez and other old settlers. No one has until now shown any documentary proof.

[40] Verdugo enlisted at Loreto on Dec. 15, 1766, serving as private, corporal, and sergeant, seven years in each capacity. He came with Capt. Rivera y Moncada in the first expedition of 1769, and served in several Indian campaigns. His name appears among the godfathers at the first baptisms in San

Alcalde Francisco Reyes had a house and where he kept his own live-stock as well as that of Cornelio Ávila and others. This was where San Fernando was established in 1797, the friars taking possession of Reyes' house, a fact that illustrates the slight tenure by which these early grants were held. Between 1795 and 1800 there were perhaps granted two other ranchos within this jurisdiction, San José de Gracia de Simí to Javier, Patricio, and Miguel Pico in or about 1795; and El Refugio to Captain José Francisco Ortega or his sons a year or two later.[41]

San Gabriel, belonging throughout the decade to

Diego, and he commanded the guard at San Luis Obispo in 1773. He was temporarily in command at San Diego in November 1775 at the time of the massacre, being the first to reach the mission and report the terrible event. He accompanied Gov. Neve to the Colorado in 1782. His wife, Doña María Guadalupe Lugo, was buried by Lasuen at San Diego April 15, 1780, and he subsequently married Gregoria Espinosa. From about 1780 he was sergeant of the Monterey company till 1787 when he was probably retired as an invalid. *Prov. St. Pap., Ben. Mil.*, MS., ii. 14; viii. 8, 9; xiv. 1, 2; xxii. 7; *Prov. St. Pap.*, MS., i. 2, 4, 5; *S. Diego, Lib. de Mision*, MS., 10, 77; *San Luis Obispo, Lib. de Mision*, MS., 29.

[41] The Simí Rancho, according to *Reg. Brands*, MS., 33, and *Hoffman's Land Cases*, was granted by Borica in 1795, being regranted, or at least petitioned for, in 1821, and also by Alvarado in 1842. According to *Reg. Brands*, MS., 32, El Refugio was granted by Borica, therefore before 1800, to Capt. Ortega, therefore before 1798 when Ortega died. I think there is room for doubt about one or both of these grants. Respecting both it may be said that Borica does not seem to have favored such grants. As to Simí, when an exploring party visited the valley in August 1795 they did not mention any rancho as they did Reyes' and Verdugo's; and not only this but in April 1796 Borica expressly refused to grant Pico (no given name) permission to leave the pueblo and settle on a rancho. As to El Refugio, we know that Ortega in 1796 was in trouble about a deficit in his Loreto accounts, *Prov. Rec.*, MS., iv. 68, 72, 81–2, 86; his son José María wished to take a land-grant on which to work and pay his father's indebtedness, and although Borica advised him against the scheme, still a grant was ordered to be made to him of the Zanja de Cota lands if unoccupied. The author of *Los Angeles, Hist.*, 8, 9, thinks that Santiago de Santa Ana was one of these early grants. His reasons are: A popular belief that this was one of the oldest ranchos; testimony in the district court that the original occupant was Grijalva; the probability that the grant to Yorba in 1810 was a regrant to Grijalva's son-in-law; and finally a recognition by the court of the Peraltas' claims as descendants of the original occupant. This is an ingenious but probably erroneous argument. Lieut. Grijalva was a pensioner of the San Diego company after 1796 as was Sergt. Yorba, his son-in-law, after 1798; but Grijalva, dying at San Diego in 1806, named no land in his will though he did name cattle; and moreover he refused to give his daughters anything, on the ground that they had been provided for at their marriage—one with Yorba in 1782 and the other with Peralta in 1785. Peralta's claims resulted from the fact that Arrillaga's grant of July 1, 1810, was to Yorba and Peralta in company. In his petition of Nov. 24, 1809, Yorba says nothing of any previous occupancy by himself or others. *Reg. Brands*, MS., 34.

the jurisdiction of San Diego, was one of the most flourishing of the missions, but its annals may be very briefly disposed of. Cruzado and Sanchez still toiled together as ministers. Calzada remained until 1792. Cristóbal Orámas served here in 1792–3;[42] Juan Martin in 1794–6; Juan Lope Cortés in 1796–8; and Pedro de San José Estévan to 1800 and later, so that the mission had always three padres. They baptized 1,267 natives, but they buried 1,124,[43] so that the community was increased only from 1,040 to 1,140, standing now third instead of second in the list. In large stock San Gabriel stood fourth, with a gain from 4,220 to 7,090 head; while in sheep it was second to San Juan only, its flocks having increased from 6,000 to 12,360. In agricultural products San Gabriel was a tie with San Buenaventura in 1800, with a crop of 9,400 bushels, the smallest having been 3,600 in 1793, and the average about 6,400.

José María Verdugo, owner of a rancho in the vicinity, was corporal of the mission guard much of the time down to 1798, and his successor was Pedro Poyorena. José Miguel Flores, a discharged soldier, was majordomo down to his death in 1796.[44] A stone church was half finished in 1794, but in 1800 it had not yet been completed. There is no record of manufacturing industries save that a little cotton obtained from San Blas was woven; but I suppose that a beginning of weaving woollen stuffs or of some

[42] Of Cristóbal Orámas we only know that he had been for five years assistant curate and became a friar only a year before coming to California, whither he brought in 1786 a most flattering reputation from the guardian for genius and exemplary conduct. *Arch. Sta Bárbara*, MS., xii. 26–7. He served at Santa Bárbara, of which mission he was a founder, from December 1786 to December 1789; at Purísima until November 1792; and at San Gabriel until September 1793, when broken down in health he retired to the college.

[43] This death-rate of 90 per cent of baptisms and doubtless 500 per cent and more of births was not caused by any great epidemic in one year, for the deaths run quite evenly as follows: 104, 84, 98, 65, 80, 87, 92, 96, 138, and 230.

[44] *San Gabriel, Lib. de Mision*, MS., passim. The mission-books contain but little beyond the names of padres and of persons baptized, married, or buried. The original registers are also imperfect, parts of several books having disappeared.

other branch of primitive manufactures must have
been made at this period, for San Gabriel, so flourishing and so prominent in later years, would naturally
have been among the first to make experiments.
Events important or petty there are none to record.
San Fernando, the new establishment in Encino Valley belonging to the jurisdiction of Santa Bárbara, I
have already noticed in another chapter.[45]

Santa Bárbara presidio remained under the able
command of Lieutenant Felipe de Goycoechea, who
was also habilitado, and was in 1798 promoted to be
brevet captain. Pablo Antonio Cota was promoted to
fill the vacant post of alférez, and served throughout
the decade, dying at the end of 1800.[46] José María
Ortega, son of the lieutenant, took Cota's place as sergeant with Olivera and Carrillo; and when the latter
went to Monterey in 1795 he was replaced by Francisco María Ruiz. The presidial force was fifty-nine
men, from which number guards were supplied to San
Buenaventura, San Fernando, Santa Bárbara, and
Purísima missions. The number of pensioners increased from one to seventeen, and all, with their
families, constituted a population *de razon* which in-

---

[45] Church-building. *St. Pap., Miss.*, MS., ii. 5, 29, 100, 110. Cotton-weav-
ing. *Id.*, ii. 6, 100; *Arch. Arzobispado*, MS., i. 30–2. July, 1796, 200 arrobas
of wool can be had at 20 reals. *St. Pap., Sac.*, MS., vi. 6. Due mission
from presidio of San Diego, 1797, $2,881. *Prov. St. Pap.*, MS., xvi. 265. For
1798, $2,597. *Id.*, xvi. 195. Due from Santa Bárbara, 1797, $3,311. *Id.*,
xvii. 78–81. Two runaway neophytes from San Gabriel brought in by the
Pápagos to Tucson. *Prov. Rec.*, MS., iv. 58.

[46] Pablo Antonio Cota was born in 1744, and enlisted in 1768, coming to
California probably in 1769, and certainly before 1774. He seems to have
commanded the guard at San Buenaventura from its foundation in 1782 until
1787, when he was removed on complaint of the padres. He subsequently
commanded at Purísima until replaced by Corporal Ortega in September
1788. During this time he was engaged in one or two minor explorations
and Indian campaigns. His commission as alférez was signed in Mexico Jan.
13, 1788. *St. Pap., Sac.*, MS., i. 55. His wife was Doña María Rosa de Lugo,
who died Jan. 10, 1797. *S. Buenaventura, Lib. de Mision*, MS., 2, 5, 9; *Sta
Bárbara, Lib de Mision*, MS., 30. In August 1795 he commanded the party
exploring for the mission site of San Fernando. *Sta María, Registro*, MS.
He died Dec. 30, 1800, *Prov. St. Pap.*, MS., xviii. 87; xxi. 56, of pleurisy,
which during this cold rainy winter attacked many persons at Santa Bárbara.
Prov. St. Pap., Ben. Mil., MS., xxix. 3.

creased from 200 to 370.[47] The total white population of this district, including Los Angeles and the ranchos, was 675, and neophytes, including San Gabriel and San Fernando, numbered almost 4,000. Having no fort,[48] Santa Bárbara obtained no part of the reënforcement of artillerymen and infantry sent to California in 1796, and was garrisoned by cuera cavalrymen only. The annual appropriation for this presidio from the royal treasury did not vary much from $15,000.[49]

It has been seen that new presidio buildings had been completed or nearly so by 1790; but some of the roofs were constructed of tules; some of the timbers supporting tile roofs were bad; the family kitchens were inside the houses and not detached as was best; a fire did considerable damage in August 1789; and it seems that no new chapel had been built. Fages in

[47] Company rosters in *Prov. St. Pap.*, *Ben. Mil.*, MS., xiii.–xxvi.; *St. Pap.*, *Sac.*, MS., i.–iii. List of about 100 persons in 1797 who have complied with religious obligations. *Prov. St. Pap.*, MS., xv. 89–93. List of 14 young men fit for military service, but whose parents need their care. *Id.*, xv. 102–4. Full list of officers and men in 1798. *Prov. St. Pap.*, *Ben. Mil.*, MS., xvii. 20–1. Four foundlings came here to live in 1800. *Id.*, xxviii. By Borica's order each mission escolta was reduced by one man in 1795. *Prov. Rec.*, MS., iv. 25; *Prov. St. Pap.*, MS., xiii. 171.

[48] One brass 6-pounder and three smaller iron pieces at the presidio with four iron guns at the three coast missions were the armament in 1798. *Prov. St. Pap.*, *Ben. Mil.*, MS., xvii. 5. Paper supplied to school and collected again for cartridges. *Prov. Rec.*, MS., iv. 32.

[49] Company accounts in *Prov. St. Pap.*, *Ben. Mil.*, MS., xv. xvii.–viii. xxi. xxiii. xxviii.; *St. Pap.*, *Sac.*, MS., ii. iv. The memorias of supplies were from $13,000 to $17,000. Account of 1794, credit, $39,737; debit, $38,634. *Prov. St. Pap.*, *Presid.*, MS., i. 3. Id. for 1797, cr., $42,377; dr., $43,095. *St. Pap.*, *Sac.*, MS., ii. 68. Id. for 1798, cr., $40,520; dr., $40,658. *Prov. St. Pap.*, *Ben. Mil.*, MS., xvii. 9–11. Total receipts of supplies in 1795, including $6,830 from missions, $22,057. *Id.*, xxi. 9. Waste in last memoria 1796, $690. *Prov. Rec.*, MS., iv. 80. Mission supplies in 1797, $4,623; in 1798, $756. *Prov. St. Pap.*, *Ben. Mil.*, MS., xvii. 10, 11. Inventory of goods on hand. Dec. 31, 1798, $9,758. *Id.*, xvii. 9. Account of 1799, cr., $45,728; dr., $46,148. *Prov. St. Pap.*, *Ben.*, MS., ii. 18, 19. Postal revenue from $56 to $105. *Prov. St. Pap.*, *Ben. Mil.*, MS., xxi. 6, 9; xxiii. 8; xxv. 14; *St. Pap.*, *Sac.*, MS., vi. 61. Tithes collected from $200 to $800 per year, the expense of collecting being from 15 to 20 per cent. *Prov. St. Pap.*, *Ben. Mil.*, MS., xix. 4; xxi. 6; *Prov. Rec.*, MS., iv. 45–6; vi. 2; *Dept. St. Pap.*, MS., x. 3, 4; *St. Pap.*, *Sac.*, MS., i. 124. In 1792–3, the papal bulls sold amounted to $62. *Prov. St. Pap.*, *Ben. Mil.*, MS., xxi. 6. From 1790 to 1795, only $8 out of $1,177 worth sent. *Id.*, xiii. 4; xxi. 9. In 1797, $87 worth sold, and those remaining ordered burned. *Prov. Rec.*, MS., iv. 87. It seems that this sale was a special one of bulls of the holy crusade. *Prov. St. Pap.*, MS., xv. 79–80.

his instructions to Romeu of February 1791 reported this state of things and hoped all would be completed that year.   In August 1793 the governor pronounced the presidio buildings the best in California owing to Goycoechea's activity, but still some roofs needed repairs.   All would be done that year except the new chapel and a cemetery outside the square.   Vancouver in November found here "the appearance of a

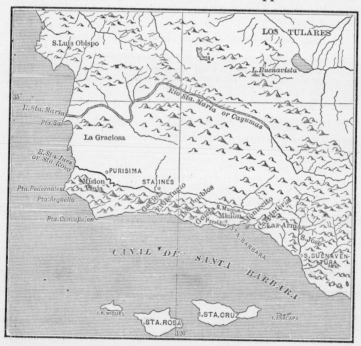

MAP OF SANTA BÁRBARA DISTRICT, 1800.

far more civilized place than any other of the Spanish establishments had exhibited.   The buildings appeared to be regular and well constructed, the walls clean and white, and the roofs of the houses were covered with a bright red tile.   The presidio excels all the others in neatness, cleanliness, and other smaller though essential comforts; it is placed on an elevated part of the plain and is raised some feet from the ground by a basement story, which adds much to its pleasantness." In October 1794 the commandant certified that to complete the buildings fifteen laborers for six months were necessary at a cost of $561. Thereupon work was stopped except upon the church and the most necessary repairs; and at the end of 1796 the viceroy declared that the sailor-workmen could no longer be employed at royal expense; but the chapel was blessed on Guadalupe day in 1797.[50]

Though Santa Bárbara seems to have had as yet no branch of the rancho del rey like those at the other presidios, yet it is credited in statistical reports with from 1,000 to 4,000 horses and cattle, and from 200 to 600 sheep. This live-stock is not to be confounded with that of the mission, but it was probably identical to some extent with that of the rancheros within the jurisdiction already referred to. There were also agricultural operations carried on by the soldiers distinct from those of the mission neophytes. Records of results are very meagre, but in 1797 they reached 1,650 bushels of wheat, corn, and beans.[51] Of mechanical industries there is nothing to record save that the attempt to obtain white apprentices was more

[50] Fages, Papel de Puntos, MS., 166. Aug. 20, 1793, governor to viceroy. Prov. St. Pap., MS., xxi. 115; Vancouver's Voyage, ii. 451, 495. Oct. 11, 1794, 15 men at 18 cents per day and 34 fanegas of maize at 13 reals, necessary to complete the buildings. Prov. St. Pap., MS., xii. 62. Oct. 24th, building expenses to stop. Id., xii. 98. Dec. 13th, Borica says the church is to be enlarged at cost of the fondo de gratificacion. Id., xii. 58. Expenses from 1784 to 1794, $2,256. Prov. St. Pap., Ben. Mil., MS., xxi. 12. Dec. 16th, viceroy to governor, the 8 ship-boys and other workmen can no longer be paid from treasury of San Blas. St. Pap., Sac., MS., vii. 57–8. Chapel to be blessed on Guadalupe day. Prov. Rec., MS., iv. 87. The $2,256 charged to fondo de gratificacion by order of April 26, 1797. Id., iv. 89.

[51] Jan. 15, 1794, governor orders that each soldier be allowed only four cows. These to be branded and the rest slaughtered. Prov. Rec., MS., i. 208. 1794–5, commandant asks for and obtains from governor 200 steers for rations. Id., iv. 16; Prov. St. Pap., MS., xii. 97. Oct. 22, 1795, Borica orders Goycoechea, Ortega, and other officers to fence their gardens; and reads them a lecture for complaining of the poor soldiers' cattle. Why should so many suffer for the convenience of a few? Prov. Rec., MS., iv. 33–4. In 1796 an effort was made here as elsewhere to promote sheep-raising. Let Peña have some land, says the governor June 9, 1796, if he will take Pico as a partner and raise twice as many sheep as other stock. Rancheros must go to the pueblo to live he says, Dec. 29th, unless they will raise sheep. Prov. Rec., MS., iv. 66, 86.

successful here than at San Diego, since six boys were taught by the weaver Enriquez during his southern tour in 1798.[52]

Vancouver's visit in 1793 was first in the slight chain of local events to be recorded in this decade. He anchored here November 10th and sailed the 18th. His reception in comparison with that at Monterey and San Francisco seemed to him agreeable, though the difference was chiefly imaginary. Goycoechea was courteous and hospitable, and Vancouver had learned not to expect too much. Little was done except to obtain wood and water, purchase supplies from private individuals, and take required exercise within sight of the presidio, retiring on board at night. An excellent spring, said to have been unknown to the Spaniards, was found near the old wells. Fathers Miguel and Tapis were particularly affable and anxious to entertain and aid the foreigners, who carried away a flattering opinion of Santa Bárbara and its people.[53] January 10, 1794, there was a public execution. Ignacio Rochin was shot, there being no hangman in the country, for the murder of one Álvarez. The wife of the victim, Rochin's accomplice, was condemned to hard work as a servant, the sentences coming finally from the audiencia of Guadalajara.[54]

In August 1795 the English merchant ship *Phœnix*, Captain Moore, touched here for supplies and left a 'Boston boy' who was soon sent to San Blas as already related.[55] The same year the inhabitants contributed nearly one thousand dollars toward paying the expenses of the war with France.

[52] *Prov. Rec.*, MS., iv. 99. July 21, 1796, Borica to Goycoechea. The sons of soldiers and settlers must be urged to learn weaving, tailoring, and pottery. *Id.*, iv. 72–3. A bricklayer, a carpenter, and a *violinista* in the company in 1798. *Id.*, iv. 95. Timber for oars sent to San Diego. *Id.*, iv. 88.

[53] *Vancouver's Voyage*, ii. 451–6, 493, 497, 500. The English navigator was surprised at the failure of the Spaniards to fortify so strong and important a position. He mentions two brass nine-pounders before the presidio entrance.

[54] *Sta Bárbara, Lib. de Mision*, MS., 29; *Prov. Rec.*, MS., iv. 5, 7; *Prov. St. Pap.*, MS., xii. 92; xiii. 176; *Id.*, *Ben. Mil.*, xxi. 8; *García, Hechos*, MS., 1, 2.

[55] See p. 536, this volume. *Prov. St. Pap., Ben. Mil.*, MS., xxi. 9.

The year 1796 was marked by the discovery of what was thought to be a quicksilver mine in the black mire at the Punta del Cerro de la Laguna. A load of the metal-bearing mud was taken to the presidio for examination by Borica's orders, but nothing further is heard of it.[56] In February 1797 a soldier named Gonzalez is said to have been poisoned by the natives, who thus revenged themselves for what they regarded as cruel treatment.[57] In March and April came the alarm of war with England. Couriers were despatched, sentinels posted, guns made ready, the natives exhorted, and abundant reasons given for not doing more.[58] In May the *Princesa* arrived off the mouth of the Rio Purísima and landed thirty of her hundred and sixty men, who were suffering from scurvy, but who rapidly recovered.[59] In December there arrived the *Magallanes,* a full-rigged ship of war, which had come over from Manila to make observations and if necessary convoy the San Blas vessels southward.[60] On February 3, 1798, occurred the death of the old pioneer of 1769, Brevet Captain José Francisco Ortega, former commandant of Santa Bárbara and for several years living as a retired pensioner in this vicinity. He left many sons and daughters, and many of his grandchildren still live in California.[61]

[56] *Prov. Rec.*, MS., iv. 57.

[57] The death of Rafael Gerardo Gonzalez on Feb. 14th is recorded in *Sta Bárbara, Lib. de Mision*, MS., 30. The fact that he was poisoned rests on the statement of his son Rafael Gonzalez, still living at Santa Bárbara, *Gonzalez, Experiencias*, MS., 1, 2, who was born a few days after his father's death. He flogged some boys who allowed the crows to eat his corn, and the natives soon invited him to a feast of poisoned fish.

[58] Goycoechea to Borica, March 28, April 10, 1797, in *Prov. St. Pap.*, MS., xv. 43–5, 188–9.

[59] *Id.*, xv. 52; *Prov. Rec.*, MS., iv. 90–1.

[60] *Prov. St. Pap.*, MS., xv. 113–14; xvi. 185; xvii. 1, 6.

[61] José Francisco Ortega was a native of the town of Zelaya in what is now the State of Guanajuato, where in his early youth he was employed as a warehouse clerk. Enlisting Oct. 1, 1755, he served in the cuera company of Loreto ten months as private, two years and a half as corporal, and fourteen and a half as sergeant. Some time after he was first made sergeant he obtained his discharge and gave his attention to mining in Baja California, where he was for a time a kind of alcalde of all the mining-camps of the peninsula. When Portolá came as governor, Ortega was readmitted as sergeant and for a year or more attended to the accounts of the royal warehouse. He accompanied the second land expedition northward in 1769 under Portolá and with

At Santa Bárbara mission adjoining the presidio,
Padre Antonio Paterna, the founder, and an old

Junípero Serra. On the way he received a letter from Don José de Galvez
promising him the place of lieutenant at Loreto on his return. On this march
he distinguished himself by his tireless activity, always going ahead to explore
the way and traversing the route three times before he reached San Diego.
Then he went on with the first expedition to Monterey, and was perhaps the
first to discover San Francisco Bay, probably the first to visit the site of the
present city, and certainly the one who explored the bay region most extensively on this trip. Back at San Diego he was for a time in command of the
guard, but soon returned to Loreto where the governor kept him busy in constant journeys to Sinaloa and to San Diego, and in explorations. By his zeal
in these early expeditions, Ortega made himself a great favorite with the missionaries and especially with Junípero Serra, who in 1773 urged his appointment as commandant in California to succeed Fages. *Serra, Representacion de
13 de Mayo 1773*, MS. It is from this document that we obtain many of the
facts about his earlier life and services. Much is also gathered from his own
later narratives. *Ortega, Memorial al Comandante General sobre méritos y servicios militares, 8 de Junio 1786*, MS., and *Ortega, Fragmento*, MS., both of
which are very important documents on early history. Serra's efforts could
not make him commandant, but he was made lieutenant and commanded at
San Diego for over eight years. His services in the exciting times which followed the massacre of 1775 have been already recorded. In 1781 he founded
Santa Bárbara, planning the buildings, fortifications, and irrigating works in a
manner which gained him great credit, and serving as commandant and habilitado until 1784, when he was transferred to the frontier. Here in 1786 he
petitioned for pecuniary relief and for retirement, being unfitted for duty by
30 years of active service and by increasing obesity. His petition was not
granted, but he was transferred back to California and was in command at
Monterey from September 1787 to March 1791. A year later he went down
to Loreto and was commandant there during Arrillaga's absence until 1795,
when he was retired as brevet captain on half lieutenant's pay, attached to the
Santa Bárbara company. *Prov. St. Pap., Ben. Mil.*, MS., xxii. 4; xxiii. 2.
Like most other officers who served as habilitados Ortega was in some trouble
with his accounts during this last term at Loreto, and was oppressed by debt
in the last years of his life. The deficit was $2,597. *St. Pap., Sac.*, MS., ix.
73. José María Ortega, his son, asked to be discharged from military service
or retired as invalid, and to be granted lands that he might pay off the deficit.
Borica wrote July 11, 1796, approving the son's desire to clear his father, but
disapproving the scheme as not likely to succeed because the missions would
have the preference in selling grain. He thought the captain would be
allowed to keep a portion of his pay. Oct. 28th, he sent the discharge of
the captain's sons, and ordered their grain to be bought to pay the deficit.
A strict watch was to be kept on the property to prevent other creditors from
being favored. The sons finally paid up the deficit. *Prov. Rec.*, MS., iv.
69-72, 81-2, 86. It is possible, though not certain, that there was provisionally granted to the family at this time or before 1800, the rancho de Nuestro
Señora del Refugio, which remained long in the family and was famous in
connection with smuggling operations during the Mexican rule. Capt. Ortega
died suddenly on Feb. 3, 1798, at the Casil ranchería while on his way to the
presidio, and was buried next day in the mission cemetery by Tapis. *Prov.
St. Pap., Ben. Mil.*, MS., xxvi. 3; *Prov. Rec.*, MS., iv. 97; *Sta Bárbara, Lib.
de Mision*, MS., 31. Ortega's wife was Doña María Antonia Victoria Carrillo, who died very suddenly and was buried in the presidio church on May
8, 1803. *Id.*, 33. In 1802 she received a pension of $9,150. *Prov. St. Pap.,
Ben. Mil.*, xxx. 4. They had several children when they came to San Diego,
Ignacio, José María, Vicente, Francisco, Juan, María Luisa, and María, according to Taylor, and there were born at San Diego, José Francisco María,

pioneer of 1771, died in 1793[62] and was succeeded
by Estévan Tapis.   José de Miguel had served since
1790, and was succeeded in 1798 by Juan Lope Cortés.
By this missionary force 1,237 natives were baptized,
634 were buried, and the number of neophytes was
increased from 438 to 864 in the ten years.[63]   Meanwhile horses and cattle had multiplied from 296 to
2,492, and sheep from 503 to 5,615.   Crops were
3,000 bushels in 1800; 5,400 in 1797; and only 150
bushels of wheat in 1795.[64]

Juan Capistrano María Hermógenes, María Antonio de Jesus, and José María
Martin. *San Diego, Lib. de Mision*, MS., 12, 14, 17, 19, 27, 50; *Loreto, Lib.
Mision*, MS., 198; *Taylor's Discoverers and Founders*, ii. No. 27.

[62] Antonio Paterna was a native of Seville, and served 20 years in the
Sierra Gorda missions before coming to California.   He left his college in
October 1770; sailed from San Blas in the *San Antonio* Jan. 21, 1771; arrived
at San Diego March 12th, at Monterey May 21st, and back at San Diego
July 14th.   He was supernumerary at San Gabriel until May 1772, and minister until September 1777.   During this time he was acting president in
1772-3 until Palou's arrival.   He was minister at San Luis Obispo from 1777
to 1786; and at Santa Bárbara from its foundation, Dec. 4, 1786, until his
death on Feb. 13, 1793. *Sta Bárbara, Lib. de Mision*, MS., 44-5; *Arch. Sta
Bárbara*, MS., vii. 5, 6; xi. 221.   He had been a zealous and faithful worker.
His body was buried in the mission church on Feb. 14th.   Whether it was
subsequently transferred to the new church does not appear from the records.

[63] The discrepancy of about 200 may result from the baptism of certain
natives who were allowed to remain in their rancherías and not included on
the mission registers.   There was some correspondence in 1796 about the rancherías of the channel, and their willingness to become Christians if not compelled to leave their lands and fisheries and live at the missions.   Borica
favored allowing them to remain and adding an extra friar to Santa Bárbara
and Purísima to attend to their instruction, houses or stations being established
at suitable points. *St. Pap., Miss.*, MS., ii. 92-8; *Prov. Rec.*, MS., iv. 55-6.
In August 1797, 300 natives near the presidio were given over to Lasuen for
baptism on condition of not leaving their ranchería. *Id.*, iv. 92; vi. 54-5.
According to a report of Goycoechea, March 12, 1796, the rancherías from San
Buenaventura to Purísima were as follows: Sisolopó at San Buenaventura; El
Rincon, 5 leagues; La Carpintería, 1 l.; El Paredon, 1¼ l.; Montecito, 1¼ l.;
Yuctu, at presidio, 1½ l.; Sacpili, 2½ l.; Alcas; Gelijec; Geloó; Miguigui, 3 l.,
Casil, 3 l. ; Quemada, 1 l.; Gaviota, 3 l.; El Bulito Estait. 2 l.; Sta Texas (?),
2 l.; El Cojo Sisilopo, 1½ l.; Espada, 1½ l.; Pedernales, 1½ l.   Total number
of gentiles, 1783. *St. Pap., Miss.*, MS., ii. 94.   Najalayegua, Matita, and
Somes are also named.

[64] Weather reports at Santa Bárbara.   Much complaint in 1795, 1797, and
1800. *Prov. St. Pap.*, MS., vii. 65; x. 117; *Arch. Sta Bárbara*, MS., xii. 62;
St. Pap., Sac., MS., vi. 100-1; *St. Pap., Miss.*, MS., ii. 103-6; *Prov. St. Pap.,
Ben. Mil.*, MS., xvii. 22; *Prov. Rec.*, MS., xi. 136.   According to accounts in
Arch. Sta Bárbara, MS., ii. 133-9; ix. 476-83, 494-6, the mission had in
1800 a credit balance in Mexico of $528; a draft from the habilitado for
$1,267; $309 in money at the mission; $1,061 due from presidio; and $416 due
from private individuals; total, $3,581 in addition to buildings, etc.   Supplies
furnished to presidio from 1793 to 1800, $5,179.   Otter-skins sent to Mexico,
$1,624.   A full account of mission supplies purchased in Mexico is given in
Santa Bárbara, Memorias de los Efectos remitidos á la Mision para los años

Much progress was made in mission buildings during this decade. In 1791 a guard-house and three tool-houses were added; in 1792 two large stone corrals. In 1793–4 a new church of adobes, tiled and plastered, 28 x 135 feet, with a sacristy 15 x 28 feet, and a brick portico in front, was erected; and in 1794 the improvements were a granary and spinnery on stone foundations, a cemetery enclosure 48 x 135 feet, and a sheep-corral. In 1795 a corridor with tile roof and brick pillars was added on the side of the square next the presidio, and another to the spinnery; four new rooms for the friars were completed; and beams of alder and poplar were replaced with pine wherever they had been used. In 1797 several rooms for granaries, store-rooms, and offices were completed. In 1799 there were built nineteen adobe houses for natives, each 12 x 19 feet, plastered, whitewashed, and roofed with tiles; and an adobe wall nine feet high was extended for 1,200 yards round the garden and vineyard. In 1799 was added a warehouse, and in 1800 thirty-one more dwellings in a row, and corridors on brick pillars round the three remaining sides of the square were completed; while preparations were made for the construction of a reservoir for drinking-water, to be made of stone, brick, and mortar.[65] In 1800 sixty neophytes were engaged in weaving and other work connected with that branch of industry. The carpenter of the presidio was engaged at one dollar per day to teach the natives his trade; and a corporal taught tanning at $150 per year. Of the two soldiers that constituted the guard one was employed by the friars as majordomo.[66]

1786 hasta 1810, MS. These supplies were purchased by the padres with their salaries and with the products of sales of produce. They consist of implements, groceries, church vestments, and vessels, clothing, etc. The total amount for this decade was $10,500, of which $8,000 was paid by the sínodos, and the rest by drafts from the habilitado. In 1800, as I have said, the mission was $528 ahead; but before it owed from $100 to $2,000.

[65] Arch. Sta Bárbara, MS., v. 26–30, 39, 42–5, 49, 53, 58, 61–2; ii. 99, 138–40; St. Pap., Miss., MS., i. 117; ii. 71, 79.

[66] Arch. Sta Bárbara, MS., ii. 96–7, 129, 137–8. Before October, 165 naguas of home manufacture had been distributed, 800 yds. of cotton and

San Buenaventura, the southernmost of the channel establishments, remained under the care of its founders, Francisco Dumetz and Vicente de Santa María, until 1797, when the former was succeeded by José Francisco de Paula Señan. Though its population was smaller than that of any other mission except San Francisco and the new establishments, it had more cattle and raised more grain in 1800 than any other place in California.[67] Vancouver landed here November 20, 1793, having brought Padre Santa María from Santa Bárbara, and spent a few hours very pleasantly at the mission, which he found to be "in a very superior style to any of the new establishments yet seen." "The garden of Buena Ventura far exceeded anything I had before met with in these regions, both in respect of the quantity, quality, and variety of its excellent productions, not only indigenous to the country, but appertaining to the temperate as well as torrid zone; not one species having yet been sown or planted that had not flourished. These have principally consisted of apples, pears, plumbs, figs, oranges, grapes, peaches, and pomegranates, together with the plantain, banana, cocoa nut, sugar cane, indigo, and a great variety of the necessary and useful kitchen herbs, plants, and roots. All these were flourishing in the greatest health and perfection, though separated from the sea-side only by two or three fields of corn; that were cultivated within a few yards of the surf."

The buildings were also of a superior class, a previous destruction by fire, noted only by Vancouver, having caused them to be rebuilt.[68] The church was

taparabo woven, 700 yds. of blanketing. One thousand and twenty dollars worth of soap furnished to Monterey, perhaps by the presidio, in 1798. *Prov. Rec.*, MS., iv. 105.

[67] Increase of neophytes, 385 to 715; baptisms, 757; burials, 412; cattle and horses, 961 to 10,013; sheep, 1,503 to 4,622; crops in 1850, 9,400 bushels; 1,500 bushels in 1797 was the smallest crop; average yield, 4,800 bushels; wheat was not largely raised until 1798, when it became the chief crop, over 8,000 bushels per year.

[68] *Vancouver's Voyage*, ii. 457-61, 494, 497. One reason of Santa María for going on board the ship was to remove a prejudice among the natives against foreigners. They begged him for God's sake not to intrust himself

not yet built, but it was begun about this time and half finished in 1794, all the rest of the square being complete. The new church was of stone, and in 1797 is spoken of as nearly finished. It was not, however, completed before 1800.[69] A fight between the neophytes and pagans in 1795 seems to have afforded the only excitement of the period. The Christians were victorious, killing two chiefs and taking six or seven captives, but having several wounded. The leaders on both sides were admonished or punished, the neophyte Domingo being put to work in chains.[70]

Purísima is the last mission of this district. Here Father Arroita served until 1796 when he was permitted to retire, having completed his term of ten years.[71] Orámas remained until 1792; José Antonio Calzada from October 1792 until August 1796, returning in May 1798; Juan Martin served in 1796–7; and Gregorio Fernandez from 1796. Baptizing 1,079 and burying 397, the missionaries increased the neophyte community from 234 to 959. This was the largest proportional gain and the smallest death-rate in California. Live-stock, large and small, increased to 1,900 and 4,000 head respectively; and crops in 1800

to the stranger's care, and were positive he would never return. On arrival the surf prevented landing at the first attempt, and the padre was not a little frightened as he had not his prayer-book with him. When the natives brought the book his courage returned and he laughed at his former fears as the sailors had laughed before. On landing finally, the natives crowded round their padre to welcome him home and receive his blessing. Vancouver was deeply impressed with the missionary's piety and the earnest devotion of his neophytes. He noted that the natives were always addressed in their own language, and there is other evidence of this. *Prov. St. Pap.*, MS., xvii. 71.

[69] *St. Pap., Miss.*, MS., ii. 5, 24, 29, 71, 100. In 1791 there were two bells here belonging to Santa Bárbara, which the friars refused to give up. *Prov. St. Pap.*, MS., x. 171. In *San Buenaventura, Memorias de Efectos remitidos á la Mision, 1790–1810*, MS., we have the mission accounts of supplies from Mexico, but not so complete nor so clearly stated as in the case of Santa Bárbara. The mission was from $200 to $1,200 in debt during this decade, but cleared itself early in the next. Due mission from the presidio in 1797, $1,612. *Prov. St. Pap.*, MS., xvii. 78–81.

[70] *Prov. Rec.*, MS., iv. 35–6.

[71] Francisco José de Arroita came from Spain to Mexico in 1785, was appointed to California in April 1786, and came to his post with a reputation from the guardian of being, like his companions, a good man, though somewhat lively (*vivo*) and without much experience. He served at San Luis Obispo from April to December 1787, and at Purísima from its establishment till June 1796, about which time he sailed for San Blas.

were 2,250 bushels, 4,000 in 1799 being the largest, and 1,200 in 1795 the smallest. Wheat and corn were the chief productions. Mission buildings were of adobes and tiles, and the houses had after 1794 corridors of brick. In 1795 the old church was in a bad condition and materials were being collected for a new one, there being no record of further progress.[72] Bears and rattlesnakes were a prominent feature in the region of Purísima. Two of the latter bit a neophyte at the same time, writes the minister on June 3, 1799.[73]

[72] *St. Pap., Miss.*, MS., ii. 22, 71. Due mission from the presidio 1797, $405. *Prov. St. Pap.*, MS., xvii. 78–81. List of members of the guard, 1797, 6 married soldiers and 3 bachelors. *Id.*, xv. 93. Antonio Enriquez, the weaver, taught the natives at Purísima in 1797. *Prov. St. Pap., Ben. Mil.*, MS., xxv. 14; *Prov. Rec.*, MS., vi. 185–6.

[73] *Arch. Arzobispado*, MS., i. 59.

CHAPTER XXXI.

LOCAL EVENTS AND PROGRESS—MONTEREY DISTRICT.

1791-1800.

MONTEREY PRESIDIO—MILITARY FORCE AND INHABITANTS—OFFICERS—LEON PARRILLA—HERMENEGILDO SAL—PEREZ FERNANDEZ—PRESIDIO BUILDINGS—BATTERY—RANCHO DEL REY—PRIVATE RANCHOS—INDUSTRIES—COMPANY ACCOUNTS—INDIAN AFFAIRS—SAN CÁRLOS MISSION—MISSIONARY CHANGES—PASCUAL MARTINEZ DE ARENAZA—STATISTICS OF AGRICULTURE, LIVE-STOCK, AND POPULATION—VANCOUVER'S DESCRIPTION—A NEW STONE CHURCH—A WIFE-MURDER—SAN ANTONIO DE PADUA DE LOS ROBLES—MIGUEL PIERAS—BENITO CATALAN—SAN LUIS OBISPO—MIGUEL GIRIBET—BARTOLOMÉ GILI—INDIAN TROUBLES.

THE presidial cavalry company of Monterey contained from sixty-two to eighty-five men, including two officers, six non-commissioned officers, a surgeon, a phlebotomist, two or three mechanics, fifty privates, and from two to twenty-four pensioners. After 1796 there were also stationed here seven artillerymen and twenty Catalan volunteers of Alberni's company, increasing the total force to about one hundred and ten, who with their families constituted a population *de razon* in the jurisdiction of about four hundred, or four hundred and ninety including Branciforte and Santa Cruz. About thirty of the cavalrymen were stationed at the six missions subject to Monterey—San Cárlos, San Miguel, Soledad, San Antonio, San Luis Obispo, and San Juan Bautista, in which the total population of christianized natives was four thousand.[1]

---

[1] See company rolls in *Prov. St. Pap., Ben. Mil.*, MS., xiii. 9; xiv. 2; xvii. 6; xviii. 1; xx. 1; xxi. 2, 11; xxii. 5; xxiii. 2; xxvi. 3, 4, 15; xxvii. 4; *St. Pap., Sac.*, MS., i. 10–13; iii. 14; iv. 20. Missions included in the jurisdiction. Sal's report of 1798, in *Prov. St. Pap.*, MS., xvii. 63. White population in 1800, 518; Indian population, 3,949. *St. Pap., Miss.*, MS., iii. 15.

Diego Gonzalez kept his place on the rolls as nominal lieutenant of the Monterey company until August 1792, although he had long been absent; and his successor was Leon Parrilla, who held the place until September 1795, although from incompetency, ill-health, and partial insanity he never exercised any authority.[2]

Meanwhile the commandants were Ortega of the Loreto company until March 1791, and Argüello of the San Francisco company until March 1796.[3] Then Sal, who in September 1795 had been promoted from alférez to lieutenant, took the command which he held until his death in 1800,[4] when he was succeeded by

Twelve sailors from the *Concepcion* and *San Cárlos* remained at Monterey as laborers in 1795, two of them as soldiers. *Prov. Rec.*, MS., vi. 62. Two foundlings in 1800. *Prov. St. Pap., Ben. Mil.*, MS., xxviii. 22. List of 16 workmen who came in 1798 on the *Concepcion. Prov. St. Pap.*, MS., xviii. 19–20. List of company in 1798. *Id., Ben. Mil.*, MS., xvii. 17–19. List of Catalan volunteers in 1799. *St. Pap., Miss.*, MS., iii. 7.

[2] Leon Parrilla was promoted to be lieutenant of the Monterey company on Aug. 8, 1792. His past service had been three years as cadet, three years as guidon-bearer, and four years as alférez, first in the dragoons and later in the regiment of España. He had never given proof of courage or application, and his natural abilities were deemed only medium. *Parrilla, Hoja de Servicios*, MS., in *Prov. St. Pap., Ben. Mil.*, MS., xxi. 4. He arrived in San Francisco July 25, 1793, and soon proceeded to Monterey. *St. Pap., Sac.*, MS., iv. 18. Here he immediately became unfit to perform the duties of commandant and habilitado by reason of fits of insanity; consequently Argüello continued to discharge those duties by the governor's order and the viceroy's approval. *Prov. Rec.*, MS., ii. 165; viceroy to governor, April 26, 1794, in *Prov. St. Pap.*, MS., xi. 169. · August 13, 1794, Arrillaga, *Papel de Puntos*, MS., 196–7, says to Borica that Parrilla is incapable, apparently demented, and has to be confined to his house under guard. He sometimes escaped at night and had to be brought back by force. Once he tried to escape by sea in a boat. Dec. 13, 1794, Sal pronounces him incapable of keeping books. *Prov. St. Pap.*, MS., xii. 140. At the end of 1794 Borica declares him useless for any services, and proposes to send him away in the first vessel for San Blas. This was done, and approved by the viceroy. Parrilla was put on the retired list with a pension from July 1, 1795. *Prov. St. Pap.*, MS., xxi. 213; xiii. 123, 270; *Id., Ben. Mil.*, MS., xxi. 4.

[3] Ortega did not, however, leave Monterey until May 1792. Argüello in 1794 was administrator of tobacco revenues and had a kind of supervision over all presidio accounts. Sal in 1799 was called administrador general de real hacienda for New California. *Prov. St. Pap.*, MS., xii. 136–7; xvii. 285, 315; *Prov. Rec.*, MS., iv. 176.

[4] Hermenegildo Sal seems to have come to California as a private soldier with Anza's expedition in 1776. This would be remarkable for a man of his ability were it not for certain hints that he came under pardon for some offence not specified which may have reduced him to the ranks. *Prov. Rec.*, MS., ii. 74. He was a native of the Villa de Valdemoro, Castilla la Nueva. *San Francisco, Lib. de Mision*, MS., 10; *St. Pap., Sac.*, MS., iii. 1, 2. He was with Capt. Rivera at San Diego in 1776, *Prov. St. Pap.*, MS., i. 219, and was

Raimundo Carrillo. It must be noted, however, that while Sal and Carrillo were commanders of the presidial company, Lieutenant-colonel Alberni came down from San Francisco early in 1800 and by virtue of his superior rank became comandante of the post.

by that officer put in charge of the military warehouse of San Francisco. Here Gov. Neve noticed his intelligent management of financial affairs in May 1777, and the next year obtained his appointment as guarda-almacen, which position he held until February 1782, when he was called to Monterey to settle the accounts of the defunct store-keeper. *Prov. Rec.*, MS., i. 69, 119; ii. 75; *San Francisco, Lib. de Mision*, MS., 6. May 19, 1782, he was made sergeant of the Santa Bárbara Company, and in August received his commission as alférez of Monterey, dated May 29th. His commission as lieutenant was dated April 27, 1795, and was received in August or September. *Prov. St. Pap.*, MS., iii. 209; *Prov. Rec.*, MS., ii. 65; iv. 232; *St. Pap., Sac.*, MS., iii. 1, 2, 55. He was at Monterey from 1782 to 1791, and from 1794 to 1800, being habilitado from 1782 to 1787 and from 1797 to 1800, and commandant from 1785 to 1787 and 1796 to 1800. He was at San Francisco as habilitado and acting commandant from 1791 to 1794. In addition to his other duties Sal acted as governor's secretary during a large part of Borica's administration. He was present at the founding of Santa Cruz in 1791 and at the consecration of its church in 1794. In 1795 he accompanied Dantí in a search for mission sites. Don Hermenegildo had a good education for his time, wrote a fine hand, and was probably the best accountant and the clearest headed business man in California. Only once was fault found with his accounts, and an investigation showed that instead of his owing the company $3,000 as was charged, the company was in debt to him. He was a hasty, quick-tempered man, prone as a commander to order severe penalties for offences against his strict discipline, and then to countermand the order when his anger had passed away. Stung by the taunts of an anonymous letter he once made a personal attack upon Capt. Nicolás Soler, accusing him of an intrigue with his wife. Sal married at San Francisco on May 16, 1777, María José Amézquita, *San Francisco, Lib. de Mision*, MS., 10, 55, 72, by whom he had several children, some of whom died in infancy. Vancouver, who speaks in the highest terms of Sal and his wife, was also delighted with the decorous behavior of their two daughters and son, and the attention that had evidently been paid to their education. *Vancouver's Voyage*, ii. 8. One daughter, Rafaela, was the first wife of Luis Antonio Argüello and died at San Francisco Feb. 6, 1814, as shown by the mission records. Another, Josefa, was the wife of Sergt. Roca who commanded the artillery at San Diego, and was left a widow in 1814. *S. Diego, Lib. de Mision*, MS., 94. A third, unmarried, was the guest of R. C. Hopkins of San Francisco in 1863, and died before 1867. *Dwinelle's Colon. Hist.*, xvii. José María Amador speaks of a son, Domingo, who was a *soldado distinguido* in the San Francisco company and died young. *Amador, Mem.*, MS., 121. Another son, Meliton, was buried at San Diego, Aug. 21, 1810. *San Diego, Lib. de Mision*, MS., 42. Suffering from phthisis and unable to discharge efficiently his duties, on March 18, 1800, Sal petitioned the king for retirement with rank of captain. The viceroy granted the request provisionally on Aug. 1st, with encouragement to hope for success at court. *St. Pap., Sac.*, MS., iv. 32; ix. 60. In September a settler named Borbosa attempted to murder him with a dagger, but was prevented by Surgeon Soler. *Prov. Rec.*, xi. 145–6. Finally he died at Monterey. Dec. 8, 1800, and his remains were interred at San Cárlos mission with military honors. His executors were Lieut. Argüello and Sergt. Roca. *Prov. St. Pap.*, MS., xviii. 10–17; *Id., Ben. Mil.*, MS., xxviii. 3; xxxii. 7; *Prov. Rec.*, MS., x. 9. His disease was in those days regarded as contagious, and therefore, at the

The position of habilitado accompanied that of commandant, except that José Perez Fernandez held it from April 1796 to June 1797.[5]   The company alférez was Sal down to 1795 and Carrillo down to 1800. Pablo Soler held the place of surgeon throughout the decade.   Manuel Rodriguez was connected with the company as cadet from 1794 to 1797.   Manuel Vargas was the sergeant until 1794, when he became an invalid, and Macario Castro took the position.[6]

The ravages caused by the fire of 1789 had been nearly repaired before Fages left the country, and, with the exception of the chapel, the buildings seem to have been completed in 1791,[7] though another fire

recommendation of the surgeon, all his clothing and bedding were burned as was the roof of his house after the plastering had been removed from the walls. *St. Pap., Sac.*, MS., iv. 29; *Prov. Rec.*, MS., xi. 149.

[5] José Perez Fernandez was in 1791 a sergeant attached to the Loreto company, having come there that year after 16 years' service in the España dragoons.   In 1791 he was recommended by the governor in a *terna* with Carrillo and Amador—but with a preference by reason of his skill in accounts—for alférez of San Francisco. He was commissioned Aug. 17, 1792, and held the place until 1797, being habilitado and acting commandant from July 1794 to April 1796.   Then he served as habilitado at Monterey, though still belonging to the San Francisco company, until June 1797, and two months later he was transferred to Loreto.   He was born in 1749. *St. Pap., Sac.*, MS., i. 55; v. 76; *Prov. Rec.*, MS., v. 268; vi. 78.

[6] It would serve no good purpose to give all the multitudinous references from which I have formed the preceding account of Monterey officials.   The following are a few of the most important, or at least the most definite: Ortega gives up habilitacion to Argüello March 31, 1791. *Prov. St. Pap., Ben. Mil.*, MS., xv. 3.   Argüello commandant as early as July 1791. *Arch. Arzobispado*, MS., i. 20, 63.   But in *Prov. St. Pap., Ben. Mil.*, MS., xiii. 9, Ortega is called commandant until May 1792.   There are indications that Parrilla may have attempted to perform the functions of his office in 1794. *Prov. Rec.*, MS., ii. 152, 165.   There is some confusion about the *habilitacion* of Sal and Perez Fernandez in 1796–7. *St. Pap., Sac.*, MS., iv. 20; vii. 38–9, 47; *Prov. Rec.*, MS., iv. 206–7; v. 77, 268; vi. 2, 4.   Argüello is spoken of as commandant in April 1797, in *Prov. St. Pap.*, MS., xvi. 212.   Sal called justicia mayor of the partido. *S. José Arch.*, MS., iv. 22.

[7] The total cost of the restoration was $2,609, and Fages, in a report dated Aug. 12, 1793, took great credit to himself for having done the work so cheaply by means of voluntary labor of gentiles, soldiers, and sailors. *Prov. St. Pap.*, MS., xiii. 191.   Elsewhere the expense exclusive of the church is given as $2,362. *Id.*, xxi. 125.   Jan. 23, 1794, viceroy approves account of $2,609. *Id.*, xi. 159.   Oct. 31, 1795, Argüello to habilitado general, $1,600 in effects received in 1792 given to persons who worked on presidio to end of 1792.   These were 3 sergeants, 9 corporals, and 103 soldiers, whose gratuity amounts to $1,181. *Prov. St. Pap., Presid.*, MS., ii. 2, 3.   Dec. 1795, $3,122 paid over for building expenses. *St. Pap., Sac.*, MS., vii. 41; *Prov. Rec.*, MS., iv. 182.   March 12, 1795, Borica to viceroy, the buildings would have cost very heavily had it not been for the convenient supply of stone, lime, sand, and timber.   The other presidios have not such advantages. *St.*

did some damage in October 1792. Vancouver describes and gives a view of the presidio as it appeared in 1792. It was like that of San Francisco[8] except that the enclosure was complete. There was a circular block-house at each corner raised a little above the top of the wall; there were two or three small doors besides the main gate-way, and the commandant's house had boarded floors. He is in error when he states that the square was 300 x 250 yards, and that the structure had not undergone the slightest change or improvement since the foundation.[9]

According to a report of Carrillo at the end of 1800 each side of the square measured one hundred and ten yards, the four walls were built of adobes and stone, and the buildings were roofed with tiles. On the north were the main entrance, the guard-house, and the warehouses; on the west the houses of the governor, commandant, and other officers, some fifteen apartments in all; on the east nine houses for the soldiers, and a blacksmith shop; and on the south besides nine similar houses was the presidio church opposite the main gate-way.[10] All the structures were again in bad condition; the walls were cracked, having been built on insufficient foundations after the fire; and

---

Pap., Sac., MS., xvii. 3. Three thousand one hundred and twenty-two dollars was the total expense down to Dec. 31, 1795. *Prov. St. Pap.*, MS., xiii. 196, 201. Aug. 20, 1793, bastions unfinished, and house of the alférez needs repairs like some of the soldiers' dwellings. Total cost of repairs to date, $2,000. *Id.*, xxi. 115. Fire of Oct. 15, 1792. *Id.*, xxi. 90.

[8] See next chapter for plan and description of San Francisco Presidio.

[9] *Vancouver's Voyage*, ii. 43-4: View of presidio, ii. 440; view of scene in Salinas Valley, iii. 334. Vancouver deemed the site chosen by no means the best in the vicinity. There was low marshy ground between the square and the beach.

[10] Aug. 6-9, 1791, instructions addressed to Argüello about building the church. *Prov. St. Pap.*, MS., x. 42. March 1, 1792, viceroy orders work suspended until further orders. *St. Pap., Sac.*, MS., iv. 1. April 4th, viceroy sends a plan for church, made by the directors of the academy of architecture of San Cárlos, Mexico. *Id.*, i. 112. Fages says he followed such a plan, but this must have been an earlier one. *Prov. St. Pap.*, MS., xiii. 191. Vancouver's picture represents the church as completed. The cost was $1,500, which was refunded to the company by the government. *Prov. Rec.*, MS., iv. 206; *St. Pap., Sac.*, MS., vii. 58; *Prov. St. Pap.*, MS., xvi. 227. Had it been built by day-laborers in the usual way the expense would have been at least $5,000, as Borica believed. It was done by troops, sailors, Indians, and convicts. *Id.*, xxi. 267-8.

further delay would greatly increase the cost of prospective repairs.[11] The armament of Monterey at the time of Vancouver's first visit consisted of seven small guns planted outside the presidio walls without breastwork or protection from the weather. At the same time Bodega y Cuadra left some material, and men were set at work on a battery to be erected on a neighboring eminence. Accordingly on Vancouver's return in 1793 he found the guns mounted on a "sorry kind of barbet battery, consisting chiefly of a few logs of wood, irregularly placed; behind which those cannon, about eleven in number, are opposed to the anchorage, with very little protection in the front, and on their rear and flanks intirely open and exposed." This work cost $450, and, while it might serve to prevent a foe from cutting out vessels at anchor, was entirely useless, as Córdoba reported in 1796, for the defence of the port. It does not appear that anything was done for its improvement before 1800.[12]

Connected with this presidio was the main establishment of the rancho del rey, located where now stands Salinas City; or at least that was its location in later years, and I find no record of any transfer. At the beginning of the decade there were 5,000 cattle and 2,000 horses in this royal establishment, and during the first half of the period the net annual proceeds of sales were from $3,000 to $2,000; but subsequently the sum was diminished to but little over $500, and in 1800 the cattle had dwindled to 1,600

[11] *Carrillo, Los Edificios de Monterey, 1800,* MS. Alberni on coming to the 'Corte Californiana' in 1800 found things in a deplorable state, and built four houses for married soldiers at his own expense. *Prov. St. Pap.,* MS., xviii. 11.

[12] 1792, slight description of presidio buildings in *Sutil y Mexicana, Viage,* 162. Cuadra's battery of four guns on the hill. *Prov. St. Pap.,* MS., xxi. 89, 164; *Prov. Rec.,* MS., ii. 158; *Vancouver's Voyage,* ii. 500. 1796, battery of ten guns of small calibre. Vessels could easily anchor beyond their range. Córdoba's report, in *Prov. St. Pap.,* MS., xiv. 83. Lists of munitions, 1796–7. *St. Pap., Sac.,* MS., vi. 91; viii. 76–7; ix. 34. Esplanade, casamata, and barrack cost $450, built very economically. *Prov. St. Pap.,* MS., xxi. 267–8. Viceroy ordered $444 paid in 1797. *Prov. Rec.,* MS., iv. 205. Three hundred and eighty-one dollars spent in repairs before February 1798. *Prov. St. Pap.,* MS., xvii. 11.

while the horses had increased to 6,000.[13] Besides
the king's live-stock the company or its members had
in 1800 over 1,000 horses, 700 cattle, 250 mules and
asses, and 400 sheep. The horses had increased very
rapidly and subsequently decreased as abruptly so far
as we may trust the meagre statistics. Sheep had
decreased from 700 in 1794, in spite of special efforts
made in 1796 to foster this branch of industry. These
last figures include, I suppose, the live-stock kept on
the half-dozen private ranchos in the Monterey region.
These ranchos, like those already referred to in the
south, were provisionally granted to settlers and pensioners; but unlike the former none of them seem to
have been rendered permanent by subsequent re-
grants.[14]

In the early part of the decade industrial operations were confined for the most part to the labors of
carpenters, bricklayers, and masons on the presidio
buildings; but later, a tailor, saddler, and one or more

[13] In 1798 the change was still more marked, when there are said to have
been 7,491 horses and 1,200 cattle. This result was attributed to droughts,
thefts, export of females to Baja California, ravages of bears and wolves, foundation of the branch at San Francisco, and the lack of a market for horses.
Sergt. Macario Castro had charge of the rancho as majordomo, with six soldiers. Gov. to viceroy, Dec. 3, 1798. Prov. Rec., MS., vi. 104, 109. Accounts
of the rancho in Prov. St. Pap., Ben. Mil., MS., xiii. 1, 4; xviii. 1, 2, 7;
xxiii. 3; xxv. 2, 3; xxviii. 4. Two hundred fat cattle to be killed annually;
no tallow to come from San Blas; Sta Bárbara to be supplied—1792. Prov.
Rec., MS., ii. 156. Cattle very numerous in 1794. Prov. St. Pap., MS., xii.
189–91. Bears very numerous and troublesome in 1792, doing great harm
both to live-stock and to gardens. Prov. Rec., MS., ii. 159. Sheep-raising fos-
tered, 1796. Id., vi. 79; iv. 62.

[14] The ranchos were six in number in January 1795: Buenavista, 5
leagues from Monterey, held by José Soberanes and Joaquin Castro; Salina,
4 leagues, by Antonio Aceves and Antonio Romero; Bajada á Huerta Vieja,
½ league, by Antonio Montaño; Cañada de Huerta Vieja, ¾ league, by Antonio Buelna; Mesa de la Pólvora, a musket-shot, by Eugenio Rosalío; and
Chupadero, 1 mile, by Bernardo Heredia and Juan Padilla. There were on
these ranchos 277 cattle, 112 horses, 110 sheep, and 9 mules. Monterey,
Ranchos existentes en 1795, MS. But this very year, according to Calleja,
Respuesta, MS., 12, one of these ranchos, that of Aceves and Romero, was destroyed by Indians; and also another not in the list belonging to Osuna and
Alegre. Lands were granted provisionally to invalids and settlers on the
river (Salinas) near Monterey before 1793. Id., xxi. 132; xii. 189; Prov. Rec.,
MS., vi. 40–1. A small piece of land had been granted by Rivera in 1775 to
Manuel Butron; but Butron was now an inhabitant of San José, and there is
no evidence of any lands whatever held by the soldiers, except the six or
seven ranchos mentioned.

weavers were kept at work. The looms turned out only the coarsest varieties of blankets and woollen stuffs; and so unsatisfactory were the results, due largely to the poor quality of the wool, that Sal in 1800 determined to stop the work, employing the workmen in sweeping the plaza and serving the officers.[15]

The subject of presidial finances and supplies at Monterey as capital of the province is naturally more important and also more complicated than at the other jurisdictions; but unfortunately the preserved records, though bulky, are far less complete and satisfactory here than elsewhere. The pay-rolls and ordinary expenses of the Monterey company were about $15,000 per year; a sum which was increased by the salaries of provincial officers and other government expenses to a total varying from $19,000 to $25,000; and the annual supplies from Mexico and San Blas, though varying considerably, do not seem to have fallen short of the total appropriation for expenses, although supplies to the average amount of $5,000 were obtained from the missions, and others from San José. In fact these supplies were purchased with articles sent from Mexico or with drafts on Mexico, so that in either case the amounts were included in the *memorias*. Tithes and postage in this district

[15] Aug. 1791, four mechanics came. Tailors did $125 of work for private parties. *St. Pap., Sac.*, MS., v. 95; xiii. 3. 1792, stone-cutters and masons, Santiago Ruiz, Salvador Rivera, and Pedro Alcántara. *Id.*, ii. 9, 10. Six mechanics arrived in July. *Prov. St. Pap.*, MS., xxi. 73–4. 1793, the armorer Pedro Gonzalez García ordered to remain at Monterey. *Id.*, xiii. 56–8. 1794, one bricklayer and a carpenter, also three masons to work on church. *Id.*, xii. 192–3; xxi. 128–9. 1796, a tailor and a *listonero* to remain. *Prov. Rec.*, MS., v. 78. Alcántara left this year. *Prov. St. Pap.*, MS., xxi. 236. Salvador Béjar engaged as carpenter in April. *Id.*, xxi. 238. Antonio Hernandez, a saddler, in August. *Id.*, xxi. 44. April 28, 1797, weavers Mendoza and Enriquez must be sent to Monterey; 200 *arrobas* of wool to be bought in the south. *Prov. Rec.*, MS., iv. 89. July 20, 1797, a manufactory of blankets renders importation unnecessary. Sal to Borica, in *Prov. St. Pap.*, MS., xvi. 233. In 1797 the tailoring account was as follows: work done, $573; expense of supporting six apprentices, $295; paid to the tailor ⅓ of proceeds, $34; net proceeds, $244. *Prov. St. Pap., Ben. Mil.*, MS., xxv. 5, 6. Proceeds in 1800, $225. *Id.*, xxviii. 3. The weaver and saddler earned in 1800, down to the time of discharge, $1,365. *Id.*, xxviii. 6. Weaving suspended by Sal. *Prov. St. Pap.*, MS., xviii. 18, 19.

yielded to the royal treasury about $400 each per year, while the tobacco revenue was from $1,000 to $2,000, and the sale of papal indulgences yielded from $75 to $125. The annual inventory showed the contents of the warehouses to be usually about $40,000.[16] In addition to the foregoing statistics Monterey annals from 1791 to 1800 present nothing of interest which has not been recorded in preceding chapters devoted to gubernatorial changes, precautions against foreigners, and the movements of vessels. The only foreign craft that touched at Monterey during the decade were those of Vancouver in 1792–4; the English *Providence* under Broughton in 1796; the American *Otter* under Dorr in the same year; and an unknown vessel that anchored in the bay in 1800. The only Indian troubles in this district that require notice were those at San Juan and have already been described.[17]

The mission of the Monterey jurisdiction, besides the new establishments, San Miguel, Soledad, and San Juan Bautista, were San Cárlos, San Antonio, and San Luis Obispo. At San Cárlos Father Arenaza served as minister until 1797, when he left the country.[18] Señan was permitted to retire in 1795 to the

[16] Monterey presidial accounts in *Prov. St. Pap.*, *Ben. Mil.*, MS., xiii. 2, 20; xiv. 4, 8; xvi. 5; xvii. 8, 9; xviii. 1, 5–7, 8–11; xix. 7–9; xxiii. 7–9, 11; xxiv. 17; xxv. 3–5, 8–9, 11–13; xxvi. 5–7; xxvii. 1, 5, 6; xxviii. 6, 8, 9, 20; xxxiii. 13, 14; *St. Pap., Sac.*, MS., i. 1–4; ii. 36, 64; v. 71; vi. 118–20; vii. 59, 81–8; ix. 48; *Prov. St. Pap., Ben.*, MS., i. 13; ii. 17, 18; *Prov. St. Pap.*, MS., xvii. 8, 11, 36–43, 68; xxi. 120; and *Perez Fernandez, Cuenta General de la Habilitacion de Monterey, 1796*, MS., which is a very complete report rendered on turning over the company accounts to Sal. In 1793 the governor pointed out an error in the treasury accounts of about $30,000. The totals of the habilitado's accounts varied from $60,000 to $85,000. The balance due the treasury or the company was usually only a few hundred dollars. The company applied to its use the proceeds of tithes, postage, and tobacco, and paid the amounts by drafts in Mexico, which were charged on the next *memoria*. The habilitado's commission in 1796 was $2,780. Debt of company in 1796, $9,788. In 1799 a robbery of $800 from the warehouse is noted. The *fondo de retencion* amounted in 1799 to $3,037 after $587 had been paid out. This fund was due to 36 men, or not quite $100 to each.

[17] See chapter xxvi., this volume.

[18] Pascual Martinez de Arenaza came to Mexico from his native Basque province of Álava in 1785. He volunteered and was assigned to California in 1786, with a good reputation from the guardian, though his experience was limited and his character somewhat *vivo. Arch. Sta Bárbara*, MS., xii. 26–7. After a term as supernumerary he served as minister at San Cárlos

college, though he subsequently came back to California. Arenaza was followed in the ministry by Francisco Pujol who completed the decade; Señan by Antonio Jaime in 1795–6, Mariano Payeras in 1796–8, and José Viñals from 1798, Carnicer serving also for a short period in 1798–9. Throughout the decade, moreover, President Lasuen made San Cárlos his home when not absent on one of his frequent tours through the province. Although the baptisms, 790 in number, exceeded the deaths by 220, yet the neophyte population increased during this decade only from 733 to 758. San Cárlos had reached its highest figure, 927, in 1794, and was now on the retrograde. Meanwhile horses and cattle had increased from 1,378 to 2,180, and smaller live-stock from 1,263 to 4,160. The crop in 1800 was about 6,000 bushels; the largest in 1797, 7,400 bushels; the smallest in 1795, 1,100 bushels;[19] average 3,700 bushels.

Vancouver was at San Cárlos on Sunday, December 2, 1792, and while he gives no detailed description of the establishment, contenting himself with the remark that the buildings, though smaller, were similar in architecture and material to those of San Francisco and Santa Clara previously visited, he presents a drawing which shows four buildings irregularly arranged and partially enclosing a square. The old

from 1788 to 1797. On the expiration of his 10 years of service he was granted permission to retire on July 8, 1797. The last trace of his presence in California is on Oct. 3d of the same year when he officiated at Soledad. *Soledad, Lib. de Mision*, MS., 20. After his arrival in Mexico he died of phthisis before May 14, 1799, as we learn from a letter of the guardian in *Arch. Sta Bárbara*, MS., xi. 281–2.

[19] Barley was usually produced in as large quantities as wheat, and maize was not far behind. In 1795 both were a total failure. This year supplies had to be obtained from Santa Clara. *Arch. Sta Bárbara*, MS., ii. 229–30. 1796 was not much better than 1795, and in 1792 the crops had been very light, and heavy rains after the harvest not only injured much grain in the warehouses, but prevented the hauling of supplies from abroad. *St. Pap., Sac.*, MS., vii. 68. April 2, 1796, governor says the troops are suffering want in consequence of droughts for three successive years. *Prov. St. Pap.*, MS., xxi. 235. Aug. 12, 1797, he rejoices at a surplus of 1,700 fanegas of barley and 200 of pease at San Cárlos. *Prov. Rec.*, MS., vi. 194. There was a general drought in 1800, but San Cárlos had good crops. *Id.*, ix. 7; *St. Pap., Sac.*, MS., vii. 69. Supplies furnished to the presidio in 1795–6, $1,768 and $1,334. *Prov. St. Pap.*, MS., xvi. 203, 206.

church, partly thatched and partly tiled, stands on the left of the picture, and probably on the west side of the square. Three bells hang on a frame raised on a stone foundation; a lofty cross, bearing a close resemblance to a modern telegraph-pole, rears its head near the centre of the plaza, and just beyond, almost in contact with, and apparently north-eastward from, the old church, are the rising stone walls of a new one. Beyond, on an eminence, may be seen a corral for cattle, while at the right are the conical huts of the neophytes. The new church was being built of a soft, straw-colored stone, which was said to harden on exposure to the air. The lime used was made from sea-shells. This church, the ruins of which are still to be seen on the banks of the Carmelo, was completed and dedicated in September 1797.[20] Nothing occurred to vary the monotonous routine of mission life at San Cárlos, unless a rather curious illustration of the method in which justice was administered be worth a place in the record. Estanislao, a neophyte, did not live happily with his

[20] There is some confusion among the different authorities respecting this church. Vancouver, *Voyage*, ii. 10, 34–6, gives the views alluded to, and says distinctly that the natives were at work on the new church at the time of his visit in 1792, the only visit mentioned in his work. But President Lasuen, in two letters of June 7 and Dec. 10, 1794, *Arch. Sta Bárbara*, MS., vi. 219–20; *Arch. Arzobispado*, MS., i. 38, says that the first stone was laid on July 7, 1793, or a year after Vancouver's visit. He says that the mason Ruiz came to San Cárlos in December 1792, but that *no materials were ready*, and he had to wait until the rainy season was past. It is impossible to reconcile these two statements; the difficulty may, however, be partially removed by supposing that Vancouver's picture was made at his third visit, in 1794. *Taylor, Discov. and Founders*, ii., No. 28, 167, tells us that the new church was dedicated Feb. 2, 1793; while David Spence, *Id.*, ii., No. 24, 3, says it was finished in 1786; that it stood north and south, forming the west side of the square, and coming up nearly to the west end of the present church; that the foundations were still visible in 1851; and that Serra's remains were removed on the day of dedication, being buried at the foot of the altar. 1794, masonry church half finished; 1797, 'muy adelantada.' *St. Pap., Miss.*, MS., ii. 5, 29, 100. 1797, finished, with tile roof. *Id.*, 120. Consecrated in September 1797. Lasuen, in *Arch. Sta Bárbara*, MS., xii. 66. In 1798 the Indians still lived in miserable grass huts. Sal's Report, in *Prov. St. Pap.*, MS., xvii. 65. 1793–4, several Indians work as carpenters, bricklayers, and stone-cutters under the instruction of the king's artisans. *Arch. Sta Bárbara*, MS., xii. 59. 1794, one master of each of the trades mentioned assigned to San Cárlos. *Prov. St. Pap.*, MS., xii. 192–3. 1799, hemp used to some extent for clothing for neophytes. *Prov. Rec.*, MS., vi. 117.

wife, and finally left her in the woods, after having administered some severe blows. So he confessed to his mistress, and so he testified before Sergeant Vargas, who was sent to investigate after the dead body of the woman had been found. But Estanislao's testimony was somewhat conflicting as to the force and manner of his blows, and he was acquitted on the theory that his spouse might have been killed by a bear.[21]

At San Antonio de Padua de los Robles the gain in neophyte population was from 1,076 to 1,118, with 767 baptisms and 656 deaths, this mission thus receding from the first to the fourth place, behind Santa Clara, San Diego, and San Gabriel. Cattle and horses had decreased from 2,232 to 2,217, having been as low as 1,175 in 1795. Small stock had increased only from 1,984 to 2,075; but 240 goats had disappeared altogether. Crops were 1,700 bushels in 1800, 4,200 bushels in 1799 and 420 bushels in 1795 being the extremes, and the average 2,200 bushels.[22] In 1787 the San Antonio church was mentioned as one of the best in California; in 1793 a block eighty varas long and one vara thick was built for friars' houses, church, and storehouse; and in 1797 the church is mentioned as of adobes with tile roof. The huts of the neophytes were of a more substantial character than at San Cárlos.[23] The two venerable founders Pieras and Sitjar served together until 1794, when

[21] *Arch. Arzobispado*, MS., i. 20-7. Estanislao was freed by an order of Arrillaga dated Loreto, Sept. 13, 1792.

[22] Wheat was the leading crop, barley and corn varying greatly, but the latter generally in excess. 1794-6 were very hard years. In 1795-6 the Indians killed a good deal of stock, and Lasuen favored severe measures, to dispel the Indians' prevalent idea that Spanish forbearance proceeded from weakness. *Arch. Sta Bárbara*, MS., xii. 64-5. Supplies to the presidio in 1795-6, $1,490 and $483. *Prov. St. Pap.*, MS., xvi. 203, 206. Hard times in respect of church vestments in 1795-1800. *Arch. Sta Bárbara*, MS., xii. 62, 64.

[23] *Fages, Informe Gen.*, MS., 146; *St Pap., Miss.*, MS., i. 121; ii. 120-1; Sal's Report in *Prov. St. Pap.*, MS., xvii. 65. The exact meaning of the report of 1793 is not clear. In 1794 an adobe room 14 x 9 varas, and a tile-roofed *pozolera*, or porridge-room, were completed.

the former, worn out with his long labors, retired to his college,[24] and was succeeded by José de la Cruz Espí in 1793–4, José Manuel Martiarena in 1794–5, and Marcelino Ciprés from 1795. Sitjar was absent at San Miguel from July 1797 to August 1798, and his place was filled by Benito Catalan, who served here from 1796 to 1799.[25]

At San Luis Obispo Miguel Giribet continued as senior missionary until 1799, when he left California for his college;[26] and President Lasuen seems to have acted as senior minister after Giribet's departure until August 1800, when José Miguel came. The position of associate was held successfully by Estévan Tapis in 1790–3, Gregorio Fernandez in 1794–6, Antonio Peyri in 1796–8, and Luis Antonio Martinez, who began his long ministry in 1798. Bartolomé Gili spent some time here before his departure in 1794.[27]

[24] Miguel Pieras was a native of the island of Mallorca; was appointed to the California missions in August 1770; left the college in October; sailed from San Blas in January 1771; arrived at San Diego March 12th, and at Monterey May 21st. His only service as regular minister was at San Antonio where he served from the foundation July 14, 1772, to April or May 1794. His last signature in the mission-books was April 27th. His license from the viceroy was dated Jan. 10th, and that of the governer on May 31st. I have found nothing in the records bearing upon his character. For his handwriting and autograph see *San Antonio, Doc. Sueltos*, MS., 18, 22.

[25] Nothing is known of Padre Benito Catalan beyond the fact that he served at San Antonio, was one of the unfortunate padres afflicted with insanity, *Lasuen*, in *Arch. Arzobispado*, MS., i. 56, and sailed from San Diego on the *Concepcion* in January 1800.

[26] Miguel Giribet came to California in 1785 where he served two years at San Francisco and 12 at San Luis Obispo. It is noticeable that President Lasuen in a letter of Aug. 13, 1799, to Borica, credits Giribet with only 12 years of service in California. He was zealous and successful, but as was so frequently the case his health was unequal to his task. His last signature on the San Luis books was on Oct. 2, 1799. His license from the governor was dated Aug. 22d, and he sailed from San Diego on Jan. 16, 1800. He died in 1804 at the college. *Arch. Sta Bárbara*, MS., xi. 60–1, 283, 294; *Arch. Arzobispado*, MS., i. 56; *S. Francisco, Lib. de Mision*, MS.; *S. Luis Obispo, Lib. de Mision*, MS.

[27] Bartolomé Gili came to California in 1791, and served irregularly, as supernumerary for the most part, at San Antonio, Soledad, and San Luis, from 1791 to 1794. He was one of the few black sheep in the missionary fold. He asked leave to retire in 1793 on a plea of ill-health, but his request was denied until a full report could be rendered respecting the peculiar nature of his illness and his immoral excesses for a period of five years. The full results of the investigation are not known; but Gili sailed as chaplain of the *Concepcion* in August 1794.

San Luis with 675 baptisms and 523 deaths had gained in neophyte population from 605 in 1790 to 726 in 1800; but this mission had reached its highest figure of population in 1794 with 946 souls. Cattle and horses had increased to 6,500 head; sheep to 6,150; and 2,700 bushels of grain were raised in 1800, 4,100 bushels in 1798 being the largest yield, 1,800 in 1791 the smallest, and 3,200 bushels the average. No barley was raised at this mission.[28] A water-power mill was finished early in 1798; a miller, smith, and carpenter of the king's artisan instructors were sent here in 1794; and a small quantity of cotton from San Blas was woven on the mission looms.[29] The church, of adobes with tile roof, was built before 1793, in which year a portico was added to the front. In 1794 the ministers' house, work-room, barrack, and guard-house were completed. The native huts here were well built and afforded sufficient protection against everything but fire.[30]

In 1794 a slight ripple of excitement was caused by what seems to have been an attempt to incite an Indian revolt at San Luis. Four or five gentile chiefs were the guilty parties, and they sent agents with presents to enlist the neophytes of Purísima. Indeed this sending of agents was apparently the only overt act committed; but the neophytes refused to attack their Christian friends for any such paltry presents as were offered, and the matter ended with the condemnation of five ringleaders to hard work at the presidios.[31] Subsequently in the beginning of 1797 the natives were in an excited condition over the murder of a neophyte by two gentiles, but the presence of Captain Ortega served to restore quiet.

[28] Supplies to Monterey presidio in 1795–6, $2,504 and $1,131. *Prov. St. Pap.*, MS., xvi. 203, 206; *Prov. Rec.*, MS., iv. 222. The governor granted a piece of land at Santa Margarita to the invalid corporal Cayuelas in the name of his neophyte wife, but Lasuen objected. *Arch. Sta Bárbara*, MS., xi. 398.
[29] *Prov. Rec.*, MS., iv. 177; vi. 68; *Prov. St. Pap.*, MS., xii. 192–3; *St. Pap., Miss.*, MS., ii. 6, 108; *Arch. Arzobispado*, MS., i. 30–2.
[30] *St. Pap., Miss.*, MS., i. 119; ii. 21, 120; *Prov. St. Pap.*, MS., xvii. 65.
[31] *Prov. St. Pap.*, MS., xii. 100–3, 194.

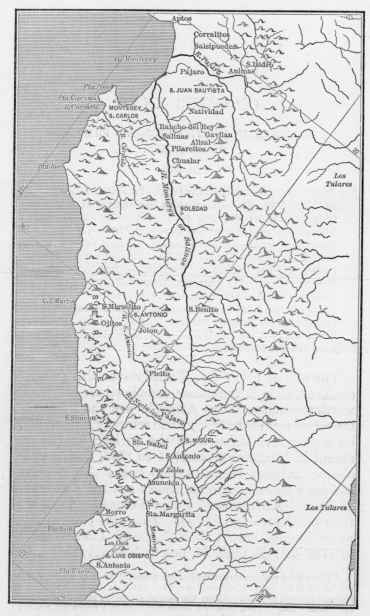

MAP OF MONTEREY.

CHAPTER XXXII.

LOCAL EVENTS AND PROGRESS—SAN FRANCISCO JURISDICTION.

1791–1800.

The official list of San Francisco for this decade is confused, though the minor complications are hardly worth recording. José Argüello was the lieutenant, brevetted captain in 1798, of the company, and properly its commander throughout the period; but he was absent in Monterey from 1791 to 1796, during which absence Alférez Hermenegildo Sal of the Monterey company was acting comandante until the middle of 1794, and Alférez José Perez Fernandez from that time till the spring of 1796. The same persons acted as habilitados, except that Raimundo Carrillo served in 1796–7.[1] It must be noted, however, that Lieu-

---

[1] These brief statements are made from a careful study of the 65 distinct references to different archives which are before me, but which it would serve no good purpose to print. About the date of Argüello's return there is some confusion. May 2, 1795, viceroy's order that Argüello rejoin his company. *Prov. St. Pap.*, MS., xiii. 85, 91. Ordered by governor in January 1796 to

tenant-colonel Pedro de Alberni, captain of the Catalan volunteers, by reason of his superior rank in the
army, was commandant of the military post from
April 1796. The alférez of the presidial company
was Ramon Lasso de la Vega until the end of 1791,
José Perez Fernandez from 1792 until 1797, and
Manuel Rodriguez from 1797 to 1800, although he
never served at San Francisco, and the place was
practically vacant. The position of sergeant was held
throughout the decade by Pedro Amador.

The company was composed of thirty-one privates,
besides the sergeant and four corporals. After the
middle of 1796 the military force was augmented by
detachments of twenty-five Catalan volunteers and
seven or eight artillerymen. There were also from
three to eight pensioners, making 79 men in all, who
with their families constituted a population, not including San José and Branciforte, of 225 within the jurisdiction. With the two pueblos the population was
460, and the christianized natives numbered 2,670.
Not less than twenty of the soldiers were usually
scattered in the mission and pueblo guards, so that
before the infantry reënforcement came the presidio
had but a very small force, and when parties had to
be sent with despatches, or against the natives, or for

turn over command at Monterey and go to San Francisco. *St. Pap., Sac.*,
MS., vii. 38-9; *Prov. Rec.*, MS., iv. 178. Took command in April. *Id.*, v.
85. But there are indications that Argüello went again to Monterey to command for a short time in the spring of 1797. He returned to San Francisco
April 18th. *Prov. St. Pap.*, MS., xvi. 57, 212. Sal gave up the command to
Perez on June 30, 1794. *Id.*, xvi. 84; *Prov. Rec.*, MS., ii. 149. Perez retained
the command until November 1795, when Sal seems to have resumed it for a
few months until Argüello's arrival. *Id.*, iv. 237; v. 75. But Sal did not
resume the *habilitacion*, which Perez gave up to Carrillo in April 1796, according to orders dated Nov. 8, and Dec. 11, 1795, transferring him to Monterey.
Id., iv. 237; v. 74. Carrillo gave up the *habilitacion* to Argüello on Sept. 1,
1797. *Id.*, vi. 7. Carrillo's accounts at the end of August showed a deficit of
$1,823. Figures given *Prov. St. Pap., Presid.*, MS., i. 81-2, 84-7. Also stated
to have been $1,425, and $1,946. *Prov. Rec.*, MS., v. 265, 267; *Prov. St. Pap.*,
MS., xvi. 80-1. This amount was charged to the company, until it could be
repaid from half of Carrillo's pay as alférez. It was a great hardship to the
soldiers and their families; and Argüello thought it particularly unjust that
the presidal company should have to bear the whole burden while the volunteers and artillerymen were exempt, and also while Lasso de la Vega was receiving half-pay and was not required to pay up his old indebtedness. *Id.*,
xvi. 40-1.

supplies, the post was left almost deserted.[2] From
the fragmentary company accounts that have been
preserved we learn that the annual appropriation for
pay-roll and contingent fund of San Francisco was
a little less than $10,000;. supplies from Mexico
amounted on an average to about $7,000; and sup-
plies from the missions about $3,000. At the end of
each year an inventory showed from $11,000 to $16,-
000 worth of goods in the presidial warehouse.[3]

The subject of presidio buildings received a large
share of attention and correspondence between 1791

[2] March 4, 1792. Nov. 1, 1794, complaints of commandant. *Prov. St. Pap.*,
MS., xi. 51–2, 56; xii. 42.   Thirty soldiers were left at San Francisco in April
1797 as a temporary expedient, *Id.*, xxi. 255–6; *Prov. Rec.*, MS., viii. 178;
and there were also workmen left at other times not included in the statistics
of population. The guard at San Francisco mission was four men. *Prov. St.
Pap.*, MS., xii. 25, 77; xiii. 231.   List of the cuera soldiers and their families
in 1795. *Prov. St. Pap.*, MS., xiii. 236–7, 242–4. List of the artillerymen.
Id., xiii. 75. List of volunteers. *Id.*, *Ben. Mil.*, xxiv. 1, 2. List of presidial
company in 1798. *Id.*, xvi. 16, 17. Company rolls and statement, in *Prov.
St. Pap.*, *Ben. Mil.*, MS., xiii. xxviii.; *St. Pap.*, *Sac.*, MS., i. v.
[3] Company accounts in *Prov. St. Pap.*, *Ben. Mil.*, MS., xiii.–xviii. passim;
St. Pap., *Sac.*, MS., i. 52; ii. 36; v. 60, 73–4; vi. 120. Argüello's account as
habilitado for 1800 is as follows: charges himself with effects on hand Dec.
31, 1799, $14,748; supplies from Mexico and San Blas, 1800, $10,876; balances
due soldiers, $3,299; funds of *montepio*, *inválidos*, and *retencion* (amounts
held for the soldiers), $604; proceeds of tobacco, post-office, and tithes, $1,403;
debt to presidio of Monterey, $881; supplies received from missions, $3,417;
draft on habilitado general, $680.   Total, $35,748.   Credits himself with:
pay-roll of company and pensioners, $9,504; amount paid company on old
account, $3,573; other sums paid, $565; paid debt of 1799 to Monterey,
$2,593; paid missions for supplies of 1799, $3,776; amount charged by habilitado general, $3,081; effects on Dec. 31, 1800, $12,885.   Total, $35,977.   Balance
in favor of Argüello, $229.   The *fondo de retencion* (money held back from a
soldier's pay to be given him at discharge) amounted in the early years to
about $1,200, but later, when added to the *fondo de inválidos* (percentage on
pay reserved with which to pay pensions), and the *fondo de montepio* (per-
centage on officers' pay for their widows), it amounted to only about $700.
St. Pap., *Sac.*, MS., v. 60, 73–4; *Prov. St. Pap.*, MS., xvi. 202–3.   In 1795
the habilitado reports only $3,490 to pay for the next year's supplies. *St. Pap.*,
Sac., MS., i. 52.   Of $1,122 in coin sent up in 1796, $266 was paid to soldiers,
$300 to the mission, and $400 to Argüello; so that the sergeant applying for
money was told to wait. *Prov. St. Pap.*, MS., xiv. i.   In 1798 the presidio
got $6,404 in supplies from the missions. *Id.*, *Ben. Mil.*, xvii. 12, 13. In
1797 the amount was $8,973. *Id.*, xxv. 9, 10.   In 1799 it was $3,776. *Id.*,
xxvi. 7, 8.   In 1800 it was $3,417. *Id.*, xxviii. 18, 19.   Accounts of tithes are
neither complete nor altogether intelligible.   For some years the proceeds are
given as $500 and in others $80, some reports perhaps including the whole
jurisdiction and others not. Papal bulls yielded in 1797 only $2. The net
proceeds of the post-office averaged $83 per year for the decade. Revenues from
tobacco sales were from $500 to $1,500, averaging $1,100. *Prov. St. Pap.*, MS.,
xxi. 193; *Id.*, *Ben. Mil.*, xiii. 7; xiv. 5; viii. 14; ix. 1; xvii. 12; xviii. 2, 3;
xxi. 1; xxv. 9; xxvi. 7; xxvii. 2; xxviii. 14, 15.

and 1800, with but meagre results so far as the
presidio proper was concerned.   On March 4, 1792,
Comandante Sal sent the governor a description
accompanied by a plan which I reproduce.[4]   Three
sides of the square of 120 yards were occupied by
adobe walls and houses, both of adobes and of rough
stones laid in mud; and the fourth side was protected
by a primitive palisade fence.   All the structures
were roofed with straw and tules, exposed to fire and
at the mercy of the winds.   All, except the com-

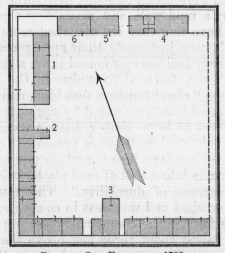

PLAN OF SAN FRANCISCO, 1792.

mandant's house lately completed and two or three of
the soldiers' houses, were, through the poor quality
of materials and want of knowledge and care on the
part of the builders, liable to fall at any moment, the
church being in a particularly precarious condition.
None of the structures were those originally built;
each year some of them had fallen and been restored
in the same faulty manner with the same perishable

[4] Sal, Informes sobre los Edificios de San Francisco, 1792, MS.   1. Commandant's house, 4 rooms and yard, 37 x 6 varas, of adobes.   2. Sergeant's
house, of stone, without mortar.   3. Chapel 19 x 8 varas.   4. Barracks,
guard-house, and calabooses, of adobe and stones.   5, 6. Warehouses for food
and clothing, of stones and mud.   The other structures are the soldiers'
dwellings.

material.   Timber had to be brought thirty miles, and tules nine miles.   The garrison was so small and its duties so many that Sal deemed it impossible to accomplish the necessary repairs.   At the end of the year the same condition of affairs existed, and Sal urged the government to send eight or ten sailor-workmen and a bricklayer; otherwise an appropriation of $3,000 would be required to hire Indian laborers.   Meanwhile Vancouver visited and described the presidio in November, and he describes it as a "square area whose sides were about two hundred yards in length enclosed by a mud wall, and resembling a pound for cattle.   Above this wall the thatched roofs of their low small houses just made their appearance."   One side was " very indifferently fenced in by a few bushes here and there, fastened to stakes in the ground."   The wall was " about fourteen feet high, and five feet in breadth, and was first formed by uprights and horizontal rafters of large timber, between which dried sods and moistened earth were pressed as close and hard as possible, after which the whole was cased with the earth made into a sort of mud plaster, which gave it the appearance of durability."   The church had been whitewashed and was neat in comparison to the rest.   The floor in the commandant's house was the native soil raised about three feet above the original level.   The windows were mere holes in the thick walls, without glass.[5]

In 1793–4 complaints and calls for aid continued, but attention was given almost exclusively to new fortifications on the shore to the neglect of the presidio

[5] *Vancouver's Voyage*, ii. 7–9. There is a communication from Sal to Arrillaga dated Nov. 29th, stating that work on the building was finished, tile roofs on the church, warehouses, and nine new houses for soldiers; but this does not agree with the other records, and I am at a loss to know why such a letter was written. *St. Pap., Sac.*, MS., i. 118. August 20, 1793, the governor informs the viceroy of the bad condition of the buildings, although $1,400 have been spent on repairs since the foundation. *Prov. St. Pap.*, MS., xxi. 114–15. Dec. 29th, Sal to Borica, the $1,200 gratuity for the troops for building the presidio not yet received; nor are there any lists. Hints that the other presidios get $4,000. *Id.*, xi. 54, 57.

square.[6] Late in 1794 Sal proposed removal to a better site near Fort Point. Borica would not consent until he had made a personal examination; but in June 1795 he reported in favor of the scheme and estimated the cost of the new presidio at $11,716. The viceroy disapproved so large an outlay for buildings of doubtful utility, the matter was dropped, and the rains and winds continued their ravages,[7] the drifting sand contributing to the devastation by covering the powder-magazine, notwithstanding the soldiers' efforts. Quarters of some kind must have been built for the volunteers and artillerymen,[8] but I find no evidence that there was any material improvement within the presidio square from the date of Vancouver's visit to 1800.

Still there was some building done in the way of fortifications. In the general movement already

[6] Aug. 8, 1794, Perez Fernandez and others state that nothing has been done, and the soldiers are overburdened with work. The buildings should be solidly constructed to avoid later repairs, and he and the commandant will guarantee to complete the work economically and well if a few mechanics can be furnished. *St. Pap., Sac.*, MS., v. 108–10. Arrillaga informs Borica of the needs of San Francisco in 1794. *Papel de Puntos*, MS., 192. Jan. 31, 1794, commandant to governor; house of 2d officer in a bad state; adobes and tiles melting away; will try to save the timbers. *Prov. St. Pap.*, MS., xii. 66. Feb. 1, 1794, rain came near spoiling the powder, but hides and tiles were arranged to save it. *Id.*, xii. 56.

[7] Nov. 1, 1794, commandant to governor. *Prov. St. Pap.*, MS., xii. 35–6. Dec. 3, Borica's reply. *Prov. Rec.*, MS., v. 28, 54–5. June 27, 1795, B. to viceroy, old buildings ready to fall; total expenses since 1776, $8,188; presidio, 2,889 varas from fort; new one, 481 varas. *Id.*, vi. 51. Dec. 4, 1795, V. R. to B., advises that the new structures be not undertaken, but wants additional information. *Prov. St. Pap.*, MS., xiii. 32–6. Jan. 22, 1796, a heavy gale did much damage to church and one house. *Prov. St. Pap., Ben. Mil.*, MS., xxiii. 6, 7; *Prov. Rec.*, MS., v. 81. June 16, B. calls for a report from Alberni. *Prov. St. Pap., Ben. Mil.*, MS., xxiv. 7. June 30th, Alberni to B., he disapproves the removal, because the San Joaquin hill has no water and is less sheltered; but the coming rains will bring the old buildings down, and a new presidio should be begun. Córdoba agrees with Alberni. *St. Pap., Sac.*, MS., iv. 36–7. July 20, 1797, Argüello to B. The old complaints. Nothing done yet. *Prov. St. Pap.*, MS., xv. 11, 12. Aug. 8, Id. to Id. Warehouses badly built and in great danger from fire. *Id.*, xvi. 39. Aug. 19, B. orders Argüello to have warehouses of stone or adobe built. *Prov. Rec.*, MS., v. 267. In January 1800 a huricane tore off several roofs; $1,799 were spent in repairs during the year; and complaints continued. *Prov. St. Pap.*, MS., xviii. 24–7; xxi. 31.

[8] One hundred and ninety-two dollars spent on quarters for volunteers. Expenditure approved by viceroy Feb. 28, 1798. *Prov. St. Pap.*, MS., xvii. 10, 11.

noticed towards the strengthening of coast defences San Francisco could not be neglected, since it was recognized as the strongest and most important natural position in California. Vancouver as he entered the bay was saluted by a brass three-pounder lashed to a log at Fort Point, and he found another mounted on a rotten carriage before the presidio. There had been two guns here, but one had burst shortly before in firing a salute on a saint's day. No wonder the Englishman was surprised at the unprotected condition of so important a point. When he returned in 1793, eleven brass nine-pounders were lying on the beach, and a number of natives were erecting what seemed to be a platform or barbette battery at Fort Point; but this was intended by the Spaniards to be a much more formidable work, the Castillo de San Joaquin, to command the entrance to San Francisco Bay. The guns had been sent from San Blas in the *Aranzazu*, and a gunner's mate, master-carpenter, and one or two workmen had begun work on the fort in August.[9] Thirty neophytes were hired from the mission, and as many more gentiles from San José. Choppers were sent to the distant forests down the peninsula; twenty-three yoke of oxen were employed in hauling the timber; adobes, bricks, and tiles were rapidly prepared, and the work was pushed forward until interrupted by the rains. Soon after its resumption in the spring of 1794 there came an order from the viceroy that the works here and elsewhere were to be constructed of fascines, to avoid heavy expenses; but so much progress had been made that it was deemed best to complete the fortification as begun,

[9] *Vancouver's Voyage*, ii. 9, 500. Sept. 30, 1792, Sal reports the bursting of the gun into 10 pieces, nobody hurt. *St. Pap., Sac.*, MS., vi. 74; i. 117. Although Vancouver says a gun was fired, Sal reports to the governor that the *Chatham* got no salute for want of a cannon. *Id.*, iii. 23. Oct. 31st, Sal to Arrillaga. Only one cannon, and that burst several years ago. Cuadra gave some powder and promised four or five guns. So it seems that the presidio gun was not so effective even as Vancouver supposed. *Id.*, i. 119. Aug. 20, 1793, Arrillaga to viceroy, announcing that work had been begun on a fort. After completing it the men will go to Monterey. *Prov. St. Pap.*, MS., xxi. 113. Dec. 31, 1793, statement of munitions. *St. Pap., Sac.*, MS. v. 61.

especially as earthworks and fascines were thought to
be useless here. The fort was completed and blessed
under the name of San Joaquin on December 8, 1794,
the eight guns of the battery being mounted, the
sentry-box, casemate, and other necessary buildings
being attached, and nothing more being required but
a garrison to prevent any hostile vessel from entering

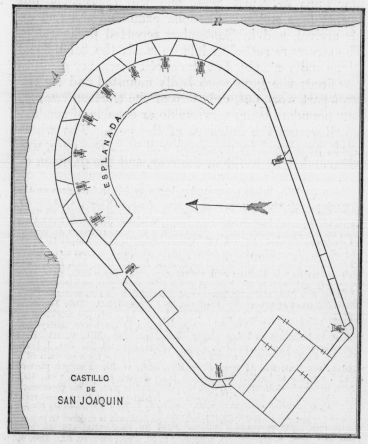

CASTILLO
DE
SAN JOAQUIN

the port—so at least Arrillaga believed. We have
no detailed description of this fort, but its main walls
were of adobes, faced in the embrasures with bricks.
The annexed plan is from an original in my possession.

The castillo was of horseshoe shape, about one hundred by one hundred and twenty feet. Its cost was $6,000, which was paid with some reluctance by the royal treasury.[10]

The elements had now another object on which to exert their destructive power, and repairs kept pace as nearly as possible. The *San Cárlos* brought some new guns in. April 1796, and the *Concepcion* left twenty-four sailors. Córdoba examined the fort on his arrival, and in September reported unfavorably. The structure rested mainly on sand; the brick-faced adobe walls crumbled at the shock whenever a salute was fired; the guns were badly mounted and for the most part worn out, only two of the thirteen twenty-four pounders being serviceable or capable of sending a ball across the entrance of the port. The whole work, protected by an adobe wall with one gate, was commanded by a hill in the rear, and the garrison of

[10] Jan. 30, 1794, Sal to governor, has begun to fell timber; guns on the esplanade. *Prov. St. Pap.*, MS., xii. 47–51. Jan. 31st, 6 guns in the battery facing the harbor. *Id.*, xii. 67. The padres endeavored to obtain an extra blanket and pair of breeches for each neophyte laborer per month but failed; 1,500 adobes being made daily. April 30th, a sergeant and four soldiers in charge of the laborers. *Id.*, xii. 74. Twenty-two Indians ran away in April. *Id.*, xii. 53. June 9th, viceroy acknowledges receipt of advices on measures taken to complete the provisional esplanade. *Id.*, xi. 174. Jan. 10th, viceroy's orders to use fascines and reduce expenses. June 12th, governor's reply. *Id.*, xxi. 143–4; xii. 120. A *condestable*, carpenter, and two sawyers sent from San Blas, and a bricklayer and tile-maker were also retained. The troops did most of the work. *Arrillaga*, in *Id.*, xii. 191–2. Dec. 1st, commandant says the work is almost finished, and he sends the workmen to Monterey. *Id.*, xii. 31. Dec. 3d, governor refers to the tower, sentry-box, and other buildings as being nearly done. *Prov. Rec.*, MS., v. 29. Fort blessed on Dec. 8th. *Id.*, v. 31–2; *Prov. St. Pap.*, MS., xii. 26. Jan. 1, 1795, governor sends the viceroy a plan of the work, and asks for a garrison of a captain, sergeant, and 11 men. *Prov. Rec.*, MS., vi. 35. I copy a plan of what I suppose to be this fortification from *Alviso, Doc. Hist. Cal.*, 156. Elliot, in *Overland Monthly*, iv. 344, says he has the plan in his possession. One of the old guns, four of which serve as fender-posts of the present fort, bears the inscription '*Governando los señores de la Real Audiencia de Lima.*' Cost of building the *castillo*, $6,491, which real hacienda is ordered to pay on Oct. 8, 1795, as V. R. informs the gov. *Prov. St. Pap.*, MS., xiii. 45, 162; *Prov. Rec.*, MS., v. 35. $6,503, according to *St. Pap., Sac.*, iv. 52. Dec. 4, 1795, viceroy to Borica, $1,482 have been paid over to habilitado general in favor of company fund. *Prov. St. Pap.*, MS., xiii. 32. May 16, 1795, José Garaycoechea, *condestable distinguido de artillería de marina*, employed on the fort, discharged, his work being done. *Prov. Rec.*, MS., vi. 46. Dec. 4th, the viceroy complains that a fort, costly and not needed (?), has been improperly constructed, without investigation or skill. *Prov. St. Pap.*, MS., xiii. 32–6.

a corporal and six artillerymen was altogether insufficient. There were several places between Monterey and San Francisco where an enemy might land, therefore the cavalry force should be increased. To repair Fort San Joaquin would be very costly; but a new fort should be built on the hill just back of it, and another across the channel at San Cárlos.[11]

Beyond the constant repairs by which Fort San Joaquin was kept as nearly in its original state as possible, and some changes in the disposition of the guns under Córdoba's instructions, I find no evidence of further progress at Fort Point during this decade. There was, however, still another battery established in 1797. This was to the east on Point Médanos, later called Point San José and Black Point, renamed Mason, and long occupied by a battery. It was

[11] Córdoba, Informe al Virey, MS., 82-3. The point across the channel is called Punto de Bonetes in 1776. Arch. Sta B., MS., iv. 153. Feb. 22, 1796, damage to fort by a storm from the north. Prov. St. Pap., MS., xxi. 234. Mar. 22d, reference to a sentry-box erected. April, Borica orders mortar to be used in the roofing, and the powder-house to have a new adobe wall at some distance. Prov. Rec., MS., v. 83, 85. Arrival of guns and sailors. Prov. St. Pap., MS., xiv. 86, 175; Id., Ben. Mil., xxiv. 12. July 9th, Alberni to have charge of the work, 41 Indians from Santa Clara at work. Prov. Rec., MS., v. 87-8. July 16th, Córdoba has been at work on repairs. St. Pap., Sac., MS., xvii. 8. Nov. 29th, 6,000 ball-cartridges being made. Prov. St. Pap., MS., xiv. 119. Dec. 6th, Borica to V. R., announces damages caused by rains. St. Pap., Sac., MS., iv. 69. Dec. 27th, V. R. to B., will send the needed armament of heavy guns; meanwhile let guns be taken from other places where they are less needed. Id., vii. 32-5; Prov. St. Pap., MS., xxi. 251. Jan. 30, 1797, Habilitado Carrillo asks for reimbursement of $468 spent on casemate, etc. Prov. St. Pap., MS., xvi. 69. March 26th, Córdoba wants 11 24-pounders; smaller guns of no use here. Prov. Rec., MS., vi. 86. April 4th, B. forwards V. R.'s orders for repairs, etc. Prov. St. Pap., MS., xxi. 251-2; Prov. Rec., MS., v. 103. April 30th, work on fort not yet begun. Prov. St. Pap., MS., xvii. 148. June, fort repaired, with 6 guns in front and 3 on each side. Id., xxi. 264. Oct. 24th, 24 sailors left on the San Cárlos for San Blas. Prov. Rec., MS., vi. Feb. 1, 1798, B. asks the V. R. for a new fort on the other shore, an increase of armament to 26 24-pounders, an increase of 128 infantry and 19 gunners in the garrisons, and a boat with a patron and 10 sailors. Prov. Rec., MS., vi. 69. March 15, 1799, another appeal for a boat. Id., vi. 120. December 31, 1798, there were 3 iron 24-pounders, 1 iron 12-pounder, and 8 brass 8-pounders. Prov. St. Pap., Ben. Mil., MS., xvii. 7. Expenses of the year for repairs $661. Id., xvii. 13. March 2, 1799, B. informs V. R. that a rainstorm caused the walls of the fort to fall, also the new casemate wall, and the barracks are threatened. Prov. Rec., MS., vi. 119. July 15th, V. R. will attend to the matter. Meanwhile let the works be repaired with adobes, fascines, and earth. Prov. St. Pap., MS., xvii. 341. In January 1800 a hurricane broke the flag-staff which fell on the barracks of the garrison and smashed some tiles. Id., xxiii. 24; xxi. 31.

known as the Battery at Yerba Buena, designed to command the shore stretching westward to Fort Point, and that stretching eastward to what was called later North Point, together with the body of water between that shore and Alcatraz Island, already so called, known as the anchorage of Yerba Buena, though it does not appear that any vessel except that of Vancouver ever had anchored there. Thus it will be seen that the name Yerba Buena, while it may have been given in a general way to the whole eastern part of the peninsula from Black Point to Rincon Point, was applied in these early times particularly to the North Beach region and not, as is commonly supposed and as was the case after 1830, to the cove south of Telegraph Hill. Of the battery we know but little save that it was a less elaborate work than Fort San Joaquin, being hastily constructed of brushwood fascines for the most part, with eight embrasures and five eight-pound guns not needed at the fort. No permanent garrison was kept here, but at least until after 1800 the works were visited daily by a sentinel, and to a certain extent kept in order.[12]

I have spoken several times of Vancouver's voyages and his observations in California; but as his was the first visit of a foreigner to San Francisco Bay, as it

[12] The battery is first mentioned by the governor in communications of April 4, 1797. On April 19th Argüello received Borica's orders to furnish aid. April 30th, Córdoba objected on account of small garrisons and distance from the fort. But May 3d he was ordered by Borica to begin work, and in June it was almost finished. *Prov. St. Pap.*, MS., xvi. 55; xvii. 148–9; xviii. 28; xxi. 251–2, 256, 264; *Prov. Rec.*, MS., v. 103, 107; vi. 53, 69. The first use of the name Yerba Buena that I have seen is in Sal's letter of Nov. 14, 1792, announcing Vancouver's arrival. He is said to have anchored 'como á una legua mas abajo del presidio frente del parage que llamamos la Yerba Buena.' *St. Pap., Sac.*, MS., i. 116. It is also used in Sal's letter of Nov. 30th. *Id.*, iii. 21. Vancouver's anchorage was about midway between Black Point and North Point. *Vancouver's Voyage, Atlas.* The name is that of a species of mint. Whether it was first applied to the island and from that to the eastern part of the peninsula, or *vice versa*, I am uncertain. The name Isla del Alcatraz is used by Borica in July 1797. *Prov. St. Pap.*, MS., xxi. 264. I mention this fact because it has often been stated that the original and correct form was Alcatraces in the plural. The name is that applied by Californians and Mexicans to the pelican, though more properly belonging to the albatross.

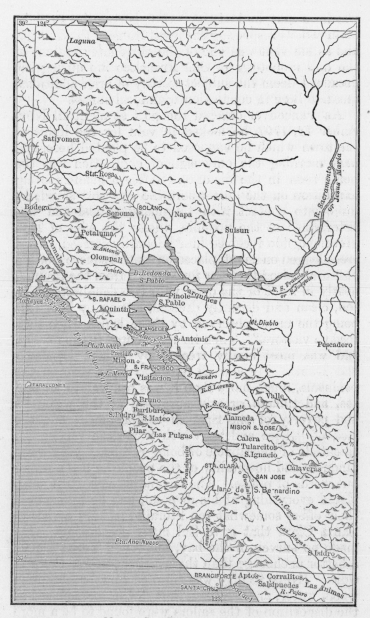

MAP OF SAN FRANCISCO DISTRICT.

was here that he had the best opportunities to make observations respecting the institutions of the country, and as his visit was one of the chief interruptions of the dull monotony of San Francisco life during the decade, I deem the subject worthy of brief additional mention here in connection with local annals.

As Vancouver entered the port at nightfall November 14, 1792, he looked in vain for the lights of the town which he supposed to be planted here, and next morning the only sign of civilization was the herds seen in the distance. After a quail-shooting expedition on the hills where the city now stands he came into contact with Commandant Sal and was entertained at the presidio, where the wife of Don Hermenegildo received him "decently dressed, seated cross-legged on a mat, placed on a small square wooden platform raised three or four inches from the ground, nearly in front of the door, with two daughters and a son, clean and decently dressed, sitting by her; this being the mode observed by these ladies when they receive visitors." Then he was invited to the mission and was most kindly treated by fathers Landaeta and Dantí. He saw all that was to be seen on the peninsula, much more than it was prudent to let him see, and though greatly surprised at the weakness and poverty of the Spanish establishment and the lack of "those articles which alone can render the essentials of life capable of being relished," yet for the kindness and hospitality of the people he had nothing but words of praise. The Spaniards as is their wont placed everything at his disposal, and he interpreted their offers somewhat too literally, making a visit to Santa Clara that gave Sal many forebodings. He made no survey of the bay, but found Yerba Buena a better anchorage than the usual one nearer the presidio. Every facility was afforded him for obtaining wood, water, and supplies, though the carts placed at the disposition of the sailors were found to be a more clumsy and useless contrivance on land than the rude balsas of the natives as water craft. Vancouver sailed for Monterey on the 25th of November. He came back in October of the next year, but was obliged to put up with the ordinary courtesies allowed to foreigners in Spanish colonial ports, and so great was the contrast that he left in disgust after a few days' stay at anchor.[13]

The 13th of March 1793 a strange vessel was announced at the entrance of the port. A guard was posted and the live-stock driven in. A boat came to land in the afternoon, with six men who said the vessel was English and the captain's name Brown, in need of water, wood, and meat, for which he would send the next day. The vessel anchored beyond Point Almejas, opposite San Pedro rancho, fired a gun, and displayed the English flag. On the 15th she was seen near the Farallones, and on the 16th Sal reported these facts with his opinion that the foreign craft meant mischief, though pretending to be bound for Nootka.[14]

In 1795 three mines were discovered somewhere within the jurisdiction of San Francisco, called San Diego, Cármen, and San José, with the respective aliases of Descubridora, Buenavista, and Esperanza. One of them was expected to yield gold, and the others silver or quicksilver. Specimens of the ore were sent by Perez Fernandez to the governor, but Monterey experts failed to discover metal except in one specimen.[15] The coming of Alberni and his company of volunteers was the event of 1796, but beyond a bare mention and the enrolment of the reënforcements on the military records it left no trace in local annals; yet as almost doubling the population of San Fran-

[13] *Vancouver's Voyage*, ii. 1–27, 433–4. For further account of this voyage, and a map published in Vancouver's work, see chapter xxiv., this volume.

[14] March 16th, Sal to Borica, in *St. Pap., Sac.*, MS., ii. 131–2.

[15] Sept. 28, 1795, Perez Fernandez to Borica. *St. Pap., Sac.*, MS., vii. 66–7. Sept. 30th, B.'s reply authorizing ore to be sent to San Blas for assaying. *Prov. Rec.*, MS., v. 70.

cisco it merits mention.[16] In 1797 there was a proposition to establish a Carmelite convent and hospice at San Francisco, but it was disapproved by both the guardian and the fiscal, and consequently was abandoned.[17] The leading event of this year was the wreck of the transport vessel *San Cárlos* in the bay on the night of the 23d of March. No details are known except that little of the cargo was lost.[13] The *Concepcion* as a coast guard spent a large part of the year in this port. At the end of May 1799 the American ship *Eliza* of 136 tons and carrying twelve guns, bound for Boston with hides, under James Rowan, obtained supplies under the prescribed restrictions.[19]

There were two topics of local interest at San Francisco during the decade which affected the mission not less than the presidio. These were the establishment of the rancho del rey, and Indian affairs. The royal rancho had been founded here in 1777, with 115 head of cattle, which were pastured on the hills about the presidio. The animals multiplied rapidly notwithstanding annual slaughters in the later years and the

[16] It is implied by Borica, *Prov. St. Pap.*, MS., xxi. 241, that Alberni's men had lands granted them at San Francisco and the Alameda; but such was probably not the case. Alberni and his company arrived May 7, 1796, on the *San Cárlos. Prov. St. Pap., Ben. Mil.*, MS., xxiii. 83.

[17] *Arch. Sta Bárbara*, MS., iv. 186–93; ix. 10–14; xiii. 84.

[18] *Prov. St. Pap.*, MS., xvi. 57–8, 181; xvii. 242; xxi. 251, 263; *Prov. Rec.*, MS., vi. 86, 92, 95. This was not the original *San Cárlos* of 1769, but her successor surnamed *El Filipino*. The crew were obliged to remain for some time in California. The only stores specially named as lost are 4 boxes of cigars and 15 lbs. of powder. April 26th, Capt. Saavedra says to Argüello that most of his men lost their clothes, tobacco, and soap in the wreck. He asks for them the advance of a month's pay, which was granted to the amount of $1,026. The troops with 55 natives worked to save the cargo. April 24th, the padres answer the complaint that they failed to render aid, by stating that Fernandez was absent, but Landaeta sent all his disposable Indians, who worked waist-deep in water for three days and nights. *St. Pap., Sac.*, MS., vi. 108–9. April 14th, the finding of a white man's body in the surf at Pt Reyes is reported, and the mission majordomo had seen a vessel off the Farallones shortly before. *Prov. St. Pap.*, MS., xv. 116. Alberni at the same time wished to send natives to see if there were any vessels at Bodega; but they refused from fear of their enemies. *Id.*, xvii. 152.

[19] May 27th, Rowan to Argüello, will obey the governor's orders to sail as soon as possible and not to enter any other port. *Prov. St. Pap.*, xvii. 206–8, 238; xviii. 26. June 3d, Borica to viceroy, Rowan left a draft for $24 on Boston. *Prov. Rec.*, MS., vi. 125–6.

ravages of wild beasts,[20] so that in 1791 they numbered over 1,200. At the end of March of this year the cattle were transferred to Monterey, except a few milch cows which the soldiers were allowed to keep. This change seems to have been made by order of the comandante general at the petition of the padres who represented that injury was done to the interests of the mission. Subsequently the garrison was obliged to obtain meat from Monterey.[21] In 1796, at the suggestion of Sal, Borica determined to reëstablish a branch of the rancho del rey, and this was accomplished in September 1797, two hundred and sixty-five cattle being purchased from the missions and placed at Buriburi between San Bruno and San Mateo.[22]

When the news reached Mexico it brought out a protest of the guardian, in which he narrated the past history of the rancho, claimed that Borica had acted in opposition to the king's wishes that the mission lands should not be encroached upon, and demanded an order to remove not only the rancho but the cattle owned by the soldiers. The pasturage it was claimed was all needed for the mission herds, which now must be driven far down the peninsula; and the natives were suffering great injury in their

[20] In the cattle account of 1782 appears an item of three arrobas of *yerba de Puebla* with which to poison wolves. *Prov. Rec.*, MS., iii. 115. April and May 1790, commandant refers to ravages of bears and savages. *Prov. St. Pap.*, MS., ix. 213–14. Bears numerous in 1798. *Id.*, xvii. 103.

[21] Cattle of the rancho in 1790, 1,174 head. *Prov. St. Pap., Ben. Mil.*, MS., xiii. 6, 7. Net proceeds of sales, $91. *Id.* Sales in 1791, $81. *Id.*, xv. 5. Number of cattle at transfer on March 31, 1791, 1,215 head. *St. Pap., Miss. and Colon.*, MS., i. 68. The rancho was moved by order of Fages, *Id.*, or by order of commandant general at request of padres. *Prov. St. Pap.*, MS., xvii. 14–16. Statistical reports show that the soldiers had from 96 to 147 cattle down to 1797 and then the number increased to 500 or 600, not including the king's cattle. In 1793 the number was 115, and the names of 14 owners, 23 credited to Juan Bernal being the largest number, are given from an old inventory in *Halley's Centennial Year Book of Alameda County*, 27. There is quite a mass of information from the archives given in this work, but there are nearly as many blunders as words in the translation, copying, and printing. In 1794, 75 cattle for food were sent up from Monterey. *Prov. St. Pap.*, MS., xii. 30.

[22] Borica to commandants April 30, 1796, Aug. 15, Sept. 1, 1797. *Prov. Rec.*, MS., v. 85, 269; iv. 255–6. Argüello to B. Sept. 29th. *Prov. St. Pap.*, MS., xvi. 92.

natural and legal rights.[23]   Borica, being called upon
for an explanation, asked Argüello for a report in
which the governor's eleven question were clearly
answered. According to this report the mission was
in no respect injured by the king's cattle at Buriburi,
feeding on the hills westward to the Cañada de San
Andrés and south-westward for two leagues, nor
would it be injured even should its cattle greatly increase, for it still had several large *sitios:* San Pedro,
five leagues southward on the coast, where horned
cattle were kept; another two leagues to the south,
where were the herds of mares; El Pilar,[24] where
there was abundant pasturage for the oxen; San
Mateo, five leagues from the mission, stretching to
Santa Clara on the south-east and to San Pedro on
the west; besides the smaller and nearer tracts of La
Visitacion, San Bruno, and Lake Merced. Argüello
also proved that the mission had been accustomed to
sell to the presidio and the vessels cattle about one
third smaller than those of Monterey at prices exceeding those of the tariff, besides obliging the purchaser to go long distances after the animals.[25]   His
arguments seemed conclusive to the viceroy, who in
March 1799 ordered the rancho maintained, notwithstanding the opposition of the friars.[26]

The natives, Christian and gentile, caused more
trouble in the region of San Francisco than in any
other part of California, the troublesome gentiles
being chiefly those inhabiting what is now known as

[23] Feb. 5, 1798, guardian to viceroy, in *Prov. St. Pap.*, MS., xvii. 14–16.
Horses were kept 10 leagues distant; sheep under a salaried man six leagues
away; and the oxen not actually at work were also pastured at a long distance.
[24] But according to *Prov. Rec.*, MS., v. 103, Argüello himself had received
a provisional grant of El Pilar in 1797.
[25] June 14, 1798, Borica to Argüello. *St. Pap., Miss. and Colon*, MS., i.
68–70. *Argüello, Informe sobre el Rancho del Rey y su influencia y relacion con
la Mision de San Francisco, 24 de Julio 1798*, MS. Salazar speaks of S. Pedro
or Punta de Almejas. *Arch. Sta Bárbara*, ii. 75.
[26] March 13, 1799, Viceroy Azanza to Borica. *Prov. St. Pap.*, MS., xvii.
220.   June 5th, to commandant. *Prov. Rec.*, MS., iv. 298.   Dec. 31st, number of cattle in the rancho, 879. Net yield from sales, $179. *Prov. St. Pap.*,
Ben. Mil., MS., xxviii. 5.

Alameda and Contra Costa counties, acting in conjunction with deserters from San Francisco mission, but threatening more seriously Mission San José. All was quiet, however, until 1795.[27] In March of that year Father Dantí sent a party of fourteen neophytes to the rancherías of the Chaclanes, or Sacalanes, to bring in some fugitives, but they were attacked by gentiles and Christians combined, and at least seven of the number were killed. The affair was reported to Borica, who informed the viceroy, but ordered no retaliation as the Sacalanes were a brave people and would be troublesome as foes, and the friars were directed to send out no more such parties.[28] In September of the same year over two hundred natives deserted from San Francisco, different parties in different directions, the number including many old neophytes who had always been faithful before. In the correspondence which followed, Borica indicated his belief that the disaster was due largely to cruelty on the part of the padres. He ordered a strict investigation; instructed the soldiers to afford no aid in the infliction of punishments unless at the request of both padres, for it seems that Dantí was much more severe than his associate, and finally protested to the president that rigorous steps must be taken to insure better

[27] In February 1793 a new convert named Charquin ran away and waged war on all aborigines who favored christianity, holding 20 women and children captives in the mountains. *St. Pap., Sac.*, MS., vii. 24–5. In February 1795 the governor reported the prospects for new converts excellent at San Francisco and Santa Clara, on account of a scarcity of seeds. *Prov. Rec.*, MS., vi. 37.

[28] March 3, May 3, May 29, 1795, commandant to Borica. June 23d, B. to viceroy. *Prov. St. Pap.*, MS., xiii. 241–2, 275–6; *Prov. Rec.*, MS., v. 50, 56; vi. 48–50. I suppose the Sacalanes lived in what is now Alameda County, somewhere between Oakland and Mission San José. The messengers are said to have travelled two nights and one day before reaching the rancherías. Borica says the Chimenes did the killing and lived 30 leagues from Bodega on the coast. Subsequent expeditions show, however, that the Sacalanes, the guilty parties, did not at any rate live north of the bay. The commandant charges Dantí with having at first pronounced the story of the survivors a lie, and with attempting later to keep it from the knowledge of the officers. July 6th, Borica to friars, regrets that they continue sending Indians to the other side of the bay. It must be stopped. *Prov. Rec.*, MS., vi. 146. Sept. 18th, V. R. approves B.'s policy of avoiding war. *Prov. St. Pap.*, MS., xiii. 82.

treatment and better food, to which Lasuen gave assent.[29]

In June 1797 a new mishap occurred. A large part of the fugitives belonged to the Cuchillones across the bay. Notwithstanding the governor's orders the missionaries sent one Raimundo, a Californian—a name still applied exclusively to the natives of Baja California—with thirty natives to bring back the runaways. They crossed in balsas and fell into a difficulty with the Cuchillones which is not clearly described, though it appears that no life was lost and no fugitive recovered. This affair gave rise to a new correspondence and to earnest protests from the friars, who were inclined to think that the quarrel, if any occurred, had been greatly exaggerated.[30] Now the Sacalanes assumed a threatening attitude toward Mission San Jose, and Sergeant Amador was sent to investigate. He found that the gentiles were threatening to kill the Christians if they continued to work, and the soldiers if they dared to interfere. He accordingly recommended to Borica that an expedition be sent to punish them, to collect fugitives, and to dispel the idea of the Sacalanes that the Spaniards were afraid of them. Borica assented and ordered Amador to take twenty-two men and fall upon the ranchería at dawn, capturing the head men and deserters, but avoiding bloodshed if possible. They set out July 13th, and on the 15th the troops under Amador and Vallejo reached the hostile camp. The Sacalanes would listen to nothing; they had digged pits, so that the Spaniards were forced to dismount and attack with sword and lance. In the fight two soldiers were

---

[29] Correspondence on the subject during 1795–6. In *Prov. St. Pap.*, MS., xiii. 147–8; xiv. 176; *Id.*, *Ben. Mil.*, xxiv. 8–10; *Prov. Rec.*, MS., v. 69, 80, 91; vi. 172, 176.

[30] Letters of Argüello, Espí, Fernandez, and Landaeta in *Prov. St. Pap.*, MS., xv. 19–25. July 16th, Argüello assembled the natives and made known to them the governor's orders that they were not to go after fugitives even if told to do so by the padres. Then the padres received a lecture on the evils that might have resulted. Landaeta insisted that the natives had gone of their own accord and had not been sent. Argüello to Borica, in *Id.*, xv. 25–7.

wounded and seven natives killed. The Cuchillones were subsequently attacked and retreated after one had been killed. On the 18th Amador returned to San José with eighty-three Christians and nine gentiles, including five Sacalanes implicated in the affair of 1795 and three Cuchillones in that of Raimundo.[31]

The testimony and confessions of fourteen of the captives were taken the 9th of August, and nine of them having been proved guilty, were subsequently sentenced by Borica to receive from twenty-five to seventy-five lashes and to work in shackles at the presidio from two months to a year.[32] In this examination and in another held the 12th of August with a view to learn why the neophytes had run away, nearly all the witnesses gave as their reasons excessive flogging, hunger, and the death of relatives.[33] Borica subsequently announced that in consequence of his efforts and especially of the kindness of Father Fernandez, the natives were treated better than before; but Lasuen declared that the charges of cruelty were unfounded, as proved by the large number of conversions. The neophytes fled, not because they were flogged or overworked, but because of the rav-

[31] *Amador, Expedicion contra los gentiles Sacalanes, con Correspondencia perteneciente al asunto, 1796*, MS.; *Prov. St. Pap.*, MS., xv. 176-8; xvi. 38-9, 70-1, 88, 90; *Prov. Rec.*, MS., v. 206-7. The diary is dated San José, July 19th, and the papers include: July 6th, Argüello to Borica; July 8th, Amador to B.; July 10th, B. to A.; July 19th, A. to B.; July 21st, B. to A. Christians not to be punished, but gentiles kept at work on presidio; July 26th, receipt of Espí and Landaeta for 79 returned neophytes. Returning natives have never been punished. July 30th, Argüello to B., has given up the neophytes and will try the gentiles.

[32] *Argüello, Relacion de lo que declararon los Gentiles Sacalanes, 1797*, MS.; *Borica, Castigos que han de sufrir los Indios, 1797*, MS.

[33] *Argüello, Relacion que formó de las declaraciones de los Indios Cristianos huidos de la Mision de San Francisco, 1797*, MS. Tiburcio was flogged five times by Dantí for crying at the death of his wife and child. Magin was put in the stocks when ill. Tarazon visited his country and felt inclined to stay. Claudio was beaten by the alcalde with a stick and forced to work when ill. José Manuel was struck with a bludgeon. Liberato ran away to escape dying of hunger as his mother, two brothers, and three nephews had done. Otolon was flogged for not caring for his wife after she had sinned with the vaquero. Milan had to work with no food for his family and was flogged because he went after clams. Patabo had lost his family and had no one to take care of him. Orencio's niece died of hunger. Toribio was always hungry. Magno received no ration because, occupied in tending his sick son, he could not work.

ages of an epidemic.[34]   No further troubles occurred
at San Francisco, but the Sacalanes-and other gentiles
continued their hostile influence at San José mission,
several times requiring the presence of Amador, who
in April 1800 made another raid, killing a chief, capturing twenty fugitives, and breaking all the bows
and arrows of the foe.[35]

Something remains to be said of San Francisco Mission, where we left Cambon and Dantí in charge as
ministers at the end of 1790.   Cambon, one of the
few remaining pioneer missionaries, and a founder of
San Francisco, retired to his college entirely broken
down in health at the end of 1791,[36] and was succeeded
by Martin Landaeta, a new-comer, who however was
absent from October 1798 to September 1800, Espí
serving in 1797–9, and Merelo in 1799–1800.   Diego
García remained until October 1791, and returned in
1796–7.   Dantí retired in the summer of 1796; Padre
Fernandez took his place in 1796–7 with García as a
supernumerary, and Rámon Abella came in July 1798.
Padre Martiarena was also supernumerary from
August 1800, and the names of several others appear
on the mission-books as having officiated here at different dates.[37]

[34] July 1, 1798, Borica to viceroy, in *Prov. Rec.*, MS., vi. 97–8; *Lasuen, Representacion, 1801*, MS., in *Arch. Sta Bárbara*, ii. 202–5.

[35] *Amador, Salida contra Indios Gentiles, 1800*, MS.   Also on slight previous troubles at San José. *Prov. St. Pap.*, MS., xvi. 173–4; xvii. 97, 100–1, 106–7.

[36] Pedro Benito Cambon, a native of Santiago in Galicia, Spain, was ordered to California from the college in August 1770, setting out in Oct., sailing from San Blas in January 1771, and arriving at San Diego March 12, and Mon-
terey May 21st.   He was a founder of San Gabriel in September 1771, and served there until April 1772.   He then spent several years at Velicatá in Baja California for the benefit of his health, and to look after Franciscan property.   He went to San Francisco in Oct. 1776, but was absent from Oct. 1779 until May 1782, during which time he made a trip from San Blas to Manila as chaplain of the *San Cárlos*, devoting his pay to the purchase of supplies for his neophytes, and also founded San Buenaventura in March 1782.
He was a zealous and able man, but his health repeatedly broke down, and
finally in November 1791, at the request of Lasuen, and on a certificate signed
by three surgeons, he was permitted to depart without waiting for the viceroy's license.   His last signature on the mission-books was on Sept. 10th. *S.
Francisco, Lib. Mision*, MS., i, 61, 69; *Arch. Arzobispado*, MS., i. 18, 19.

[37] José de la Cruz Espí, possibly Espi as written by himself, a native of
Valencia, came to Mexico in 1786, and two years later went to Nootka as
chaplain with the expedition of Martinez, which touched on the California

During the decade 1,213 natives were baptized,
1,031 were buried, 203 of them in 1795, and the neophyte population as registered grew from 438 to 644,
from which it would appear that most of the fugitive
cimarrones had been recovered before 1800. Large
stock increased from 2,000 to 8,200, and sheep from
1,700 to 6,200.[38] Crops in 1800 amounted to 4,100
bushels, one half wheat, the largest yield having been

coast. He came to California as a missionary in 1793, serving at San Antonio
from September of that year until September 1794; at Soledad until Decem-
ber 1795; at Santa Cruz until 1797; and at San Francisco from June 1797
until August 1799, when he obtained leave to retire and sailed from San
Diego Jan. 16, 1800. He had served 10 years and refused to remain longer.
His signature appears on the San Francisco books until Aug. 19, 1799. *S.
Francisco, Lib. de Mision*, MS., 44; *Arch. Sta Bárbara*, MS., xi. 60, 220;
Arch. Arzobispado, MS., i. 57.

Of Antonio Danti we only know that he was minister at San Francisco
from October 1790 until July 1796; that he had a fiery temperament—*genio
de pólvora*, as Borica termed it—and was disposed to be unduly severe to his
Indians; and that he was finally allowed to retire, suffering from some trouble
with his legs and with inflammation of the eyes threatening blindness. *San
Francisco, Lib. de Mision*, MS., 41; *Arch. Sta Bárbara*, MS., vi. 227; xi.
56–7; *Prov. Rec.*, MS., vi. 149, 157, 163.

Diego García came to California in 1787, serving at San Francisco from
September of that year until October 1791; at Soledad until February 1792;
at San Antonio until November 1792; again at Soledad until March 1796; and
again at San Francisco until May 1797. He was generally a supernumerary
and his services as minister were not in great demand. One year on some
frivolous pretext he neglected to sow any grain; he made himself obnoxious
to each successive associate; and once when assigned to San José refused
obedience. Naturally no objection was made to his retiring at the end of his
term of 10 years, the coming of which probably saved him from dismissal by
Lasuen. His license was dated July 8, 1797; his last signature at San Francisco was on May 18th. *San Francisco, Lib. de Mision*, MS., 40, 61; *Soledad,
Lib. de Mision*, MS.; *Arch. Sta Bárbara*, MS., xi. 227–8; *Prov. Rec.*, MS., vi.
115.

José María Fernandez left his college in February and arrived at San
Francisco in September 1796, serving until May 1797 as minister, receiving
his license in July, and leaving California a little later. He was a very kind-
hearted man, and as we have seen Borica gave him great credit for having
secured better treatment for the natives at San Francisco; but a blow on
the head accidentally received affected his health and especially his mind to
such an extent as to incapacitate him for missionary labor. *San Francisco, Lib.
de Mision*, MS.; *Arch. Sta Bárbara*, xi. 57–8; *Prov. Rec.*, MS. vi. 98.

[38] May 28, 1791, Fages informed Romeu that the padres of San Francisco
had formed a new establishment seven leagues away, where they kept most
of their neophytes. *Prov. St. Pap.*, MS., x. 149; but we hear no more of the
subject. The controversies between mission and presidio about pasturage, and
the alleged inferiority of San Francisco cattle, have been already noticed. In
Prov. Rec., MS., vi. 79, it is stated that sheep-raising was introduced in
1796, but no special increase appears in the statistics for that year. May 19,
1797, Argüello says the San Francisco sheep being of Merino stock may be a
little better than elsewhere. He wanted to buy 100, but Landaeta refused to
sell. *Prov. St. Pap.*, MS., xv. 8, 9.

5,800 bushels in 1796; the smallest 1,200 in 1792,[39] and the average 3,600 bushels. The mission buildings were described by Vancouver as forming two sides of a square, without any apparent intention of completing the quadrangle, the architecture and material being as at the presidio, but the apartments larger, better constructed, and cleaner. At this time all roofs were of thatch, and the dwellings of the Indians were huts of willow poles, basket-work of twigs, and thatch of grass and tules, about twelve feet high, six or seven feet in diameter, and "abominably infested with every kind of filth and nastiness." In 1793 nineteen adobe houses were built, which number was subsequently increased until in 1798 there were enough for most of the married neophytes. In 1794 a new storehouse 150 feet long was built and roofed with tiles as were some of the old buildings, and half a league of ditch was dug round the *potrero* and fields. In 1795 another adobe building 180 feet long was erected; and tile roofs were completed for all the structures, including the church, about which from the laying of the corner-stone in 1782 nothing more is recorded down to 1800.[40] At the time of Vancouver's visit one large room was occupied by manufacturers of a coarse sort of blanketing, made from wool produced in the neighborhood. "The looms, though rudely wrought, were tolerably well contrived, and had been made by the Indians. The produce is wholly applied to the clothing of the converted Indians. I saw some of the cloth, which was by no

[39] Where the cultivated fields were situated at this time does not appear. In 1795 supplies furnished to the presidio amounted to $2,831. *Prov. Rec.*, MS., v. 26. In January 1795 cold weather prevented the padres from saying mass. *Id.*, v. 40–1. From 1797 to 1800 regular weather reports were rendered at the end of each year. 1797 was cold, windy, and foggy. *St. Pap., Sac.*, MS., vi. 100. In 1798 the summer began with 'terrible and continuous wind' and fog, and the winter with frost, heavy rains, and roof-damaging winds. *Prov. St. Pap., Ben. Mil.*, MS., xvii. 22–3. In 1799 little rain, heavy north winds, and much frost. *Id.*, xxvii. 2. 1800, heavy rains, some frost, strong winds. *Id.*, xxviii. 12–13.

[40] *Vancouver's Voyage*, ii. 10–14; *St. Pap., Miss.*, MS., i. 124; ii. 15, 78; *Prov. St. Pap.*, MS., xvii. 59–60. Fages states that in 1787 there was but a suplemento de iglesia, a temporary affair. *Fages, Informe Gen.*, MS., 146.

means despicable; and, had it received the advantage
of fulling, would have been a very decent sort of
clothing." In 1797 Borica ordered that mission
blankets should be used at the presidio, and no more
obtained from Mexico; but in 1799 he disapproved
the friars' scheme of building a fulling-mill. In 1796
a manufacture of coarse pottery was established under Mariano Tapia.[41]

The new establishments of Branciforte, Santa Cruz,
and Mission San José having been elsewhere noticed,
there remain the annals of Santa Clara and the pueblo
of San José, the former within this northern jurisdiction, and the latter most conveniently included in it,
though it really belonged to the military jurisdiction
of Monterey. At the pueblo population increased in
general terms from eighty to one hundred and seventy, though the variation from year to year is so

[41] White apprentices were to come to San Francisco to learn to make pottery. *Prov. Rec.*, MS., iv. 53–4; v. 78, 206; vi. 230. Some cotton from San
Blas was woven before 1797. *St. Pap., Miss.*, MS., ii. 100. In 1798 the mission contracted to furnish tiles to the presidio at $20 per thousand. *Prov. St.
Pap.*, MS., xvii. 97; xvi. 25, 42.

Such are the facts briefly stated in 23 pages that I have to present respecting San Francisco from 1791 to 1800. Most of the facts are in themselves not
very startling or important, but they constitute the annals for ten years of
what is now a great city; and they have been recorded not diffusely, I believe,
but with due condensation. As I write, a *History of the City of San Francisco* comes from the press. It was written in accordance with a resolution of
congress calling for a historical sketch of each town from its foundation, as a
centennial memorial; it was written by a pioneer, an editor, the author of
several good works, the historian of the Society of California Pioneers; in
fact by a man generally supposed, and with much reason, to be better qualified
than any other for the task, for which he was paid by the city. Being a history of a town the work might naturally be expected to deal largely in local
details whose absence in a history of California would be excusable. The
work has received no unfavorable criticism, except for its rendering of modern
events involving personal and political prejudices. For the Spanish period
there is nothing but praise. The leading journals of the city credit the
author with immense research among the records of the past, and with an
exhaustive treatment of his subject. Naturally, therefore, it was with some
trembling that I compared the results with those of my own labors; but I
breathe more freely and am encouraged, when I see that respecting this decade the work alluded to contains the following, and nothing more: 'Cambon
was soon superseded by Danti, and he by Avella, who served 20 years, com-
mencing in 1797;' the mission had in '1793, 704 Indians, 2,700 cattle, 2,300
sheep, and 314 horses.' For four decades, from 1780 to 1820, all that the work
contains will barely fill one page of foolscap manuscript. This is but a sample
of the record of early California events hitherto called history, and yet the
work to which I refer is one of the best of its class.

great and inexplicable as to inspire doubts of entire accuracy.[42] Of the nine original settlers six were still left in 1797, the latest complete report extant, and about fifty new names of settlers, pensioners, and soldiers appear during the decade. Ignacio Vallejo held the office of comisionado until November 1792, and from May 1797 to November 1799; Macario Castro from 1792 to 1794, and from 1799 to 1807; and Gabriel Moraga from 1794 to 1797, the same men being corporals of the guard. Marcos Chabolla was alcalde in 1796, José María Martinez in 1797, Jacobo Velarde in 1798, Ignacio Castro in 1799, and Francisco Castro in 1800.

Cattle and horses increased from less than 1,000 head to 6,580, while sheep, notwithstanding Borica's efforts, decreased to less than 400.[43] Agricultural products were 4,300 bushels in 1800, the largest crop having been 6,700 bushels in 1797, and the smallest

[42] According to the statistics the population in 1791 was 82; in 1792, 122; in 1794, 80; in 1795, 187; in 1796, 208; in 1798, 152; and in 1800, 171, from 10 to 20 natives being included in each number. Of the 26 names given in a former chapter (xvi.) for 1790, there disappeared before 1797, Antonio Romero and Francisco Ávila (sent away in 1792) of the *pobladores*, Juan Antonio Amézquita, invalid; and Higuera, Cayuelas, and Joaquin Castro, *agregados*. The new names that appear during the decade, most of them on the list of 1797, are as follows: Francisco Alvirez, Javier Alviso, Francisco Alviso, José Águila, Francisco Arias, Justo Altamirano, José Ávila, Nicolás Berreyesa, Pedro Bojorques, José María Benavides, Antonio Buelna, Francisco Béjar, Marcos Chabolla, Francisco Castro, Macario Castro, Leocadio Cibrian, Pablo Cibrian, Ignacio Cantua, Nicolás Camareno, Bernardo Flores, Bernardo Gonzalez, Francisco Gonzalez, Nicolás Galindo, Bernardo Heredia, Salvador Higuera, Ramon Lasso de la Vega, José Larios, José María Martinez, Leocadio Martinez, Dolores Mesa, Joaquin Mesa, Gabriel Moraga, Juan·Mejía, Miguel Osuna, Ignacio Pacheco, Miguel Pacheco, Luis Peralta, José Pliego, Pedro Romero, José María Ruiz, Juan Rosas, José Saez, Miguel Saez, Justo Saez, José Antonio Sanchez, Albino Tobar, Rafael Villavicencio, Jacobo Velarde, Antonio Soto. List of 1793, in *Prov. Rec.*, MS., v. 410–14. Lists of 1797, in *Prov. St. Pap.*, MS., xv. 130–1; *Id., Ben. Mil.*, MS., xxv. 6, 7.

[43] Three thousand three hundred and forty-seven cattle, horses, and mules, the number for 1799, would probably be a fairer estimate, for the statistics are very irregular. An increase from 945 cattle in 1799 to 3,311 in 1800 is inexplicable, the number given for 1801 being 1,841. Sheep-raising introduced in 1796, according to *Prov. Rec.*, MS., vi. 79. May 18, 1796, Sal to comisionado, transcribing Borica's orders. Many vecinos have not a single sheep. This is bad and contrary to the reglamento. Each settler must at once obtain a ram and 10 sheep, and the government will at once advance the means to the poor. *S. José, Arch.*, MS., ii. 87. A settler must not keep more than 50 cattle, and should keep sheep in the proportion of three to one. *Prov. Rec.*, MS., iv. 204; *Dep. St. Pap., S. José*, MS., i. 73–4.

1,800 in 1799.[44] These figures include wheat, corn,
and beans, but not hemp, the culture of which was
introduced into California in 1795, San José being
selected as the place for the experiment, and Ignacio
Vallejo as the man to superintend it. Small crops of
this staple were raised nearly every year during the
last half of the decade. Some rude machinery was
constructed for its preparation, and several small lots
of the prepared fibre were sent to Monterey for shipment to San Blas.[45]

Outside of the pueblo limits, there is no evidence of
any agricultural or stock-raising operations in this
region or in the San Francisco jurisdiction, where no
land-grants even of a provisional nature had been
made, except perhaps El Pilar on the peninsula to José
Argüello in 1797, about which there is some uncertainty.[46] The slight structures of the town had, as

[44] Jan. 15, 1795, Borica urges increased attention to agriculture and promises preference in the purchase of supplies. *Dept. St. Pap., S. José*, MS., i.
45–6. March 29, 1796, Borica is glad to know the reservoir is finished and
he offers a premium of $25 to the man who shall raise the biggest crop. *Prov.
Rec.*, MS., iv. 186. Sept. 1796, Borica congratulates San José on her wheat
crop. In May he had soundly rated the comisionado for not planting more
corn. *Id.*, iv. 188–9, 196, 202. May 2, 1796, 10 sacks seed-corn sent from
Monterey. *S. José, Arch.*, MS., ii. 87. Sept. 15, 1797, complaints of bad
quality of San José flour. *Id.*, v. 32. May 30, 1798, Borica orders the settlers
to enclose their fields. *Prov. Rec.*, MS., iv. 272, 293. Aug. 31, 1799, Vallejo
to B., very poor wheat crops caused by *chahuiste*. Asks for time to pay
loans and tithes. *Prov. St. Pap.*, MS., xvii. 229.

[45] Dec. 23, 1795, Borica to Moraga ordering him to afford Vallejo aid in the
way of grain with which to pay native laborers. *Prov. Rec.*, MS., iv. 241.
Dec. 4th, Argüello to Moraga, transcribes B.'s note of Dec. 1st, with viceroy's
order of Aug. 26th, in reply to Borica's of Feb. 1st, with instructions on preparation of hemp, and promise of instruments. *S. José, Arch.*, MS., iv. 28.
Lands of Linares taken and others given him. *Prov. Rec.*, MS., iv. 177–80.
July 3, 1796, B. regrets loss of first crop; but five fanegas of seed were saved.
Id., iv. 192, 199. August 13th, B. to Vallejo, carpenter Béjar to make machinery. Grain to be sown for rations of native laborers. *Id.*, iv. 197. About 30
fanegas of seed harvested in 1796–7. Twenty-five arrobas (625 lbs.) sent to
San Blas in 1798. *Id.*, vi. 103; *St. Pap., Sac.*, MS., iv. 70. Numerous minor
communications on the subject during 1797, showing great interest on the
part of Borica and even the V. R. *Prov. St. Pap.*, MS., xv. Seven bales
shipped in September 1800. Crop in 1800–1 not good. *Prov. Rec.*, MS., iv.
15; *S. José, Arch.*, MS., iii. 59, 66, 70.

[46] Application and grant recorded in *Prov. Rec.*, MS., v. 103; but in 1798 Argüello himself names El Pilar as belonging to the mission. *Argüello, Informe
sobre Rancho del Rey*, MS. In his report of 1794 Arrillaga says that the settlers
of San José formerly did not possess their lands in property, and the land annually assigned them by the comisionado was not properly cultivated because liable
next year to fall into the hands of another. The comisionado was therefore or-

we have seen, been removed before 1791 to a short distance from the original site, but there is nothing to show that the buildings on the new site were of a more substantial character;[47] neither was there anything noticeable accomplished in the way of manufactures.[48]

The settlers showed a spirit of insubordination early in 1792, owing to popular dissatisfaction with Vallejo as comisionado, but on his removal quiet was restored, not to be disturbed in the same way until 1800 under Castro's administration. At this time a gang of idle vagabonds committed all kinds of depredations, and finally set the comisionado's house on fire one night when a "peaceable and lawful ball" was in progress. A detachment of soldiers was sent from San Francisco to restore order, which it is to be presumed they accomplished, though we have no particulars.[49] Meanwhile in 1794 there had been fears of an Indian outbreak which gave rise to much correspondence and caused unusual precautions. Father Fernandez of Santa Clara was accused of undue severity in connection with this affair, a charge not fully sustained when Alférez Sal was sent to make investigations. No out-

dered to distribute four *suertes* to each on condition of paying a fee of reconocimiento to the king, and of not selling without consent of the authorities. *Prov. St. Pap.*, MS., xii. 188–9. Dec. 29, 1793, governor to comisionado, each lot to be 200 yards square, for which half a fanega of maize must be paid. New settlers must pay same as old pobladores, and will get a title. After a year and a day they may hold office. He who abandons his land loses all improvements. Retired soldiers pay no reconocimiento, but their heirs must pay. *Id.*, xxi. 177–8. Feb. 7, 1800, some settlers disposed to abandon their lands or part of them. This must not be allowed. *S. José, Arch.*, MS., iii. 63.

[47] Sept. 25, 1797, reference to a bridge over the creek. *Prov. Rec.*, MS., iv. 257. April 3, 1799, if the people want a chapel they may use the community grain to build it. *Id.*, iv. 292.

[48] Jan. 1795, Borica urges the people to tan hides and make saddles, boots, and shoes, etc., which will be purchased at fair prices if of good quality. He will have no idleness. *Prov. Rec.*, MS., iv. 220. Leocadio Martinez, carpenter, was exiled here in 1796. *San José, Arch.*, MS., ii. 79. Oct. 28, 1798, Larios and Balesteros allowed to build a water-mill. *Prov. Rec.*, MS., iv. 283. July 1799, reference to Villavicencio's weavery at San José. *Id.*, iv. 300.

[49] *Arrillaga, Papel de Puntos*, MS., 188. Sept. 30, 1800, Castro to Sal, with certificate of alcalde and Ramon Lasso. Oct. 2d, Sal to Arrillaga transmitting the complaint. Dec. 13th, governor's orders to Sal and Alberni. *Prov. St. Pap.*, MS., xviii. 4–8, 16.

break occurred.[50] After 1797 a large part of the military guard was withdrawn to provide for the new foundations.

In 1797 there was a proposition to move the pueblo to the western bank of the river, with a view to escape the danger of inundation. It was favored by Moraga, Vallejo, Alcalde Chabolla, and in fact by all the settlers except four. Borica ordered Córdoba to examine the proposed site and make a plan for the town, and the change seemed likely to be effected; but after September the whole subject was dropped,[51] probably in consequence of a controversy between the pueblo and mission about boundaries. This quarrel was the most notable local event of the decade. In April 1797 Father Sanchez of Santa Clara complained that the townsmen were encroaching on the mission lands. Borica thereupon sent the engineer Córdoba to make a survey and establish the boundaries, taking into account the views of both friars and vecinos and also the former survey of Moraga. Córdoba reported in August that the bound, so far as it could be determined from Moraga's rather vague survey by measuring 1,950 varas down the river from where the old dam was said to have been, was within the mission *potrero*, and that the padres refused to accept it in a representation enclosed in the report. In this document, addressed by Catalá and Viader to Borica, great stress was placed on the rights of the natives, and to the fact that some time in the future the lands must be divided among the 5,000 native owners. It

[50] Correspondence between Moraga, Argüello, and Sal in *Prov. St. Pap.*, MS., xii. 33, 49–53, 124–32, 189–91. May 16, 1797, guard to be withdrawn. *Prov. Rec.*, MS., iv. 213. Aug. 2, 1794, troops ordered to be drawn up under arms, and all citizens to assemble with officials to formally recognize Borica as governor. *S. José, Arch.*, MS., iii. 23. May 20, 1797, Moraga to Vallejo, statement of armament and ammunition. There was one mounted cannon. *Prov. St. Pap.*, MS., xv. 168–9; *S. José, Arch.*, MS., iii. 48–9.

[51] Jan. 8, 1797, Moraga to Borica. *Prov. St. Pap.*, MS., xv. 4. Jan. 10th, Chabolla to B. *Id.*, xvi. 24. May 11th, B. to Córdoba. *Id.*, xxi. 257. Sept. 7th, Vallejo to B. *Id.*, xv. 145. Sept. 26th, Vallejo says the alcalde has directed the people to build across the river. *Id.*, xvii. 241. No date, José María Martinez says the settlers did not desire the removal. *Id.*, xvii. 241.

was claimed that the mission had been in actual possession of the lands in dispute for twelve years, and instances were cited where controversies with individuals had been decided by Moraga and others in favor of the mission. Moreover, the natives, both Christian and gentile, were beginning to complain that they were robbed of their lands.

Nothing more is heard of the matter for a year.[52] In July 1798 the guardian of San Fernando college, who was no other than Padre Tomás de la Peña, formerly minister of Santa Clara, and to whom the matter had naturally been referred by the missionaries, addressed a petition to the viceroy. In it he states that Moraga founded the pueblo nearer the mission than Neve had intended it to be. Neve had subsequently admitted this and promised to move the town; but as during his administration no lands were assigned, no landmarks fixed, and no pueblo cattle sent across the river, there had been no trouble.[53] When Fages came he determined to grant lands and fix boundaries, and he did so notwithstanding the friars' verbal and written protest and Junípero Serra's entreaties, to which he paid not the slightest respect. From that time troubles were frequent, and Fages, the archenemy of the friars, seemed to take pleasure in annoying them. In 1786, however, Palou on his return to Mexico laid the matter before the viceroy and obtained a promise of relief or at least of investigation; the river to be the boundary until a definite settlement should be made. Owing to the death of the viceroy followed by that of Palou, the promise

<hr />

[52] In the mean time, however, the padres of Mission San José complained of damage done by pueblo horses, and Vallejo gave orders to remedy the evil, though it was difficult to keep the horses off the lands where they had been born and raised. Oct. 9, 1798, P. Barcenilla to Vallejo. Oct. 18th, Vallejo to Borica. *Prov. St. Pap.*, MS., xv. 156–7.

[53] Neve, *Instruccion que dá á Fages*, MS., 147, seems to have pronounced in favor of the half-way mark between pueblo and mission as the boundary. 'Declaro que la guardiaraya ó lindero que divide los dos términos de Oriente á Poniente es la mediacion del terreno que intermedia entre las dos poblaciones, correspondiendo á la mision la parte del Norte, y al Pueblo la del Sur, donde pueden ponerse desde luego mojoneras.'

was not fulfilled; but during the time of Romeu and Arrillaga, the mission had never recognized the old landmarks, and without hinderance had built their fences and used the land beyond those old bounds. Now, however, the settlers were encroaching on the lands thus occupied, and insisting on the limits fixed by Fages. The petition calls for the river Guadalupe as a dividing line, which will leave to the pueblo land enough, and with which the mission will be content, though its lands be less in extent and of inferior quality.

This petition was referred to Borica, who in December 1798 reported in favor of the padres, but suggested that a part of the mountains toward the coast should be reserved to the pueblo for a source of wood-supply. On this basis the matter was settled, after some unimportant correspondence between local authorities, by a viceregal decree of September 1, 1800, in favor of the Guadalupe as a boundary, with a reservation of mountain woodland to be agreed upon and clearly marked to prevent future disputes. Captain Argüello was appointed commissioner for the pueblo, and Padre Landaeta for the mission, and in July 1801 the boundaries were surveyed and landmarks fixed. Thus the missionaries were victorious.[54] I append in a note a slight résumé of pueblo regulations at San José as expressed in the correspondence of this decade.[55]

[54] San José, Cuestion de Límites entre el Pueblo y la Mision de Santa Clara, 1797–1801. Varios Papeles tocantes al Asunto., MS. These papers include April 30, 1797, complaint of P. Sanchez to Borica; May 11th, decree of B. with instructions to Córdoba; July 29th, examination of witnesses at San José; Aug. 7th, Córdoba's report; Aug. 6th, representation of Catalá and Viader to B.; July 27, 1798, Peña, Peticion del P. Guardian sobre límites de San José y Santa Clara, 1798, MS. Aug. 7th, Viceroy Azanza to B.; Dec. 3d, B. to V. R., approving padre's claims, in Prov. Rec., MS. vi. 110; Jan. 3d, April 1, 1800, Sal to comisionado of S. José. S. José, Arch., MS., iii. 50, 56. Feb. 9th, Gov. to Sal. Prov. Rec., MS., xi. 134. Sept. 1st, V. R.'s decree of settlement. St. Pap., Sac., MS., ix. 10, 11. Aug. 1, 1801, Carrillo to Arrillaga, has received Argüello's report of July 31st. St. Pap., Miss. and Colon., MS., i. 44. Aug. 31st, Gov. to Carrillo, is advised of the establishment of the line and of the settlers' discontent. Governor to president to same effect. Prov. St. Pap., Ben. Mil., MS., xxxii. 3; Prov. Rec., MS., vi. 15. Oct. 20, 1803, padre asks permission to mark the boundaries with trenches. S. José, Arch., MS., iv. 100. See also Hall's Hist. S. José, 57–80.

[55] June 12, 1792, Argüello to governor, only soldiers, justices, and travellers may carry arms; boys must not go into the country without a guardian;

At the mission of Santa Clara Peña and Noboa
served as ministers until August 1794, when both
retired to their college, the former on account of ill-
health, the latter at the expiration of his term of ten
years.[56] Padre Peña during the later years of his

all single males over 12 years old must sleep in the guard-house, for the protection of family peace; severe punishment for gaming. *St. Pap., Sac.*, MS.,
i. 111. 1794, troops had to take care of their animals or pay for it, the settlers objecting. *Arrillaga, Papel de Puntos*, MS., 189. Dec. 4, 1795, Borica
approves that no grain be sown in community, but each settler contribute two
fanegas of wheat and two of corn each year. *Prov. Rec.*, MS., iv. 239. April
29, 1796, neither gentiles nor Christian Indians must be allowed to ride. *S.
José, Arch.*, MS., ii. 65, 86. Nov. 5, 1796, B.'s orders that no gambling,
drinking, or illicit sexual relations are to be allowed, and Moraga must prevent them or be dismissed. *Id.*, ii. 72. Sept. 3, 1796, no neophyte to be
allowed in the pueblo without a paper from the padre. *Dept. St. Pap., S.
José*, MS.. i. 67. Jan. 3, 1798, three keys to community granary, one kept
by comisionado, one by alcalde, and one by senior regidor. *Prov. Rec.*, MS.,
iv. 263. April 30, 1798, comisionado not to meddle in administration of justice. *Id.*, iv., 269-70. Dec. 13th, each invalid and settler, according to reglamento, must keep two horses and equipments. *Id.*, iv. 286. Nov. 21, 1799,
Borica's instructions to Castro on relieving Vallejo as comisionado. Details
on inventories, tithes, loan of seed, and moral supervision. *San José, Arch.*,
MS., vi. 40. August 22, 1800, Sol to comisionado. No one from Branciforte
to sow grain at San José. Alcalde has been instructed about those who beat
children. Comisionado to look after crops which are being neglected. Mules
won't sell at any price. If Larios will not pay tithes he must not sow. *San
José, Arch.*, MS., iii. 68. Oct. 4th, patrol after 11 P. M. to prevent disorders
and fires and arrest any one abroad without cause. A scouting party to be
organized for the country. *Id.*, iii. 65. Oct. 7th, if Heredia refuses to aid in
repairs to the *depósito*, give him 40 days to leave the jurisdiction with all his
family and belongings. *Id.*, iii. 64. Only those duly registered as vecinos can
sow without special license. *Id.*, iii. 58. Oct. 15th, petitions can be sent only
through the comisionado. *Id.*, iii. 48. Oct. 25th, if Hernandez is found with
a knife he is to get 50 lashes; neither must he get drunk nor create scandal.
Id., iii. 71.

[56] Tomás de la Peña y Saravia, a native of Spain, left Mexico in October
1770, sailed from San Blas in February 1771, was driven to Manzanillo, came
back to Sinaloa by land, and finally reached Loreto November 24, 1771, being
assigned to Comondú Mission. He came up to San Diego on September 1772,
serving there for a year, and subsequently as a supernumerary for short periods
at San Luis Obispo and San Cárlos. From June to August 1774 he made a
voyage with Perez to the north-west coast, keeping a diary of the expedition.
After his return he remained as supernumerary at San Cárlos and neighboring
missions until January 1777, when he became a founder of Santa Clara,
serving there until August 11, 1794, when he sailed for San Blas in the *Santiago*. In 1795 he received some votes for guardian of the college, and was
subsequently elected, since he held the position in 1798. He was also sindic
of the college from 1800 to Feb. 9, 1806, the date of his death. P. Peña was
an able and successful missionary, but hot-tempered and occasionally harsh
in his treatment of the neophytes. He was accused before 1790 of having
caused the death of two boys by his blows; but after a full investigation the
charge was proven false, the Indian witnesses confessing that they had testified falsely, and some evidence being adduced to show that Commandant
Gonzalez, whom the padre had reproved for his immorality, had used his
influence in favor of the accusation. The formal decision was not reached
until 1795, after the padre had retired to Mexico; but he interceded with

stay in California was a prey to that peculiar hypochondria which affected so many of the early missionaries, amounting at the last almost to insanity. It is possible that in his case this condition was aggravated by serious but unfounded charges of having killed two Indian boys by ill-treatment. The successors in the ministry were Magin Catalá,[57] and Manuel Fernandez, but the latter served only a year, being accused of excessive severity toward the natives, and then came José Viader. For three decades I shall have no further changes in ministers to record at Santa Clara.

In 1800 this mission had a larger neophyte population than any other in California, showing a gain from 927 to 1,247, baptisms having numbered 2,288, and deaths 1,682, so that a margin of nearly 300 is left for runaways. The baptisms in 1794 had been 500, and 235 in 1796 had been the largest number of deaths. Live-stock, large and small, had increased to about 5,000 each, Santa Clara being behind San Francisco in this respect, and barely equal in agricultural products, which in 1800 amounted to 4,200 bushels. The best crop was 8,300 bushels in 1797, the worst 3,200 in 1792, the average being 4,600 bushels. Wheat was

the authorities in behalf of his Indian accusers, who were released after publicly apologizing to the ministers for their attempt to bring dishonor on the order. President Lasuen in May 1794 spoke of his condition as being pitiable, for he had became emaciated, talked to himself, appeared constantly afraid, and showed other symptoms which caused fears that he might lose his reason. Peña had a patent as president in case of accident to Lasuen. See *Arch. Sta. Bárbara*, MS., x. 150, 289; xi. 52, 220, 240; xii. 436; *Sta Clara, Lib. de Mision*, MS.; *Sta Cruz, Lib. de Mision*, MS., 10; *Arch. Arzobispado*, MS., i. 39; *Prov. Rec.*, MS., iii. 33–5; iv. 234; *Prov. St. Pap., Ben. Mil.*, MS., xix. 6; and *Peña, Cargo de Homicidio contra el Padre Tomás de la Peña*, 1786–95, MS. Of Diego de Noboa nothing is known save that he arrived at San Francisco from Mexico on June 2, 1783, remained unattached at San Francisco and Santa Clara until June 1784, when he became minister of the latter mission and continued to serve there until he sailed with his associate on Aug, 11, 1794.

[57] Sept. 3, 1796, Borica says that it is reported that Catalá has threatened the comandante of San José to destroy the houses if he admits Christian natives to the pueblo. He does not believe any such reports. Magin is a friar, not a Robespierre. *Prov. Rec.*, MS., vi. 169–70. Jan. 7, 1797, B. orders Moraga and Vallejo to give satisfaction to Catalá for their rudeness, and asks the padre to bear a little with the manners of men who were not educated 'en el colegio de nobles ni en el Romano.' *Id.*, vi. 179–80.

the leading product, and no barley was raised as a rule.[58]

Vancouver describes the mission buildings as on the same general plan as at San Francisco, forming an incomplete square of about 100 by 170 feet. The structures were somewhat superior to those of San Francisco, the church being long, lofty, and as well built as the rude materials would permit. The upper stories, or garrets, of the buildings and some of the lower rooms were used as granaries, and there were also two detached storehouses recently erected. Close to the padres' house ran a fine stream of water, but in order to be near this stream the site had been selected in a low marshy spot only a few hundred yards from dry and comfortable eminences.[59] In fact this very year of 1792 the friars had been confined for a long time to their house by a flood, and it had been resolved to move the mission buildings some five hundred yards to higher ground.[60] There is no further direct record of the removal, and it is not likely that the new church was ever moved, but a report of 1797 that the ministers' houses, guard-room, storehouse, and soldiers' dwellings had been completed indicates a transfer of such buildings as were on the lowest ground.[61] The church had a roof of tiles and had

[58] Supplies furnished to Monterey in 1795, $1,439; to S. Francisco, $212; to Monterey in 1796, $2,147; in 1798, $800. In December 1797 had a draft from Argüello for $1,643. Ordered a bill of goods of $4,000 from Mexico. *Prov. St. Pap.*, MS., xvi. 203, 206; xvii. 62; *Prov. Rec.*, MS., v. 76. Furnished supplies to San Cárlos in the hard year of 1795. *Arch. Sta Bárbara*, MS., ii. 229–30. Bean crop failed in 1795, raising price from $2.50 to $3.50. *Prov. St. Pap.*, MS., xvii. 67–8. The following items are from Vancouver's observations in 1792. Many thousand bushels of different grains in store. Hemp and flax succeed well. Wheat yields 25 and 30 fold. Barley and oats not raised because the superior grain could be produced with the same labor. In the garden were peaches, apricots, apples, pears, figs and vines, though the latter do not flourish. Immense herds of cattle; 24 oxen killed every Saturday for food. *Vancouver's Voyage*, ii., 19–24.

[59] *Vancouver's Voyage*, ii., 18, 19.

[60] June 30, 1792, Sal to Arrillaga, in *St. Pap.*, *Sac.*, MS., iii., 23. May 28, 1791, Fages to Romeu, the padres are forming a new establishment *Prov. St. Pap.*, MS., x. 150.

[61] Aug. 17, 1796, Amador to Borica, in *Prov. St. Pap.*, MS., xv., 170–1. The padres' houses had 8 rooms of 5 yds. each; guard-house, 8 x 5; storehouse, 5 yds. square; 5 soldiers' houses, each 5½ yds. There was also a corral

been lengthened twenty-four feet in 1795. At the time of Vancouver's visit some of the natives were at work on adobe houses for themselves. Fourteen of these dwellings, thatched, were completed in 1793, nine more in 1794, and before 1798 nearly all the married neophytes were thus accommodated.[62] The cloth woven at Santa Clara seemed to Vancouver of a better quality than at San Francisco. In 1792 two thousand hides were tanned, but very few of them could be sold. Miguel Sangrador was the master tanner and shoemaker; Cayetano Lopez the master carpenter and mill-maker. It does not appear that there was any water-power mill either at Santa Clara or San José before 1800.[63]

36 yds. square with walls 6 feet high, built of stout timbers and adobes *de cajon*.

[62] Besides enlarging the church, a trench was dug in 1795, half a league long, nine feet wide, and five feet deep. *St. Pap., Miss.*, MS., ii. 78, 122. Adobe houses for neophytes. *Id.*, ii. 16, 123. In 1798 they seem to have had tile roofs. Argüello's report in *Prov. St. Pap.*, MS., xvii. 59–60. Guardhouse finished in 1796. *Prov. Rec.*, MS., v. 92. Vancouver was shown by Peña a ponderous black stone which was to be used for building and for mill stones as soon as any one could be found capable of working it. *Voyage*, ii. 35.

[63] *Arch. Sta Bárbara*, MS., ii. 72–3; *St. Pap., Sac.*, MS., ii. 9, 10; *Prov. St. Pap.*, MS., xxi. 128–9. Aug. 1797, *rastras* made at San José for grinding wheat. *Prov. Rec.*, MS., iv. 253. April 18, 1796, Borica orders Vallejo to seek suitable stones for a mill; but on May 2d he was directed to suspend the work. *Id.*, vi. 187–8.

CHAPTER XXXIII.

CLOSE OF BORICA'S RULE.

1800.

END OF A DECADE AND CENTURY—BORICA'S POLICY AND CHARACTER—INDUS-
TRIAL REVIVAL—FRUITLESS EFFORTS—GOVERNOR'S RELATIONS WITH
FRIARS, SOLDIERS, NEOPHYTES, AND SETTLERS—EFFORTS FOR PROMO-
TION—A KNIGHT OF SANTIAGO—FAMILY RELATIONS—LEAVE OF ABSENCE,
DEPARTURE, AND DEATH—ARRILLAGA AND ALBERNI IN COMMAND—LIST
OF SECONDARY AUTHORITIES ON EARLY CALIFORNIA HISTORY—LIST OF
INHABITANTS OF CALIFORNIA FROM 1769 TO 1800.

THE rule of Diego de Borica from 1794 to 1800
was a period rather of progress, or of effort toward
progress, than of events. Going beyond the routine
duties of his position, the governor devoted himself
faithfully and intelligently to the general advancement
of his province. No one of California's few classes of
inhabitants was slighted or specially favored. Missionaries, neophytes, pagans, soldiers, and settlers,
each received sympathy, encouragement, and aid from
the government. No industry or institution was
neglected. Missions and pueblos, conversion and
colonization, agriculture and trade, civil and military
and ecclesiastical government, all received close attention. The neophytes were the weakest class and
received the most sympathy; the padres were the
strongest and required least protection; the settlers
were the most difficult to manage and received attention proportionate to the magnitude of interests involved in the future prosperity of the country. If
the results of Borica's efforts as presented in the preceding chapters were slight and unsatisfactory in

many respects as viewed from an Anglo-American standpoint, this fact was due to inherent difficulties in the problems presented for solution, to the spirit of the times, to the nature of the raw material both native and foreign, rather than to Borica's shortcomings or to inadequate royal provisions. Don Diego was not a genius; he was a prudent, sensible man, honest and zealous in the discharge of his public duties.

I have already noted Borica's arrival with his family at Loreto, and in the autumn of 1794, at Monterey. Fortunately a quantity of his private letters or blotters of the same, were left in California and have been preserved in the archives giving us a brief glance at the man in his private capacity, as an agreeable companion, a *bon vivant*, jovial and witty. The letters also gave us Borica's early impressions of California, enthusiastically eulogized as the best country in the world in which to live long and well.[1] Unfortunately the governor took better care of private correspondence in later years, and from the beginning of 1795 his individuality is well nigh sunk in the generalities of official communications, which nevertheless continue to show the good-humor, kindness of heart, sympathy for all suffering, invariable courtesy, and business-like good sense which always characterized the man.[2] His relations with the friars were always friendly and mutually respectful. At the first he assured President Lasuen of his desire to avoid all controversy between the secular and the missionary authorities, a desire reciprocated by Lasuen,[3] and subsequently kept in view by both parties. Lasuen

---

[1] See chapter xxv. of this volume.

[2] García, in *Taylor's Discov. and Found.*, No. 25, ii. 145, speaks of Borica as not liked by the people on account of his stiff and formal manners; but there is nothing in contemporary records to show that such was the feeling toward him. Romero, *Memorias*, MS., 18, speaks of him as noted for kindness and courtesy in his intercourse with subordinates, though never permitting neglect of duty to pass unrebuked.

[3] *Arch. Arzobispado*, MS., i. 36. Yet in 1791 the bishop of Durango in a letter to the viceroy had spoken very bitterly and sarcastically of Borica's mission policy in the Provincias Internas. *Pinart, Col. Doc.*, MS., 7.

often deemed Borica too much disposed to hear and credit the complaints of lying neophytes, but no noticeable coolness ensued. Still Borica's success in maintaining harmony with the padres should not be compared with the failure of his predecessors to their disadvantage; for to a certain extent that success resulted from the fact that Neve and Fages had fought the battle, and the missionaries had learned from experience that it was not wise as yet to renew the conflict.

I find no evidence that Borica ever left the capital during his rule of six years, though it is not unlikely that he may have visited San José and San Francisco. In July 1794, before coming north, he sent a petition to the king for promotion, and in October 1795 received his commission as colonel of cavalry.[4] In these early years he also cherished the hope of still further promotion to a generalship, or at least to the governorship of Sonora, Durango, or Zacatecas. To this end he sent large sums of money to Spain to be used at court, but his agent Miranda seems to have spent the money to no purpose.[5] He seems to have been a man of wealth, or at all events his wife, Doña María Magdalena de Urquides, had large estates in Nueva Vizcaya.[6] Being a knight of the order of Santiago he acted on May 5, 1796, as grand master at the initiation of the Spanish naval officer Don Ramon de Saavedra, at Monterey. President Lasuen served as prelate on

[4] *Prov. Rec.*, MS., v. 71; vi. 26; *Prov. St. Pap.*, MS., xi. 197; xiii. 55; xiv. 29; xvii. 2. Previous to his appointment as governor he had been adjutant-inspector in Chihuahua, his pay in that position running to May 13, 1794. *Id.*, xii. 174.

[5] *Prov. St. Pap.*, MS., xxi. 206, 215–16, 222–4, 227.

[6] *Prov. Rec.*, MS., vi. 124. His wife and daughter, a beauty of 16, were very popular. *García*, in *Taylor's Discov. and Found.*, No. 25, 11. José María Romero, *Memorias*, MS., 18, says Borica had a son of the age of about 15, whom he knew, and whose name he thinks was Cosme. He may indeed have had a son, for he wrote to the president on July 23, 1795, that his wife was about to bear him 'un Califórnico ó una Califórnica,' *Prov. Rec.*, MS., vi. 147, but he could not have been 15 years old in California. He had a sister, Bernarda de Borica, in Victoria, province of Álava, Spain, his native place; and he sent her, April 27, 1795, a bill of exchange for 105 pounds sterling. *Prov. St. Pap.*, MS., xxi. 210, 225.

that occasion, and it was probably the only ceremony of the kind that ever occurred in California.[7]

In April 1799 Governor Borica applied to the viceroy for leave of absence to recuperate his health. He said he had served thirty-six years, twenty-five of which had been spent in active campaigns against Indian tribes and in tours of inspection of presidios, mining-camps, and other settlements in the Provincias Internas. Journeyings aggregating ten thousand four hundred and seventy-five leagues almost exclusively on horseback had given rise to a malady which demanded medical treatment. Either a leave of absence or a permanent transfer to an easier position in New Spain would be satisfactory as he had no wish to return to Spain. The result was a grant of eight months' leave signed by the viceroy in June and made known in California in September.[8] The document provided that Arrillaga, remaining at Loreto, should be governor *ad interim*, while Alberni, presumably by virtue of his seniority of military rank over Arrillaga, was to take the position of comandante de armas for Alta California. It was the governor's intention to depart in October, but he was delayed by new orders from Mexico until the beginning of the next year. The viceroy instructed him, owing to the hostile attitude of British vessels in the Pacific, not to avail himself of his leave of absence "until the aspect of things should change."[9]

The 3d of January 1800 Borica announced his intention to depart on the 12th or 15th, and the commandants were notified to publish the accession of

---

[7] *St. Pap., Sac.*, MS., vi. 84–5; *Prov. St. Pap., Ben. Mil.*, MS., xxiii. 3.

[8] April 1, 1799, Borica to viceroy, in *Prov. Rec.*, MS., vi. 123–4. Sept. 19th, B. to Arrillaga, Alberni, and the commandants. *Prov. St. Pap.*, MS., xvii. 318; *Id., Ben. Mil.*, xxiv. 12; *Prov. Rec.*, MS., iv. 174–5. Nov. 8th, Arrillaga's reply. *Prov. St. Pap.*, MS., xvii. 291.

[9] July 6, 1799, viceroy to Borica. *Prov. St. Pap.*, MS., xvii. 344. Dec. 31st, the V. R. ordered him to use his own discretion as to the need of his presence in California. *St. Pap., Sac.*, MS., iv., 73; but this communication could not have been received before B.'s departure, and possibly the preceding one also failed to arrive.

Arrillaga and Alberni.[10] On the 16th of the same month he sailed on the *Concepcion* from San Diego with his family, Captain Grajera, and four retiring padres. Grajera, as we have seen, died two days out from port; of Colonel Borica after his departure we know only by a brief note in a subsequent communication of the viceroy that he died at Durango July 19, 1800.[11] January 16th, the date of Borica's departure from California, may be regarded as the day when Arrillaga's third term of rule *ad interim* began. There were no events connected with his rule for the rest of 1800 that require mention here.

A Spanish account of California published in 1799, though relating chiefly to the peninsula, contains a tolerably complete and accurate sketch of the northern establishments; and the instructions left by Viceroy Azanza to his successor in 1800 contain frequent allusions to Californian affairs and have already been cited on special topics.[12] It will have been noticed that my foot-notes form an index of authorities on each succesive phase of the historic record—that is of original authorities in manuscript and print; but I have not deemed it best or worth the space required to extend this indexing process to the secondary authorities. Seven eighths of the events recorded in

[10] Jan. 3, 1800, Borica to commandants. *Prov. Rec.*, MS., iv. 114. March 5th, Goycoechea to Arrillaga. *Prov. St. Pap.*, MS., xviii. 23–4. March 8th, Arrillaga and Alberni ordered to be recognized by Sal. *S. José, Arch.*, MS., iii. 51.

[11] Departure on the *Concepcion*. *Prov. St. Pap.*, MS., xxi. 30; *Prov. Rec.*, MS., xii. 1. He seems to have gone to San Diego by land after Jan. 3d, or at least such had been his plan in September, when Sal had sent an order to San José for pack-animals for the governor's journey. *S. José Arch.*, vi. 43. Notice of Borica's death in V. R.'s communication of August 14th. *St. Pap., Sac.*, MS., ix. 70; *Vireyes, Instrucciones*, 201. In a letter of Padre Cortés from Mexico dated April 1st, the V. R. is said to have advised the king to continue Borica in office in California for five years longer. *Arch. Sta Bárbara*, MS., xii. 307. There is a vague reference to a settler who was severely punished for an attempt to take Borica's life. Gov. to V. R., Dec. 5, 1800. *Prov. St. Pap.*, MS., xxi. 50.

[12] *California*, in *Viagero (El) Universal, ó Noticia del Mundo Antiguo y Nuevo. Obra recopilada de los mejores viageros por D. P. E. P.* Madrid, 1799, tom. xxvi. 1–189. See also an article on California in *Cancelada, Telégrafo Mex.*, 99–103.

this and the following volumes are here mentioned for the first time; but the other eighth have been often repeated on the authority of Palou, the old voyagers, and a few documents, by modern writers. The works of such writers I have fully studied and utilized, citing them whenever there has been any reason for so doing, but have not, as before stated, given a complete index in my notes. Omitting many books that contain a superficial account of early events or a mere reference to them, I append in a note a list of works that have some merit, many of them standard works of real and recognized value, as the reader will see at a glance. They are grouped here as secondary authorities only because on the earliest period of history they add nothing to the original records in my collection.[13]

Having thus reached the end of the decade and century, I close my first volume of California's annals with a list containing the names of over 1,700 male inhabitants of the province down to the year 1800. The names have been collected with great care and labor from mission registers of baptisms, marriages, and deaths; from company rosters, pueblo *padrones*, and from thousands of miscellaneous documents in the archives. That the list is absolutely complete and accurate I cannot pretend, for a few of the registers have been lost, and some names, especially of

[13] *Alvarado, Hist. Cal.*, MS.; *Bartlett's Person. Nar.*; *Browne's Lower Cal.*; *Bustamante, Suplemento; Cal., Past, Present, etc.; Capron's Hist. Cal.; Cronise's Nat. Wealth; Diccionario Universal; Dwinelle's Col. Hist. S. F.; Farnham's Life in Cal.; Forbes' Hist. Cal.; Frignet, La Californie; Hartmann, Californien; Hayes' Emigrant Notes; Hayes' Mission Books; Hayes' Scrap-books; Hittell's Hist. S. Francisco; Hughes' Cal.; Humboldt, Essai Pol.; Gleeson's Hist. Cath. Ch.; Greenhow's Or. and Cal.; Lassépas, Baja Cal.; Life of St. Francis; Lorenzana, in Cortés, Hist.; Los Angeles, Hist.; Mayer MSS.; Mofras, Exploration; Morse's Illust. Sketches; Payno, in Revista Científica; Randolph's Oration; Ryan, in Golden Era; Shea's Cath. Missions; Shuck's Cal. Scrap-book; Soulé's Annals of S. F.; Sutil y Mexicana, Viage; Taylor, in Farmer, and Bulletin; Taylor's Discov. and Founders; Taylor's Odds and Ends; Tuthill's Hist. Cal.; Vallejo's Hist. Cal.*, MS.; *Vischer's Missions of Cal.* Also 40 or 50 county histories published within the past ten years; and numerous newspaper articles, especially in *S. F. Bulletin, Call*, and *Alta*, and *Sacramento Union*. There is hardly a paper in the state that has not published some valuable matter with much of no value.

children, in the later years, are therefore missing. Again some of the persons mentioned in connection with the earliest expedition, especially those to whom no special occupation is assigned, never came to Alta California at all, or only came as vaqueros or escorts to return immediately. Another source of error is the uniformity of Spanish given names and the fact that men were known at different times by different names or combination of names to avoid confusion; hence there is no doubt that my list contains a certain number of repetitions. Yet it may well be doubted if so complete a list of the earliest inhabitants can be formed for any other state of the United States or Mexico. My attempts at chronology are limited to the separation of the names into four classes, putting each person in the class in which his name first appears in the records. Number 1 includes the earliest pioneers who came in 1769–73; number 2 those of 1774–80; number 3 those of 1780–90; and number 4 those of 1790–1800.

INHABITANTS OF CALIFORNIA, 1769–1800.

Abella, Ramon, padre.[4]
Acebedo, Francisco Ant., soldier.[2]
Acebedo, José Antonio, soldier.[2]
Acebedo, Julian, soldier.[2]
Acedo, José, settler.[4]
Aceves, Antonio, child.[2]
Aceves, José María, child.[2]
Aceves, Antonio Quiterio, soldier.[2]
Aceves, Pablo, soldier.[4]
Acosta, Antonio, soldier.[3]
Acosta, José, Cat. vol.[4]
Aguiar, Francisco.[1]
Aguila, José, settler.[4]
Aguila, Juan José, child.[4]
Aguilar, Francisco Javier.[1]
Aguilar, Luis Antonio.[1]
Alanis, Antonio, child.[3]
Alanis, Eugenio Nicolás, child.[3]
Alanis, Isidro.[4]
Alanis, Máximo, soldier.[3]
Alari, José, Cat. vol.[4]
Alberni, Pedro, lieutenant-colonel.[4]
Alcántara, Pedro, mason.[4]
Alegre, Antonio, soldier.[2]
Alegría, Norberto, soldier.[3]

Alipás, Juan N., soldier.[4]
Altamirano, José Antonio, soldier.[3]
Altamirano, Lúcas Domingo, child.[2]
Altamirano, José Marcos, child.[2]
Altamirano, Justo Roberto, soldier.[2]
Altamirano, Lúcas, soldier.[4]
Altamirano, Juan, soldier.[4]
Alvarado, Juan B.[1]
Alvarado, Bernardino.[1]
Alvarado, Ignacio, soldier.[2]
Alvarado, Francisco Javier, soldier.[3]
Alvarado, Juan B., child.[3]
Alvarado, Fran. Ma. D. C., child.[4]
Alvarado, José Vicente, child.[4]
Alvarado, Juan José, soldier.[4]
Alvarado, Juan N. D., child.[4]
Álvarez, Juan, soldier.[2]
Álvarez, Joaquin, soldier.[2]
Álvarez, Luis, soldier.[2]
Álvarez, Pedro, soldier.[2]
Álvarez, Felipe, convict.[4]
Álvarez, Doroteo.[4]
Álvarez, José, artilleryman.[4]
Álvarez, Juan, artilleryman.[4]
Álvarez, José, child.[4]

Alvires, Claudio, servant.[2]
Alvires, Juan, soldier.[3]
Alvires, Estévan.[4]
Alviso, Francisco, settler.[2]
Alviso, Domingo, soldier.[2]
Alviso, Anastasio Gerónimo, child.[4]
Alviso, Francisco Javier, soldier.[4]
Alviso, Francisco Solano, child.[4]
Alviso, Gerónimo Antonio, child.[4]
Alviso, Ignacio, soldier.[4]
Alviso, Javier, settler.[4]
Alviso, José Antonio, child.[4]
Alviso, José Gabriel L., child.[4]
Alvitre, Sebastian, soldier.[1]
Alvitre, Juan José Ma., child.[4]
Amador, Pedro, soldier.[1]
Amador, José Sinforoso, child.[3]
Amador, José Fructuoso.[3]
Amador, Juan Pablo.[3]
Amador, José María, child.[4]
Amador, Marcos Antonio, child.[4]
Amarrillas, Juan Angel, soldier.[2]
Amézquita, José Gabriel, child.[2]
Amézquita, Juan Antonio, soldier.[2]
Amézquita, Manuel Dom., settler.[2]
Amézquita, Florentino, settler.[4]
Amézquita, Gregorio, settler.[4]
Amézquita, Francisco Ma., settler.[4]
Amézquita, José, soldier.[4]
Amézquita, José Miguel, settler.[4]
Amézquita, José Reyes, settler.[4]
Amézquita, Serafin, settler.[4]
Amurrio, Gregorio, padre.[1]
Antonio, Manuel, servant.[2]
Antonio, José Crispin, child.[4]
Antonio, Macedonio, soldier.[4]
Antuña, Manuel, soldier.[2]
Arana, José, soldier.[3]
Aranguren, José, soldier.[3]
Arce, José G.[1]
Arce, Sebastian.[1]
Arce, Joaquin, child.[2]
Arcés, José, settler.[4]
Archuleta, José Ignacio, servant.[2]
Archuleta, José Norberto, child.[2]
Archuleta, Miguel Gerónimo, child.[2]
Archuleta, Gregorio, soldier.[4]
Arellanes, Teodoro.[4]
Arellano, Man. J. R., soldier.[2]
Arenaza, Pascual M., padre.[3]
Argüelles, Francisco, artilleryman.[4]
Argüello, Francisco Rafael, child.[4]
Argüello, José Dario, alférez.[3]
Argüello, José Gervacio, child.[3]
Argüello, Luis Antonio, child.[3]
Argüello, José Ignacio M., child.[4]
Armenta, Cristóbal, settler.[2]
Armenta, Joaquin, soldier.[2]
Arriola, Alejandro, soldier.[3]
Arias, Francisco, settler.[4]

Armenta, José Ma., soldier.[4]
Arriola, José Francisco, mechanic.[4]
Arriola, José Rafael B., child.[4]
Arriola, Rafael, convict.[4]
Arriz, Ignacio.[1]
Arroita, Francisco José, padre.[3]
Arroyo, José Manuel, smith.[2]
Arroyo, Juan Isidro, child.[3]
Arroyo, Vicente, soldier.[3]
Arroyo, Félix, child.[3]
Arroyo, José, sailor.[4]
Aruz, Domingo, soldier.[2]
Aruz, Martin, settler.[4]
Arvallo, Feliciano, settler.[2]
Ávalos, Nicolás.[1]
Ávalos, Joaquin, tanner.[4]
Ávila, Francisco.[4]
Ávila, Adanto, child.[4]
Ávila, Anastasio.[4]
Ávila, Antonio Ignacio.[4]
Ávila, Cornelio, settler.[4]
Ávila, Ignacio.[4]
Ávila, José, convict.[4]
Ávila, José Antonio, settler.[4]
Ávila, José María.[4]
Ávila, Miguel.[4]
Ávila, Santa Ana, soldier.[4]
Avis, Fructuoso, soldier.[4]
Ayala, José, soldier.[3]
Ayala, José C. D., child.[4]
Ayala, José Salvador, child.[4]
Ayala, Juan José G., child.[4]
Ayala, Juan P. M., child.[4]
Bacilio, Antonio, Cat. vol.[4]
Badiola, Manuel Antonio.[1]
Balderrama, convict.[4]
Ballesteros, Juan, soldier.[3]
Ballesteros, Juan Antonio, child.[3]
Ballesteros, Javier Antonio, child.[4]
Banderas, José F. de la Cruz.[4]
Barajas, José, sailor.[4]
Barbosa, José, settler.[4]
Bárcena, José, convict.[4]
Bárcenas, Marcos, settler.[4]
Barcenilla, Isidoro, padre.[4]
Barona, José, Padre.[4]
Barraza, Macedonio, soldier.[3]
Barrera, Juan Antonio, soldier.[3]
Barrientos, José, Cat. vol.[4]
Basadre y Vega, Vicente, settler.[3]
Belen, Miguel, servant.[2]
Bello, Mateo, Cat. vol.[4]
Beltran, Francisco Javier, soldier.[2]
Beltran, Joaquin, soldier.[2]
Beltran, Nicolás, soldier.[2]
Benavides, José Ma., settler.[4]
Beranzuela, Pedro, soldier.[4]
Bermudez, José, soldier.[4]
Bermudez, José S., child.[4]
Bermudez, Manuel Antonio, child.[4]

Bernal, Francisco, servant.[1]
Bernal, José Dionisio, soldier.[2]
Bernal, Juan Francisco, soldier.[2]
Bernal, Manuel Ramon, soldier.[2]
Bernal, Apolinario, child.[3]
Bernal, Juan, child.[3]
Bernal, Ramon, settler.[3]
Bernal, Bruno, child.[4]
Bernal, Joaquin, soldier.[4]
Bernal, José Agustin, child.[4]
Bernal, José Cipriano, child.[4]
Bernal, José C. Cipriano, child.[4]
Bernardo, José, settler.[4]
Berreyesa, Nicolás A., settler.[2]
Berreyesa, Juan José, child.[4]
Berreyesa, José Nazario, settler.[4]
Berreyesa, José de los Reyes, settler.[4]
Blanco, Juan, smith.[4]
Blanco, Miguel.[4]
Bojorges, José Ramon, soldier.[2]
Bojorges, Hermenegildo, child.[2]
Bojorges, Pedro Antonio, soldier.[2]
Bojorges, Francisco H., settler.[4]
Bonnel, Ramon, Cat. vol.[1]
Borica, Diego de, governor.[4]
Boronda, Manuel, soldier.[3]
Boronda, Canuto José, child.[4]
Bosch, Buenaventura, settler.[3]
Botello, Joaquin, tailor.[4]
Bravo, José Marcelino, soldier.[1]
Briones, Ignacio Vicente, soldier.[2]
Briones, José Antonio, soldier.[1]
Briones, Ignacio Vicente, child.[3]
Briones, José Joaquin, child.[2]
Briones, Felipe Santiago, child.[3]
Briones, Nicolás María, child.[2]
Briones, Marcos, soldier.[3]
Briones, Manuel, soldier.[4]
Brito, Mariano, artilleryman.[4]
Brito, Miguel, artilleryman.[4]
Bruno, Francisco, soldier.[2]
Buelna, Eusebio José J., child.[2]
Buelna, José Antonio, soldier.[2]
Buelna, Ramon, soldier.[2]
Buelna, Eusebio J. J., child.[4]
Buelna, José Raim, child.[3]
Buelna, José María, child.[4]
Bulferig, Gerónimo, Cat. vol.[1]
Bumbau, Francisco, Cat. vol.[1]
Bustamante, José, soldier.[3]
Bustamante, Manuel, soldier.[3]
Butron, Manuel, soldier.[2]
Butron, Sebastian, settler.[4]
Caballero, José, Cat. vol.[4]
Calixto, José, soldier.[4]
Calvo, Francisco, soldier.[3]
Calzada, José Antonio, padre.[3]
Calzada, José, convict.[4]
Calzada, José Dionisio, settler.[4]
Camacho, José Antonio, soldier.[1]

Camacho, Tomás M., servant.[1]
Camacho, Juan Miguel, soldier.[1]
Camacho, Anastasio, soldier.[2]
Camacho, Antonio, soldier.[2]
Camarena, Nicolás, settler.[4]
Cambon, Pedro Benito, padre.[1]
Camero, Manuel, settler.[3]
Campa, Pedro, sailor.[2]
Campa y Coz, Miguel, padre.[1]
Campo, José, Cat. vol.[4]
Campos, Francisco, soldier.[3]
Cañedo, Albino, soldier.[2]
Cañedo, José Manuel, settler.[2]
Cañedo, Juan Ignacio, soldier.[4]
Cañizares, José, piloto.[1]
Cano, José, artilleryman.[4]
Cantua, Ignacio, soldier.[2]
Capinto, José Ma., tailor.[4]
Capinto, Mariano, tailor.[4]
Carabanas, Joaquin, soldier.[3]
Carabanas, Nicolás, soldier.[2]
Caravantes, José Salvador, soldier.[3]
Caravantes, Ventura, settler.[4]
Carcamo, José, Cat. vol.[4]
Cárdenas, Melchor, servant.[2]
Cárdenas, Cristóbal, servant.[1]
Cárdenas y Rivera, Tadeo.[1]
Cariaga, Salvador, soldier.[2]
Carlon, Hilario Ignacio, soldier.[3]
Carnicer, Baltasar, padre.[4]
Carranza, Domingo, padre.[4]
Carrillo, Guillermo, soldier.[1]
Carrillo, Mariano, sergeant.[1]
Carrillo, José Raimundo, soldier.[1]
Carrillo, Anastasio José, child.[3]
Carrillo, Cárlos Antonio, child.[3]
Carrillo, Domingo Ant. Igna., child.[4]
Carrillo, José Antonio E., child.[4]
Carrillo, Luis, sailor.[4]
Casasallas, Simon, Cat. vol.[4]
Casillas, Juan Manuel.[1]
Castañeda, José.[3]
Castañeda, José Ruiz, soldier.[3]
Castelo, Agustin, soldier.[1]
Castillo, José, phlebotomist.[4]
Castillo, José, soldier.[4]
Castro, Antonio, soldier.[2]
Castro, Ignacio, soldier.[2]
Castro, Joaquin, soldier.[2]
Castro, José, servant.[2]
Castro, Isidro.[2]
Castro, José Macario, soldier.[3]
Castro, José Simon J. N., child.[3]
Castro, Mariano, soldier.[3]
Castro, Mariano de la Cruz, child.[3]
Castro, Agapito, settler.[4]
Castro, Francisco, settler.[4]
Castro, José Joaquin, settler.[4]
Castro, José S. T., child.[4]
Castro, Simeon, settler.[4]

Cavaller, José, padre.[1]
Cayuelas, Francisco, Cat. vol.[1]
Cayuelas, Francisco, soldier.[3]
Cayuelas, Pedro, soldier.[3]
Cervantes, Juan Pablo.[1]
Cervantes, Guadalupe, soldier.[4]
Cervantes, Pablo Victoriano, soldier.[3]
Chabolla, Márcos, soldier.[3]
Chabolla, Pedro R., child.[3]
Chabolla, José, child.[4]
Chabolla, José Luis, child.[4]
Chabolla, Salvador.[4]
Chamorro, smith.[2]
Chaves, José Mateo, settler.[4]
Chaves, José, convict.[4]
Chavira, José Antonio, settler.[4]
Chavira, Jose, convict.[4]
Cibrian, Pablo, soldier.[4]
Cibrian, Leocadio, soldier.[3]
Cibrian, Pablo Antonio, smith.[4]
Ciprés, Marcelino, padre.[4]
Cisneros, José, servant.[3]
Clua, Domingo, Cat. vol.[2]
Contreras, Luis, muleteer.[2]
Contreras, José, soldier.[4]
Cordero, Joaquin Ignacio.[1]
Cordero, Francisco.[1]
Cordero, Mariano Antonio, soldier.[1]
Cordero, José E., child.[2]
Cordero, Fermin, settler.[4]
Cordero, Manuel, soldier.[2]
Cordero, José Dom., child.[4]
Cordero, Miguel E., child.[4]
Cordero, Pedro, settler.[4]
Córdoba, Alberto, engineer.[4]
Cornejo, Casimiro, settler.[4]
Cornejo, Casimiro, convict.[4]
Corona, Francisco, soldier.[4]
Coronel, Juan Antonio, muleteer.[2]
Cortés, Juan Lope, padre.[4]
Cortés, José Antonio, soldier.[3]
Cortés, Nicolás, soldier.[4]
Cortés, Nicolás Felipe, soldier.[4]
Costansó, Miguel, engineer.[1]
Cota, Antonio, soldier.[1]
Cota, Pablo Antonio, soldier.[1]
Cota, Manuel Antonio, child.[2]
Cota, Roque, soldier.[2]
Cota, Guillermo, sergeant.[3]
Cota, Juan Ignacio, soldier.[3]
Cota, Mariano, soldier.[3]
Cota, Nabor Antonio, child.[3]
Cota, Bartolomé José, child.[4]
Cota, Francisco Atanasio, child.[4]
Cota, José Manuel Ma., child.[4]
Cota, José Valentin, child.[4]
Cota, Juan Francisco, child.[4]
Cota, Manuel, soldier.[4]
Cota, Pedro Antonio, child.[4]
Crespí, Juan, padre.[1]

Cruzado, Antonio, padre.[1]
Cruz, Faustino José, soldier.[3]
Cruz y Sotomayor, Juan, soldier.[3]
Cuevas, Luis, settler.[4]
Dandricu, Andrés, soldier.[4]
Dantí, Antonio, padre.[3]
Dávila, José, surgeon.[2]
Dávila, Manuel, carpenter.[3]
Dávila, J., soldier.[3]
Dávila, José Antonio, smith.[4]
Delgado, Alonzo, Cat. vol.[4]
Diaz, Joaquin, soldier.[2]
Dominguez, Juan José, soldier.[1]
Dominguez, José Dolores, soldier.[2]
Dominguez, José Antonio, child.[3]
Dominguez, José Ma. D., child.[3]
Dominguez, Cristóbal, soldier.[4]
Dominguez, José Antonio, child.[4]
Dominguez, José Asuncion, child.[4]
Dominguez, José Francisco, child.[4]
Dominguez, Remesio, settler.[4]
Duarte, Alejo Antonio, soldier.[1]
Duarte, José Ma., soldier.[1]
Duarte, Pascual.[1]
Duarte, Francisco Javier, child.[4]
Duarte, Juan José, servant.[4]
Duarte, Leandro, soldier.[4]
Ducil, Sebastian, Cat. vol.[4]
Dumetz, Francisco, padre.[1]
Encarnacion, José, soldier.[3]
Enriquez, Antonio, servant.[3]
Enriquez, Antonio Domingo, weaver.[4]
Enriquez, Sebastian, child.[4]
Escamilla, Antonio Santos, child.[4]
Escamilla, José, soldier.[4]
Escamilla, Tomás, convict.[4]
Escribano, Sebastian, Cat. vol.[4]
Esparza, José Lorenzo, mechanic.[1]
Espí, José de la C., padre.[4]
Espinosa, Antonio, soldier.[2]
Espinosa, Joaquin, soldier.[2]
Espinosa, Juan, servant.[2]
Espinosa, Gabriel, soldier.[3]
Espinosa, José Miguel, soldier.[3]
Espinosa, Salvador, soldier.[3]
Espinosa, Tomás, soldier.[3]
Espinosa, Cayetano, soldier.[4]
Espinosa, José Gabriel S.[4]
Espinosa, José Ma. E., child.[4]
Espinosa, José Fio, Cat. vol.[4]
Espinosa, Juan Antonio J., child.[4]
Estévan, Pedro de S. José, padre.[4]
Estévan, Antonio, sailor.[4]
Estrada, José Bonifacio, soldier.[2]
Estudillo, José María, soldier.[4]
Fages, Pedro, lieutenant.[1]
Faura, José, padre.[4]
Feliciano, Alejo, settler.[2]
Feliciano, Hilario, child.[3]
Félix, Claudio Victor.[1]

Félix, Anast. Ma., soldier.[2]
Félix, Doroteo, soldier.[2]
Félix, José Vicente, soldier.[2]
Félix, José Francisco, soldier.[3]
Felix, Juan José Ignacio, child.[3]
Félix, Antonio Rafael, child.[4]
Félix, Victorino, soldier.[3]
Félix, Fernando de la T., child.[4]
Félix, José, child.[4]
Félix, José Luciano, child.[4]
Félix, José Vicente Valentin, child.[4]
Félix, Juan.[4]
Félix, Juan Jose de G., child.[4]
Félix, Leonardo Ma., child.[4]
Félix, Pedro Antonio, child.[4]
Fernandez, Gaspar Antonio, child.[3]
Fernandez, José Rosalino, soldier.[3]
Fernandez, Pedro Ignacio, child.[4]
Fernandez, Rafael Ma. de la C., child.[4]
Fernandez, Victor, Cat. vol.[4]
Fernandez, Gregorio, padre.[4]
Fernandez, José Ma., padre.[4]
Fernandez, Manuel, padre.[4]
Feyjoo, José, soldier.[3]
Ferrer, Pablo, Cat. vol.[1]
Figuer, Juan, padre.[1]
Figueroa, Manuel, soldier.[2]
Figueroa, Salvador Ignacio, child.[4]
Flores, Hermenegildo, soldier.[2]
Flores, Victoriano, servant.[2]
Flores, José Miguel, soldier.[2]
Flores, José María, soldier.[3]
Flores, José Teodosio, child.[3]
Flores, Bernardo, settler.[4]
Flores, Diego.[4]
Flores, Francisco, soldier.[4]
Flores, Isidro, soldier.[4]
Flores, José Ma. de la T., child.[4]
Flores, Leandro José, child.[4]
Flores, Pedro, soldier.[4]
Font, José, lieutenant.[4]
Fontes, Luis Ma., soldier.[3]
Fontes, Pedro, servant.[2]
Fragoso, Luis Ma., soldier.[3]
Fragoso, Rafael, Cat. vol.[4]
Franco, Juan, servant.[3]
Franco, José, convict.[4]
Franco, Pablo, convict.[4]
Fuster, Vicente, padre.[1]
Galindo, Nicolás, settler.[2]
Galindo, Francisco A., child.[2]
Galindo, José Rafael, child.[2]
Galindo, Alejandro Fidel, child.[3]
Galindo, José Leandro, child.[3]
Galindo, Juan Crisóstomo, child.[3]
Galindo, Claudio, Cat. vol.[4]
Galindo, José Cárlos H., child.[4]
Galindo, Venancio, soldier.[4]
Gallego, Cárlos, soldier.[2]
Galvez, Diego, Cat. vol.[4]

Gámez, Teodoro, soldier.[4]
Garaicoechea, José, corporal.[4]
García, Diego, padre.[3]
García, Felipe, smith.[2]
García, Francisco Bruno, soldier.[2]
García, Francisco Ma., child.[2]
García, Francisco P., soldier.[2]
García, José Reyes, child.[2]
García, Juan José, child.[2]
García, José Antonio, soldier.[2]
García, Pedro, settler.[3]
García, Pedro Gonzalez, smith.[4]
García, Cárlos Ma.[4]
García, José Antonio Inoc., child.[4]
García, José Hilario Ramon, child.[4]
García, José de las Llagas, child.[4]
García, José Ma. Cancio, child.[4]
García, José Ma. Desiderio, child.[4]
García, Julian.[4]
García, Luz, soldier.[4]
García, Nicolás, Cat. vol.[4]
García, Pedro Antonio, child.[4]
García, Pedro Gonz., smith.[4]
Garibay, Jose Joaquin, child.[4]
Garibay, Vicente, soldier.[4]
Garracino, Pedro, soldier.[2]
Gerardo.   (See Gonzalez G.)
German, Cris. Ant., child.[3]
German, Isidro, soldier.[3]
German, Faustin J., child.[4]
German, Manuel Ignacio, child.[4]
German, Juan, soldier.[4]
German, Juan, child.[4]
Gíol, José, servant.[2]
Gili, Bartolomé, padre.
Giribet, Miguel, padre.[3]
Gloria, Jacinto, soldier.[2]
Gloria, José Ma., soldier.[2]
Gomez, Francisco, padre.[1]
Gomez, Nicolás, settler.[2]
Gomez, Francisco, soldier.[4]
Gomez, José Antonio, Cat. vol.[4]
Gomez, Rafael, settler.[4]
Gomez, Rafael, convict.[4]
Gomez, Francisco, carpenter.[4]
Góngora, José Ma., soldier.[1]
Góngora, José Antonio, child.[2]
Gonopra, José Ma., soldier.[4]
Gonzalez, Antonio Alejo., soldier.[1]
Gonzalez, Inocencio, sailor.[1]
Gonzalez, Cirilo, servant.[2]
Gonzalez, José Antonio, soldier.[2]
Gonzalez, José Romualdo, child.[2]
Gonzalez, José Manuel, settler.[2]
Gonzalez, Mateo Jacobo, child.[2]
Gonzalez, Ramon.[2]
Gonzalez, Nicolás, soldier.[2]
Gonzalez, Alejandro, soldier.[3]
Gonzalez, Bernardo, soldier.[2]
Gonzalez, Diego, lieutenant.[2]

Gonzalez, Felipe, soldier.[3]
Gonzalez, José Eusebio, child.[3]
Gonzalez, José Feliciano, soldier.[3]
Gonzalez, Mateo Jacobo, child.[3]
Gonzalez, Tomás, soldier.[3]
Gonzalez, Alejo., Cat. vol.[4]
Gonzalez, Francisco, soldier.[4]
Gonzalez, Francisco, padre.[4]
Gonzalez, José, Cat. vol.[4]
Gonzalez, José Rafael M., child.[4]
Gonzalez, Man. Ciriaco, child.[4]
Gonzalez, Juan, soldier.[4]
Gonzalez, Pedro, mechanic.[4]
Gonzalez, Rafael, child.[4]
Gonzalez Gerardo, Rafael.[1]
Gonzalez, José Leandro, child.[4]
Goycoechea, Felipe, lieutenant.[4]
Grajera, Antonio, lieutenant.[4]
Grijalva, Juan Pablo, sergeant.[2]
Guerrero, Juan José.[1]
Guerrero, Joaquin, soldier.[2]
Guerrero, José, servant.[2]
Guerrero, José Antonio, soldier.[2]
Guerrero, Julian, soldier.[2]
Guerrero, Mateo, artilleryman.[4]
Guevara, José, soldier.[3]
Guevara, José Canuto, child.[4]
Guevara, José Sebastian, child.[4]
Guevara, Sebastian, Cat. vol.[4]
Guevara, José Francisco, child.[4]
Gutierrez, Ignacio Ma., soldier.[2]
Gutierrez, Felipe, soldier.[3]
Gutierrez, Manuel, servant.[3]
Gutierrez, Francisco, Cat. vol.[4]
Guzman, Isidro, soldier.[3]
Guzman, Juan Ma., child.[4]
Guzman, Toribio, soldier.[3]
Guztinzar, Manuel, servant.[4]
Haro, Felipe, Cat. vol.[4]
Hechedo, José Francisco.[4]
Henriquez, Antonio Dom., weaver.[4]
Heredia, Bernardino, soldier.[2]
Heredia, José Bernardo, soldier.[2]
Hernandez, José Rafael.[1]
Hernandez, Vicente Antonio.[2]
Hernandez, Justo, soldier.[3]
Hernandez, Juan José Antonio, child.[3]
Hernandez, Felipe, settler.[4]
Hernandez, Felipe, convict.[4]
Hernandez, José Antonio, settler.[4]
Hernandez, José, convict.[4]
Hernandez, J. José de la Luz, soldier.[4]
Hernandez, Antonio, saddler.[4]
Hernandez, Juan María, saddler.[4]
Hernandez, Juan, convict.[4]
Herrera, José, soldier.[4]
Higuera, Joaquin, soldier.[2]
Higuera, José Atanasio, soldier.[2]
Higuera, José Loreto, child.[2]
Higuera, José Manuel, soldier.[2]

Higuera, Juan José, soldier.[2]
Higuera, José Ignacio, soldier.[2]
Higuera, Bernardo de la Luz, child.[3]
Higuera, Juan José, child.[3]
Higuera, Salvador, soldier.[3]
Higuera, Tiburcio, child.[3]
Higuera, Tiburcio Javier, child.[4]
Higuera, Gregorio Ignacio Ma., child.[4]
Higuera, Hilario.[4]
Higuera, José 1°, soldier.[4]
Higuera, José 2°, soldier.[4]
Higuera, José Cárlos Salv., child.[4]
Higuera, José Gerónimo, child.[4]
Higuera, José Ma., child.[4]
Higuera, José Policarpo, child.[4]
Higuera, José Antonio.[4]
Higuera, José Joaquin.[4]
Higuera, Manuel, soldier.[4]
Higuera, Nicolás Antonio.[4]
Higuera, Salvador, soldier.[4]
Horchaga, José Hilario, child.[3]
Horchaga, José Manuel, child.[3]
Horchaga, Manuel, soldier.[3]
Hores, José, settler.[3]
Horra, Antonio de la C., padre.[4]
Hortel, Juan, Cat. vol.[4]
Ibarra, Francisco, servant.[2]
Ibarra, Andrés Dolores, child.[2]
Ibarra, Gil María, child.[3]
Ibarra, José Desiderio, child.[3]
Ibarra, Juan Antonio, soldier.[3]
Ibarra, Ramon, soldier.[3]
Ibarra, Albino, soldier.[4]
Ibarra, Antonio, child.[4]
Ibarra, Calixto José Antonio, child.[4]
Igadera, José, convict.[4]
Igareda, José Gordiano, settler.[4]
Iñiquez, Juan, Cat. vol.[4]
Islas, Miguel, soldier.[1]
Isvan, José Albino, soldier.[4]
Iturrate, Domingo S., padre.[4]
Izquierdo, José, soldier.[2]
Jaime, Antonio, padre.[4]
Jaume, Luis, padre.[1]
Jimenez, Francisco, Cat. vol.[4]
Jimenez, Hilario, soldier.[4]
Jimenez, Pascual Antonio, child.[4]
Juarez, Francisco, soldier.[3]
Juarez, José Joaquin, child.[4]
Juncosa, Dom, padre.[1]
Labra, Juan Antonio, soldier.[1]
Ladron de Guevara, José I., soldier.[4]
Landaeta, Martin, padre.[4]
Lasuen, Fermin Francisco, padre.[1]
Lara, José, settler.[3]
Lara, José Sostenes, child.[4]
Lara, Julian, soldier.[4]
Lara, José Antonio Seferino, child.[4]
Larios, José Ma., soldier.[3]
Lasso de la Vega, Ramon, alférez.[3]

Leal, Isidro José, servant.[2]
Leiva, Anastasio, soldier.[2]
Leiva, Agustin, soldier.[3]
Leiva, José Andrés, child.[3]
Leiva, José Antonio Ma., soldier.[1]
Leiva, Juan, soldier.[3]
Leiva, Miguel, soldier.[3]
Leiva, José Antonio.[4]
Leiva, José Rafael, child.[4]
Leiva, Manuel Ramon, child.[4]
Leiva, Rufino, soldier.[4]
Leon, José Ma., soldier.[2]
Leon, José Manuel, soldier.[2]
Lima, José, soldier.[3]
Linares, Ignacio, soldier.[2]
Linares, José de los S., child.[3]
Linares, Mariano de Dolores, child.[3]
Linares, Francisco, settler.[4]
Linares, Ramon, soldier.[4]
Linares, Salvador, soldier.[4]
Lineza, Miguel, Cat. vol.[1]
Lisalde, Diego.[4]
Lisalde, Félix, soldier.[4]
Lisalde, Juan Crisos. Antonio, child.[4]
Lizalda, Pedro Antonio, soldier.[2]
Llamas, Antonio, Cat. vol.[4]
Lledo, Rafael, carpenter.[4]
Llepis, José Mariano, servant.[2]
Lobo, José, soldier.[2]
Lobo, José Basilio, child.[3]
Lobo, Cecilio.[4]
Lobo, Pedro.[4]
Lopez, Baldomero, padre.[4]
Lopez, Jacinto, padre.[4]
Lopez, Juan Francisco, soldier.[1]
Lopez, Francisco, soldier.[2]
Lopez, Ignacio Ma. de Jesus.[2]
Lopez, Gaspar, soldier.[2]
Lopez, Joaquin, soldier.[2]
Lopez, José Ma., soldier.[2]
Lopez, Luis, soldier.[2]
Lopez, Pedro, servant.[2]
Lopez, Sebastian A., soldier.[2]
Lopez, José Antonio Gil, child.[3]
Lopez, José Ma. Ramon, child.[3]
Lopez, Juan José, child.[3]
Lopez, Melchor, soldier.[3]
Lopez, Juan, convict.[4]
Lopez, Cayetano, carpenter.[4]
Lopez, Claudio, soldier.[4]
Lopez, Cornelio Ma., child.[4]
Lopez, Ignacio, soldier.[4]
Lopez, Estévan Ignacio, child.[4]
Lopez, Juan José Trinidad, settler.[4]
Lozano, Pedro, Cat. vol.[4]
Lugo, Luis Gonzaga, soldier.[1]
Lugo, Francisco, soldier.[2]
Lugo, Ignacio, soldier.[2]
Lugo, José Ignacio, child.[2]
Lugo, Seferino, soldier.[2]

Lugo, José Antonio, soldier.[3]
Lugo, Salvador, soldier.[3]
Lugo, Ant. Ma., soldier.[4]
Lugo, José, Cat. vol.[4]
Lugo, José Antonio, child.[4]
Lugo, Juan Ma., child.[4]
Lugo, Juan, servant.[4]
Lugo, Miguel, soldier.[4]
Lugo, Pablo José, child.[4]
Lugo, Ramon Lorenzo, child.[4]
Lujan, José, alférez.[4]
Machado, José Antonio, child.[3]
Machado, José Manuel, soldier.[3]
Machado, José Agustin Ant., child.[4]
Machado, José Hilario.[4]
Machado, José Ignacio Ant., child.[4]
Machuca, José, settler.[4]
Malaret, Domingo, Cat. vol.[1]
Maldonado, Juan, Cat. vol.[4]
Mallen, Manuel, Cat. vol.[4]
Manrique, Sebastian, soldier.[1]
Manriquez, Luis, soldier.[2]
Manzana, Miguel A., Cat. vol.
Marin, Antonio, Cat. vol.[4]
Mariné y Salvatierra, J., artilleryman.[4]
Mariner, Juan, padre.[3]
Mario, Tomás, soldier.[2]
Marquez, Francisco Rafael, soldier.[2]
Marquez, José, soldier.[4]
Marron, Rafael, soldier.[3]
Martiarena, José Manuel, padre.[4]
Martin, Juan, padre.[4]
Martinez, Luis Antonio, padre.[4]
Martinez, Pedro Adriano, padre.[4]
Martinez, Luis María, soldier.[2]
Martinez, Toribio, soldier.[2]
Martinez, Dionisio, servant.[3]
Martinez, José Ma., soldier.[3]
Martinez, Juan Ignacio, soldier.[3]
Martinez, Norberto, child.[3]
Martinez, Antonio, soldier.[4]
Martinez, Bartolomé Mateo.[4]
Martinez, Gregorio, artilleryman.[4]
Martinez, José, Cat. vol.[4]
Martinez, José Leocadio, settler.[4]
Martinez, José Ma., settler.[4]
Martinez, Manuel, Cat. vol.[4]
Martinez, Máximo.[4]
Martinez, Máximo Ramon, child.[4]
Martinez, Reyes.[4]
Medina, José, artilleryman.[4]
Mejía, Pedro.[2]
Mejía, Francisco Javier, soldier.[3]
Mejía, Juan, soldier.[3]
Melecio, José, soldier.[3]
Mendoza, Manuel, soldier.[2]
Mendoza, José de los Reyes, child.[4]
Mendoza, Manuel, Cat. vol.[4]
Mendoza, Mariano, tilemaker.[4]
Mendoza, Mariano, José, weaver.[4]

Mendoza, Miguel, Cat. vol.[4]
Mequías, Juan Alberto, soldier.[3]
Mercado, Mariano, artilleryman.[4]
Merelo, Lorenzo, padre.[4]
Merino, Agustin, padre.[4]
Mesa, Nicolás Ma., child.[2]
Mesa, Valerio, soldier.[2]
Mesa, Dolores, soldier.[3]
Mesa, Ignacio, soldier.[3]
Mesa, Juan Antonio, soldier.[3]
Mesa, Luis Ma., child.[3]
Mesa, José Antonio, soldier.[4]
Mesa, José Julian Antonio, child.[4]
Mesa, Juan José, servant.[4]
Miguel, José, padre.[3]
Miranda, Juan Ma., soldier.[1]
Miranda, Alejo, soldier.[3]
Miranda, Antonio, soldier.[3]
Miranda, José Antonio, child.[3]
Miranda, Apolinario, child.[4]
Miranda, José Hilario, soldier.[4]
Miranda, José Mariano, Cat. vol.[4]
Miranda, José Santiago, child.[4]
Miranda, Juan Crisóstomo, child.[4]
Miranda, Vicente Manuel, child.[4]
Mojica, José Ma., settler.[4]
Mojica, Vicente, settler.[4]
Molas, José, Cat. vol.[1]
Molina, Joaquin, settler.[2]
Molina, Pedro, soldier.[2]
Monreal, José Antonio Nicolás, child.[4]
Monroy, José, soldier.[4]
Montaloan, Laureano, soldier.[3]
Montaña, Antonio, Cat. vol.[1]
Montaño, Antonio, soldier.[3]
Montero, Cesareo Antonio, child.[3]
Montero, Manuel, soldier.[4]
Monteverde, Francisco, artilleryman.[4]
Montial, Juan Andrés, soldier.[3]
Moraga, José Joaquin, alférez.[2]
Moraga, Gabriel, soldier.[3]
Moraga, Vicente José, child.[3]
Moreno, F. S., soldier.[4]
Moreno, Felipe Santiago, smith.[4]
Moreno, Felipe, settler.[3]
Moreno, José, settler.[3]
Moreno, Juan Francisco, child.[4]
Moreno, Manuel, soldier.[4]
Morillo, José Julian, soldier.[1]
Moumarus, Luis, Cat. vol.[1]
Muñoz, Manuel, mechanic.[3]
Mugártegui, Pablo, padre.[1]
Murguía, José Ant., padre.[1]
Murillo, Loreto, soldier.[2]
Murillo, Francisco, carpenter.[3]
Murillo, Juan, smith.[3]
Muruato, José, Cat. vol.[4]
Navarro, José Antonio, settler.[3]
Navarro, José Clemente, child.[3]
Navarro, José María, child.[3]

Nieto, José Manuel, soldier.[1]
Nieto, Juan José Ma., child.[3]
Nieto, Manuel Perez, soldier.[3]
Nieto, José Antonio Ma., soldier.[4]
Noriega, José Ramon, soldier.[1]
Noriega, José Raimundo, soldier.[2]
Noboa, Diego, padre.[3]
Nocedal, José, padre.[2]
Obaye, José Antonio, soldier.[2]
Oceguera, Faustino, Cat. vol.[4]
Ochoa, Francisco Javier.[1]
Ochoa, Felipe, soldier.[2]
Ojeda, Gabriel.[1]
Olivares, José Miguel, soldier.[2]
Olivares, José Francisco B., child.[3]
Olivares, Pedro Alcántara, child.[3]
Olivas, Juan Matias, soldier.[3]
Olivas, Cosme.[4]
Olivas, José Herculano, child.[4]
Olivas, José Lázaro Ma., child.[4]
Olivas, José Nicolás, child.[4]
Olivas, Pablo, settler.[4]
Olivera, José Ignacio, soldier.[1]
Olivera, Juan María, soldier.[1]
Olivera, Ignacio, servant.[1]
Olivera, Antonio Lúcas Ma., child.[2]
Olivera, Diego Ant. de la Luz, child.[3]
Olivera, José Desiderio, child.[3]
Olivera, José, soldier.[3]
Olivera, José Leonardo M., child.[3]
Olivera, José Ma. Matias, child.[3]
Olivera, Maximo José, child.[3]
Olivera, Tomás Antonio, child.[3]
Olivera, Higinio, soldier.[4]
Olivera, José Ant. Secundino, child.[4]
Olivera, Rosalina Ma., child.[4]
Oliveros, Lúcas.[4]
Olvera, Diego, servant.[2]
Olvera, Francisco, servant.[2]
Ontiveros, José Antonio, soldier.[1]
Ontiveros, Francisco, soldier.[3]
Ontiveros, Juan de Dios, settler.[4]
Ontiveros, Juan Ma.[4]
Ontiveros, Pacífico Juan, child.[4]
Ontiveros, Patricio, soldier.[4]
Orámas, Cristóbal, padre.[3]
Oribe, Tomás C., soldier.[3]
Orozco, José Manuel, servant.[1]
Ortega, José Francisco, sergeant.[1]
Ortega, Ignacio, soldier.[2]
Ortega, José Francisco Ma., child.[2]
Ortega, José Ma., soldier.[2]
Ortega, Juan, soldier.[2]
Ortega, Juan Cap. Ant. M. H., child.[2]
Ortega, José Ma. Martin, child.[3]
Ortega, Juan Cap., child.[3]
Ortega, Miguel, servant.[3]
Ortega, Francisco.[4]
Ortega, José Miguel, child.[4]
Ortega, José Quintin de los S., child.[4]

Ortega, José Vicente, soldier.[4]
Ortega, Antonio, convict.[4]
Ortega, Matias.[4]
Ortega, Miguel, Cat. vol.[4]
Ortel, Juan, Cat. vol.[4]
Osequera, Faustino, soldier.[4]
Osio, José Ma., Cat. vol.[4]
Osorio, José, artilleryman.[4]
Osorno, Pedro, convict.[4]
Osuna, Juan Ismerio.[1]
Osuna, Juan Luis, soldier.[2]
Osuna, Miguel, tailor.[3]
Osuna, José Joaquin, soldier.[3]
Osuna, José Ma.[4]
Osuna, Juan Nepomuceno, child.[4]
Otondo, Felipe, settler.[2]
Pacheco, Juan Salvio, soldier.[2]
Pacheco, Bartolomé Ignacio, settler.[2]
Pacheco, Rafael, convict.[4]
Pacheco, Miguel, soldier.[2]
Pacheco, Bartolo, soldier.[4]
Pacheco, Francisco, Cat. vol.[4]
Pacheco, Ignacio, child.[2]
Padilla, Juan, soldier.[3]
Padilla, Jacinto, Cat. vol.[4]
Pajarrales, settler.[4]
Palafox, José, Cat. vol.[4]
Palomares, José Cristóbal, soldier.[4]
Palomares, José Ramirez, soldier.[3]
Palou, Francisco, padre.[1]
Panella, José, padre.[4]
Parron, Fernando, padre.[1]
Paterna, Antonio, padre.[1]
Parrilla, Leon, lieutenant.[4]
Patron, Antonio José, soldier.[2]
Parra, José, soldier.[3]
Parra, José, child.[3]
Parra, José Antonio, settler.[3]
Parra, José Miguel Sabino, child.[3]
Patiño, José Victoriano, soldier.[3]
Payeras, Mariano, padre.[4]
Pedraza, José Antonio, settler.[3]
Pedro, José Antonio Ma. de S. T., child.[2]
Pedro, José Francisco de S. T., child.[2]
Pedro y Gil, Rafael, storekeeper.[2]
Peña, Francisco Ma., soldier.[1]
Peña, José Antonio, soldier.[1]
Peña, Gerardo, soldier.[2]
Peña, Luis, soldier.[2]
Peña, Eustaquio, child.[4]
Peña, José, artilleryman.[4]
Peña, Teodoro, Cat. vol.[4]
Peña y Saravia, Tomás, padre.[1]
Pengues, Miguel Sobrevía, Cat. vol.[1]
Peralta, Gabriel, soldier.[2]
Peralta, Juan José, soldier.[2]
Peralta, Luis Ma., soldier.[2]
Peralta, Pedro Regalado, soldier.[3]
Peralta, Hermenegildo Ignacio, child.[4]
Peralta, Juan.[4]

Peralta, Pantaleon, child.[4]
Perez, Juan, captain of vessel.[1]
Perez, Crispin, soldier.[2]
Perez, José Ignacio, soldier.[2]
Perez, Antonio Irimeo, child.[4]
Perez, Antonio Ma., child.[4]
Perez, Estévan.[4]
Perez, José Ma., soldier.[4]
Perez, José Ma., convict.
Perez, Juan Bautista, Cat. vol.[4]
Perez, Luis, soldier.[4]
Perez, Manuel, Cat. vol.[4]
Perez Fernandez, José, alférez.[4]
Perez de la Fuente, Pedro, settler.[3]
Pericas, Miguel, Cat. vol.[1]
Peyri, Antonio, padre.[4]
Pico, Santiago de la Cruz, soldier.[2]
Pico, Francisco Javier, soldier.[3]
Pico, José Dolores, soldier.[3]
Pico, José Ma., soldier.[3]
Pico, Juan Patricio, child.[3]
Pico, Joaquin, soldier.[4]
Pico, José Antonio Bernardo, child.[4]
Pico, José Vicente, child.[4]
Pico, Mariano.[4]
Pico, Miguel, soldier.[4]
Pico, Patricio, servant.[4]
Pieras, Miguel, padre.[1]
Piña, Juan Máximo, soldier.[3]
Piña, Mariano, servant.[3]
Piña, Pedro Rafael, child.[3]
Pinto, Juan María, soldier.[2]
Pinto, Pablo, soldier.[2]
Pinto, Marcelo, soldier.[3]
Planes, Gerónimo, Cat. vol.[1]
Plenelo, Valentin, Cat. vol.[1]
Pliego, José, settler.[4]
Palanco, José, soldier.[3]
Pollorena, Pedro.[2]
Pollorena, Juan, child.[4]
Pollorena, Rafael Eugenio, child.[4]
Portella, Francisco, Cat. vol.[1]
Portolá, Gaspar de, governor.[1]
Preciado, Venancio, servant.[3]
Prestamero, Juan, padre.[1]
Puga, Joaquin, servant.[2]
Puyol, Francisco, padre.[4]
Prat, Pedro, surgeon.[1]
Puig, Juan, sergt. Cat. vol.[1]
Quesada, Manuel, soldier.[4]
Quesada, Manuel, Cat. vol.[4]
Quijada, Ignacio Ma., child.[3]
Quijada, Vicente, soldier.[3]
Quijada, José Nazario de la T., child.[4]
Quijada, José Lorenzo, child.[4]
Quijada, Simon, child.[4]
Quintero, Luis, settler.[3]
Quintero, Clemente.[4]
Quintero, Teodosio.[4]
Quinto, Simon Tadeo.[4]

Ramirez, Francisco, soldier.[2]
Ramirez, Bernardo, soldier.[3]
Ramirez, José Antonio, carpenter.[4]
Ramirez, José Guadalupe.[4]
Ramos, José, smith.[3]
Ramos, José, convict.[4]
Ramos, Pablo Antonio, child.[3]
Resa, Lorenzo, sailor.[2]
Rey, Cristóbal, Cat. vol.[4]
Rey, José, Cat. vol.[4]
Rey, Juan del, soldier.[4]
Reyes, Juan Francisco.[1]
Reyes, Martin, soldier.[1]
Reyes, Francisco, settler.[3]
Reyes, José Jacinto, child.[3]
Reyes, José, convict.[4]
Reyes, José, saddler.[4]
Reyes, Máximo Julian, child.[4]
Rio, Francisco del.[2]
Rioboo, Juan Antonio García, padre.[3]
Rios, Feliciano, soldier.[2]
Rios, Julian, soldier.[2]
Rios, Cayetano, child.[3]
Rios, Silverio Antonio Juan, child.[4]
Rivera, Tadeo, soldier.[2]
Rivera, Joaquin, stone-cutter.[4]
Rivera, Salvador, stone-cutter.[4]
Rivera y Moncada, Fernando, captain.[1]
Roberto, Justo, soldier.[3]
Roberto, Matias, child.[3]
Robles, Juan José, soldier.[1]
Robles, Manuel Ma., soldier.[2]
Robles, José Antonio, settler.[4]
Roca, Cárlos Pedro José, child.[4]
Roca, José, sergeant artilleryman.[4]
Rocha, Juan Estévan, soldier.[1]
Rocha, Cornelio, settler.[4]
Rocha, Cornelio, convict.[4]
Rocha, José, Cat. vol.[4]
Rocha, Juan José Lor., child.[4]
Rochin, Ignacio, soldier.[3]
Rodriguez, Manuel, carpenter.[1]
Rodriguez, José, servant.[2]
Rodriguez, Pablo, settler.[2]
Rodriguez, Vicente, soldier.[2]
Rodriguez, Alejo Máximo, child.[3]
Rodriguez, Inocencio José, child.[3]
Rodriguez, Joaquin, soldier.[3]
Rodriguez, José Antonio, soldier.[3]
Rodriguez, José Fran. Ant. L., child.[3]
Rodriguez, José Ignacio, soldier.[3]
Rodriguez, José de Jesus I., child.[3]
Rodriguez, José Leon, child.[3]
Rodriguez, José Ma., child.[3]
Rodriguez, Sebastian, child.[3]
Rodriguez, Alejandro, child.[4]
Rodriguez, Felipe Antonio, child.[4]
Rodriguez, José del Cármen S., child.[4]
Rodriguez, José Brigido, child.[4]
Rodriguez, Juan, child.[4]

Rodriguez, Juan Francisco, child.[4]
Rodriguez, Juan de Dios, child.[4]
Rodriguez, Manuel, cadet.[4]
Rodriguez, Matias, servant.[4]
Roman, José Joaquin, settler.[4]
Romero, Antonio, servant.[2]
Romero, Felipe, smith.[2]
Romero, Anselmo José Ignacio, child.[3]
Romero, José Domingo, child.[3]
Romero, José Estévan, soldier.[3]
Romero, José Ma. Basilio F., child.[3]
Romero, Juan María, child.[3]
Romero, Pedro, soldier.[3]
Romero, José Ant. Estévan, child.[4]
Romero, José Gregorio, child.[4]
Romero, José Man. Secundino, child.[4]
Romero, Juan Ma., soldier.[3]
Romero, Luis, soldier.[4]
Romero, Rafael, Cat. vol.[4]
Rosales, Bernardo, muleteer.[1]
Rosales, Cornelio, child.[2]
Rosales, José Cornelio, soldier.[4]
Rosalío, Eugenio, soldier.[2]
Rosas, Juan Estévan.[2]
Rosas, Alejo, settler.[3]
Rosas, Baltasar Juan José, child.[3]
Rosas, Basilio, settler.[3]
Rosas, Cárlos, soldier.[3]
Rosas, José Alejandro, settler.[3]
Rosas, José Máximo, settler.[3]
Rosas, José Máximo, child.[3]
Rosas, Gil Antonio, child.[4]
Rosas, José Darío, settler.[4]
Rosas, José, convict.[4]
Rosas, José Antonio, child.[4]
Rosas, José Antonio, soldier.[4]
Rosas, José Antonio Doroteo, child.[4]
Rosas, Leon María, child.[4]
Rosas, Luis María, child.[4]
Rubio, Ascensio Álvarez.[1]
Rubio, Bernardo.[1]
Rubio, José Cárlos.[1]
Rubio, Juan Antonio, soldier.[1]
Rubio, Cárlos, soldier.[3]
Rubio, Fran. Ramon de la L., child.[3]
Rubio, Mateo, soldier.[3]
Rubio, José Antonio, child.[4]
Rubio, Luis Ma., child.[4]
Rubio, Rafael Felipe, child.[4]
Rubiol, Francisco, Cat. vol.[4]
Rubi, Mariano, padre.[3]
Rueda, Pedro.
Ruelas, Fernando, soldier.[1]
Ruelas, Francisco, soldier.[3]
Ruelas, Venancio, Cat. vol.[4]
Ruiz, Antonio Vicente.[1]
Ruiz, Alejandro, soldier.[1]
Ruiz, Juan Ma., soldier.[1]
Ruiz, Diego Ma., soldier.[2]
Ruiz, Francisco Ma., soldier.[2]

Ruiz, Efigenio, soldier.[3]
Ruiz, Fructuoso Ma., soldier.[3]
Ruiz, Juan Pedro Jacinto, child.[3]
Ruiz, Nervo Pedro.[3]
Ruiz, Pedro José.[3]
Ruiz, Estévan, bricklayer.[4]
Ruiz, Ignacio, soldier.[4]
Ruiz, José Hilario, child.[4]
Ruiz, José Joaquin, child.[4]
Ruiz, Manuel, mechanic.[4]
Ruiz, Santiago, mason.[4]
Ruiz, Toribio, mason.[4]
Saez, Nazario, settler.[2]
Saez, Justo, soldier.[3]
Saez, Juan, settler.[4]
Saez, Miguel.[4]
Saenz, Ignacio, convict.[4]
Sajo, José, soldier.[3]
Sal, Hermenegildo, soldier.[2]
Sal, Ignacio Francisco, child.[4]
Sal, Domingo, child.[4]
Sal, Meliton, child.[4]
Salazar, Alonso Isidro, padre.[4]
Salazar, Doroteo de la Luz, child.[3]
Salazar, Doroteo, soldier.[3]
Salazar, José Loreto, soldier.[3]
Salazar, Juan José, child.[3]
Salazar, Miguel, soldier.[4]
Salas, Francisco, Cat. vol.[4]
Salazar, José Marcos, settler.[4]
Salazar, José, convict.[4]
Salazar, Miguel, soldier.[4]
Samaniego, José Ma. Gil, soldier.[3]
Samaniego, Pablo Ant. Nemesio, child.[3]
Samaniego, Tiburcio Antonio, child.[3]
Samaniego, José del Cármen, child.[4]
Sanchez, Francisco Miguel, padre.[1]
Sanchez, Joaquin, servant.[2]
Sanchez, José Antonio, soldier.[2]
Sanchez, Juan, sailor.[4]
Sanchez, Francisco, soldier.[3]
Sanchez, José Tadeo, soldier.[3]
Sanchez, José Segundo, soldier.[4]
Sanchez, José Antonio, child.[4]
Sanchez, Juan, soldier.[4]
Sanchez, Juan Ma., child.[4]
Sanchez, Vicente.[4]
Sanchez, Vicente Anastasio, child.[4]
Sangrador, Miguel, tanner.[4]
Sandoval, Antonio, servant.[2]
Sandoval, Gregorio Antonio, soldier.[3]
Santa Ana, José Francisco, child.[4]
Santa Catarina y Noriega, M., padre.[2]
Santa María, Vicente, padre.[2]
Santiago, Juan José M., padre.[3]
Sarmiento, Francisco, Cat. vol.[4]
Sarco, José Joaquin, artilleryman.[4]
Segundo, Angel, settler.[2]
Segura, Gregorio, smith.[3]
Señan, José Francisco de P., padre.[3]

Sepúlveda, Rafael, soldier.[2]
Sepúlveda, Juan José, soldier.[2]
Sepúlveda, Francisco Javier, soldier.[3]
Sepúlveda, Enrique.[4]
Sepúlveda, Francisco Javier, child.[4]
Sepúlveda, José Dolores, child.[4]
Sepúlveda, José Enrique A., child.[4]
Sepúlveda, José de los Dolores, child.[4]
Sepúlveda, Patricio.[4]
Sepúlveda, Sebastian, soldier.[4]
Serra, Junípero, padre.[1]
Serrano, Francisco, soldier.[3]
Serrano, Leandro José, child.[3]
Serrano, José María, Cat. vol.[4]
Servin, José Isidro, Cat. vol.[4]
Sierra, Benito, padre.[2]
Silva, José, settler.[2]
Silva, Hilario Leon José, child.[2]
Silva, José Manuel, servant.[2]
Silva, José Miguel, soldier.[2]
Silva, Juan de Dios J. S., child.[3]
Silva, Rafael, child.[3]
Silva, Hilario Leon José, child.[4]
Silva, José de los Santos, child.[4]
Silva, José Ma., child.[4]
Silva, José Manuel Victor, child.[4]
Silva, Teodoro.[4]
Sinova, José, soldier.[2]
Sinova, José Francisco, servant.[2]
Sitjar, Buenaventura, padre.[1]
Sola, Faustino, padre.[3]
Soberanes, José Ma., soldier.[1]
Soberanes, Agustin, servant.[2]
Soberanes, José Ma., soldier.[2]
Soler, Juan, store-keeper.[2]
Soler, Nicolás, captain.[3]
Soler, Pablo, surgeon.[4]
Solis, Alejandro, soldier.[2]
Solórzano, Francisco, soldier.[4]
Solórzano, Juan, soldier.[4]
Solórzano, Juan Mateo, child.[4]
Solórzano, Pio Antonio, child.[4]
Somera, José Antonio F., padre.[1]
Sorno, José Nolasco, settler.[4]
Sorde, José, Cat. vol.[1]
Sotelo, Francisco Antonio, soldier.[3]
Sotelo, José Antonio, soldier.[2]
Sotelo, José Gabriel, child.[3]
Sotelo, José Ma., child.[3]
Sotelo, José Antonio, child.[4]
Sotelo, José Ma. Tiburcio, child.[4]
Sotelo, Ramon, soldier.[4]
Soto, Mateo Ignacio.[1]
Soto, Alejandro, soldier.[2]
Soto, Damaso, child.[2]
Soto, Francisco José Dolores, child.[2]
Soto, Francisco Ma., child.[2]
Soto, Ignacio, soldier.[2]
Soto, Isidro, child.[2]
Soto, Francisco Rexis, soldier.[3]

Soto, Guillermo, soldier.[3]
Soto, Ignacio Javier.[3]
Soto, José Joaquin, child.[3]
Soto, Mariano, servant.[3]
Soto, Antonio, settler.[4]
Soto, José Ma. Ant., child.[4]
Soto, Juan.[4]
Soto, Miguel, soldier.[4]
Soto, Rafael.[4]
Soto, Tomás.[4]
Sotomayor, Alejandro, soldier.[1]
Sotomayor, José Crisógono.
Sotomayor, José Doroteo.
Suarez, Simon, lieutenant.[4]
Talamantes, soldier.[4]
Tapia, Felipe Santiago, soldier.[2]
Tapia, Bartolomé, servant.[3]
Tapia, Cristóbal.[3]
Tapia, José Bartolo, settler.[3]
Tapia, José Francisco, soldier.[3]
Tapia, Francisco, soldier.[4]
Tapia, José Antonio, child.[4]
Tapia, Mariano, potter.[4]
Tapinto, Mariano, tailor.[4]
Tapis, Estévan, padre.[3]
Tejo, Ignacio Antonio, Cat. vol.[4]
Ticó, José Joaquin, sergeant Cat. vol.[4]
Ticó, Fern. José Ma. Ign. M., child.[4]
Tobar, Albino, settler.[4]
Toca, José Manuel, teacher.[4]
Toral, José Perez, cadet.[4]
Torres, Victoriano, settler.[2]
Torres, Narciso, Cat. vol.[4]
Torres, Nicolás.[4]
Torrens, Hilario, padre.[3]
Trasviñas, Antonio, soldier.[1]
Trujillo, José, Cat. vol.[4]
Ulloa, José Santos, smith.[3]
Uribes, Miguel, settler.[4]
Ursetino, José, carpenter.[2]
Uría, José Antonio, padre.[4]
Usson, Ramon, padre.[1]
Valderrama, José Cornelio, settler.[4]
Valdés, Juan Bautista, soldier.[2]
Valdés, Antonio Albino, child.[3]
Valdés, Antonio Ma. de Sta M., child.[3]
Valdés, Eugenio, soldier.[3]
Valdés, José Basilio, child.[3]
Valdés, José Lorenzo, servant.[3]
Valdés, José Melesio, soldier.[3]
Valdés, Juan Melesio, soldier.[3]
Valdés, Luciano José, child.[3]
Valdés, Máximo Tomás, child.[3]
Valdés, Antonio.[4]
Valdés, Crecencio.[4]
Valdés, Francisco, Cat. vol.[4]
Valdés, Gregorio.[4]
Valdés, José Rafael, child.[4]
Valencia, José Manuel, soldier.[2]
Valencia, Francisco, soldier.[3]

Valencia, Ignacio.[3]
Valencia, Juan Ignacio, soldier.[3]
Valencia, Juan Vicente Cris., child.[3]
Valencia, Manuel, settler.[3]
Valencia, Miguel Antonio, child.[3]
Valencia, José Antonio, child.[4]
Valencia, José Manuel, child.[4]
Valenzuela, Agustin, soldier.[2]
Valenzuela, José Julian, child.[2]
Valenzuela, Rafael, soldier.[2]
Valenzuela, Angel, soldier.[3]
Valenzuela, Antonio Ma., child.[3]
Valenzuela, Gaspar José, child.[3]
Valenzuela, José.[3]
Valenzuela, José Antonio Ma., child.[3]
Valenzuela, José Manuel, soldier.[3]
Valenzuela, Antonio de Gr., child.[4]
Valenzuela, Joaquin, child.[4]
Valenzuela, José Antonio Ma., child.[4]
Valenzuela, José Candelario, child.[4]
Valenzuela, José Ignacio.[4]
Valenzuela, José Rafael, child.[4]
Valenzuela, Juan, soldier.[4]
Valenzuela, Juan Angel, child.[4]
Valenzuela, Juan Ma., child.[4]
Valenzuela, Máximo.[4]
Valenzuela, Pedro, soldier.[4]
Valenzuela, Simeon Máximo, child.[4]
Valenzuela, Vicente, soldier.[4]
Valenzuela, Vicente Antonio, child.[4]
Valenzuela, José Ma., child.[3]
Valenzuela, José Matías, child.[3]
Valenzuela, José Miguel, child.[3]
Valenzuela, José Pedro, soldier.[3]
Valenzuela, José Ramon, child.[3]
Valenzuela, Segundo, soldier.[3]
Valero, Ignacio, soldier.[4]
Vallejo, Ign. Vicente Ferrer, soldier.[2]
Vallejo, Juan José, soldier.[2]
Vallejo, José de Jesus, child.[4]
Vanegas, Cosme.[4]
Varelas, Casimiro, settler.[2]
Varelas, Juan, child.[2]
Varelas, José Cayetano, child.[3]
Varelas, José Manuel, child.[4]
Varelas, Juan, soldier.[4]
Vargas, Manuel, sergeant.[3]
Vazquez, Gil Anastasio, soldier.[2]
Vazquez, José Francisco, child.[2]
Vazquez, Juan Atanasio, soldier.[2]
Vazquez, Juan Silverio, child.[2]
Vazquez, José Tiburcio, settler.[2]
Vazquez, Antonio, soldier.[4]
Vazquez, José, convict.[4]
Vazquez, Faustino.[4]
Vazquez, Felipe.[4]
Vazquez, Félix.[4]
Vazquez, Hermenegildo.[4]
Vazquez, José Antonio Pablo, child.[4]
Vazquez, José Timoteo, settler.[4]

Vazquez, Julio Ma., child.[4]
Vega, José Manuel, Cat. vol.[4]
Vegas, Matías, soldier.[2]
Véjar, Pablo, carpenter.[4]
Véjar, Salv., carpenter.[4]
Velarde, José Jacobo, soldier.[2]
Velarde, José Ma., soldier.[3]
Velarde, Agustin.[4]
Velarde, José Luciano.[4]
Vegerano, José Ma., muleteer.[1]
Velasco, Fernando, soldier.[3]
Velasco, José Ignacio Mateo, child.[3]
Velazquez, José.[1]
Velazquez, José Ma., convict.[4]
Velez, José Miguel, settler.[2]
Velis, José, Cat. vol.[4]
Verdugo, Joaquin.[1]
Verdugo, José Ma., soldier.[1]
Verdugo, Francisco Ma. de la Cruz.[1]
Verdugo, Mariano de la Luz, soldier.[1]
Verdugo, Florencio, soldier.[2]
Verdugo, Ignacio Leonardo Ma.[2]
Verdugo, Juan Diego, soldier.[2]
Verdugo, Juan Ma., soldier.[3]
Verdugo, Leonardo, soldier.[3]
Verdugo, Manuel José, child.[3]
Verdugo, Anselmo José, child.[4]
Verdugo, Joaquin.[4]
Verdugo, José Francisco, child.[4]
Verdugo, Juan Andrés Dolores, child.[4]
Verdugo, Julio Antonio José, child.[4]
Verdugo, Meliton José.[4]
Verduzco, Anastasio Javier.[1]
Viader, José, padre.[4]
Victoriano, soldier.[1]
Vila, Vicente, captain of vessel.[1]
Villa, José, settler.[3]
Villa, Vicente Ferrer, child.[3]
Villa, Eleuterio.[4]

Villa, José Antonio Doroteo, child.[4]
Villa, José Francisco Antonio, child.[4]
Villa, Pascual, soldier.[4]
Villa, Rafael.[4]
Villalba, Onofre, Cat. vol.[4]
Villagomez, Francisco, soldier.[2]
Villalobos, José, soldier.[2]
Villalobos, José Ma., child.[4]
Villaseñor, José, artilleryman.[4]
Villavicencio, Rafael, soldier.[1]
Villavicencio, José Antonio, child.[2]
Villavicencio, Antonio, settler.[3]
Villavicencio, Félix, settler.[3]
Villavicencio, Pascual, settler.[4]
Villavicencio, José, soldier.[4]
Villarino, Félix Antonio, settler.[4]
Villela, Juan Manuel, soldier.[2]
Villela, Marcos, soldier.[4]
Viñals, José, padre.[4]
Virjan, Manuel, muleteer.[2]
Vizcaino, Juan, padre.[1]
Vizcarra, José, soldier.[4]
Yorba, Antonio, Cat. vol.[1]
Yorba, Francisco Javier, soldier.[1]
Yorba, José Antonio.[4]
Yorba, José Domingo, child.[4]
Yorba, Tomás.[4]
Zambrano, Nicolás, soldier.[1]
Zayas, José Salvador, soldier.[3]
Zúñiga, Pedro B., child.[2]
Zúñiga, Pio Quinto, soldier.[2]
Zúñiga, José, lieutenant.[3]
Zúñiga, José Antonio, child.[3]
Zúñiga, José Valentin Q., child.[3]
Zúñiga, Serapio Ma., child.[3]
Zúñiga, Guillermo A., child.[4]
Zúñiga, José Manuel, child.[4]
Zúñiga, Ventura.[4]